THE COMPLETE

ELFQUEST®

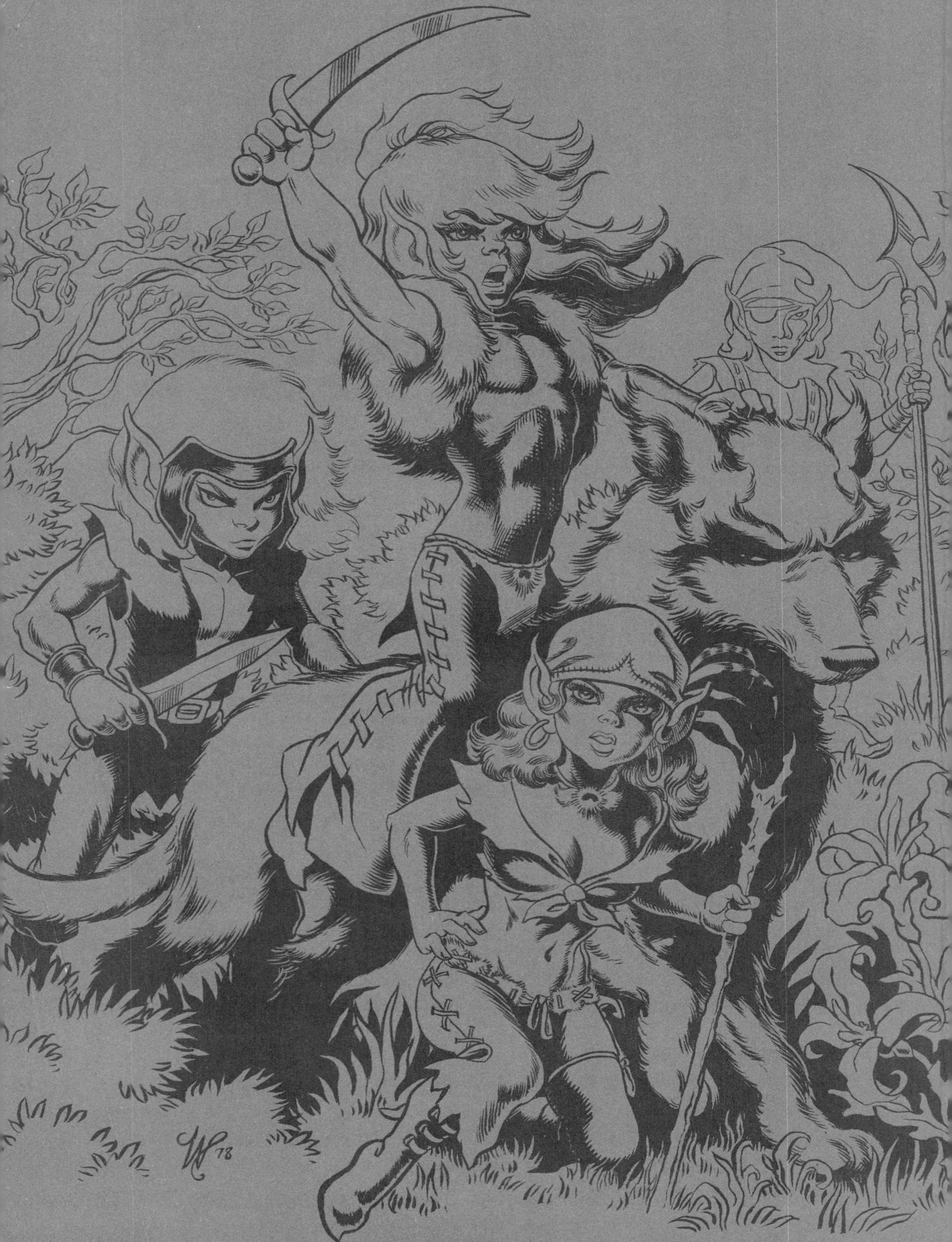

THE COMPLETE

ElfQuest®

VOLUME ONE

BY WENDY AND RICHARD PINI

DARK HORSE BOOKS

President & Publisher MIKE RICHARDSON

Collection Editor SIERRA HAHN

Collection Assistant Editor SPENCER CUSHING

Digital Production ALLYSON HALLER

Collection Designer TINA ALESSI

Special thanks to Phil Seuling and Bud Plant, whose faith and fearlessness
gave ElfQuest its opening shot into the nascent direct market.

NEIL HANKERSON Executive Vice President - TOM WEDDLE Chief Financial Officer - DALE LAFOUNTAIN Chief Information
Officer - TIM WIESCH Vice President of Licensing - MATT PARKINSON Vice President of Marketing - VANESSA TODD-
HOLMES Vice President of Production and Scheduling - MARK BERNARDI Vice President of Book Trade and Digital Sales
- RANDY LAHRMAN Vice President of Product Development - KEN LIZZI General Counsel - DAVE MARSHALL Editor in Chief
- DAVEY ESTRADA Editorial Director - CHRIS WARNER Senior Books Editor - CARY GRAZZINI Director of Specialty Projects
- LIA RIBACCHI Art Director - MATT DRYER Director of Digital Art and Prepress - MICHAEL GOMBOS Senior Director of
Licensed Publications - KARI YADRO Director of Custom Programs - KARI TORSON Director of International Licensing

Published by Dark Horse Books
A division of Dark Horse Comics LLC
10956 SE Main Street
Milwaukie, OR 97222

First edition: August 2014
ISBN 978-1-61655-407-1
13 15 17 19 20 18 16 14 12
Printed in China

To find a comic shop in your area, visit comicshoplocator.com

LIBRARY OF CONGRESS CATALOGING-IN-PUBLICATION DATA

Pini, Wendy.
The Complete Elfquest Volume 1 / Wendy Pini, Richard Pini.
pages cm
Summary: "ElfQuest is an epic fantasy comic series started by Wendy and Richard Pini first appearing in 1978.
Following a tribe of elves called the Wolfriders readers follow their journey on a new world. Complete ElfQuest
Volume One collects Issues #1 through #20 of ElfQuest: The Original Quest"– Provided by publisher.
ISBN 978-1-61655-407-1 (paperback)
1. Graphic novels. I. Pini, Richard. II. Title.
PN6728.E45P53 2014
741.5'973–dc23
2014014517

This volume collects and reprints the comic book series ElfQuest: The Original Quest #1–#20.

TO OUR FANS, WHOSE YEARNING

KEEPS THE ADVENTURE GOING,

AND WHOSE LOVE KEEPS US GOING.

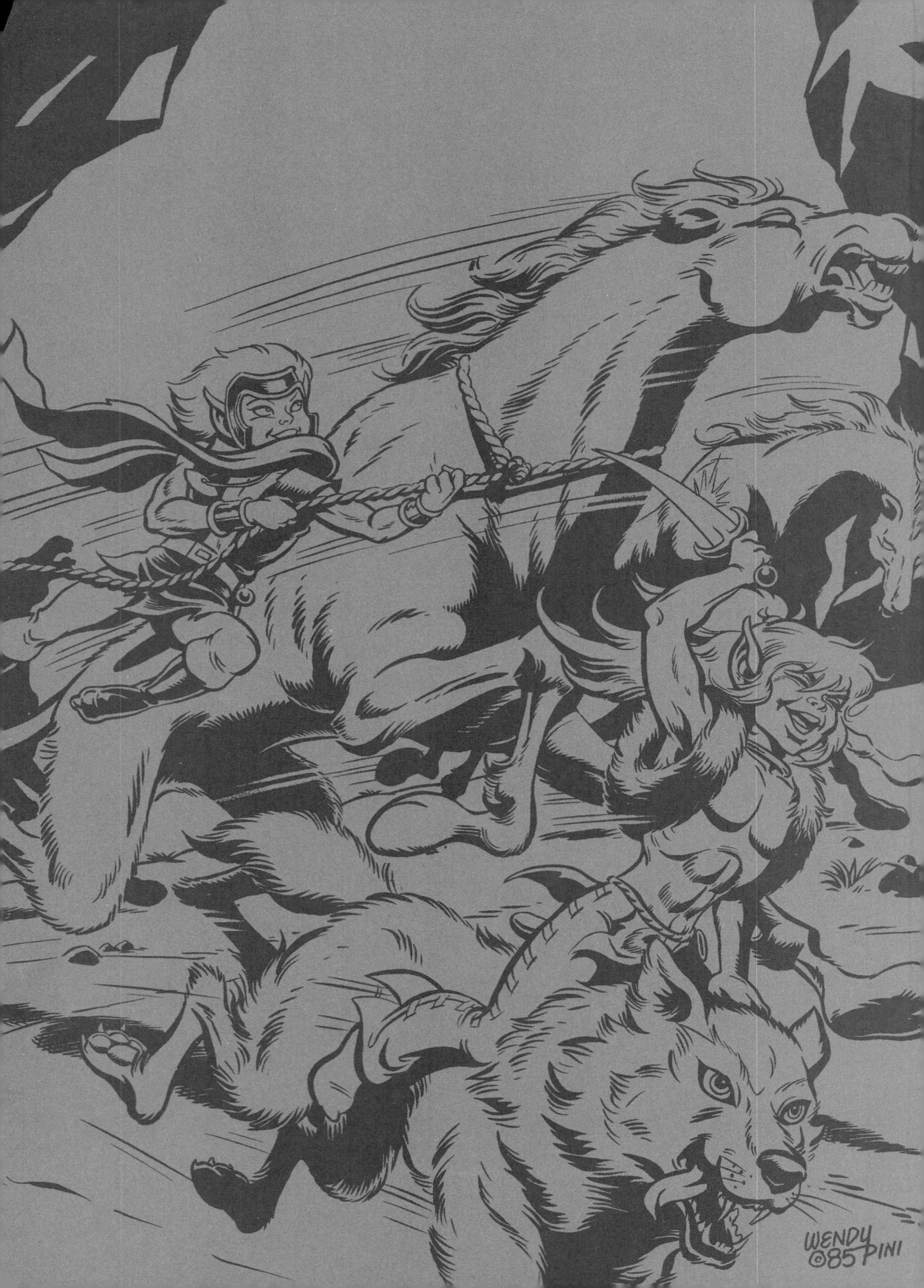
WENDY PINI
©85

CONTENTS

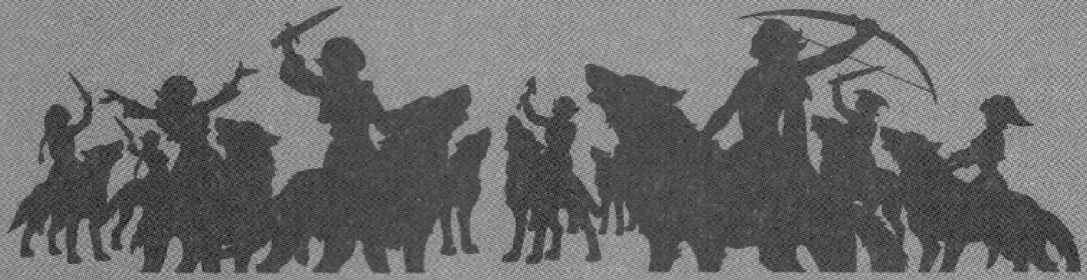

INTRODUCTION

BY ROB BESCHIZZA

ElfQuest is the longest-running indie comic fantasy series in America, exquisitely spun from sources Western and Eastern, spiritual and secular.

ElfQuest is a fairy tale about cute little elves living in the forest.

ElfQuest is a story about savage, wolf-riding demons that corrupt God's green land, doing stuff your parents would never guess just by looking at the cover.

ElfQuest is a tale about an inexperienced leader's desperate effort to save his people, his tribe, his family. The galling failure of every venerated ancestor rests heavy in his heart.

ElfQuest is about the final victory over ignorance, the awareness of one's own capacity for knowledge.

ElfQuest is about life, love, and the pursuit not merely of happiness, but of peace—and power.

ElfQuest is about death's final calm, lurking beyond the last comforting shadow of dawn. It is the blood on the leaves, reminding you not only that one you love is gone forever, but that all that you are has dwindled yet again, closing inexorably to zero.

ElfQuest is about infinity, the stars' own time.

ElfQuest is about the Now, the sharp intake of breath, the fight and the fire.

ElfQuest is the strength that drives us to embrace the otherness within ourselves and those we know.

ElfQuest is our weakness, the unrestrained hopes and dreams that lead us to despair and ruin.

The message *ElfQuest* shouts: "Change! Seek the power of growth, the evolutionary aspiration that leads us to the truth."

ElfQuest's unintended admonition: "Hide! Sing the song in your hearts—but quietly, lest humanity harm once again the spirit that guides it."

ElfQuest is paradox, the first dawn and the final sunset.

ElfQuest is escapist fluff. Just look at those hairstyles!

ElfQuest is the rebirth of utopian fantasy, the antidote to way too much Tolkien.

ElfQuest is a silly girl's book that any self-respecting comic book guy will tell you was, like, ahead of its time back in the seventies, but totally doesn't hold up now.

It's that whisper
   the susurration
      maybe just the high wind in the trees
         inviting you somewhere
           dangerous

Rob Beschizza is managing editor of the arts and culture webzine Boing Boing. He is a storyteller, deceiver, and artificer.

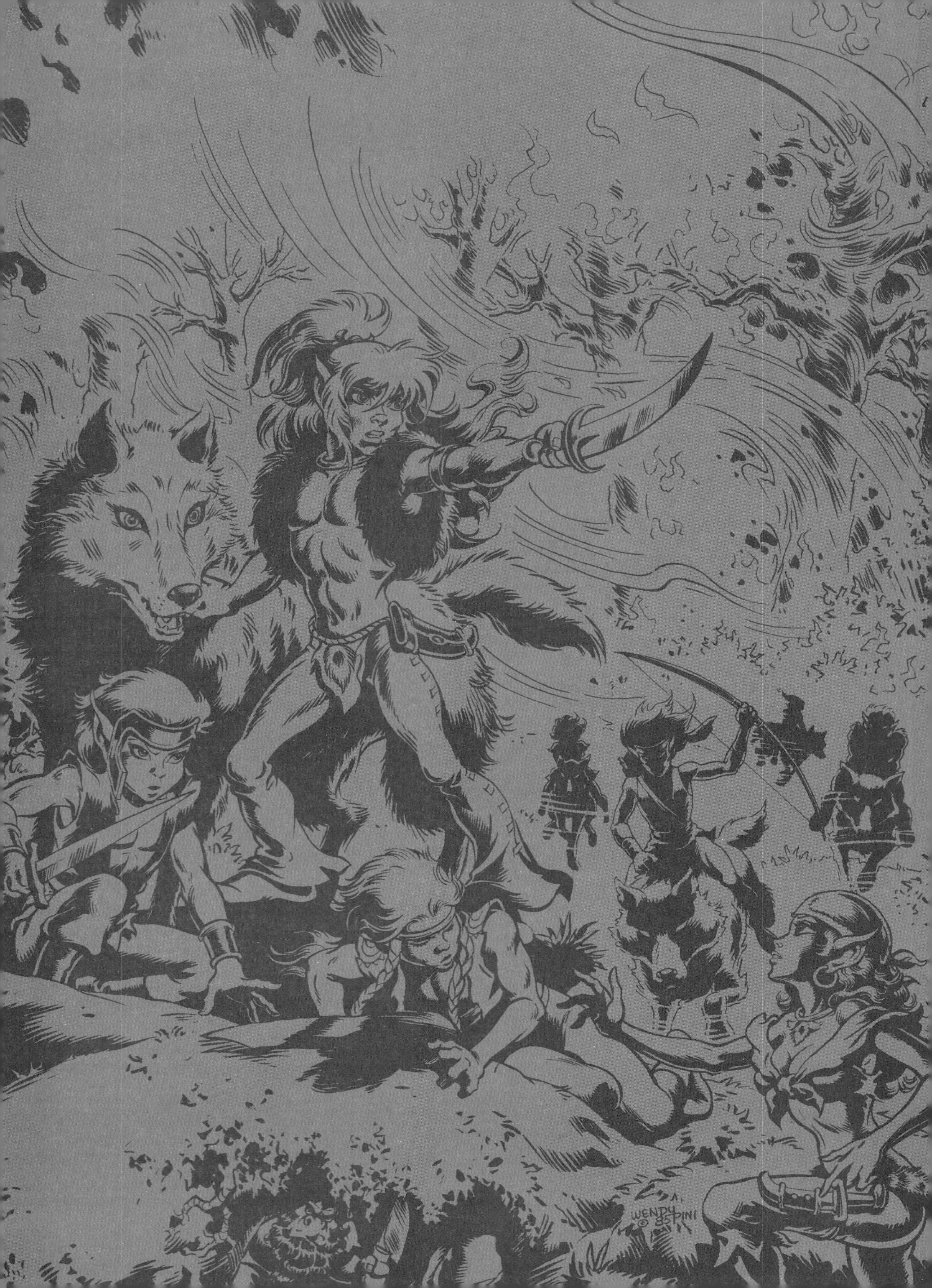
WENDY PINI
© 85

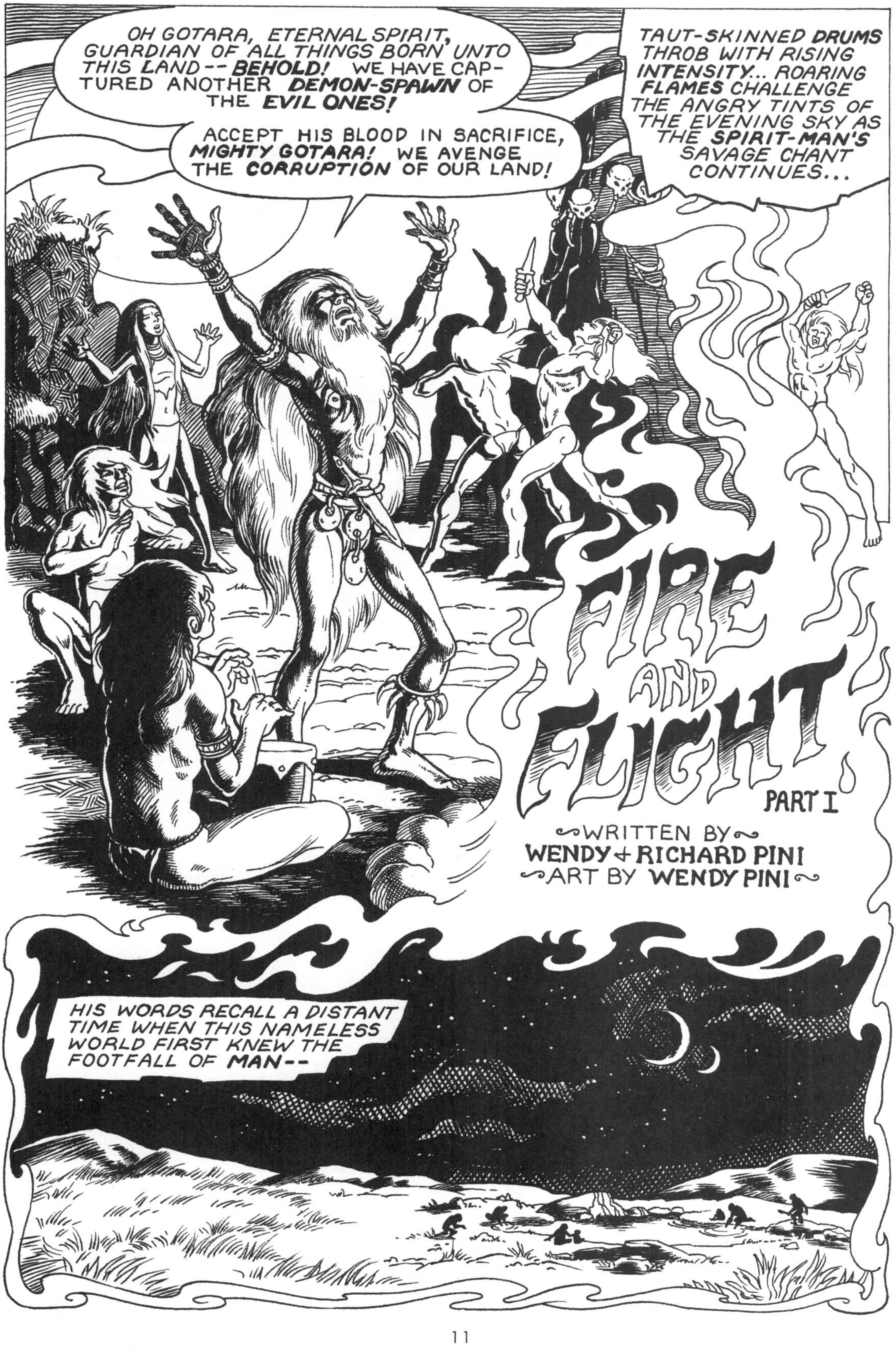
OH GOTARA, ETERNAL SPIRIT, GUARDIAN OF ALL THINGS BORN UNTO THIS LAND -- BEHOLD! WE HAVE CAPTURED ANOTHER DEMON-SPAWN OF THE EVIL ONES!
ACCEPT HIS BLOOD IN SACRIFICE, MIGHTY GOTARA! WE AVENGE THE CORRUPTION OF OUR LAND!
TAUT-SKINNED DRUMS THROB WITH RISING INTENSITY... ROARING FLAMES CHALLENGE THE ANGRY TINTS OF THE EVENING SKY AS THE SPIRIT-MAN'S SAVAGE CHANT CONTINUES...
FIRE AND FLIGHT
PART I
WRITTEN BY WENDY + RICHARD PINI
ART BY WENDY PINI
HIS WORDS RECALL A DISTANT TIME WHEN THIS NAMELESS WORLD FIRST KNEW THE FOOTFALL OF MAN--

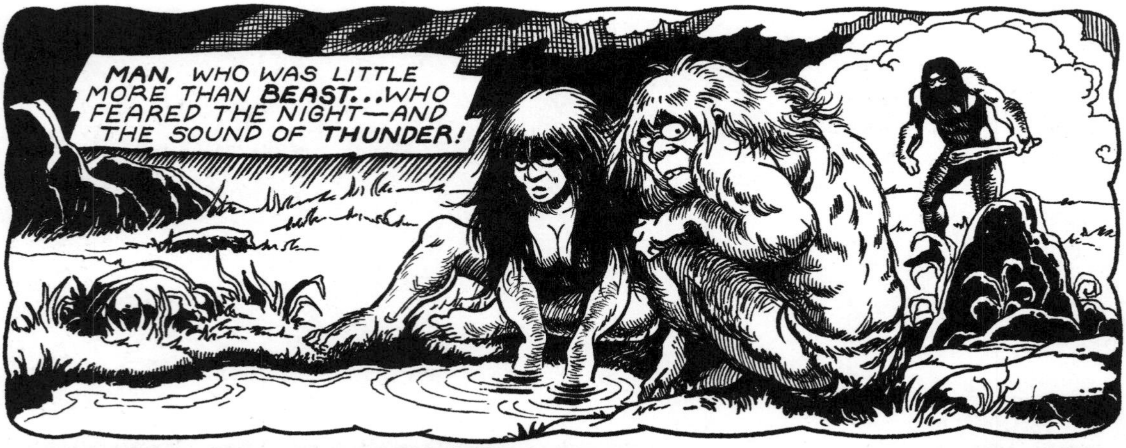
MAN, WHO WAS LITTLE MORE THAN BEAST...WHO FEARED THE NIGHT—AND THE SOUND OF THUNDER!

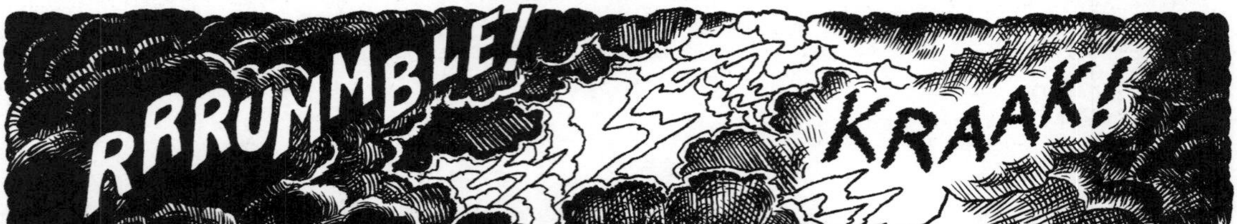
RRRUMMBLE!
KRAAK!

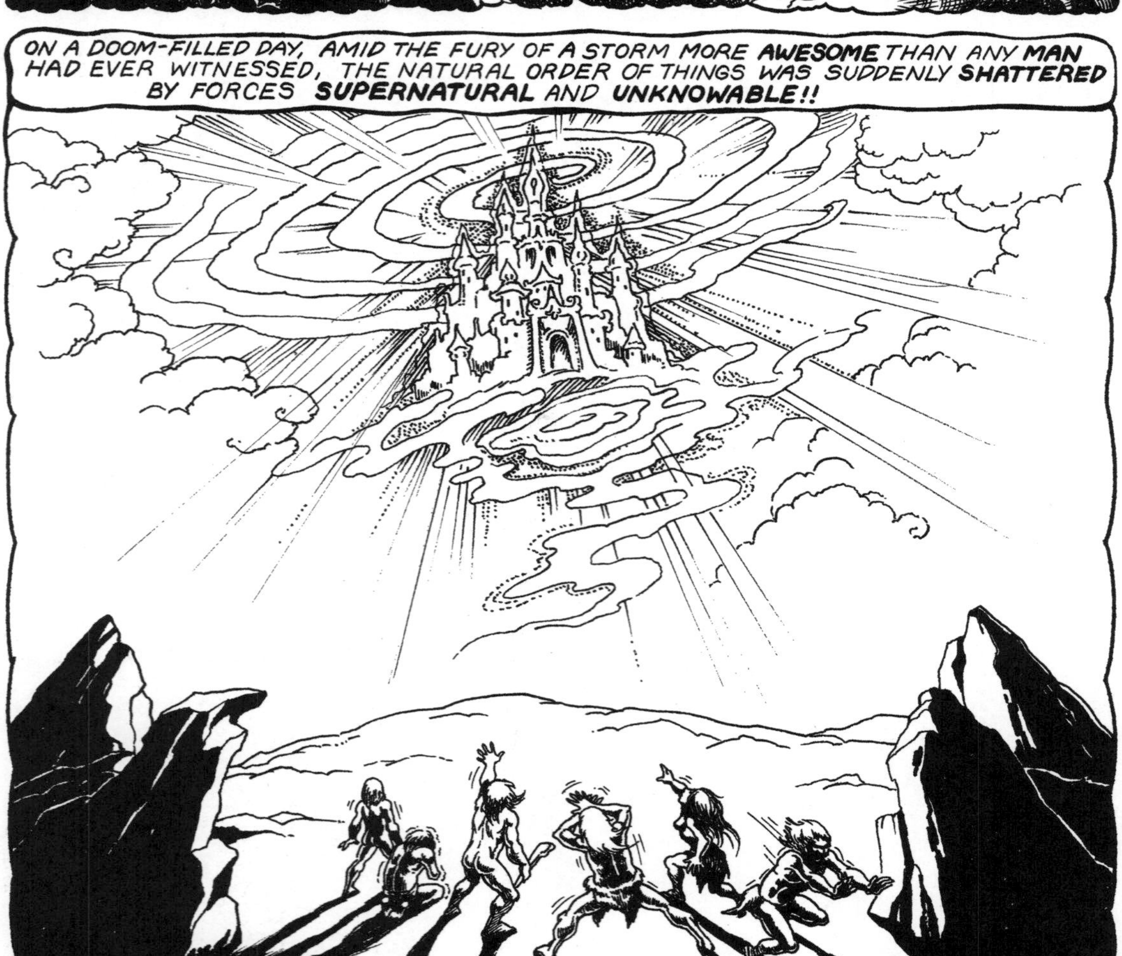
ON A DOOM-FILLED DAY, AMID THE FURY OF A STORM MORE AWESOME THAN ANY MAN HAD EVER WITNESSED, THE NATURAL ORDER OF THINGS WAS SUDDENLY SHATTERED BY FORCES SUPERNATURAL AND UNKNOWABLE!!

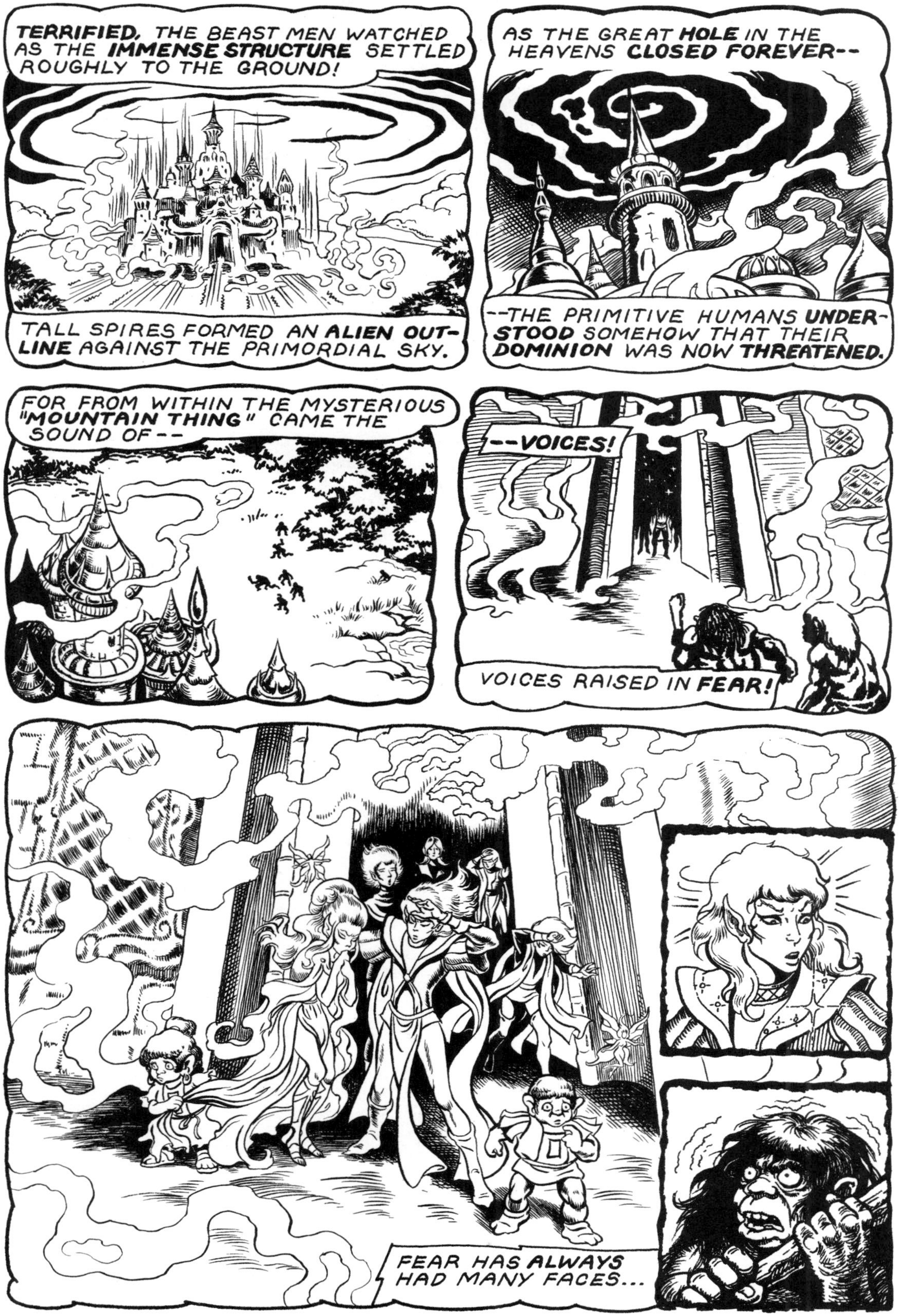
TERRIFIED, THE BEAST MEN WATCHED AS THE IMMENSE STRUCTURE SETTLED ROUGHLY TO THE GROUND!
TALL SPIRES FORMED AN ALIEN OUT-LINE AGAINST THE PRIMORDIAL SKY.
AS THE GREAT HOLE IN THE HEAVENS CLOSED FOREVER--
--THE PRIMITIVE HUMANS UNDER-STOOD SOMEHOW THAT THEIR DOMINION WAS NOW THREATENED.
FOR FROM WITHIN THE MYSTERIOUS "MOUNTAIN THING" CAME THE SOUND OF--
--VOICES!
VOICES RAISED IN FEAR!
FEAR HAS ALWAYS HAD MANY FACES...

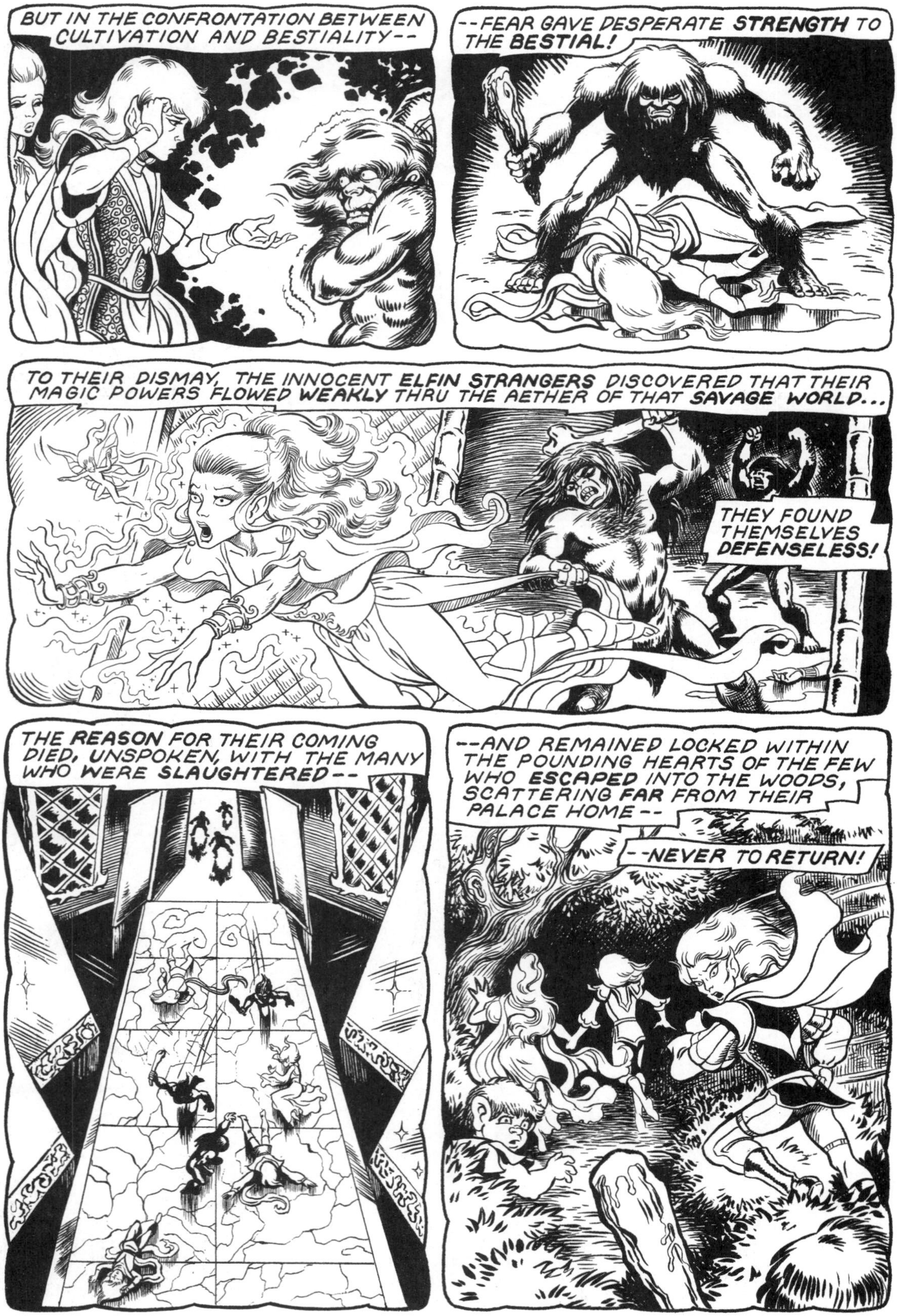
BUT IN THE CONFRONTATION BETWEEN CULTIVATION AND BESTIALITY--
--FEAR GAVE DESPERATE STRENGTH TO THE BESTIAL!
TO THEIR DISMAY, THE INNOCENT ELFIN STRANGERS DISCOVERED THAT THEIR MAGIC POWERS FLOWED WEAKLY THRU THE AETHER OF THAT SAVAGE WORLD...
THEY FOUND THEMSELVES DEFENSELESS!
THE REASON FOR THEIR COMING DIED, UNSPOKEN, WITH THE MANY WHO WERE SLAUGHTERED--
--AND REMAINED LOCKED WITHIN THE POUNDING HEARTS OF THE FEW WHO ESCAPED INTO THE WOODS, SCATTERING FAR FROM THEIR PALACE HOME--
--NEVER TO RETURN!

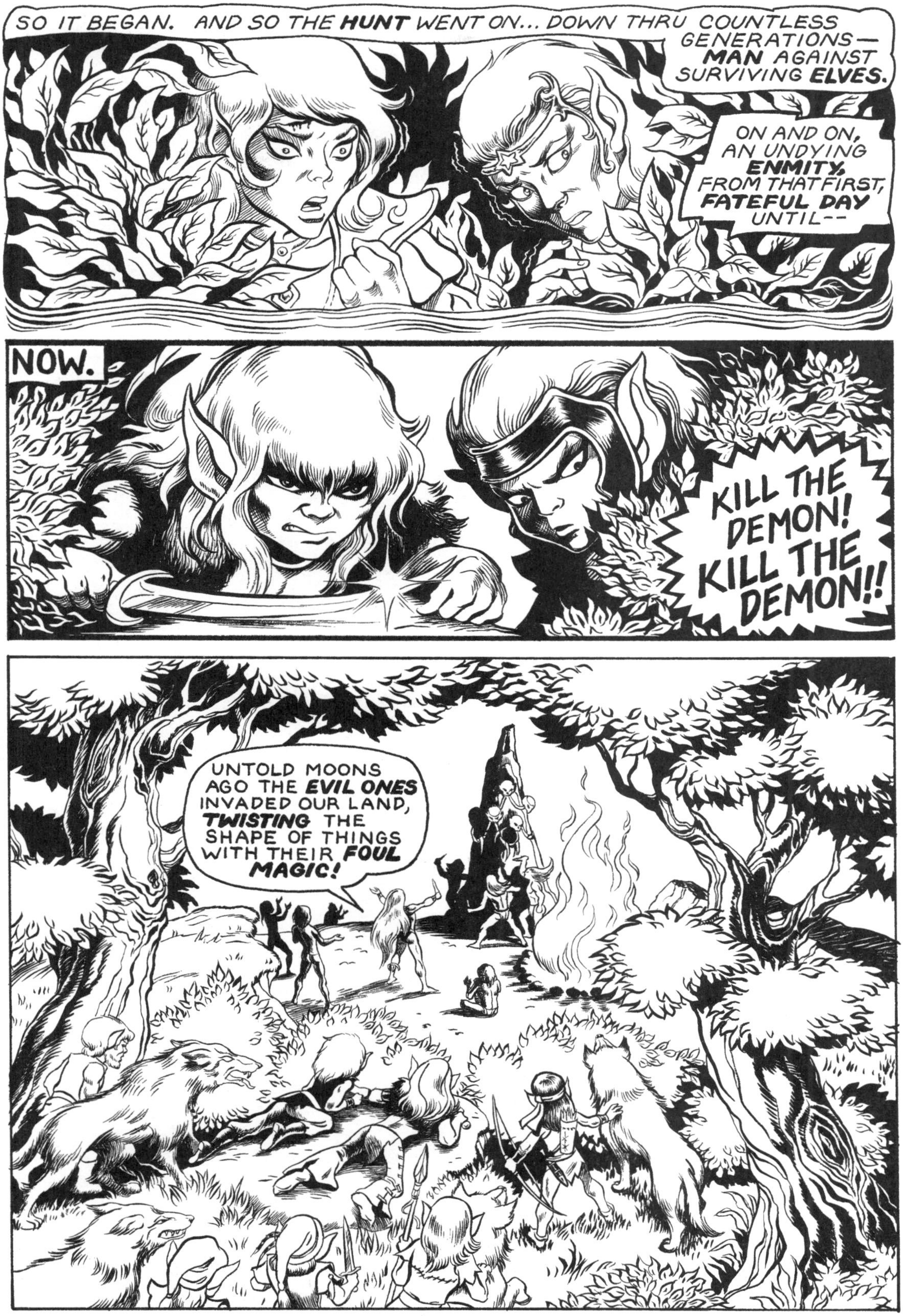
SO IT BEGAN. AND SO THE HUNT WENT ON... DOWN THRU COUNTLESS GENERATIONS— MAN AGAINST SURVIVING ELVES.
ON AND ON, AN UNDYING ENMITY. FROM THAT FIRST, FATEFUL DAY UNTIL--
NOW.
KILL THE DEMON! KILL THE DEMON!!
UNTOLD MOONS AGO THE EVIL ONES INVADED OUR LAND, TWISTING THE SHAPE OF THINGS WITH THEIR FOUL MAGIC!

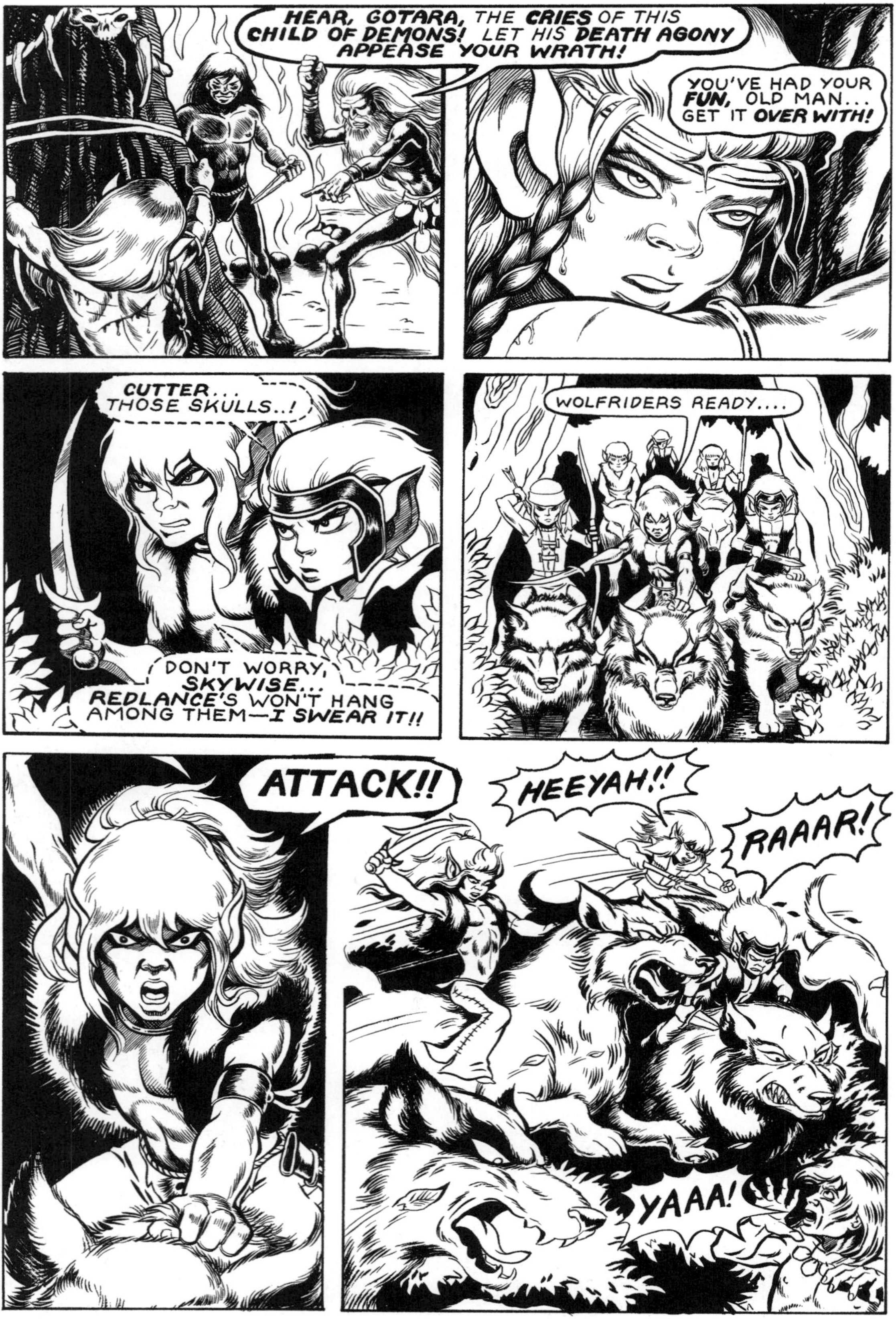
HEAR, GOTARA, THE CRIES OF THIS CHILD OF DEMONS! LET HIS DEATH AGONY APPEASE YOUR WRATH!
YOU'VE HAD YOUR FUN, OLD MAN... GET IT OVER WITH!
CUTTER... THOSE SKULLS..!
DON'T WORRY, SKYWISE... REDLANCE'S WON'T HANG AMONG THEM—I SWEAR IT!!
WOLFRIDERS READY....
ATTACK!!
HEEYAH!!
RAAAR!
YAAA!

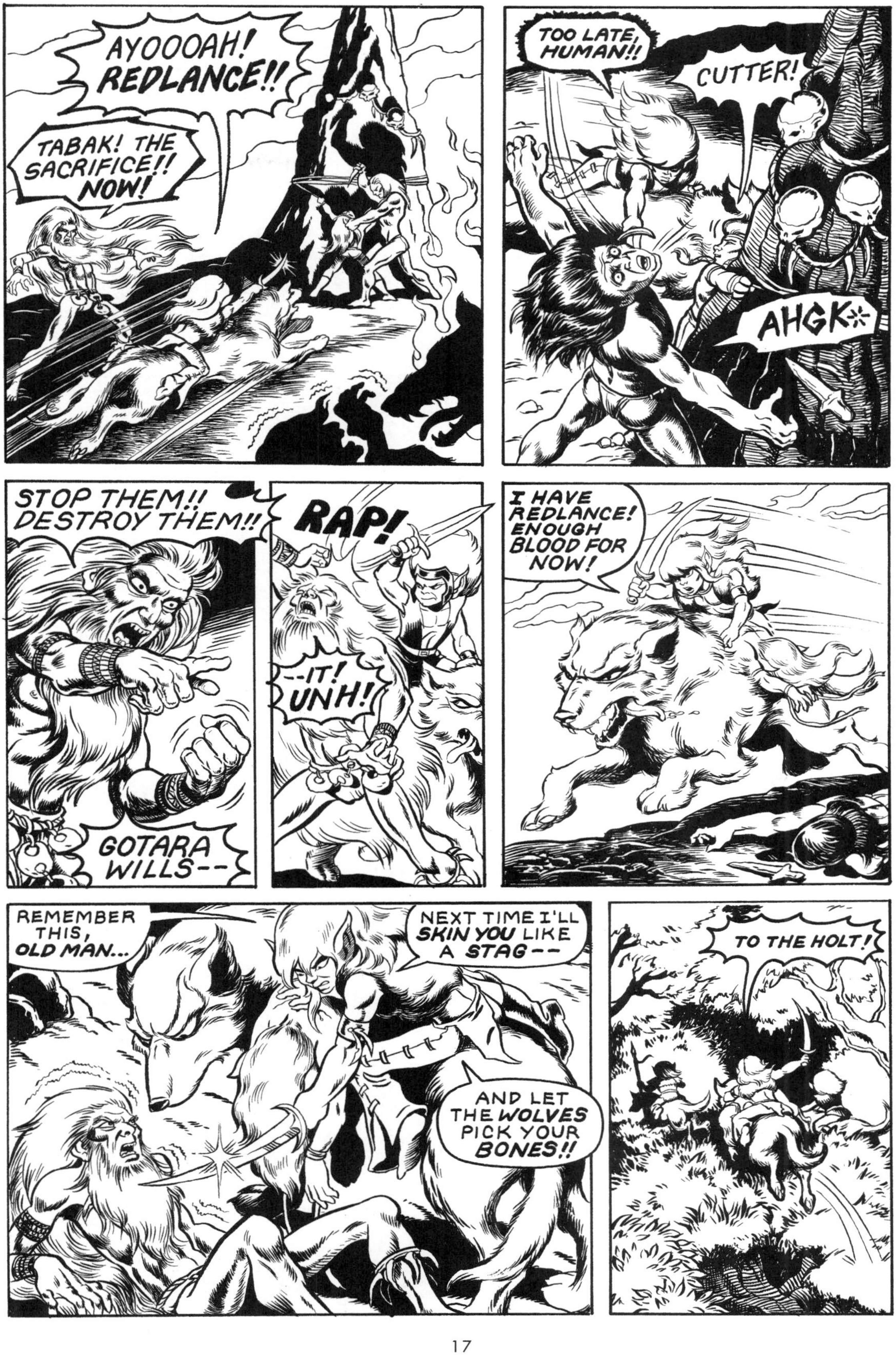
AYOOOAH! REDLANCE!!
TABAK! THE SACRIFICE!! NOW!
TOO LATE, HUMAN!!
CUTTER!
AHGK
STOP THEM!! DESTROY THEM!!
GOTARA WILLS--
RAP!
--IT! UNH!
I HAVE REDLANCE! ENOUGH BLOOD FOR NOW!
REMEMBER THIS, OLD MAN...
NEXT TIME I'LL SKIN YOU LIKE A STAG--
AND LET THE WOLVES PICK YOUR BONES!!
TO THE HOLT!

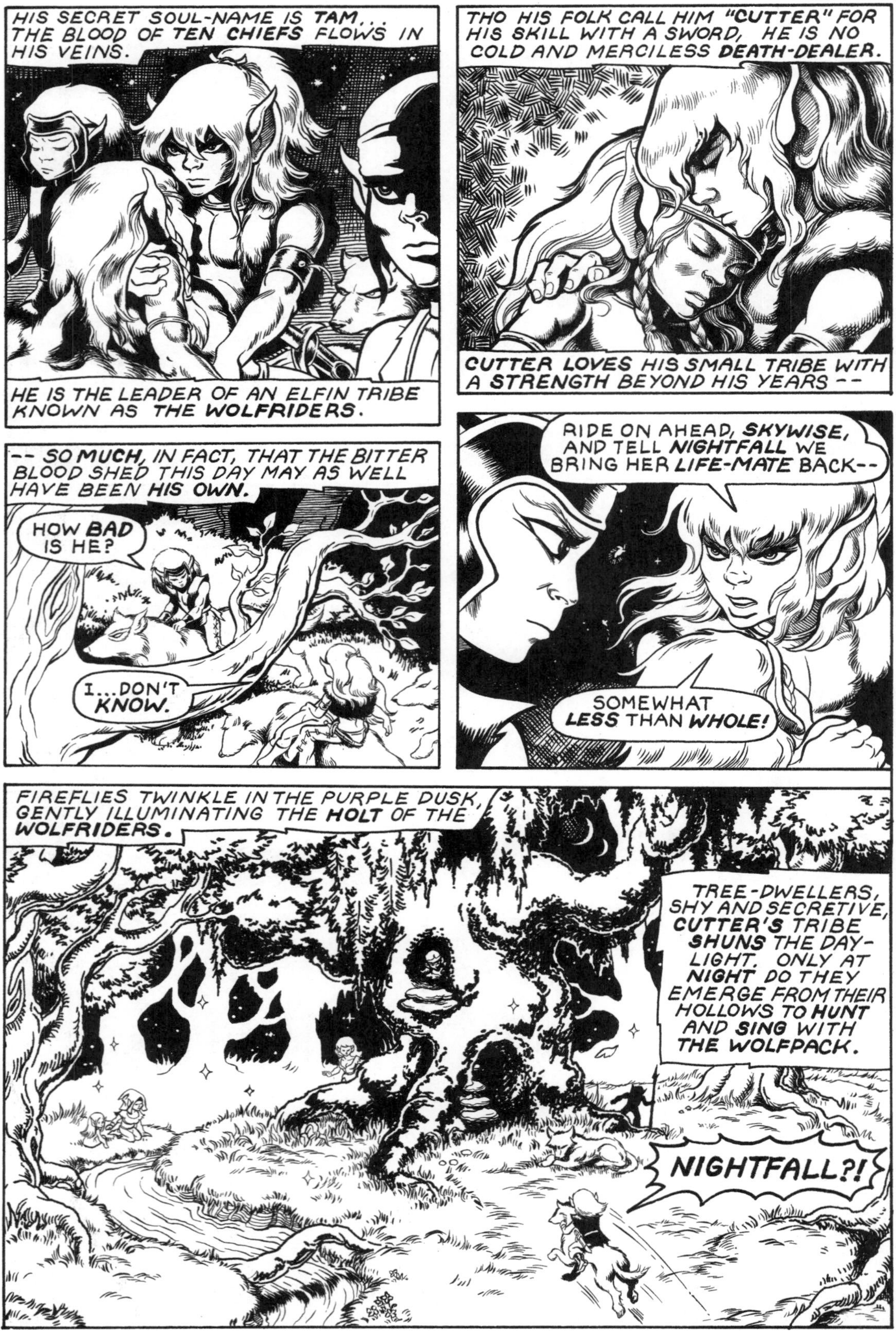
HIS SECRET SOUL-NAME IS TAM... THE BLOOD OF TEN CHIEFS FLOWS IN HIS VEINS.
HE IS THE LEADER OF AN ELFIN TRIBE KNOWN AS THE WOLFRIDERS.
THO HIS FOLK CALL HIM "CUTTER" FOR HIS SKILL WITH A SWORD, HE IS NO COLD AND MERCILESS DEATH-DEALER.
CUTTER LOVES HIS SMALL TRIBE WITH A STRENGTH BEYOND HIS YEARS --
-- SO MUCH, IN FACT, THAT THE BITTER BLOOD SHED THIS DAY MAY AS WELL HAVE BEEN HIS OWN.
HOW BAD IS HE?
I...DON'T KNOW.
RIDE ON AHEAD, SKYWISE, AND TELL NIGHTFALL WE BRING HER LIFE-MATE BACK--
SOMEWHAT LESS THAN WHOLE!
FIREFLIES TWINKLE IN THE PURPLE DUSK, GENTLY ILLUMINATING THE HOLT OF THE WOLFRIDERS.
TREE-DWELLERS, SHY AND SECRETIVE, CUTTER'S TRIBE SHUNS THE DAY-LIGHT. ONLY AT NIGHT DO THEY EMERGE FROM THEIR HOLLOWS TO HUNT AND SING WITH THE WOLFPACK.
NIGHTFALL?!

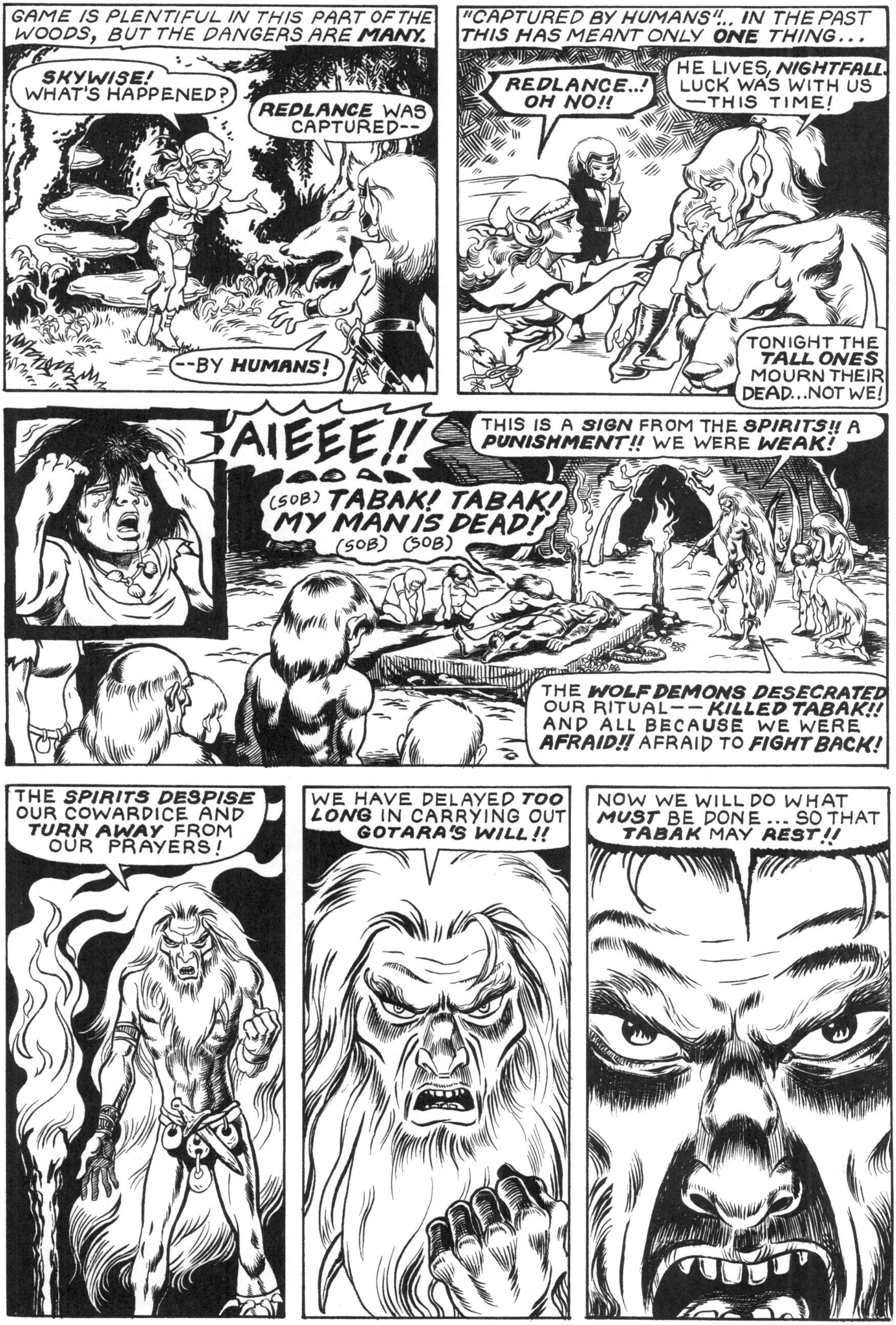
GAME IS PLENTIFUL IN THIS PART OF THE WOODS, BUT THE DANGERS ARE MANY.
SKYWISE! WHAT'S HAPPENED?
REDLANCE WAS CAPTURED--
--BY HUMANS!
"CAPTURED BY HUMANS"... IN THE PAST THIS HAS MEANT ONLY ONE THING...
REDLANCE..! OH NO!!
HE LIVES, NIGHTFALL. LUCK WAS WITH US —THIS TIME!
TONIGHT THE TALL ONES MOURN THEIR DEAD...NOT WE!
AIEEE!!
(SOB) TABAK! TABAK! MY MAN IS DEAD! (SOB) (SOB)
THIS IS A SIGN FROM THE SPIRITS!! A PUNISHMENT!! WE WERE WEAK!
THE WOLF DEMONS DESECRATED OUR RITUAL-- KILLED TABAK!! AND ALL BECAUSE WE WERE AFRAID!! AFRAID TO FIGHT BACK!
THE SPIRITS DESPISE OUR COWARDICE AND TURN AWAY FROM OUR PRAYERS!
WE HAVE DELAYED TOO LONG IN CARRYING OUT GOTARA'S WILL!!
NOW WE WILL DO WHAT MUST BE DONE ... SO THAT TABAK MAY REST!!

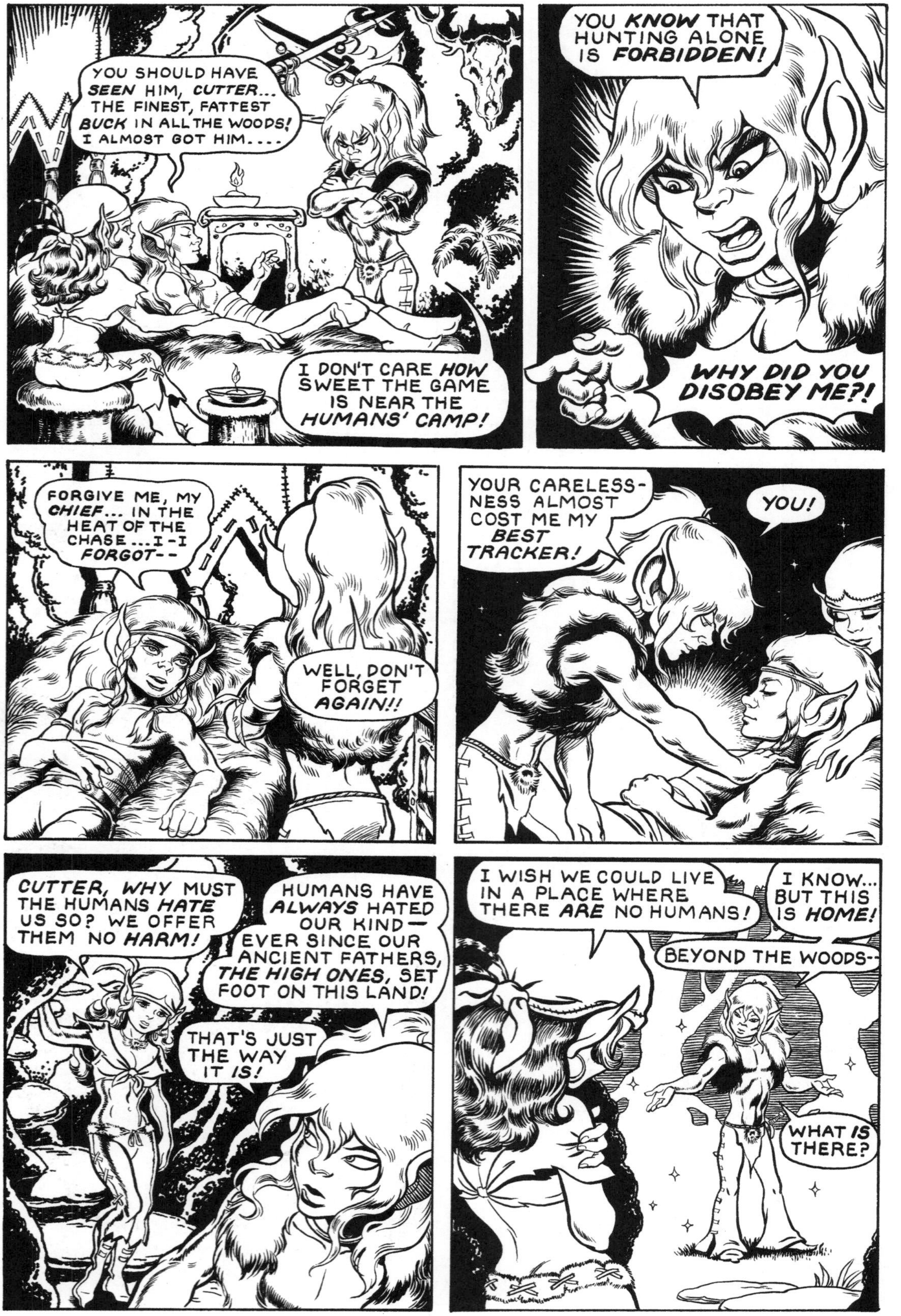
YOU SHOULD HAVE SEEN HIM, CUTTER... THE FINEST, FATTEST BUCK IN ALL THE WOODS! I ALMOST GOT HIM....
I DON'T CARE HOW SWEET THE GAME IS NEAR THE HUMANS' CAMP!
YOU KNOW THAT HUNTING ALONE IS FORBIDDEN!
WHY DID YOU DISOBEY ME?!
FORGIVE ME, MY CHIEF... IN THE HEAT OF THE CHASE...I-I FORGOT--
WELL, DON'T FORGET AGAIN!!
YOUR CARELESS-NESS ALMOST COST ME MY BEST TRACKER!
YOU!
CUTTER, WHY MUST THE HUMANS HATE US SO? WE OFFER THEM NO HARM!
HUMANS HAVE ALWAYS HATED OUR KIND— EVER SINCE OUR ANCIENT FATHERS, THE HIGH ONES, SET FOOT ON THIS LAND!
THAT'S JUST THE WAY IT IS!
I WISH WE COULD LIVE IN A PLACE WHERE THERE ARE NO HUMANS!
I KNOW... BUT THIS IS HOME!
BEYOND THE WOODS--
WHAT IS THERE?

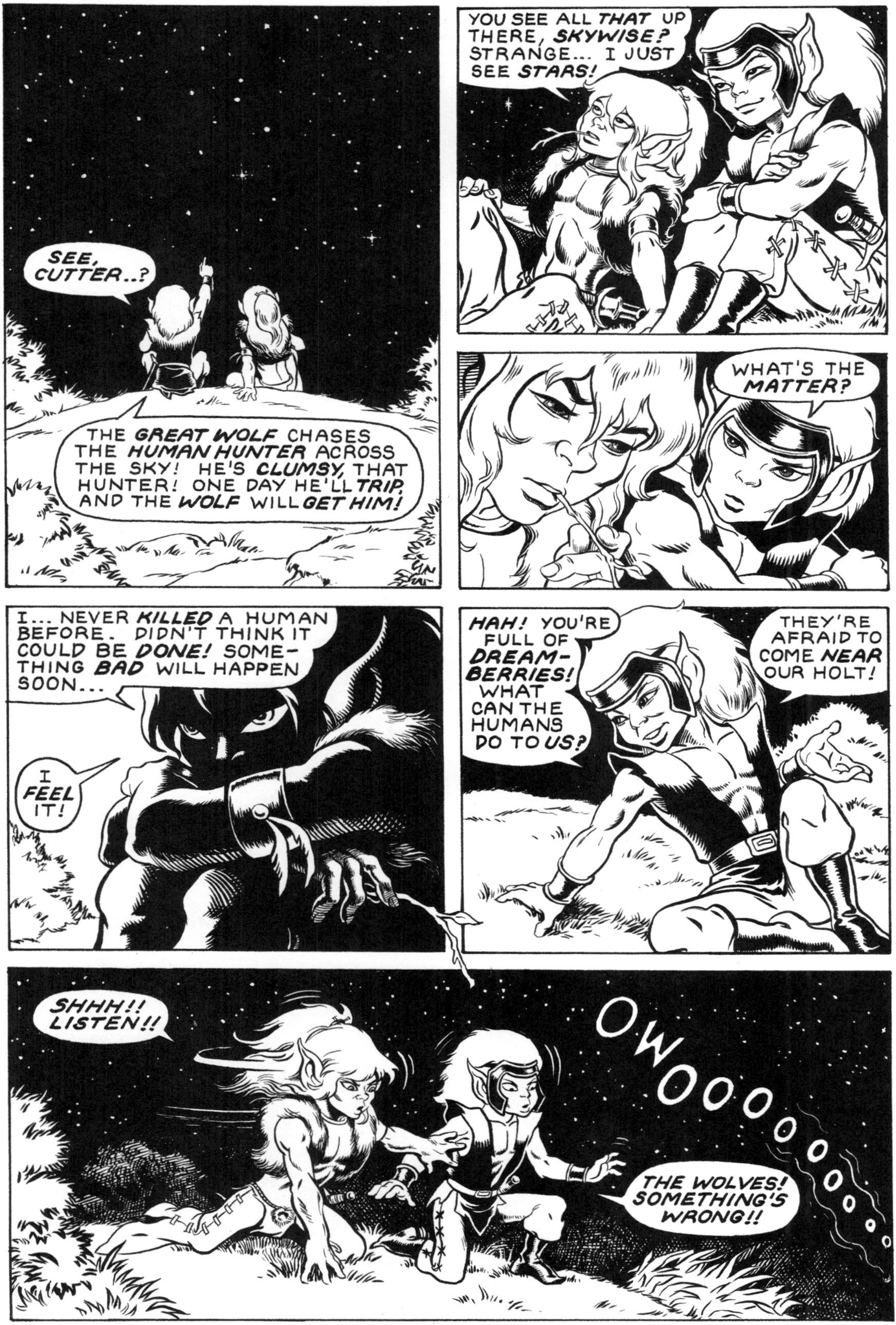
SEE, CUTTER..?
THE GREAT WOLF CHASES THE HUMAN HUNTER ACROSS THE SKY! HE'S CLUMSY, THAT HUNTER! ONE DAY HE'LL TRIP, AND THE WOLF WILL GET HIM!
YOU SEE ALL THAT UP THERE, SKYWISE? STRANGE... I JUST SEE STARS!
WHAT'S THE MATTER?
I... NEVER KILLED A HUMAN BEFORE. DIDN'T THINK IT COULD BE DONE! SOMETHING BAD WILL HAPPEN SOON...
I FEEL IT!
HAH! YOU'RE FULL OF DREAMBERRIES! WHAT CAN THE HUMANS DO TO US?
THEY'RE AFRAID TO COME NEAR OUR HOLT!
SHHH!! LISTEN!!
OWOOOOOOOOOOO
THE WOLVES! SOMETHING'S WRONG!!

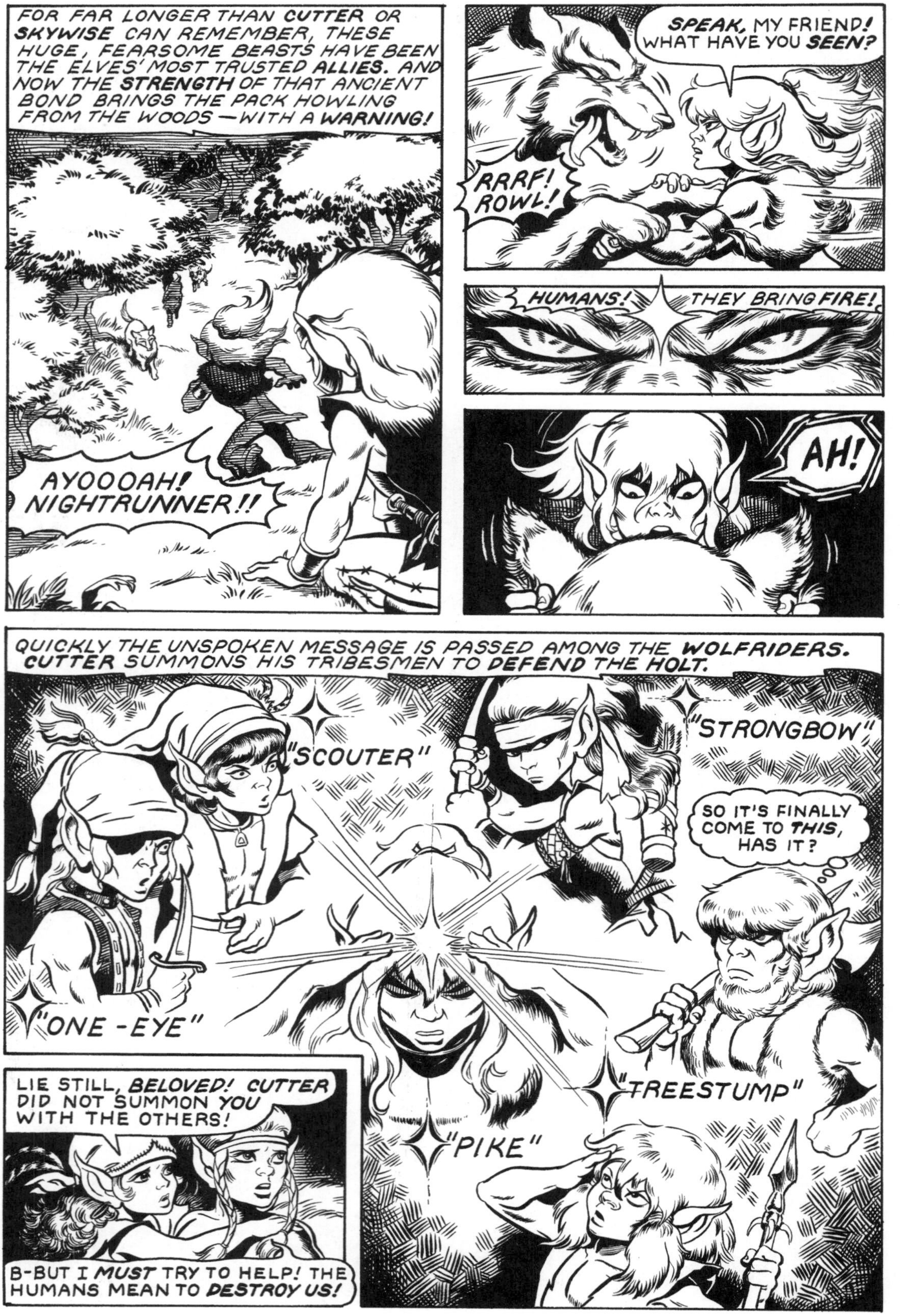
FOR FAR LONGER THAN CUTTER OR SKYWISE CAN REMEMBER, THESE HUGE, FEARSOME BEASTS HAVE BEEN THE ELVES' MOST TRUSTED ALLIES. AND NOW THE STRENGTH OF THAT ANCIENT BOND BRINGS THE PACK HOWLING FROM THE WOODS — WITH A WARNING!
AYOOOAH! NIGHTRUNNER!!
SPEAK, MY FRIEND! WHAT HAVE YOU SEEN?
RRRF! ROWL!
HUMANS! THEY BRING FIRE!
AH!
QUICKLY THE UNSPOKEN MESSAGE IS PASSED AMONG THE WOLFRIDERS. CUTTER SUMMONS HIS TRIBESMEN TO DEFEND THE HOLT.
"SCOUTER"
"STRONGBOW"
SO IT'S FINALLY COME TO THIS, HAS IT?
"ONE-EYE"
"TREESTUMP"
"PIKE"
LIE STILL, BELOVED! CUTTER DID NOT SUMMON YOU WITH THE OTHERS!
B-BUT I MUST TRY TO HELP! THE HUMANS MEAN TO DESTROY US!

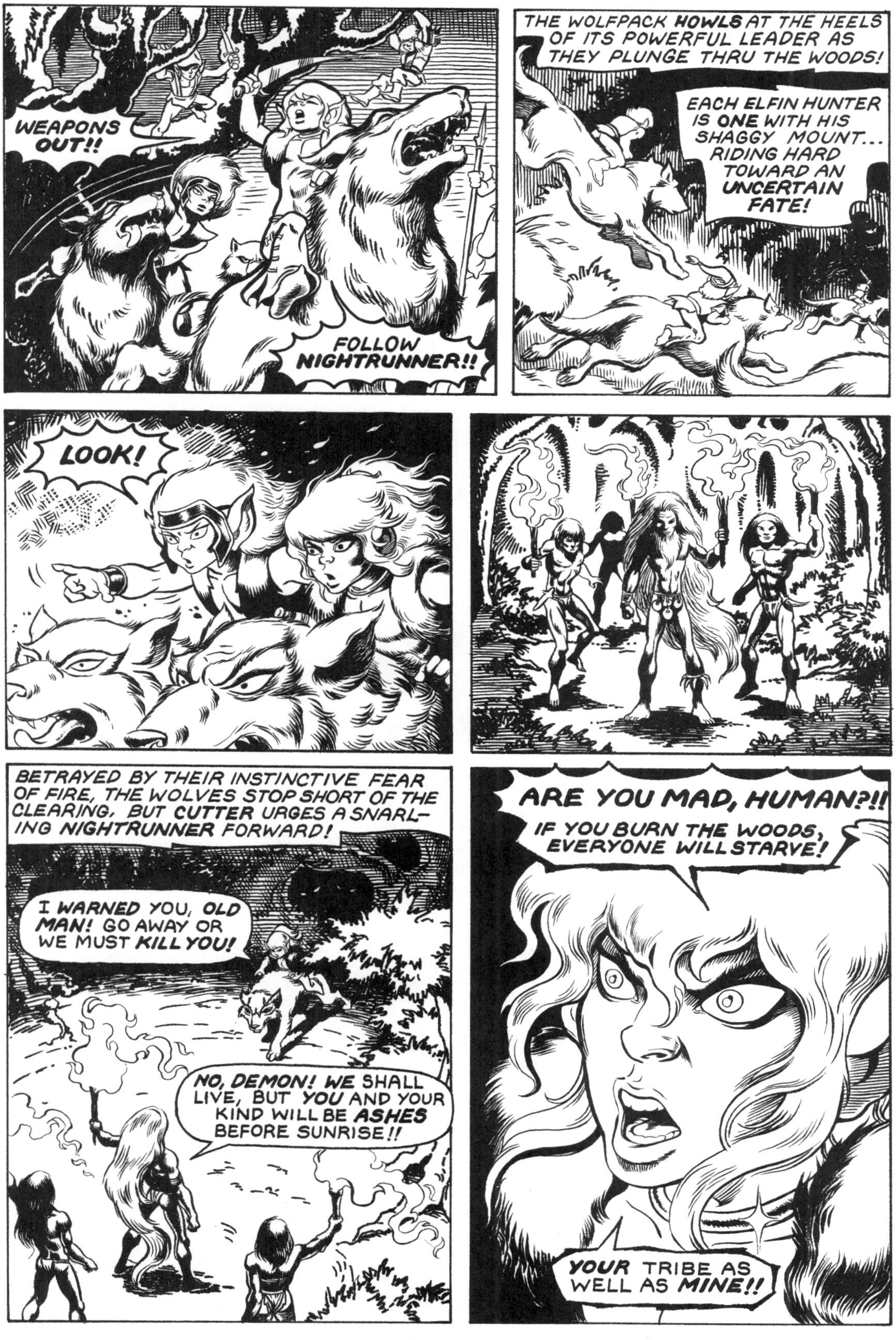
WEAPONS OUT!!
FOLLOW NIGHTRUNNER!!
THE WOLFPACK HOWLS AT THE HEELS OF ITS POWERFUL LEADER AS THEY PLUNGE THRU THE WOODS!
EACH ELFIN HUNTER IS ONE WITH HIS SHAGGY MOUNT... RIDING HARD TOWARD AN UNCERTAIN FATE!
LOOK!
BETRAYED BY THEIR INSTINCTIVE FEAR OF FIRE, THE WOLVES STOP SHORT OF THE CLEARING, BUT CUTTER URGES A SNARLING NIGHTRUNNER FORWARD!
I WARNED YOU, OLD MAN! GO AWAY OR WE MUST KILL YOU!
NO, DEMON! WE SHALL LIVE, BUT YOU AND YOUR KIND WILL BE ASHES BEFORE SUNRISE!!
ARE YOU MAD, HUMAN?!!
IF YOU BURN THE WOODS, EVERYONE WILL STARVE!
YOUR TRIBE AS WELL AS MINE!!

NO MATTER! GOTARA WILLS A *CLEANSING!* ONLY MAN MUST RULE THIS LAND! *ALL DEMONS MUST BURN!!*

NO!!

GOTARAAAA*

WHUNK!

ELFIN ARROWS, HOWEVER SWIFT, FAIL TO PREVENT THE *INEVITABLE...*

SKREEE!

MADMEN!! THEY'LL PAY FOR THIS WITH THEIR CURSED BLOOD!!

NO TIME! (KOFF) THE FIRE IS SPREADING!

WE MUST GET BACK TO THE *HOLT!*

COME, FATHER! MOTHER *NEEDS* US! AND I MUST SAVE *DEWSHINE!*

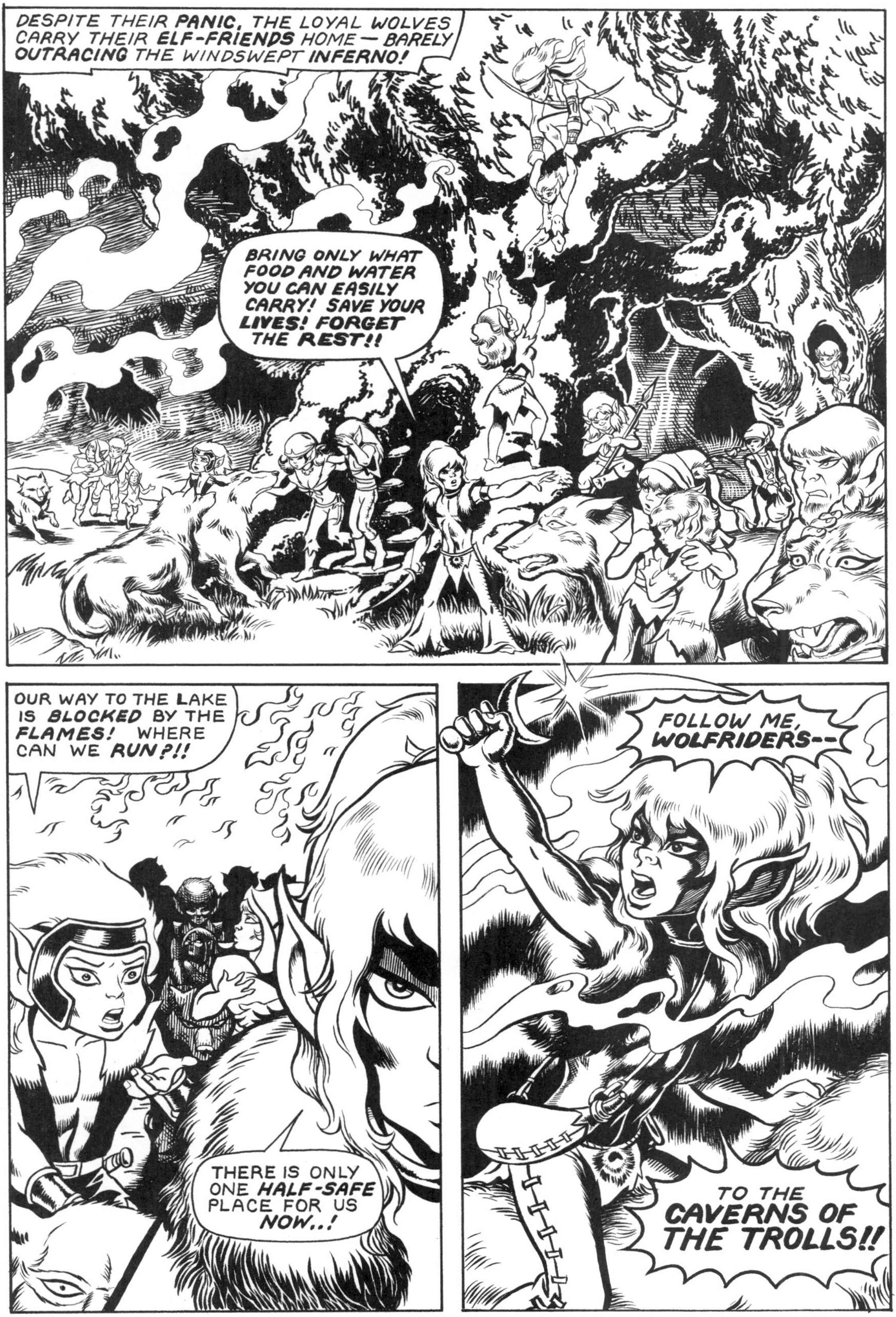
DESPITE THEIR PANIC, THE LOYAL WOLVES CARRY THEIR ELF-FRIENDS HOME — BARELY OUTRACING THE WINDSWEPT INFERNO!
BRING ONLY WHAT FOOD AND WATER YOU CAN EASILY CARRY! SAVE YOUR LIVES! FORGET THE REST!!
OUR WAY TO THE LAKE IS BLOCKED BY THE FLAMES! WHERE CAN WE RUN?!!
THERE IS ONLY ONE HALF-SAFE PLACE FOR US NOW..!
FOLLOW ME, WOLFRIDERS--
TO THE CAVERNS OF THE TROLLS!!

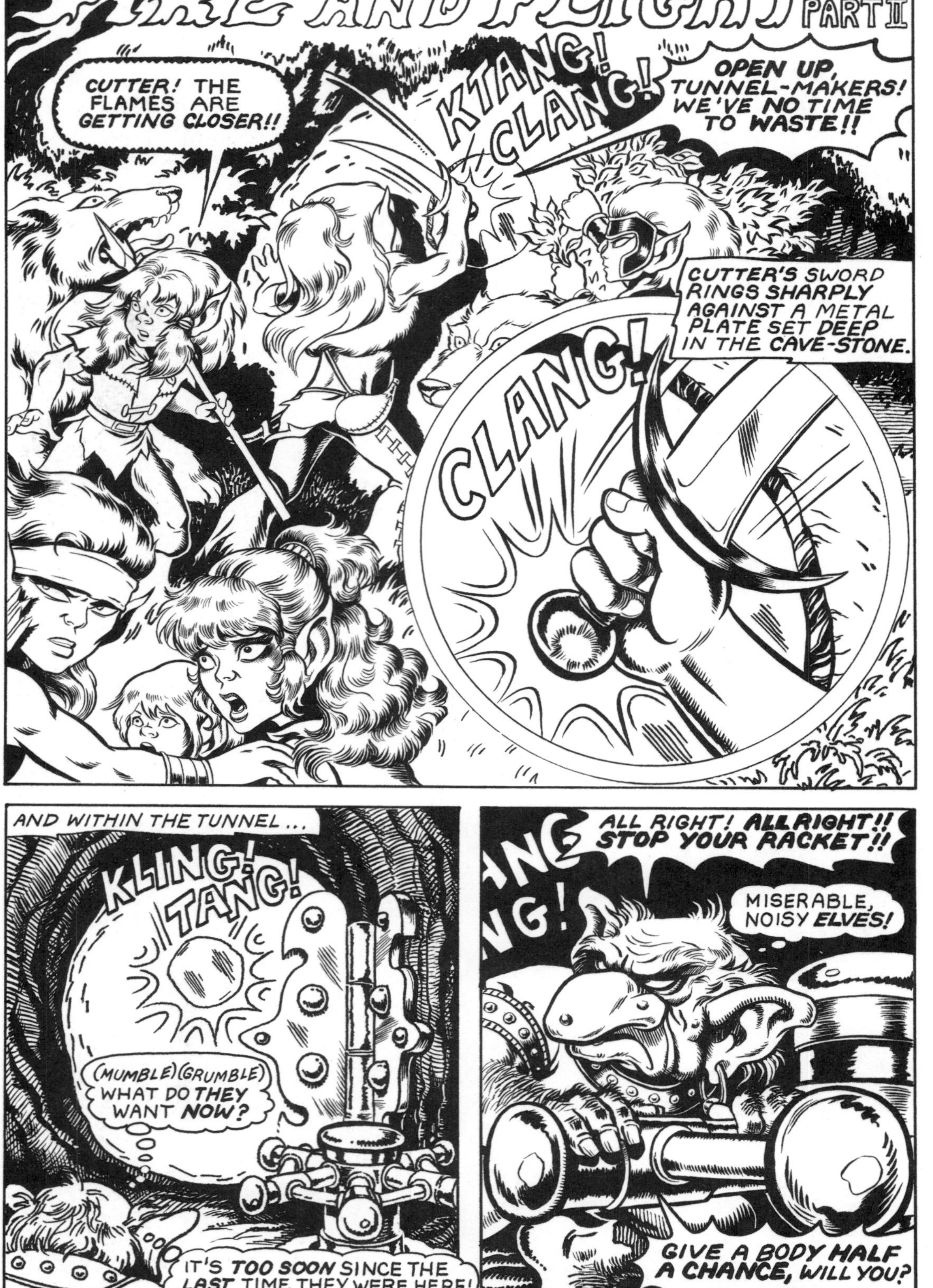
FIRE AND FLIGHT PART II
CUTTER! THE FLAMES ARE GETTING CLOSER!!
KTANG! CLANG!
OPEN UP, TUNNEL-MAKERS! WE'VE NO TIME TO WASTE!!
CUTTER'S SWORD RINGS SHARPLY AGAINST A METAL PLATE SET DEEP IN THE CAVE-STONE.
CLANG!
AND WITHIN THE TUNNEL...
KLING! TANG!
(MUMBLE)(GRUMBLE) WHAT DO THEY WANT NOW?
IT'S TOO SOON SINCE THE LAST TIME THEY WERE HERE!
ALL RIGHT! ALL RIGHT!! STOP YOUR RACKET!!
MISERABLE, NOISY ELVES!
GIVE A BODY HALF A CHANCE, WILL YOU?

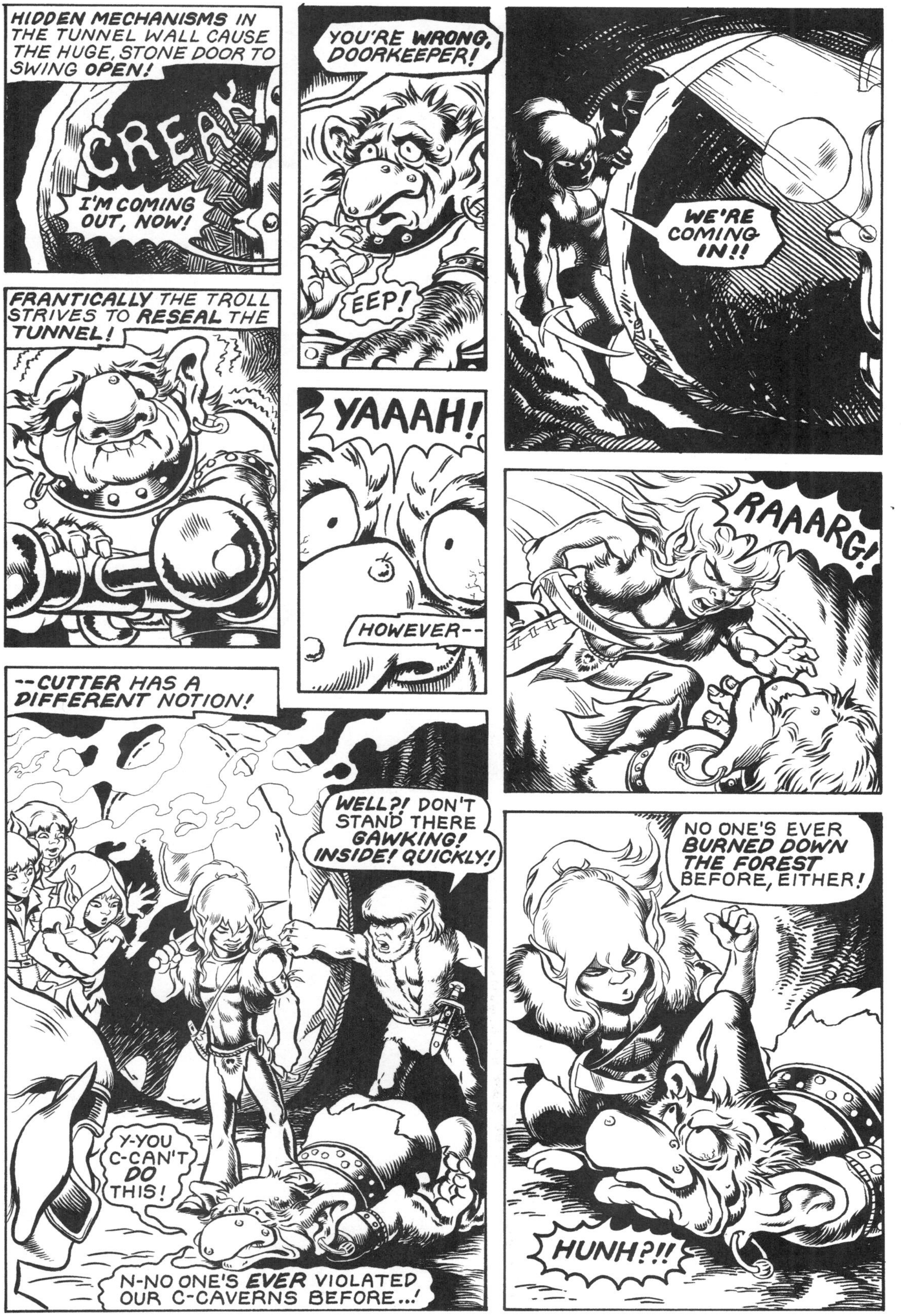
HIDDEN MECHANISMS IN THE TUNNEL WALL CAUSE THE HUGE, STONE DOOR TO SWING OPEN!
CREAK!
I'M COMING OUT, NOW!
YOU'RE WRONG, DOORKEEPER!
EEP!
WE'RE COMING IN!!
FRANTICALLY THE TROLL STRIVES TO RESEAL THE TUNNEL!
YAAAH!
HOWEVER--
RAAARG!
--CUTTER HAS A DIFFERENT NOTION!
WELL?! DON'T STAND THERE GAWKING! INSIDE! QUICKLY!
Y-YOU C-CAN'T DO THIS!
N-NO ONE'S EVER VIOLATED OUR C-CAVERNS BEFORE..!
NO ONE'S EVER BURNED DOWN THE FOREST BEFORE, EITHER!
HUNH?!!

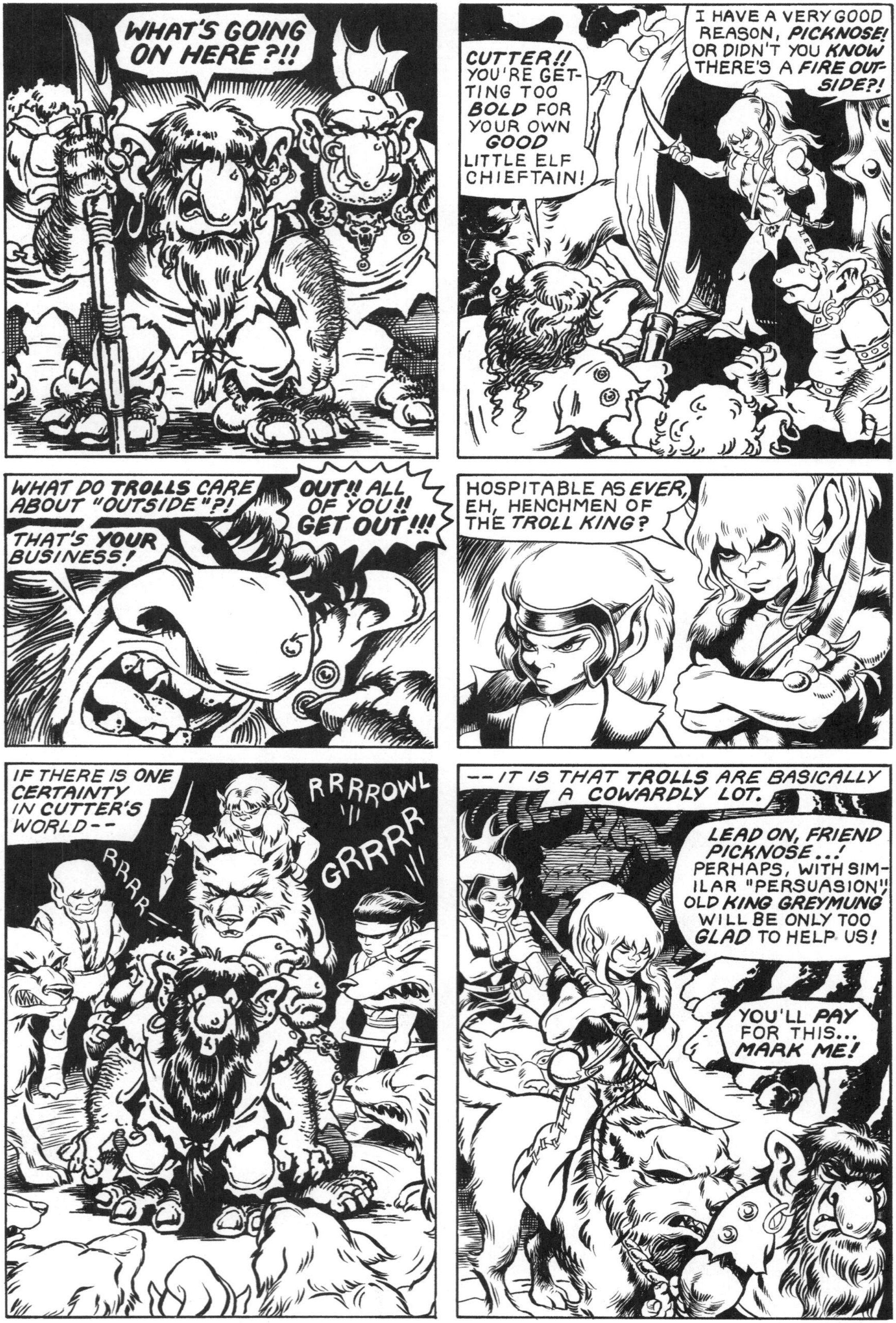

WHAT'S GOING ON HERE?!!
CUTTER!! YOU'RE GETTING TOO BOLD FOR YOUR OWN GOOD LITTLE ELF CHIEFTAIN!
I HAVE A VERY GOOD REASON, PICKNOSE! OR DIDN'T YOU KNOW THERE'S A FIRE OUTSIDE?!
WHAT DO TROLLS CARE ABOUT "OUTSIDE"?!
THAT'S YOUR BUSINESS!
OUT!! ALL OF YOU!! GET OUT!!!
HOSPITABLE AS EVER, EH, HENCHMEN OF THE TROLL KING?
IF THERE IS ONE CERTAINTY IN CUTTER'S WORLD--
RRRROWL
RRRR
GRRRR
--IT IS THAT TROLLS ARE BASICALLY A COWARDLY LOT.
LEAD ON, FRIEND PICKNOSE...! PERHAPS, WITH SIMILAR "PERSUASION", OLD KING GREYMUNG WILL BE ONLY TOO GLAD TO HELP US!
YOU'LL PAY FOR THIS... MARK ME!

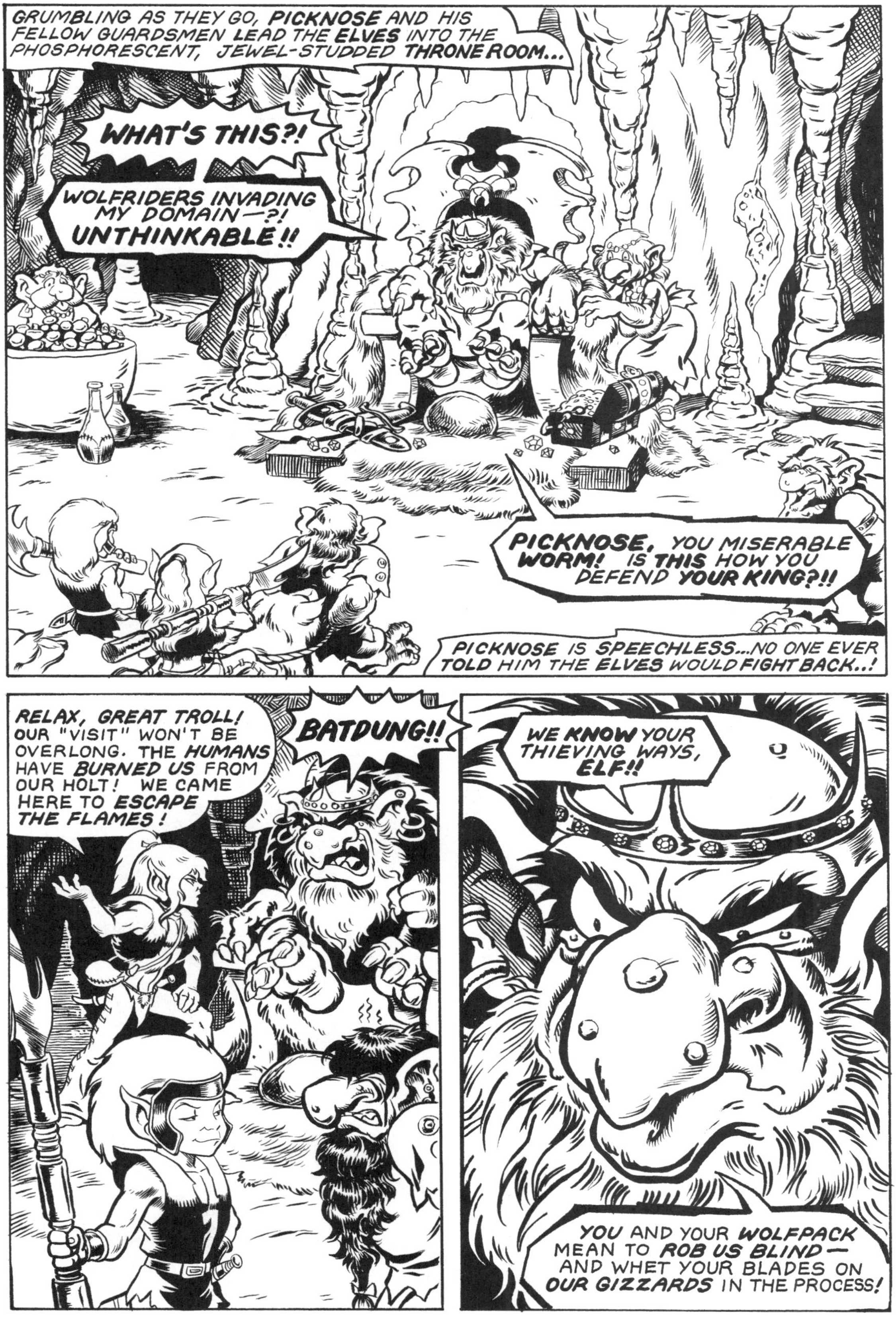
GRUMBLING AS THEY GO, PICKNOSE AND HIS FELLOW GUARDSMEN LEAD THE ELVES INTO THE PHOSPHORESCENT, JEWEL-STUDDED THRONE ROOM...
WHAT'S THIS?!
WOLFRIDERS INVADING MY DOMAIN—?! UNTHINKABLE!!
PICKNOSE, YOU MISERABLE WORM! IS THIS HOW YOU DEFEND YOUR KING?!!
PICKNOSE IS SPEECHLESS...NO ONE EVER TOLD HIM THE ELVES WOULD FIGHT BACK..!
RELAX, GREAT TROLL! OUR "VISIT" WON'T BE OVERLONG. THE HUMANS HAVE BURNED US FROM OUR HOLT! WE CAME HERE TO ESCAPE THE FLAMES!
BATDUNG!!
WE KNOW YOUR THIEVING WAYS, ELF!!
YOU AND YOUR WOLFPACK MEAN TO ROB US BLIND— AND WHET YOUR BLADES ON OUR GIZZARDS IN THE PROCESS!

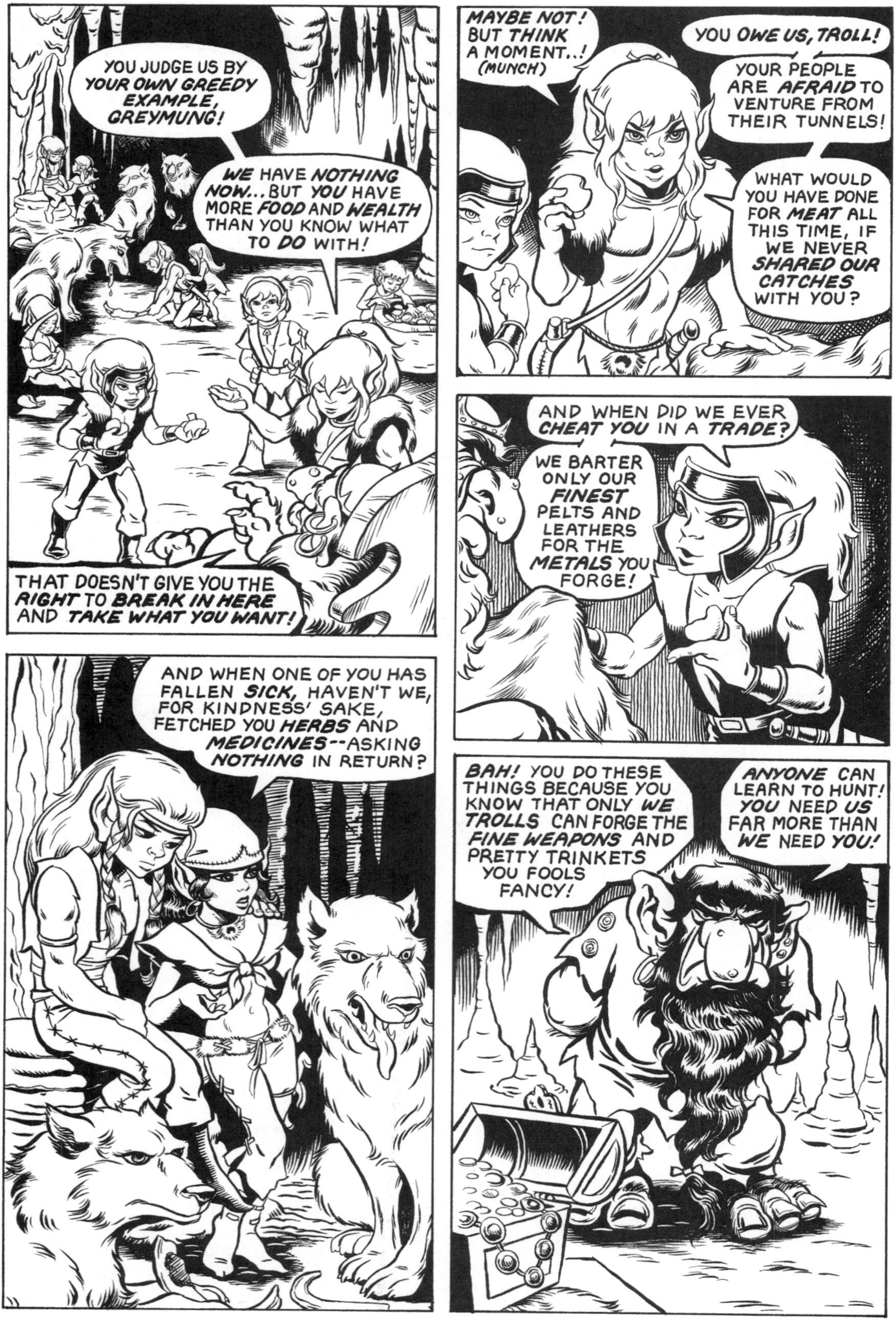
YOU JUDGE US BY YOUR OWN GREEDY EXAMPLE, GREYMUNG!
WE HAVE NOTHING NOW... BUT YOU HAVE MORE FOOD AND WEALTH THAN YOU KNOW WHAT TO DO WITH!
THAT DOESN'T GIVE YOU THE RIGHT TO BREAK IN HERE AND TAKE WHAT YOU WANT!
MAYBE NOT! BUT THINK A MOMENT..! (MUNCH)
YOU OWE US, TROLL!
YOUR PEOPLE ARE AFRAID TO VENTURE FROM THEIR TUNNELS!
WHAT WOULD YOU HAVE DONE FOR MEAT ALL THIS TIME, IF WE NEVER SHARED OUR CATCHES WITH YOU?
AND WHEN DID WE EVER CHEAT YOU IN A TRADE?
WE BARTER ONLY OUR FINEST PELTS AND LEATHERS FOR THE METALS YOU FORGE!
AND WHEN ONE OF YOU HAS FALLEN SICK, HAVEN'T WE, FOR KINDNESS' SAKE, FETCHED YOU HERBS AND MEDICINES--ASKING NOTHING IN RETURN?
BAH! YOU DO THESE THINGS BECAUSE YOU KNOW THAT ONLY WE TROLLS CAN FORGE THE FINE WEAPONS AND PRETTY TRINKETS YOU FOOLS FANCY!
ANYONE CAN LEARN TO HUNT! YOU NEED US FAR MORE THAN WE NEED YOU!

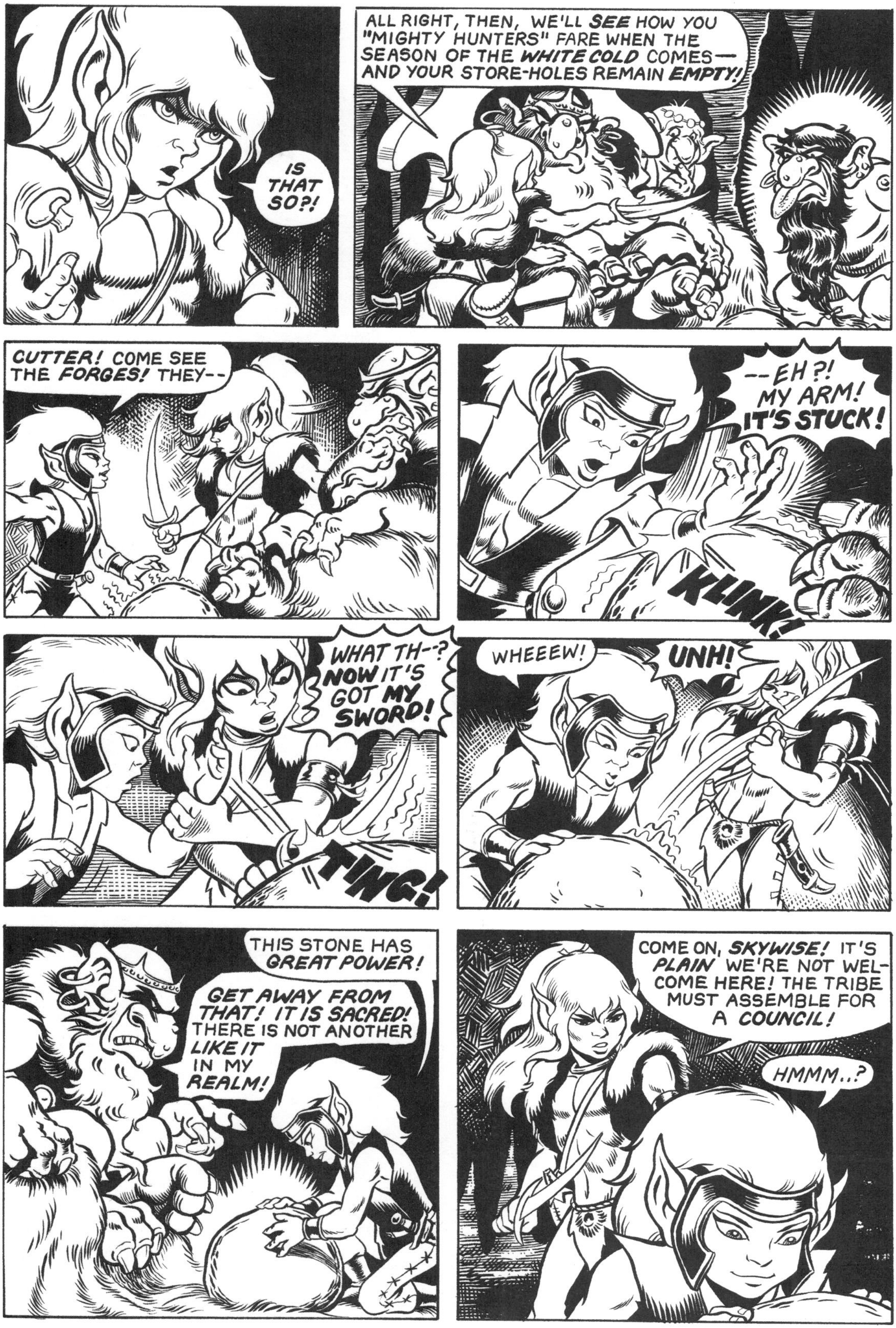
IS THAT SO?!
ALL RIGHT, THEN, WE'LL SEE HOW YOU "MIGHTY HUNTERS" FARE WHEN THE SEASON OF THE WHITE COLD COMES— AND YOUR STORE-HOLES REMAIN EMPTY!
CUTTER! COME SEE THE FORGES! THEY--
--EH?! MY ARM! IT'S STUCK!
KLINK!
WHAT TH--? NOW IT'S GOT MY SWORD!
TING!
WHEEEW!
UNH!
THIS STONE HAS GREAT POWER!
GET AWAY FROM THAT! IT IS SACRED! THERE IS NOT ANOTHER LIKE IT IN MY REALM!
COME ON, SKYWISE! IT'S PLAIN WE'RE NOT WEL-COME HERE! THE TRIBE MUST ASSEMBLE FOR A COUNCIL!
HMMM..?

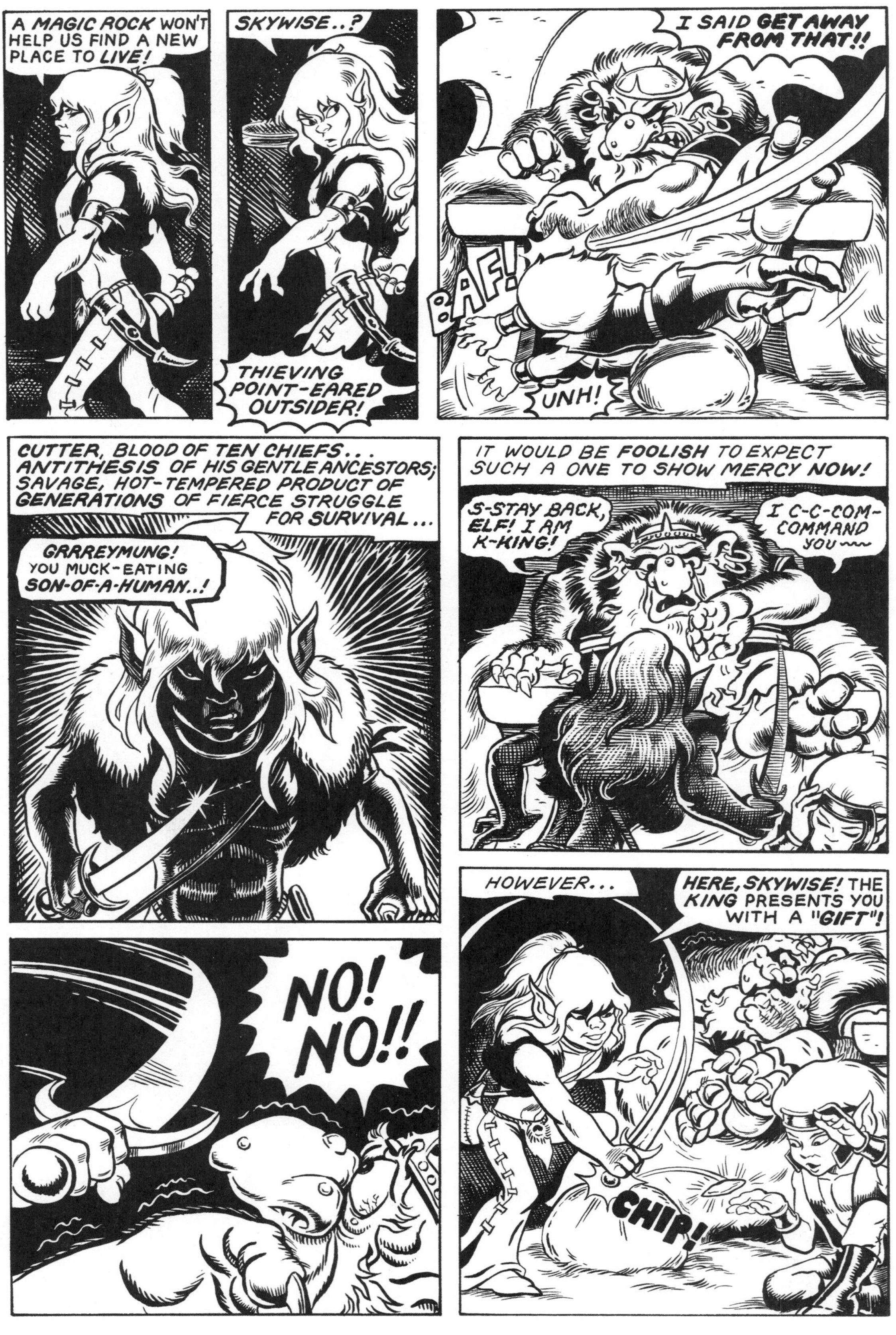
A MAGIC ROCK WON'T HELP US FIND A NEW PLACE TO LIVE!
SKYWISE..?
THIEVING POINT-EARED OUTSIDER!
I SAID GET AWAY FROM THAT!!
BAF!
UNH!
CUTTER, BLOOD OF TEN CHIEFS... ANTITHESIS OF HIS GENTLE ANCESTORS; SAVAGE, HOT-TEMPERED PRODUCT OF GENERATIONS OF FIERCE STRUGGLE FOR SURVIVAL...
GRRREYMUNG! YOU MUCK-EATING SON-OF-A-HUMAN..!
IT WOULD BE FOOLISH TO EXPECT SUCH A ONE TO SHOW MERCY NOW!
S-STAY BACK, ELF! I AM K-KING!
I C-C-COM-COMMAND YOU~~~
NO! NO!!
HOWEVER...
HERE, SKYWISE! THE KING PRESENTS YOU WITH A "GIFT"!
CHIP!

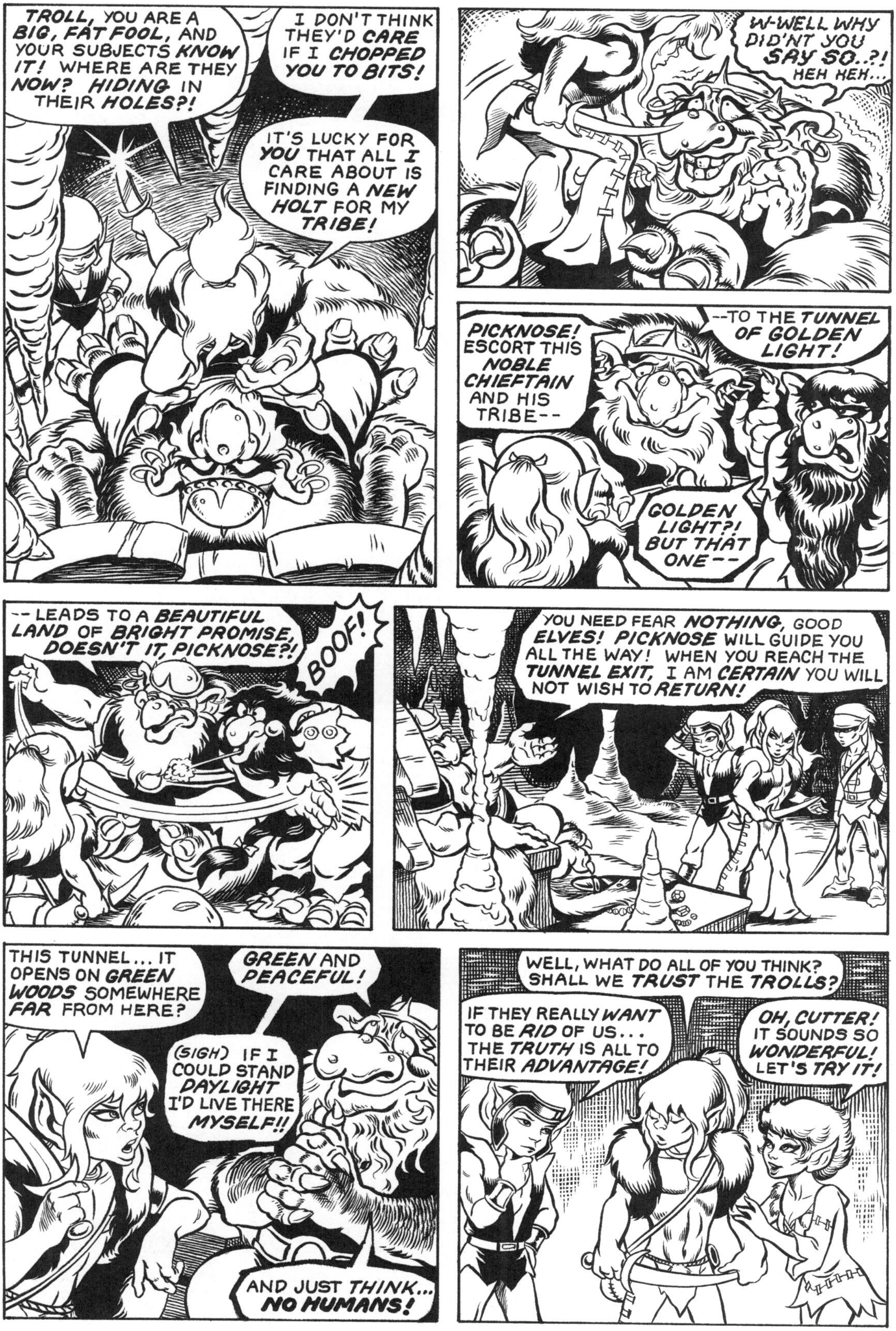
TROLL, YOU ARE A BIG, FAT FOOL, AND YOUR SUBJECTS KNOW IT! WHERE ARE THEY NOW? HIDING IN THEIR HOLES?!
I DON'T THINK THEY'D CARE IF I CHOPPED YOU TO BITS!
IT'S LUCKY FOR YOU THAT ALL I CARE ABOUT IS FINDING A NEW HOLT FOR MY TRIBE!
W-WELL WHY DID'NT YOU SAY SO..?! HEH HEH...
PICKNOSE! ESCORT THIS NOBLE CHIEFTAIN AND HIS TRIBE--
--TO THE TUNNEL OF GOLDEN LIGHT!
GOLDEN LIGHT?! BUT THAT ONE--
--LEADS TO A BEAUTIFUL LAND OF BRIGHT PROMISE, DOESN'T IT, PICKNOSE?!
BOOF!
YOU NEED FEAR NOTHING, GOOD ELVES! PICKNOSE WILL GUIDE YOU ALL THE WAY! WHEN YOU REACH THE TUNNEL EXIT, I AM CERTAIN YOU WILL NOT WISH TO RETURN!
THIS TUNNEL... IT OPENS ON GREEN WOODS SOMEWHERE FAR FROM HERE?
GREEN AND PEACEFUL!
(SIGH) IF I COULD STAND DAYLIGHT I'D LIVE THERE MYSELF!!
AND JUST THINK... NO HUMANS!
WELL, WHAT DO ALL OF YOU THINK? SHALL WE TRUST THE TROLLS?
IF THEY REALLY WANT TO BE RID OF US... THE TRUTH IS ALL TO THEIR ADVANTAGE!
OH, CUTTER! IT SOUNDS SO WONDERFUL! LET'S TRY IT!

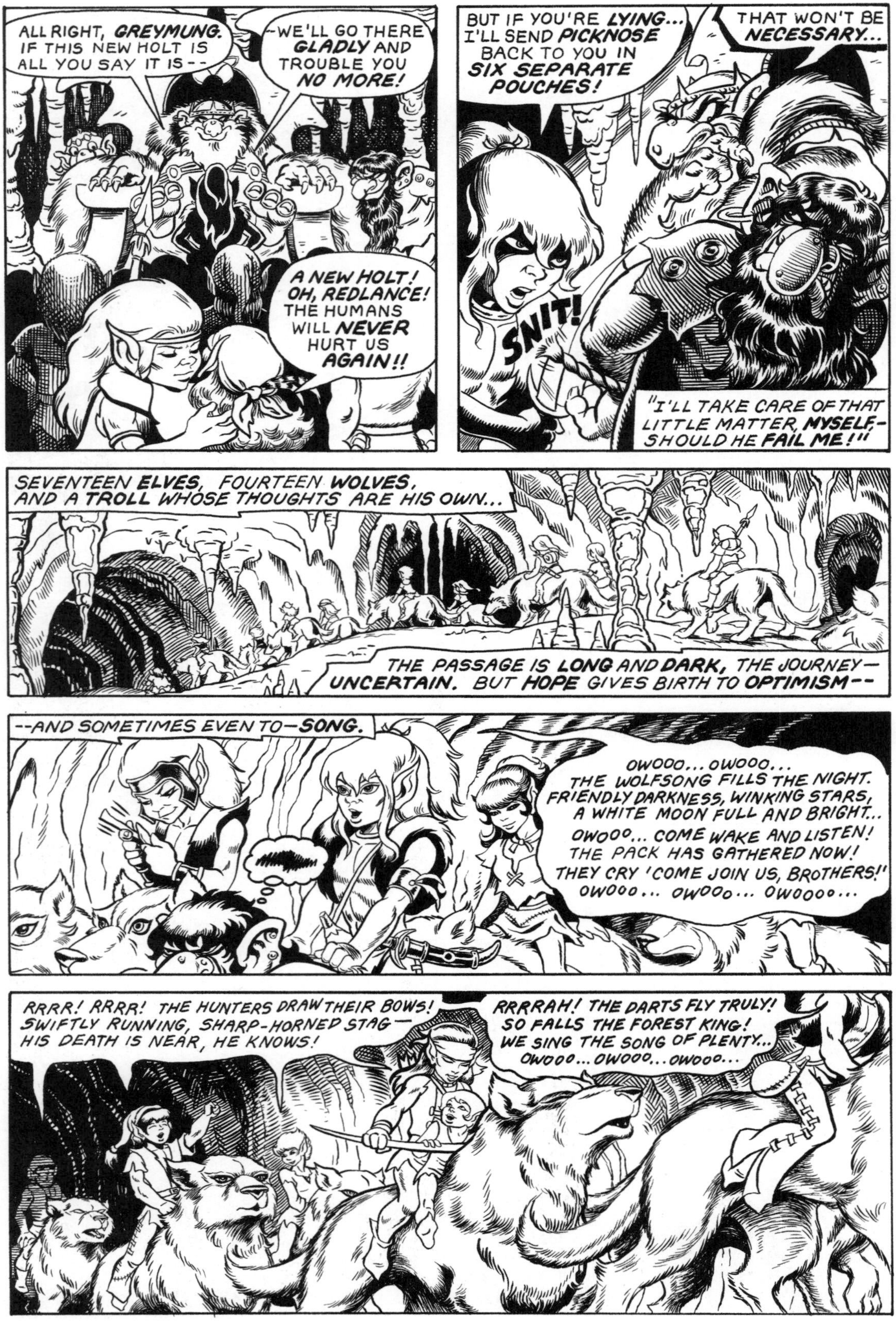
ALL RIGHT, GREYMUNG. IF THIS NEW HOLT IS ALL YOU SAY IT IS--
-WE'LL GO THERE GLADLY AND TROUBLE YOU NO MORE!
A NEW HOLT! OH, REDLANCE! THE HUMANS WILL NEVER HURT US AGAIN!!
BUT IF YOU'RE LYING... I'LL SEND PICKNOSE BACK TO YOU IN SIX SEPARATE POUCHES!
THAT WON'T BE NECESSARY...
SNIT!
"I'LL TAKE CARE OF THAT LITTLE MATTER, MYSELF-SHOULD HE FAIL ME!"
SEVENTEEN ELVES, FOURTEEN WOLVES, AND A TROLL WHOSE THOUGHTS ARE HIS OWN...
THE PASSAGE IS LONG AND DARK, THE JOURNEY—UNCERTAIN. BUT HOPE GIVES BIRTH TO OPTIMISM--
--AND SOMETIMES EVEN TO—SONG.
OWOOO... OWOOO... THE WOLFSONG FILLS THE NIGHT. FRIENDLY DARKNESS, WINKING STARS, A WHITE MOON FULL AND BRIGHT... OWOOO... COME WAKE AND LISTEN! THE PACK HAS GATHERED NOW! THEY CRY 'COME JOIN US, BROTHERS!' OWOOO... OWOOO... OWOOOO...
RRRR! RRRR! THE HUNTERS DRAW THEIR BOWS! SWIFTLY RUNNING, SHARP-HORNED STAG— HIS DEATH IS NEAR, HE KNOWS!
RRRRAH! THE DARTS FLY TRULY! SO FALLS THE FOREST KING! WE SING THE SONG OF PLENTY... OWOOO... OWOOO... OWOOO...

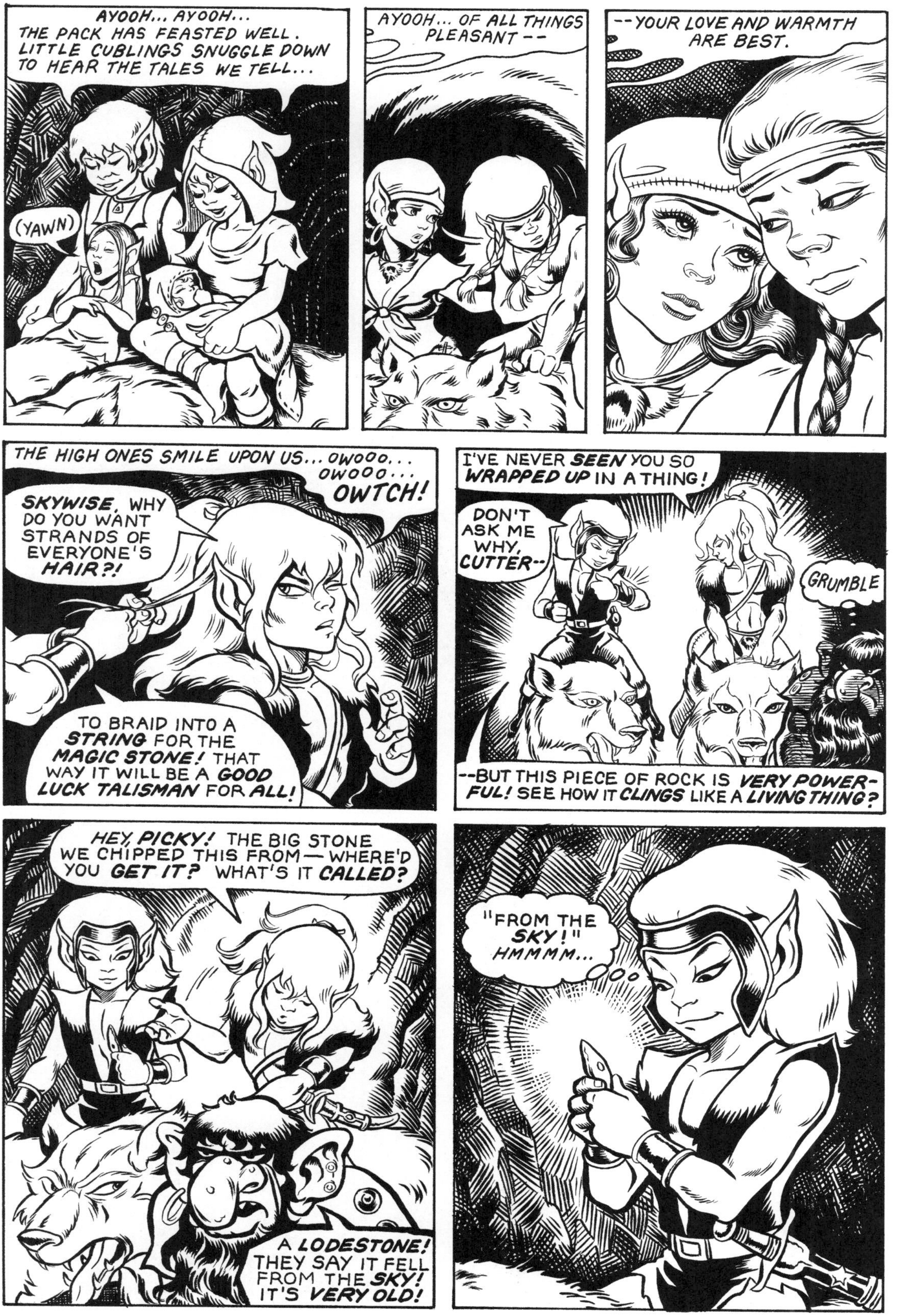

AYOOH... AYOOH... THE PACK HAS FEASTED WELL. LITTLE CUBLINGS SNUGGLE DOWN TO HEAR THE TALES WE TELL...
(YAWN)
AYOOH... OF ALL THINGS PLEASANT --
-- YOUR LOVE AND WARMTH ARE BEST.
THE HIGH ONES SMILE UPON US... OWOOO... OWOOO... OWTCH!
SKYWISE, WHY DO YOU WANT STRANDS OF EVERYONE'S HAIR?!
TO BRAID INTO A STRING FOR THE MAGIC STONE! THAT WAY IT WILL BE A GOOD LUCK TALISMAN FOR ALL!
I'VE NEVER SEEN YOU SO WRAPPED UP IN A THING!
DON'T ASK ME WHY, CUTTER--
GRUMBLE
--BUT THIS PIECE OF ROCK IS VERY POWERFUL! SEE HOW IT CLINGS LIKE A LIVING THING?
HEY, PICKY! THE BIG STONE WE CHIPPED THIS FROM— WHERE'D YOU GET IT? WHAT'S IT CALLED?
A LODESTONE! THEY SAY IT FELL FROM THE SKY! IT'S VERY OLD!
"FROM THE SKY!" HMMMM...

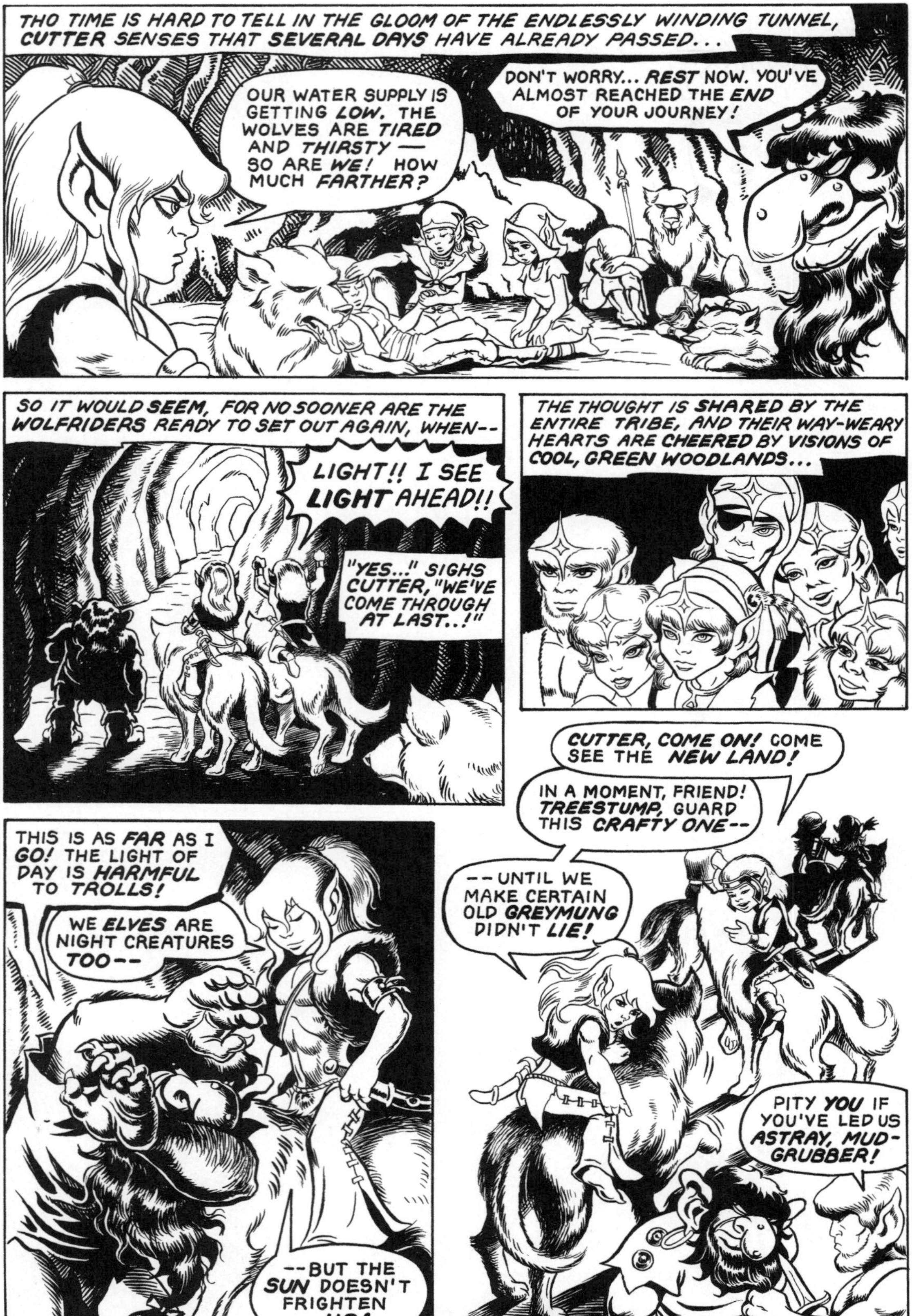
THO TIME IS HARD TO TELL IN THE GLOOM OF THE ENDLESSLY WINDING TUNNEL, CUTTER SENSES THAT SEVERAL DAYS HAVE ALREADY PASSED...
OUR WATER SUPPLY IS GETTING LOW. THE WOLVES ARE TIRED AND THIRSTY — SO ARE WE! HOW MUCH FARTHER?
DON'T WORRY... REST NOW. YOU'VE ALMOST REACHED THE END OF YOUR JOURNEY!
SO IT WOULD SEEM, FOR NO SOONER ARE THE WOLFRIDERS READY TO SET OUT AGAIN, WHEN--
LIGHT!! I SEE LIGHT AHEAD!!
"YES..." SIGHS CUTTER, "WE'VE COME THROUGH AT LAST..!"
THE THOUGHT IS SHARED BY THE ENTIRE TRIBE, AND THEIR WAY-WEARY HEARTS ARE CHEERED BY VISIONS OF COOL, GREEN WOODLANDS...
THIS IS AS FAR AS I GO! THE LIGHT OF DAY IS HARMFUL TO TROLLS!
WE ELVES ARE NIGHT CREATURES TOO--
--BUT THE SUN DOESN'T FRIGHTEN US!
CUTTER, COME ON! COME SEE THE NEW LAND!
IN A MOMENT, FRIEND! TREESTUMP, GUARD THIS CRAFTY ONE--
--UNTIL WE MAKE CERTAIN OLD GREYMUNG DIDN'T LIE!
PITY YOU IF YOU'VE LED US ASTRAY, MUD-GRUBBER!

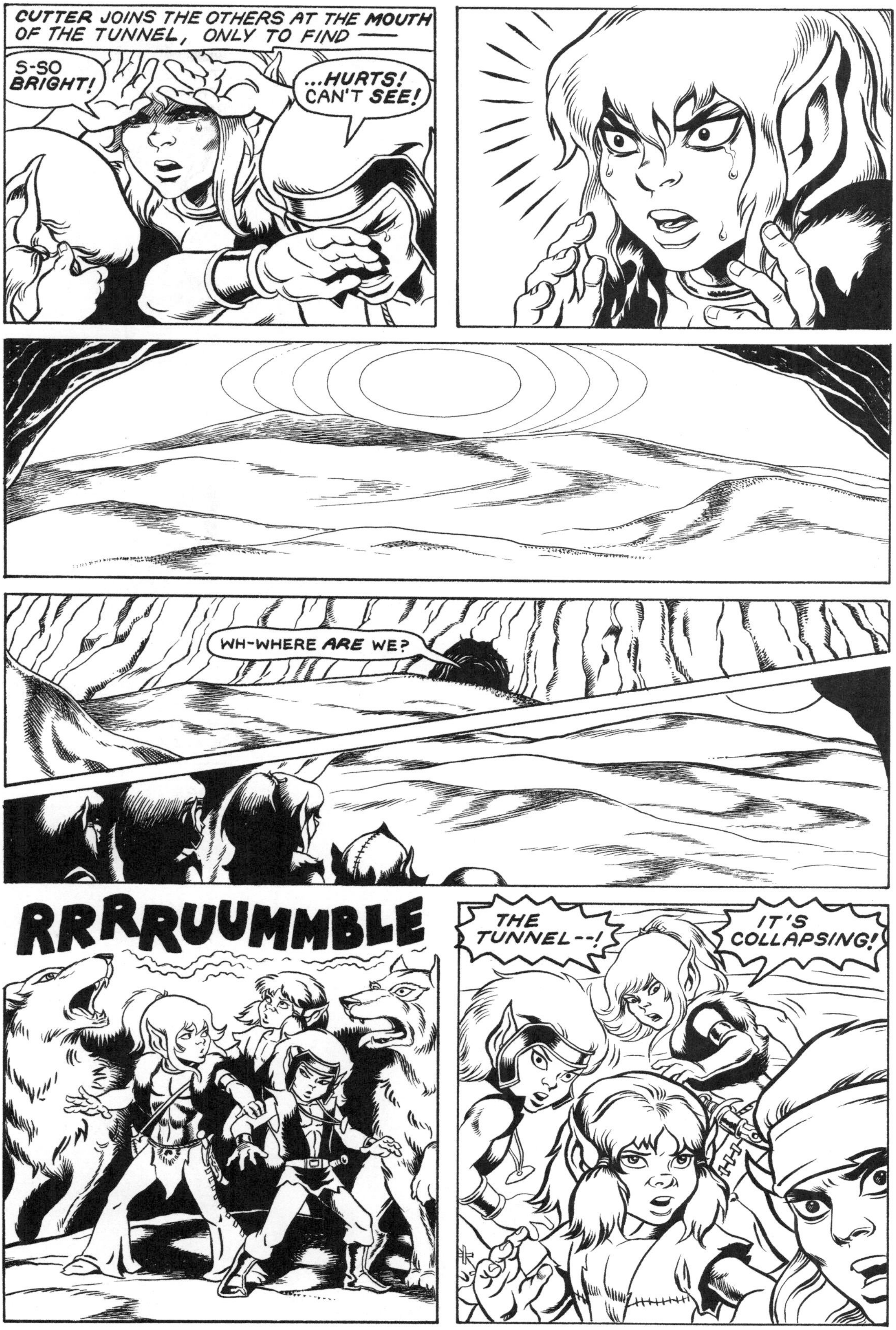
CUTTER JOINS THE OTHERS AT THE MOUTH OF THE TUNNEL, ONLY TO FIND —
S-SO BRIGHT!
...HURTS! CAN'T SEE!
WH-WHERE ARE WE?
RRRRUUMMBLE
THE TUNNEL--!
IT'S COLLAPSING!

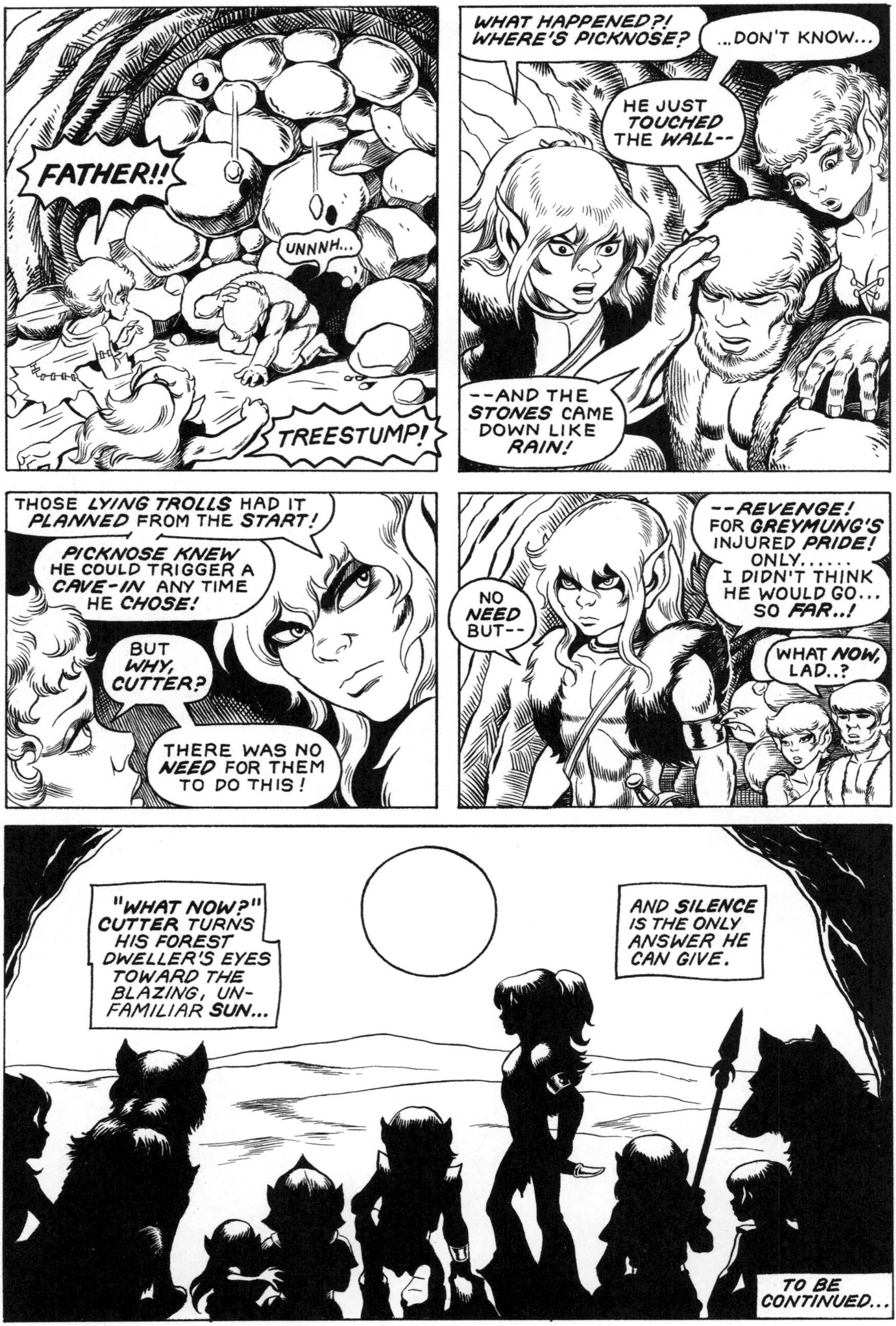
FATHER!!
UNNNH...
TREESTUMP!
WHAT HAPPENED?! WHERE'S PICKNOSE?
...DON'T KNOW...
HE JUST TOUCHED THE WALL--
--AND THE STONES CAME DOWN LIKE RAIN!
THOSE LYING TROLLS HAD IT PLANNED FROM THE START!
PICKNOSE KNEW HE COULD TRIGGER A CAVE-IN ANY TIME HE CHOSE!
BUT WHY, CUTTER?
THERE WAS NO NEED FOR THEM TO DO THIS!
NO NEED BUT--
--REVENGE! FOR GREYMUNG'S INJURED PRIDE! ONLY...... I DIDN'T THINK HE WOULD GO... SO FAR..!
WHAT NOW, LAD..?
"WHAT NOW?" CUTTER TURNS HIS FOREST DWELLER'S EYES TOWARD THE BLAZING, UN-FAMILIAR SUN...
AND SILENCE IS THE ONLY ANSWER HE CAN GIVE.
TO BE CONTINUED...

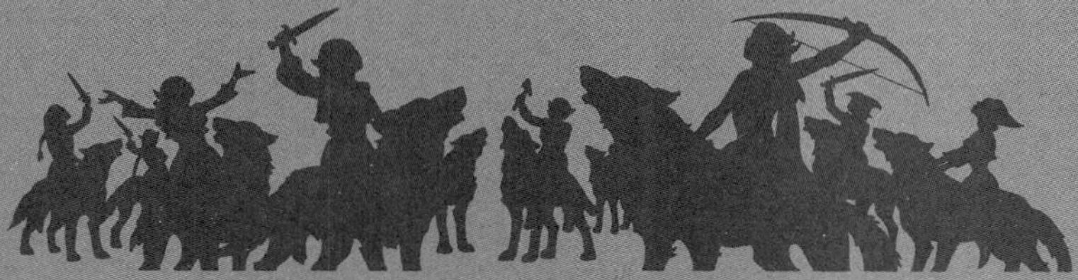

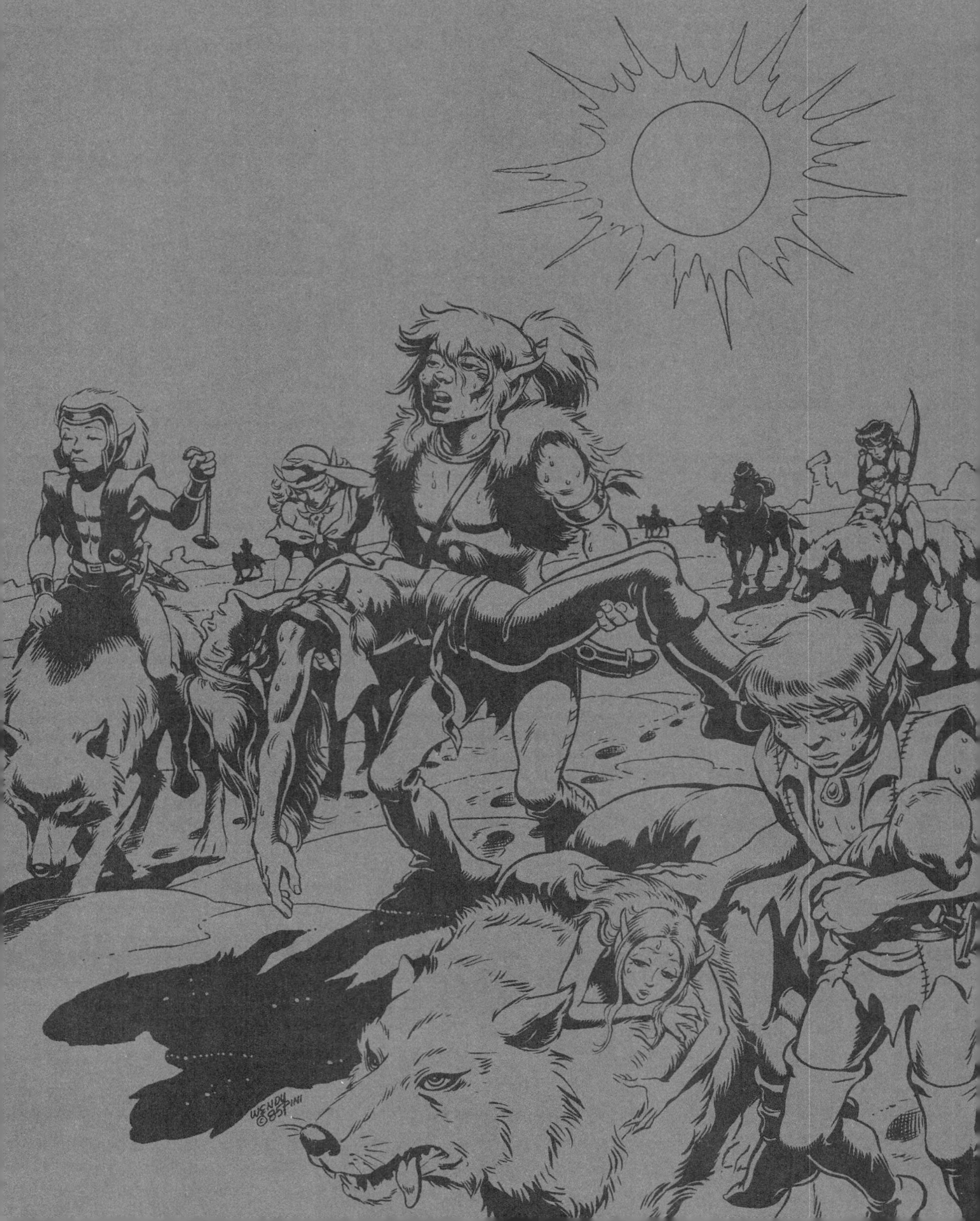
WENDY ©85 PINI

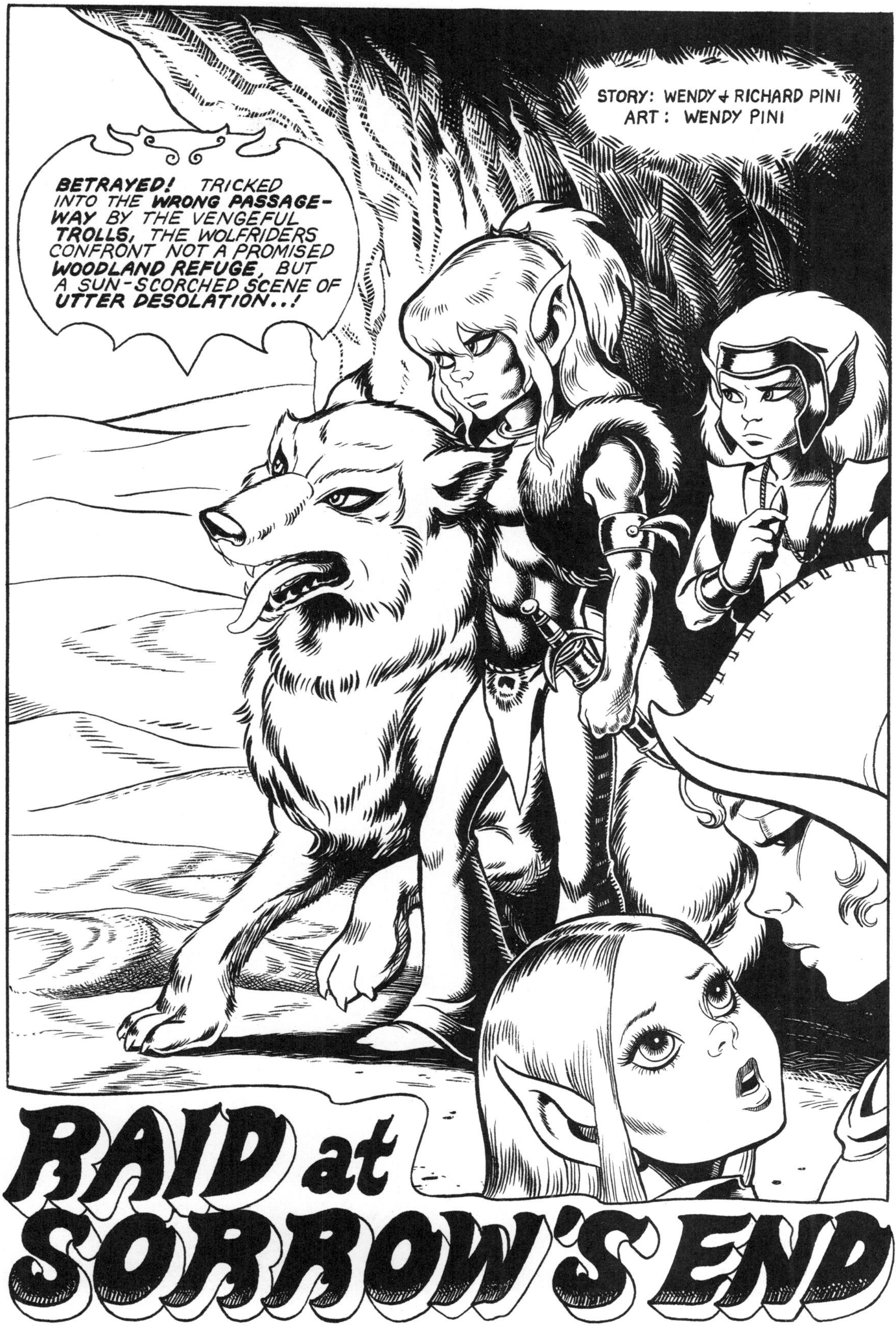
STORY: WENDY & RICHARD PINI
ART: WENDY PINI
BETRAYED! TRICKED INTO THE WRONG PASSAGEWAY BY THE VENGEFUL TROLLS, THE WOLFRIDERS CONFRONT NOT A PROMISED WOODLAND REFUGE, BUT A SUN-SCORCHED SCENE OF UTTER DESOLATION..!
RAID at SORROW'S END

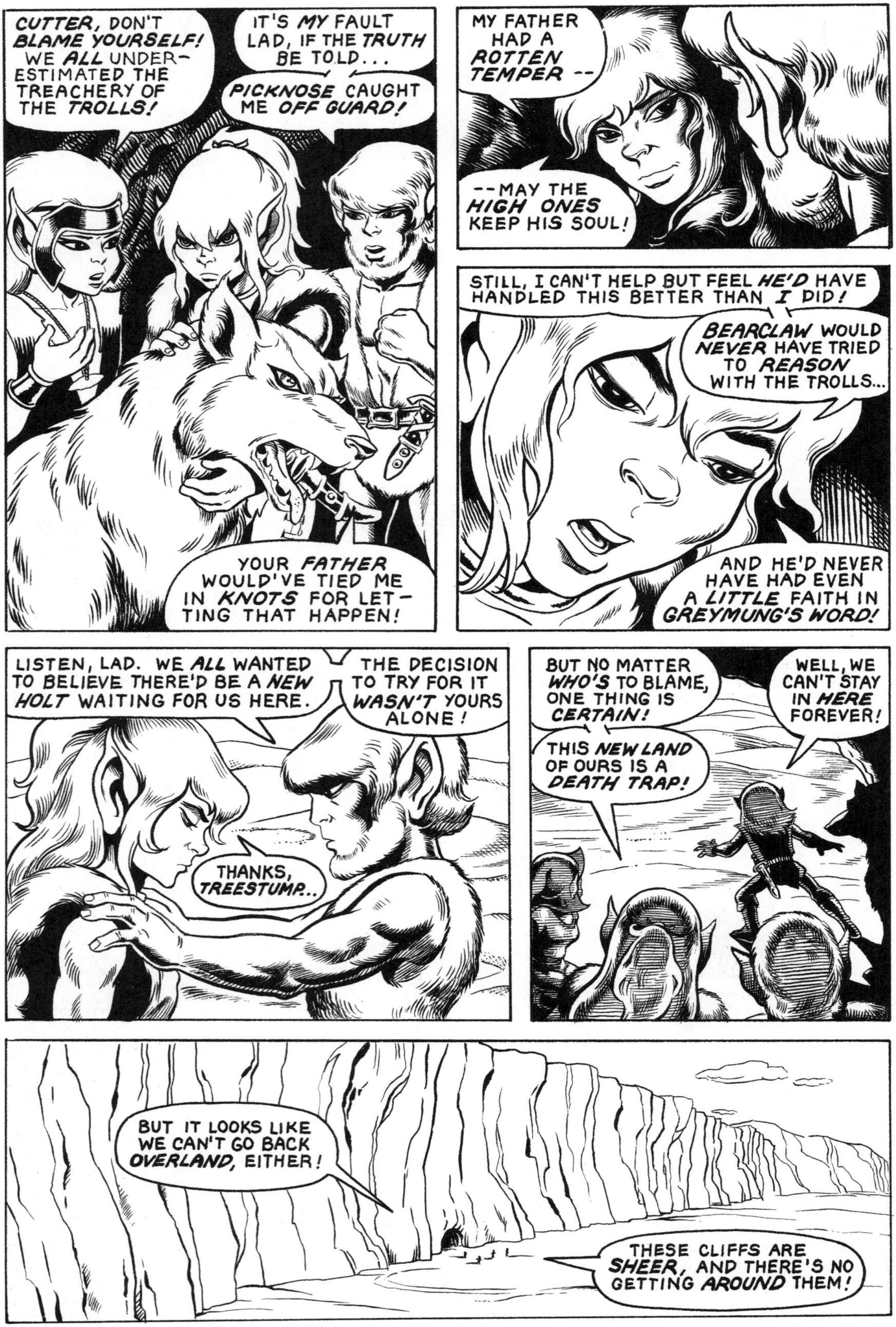
CUTTER, DON'T BLAME YOURSELF! WE ALL UNDER-ESTIMATED THE TREACHERY OF THE TROLLS!
IT'S MY FAULT LAD, IF THE TRUTH BE TOLD...
PICKNOSE CAUGHT ME OFF GUARD!
YOUR FATHER WOULD'VE TIED ME IN KNOTS FOR LET-TING THAT HAPPEN!
MY FATHER HAD A ROTTEN TEMPER --
--MAY THE HIGH ONES KEEP HIS SOUL!
STILL, I CAN'T HELP BUT FEEL HE'D HAVE HANDLED THIS BETTER THAN I DID!
BEARCLAW WOULD NEVER HAVE TRIED TO REASON WITH THE TROLLS...
AND HE'D NEVER HAVE HAD EVEN A LITTLE FAITH IN GREYMUNG'S WORD!
LISTEN, LAD. WE ALL WANTED TO BELIEVE THERE'D BE A NEW HOLT WAITING FOR US HERE.
THE DECISION TO TRY FOR IT WASN'T YOURS ALONE!
THANKS, TREESTUMP...
BUT NO MATTER WHO'S TO BLAME, ONE THING IS CERTAIN!
THIS NEW LAND OF OURS IS A DEATH TRAP!
WELL, WE CAN'T STAY IN HERE FOREVER!
BUT IT LOOKS LIKE WE CAN'T GO BACK OVERLAND, EITHER!
THESE CLIFFS ARE SHEER, AND THERE'S NO GETTING AROUND THEM!

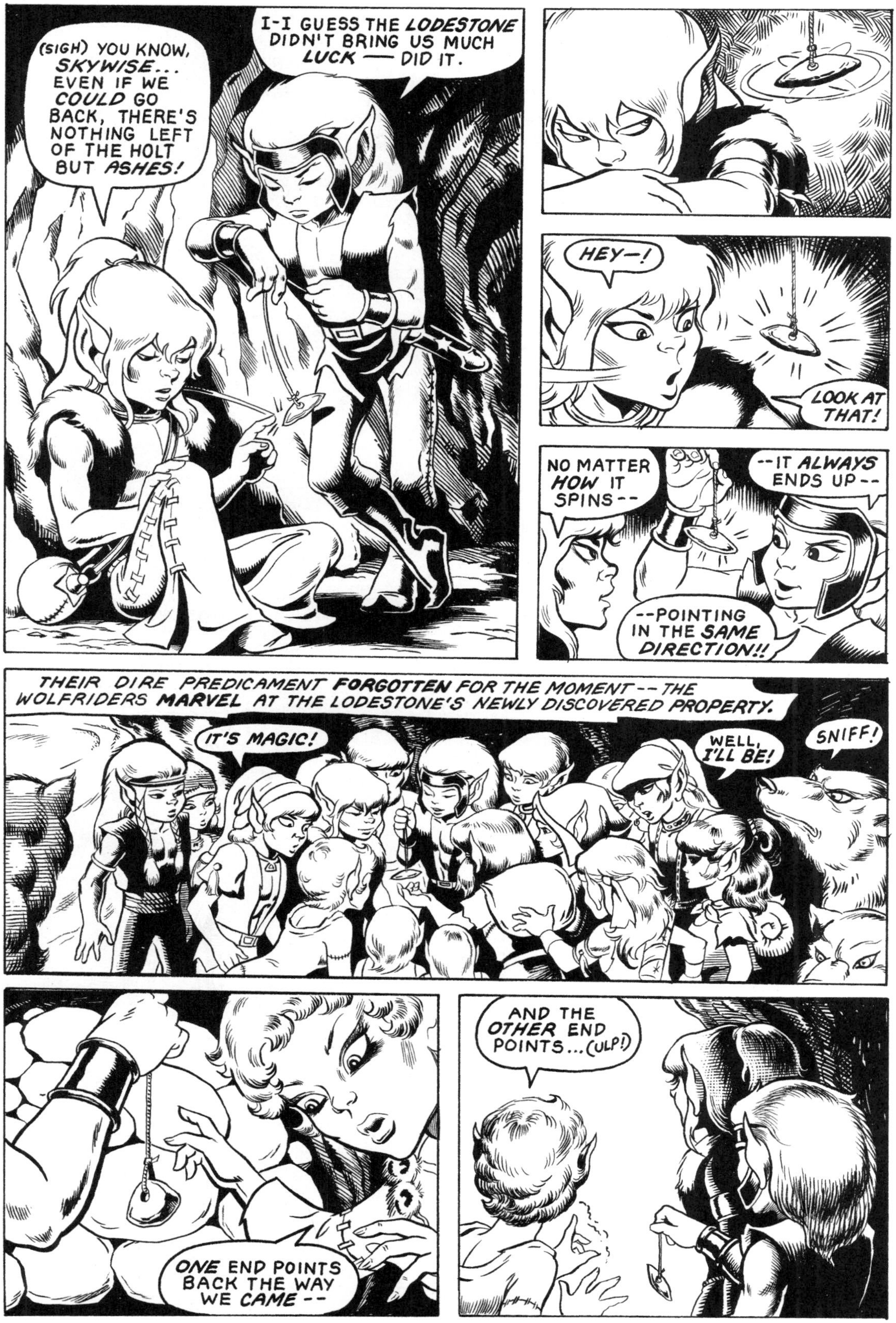

(SIGH) YOU KNOW, SKYWISE... EVEN IF WE COULD GO BACK, THERE'S NOTHING LEFT OF THE HOLT BUT ASHES!
I-I GUESS THE LODESTONE DIDN'T BRING US MUCH LUCK — DID IT.
HEY—!
LOOK AT THAT!
NO MATTER HOW IT SPINS--
--IT ALWAYS ENDS UP--
--POINTING IN THE SAME DIRECTION!!
THEIR DIRE PREDICAMENT FORGOTTEN FOR THE MOMENT-- THE WOLFRIDERS MARVEL AT THE LODESTONE'S NEWLY DISCOVERED PROPERTY.
IT'S MAGIC!
WELL, I'LL BE!
SNIFF!
ONE END POINTS BACK THE WAY WE CAME--
AND THE OTHER END POINTS... (ULP!)

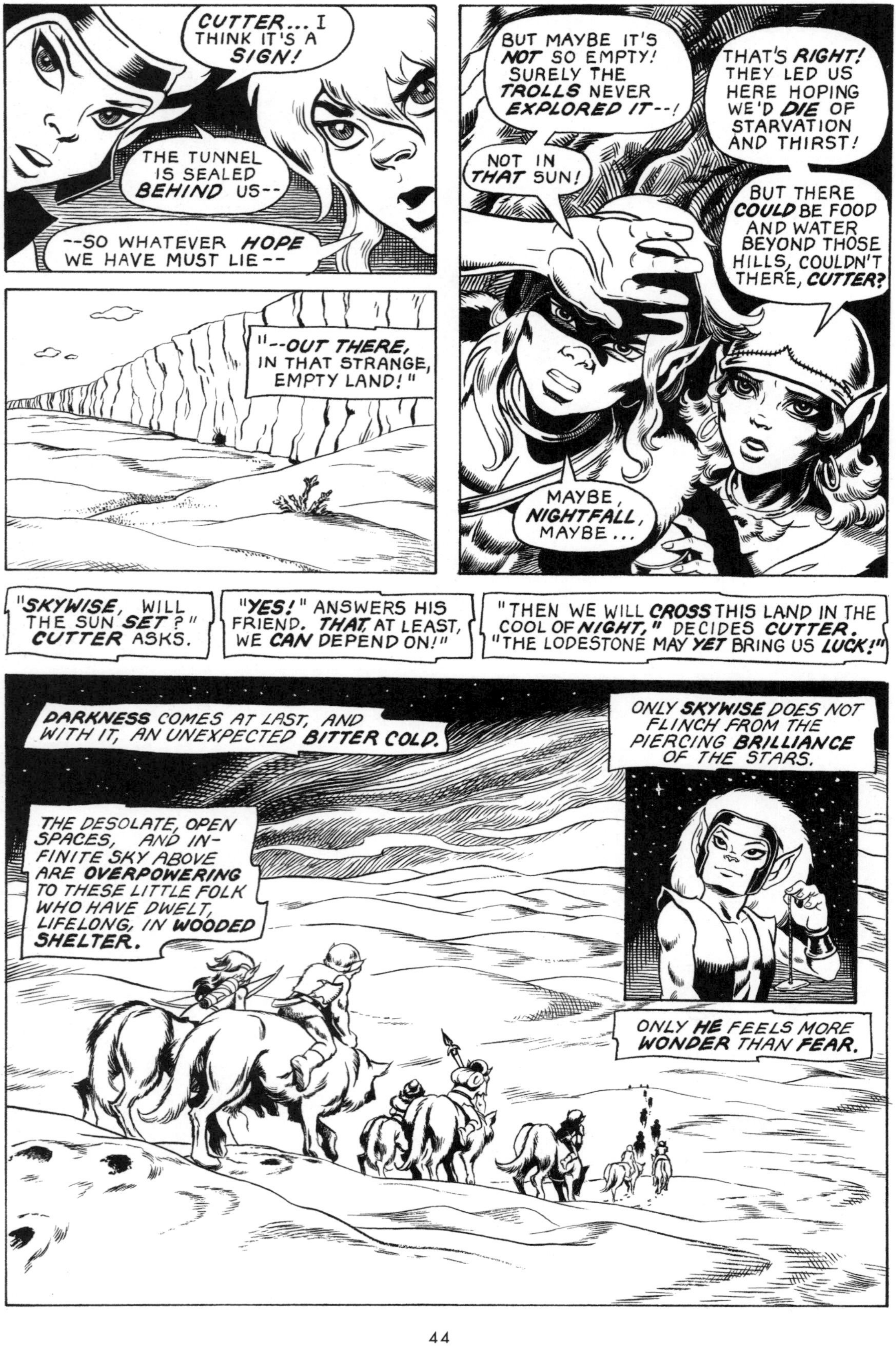
CUTTER... I THINK IT'S A SIGN!
THE TUNNEL IS SEALED BEHIND US--
--SO WHATEVER HOPE WE HAVE MUST LIE--
"--OUT THERE, IN THAT STRANGE, EMPTY LAND!"
BUT MAYBE IT'S NOT SO EMPTY! SURELY THE TROLLS NEVER EXPLORED IT--!
NOT IN THAT SUN!
THAT'S RIGHT! THEY LED US HERE HOPING WE'D DIE OF STARVATION AND THIRST!
BUT THERE COULD BE FOOD AND WATER BEYOND THOSE HILLS, COULDN'T THERE, CUTTER?
MAYBE, NIGHTFALL, MAYBE...
"SKYWISE, WILL THE SUN SET?" CUTTER ASKS.
"YES!" ANSWERS HIS FRIEND. THAT, AT LEAST, WE CAN DEPEND ON!"
"THEN WE WILL CROSS THIS LAND IN THE COOL OF NIGHT," DECIDES CUTTER. "THE LODESTONE MAY YET BRING US LUCK!"
DARKNESS COMES AT LAST, AND WITH IT, AN UNEXPECTED BITTER COLD.
ONLY SKYWISE DOES NOT FLINCH FROM THE PIERCING BRILLIANCE OF THE STARS.
THE DESOLATE, OPEN SPACES, AND INFINITE SKY ABOVE ARE OVERPOWERING TO THESE LITTLE FOLK WHO HAVE DWELT, LIFELONG, IN WOODED SHELTER.
ONLY HE FEELS MORE WONDER THAN FEAR.

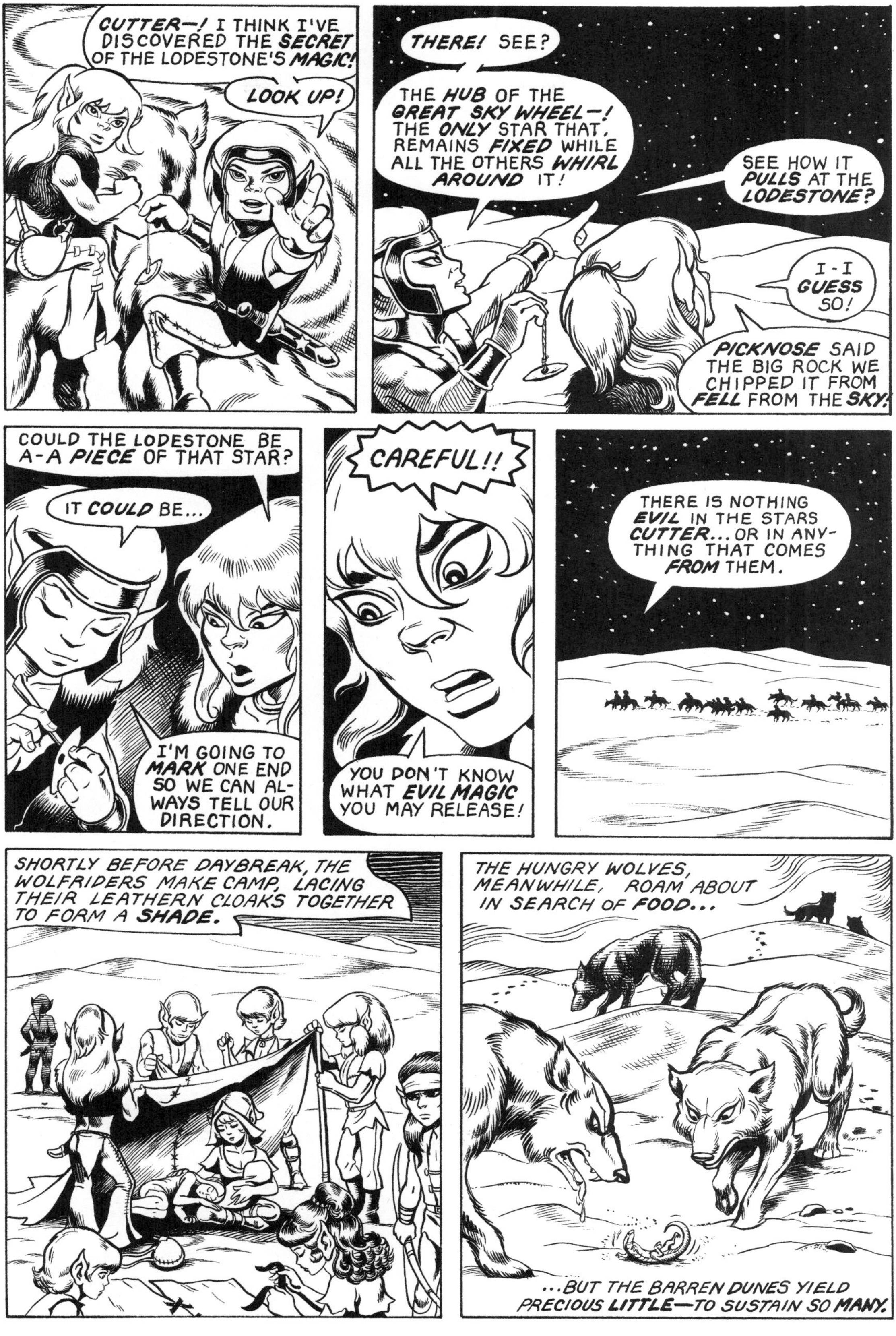
CUTTER—! I THINK I'VE DISCOVERED THE SECRET OF THE LODESTONE'S MAGIC!
LOOK UP!
THERE! SEE?
THE HUB OF THE GREAT SKY WHEEL—! THE ONLY STAR THAT, REMAINS FIXED WHILE ALL THE OTHERS WHIRL AROUND IT!
SEE HOW IT PULLS AT THE LODESTONE?
I-I GUESS SO!
PICKNOSE SAID THE BIG ROCK WE CHIPPED IT FROM FELL FROM THE SKY!
COULD THE LODESTONE BE A-A PIECE OF THAT STAR?
IT COULD BE...
I'M GOING TO MARK ONE END SO WE CAN ALWAYS TELL OUR DIRECTION.
CAREFUL!!
YOU DON'T KNOW WHAT EVIL MAGIC YOU MAY RELEASE!
THERE IS NOTHING EVIL IN THE STARS CUTTER... OR IN ANYTHING THAT COMES FROM THEM.
SHORTLY BEFORE DAYBREAK, THE WOLFRIDERS MAKE CAMP, LACING THEIR LEATHERN CLOAKS TOGETHER TO FORM A SHADE.
THE HUNGRY WOLVES, MEANWHILE, ROAM ABOUT IN SEARCH OF FOOD...
...BUT THE BARREN DUNES YIELD PRECIOUS LITTLE—TO SUSTAIN SO MANY.

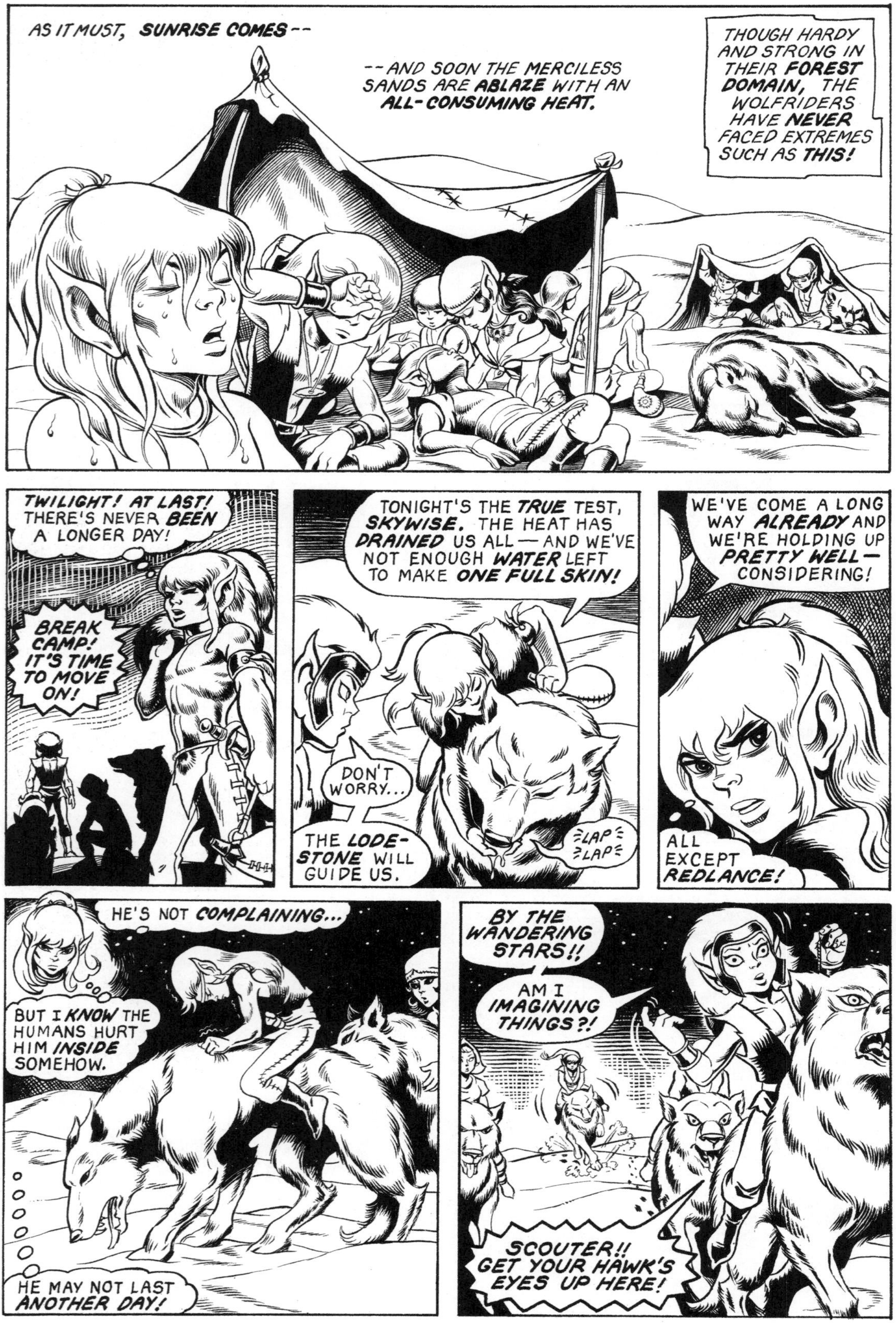

AS IT MUST, SUNRISE COMES --
-- AND SOON THE MERCILESS SANDS ARE ABLAZE WITH AN ALL-CONSUMING HEAT.
THOUGH HARDY AND STRONG IN THEIR FOREST DOMAIN, THE WOLFRIDERS HAVE NEVER FACED EXTREMES SUCH AS THIS!
TWILIGHT! AT LAST! THERE'S NEVER BEEN A LONGER DAY!
BREAK CAMP! IT'S TIME TO MOVE ON!
TONIGHT'S THE TRUE TEST, SKYWISE. THE HEAT HAS DRAINED US ALL — AND WE'VE NOT ENOUGH WATER LEFT TO MAKE ONE FULL SKIN!
DON'T WORRY...
THE LODE-STONE WILL GUIDE US.
LAP LAP
WE'VE COME A LONG WAY ALREADY AND WE'RE HOLDING UP PRETTY WELL — CONSIDERING!
ALL EXCEPT REDLANCE!
HE'S NOT COMPLAINING...
BUT I KNOW THE HUMANS HURT HIM INSIDE SOMEHOW.
HE MAY NOT LAST ANOTHER DAY!
BY THE WANDERING STARS!!
AM I IMAGINING THINGS?!
SCOUTER!! GET YOUR HAWK'S EYES UP HERE!

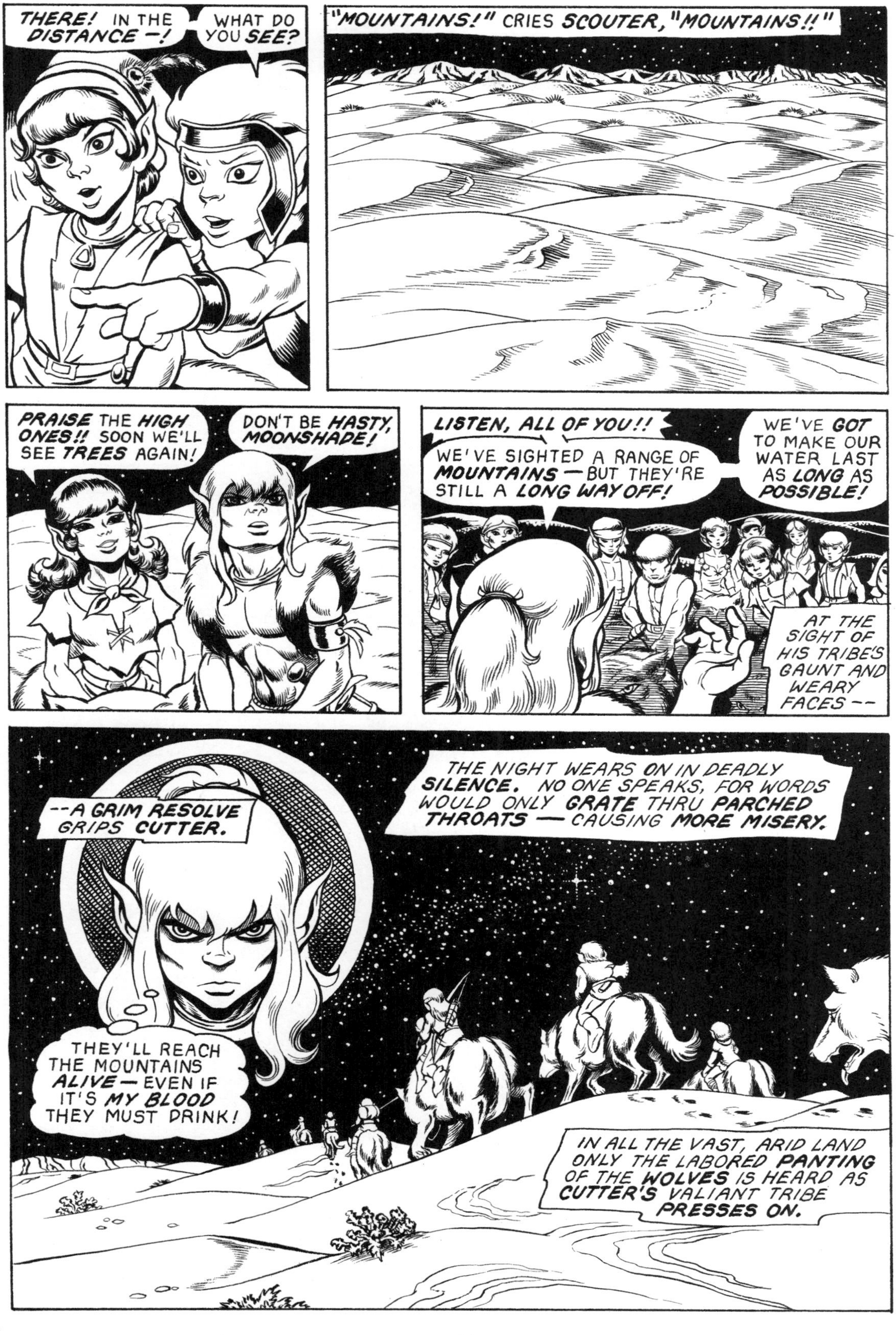
THERE! IN THE DISTANCE --!
WHAT DO YOU SEE?
"MOUNTAINS!" CRIES SCOUTER, "MOUNTAINS!!"
PRAISE THE HIGH ONES!! SOON WE'LL SEE TREES AGAIN!
DON'T BE HASTY, MOONSHADE!
LISTEN, ALL OF YOU!!
WE'VE SIGHTED A RANGE OF MOUNTAINS -- BUT THEY'RE STILL A LONG WAY OFF!
WE'VE GOT TO MAKE OUR WATER LAST AS LONG AS POSSIBLE!
AT THE SIGHT OF HIS TRIBE'S GAUNT AND WEARY FACES --
--A GRIM RESOLVE GRIPS CUTTER.
THE NIGHT WEARS ON IN DEADLY SILENCE. NO ONE SPEAKS, FOR WORDS WOULD ONLY GRATE THRU PARCHED THROATS -- CAUSING MORE MISERY.
THEY'LL REACH THE MOUNTAINS ALIVE -- EVEN IF IT'S MY BLOOD THEY MUST DRINK!
IN ALL THE VAST, ARID LAND ONLY THE LABORED PANTING OF THE WOLVES IS HEARD AS CUTTER'S VALIANT TRIBE PRESSES ON.

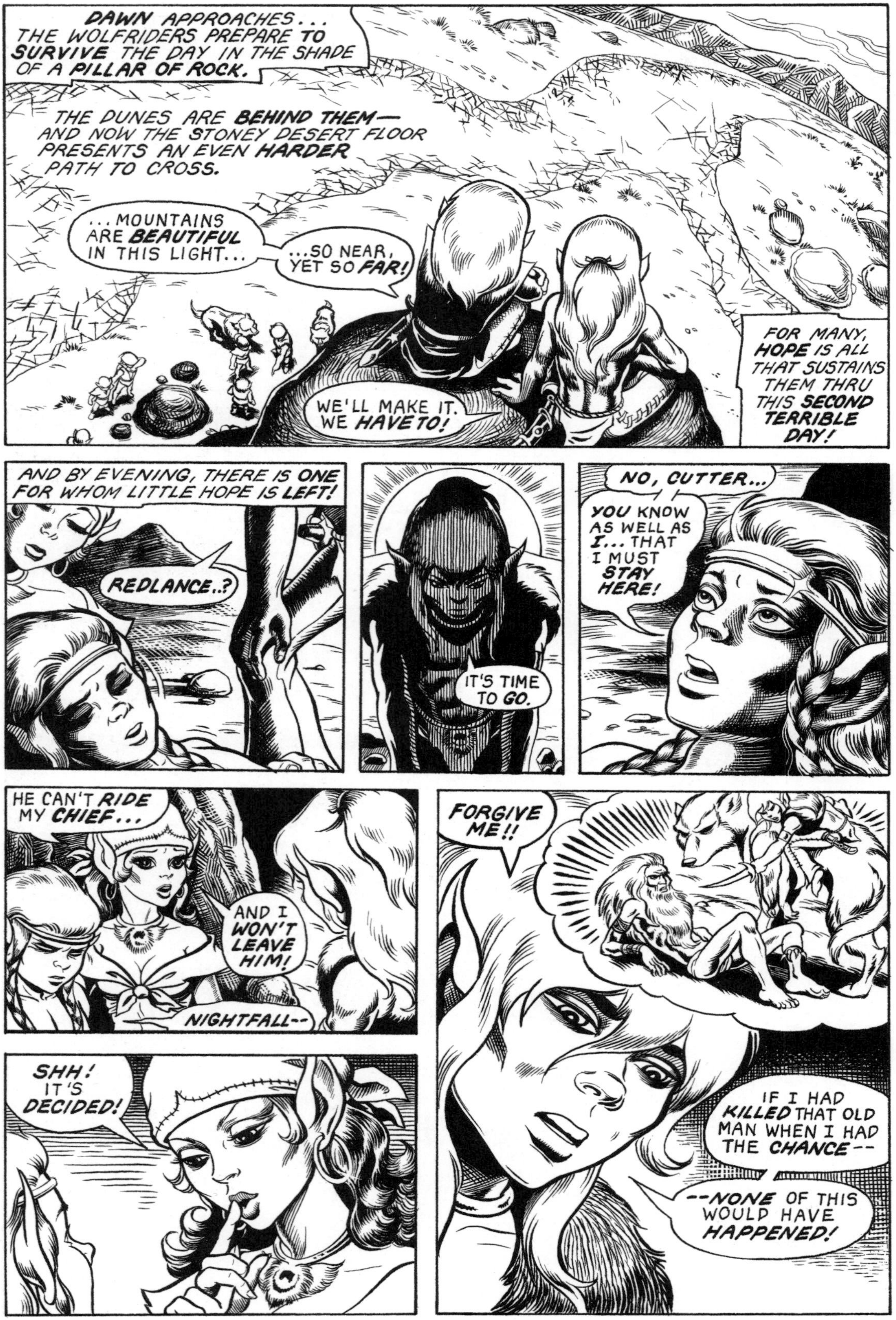
DAWN APPROACHES... THE WOLFRIDERS PREPARE TO SURVIVE THE DAY IN THE SHADE OF A PILLAR OF ROCK.
THE DUNES ARE BEHIND THEM— AND NOW THE STONEY DESERT FLOOR PRESENTS AN EVEN HARDER PATH TO CROSS.
...MOUNTAINS ARE BEAUTIFUL IN THIS LIGHT...
...SO NEAR, YET SO FAR!
WE'LL MAKE IT. WE HAVE TO!
FOR MANY, HOPE IS ALL THAT SUSTAINS THEM THRU THIS SECOND TERRIBLE DAY!
AND BY EVENING, THERE IS ONE FOR WHOM LITTLE HOPE IS LEFT!
REDLANCE..?
IT'S TIME TO GO.
NO, CUTTER...
YOU KNOW AS WELL AS I... THAT I MUST STAY HERE!
HE CAN'T RIDE MY CHIEF...
AND I WON'T LEAVE HIM!
NIGHTFALL--
SHH! IT'S DECIDED!
FORGIVE ME!!
IF I HAD KILLED THAT OLD MAN WHEN I HAD THE CHANCE--
--NONE OF THIS WOULD HAVE HAPPENED!

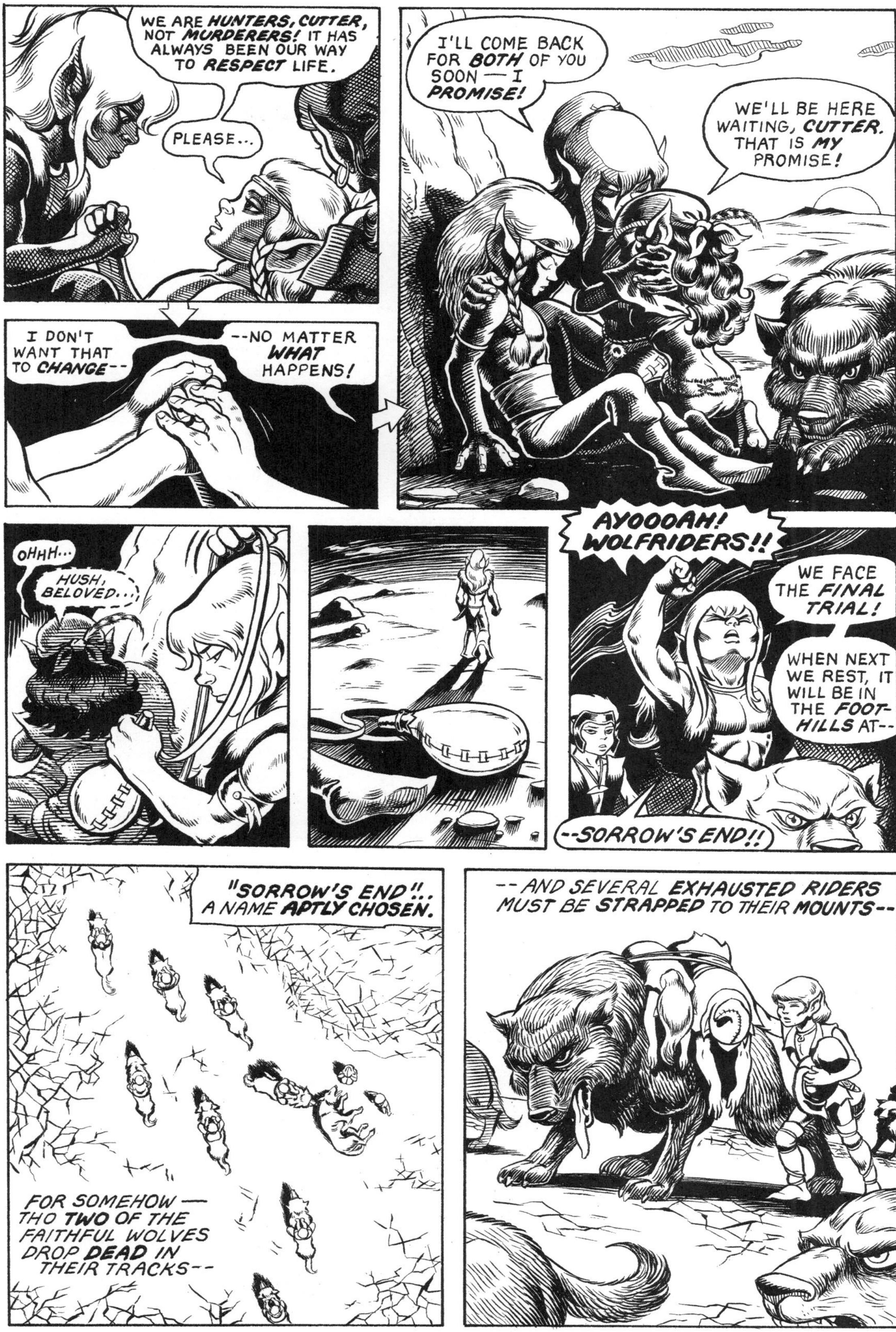
WE ARE HUNTERS, CUTTER, NOT MURDERERS! IT HAS ALWAYS BEEN OUR WAY TO RESPECT LIFE.
PLEASE...
I DON'T WANT THAT TO CHANGE--
--NO MATTER WHAT HAPPENS!
I'LL COME BACK FOR BOTH OF YOU SOON — I PROMISE!
WE'LL BE HERE WAITING, CUTTER. THAT IS MY PROMISE!
OHHH...
HUSH, BELOVED...
AYOOOAH! WOLFRIDERS!!
WE FACE THE FINAL TRIAL!
WHEN NEXT WE REST, IT WILL BE IN THE FOOT-HILLS AT--
--SORROW'S END!!
"SORROW'S END"... A NAME APTLY CHOSEN.
FOR SOMEHOW — THO TWO OF THE FAITHFUL WOLVES DROP DEAD IN THEIR TRACKS--
--AND SEVERAL EXHAUSTED RIDERS MUST BE STRAPPED TO THEIR MOUNTS--

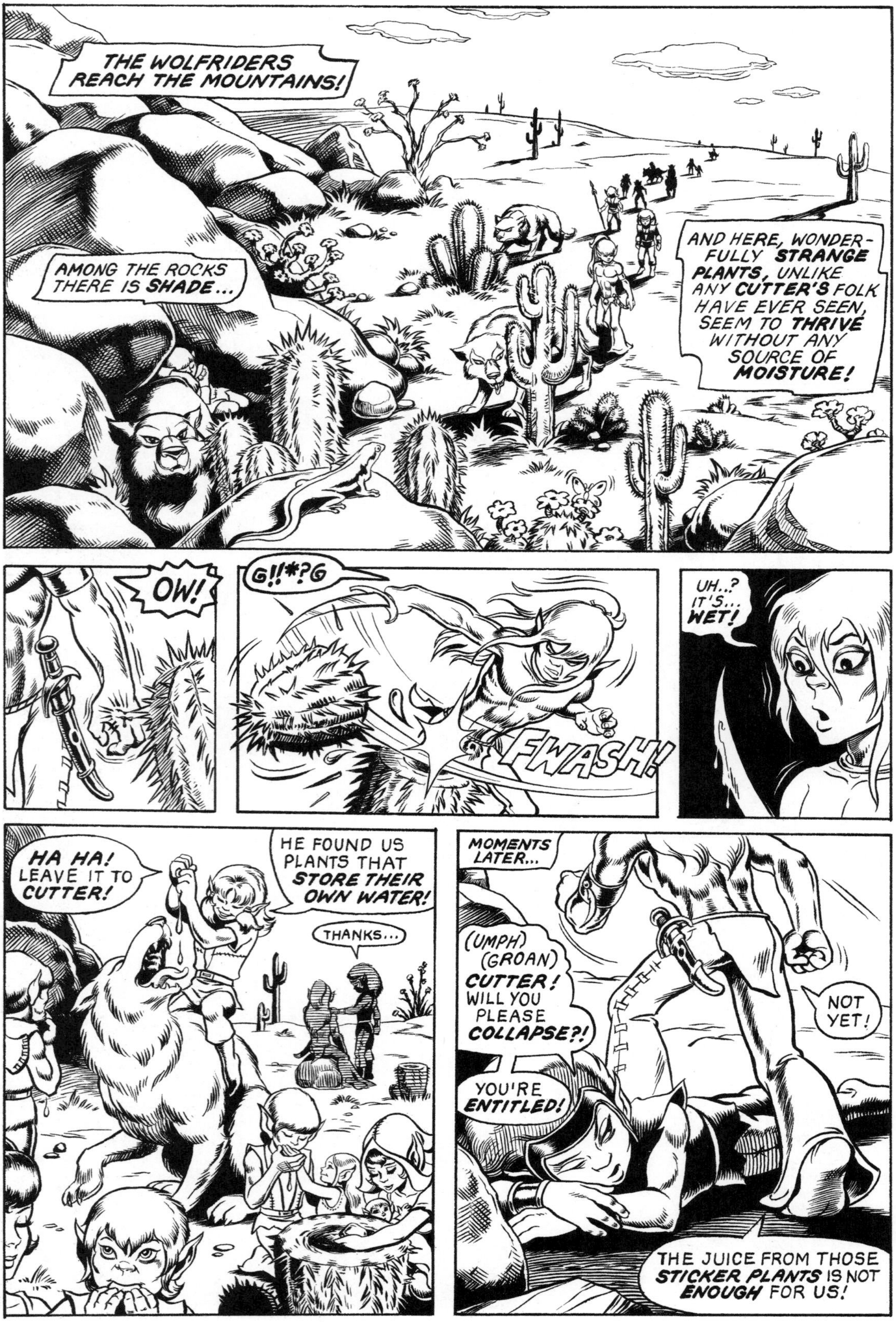

THE WOLFRIDERS REACH THE MOUNTAINS!
AMONG THE ROCKS THERE IS SHADE...
AND HERE, WONDERFULLY STRANGE PLANTS, UNLIKE ANY CUTTER'S FOLK HAVE EVER SEEN, SEEM TO THRIVE WITHOUT ANY SOURCE OF MOISTURE!
OW!
G!!*?G
FWASH!
UH..? IT'S... WET!
HA HA! LEAVE IT TO CUTTER!
HE FOUND US PLANTS THAT STORE THEIR OWN WATER!
THANKS...
MOMENTS LATER...
(UMPH) (GROAN) CUTTER! WILL YOU PLEASE COLLAPSE?!
NOT YET!
YOU'RE ENTITLED!
THE JUICE FROM THOSE STICKER PLANTS IS NOT ENOUGH FOR US!

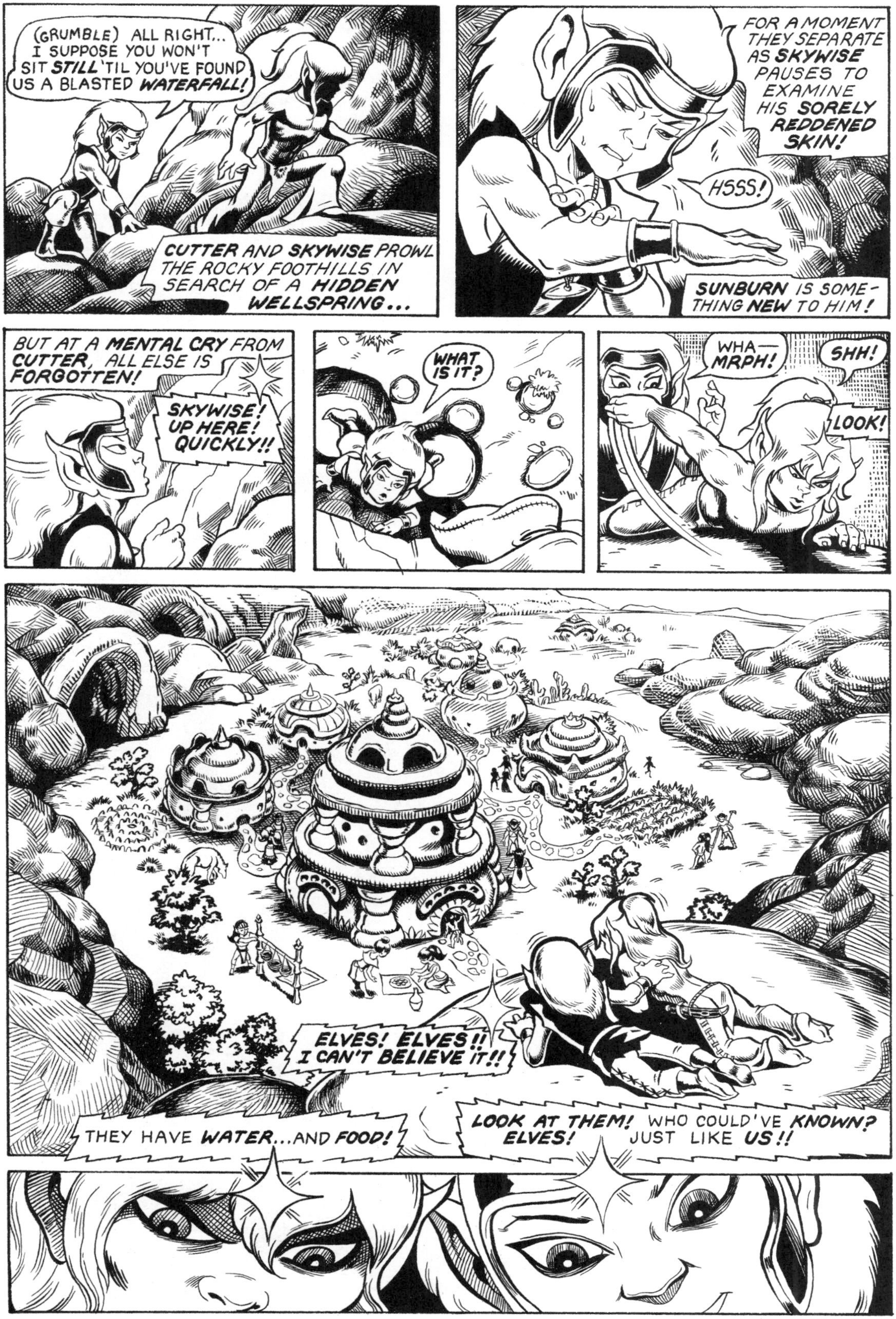
(GRUMBLE) ALL RIGHT... I SUPPOSE YOU WON'T SIT STILL 'TIL YOU'VE FOUND US A BLASTED WATERFALL!
CUTTER AND SKYWISE PROWL THE ROCKY FOOTHILLS IN SEARCH OF A HIDDEN WELLSPRING...
FOR A MOMENT THEY SEPARATE AS SKYWISE PAUSES TO EXAMINE HIS SORELY REDDENED SKIN!
HSSS!
SUNBURN IS SOMETHING NEW TO HIM!
BUT AT A MENTAL CRY FROM CUTTER, ALL ELSE IS FORGOTTEN!
SKYWISE! UP HERE! QUICKLY!!
WHAT IS IT?
WHA— MRPH!
SHH!
LOOK!
ELVES! ELVES!! I CAN'T BELIEVE IT!!
THEY HAVE WATER...AND FOOD!
LOOK AT THEM! WHO COULD'VE KNOWN? ELVES! JUST LIKE US!!

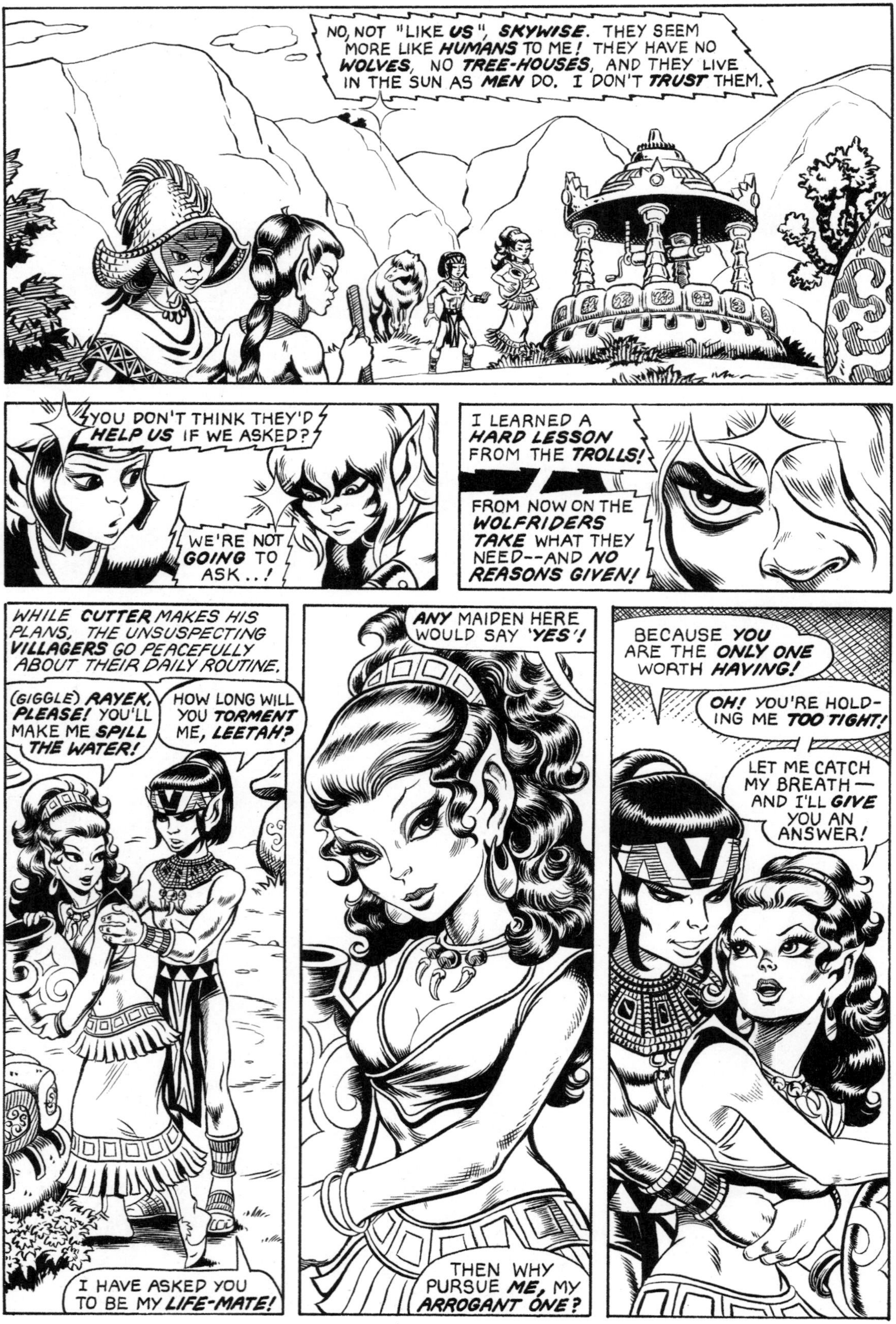

NO, NOT "LIKE US", SKYWISE. THEY SEEM MORE LIKE HUMANS TO ME! THEY HAVE NO WOLVES, NO TREE-HOUSES, AND THEY LIVE IN THE SUN AS MEN DO. I DON'T TRUST THEM.
YOU DON'T THINK THEY'D HELP US IF WE ASKED?
WE'RE NOT GOING TO ASK..!
I LEARNED A HARD LESSON FROM THE TROLLS!
FROM NOW ON THE WOLFRIDERS TAKE WHAT THEY NEED--AND NO REASONS GIVEN!
WHILE CUTTER MAKES HIS PLANS, THE UNSUSPECTING VILLAGERS GO PEACEFULLY ABOUT THEIR DAILY ROUTINE.
(GIGGLE) RAYEK, PLEASE! YOU'LL MAKE ME SPILL THE WATER!
HOW LONG WILL YOU TORMENT ME, LEETAH?
I HAVE ASKED YOU TO BE MY LIFE-MATE!
ANY MAIDEN HERE WOULD SAY 'YES'!
THEN WHY PURSUE ME, MY ARROGANT ONE?
BECAUSE YOU ARE THE ONLY ONE WORTH HAVING!
OH! YOU'RE HOLDING ME TOO TIGHT!
LET ME CATCH MY BREATH — AND I'LL GIVE YOU AN ANSWER!

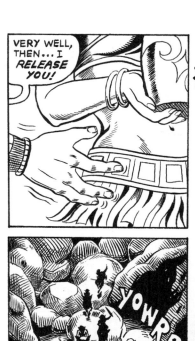

VERY WELL, THEN... I *RELEASE* YOU!

WHA-?! LEETAH!

HA HA HA HA HA HA HA!

(GASP!)

OWOOOO

YOWRR!

HEEYAH!

GRRAARR!

IT IS TRUE THAT DESPERATION GIVES RISE TO *DESPERATE ACTION,* --

EEEE!!

--SOMETIMES, SADLY, EVEN WHEN THERE IS NO *NEED..!*

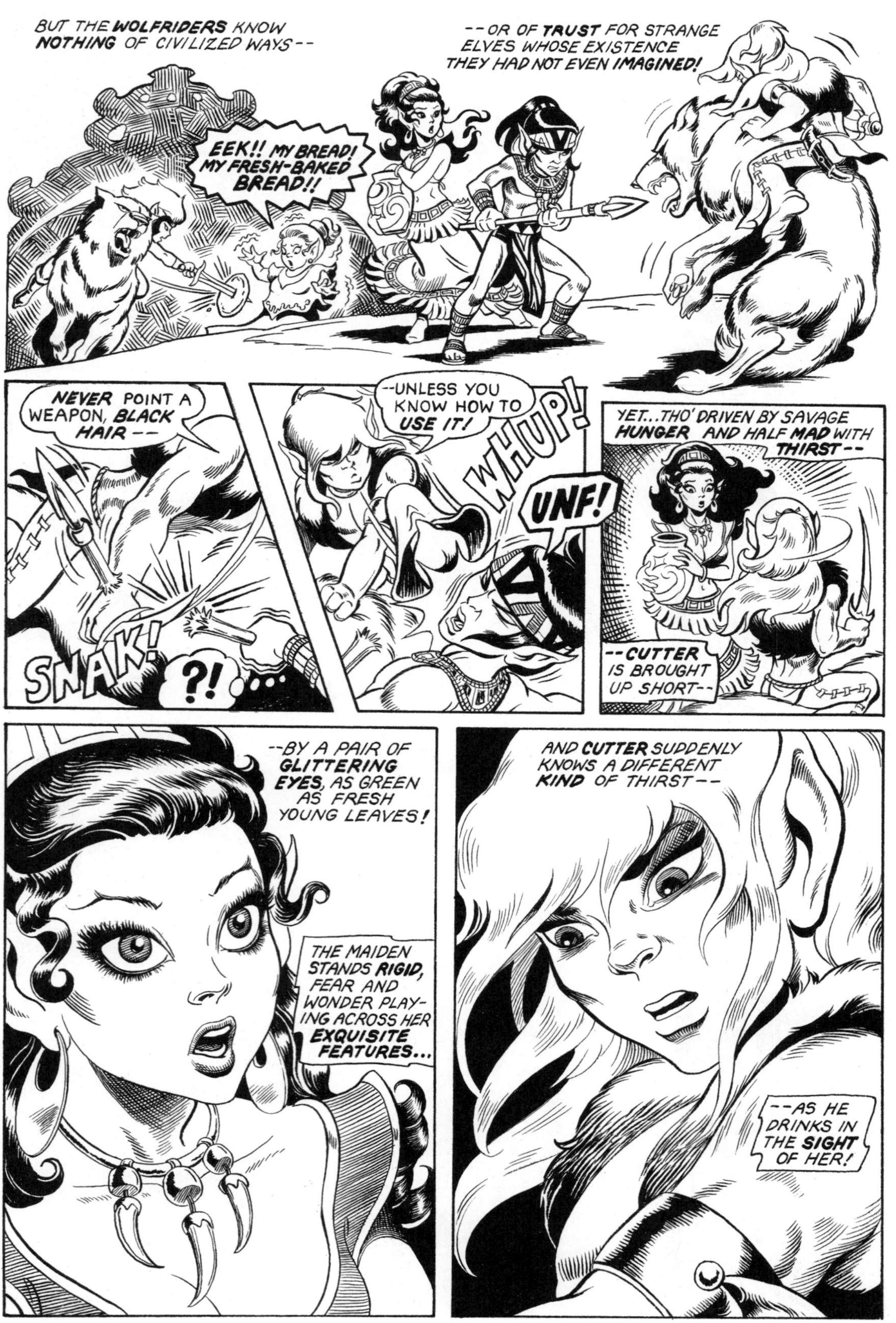
BUT THE WOLFRIDERS KNOW NOTHING OF CIVILIZED WAYS--
--OR OF TRUST FOR STRANGE ELVES WHOSE EXISTENCE THEY HAD NOT EVEN IMAGINED!
EEK!! MY BREAD! MY FRESH-BAKED BREAD!!
NEVER POINT A WEAPON, BLACK HAIR--
SNAK!
?!
--UNLESS YOU KNOW HOW TO USE IT!
WHUP!
UNF!
YET...THO' DRIVEN BY SAVAGE HUNGER AND HALF MAD WITH THIRST--
--CUTTER IS BROUGHT UP SHORT--
--BY A PAIR OF GLITTERING EYES, AS GREEN AS FRESH YOUNG LEAVES!
THE MAIDEN STANDS RIGID, FEAR AND WONDER PLAYING ACROSS HER EXQUISITE FEATURES...
AND CUTTER SUDDENLY KNOWS A DIFFERENT KIND OF THIRST--
--AS HE DRINKS IN THE SIGHT OF HER!

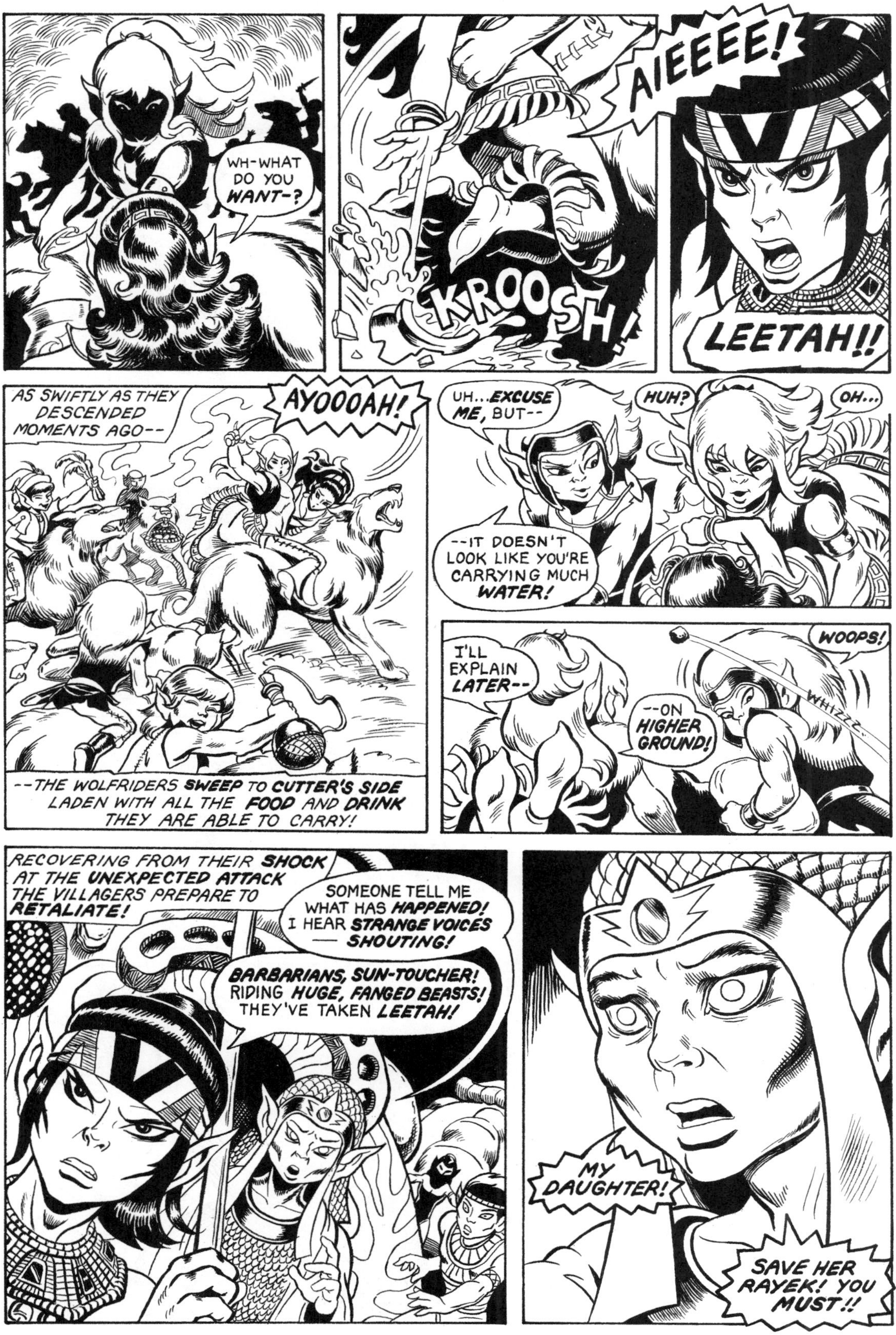
WH-WHAT DO YOU WANT-?
KROOSH!
AIEEEE!
LEETAH!!
AS SWIFTLY AS THEY DESCENDED MOMENTS AGO--
AYOOOAH!
--THE WOLFRIDERS SWEEP TO CUTTER'S SIDE LADEN WITH ALL THE FOOD AND DRINK THEY ARE ABLE TO CARRY!
UH...EXCUSE ME, BUT--
HUH?
OH...
--IT DOESN'T LOOK LIKE YOU'RE CARRYING MUCH WATER!
I'LL EXPLAIN LATER--
WOOPS!
WHIZZZ
--ON HIGHER GROUND!
RECOVERING FROM THEIR SHOCK AT THE UNEXPECTED ATTACK THE VILLAGERS PREPARE TO RETALIATE!
SOMEONE TELL ME WHAT HAS HAPPENED! I HEAR STRANGE VOICES — SHOUTING!
BARBARIANS, SUN-TOUCHER! RIDING HUGE, FANGED BEASTS! THEY'VE TAKEN LEETAH!
MY DAUGHTER!
SAVE HER RAYEK! YOU MUST!!

RAID AT SORROW'S END PART 2

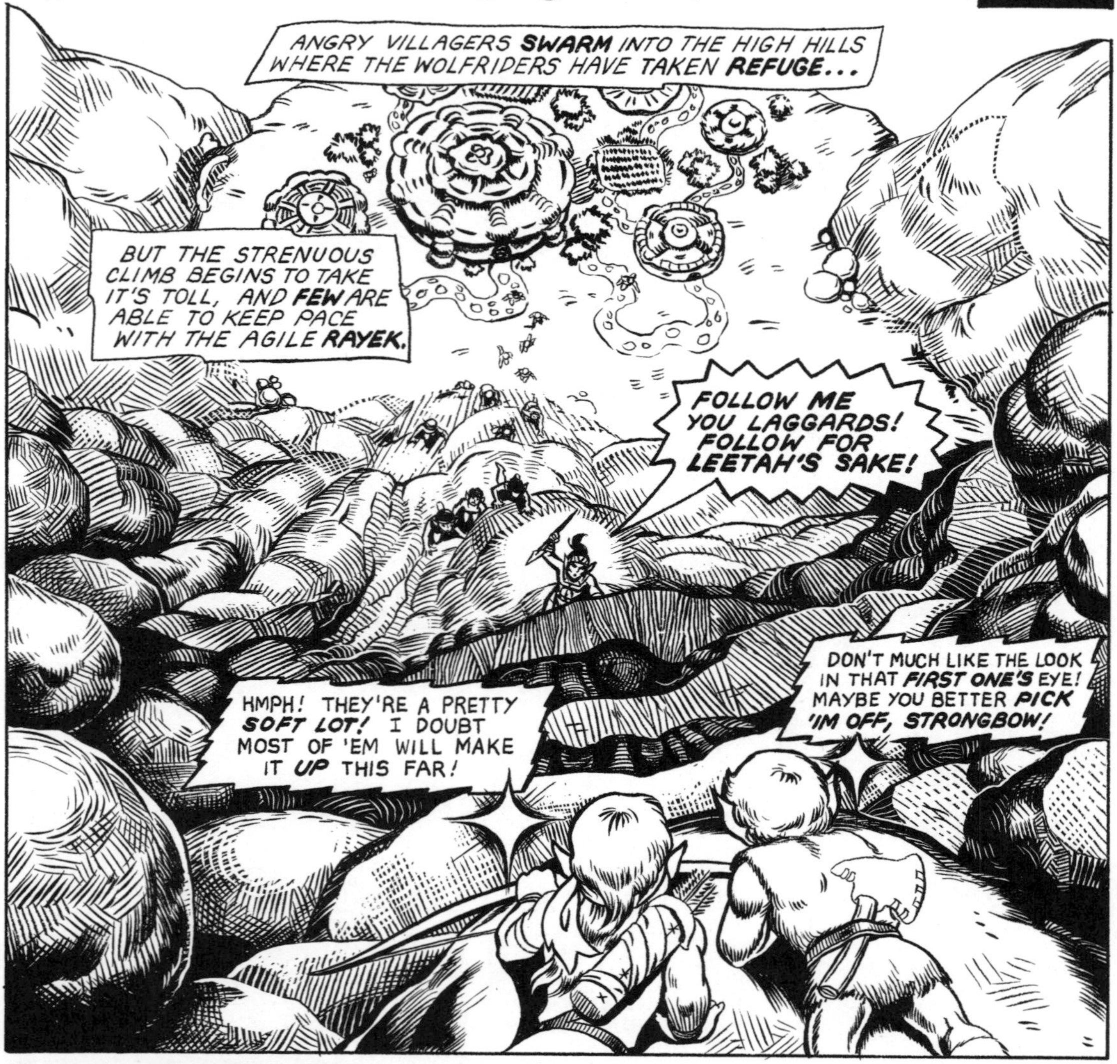
ANGRY VILLAGERS SWARM INTO THE HIGH HILLS WHERE THE WOLFRIDERS HAVE TAKEN REFUGE...
BUT THE STRENUOUS CLIMB BEGINS TO TAKE IT'S TOLL, AND FEW ARE ABLE TO KEEP PACE WITH THE AGILE RAYEK.
FOLLOW ME YOU LAGGARDS! FOLLOW FOR LEETAH'S SAKE!
HMPH! THEY'RE A PRETTY SOFT LOT! I DOUBT MOST OF 'EM WILL MAKE IT UP THIS FAR!
DON'T MUCH LIKE THE LOOK IN THAT FIRST ONE'S EYE! MAYBE YOU BETTER PICK 'IM OFF, STRONGBOW!

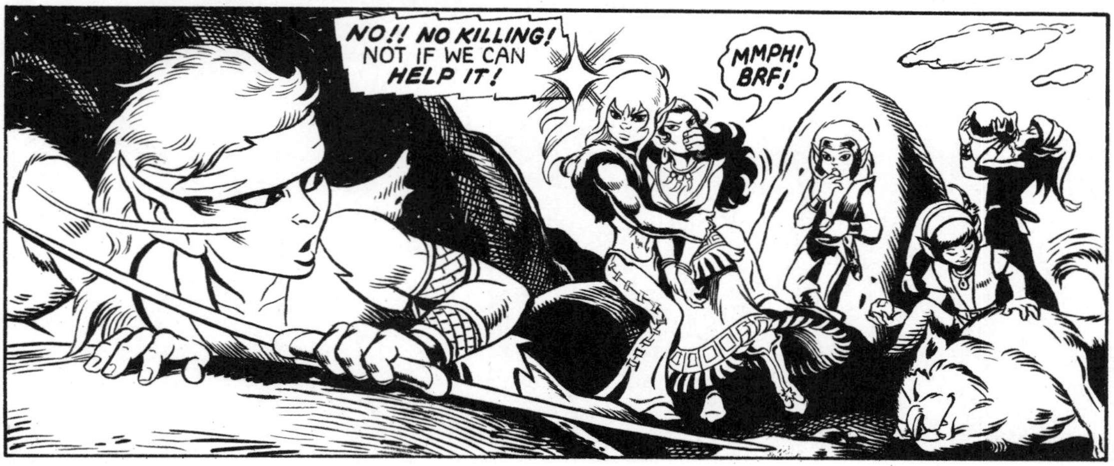
NO!! NO KILLING! NOT IF WE CAN HELP IT!
MMPH! BRF!

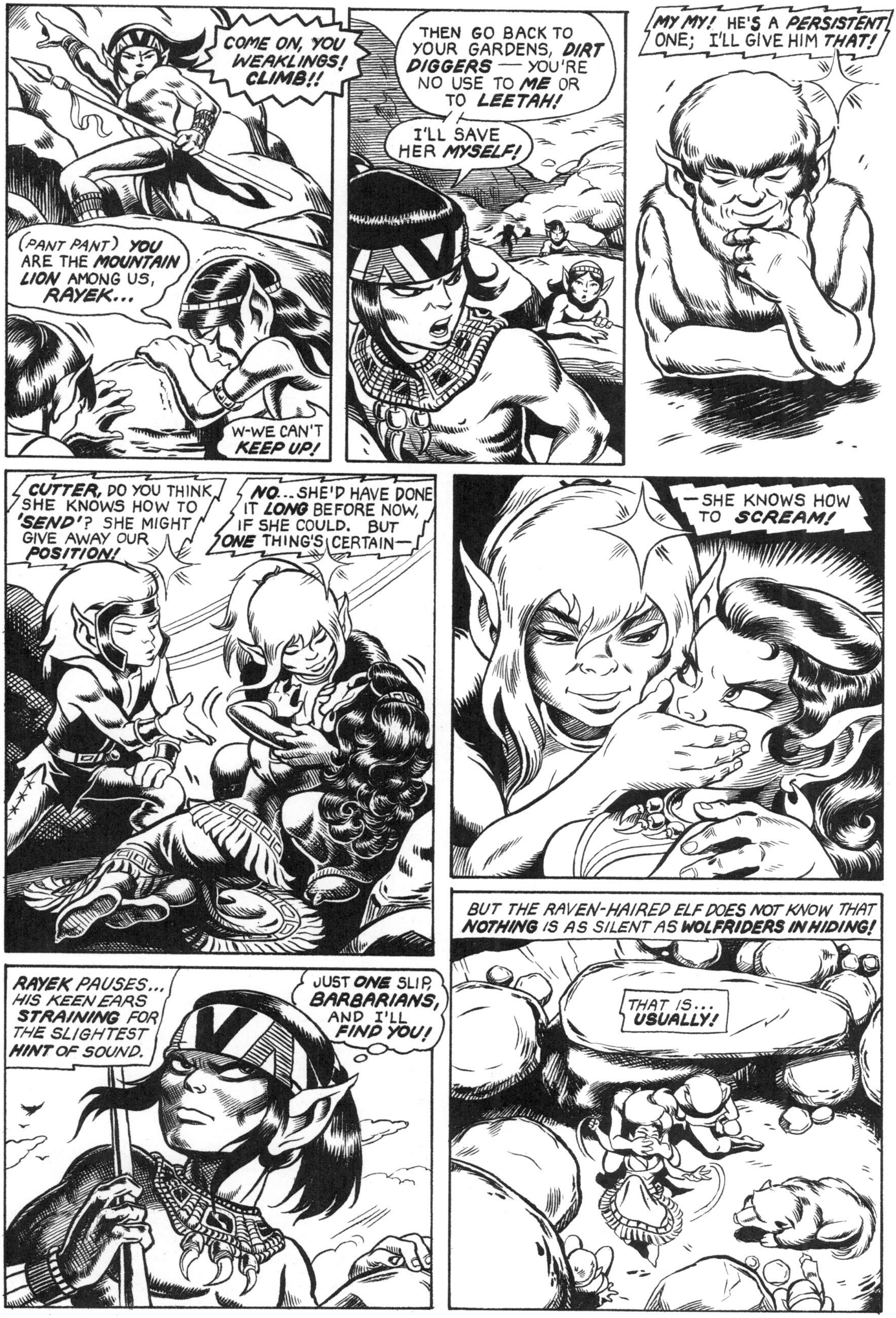
COME ON, YOU WEAKLINGS! CLIMB!!
(PANT PANT) YOU ARE THE MOUNTAIN LION AMONG US, RAYEK...
W-WE CAN'T KEEP UP!
THEN GO BACK TO YOUR GARDENS, DIRT DIGGERS — YOU'RE NO USE TO ME OR TO LEETAH!
I'LL SAVE HER MYSELF!
MY MY! HE'S A PERSISTENT ONE; I'LL GIVE HIM THAT!
CUTTER, DO YOU THINK SHE KNOWS HOW TO 'SEND'? SHE MIGHT GIVE AWAY OUR POSITION!
NO... SHE'D HAVE DONE IT LONG BEFORE NOW, IF SHE COULD. BUT ONE THING'S CERTAIN—
—SHE KNOWS HOW TO SCREAM!
RAYEK PAUSES... HIS KEEN EARS STRAINING FOR THE SLIGHTEST HINT OF SOUND.
JUST ONE SLIP, BARBARIANS, AND I'LL FIND YOU!
BUT THE RAVEN-HAIRED ELF DOES NOT KNOW THAT NOTHING IS AS SILENT AS WOLFRIDERS IN HIDING!
THAT IS... USUALLY!

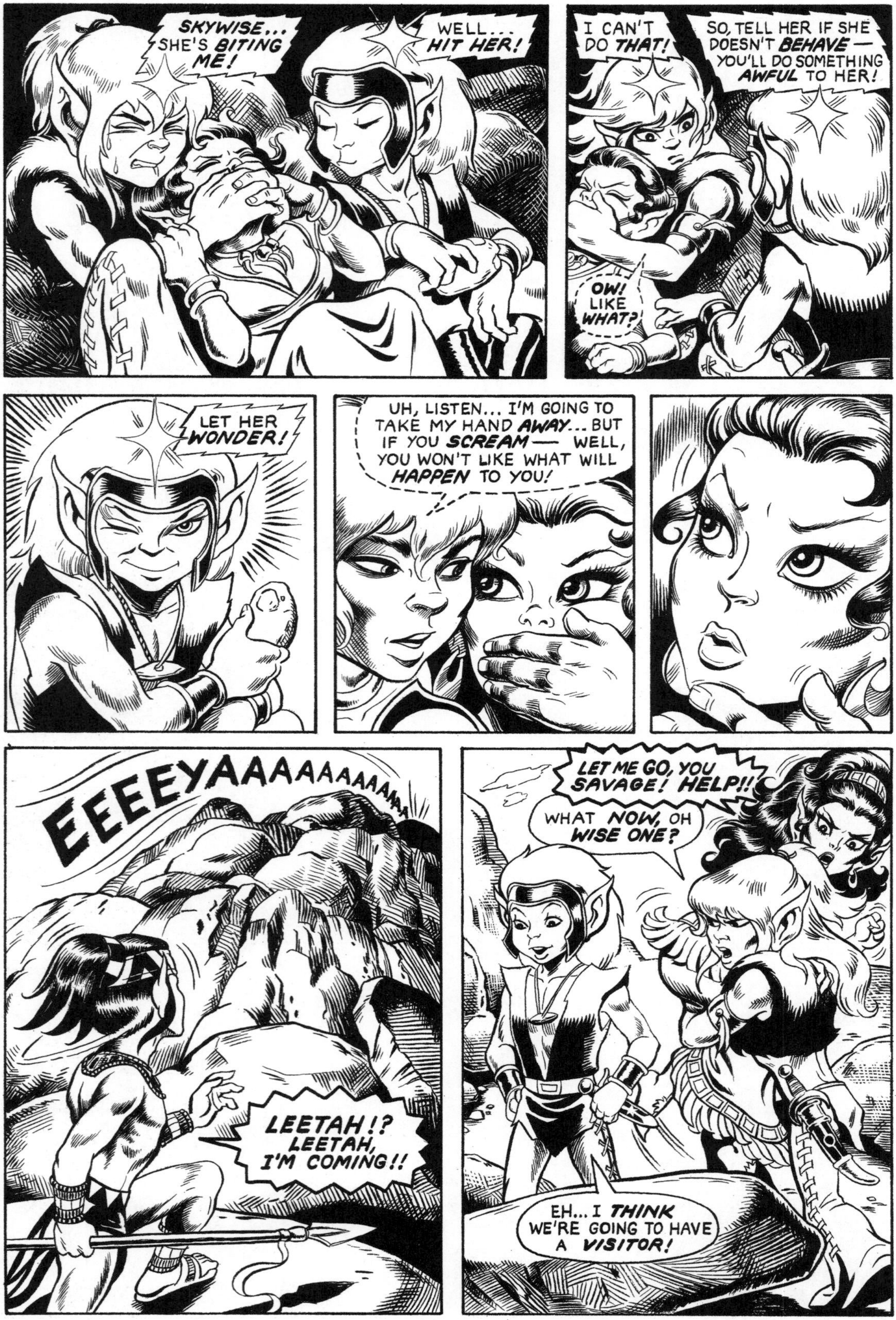
SKYWISE... SHE'S BITING ME!
WELL... HIT HER!
I CAN'T DO THAT!
SO, TELL HER IF SHE DOESN'T BEHAVE— YOU'LL DO SOMETHING AWFUL TO HER!
OW! LIKE WHAT?
LET HER WONDER!
UH, LISTEN... I'M GOING TO TAKE MY HAND AWAY... BUT IF YOU SCREAM— WELL, YOU WON'T LIKE WHAT WILL HAPPEN TO YOU!
EEEEYAAAAAAAAAAA
LEETAH!? LEETAH, I'M COMING!!
LET ME GO, YOU SAVAGE! HELP!!
WHAT NOW, OH WISE ONE?
EH... I THINK WE'RE GOING TO HAVE A VISITOR!

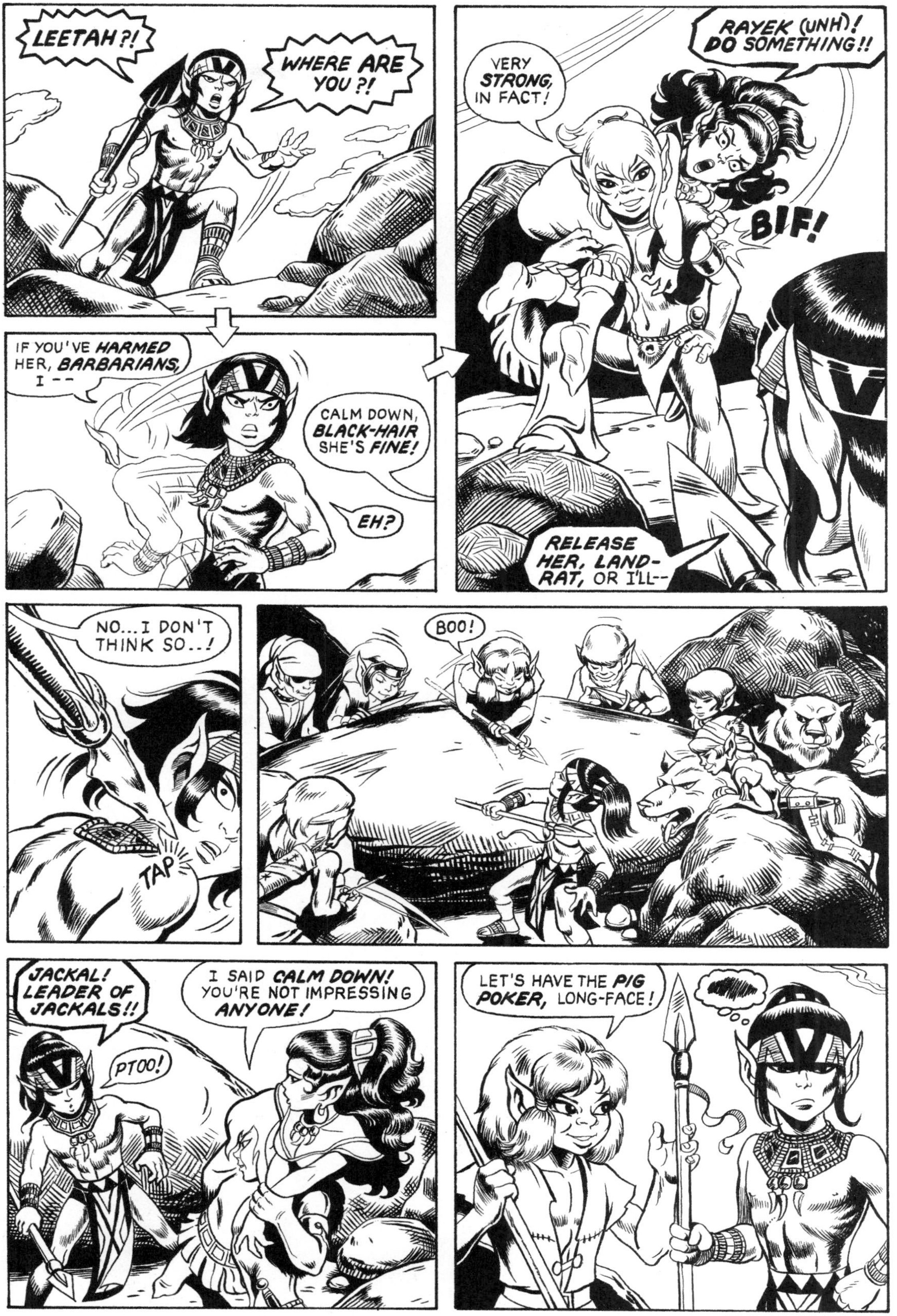
LEETAH?!
WHERE ARE YOU?!
IF YOU'VE HARMED HER, BARBARIANS, I --
CALM DOWN, BLACK-HAIR SHE'S FINE!
EH?
VERY STRONG, IN FACT!
RAYEK (UNH)! DO SOMETHING!!
BIF!
RELEASE HER, LAND-RAT, OR I'LL--
NO...I DON'T THINK SO..!
TAP
BOO!
JACKAL! LEADER OF JACKALS!!
PTOO!
I SAID CALM DOWN! YOU'RE NOT IMPRESSING ANYONE!
LET'S HAVE THE PIG POKER, LONG-FACE!

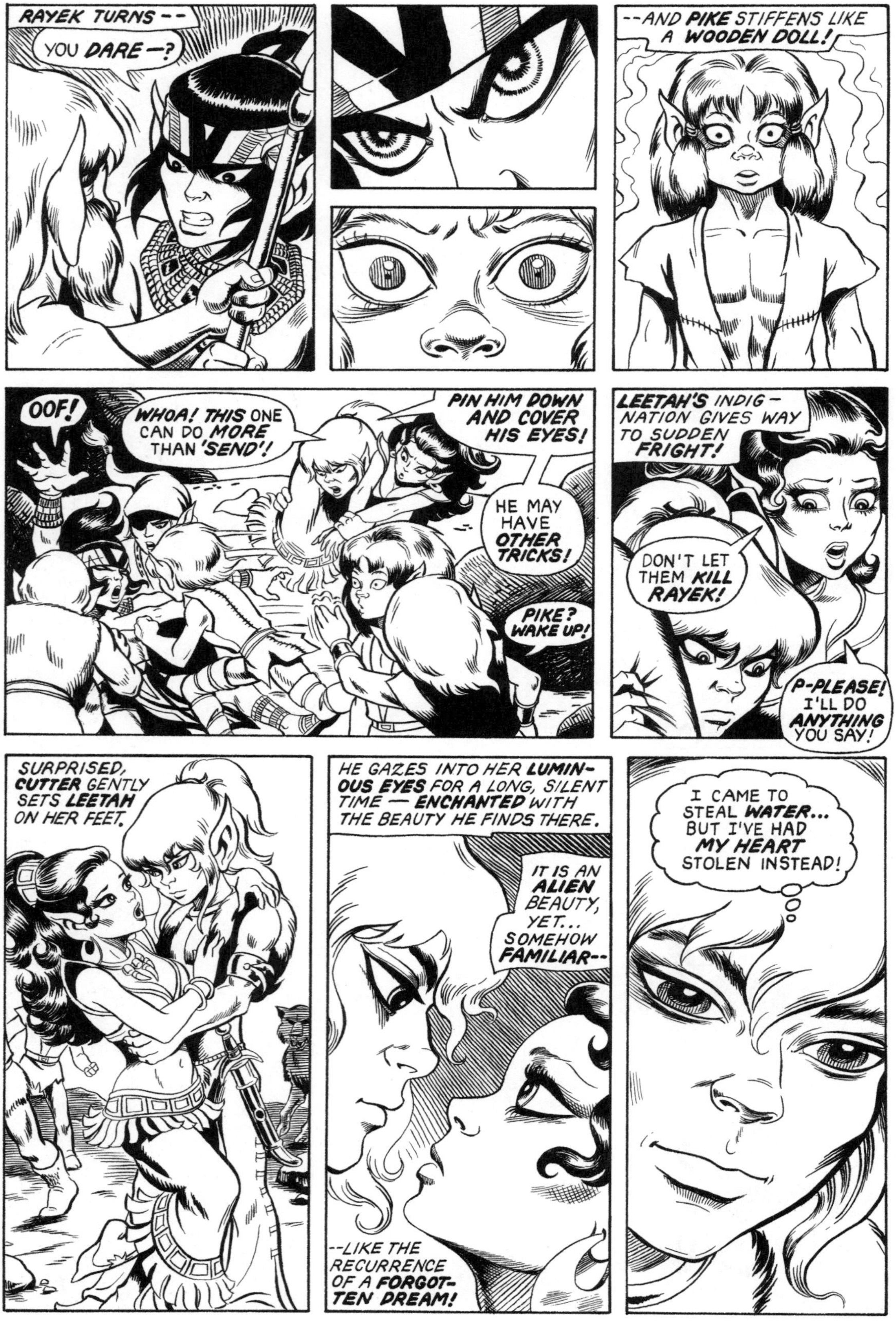
RAYEK TURNS --
YOU DARE --?
--AND PIKE STIFFENS LIKE A WOODEN DOLL!
OOF!
WHOA! THIS ONE CAN DO MORE THAN 'SEND'!
PIN HIM DOWN AND COVER HIS EYES!
HE MAY HAVE OTHER TRICKS!
PIKE? WAKE UP!
LEETAH'S INDIGNATION GIVES WAY TO SUDDEN FRIGHT!
DON'T LET THEM KILL RAYEK!
P-PLEASE! I'LL DO ANYTHING YOU SAY!
SURPRISED, CUTTER GENTLY SETS LEETAH ON HER FEET.
HE GAZES INTO HER LUMINOUS EYES FOR A LONG, SILENT TIME — ENCHANTED WITH THE BEAUTY HE FINDS THERE.
IT IS AN ALIEN BEAUTY, YET... SOMEHOW FAMILIAR--
--LIKE THE RECURRENCE OF A FORGOTTEN DREAM!
I CAME TO STEAL WATER... BUT I'VE HAD MY HEART STOLEN INSTEAD!

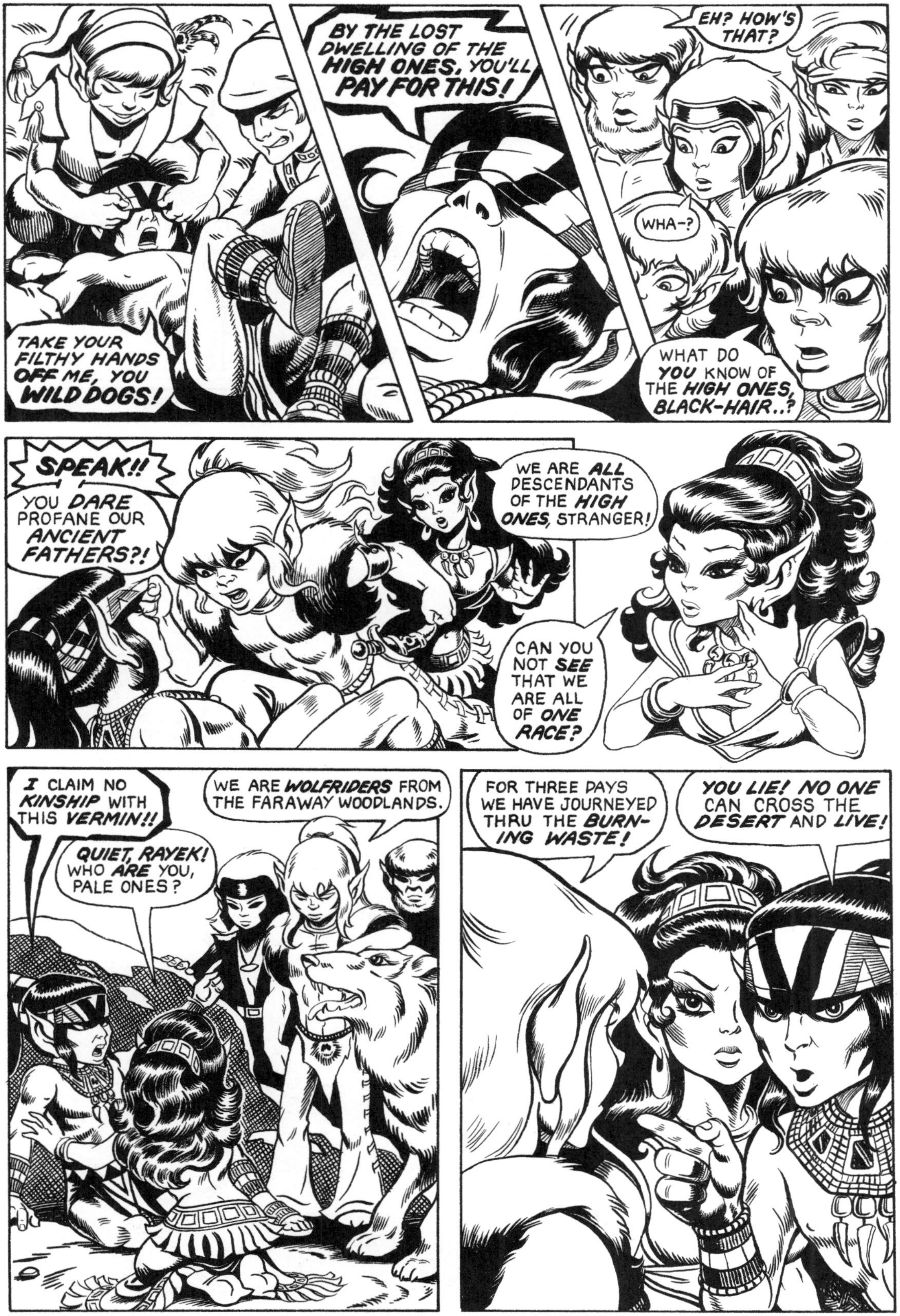
TAKE YOUR FILTHY HANDS OFF ME, YOU WILD DOGS!
BY THE LOST DWELLING OF THE HIGH ONES, YOU'LL PAY FOR THIS!
EH? HOW'S THAT?
WHA-?
WHAT DO YOU KNOW OF THE HIGH ONES, BLACK-HAIR..?
SPEAK!!
YOU DARE PROFANE OUR ANCIENT FATHERS?!
WE ARE ALL DESCENDANTS OF THE HIGH ONES, STRANGER!
CAN YOU NOT SEE THAT WE ARE ALL OF ONE RACE?
I CLAIM NO KINSHIP WITH THIS VERMIN!!
WE ARE WOLFRIDERS FROM THE FARAWAY WOODLANDS.
QUIET, RAYEK! WHO ARE YOU, PALE ONES?
FOR THREE DAYS WE HAVE JOURNEYED THRU THE BURNING WASTE!
YOU LIE! NO ONE CAN CROSS THE DESERT AND LIVE!

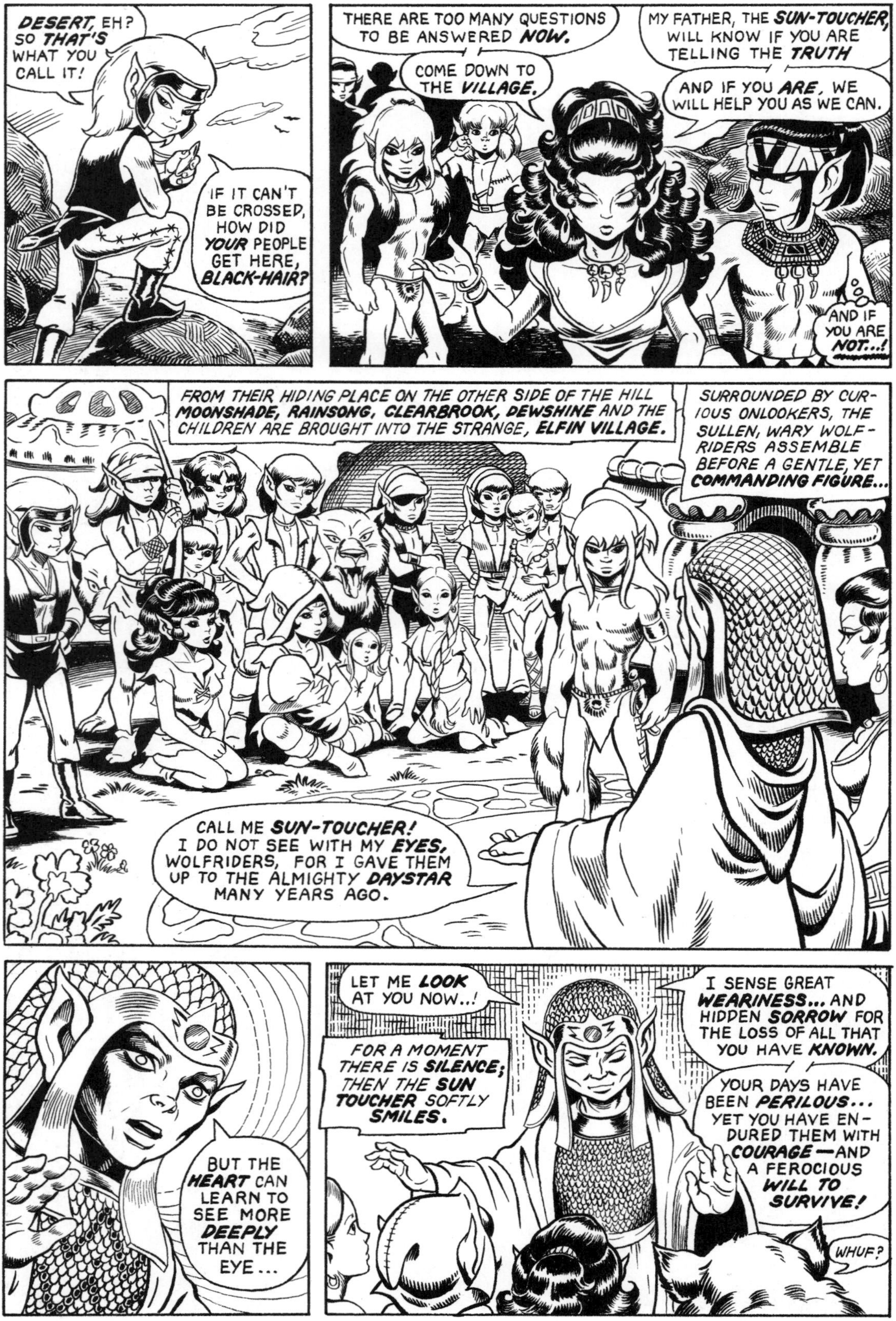
DESERT, EH? SO THAT'S WHAT YOU CALL IT!
IF IT CAN'T BE CROSSED, HOW DID YOUR PEOPLE GET HERE, BLACK-HAIR?
THERE ARE TOO MANY QUESTIONS TO BE ANSWERED NOW.
COME DOWN TO THE VILLAGE.
MY FATHER, THE SUN-TOUCHER, WILL KNOW IF YOU ARE TELLING THE TRUTH
AND IF YOU ARE, WE WILL HELP YOU AS WE CAN.
AND IF YOU ARE NOT...!
FROM THEIR HIDING PLACE ON THE OTHER SIDE OF THE HILL MOONSHADE, RAINSONG, CLEARBROOK, DEWSHINE AND THE CHILDREN ARE BROUGHT INTO THE STRANGE, ELFIN VILLAGE.
SURROUNDED BY CURIOUS ONLOOKERS, THE SULLEN, WARY WOLF-RIDERS ASSEMBLE BEFORE A GENTLE, YET COMMANDING FIGURE...
CALL ME SUN-TOUCHER! I DO NOT SEE WITH MY EYES, WOLFRIDERS, FOR I GAVE THEM UP TO THE ALMIGHTY DAYSTAR MANY YEARS AGO.
BUT THE HEART CAN LEARN TO SEE MORE DEEPLY THAN THE EYE...
LET ME LOOK AT YOU NOW...!
FOR A MOMENT THERE IS SILENCE; THEN THE SUN TOUCHER SOFTLY SMILES.
I SENSE GREAT WEARINESS... AND HIDDEN SORROW FOR THE LOSS OF ALL THAT YOU HAVE KNOWN.
YOUR DAYS HAVE BEEN PERILOUS... YET YOU HAVE ENDURED THEM WITH COURAGE—AND A FEROCIOUS WILL TO SURVIVE!
WHUF?

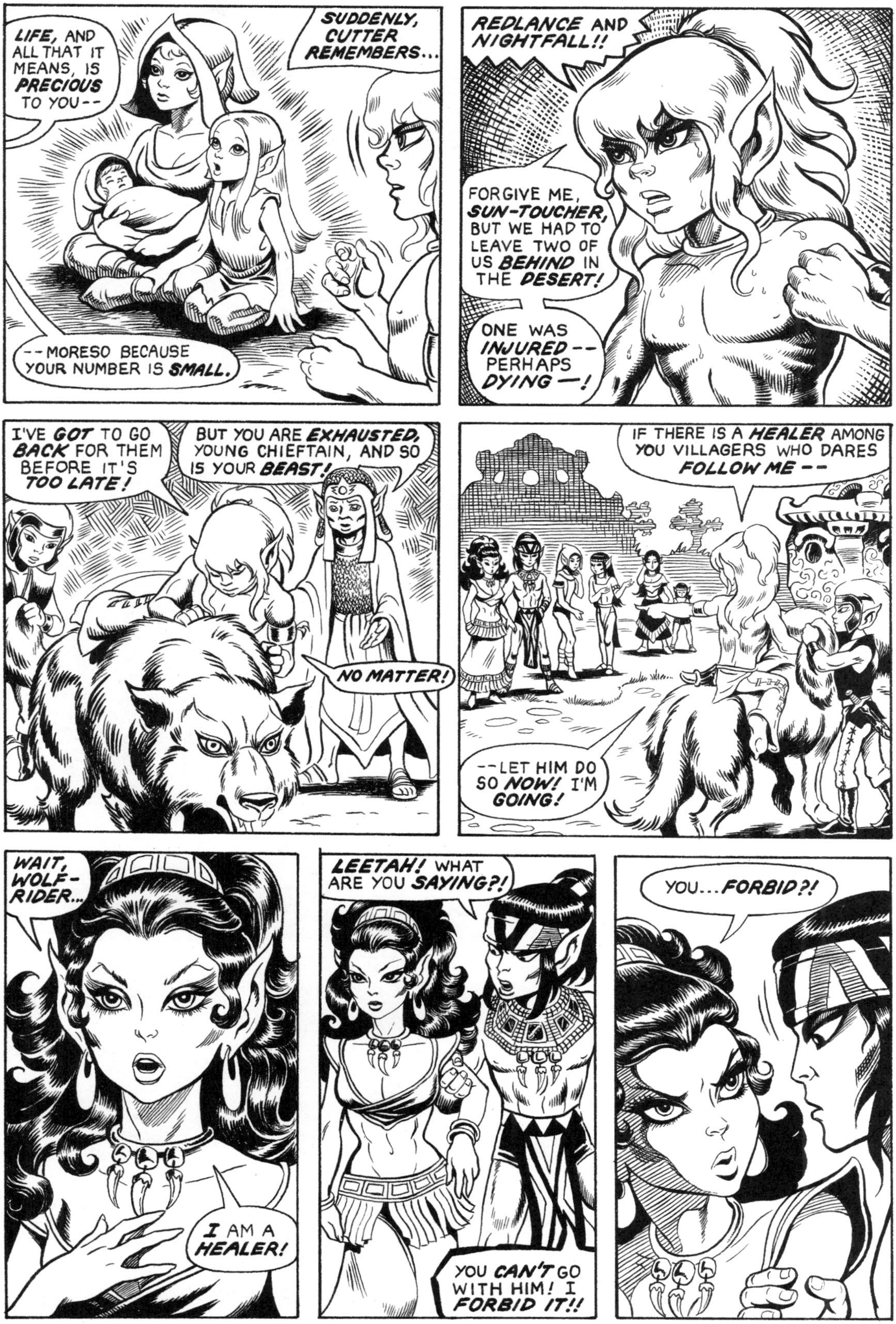
LIFE, AND ALL THAT IT MEANS, IS PRECIOUS TO YOU--
--MORESO BECAUSE YOUR NUMBER IS SMALL.
SUDDENLY, CUTTER REMEMBERS...
REDLANCE AND NIGHTFALL!!
FORGIVE ME, SUN-TOUCHER, BUT WE HAD TO LEAVE TWO OF US BEHIND IN THE DESERT!
ONE WAS INJURED -- PERHAPS DYING --!
I'VE GOT TO GO BACK FOR THEM BEFORE IT'S TOO LATE!
BUT YOU ARE EXHAUSTED, YOUNG CHIEFTAIN, AND SO IS YOUR BEAST!
NO MATTER!
IF THERE IS A HEALER AMONG YOU VILLAGERS WHO DARES FOLLOW ME --
--LET HIM DO SO NOW! I'M GOING!
WAIT, WOLF-RIDER...
I AM A HEALER!
LEETAH! WHAT ARE YOU SAYING?!
YOU CAN'T GO WITH HIM! I FORBID IT!!
YOU... FORBID?!

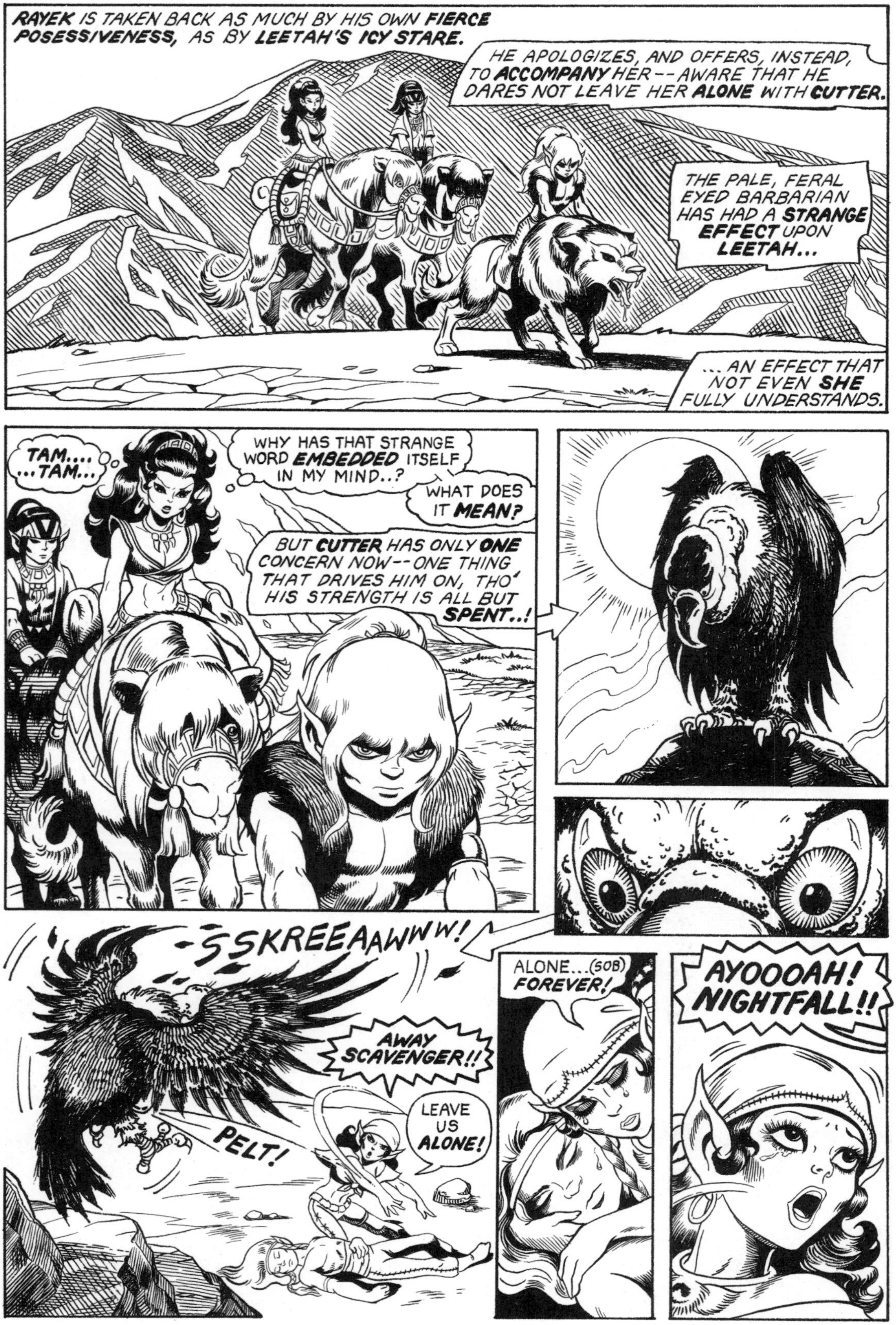
RAYEK IS TAKEN BACK AS MUCH BY HIS OWN FIERCE POSESSIVENESS, AS BY LEETAH'S ICY STARE.
HE APOLOGIZES, AND OFFERS, INSTEAD, TO ACCOMPANY HER-- AWARE THAT HE DARES NOT LEAVE HER ALONE WITH CUTTER.
THE PALE, FERAL EYED BARBARIAN HAS HAD A STRANGE EFFECT UPON LEETAH...
...AN EFFECT THAT NOT EVEN SHE FULLY UNDERSTANDS.
TAM.... ...TAM...
WHY HAS THAT STRANGE WORD EMBEDDED ITSELF IN MY MIND..?
WHAT DOES IT MEAN?
BUT CUTTER HAS ONLY ONE CONCERN NOW-- ONE THING THAT DRIVES HIM ON, THO' HIS STRENGTH IS ALL BUT SPENT..!
-SSKREEAAWWW!
AWAY SCAVENGER!!
LEAVE US ALONE!
PELT!
ALONE...(SOB) FOREVER!
AYOOOAH! NIGHTFALL!!

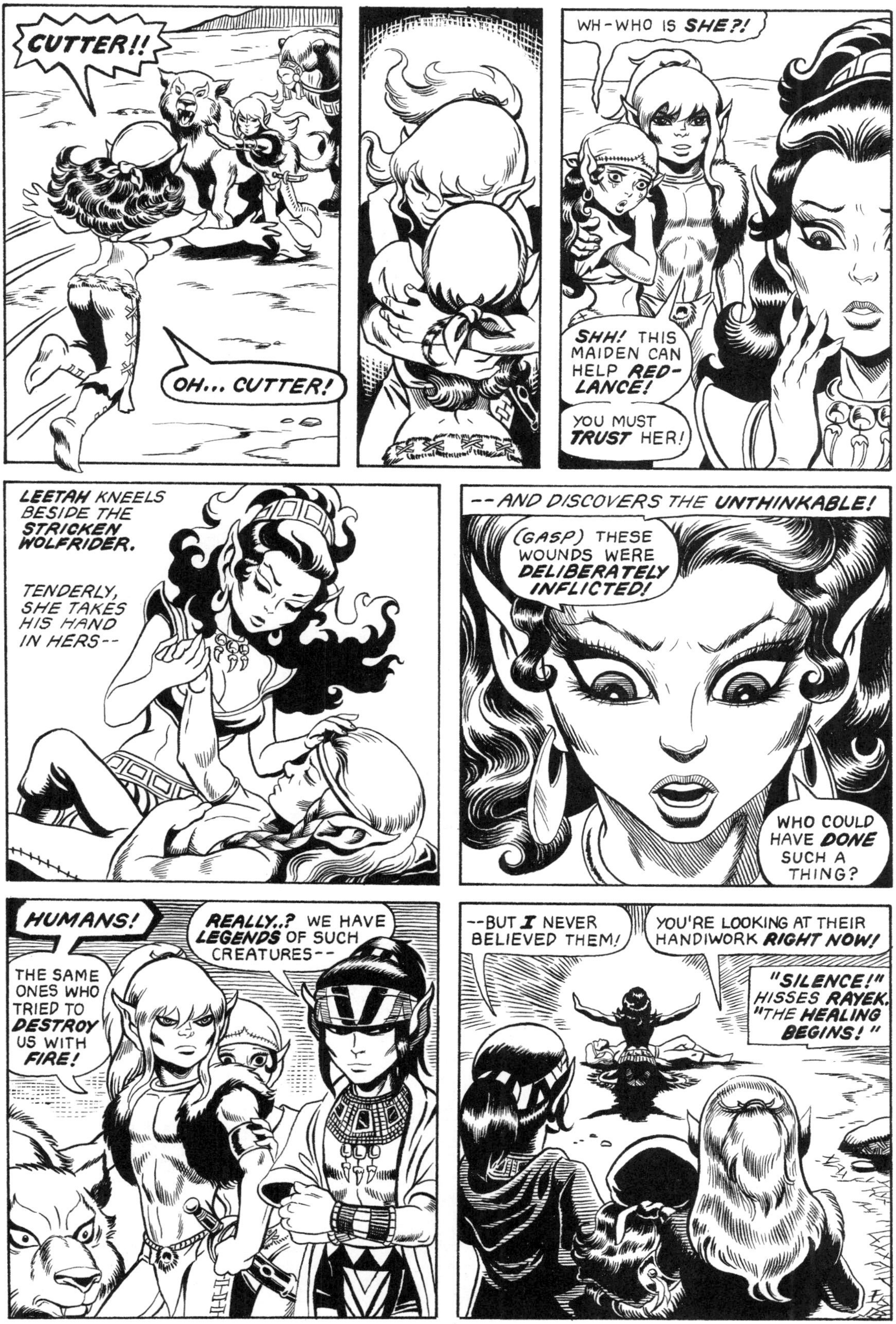
CUTTER!!
OH... CUTTER!
WH-WHO IS SHE?!
SHH! THIS MAIDEN CAN HELP REDLANCE!
YOU MUST TRUST HER!
LEETAH KNEELS BESIDE THE STRICKEN WOLFRIDER.
TENDERLY, SHE TAKES HIS HAND IN HERS--
--AND DISCOVERS THE UNTHINKABLE!
(GASP) THESE WOUNDS WERE DELIBERATELY INFLICTED!
WHO COULD HAVE DONE SUCH A THING?
HUMANS!
THE SAME ONES WHO TRIED TO DESTROY US WITH FIRE!
REALLY..? WE HAVE LEGENDS OF SUCH CREATURES--
--BUT I NEVER BELIEVED THEM!
YOU'RE LOOKING AT THEIR HANDIWORK RIGHT NOW!
"SILENCE!" HISSES RAYEK. "THE HEALING BEGINS!"

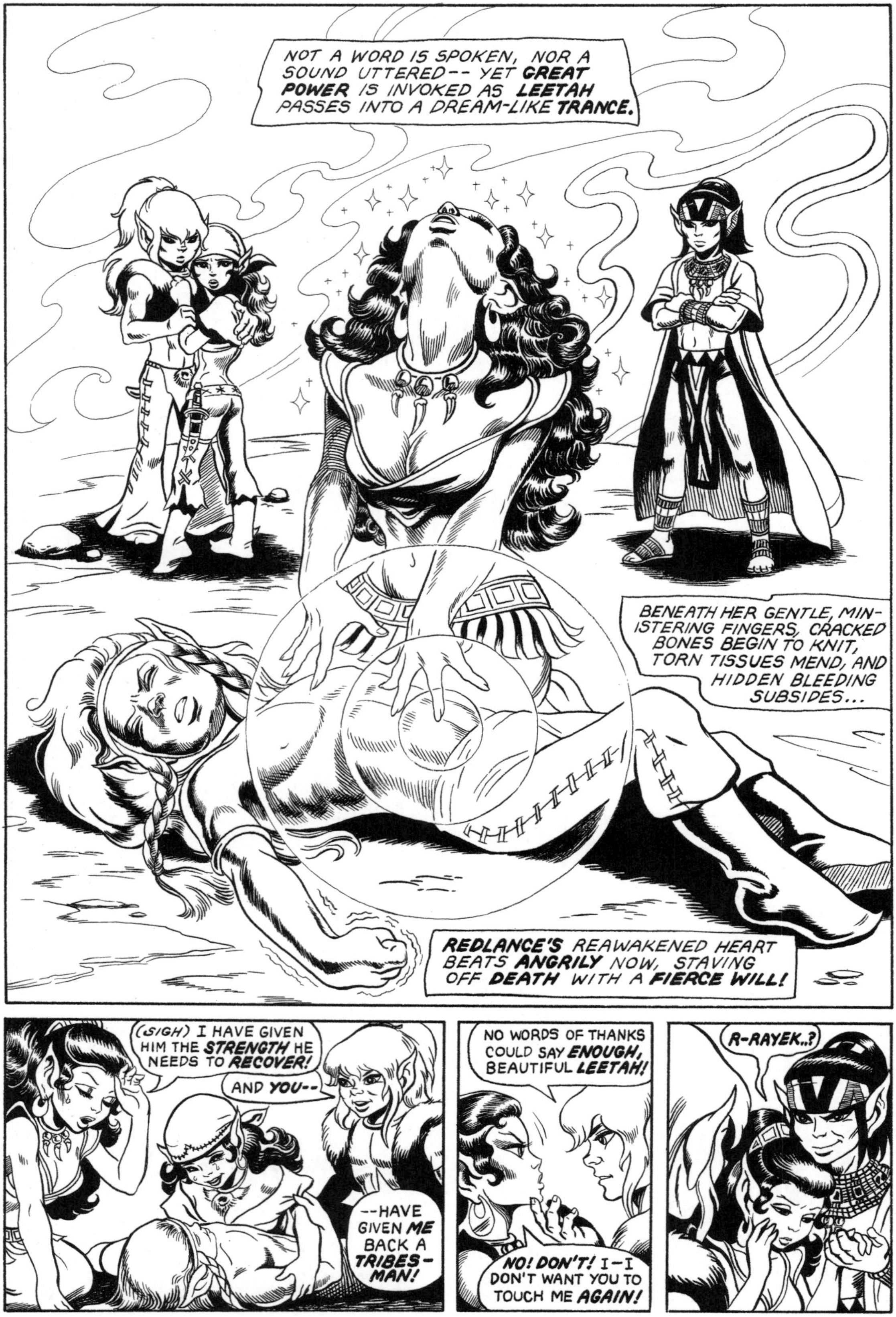

NOT A WORD IS SPOKEN, NOR A SOUND UTTERED-- YET **GREAT POWER** IS INVOKED AS **LEETAH** PASSES INTO A DREAM-LIKE **TRANCE.**
BENEATH HER GENTLE, MINISTERING FINGERS, CRACKED BONES BEGIN TO KNIT, TORN TISSUES MEND, AND HIDDEN BLEEDING SUBSIDES...
REDLANCE'S REAWAKENED HEART BEATS **ANGRILY** NOW, STAVING OFF **DEATH** WITH A **FIERCE WILL!**
(*SIGH*) I HAVE GIVEN HIM THE **STRENGTH** HE NEEDS TO **RECOVER!**
AND **YOU**--
--HAVE GIVEN **ME** BACK A **TRIBESMAN!**
NO WORDS OF THANKS COULD SAY **ENOUGH,** BEAUTIFUL **LEETAH!**
NO! DON'T! I--I DON'T WANT YOU TO TOUCH ME **AGAIN!**
R-RAYEK..?

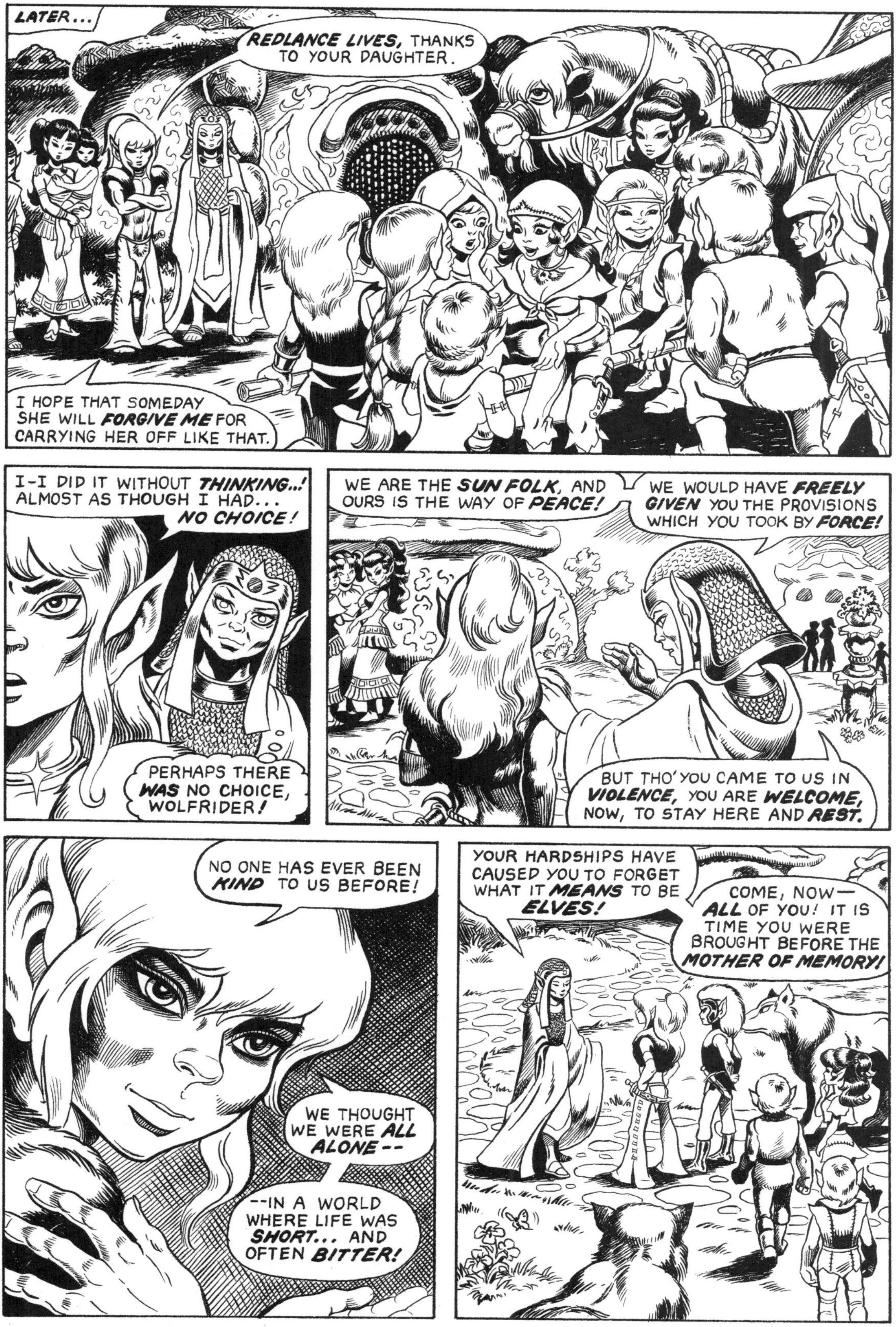

LATER...
REDLANCE LIVES, THANKS TO YOUR DAUGHTER.
I HOPE THAT SOMEDAY SHE WILL FORGIVE ME FOR CARRYING HER OFF LIKE THAT.
I-I DID IT WITHOUT THINKING...! ALMOST AS THOUGH I HAD... NO CHOICE!
PERHAPS THERE WAS NO CHOICE, WOLFRIDER!
WE ARE THE SUN FOLK, AND OURS IS THE WAY OF PEACE!
WE WOULD HAVE FREELY GIVEN YOU THE PROVISIONS WHICH YOU TOOK BY FORCE!
BUT THO' YOU CAME TO US IN VIOLENCE, YOU ARE WELCOME, NOW, TO STAY HERE AND REST.
NO ONE HAS EVER BEEN KIND TO US BEFORE!
WE THOUGHT WE WERE ALL ALONE--
--IN A WORLD WHERE LIFE WAS SHORT... AND OFTEN BITTER!
YOUR HARDSHIPS HAVE CAUSED YOU TO FORGET WHAT IT MEANS TO BE ELVES!
COME, NOW— ALL OF YOU! IT IS TIME YOU WERE BROUGHT BEFORE THE MOTHER OF MEMORY!

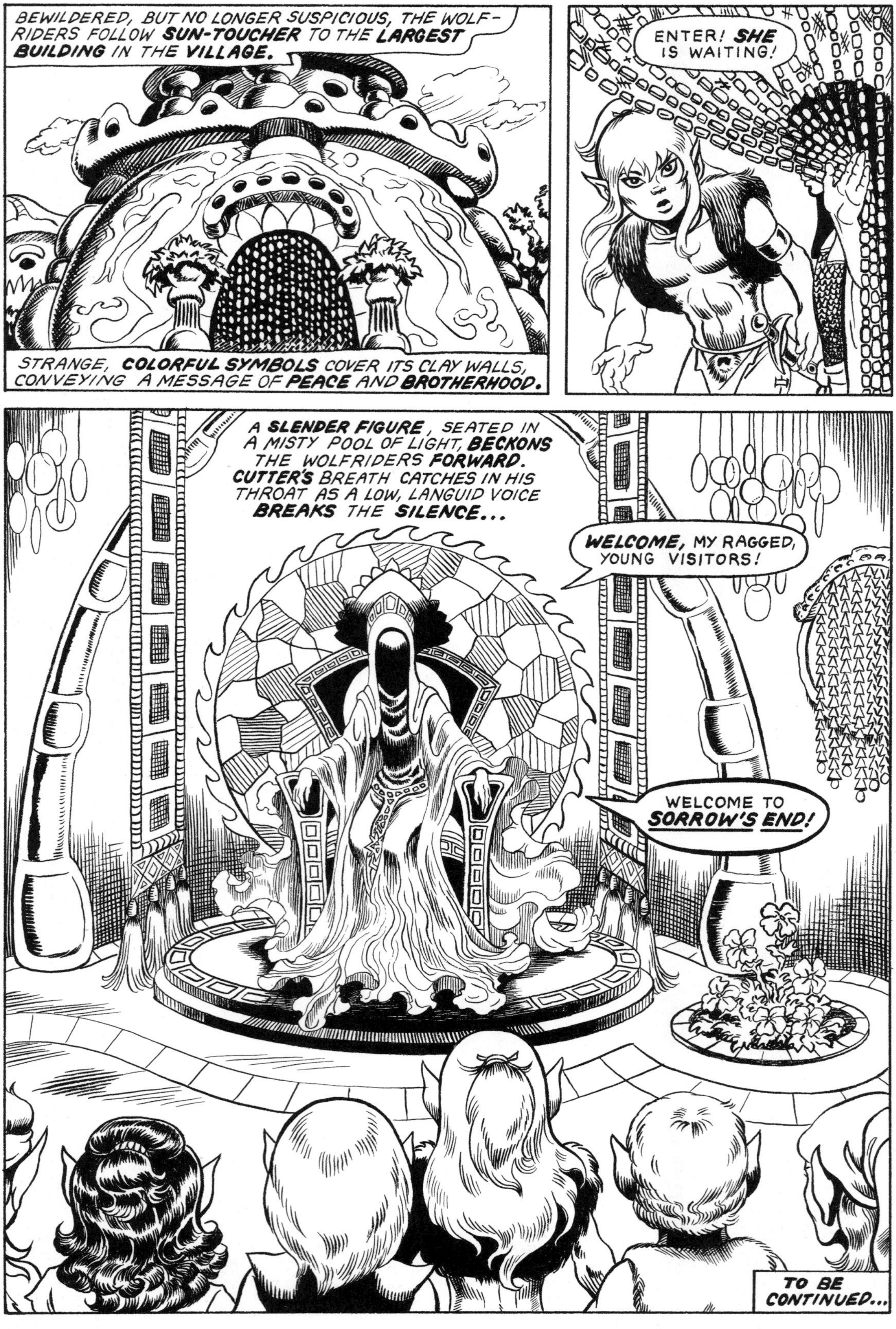
BEWILDERED, BUT NO LONGER SUSPICIOUS, THE WOLF-RIDERS FOLLOW SUN-TOUCHER TO THE LARGEST BUILDING IN THE VILLAGE.
STRANGE, COLORFUL SYMBOLS COVER ITS CLAY WALLS, CONVEYING A MESSAGE OF PEACE AND BROTHERHOOD.
ENTER! SHE IS WAITING!
A SLENDER FIGURE, SEATED IN A MISTY POOL OF LIGHT, BECKONS THE WOLFRIDERS FORWARD. CUTTER'S BREATH CATCHES IN HIS THROAT AS A LOW, LANGUID VOICE BREAKS THE SILENCE...
WELCOME, MY RAGGED, YOUNG VISITORS!
WELCOME TO SORROW'S END!
TO BE CONTINUED...

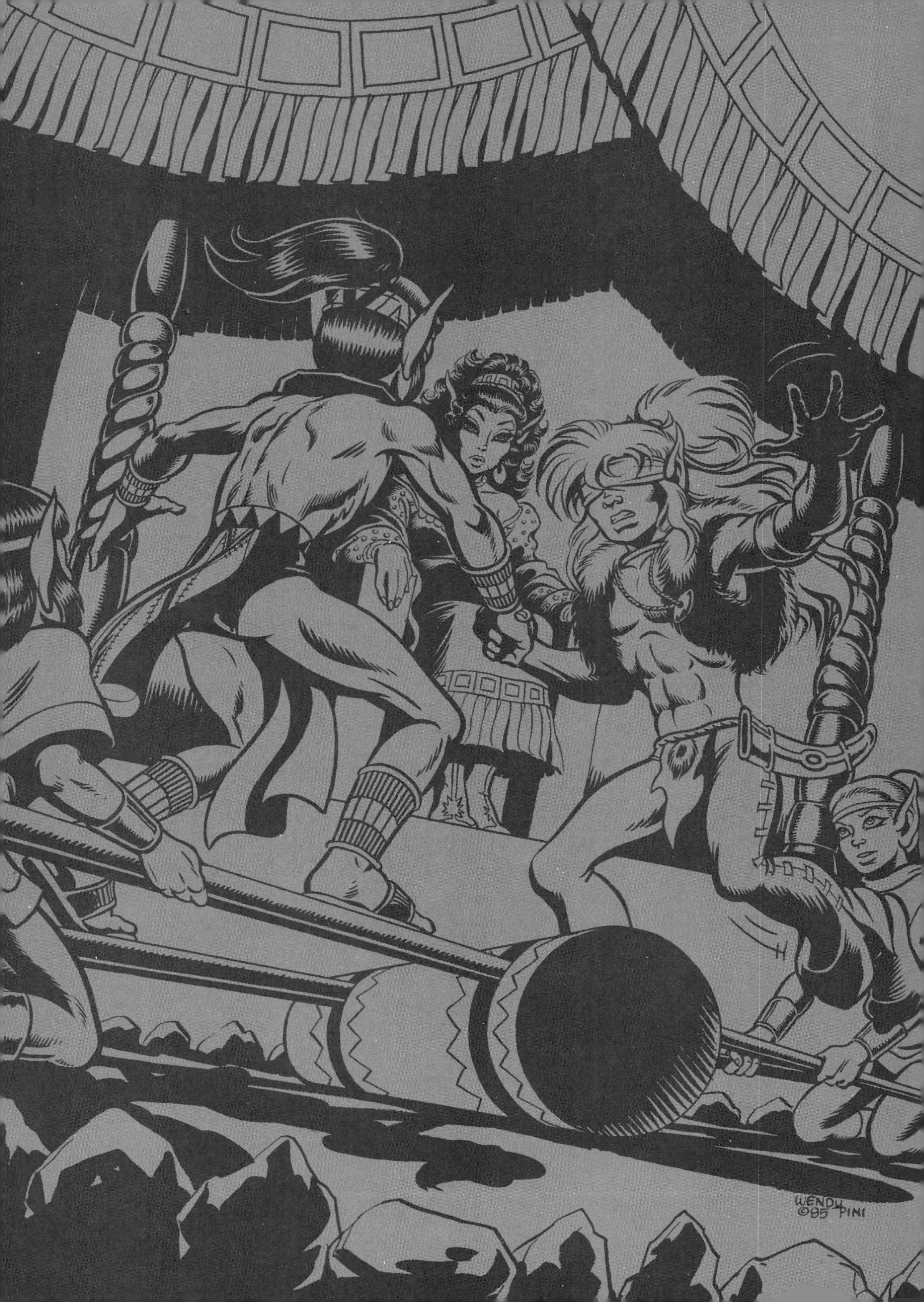
WENDY
©85 PINI

THE CHALLENGE

SURVIVING A CRUEL, THREE-DAY JOURNEY THROUGH SCORCHING DESERT SANDS, THE **WOLFRIDERS** COME UPON A WONDROUS **ELFIN VILLAGE** FLOURISHING IN THE MIDST OF THE WILDERNESS...

STORY BY WENDY+RICHARD PINI
ART BY WENDY PINI

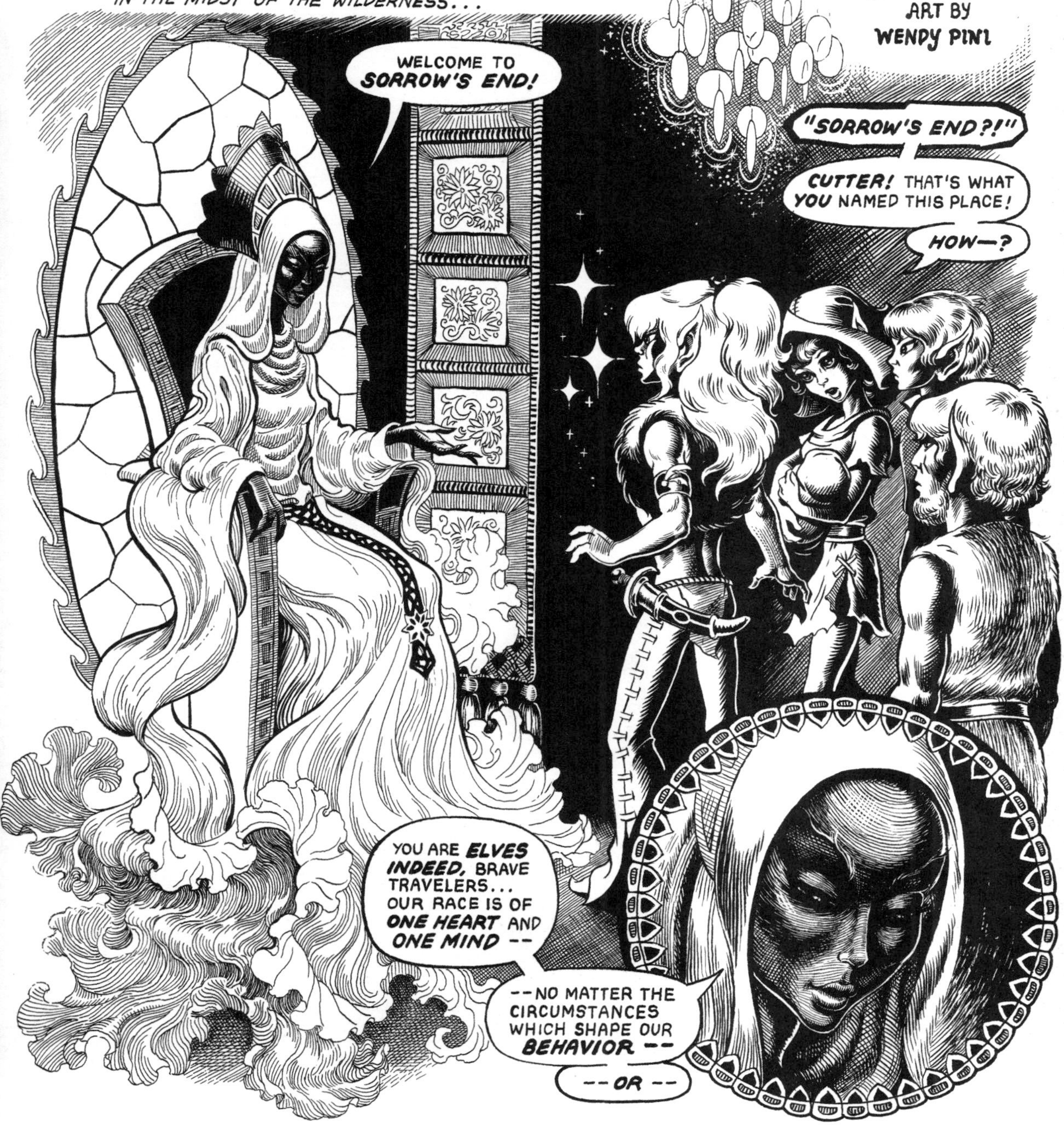
WELCOME TO SORROW'S END!
"SORROW'S END?!"
CUTTER! THAT'S WHAT YOU NAMED THIS PLACE!
HOW—?
YOU ARE ELVES INDEED, BRAVE TRAVELERS... OUR RACE IS OF ONE HEART AND ONE MIND --
--NO MATTER THE CIRCUMSTANCES WHICH SHAPE OUR BEHAVIOR --
-- OR --

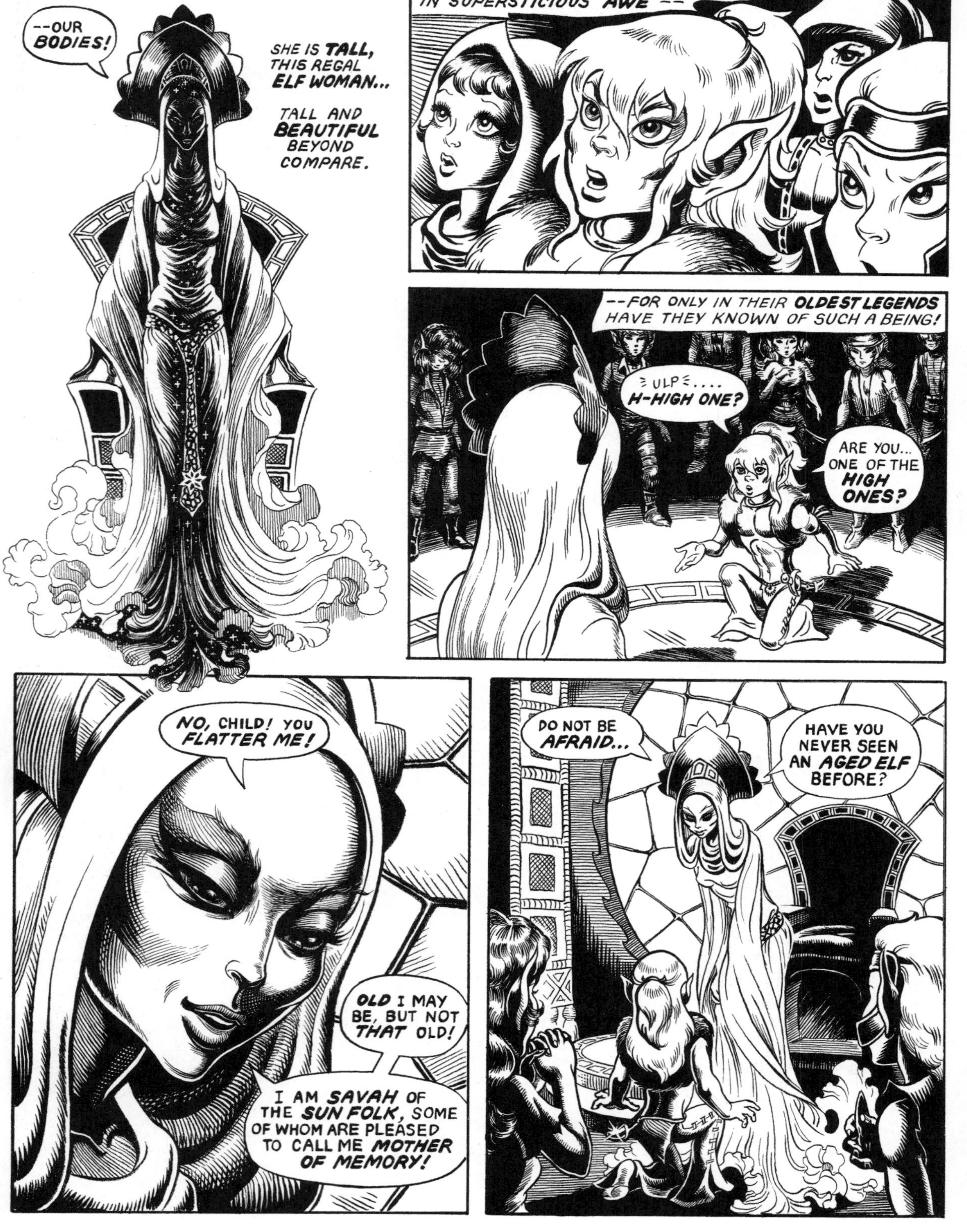
--OUR BODIES!
SHE IS TALL, THIS REGAL ELF WOMAN...
TALL AND BEAUTIFUL BEYOND COMPARE.
THE WOLFRIDERS SHRINK FROM HER IN SUPERSTICIOUS AWE --
--FOR ONLY IN THEIR OLDEST LEGENDS HAVE THEY KNOWN OF SUCH A BEING!
ULP.... H-HIGH ONE?
ARE YOU... ONE OF THE HIGH ONES?
NO, CHILD! YOU FLATTER ME!
OLD I MAY BE, BUT NOT THAT OLD!
I AM SAVAH OF THE SUN FOLK, SOME OF WHOM ARE PLEASED TO CALL ME MOTHER OF MEMORY!
DO NOT BE AFRAID...
HAVE YOU NEVER SEEN AN AGED ELF BEFORE?

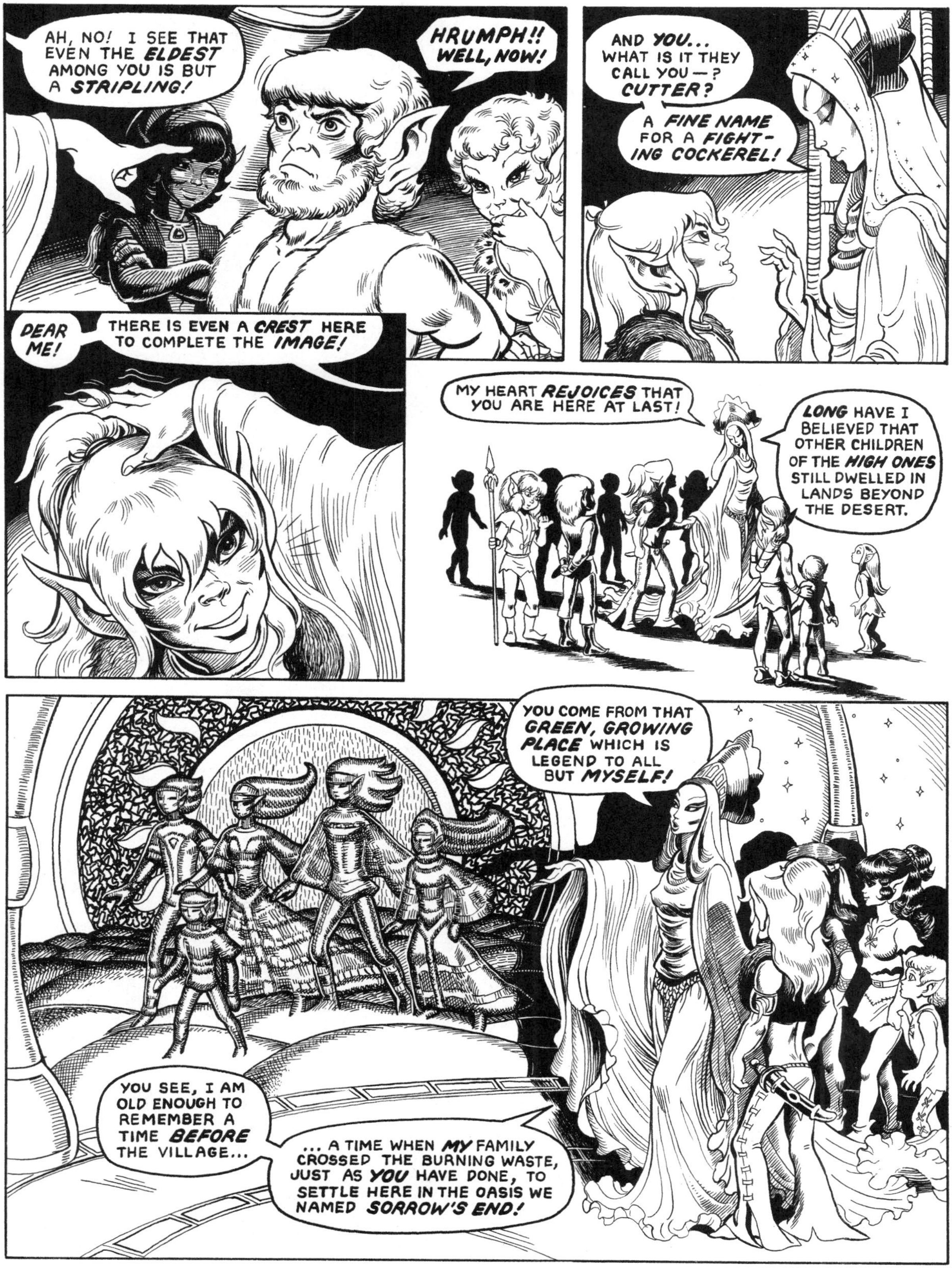

AH, NO! I SEE THAT EVEN THE ELDEST AMONG YOU IS BUT A STRIPLING!
HRUMPH!! WELL, NOW!
AND YOU... WHAT IS IT THEY CALL YOU —? CUTTER?
A FINE NAME FOR A FIGHT-ING COCKEREL!
DEAR ME!
THERE IS EVEN A CREST HERE TO COMPLETE THE IMAGE!
MY HEART REJOICES THAT YOU ARE HERE AT LAST!
LONG HAVE I BELIEVED THAT OTHER CHILDREN OF THE HIGH ONES STILL DWELLED IN LANDS BEYOND THE DESERT.
YOU COME FROM THAT GREEN, GROWING PLACE WHICH IS LEGEND TO ALL BUT MYSELF!
YOU SEE, I AM OLD ENOUGH TO REMEMBER A TIME BEFORE THE VILLAGE...
... A TIME WHEN MY FAMILY CROSSED THE BURNING WASTE, JUST AS YOU HAVE DONE, TO SETTLE HERE IN THE OASIS WE NAMED SORROW'S END!

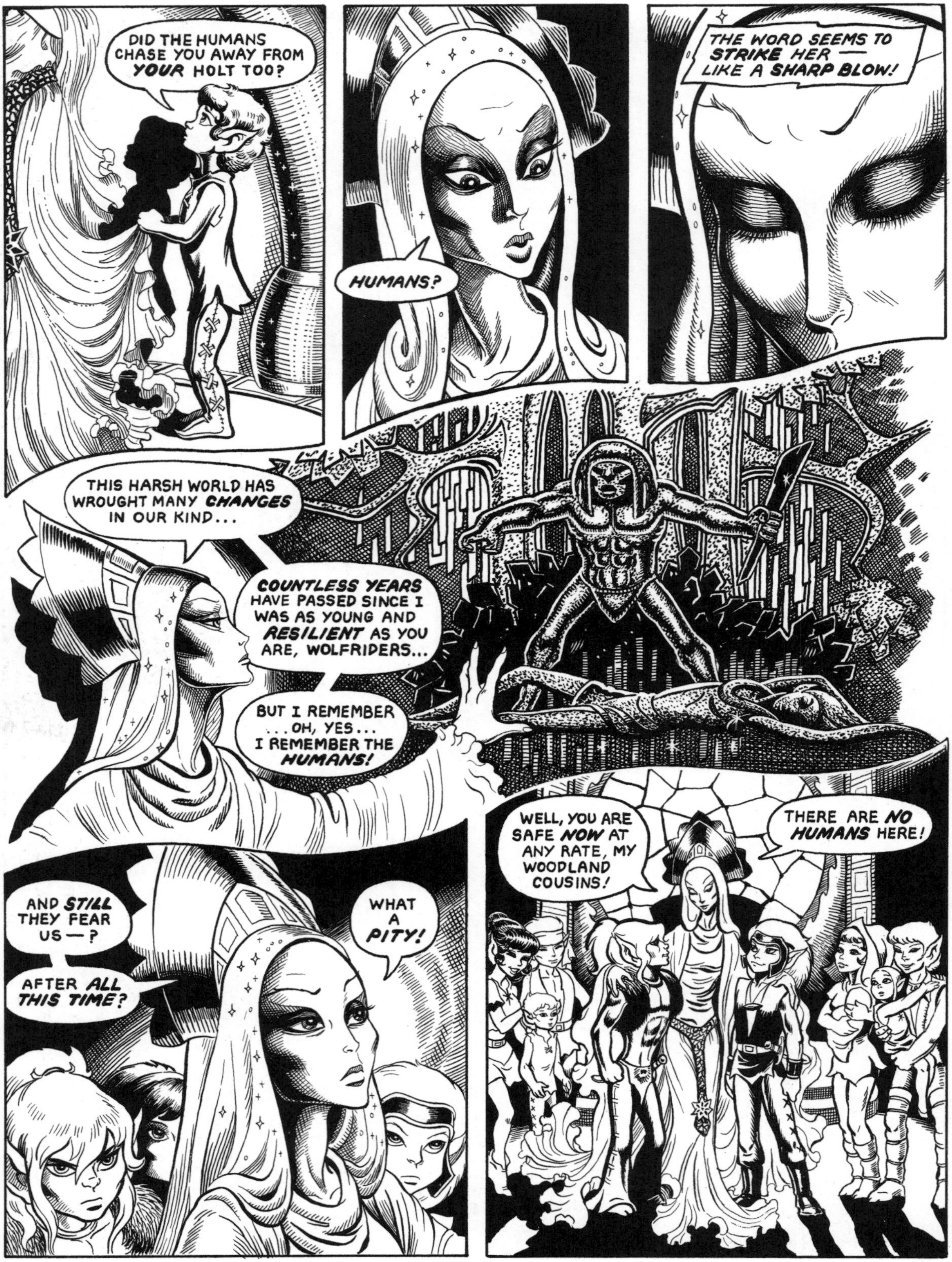
DID THE HUMANS CHASE YOU AWAY FROM YOUR HOLT TOO?
HUMANS?
THE WORD SEEMS TO STRIKE HER — LIKE A SHARP BLOW!
THIS HARSH WORLD HAS WROUGHT MANY CHANGES IN OUR KIND...
COUNTLESS YEARS HAVE PASSED SINCE I WAS AS YOUNG AND RESILIENT AS YOU ARE, WOLFRIDERS...
BUT I REMEMBER ...OH, YES... I REMEMBER THE HUMANS!
AND STILL THEY FEAR US—?
AFTER ALL THIS TIME?
WHAT A PITY!
WELL, YOU ARE SAFE NOW AT ANY RATE, MY WOODLAND COUSINS!
THERE ARE NO HUMANS HERE!

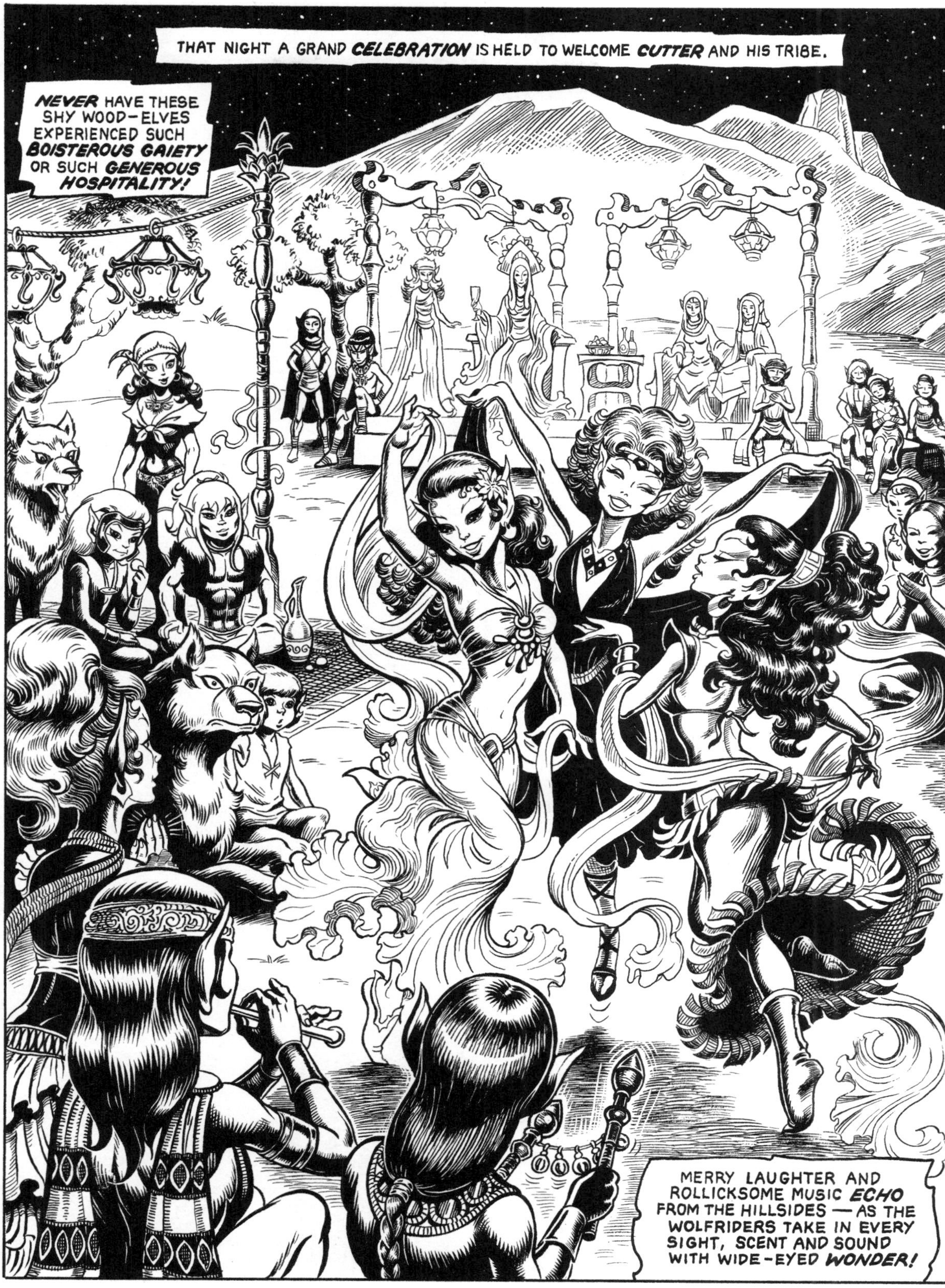
THAT NIGHT A GRAND CELEBRATION IS HELD TO WELCOME CUTTER AND HIS TRIBE.
NEVER HAVE THESE SHY WOOD-ELVES EXPERIENCED SUCH BOISTEROUS GAIETY OR SUCH GENEROUS HOSPITALITY!
MERRY LAUGHTER AND ROLLICKSOME MUSIC ECHO FROM THE HILLSIDES — AS THE WOLFRIDERS TAKE IN EVERY SIGHT, SCENT AND SOUND WITH WIDE-EYED WONDER!

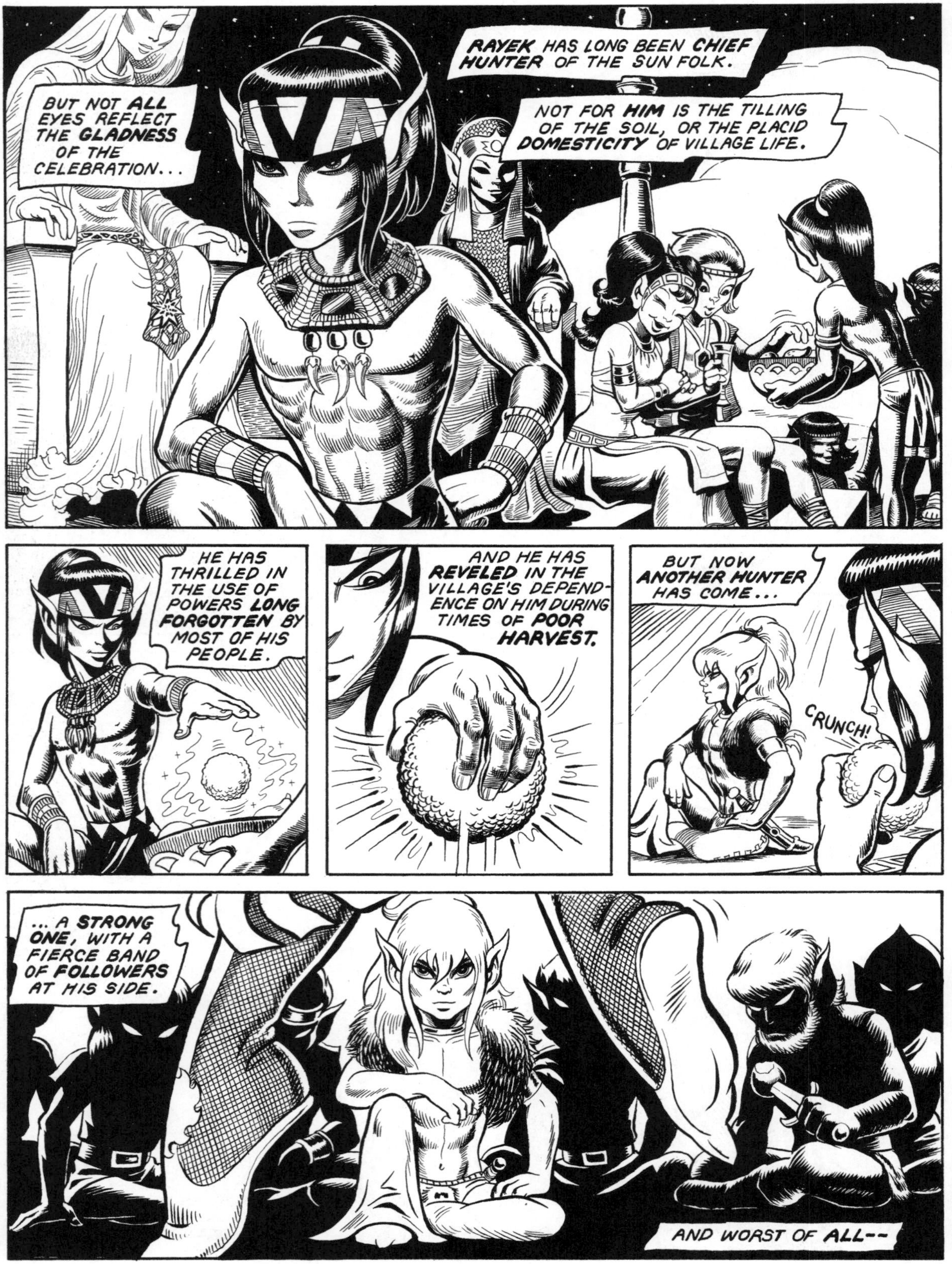

BUT NOT ALL EYES REFLECT THE GLADNESS OF THE CELEBRATION...
RAYEK HAS LONG BEEN CHIEF HUNTER OF THE SUN FOLK.
NOT FOR HIM IS THE TILLING OF THE SOIL, OR THE PLACID DOMESTICITY OF VILLAGE LIFE.
HE HAS THRILLED IN THE USE OF POWERS LONG FORGOTTEN BY MOST OF HIS PEOPLE.
AND HE HAS REVELED IN THE VILLAGE'S DEPENDENCE ON HIM DURING TIMES OF POOR HARVEST.
BUT NOW ANOTHER HUNTER HAS COME...
CRUNCH!
... A STRONG ONE, WITH A FIERCE BAND OF FOLLOWERS AT HIS SIDE.
AND WORST OF ALL--

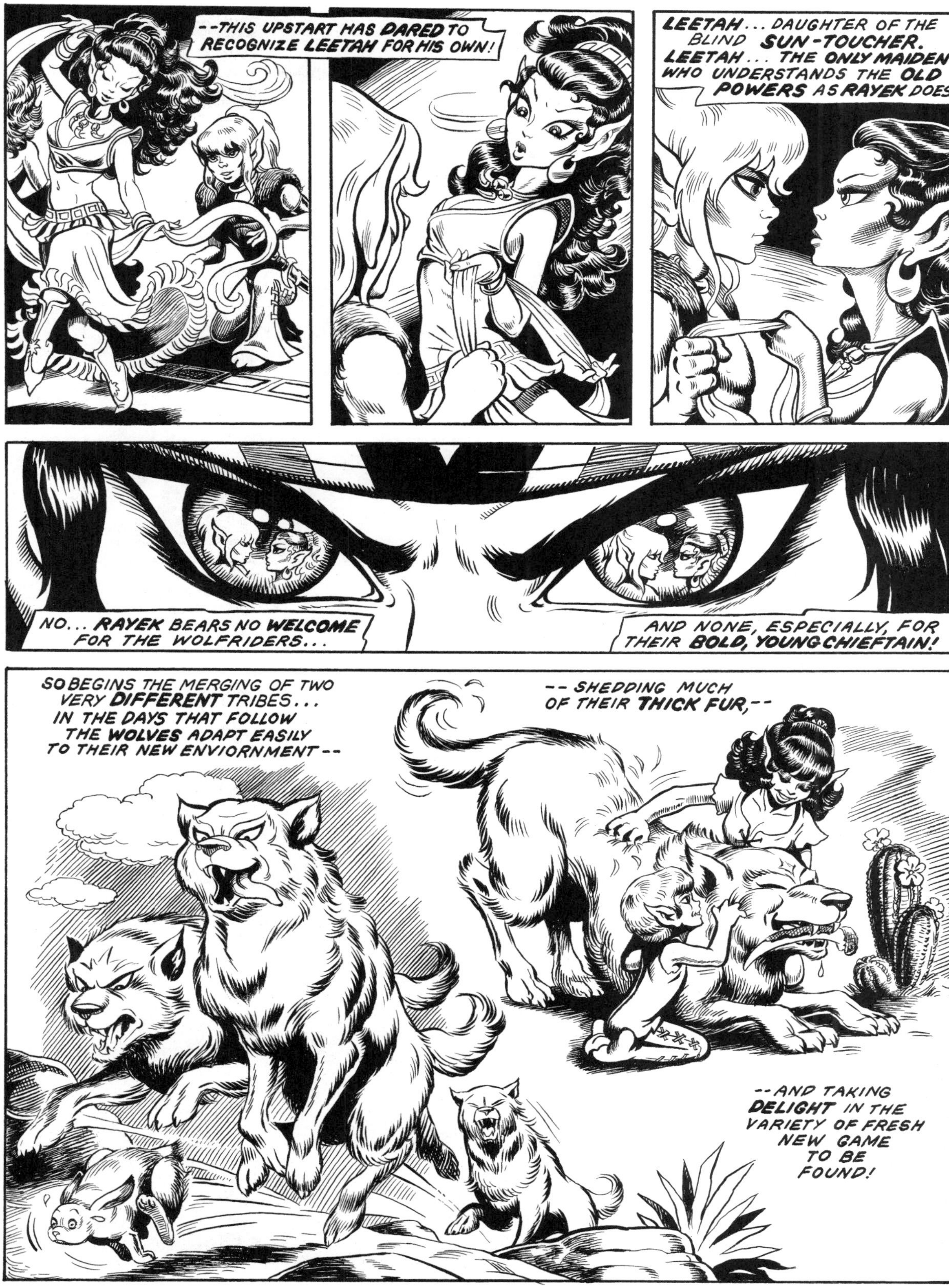
--THIS UPSTART HAS DARED TO RECOGNIZE LEETAH FOR HIS OWN!
LEETAH... DAUGHTER OF THE BLIND SUN-TOUCHER. LEETAH... THE ONLY MAIDEN WHO UNDERSTANDS THE OLD POWERS AS RAYEK DOES.
NO... RAYEK BEARS NO WELCOME FOR THE WOLFRIDERS...
AND NONE, ESPECIALLY, FOR THEIR BOLD, YOUNG CHIEFTAIN!
SO BEGINS THE MERGING OF TWO VERY DIFFERENT TRIBES... IN THE DAYS THAT FOLLOW THE WOLVES ADAPT EASILY TO THEIR NEW ENVIORNMENT--
--SHEDDING MUCH OF THEIR THICK FUR,--
--AND TAKING DELIGHT IN THE VARIETY OF FRESH NEW GAME TO BE FOUND!

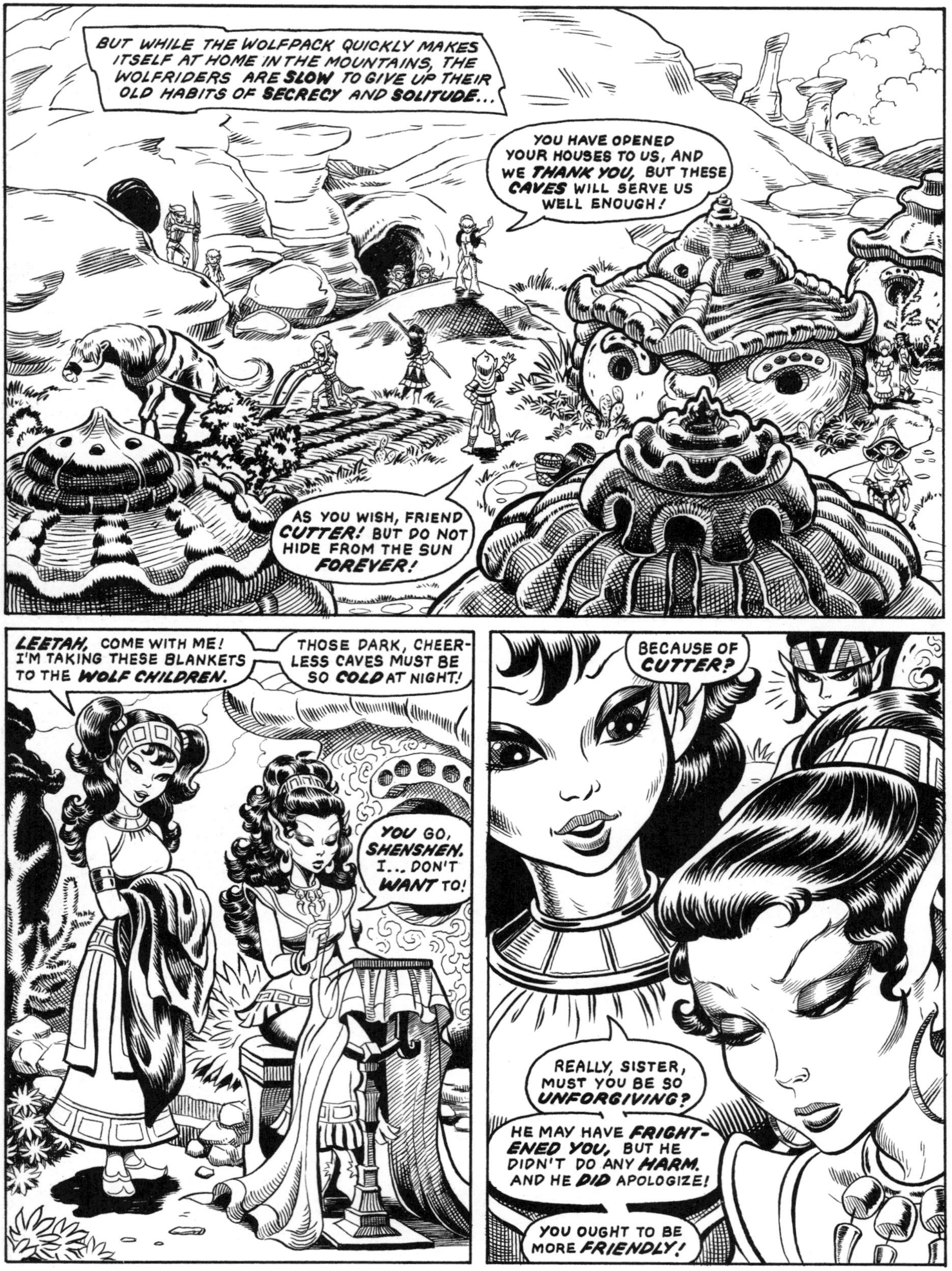
BUT WHILE THE WOLFPACK QUICKLY MAKES ITSELF AT HOME IN THE MOUNTAINS, THE WOLFRIDERS ARE SLOW TO GIVE UP THEIR OLD HABITS OF SECRECY AND SOLITUDE...
YOU HAVE OPENED YOUR HOUSES TO US, AND WE THANK YOU, BUT THESE CAVES WILL SERVE US WELL ENOUGH!
AS YOU WISH, FRIEND CUTTER! BUT DO NOT HIDE FROM THE SUN FOREVER!
LEETAH, COME WITH ME! I'M TAKING THESE BLANKETS TO THE WOLF CHILDREN.
THOSE DARK, CHEERLESS CAVES MUST BE SO COLD AT NIGHT!
YOU GO, SHENSHEN. I... DON'T WANT TO!
BECAUSE OF CUTTER?
REALLY, SISTER, MUST YOU BE SO UNFORGIVING?
HE MAY HAVE FRIGHTENED YOU, BUT HE DIDN'T DO ANY HARM. AND HE DID APOLOGIZE!
YOU OUGHT TO BE MORE FRIENDLY!

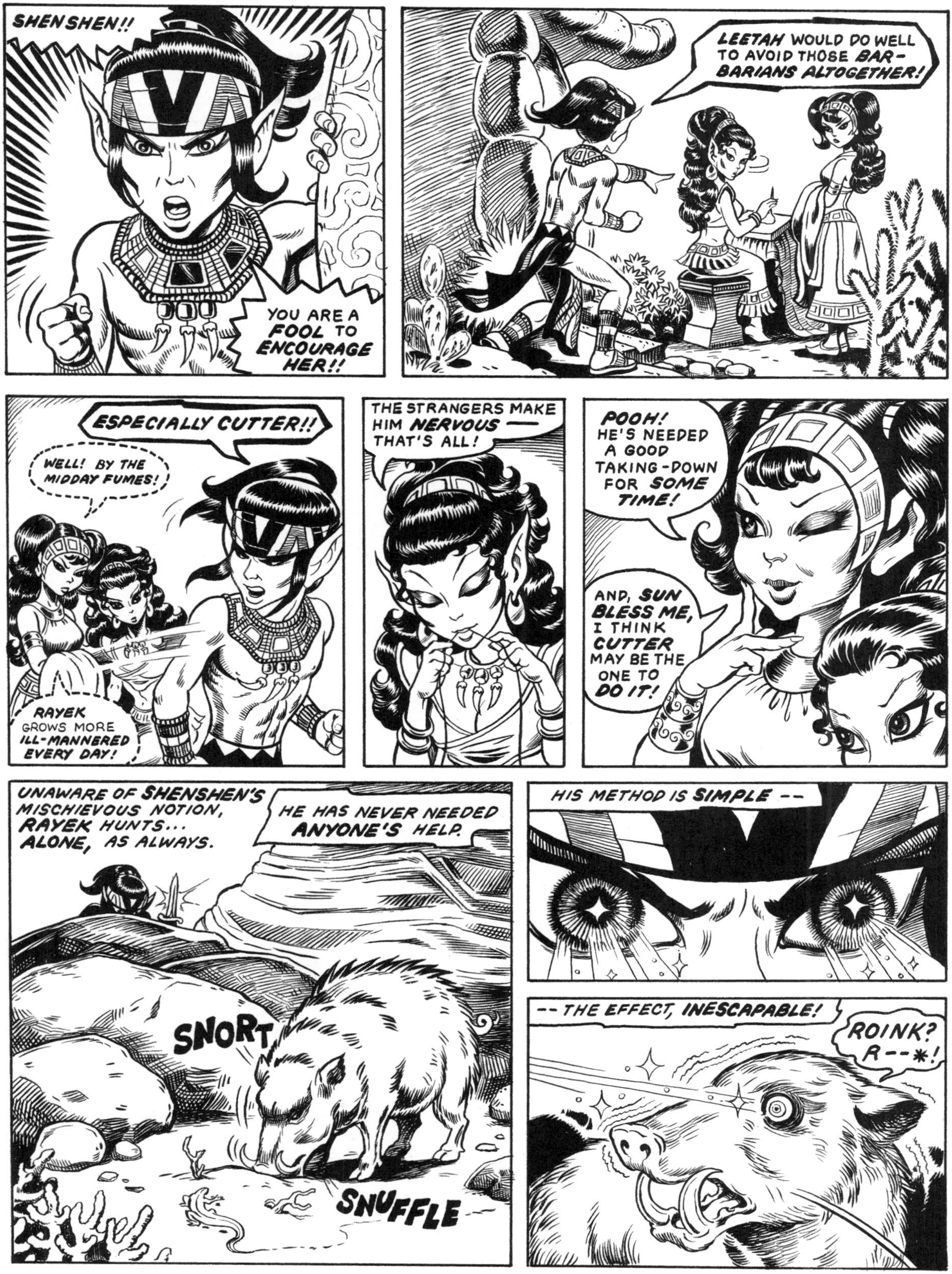
SHENSHEN!!
YOU ARE A FOOL TO ENCOURAGE HER!!
LEETAH WOULD DO WELL TO AVOID THOSE BAR-BARIANS ALTOGETHER!
ESPECIALLY CUTTER!!
WELL! BY THE MIDDAY FUMES!
RAYEK GROWS MORE ILL-MANNERED EVERY DAY!
THE STRANGERS MAKE HIM NERVOUS — THAT'S ALL!
POOH! HE'S NEEDED A GOOD TAKING-DOWN FOR SOME TIME!
AND, SUN BLESS ME, I THINK CUTTER MAY BE THE ONE TO DO IT!
UNAWARE OF SHENSHEN'S MISCHIEVOUS NOTION, RAYEK HUNTS... ALONE, AS ALWAYS.
HE HAS NEVER NEEDED ANYONE'S HELP.
SNORT
SNUFFLE
HIS METHOD IS SIMPLE --
-- THE EFFECT, INESCAPABLE!
ROINK? R--*!

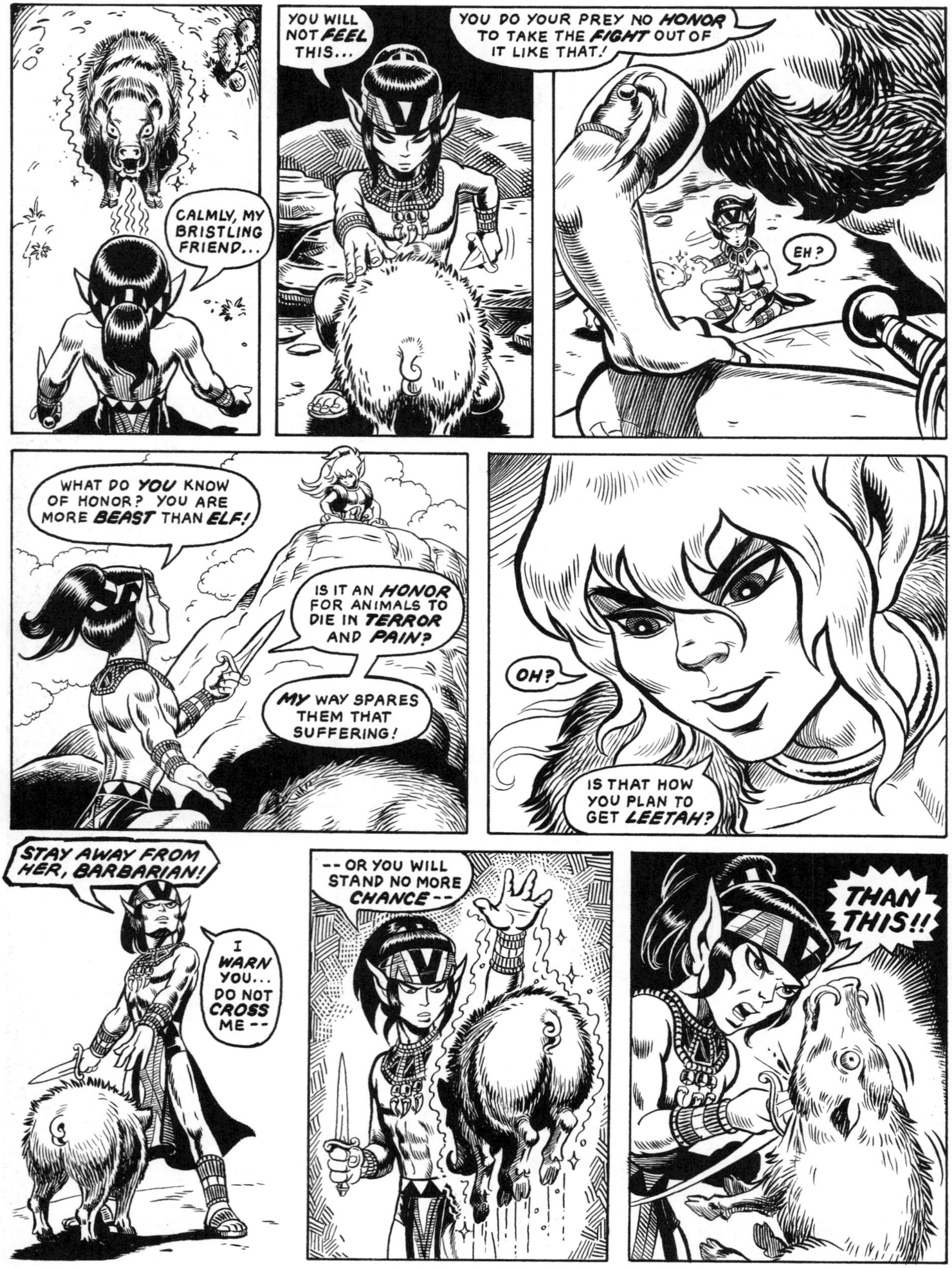

CALMLY, MY BRISTLING FRIEND...
YOU WILL NOT FEEL THIS...
YOU DO YOUR PREY NO HONOR TO TAKE THE FIGHT OUT OF IT LIKE THAT!
EH?
WHAT DO YOU KNOW OF HONOR? YOU ARE MORE BEAST THAN ELF!
IS IT AN HONOR FOR ANIMALS TO DIE IN TERROR AND PAIN?
MY WAY SPARES THEM THAT SUFFERING!
OH?
IS THAT HOW YOU PLAN TO GET LEETAH?
STAY AWAY FROM HER, BARBARIAN!
I WARN YOU... DO NOT CROSS ME --
-- OR YOU WILL STAND NO MORE CHANCE --
THAN THIS!!

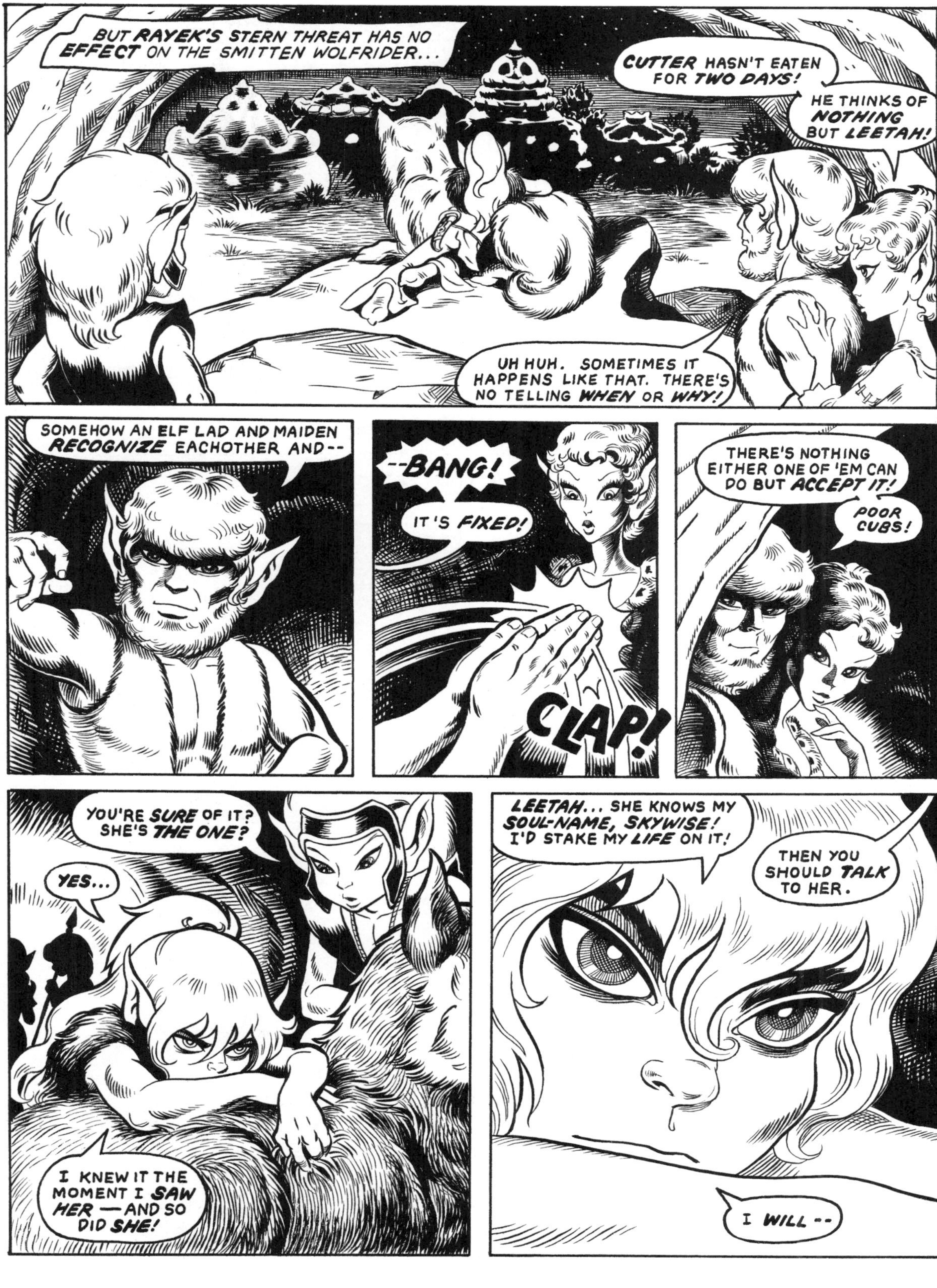

BUT RAYEK'S STERN THREAT HAS NO EFFECT ON THE SMITTEN WOLFRIDER...
CUTTER HASN'T EATEN FOR TWO DAYS!
HE THINKS OF NOTHING BUT LEETAH!
UH HUH. SOMETIMES IT HAPPENS LIKE THAT. THERE'S NO TELLING WHEN OR WHY!
SOMEHOW AN ELF LAD AND MAIDEN RECOGNIZE EACHOTHER AND--
--BANG!
IT'S FIXED!
CLAP!
THERE'S NOTHING EITHER ONE OF 'EM CAN DO BUT ACCEPT IT!
POOR CUBS!
YOU'RE SURE OF IT? SHE'S THE ONE?
YES...
I KNEW IT THE MOMENT I SAW HER —AND SO DID SHE!
LEETAH... SHE KNOWS MY SOUL-NAME, SKYWISE! I'D STAKE MY LIFE ON IT!
THEN YOU SHOULD TALK TO HER.
I WILL--

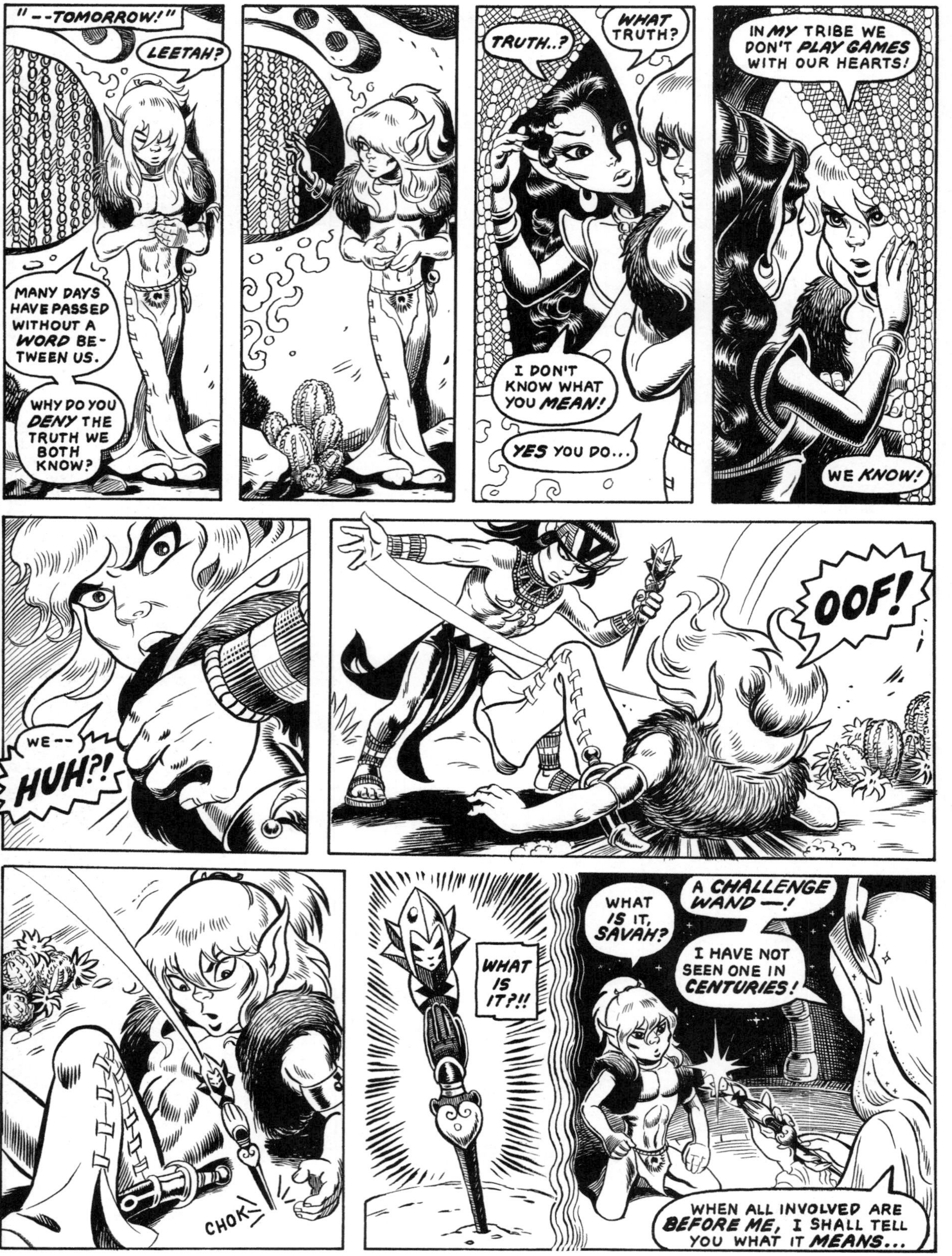

"--TOMORROW!"
LEETAH?
MANY DAYS HAVE PASSED WITHOUT A WORD BETWEEN US.
WHY DO YOU DENY THE TRUTH WE BOTH KNOW?
TRUTH..?
WHAT TRUTH?
I DON'T KNOW WHAT YOU MEAN!
YES YOU DO...
IN MY TRIBE WE DON'T PLAY GAMES WITH OUR HEARTS!
WE KNOW!
WE--
HUH?!
OOF!
CHOK
WHAT IS IT?!!
WHAT IS IT, SAVAH?
A CHALLENGE WAND--!
I HAVE NOT SEEN ONE IN CENTURIES!
WHEN ALL INVOLVED ARE BEFORE ME, I SHALL TELL YOU WHAT IT MEANS...

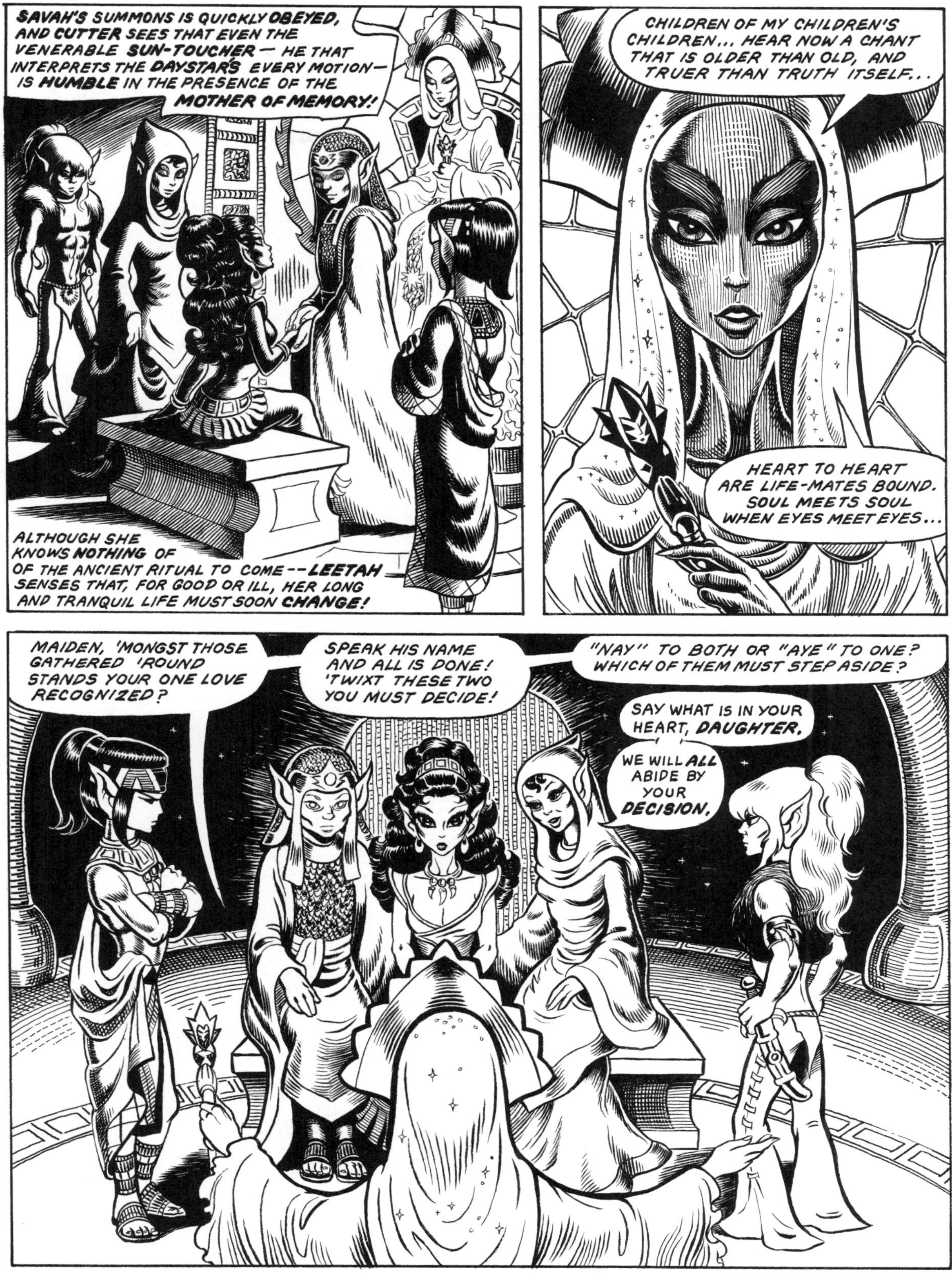
SAVAH'S SUMMONS IS QUICKLY OBEYED, AND CUTTER SEES THAT EVEN THE VENERABLE SUN-TOUCHER — HE THAT INTERPRETS THE DAYSTAR'S EVERY MOTION — IS HUMBLE IN THE PRESENCE OF THE MOTHER OF MEMORY!
ALTHOUGH SHE KNOWS NOTHING OF OF THE ANCIENT RITUAL TO COME -- LEETAH SENSES THAT, FOR GOOD OR ILL, HER LONG AND TRANQUIL LIFE MUST SOON CHANGE!
CHILDREN OF MY CHILDREN'S CHILDREN... HEAR NOW A CHANT THAT IS OLDER THAN OLD, AND TRUER THAN TRUTH ITSELF...
HEART TO HEART ARE LIFE-MATES BOUND. SOUL MEETS SOUL WHEN EYES MEET EYES...
MAIDEN, 'MONGST THOSE GATHERED 'ROUND STANDS YOUR ONE LOVE RECOGNIZED?
SPEAK HIS NAME AND ALL IS DONE! 'TWIXT THESE TWO YOU MUST DECIDE!
"NAY" TO BOTH OR "AYE" TO ONE? WHICH OF THEM MUST STEP ASIDE?
SAY WHAT IS IN YOUR HEART, DAUGHTER.
WE WILL ALL ABIDE BY YOUR DECISION.

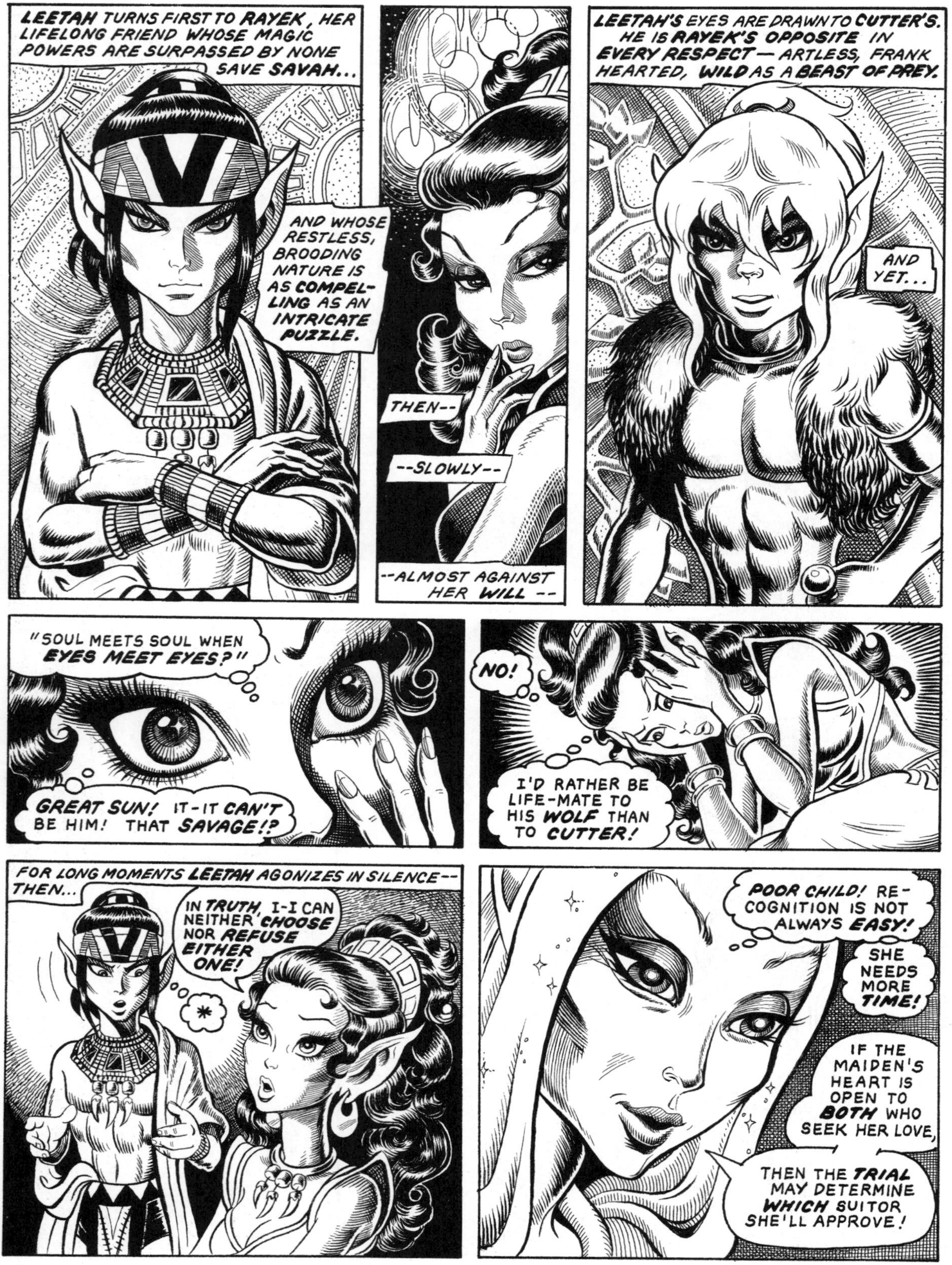
LEETAH TURNS FIRST TO RAYEK, HER LIFELONG FRIEND WHOSE MAGIC POWERS ARE SURPASSED BY NONE SAVE SAVAH...
AND WHOSE RESTLESS, BROODING NATURE IS AS COMPELLING AS AN INTRICATE PUZZLE.
THEN--
--SLOWLY--
--ALMOST AGAINST HER WILL --
LEETAH'S EYES ARE DRAWN TO CUTTER'S. HE IS RAYEK'S OPPOSITE IN EVERY RESPECT — ARTLESS, FRANK HEARTED, WILD AS A BEAST OF PREY.
AND YET...
"SOUL MEETS SOUL WHEN EYES MEET EYES?"
GREAT SUN! IT-IT CAN'T BE HIM! THAT SAVAGE!?
NO!
I'D RATHER BE LIFE-MATE TO HIS WOLF THAN TO CUTTER!
FOR LONG MOMENTS LEETAH AGONIZES IN SILENCE-- THEN...
IN TRUTH, I-I CAN NEITHER CHOOSE NOR REFUSE EITHER ONE!
*
POOR CHILD! RECOGNITION IS NOT ALWAYS EASY!
SHE NEEDS MORE TIME!
IF THE MAIDEN'S HEART IS OPEN TO BOTH WHO SEEK HER LOVE,
THEN THE TRIAL MAY DETERMINE WHICH SUITOR SHE'LL APPROVE!

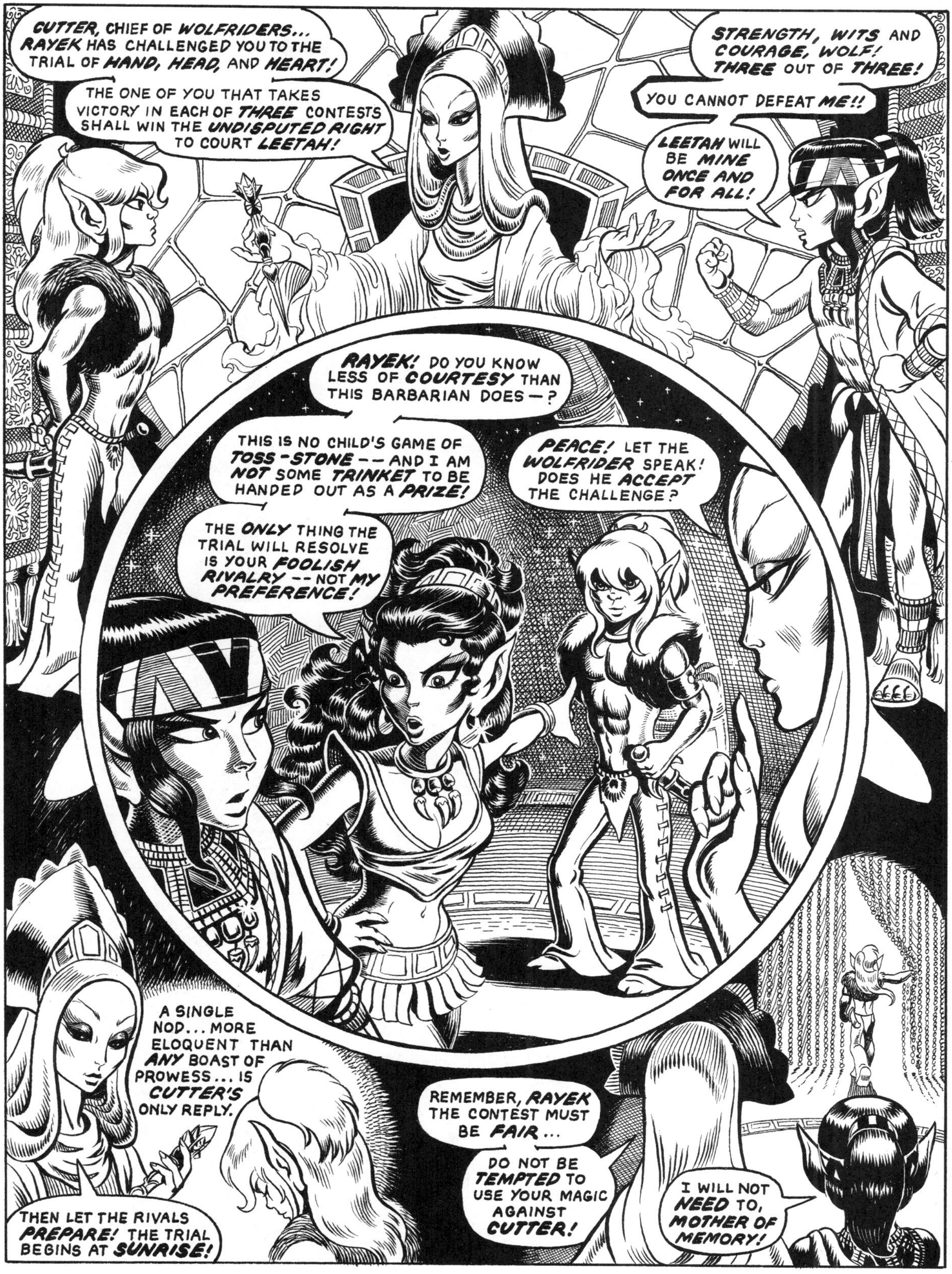
CUTTER, CHIEF OF WOLFRIDERS... RAYEK HAS CHALLENGED YOU TO THE TRIAL OF HAND, HEAD, AND HEART!
THE ONE OF YOU THAT TAKES VICTORY IN EACH OF THREE CONTESTS SHALL WIN THE UNDISPUTED RIGHT TO COURT LEETAH!
STRENGTH, WITS AND COURAGE, WOLF! THREE OUT OF THREE!
YOU CANNOT DEFEAT ME!!
LEETAH WILL BE MINE ONCE AND FOR ALL!
RAYEK! DO YOU KNOW LESS OF COURTESY THAN THIS BARBARIAN DOES—?
THIS IS NO CHILD'S GAME OF TOSS-STONE -- AND I AM NOT SOME TRINKET TO BE HANDED OUT AS A PRIZE!
THE ONLY THING THE TRIAL WILL RESOLVE IS YOUR FOOLISH RIVALRY -- NOT MY PREFERENCE!
PEACE! LET THE WOLFRIDER SPEAK! DOES HE ACCEPT THE CHALLENGE?
A SINGLE NOD... MORE ELOQUENT THAN ANY BOAST OF PROWESS... IS CUTTER'S ONLY REPLY.
THEN LET THE RIVALS PREPARE! THE TRIAL BEGINS AT SUNRISE!
REMEMBER, RAYEK THE CONTEST MUST BE FAIR...
DO NOT BE TEMPTED TO USE YOUR MAGIC AGAINST CUTTER!
I WILL NOT NEED TO, MOTHER OF MEMORY!

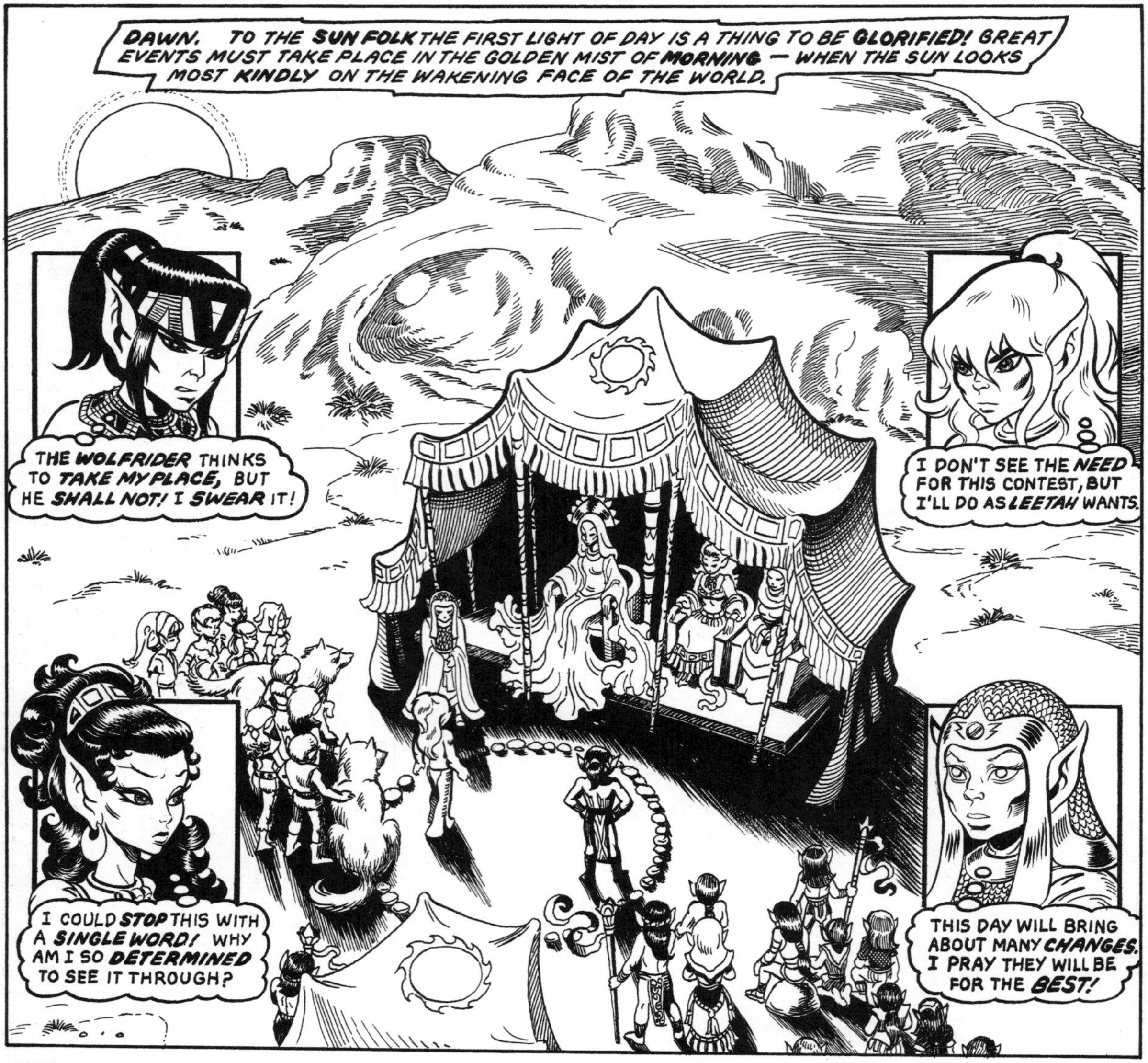
DAWN. TO THE SUN FOLK THE FIRST LIGHT OF DAY IS A THING TO BE GLORIFIED! GREAT EVENTS MUST TAKE PLACE IN THE GOLDEN MIST OF MORNING — WHEN THE SUN LOOKS MOST KINDLY ON THE WAKENING FACE OF THE WORLD.
THE WOLFRIDER THINKS TO TAKE MY PLACE, BUT HE SHALL NOT! I SWEAR IT!
I DON'T SEE THE NEED FOR THIS CONTEST, BUT I'LL DO AS LEETAH WANTS.
I COULD STOP THIS WITH A SINGLE WORD! WHY AM I SO DETERMINED TO SEE IT THROUGH?
THIS DAY WILL BRING ABOUT MANY CHANGES. I PRAY THEY WILL BE FOR THE BEST!

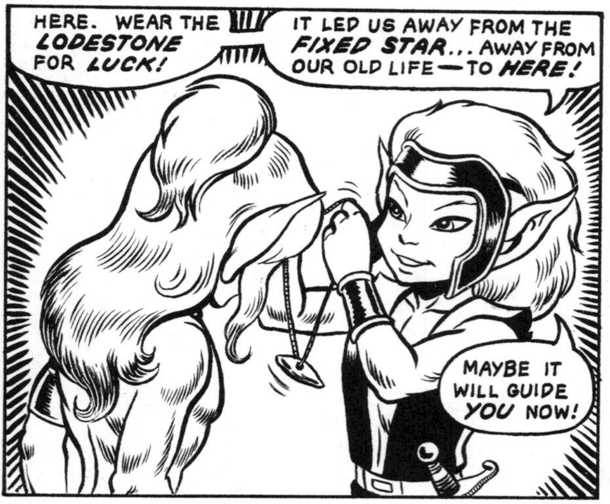
HERE. WEAR THE LODESTONE FOR LUCK!
IT LED US AWAY FROM THE FIXED STAR... AWAY FROM OUR OLD LIFE—TO HERE!
MAYBE IT WILL GUIDE YOU NOW!

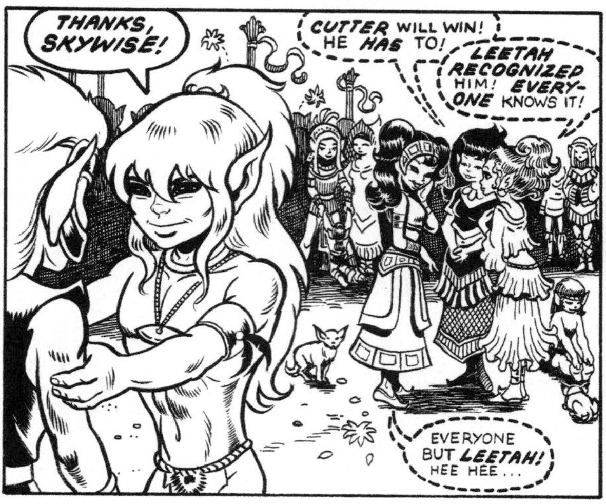
THANKS, SKYWISE!
CUTTER WILL WIN! HE HAS TO!
LEETAH RECOGNIZED HIM! EVERYONE KNOWS IT!
EVERYONE BUT LEETAH! HEE HEE...

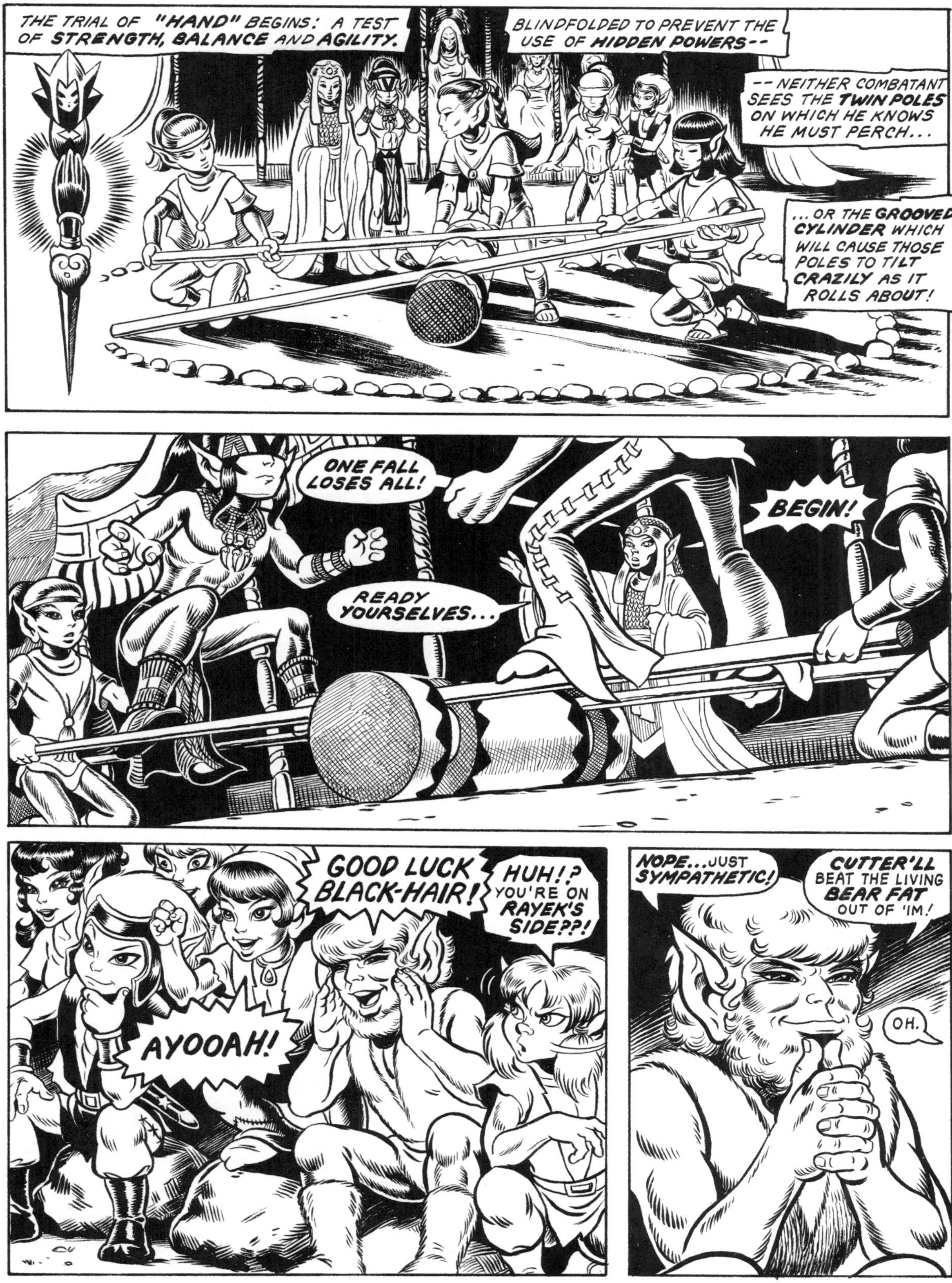
THE TRIAL OF "HAND" BEGINS: A TEST OF STRENGTH, BALANCE AND AGILITY.
BLINDFOLDED TO PREVENT THE USE OF HIDDEN POWERS--
--NEITHER COMBATANT SEES THE TWIN POLES ON WHICH HE KNOWS HE MUST PERCH...
...OR THE GROOVED CYLINDER WHICH WILL CAUSE THOSE POLES TO TILT CRAZILY AS IT ROLLS ABOUT!
ONE FALL LOSES ALL!
READY YOURSELVES...
BEGIN!
GOOD LUCK BLACK-HAIR!
AYOOAH!
HUH!? YOU'RE ON RAYEK'S SIDE??!
NOPE...JUST SYMPATHETIC!
CUTTER'LL BEAT THE LIVING BEAR FAT OUT OF 'IM!
OH.

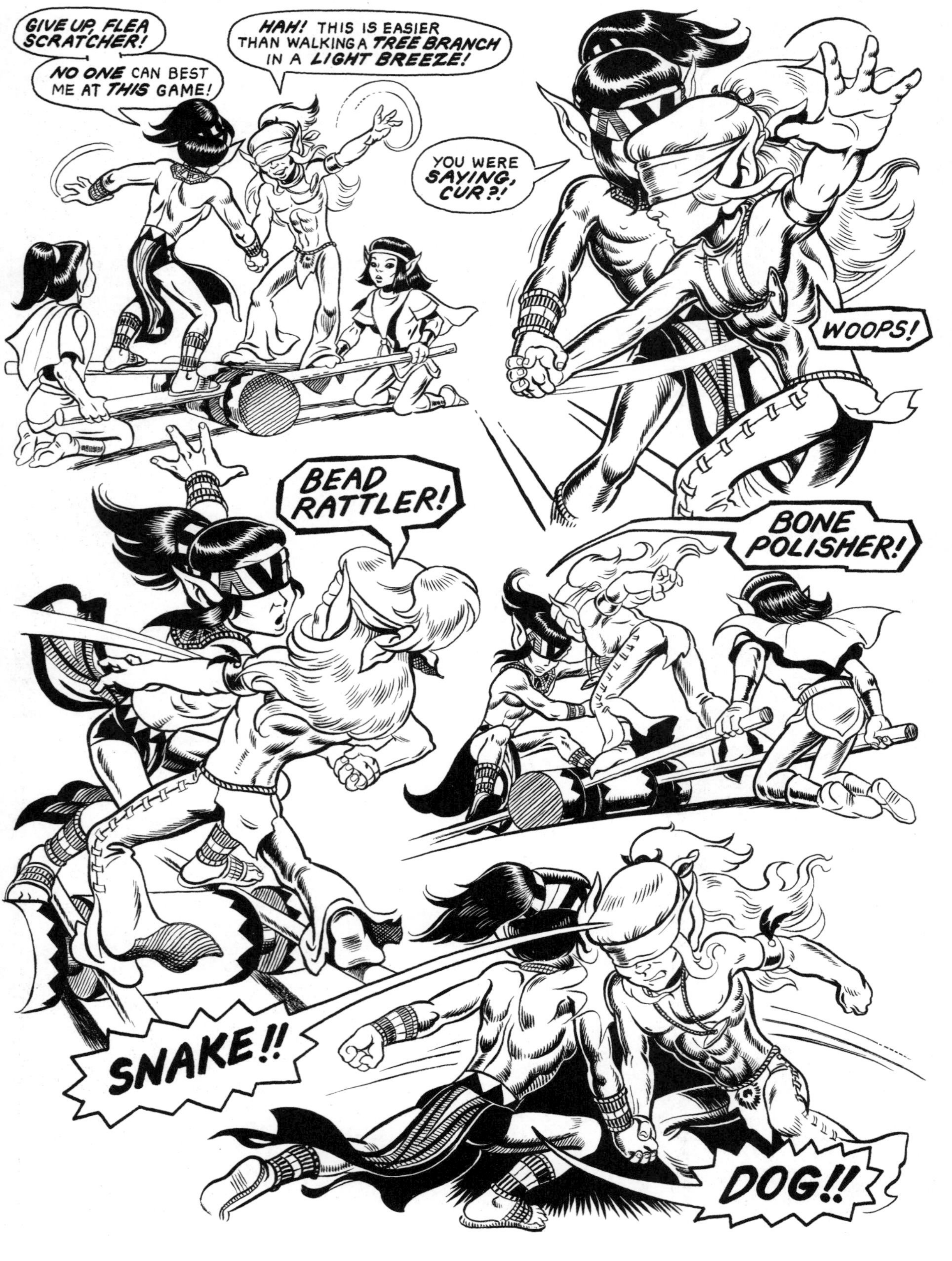

GIVE UP, FLEA SCRATCHER!
NO ONE CAN BEST ME AT THIS GAME!
HAH! THIS IS EASIER THAN WALKING A TREE BRANCH IN A LIGHT BREEZE!
YOU WERE SAYING, CUR?!
WOOPS!
BEAD RATTLER!
BONE POLISHER!
SNAKE!!
DOG!!

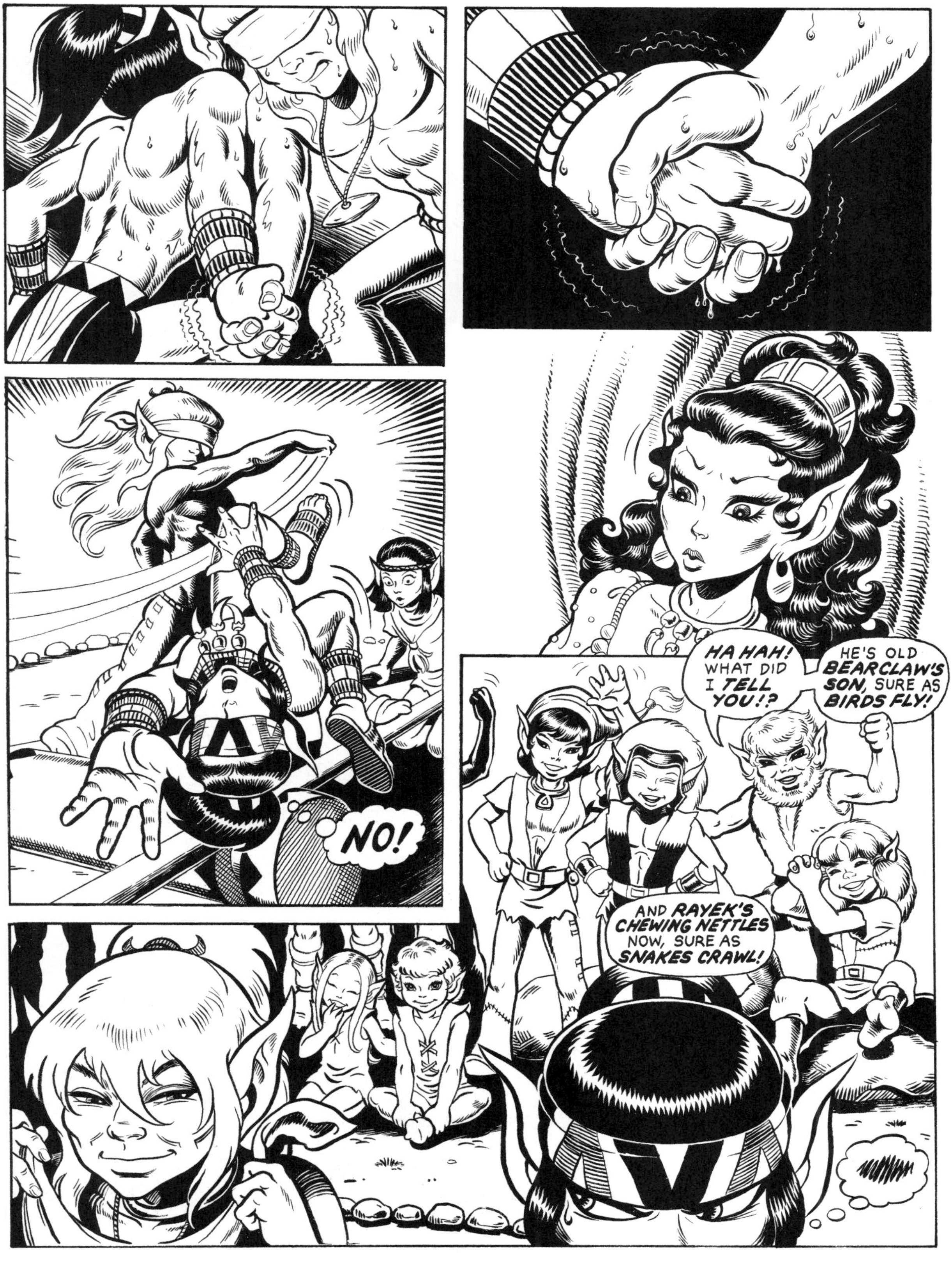
NO!
HA HAH! WHAT DID I TELL YOU!?
HE'S OLD BEARCLAW'S SON, SURE AS BIRDS FLY!
AND RAYEK'S CHEWING NETTLES NOW, SURE AS SNAKES CRAWL!

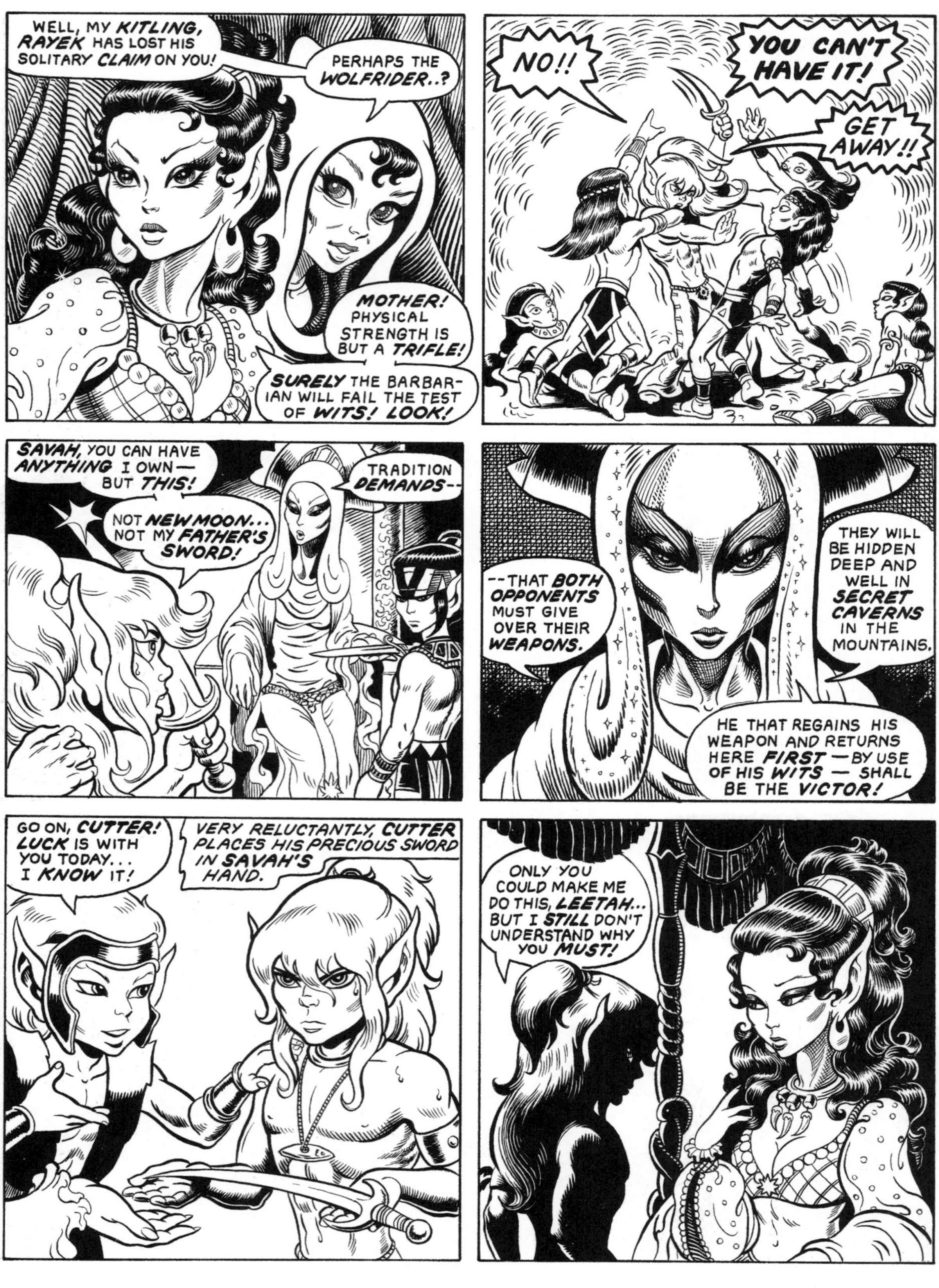
WELL, MY KITLING, RAYEK HAS LOST HIS SOLITARY CLAIM ON YOU!
PERHAPS THE WOLFRIDER..?
MOTHER! PHYSICAL STRENGTH IS BUT A TRIFLE!
SURELY THE BARBARIAN WILL FAIL THE TEST OF WITS! LOOK!
NO!!
YOU CAN'T HAVE IT!
GET AWAY!!
SAVAH, YOU CAN HAVE ANYTHING I OWN— BUT THIS!
NOT NEW MOON... NOT MY FATHER'S SWORD!
TRADITION DEMANDS--
--THAT BOTH OPPONENTS MUST GIVE OVER THEIR WEAPONS.
THEY WILL BE HIDDEN DEEP AND WELL IN SECRET CAVERNS IN THE MOUNTAINS.
HE THAT REGAINS HIS WEAPON AND RETURNS HERE FIRST — BY USE OF HIS WITS — SHALL BE THE VICTOR!
GO ON, CUTTER! LUCK IS WITH YOU TODAY... I KNOW IT!
VERY RELUCTANTLY, CUTTER PLACES HIS PRECIOUS SWORD IN SAVAH'S HAND.
ONLY YOU COULD MAKE ME DO THIS, LEETAH... BUT I STILL DON'T UNDERSTAND WHY YOU MUST!

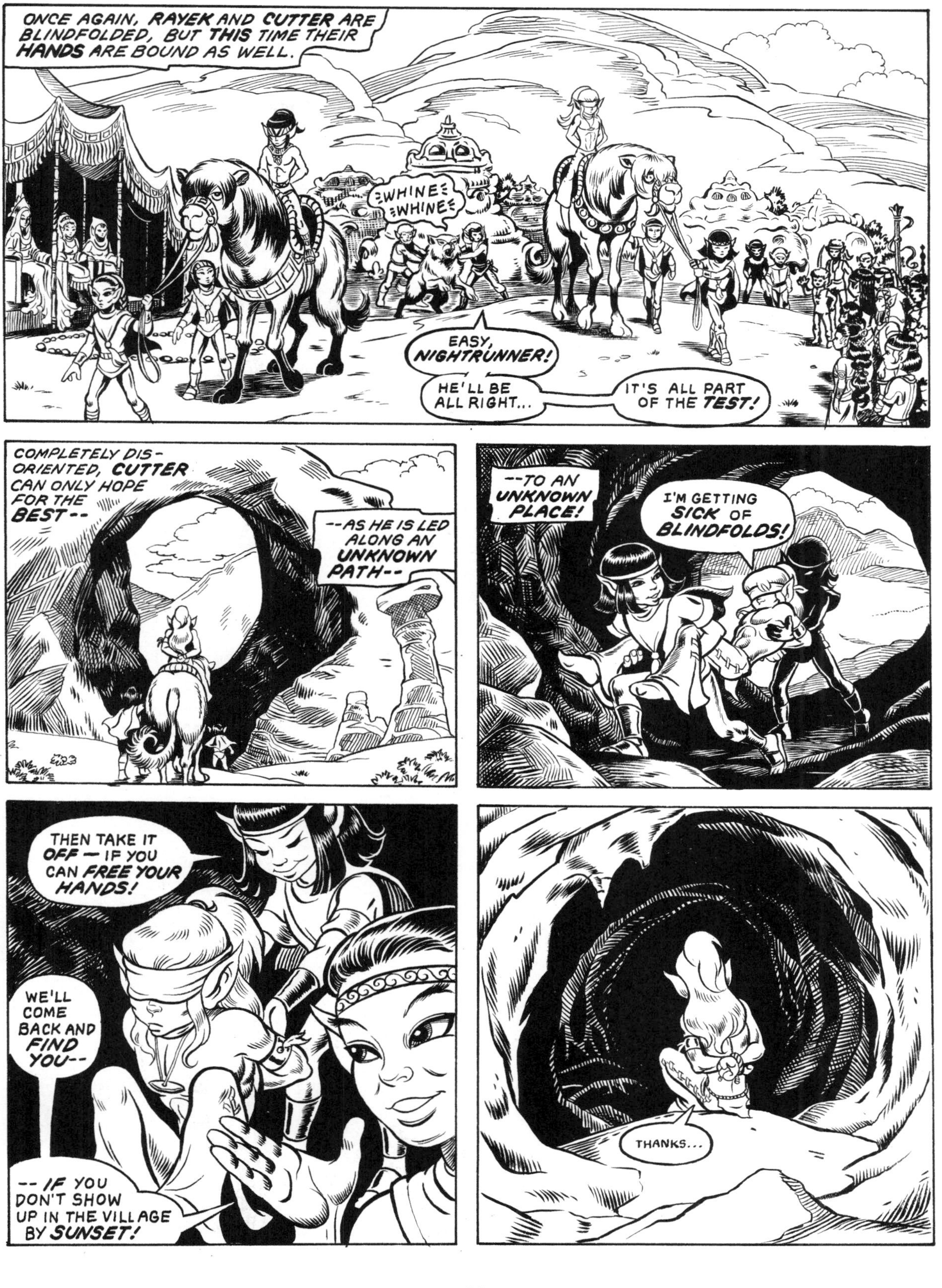
ONCE AGAIN, RAYEK AND CUTTER ARE BLINDFOLDED, BUT THIS TIME THEIR HANDS ARE BOUND AS WELL.
WHINE WHINE
EASY, NIGHTRUNNER!
HE'LL BE ALL RIGHT...
IT'S ALL PART OF THE TEST!
COMPLETELY DIS-ORIENTED, CUTTER CAN ONLY HOPE FOR THE BEST--
--AS HE IS LED ALONG AN UNKNOWN PATH--
--TO AN UNKNOWN PLACE!
I'M GETTING SICK OF BLINDFOLDS!
THEN TAKE IT OFF — IF YOU CAN FREE YOUR HANDS!
WE'LL COME BACK AND FIND YOU--
--IF YOU DON'T SHOW UP IN THE VILLAGE BY SUNSET!
THANKS...

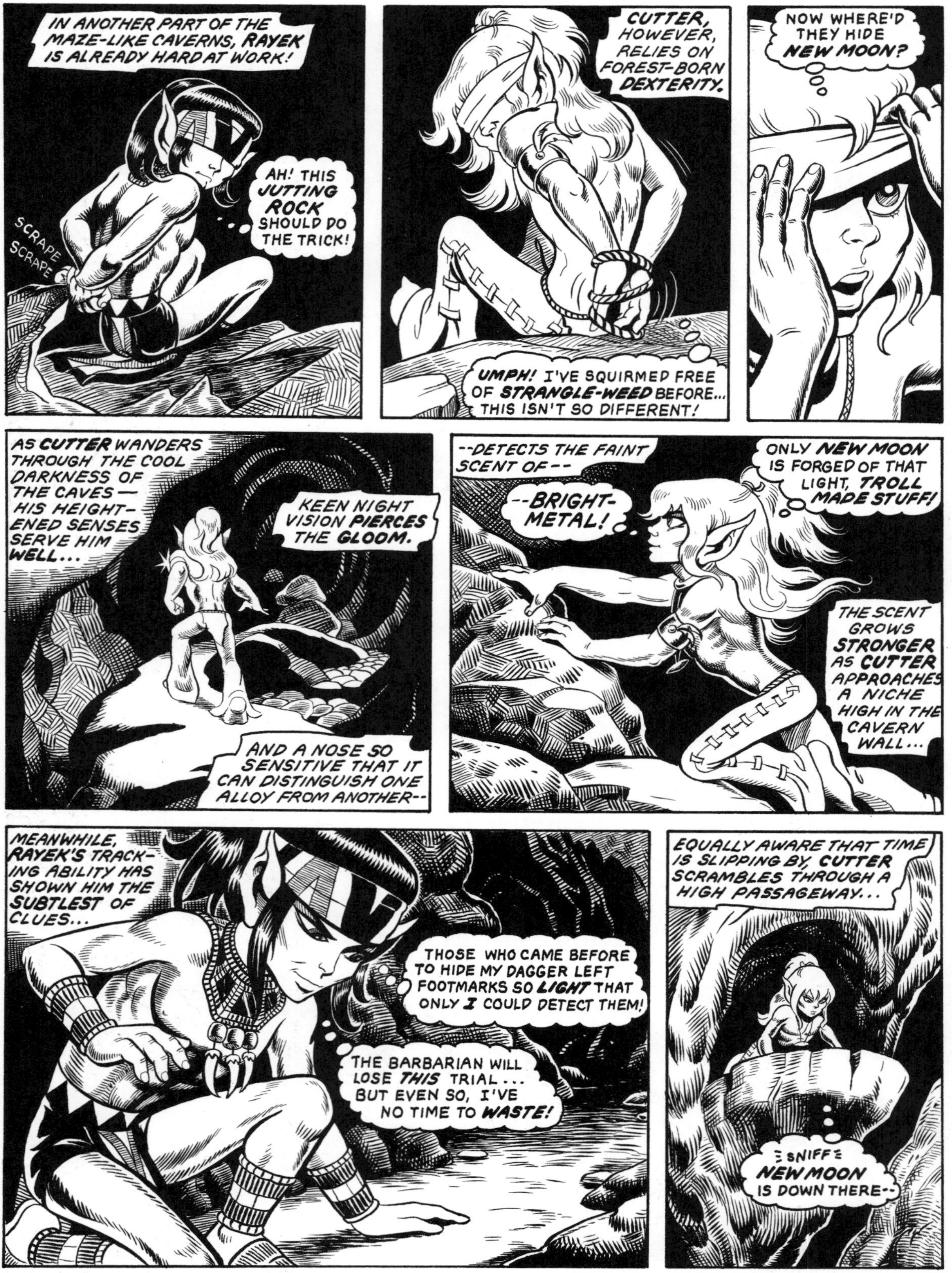
IN ANOTHER PART OF THE MAZE-LIKE CAVERNS, RAYEK IS ALREADY HARD AT WORK!
AH! THIS JUTTING ROCK SHOULD DO THE TRICK!
SCRAPE SCRAPE
CUTTER, HOWEVER, RELIES ON FOREST-BORN DEXTERITY.
UMPH! I'VE SQUIRMED FREE OF STRANGLE-WEED BEFORE... THIS ISN'T SO DIFFERENT!
NOW WHERE'D THEY HIDE NEW MOON?
AS CUTTER WANDERS THROUGH THE COOL DARKNESS OF THE CAVES— HIS HEIGHTENED SENSES SERVE HIM WELL...
KEEN NIGHT VISION PIERCES THE GLOOM.
AND A NOSE SO SENSITIVE THAT IT CAN DISTINGUISH ONE ALLOY FROM ANOTHER--
--DETECTS THE FAINT SCENT OF--
--BRIGHT-METAL!
ONLY NEW MOON IS FORGED OF THAT LIGHT, TROLL MADE STUFF!
THE SCENT GROWS STRONGER AS CUTTER APPROACHES A NICHE HIGH IN THE CAVERN WALL...
MEANWHILE, RAYEK'S TRACKING ABILITY HAS SHOWN HIM THE SUBTLEST OF CLUES...
THOSE WHO CAME BEFORE TO HIDE MY DAGGER LEFT FOOTMARKS SO LIGHT THAT ONLY I COULD DETECT THEM!
THE BARBARIAN WILL LOSE THIS TRIAL... BUT EVEN SO, I'VE NO TIME TO WASTE!
EQUALLY AWARE THAT TIME IS SLIPPING BY, CUTTER SCRAMBLES THROUGH A HIGH PASSAGEWAY...
SNIFF NEW MOON IS DOWN THERE--

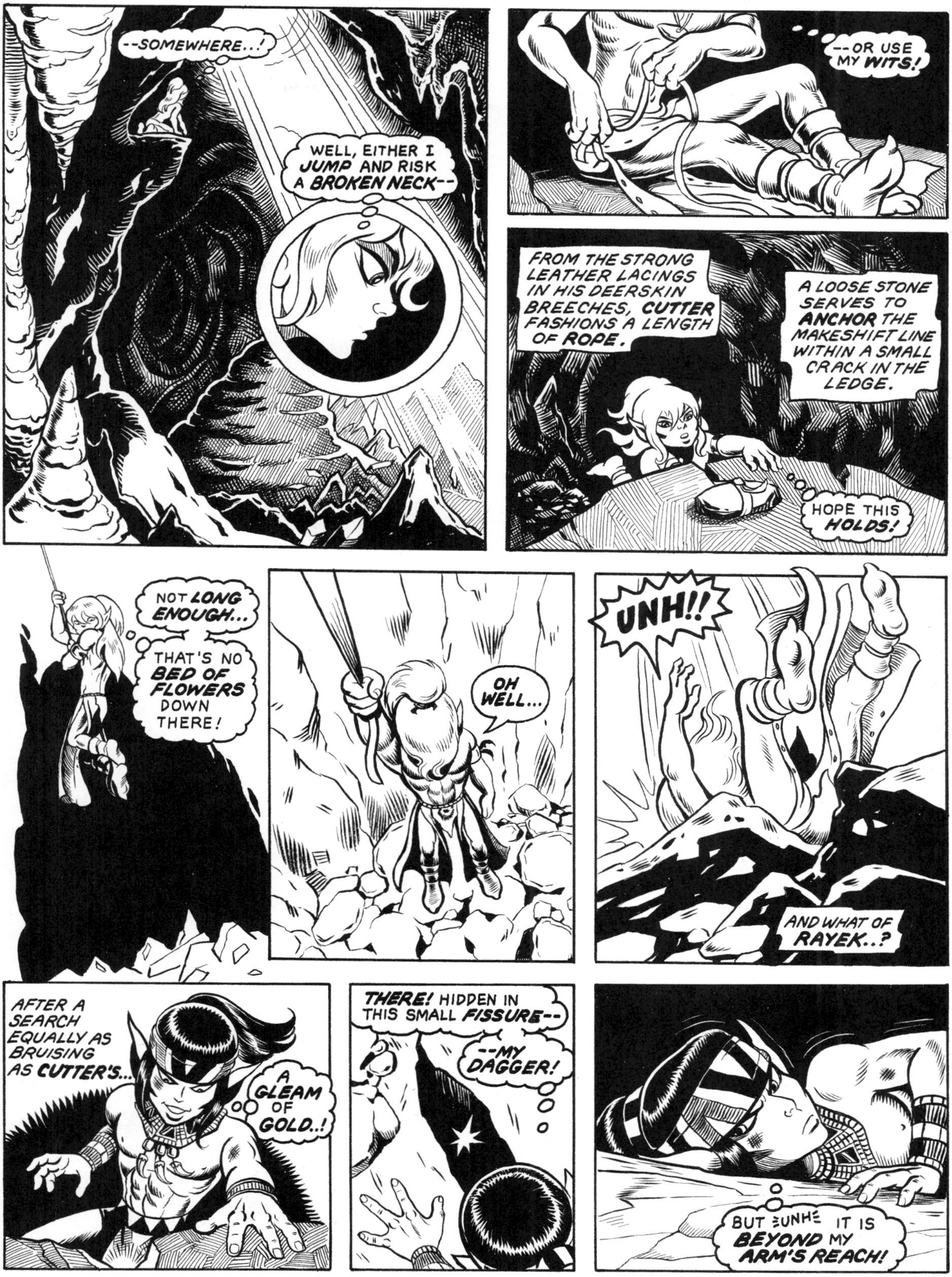
--SOMEWHERE..!
WELL, EITHER I JUMP AND RISK A BROKEN NECK--
--OR USE MY WITS!
FROM THE STRONG LEATHER LACINGS IN HIS DEERSKIN BREECHES, CUTTER FASHIONS A LENGTH OF ROPE.
A LOOSE STONE SERVES TO ANCHOR THE MAKESHIFT LINE WITHIN A SMALL CRACK IN THE LEDGE.
HOPE THIS HOLDS!
NOT LONG ENOUGH...
THAT'S NO BED OF FLOWERS DOWN THERE!
OH WELL...
UNH!!
AND WHAT OF RAYEK..?
AFTER A SEARCH EQUALLY AS BRUISING AS CUTTER'S...
A GLEAM OF GOLD..!
THERE! HIDDEN IN THIS SMALL FISSURE--
--MY DAGGER!
BUT UNH IT IS BEYOND MY ARM'S REACH!

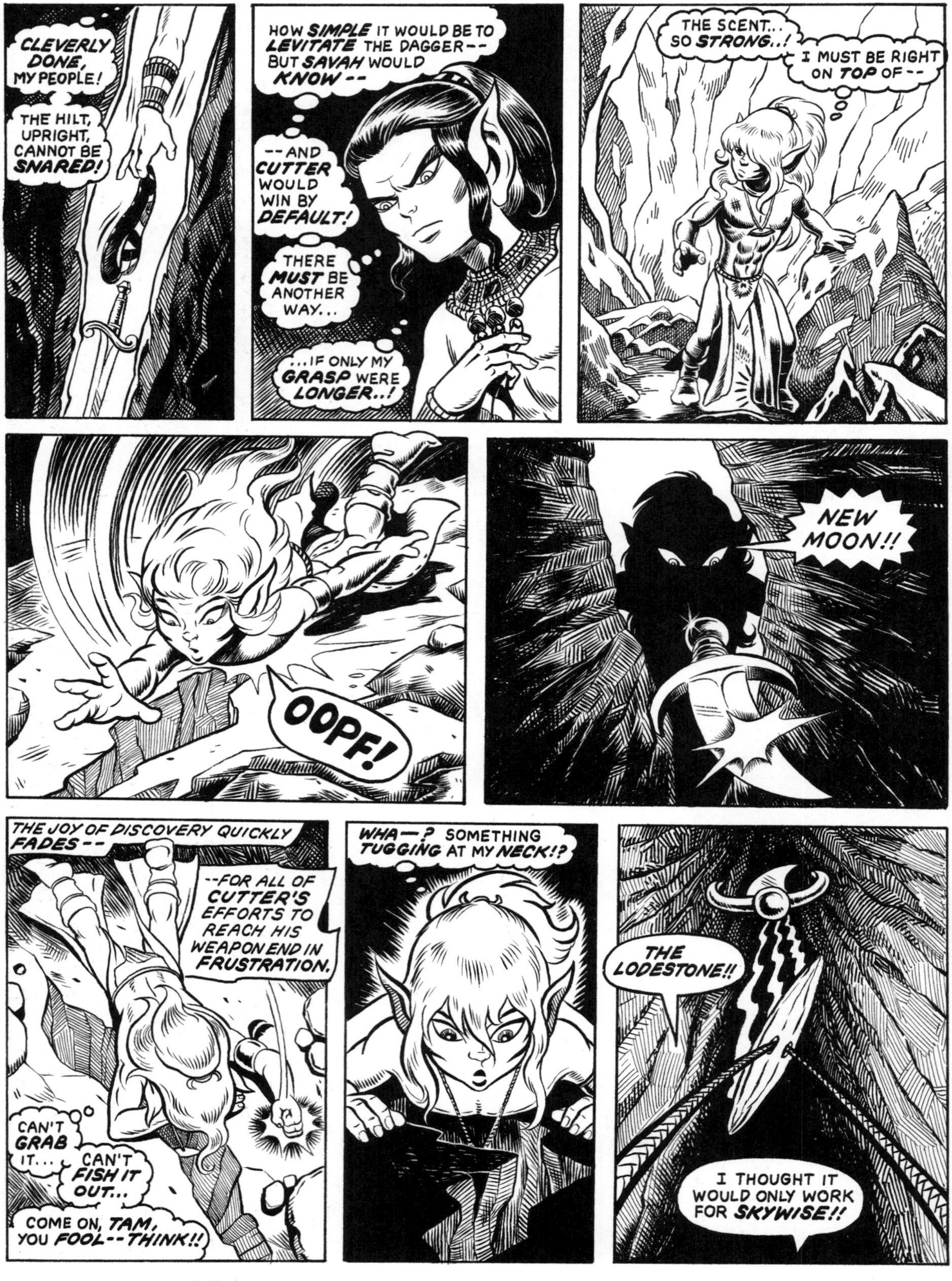
CLEVERLY DONE, MY PEOPLE!
THE HILT, UPRIGHT, CANNOT BE SNARED!
HOW SIMPLE IT WOULD BE TO LEVITATE THE DAGGER-- BUT SAVAH WOULD KNOW--
--AND CUTTER WOULD WIN BY DEFAULT!
THERE MUST BE ANOTHER WAY...
...IF ONLY MY GRASP WERE LONGER..!
THE SCENT... SO STRONG..!
I MUST BE RIGHT ON TOP OF--
OOPF!
NEW MOON!!
THE JOY OF DISCOVERY QUICKLY FADES--
--FOR ALL OF CUTTER'S EFFORTS TO REACH HIS WEAPON END IN FRUSTRATION.
CAN'T GRAB IT...
CAN'T FISH IT OUT...
COME ON, TAM, YOU FOOL--THINK!!
WHA--? SOMETHING TUGGING AT MY NECK!?
THE LODESTONE!!
I THOUGHT IT WOULD ONLY WORK FOR SKYWISE!!

AT THE SAME TIME...

THIS SLIVER OF **CLEARSTONE** WILL HOLD THE TEETH *APART,--*

IT SHOULD WORK AS WELL AS *MAGIC!*

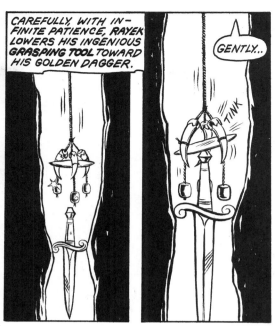

CAREFULLY, WITH IN-FINITE PATIENCE, RAYEK LOWERS HIS INGENIOUS *GRASPING TOOL* TOWARD HIS GOLDEN DAGGER.

GENTLY...

TINK

AH!

CLICK!

CLACK!

HEH HEH HEH

I'D LIKE TO SEE --

--THE *WOLF-RIDER* FIGURE THIS OUT!

RAYEK EMERGES TO WELCOME AFTER-NOON SUNLIGHT, *CERTAIN* OF HIS TRIUMPH!

WHAT MATTERS THE **LOSS** OF ONE PALTRY *TRIAL* OF *HAND?*

LEETAH KNOWS THAT *WIT* IS BETTER THAN *STRENGTH!* SHE WILL CHOOSE *ME!*

BUT THE ELATED HUNTER'S *RETURN* TO HIS VILLAGE IS MARRED BY AN UN-PLEASANT *SURPRISE...*

WHAT *KEPT* YOU, O MIGHTY SLAYER OF *TOADS?*

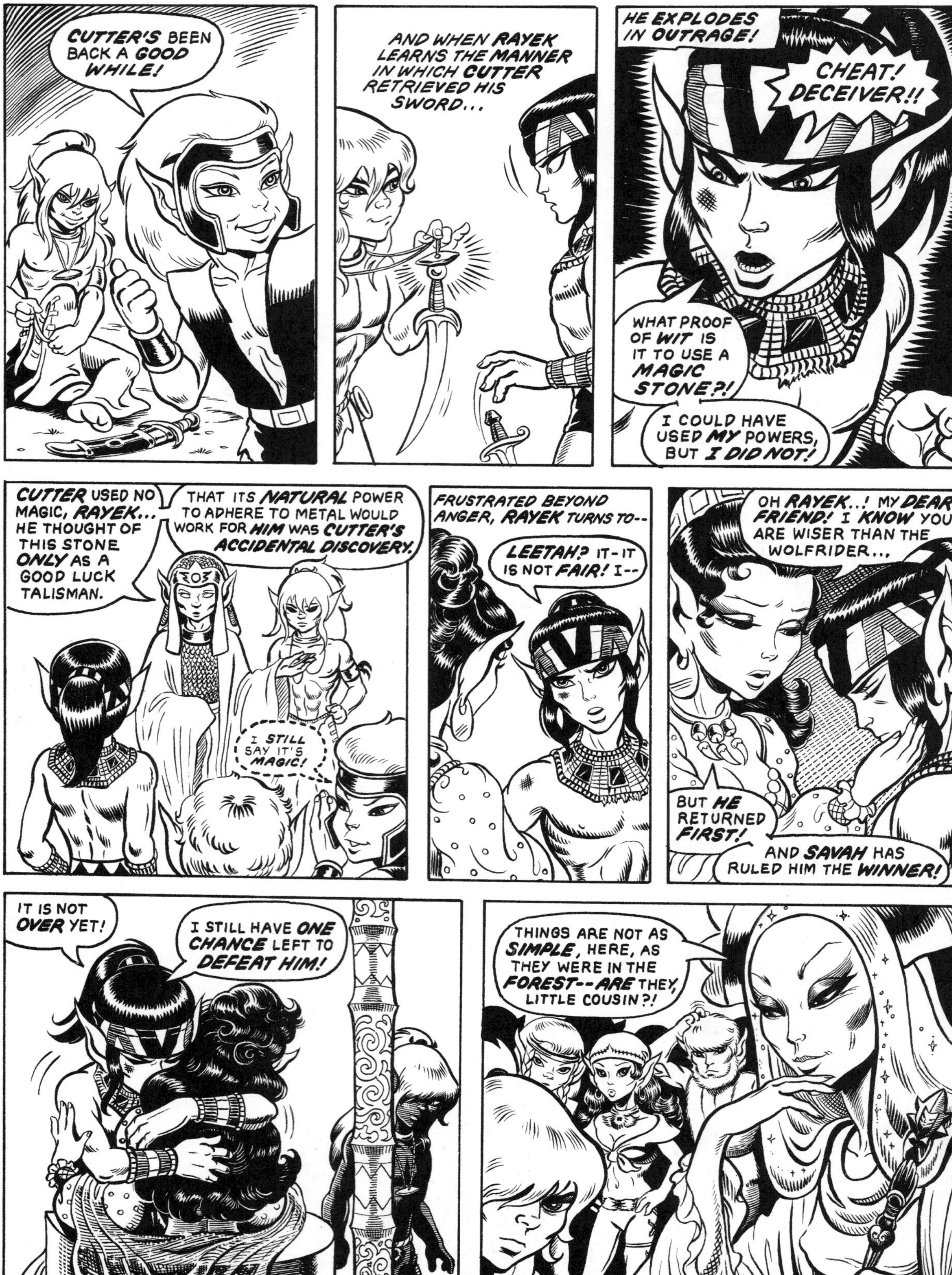
CUTTER'S BEEN BACK A GOOD WHILE!
AND WHEN RAYEK LEARNS THE MANNER IN WHICH CUTTER RETRIEVED HIS SWORD...
HE EXPLODES IN OUTRAGE!
CHEAT! DECEIVER!!
WHAT PROOF OF WIT IS IT TO USE A MAGIC STONE?!
I COULD HAVE USED MY POWERS, BUT I DID NOT!
CUTTER USED NO MAGIC, RAYEK... HE THOUGHT OF THIS STONE ONLY AS A GOOD LUCK TALISMAN.
THAT ITS NATURAL POWER TO ADHERE TO METAL WOULD WORK FOR HIM WAS CUTTER'S ACCIDENTAL DISCOVERY.
I STILL SAY IT'S MAGIC!
FRUSTRATED BEYOND ANGER, RAYEK TURNS TO--
LEETAH? IT-IT IS NOT FAIR! I--
OH RAYEK...! MY DEAR FRIEND! I KNOW YOU ARE WISER THAN THE WOLFRIDER...
BUT HE RETURNED FIRST!
AND SAVAH HAS RULED HIM THE WINNER!
IT IS NOT OVER YET!
I STILL HAVE ONE CHANCE LEFT TO DEFEAT HIM!
THINGS ARE NOT AS SIMPLE, HERE, AS THEY WERE IN THE FOREST--ARE THEY, LITTLE COUSIN?!

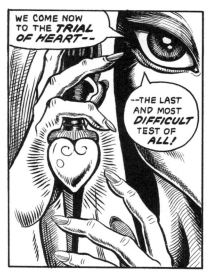

WE COME NOW TO THE *TRIAL OF HEART*--

--THE LAST AND MOST *DIFFICULT* TEST OF *ALL!*

FOR *EITHER* OF YOU TO *WIN* YOU MUST OVERCOME YOUR *GREATEST FEAR!!*

THEN THE CONTEST IS *ENDED!*

MY GREATEST FEAR IS FOR THE *SAFETY* OF MY *TRIBE* —!

I WOULD NOT CHANGE *THAT* IF I *COULD!!*

HOW *LITTLE* YOU KNOW YOURSELF!

BURIED DEEP IN YOUR MIND ARE FEARS THAT YOU NEVER *IMAGINED* WERE YOURS!

IT IS FROM *THOSE* THAT I SHALL SELECT THE APPROPRIATE TEST FOR *EACH* OF YOU!

SAVAH PLACES HER WARM, DRY FINGERTIPS AGAINST *CUTTER'S* SWEATING BROW.

HE IS AWARE THAT SHE WALKS QUIETLY IN THE SHADOWED TUNNELS OF HIS MIND—SEARCHING FOR...

... SHE HAS *FOUND* IT!! AND *CUTTER* IS CHILLED BY A *SUDDEN, NAMELESS DREAD!*

SHE *KNOWS!*

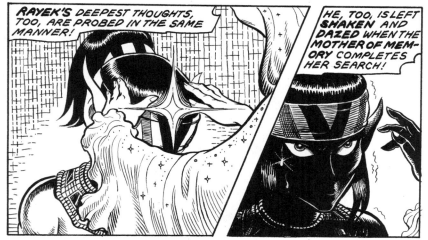

RAYEK'S DEEPEST THOUGHTS, TOO, ARE PROBED IN THE SAME MANNER!

HE, TOO, IS LEFT *SHAKEN* AND *DAZED* WHEN THE MOTHER OF MEMORY COMPLETES HER SEARCH!

FOR *CUTTER'S* TRIAL, WE MUST GO WHERE THE *CARRION BIRDS* NEST--

--AND WHERE THE WIND MOANS SADLY... LIKE A *BEAST* IN *PAIN!*

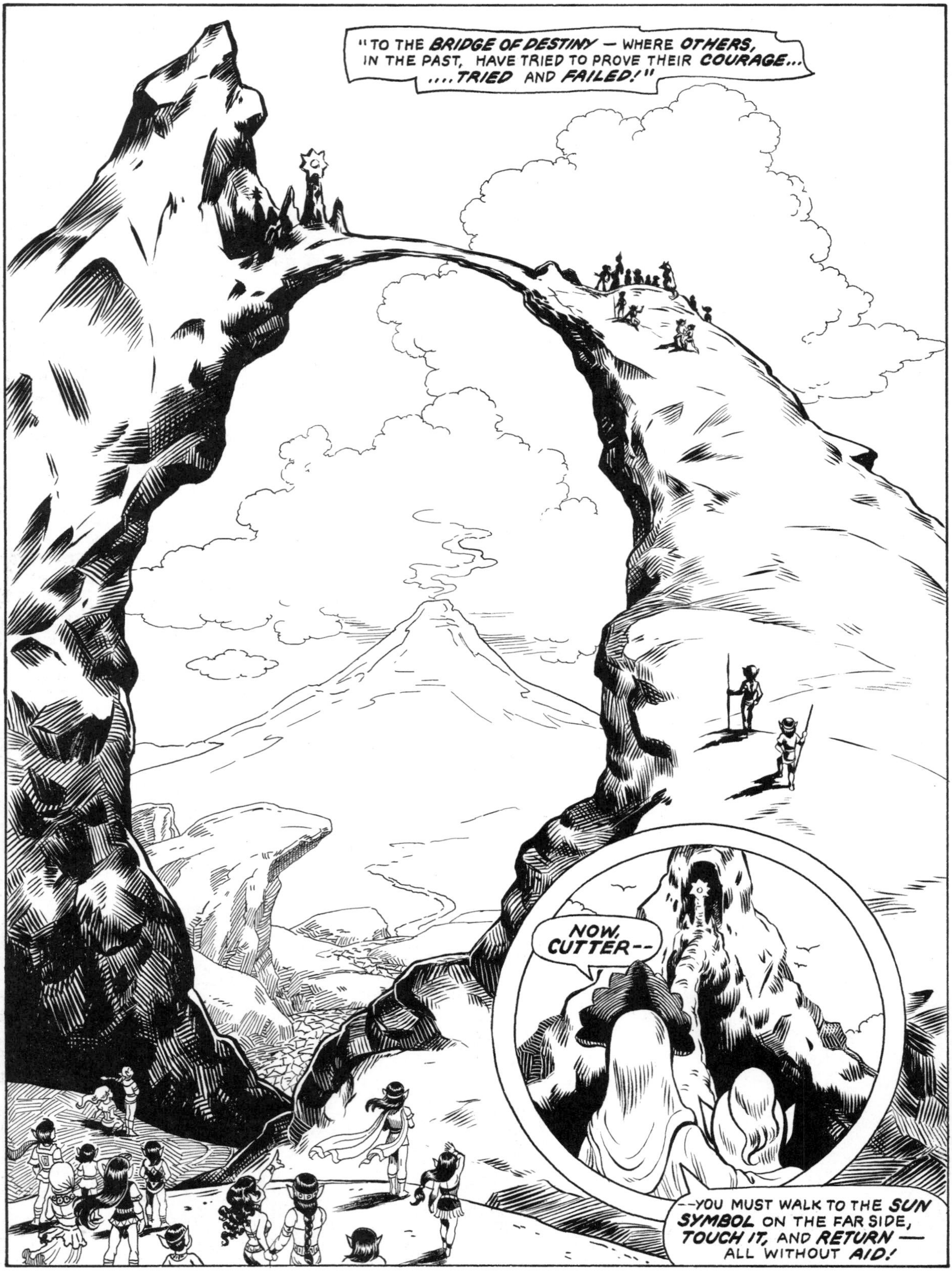
"TO THE BRIDGE OF DESTINY — WHERE OTHERS, IN THE PAST, HAVE TRIED TO PROVE THEIR COURAGE... ....TRIED AND FAILED!"
NOW, CUTTER--
--YOU MUST WALK TO THE SUN SYMBOL ON THE FAR SIDE, TOUCH IT, AND RETURN — ALL WITHOUT AID!

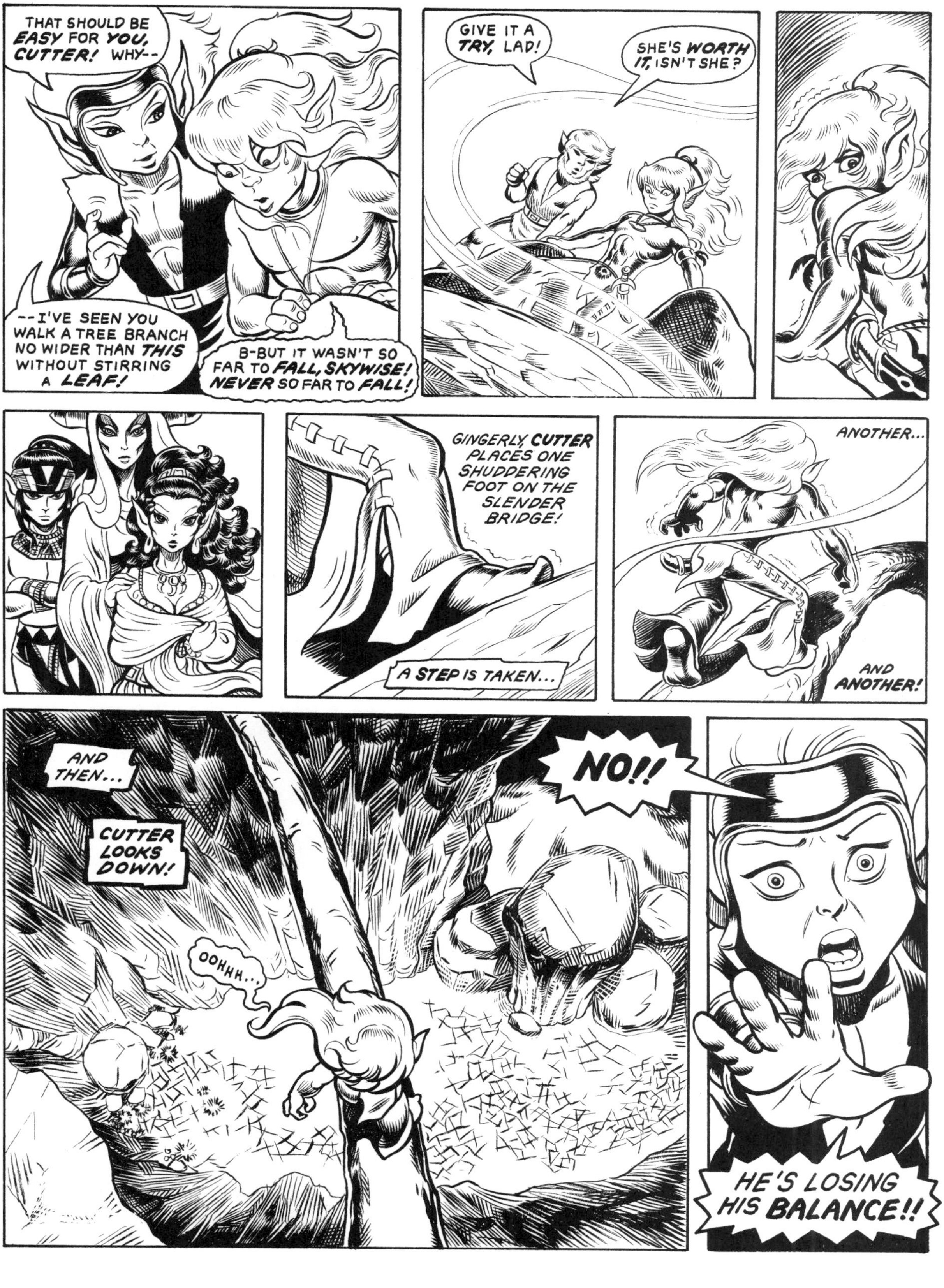
THAT SHOULD BE EASY FOR YOU, CUTTER! WHY--
--I'VE SEEN YOU WALK A TREE BRANCH NO WIDER THAN THIS WITHOUT STIRRING A LEAF!
B-BUT IT WASN'T SO FAR TO FALL, SKYWISE! NEVER SO FAR TO FALL!
GIVE IT A TRY, LAD!
SHE'S WORTH IT, ISN'T SHE?
GINGERLY, CUTTER PLACES ONE SHUDDERING FOOT ON THE SLENDER BRIDGE!
A STEP IS TAKEN...
ANOTHER...
AND ANOTHER!
AND THEN...
CUTTER LOOKS DOWN!
OOHHH...
NO!!
HE'S LOSING HIS BALANCE!!

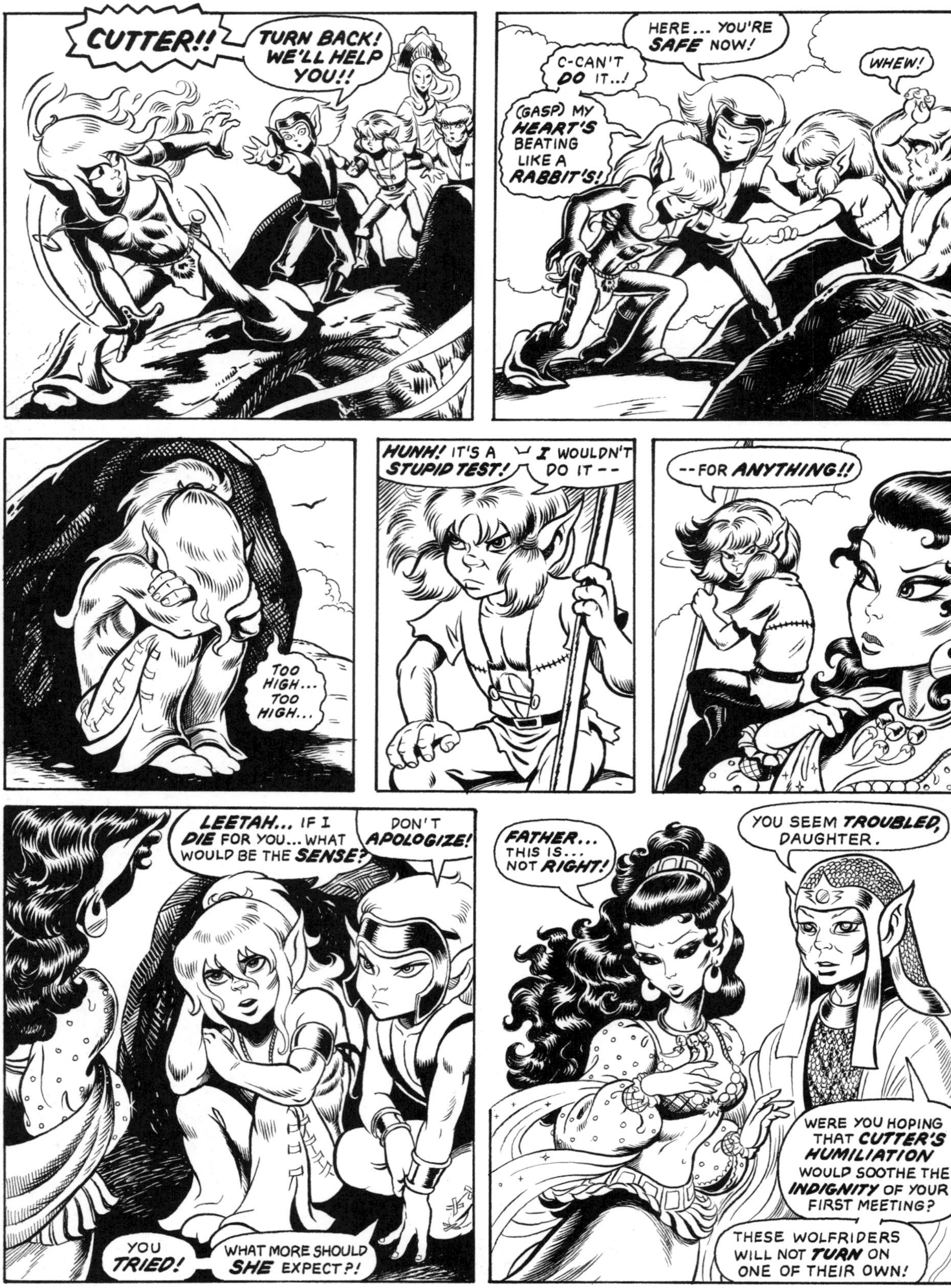
CUTTER!!
TURN BACK! WE'LL HELP YOU!!
HERE... YOU'RE SAFE NOW!
C-CAN'T DO IT...!
(GASP) MY HEART'S BEATING LIKE A RABBIT'S!
WHEW!
TOO HIGH... TOO HIGH...
HUNH! IT'S A STUPID TEST!
I WOULDN'T DO IT --
--FOR ANYTHING!!
LEETAH... IF I DIE FOR YOU... WHAT WOULD BE THE SENSE?
DON'T APOLOGIZE!
YOU TRIED!
WHAT MORE SHOULD SHE EXPECT?!
FATHER... THIS IS... NOT RIGHT!
YOU SEEM TROUBLED, DAUGHTER.
WERE YOU HOPING THAT CUTTER'S HUMILIATION WOULD SOOTHE THE INDIGNITY OF YOUR FIRST MEETING?
THESE WOLFRIDERS WILL NOT TURN ON ONE OF THEIR OWN!

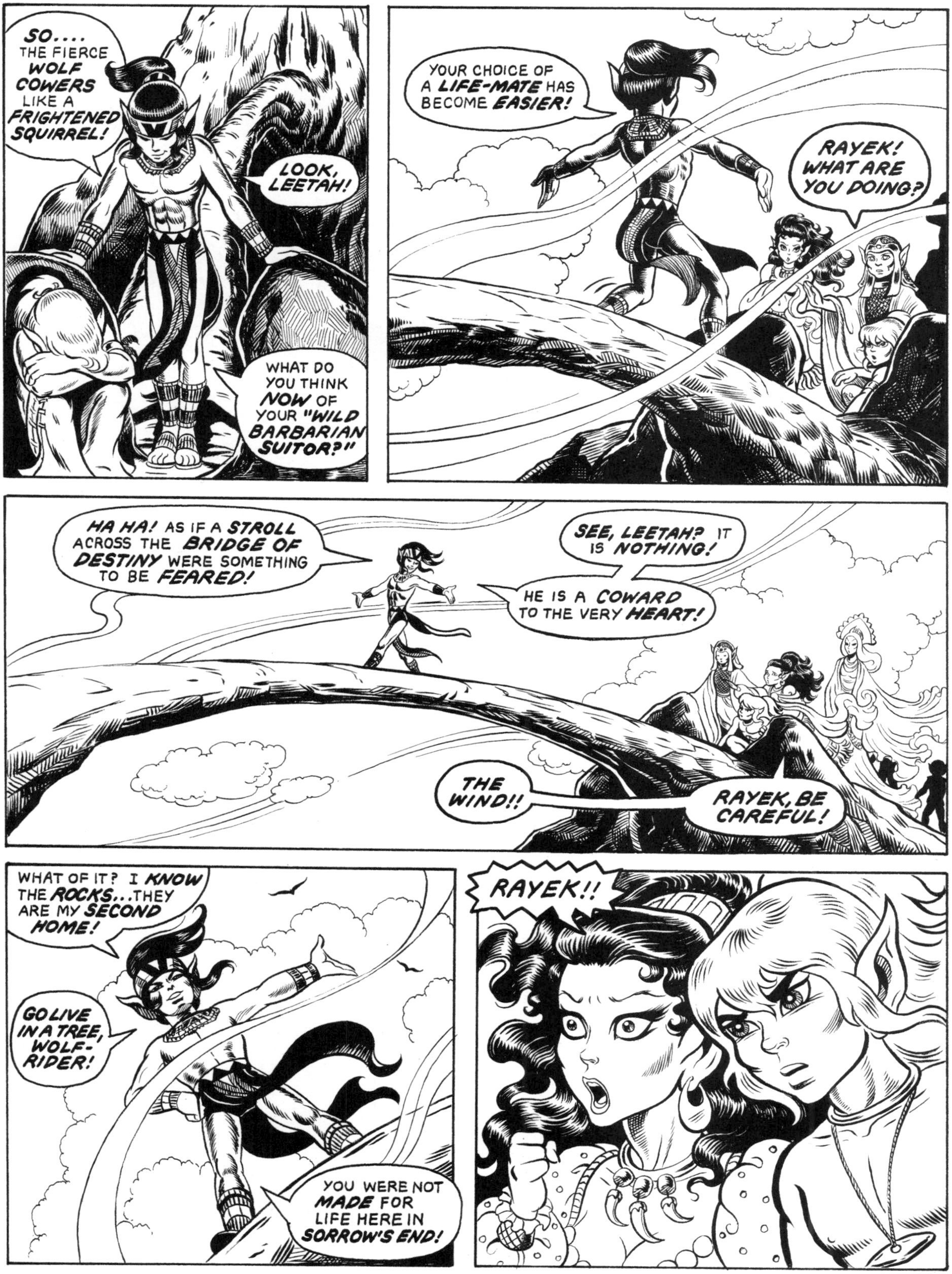
SO.... THE FIERCE WOLF COWERS LIKE A FRIGHTENED SQUIRREL!
LOOK, LEETAH!
WHAT DO YOU THINK NOW OF YOUR "WILD BARBARIAN SUITOR?"
YOUR CHOICE OF A LIFE-MATE HAS BECOME EASIER!
RAYEK! WHAT ARE YOU DOING?
HA HA! AS IF A STROLL ACROSS THE BRIDGE OF DESTINY WERE SOMETHING TO BE FEARED!
SEE, LEETAH? IT IS NOTHING!
HE IS A COWARD TO THE VERY HEART!
THE WIND!!
RAYEK, BE CAREFUL!
WHAT OF IT? I KNOW THE ROCKS...THEY ARE MY SECOND HOME!
GO LIVE IN A TREE, WOLF-RIDER!
YOU WERE NOT MADE FOR LIFE HERE IN SORROW'S END!
RAYEK!!

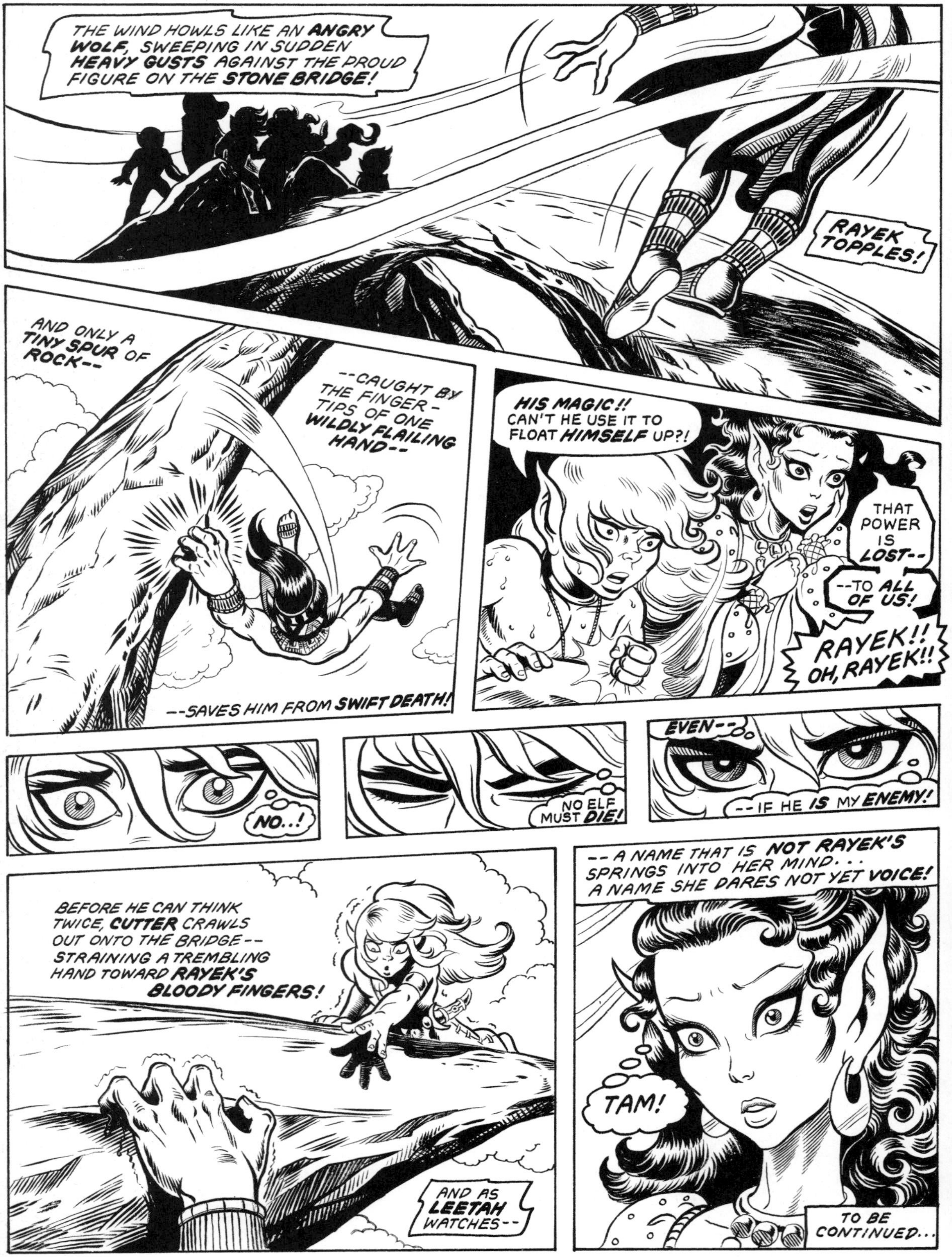
THE WIND HOWLS LIKE AN ANGRY WOLF, SWEEPING IN SUDDEN HEAVY GUSTS AGAINST THE PROUD FIGURE ON THE STONE BRIDGE!
RAYEK TOPPLES!
AND ONLY A TINY SPUR OF ROCK--
--CAUGHT BY THE FINGER-TIPS OF ONE WILDLY FLAILING HAND--
--SAVES HIM FROM SWIFT DEATH!
HIS MAGIC!! CAN'T HE USE IT TO FLOAT HIMSELF UP?!
THAT POWER IS LOST--
--TO ALL OF US!
RAYEK!! OH, RAYEK!!
NO..!
NO ELF MUST DIE!
EVEN--
--IF HE IS MY ENEMY!
BEFORE HE CAN THINK TWICE, CUTTER CRAWLS OUT ONTO THE BRIDGE-- STRAINING A TREMBLING HAND TOWARD RAYEK'S BLOODY FINGERS!
AND AS LEETAH WATCHES--
--A NAME THAT IS NOT RAYEK'S SPRINGS INTO HER MIND... A NAME SHE DARES NOT YET VOICE!
TAM!
TO BE CONTINUED...

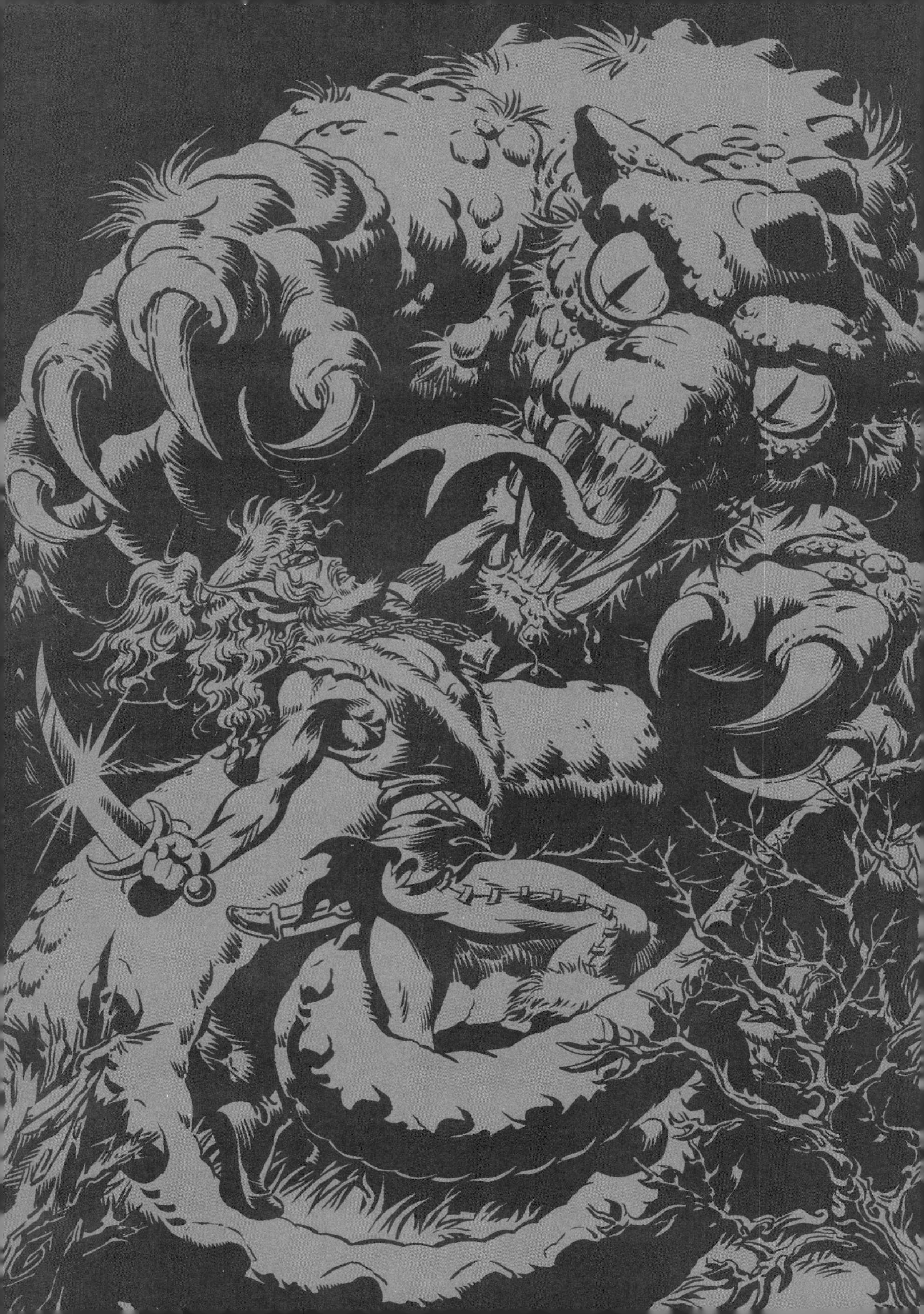

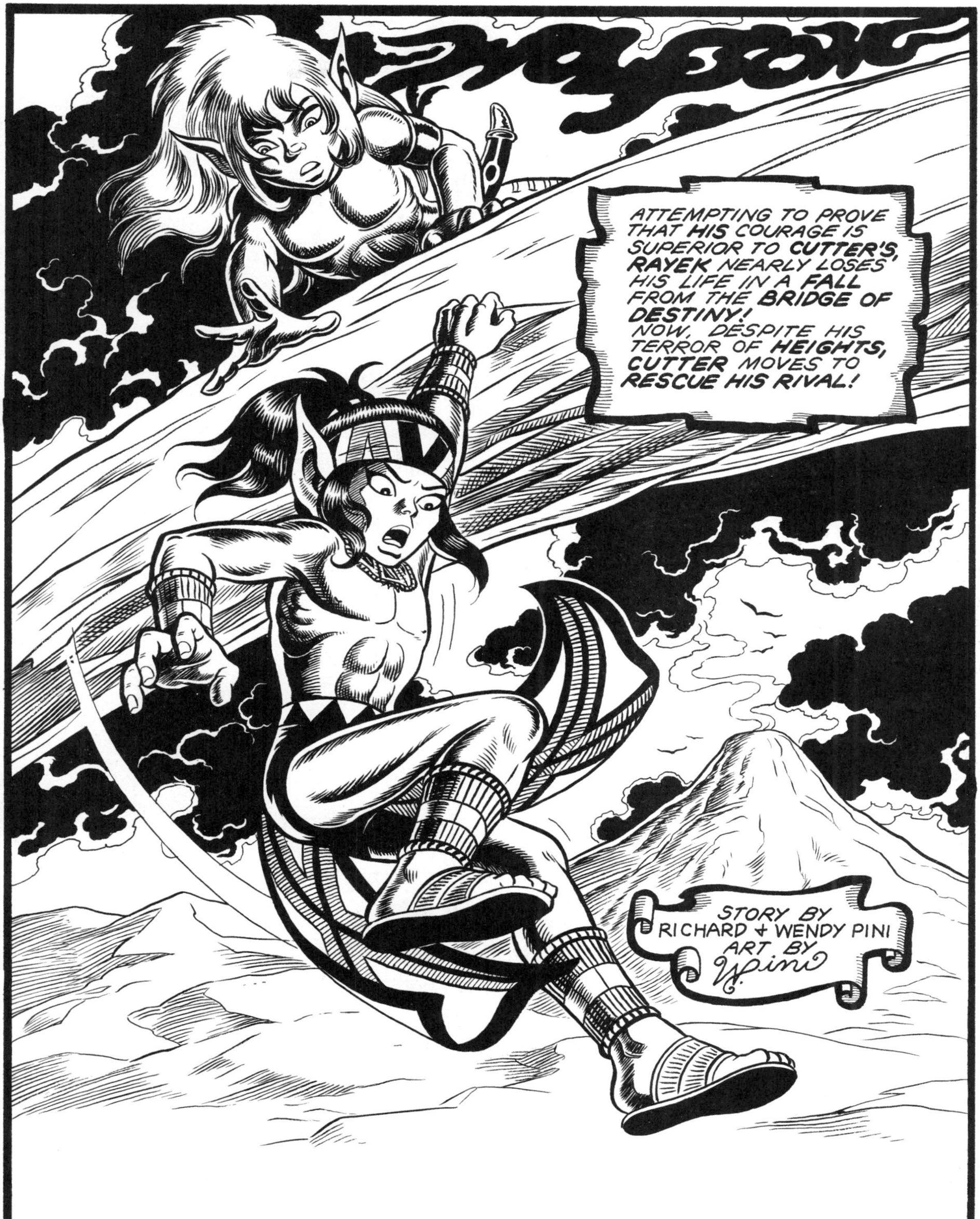
ATTEMPTING TO PROVE THAT HIS COURAGE IS SUPERIOR TO CUTTER'S, RAYEK NEARLY LOSES HIS LIFE IN A FALL FROM THE BRIDGE OF DESTINY!
NOW, DESPITE HIS TERROR OF HEIGHTS, CUTTER MOVES TO RESCUE HIS RIVAL!
STORY BY RICHARD + WENDY PINI ART BY W. Pini

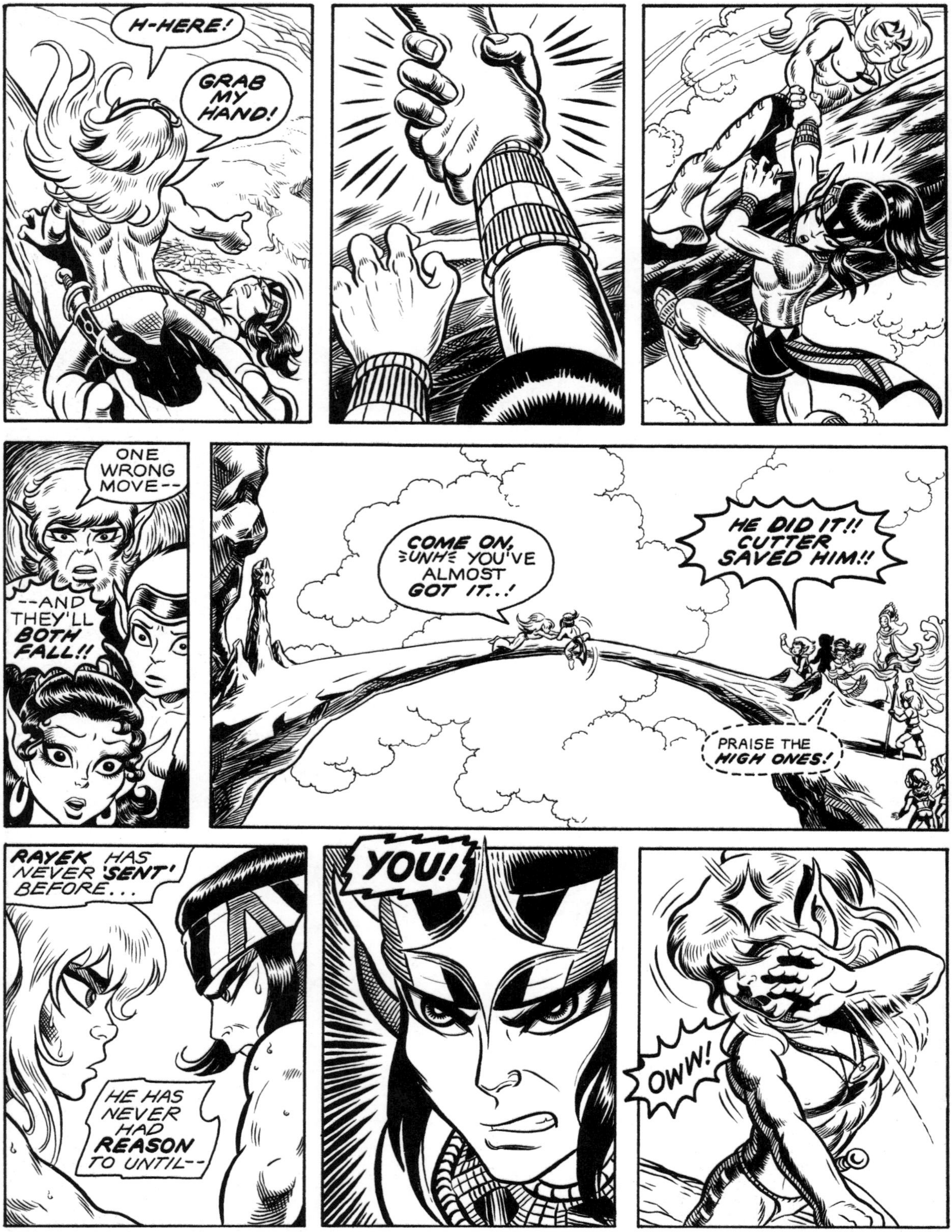
H-HERE!
GRAB MY HAND!
ONE WRONG MOVE--
--AND THEY'LL BOTH FALL!!
COME ON, UNH YOU'VE ALMOST GOT IT..!
HE DID IT!! CUTTER SAVED HIM!!
PRAISE THE HIGH ONES!
RAYEK HAS NEVER 'SENT' BEFORE...
HE HAS NEVER HAD REASON TO UNTIL--
YOU!
OWW!

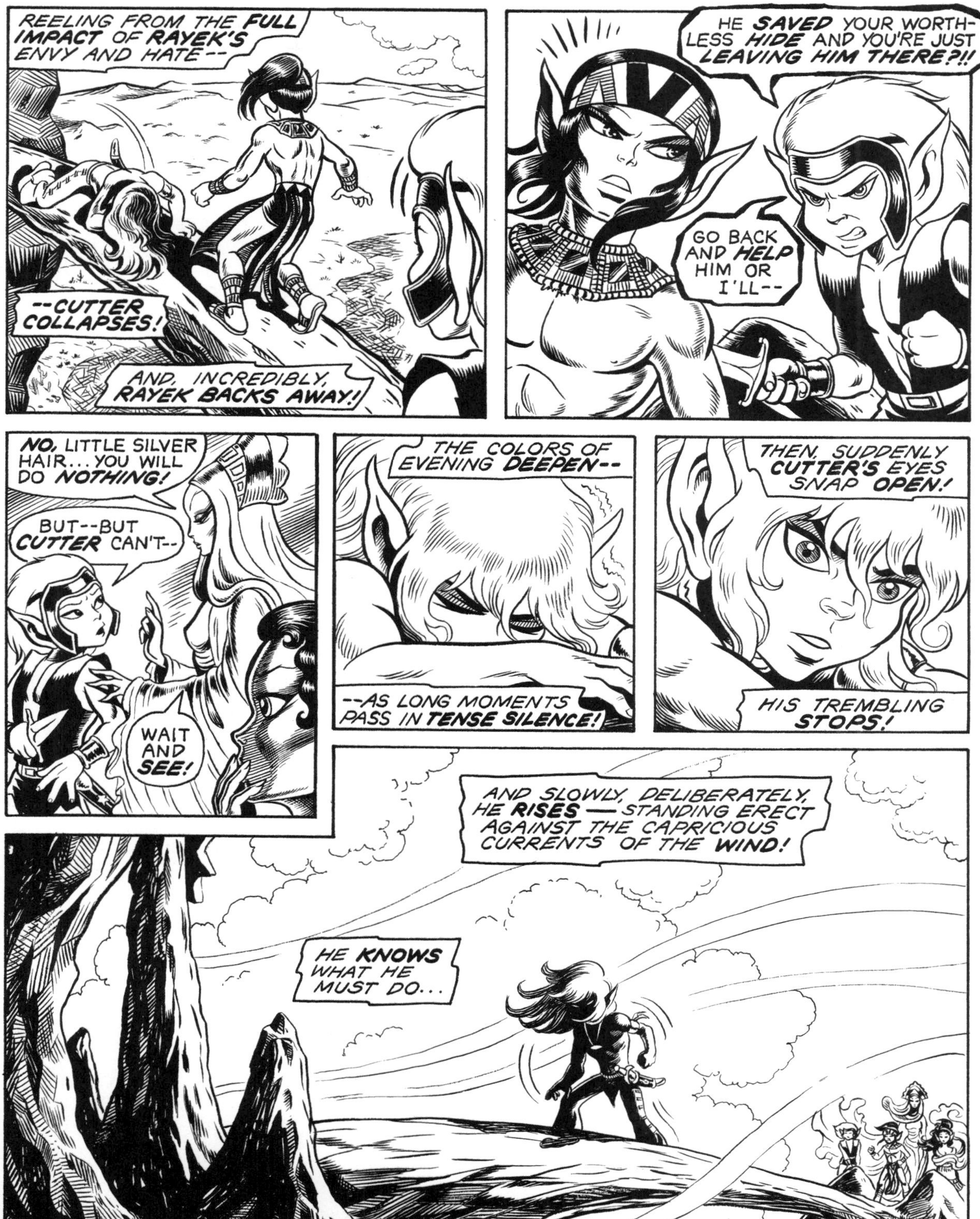

REELING FROM THE FULL IMPACT OF RAYEK'S ENVY AND HATE--
--CUTTER COLLAPSES!
AND, INCREDIBLY, RAYEK BACKS AWAY!
HE SAVED YOUR WORTH-LESS HIDE AND YOU'RE JUST LEAVING HIM THERE?!!
GO BACK AND HELP HIM OR I'LL--
NO, LITTLE SILVER HAIR... YOU WILL DO NOTHING!
BUT--BUT CUTTER CAN'T--
WAIT AND SEE!
THE COLORS OF EVENING DEEPEN--
--AS LONG MOMENTS PASS IN TENSE SILENCE!
THEN, SUDDENLY CUTTER'S EYES SNAP OPEN!
HIS TREMBLING STOPS!
AND SLOWLY, DELIBERATELY, HE RISES — STANDING ERECT AGAINST THE CAPRICIOUS CURRENTS OF THE WIND!
HE KNOWS WHAT HE MUST DO...

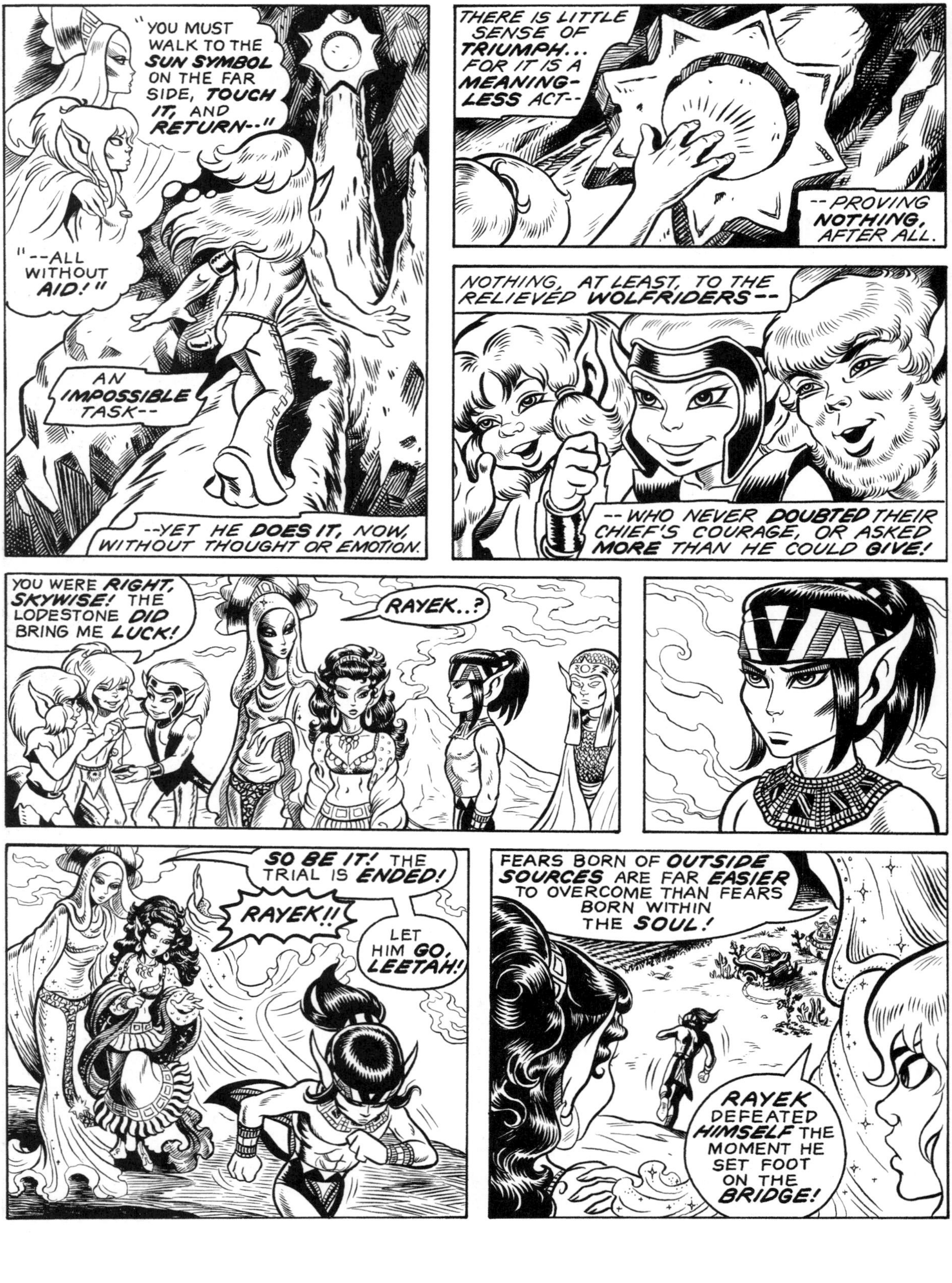
"YOU MUST WALK TO THE SUN SYMBOL ON THE FAR SIDE, TOUCH IT, AND RETURN--"
"--ALL WITHOUT AID!"
AN IMPOSSIBLE TASK--
--YET HE DOES IT, NOW, WITHOUT THOUGHT OR EMOTION.
THERE IS LITTLE SENSE OF TRIUMPH... FOR IT IS A MEANINGLESS ACT--
--PROVING NOTHING, AFTER ALL.
NOTHING, AT LEAST, TO THE RELIEVED WOLFRIDERS--
--WHO NEVER DOUBTED THEIR CHIEF'S COURAGE, OR ASKED MORE THAN HE COULD GIVE!
YOU WERE RIGHT, SKYWISE! THE LODESTONE DID BRING ME LUCK!
RAYEK..?
SO BE IT! THE TRIAL IS ENDED!
RAYEK!!
LET HIM GO, LEETAH!
FEARS BORN OF OUTSIDE SOURCES ARE FAR EASIER TO OVERCOME THAN FEARS BORN WITHIN THE SOUL!
RAYEK DEFEATED HIMSELF THE MOMENT HE SET FOOT ON THE BRIDGE!

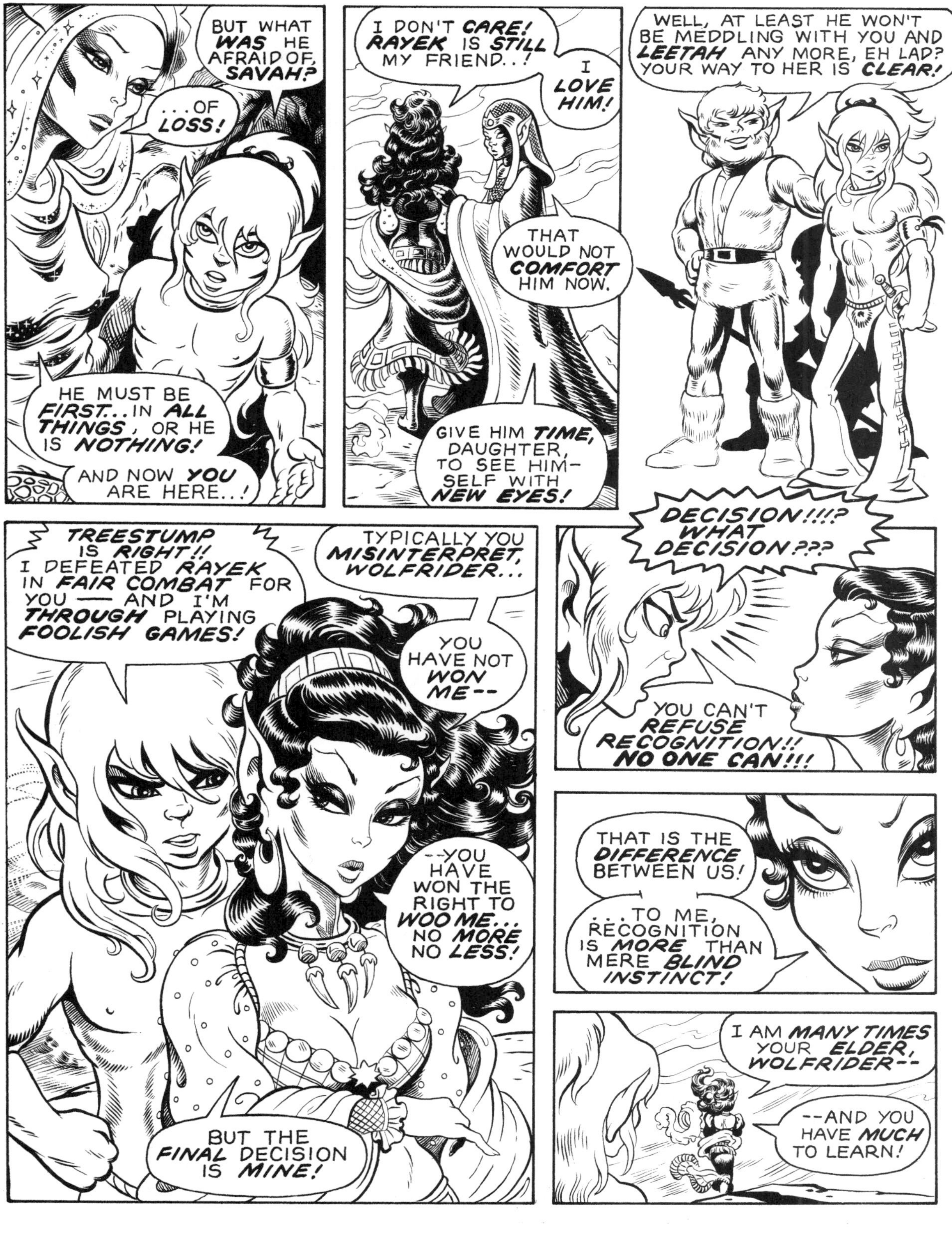
BUT WHAT WAS HE AFRAID OF, SAVAH?
...OF LOSS!
HE MUST BE FIRST...IN ALL THINGS, OR HE IS NOTHING!
AND NOW YOU ARE HERE...!
I DON'T CARE! RAYEK IS STILL MY FRIEND..!
I LOVE HIM!
THAT WOULD NOT COMFORT HIM NOW.
GIVE HIM TIME, DAUGHTER, TO SEE HIMSELF WITH NEW EYES!
WELL, AT LEAST HE WON'T BE MEDDLING WITH YOU AND LEETAH ANY MORE, EH LAD? YOUR WAY TO HER IS CLEAR!
TREESTUMP IS RIGHT!! I DEFEATED RAYEK IN FAIR COMBAT FOR YOU — AND I'M THROUGH PLAYING FOOLISH GAMES!
TYPICALLY YOU MISINTERPRET, WOLFRIDER...
YOU HAVE NOT WON ME--
--YOU HAVE WON THE RIGHT TO WOO ME... NO MORE NO LESS!
BUT THE FINAL DECISION IS MINE!
DECISION!!!? WHAT DECISION???
YOU CAN'T REFUSE RECOGNITION!! NO ONE CAN!!!
THAT IS THE DIFFERENCE BETWEEN US!
...TO ME, RECOGNITION IS MORE THAN MERE BLIND INSTINCT!
I AM MANY TIMES YOUR ELDER, WOLFRIDER--
--AND YOU HAVE MUCH TO LEARN!

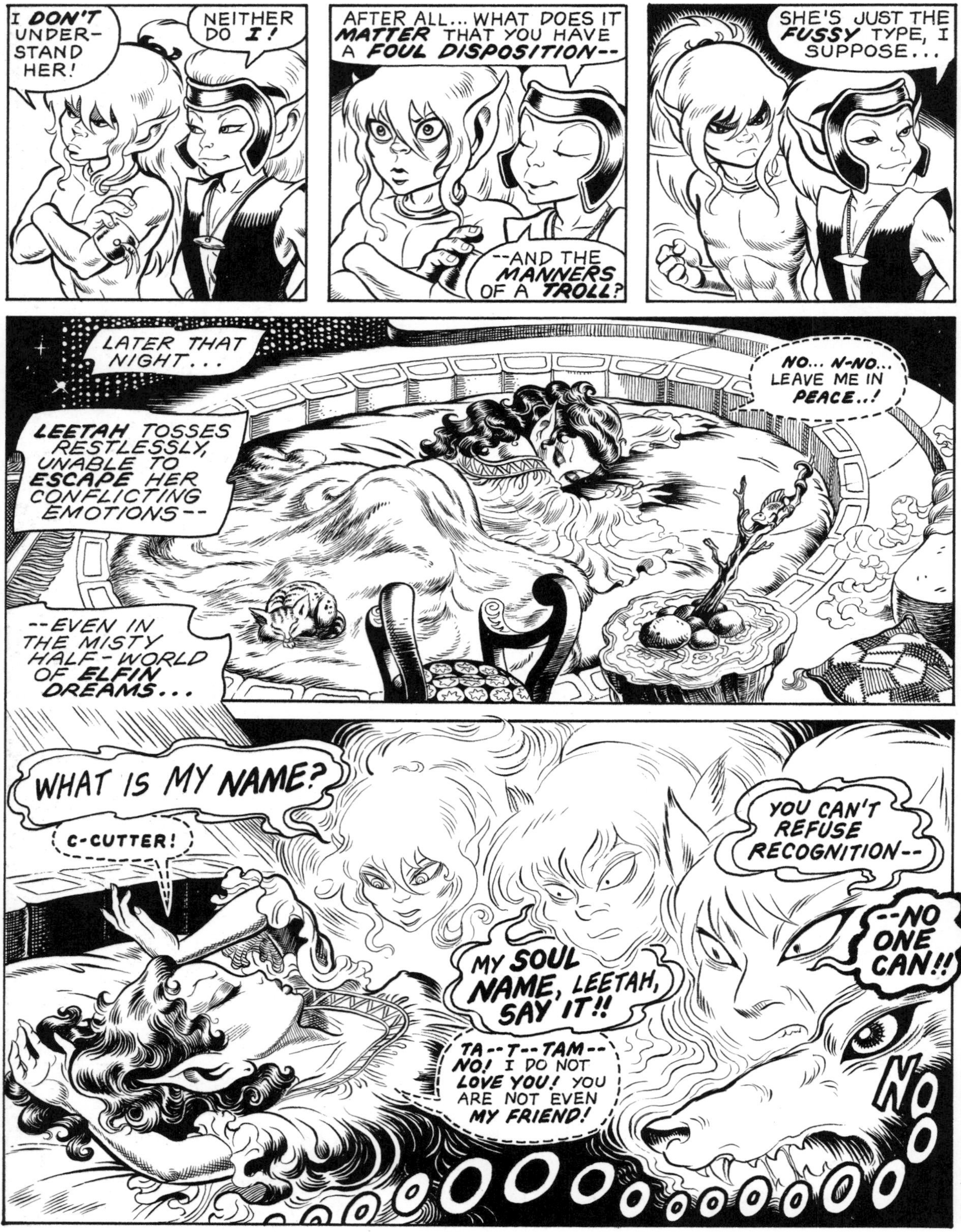
I DON'T UNDERSTAND HER!
NEITHER DO I!
AFTER ALL... WHAT DOES IT MATTER THAT YOU HAVE A FOUL DISPOSITION--
--AND THE MANNERS OF A TROLL?
SHE'S JUST THE FUSSY TYPE, I SUPPOSE...
LATER THAT NIGHT...
NO... N-NO... LEAVE ME IN PEACE..!
LEETAH TOSSES RESTLESSLY, UNABLE TO ESCAPE HER CONFLICTING EMOTIONS--
--EVEN IN THE MISTY HALF-WORLD OF ELFIN DREAMS...
WHAT IS MY NAME?
C-CUTTER!
YOU CAN'T REFUSE RECOGNITION--
--NO ONE CAN!!
MY SOUL NAME, LEETAH, SAY IT!!
TA--T--TAM-- NO! I DO NOT LOVE YOU! YOU ARE NOT EVEN MY FRIEND!
NOOOOOOOOOOOOOOOOOOOO

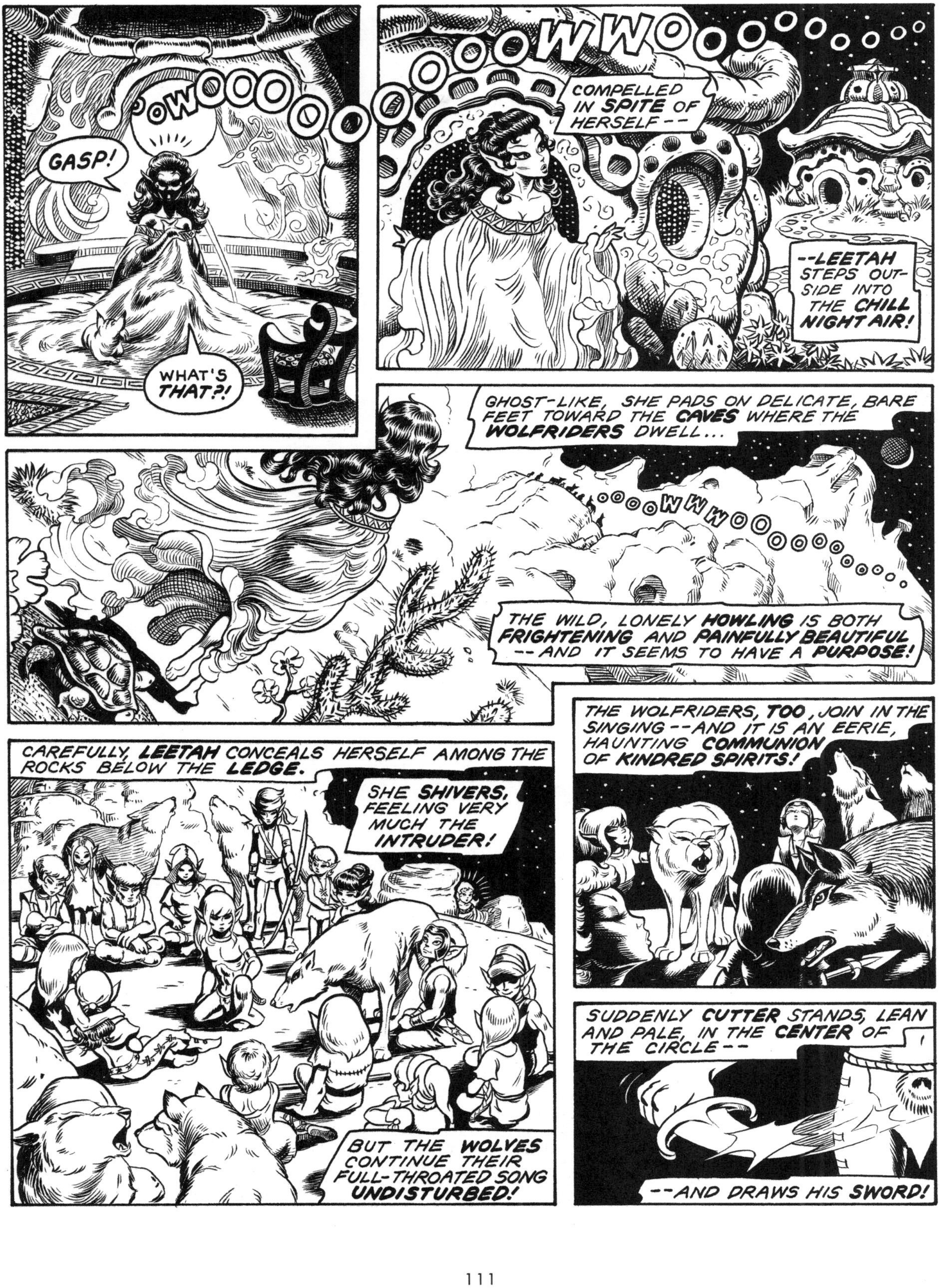

OWOOOOOOOOOOOWWWOOOOOOOOO
GASP!
WHAT'S THAT?!
COMPELLED IN SPITE OF HERSELF--
--LEETAH STEPS OUTSIDE INTO THE CHILL NIGHT AIR!
GHOST-LIKE, SHE PADS ON DELICATE, BARE FEET TOWARD THE CAVES WHERE THE WOLFRIDERS DWELL...
OOOOWWWOOOOOOOOOOOO
THE WILD, LONELY HOWLING IS BOTH FRIGHTENING AND PAINFULLY BEAUTIFUL --AND IT SEEMS TO HAVE A PURPOSE!
CAREFULLY, LEETAH CONCEALS HERSELF AMONG THE ROCKS BELOW THE LEDGE.
SHE SHIVERS, FEELING VERY MUCH THE INTRUDER!
BUT THE WOLVES CONTINUE THEIR FULL-THROATED SONG UNDISTURBED!
THE WOLFRIDERS, TOO, JOIN IN THE SINGING--AND IT IS AN EERIE, HAUNTING COMMUNION OF KINDRED SPIRITS!
SUDDENLY CUTTER STANDS, LEAN AND PALE, IN THE CENTER OF THE CIRCLE--
--AND DRAWS HIS SWORD!

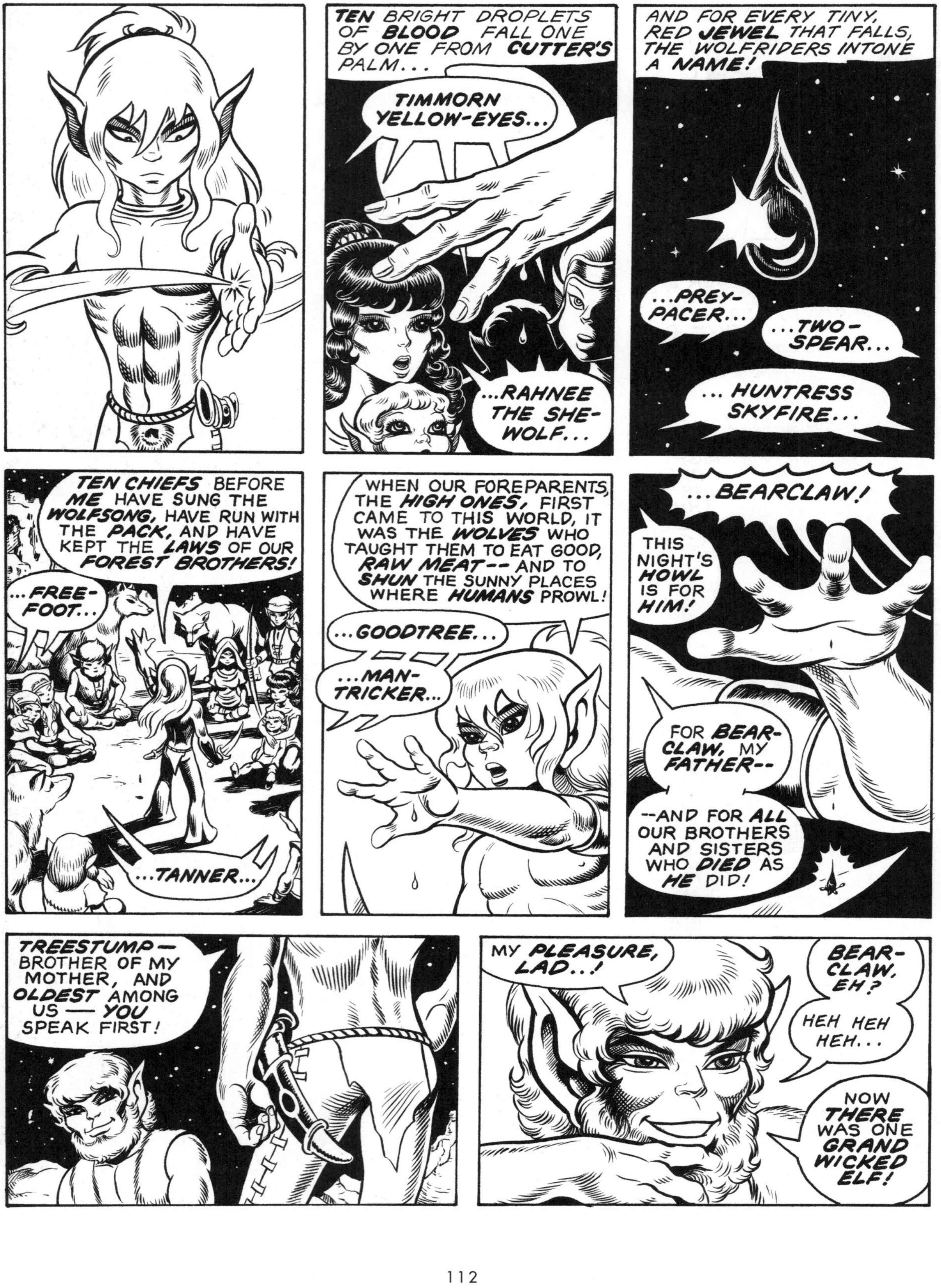
TEN BRIGHT DROPLETS OF BLOOD FALL ONE BY ONE FROM CUTTER'S PALM...
TIMMORN YELLOW-EYES...
...RAHNEE THE SHE-WOLF...
AND FOR EVERY TINY, RED JEWEL THAT FALLS, THE WOLFRIDERS INTONE A NAME!
...PREY-PACER...
...TWO-SPEAR...
... HUNTRESS SKYFIRE...
TEN CHIEFS BEFORE ME HAVE SUNG THE WOLFSONG, HAVE RUN WITH THE PACK, AND HAVE KEPT THE LAWS OF OUR FOREST BROTHERS!
...FREE-FOOT...
...TANNER...
WHEN OUR FOREPARENTS, THE HIGH ONES, FIRST CAME TO THIS WORLD, IT WAS THE WOLVES WHO TAUGHT THEM TO EAT GOOD, RAW MEAT-- AND TO SHUN THE SUNNY PLACES WHERE HUMANS PROWL!
...GOODTREE...
...MAN-TRICKER...
... BEARCLAW!
THIS NIGHT'S HOWL IS FOR HIM!
FOR BEAR-CLAW, MY FATHER--
--AND FOR ALL OUR BROTHERS AND SISTERS WHO DIED AS HE DID!
TREESTUMP— BROTHER OF MY MOTHER, AND OLDEST AMONG US — YOU SPEAK FIRST!
MY PLEASURE, LAD...!
BEAR-CLAW, EH?
HEH HEH HEH...
NOW THERE WAS ONE GRAND WICKED ELF!

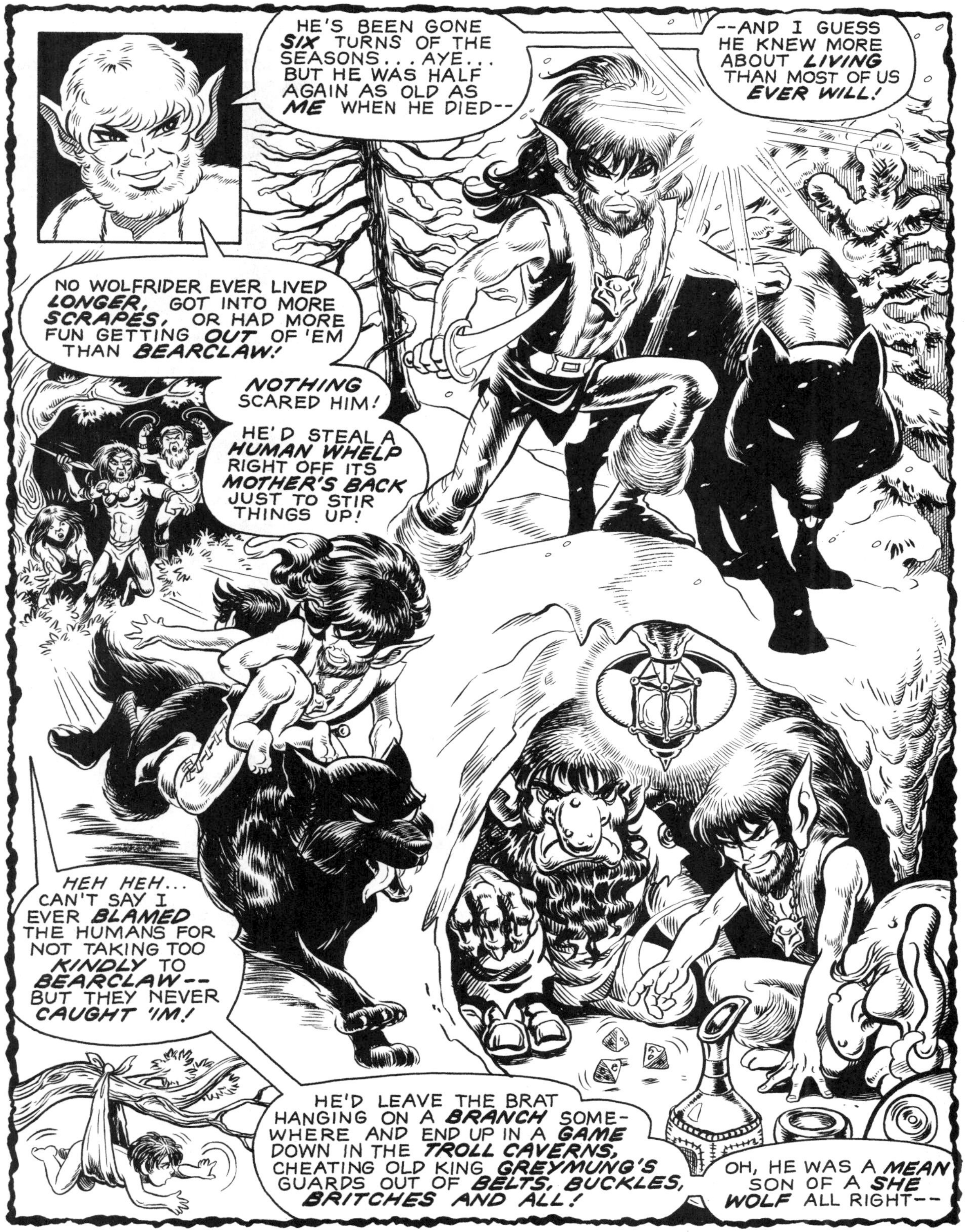
HE'S BEEN GONE SIX TURNS OF THE SEASONS... AYE... BUT HE WAS HALF AGAIN AS OLD AS ME WHEN HE DIED--
--AND I GUESS HE KNEW MORE ABOUT LIVING THAN MOST OF US EVER WILL!
NO WOLFRIDER EVER LIVED LONGER, GOT INTO MORE SCRAPES, OR HAD MORE FUN GETTING OUT OF 'EM THAN BEARCLAW!
NOTHING SCARED HIM!
HE'D STEAL A HUMAN WHELP RIGHT OFF ITS MOTHER'S BACK JUST TO STIR THINGS UP!
HEH HEH... CAN'T SAY I EVER BLAMED THE HUMANS FOR NOT TAKING TOO KINDLY TO BEARCLAW-- BUT THEY NEVER CAUGHT 'IM!
HE'D LEAVE THE BRAT HANGING ON A BRANCH SOMEWHERE AND END UP IN A GAME DOWN IN THE TROLL CAVERNS, CHEATING OLD KING GREYMUNG'S GUARDS OUT OF BELTS, BUCKLES, BRITCHES AND ALL!
OH, HE WAS A MEAN SON OF A SHE WOLF ALL RIGHT--

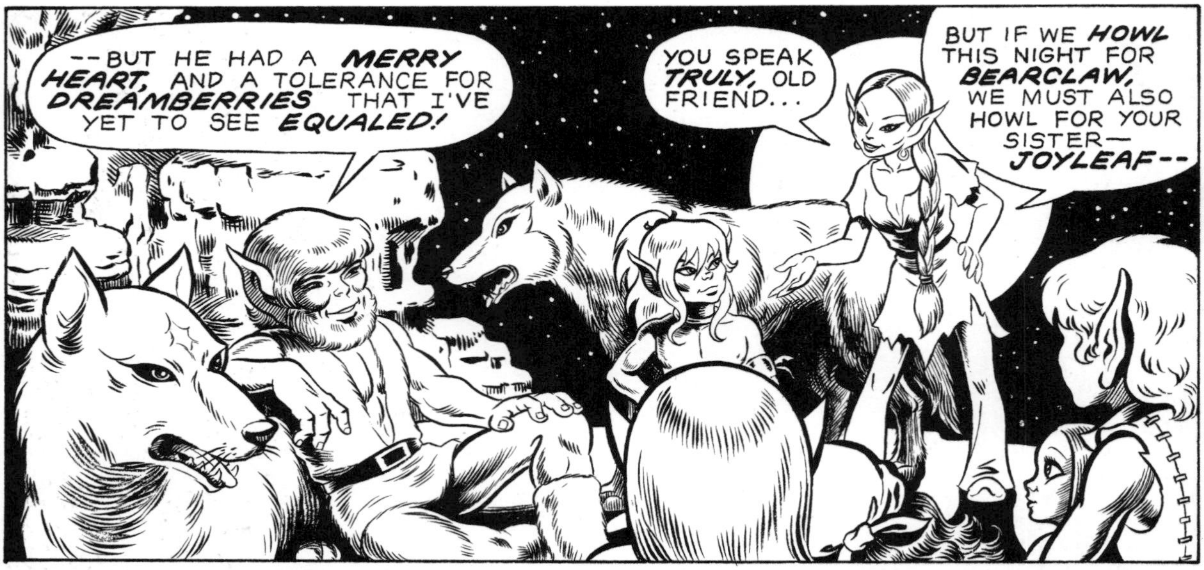
--BUT HE HAD A MERRY HEART, AND A TOLERANCE FOR DREAMBERRIES THAT I'VE YET TO SEE EQUALED!
YOU SPEAK TRULY, OLD FRIEND...
BUT IF WE HOWL THIS NIGHT FOR BEARCLAW, WE MUST ALSO HOWL FOR YOUR SISTER— JOYLEAF--

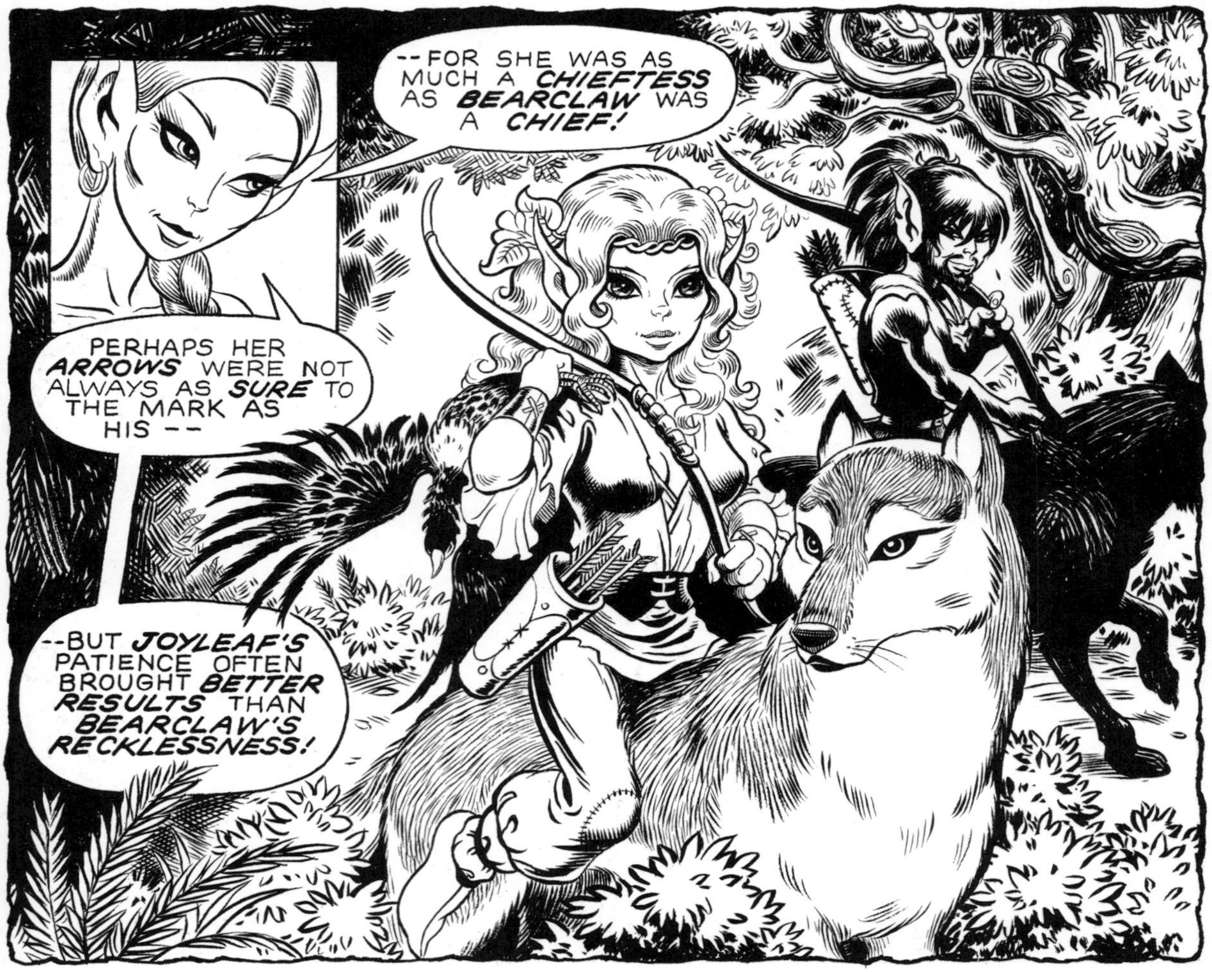
--FOR SHE WAS AS MUCH A CHIEFTESS AS BEARCLAW WAS A CHIEF!
PERHAPS HER ARROWS WERE NOT ALWAYS AS SURE TO THE MARK AS HIS --
--BUT JOYLEAF'S PATIENCE OFTEN BROUGHT BETTER RESULTS THAN BEARCLAW'S RECKLESSNESS!

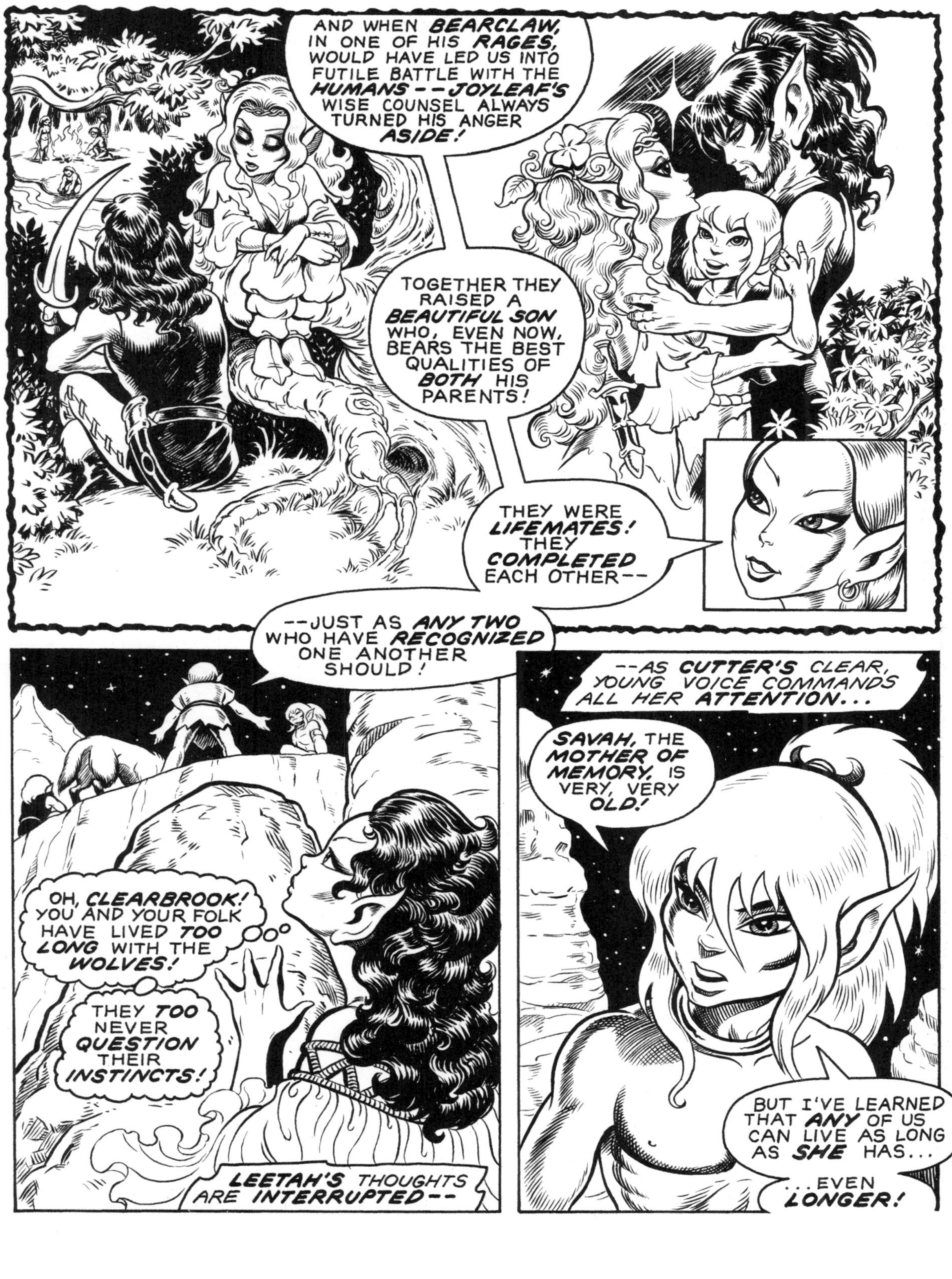
AND WHEN BEARCLAW, IN ONE OF HIS RAGES, WOULD HAVE LED US INTO FUTILE BATTLE WITH THE HUMANS--JOYLEAF'S WISE COUNSEL ALWAYS TURNED HIS ANGER ASIDE!
TOGETHER THEY RAISED A BEAUTIFUL SON WHO, EVEN NOW, BEARS THE BEST QUALITIES OF BOTH HIS PARENTS!
THEY WERE LIFEMATES! THEY COMPLETED EACH OTHER--
--JUST AS ANY TWO WHO HAVE RECOGNIZED ONE ANOTHER SHOULD!
OH, CLEARBROOK! YOU AND YOUR FOLK HAVE LIVED TOO LONG WITH THE WOLVES!
THEY TOO NEVER QUESTION THEIR INSTINCTS!
LEETAH'S THOUGHTS ARE INTERRUPTED--
--AS CUTTER'S CLEAR, YOUNG VOICE COMMANDS ALL HER ATTENTION...
SAVAH, THE MOTHER OF MEMORY, IS VERY, VERY OLD!
BUT I'VE LEARNED THAT ANY OF US CAN LIVE AS LONG AS SHE HAS...
...EVEN LONGER!

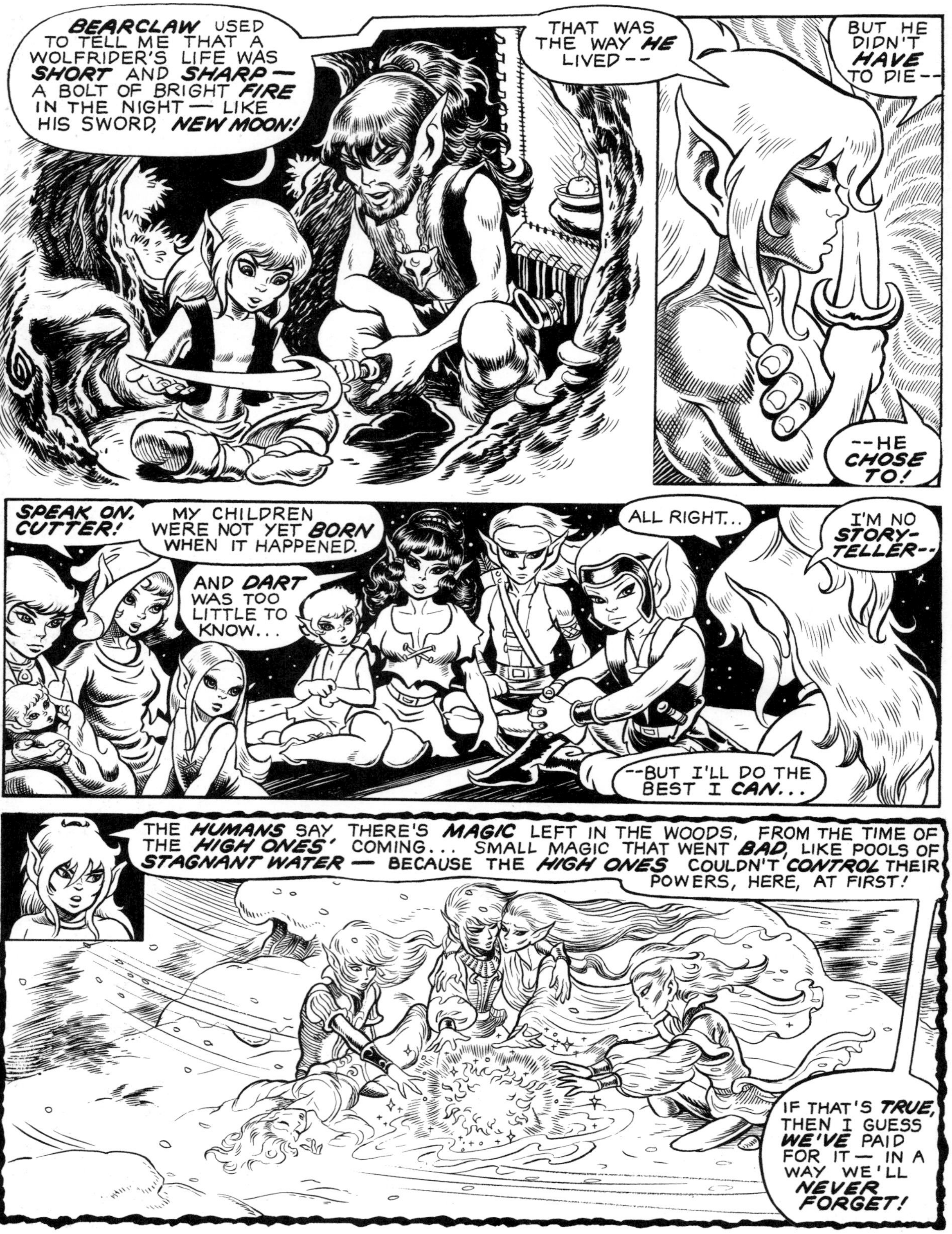
BEARCLAW USED TO TELL ME THAT A WOLFRIDER'S LIFE WAS SHORT AND SHARP — A BOLT OF BRIGHT FIRE IN THE NIGHT — LIKE HIS SWORD, NEW MOON!
THAT WAS THE WAY HE LIVED--
BUT HE DIDN'T HAVE TO DIE--
--HE CHOSE TO!
SPEAK ON, CUTTER!
MY CHILDREN WERE NOT YET BORN WHEN IT HAPPENED.
AND DART WAS TOO LITTLE TO KNOW...
ALL RIGHT...
I'M NO STORY-TELLER--
--BUT I'LL DO THE BEST I CAN...
THE HUMANS SAY THERE'S MAGIC LEFT IN THE WOODS, FROM THE TIME OF THE HIGH ONES' COMING... SMALL MAGIC THAT WENT BAD, LIKE POOLS OF STAGNANT WATER — BECAUSE THE HIGH ONES COULDN'T CONTROL THEIR POWERS, HERE, AT FIRST!
IF THAT'S TRUE, THEN I GUESS WE'VE PAID FOR IT — IN A WAY WE'LL NEVER FORGET!

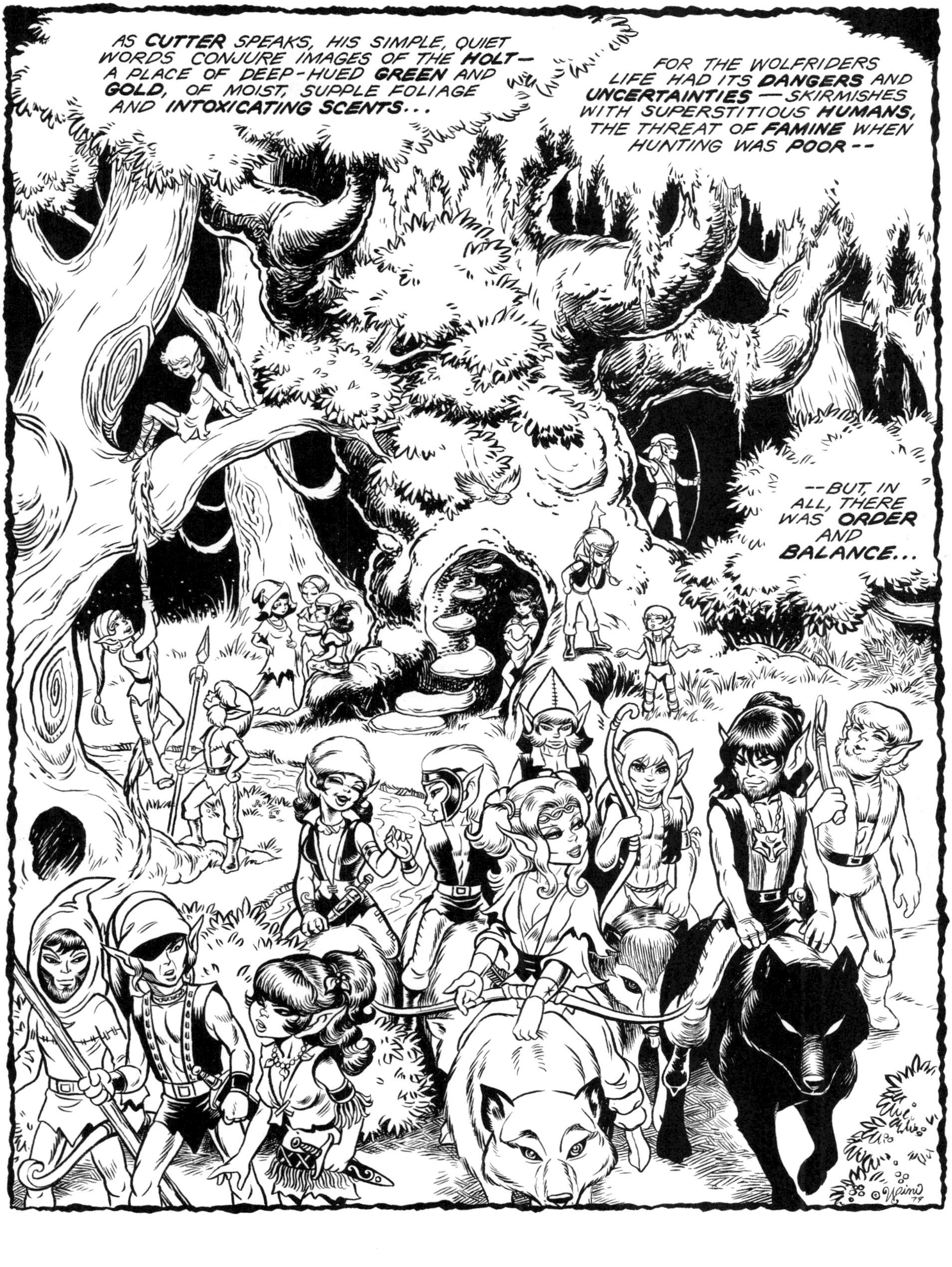
AS CUTTER SPEAKS, HIS SIMPLE, QUIET WORDS CONJURE IMAGES OF THE HOLT— A PLACE OF DEEP-HUED GREEN AND GOLD, OF MOIST, SUPPLE FOLIAGE AND INTOXICATING SCENTS...
FOR THE WOLFRIDERS LIFE HAD ITS DANGERS AND UNCERTAINTIES — SKIRMISHES WITH SUPERSTITIOUS HUMANS, THE THREAT OF FAMINE WHEN HUNTING WAS POOR --
--BUT, IN ALL, THERE WAS ORDER AND BALANCE...

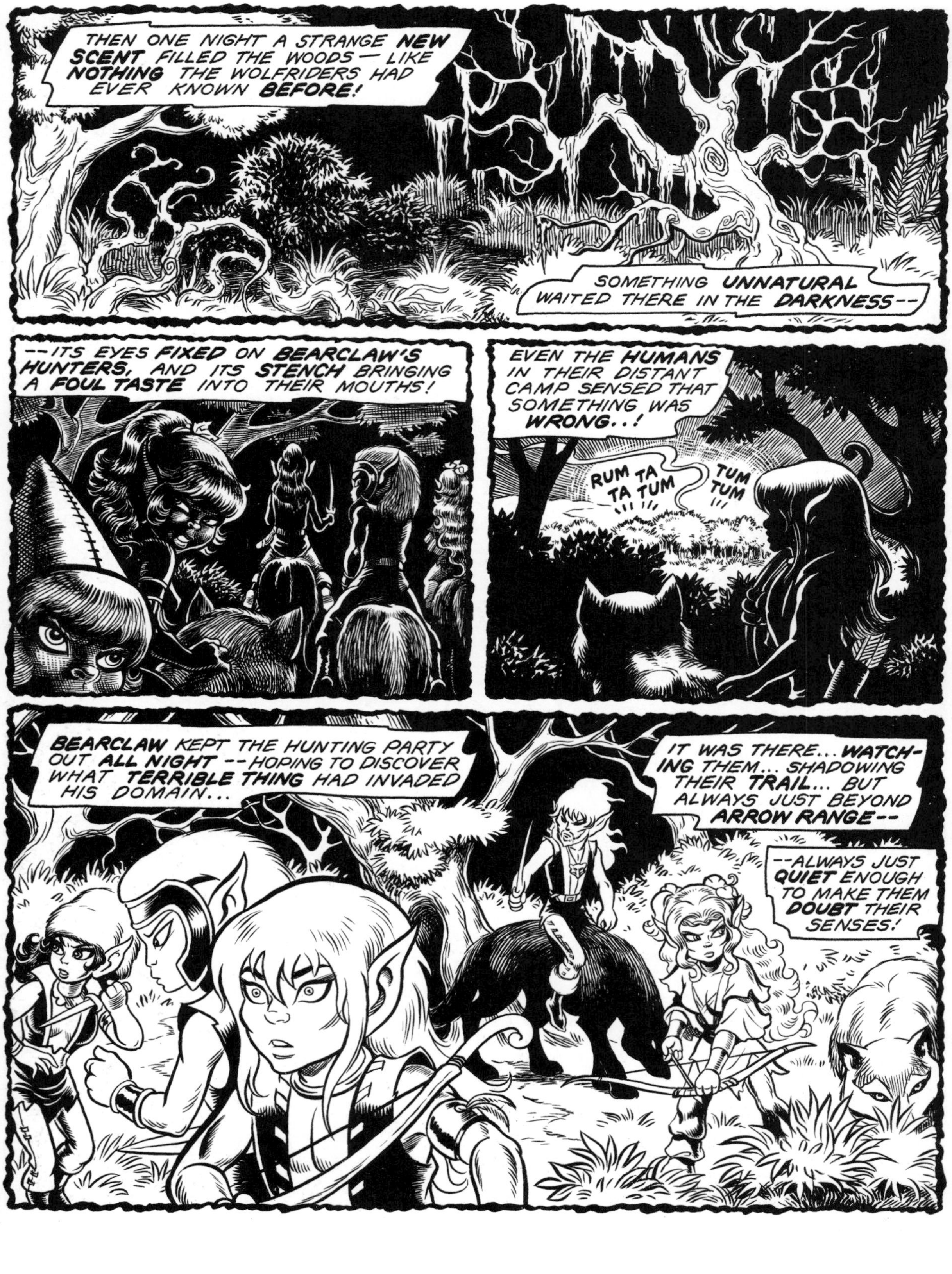
THEN ONE NIGHT A STRANGE NEW SCENT FILLED THE WOODS — LIKE NOTHING THE WOLFRIDERS HAD EVER KNOWN BEFORE!
SOMETHING UNNATURAL WAITED THERE IN THE DARKNESS--
--ITS EYES FIXED ON BEARCLAW'S HUNTERS, AND ITS STENCH BRINGING A FOUL TASTE INTO THEIR MOUTHS!
EVEN THE HUMANS IN THEIR DISTANT CAMP SENSED THAT SOMETHING WAS WRONG..!
RUM TA TA TUM
TUM TUM
BEARCLAW KEPT THE HUNTING PARTY OUT ALL NIGHT --HOPING TO DISCOVER WHAT TERRIBLE THING HAD INVADED HIS DOMAIN...
IT WAS THERE... WATCHING THEM... SHADOWING THEIR TRAIL... BUT ALWAYS JUST BEYOND ARROW RANGE--
--ALWAYS JUST QUIET ENOUGH TO MAKE THEM DOUBT THEIR SENSES!

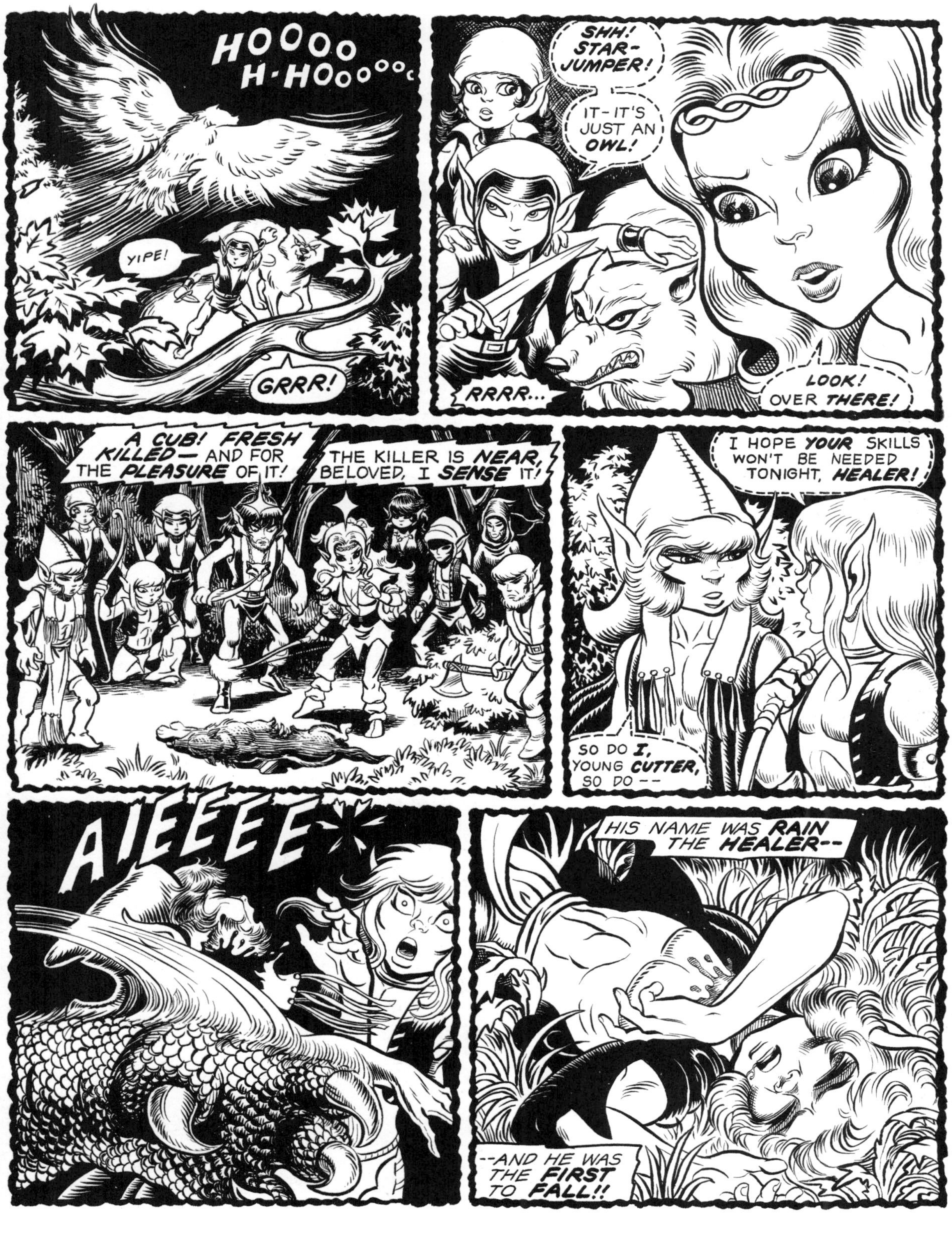
HOOOO H-HOOOOOO
YIPE!
GRRR!
SHH! STAR-JUMPER!
IT-IT'S JUST AN OWL!
RRRR...
LOOK! OVER THERE!
A CUB! FRESH KILLED— AND FOR THE PLEASURE OF IT!
THE KILLER IS NEAR, BELOVED, I SENSE IT!
I HOPE YOUR SKILLS WON'T BE NEEDED TONIGHT, HEALER!
SO DO I, YOUNG CUTTER, SO DO --
AIEEEEE
HIS NAME WAS RAIN THE HEALER--
--AND HE WAS THE FIRST TO FALL!!

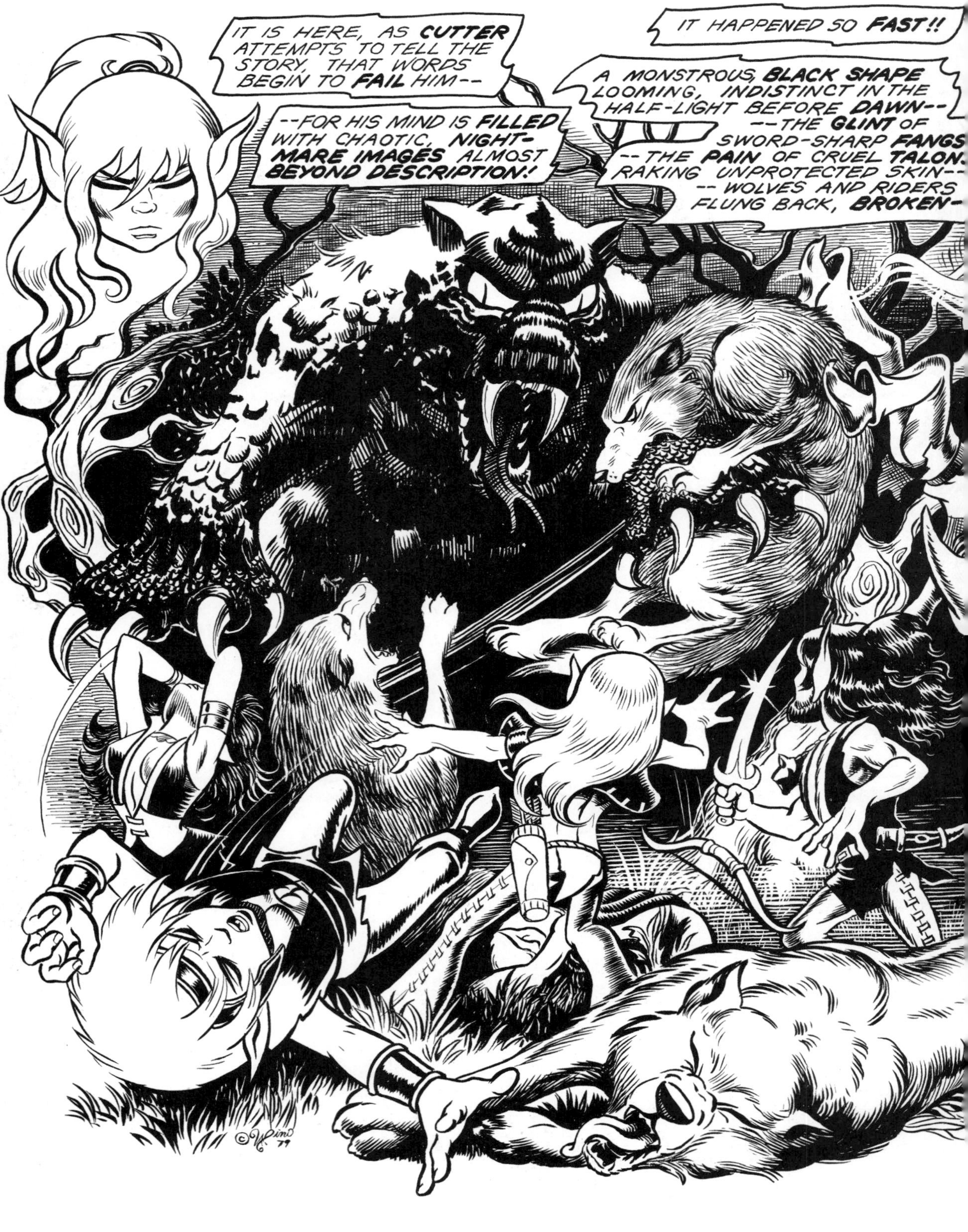
IT IS HERE, AS CUTTER ATTEMPTS TO TELL THE STORY, THAT WORDS BEGIN TO FAIL HIM--
--FOR HIS MIND IS FILLED WITH CHAOTIC, NIGHT-MARE IMAGES ALMOST BEYOND DESCRIPTION!
IT HAPPENED SO FAST!!
A MONSTROUS, BLACK SHAPE LOOMING, INDISTINCT IN THE HALF-LIGHT BEFORE DAWN-- --THE GLINT OF SWORD-SHARP FANGS --THE PAIN OF CRUEL TALONS RAKING UNPROTECTED SKIN-- --WOLVES AND RIDERS FLUNG BACK, BROKEN--

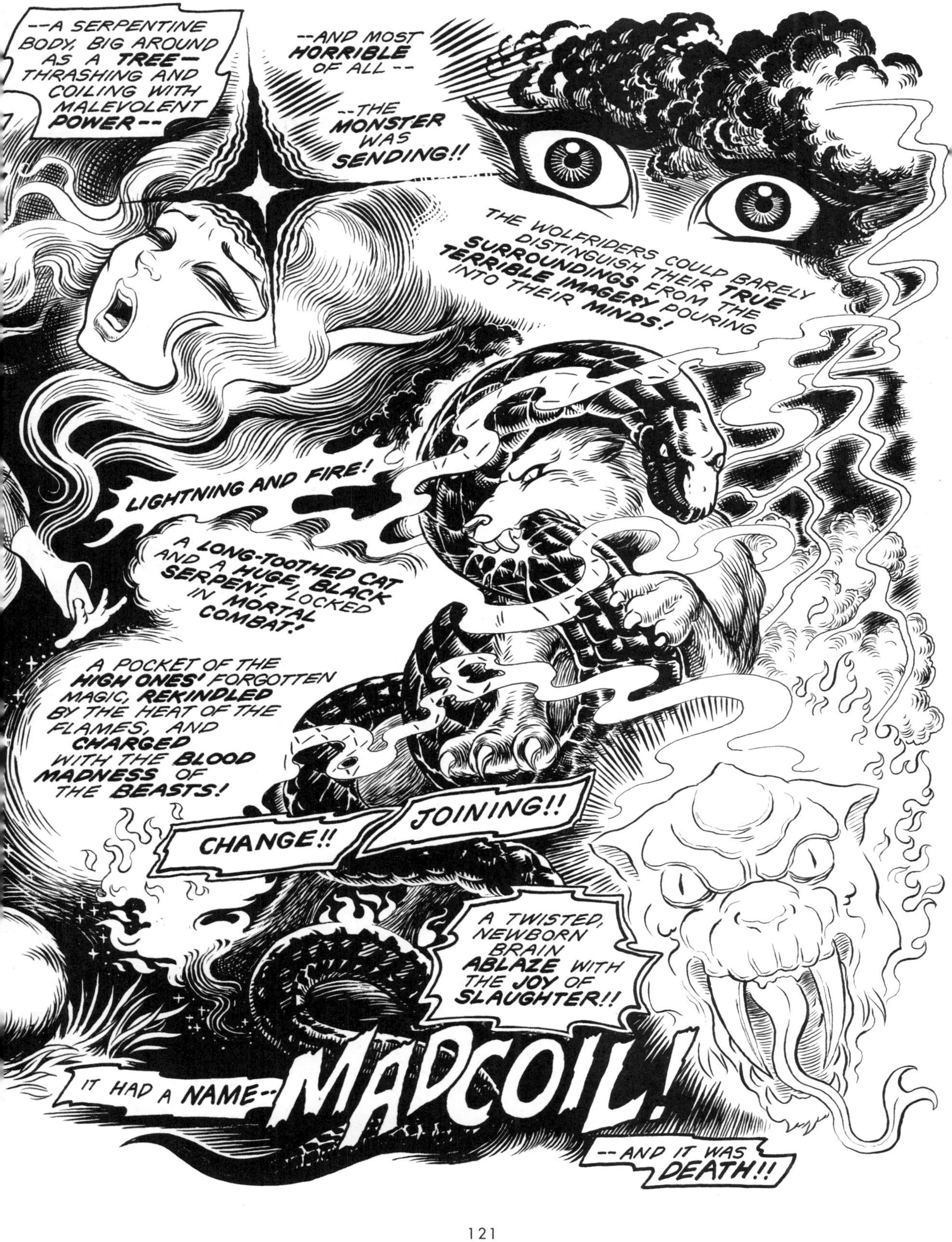
--A SERPENTINE BODY, BIG AROUND AS A TREE--THRASHING AND COILING WITH MALEVOLENT POWER--
--AND MOST HORRIBLE OF ALL--
--THE MONSTER WAS SENDING!!
THE WOLFRIDERS COULD BARELY DISTINGUISH THEIR TRUE SURROUNDINGS FROM THE TERRIBLE IMAGERY POURING INTO THEIR MINDS!
LIGHTNING AND FIRE!
A LONG-TOOTHED CAT AND A HUGE, BLACK SERPENT, LOCKED IN MORTAL COMBAT!
A POCKET OF THE HIGH ONES' FORGOTTEN MAGIC, REKINDLED BY THE HEAT OF THE FLAMES, AND CHARGED WITH THE BLOOD MADNESS OF THE BEASTS!
CHANGE!!
JOINING!!
A TWISTED, NEWBORN BRAIN ABLAZE WITH THE JOY OF SLAUGHTER!!
IT HAD A NAME--MADCOIL!
--AND IT WAS DEATH!!

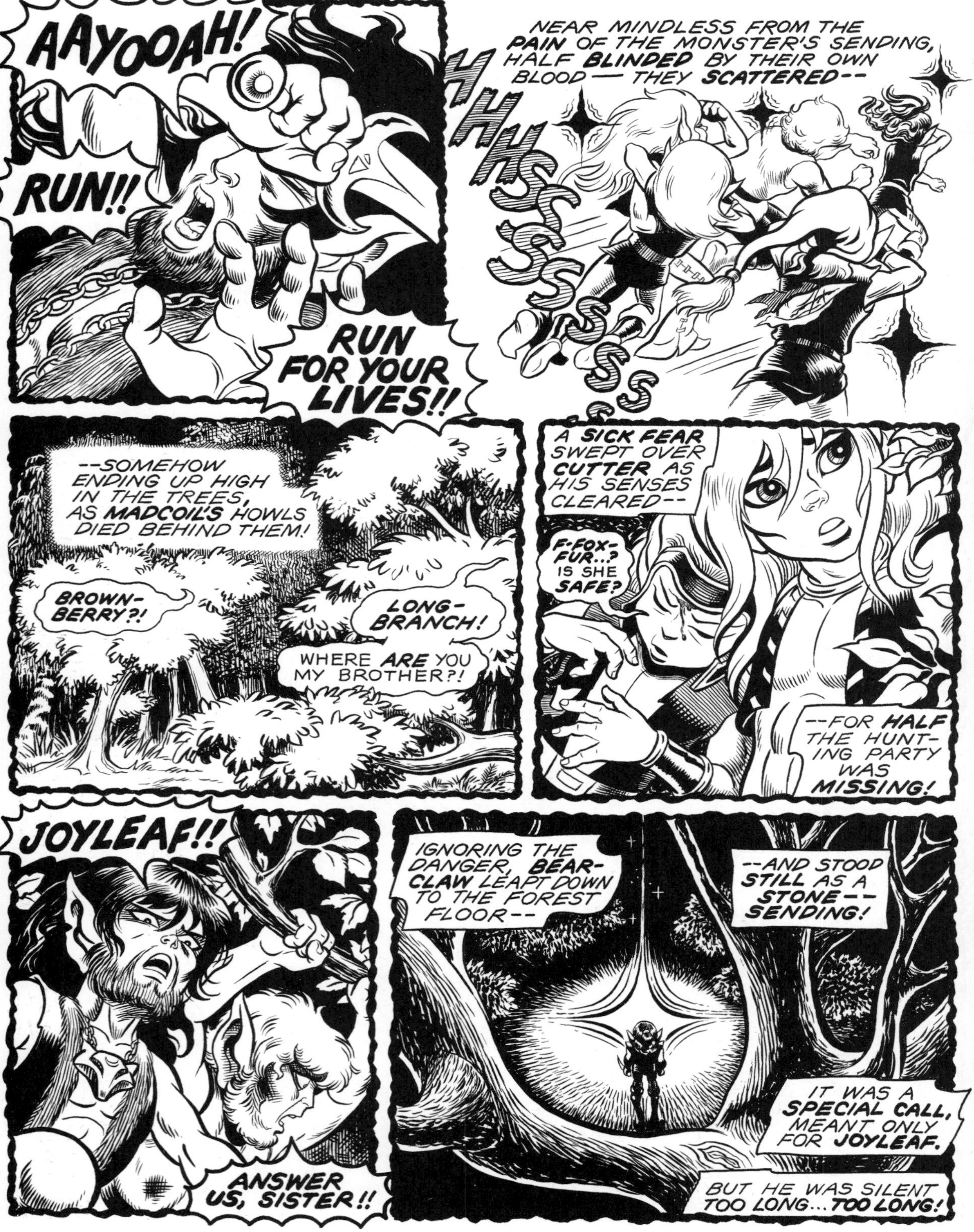
AAYOOAH!
RUN!!
RUN FOR YOUR LIVES!!
NEAR MINDLESS FROM THE PAIN OF THE MONSTER'S SENDING, HALF BLINDED BY THEIR OWN BLOOD — THEY SCATTERED--
HHHHSSSSSSSSS
--SOMEHOW ENDING UP HIGH IN THE TREES, AS MADCOIL'S HOWLS DIED BEHIND THEM!
BROWN-BERRY?!
LONG-BRANCH!
WHERE ARE YOU MY BROTHER?!
A SICK FEAR SWEPT OVER CUTTER AS HIS SENSES CLEARED--
F-FOX-FUR...? IS SHE SAFE?
--FOR HALF THE HUNTING PARTY WAS MISSING!
JOYLEAF!!
ANSWER US, SISTER!!
IGNORING THE DANGER, BEAR-CLAW LEAPT DOWN TO THE FOREST FLOOR--
--AND STOOD STILL AS A STONE--SENDING!
IT WAS A SPECIAL CALL, MEANT ONLY FOR JOYLEAF.
BUT HE WAS SILENT TOO LONG...TOO LONG!

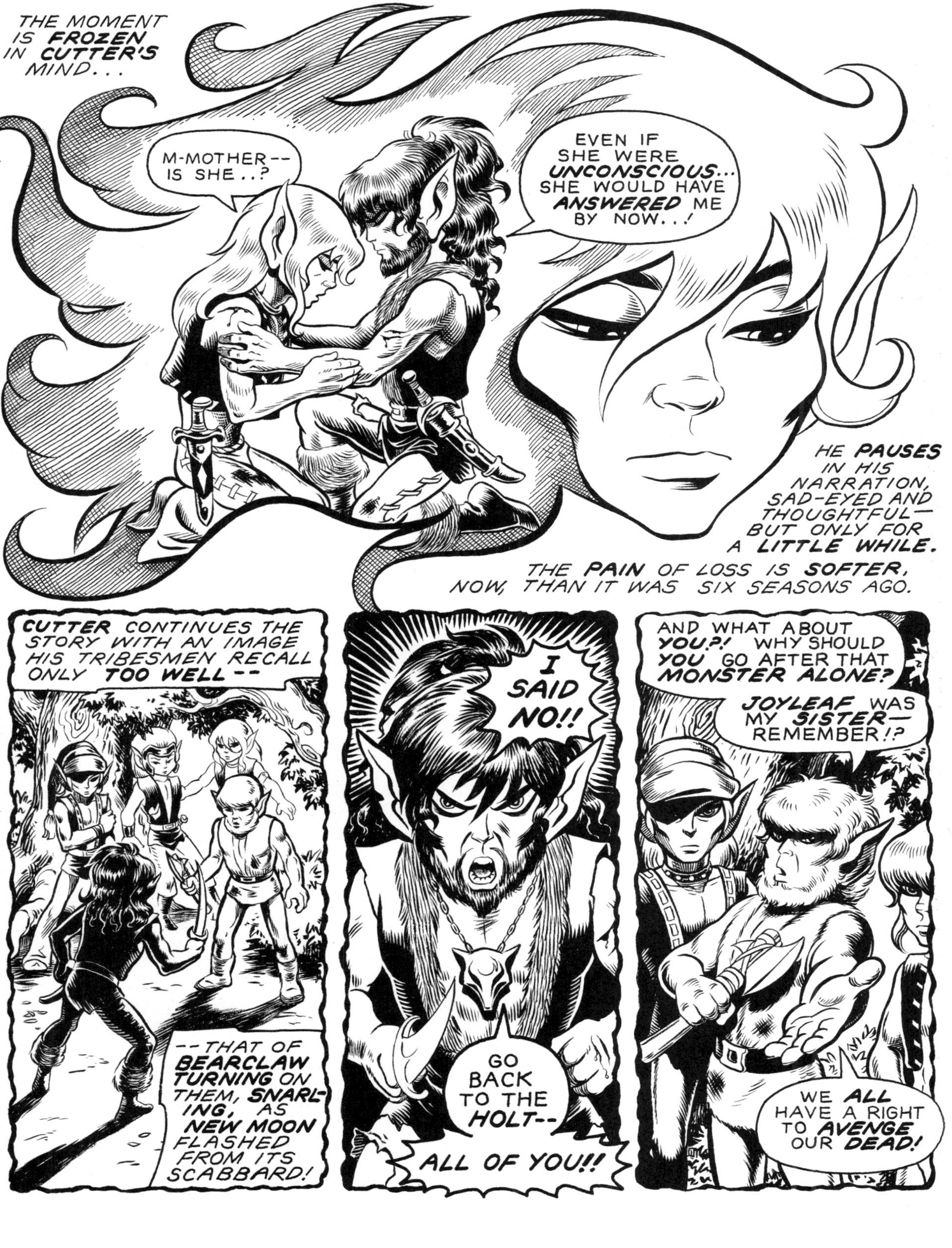

THE MOMENT IS **FROZEN** IN **CUTTER'S** MIND...
M-MOTHER-- IS SHE..?
EVEN IF SHE WERE **UNCONSCIOUS**... SHE WOULD HAVE **ANSWERED** ME BY NOW..!
HE **PAUSES** IN HIS NARRATION, SAD-EYED AND THOUGHTFUL— BUT ONLY FOR A **LITTLE WHILE**.
THE **PAIN** OF LOSS IS **SOFTER**, NOW, THAN IT WAS SIX SEASONS AGO.
CUTTER CONTINUES THE STORY WITH AN IMAGE HIS TRIBESMEN RECALL ONLY **TOO WELL**--
--THAT OF **BEARCLAW TURNING** ON THEM, **SNARLING**, AS **NEW MOON** FLASHED FROM ITS SCABBARD!
I SAID NO!!
GO BACK TO THE **HOLT**--
ALL OF YOU!!
AND WHAT ABOUT **YOU?!** WHY SHOULD **YOU** GO AFTER THAT **MONSTER ALONE?**
JOYLEAF WAS MY **SISTER**— REMEMBER!?
WE **ALL** HAVE A RIGHT TO **AVENGE** OUR **DEAD!**

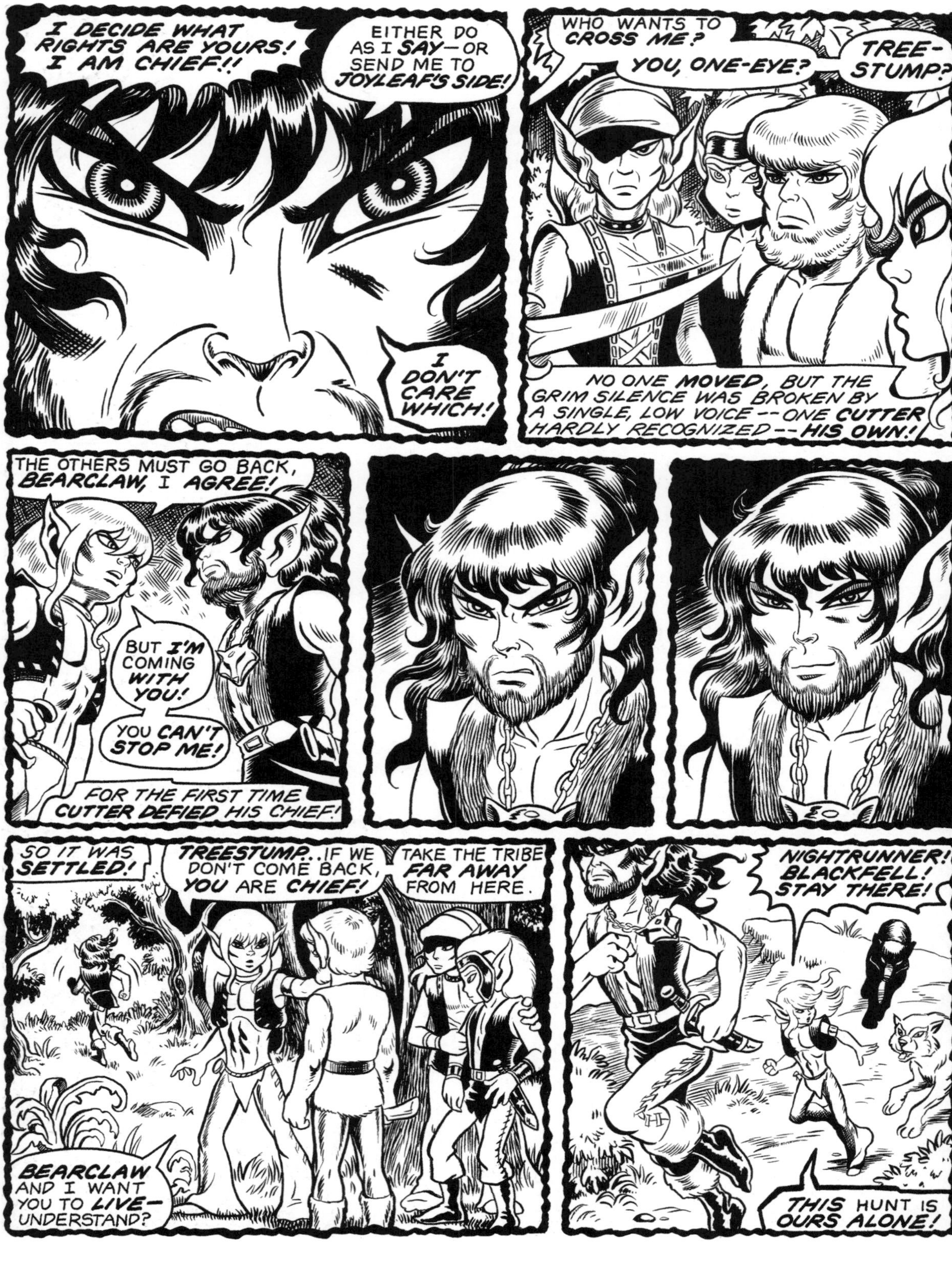

I DECIDE WHAT RIGHTS ARE YOURS! I AM CHIEF!!
EITHER DO AS I SAY—OR SEND ME TO JOYLEAF'S SIDE!
I DON'T CARE WHICH!
WHO WANTS TO CROSS ME?
YOU, ONE-EYE?
TREE-STUMP?
NO ONE MOVED, BUT THE GRIM SILENCE WAS BROKEN BY A SINGLE, LOW VOICE -- ONE CUTTER HARDLY RECOGNIZED -- HIS OWN!
THE OTHERS MUST GO BACK, BEARCLAW, I AGREE!
BUT I'M COMING WITH YOU!
YOU CAN'T STOP ME!
FOR THE FIRST TIME CUTTER DEFIED HIS CHIEF!
SO IT WAS SETTLED!
TREESTUMP.. IF WE DON'T COME BACK, YOU ARE CHIEF!
TAKE THE TRIBE FAR AWAY FROM HERE.
BEARCLAW AND I WANT YOU TO LIVE—UNDERSTAND?
NIGHTRUNNER! BLACKFELL! STAY THERE!
THIS HUNT IS OURS ALONE!

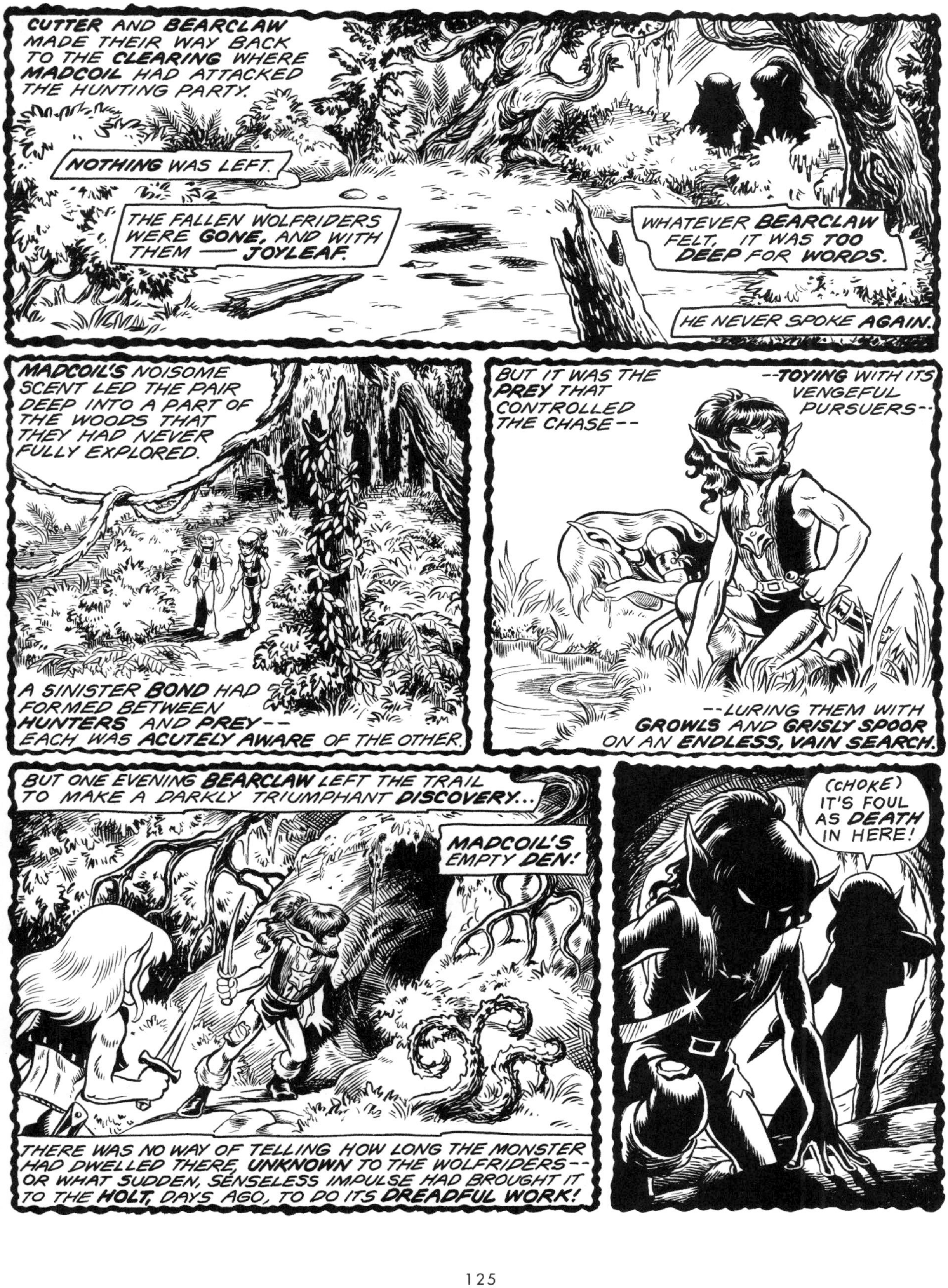

CUTTER AND BEARCLAW MADE THEIR WAY BACK TO THE CLEARING WHERE MADCOIL HAD ATTACKED THE HUNTING PARTY.
NOTHING WAS LEFT.
THE FALLEN WOLFRIDERS WERE GONE, AND WITH THEM — JOYLEAF.
WHATEVER BEARCLAW FELT, IT WAS TOO DEEP FOR WORDS.
HE NEVER SPOKE AGAIN.
MADCOIL'S NOISOME SCENT LED THE PAIR DEEP INTO A PART OF THE WOODS THAT THEY HAD NEVER FULLY EXPLORED.
A SINISTER BOND HAD FORMED BETWEEN HUNTERS AND PREY-- EACH WAS ACUTELY AWARE OF THE OTHER.
BUT IT WAS THE PREY THAT CONTROLLED THE CHASE--
--TOYING WITH ITS VENGEFUL PURSUERS--
--LURING THEM WITH GROWLS AND GRISLY SPOOR ON AN ENDLESS, VAIN SEARCH.
BUT ONE EVENING BEARCLAW LEFT THE TRAIL TO MAKE A DARKLY TRIUMPHANT DISCOVERY...
MADCOIL'S EMPTY DEN!
THERE WAS NO WAY OF TELLING HOW LONG THE MONSTER HAD DWELLED THERE, UNKNOWN TO THE WOLFRIDERS-- OR WHAT SUDDEN, SENSELESS IMPULSE HAD BROUGHT IT TO THE HOLT, DAYS AGO, TO DO ITS DREADFUL WORK!
(CHOKE) IT'S FOUL AS DEATH IN HERE!

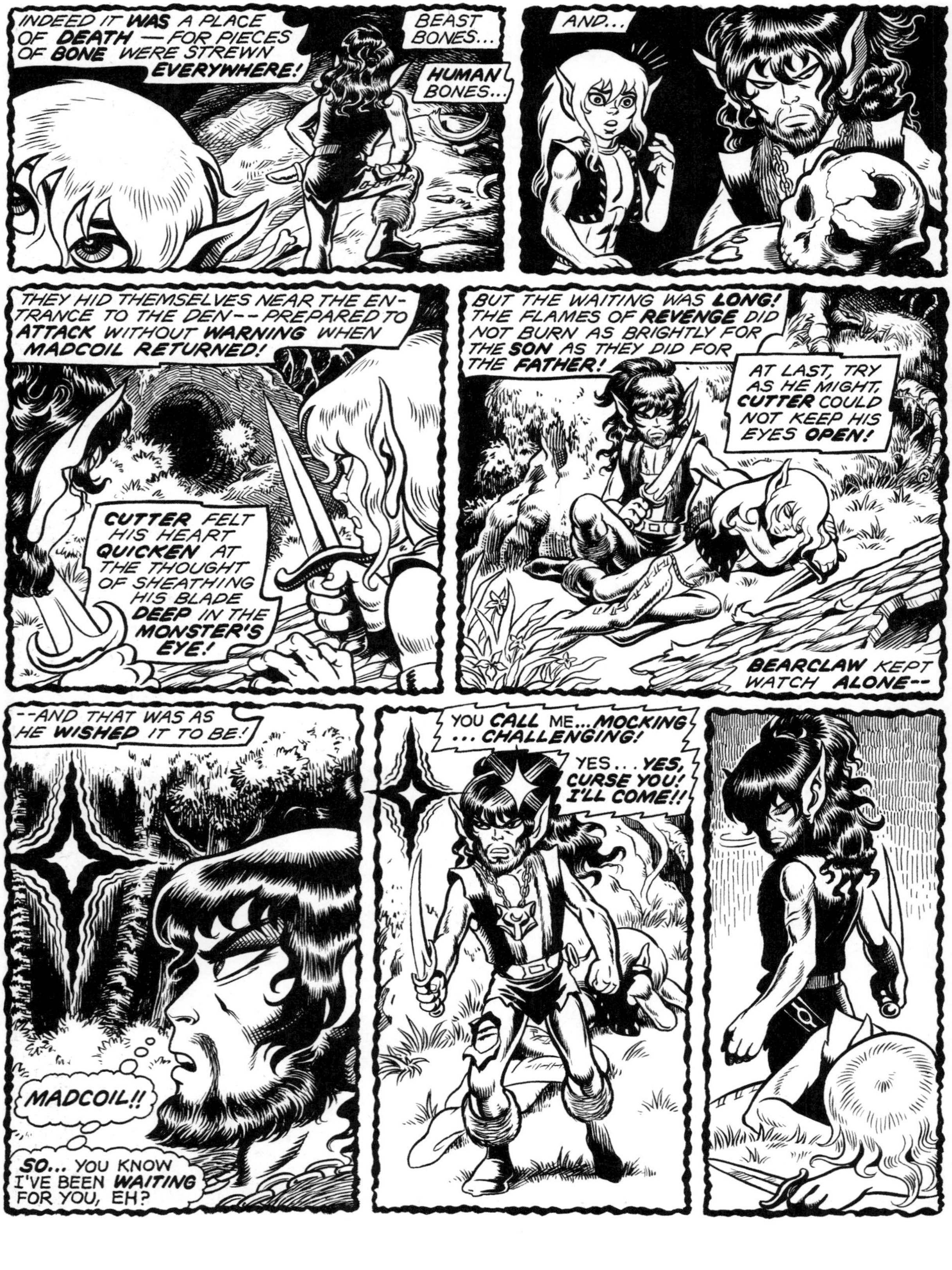
INDEED IT WAS A PLACE OF DEATH — FOR PIECES OF BONE WERE STREWN EVERYWHERE!
BEAST BONES...
HUMAN BONES...
AND...
THEY HID THEMSELVES NEAR THE ENTRANCE TO THE DEN-- PREPARED TO ATTACK WITHOUT WARNING WHEN MADCOIL RETURNED!
CUTTER FELT HIS HEART QUICKEN AT THE THOUGHT OF SHEATHING HIS BLADE DEEP IN THE MONSTER'S EYE!
BUT THE WAITING WAS LONG! THE FLAMES OF REVENGE DID NOT BURN AS BRIGHTLY FOR THE SON AS THEY DID FOR THE FATHER!
AT LAST, TRY AS HE MIGHT, CUTTER COULD NOT KEEP HIS EYES OPEN!
BEARCLAW KEPT WATCH ALONE--
--AND THAT WAS AS HE WISHED IT TO BE!
MADCOIL!!
SO... YOU KNOW I'VE BEEN WAITING FOR YOU, EH?
YOU CALL ME... MOCKING ... CHALLENGING!
YES... YES, CURSE YOU! I'LL COME!!

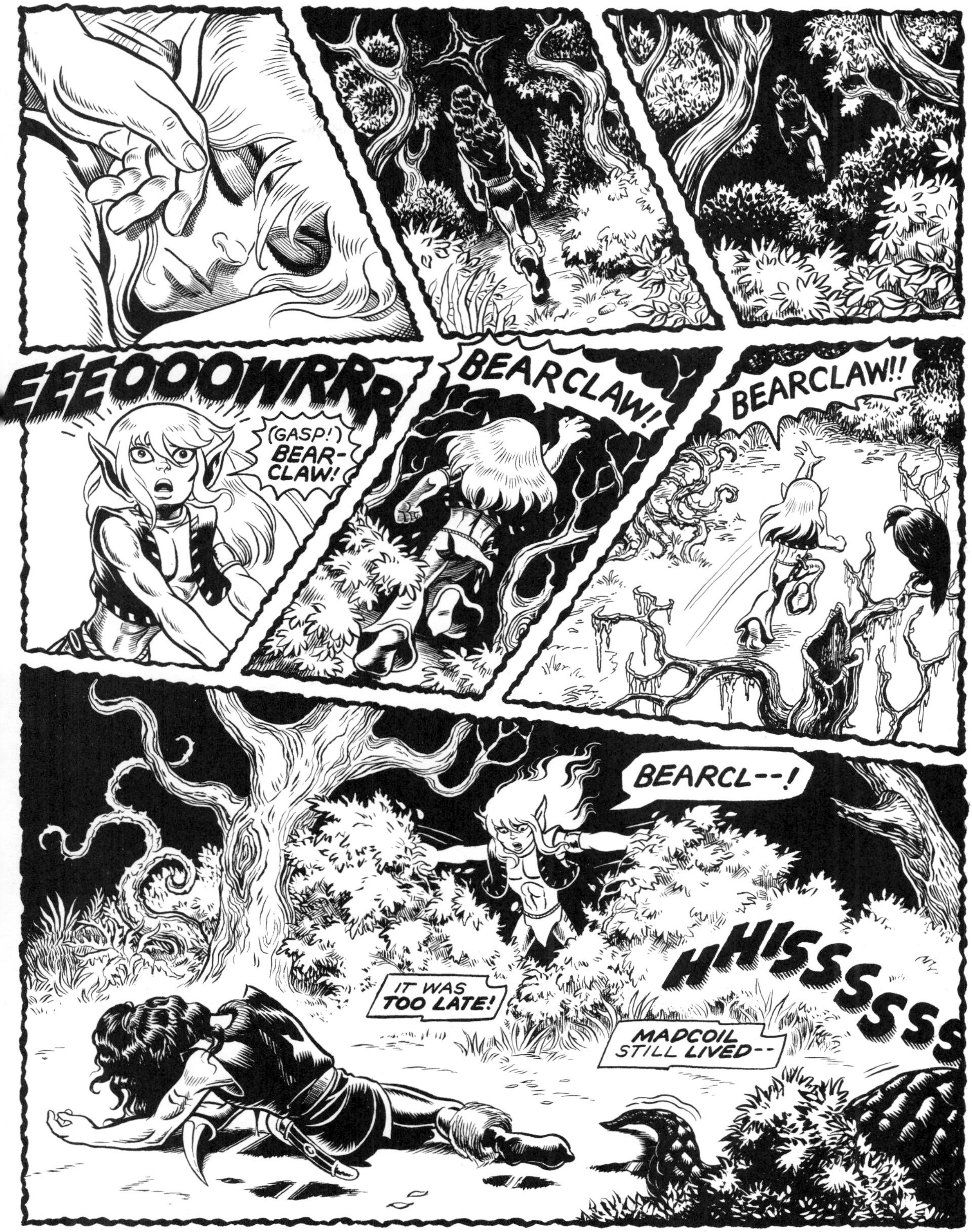
EEEOOOOWRRR
(GASP!) BEAR-CLAW!
BEARCLAW!
BEARCLAW!!
BEARCL--!
IT WAS TOO LATE!
HHISSSSSS
MADCOIL STILL LIVED--

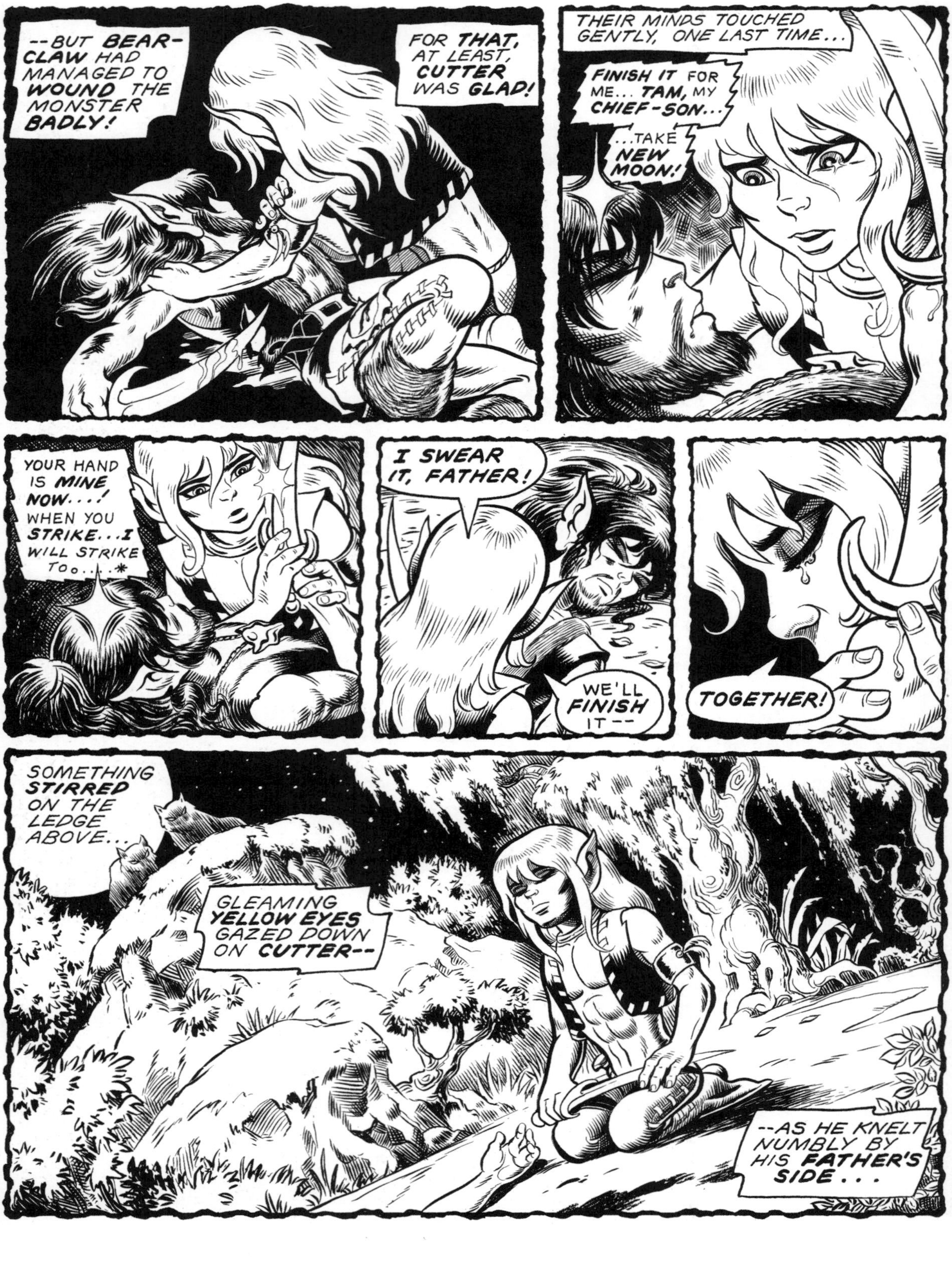

--BUT BEAR-CLAW HAD MANAGED TO WOUND THE MONSTER BADLY!
FOR THAT, AT LEAST, CUTTER WAS GLAD!
THEIR MINDS TOUCHED GENTLY, ONE LAST TIME...
FINISH IT FOR ME... TAM, MY CHIEF-SON...
...TAKE NEW MOON!
YOUR HAND IS MINE NOW...! WHEN YOU STRIKE...I WILL STRIKE TOO...*
I SWEAR IT, FATHER!
WE'LL FINISH IT--
TOGETHER!
SOMETHING STIRRED ON THE LEDGE ABOVE...
GLEAMING YELLOW EYES GAZED DOWN ON CUTTER--
--AS HE KNELT NUMBLY BY HIS FATHER'S SIDE...

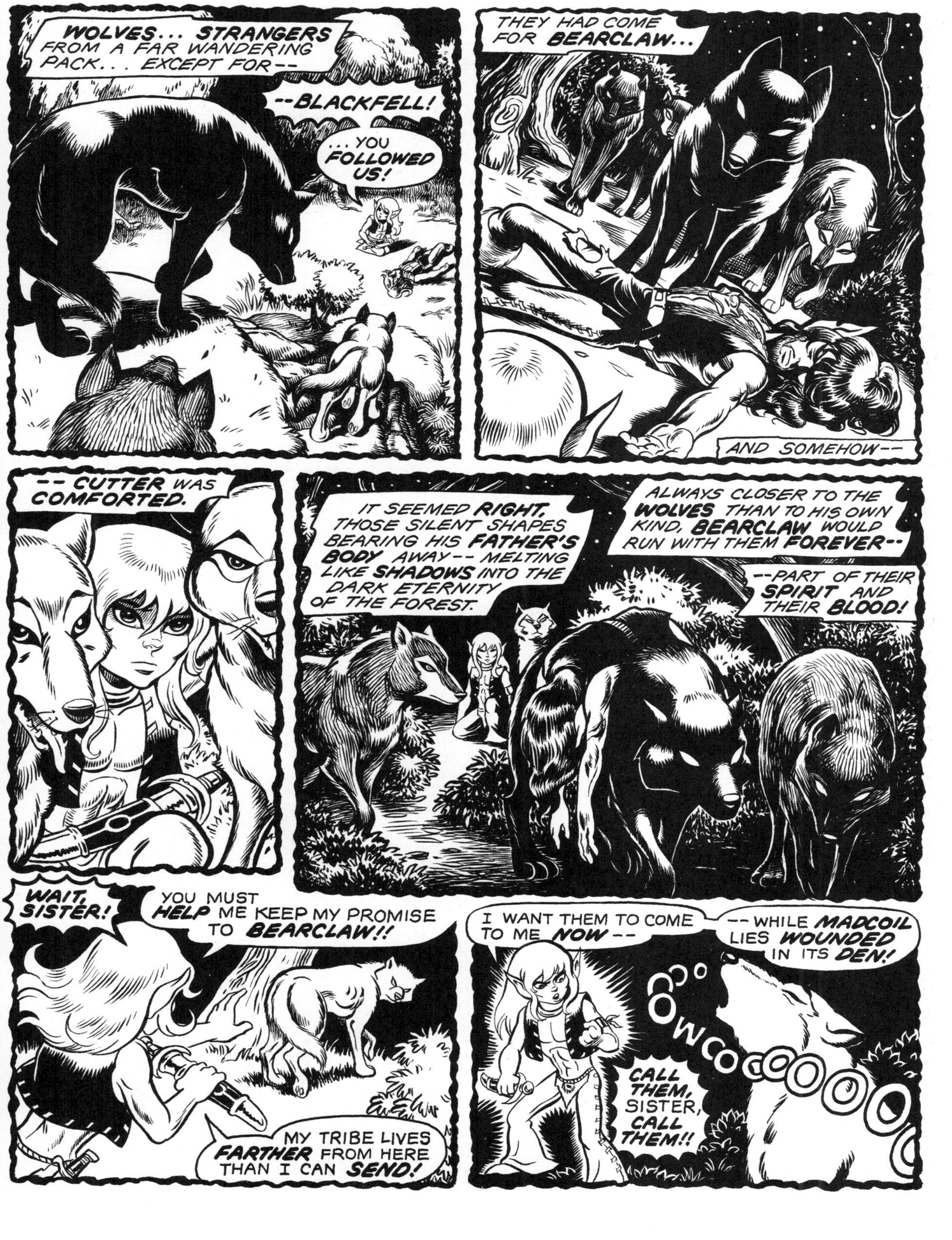
WOLVES... STRANGERS FROM A FAR WANDERING PACK... EXCEPT FOR--
--BLACKFELL!
...YOU FOLLOWED US!
THEY HAD COME FOR BEARCLAW...
AND SOMEHOW--
--CUTTER WAS COMFORTED.
IT SEEMED RIGHT, THOSE SILENT SHAPES BEARING HIS FATHER'S BODY AWAY-- MELTING LIKE SHADOWS INTO THE DARK ETERNITY OF THE FOREST.
ALWAYS CLOSER TO THE WOLVES THAN TO HIS OWN KIND, BEARCLAW WOULD RUN WITH THEM FOREVER--
--PART OF THEIR SPIRIT AND THEIR BLOOD!
WAIT, SISTER!
YOU MUST HELP ME KEEP MY PROMISE TO BEARCLAW!!
MY TRIBE LIVES FARTHER FROM HERE THAN I CAN SEND!
I WANT THEM TO COME TO ME NOW--
--WHILE MADCOIL LIES WOUNDED IN ITS DEN!
OOOWOOOOOOOOO
CALL THEM, SISTER, CALL THEM!!

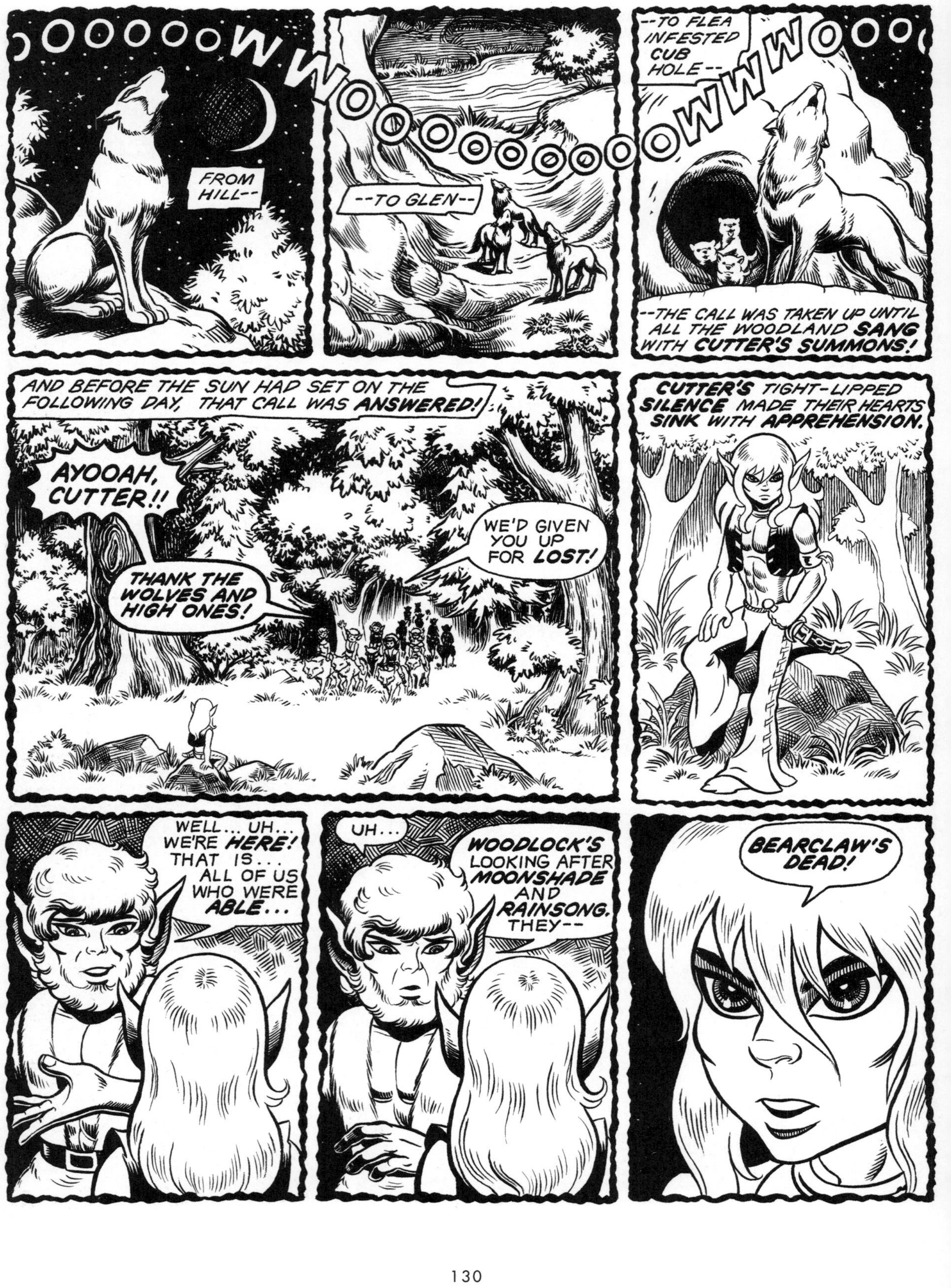
OOOOOOoWWWOOOOOOOOOOOOOOWWWWOOOO
FROM HILL--
--TO GLEN--
--TO FLEA INFESTED CUB HOLE--
--THE CALL WAS TAKEN UP UNTIL ALL THE WOODLAND SANG WITH CUTTER'S SUMMONS!
AND BEFORE THE SUN HAD SET ON THE FOLLOWING DAY, THAT CALL WAS ANSWERED!
AYOOAH, CUTTER!!
THANK THE WOLVES AND HIGH ONES!
WE'D GIVEN YOU UP FOR LOST!
CUTTER'S TIGHT-LIPPED SILENCE MADE THEIR HEARTS SINK WITH APPREHENSION.
WELL... UH... WE'RE HERE! THAT IS... ALL OF US WHO WERE ABLE...
UH...
WOODLOCK'S LOOKING AFTER MOONSHADE AND RAINSONG. THEY--
BEARCLAW'S DEAD!

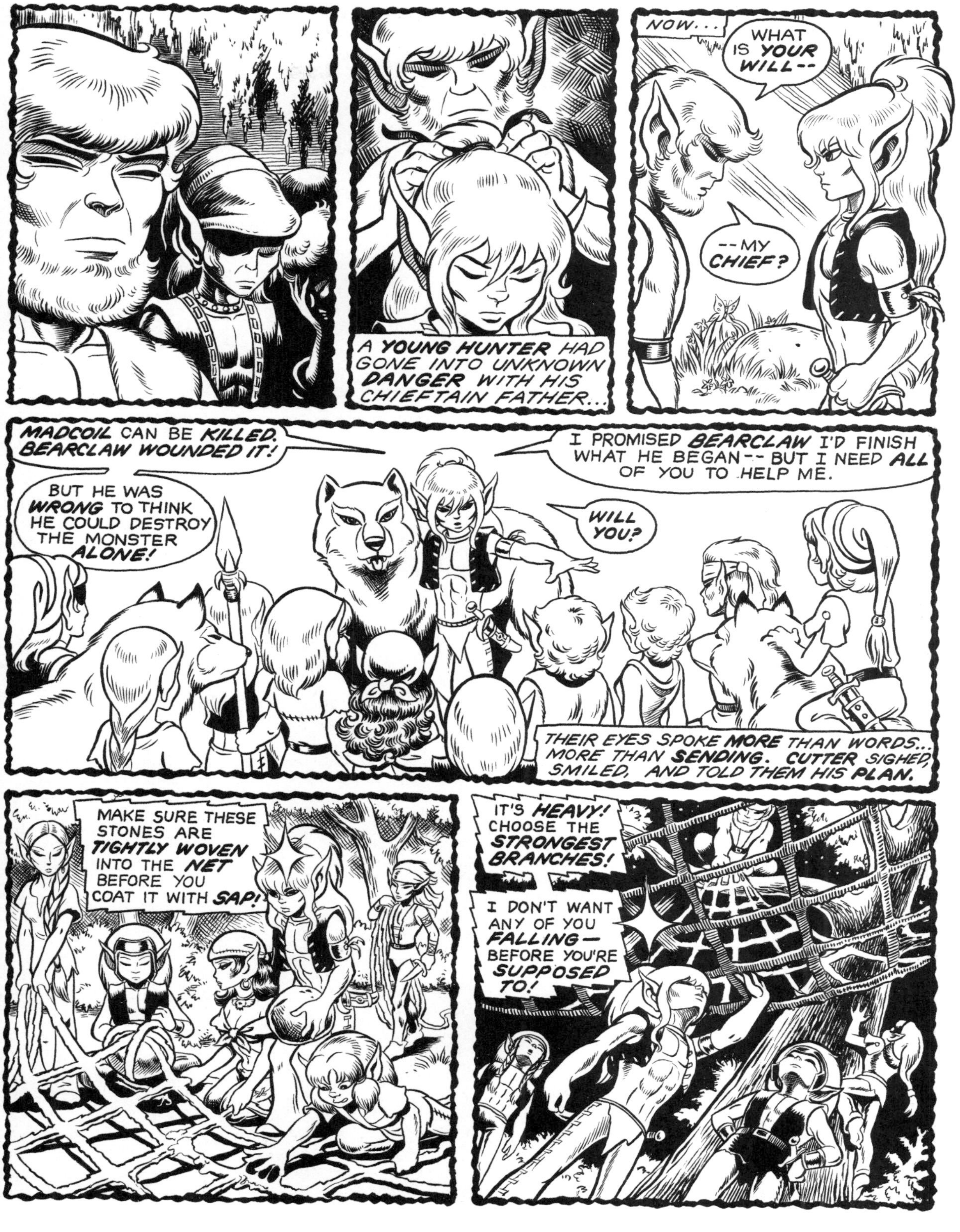
A YOUNG HUNTER HAD GONE INTO UNKNOWN DANGER WITH HIS CHIEFTAIN FATHER...
NOW...
WHAT IS YOUR WILL--
--MY CHIEF?
MADCOIL CAN BE KILLED. BEARCLAW WOUNDED IT!
BUT HE WAS WRONG TO THINK HE COULD DESTROY THE MONSTER ALONE!
I PROMISED BEARCLAW I'D FINISH WHAT HE BEGAN-- BUT I NEED ALL OF YOU TO HELP ME.
WILL YOU?
THEIR EYES SPOKE MORE THAN WORDS... MORE THAN SENDING. CUTTER SIGHED, SMILED, AND TOLD THEM HIS PLAN.
MAKE SURE THESE STONES ARE TIGHTLY WOVEN INTO THE NET BEFORE YOU COAT IT WITH SAP!
IT'S HEAVY! CHOOSE THE STRONGEST BRANCHES!
I DON'T WANT ANY OF YOU FALLING— BEFORE YOU'RE SUPPOSED TO!

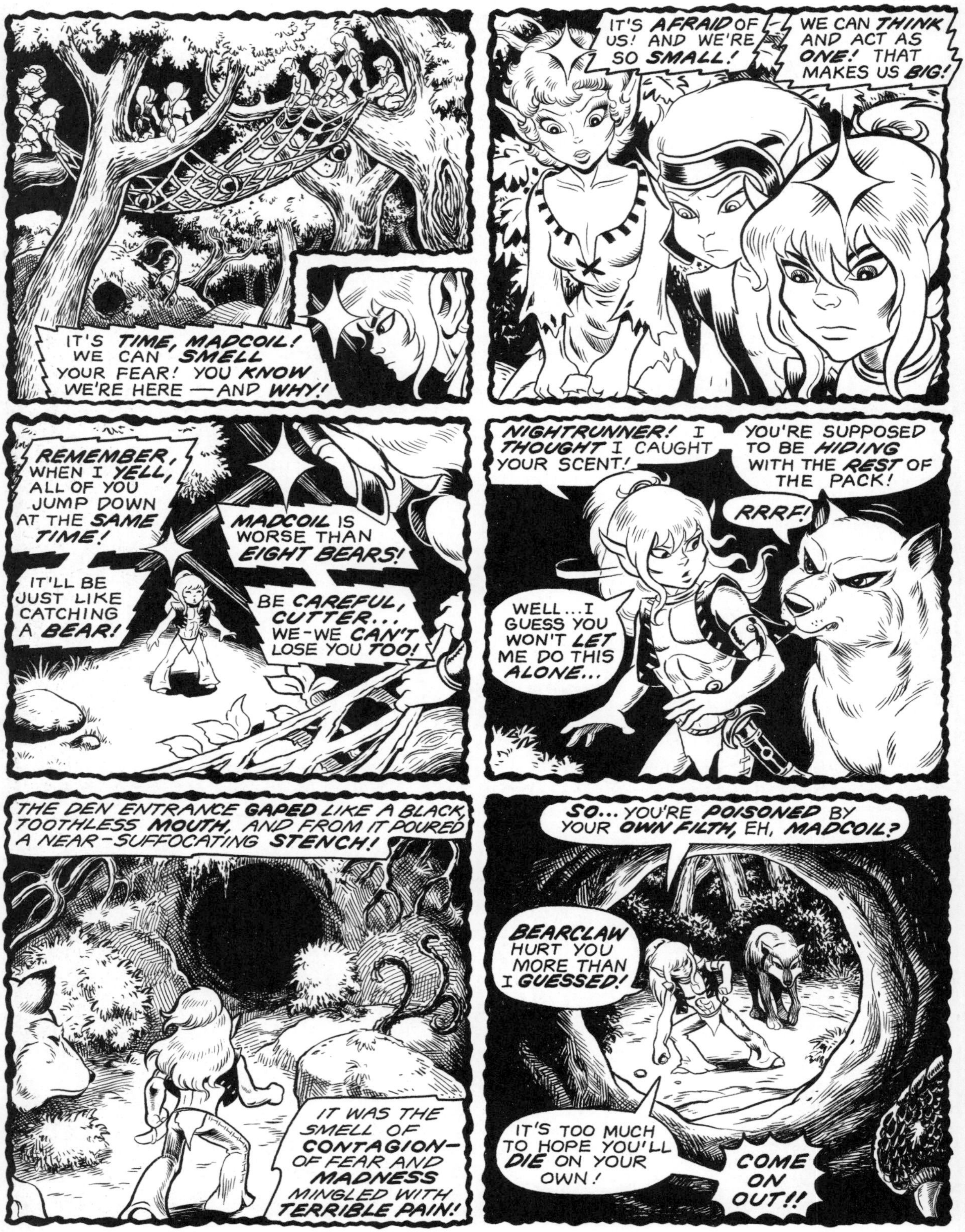
IT'S TIME, MADCOIL! WE CAN SMELL YOUR FEAR! YOU KNOW WE'RE HERE — AND WHY!
IT'S AFRAID OF US! AND WE'RE SO SMALL!
WE CAN THINK AND ACT AS ONE! THAT MAKES US BIG!
REMEMBER, WHEN I YELL, ALL OF YOU JUMP DOWN AT THE SAME TIME!
IT'LL BE JUST LIKE CATCHING A BEAR!
MADCOIL IS WORSE THAN EIGHT BEARS!
BE CAREFUL, CUTTER... WE-WE CAN'T LOSE YOU TOO!
NIGHTRUNNER! I THOUGHT I CAUGHT YOUR SCENT!
YOU'RE SUPPOSED TO BE HIDING WITH THE REST OF THE PACK!
RRRF!
WELL...I GUESS YOU WON'T LET ME DO THIS ALONE...
THE DEN ENTRANCE GAPED LIKE A BLACK, TOOTHLESS MOUTH, AND FROM IT POURED A NEAR-SUFFOCATING STENCH!
IT WAS THE SMELL OF CONTAGION— OF FEAR AND MADNESS MINGLED WITH TERRIBLE PAIN!
SO... YOU'RE POISONED BY YOUR OWN FILTH, EH, MADCOIL?
BEARCLAW HURT YOU MORE THAN I GUESSED!
IT'S TOO MUCH TO HOPE YOU'LL DIE ON YOUR OWN!
COME ON OUT!!

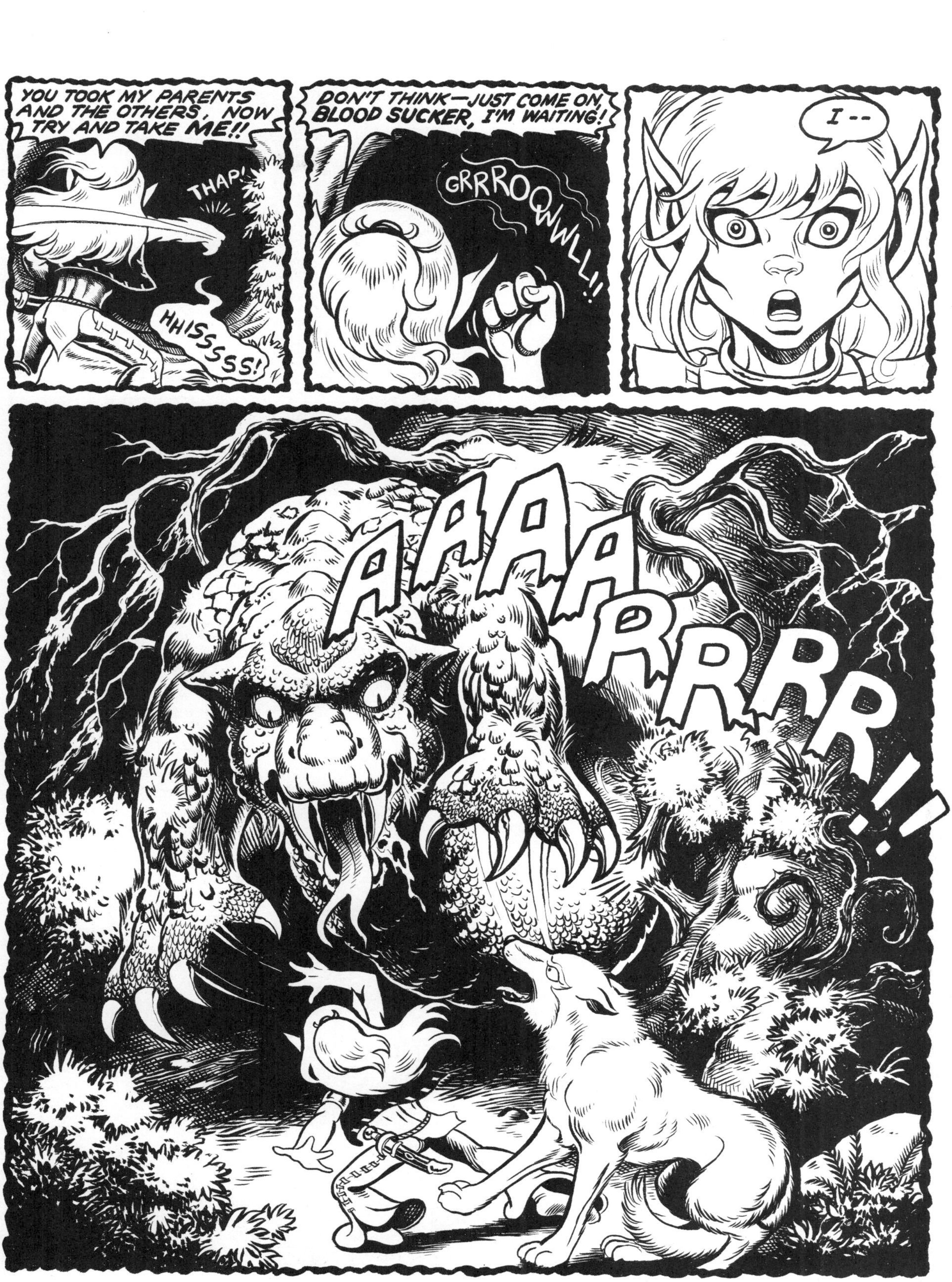
YOU TOOK MY PARENTS AND THE OTHERS, NOW TRY AND TAKE ME!!
THAP!
HHISSSSSS!
DON'T THINK—JUST COME ON, BLOOD SUCKER, I'M WAITING!
GRRROOWWLLL!!
I --
AAAARRRRR!!!

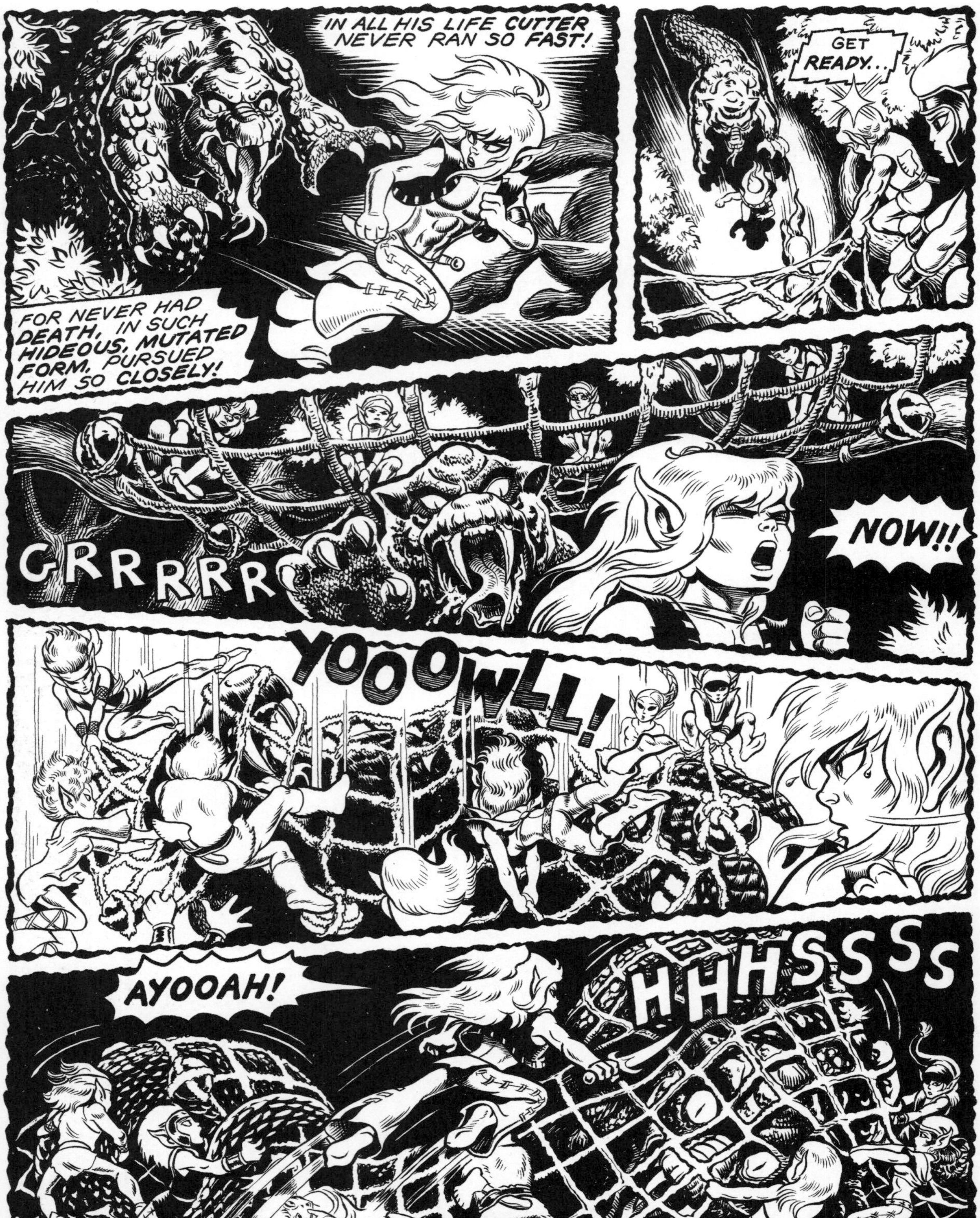

IN ALL HIS LIFE CUTTER NEVER RAN SO FAST!
FOR NEVER HAD DEATH, IN SUCH HIDEOUS, MUTATED FORM, PURSUED HIM SO CLOSELY!
GET READY...
GRRRRRR
NOW!!
YOOOWLL!
AYOOAH!
HHHSSSS

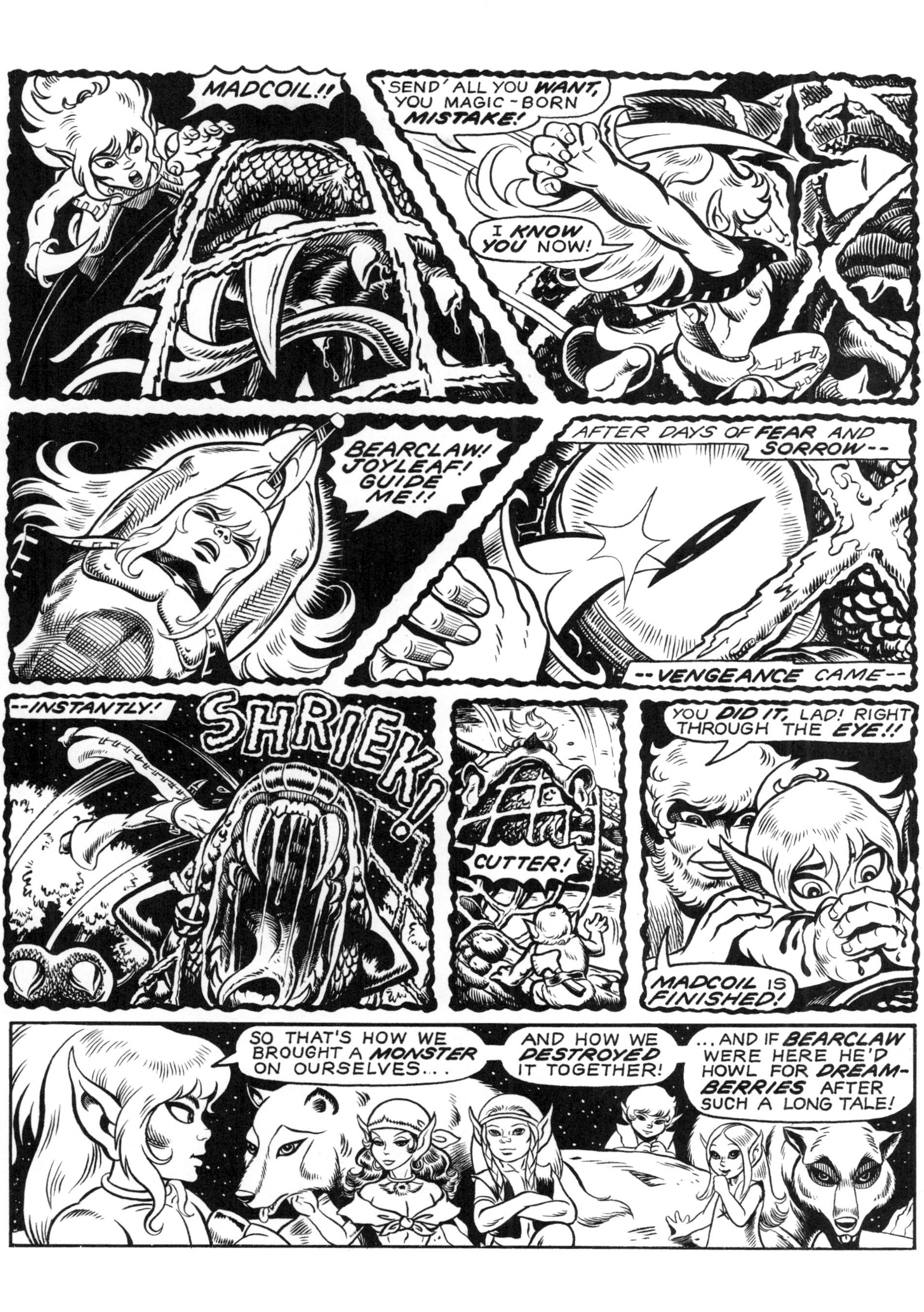

MADCOIL!!
'SEND' ALL YOU WANT, YOU MAGIC-BORN MISTAKE!
I KNOW YOU NOW!
BEARCLAW! JOYLEAF! GUIDE ME!!
AFTER DAYS OF FEAR AND SORROW--
--VENGEANCE CAME--
--INSTANTLY!
SHRIEK!
CUTTER!
YOU DID IT, LAD! RIGHT THROUGH THE EYE!!
MADCOIL IS FINISHED!
SO THAT'S HOW WE BROUGHT A MONSTER ON OURSELVES...
AND HOW WE DESTROYED IT TOGETHER!
...AND IF BEARCLAW WERE HERE HE'D HOWL FOR DREAM-BERRIES AFTER SUCH A LONG TALE!

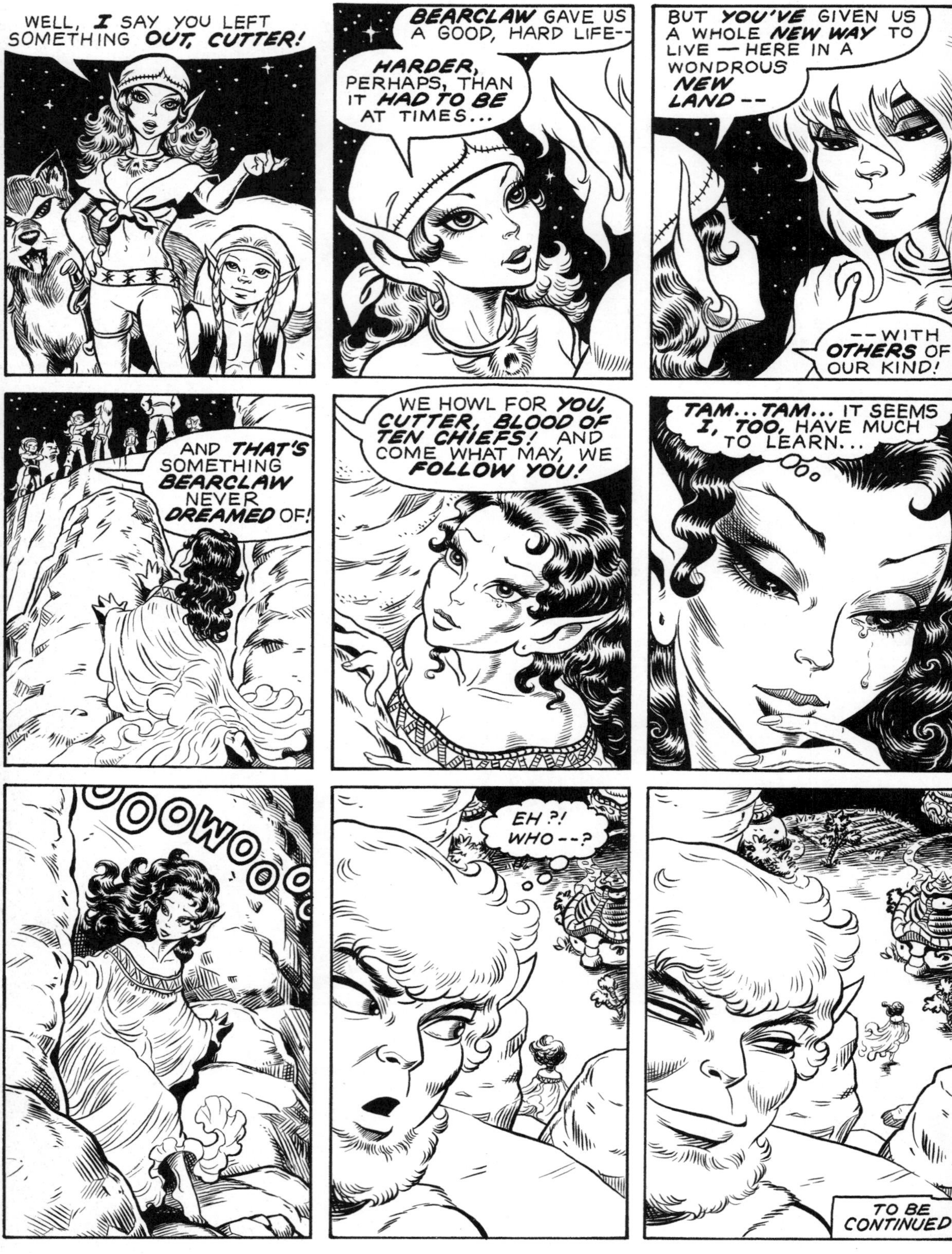
WELL, *I* SAY YOU LEFT SOMETHING *OUT, CUTTER!*
BEARCLAW GAVE US A GOOD, HARD LIFE--
HARDER, PERHAPS, THAN IT *HAD TO BE* AT TIMES...
BUT *YOU'VE* GIVEN US A WHOLE *NEW WAY* TO LIVE — HERE IN A WONDROUS *NEW LAND* --
--WITH *OTHERS* OF OUR KIND!
AND *THAT'S* SOMETHING *BEARCLAW* NEVER *DREAMED* OF!
WE HOWL FOR *YOU, CUTTER, BLOOD OF TEN CHIEFS!* AND COME WHAT MAY, WE *FOLLOW YOU!*
TAM...TAM... IT SEEMS *I, TOO,* HAVE MUCH TO LEARN...
OOOWOOOO
EH ?! WHO --?
TO BE CONTINUED

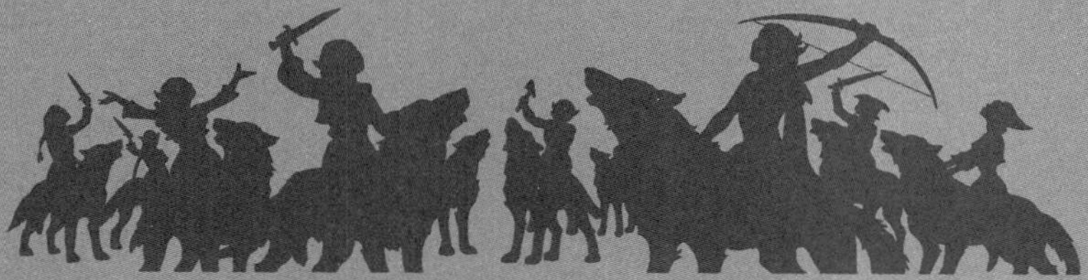

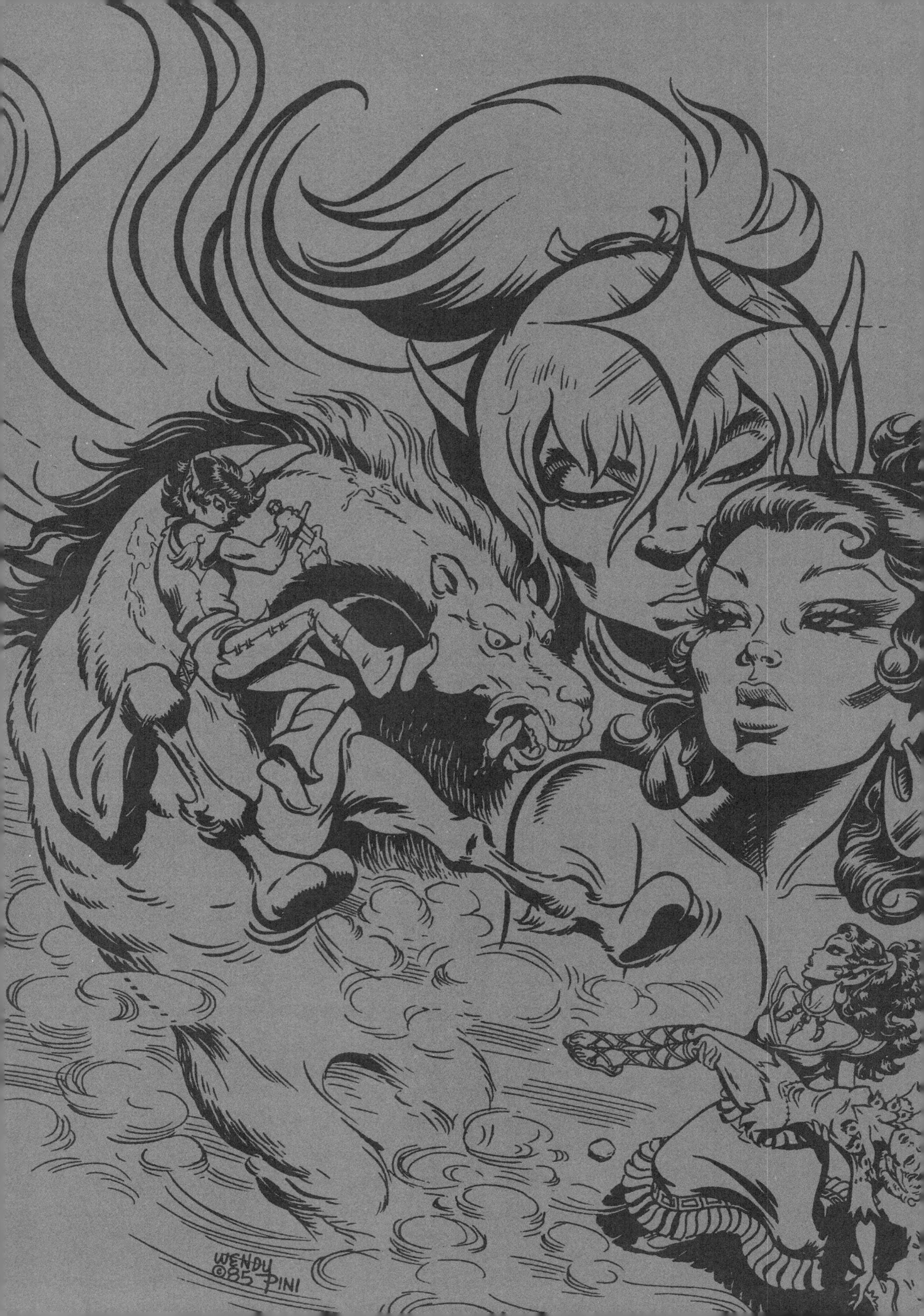
WENDY ©85 PINI

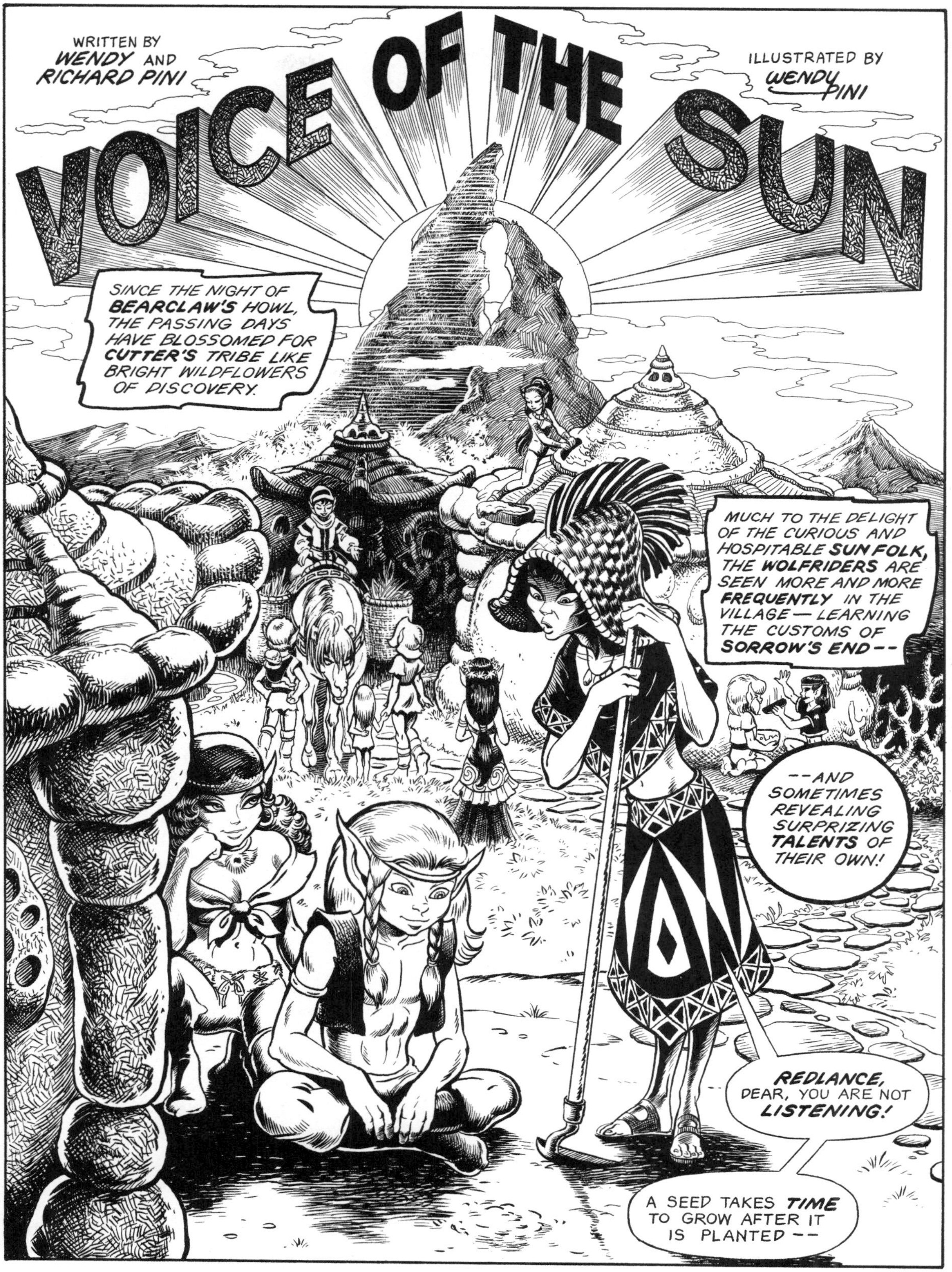

WRITTEN BY
WENDY AND
RICHARD PINI
VOICE OF THE SUN
ILLUSTRATED BY
WENDY PINI
SINCE THE NIGHT OF BEARCLAW'S HOWL, THE PASSING DAYS HAVE BLOSSOMED FOR CUTTER'S TRIBE LIKE BRIGHT WILDFLOWERS OF DISCOVERY.
MUCH TO THE DELIGHT OF THE CURIOUS AND HOSPITABLE SUN FOLK, THE WOLFRIDERS ARE SEEN MORE AND MORE FREQUENTLY IN THE VILLAGE -- LEARNING THE CUSTOMS OF SORROW'S END --
--AND SOMETIMES REVEALING SURPRIZING TALENTS OF THEIR OWN!
REDLANCE, DEAR, YOU ARE NOT LISTENING!
A SEED TAKES TIME TO GROW AFTER IT IS PLANTED --

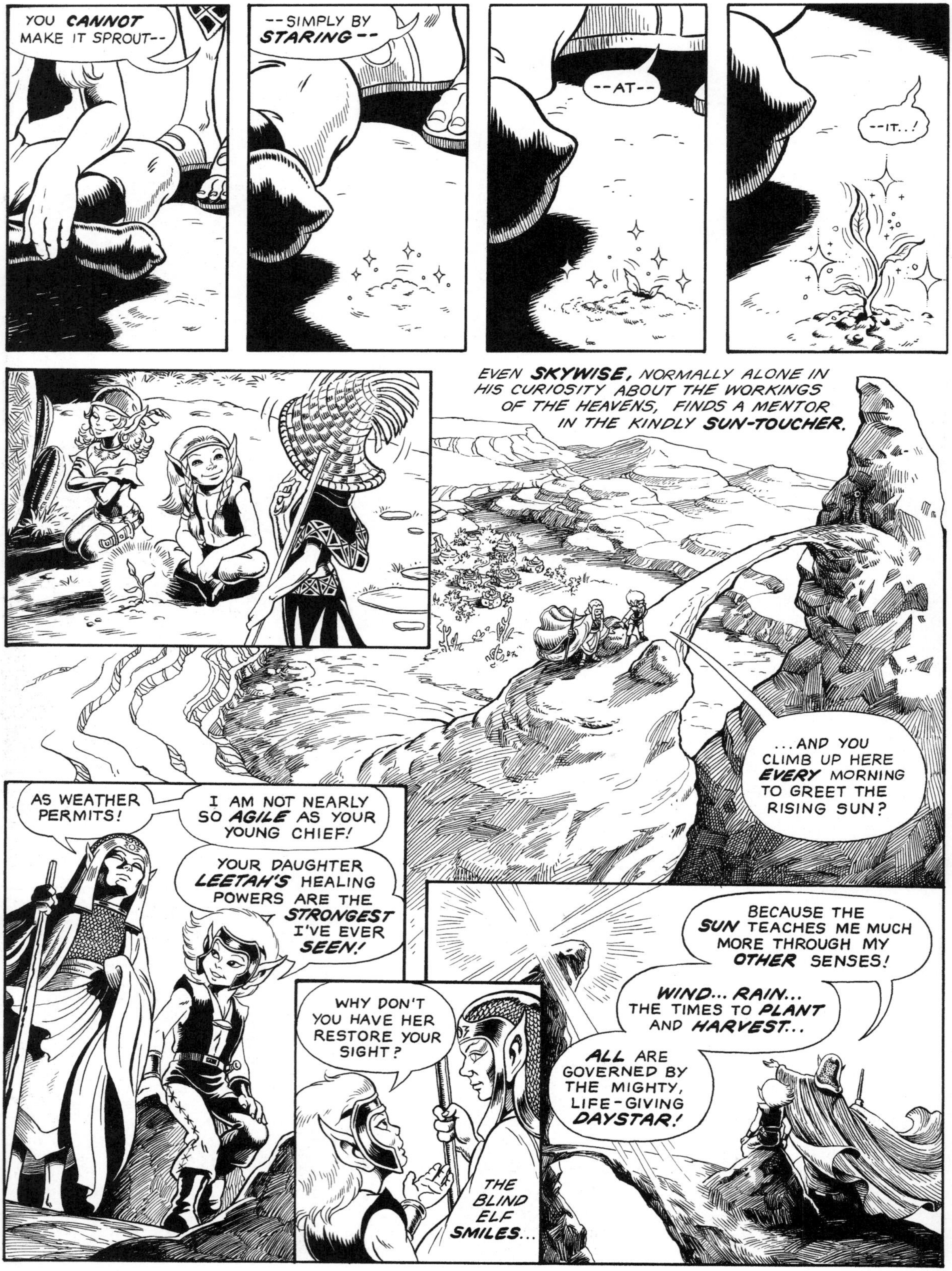
YOU CANNOT MAKE IT SPROUT--
--SIMPLY BY STARING--
--AT--
--IT..!
EVEN SKYWISE, NORMALLY ALONE IN HIS CURIOSITY ABOUT THE WORKINGS OF THE HEAVENS, FINDS A MENTOR IN THE KINDLY SUN-TOUCHER.
...AND YOU CLIMB UP HERE EVERY MORNING TO GREET THE RISING SUN?
AS WEATHER PERMITS!
I AM NOT NEARLY SO AGILE AS YOUR YOUNG CHIEF!
YOUR DAUGHTER LEETAH'S HEALING POWERS ARE THE STRONGEST I'VE EVER SEEN!
WHY DON'T YOU HAVE HER RESTORE YOUR SIGHT?
THE BLIND ELF SMILES...
BECAUSE THE SUN TEACHES ME MUCH MORE THROUGH MY OTHER SENSES!
WIND... RAIN... THE TIMES TO PLANT AND HARVEST...
ALL ARE GOVERNED BY THE MIGHTY, LIFE-GIVING DAYSTAR!

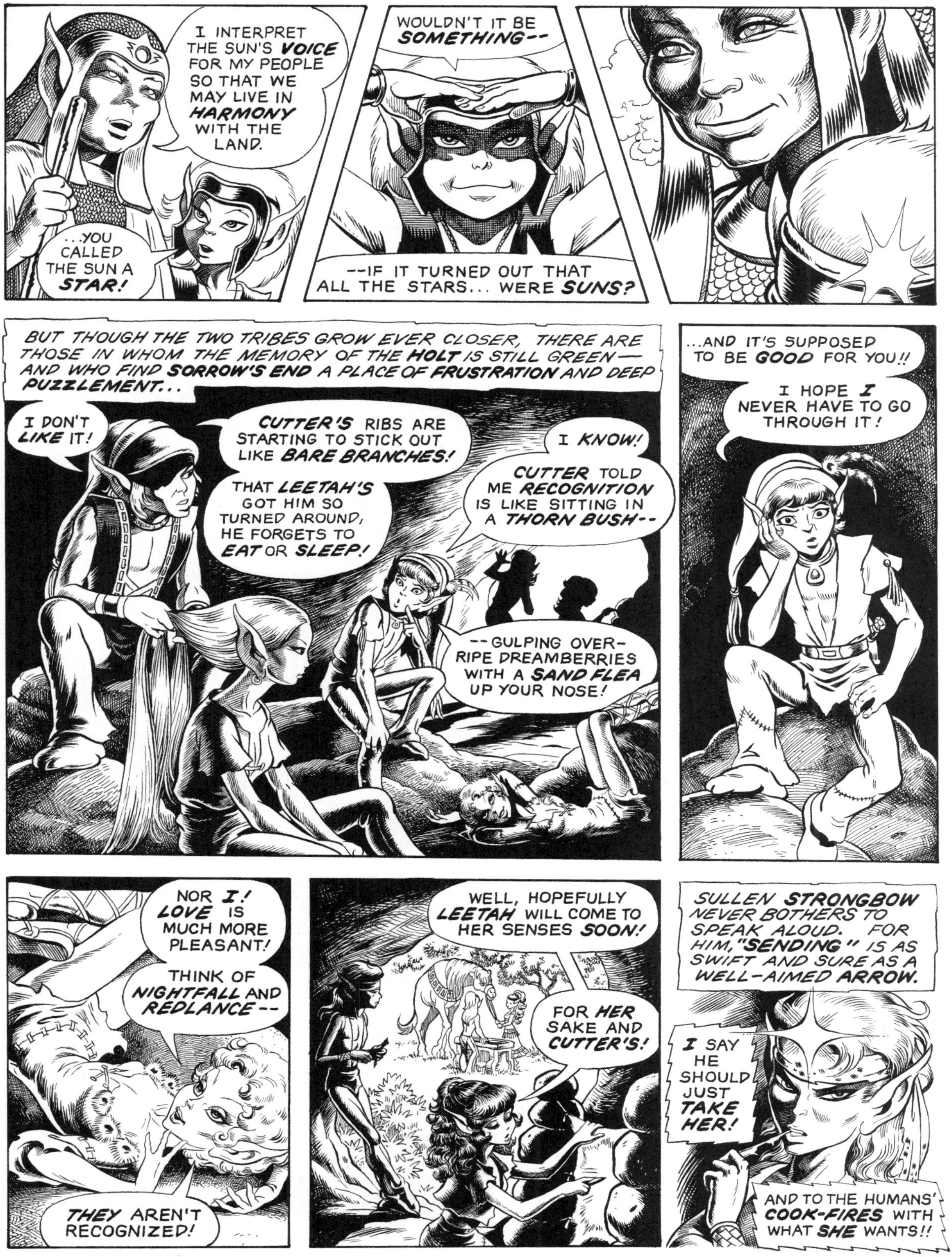
I INTERPRET THE SUN'S VOICE FOR MY PEOPLE SO THAT WE MAY LIVE IN HARMONY WITH THE LAND.
...YOU CALLED THE SUN A STAR!
WOULDN'T IT BE SOMETHING--
--IF IT TURNED OUT THAT ALL THE STARS... WERE SUNS?
BUT THOUGH THE TWO TRIBES GROW EVER CLOSER, THERE ARE THOSE IN WHOM THE MEMORY OF THE HOLT IS STILL GREEN— AND WHO FIND SORROW'S END A PLACE OF FRUSTRATION AND DEEP PUZZLEMENT...
I DON'T LIKE IT!
CUTTER'S RIBS ARE STARTING TO STICK OUT LIKE BARE BRANCHES!
THAT LEETAH'S GOT HIM SO TURNED AROUND, HE FORGETS TO EAT OR SLEEP!
I KNOW!
CUTTER TOLD ME RECOGNITION IS LIKE SITTING IN A THORN BUSH--
--GULPING OVER-RIPE DREAMBERRIES WITH A SAND FLEA UP YOUR NOSE!
...AND IT'S SUPPOSED TO BE GOOD FOR YOU!!
I HOPE I NEVER HAVE TO GO THROUGH IT!
NOR I! LOVE IS MUCH MORE PLEASANT!
THINK OF NIGHTFALL AND REDLANCE--
THEY AREN'T RECOGNIZED!
WELL, HOPEFULLY LEETAH WILL COME TO HER SENSES SOON!
FOR HER SAKE AND CUTTER'S!
SULLEN STRONGBOW NEVER BOTHERS TO SPEAK ALOUD. FOR HIM, "SENDING" IS AS SWIFT AND SURE AS A WELL-AIMED ARROW.
I SAY HE SHOULD JUST TAKE HER!
AND TO THE HUMANS' COOK-FIRES WITH WHAT SHE WANTS!!

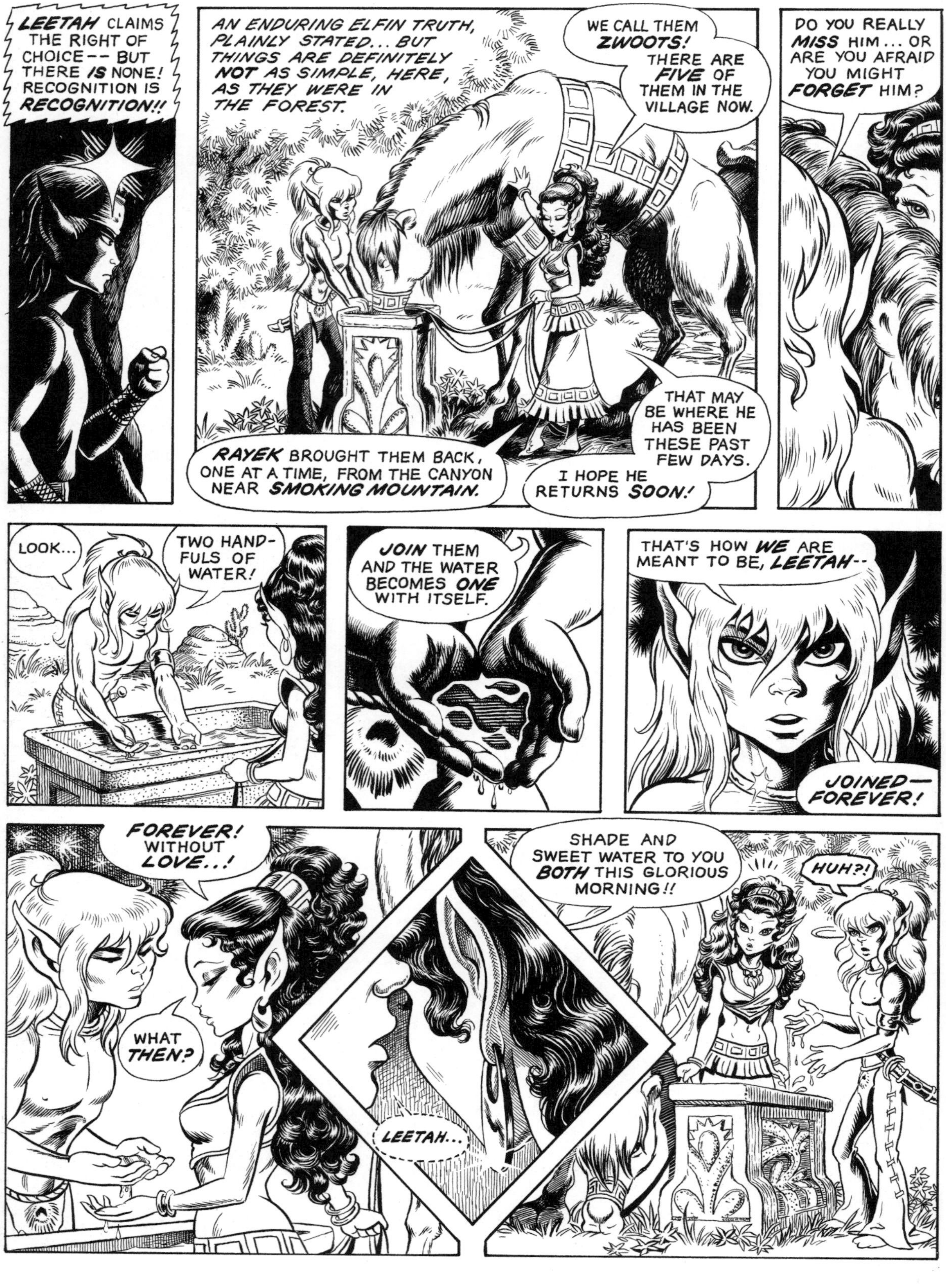
LEETAH CLAIMS THE RIGHT OF CHOICE -- BUT THERE IS NONE! RECOGNITION IS RECOGNITION!!
AN ENDURING ELFIN TRUTH, PLAINLY STATED... BUT THINGS ARE DEFINITELY NOT AS SIMPLE, HERE, AS THEY WERE IN THE FOREST.
WE CALL THEM ZWOOTS! THERE ARE FIVE OF THEM IN THE VILLAGE NOW.
RAYEK BROUGHT THEM BACK, ONE AT A TIME, FROM THE CANYON NEAR SMOKING MOUNTAIN.
THAT MAY BE WHERE HE HAS BEEN THESE PAST FEW DAYS.
I HOPE HE RETURNS SOON!
DO YOU REALLY MISS HIM... OR ARE YOU AFRAID YOU MIGHT FORGET HIM?
LOOK...
TWO HAND-FULS OF WATER!
JOIN THEM AND THE WATER BECOMES ONE WITH ITSELF.
THAT'S HOW WE ARE MEANT TO BE, LEETAH--
JOINED— FOREVER!
FOREVER! WITHOUT LOVE...!
WHAT THEN?
LEETAH...
SHADE AND SWEET WATER TO YOU BOTH THIS GLORIOUS MORNING!!
HUH?!

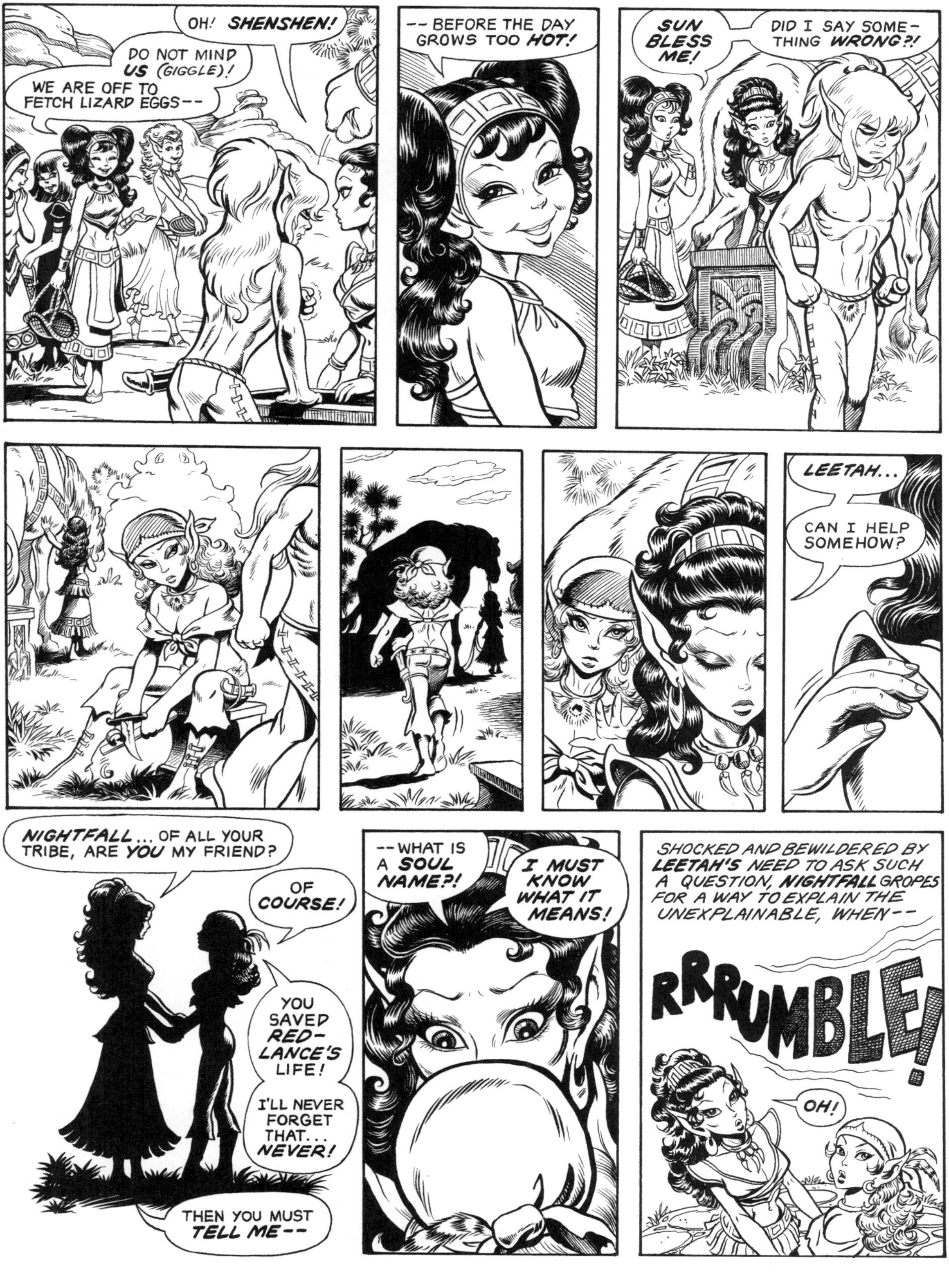
OH! SHENSHEN!
DO NOT MIND US (GIGGLE)!
WE ARE OFF TO FETCH LIZARD EGGS--
--BEFORE THE DAY GROWS TOO HOT!
SUN BLESS ME!
DID I SAY SOMETHING WRONG?!
LEETAH...
CAN I HELP SOMEHOW?
NIGHTFALL... OF ALL YOUR TRIBE, ARE YOU MY FRIEND?
OF COURSE!
YOU SAVED RED-LANCE'S LIFE!
I'LL NEVER FORGET THAT... NEVER!
THEN YOU MUST TELL ME--
--WHAT IS A SOUL NAME?!
I MUST KNOW WHAT IT MEANS!
SHOCKED AND BEWILDERED BY LEETAH'S NEED TO ASK SUCH A QUESTION, NIGHTFALL GROPES FOR A WAY TO EXPLAIN THE UNEXPLAINABLE, WHEN--
RRRUMBLE!
OH!

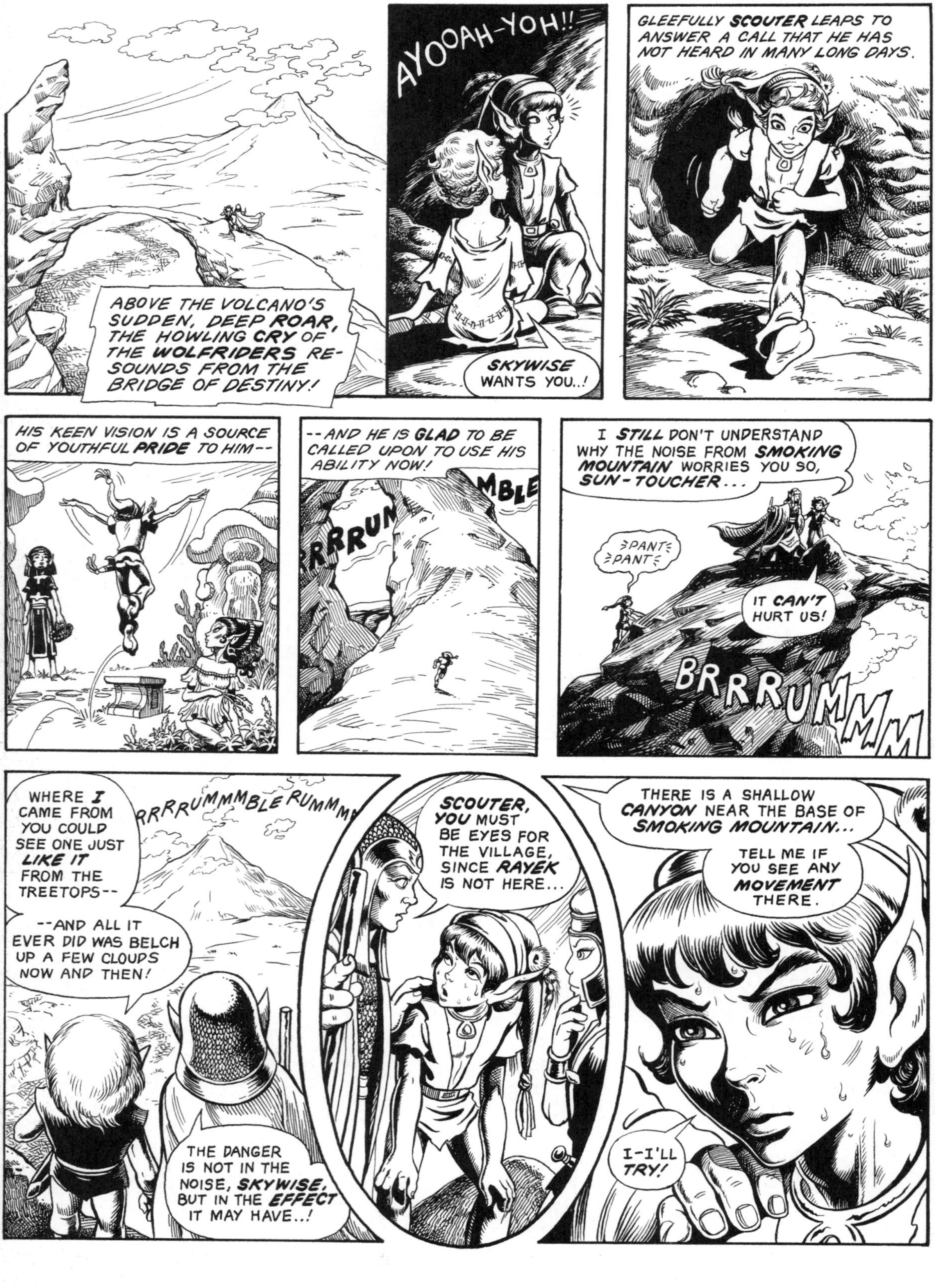
ABOVE THE VOLCANO'S SUDDEN, DEEP ROAR, THE HOWLING CRY OF THE WOLFRIDERS RESOUNDS FROM THE BRIDGE OF DESTINY!
AYOOAH-YOH!!
SKYWISE WANTS YOU..!
GLEEFULLY SCOUTER LEAPS TO ANSWER A CALL THAT HE HAS NOT HEARD IN MANY LONG DAYS.
HIS KEEN VISION IS A SOURCE OF YOUTHFUL PRIDE TO HIM--
--AND HE IS GLAD TO BE CALLED UPON TO USE HIS ABILITY NOW!
RRRRUM
MBLE
I STILL DON'T UNDERSTAND WHY THE NOISE FROM SMOKING MOUNTAIN WORRIES YOU SO, SUN-TOUCHER...
PANT PANT
IT CAN'T HURT US!
BRRRUMMMM
WHERE I CAME FROM YOU COULD SEE ONE JUST LIKE IT FROM THE TREETOPS--
RRRRUMMMBLE RUMMM
--AND ALL IT EVER DID WAS BELCH UP A FEW CLOUDS NOW AND THEN!
THE DANGER IS NOT IN THE NOISE, SKYWISE, BUT IN THE EFFECT IT MAY HAVE..!
SCOUTER, YOU MUST BE EYES FOR THE VILLAGE, SINCE RAYEK IS NOT HERE...
THERE IS A SHALLOW CANYON NEAR THE BASE OF SMOKING MOUNTAIN...
TELL ME IF YOU SEE ANY MOVEMENT THERE.
I-I'LL TRY!

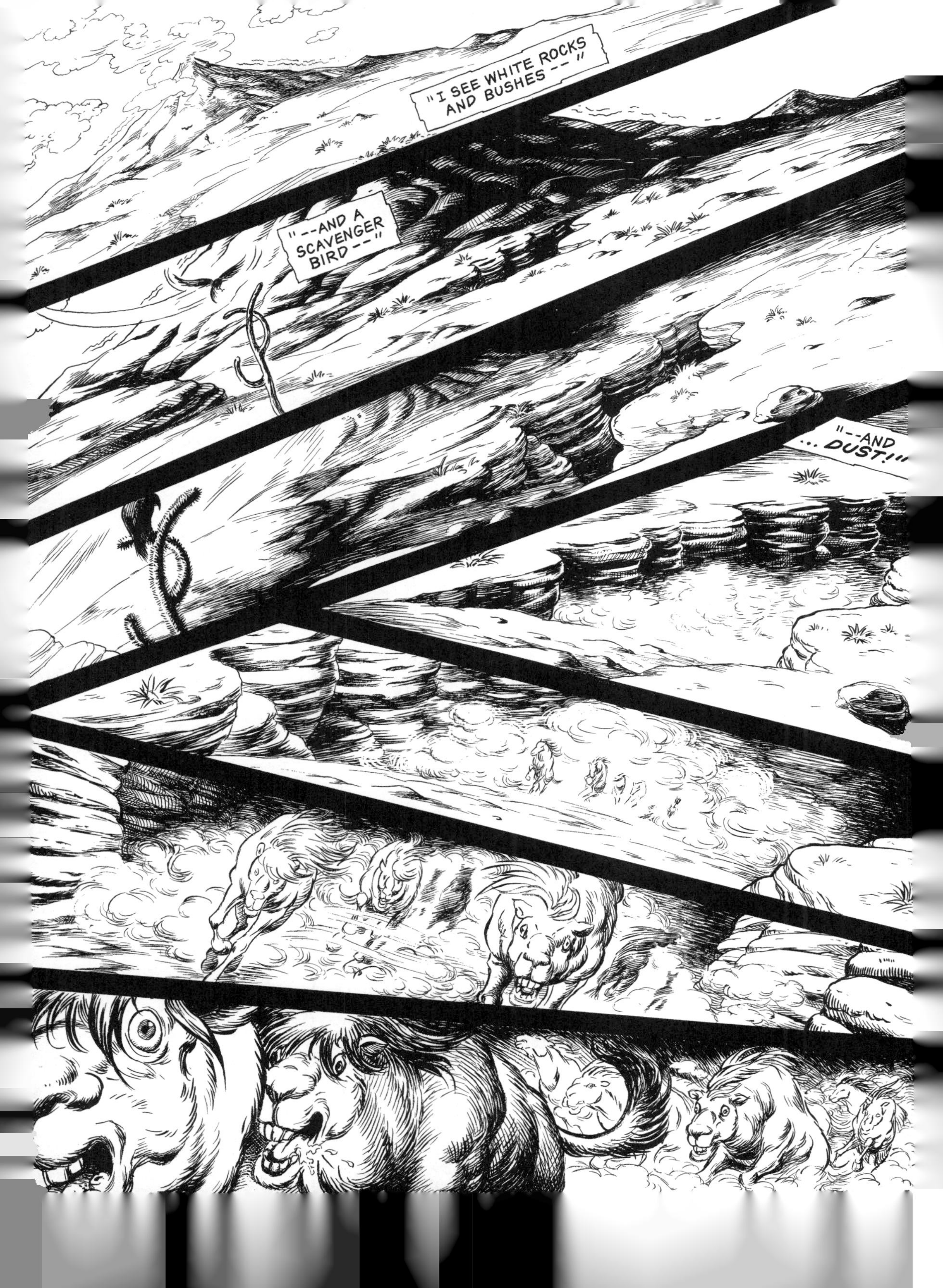

"I SEE WHITE ROCKS AND BUSHES --"
"--AND A SCAVENGER BIRD--"
"--AND ... DUST!"

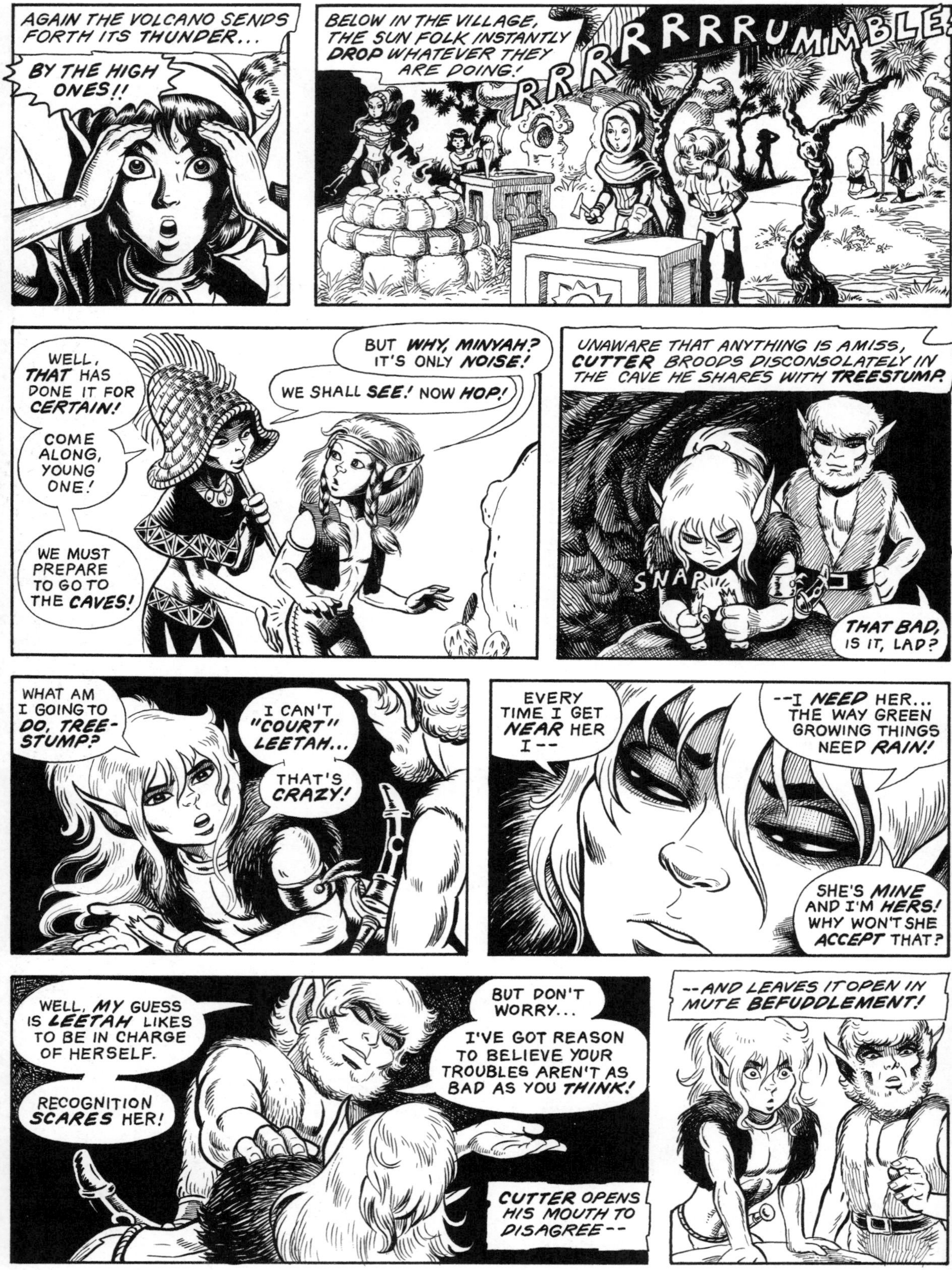
AGAIN THE VOLCANO SENDS FORTH ITS THUNDER...
BY THE HIGH ONES!!
BELOW IN THE VILLAGE, THE SUN FOLK INSTANTLY DROP WHATEVER THEY ARE DOING!
RRRRRRRRUMMBLE!
WELL, THAT HAS DONE IT FOR CERTAIN!
COME ALONG, YOUNG ONE!
WE MUST PREPARE TO GO TO THE CAVES!
BUT WHY, MINYAH? IT'S ONLY NOISE!
WE SHALL SEE! NOW HOP!
UNAWARE THAT ANYTHING IS AMISS, CUTTER BROODS DISCONSOLATELY IN THE CAVE HE SHARES WITH TREESTUMP.
SNAP
THAT BAD, IS IT, LAD?
WHAT AM I GOING TO DO, TREE-STUMP?
I CAN'T "COURT" LEETAH...
THAT'S CRAZY!
EVERY TIME I GET NEAR HER I--
--I NEED HER... THE WAY GREEN GROWING THINGS NEED RAIN!
SHE'S MINE AND I'M HERS! WHY WON'T SHE ACCEPT THAT?
WELL, MY GUESS IS LEETAH LIKES TO BE IN CHARGE OF HERSELF.
RECOGNITION SCARES HER!
BUT DON'T WORRY...
I'VE GOT REASON TO BELIEVE YOUR TROUBLES AREN'T AS BAD AS YOU THINK!
CUTTER OPENS HIS MOUTH TO DISAGREE--
--AND LEAVES IT OPEN IN MUTE BEFUDDLEMENT!

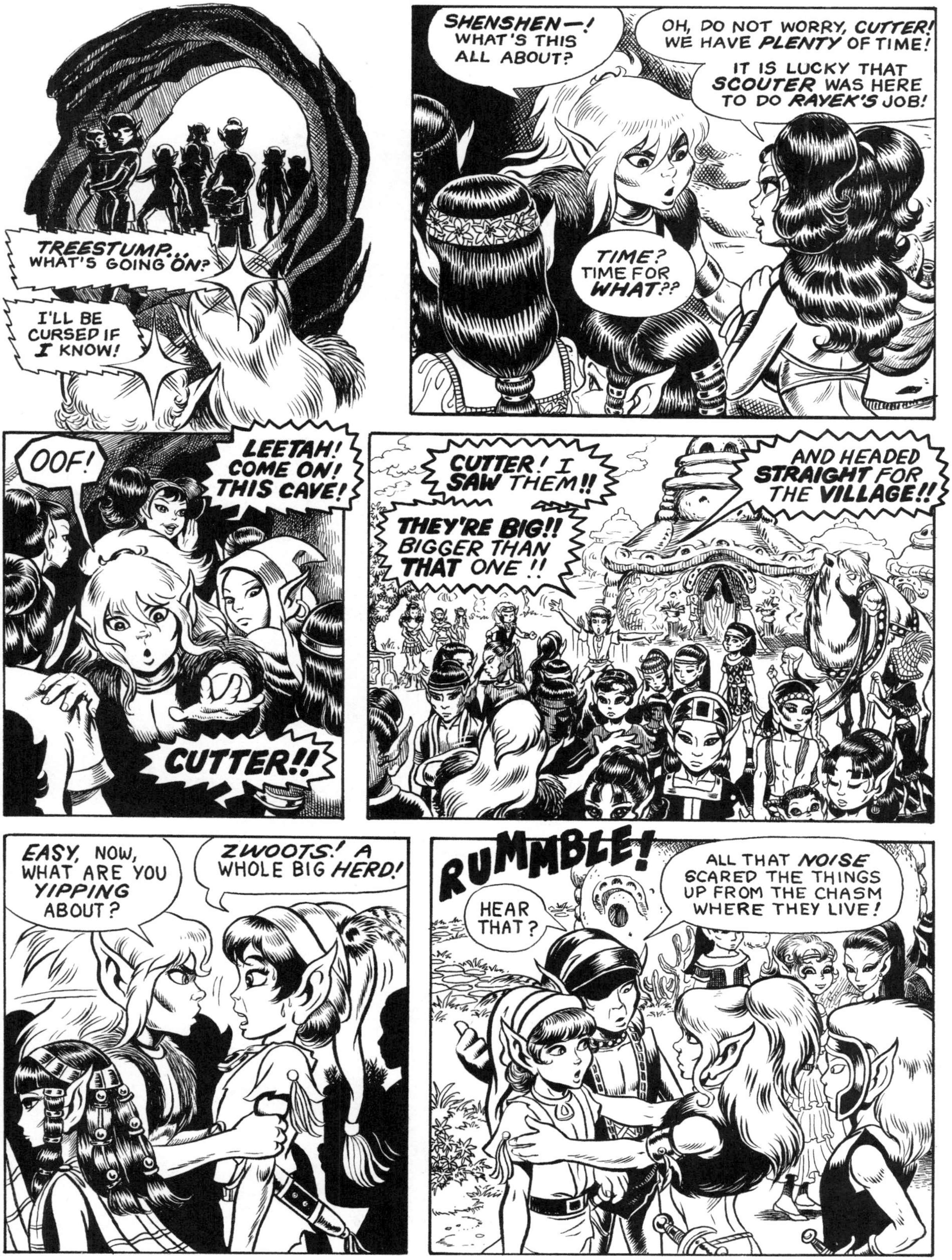
TREESTUMP... WHAT'S GOING ON?
I'LL BE CURSED IF I KNOW!
SHENSHEN—! WHAT'S THIS ALL ABOUT?
OH, DO NOT WORRY, CUTTER! WE HAVE PLENTY OF TIME!
IT IS LUCKY THAT SCOUTER WAS HERE TO DO RAYEK'S JOB!
TIME? TIME FOR WHAT??
OOF!
LEETAH! COME ON! THIS CAVE!
CUTTER!!
CUTTER! I SAW THEM!!
THEY'RE BIG!! BIGGER THAN THAT ONE!!
AND HEADED STRAIGHT FOR THE VILLAGE!!
EASY, NOW, WHAT ARE YOU YIPPING ABOUT?
ZWOOTS! A WHOLE BIG HERD!
RUMMBLE!
HEAR THAT?
ALL THAT NOISE SCARED THE THINGS UP FROM THE CHASM WHERE THEY LIVE!

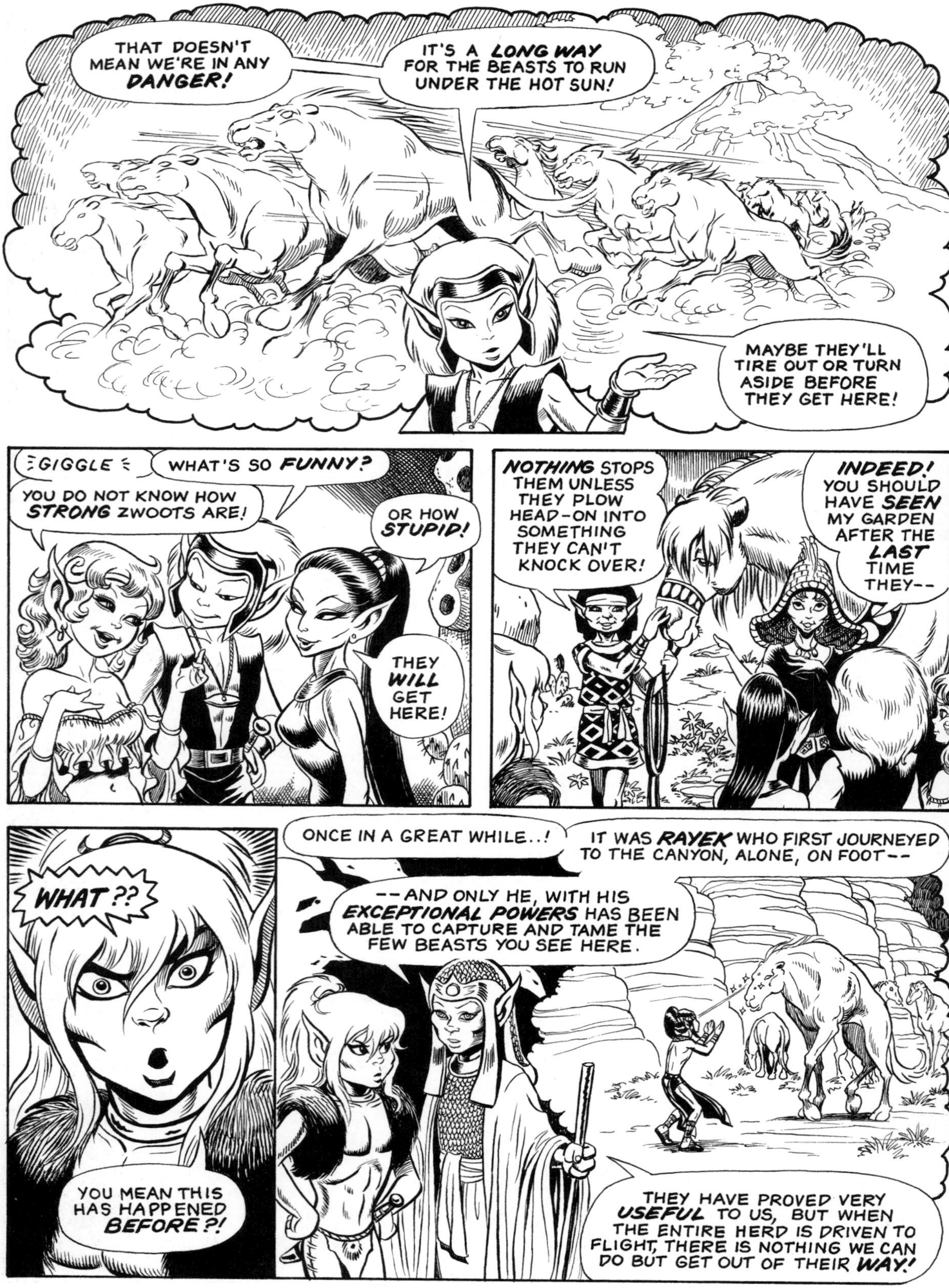
THAT DOESN'T MEAN WE'RE IN ANY DANGER!
IT'S A LONG WAY FOR THE BEASTS TO RUN UNDER THE HOT SUN!
MAYBE THEY'LL TIRE OUT OR TURN ASIDE BEFORE THEY GET HERE!
GIGGLE
WHAT'S SO FUNNY?
YOU DO NOT KNOW HOW STRONG ZWOOTS ARE!
OR HOW STUPID!
THEY WILL GET HERE!
NOTHING STOPS THEM UNLESS THEY PLOW HEAD-ON INTO SOMETHING THEY CAN'T KNOCK OVER!
INDEED! YOU SHOULD HAVE SEEN MY GARDEN AFTER THE LAST TIME THEY--
WHAT??
YOU MEAN THIS HAS HAPPENED BEFORE?!
ONCE IN A GREAT WHILE..!
IT WAS RAYEK WHO FIRST JOURNEYED TO THE CANYON, ALONE, ON FOOT--
--AND ONLY HE, WITH HIS EXCEPTIONAL POWERS HAS BEEN ABLE TO CAPTURE AND TAME THE FEW BEASTS YOU SEE HERE.
THEY HAVE PROVED VERY USEFUL TO US, BUT WHEN THE ENTIRE HERD IS DRIVEN TO FLIGHT, THERE IS NOTHING WE CAN DO BUT GET OUT OF THEIR WAY!

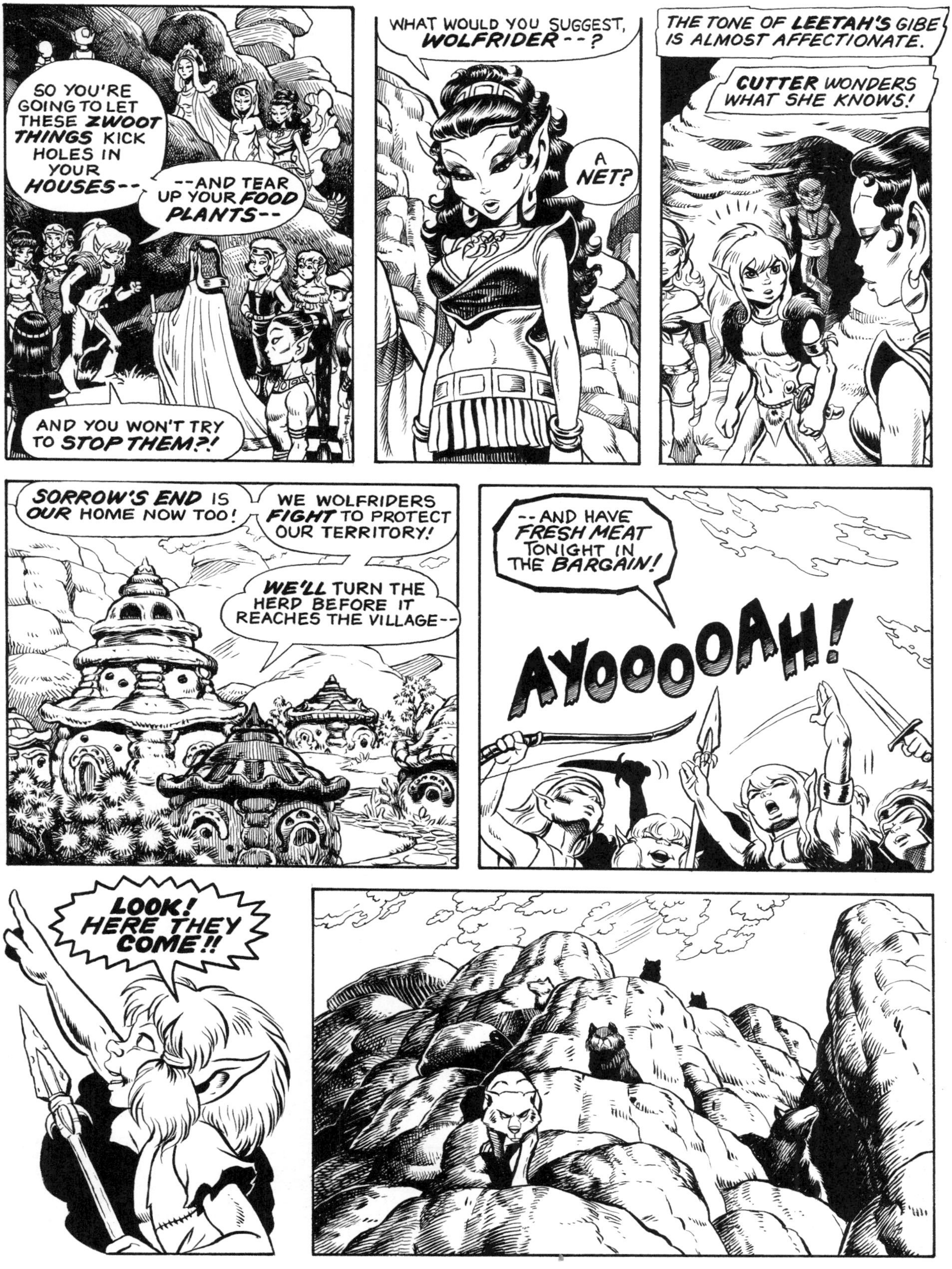
SO YOU'RE GOING TO LET THESE ZWOOT THINGS KICK HOLES IN YOUR HOUSES--
--AND TEAR UP YOUR FOOD PLANTS--
AND YOU WON'T TRY TO STOP THEM?!
WHAT WOULD YOU SUGGEST, WOLFRIDER--?
A NET?
THE TONE OF LEETAH'S GIBE IS ALMOST AFFECTIONATE.
CUTTER WONDERS WHAT SHE KNOWS!
SORROW'S END IS OUR HOME NOW TOO!
WE WOLFRIDERS FIGHT TO PROTECT OUR TERRITORY!
WE'LL TURN THE HERD BEFORE IT REACHES THE VILLAGE--
--AND HAVE FRESH MEAT TONIGHT IN THE BARGAIN!
AYOOOOOAH!
LOOK! HERE THEY COME!!

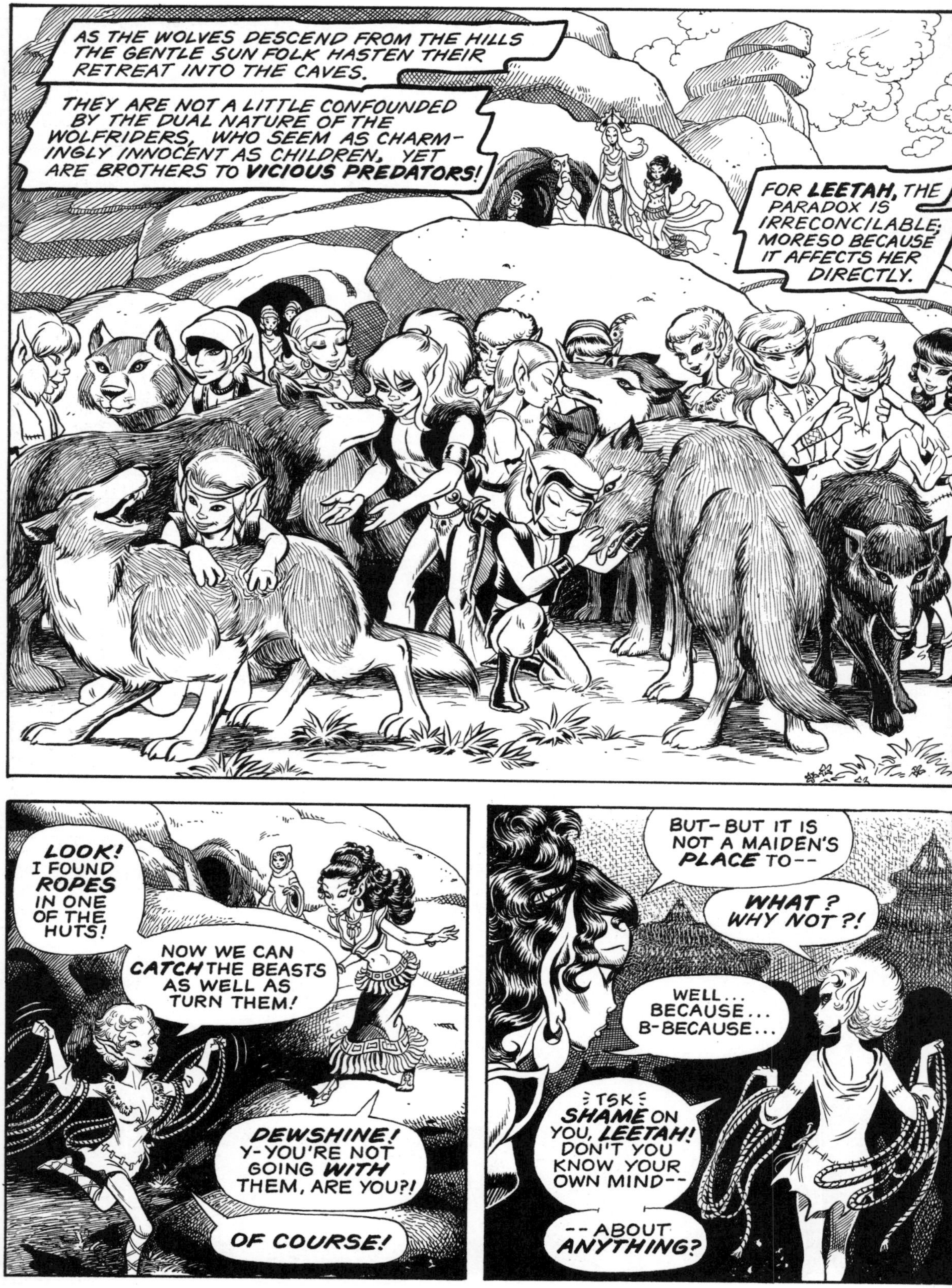
AS THE WOLVES DESCEND FROM THE HILLS THE GENTLE SUN FOLK HASTEN THEIR RETREAT INTO THE CAVES.
THEY ARE NOT A LITTLE CONFOUNDED BY THE DUAL NATURE OF THE WOLFRIDERS, WHO SEEM AS CHARMINGLY INNOCENT AS CHILDREN, YET ARE BROTHERS TO VICIOUS PREDATORS!
FOR LEETAH, THE PARADOX IS IRRECONCILABLE; MORESO BECAUSE IT AFFECTS HER DIRECTLY.
LOOK! I FOUND ROPES IN ONE OF THE HUTS!
NOW WE CAN CATCH THE BEASTS AS WELL AS TURN THEM!
DEWSHINE! Y-YOU'RE NOT GOING WITH THEM, ARE YOU?!
OF COURSE!
BUT-BUT IT IS NOT A MAIDEN'S PLACE TO--
WHAT? WHY NOT?!
WELL... BECAUSE... B-BECAUSE...
TSK SHAME ON YOU, LEETAH! DON'T YOU KNOW YOUR OWN MIND--
--ABOUT ANYTHING?

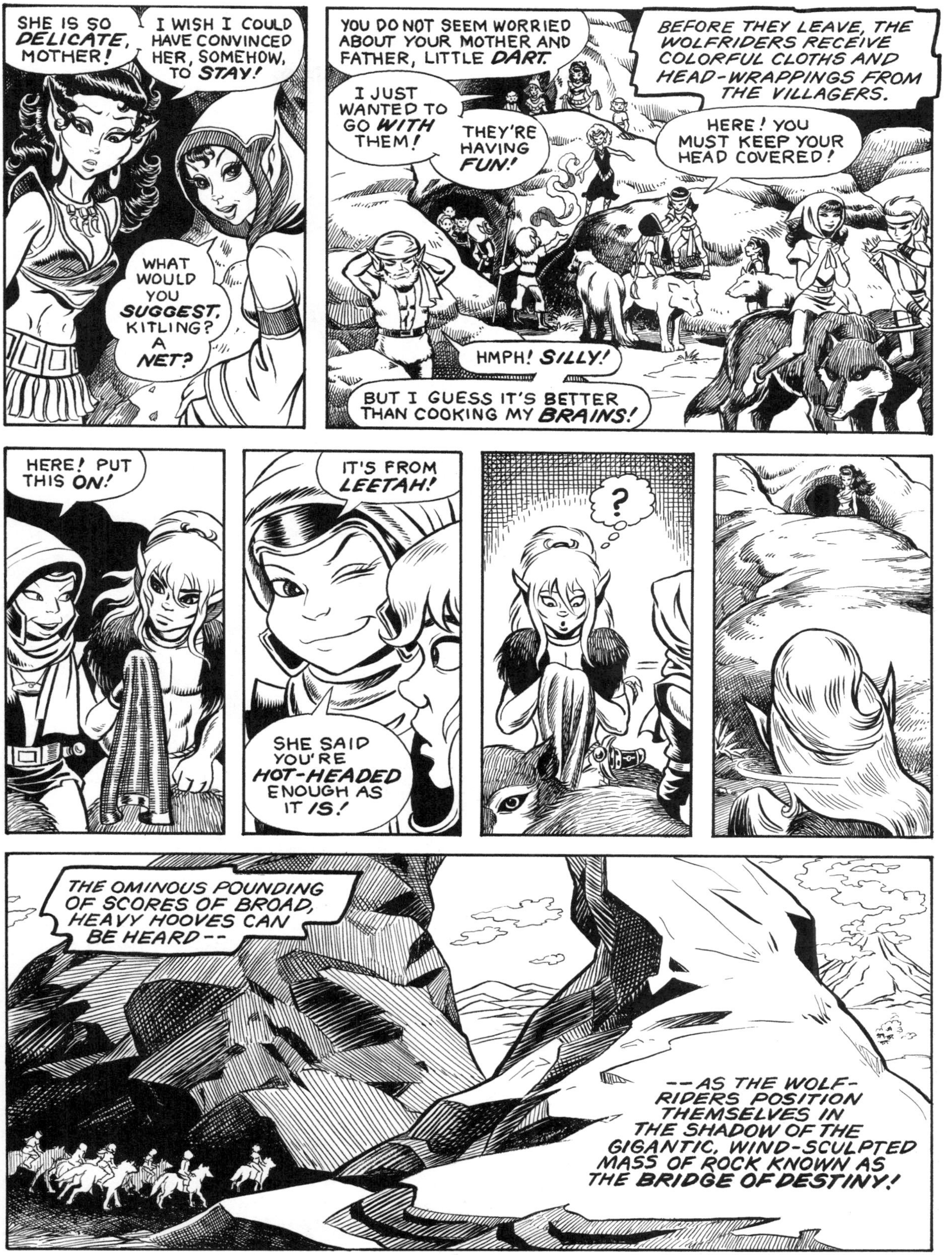
SHE IS SO DELICATE, MOTHER!
I WISH I COULD HAVE CONVINCED HER, SOMEHOW, TO STAY!
WHAT WOULD YOU SUGGEST, KITLING? A NET?
YOU DO NOT SEEM WORRIED ABOUT YOUR MOTHER AND FATHER, LITTLE DART.
I JUST WANTED TO GO WITH THEM!
THEY'RE HAVING FUN!
BEFORE THEY LEAVE, THE WOLFRIDERS RECEIVE COLORFUL CLOTHS AND HEAD-WRAPPINGS FROM THE VILLAGERS.
HERE! YOU MUST KEEP YOUR HEAD COVERED!
HMPH! SILLY!
BUT I GUESS IT'S BETTER THAN COOKING MY BRAINS!
HERE! PUT THIS ON!
IT'S FROM LEETAH!
SHE SAID YOU'RE HOT-HEADED ENOUGH AS IT IS!
?
THE OMINOUS POUNDING OF SCORES OF BROAD, HEAVY HOOVES CAN BE HEARD--
--AS THE WOLF-RIDERS POSITION THEMSELVES IN THE SHADOW OF THE GIGANTIC, WIND-SCULPTED MASS OF ROCK KNOWN AS THE BRIDGE OF DESTINY!

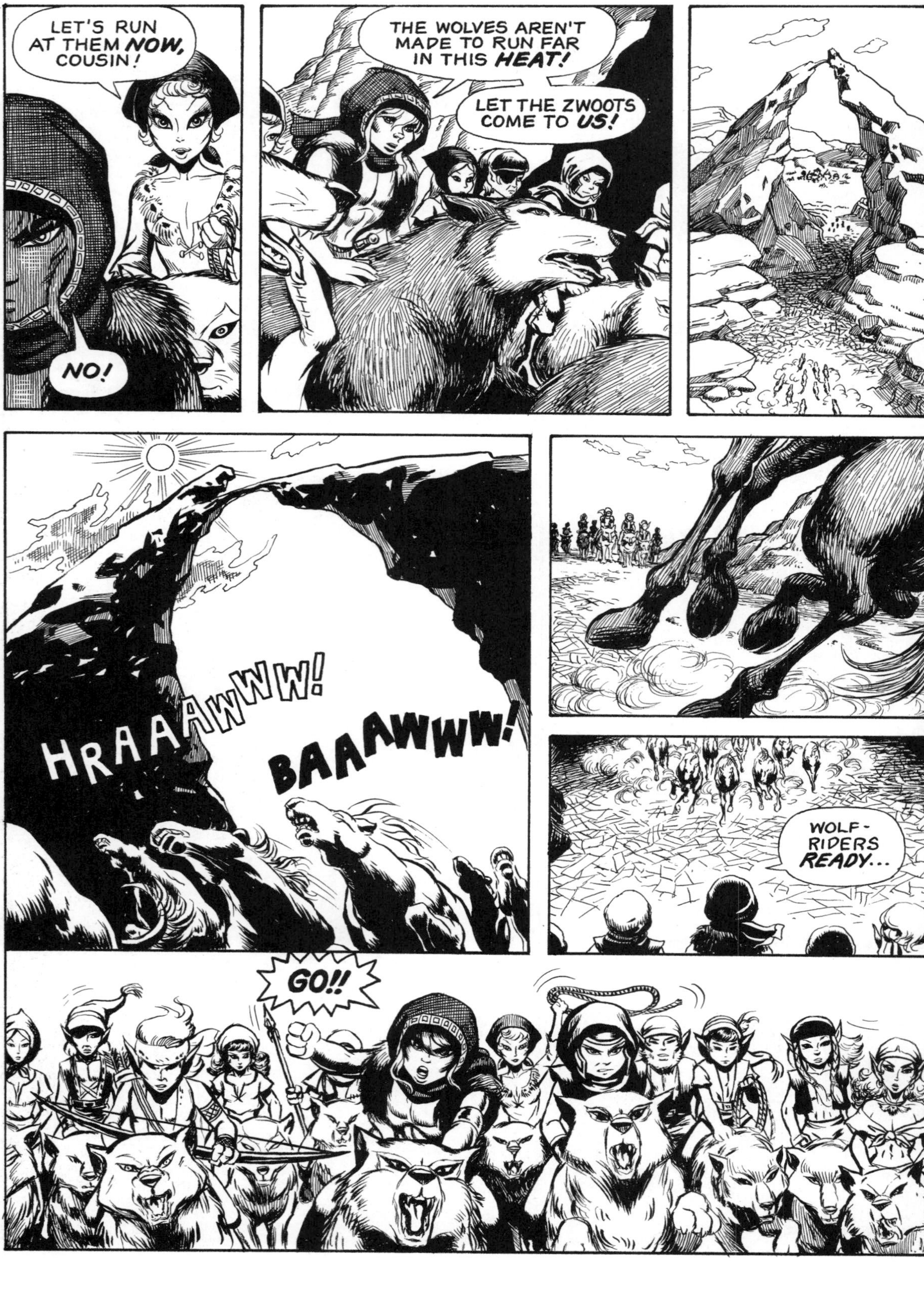
LET'S RUN AT THEM *NOW,* COUSIN!
NO!
THE WOLVES AREN'T MADE TO RUN FAR IN THIS *HEAT!*
LET THE ZWOOTS COME TO *US!*
HRAAAWWWW!
BAAAWWWW!
WOLF-RIDERS *READY...*
GO!!

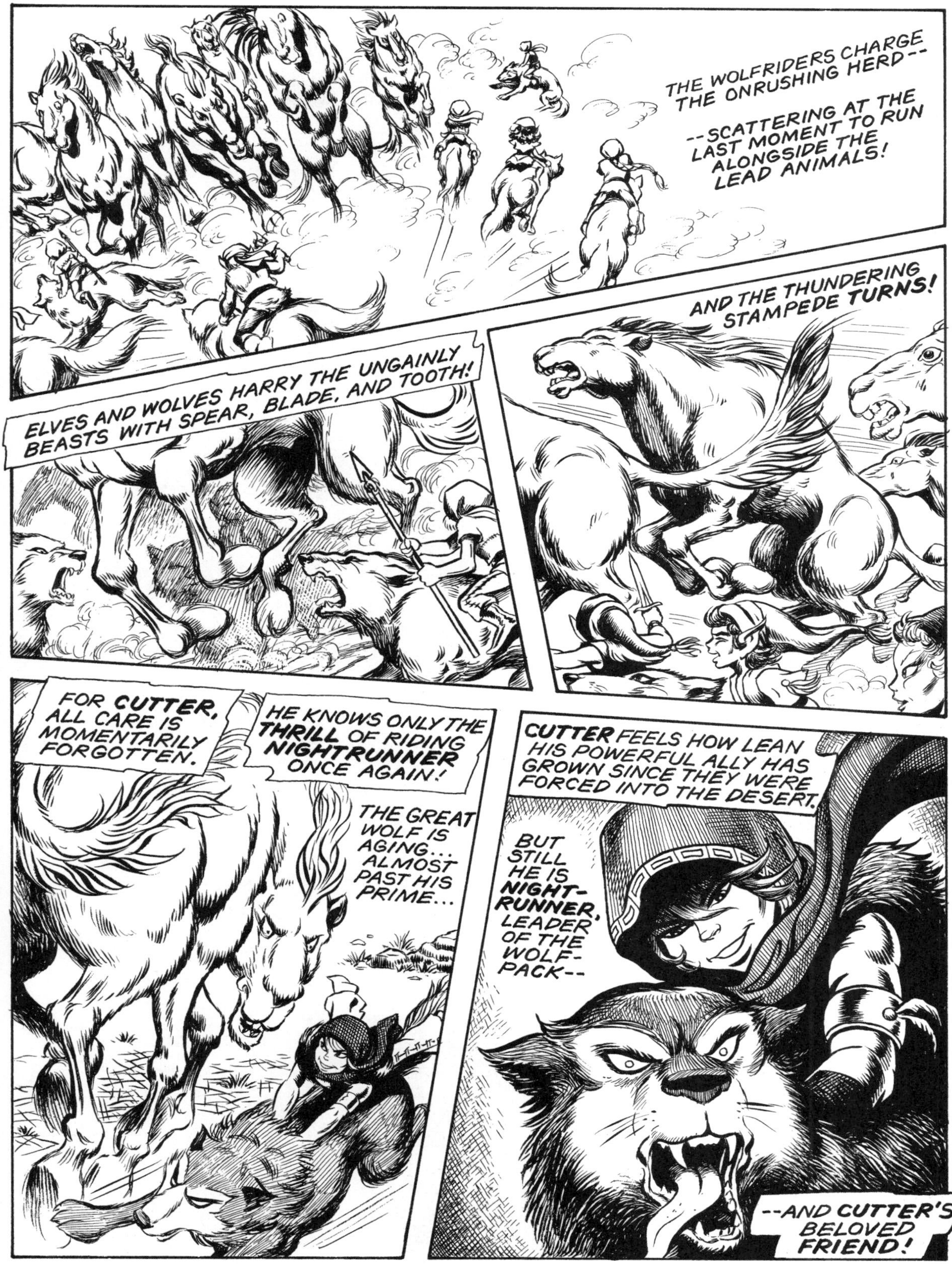
THE WOLFRIDERS CHARGE THE ONRUSHING HERD--
--SCATTERING AT THE LAST MOMENT TO RUN ALONGSIDE THE LEAD ANIMALS!
ELVES AND WOLVES HARRY THE UNGAINLY BEASTS WITH SPEAR, BLADE, AND TOOTH!
AND THE THUNDERING STAMPEDE TURNS!
FOR CUTTER, ALL CARE IS MOMENTARILY FORGOTTEN.
HE KNOWS ONLY THE THRILL OF RIDING NIGHTRUNNER ONCE AGAIN!
THE GREAT WOLF IS AGING... ALMOST PAST HIS PRIME...
CUTTER FEELS HOW LEAN HIS POWERFUL ALLY HAS GROWN SINCE THEY WERE FORCED INTO THE DESERT.
BUT STILL HE IS NIGHT-RUNNER, LEADER OF THE WOLF-PACK--
--AND CUTTER'S BELOVED FRIEND!

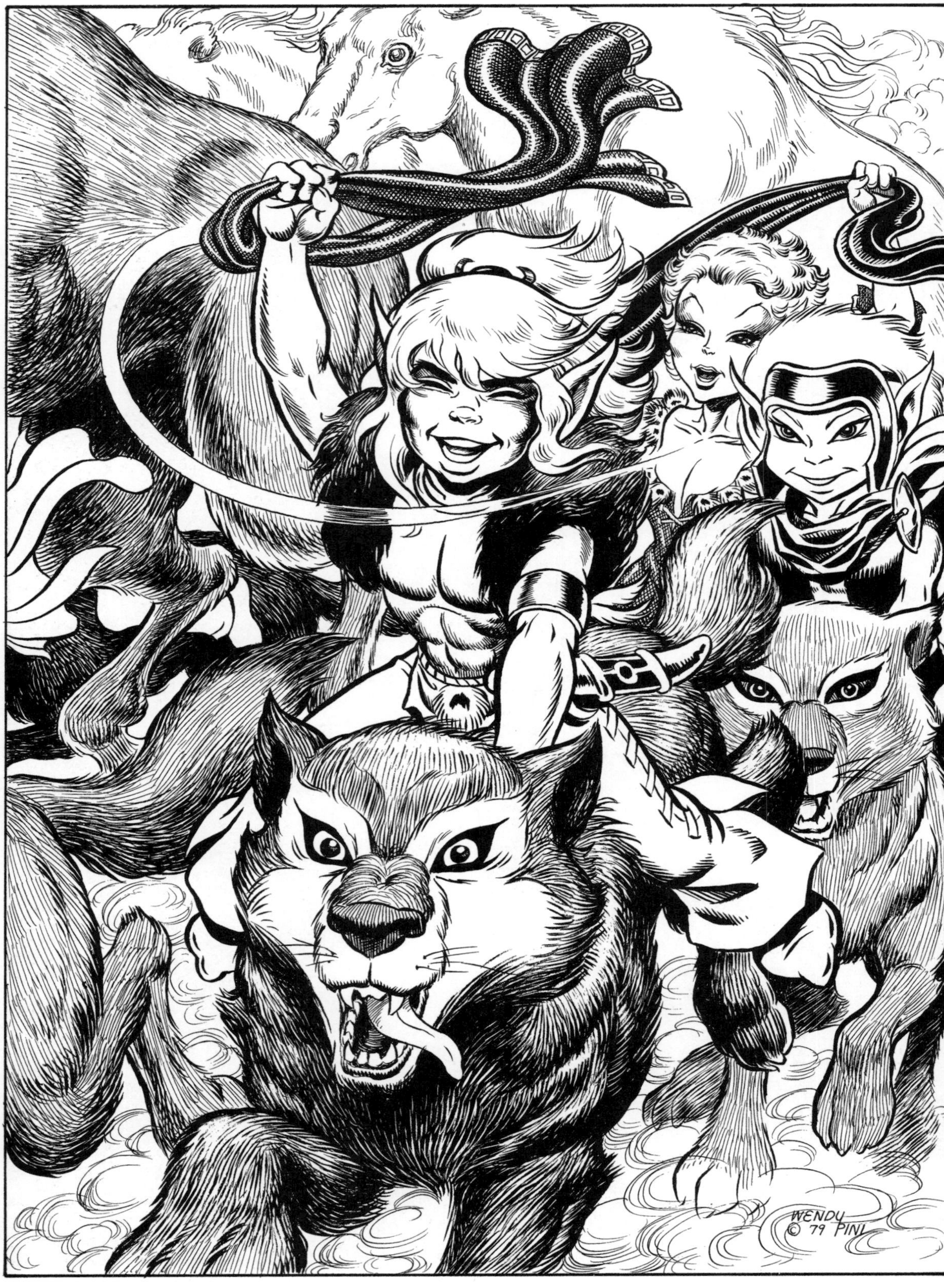
WENDY
© '79 PINI

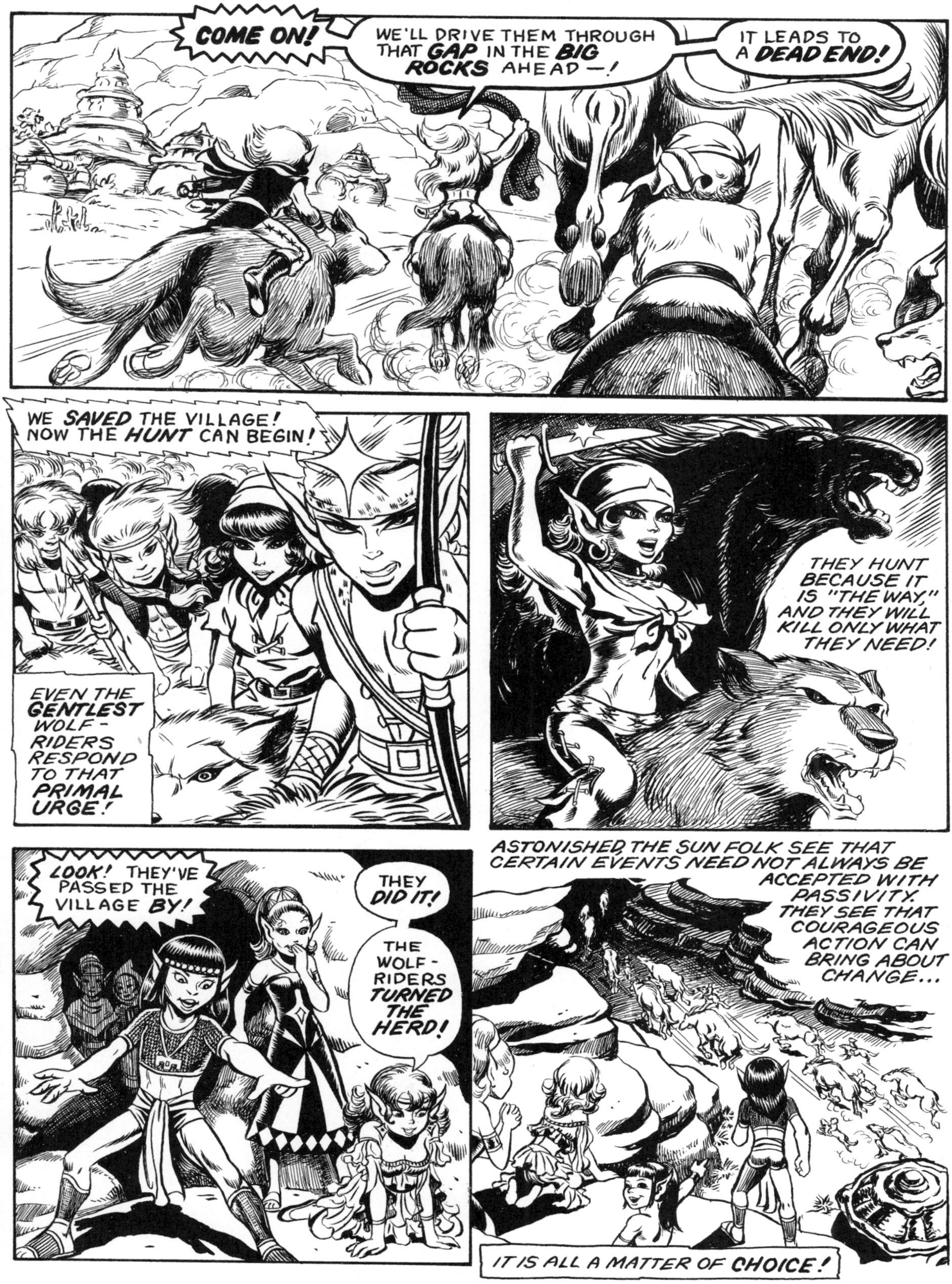
COME ON!
WE'LL DRIVE THEM THROUGH THAT GAP IN THE BIG ROCKS AHEAD—!
IT LEADS TO A DEAD END!
WE SAVED THE VILLAGE! NOW THE HUNT CAN BEGIN!
EVEN THE GENTLEST WOLF-RIDERS RESPOND TO THAT PRIMAL URGE!
THEY HUNT BECAUSE IT IS "THE WAY," AND THEY WILL KILL ONLY WHAT THEY NEED!
LOOK! THEY'VE PASSED THE VILLAGE BY!
THEY DID IT!
THE WOLF-RIDERS TURNED THE HERD!
ASTONISHED, THE SUN FOLK SEE THAT CERTAIN EVENTS NEED NOT ALWAYS BE ACCEPTED WITH PASSIVITY. THEY SEE THAT COURAGEOUS ACTION CAN BRING ABOUT CHANGE...
IT IS ALL A MATTER OF CHOICE!

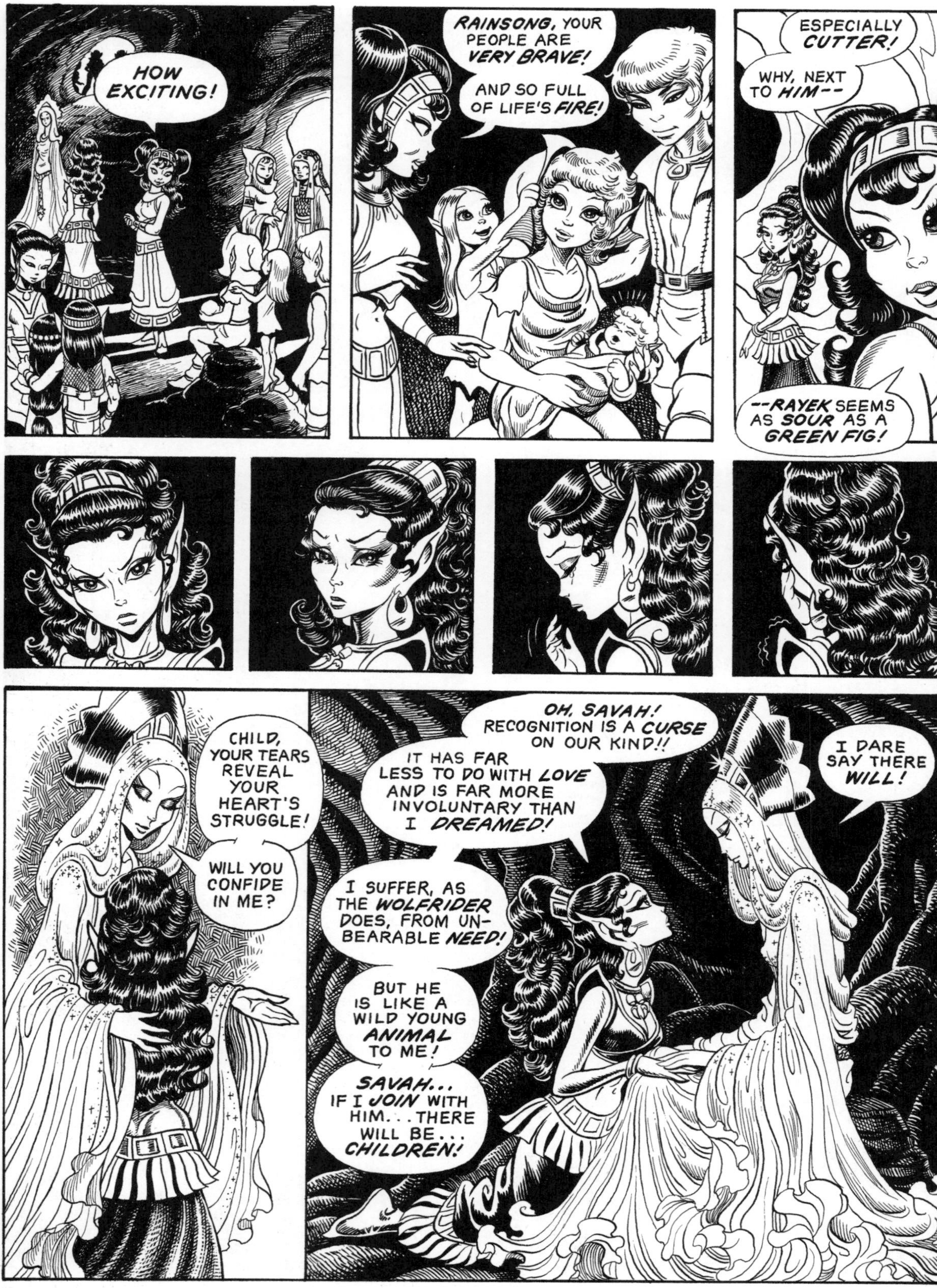

HOW EXCITING!
RAINSONG, YOUR PEOPLE ARE VERY BRAVE!
AND SO FULL OF LIFE'S FIRE!
ESPECIALLY CUTTER!
WHY, NEXT TO HIM--
--RAYEK SEEMS AS SOUR AS A GREEN FIG!
CHILD, YOUR TEARS REVEAL YOUR HEART'S STRUGGLE!
WILL YOU CONFIDE IN ME?
OH, SAVAH! RECOGNITION IS A CURSE ON OUR KIND!!
IT HAS FAR LESS TO DO WITH LOVE AND IS FAR MORE INVOLUNTARY THAN I DREAMED!
I SUFFER, AS THE WOLFRIDER DOES, FROM UN-BEARABLE NEED!
BUT HE IS LIKE A WILD YOUNG ANIMAL TO ME!
SAVAH... IF I JOIN WITH HIM... THERE WILL BE... CHILDREN!
I DARE SAY THERE WILL!

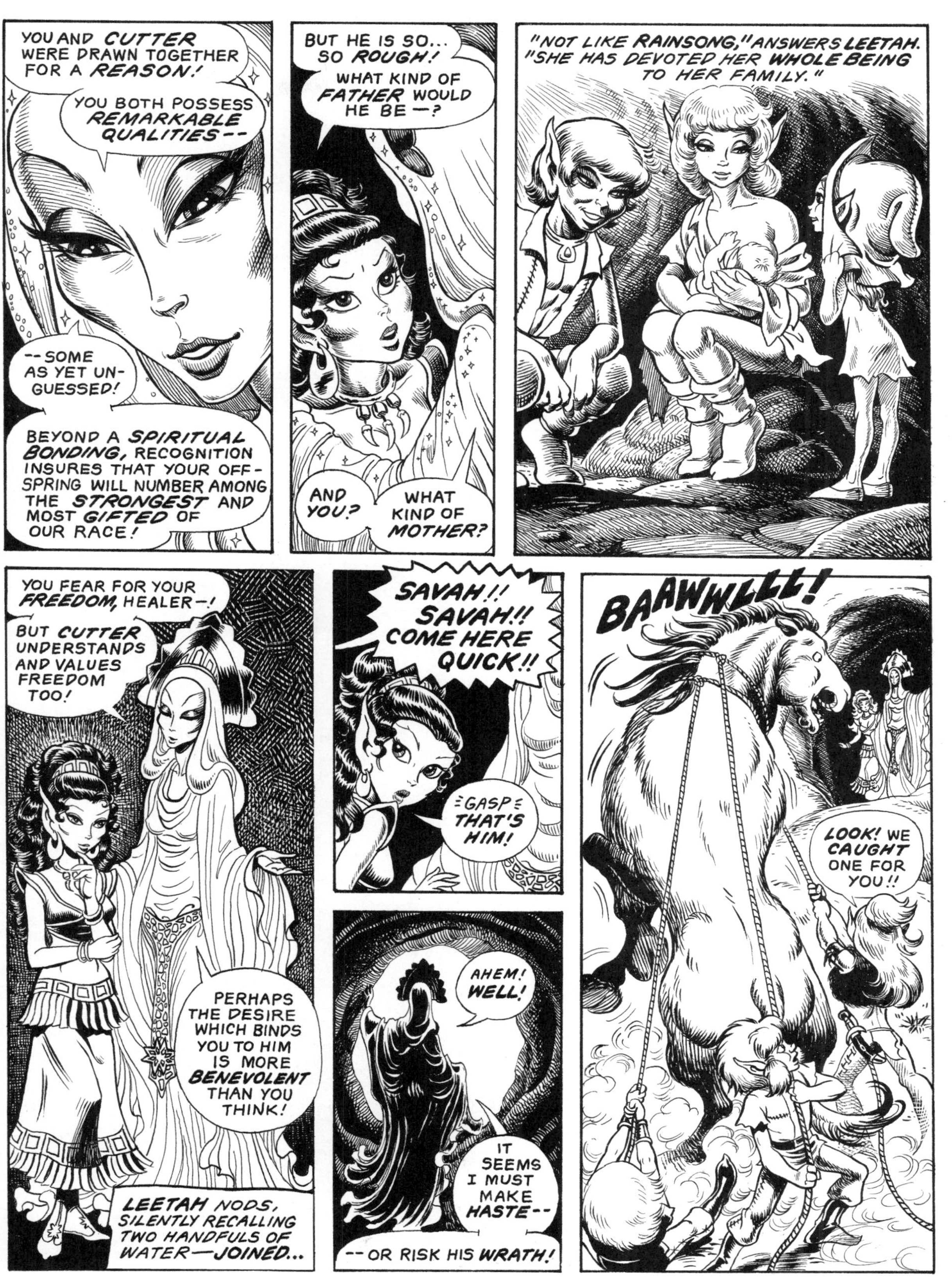
YOU AND CUTTER WERE DRAWN TOGETHER FOR A REASON!
YOU BOTH POSSESS REMARKABLE QUALITIES--
--SOME AS YET UN-GUESSED!
BEYOND A SPIRITUAL BONDING, RECOGNITION INSURES THAT YOUR OFF-SPRING WILL NUMBER AMONG THE STRONGEST AND MOST GIFTED OF OUR RACE!
BUT HE IS SO... SO ROUGH!
WHAT KIND OF FATHER WOULD HE BE--?
AND YOU?
WHAT KIND OF MOTHER?
"NOT LIKE RAINSONG," ANSWERS LEETAH. "SHE HAS DEVOTED HER WHOLE BEING TO HER FAMILY."
YOU FEAR FOR YOUR FREEDOM, HEALER--!
BUT CUTTER UNDERSTANDS AND VALUES FREEDOM TOO!
PERHAPS THE DESIRE WHICH BINDS YOU TO HIM IS MORE BENEVOLENT THAN YOU THINK!
LEETAH NODS, SILENTLY RECALLING TWO HANDFULS OF WATER—JOINED...
SAVAH!! SAVAH!! COME HERE QUICK!!
GASP THAT'S HIM!
AHEM! WELL!
IT SEEMS I MUST MAKE HASTE--
--OR RISK HIS WRATH!
BAAWWLLL!
LOOK! WE CAUGHT ONE FOR YOU!!

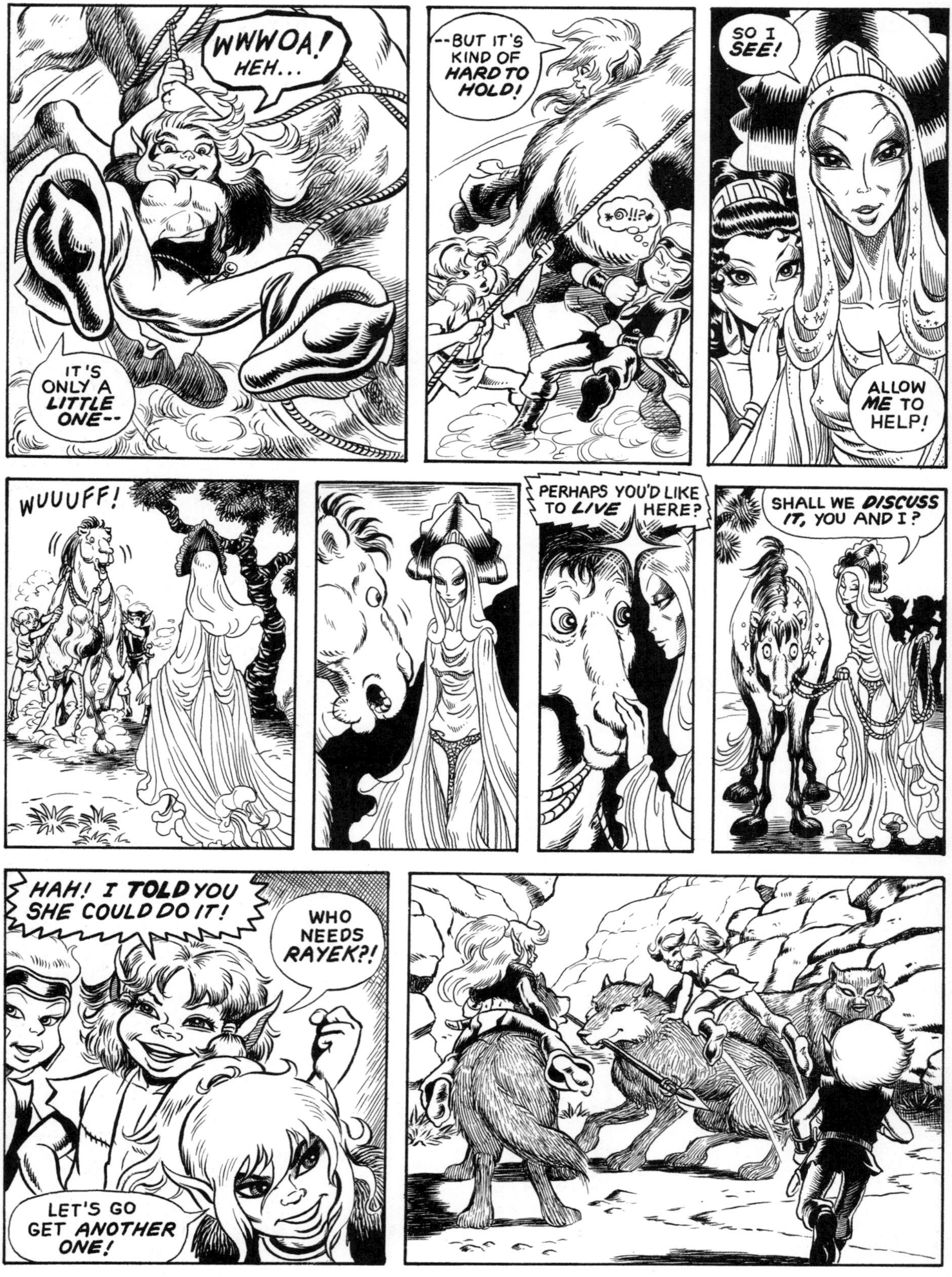
WWWOA! HEH...
IT'S ONLY A LITTLE ONE--
--BUT IT'S KIND OF HARD TO HOLD!
@!!?
SO I SEE!
ALLOW ME TO HELP!
WUUUFF!
PERHAPS YOU'D LIKE TO LIVE HERE?
SHALL WE DISCUSS IT, YOU AND I?
HAH! I TOLD YOU SHE COULD DO IT!
WHO NEEDS RAYEK?!
LET'S GO GET ANOTHER ONE!

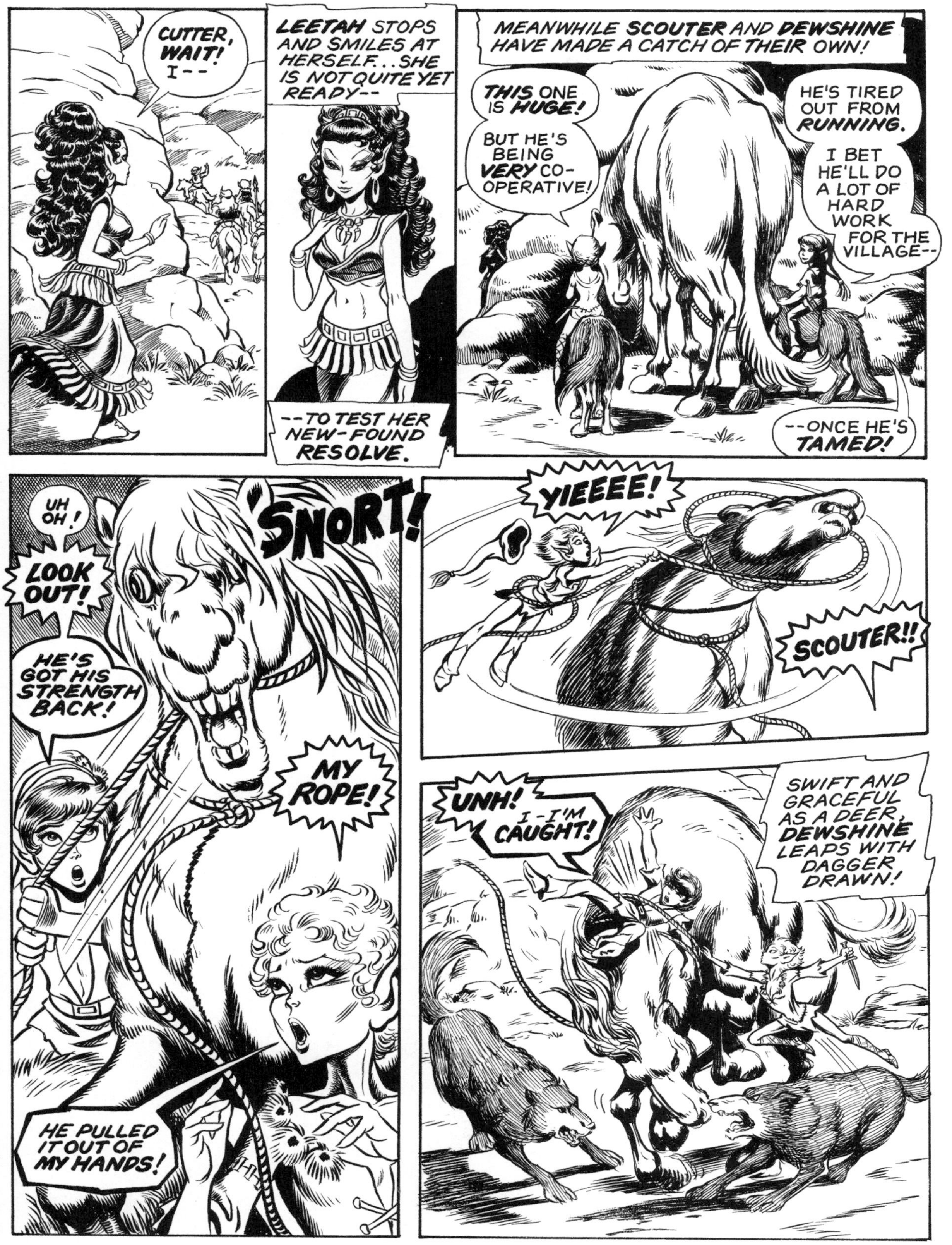
CUTTER, WAIT! I--
LEETAH STOPS AND SMILES AT HERSELF...SHE IS NOT QUITE YET READY--
--TO TEST HER NEW-FOUND RESOLVE.
MEANWHILE SCOUTER AND DEWSHINE HAVE MADE A CATCH OF THEIR OWN!
THIS ONE IS HUGE!
BUT HE'S BEING VERY CO-OPERATIVE!
HE'S TIRED OUT FROM RUNNING.
I BET HE'LL DO A LOT OF HARD WORK FOR THE VILLAGE--
--ONCE HE'S TAMED!
UH OH!
SNORT!
LOOK OUT!
HE'S GOT HIS STRENGTH BACK!
MY ROPE!
HE PULLED IT OUT OF MY HANDS!
YIEEEE!
SCOUTER!!
UNH! I-I'M CAUGHT!
SWIFT AND GRACEFUL AS A DEER, DEWSHINE LEAPS WITH DAGGER DRAWN!

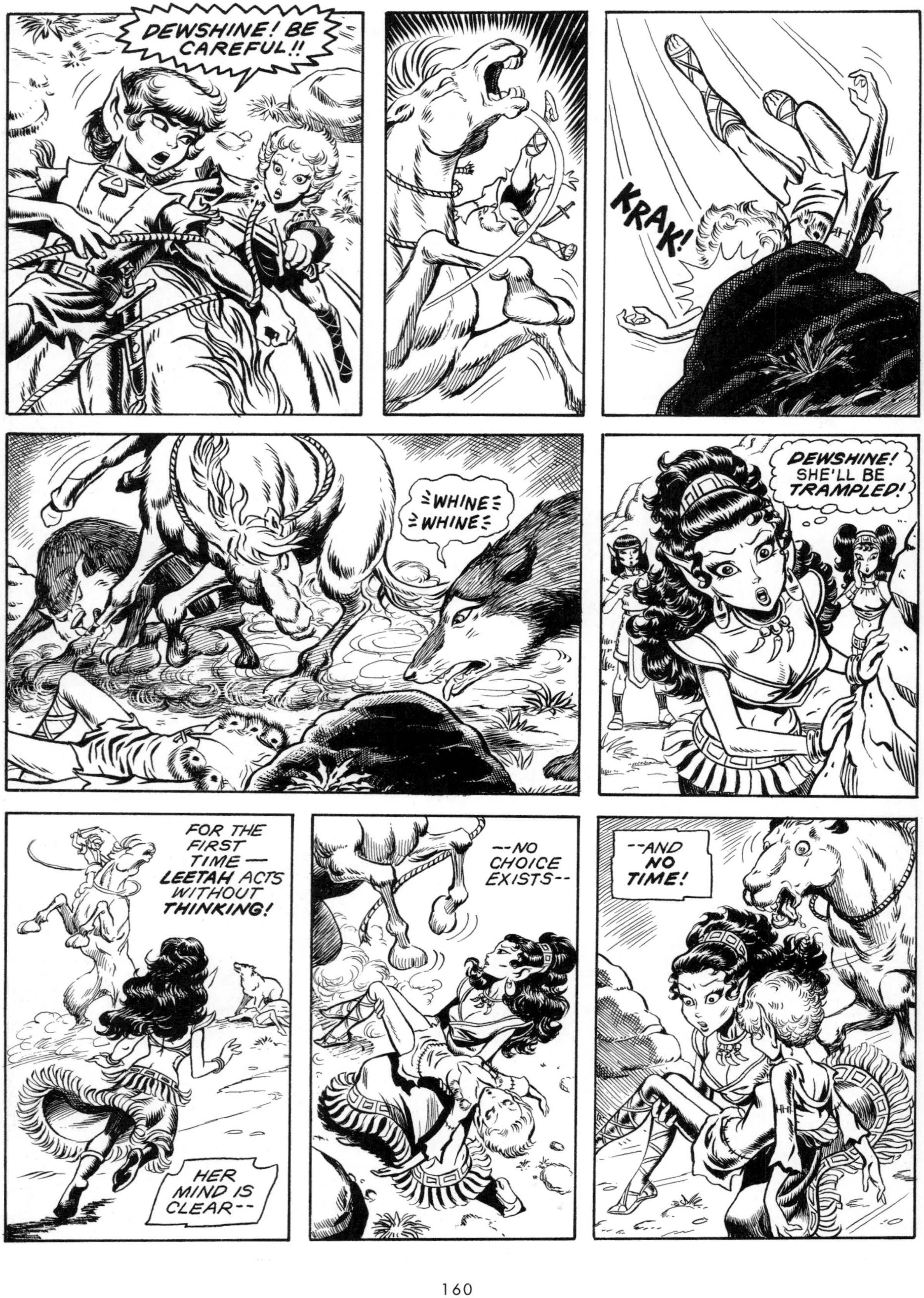
DEWSHINE! BE CAREFUL!!
KRAK!
WHINE WHINE
DEWSHINE! SHE'LL BE TRAMPLED!
FOR THE FIRST TIME— LEETAH ACTS WITHOUT THINKING!
HER MIND IS CLEAR--
--NO CHOICE EXISTS--
--AND NO TIME!

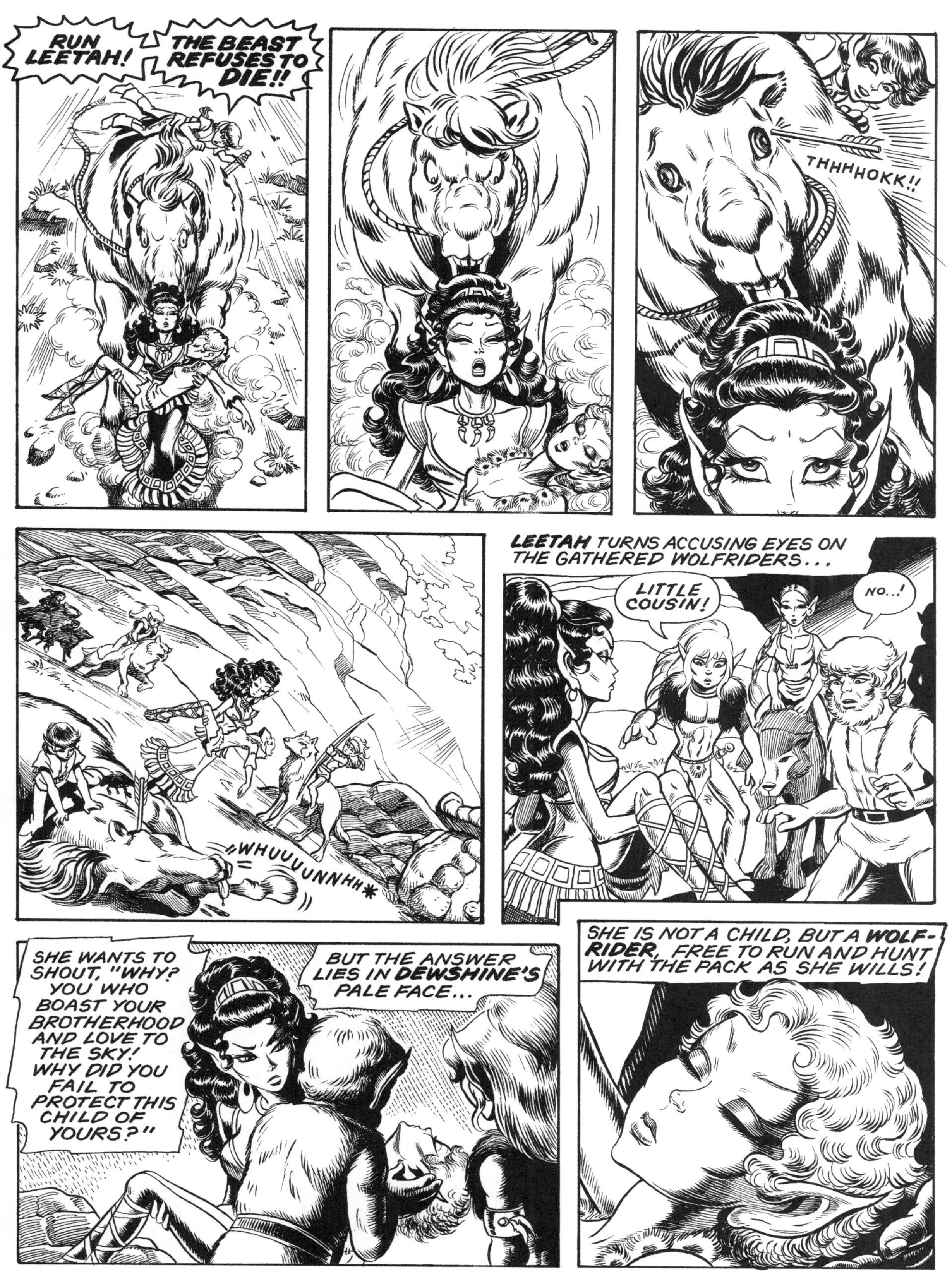
RUN LEETAH!
THE BEAST REFUSES TO DIE!!
THHHHOKK!!
LEETAH TURNS ACCUSING EYES ON THE GATHERED WOLFRIDERS...
LITTLE COUSIN!
NO..!
WHUUUUNNHH
SHE WANTS TO SHOUT, "WHY? YOU WHO BOAST YOUR BROTHERHOOD AND LOVE TO THE SKY! WHY DID YOU FAIL TO PROTECT THIS CHILD OF YOURS?"
BUT THE ANSWER LIES IN DEWSHINE'S PALE FACE...
SHE IS NOT A CHILD, BUT A WOLF-RIDER, FREE TO RUN AND HUNT WITH THE PACK AS SHE WILLS!

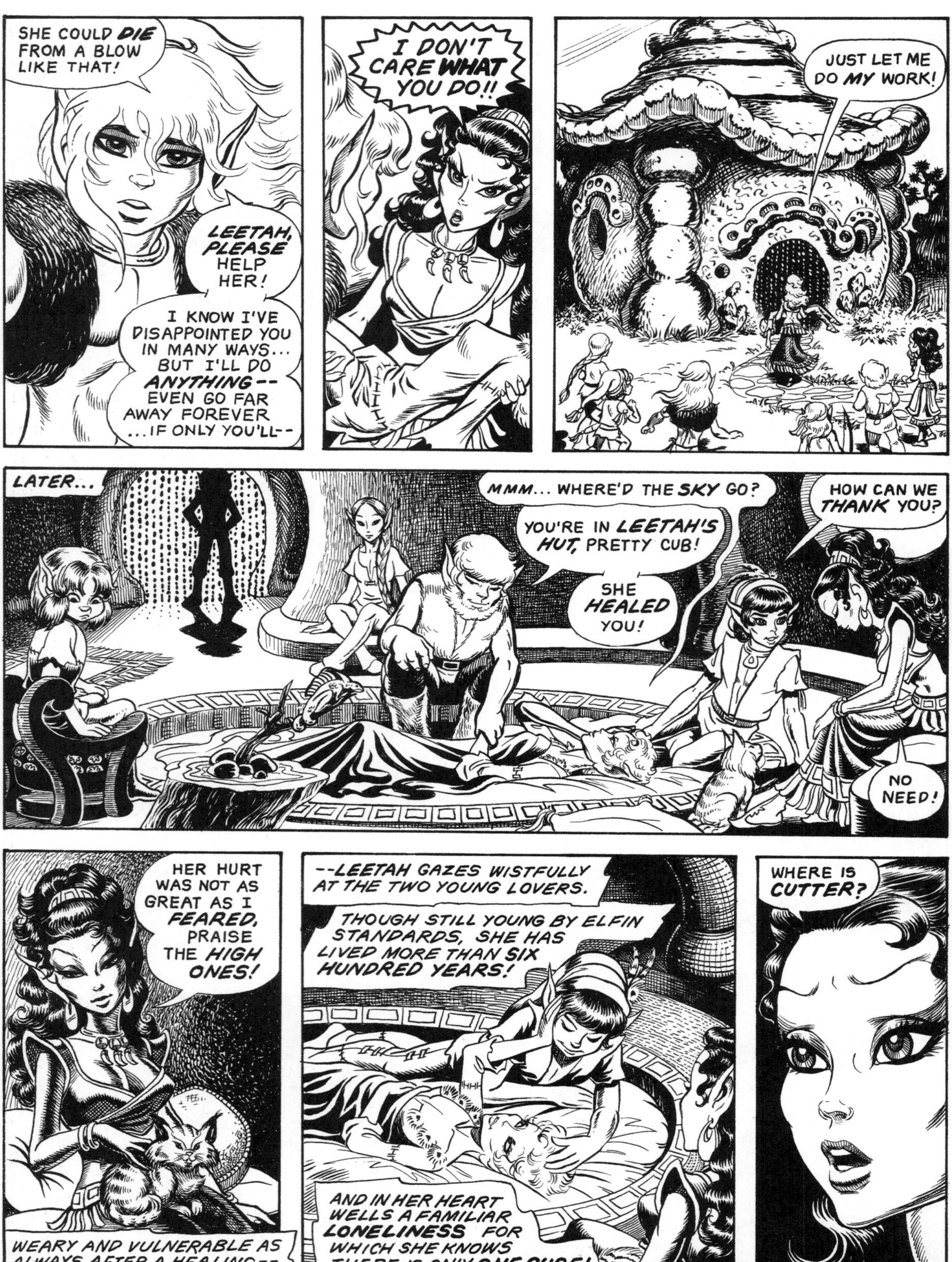
SHE COULD DIE FROM A BLOW LIKE THAT!
LEETAH, PLEASE HELP HER!
I KNOW I'VE DISAPPOINTED YOU IN MANY WAYS... BUT I'LL DO ANYTHING -- EVEN GO FAR AWAY FOREVER ...IF ONLY YOU'LL--
I DON'T CARE WHAT YOU DO!!
JUST LET ME DO MY WORK!
LATER...
MMM... WHERE'D THE SKY GO?
YOU'RE IN LEETAH'S HUT, PRETTY CUB!
SHE HEALED YOU!
HOW CAN WE THANK YOU?
NO NEED!
HER HURT WAS NOT AS GREAT AS I FEARED, PRAISE THE HIGH ONES!
WEARY AND VULNERABLE AS ALWAYS AFTER A HEALING--
--LEETAH GAZES WISTFULLY AT THE TWO YOUNG LOVERS.
THOUGH STILL YOUNG BY ELFIN STANDARDS, SHE HAS LIVED MORE THAN SIX HUNDRED YEARS!
AND IN HER HEART WELLS A FAMILIAR LONELINESS FOR WHICH SHE KNOWS THERE IS ONLY ONE CURE!
WHERE IS CUTTER?

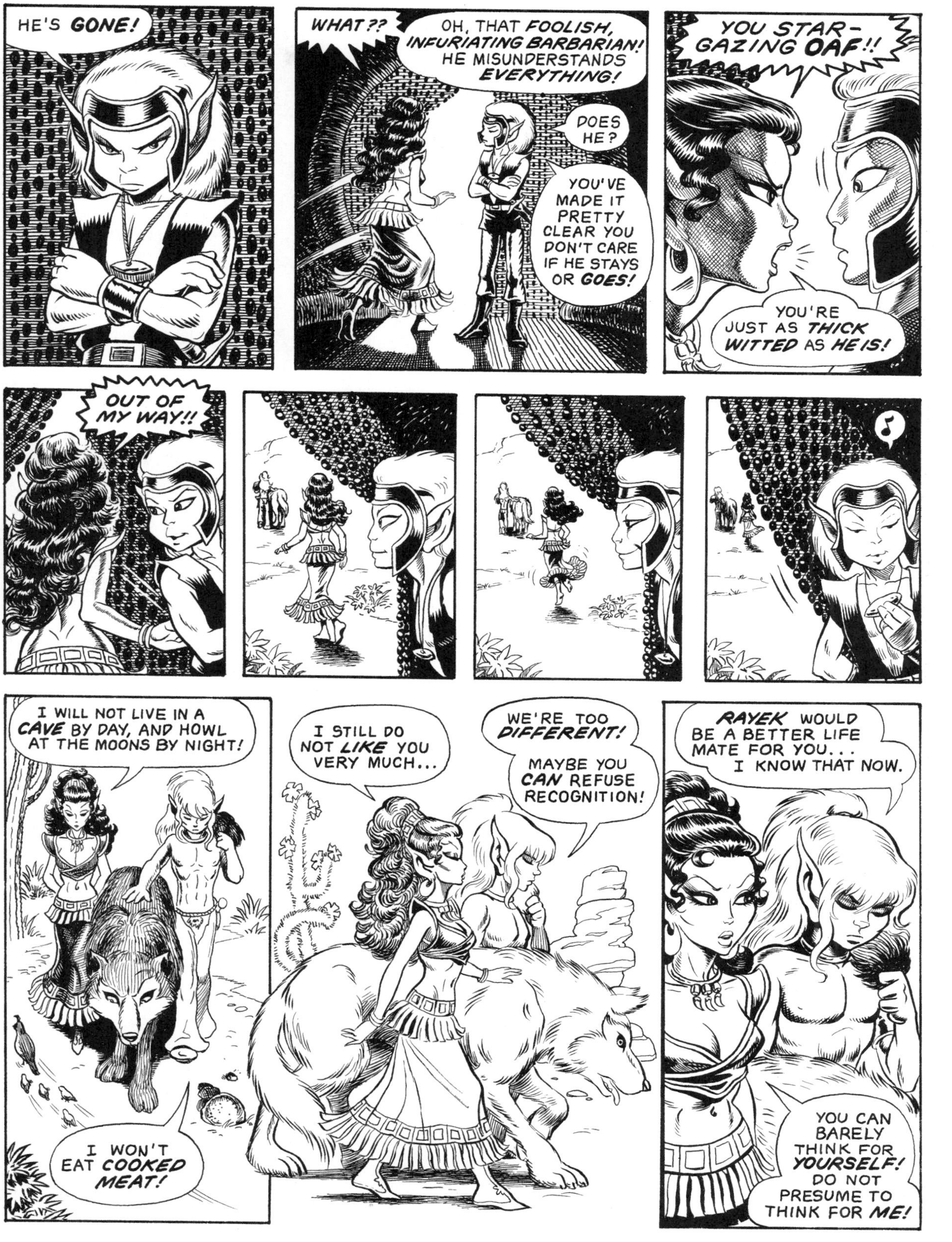
HE'S GONE!
WHAT??
OH, THAT FOOLISH, INFURIATING BARBARIAN! HE MISUNDERSTANDS EVERYTHING!
DOES HE?
YOU'VE MADE IT PRETTY CLEAR YOU DON'T CARE IF HE STAYS OR GOES!
YOU STAR-GAZING OAF!!
YOU'RE JUST AS THICK WITTED AS HE IS!
OUT OF MY WAY!!
I WILL NOT LIVE IN A CAVE BY DAY, AND HOWL AT THE MOONS BY NIGHT!
I WON'T EAT COOKED MEAT!
I STILL DO NOT LIKE YOU VERY MUCH...
WE'RE TOO DIFFERENT!
MAYBE YOU CAN REFUSE RECOGNITION!
RAYEK WOULD BE A BETTER LIFE MATE FOR YOU... I KNOW THAT NOW.
YOU CAN BARELY THINK FOR YOURSELF! DO NOT PRESUME TO THINK FOR ME!

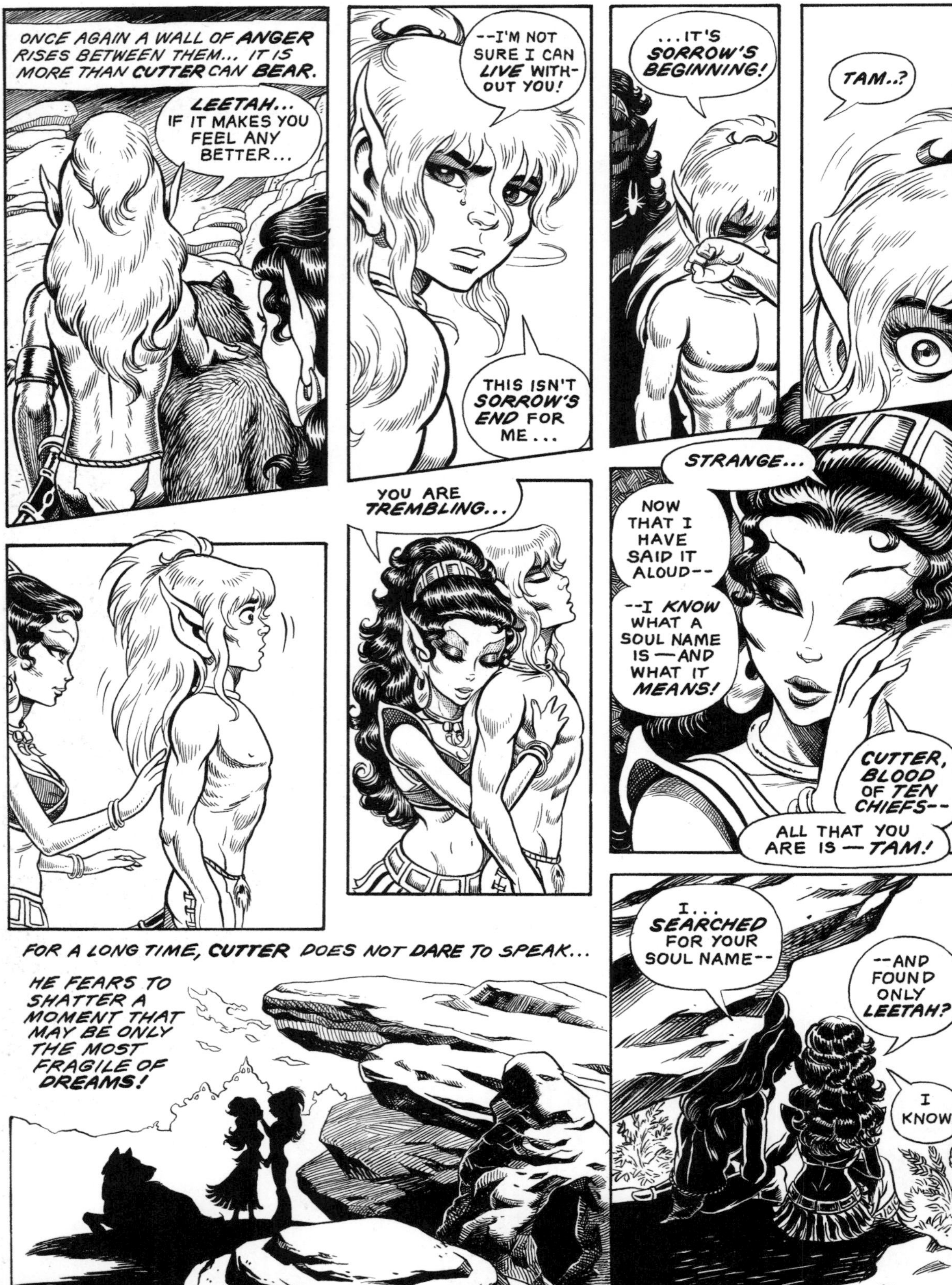

ONCE AGAIN A WALL OF ANGER RISES BETWEEN THEM... IT IS MORE THAN CUTTER CAN BEAR.
LEETAH... IF IT MAKES YOU FEEL ANY BETTER...
--I'M NOT SURE I CAN LIVE WITHOUT YOU!
THIS ISN'T SORROW'S END FOR ME...
...IT'S SORROW'S BEGINNING!
TAM..?
YOU ARE TREMBLING...
STRANGE...
NOW THAT I HAVE SAID IT ALOUD--
--I KNOW WHAT A SOUL NAME IS — AND WHAT IT MEANS!
CUTTER, BLOOD OF TEN CHIEFS--
ALL THAT YOU ARE IS — TAM!
FOR A LONG TIME, CUTTER DOES NOT DARE TO SPEAK...
HE FEARS TO SHATTER A MOMENT THAT MAY BE ONLY THE MOST FRAGILE OF DREAMS!
I... SEARCHED FOR YOUR SOUL NAME--
--AND FOUND ONLY LEETAH?
I KNOW.

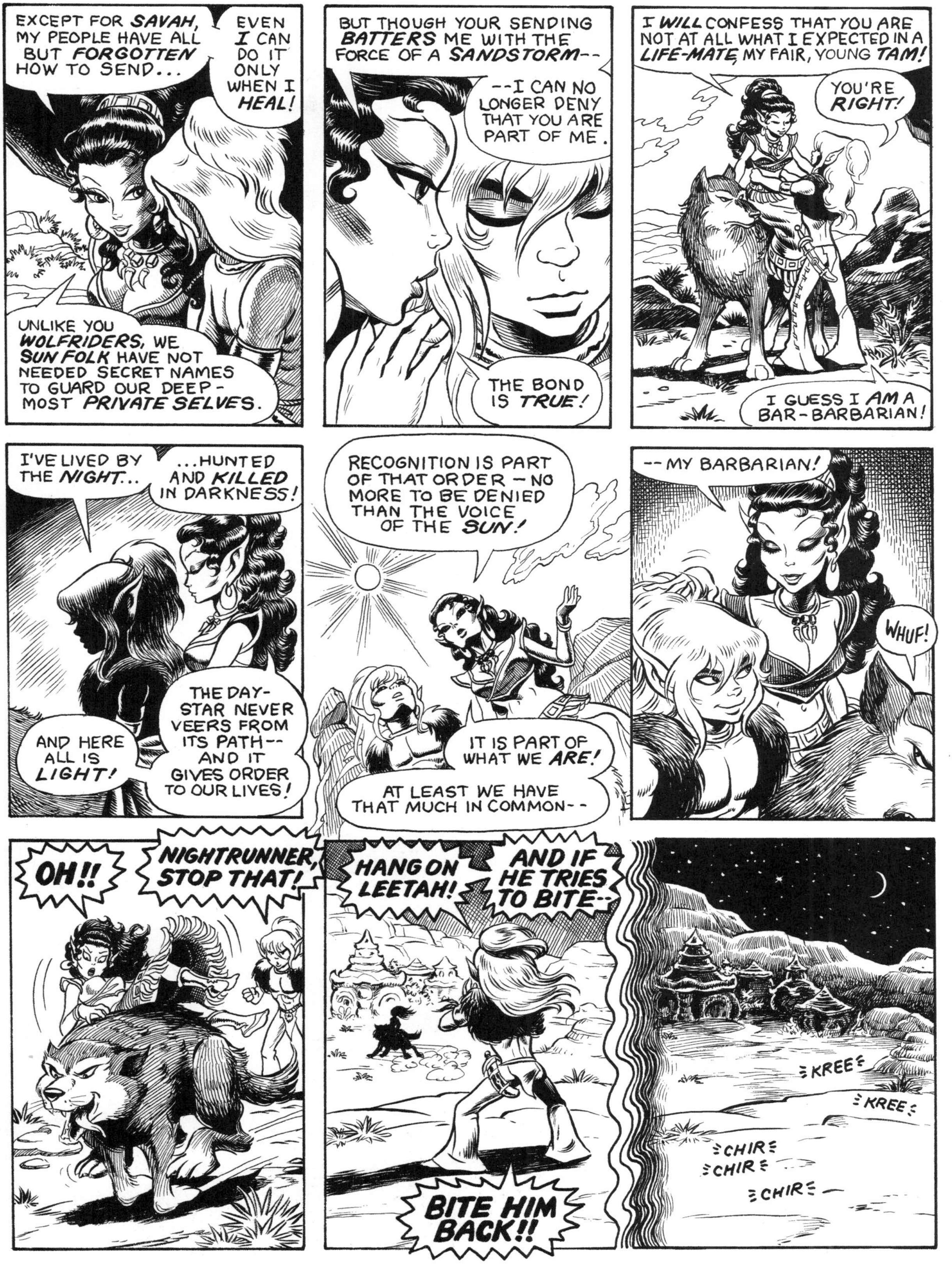
EXCEPT FOR SAVAH, MY PEOPLE HAVE ALL BUT FORGOTTEN HOW TO SEND...
EVEN I CAN DO IT ONLY WHEN I HEAL!
UNLIKE YOU WOLFRIDERS, WE SUN FOLK HAVE NOT NEEDED SECRET NAMES TO GUARD OUR DEEP-MOST PRIVATE SELVES.
BUT THOUGH YOUR SENDING BATTERS ME WITH THE FORCE OF A SANDSTORM--
--I CAN NO LONGER DENY THAT YOU ARE PART OF ME.
THE BOND IS TRUE!
I WILL CONFESS THAT YOU ARE NOT AT ALL WHAT I EXPECTED IN A LIFE-MATE, MY FAIR, YOUNG TAM!
YOU'RE RIGHT!
I GUESS I AM A BAR-BARBARIAN!
I'VE LIVED BY THE NIGHT...
...HUNTED AND KILLED IN DARKNESS!
AND HERE ALL IS LIGHT!
THE DAY-STAR NEVER VEERS FROM ITS PATH-- AND IT GIVES ORDER TO OUR LIVES!
RECOGNITION IS PART OF THAT ORDER — NO MORE TO BE DENIED THAN THE VOICE OF THE SUN!
IT IS PART OF WHAT WE ARE!
AT LEAST WE HAVE THAT MUCH IN COMMON--
-- MY BARBARIAN!
WHUF!
OH!!
NIGHTRUNNER, STOP THAT!
HANG ON LEETAH!
AND IF HE TRIES TO BITE--
BITE HIM BACK!!
KREE
KREE
CHIR
CHIR
CHIR

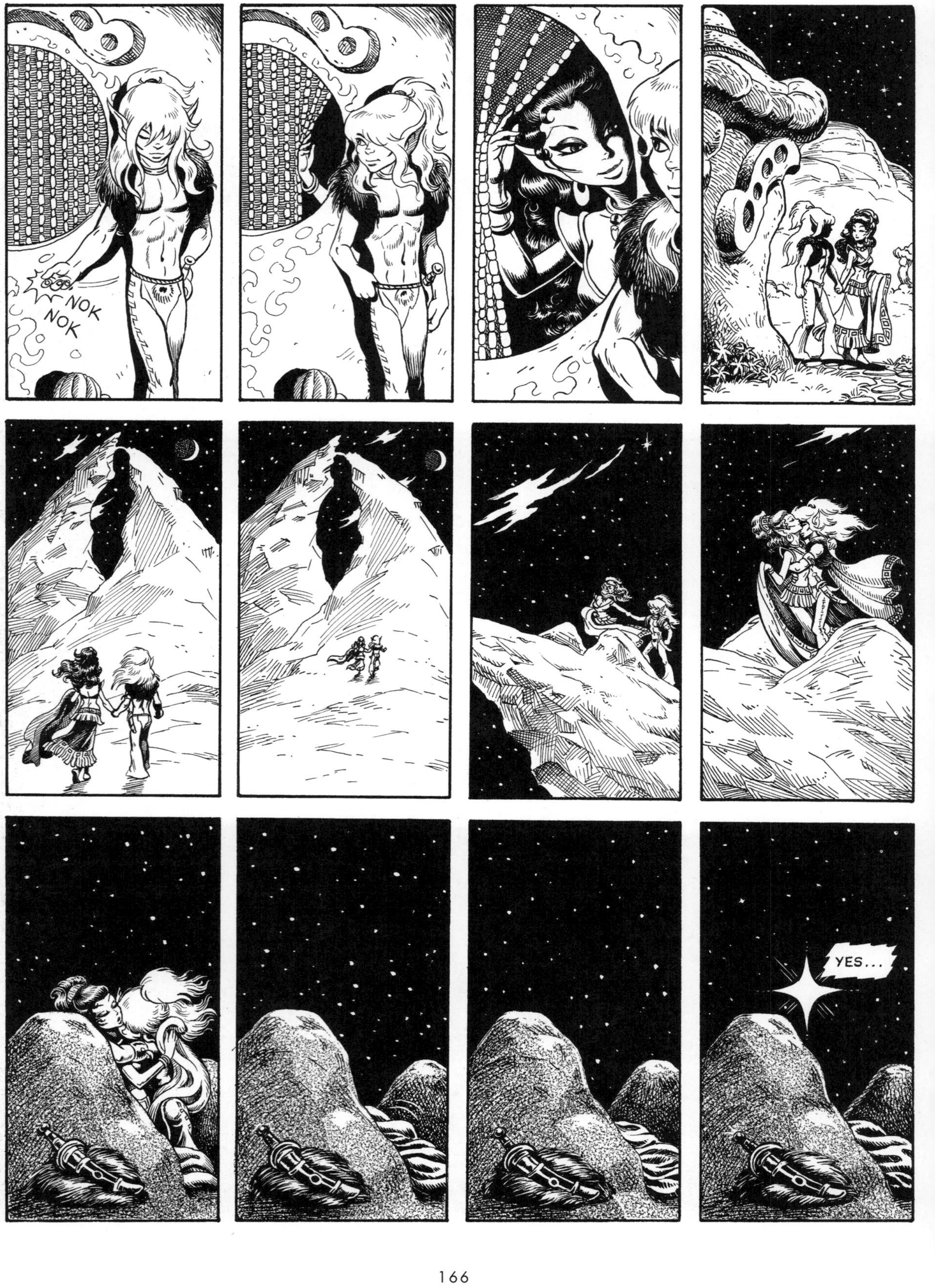
NOK
NOK
YES...

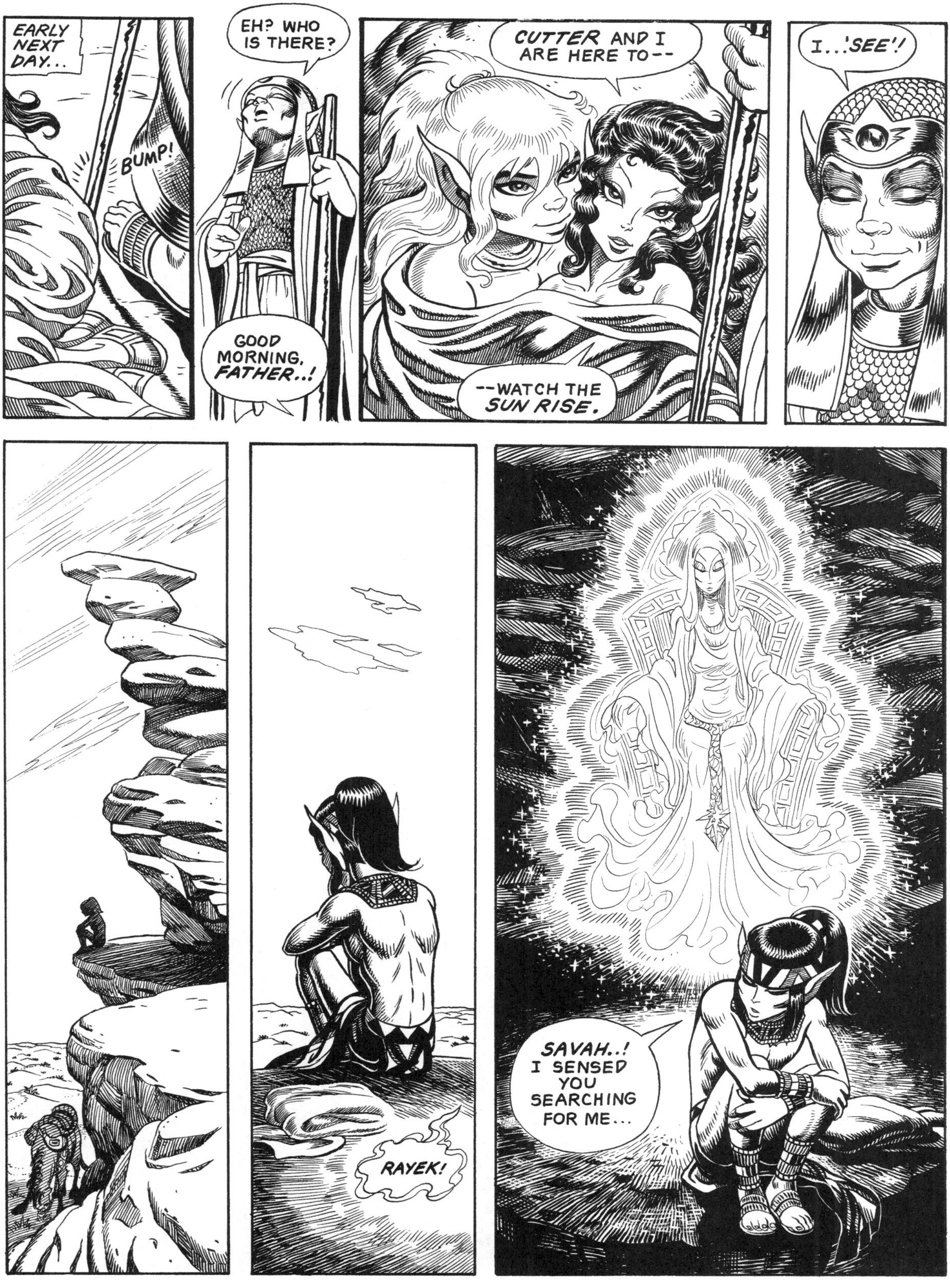
EARLY NEXT DAY...
BUMP!
EH? WHO IS THERE?
GOOD MORNING, FATHER..!
CUTTER AND I ARE HERE TO--
--WATCH THE SUN RISE.
I...'SEE'!
RAYEK!
SAVAH..! I SENSED YOU SEARCHING FOR ME...

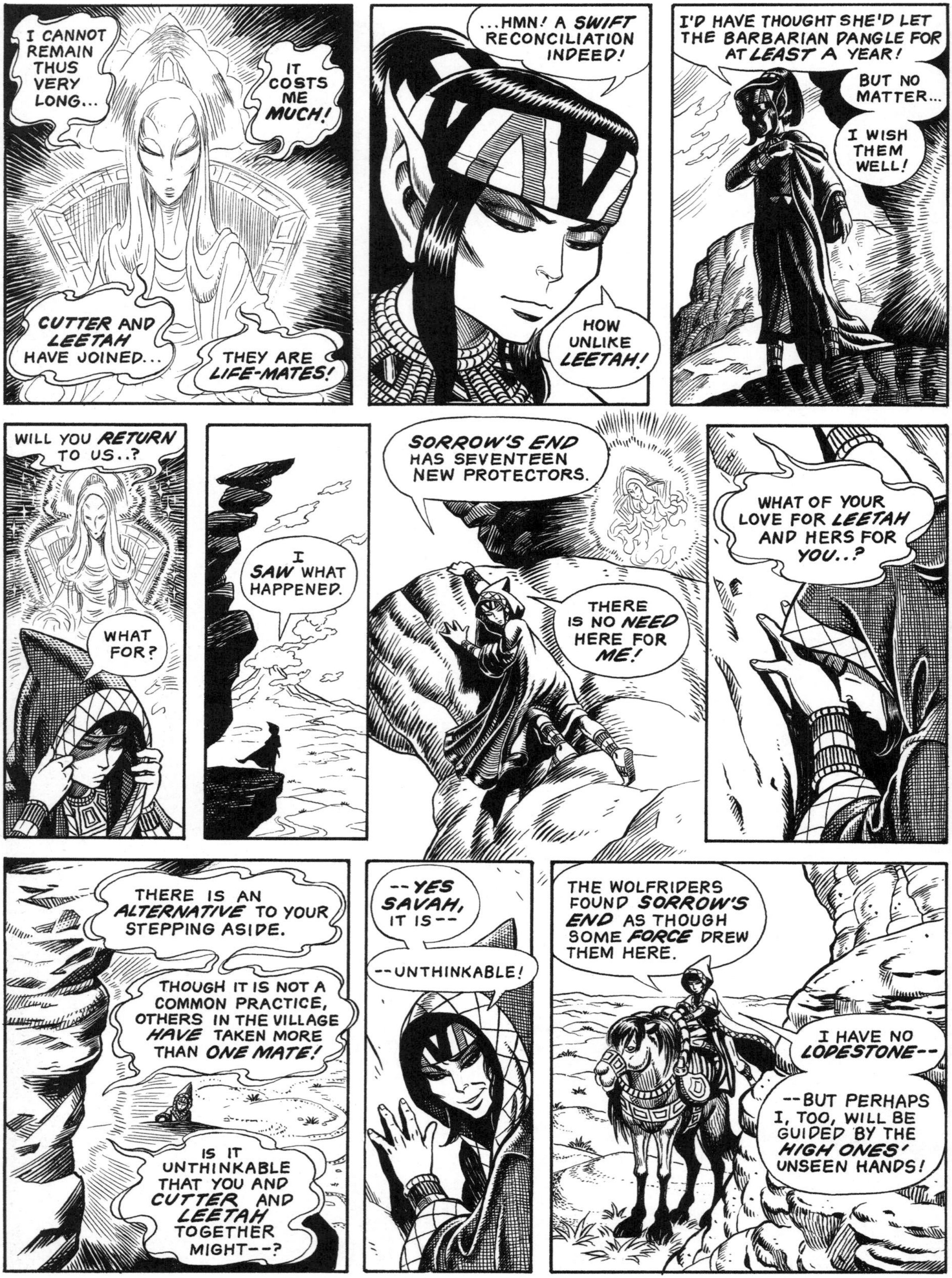
I CANNOT REMAIN THUS VERY LONG...
IT COSTS ME MUCH!
CUTTER AND LEETAH HAVE JOINED...
THEY ARE LIFE-MATES!
...HMN! A SWIFT RECONCILIATION INDEED!
HOW UNLIKE LEETAH!
I'D HAVE THOUGHT SHE'D LET THE BARBARIAN DANGLE FOR AT LEAST A YEAR!
BUT NO MATTER...
I WISH THEM WELL!
WILL YOU RETURN TO US..?
WHAT FOR?
I SAW WHAT HAPPENED.
SORROW'S END HAS SEVENTEEN NEW PROTECTORS.
THERE IS NO NEED HERE FOR ME!
WHAT OF YOUR LOVE FOR LEETAH AND HERS FOR YOU..?
THERE IS AN ALTERNATIVE TO YOUR STEPPING ASIDE.
THOUGH IT IS NOT A COMMON PRACTICE, OTHERS IN THE VILLAGE HAVE TAKEN MORE THAN ONE MATE!
IS IT UNTHINKABLE THAT YOU AND CUTTER AND LEETAH TOGETHER MIGHT--?
--YES SAVAH, IT IS--
--UNTHINKABLE!
THE WOLFRIDERS FOUND SORROW'S END AS THOUGH SOME FORCE DREW THEM HERE.
I HAVE NO LODESTONE--
--BUT PERHAPS I, TOO, WILL BE GUIDED BY THE HIGH ONES' UNSEEN HANDS!

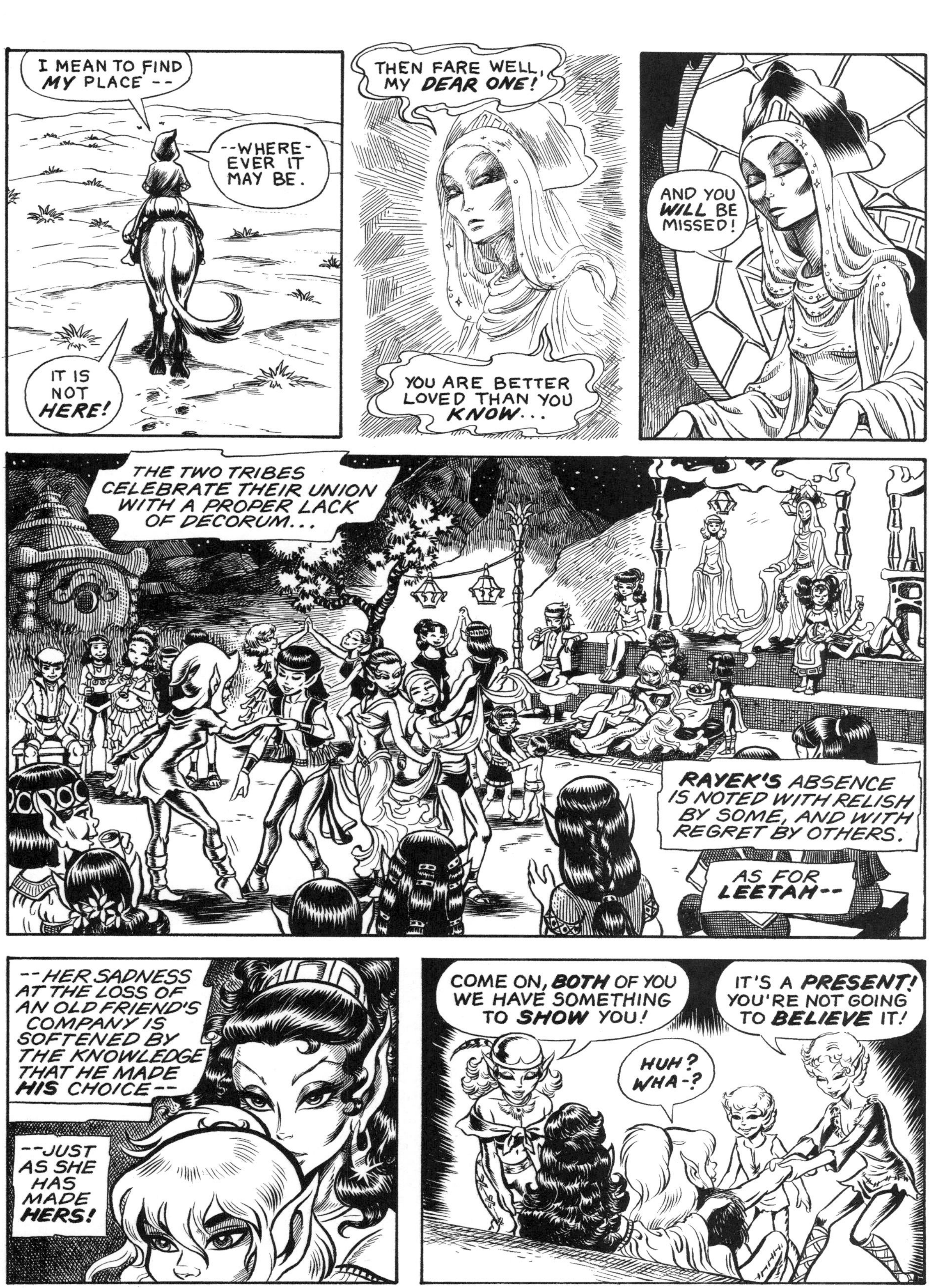
I MEAN TO FIND MY PLACE --
--WHERE-EVER IT MAY BE.
IT IS NOT HERE!
THEN FARE WELL, MY DEAR ONE!
YOU ARE BETTER LOVED THAN YOU KNOW...
AND YOU WILL BE MISSED!
THE TWO TRIBES CELEBRATE THEIR UNION WITH A PROPER LACK OF DECORUM...
RAYEK'S ABSENCE IS NOTED WITH RELISH BY SOME, AND WITH REGRET BY OTHERS.
AS FOR LEETAH--
--HER SADNESS AT THE LOSS OF AN OLD FRIEND'S COMPANY IS SOFTENED BY THE KNOWLEDGE THAT HE MADE HIS CHOICE--
--JUST AS SHE HAS MADE HERS!
COME ON, BOTH OF YOU WE HAVE SOMETHING TO SHOW YOU!
HUH? WHA-?
IT'S A PRESENT! YOU'RE NOT GOING TO BELIEVE IT!

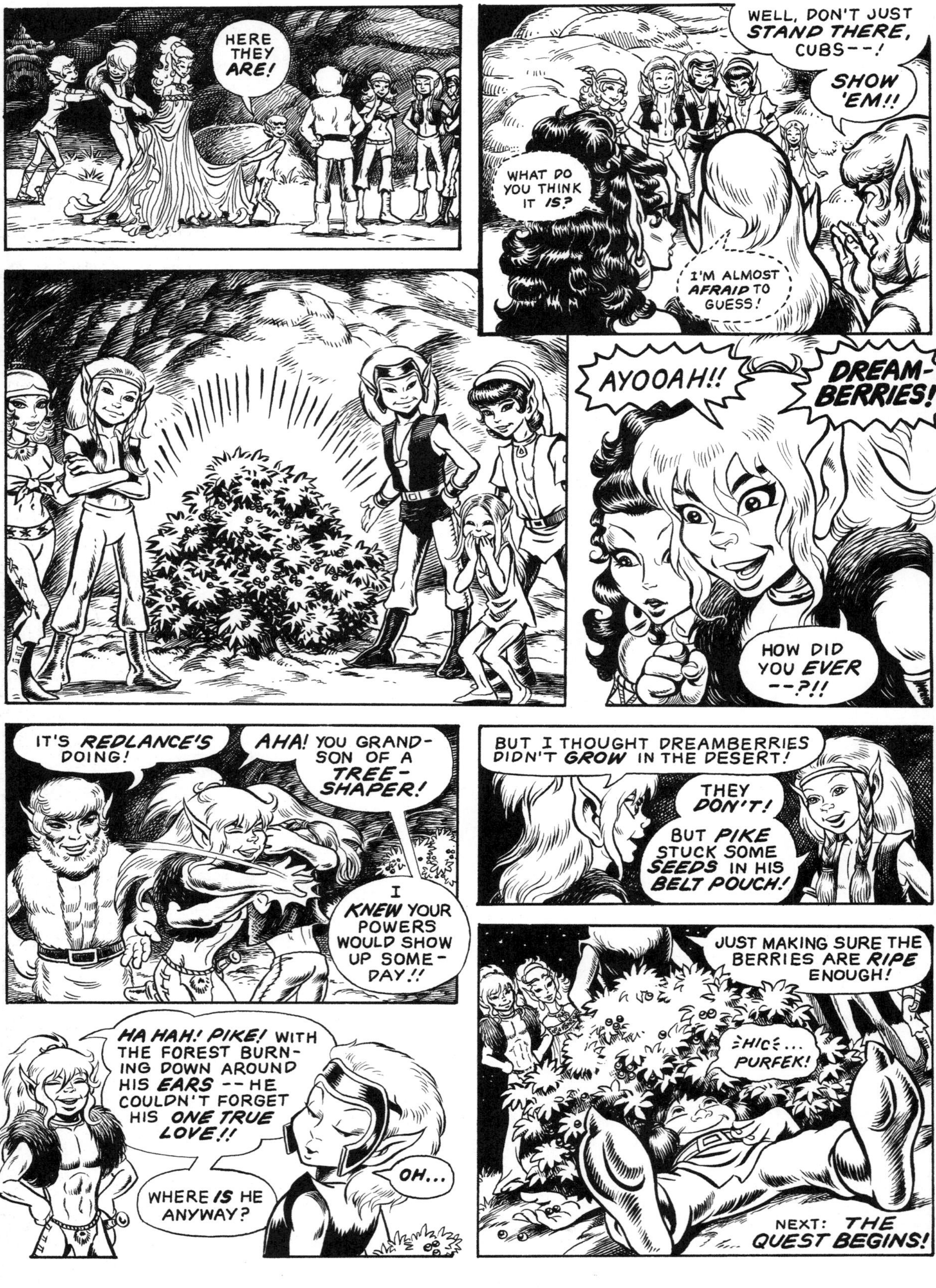
HERE THEY ARE!
WELL, DON'T JUST STAND THERE, CUBS--!
SHOW 'EM!!
WHAT DO YOU THINK IT IS?
I'M ALMOST AFRAID TO GUESS!
AYOOAH!!
DREAM-BERRIES!
HOW DID YOU EVER --?!!
IT'S REDLANCE'S DOING!
AHA! YOU GRAND-SON OF A TREE-SHAPER!
I KNEW YOUR POWERS WOULD SHOW UP SOME-DAY!!
BUT I THOUGHT DREAMBERRIES DIDN'T GROW IN THE DESERT!
THEY DON'T!
BUT PIKE STUCK SOME SEEDS IN HIS BELT POUCH!
HA HAH! PIKE! WITH THE FOREST BURN-ING DOWN AROUND HIS EARS -- HE COULDN'T FORGET HIS ONE TRUE LOVE!!
WHERE IS HE ANYWAY?
OH...
JUST MAKING SURE THE BERRIES ARE RIPE ENOUGH!
HIC... PURFEK!
NEXT: THE QUEST BEGINS!

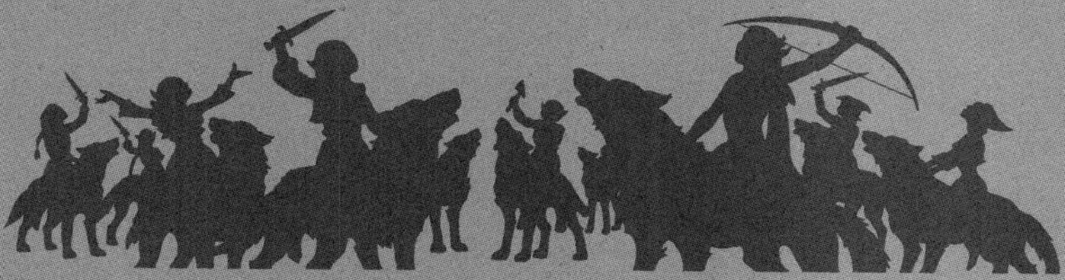

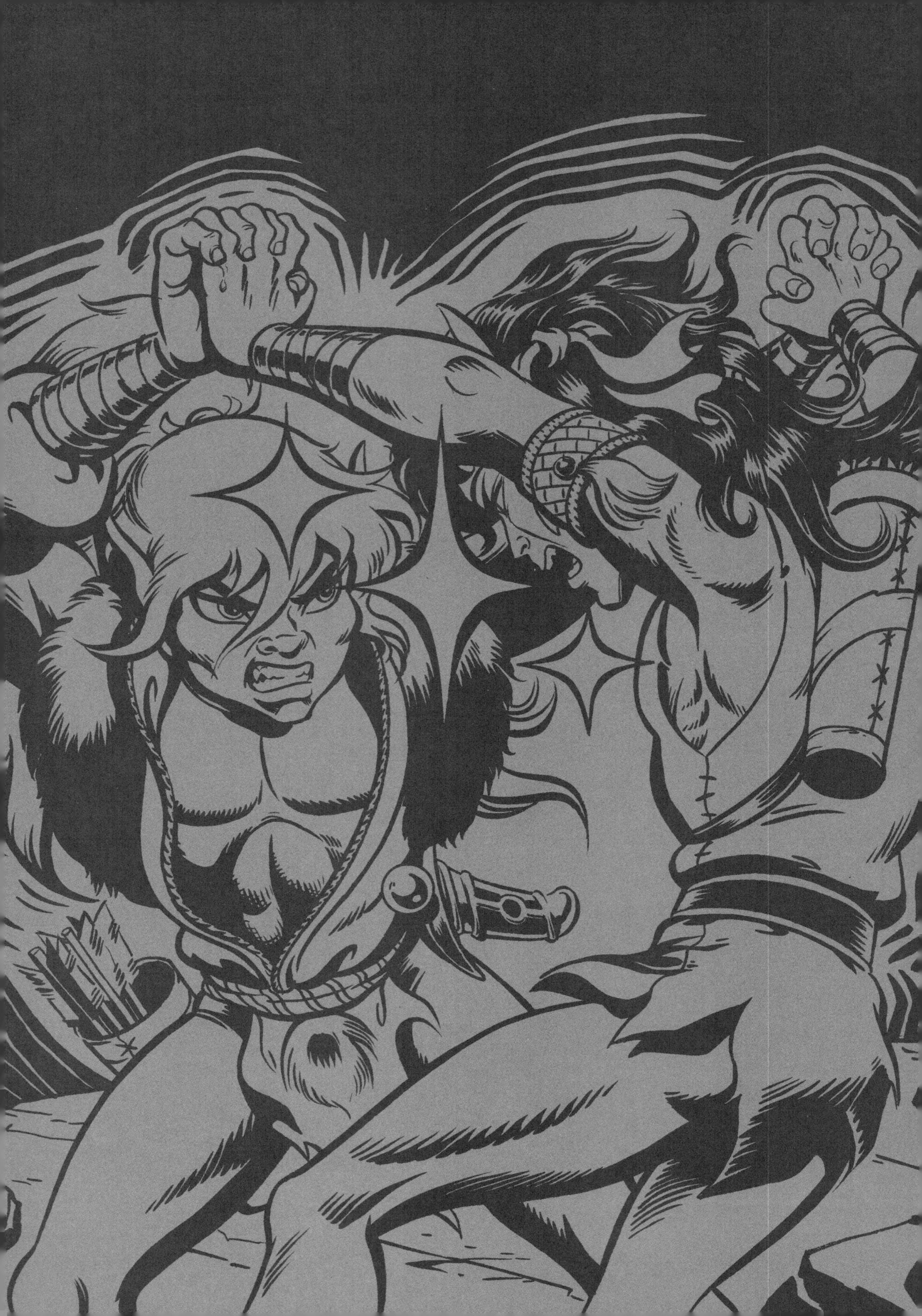

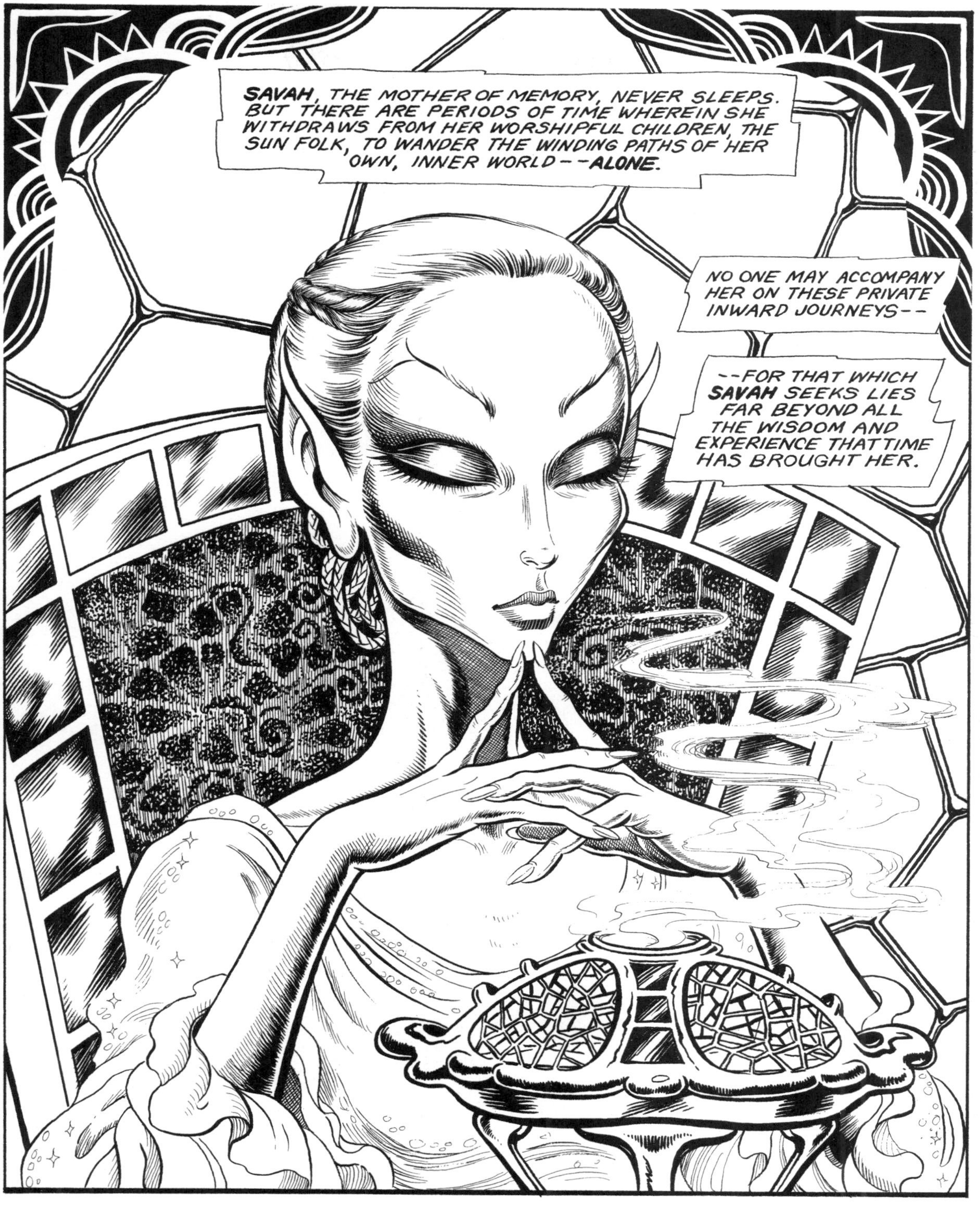
SAVAH, THE MOTHER OF MEMORY, NEVER SLEEPS. BUT THERE ARE PERIODS OF TIME WHEREIN SHE WITHDRAWS FROM HER WORSHIPFUL CHILDREN, THE SUN FOLK, TO WANDER THE WINDING PATHS OF HER OWN, INNER WORLD--ALONE.
NO ONE MAY ACCOMPANY HER ON THESE PRIVATE INWARD JOURNEYS--
--FOR THAT WHICH SAVAH SEEKS LIES FAR BEYOND ALL THE WISDOM AND EXPERIENCE THAT TIME HAS BROUGHT HER.

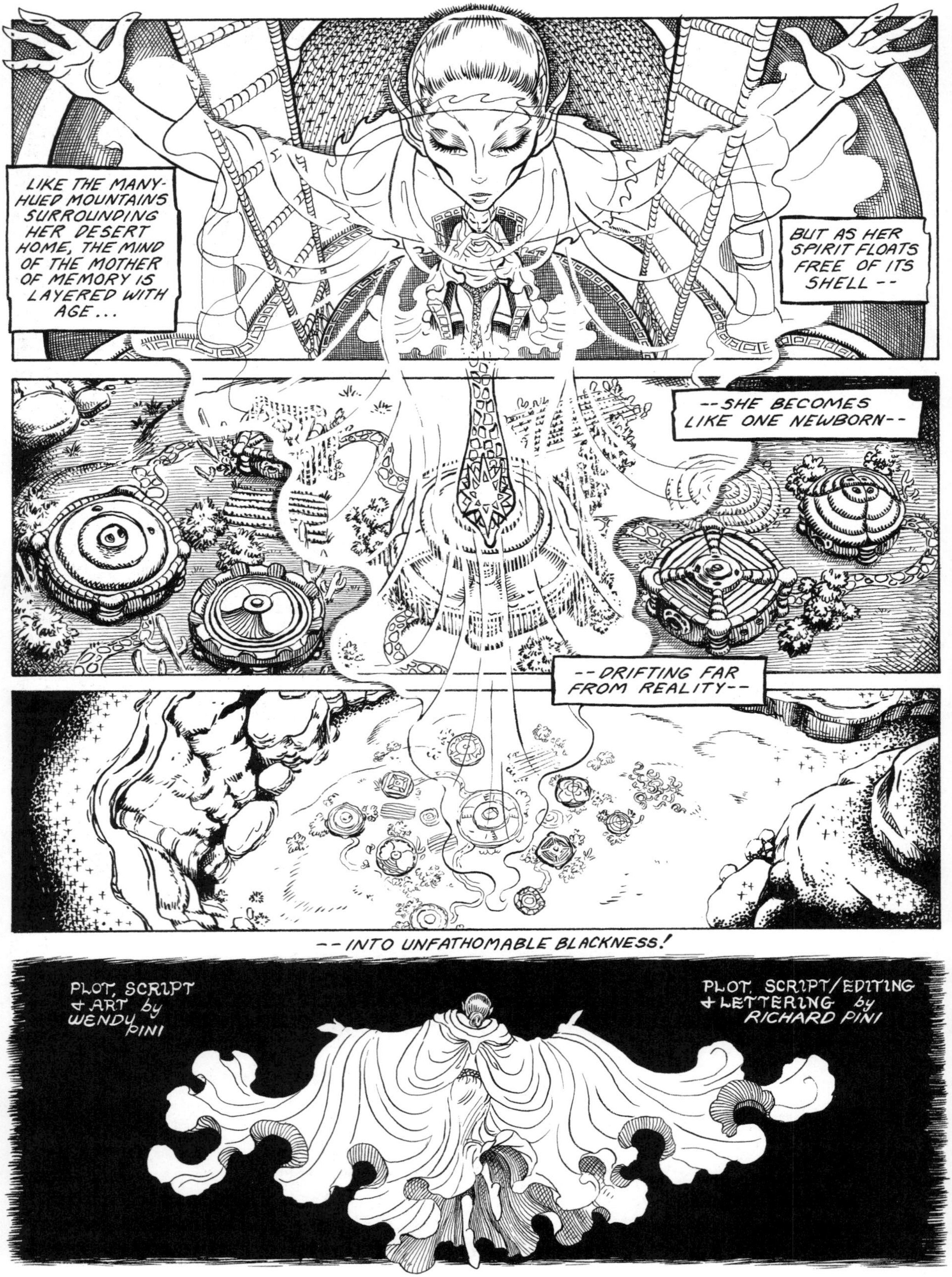
LIKE THE MANY-HUED MOUNTAINS SURROUNDING HER DESERT HOME, THE MIND OF THE MOTHER OF MEMORY IS LAYERED WITH AGE...
BUT AS HER SPIRIT FLOATS FREE OF ITS SHELL --
--SHE BECOMES LIKE ONE NEWBORN--
--DRIFTING FAR FROM REALITY--
--INTO UNFATHOMABLE BLACKNESS!
PLOT, SCRIPT & ART by WENDY PINI
PLOT, SCRIPT/EDITING & LETTERING by RICHARD PINI

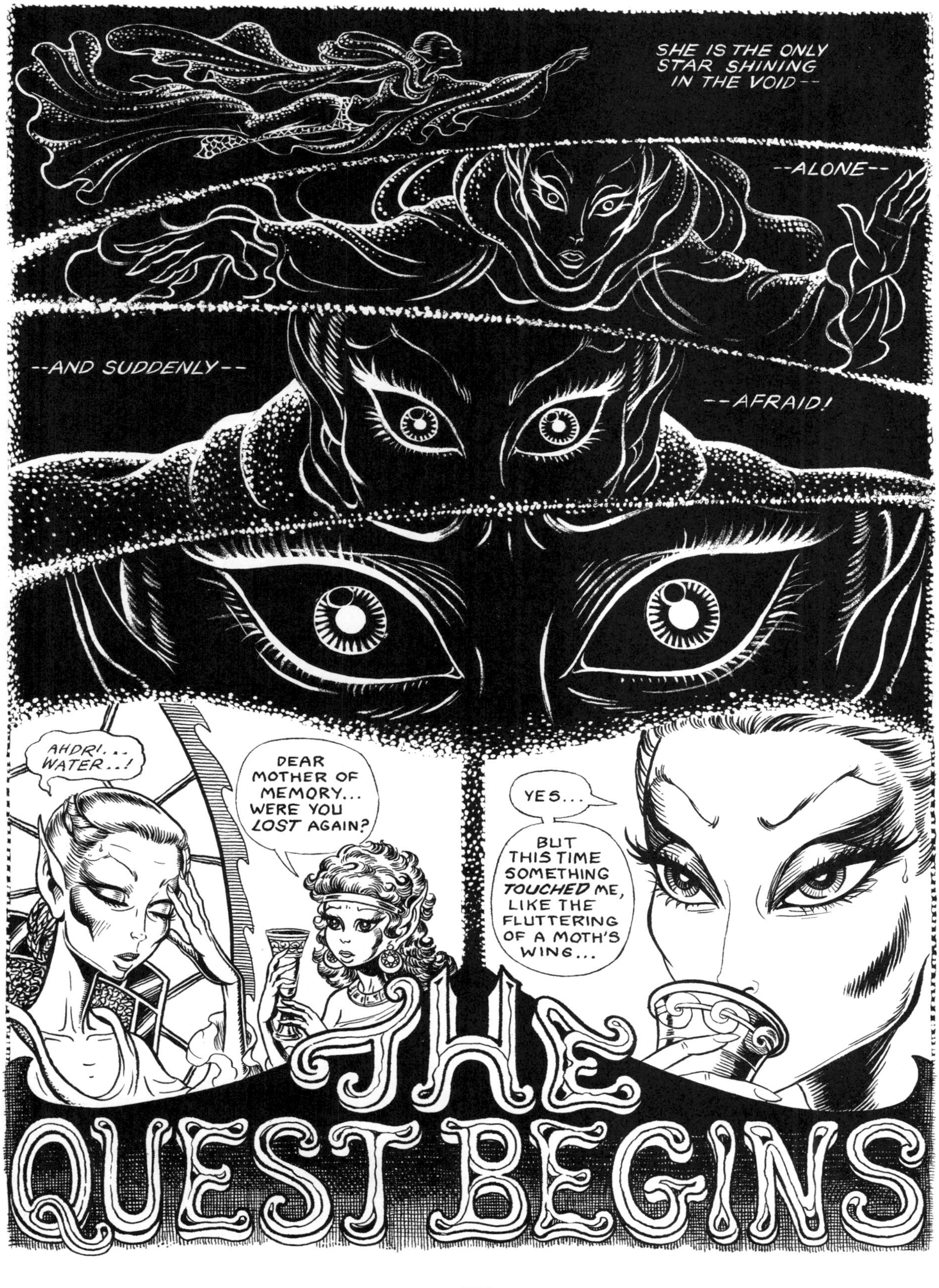
SHE IS THE ONLY STAR SHINING IN THE VOID--
--ALONE--
--AND SUDDENLY--
--AFRAID!
AHDRI... WATER..!
DEAR MOTHER OF MEMORY... WERE YOU LOST AGAIN?
YES...
BUT THIS TIME SOMETHING TOUCHED ME, LIKE THE FLUTTERING OF A MOTH'S WING...
THE QUEST BEGINS

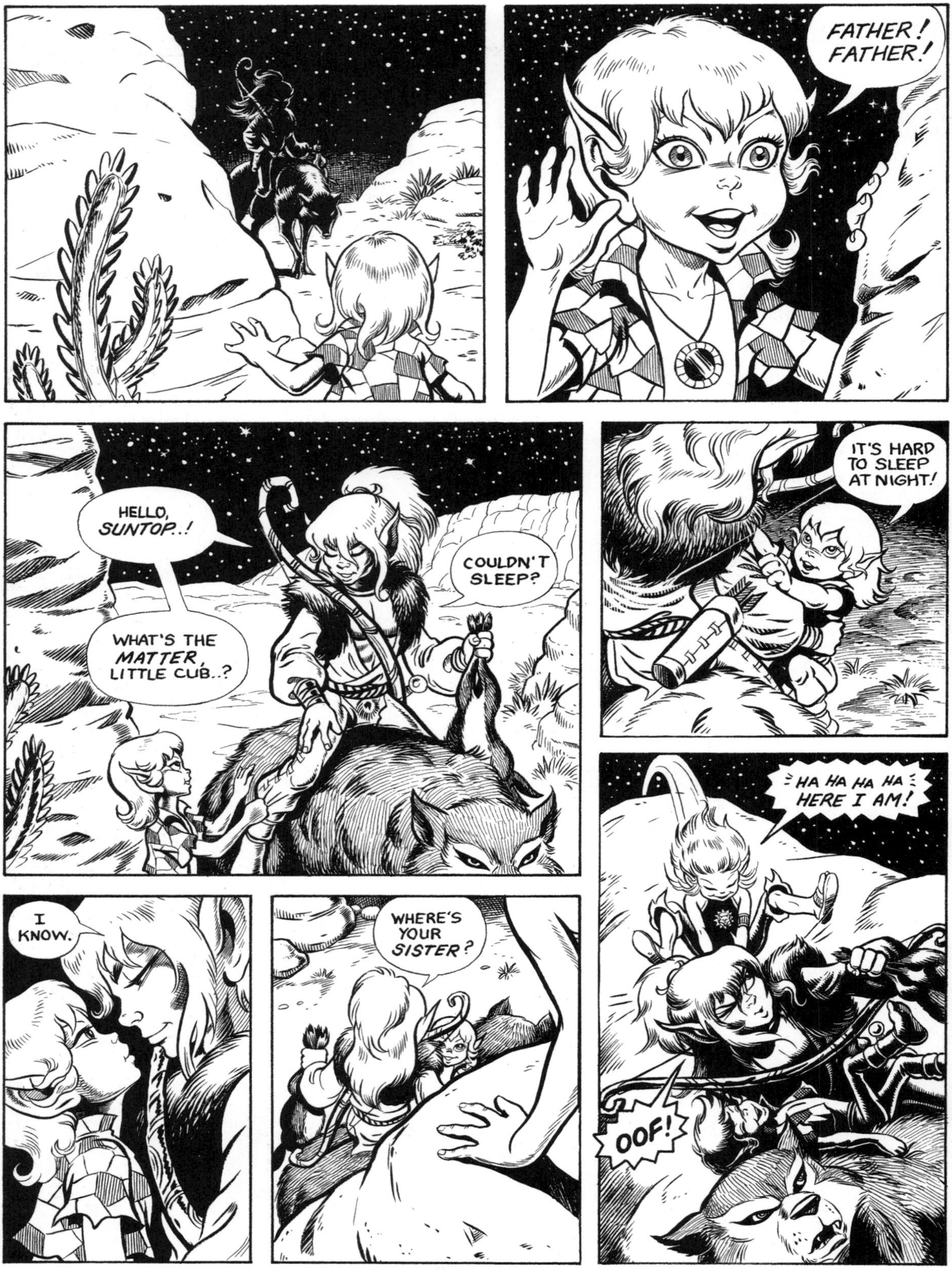
FATHER! FATHER!
HELLO, SUNTOP..!
WHAT'S THE MATTER, LITTLE CUB..?
COULDN'T SLEEP?
IT'S HARD TO SLEEP AT NIGHT!
I KNOW.
WHERE'S YOUR SISTER?
HA HA HA HA HERE I AM!
OOF!

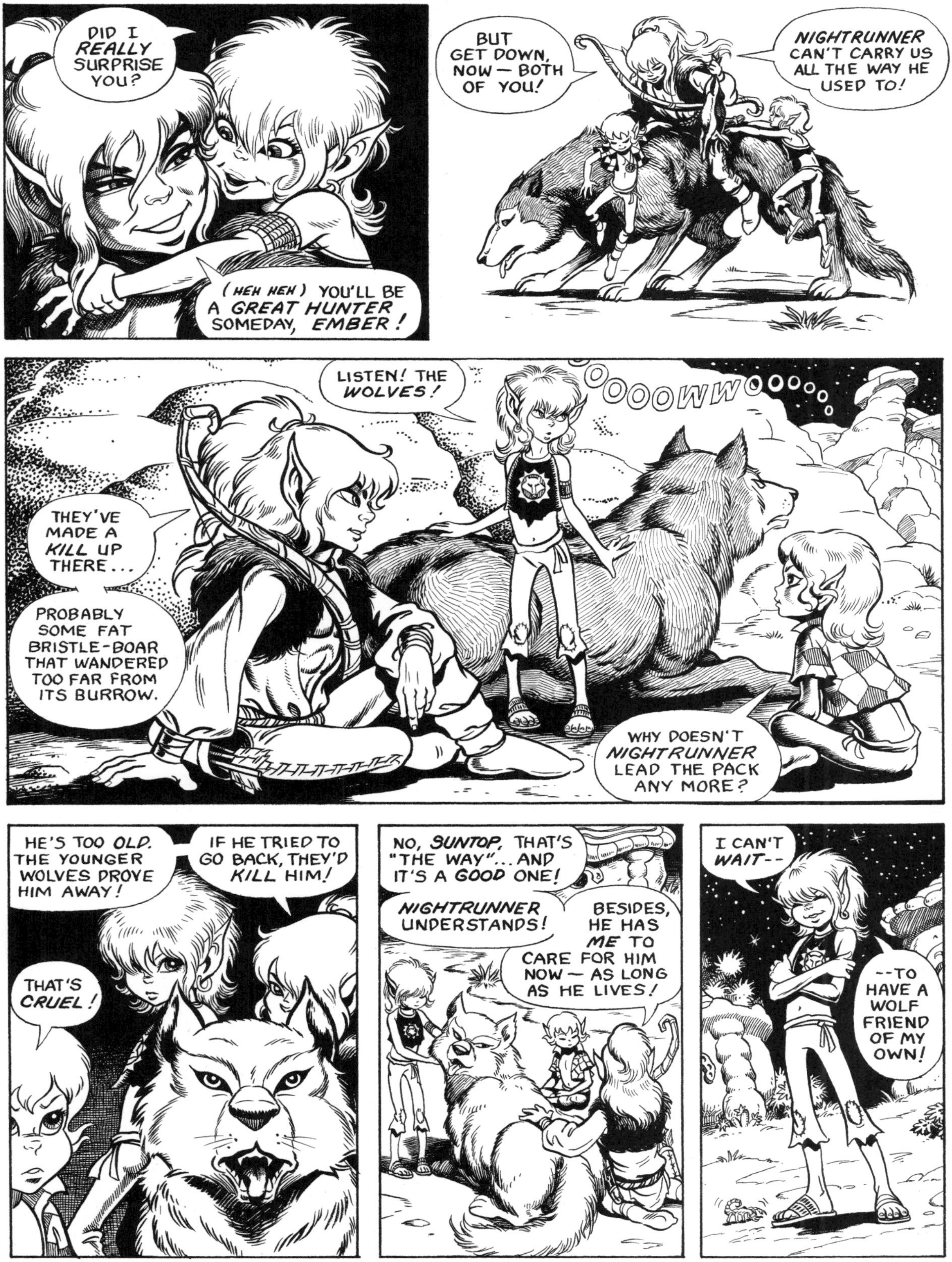
DID I REALLY SURPRISE YOU?
(HEH HEH) YOU'LL BE A GREAT HUNTER SOMEDAY, EMBER!
BUT GET DOWN, NOW — BOTH OF YOU!
NIGHTRUNNER CAN'T CARRY US ALL THE WAY HE USED TO!
LISTEN! THE WOLVES!
OOOOOWWOOOOOOO
THEY'VE MADE A KILL UP THERE...
PROBABLY SOME FAT BRISTLE-BOAR THAT WANDERED TOO FAR FROM ITS BURROW.
WHY DOESN'T NIGHTRUNNER LEAD THE PACK ANY MORE?
HE'S TOO OLD. THE YOUNGER WOLVES DROVE HIM AWAY!
IF HE TRIED TO GO BACK, THEY'D KILL HIM!
THAT'S CRUEL!
NO, SUNTOP, THAT'S "THE WAY"... AND IT'S A GOOD ONE!
NIGHTRUNNER UNDERSTANDS!
BESIDES, HE HAS ME TO CARE FOR HIM NOW — AS LONG AS HE LIVES!
I CAN'T WAIT--
--TO HAVE A WOLF FRIEND OF MY OWN!

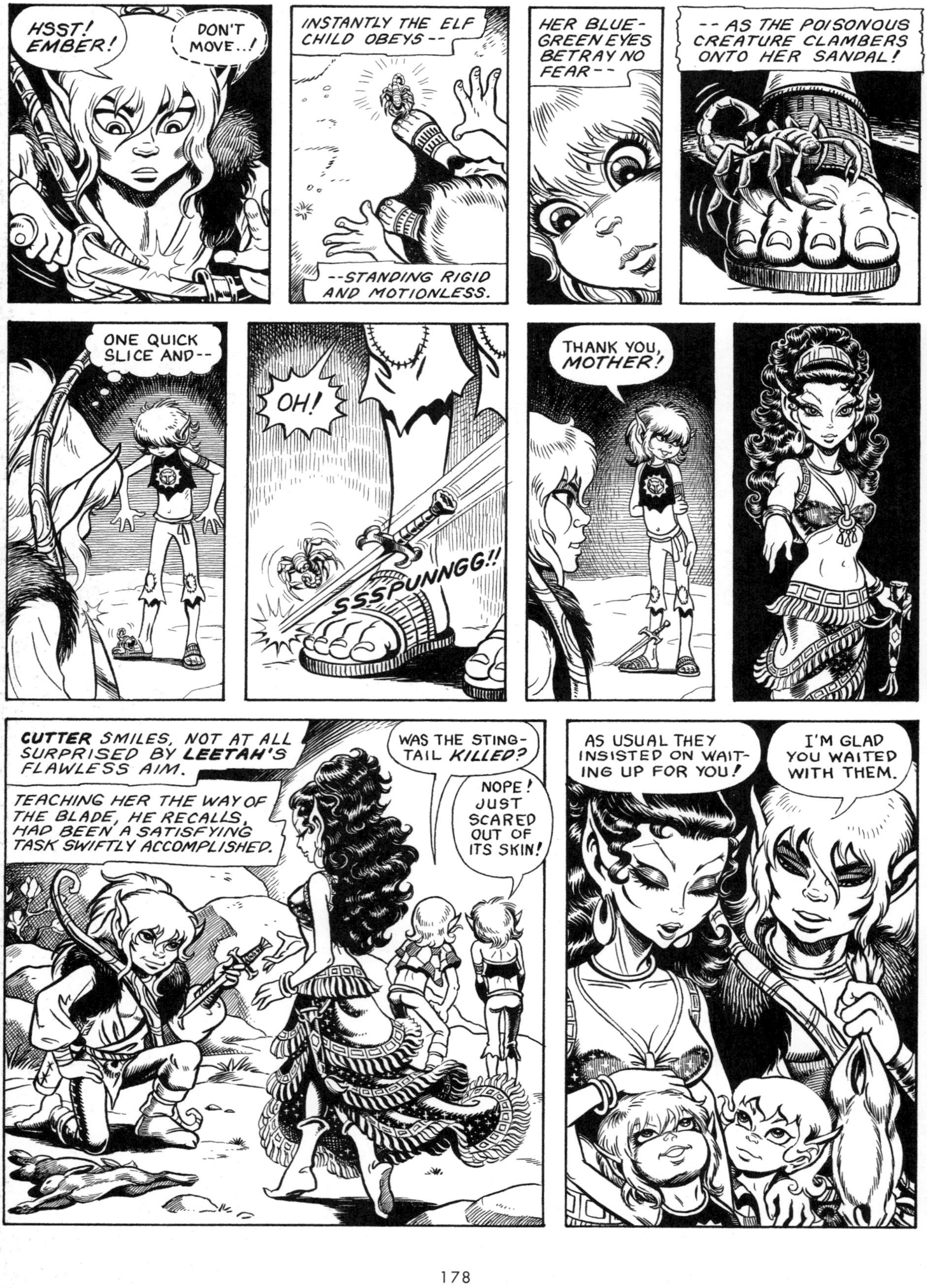
HSST! EMBER!
DON'T MOVE..!
INSTANTLY THE ELF CHILD OBEYS --
--STANDING RIGID AND MOTIONLESS.
HER BLUE-GREEN EYES BETRAY NO FEAR --
-- AS THE POISONOUS CREATURE CLAMBERS ONTO HER SANDAL!
ONE QUICK SLICE AND--
OH!
SSSPUNNGG!!
THANK YOU, MOTHER!
CUTTER SMILES, NOT AT ALL SURPRISED BY LEETAH'S FLAWLESS AIM.
TEACHING HER THE WAY OF THE BLADE, HE RECALLS, HAD BEEN A SATISFYING TASK SWIFTLY ACCOMPLISHED.
WAS THE STING-TAIL KILLED?
NOPE! JUST SCARED OUT OF ITS SKIN!
AS USUAL THEY INSISTED ON WAITING UP FOR YOU!
I'M GLAD YOU WAITED WITH THEM.

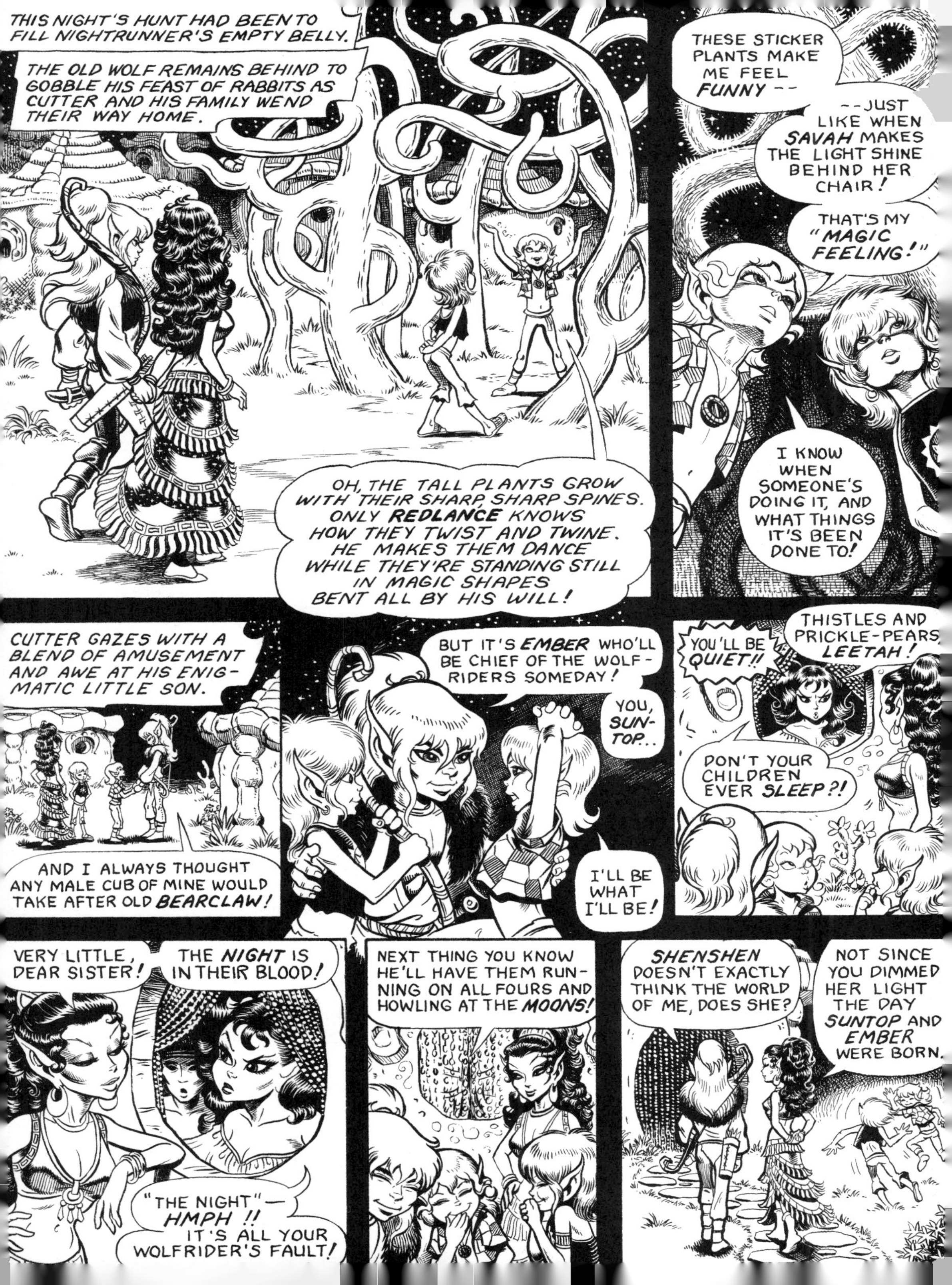
THIS NIGHT'S HUNT HAD BEEN TO FILL NIGHTRUNNER'S EMPTY BELLY.
THE OLD WOLF REMAINS BEHIND TO GOBBLE HIS FEAST OF RABBITS AS CUTTER AND HIS FAMILY WEND THEIR WAY HOME.
OH, THE TALL PLANTS GROW WITH THEIR SHARP, SHARP SPINES. ONLY REDLANCE KNOWS HOW THEY TWIST AND TWINE. HE MAKES THEM DANCE WHILE THEY'RE STANDING STILL IN MAGIC SHAPES BENT ALL BY HIS WILL!
THESE STICKER PLANTS MAKE ME FEEL FUNNY --
--JUST LIKE WHEN SAVAH MAKES THE LIGHT SHINE BEHIND HER CHAIR!
THAT'S MY "MAGIC FEELING!"
I KNOW WHEN SOMEONE'S DOING IT, AND WHAT THINGS IT'S BEEN DONE TO!
CUTTER GAZES WITH A BLEND OF AMUSEMENT AND AWE AT HIS ENIGMATIC LITTLE SON.
AND I ALWAYS THOUGHT ANY MALE CUB OF MINE WOULD TAKE AFTER OLD BEARCLAW!
BUT IT'S EMBER WHO'LL BE CHIEF OF THE WOLF-RIDERS SOMEDAY!
YOU, SUNTOP...
I'LL BE WHAT I'LL BE!
YOU'LL BE QUIET!!
THISTLES AND PRICKLE-PEARS, LEETAH!
DON'T YOUR CHILDREN EVER SLEEP?!
VERY LITTLE, DEAR SISTER!
THE NIGHT IS IN THEIR BLOOD!
"THE NIGHT"— HMPH!! IT'S ALL YOUR WOLFRIDER'S FAULT!
NEXT THING YOU KNOW HE'LL HAVE THEM RUNNING ON ALL FOURS AND HOWLING AT THE MOONS!
SHENSHEN DOESN'T EXACTLY THINK THE WORLD OF ME, DOES SHE?
NOT SINCE YOU DIMMED HER LIGHT THE DAY SUNTOP AND EMBER WERE BORN.

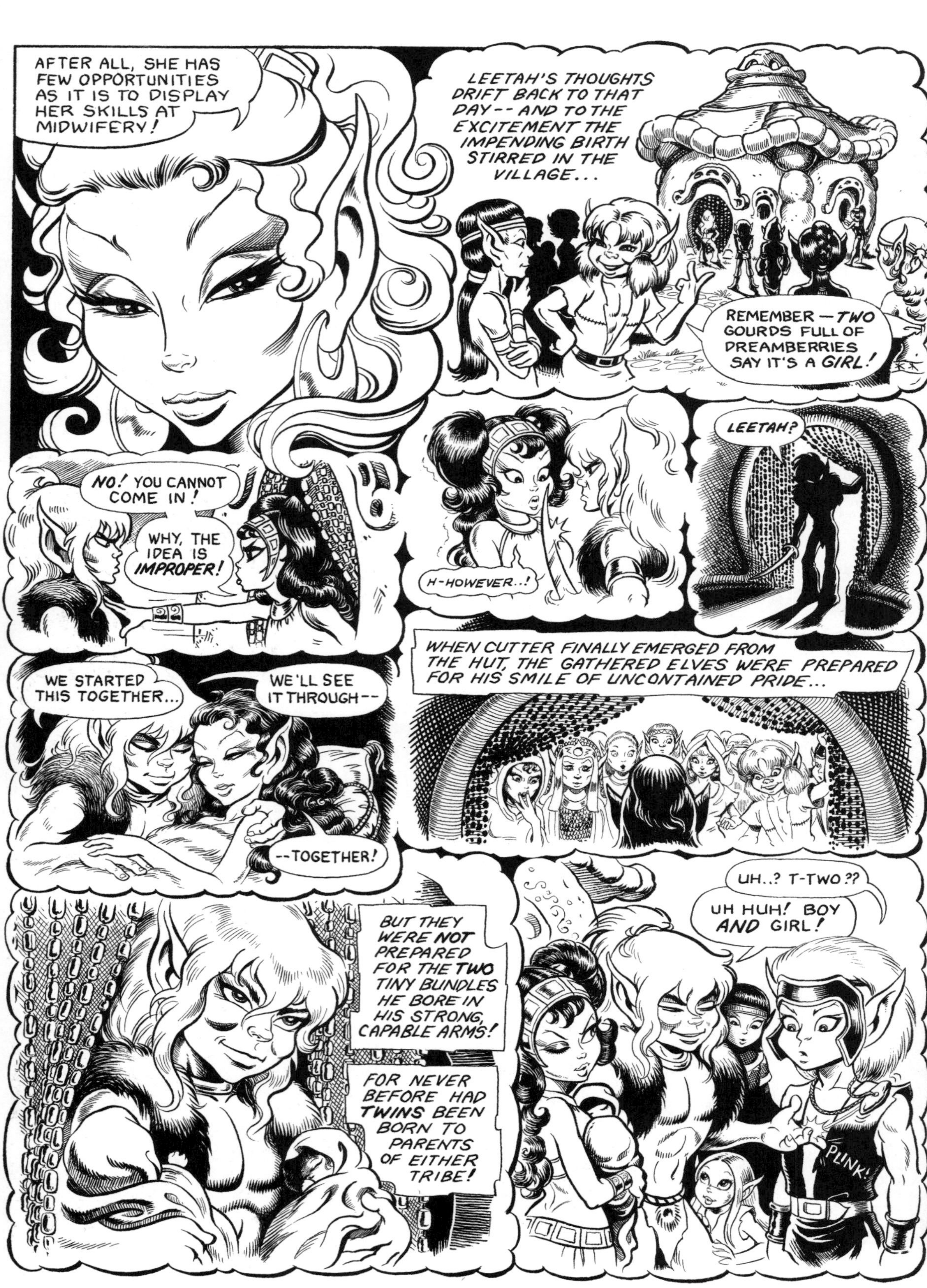

AFTER ALL, SHE HAS FEW OPPORTUNITIES AS IT IS TO DISPLAY HER SKILLS AT MIDWIFERY!
LEETAH'S THOUGHTS DRIFT BACK TO THAT DAY-- AND TO THE EXCITEMENT THE IMPENDING BIRTH STIRRED IN THE VILLAGE...
REMEMBER—TWO GOURDS FULL OF DREAMBERRIES SAY IT'S A GIRL!
NO! YOU CANNOT COME IN!
WHY, THE IDEA IS IMPROPER!
H-HOWEVER..!
LEETAH?
WE STARTED THIS TOGETHER...
WE'LL SEE IT THROUGH--
--TOGETHER!
WHEN CUTTER FINALLY EMERGED FROM THE HUT, THE GATHERED ELVES WERE PREPARED FOR HIS SMILE OF UNCONTAINED PRIDE...
BUT THEY WERE NOT PREPARED FOR THE TWO TINY BUNDLES HE BORE IN HIS STRONG, CAPABLE ARMS!
FOR NEVER BEFORE HAD TWINS BEEN BORN TO PARENTS OF EITHER TRIBE!
UH..? T-TWO??
UH HUH! BOY AND GIRL!
PLINK!

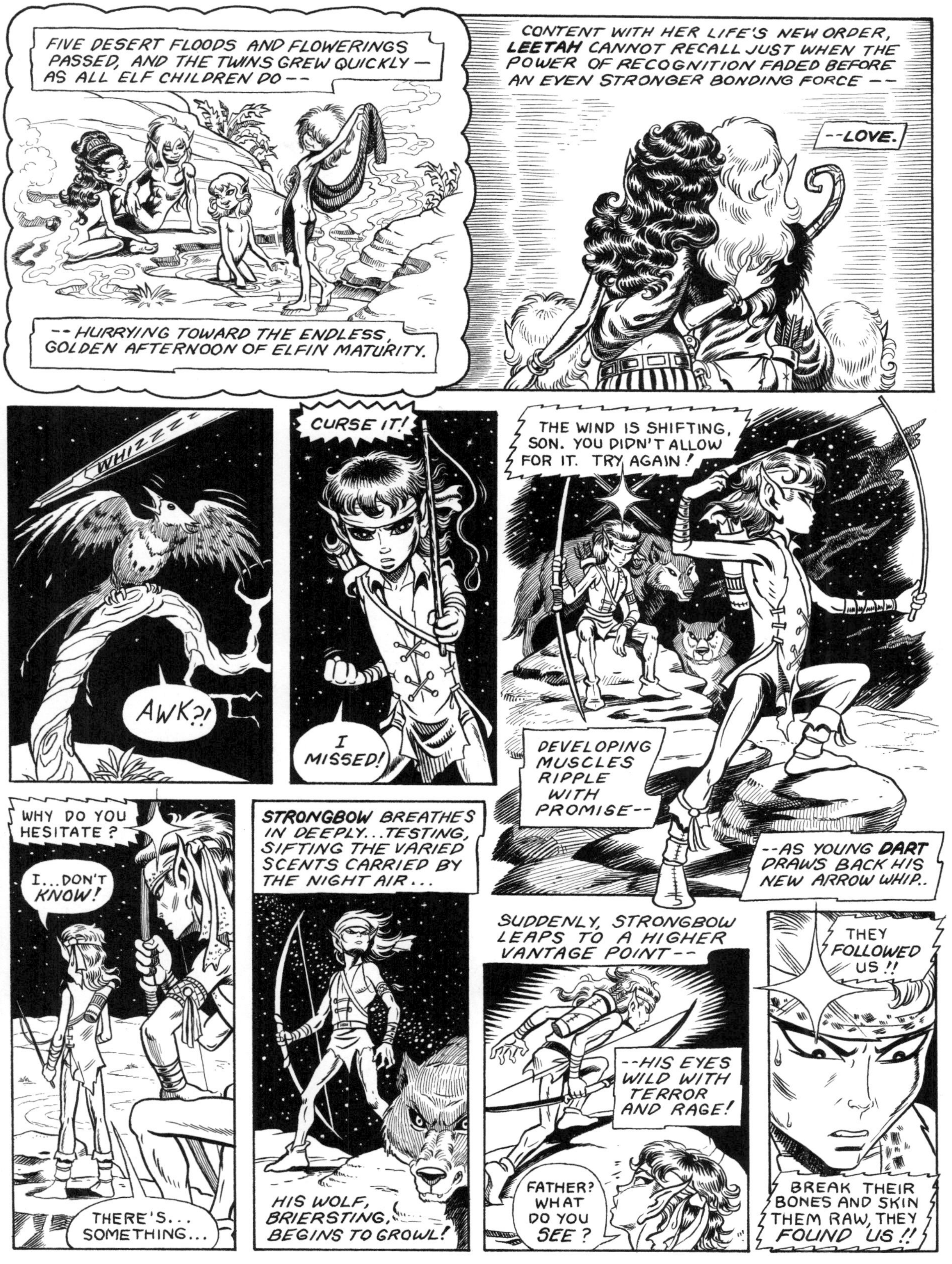

FIVE DESERT FLOODS AND FLOWERINGS PASSED, AND THE TWINS GREW QUICKLY — AS ALL ELF CHILDREN DO --
-- HURRYING TOWARD THE ENDLESS, GOLDEN AFTERNOON OF ELFIN MATURITY.
CONTENT WITH HER LIFE'S NEW ORDER, LEETAH CANNOT RECALL JUST WHEN THE POWER OF RECOGNITION FADED BEFORE AN EVEN STRONGER BONDING FORCE --
--LOVE.
WHIZZZZZ
AWK?!
CURSE IT!
I MISSED!
THE WIND IS SHIFTING, SON. YOU DIDN'T ALLOW FOR IT. TRY AGAIN!
DEVELOPING MUSCLES RIPPLE WITH PROMISE--
--AS YOUNG DART DRAWS BACK HIS NEW ARROW WHIP..
WHY DO YOU HESITATE?
I...DON'T KNOW!
THERE'S... SOMETHING...
STRONGBOW BREATHES IN DEEPLY...TESTING, SIFTING THE VARIED SCENTS CARRIED BY THE NIGHT AIR...
HIS WOLF, BRIERSTING, BEGINS TO GROWL!
SUDDENLY, STRONGBOW LEAPS TO A HIGHER VANTAGE POINT--
--HIS EYES WILD WITH TERROR AND RAGE!
FATHER? WHAT DO YOU SEE?
THEY FOLLOWED US!!
BREAK THEIR BONES AND SKIN THEM RAW, THEY FOUND US!!

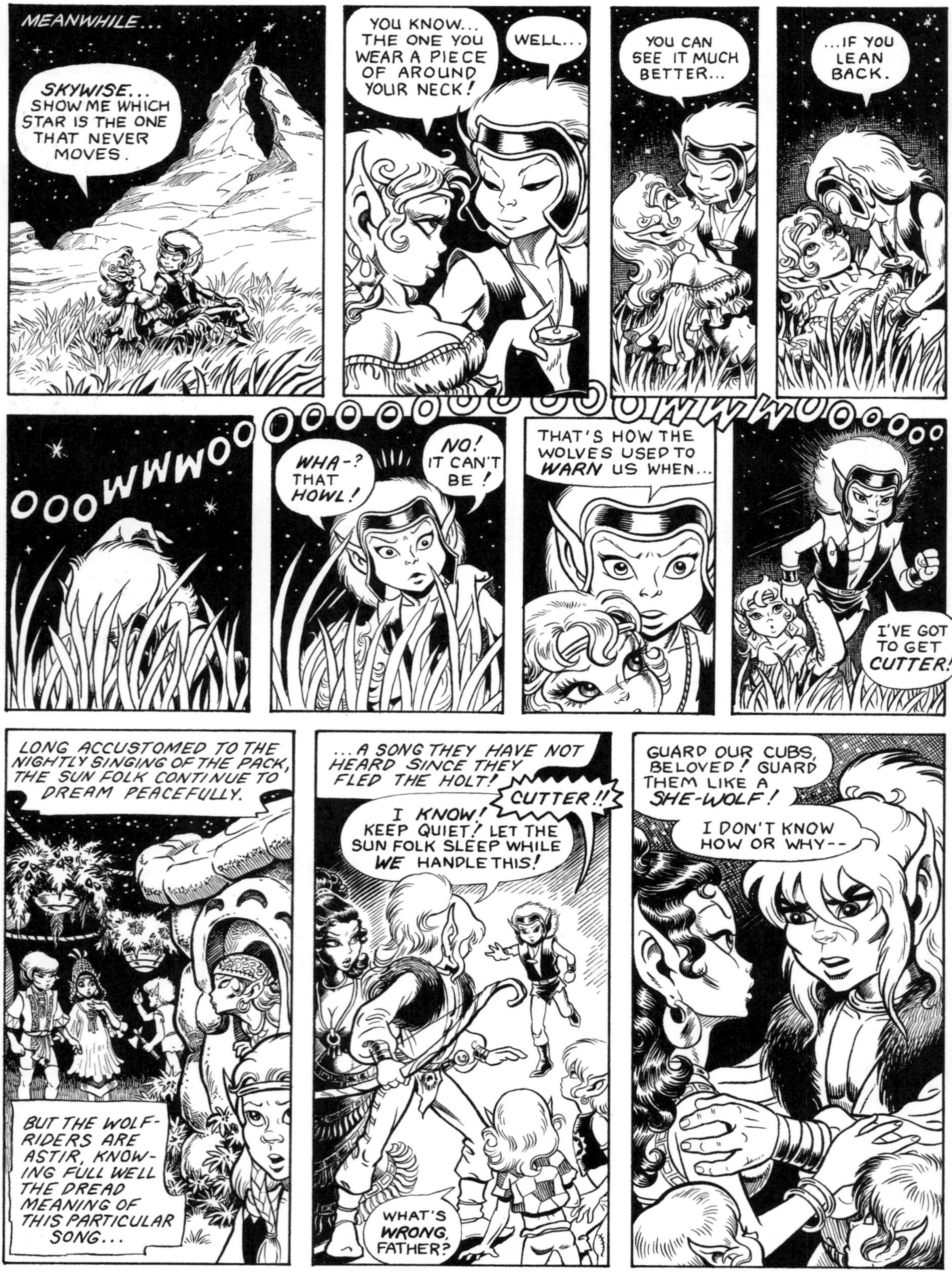
MEANWHILE...
SKYWISE... SHOW ME WHICH STAR IS THE ONE THAT NEVER MOVES.
YOU KNOW... THE ONE YOU WEAR A PIECE OF AROUND YOUR NECK!
WELL...
YOU CAN SEE IT MUCH BETTER...
...IF YOU LEAN BACK.
OOOWWWOOOOOOOOOOOOOOOWWWWOOoooo
WHA-? THAT HOWL!
NO! IT CAN'T BE!
THAT'S HOW THE WOLVES USED TO WARN US WHEN...
I'VE GOT TO GET CUTTER!
LONG ACCUSTOMED TO THE NIGHTLY SINGING OF THE PACK, THE SUN FOLK CONTINUE TO DREAM PEACEFULLY.
BUT THE WOLF-RIDERS ARE ASTIR, KNOWING FULL WELL THE DREAD MEANING OF THIS PARTICULAR SONG...
...A SONG THEY HAVE NOT HEARD SINCE THEY FLED THE HOLT!
CUTTER!!
I KNOW! KEEP QUIET! LET THE SUN FOLK SLEEP WHILE WE HANDLE THIS!
WHAT'S WRONG, FATHER?
GUARD OUR CUBS, BELOVED! GUARD THEM LIKE A SHE-WOLF!
I DON'T KNOW HOW OR WHY--

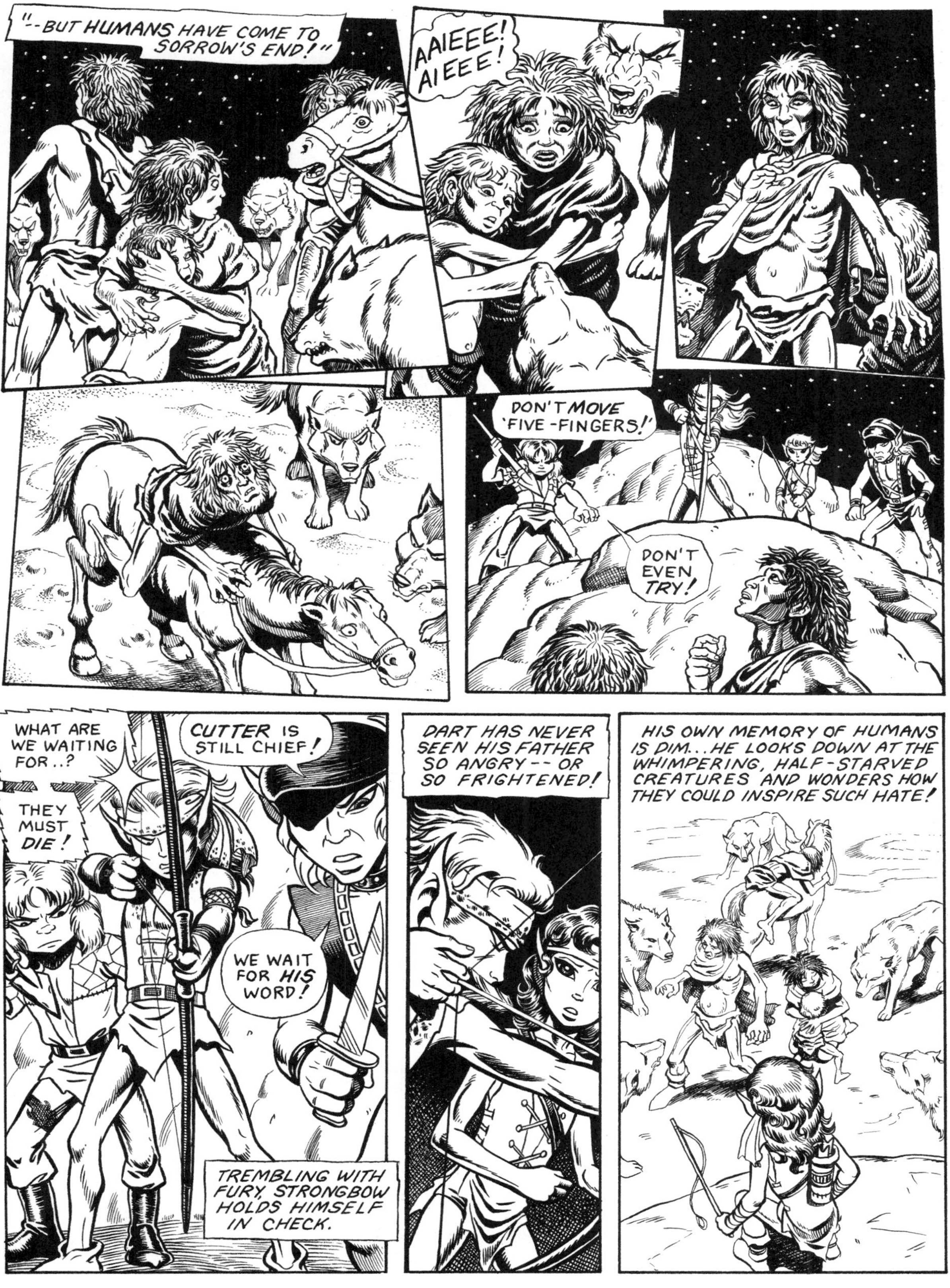
"--BUT HUMANS HAVE COME TO SORROW'S END!"
AAIEEE! AIEEE!
DON'T MOVE 'FIVE-FINGERS!'
DON'T EVEN TRY!
WHAT ARE WE WAITING FOR..?
THEY MUST DIE!
CUTTER IS STILL CHIEF!
WE WAIT FOR HIS WORD!
TREMBLING WITH FURY, STRONGBOW HOLDS HIMSELF IN CHECK.
DART HAS NEVER SEEN HIS FATHER SO ANGRY -- OR SO FRIGHTENED!
HIS OWN MEMORY OF HUMANS IS DIM... HE LOOKS DOWN AT THE WHIMPERING, HALF-STARVED CREATURES AND WONDERS HOW THEY COULD INSPIRE SUCH HATE!

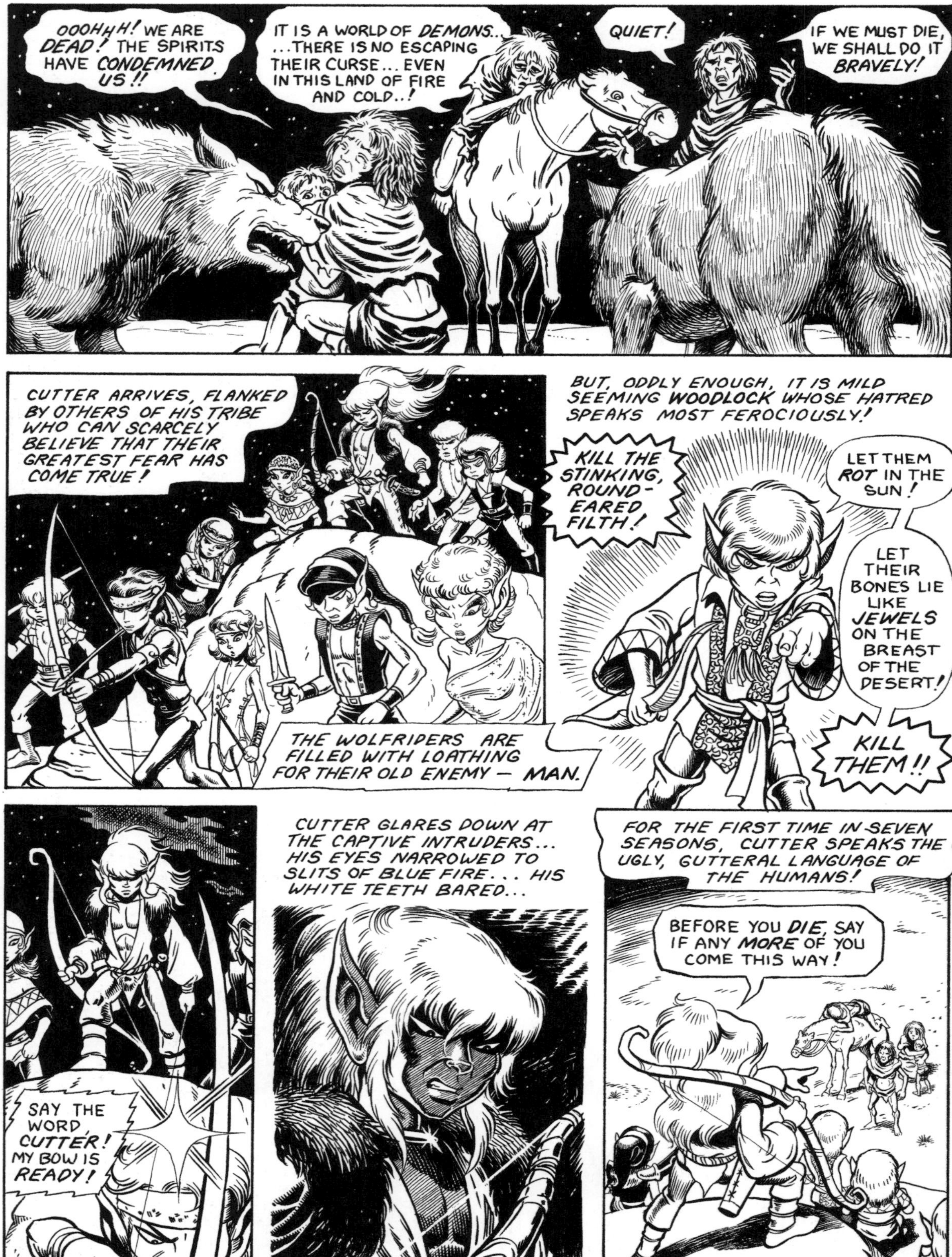
OOOHHH! WE ARE DEAD! THE SPIRITS HAVE CONDEMNED US!!
IT IS A WORLD OF DEMONS... ...THERE IS NO ESCAPING THEIR CURSE... EVEN IN THIS LAND OF FIRE AND COLD..!
QUIET!
IF WE MUST DIE, WE SHALL DO IT BRAVELY!
CUTTER ARRIVES, FLANKED BY OTHERS OF HIS TRIBE WHO CAN SCARCELY BELIEVE THAT THEIR GREATEST FEAR HAS COME TRUE!
THE WOLFRIDERS ARE FILLED WITH LOATHING FOR THEIR OLD ENEMY — MAN.
BUT, ODDLY ENOUGH, IT IS MILD SEEMING WOODLOCK WHOSE HATRED SPEAKS MOST FEROCIOUSLY!
KILL THE STINKING, ROUND-EARED FILTH!
LET THEM ROT IN THE SUN!
LET THEIR BONES LIE LIKE JEWELS ON THE BREAST OF THE DESERT!
KILL THEM!!
SAY THE WORD, CUTTER! MY BOW IS READY!
CUTTER GLARES DOWN AT THE CAPTIVE INTRUDERS... HIS EYES NARROWED TO SLITS OF BLUE FIRE... HIS WHITE TEETH BARED...
FOR THE FIRST TIME IN SEVEN SEASONS, CUTTER SPEAKS THE UGLY, GUTTERAL LANGUAGE OF THE HUMANS!
BEFORE YOU DIE, SAY IF ANY MORE OF YOU COME THIS WAY!

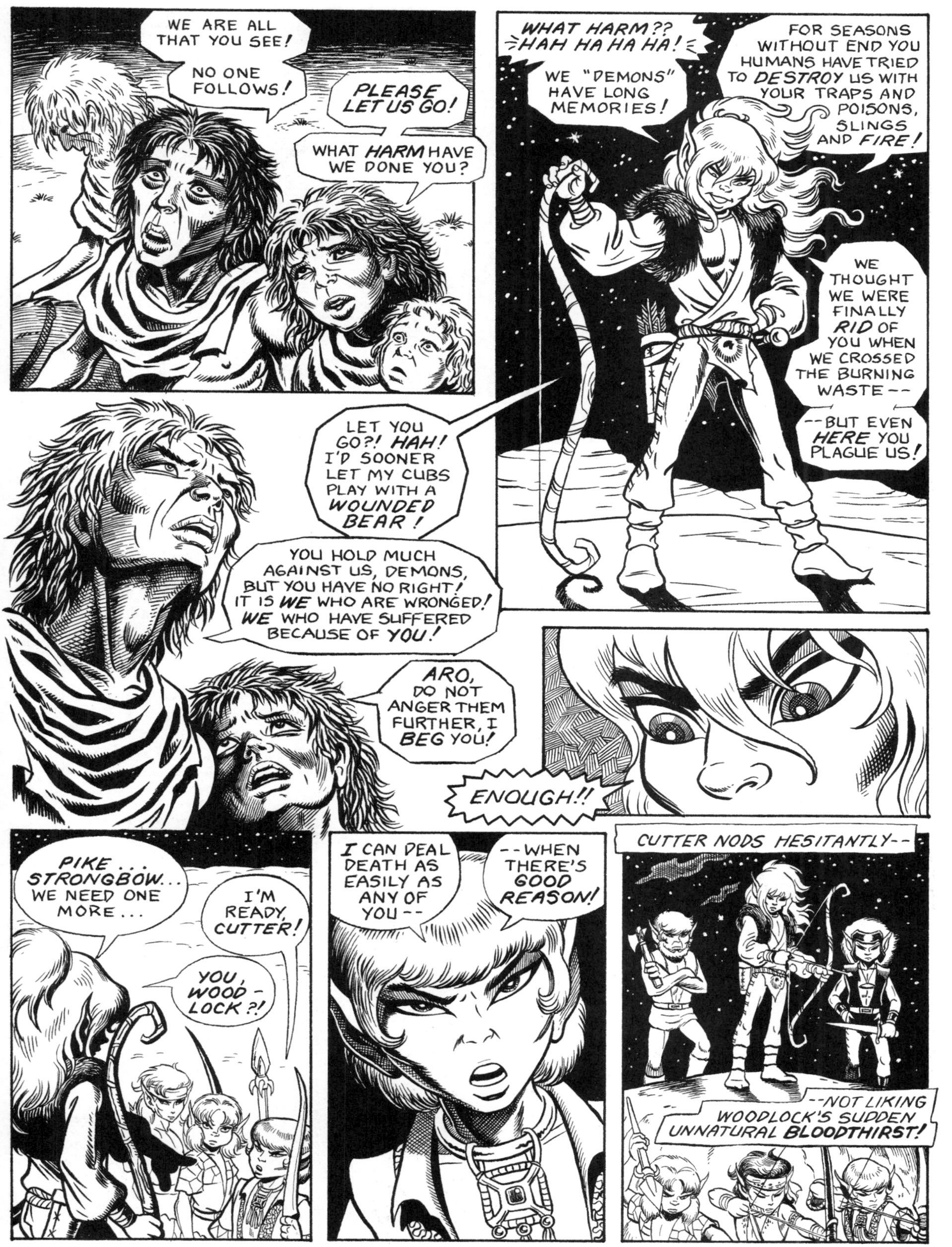

WE ARE ALL THAT YOU SEE!
NO ONE FOLLOWS!
PLEASE LET US GO!
WHAT HARM HAVE WE DONE YOU?
WHAT HARM?? HAH HA HA HA!
WE "DEMONS" HAVE LONG MEMORIES!
FOR SEASONS WITHOUT END YOU HUMANS HAVE TRIED TO DESTROY US WITH YOUR TRAPS AND POISONS, SLINGS AND FIRE!
WE THOUGHT WE WERE FINALLY RID OF YOU WHEN WE CROSSED THE BURNING WASTE--
--BUT EVEN HERE YOU PLAGUE US!
LET YOU GO?! HAH! I'D SOONER LET MY CUBS PLAY WITH A WOUNDED BEAR!
YOU HOLD MUCH AGAINST US, DEMONS, BUT YOU HAVE NO RIGHT! IT IS WE WHO ARE WRONGED! WE WHO HAVE SUFFERED BECAUSE OF YOU!
ARO, DO NOT ANGER THEM FURTHER, I BEG YOU!
ENOUGH!!
PIKE... STRONGBOW... WE NEED ONE MORE...
I'M READY, CUTTER!
YOU, WOOD-LOCK?!
I CAN DEAL DEATH AS EASILY AS ANY OF YOU--
--WHEN THERE'S GOOD REASON!
CUTTER NODS HESITANTLY--
--NOT LIKING WOODLOCK'S SUDDEN UNNATURAL BLOODTHIRST!

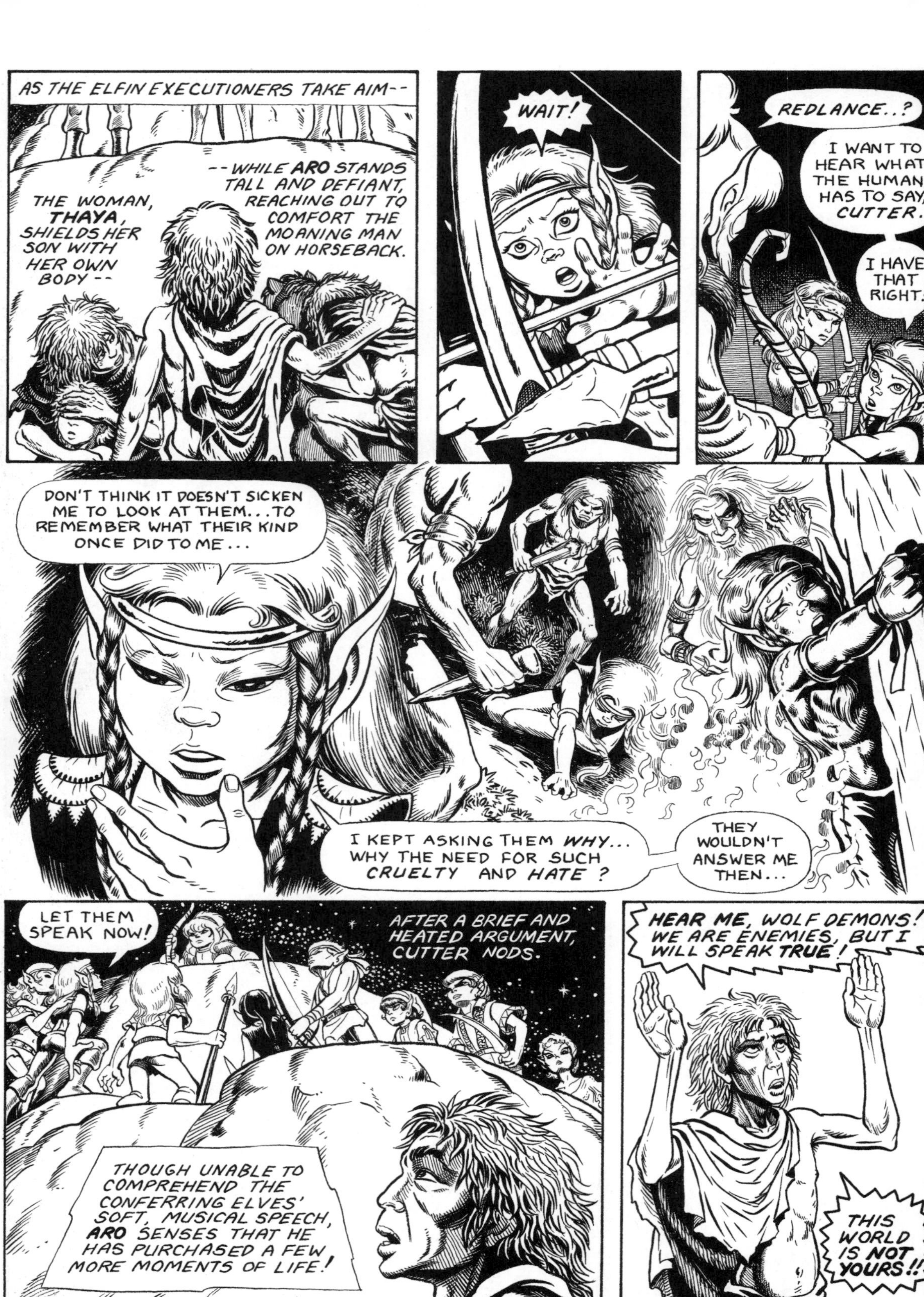

AS THE ELFIN EXECUTIONERS TAKE AIM--
THE WOMAN, THAYA, SHIELDS HER SON WITH HER OWN BODY--
--WHILE ARO STANDS TALL AND DEFIANT, REACHING OUT TO COMFORT THE MOANING MAN ON HORSEBACK.
WAIT!
REDLANCE..?
I WANT TO HEAR WHAT THE HUMAN HAS TO SAY, CUTTER.
I HAVE THAT RIGHT!
DON'T THINK IT DOESN'T SICKEN ME TO LOOK AT THEM...TO REMEMBER WHAT THEIR KIND ONCE DID TO ME...
I KEPT ASKING THEM WHY... WHY THE NEED FOR SUCH CRUELTY AND HATE?
THEY WOULDN'T ANSWER ME THEN...
LET THEM SPEAK NOW!
AFTER A BRIEF AND HEATED ARGUMENT, CUTTER NODS.
THOUGH UNABLE TO COMPREHEND THE CONFERRING ELVES' SOFT, MUSICAL SPEECH, ARO SENSES THAT HE HAS PURCHASED A FEW MORE MOMENTS OF LIFE!
HEAR ME, WOLF DEMONS! WE ARE ENEMIES, BUT I WILL SPEAK TRUE!
THIS WORLD IS NOT YOURS!!

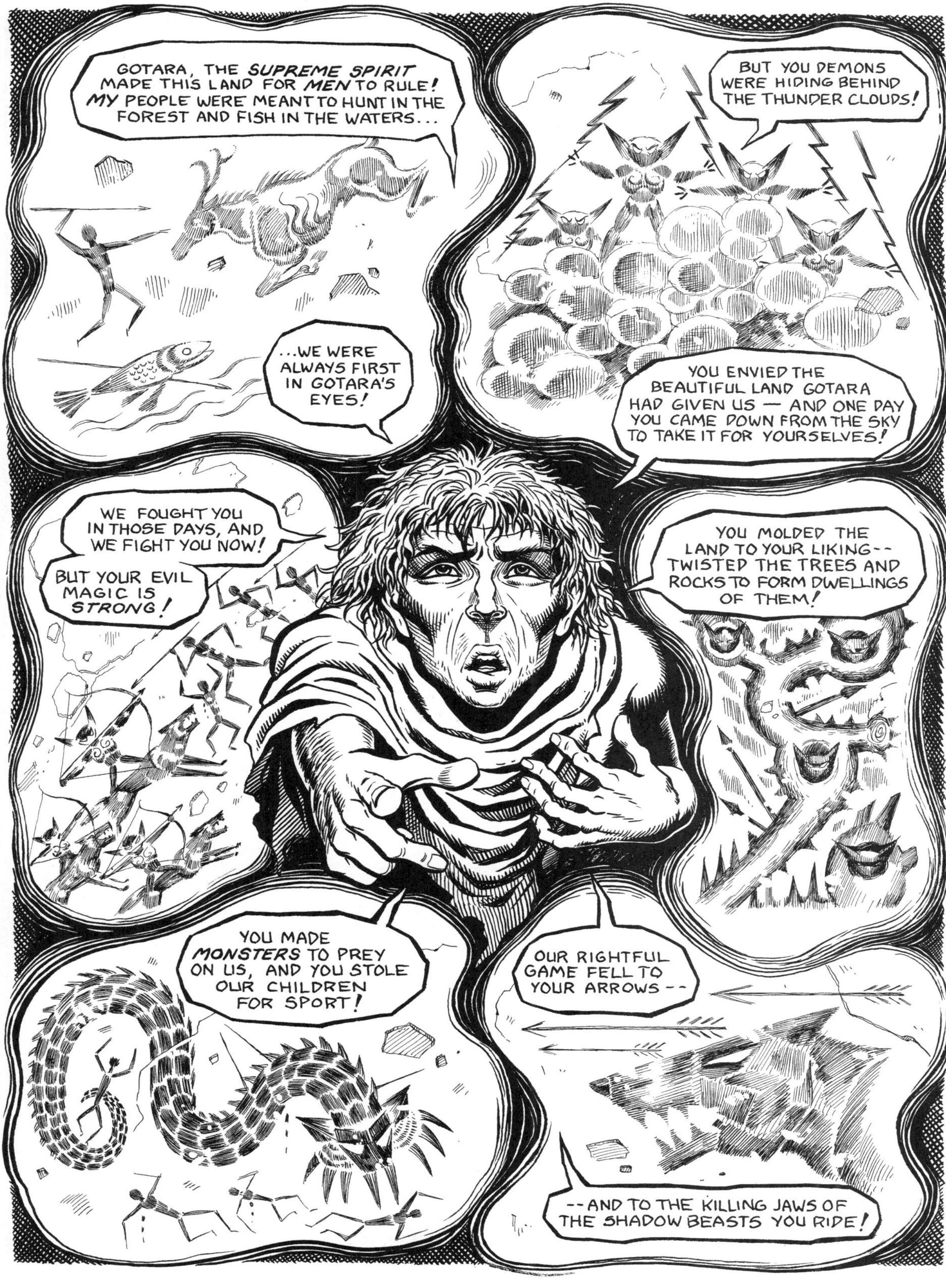
GOTARA, THE SUPREME SPIRIT MADE THIS LAND FOR MEN TO RULE! MY PEOPLE WERE MEANT TO HUNT IN THE FOREST AND FISH IN THE WATERS...
...WE WERE ALWAYS FIRST IN GOTARA'S EYES!
BUT YOU DEMONS WERE HIDING BEHIND THE THUNDER CLOUDS!
YOU ENVIED THE BEAUTIFUL LAND GOTARA HAD GIVEN US — AND ONE DAY YOU CAME DOWN FROM THE SKY TO TAKE IT FOR YOURSELVES!
WE FOUGHT YOU IN THOSE DAYS, AND WE FIGHT YOU NOW!
BUT YOUR EVIL MAGIC IS STRONG!
YOU MOLDED THE LAND TO YOUR LIKING-- TWISTED THE TREES AND ROCKS TO FORM DWELLINGS OF THEM!
YOU MADE MONSTERS TO PREY ON US, AND YOU STOLE OUR CHILDREN FOR SPORT!
OUR RIGHTFUL GAME FELL TO YOUR ARROWS --
--AND TO THE KILLING JAWS OF THE SHADOW BEASTS YOU RIDE!

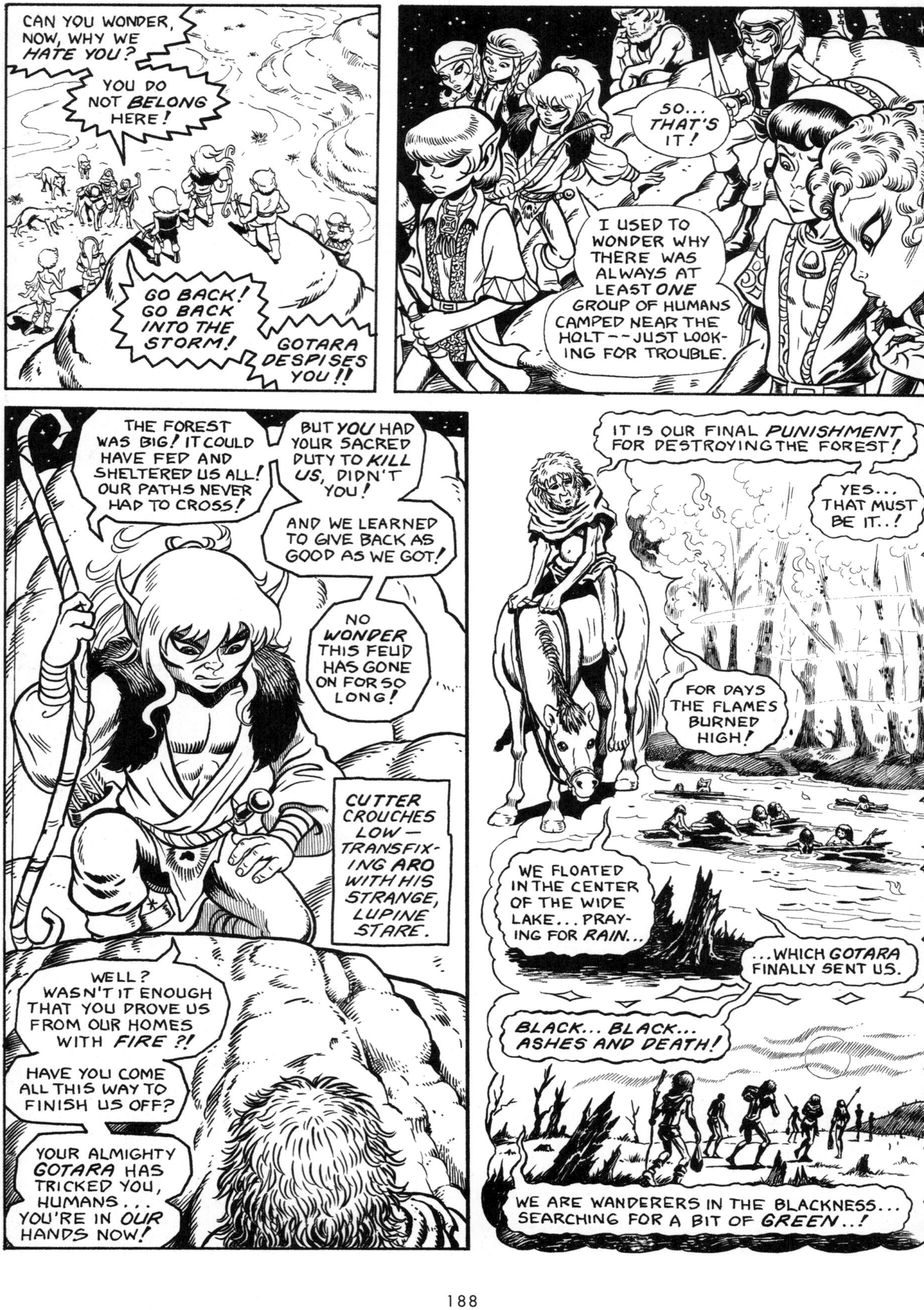
CAN YOU WONDER, NOW, WHY WE HATE YOU?
YOU DO NOT BELONG HERE!
GO BACK! GO BACK INTO THE STORM!
GOTARA DESPISES YOU!!
SO... THAT'S IT!
I USED TO WONDER WHY THERE WAS ALWAYS AT LEAST ONE GROUP OF HUMANS CAMPED NEAR THE HOLT -- JUST LOOKING FOR TROUBLE.
THE FOREST WAS BIG! IT COULD HAVE FED AND SHELTERED US ALL! OUR PATHS NEVER HAD TO CROSS!
BUT YOU HAD YOUR SACRED DUTY TO KILL US, DIDN'T YOU!
AND WE LEARNED TO GIVE BACK AS GOOD AS WE GOT!
NO WONDER THIS FEUD HAS GONE ON FOR SO LONG!
CUTTER CROUCHES LOW — TRANSFIXING ARO WITH HIS STRANGE, LUPINE STARE.
WELL? WASN'T IT ENOUGH THAT YOU DROVE US FROM OUR HOMES WITH FIRE?!
HAVE YOU COME ALL THIS WAY TO FINISH US OFF?
YOUR ALMIGHTY GOTARA HAS TRICKED YOU, HUMANS... YOU'RE IN OUR HANDS NOW!
IT IS OUR FINAL PUNISHMENT FOR DESTROYING THE FOREST!
YES... THAT MUST BE IT..!
FOR DAYS THE FLAMES BURNED HIGH!
WE FLOATED IN THE CENTER OF THE WIDE LAKE... PRAYING FOR RAIN...
...WHICH GOTARA FINALLY SENT US.
BLACK... BLACK... ASHES AND DEATH!
WE ARE WANDERERS IN THE BLACKNESS... SEARCHING FOR A BIT OF GREEN..!

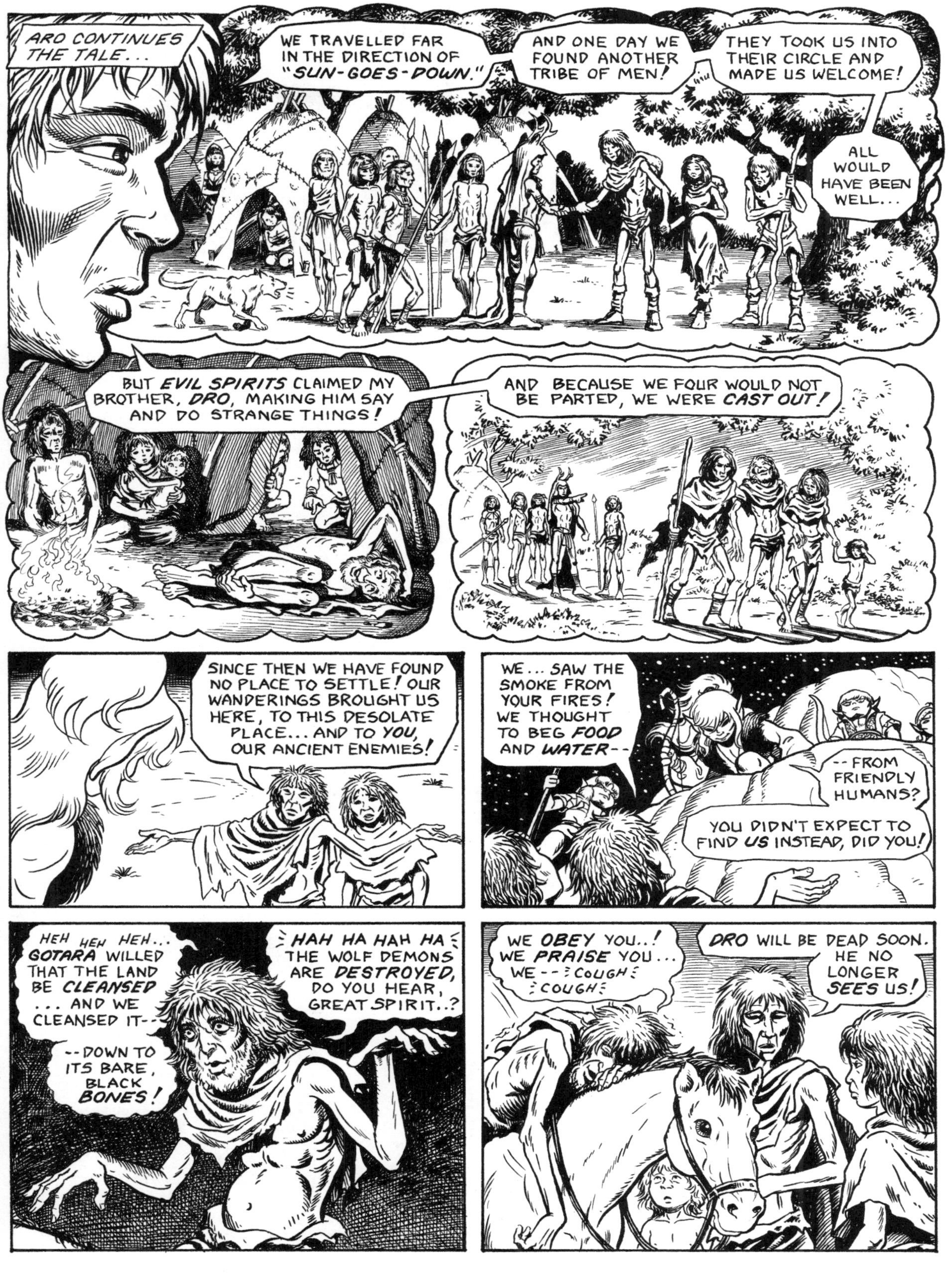

ARO CONTINUES THE TALE...
WE TRAVELLED FAR IN THE DIRECTION OF "SUN-GOES-DOWN."
AND ONE DAY WE FOUND ANOTHER TRIBE OF MEN!
THEY TOOK US INTO THEIR CIRCLE AND MADE US WELCOME!
ALL WOULD HAVE BEEN WELL...
BUT EVIL SPIRITS CLAIMED MY BROTHER, DRO, MAKING HIM SAY AND DO STRANGE THINGS!
AND BECAUSE WE FOUR WOULD NOT BE PARTED, WE WERE CAST OUT!
SINCE THEN WE HAVE FOUND NO PLACE TO SETTLE! OUR WANDERINGS BROUGHT US HERE, TO THIS DESOLATE PLACE... AND TO YOU, OUR ANCIENT ENEMIES!
WE... SAW THE SMOKE FROM YOUR FIRES! WE THOUGHT TO BEG FOOD AND WATER--
--FROM FRIENDLY HUMANS?
YOU DIDN'T EXPECT TO FIND US INSTEAD, DID YOU!
HEH HEH HEH... GOTARA WILLED THAT THE LAND BE CLEANSED ... AND WE CLEANSED IT--
--DOWN TO ITS BARE, BLACK BONES!
HAH HA HAH HA THE WOLF DEMONS ARE DESTROYED, DO YOU HEAR, GREAT SPIRIT..?
WE OBEY YOU..! WE PRAISE YOU... WE-- COUGH COUGH
DRO WILL BE DEAD SOON. HE NO LONGER SEES US!

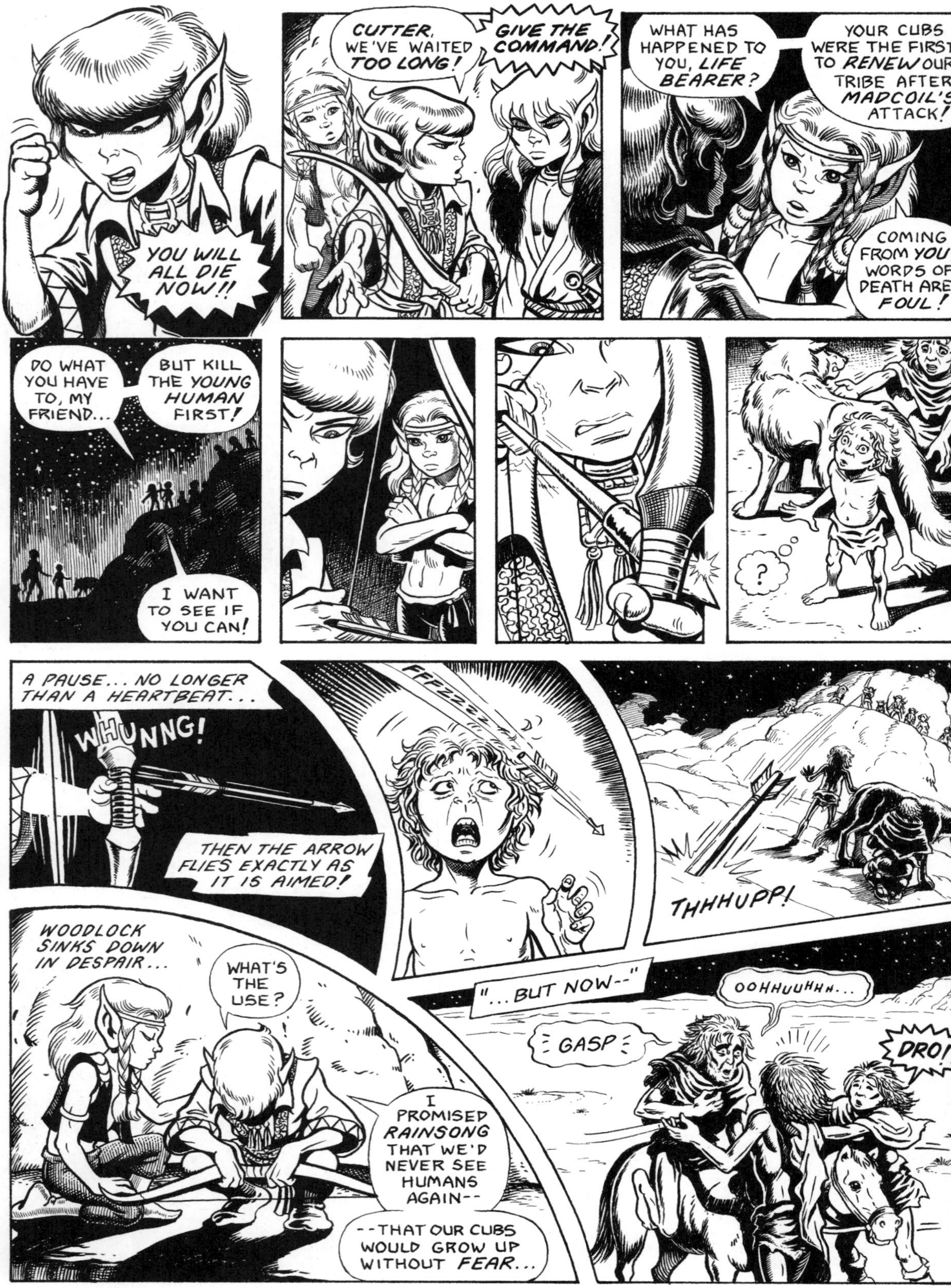
YOU WILL ALL DIE NOW!!
CUTTER, WE'VE WAITED TOO LONG!
GIVE THE COMMAND!
WHAT HAS HAPPENED TO YOU, LIFE BEARER?
YOUR CUBS WERE THE FIRST TO RENEW OUR TRIBE AFTER MADCOIL'S ATTACK!
COMING FROM YOU, WORDS OF DEATH ARE FOUL!
DO WHAT YOU HAVE TO, MY FRIEND...
BUT KILL THE YOUNG HUMAN FIRST!
I WANT TO SEE IF YOU CAN!
?
A PAUSE... NO LONGER THAN A HEARTBEAT...
WHUNNG!
THEN THE ARROW FLIES EXACTLY AS IT IS AIMED!
FFFZZZZ
THHHUPP!
WOODLOCK SINKS DOWN IN DESPAIR...
WHAT'S THE USE?
I PROMISED RAINSONG THAT WE'D NEVER SEE HUMANS AGAIN--
--THAT OUR CUBS WOULD GROW UP WITHOUT FEAR...
"...BUT NOW--"
OOHHUUHHH...
GASP
DRO!

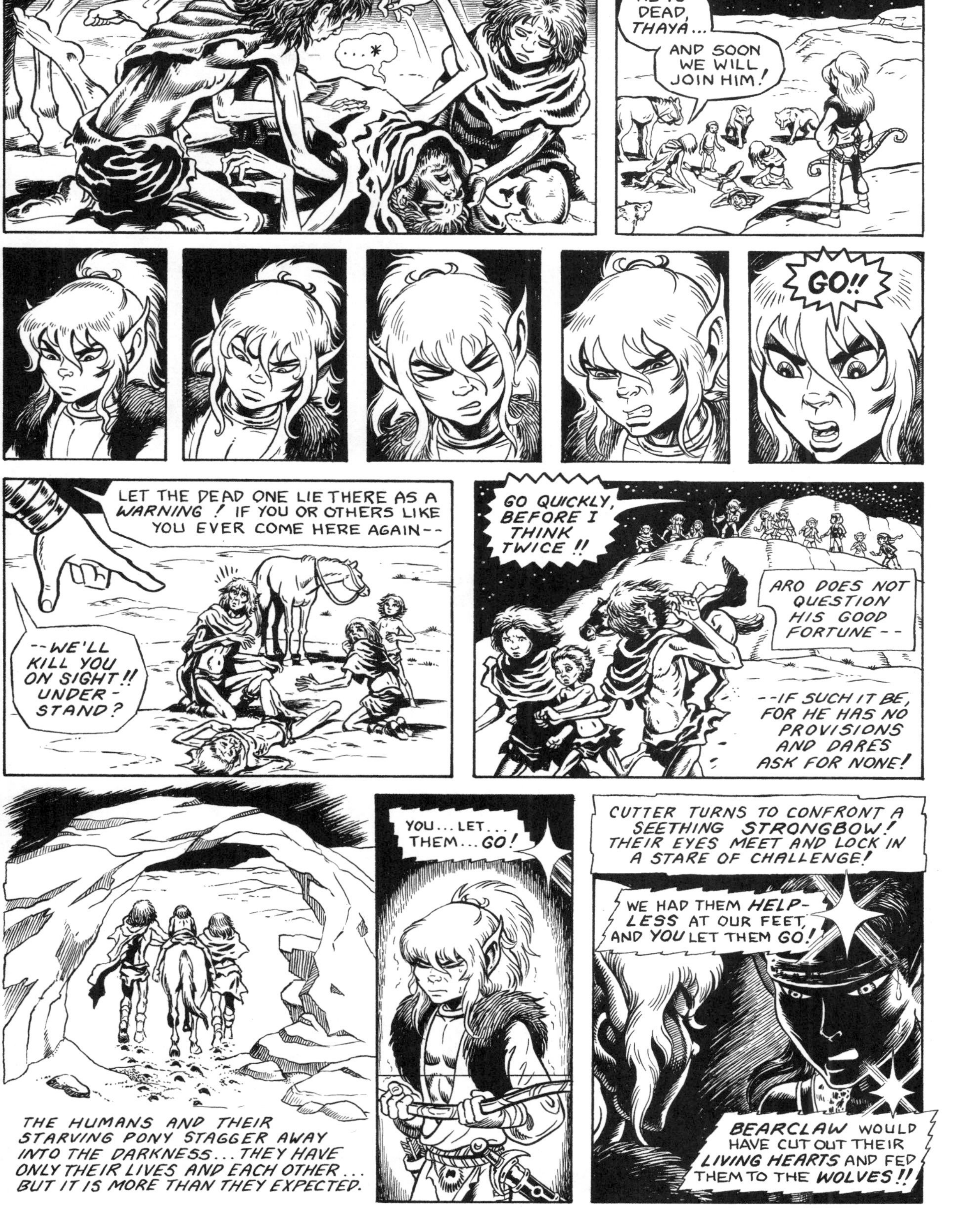

. . . *
HE IS DEAD, THAYA...
AND SOON WE WILL JOIN HIM!
GO!!
LET THE DEAD ONE LIE THERE AS A WARNING! IF YOU OR OTHERS LIKE YOU EVER COME HERE AGAIN--
--WE'LL KILL YOU ON SIGHT!! UNDER-STAND?
GO QUICKLY, BEFORE I THINK TWICE!!
ARO DOES NOT QUESTION HIS GOOD FORTUNE--
--IF SUCH IT BE, FOR HE HAS NO PROVISIONS AND DARES ASK FOR NONE!
THE HUMANS AND THEIR STARVING PONY STAGGER AWAY INTO THE DARKNESS... THEY HAVE ONLY THEIR LIVES AND EACH OTHER... BUT IT IS MORE THAN THEY EXPECTED.
YOU... LET... THEM... GO!
CUTTER TURNS TO CONFRONT A SEETHING STRONGBOW! THEIR EYES MEET AND LOCK IN A STARE OF CHALLENGE!
WE HAD THEM HELP-LESS AT OUR FEET, AND YOU LET THEM GO!
BEARCLAW WOULD HAVE CUT OUT THEIR LIVING HEARTS AND FED THEM TO THE WOLVES!!

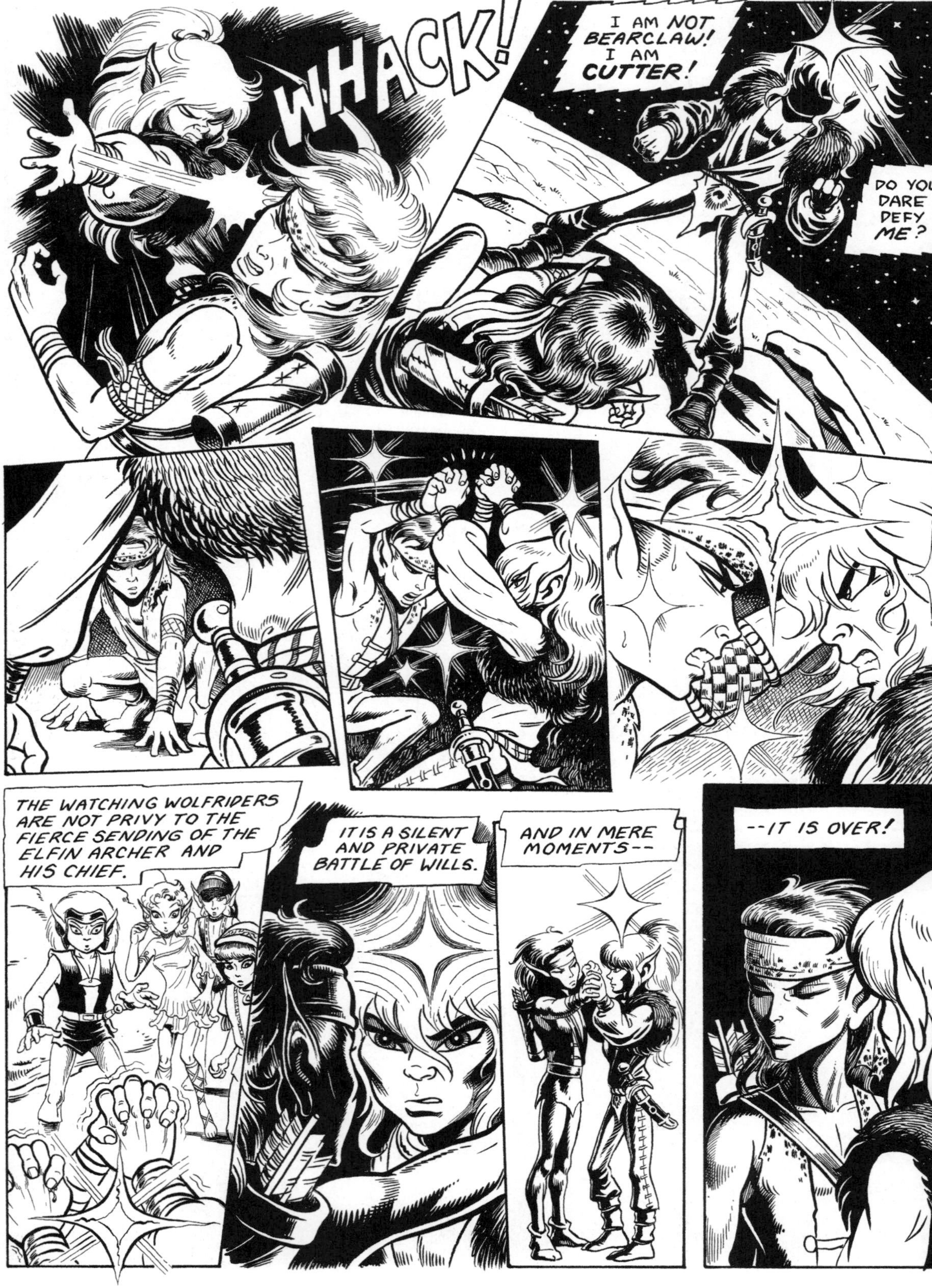
WHACK!
I AM NOT BEARCLAW! I AM CUTTER!
DO YOU DARE DEFY ME?
THE WATCHING WOLFRIDERS ARE NOT PRIVY TO THE FIERCE SENDING OF THE ELFIN ARCHER AND HIS CHIEF.
IT IS A SILENT AND PRIVATE BATTLE OF WILLS.
AND IN MERE MOMENTS--
--IT IS OVER!

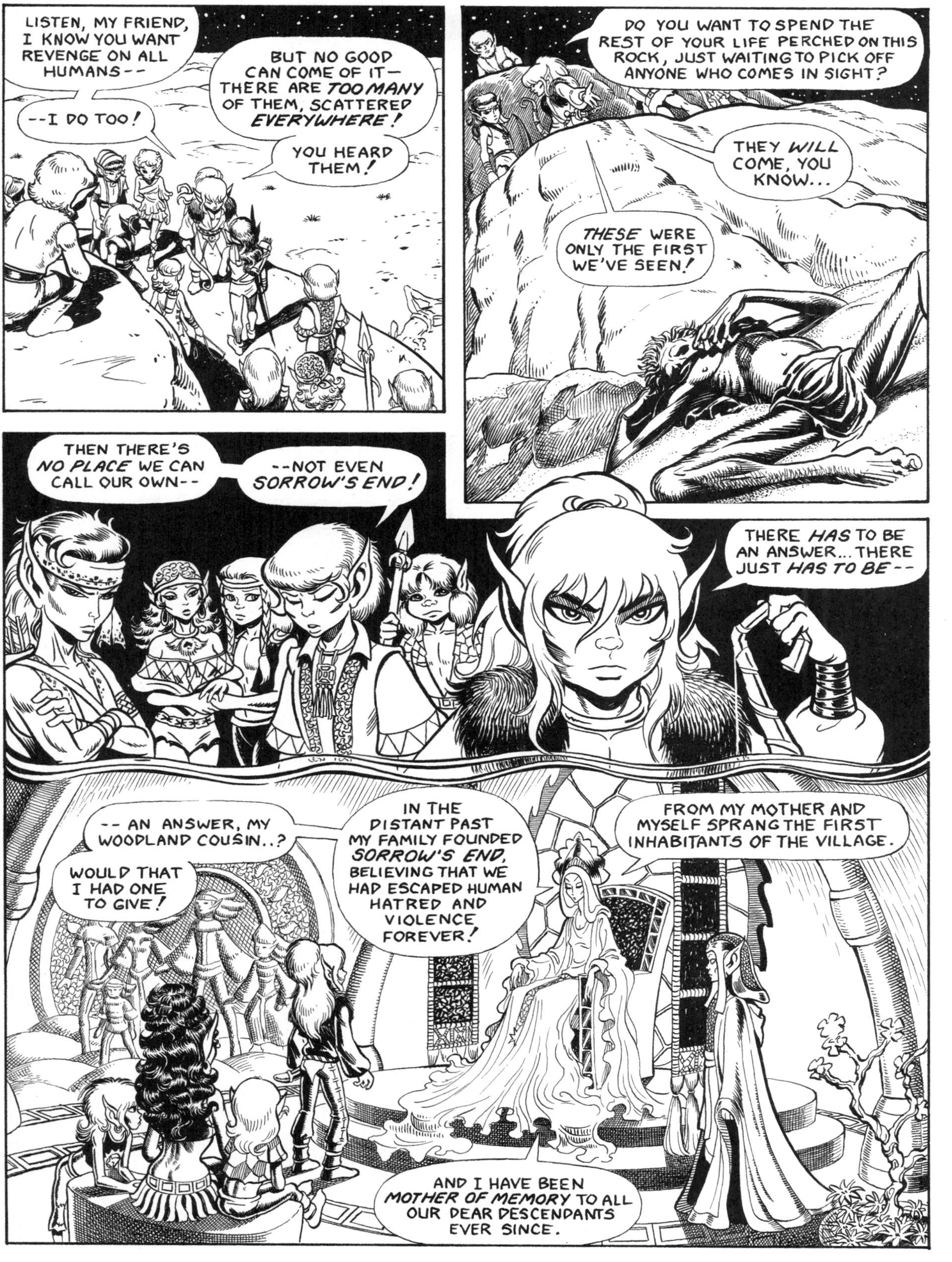
LISTEN, MY FRIEND, I KNOW YOU WANT REVENGE ON ALL HUMANS--
--I DO TOO!
BUT NO GOOD CAN COME OF IT— THERE ARE *TOO MANY* OF THEM, SCATTERED *EVERYWHERE!*
YOU HEARD THEM!
DO YOU WANT TO SPEND THE REST OF YOUR LIFE PERCHED ON THIS ROCK, JUST WAITING TO PICK OFF ANYONE WHO COMES IN SIGHT?
THEY *WILL* COME, YOU KNOW...
THESE WERE ONLY THE FIRST WE'VE SEEN!
THEN THERE'S *NO PLACE* WE CAN CALL OUR OWN--
--NOT EVEN *SORROW'S END!*
THERE *HAS* TO BE AN ANSWER... THERE JUST *HAS TO BE*--
-- AN ANSWER, MY WOODLAND COUSIN..?
WOULD THAT I HAD ONE TO GIVE!
IN THE DISTANT PAST MY FAMILY FOUNDED *SORROW'S END,* BELIEVING THAT WE HAD ESCAPED HUMAN HATRED AND VIOLENCE FOREVER!
FROM MY MOTHER AND MYSELF SPRANG THE FIRST INHABITANTS OF THE VILLAGE.
AND I HAVE BEEN *MOTHER OF MEMORY* TO ALL OUR DEAR DESCENDANTS EVER SINCE.

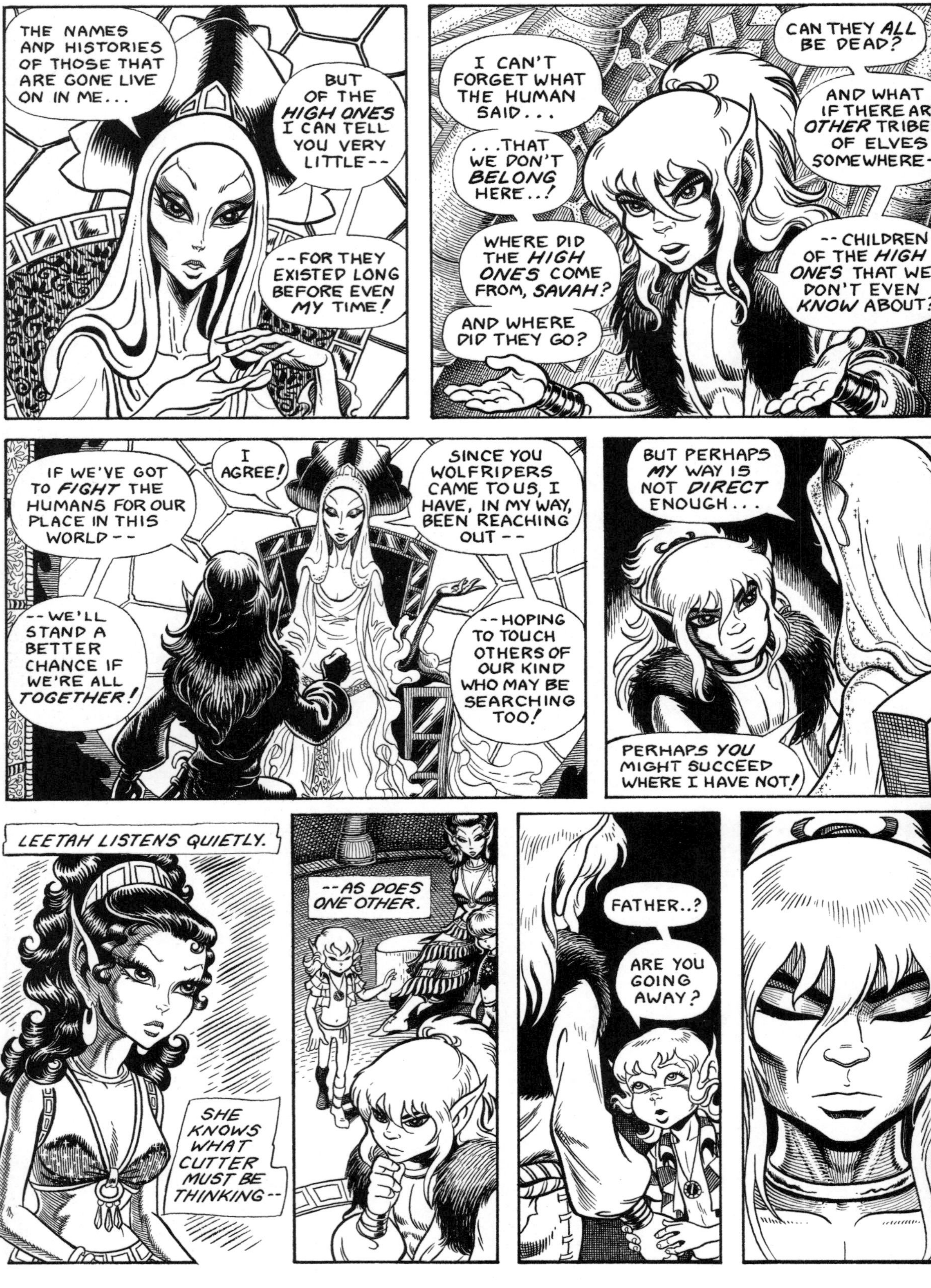
THE NAMES AND HISTORIES OF THOSE THAT ARE GONE LIVE ON IN ME...
BUT OF THE HIGH ONES I CAN TELL YOU VERY LITTLE--
--FOR THEY EXISTED LONG BEFORE EVEN MY TIME!
I CAN'T FORGET WHAT THE HUMAN SAID...
...THAT WE DON'T BELONG HERE..!
WHERE DID THE HIGH ONES COME FROM, SAVAH?
AND WHERE DID THEY GO?
CAN THEY ALL BE DEAD?
AND WHAT IF THERE ARE OTHER TRIBES OF ELVES SOMEWHERE--
--CHILDREN OF THE HIGH ONES THAT WE DON'T EVEN KNOW ABOUT?
IF WE'VE GOT TO FIGHT THE HUMANS FOR OUR PLACE IN THIS WORLD--
--WE'LL STAND A BETTER CHANCE IF WE'RE ALL TOGETHER!
I AGREE!
SINCE YOU WOLFRIDERS CAME TO US, I HAVE, IN MY WAY, BEEN REACHING OUT--
--HOPING TO TOUCH OTHERS OF OUR KIND WHO MAY BE SEARCHING TOO!
BUT PERHAPS MY WAY IS NOT DIRECT ENOUGH...
PERHAPS YOU MIGHT SUCCEED WHERE I HAVE NOT!
LEETAH LISTENS QUIETLY.
SHE KNOWS WHAT CUTTER MUST BE THINKING--
--AS DOES ONE OTHER.
FATHER..?
ARE YOU GOING AWAY?

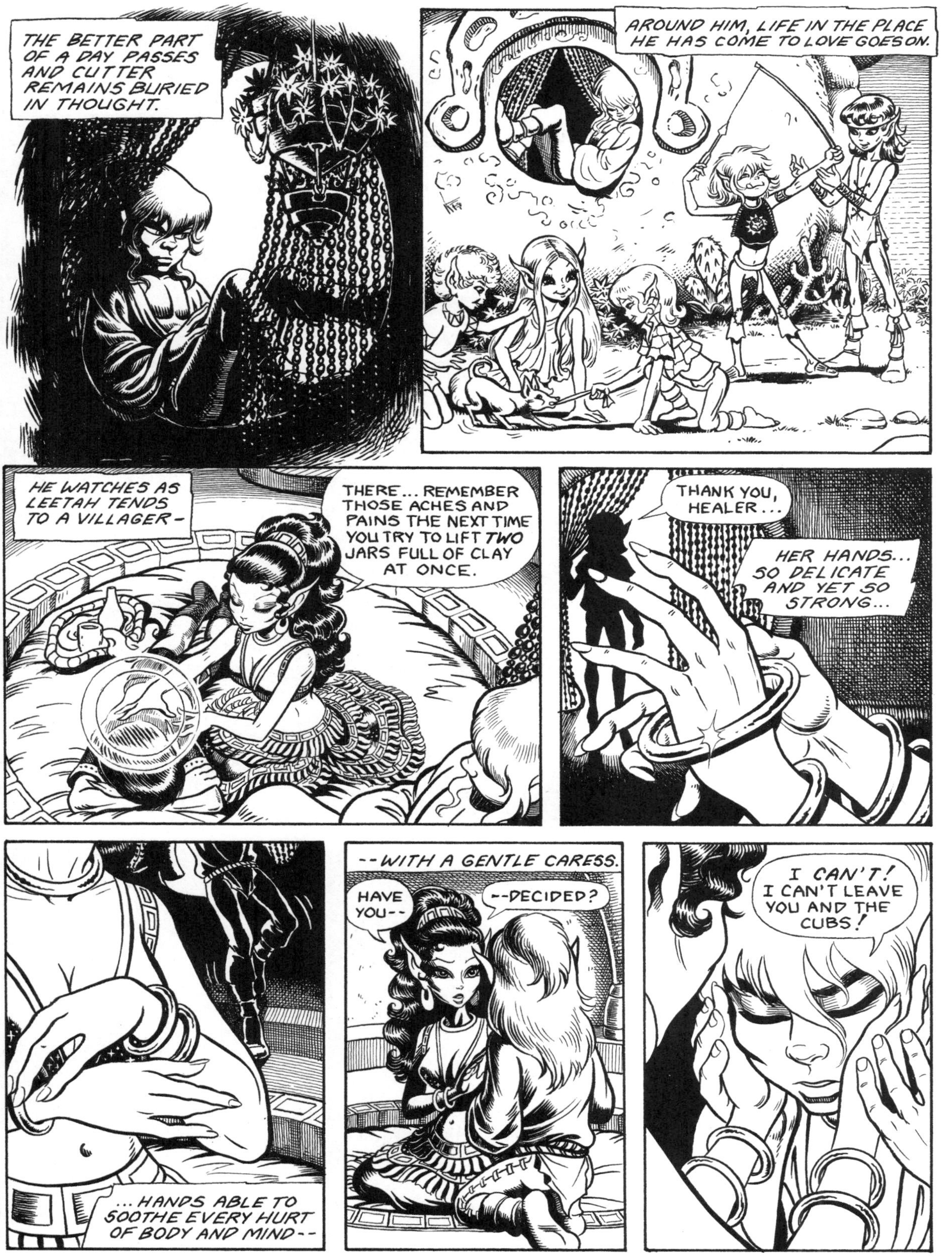
THE BETTER PART OF A DAY PASSES AND CUTTER REMAINS BURIED IN THOUGHT.
AROUND HIM, LIFE IN THE PLACE HE HAS COME TO LOVE GOES ON.
HE WATCHES AS LEETAH TENDS TO A VILLAGER--
THERE... REMEMBER THOSE ACHES AND PAINS THE NEXT TIME YOU TRY TO LIFT TWO JARS FULL OF CLAY AT ONCE.
THANK YOU, HEALER...
HER HANDS... SO DELICATE AND YET SO STRONG...
...HANDS ABLE TO SOOTHE EVERY HURT OF BODY AND MIND--
--WITH A GENTLE CARESS.
HAVE YOU--
--DECIDED?
I CAN'T! I CAN'T LEAVE YOU AND THE CUBS!

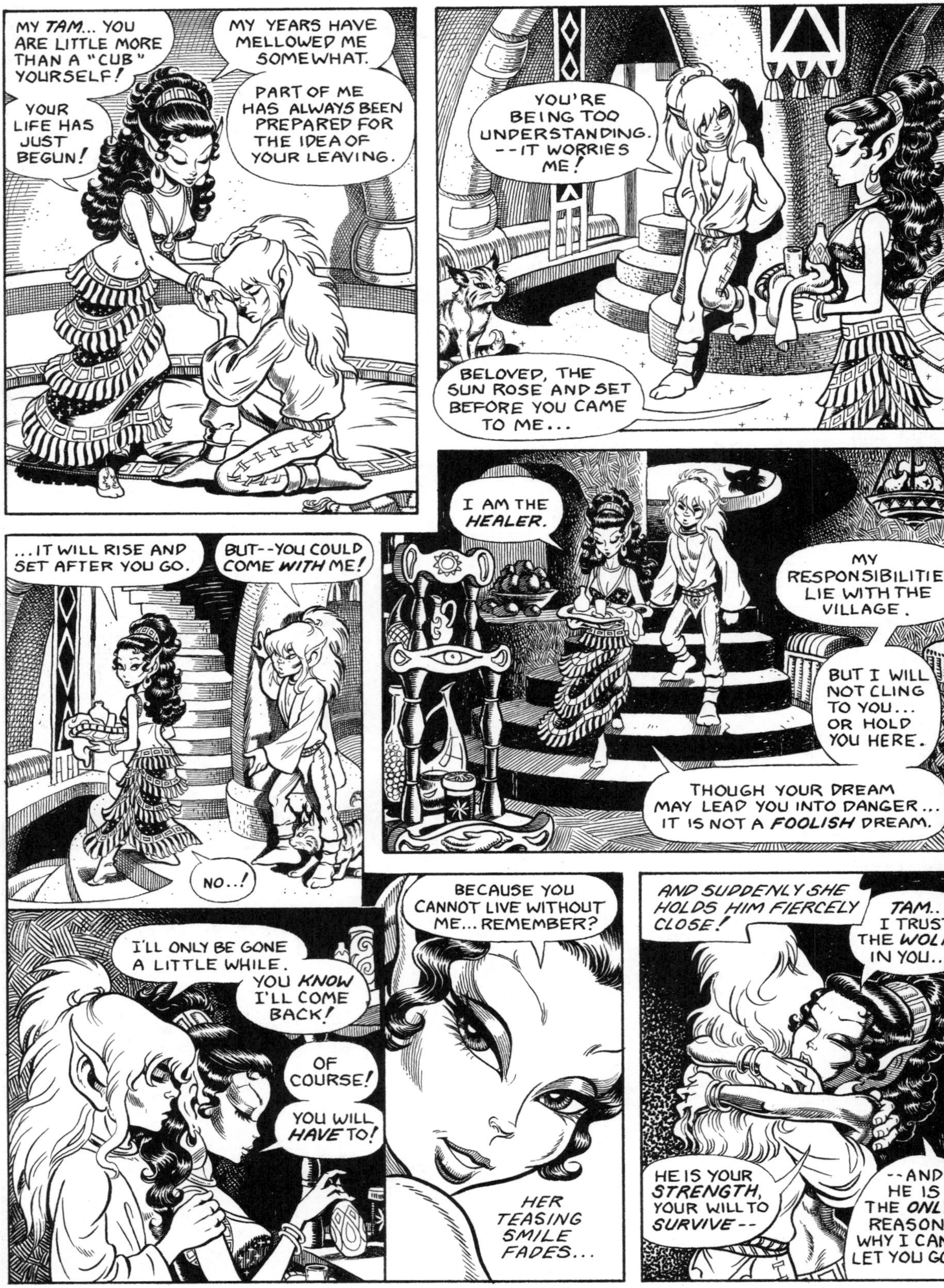
MY *TAM*... YOU ARE LITTLE MORE THAN A "CUB" YOURSELF!
YOUR LIFE HAS JUST BEGUN!
MY YEARS HAVE MELLOWED ME SOMEWHAT.
PART OF ME HAS ALWAYS BEEN PREPARED FOR THE IDEA OF YOUR LEAVING.
YOU'RE BEING TOO UNDERSTANDING. --IT WORRIES ME!
BELOVED, THE SUN ROSE AND SET BEFORE YOU CAME TO ME...
...IT WILL RISE AND SET AFTER YOU GO.
BUT--YOU COULD COME *WITH* ME!
NO..!
I AM THE *HEALER*.
MY RESPONSIBILITIES LIE WITH THE VILLAGE.
BUT I WILL NOT CLING TO YOU... OR HOLD YOU HERE.
THOUGH YOUR DREAM MAY LEAD YOU INTO DANGER... IT IS NOT A *FOOLISH* DREAM.
I'LL ONLY BE GONE A LITTLE WHILE.
YOU *KNOW* I'LL COME BACK!
OF COURSE!
YOU WILL *HAVE* TO!
BECAUSE YOU CANNOT LIVE WITHOUT ME... REMEMBER?
HER TEASING SMILE FADES...
AND SUDDENLY SHE HOLDS HIM FIERCELY CLOSE!
TAM... I TRUST THE *WOLF* IN YOU..!
HE IS YOUR *STRENGTH*, YOUR WILL TO *SURVIVE*--
--AND HE IS THE *ONLY* REASON WHY I CAN LET YOU GO!

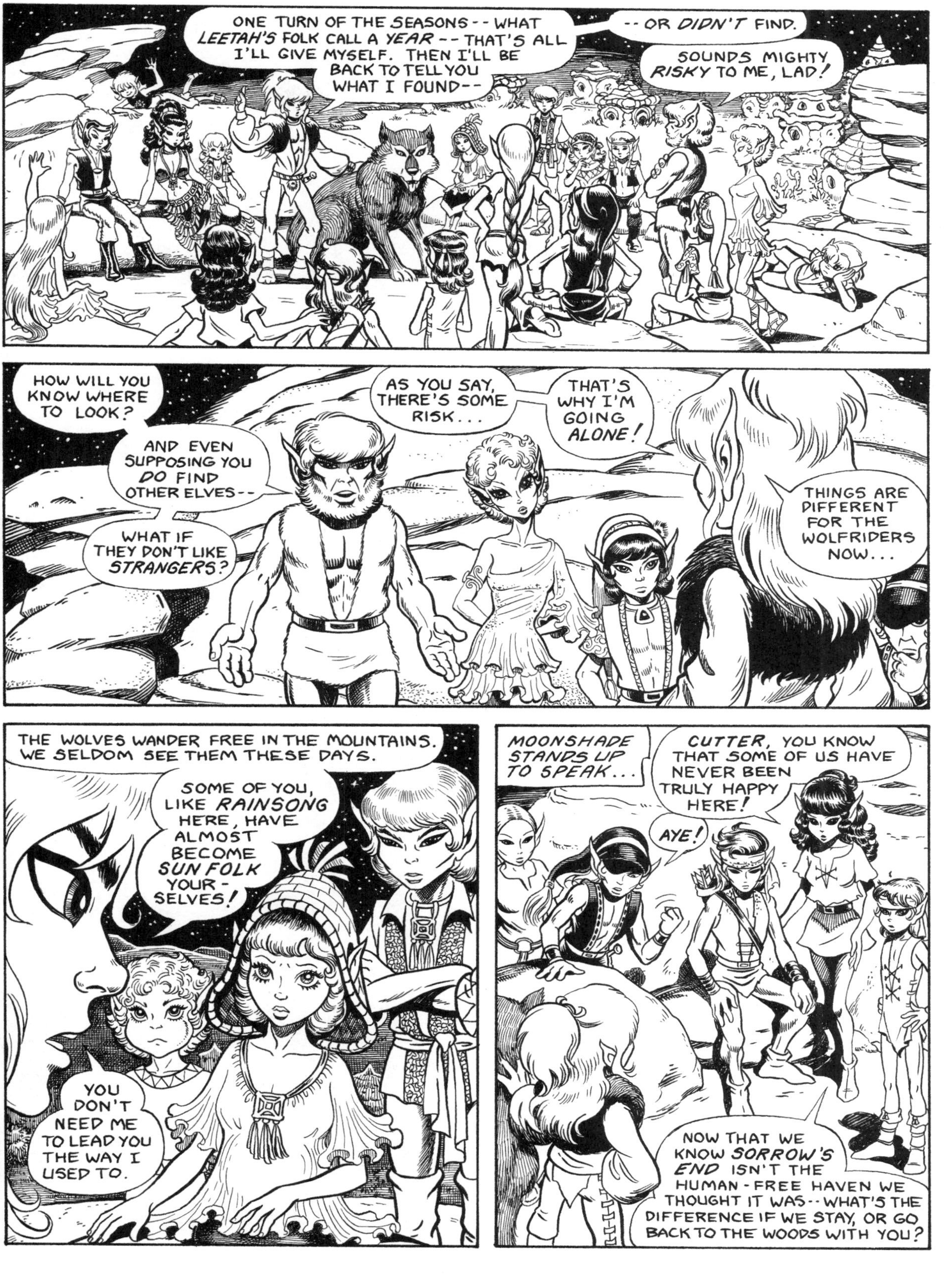
ONE TURN OF THE SEASONS - - WHAT LEETAH'S FOLK CALL A YEAR - - THAT'S ALL I'LL GIVE MYSELF. THEN I'LL BE BACK TO TELL YOU WHAT I FOUND - -
- - OR DIDN'T FIND.
SOUNDS MIGHTY RISKY TO ME, LAD!
HOW WILL YOU KNOW WHERE TO LOOK?
AND EVEN SUPPOSING YOU DO FIND OTHER ELVES - -
WHAT IF THEY DON'T LIKE STRANGERS?
AS YOU SAY, THERE'S SOME RISK...
THAT'S WHY I'M GOING ALONE!
THINGS ARE DIFFERENT FOR THE WOLFRIDERS NOW...
THE WOLVES WANDER FREE IN THE MOUNTAINS. WE SELDOM SEE THEM THESE DAYS.
SOME OF YOU, LIKE RAINSONG HERE, HAVE ALMOST BECOME SUN FOLK YOUR-SELVES!
YOU DON'T NEED ME TO LEAD YOU THE WAY I USED TO.
MOONSHADE STANDS UP TO SPEAK...
CUTTER, YOU KNOW THAT SOME OF US HAVE NEVER BEEN TRULY HAPPY HERE!
AYE!
NOW THAT WE KNOW SORROW'S END ISN'T THE HUMAN - FREE HAVEN WE THOUGHT IT WAS - - WHAT'S THE DIFFERENCE IF WE STAY, OR GO BACK TO THE WOODS WITH YOU?

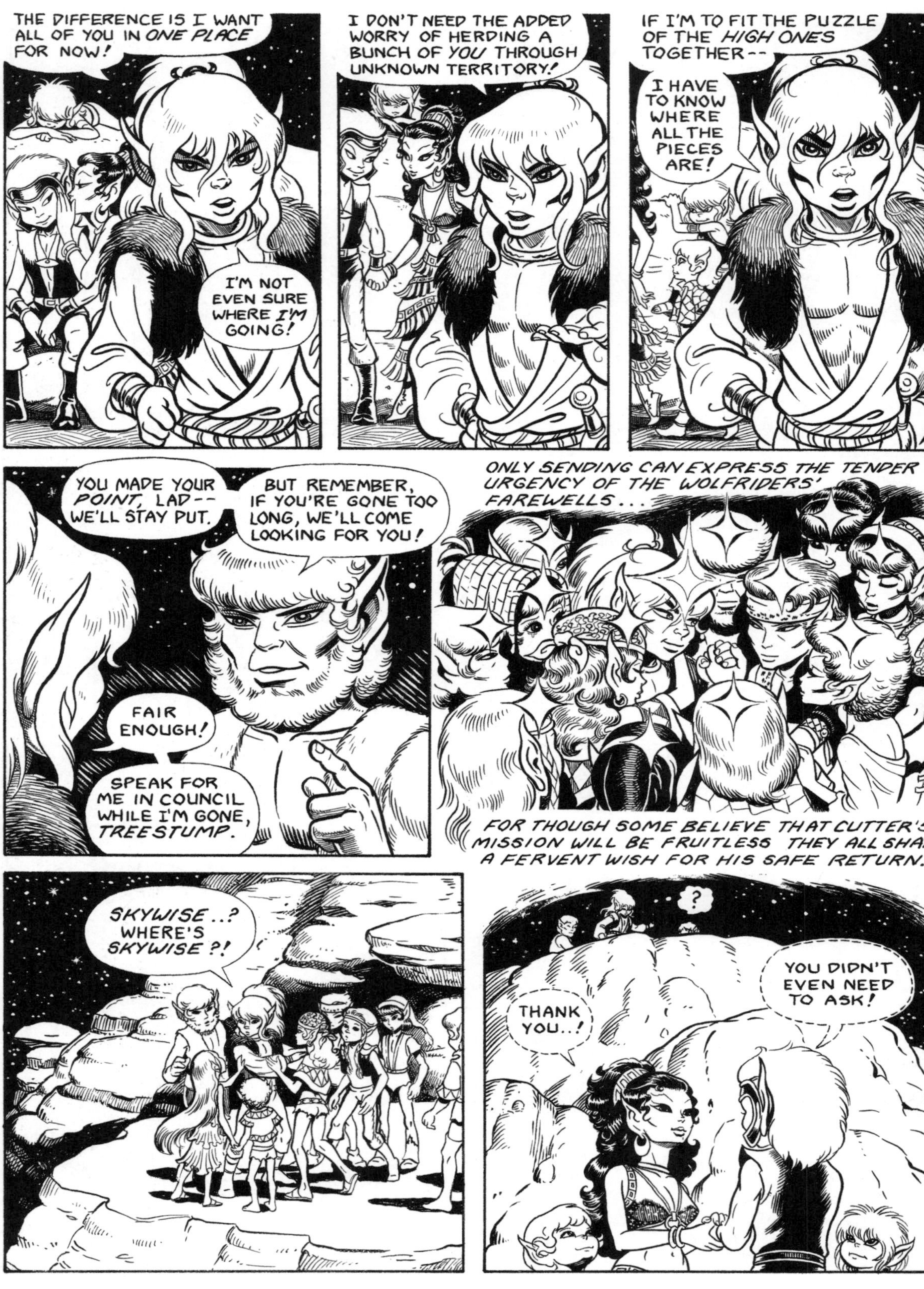
THE DIFFERENCE IS I WANT ALL OF YOU IN *ONE PLACE* FOR NOW!
I'M NOT EVEN SURE WHERE *I'M* GOING!
I DON'T NEED THE ADDED WORRY OF HERDING A BUNCH OF *YOU* THROUGH UNKNOWN TERRITORY!
IF I'M TO FIT THE PUZZLE OF THE *HIGH ONES* TOGETHER--
I HAVE TO KNOW WHERE ALL THE PIECES ARE!
YOU MADE YOUR *POINT*, LAD-- WE'LL STAY PUT.
BUT REMEMBER, IF YOU'RE GONE TOO LONG, WE'LL COME LOOKING FOR YOU!
FAIR ENOUGH!
SPEAK FOR ME IN COUNCIL WHILE I'M GONE, *TREESTUMP*.
ONLY SENDING CAN EXPRESS THE TENDER URGENCY OF THE WOLFRIDERS' FAREWELLS...
FOR THOUGH SOME BELIEVE THAT CUTTER'S MISSION WILL BE FRUITLESS THEY ALL SHARE A FERVENT WISH FOR HIS SAFE RETURN.
SKYWISE..? WHERE'S *SKYWISE*?!
?
THANK YOU...!
YOU DIDN'T EVEN NEED TO ASK!

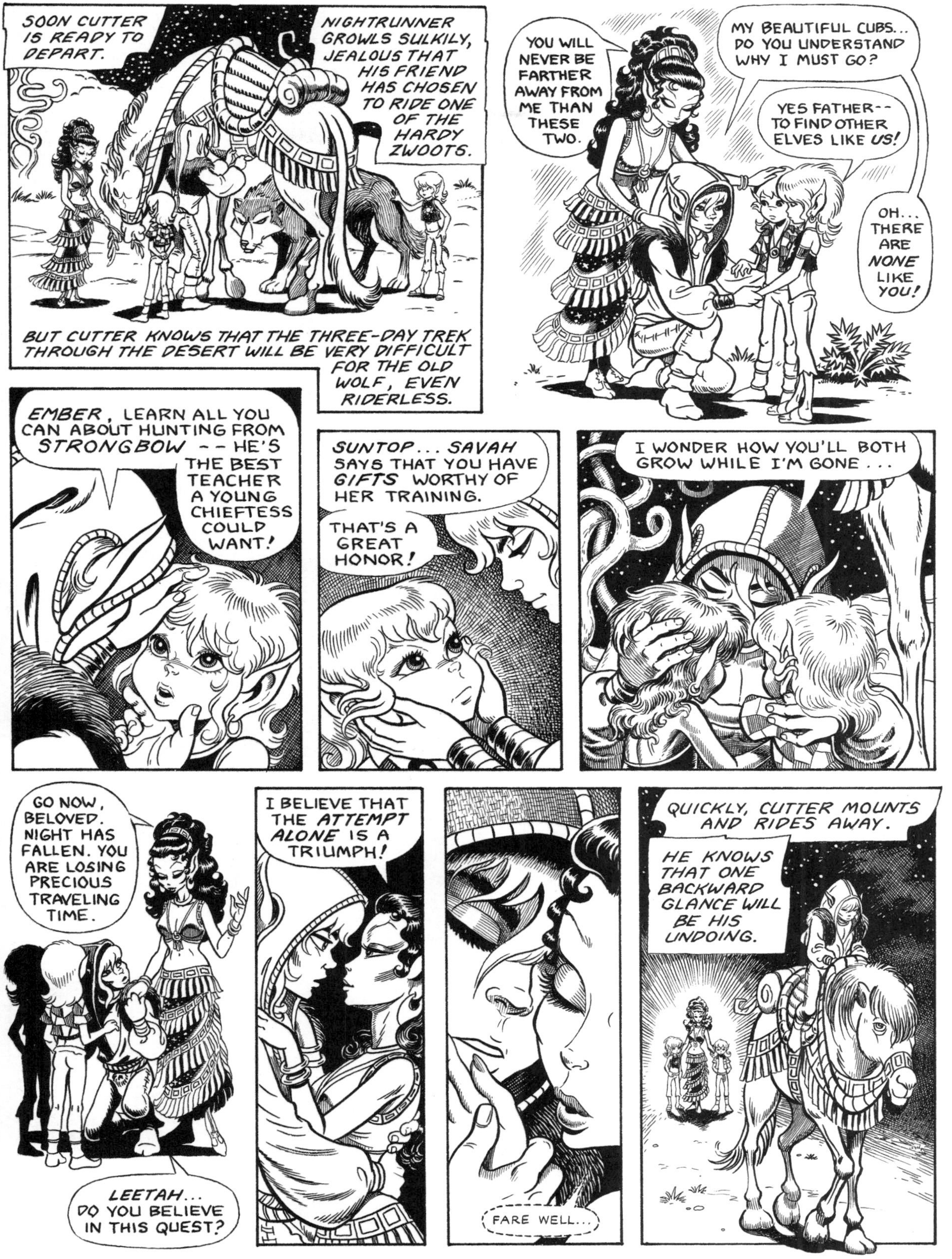
SOON CUTTER IS READY TO DEPART.
NIGHTRUNNER GROWLS SULKILY, JEALOUS THAT HIS FRIEND HAS CHOSEN TO RIDE ONE OF THE HARDY ZWOOTS.
BUT CUTTER KNOWS THAT THE THREE-DAY TREK THROUGH THE DESERT WILL BE VERY DIFFICULT FOR THE OLD WOLF, EVEN RIDERLESS.
YOU WILL NEVER BE FARTHER AWAY FROM ME THAN THESE TWO.
MY BEAUTIFUL CUBS... DO YOU UNDERSTAND WHY I MUST GO?
YES FATHER-- TO FIND OTHER ELVES LIKE US!
OH... THERE ARE NONE LIKE YOU!
EMBER, LEARN ALL YOU CAN ABOUT HUNTING FROM STRONGBOW -- HE'S THE BEST TEACHER A YOUNG CHIEFTESS COULD WANT!
SUNTOP... SAVAH SAYS THAT YOU HAVE GIFTS WORTHY OF HER TRAINING.
THAT'S A GREAT HONOR!
I WONDER HOW YOU'LL BOTH GROW WHILE I'M GONE...
GO NOW, BELOVED. NIGHT HAS FALLEN. YOU ARE LOSING PRECIOUS TRAVELING TIME.
LEETAH... DO YOU BELIEVE IN THIS QUEST?
I BELIEVE THAT THE ATTEMPT ALONE IS A TRIUMPH!
FARE WELL...
QUICKLY, CUTTER MOUNTS AND RIDES AWAY.
HE KNOWS THAT ONE BACKWARD GLANCE WILL BE HIS UNDOING.

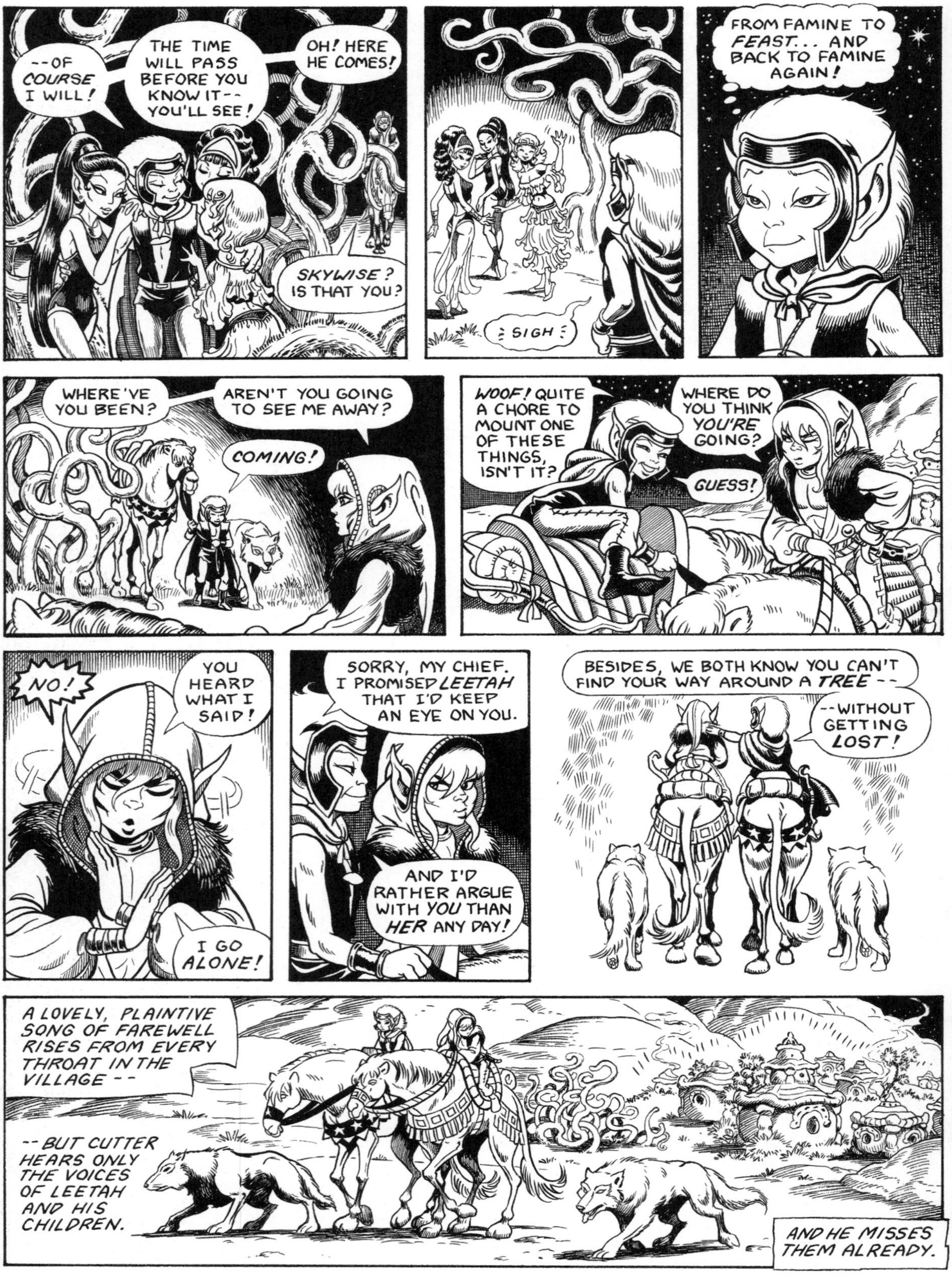
--OF COURSE I WILL!
THE TIME WILL PASS BEFORE YOU KNOW IT-- YOU'LL SEE!
OH! HERE HE COMES!
SKYWISE? IS THAT YOU?
SIGH
FROM FAMINE TO FEAST... AND BACK TO FAMINE AGAIN!
WHERE'VE YOU BEEN?
AREN'T YOU GOING TO SEE ME AWAY?
COMING!
WOOF! QUITE A CHORE TO MOUNT ONE OF THESE THINGS, ISN'T IT?
WHERE DO YOU THINK YOU'RE GOING?
GUESS!
NO!
YOU HEARD WHAT I SAID!
I GO ALONE!
SORRY, MY CHIEF. I PROMISED LEETAH THAT I'D KEEP AN EYE ON YOU.
AND I'D RATHER ARGUE WITH YOU THAN HER ANY DAY!
BESIDES, WE BOTH KNOW YOU CAN'T FIND YOUR WAY AROUND A TREE--
--WITHOUT GETTING LOST!
A LOVELY, PLAINTIVE SONG OF FAREWELL RISES FROM EVERY THROAT IN THE VILLAGE--
--BUT CUTTER HEARS ONLY THE VOICES OF LEETAH AND HIS CHILDREN.
AND HE MISSES THEM ALREADY.

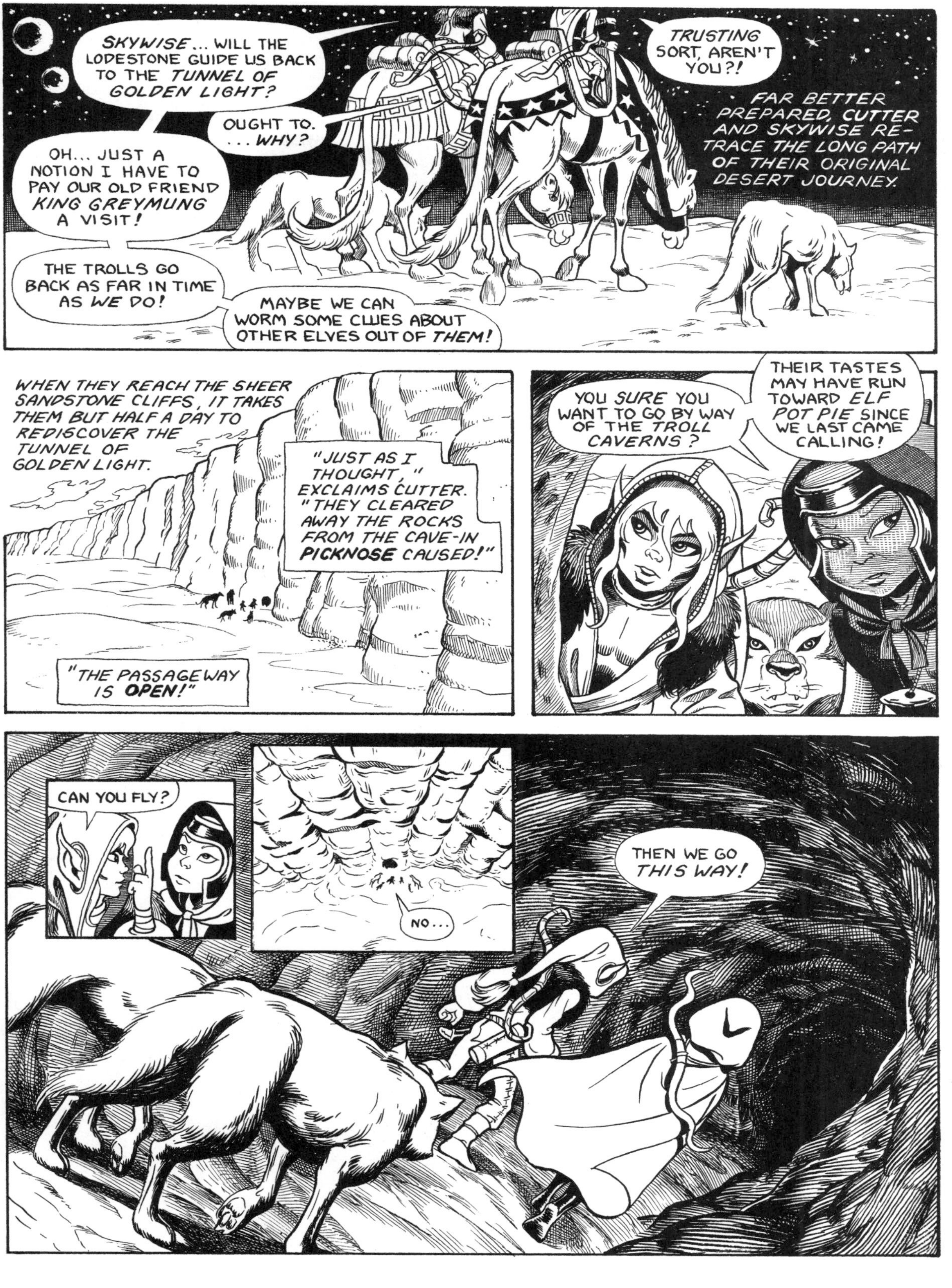
SKYWISE... WILL THE LODESTONE GUIDE US BACK TO THE TUNNEL OF GOLDEN LIGHT?
OUGHT TO. ...WHY?
OH... JUST A NOTION I HAVE TO PAY OUR OLD FRIEND KING GREYMUNG A VISIT!
THE TROLLS GO BACK AS FAR IN TIME AS WE DO!
MAYBE WE CAN WORM SOME CLUES ABOUT OTHER ELVES OUT OF THEM!
TRUSTING SORT, AREN'T YOU?!
FAR BETTER PREPARED, CUTTER AND SKYWISE RETRACE THE LONG PATH OF THEIR ORIGINAL DESERT JOURNEY.
WHEN THEY REACH THE SHEER SANDSTONE CLIFFS, IT TAKES THEM BUT HALF A DAY TO REDISCOVER THE TUNNEL OF GOLDEN LIGHT.
"JUST AS I THOUGHT," EXCLAIMS CUTTER. "THEY CLEARED AWAY THE ROCKS FROM THE CAVE-IN PICKNOSE CAUSED!"
"THE PASSAGEWAY IS OPEN!"
YOU SURE YOU WANT TO GO BY WAY OF THE TROLL CAVERNS?
THEIR TASTES MAY HAVE RUN TOWARD ELF POT PIE SINCE WE LAST CAME CALLING!
CAN YOU FLY?
NO...
THEN WE GO THIS WAY!

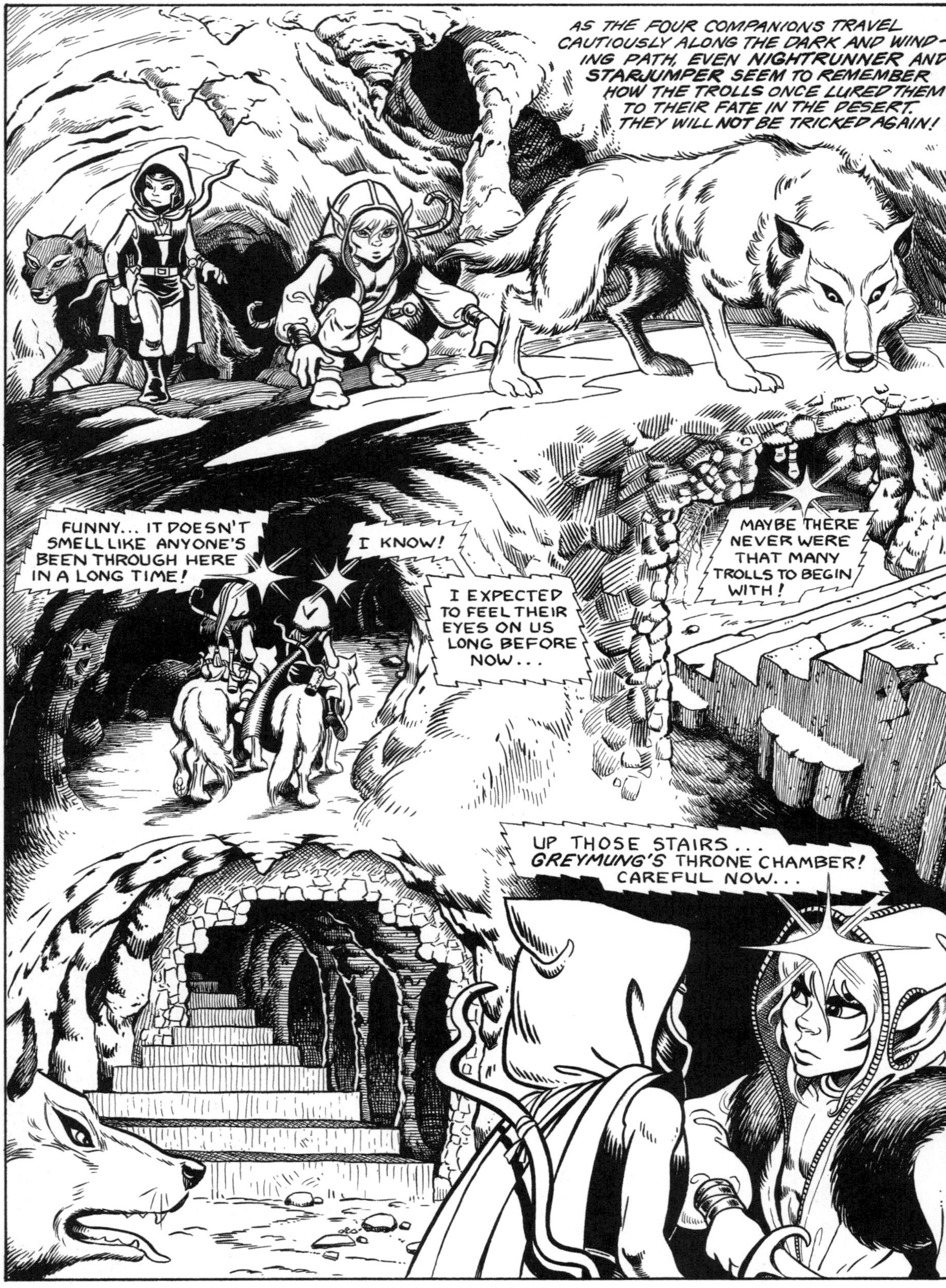

AS THE FOUR COMPANIONS TRAVEL CAUTIOUSLY ALONG THE DARK AND WINDING PATH, EVEN NIGHTRUNNER AND STARJUMPER SEEM TO REMEMBER HOW THE TROLLS ONCE LURED THEM TO THEIR FATE IN THE DESERT. THEY WILL NOT BE TRICKED AGAIN!
FUNNY... IT DOESN'T SMELL LIKE ANYONE'S BEEN THROUGH HERE IN A LONG TIME!
I KNOW!
I EXPECTED TO FEEL THEIR EYES ON US LONG BEFORE NOW...
MAYBE THERE NEVER WERE THAT MANY TROLLS TO BEGIN WITH!
UP THOSE STAIRS... GREYMUNG'S THRONE CHAMBER! CAREFUL NOW...

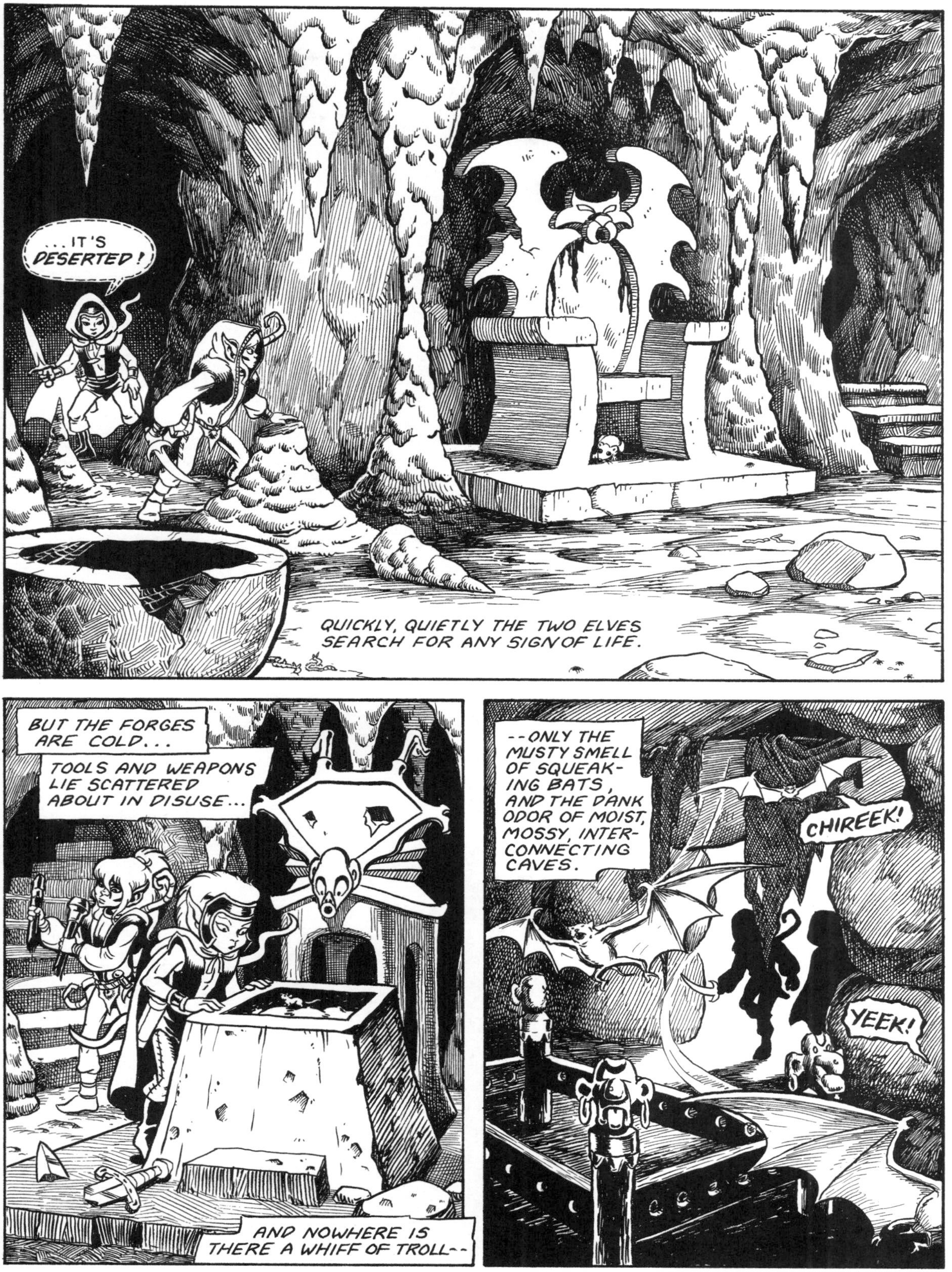
...IT'S DESERTED!
QUICKLY, QUIETLY THE TWO ELVES SEARCH FOR ANY SIGN OF LIFE.
BUT THE FORGES ARE COLD...
TOOLS AND WEAPONS LIE SCATTERED ABOUT IN DISUSE...
AND NOWHERE IS THERE A WHIFF OF TROLL--
--ONLY THE MUSTY SMELL OF SQUEAK-ING BATS, AND THE DANK ODOR OF MOIST, MOSSY, INTER-CONNECTING CAVES.
CHIREEK!
YEEK!

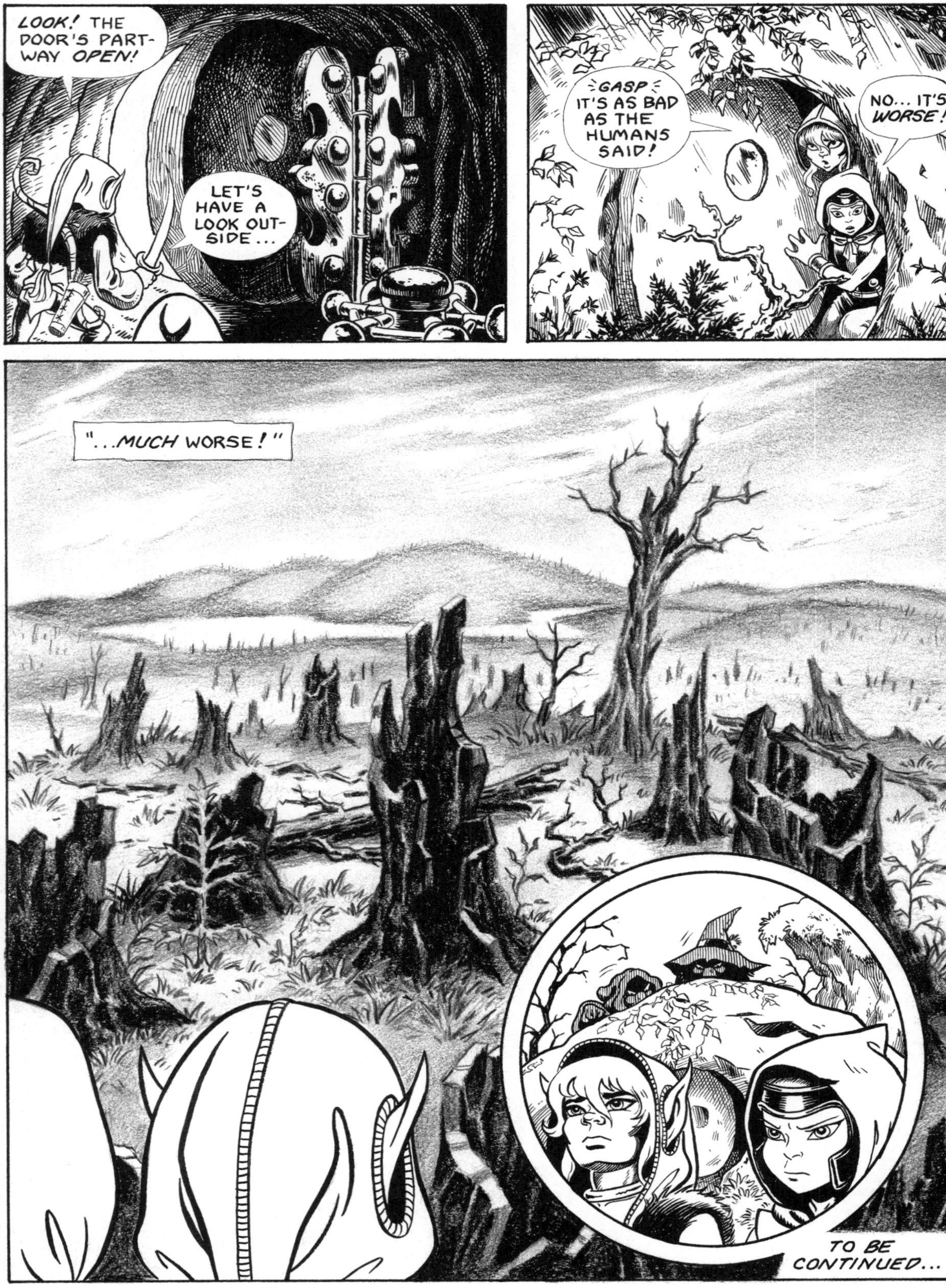
LOOK! THE DOOR'S PART-WAY OPEN!
LET'S HAVE A LOOK OUT-SIDE...
GASP IT'S AS BAD AS THE HUMANS SAID!
NO... IT'S WORSE!
"...MUCH WORSE!"
TO BE CONTINUED...

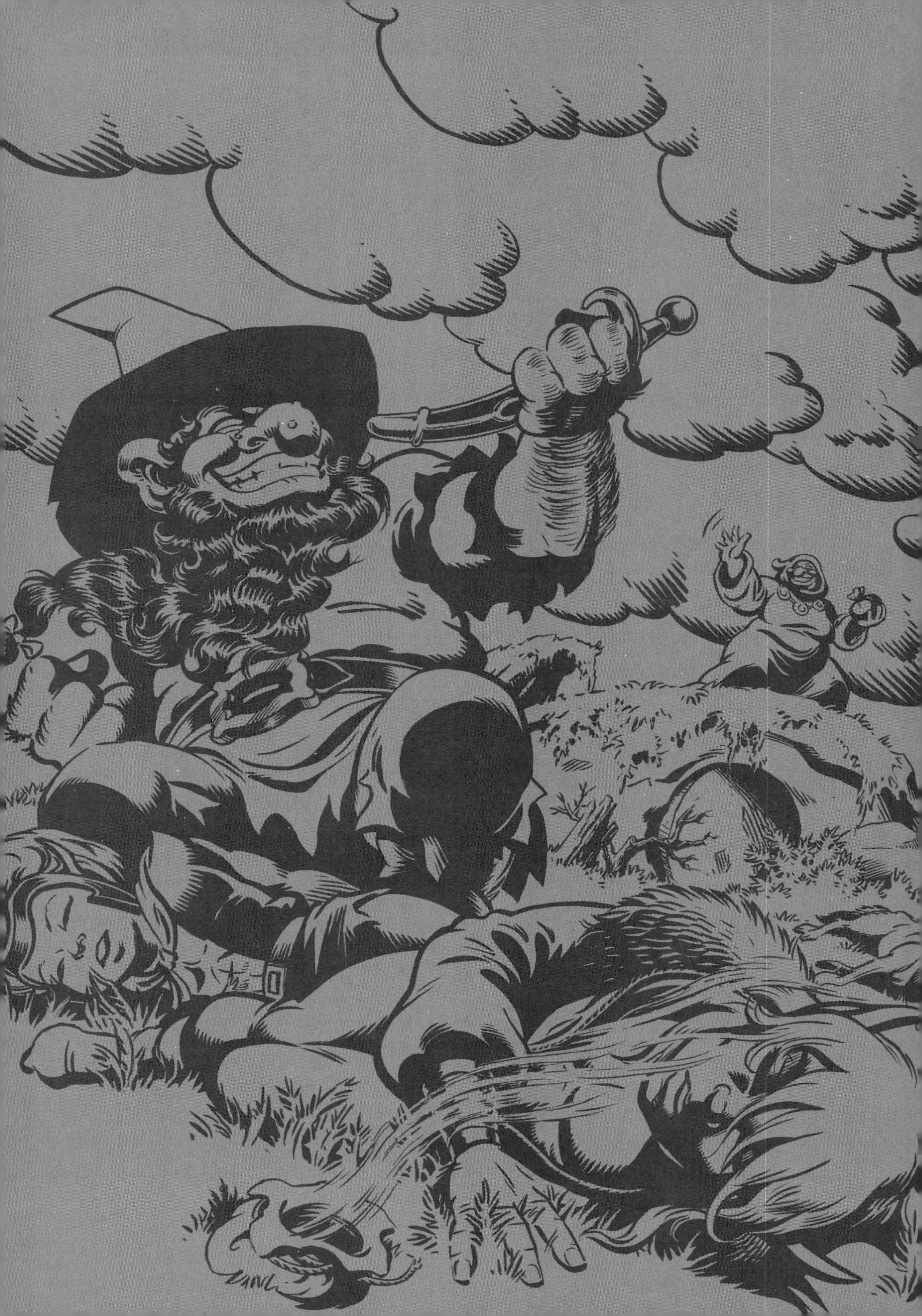

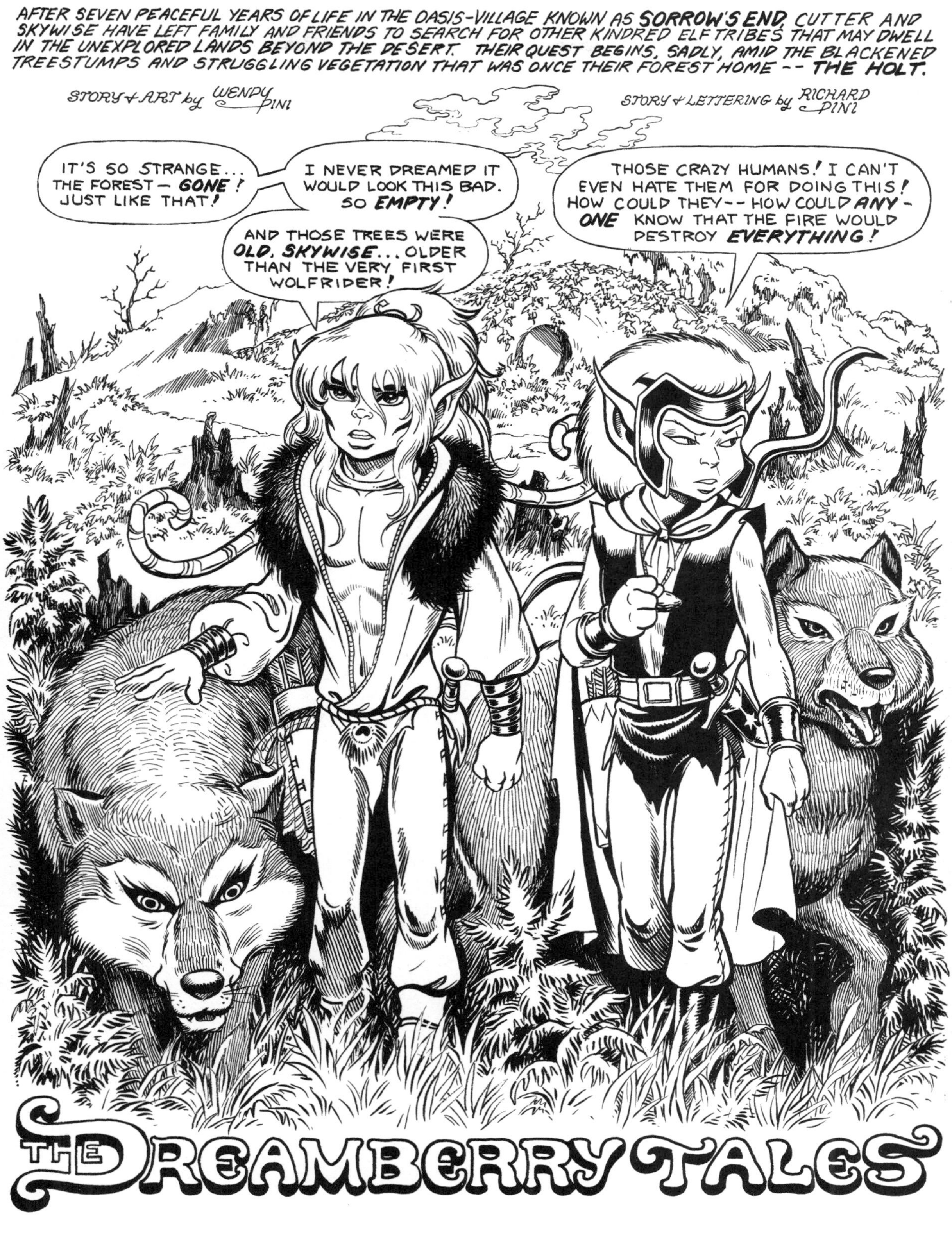
AFTER SEVEN PEACEFUL YEARS OF LIFE IN THE OASIS-VILLAGE KNOWN AS SORROW'S END, CUTTER AND SKYWISE HAVE LEFT FAMILY AND FRIENDS TO SEARCH FOR OTHER KINDRED ELF TRIBES THAT MAY DWELL IN THE UNEXPLORED LANDS BEYOND THE DESERT. THEIR QUEST BEGINS, SADLY, AMID THE BLACKENED TREESTUMPS AND STRUGGLING VEGETATION THAT WAS ONCE THEIR FOREST HOME -- THE HOLT.
STORY + ART by WENDY PINI
STORY + LETTERING by RICHARD PINI
IT'S SO STRANGE... THE FOREST — GONE! JUST LIKE THAT!
I NEVER DREAMED IT WOULD LOOK THIS BAD. SO EMPTY!
AND THOSE TREES WERE OLD, SKYWISE... OLDER THAN THE VERY FIRST WOLFRIDER!
THOSE CRAZY HUMANS! I CAN'T EVEN HATE THEM FOR DOING THIS! HOW COULD THEY-- HOW COULD ANY-ONE KNOW THAT THE FIRE WOULD DESTROY EVERYTHING!
THE DREAMBERRY TALES

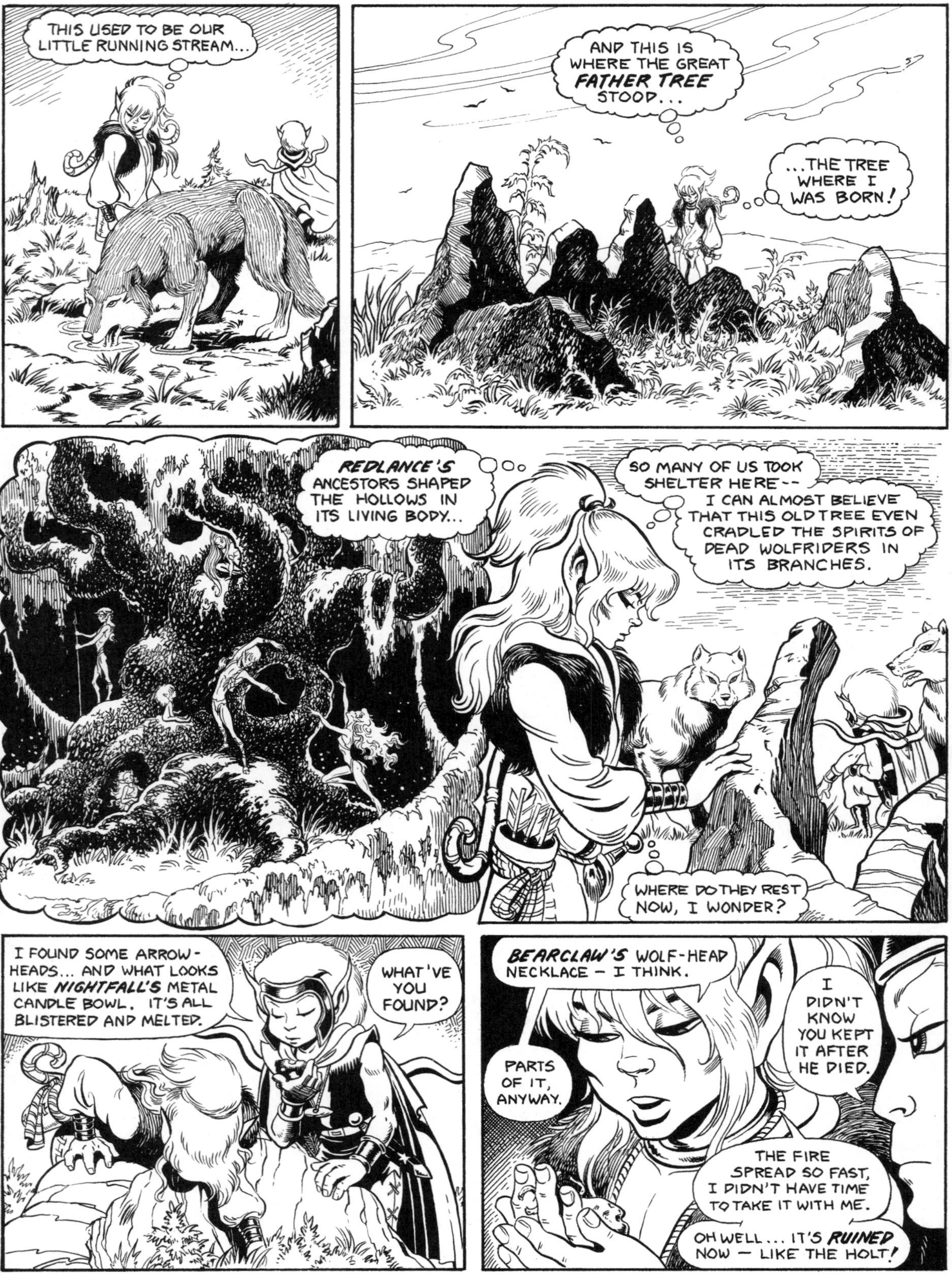

THIS USED TO BE OUR LITTLE RUNNING STREAM...
AND THIS IS WHERE THE GREAT FATHER TREE STOOD...
...THE TREE WHERE I WAS BORN!
REDLANCE'S ANCESTORS SHAPED THE HOLLOWS IN ITS LIVING BODY...
SO MANY OF US TOOK SHELTER HERE-- I CAN ALMOST BELIEVE THAT THIS OLD TREE EVEN CRADLED THE SPIRITS OF DEAD WOLFRIDERS IN ITS BRANCHES.
WHERE DO THEY REST NOW, I WONDER?
WHAT'VE YOU FOUND?
I FOUND SOME ARROW-HEADS... AND WHAT LOOKS LIKE NIGHTFALL'S METAL CANDLE BOWL. IT'S ALL BLISTERED AND MELTED.
BEARCLAW'S WOLF-HEAD NECKLACE - I THINK.
PARTS OF IT, ANYWAY.
I DIDN'T KNOW YOU KEPT IT AFTER HE DIED.
THE FIRE SPREAD SO FAST, I DIDN'T HAVE TIME TO TAKE IT WITH ME.
OH WELL... IT'S RUINED NOW - LIKE THE HOLT!

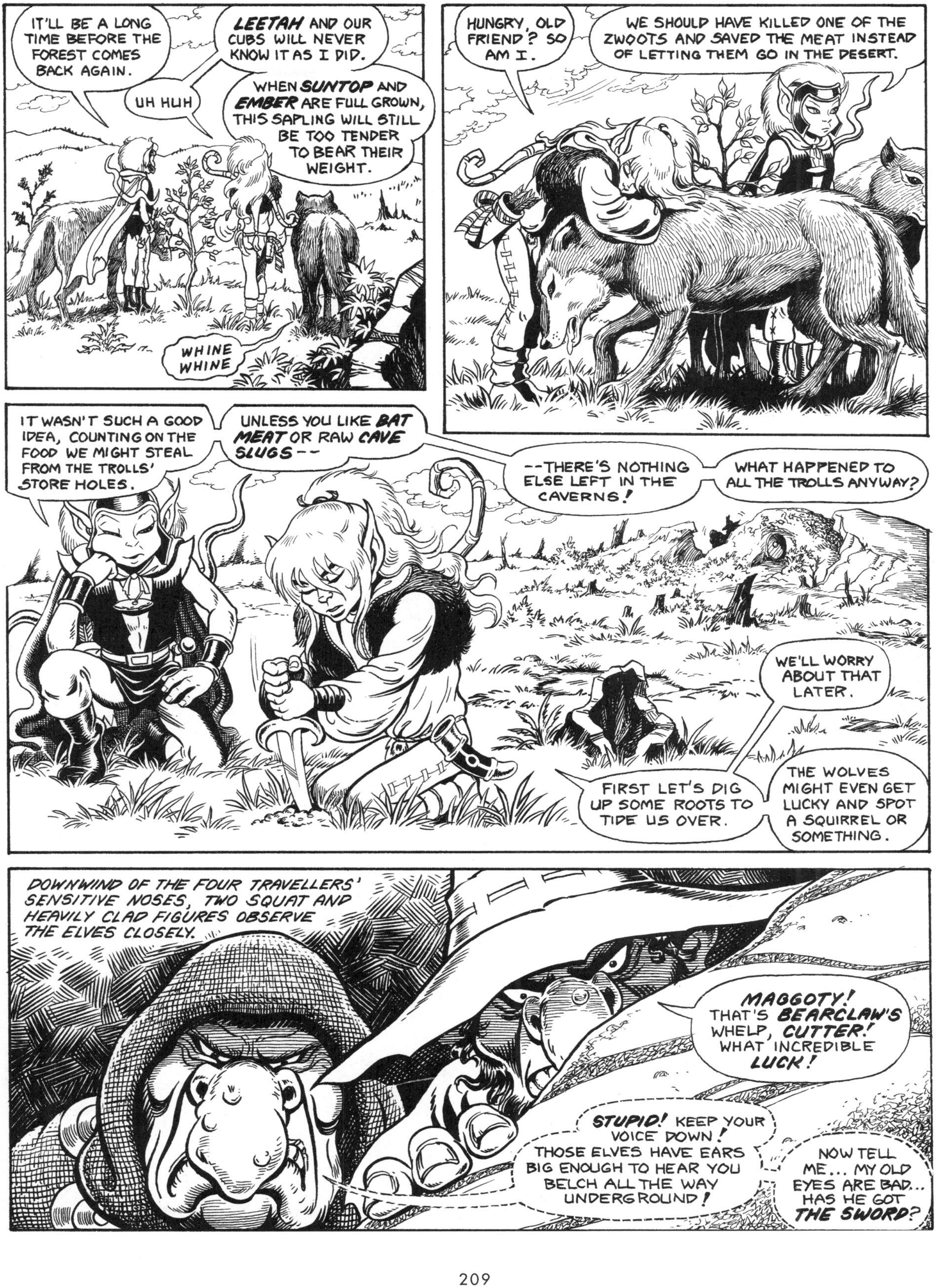
IT'LL BE A LONG TIME BEFORE THE FOREST COMES BACK AGAIN.
UH HUH
LEETAH AND OUR CUBS WILL NEVER KNOW IT AS I DID.
WHEN SUNTOP AND EMBER ARE FULL GROWN, THIS SAPLING WILL STILL BE TOO TENDER TO BEAR THEIR WEIGHT.
WHINE WHINE
HUNGRY, OLD FRIEND? SO AM I.
WE SHOULD HAVE KILLED ONE OF THE ZWOOTS AND SAVED THE MEAT INSTEAD OF LETTING THEM GO IN THE DESERT.
IT WASN'T SUCH A GOOD IDEA, COUNTING ON THE FOOD WE MIGHT STEAL FROM THE TROLLS' STORE HOLES.
UNLESS YOU LIKE BAT MEAT OR RAW CAVE SLUGS--
--THERE'S NOTHING ELSE LEFT IN THE CAVERNS!
WHAT HAPPENED TO ALL THE TROLLS ANYWAY?
WE'LL WORRY ABOUT THAT LATER.
FIRST LET'S DIG UP SOME ROOTS TO TIDE US OVER.
THE WOLVES MIGHT EVEN GET LUCKY AND SPOT A SQUIRREL OR SOMETHING.
DOWNWIND OF THE FOUR TRAVELLERS' SENSITIVE NOSES, TWO SQUAT AND HEAVILY CLAD FIGURES OBSERVE THE ELVES CLOSELY.
MAGGOTY! THAT'S BEARCLAW'S WHELP, CUTTER! WHAT INCREDIBLE LUCK!
STUPID! KEEP YOUR VOICE DOWN! THOSE ELVES HAVE EARS BIG ENOUGH TO HEAR YOU BELCH ALL THE WAY UNDERGROUND!
NOW TELL ME... MY OLD EYES ARE BAD... HAS HE GOT THE SWORD?

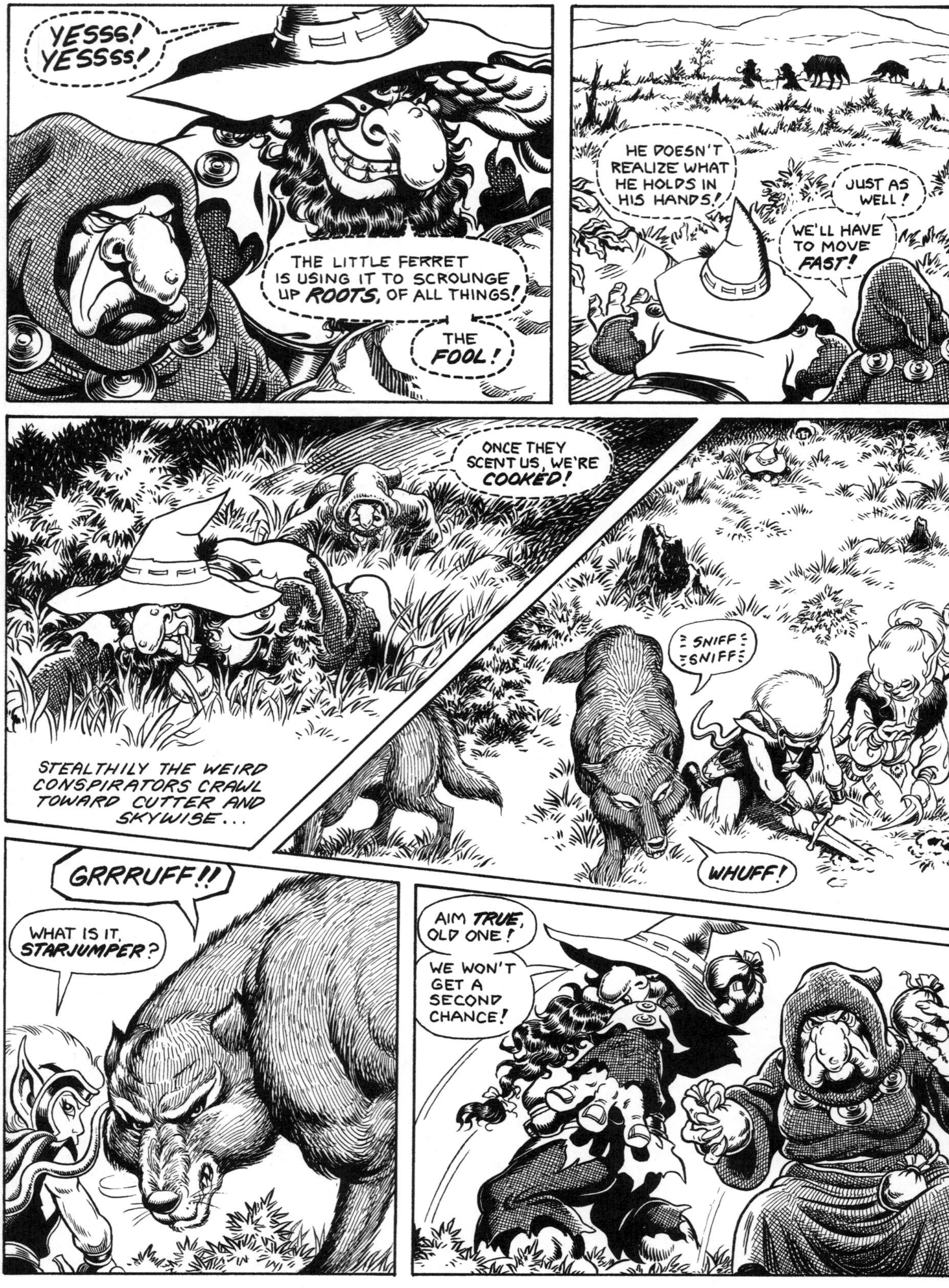
YESSS! YESSSss!
THE LITTLE FERRET IS USING IT TO SCROUNGE UP ROOTS, OF ALL THINGS!
THE FOOL!
HE DOESN'T REALIZE WHAT HE HOLDS IN HIS HANDS!
JUST AS WELL!
WE'LL HAVE TO MOVE FAST!
ONCE THEY SCENT US, WE'RE COOKED!
STEALTHILY THE WEIRD CONSPIRATORS CRAWL TOWARD CUTTER AND SKYWISE...
SNIFF SNIFF
WHUFF!
GRRRUFF!!
WHAT IS IT, STARJUMPER?
AIM TRUE, OLD ONE!
WE WON'T GET A SECOND CHANCE!

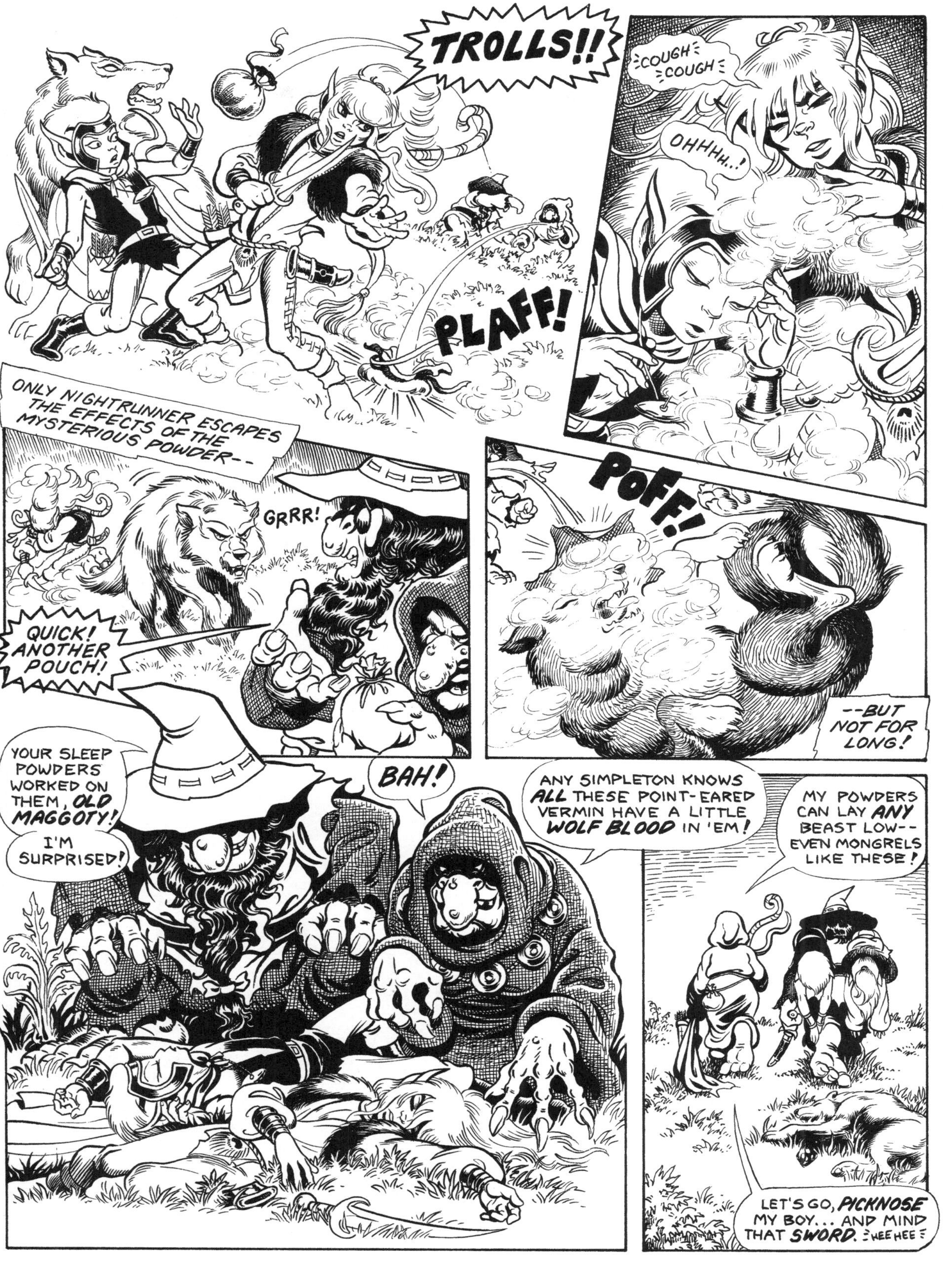
TROLLS!!
PLAFF!
COUGH COUGH
OHHHH..!
ONLY NIGHTRUNNER ESCAPES THE EFFECTS OF THE MYSTERIOUS POWDER--
GRRR!
QUICK! ANOTHER POUCH!
POFF!
--BUT NOT FOR LONG!
YOUR SLEEP POWDERS WORKED ON THEM, OLD MAGGOTY!
I'M SURPRISED!
BAH!
ANY SIMPLETON KNOWS ALL THESE POINT-EARED VERMIN HAVE A LITTLE WOLF BLOOD IN 'EM!
MY POWDERS CAN LAY ANY BEAST LOW-- EVEN MONGRELS LIKE THESE!
LET'S GO, PICKNOSE MY BOY... AND MIND THAT SWORD. HEE HEE

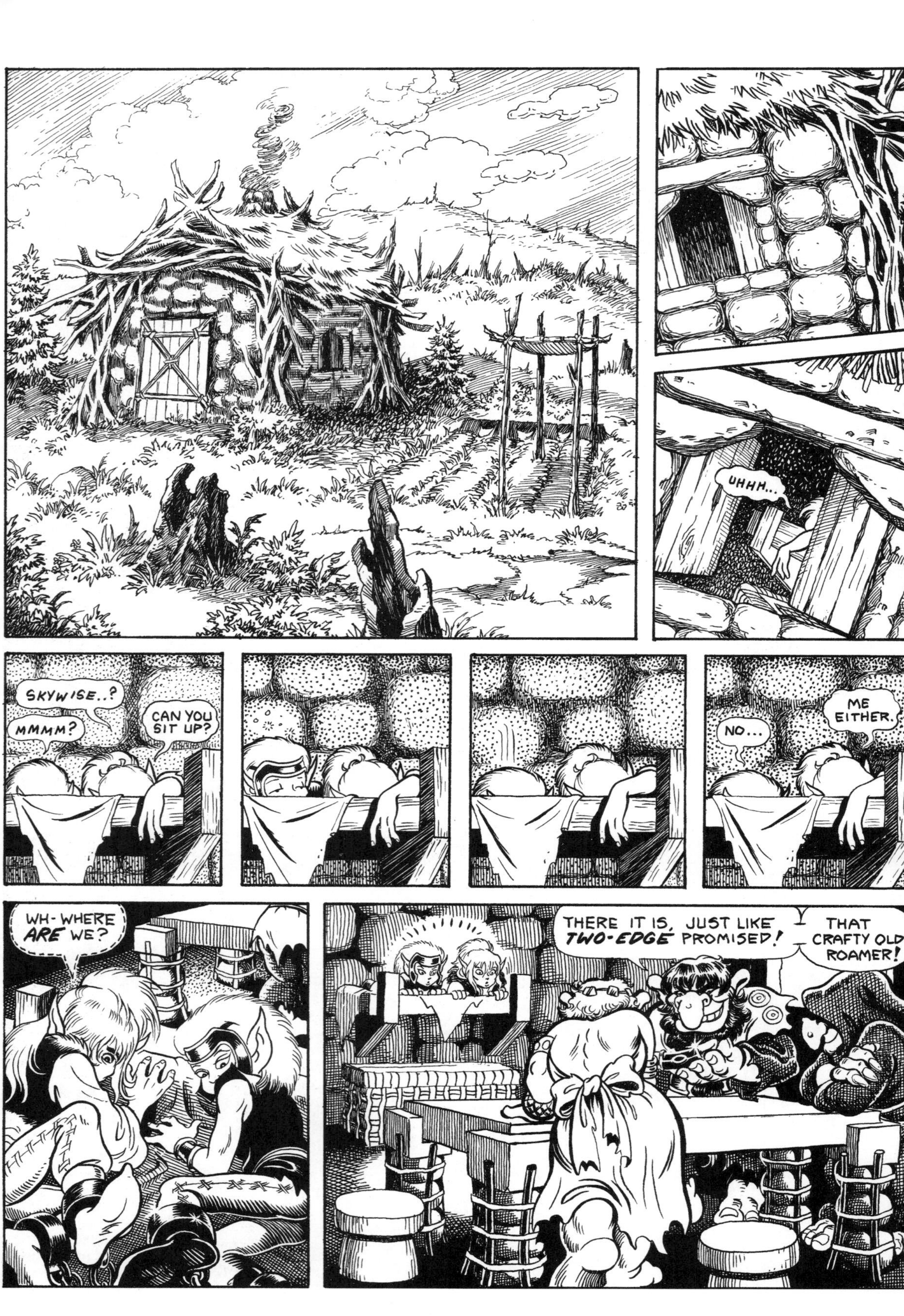
UHHH...
SKYWISE..?
MMMM?
CAN YOU SIT UP?
NO...
ME EITHER.
WH-WHERE ARE WE?
THERE IT IS, JUST LIKE TWO-EDGE PROMISED!
THAT CRAFTY OLD ROAMER!

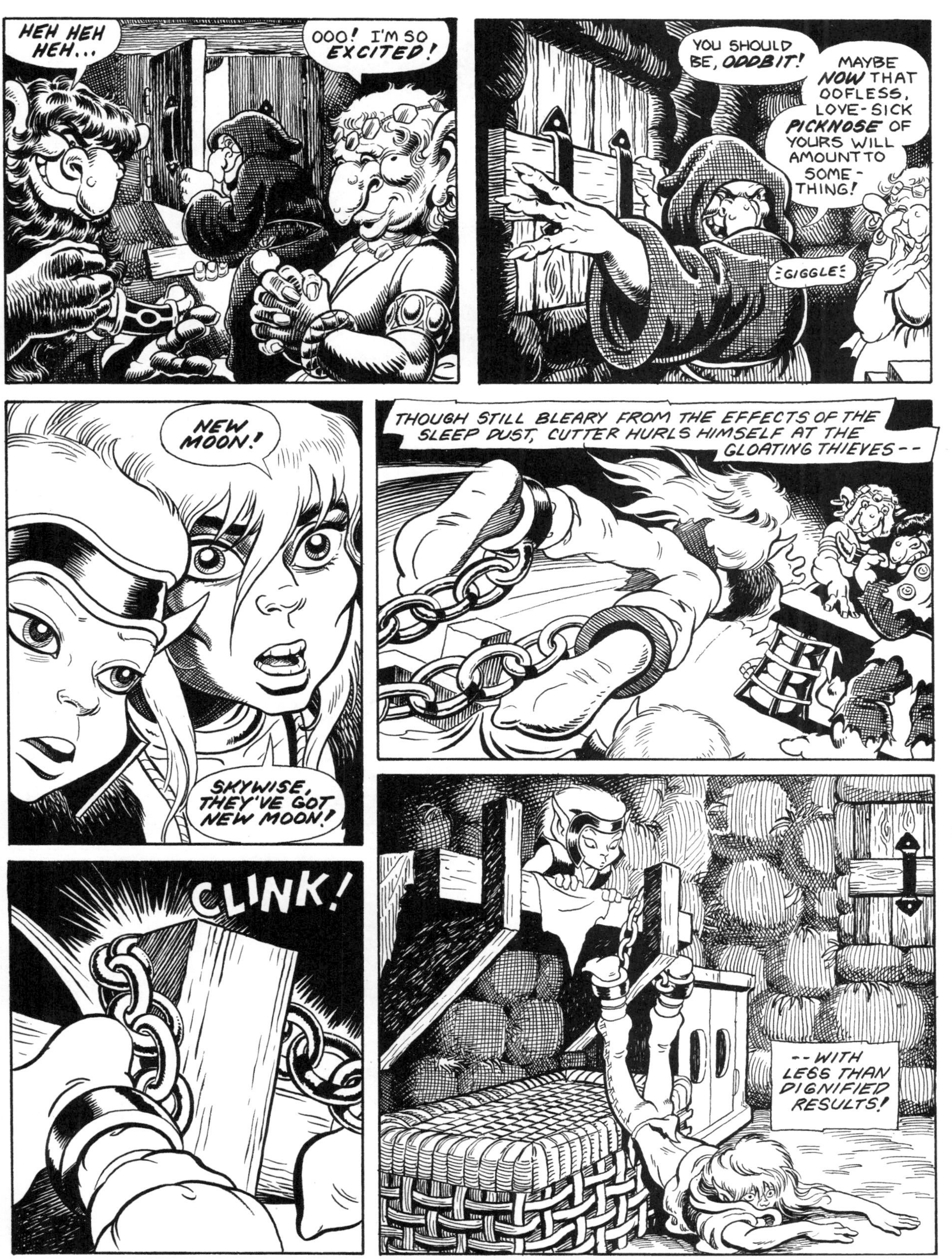
HEH HEH HEH...
OOO! I'M SO EXCITED!
YOU SHOULD BE, ODDBIT!
MAYBE NOW THAT OOFLESS, LOVE-SICK PICKNOSE OF YOURS WILL AMOUNT TO SOME-THING!
GIGGLE
NEW MOON!
SKYWISE, THEY'VE GOT NEW MOON!
THOUGH STILL BLEARY FROM THE EFFECTS OF THE SLEEP DUST, CUTTER HURLS HIMSELF AT THE GLOATING THIEVES--
CLINK!
--WITH LESS THAN DIGNIFIED RESULTS!

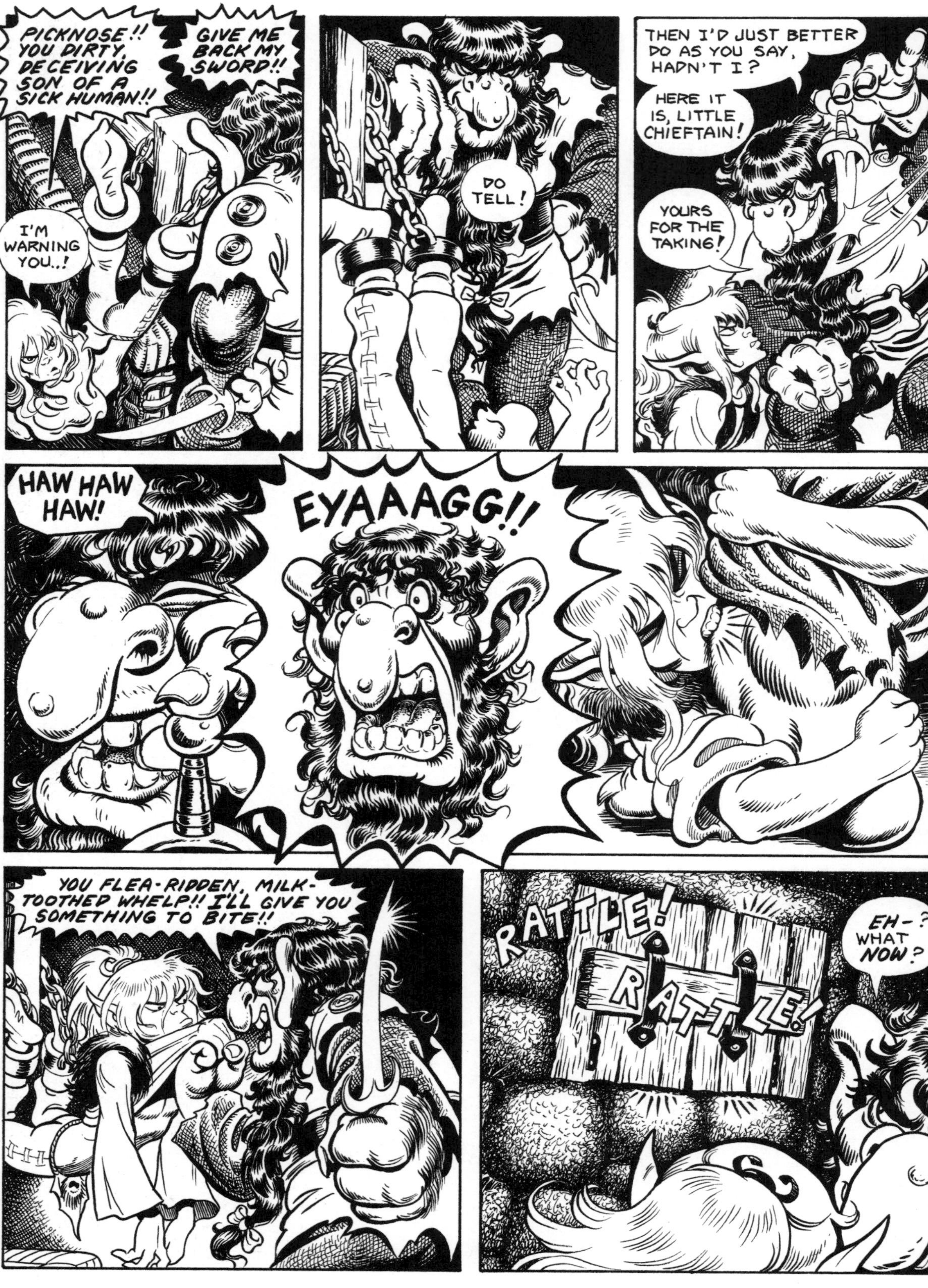
PICKNOSE!! YOU DIRTY, DECEIVING SON OF A SICK HUMAN!!
GIVE ME BACK MY SWORD!!
I'M WARNING YOU..!
DO TELL!
THEN I'D JUST BETTER DO AS YOU SAY, HADN'T I?
HERE IT IS, LITTLE CHIEFTAIN!
YOURS FOR THE TAKING!
HAW HAW HAW!
EYAAAGG!!
YOU FLEA-RIDDEN, MILK-TOOTHED WHELP!! I'LL GIVE YOU SOMETHING TO BITE!!
RATTLE! RATTLE!
EH-? WHAT NOW?

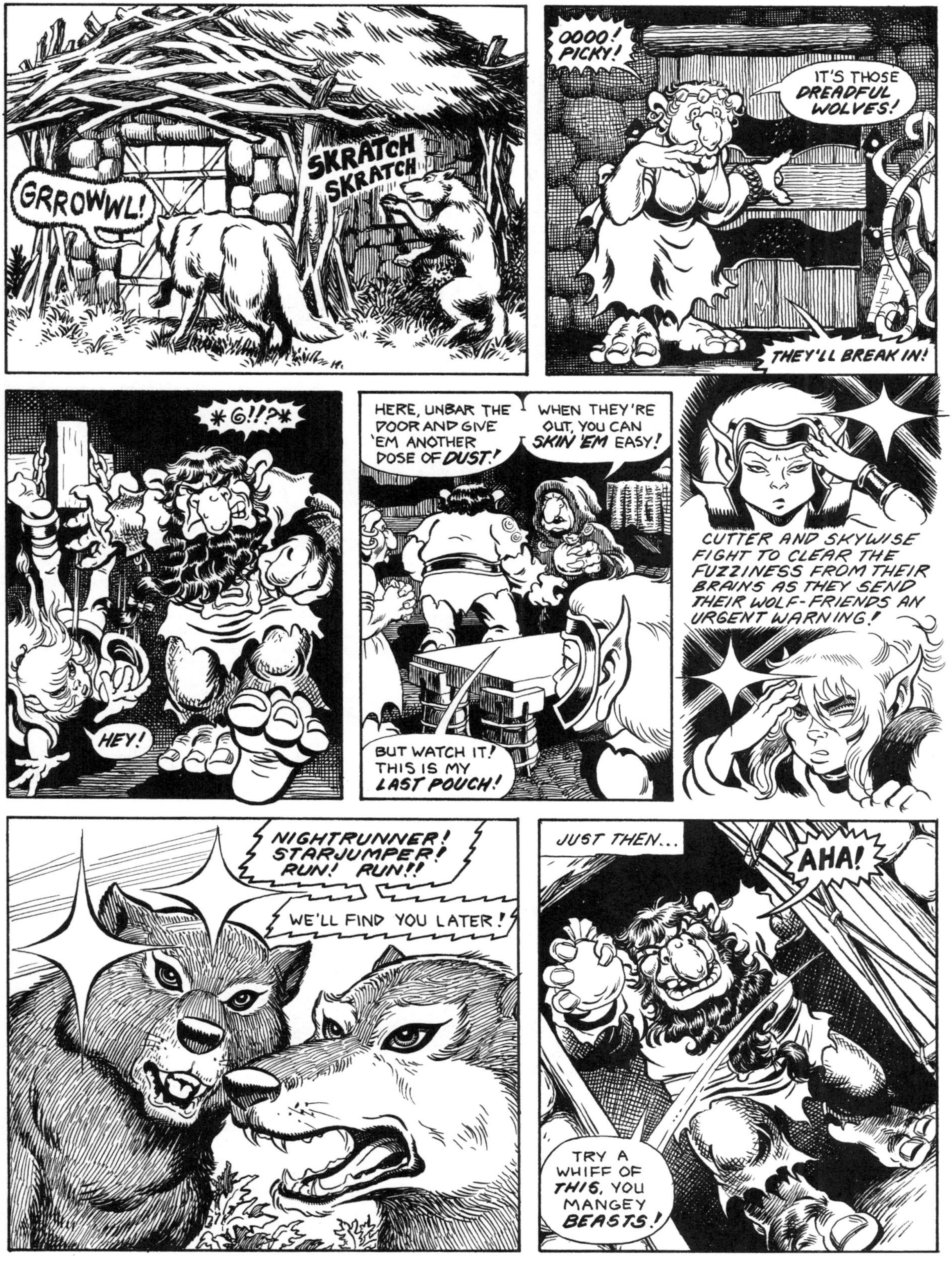
GRROWWL!
SKRATCH SKRATCH
OOOO! PICKY!
IT'S THOSE DREADFUL WOLVES!
THEY'LL BREAK IN!
6!!?
HEY!
HERE, UNBAR THE DOOR AND GIVE 'EM ANOTHER DOSE OF DUST!
WHEN THEY'RE OUT, YOU CAN SKIN 'EM EASY!
BUT WATCH IT! THIS IS MY LAST POUCH!
CUTTER AND SKYWISE FIGHT TO CLEAR THE FUZZINESS FROM THEIR BRAINS AS THEY SEND THEIR WOLF-FRIENDS AN URGENT WARNING!
NIGHTRUNNER! STARJUMPER! RUN! RUN!!
WE'LL FIND YOU LATER!
JUST THEN...
AHA!
TRY A WHIFF OF THIS, YOU MANGEY BEASTS!

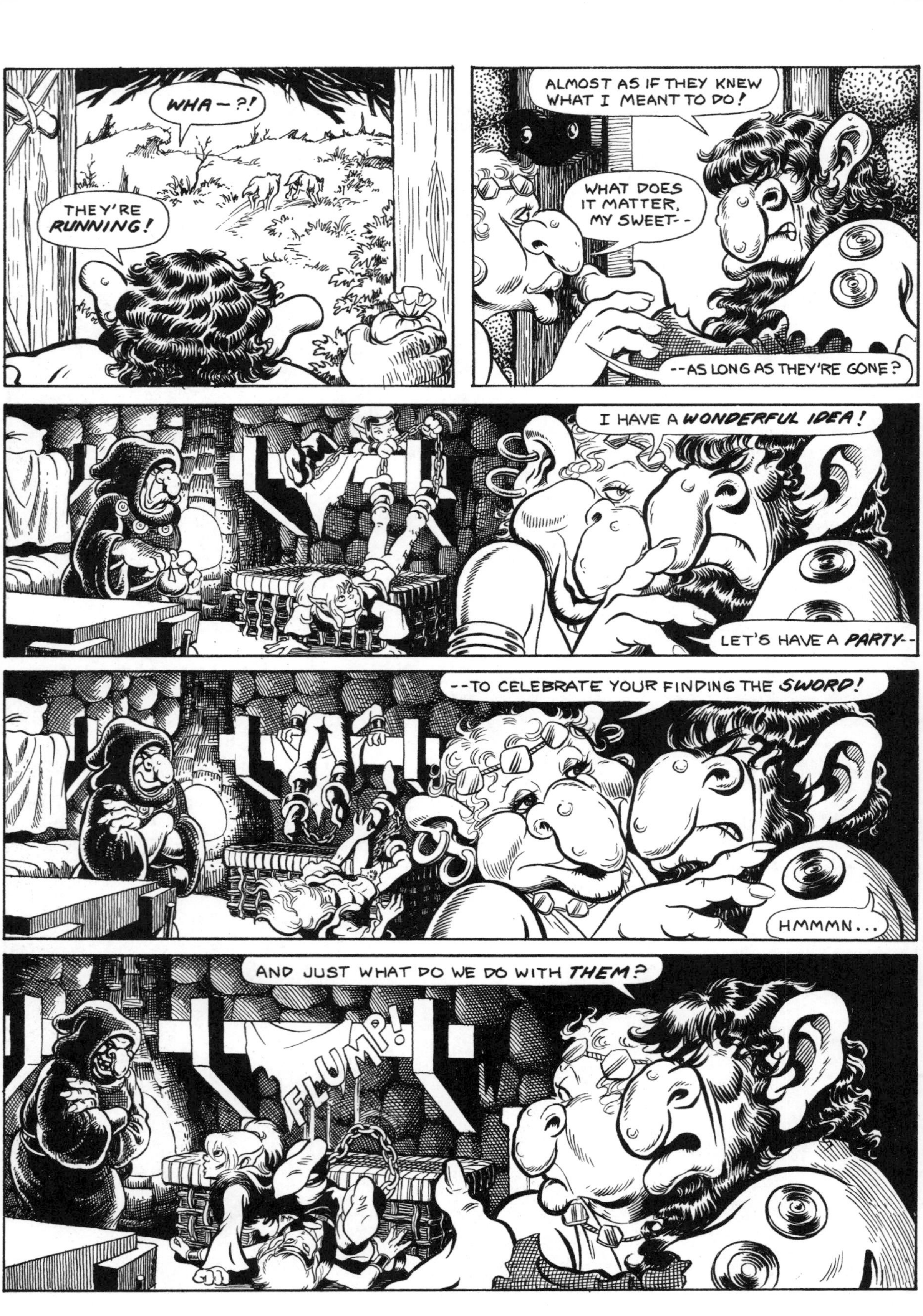
WHA--?!
THEY'RE RUNNING!
ALMOST AS IF THEY KNEW WHAT I MEANT TO DO!
WHAT DOES IT MATTER, MY SWEET--
--AS LONG AS THEY'RE GONE?
I HAVE A WONDERFUL IDEA!
LET'S HAVE A PARTY--
--TO CELEBRATE YOUR FINDING THE SWORD!
HMMMN...
AND JUST WHAT DO WE DO WITH THEM?
FLUMP!

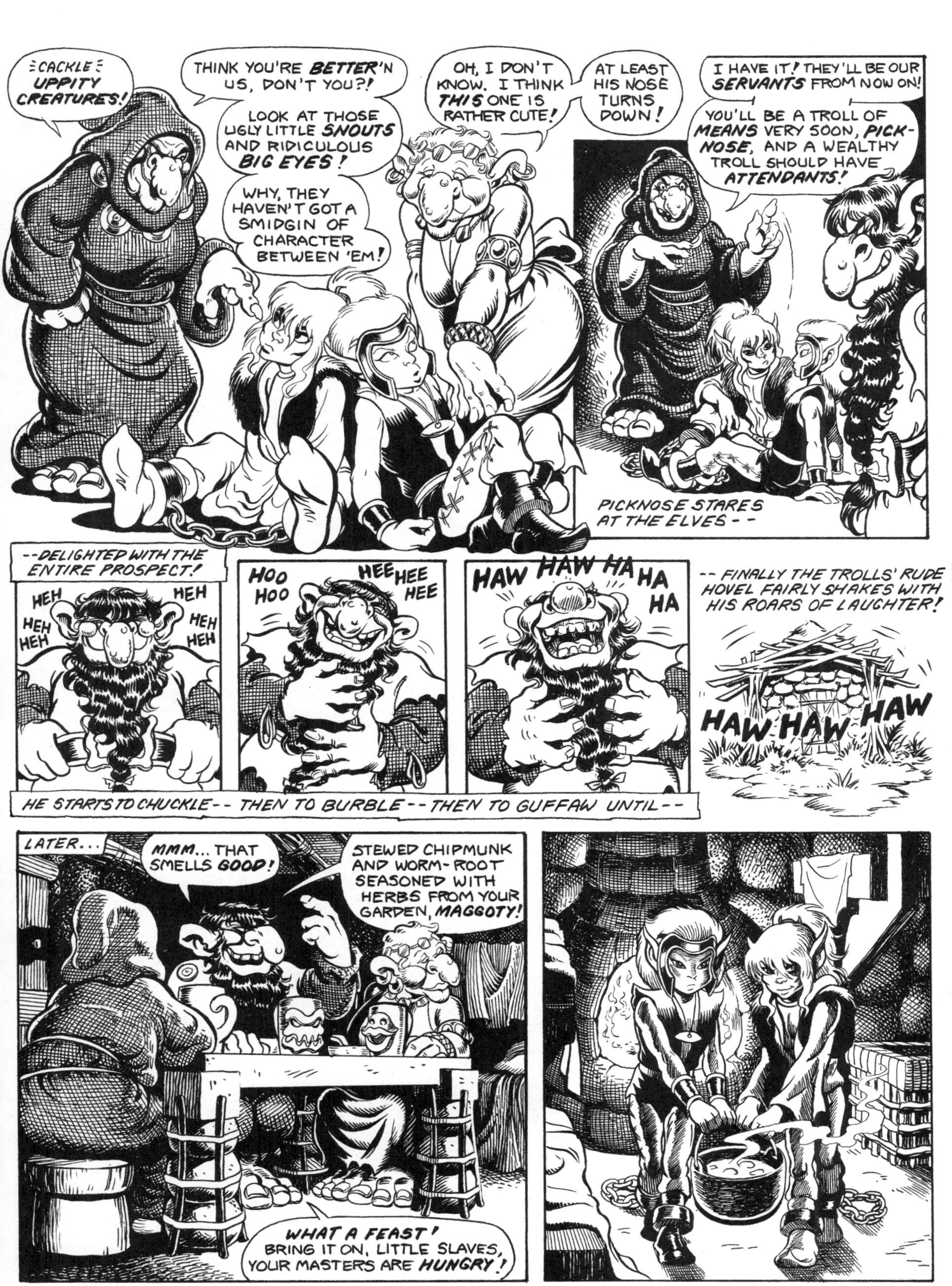
CACKLE UPPITY CREATURES!
THINK YOU'RE BETTER'N US, DON'T YOU?!
LOOK AT THOSE UGLY LITTLE SNOUTS AND RIDICULOUS BIG EYES!
WHY, THEY HAVEN'T GOT A SMIDGIN OF CHARACTER BETWEEN 'EM!
OH, I DON'T KNOW. I THINK THIS ONE IS RATHER CUTE!
AT LEAST HIS NOSE TURNS DOWN!
I HAVE IT! THEY'LL BE OUR SERVANTS FROM NOW ON!
YOU'LL BE A TROLL OF MEANS VERY SOON, PICK-NOSE, AND A WEALTHY TROLL SHOULD HAVE ATTENDANTS!
PICKNOSE STARES AT THE ELVES--
--DELIGHTED WITH THE ENTIRE PROSPECT!
HEH HEH HEH HEH HEH HEH HEH
HOO HOO HEE HEE HEE HEE
HAW HAW HA HA HA HA
--FINALLY THE TROLLS' RUDE HOVEL FAIRLY SHAKES WITH HIS ROARS OF LAUGHTER!
HAW HAW HAW
HE STARTS TO CHUCKLE-- THEN TO BURBLE--THEN TO GUFFAW UNTIL--
LATER...
MMM... THAT SMELLS GOOD!
STEWED CHIPMUNK AND WORM-ROOT SEASONED WITH HERBS FROM YOUR GARDEN, MAGGOTY!
WHAT A FEAST! BRING IT ON, LITTLE SLAVES, YOUR MASTERS ARE HUNGRY!

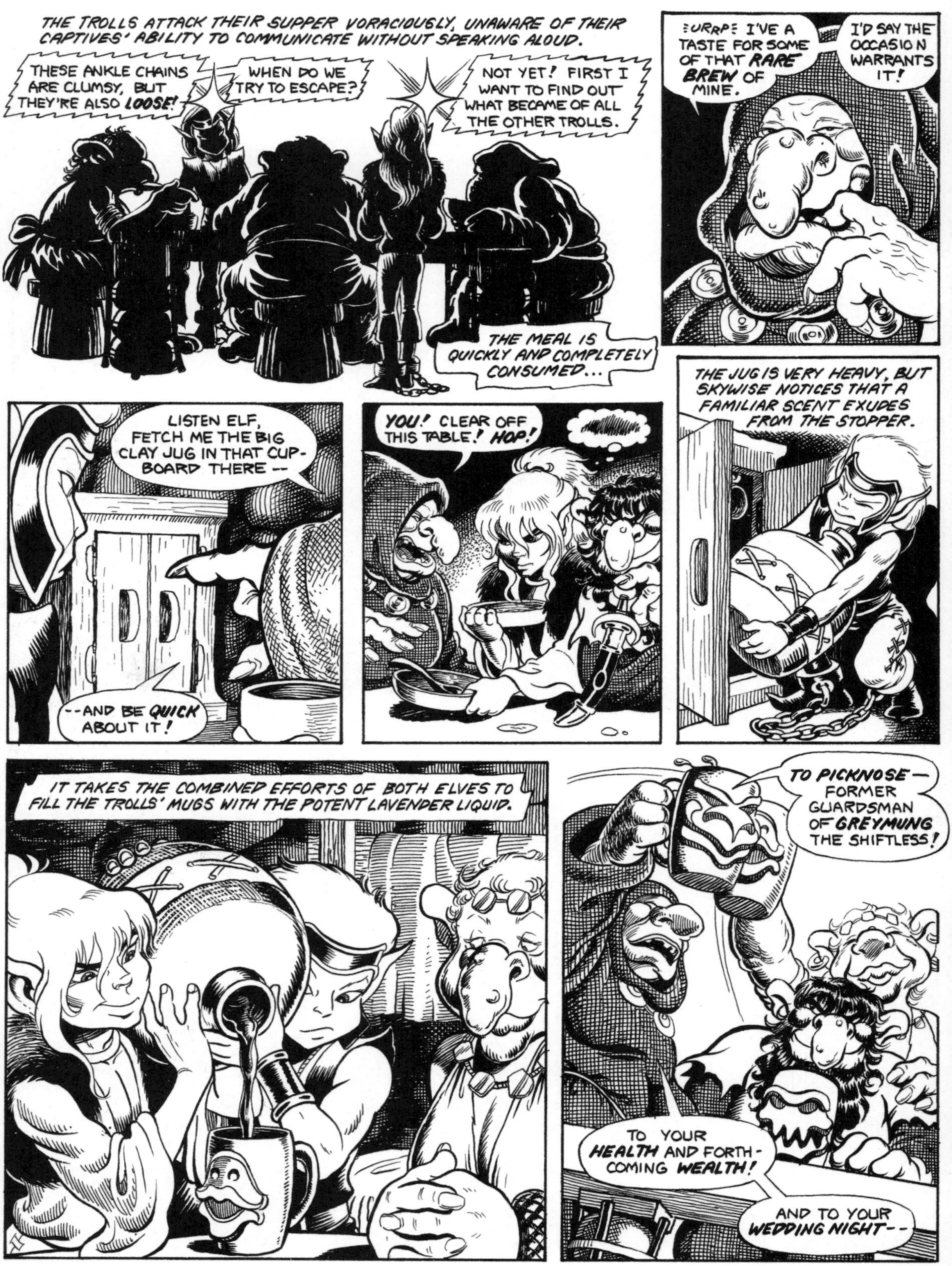
THE TROLLS ATTACK THEIR SUPPER VORACIOUSLY, UNAWARE OF THEIR CAPTIVES' ABILITY TO COMMUNICATE WITHOUT SPEAKING ALOUD.
THESE ANKLE CHAINS ARE CLUMSY, BUT THEY'RE ALSO LOOSE!
WHEN DO WE TRY TO ESCAPE?
NOT YET! FIRST I WANT TO FIND OUT WHAT BECAME OF ALL THE OTHER TROLLS.
THE MEAL IS QUICKLY AND COMPLETELY CONSUMED...
BURRP! I'VE A TASTE FOR SOME OF THAT RARE BREW OF MINE.
I'D SAY THE OCCASION WARRANTS IT!
LISTEN ELF, FETCH ME THE BIG CLAY JUG IN THAT CUPBOARD THERE --
--AND BE QUICK ABOUT IT!
YOU! CLEAR OFF THIS TABLE! HOP!
THE JUG IS VERY HEAVY, BUT SKYWISE NOTICES THAT A FAMILIAR SCENT EXUDES FROM THE STOPPER.
IT TAKES THE COMBINED EFFORTS OF BOTH ELVES TO FILL THE TROLLS' MUGS WITH THE POTENT LAVENDER LIQUID.
TO PICKNOSE — FORMER GUARDSMAN OF GREYMUNG THE SHIFTLESS!
TO YOUR HEALTH AND FORTH-COMING WEALTH!
AND TO YOUR WEDDING NIGHT--

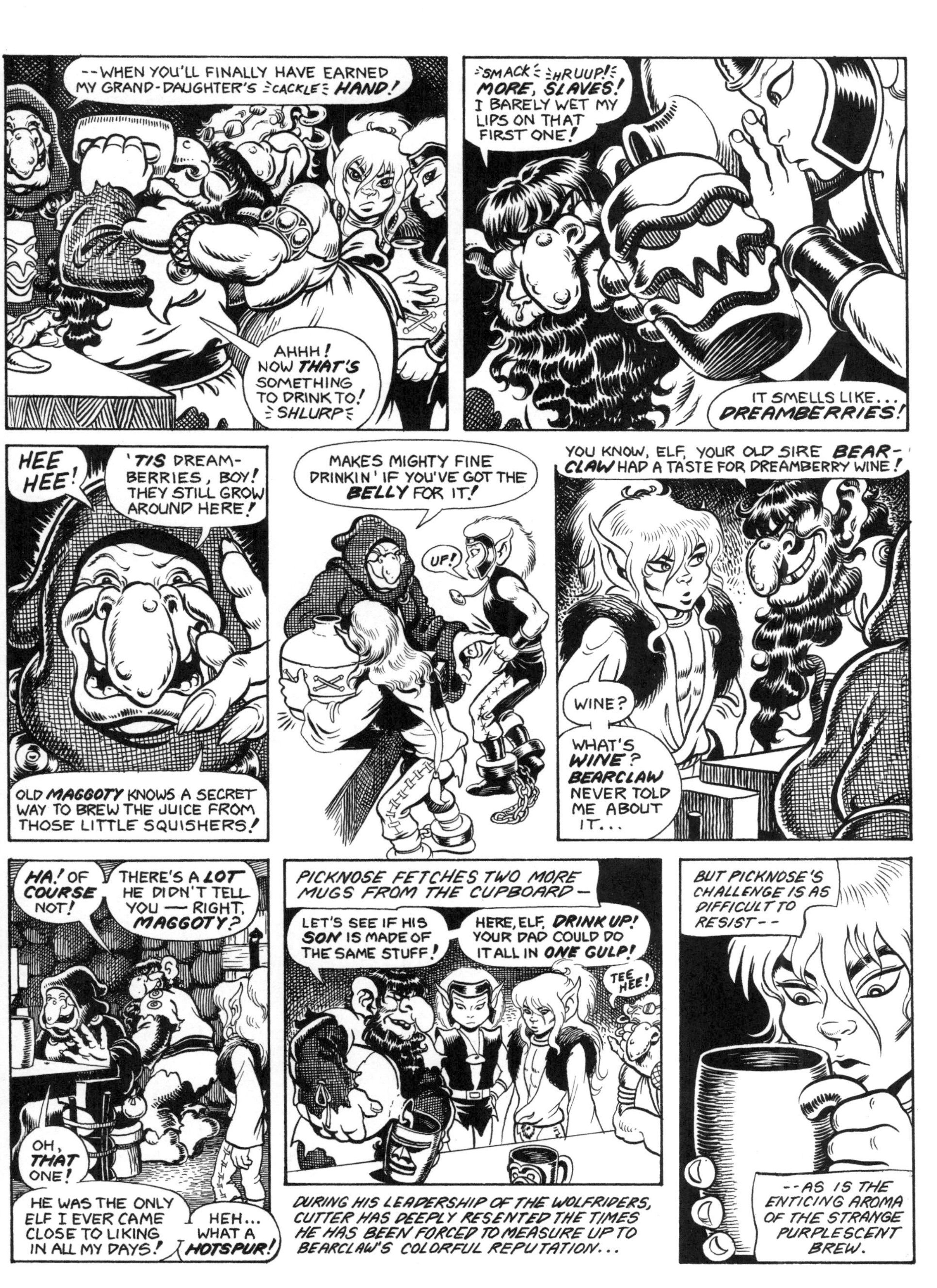
--WHEN YOU'LL FINALLY HAVE EARNED MY GRAND-DAUGHTER'S ≷CACKLE≷ HAND!
AHHH! NOW THAT'S SOMETHING TO DRINK TO! ≷SHLURP≷
≷SMACK≷ ≷HRUUP!≷ MORE, SLAVES! I BARELY WET MY LIPS ON THAT FIRST ONE!
IT SMELLS LIKE... DREAMBERRIES!
HEE HEE!
'TIS DREAM-BERRIES, BOY! THEY STILL GROW AROUND HERE!
OLD MAGGOTY KNOWS A SECRET WAY TO BREW THE JUICE FROM THOSE LITTLE SQUISHERS!
MAKES MIGHTY FINE DRINKIN' IF YOU'VE GOT THE BELLY FOR IT!
UF!
YOU KNOW, ELF, YOUR OLD SIRE BEAR-CLAW HAD A TASTE FOR DREAMBERRY WINE!
WINE?
WHAT'S WINE? BEARCLAW NEVER TOLD ME ABOUT IT...
HA! OF COURSE NOT!
THERE'S A LOT HE DIDN'T TELL YOU — RIGHT, MAGGOTY?
OH, THAT ONE!
HE WAS THE ONLY ELF I EVER CAME CLOSE TO LIKING IN ALL MY DAYS!
HEH... WHAT A HOTSPUR!
PICKNOSE FETCHES TWO MORE MUGS FROM THE CUPBOARD—
LET'S SEE IF HIS SON IS MADE OF THE SAME STUFF!
HERE, ELF, DRINK UP! YOUR DAD COULD DO IT ALL IN ONE GULP!
TEE HEE!
DURING HIS LEADERSHIP OF THE WOLFRIDERS, CUTTER HAS DEEPLY RESENTED THE TIMES HE HAS BEEN FORCED TO MEASURE UP TO BEARCLAW'S COLORFUL REPUTATION...
BUT PICKNOSE'S CHALLENGE IS AS DIFFICULT TO RESIST--
--AS IS THE ENTICING AROMA OF THE STRANGE PURPLESCENT BREW.

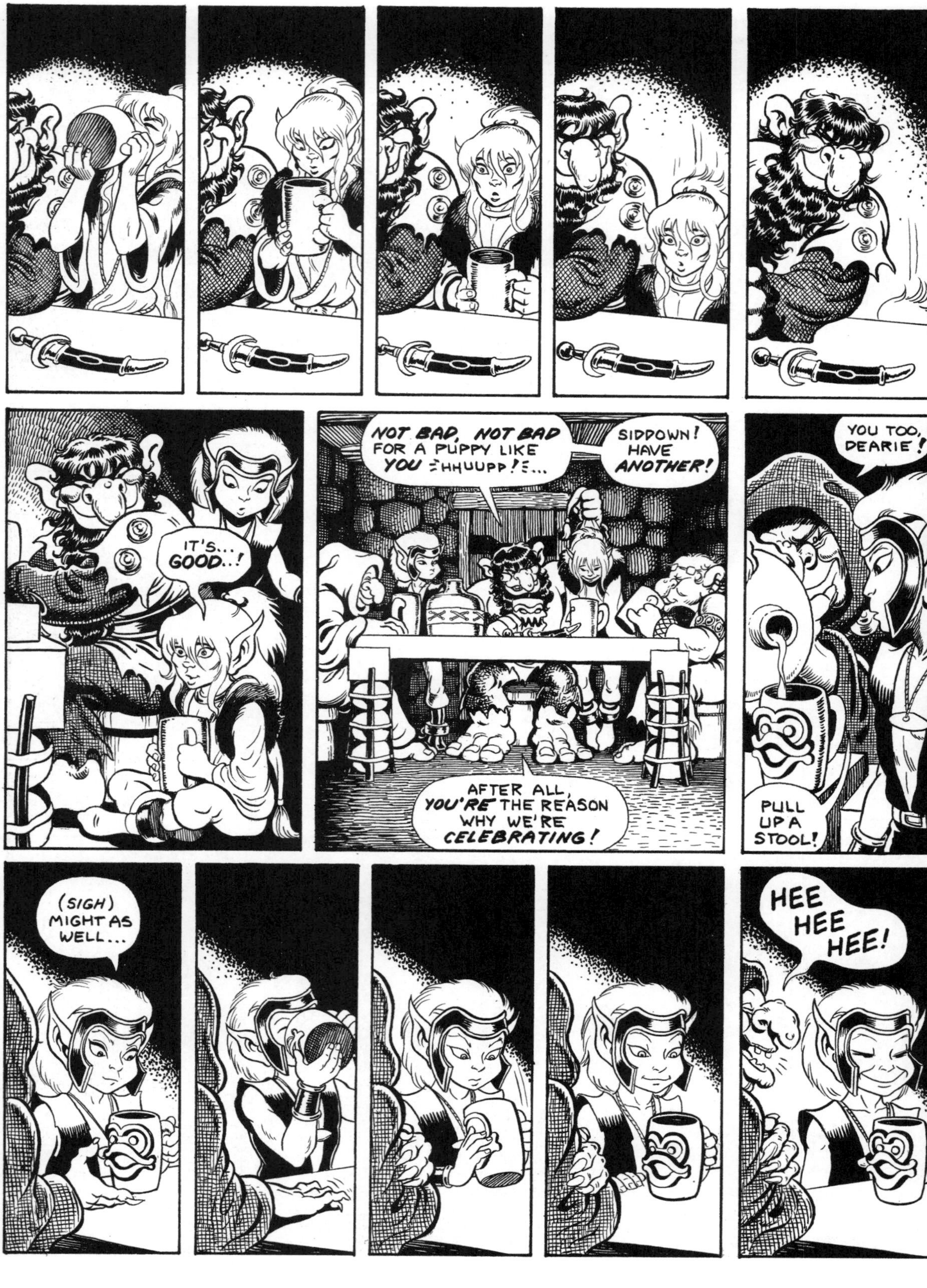
IT'S... GOOD..!
NOT BAD, NOT BAD FOR A PUPPY LIKE YOU HHUUPP!...
SIDDOWN! HAVE ANOTHER!
AFTER ALL, YOU'RE THE REASON WHY WE'RE CELEBRATING!
YOU TOO, DEARIE!
PULL UP A STOOL!
(SIGH) MIGHT AS WELL...
HEE HEE HEE!

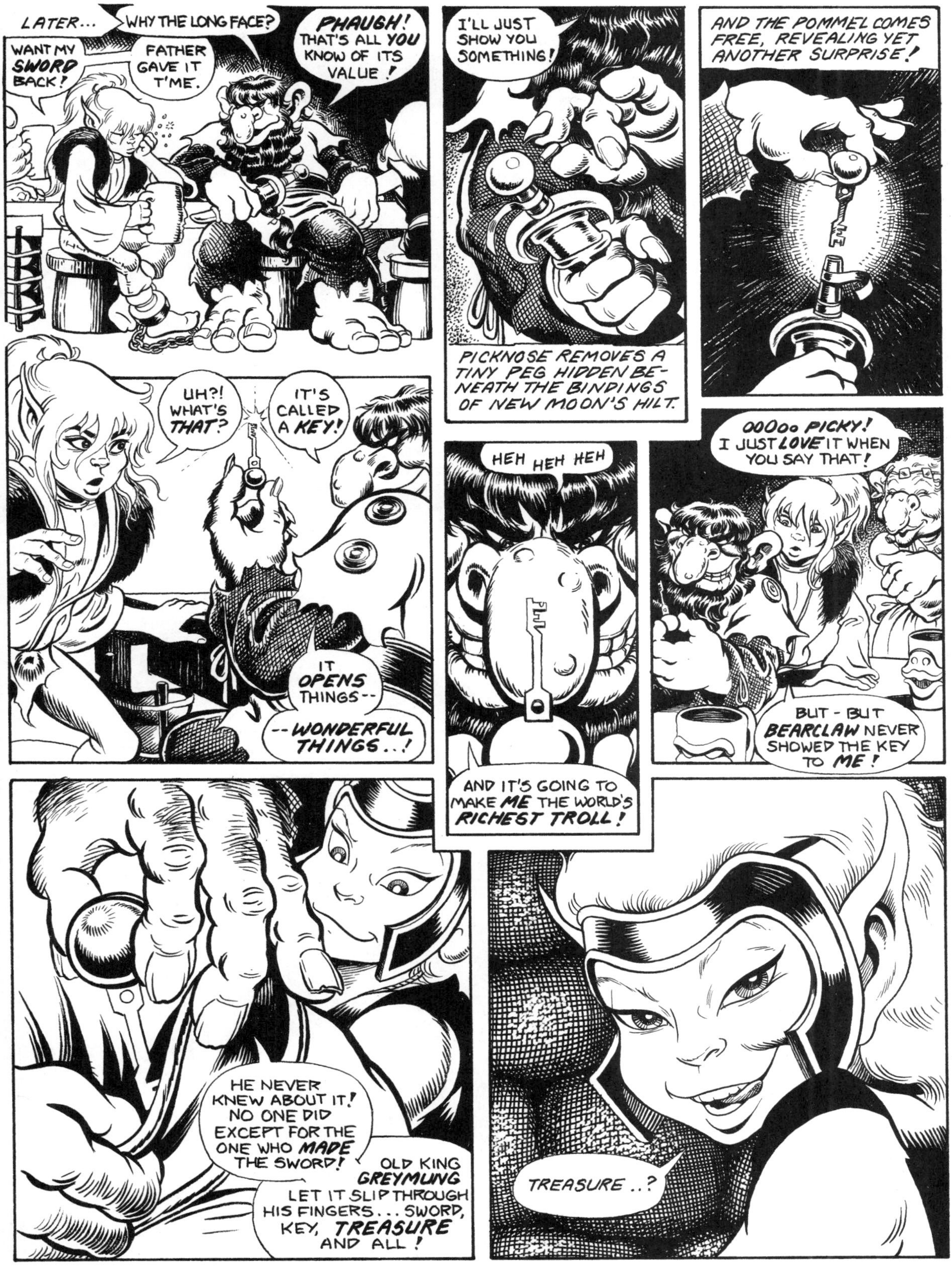
LATER...
WHY THE LONG FACE?
WANT MY SWORD BACK!
FATHER GAVE IT T'ME.
PHAUGH! THAT'S ALL YOU KNOW OF ITS VALUE!
I'LL JUST SHOW YOU SOMETHING!
PICKNOSE REMOVES A TINY PEG HIDDEN BENEATH THE BINDINGS OF NEW MOON'S HILT.
AND THE POMMEL COMES FREE, REVEALING YET ANOTHER SURPRISE!
UH?! WHAT'S THAT?
IT'S CALLED A KEY!
IT OPENS THINGS--
--WONDERFUL THINGS..!
HEH HEH HEH
AND IT'S GOING TO MAKE ME THE WORLD'S RICHEST TROLL!
OOOOo PICKY! I JUST LOVE IT WHEN YOU SAY THAT!
BUT - BUT BEARCLAW NEVER SHOWED THE KEY TO ME!
HE NEVER KNEW ABOUT IT! NO ONE DID EXCEPT FOR THE ONE WHO MADE THE SWORD!
OLD KING GREYMUNG LET IT SLIP THROUGH HIS FINGERS... SWORD, KEY, TREASURE AND ALL!
TREASURE..?

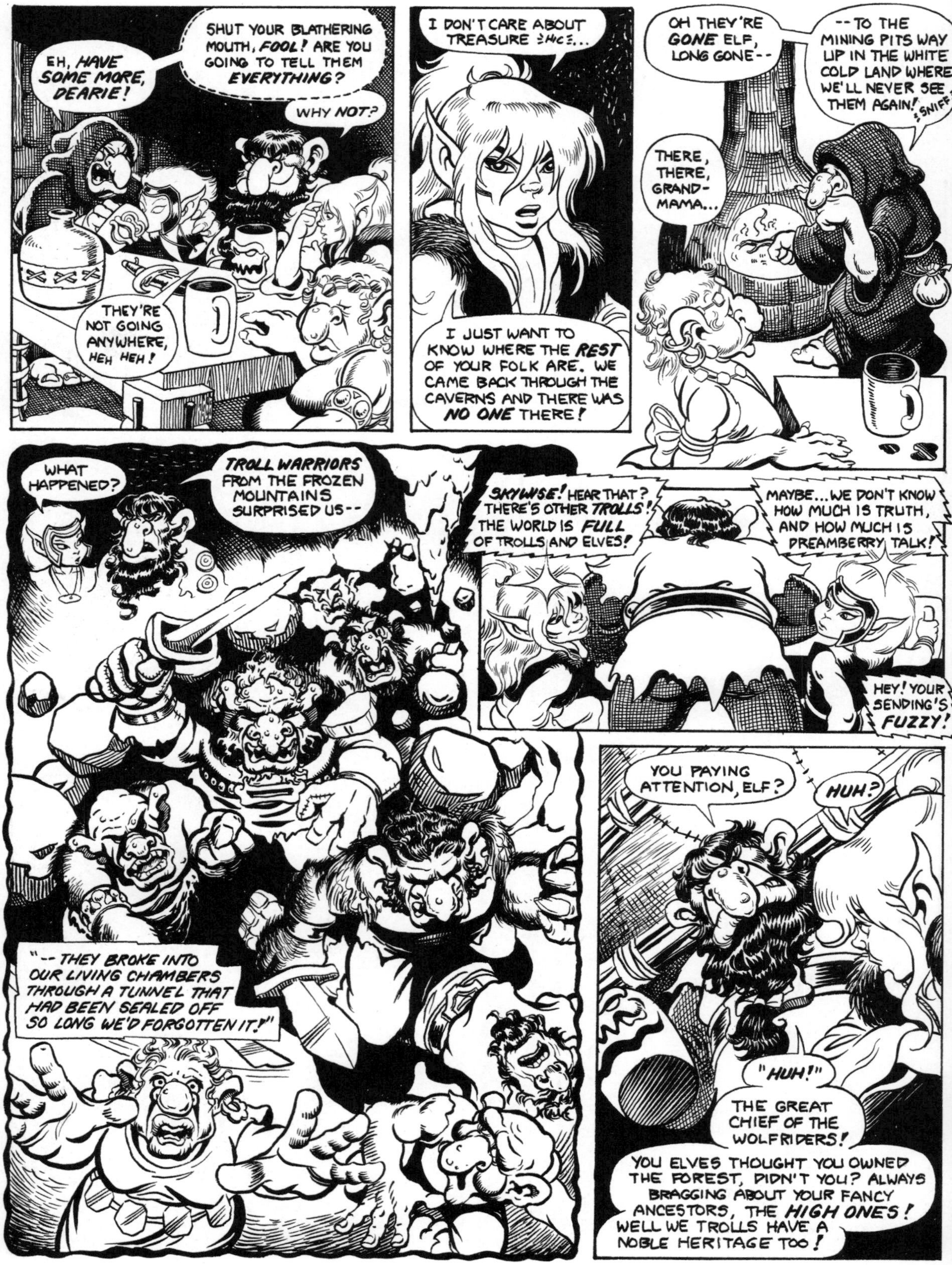

EH, HAVE SOME MORE, DEARIE!
SHUT YOUR BLATHERING MOUTH, FOOL! ARE YOU GOING TO TELL THEM EVERYTHING?
WHY NOT?
THEY'RE NOT GOING ANYWHERE, HEH HEH!
I DON'T CARE ABOUT TREASURE HIC...
I JUST WANT TO KNOW WHERE THE REST OF YOUR FOLK ARE. WE CAME BACK THROUGH THE CAVERNS AND THERE WAS NO ONE THERE!
OH THEY'RE GONE ELF, LONG GONE--
--TO THE MINING PITS WAY UP IN THE WHITE COLD LAND WHERE WE'LL NEVER SEE THEM AGAIN! SNIFF
THERE, THERE, GRAND-MAMA...
WHAT HAPPENED?
TROLL WARRIORS FROM THE FROZEN MOUNTAINS SURPRISED US--
"--THEY BROKE INTO OUR LIVING CHAMBERS THROUGH A TUNNEL THAT HAD BEEN SEALED OFF SO LONG WE'D FORGOTTEN IT!"
SKYWISE! HEAR THAT? THERE'S OTHER TROLLS! THE WORLD IS FULL OF TROLLS AND ELVES!
MAYBE... WE DON'T KNOW HOW MUCH IS TRUTH, AND HOW MUCH IS DREAMBERRY TALK!
HEY! YOUR SENDING'S FUZZY!
YOU PAYING ATTENTION, ELF?
HUH?
"HUH!"
THE GREAT CHIEF OF THE WOLFRIDERS!
YOU ELVES THOUGHT YOU OWNED THE FOREST, DIDN'T YOU? ALWAYS BRAGGING ABOUT YOUR FANCY ANCESTORS, THE HIGH ONES! WELL WE TROLLS HAVE A NOBLE HERITAGE TOO!

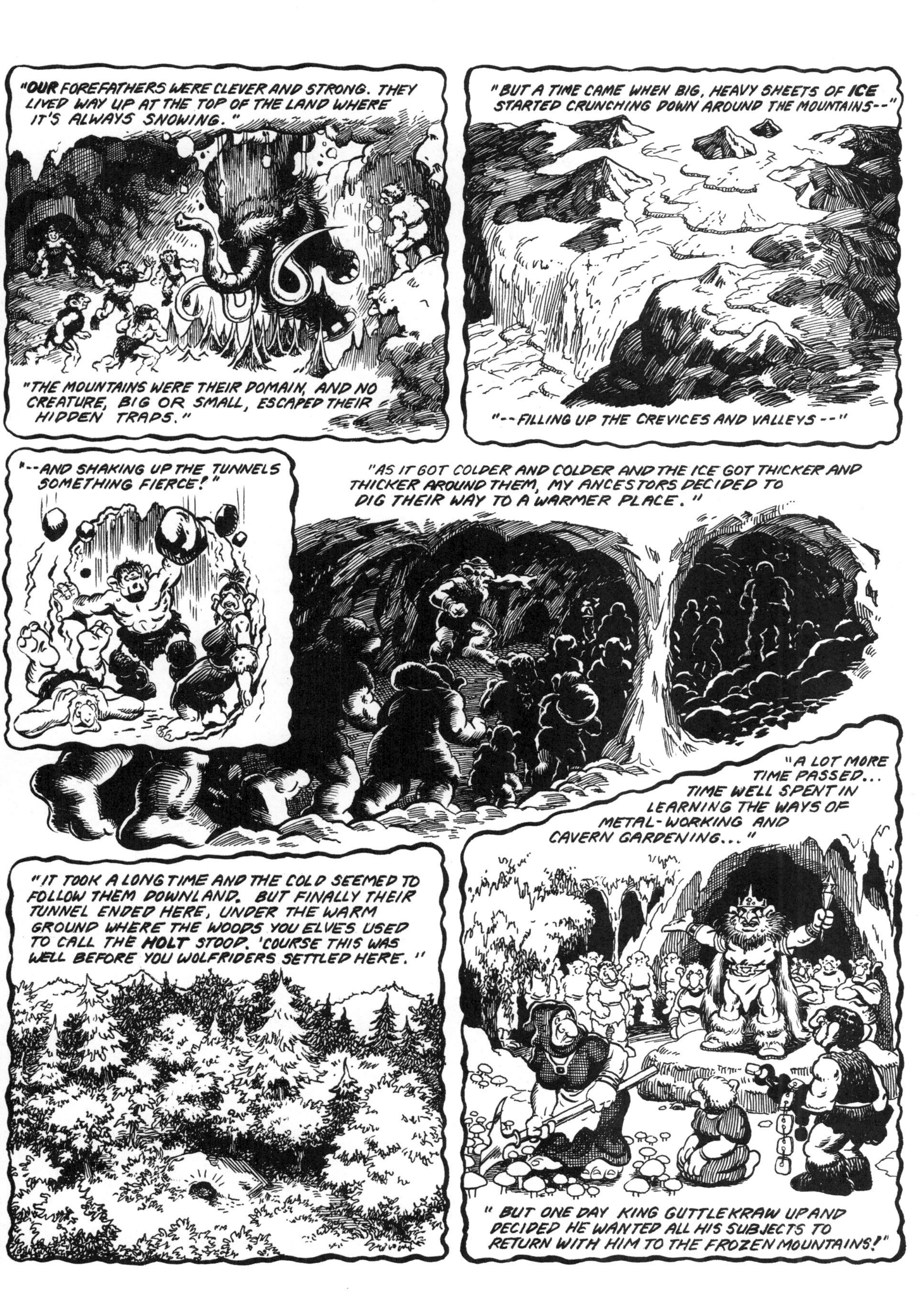
"OUR FOREFATHERS WERE CLEVER AND STRONG. THEY LIVED WAY UP AT THE TOP OF THE LAND WHERE IT'S ALWAYS SNOWING."
"THE MOUNTAINS WERE THEIR DOMAIN, AND NO CREATURE, BIG OR SMALL, ESCAPED THEIR HIDDEN TRAPS."
"BUT A TIME CAME WHEN BIG, HEAVY SHEETS OF ICE STARTED CRUNCHING DOWN AROUND THE MOUNTAINS--"
"--FILLING UP THE CREVICES AND VALLEYS--"
"--AND SHAKING UP THE TUNNELS SOMETHING FIERCE!"
"AS IT GOT COLDER AND COLDER AND THE ICE GOT THICKER AND THICKER AROUND THEM, MY ANCESTORS DECIDED TO DIG THEIR WAY TO A WARMER PLACE."
"IT TOOK A LONG TIME AND THE COLD SEEMED TO FOLLOW THEM DOWNLAND. BUT FINALLY THEIR TUNNEL ENDED HERE, UNDER THE WARM GROUND WHERE THE WOODS YOU ELVES USED TO CALL THE HOLT STOOD. 'COURSE THIS WAS WELL BEFORE YOU WOLFRIDERS SETTLED HERE."
"A LOT MORE TIME PASSED... TIME WELL SPENT IN LEARNING THE WAYS OF METAL-WORKING AND CAVERN GARDENING..."
"BUT ONE DAY KING GUTTLEKRAW UP AND DECIDED HE WANTED ALL HIS SUBJECTS TO RETURN WITH HIM TO THE FROZEN MOUNTAINS!"

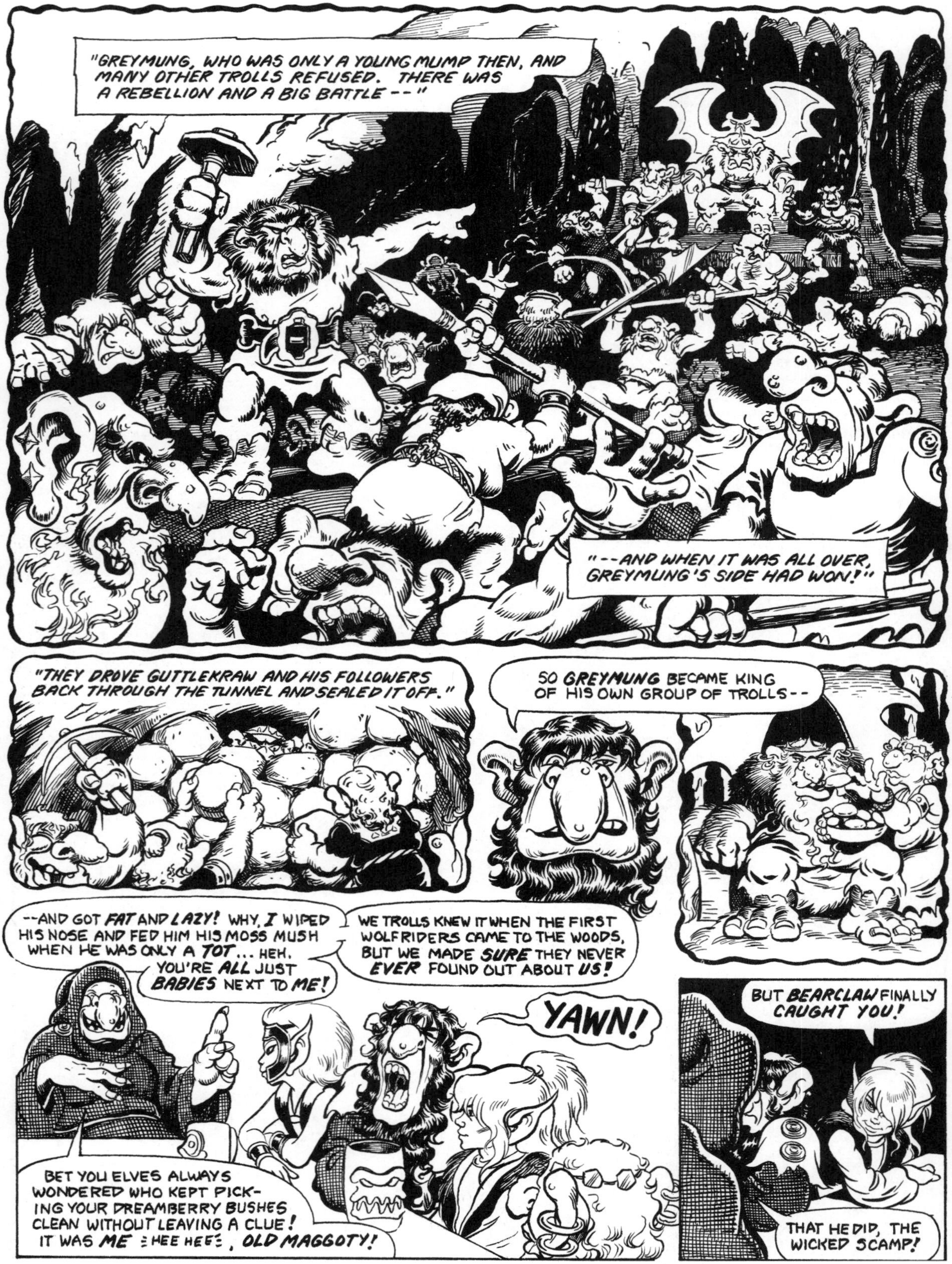
"GREYMUNG, WHO WAS ONLY A YOUNG MUMP THEN, AND MANY OTHER TROLLS REFUSED. THERE WAS A REBELLION AND A BIG BATTLE --"
"--AND WHEN IT WAS ALL OVER, GREYMUNG'S SIDE HAD WON!"
"THEY DROVE GUTTLEKRAW AND HIS FOLLOWERS BACK THROUGH THE TUNNEL AND SEALED IT OFF."
SO GREYMUNG BECAME KING OF HIS OWN GROUP OF TROLLS--
--AND GOT FAT AND LAZY! WHY, I WIPED HIS NOSE AND FED HIM HIS MOSS MUSH WHEN HE WAS ONLY A TOT... HEH. YOU'RE ALL JUST BABIES NEXT TO ME!
WE TROLLS KNEW IT WHEN THE FIRST WOLFRIDERS CAME TO THE WOODS, BUT WE MADE SURE THEY NEVER EVER FOUND OUT ABOUT US!
YAWN!
BET YOU ELVES ALWAYS WONDERED WHO KEPT PICKING YOUR DREAMBERRY BUSHES CLEAN WITHOUT LEAVING A CLUE! IT WAS ME HEE HEE, OLD MAGGOTY!
BUT BEARCLAW FINALLY CAUGHT YOU!
THAT HE DID, THE WICKED SCAMP!

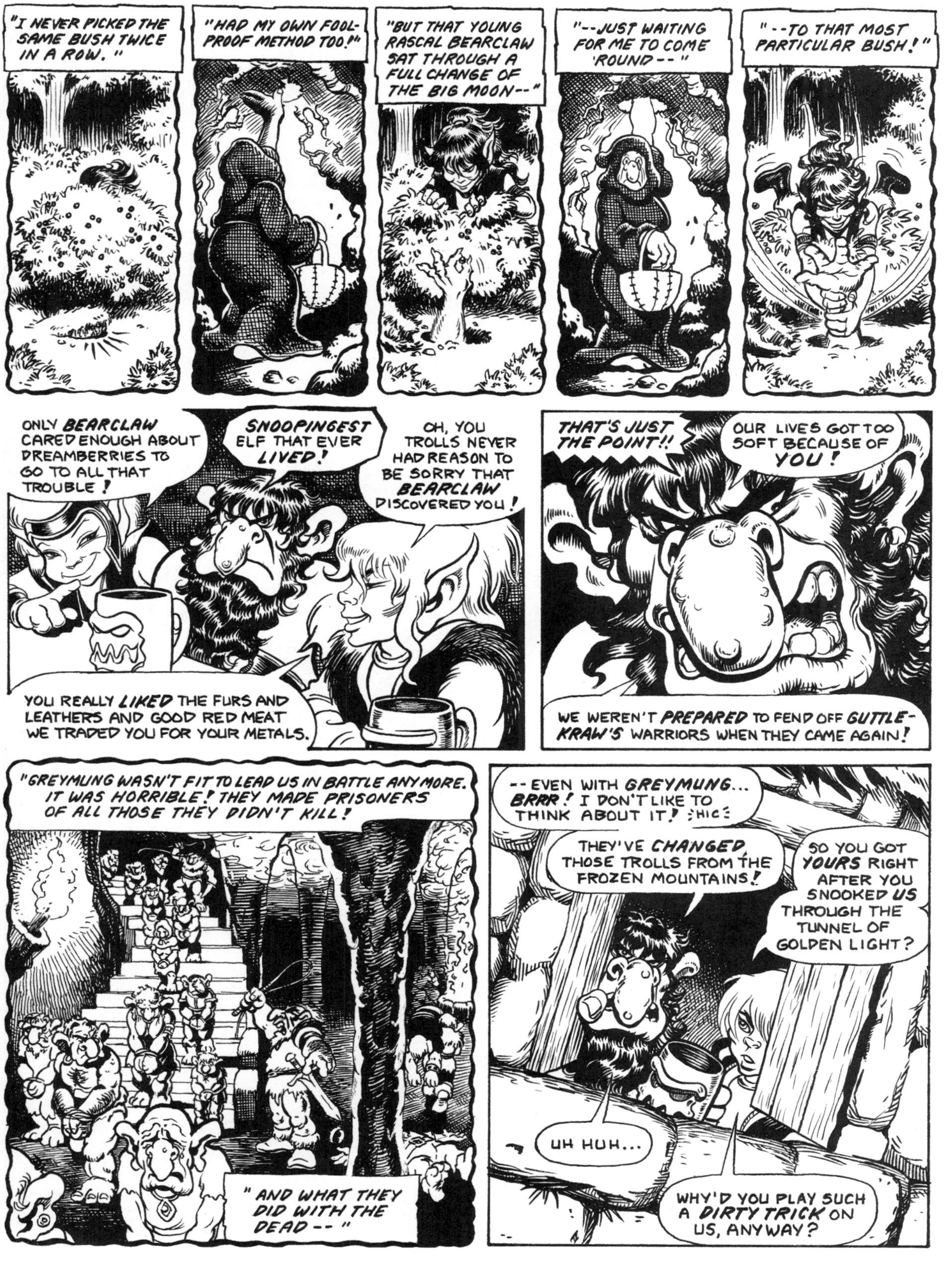
"I NEVER PICKED THE SAME BUSH TWICE IN A ROW."
"HAD MY OWN FOOL-PROOF METHOD TOO!"
"BUT THAT YOUNG RASCAL BEARCLAW SAT THROUGH A FULL CHANGE OF THE BIG MOON--"
"--JUST WAITING FOR ME TO COME 'ROUND--"
"--TO THAT MOST PARTICULAR BUSH!"
ONLY BEARCLAW CARED ENOUGH ABOUT DREAMBERRIES TO GO TO ALL THAT TROUBLE!
SNOOPINGEST ELF THAT EVER LIVED!
OH, YOU TROLLS NEVER HAD REASON TO BE SORRY THAT BEARCLAW DISCOVERED YOU!
YOU REALLY LIKED THE FURS AND LEATHERS AND GOOD RED MEAT WE TRADED YOU FOR YOUR METALS.
THAT'S JUST THE POINT!!
OUR LIVES GOT TOO SOFT BECAUSE OF YOU!
WE WEREN'T PREPARED TO FEND OFF GUTTLEKRAW'S WARRIORS WHEN THEY CAME AGAIN!
"GREYMUNG WASN'T FIT TO LEAD US IN BATTLE ANYMORE. IT WAS HORRIBLE! THEY MADE PRISONERS OF ALL THOSE THEY DIDN'T KILL!
"AND WHAT THEY DID WITH THE DEAD--"
--EVEN WITH GREYMUNG... BRRR! I DON'T LIKE TO THINK ABOUT IT! HIC
THEY'VE CHANGED THOSE TROLLS FROM THE FROZEN MOUNTAINS!
SO YOU GOT YOURS RIGHT AFTER YOU SNOOKED US THROUGH THE TUNNEL OF GOLDEN LIGHT?
UH HUH...
WHY'D YOU PLAY SUCH A DIRTY TRICK ON US, ANYWAY?

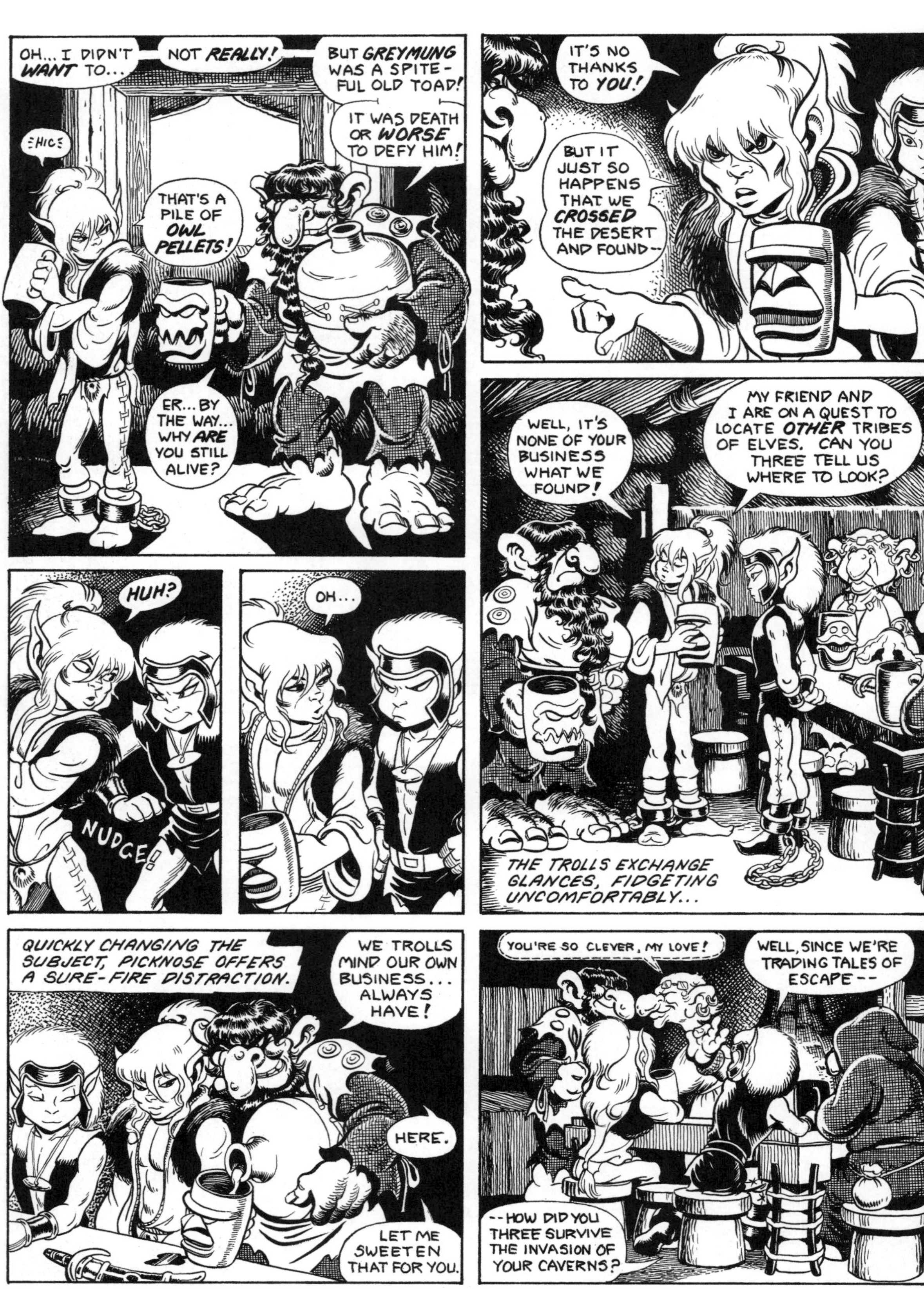

OH... I DIDN'T WANT TO...
NOT REALLY!
BUT GREYMUNG WAS A SPITE-FUL OLD TOAD!
IT WAS DEATH OR WORSE TO DEFY HIM!
HIC
THAT'S A PILE OF OWL PELLETS!
ER... BY THE WAY... WHY ARE YOU STILL ALIVE?
IT'S NO THANKS TO YOU!
BUT IT JUST SO HAPPENS THAT WE CROSSED THE DESERT AND FOUND--
HUH?
NUDGE!
OH...
WELL, IT'S NONE OF YOUR BUSINESS WHAT WE FOUND!
MY FRIEND AND I ARE ON A QUEST TO LOCATE OTHER TRIBES OF ELVES. CAN YOU THREE TELL US WHERE TO LOOK?
THE TROLLS EXCHANGE GLANCES, FIDGETING UNCOMFORTABLY...
QUICKLY CHANGING THE SUBJECT, PICKNOSE OFFERS A SURE-FIRE DISTRACTION.
WE TROLLS MIND OUR OWN BUSINESS... ALWAYS HAVE!
HERE.
LET ME SWEETEN THAT FOR YOU.
YOU'RE SO CLEVER, MY LOVE!
WELL, SINCE WE'RE TRADING TALES OF ESCAPE--
--HOW DID YOU THREE SURVIVE THE INVASION OF YOUR CAVERNS?

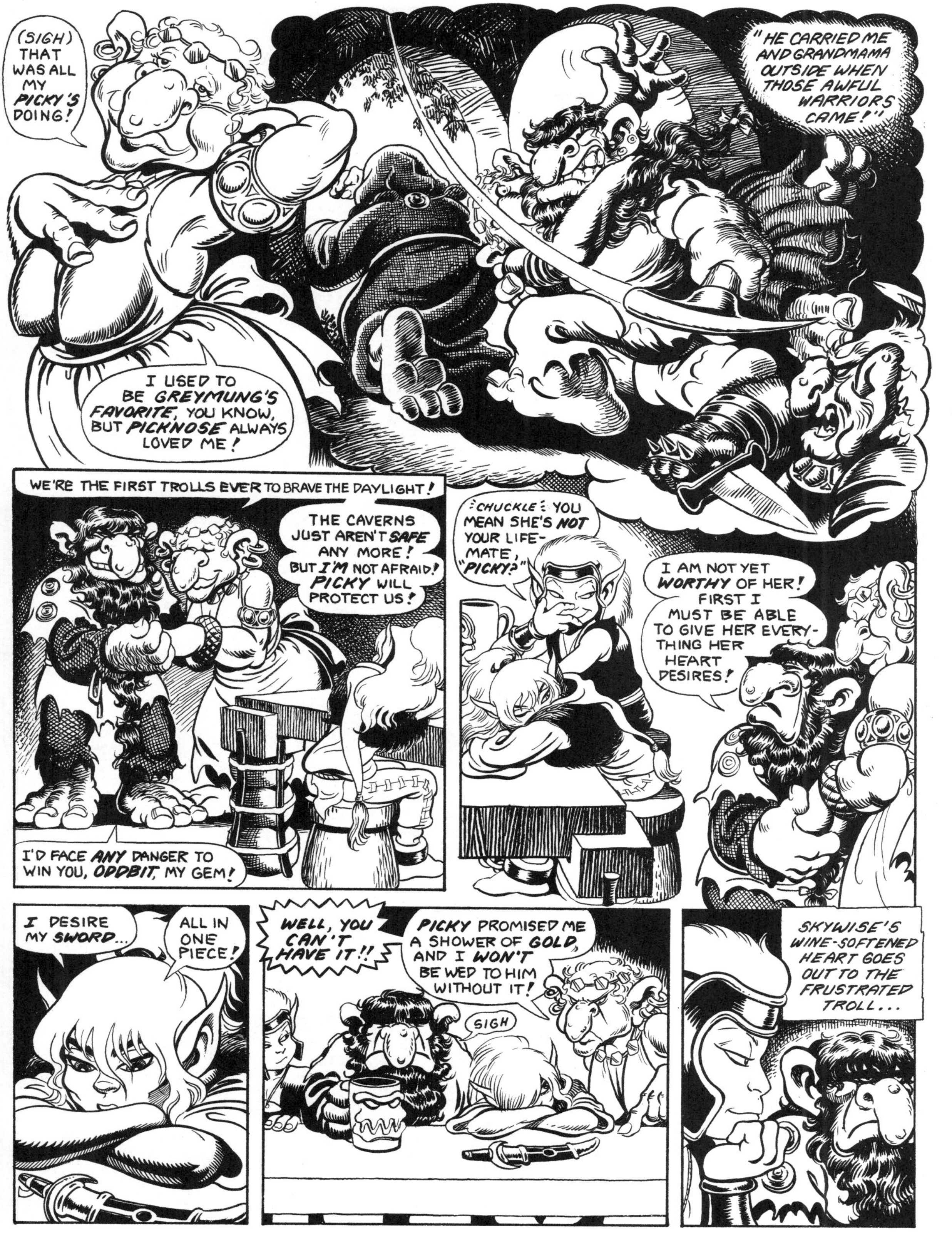
(SIGH) THAT WAS ALL MY PICKY'S DOING!
"HE CARRIED ME AND GRANDMAMA OUTSIDE WHEN THOSE AWFUL WARRIORS CAME!"
I USED TO BE GREYMUNG'S FAVORITE, YOU KNOW, BUT PICKNOSE ALWAYS LOVED ME!
WE'RE THE FIRST TROLLS EVER TO BRAVE THE DAYLIGHT!
THE CAVERNS JUST AREN'T SAFE ANY MORE! BUT I'M NOT AFRAID! PICKY WILL PROTECT US!
I'D FACE ANY DANGER TO WIN YOU, ODDBIT, MY GEM!
:CHUCKLE: YOU MEAN SHE'S NOT YOUR LIFE-MATE, "PICKY?"
I AM NOT YET WORTHY OF HER! FIRST I MUST BE ABLE TO GIVE HER EVERYTHING HER HEART DESIRES!
I DESIRE MY SWORD...
ALL IN ONE PIECE!
WELL, YOU CAN'T HAVE IT!!
PICKY PROMISED ME A SHOWER OF GOLD, AND I WON'T BE WED TO HIM WITHOUT IT!
SIGH
SKYWISE'S WINE-SOFTENED HEART GOES OUT TO THE FRUSTRATED TROLL...

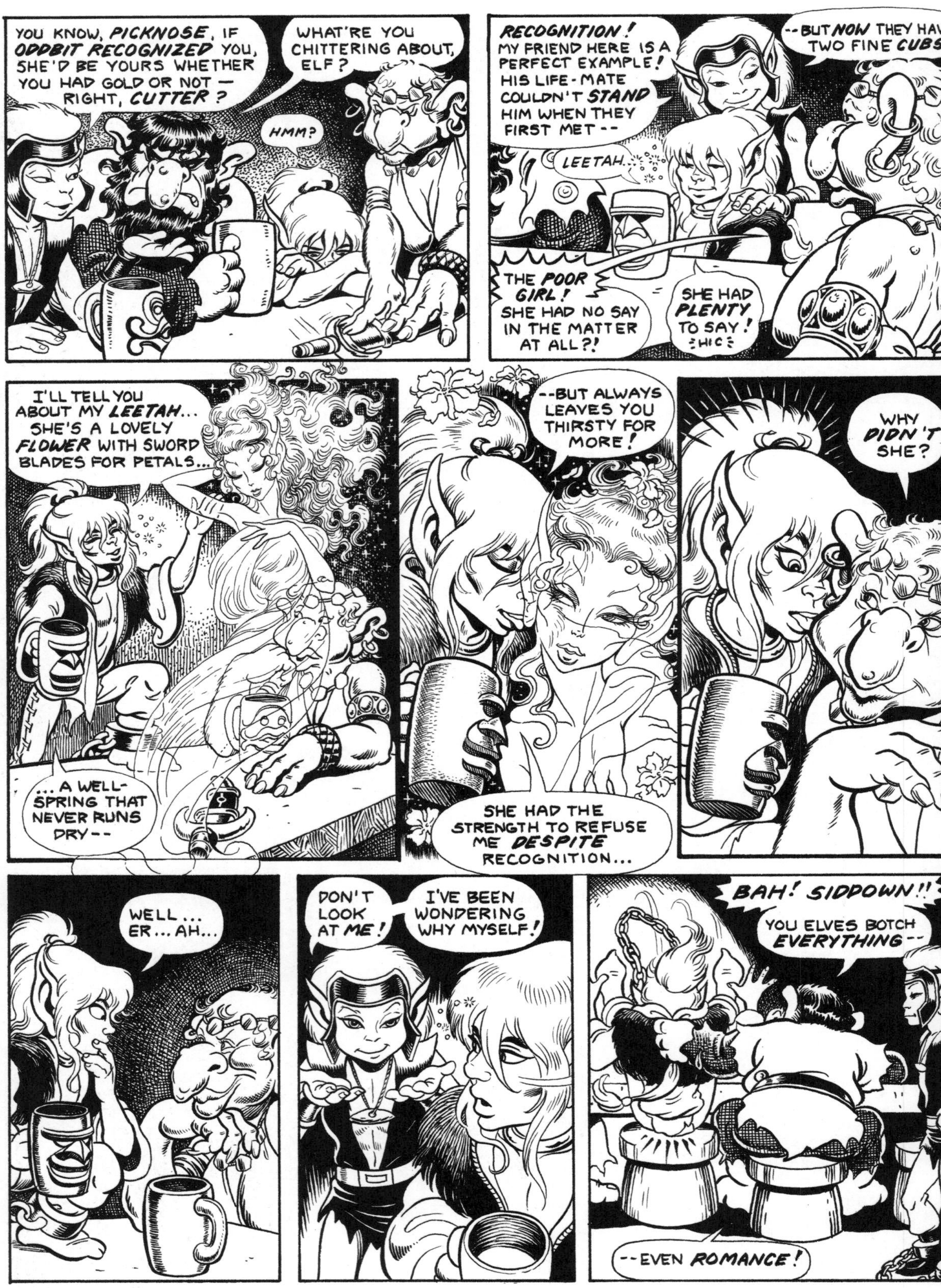

YOU KNOW, PICKNOSE, IF ODDBIT RECOGNIZED YOU, SHE'D BE YOURS WHETHER YOU HAD GOLD OR NOT — RIGHT, CUTTER?
WHAT'RE YOU CHITTERING ABOUT, ELF?
HMM?
RECOGNITION! MY FRIEND HERE IS A PERFECT EXAMPLE! HIS LIFE-MATE COULDN'T STAND HIM WHEN THEY FIRST MET --
LEETAH...
--BUT NOW THEY HAVE TWO FINE CUBS!
THE POOR GIRL! SHE HAD NO SAY IN THE MATTER AT ALL?!
SHE HAD PLENTY TO SAY! HIC
I'LL TELL YOU ABOUT MY LEETAH... SHE'S A LOVELY FLOWER WITH SWORD BLADES FOR PETALS...
... A WELL-SPRING THAT NEVER RUNS DRY --
--BUT ALWAYS LEAVES YOU THIRSTY FOR MORE!
SHE HAD THE STRENGTH TO REFUSE ME DESPITE RECOGNITION...
WHY DIDN'T SHE?
WELL... ER... AH...
DON'T LOOK AT ME!
I'VE BEEN WONDERING WHY MYSELF!
BAH! SIDDOWN!!
YOU ELVES BOTCH EVERYTHING --
-- EVEN ROMANCE!

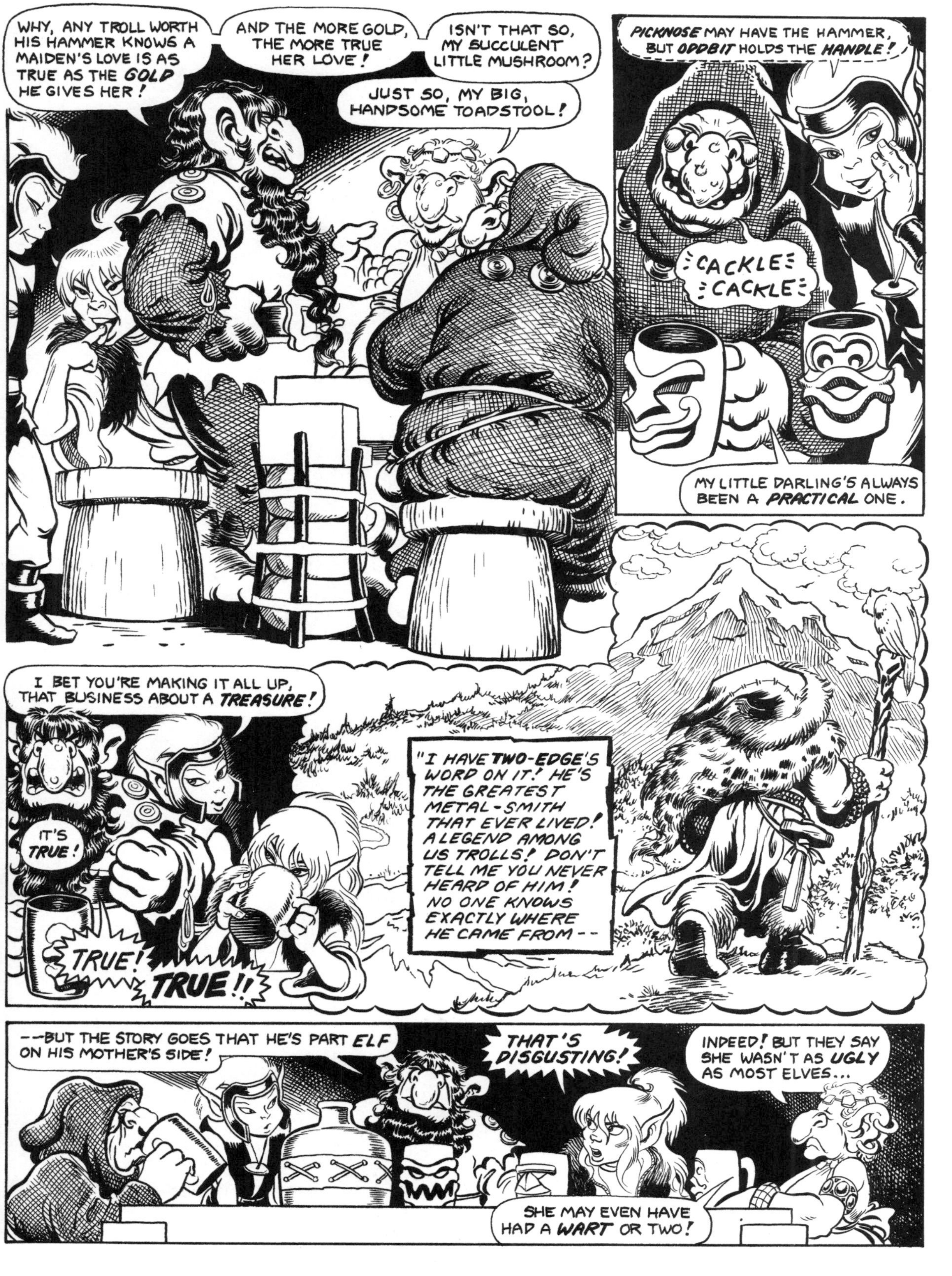
WHY, ANY TROLL WORTH HIS HAMMER KNOWS A MAIDEN'S LOVE IS AS TRUE AS THE GOLD HE GIVES HER!
AND THE MORE GOLD, THE MORE TRUE HER LOVE!
ISN'T THAT SO, MY SUCCULENT LITTLE MUSHROOM?
JUST SO, MY BIG, HANDSOME TOADSTOOL!
PICKNOSE MAY HAVE THE HAMMER, BUT ODDBIT HOLDS THE HANDLE!
CACKLE CACKLE
MY LITTLE DARLING'S ALWAYS BEEN A PRACTICAL ONE.
I BET YOU'RE MAKING IT ALL UP, THAT BUSINESS ABOUT A TREASURE!
IT'S TRUE!
TRUE! TRUE!!
"I HAVE TWO-EDGE'S WORD ON IT! HE'S THE GREATEST METAL-SMITH THAT EVER LIVED! A LEGEND AMONG US TROLLS! DON'T TELL ME YOU NEVER HEARD OF HIM! NO ONE KNOWS EXACTLY WHERE HE CAME FROM--
--BUT THE STORY GOES THAT HE'S PART ELF ON HIS MOTHER'S SIDE!
THAT'S DISGUSTING!
INDEED! BUT THEY SAY SHE WASN'T AS UGLY AS MOST ELVES...
SHE MAY EVEN HAVE HAD A WART OR TWO!

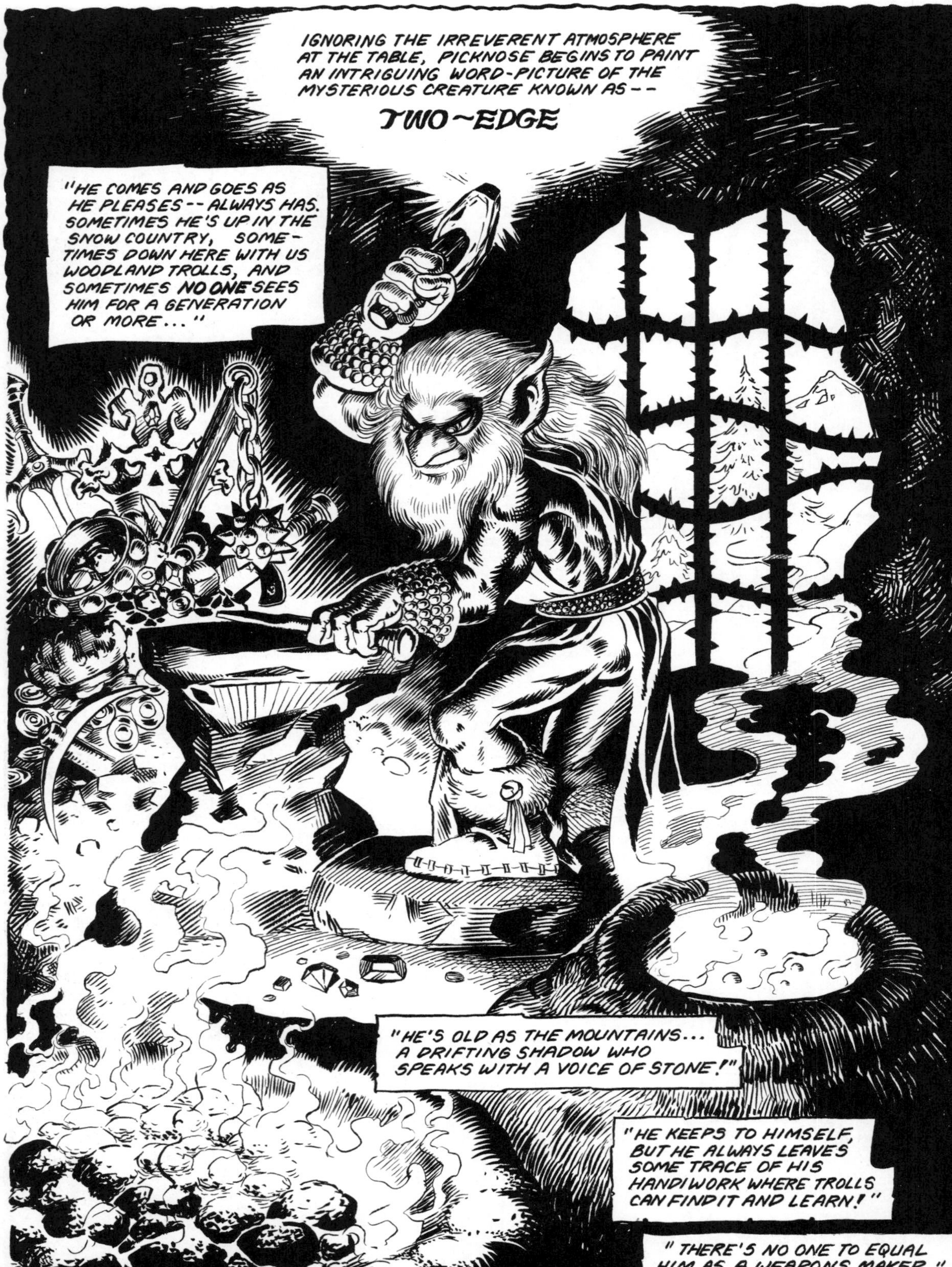

IGNORING THE IRREVERENT ATMOSPHERE AT THE TABLE, PICKNOSE BEGINS TO PAINT AN INTRIGUING WORD-PICTURE OF THE MYSTERIOUS CREATURE KNOWN AS--
TWO~EDGE
"HE COMES AND GOES AS HE PLEASES--ALWAYS HAS. SOMETIMES HE'S UP IN THE SNOW COUNTRY, SOMETIMES DOWN HERE WITH US WOODLAND TROLLS, AND SOMETIMES NO ONE SEES HIM FOR A GENERATION OR MORE..."
"HE'S OLD AS THE MOUNTAINS... A DRIFTING SHADOW WHO SPEAKS WITH A VOICE OF STONE!"
"HE KEEPS TO HIMSELF, BUT HE ALWAYS LEAVES SOME TRACE OF HIS HANDIWORK WHERE TROLLS CAN FIND IT AND LEARN!"
"THERE'S NO ONE TO EQUAL HIM AS A WEAPONS MAKER."

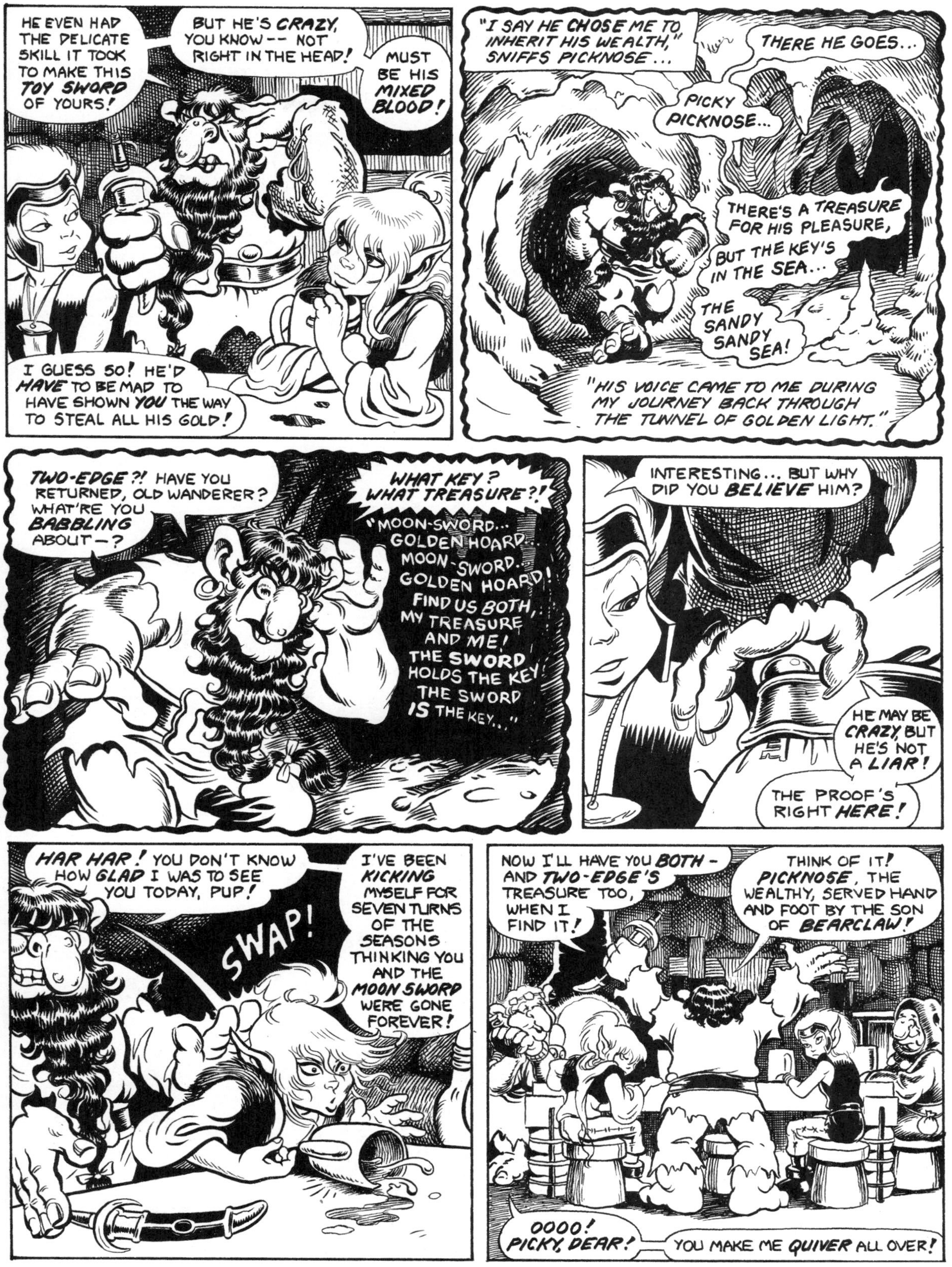
HE EVEN HAD THE DELICATE SKILL IT TOOK TO MAKE THIS TOY SWORD OF YOURS!
BUT HE'S CRAZY, YOU KNOW -- NOT RIGHT IN THE HEAD!
MUST BE HIS MIXED BLOOD!
I GUESS SO! HE'D HAVE TO BE MAD TO HAVE SHOWN YOU THE WAY TO STEAL ALL HIS GOLD!
"I SAY HE CHOSE ME TO INHERIT HIS WEALTH," SNIFFS PICKNOSE...
THERE HE GOES...
PICKY PICKNOSE...
THERE'S A TREASURE FOR HIS PLEASURE,
BUT THE KEY'S IN THE SEA...
THE SANDY SANDY SEA!
"HIS VOICE CAME TO ME DURING MY JOURNEY BACK THROUGH THE TUNNEL OF GOLDEN LIGHT."
TWO-EDGE?! HAVE YOU RETURNED, OLD WANDERER? WHAT'RE YOU BABBLING ABOUT—?
WHAT KEY? WHAT TREASURE?!
"MOON-SWORD... GOLDEN HOARD... MOON-SWORD... GOLDEN HOARD! FIND US BOTH, MY TREASURE AND ME! THE SWORD HOLDS THE KEY! THE SWORD IS THE KEY..."
INTERESTING... BUT WHY DID YOU BELIEVE HIM?
HE MAY BE CRAZY, BUT HE'S NOT A LIAR!
THE PROOF'S RIGHT HERE!
HAR HAR! YOU DON'T KNOW HOW GLAD I WAS TO SEE YOU TODAY, PUP!
SWAP!
I'VE BEEN KICKING MYSELF FOR SEVEN TURNS OF THE SEASONS THINKING YOU AND THE MOON SWORD WERE GONE FOREVER!
NOW I'LL HAVE YOU BOTH - AND TWO-EDGE'S TREASURE TOO, WHEN I FIND IT!
THINK OF IT! PICKNOSE, THE WEALTHY, SERVED HAND AND FOOT BY THE SON OF BEARCLAW!
OOOO! PICKY, DEAR!
YOU MAKE ME QUIVER ALL OVER!

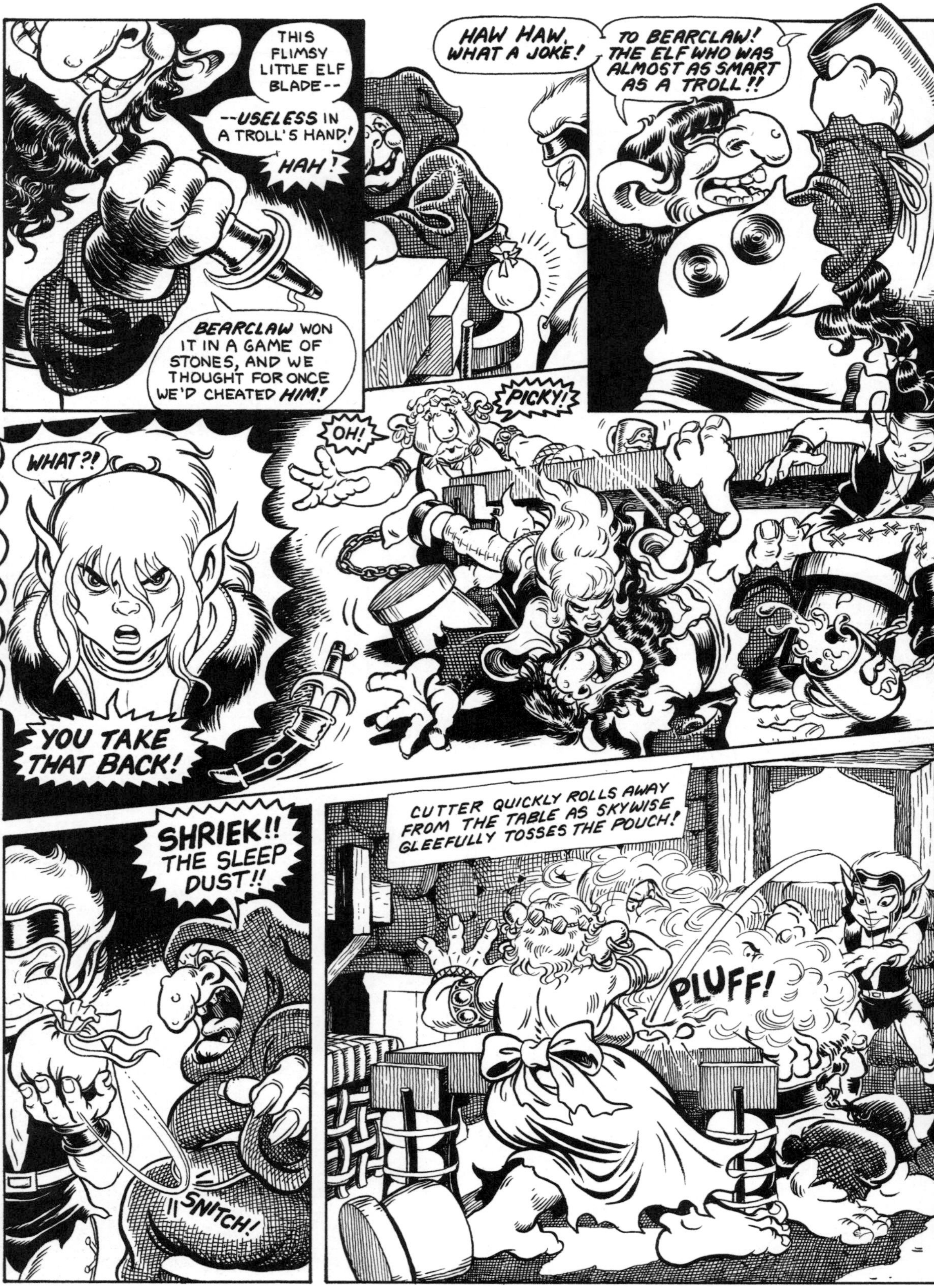

THIS FLIMSY LITTLE ELF BLADE--
--USELESS IN A TROLL'S HAND!
HAH!
BEARCLAW WON IT IN A GAME OF STONES, AND WE THOUGHT FOR ONCE WE'D CHEATED HIM!
HAW HAW, WHAT A JOKE!
TO BEARCLAW! THE ELF WHO WAS ALMOST AS SMART AS A TROLL!!
WHAT?!
YOU TAKE THAT BACK!
OH!
PICKY!
SHRIEK!! THE SLEEP DUST!!
SNITCH!
CUTTER QUICKLY ROLLS AWAY FROM THE TABLE AS SKYWISE GLEEFULLY TOSSES THE POUCH!
PLUFF!

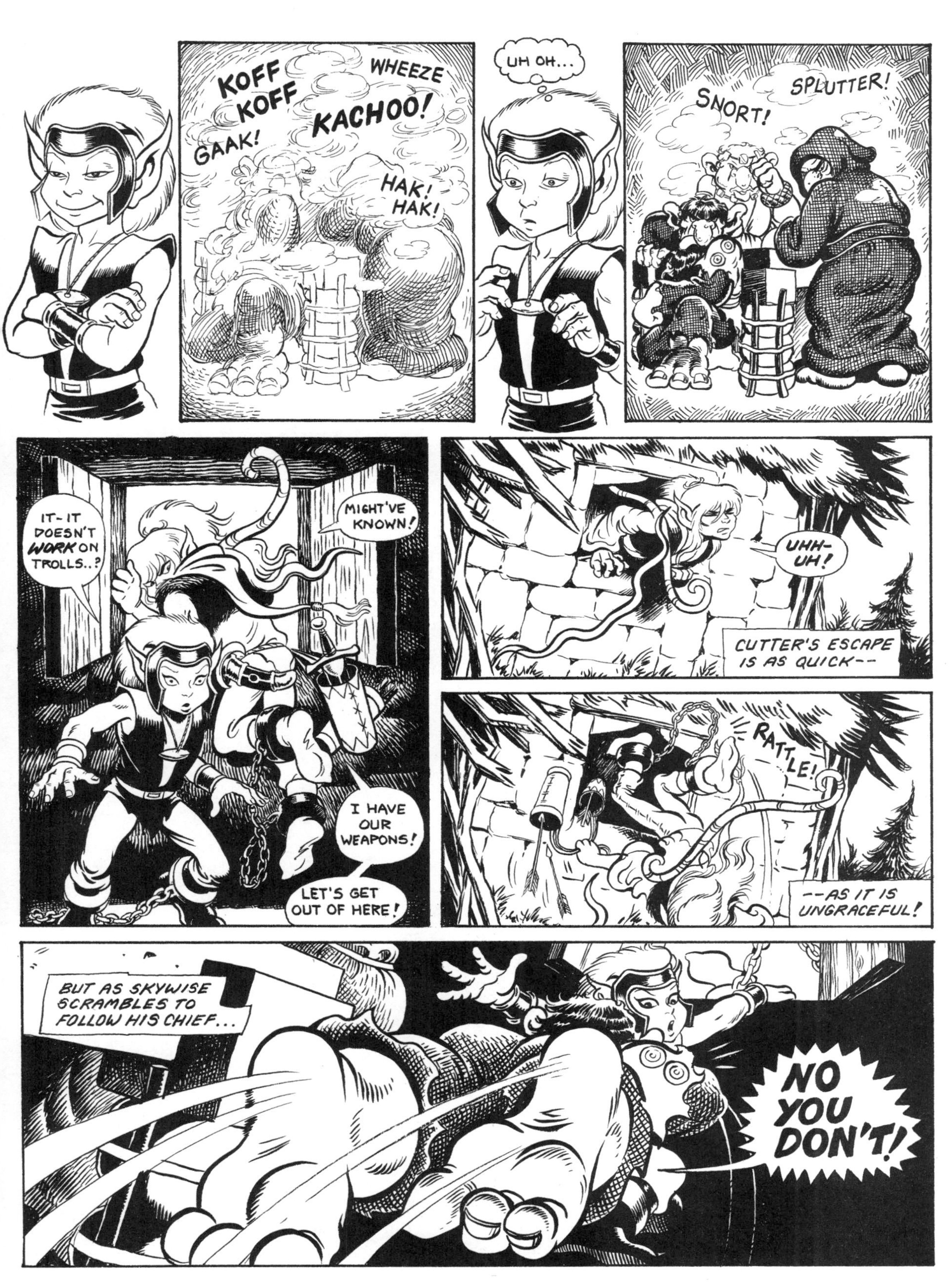
KOFF
KOFF
WHEEZE
KACHOO!
GAAK!
HAK!
HAK!
UH OH...
SNORT!
SPLUTTER!
IT-IT DOESN'T WORK ON TROLLS..?
MIGHT'VE KNOWN!
I HAVE OUR WEAPONS!
LET'S GET OUT OF HERE!
UHH-UH!
CUTTER'S ESCAPE IS AS QUICK--
RATTLE!
--AS IT IS UNGRACEFUL!
BUT AS SKYWISE SCRAMBLES TO FOLLOW HIS CHIEF...
NO YOU DON'T!

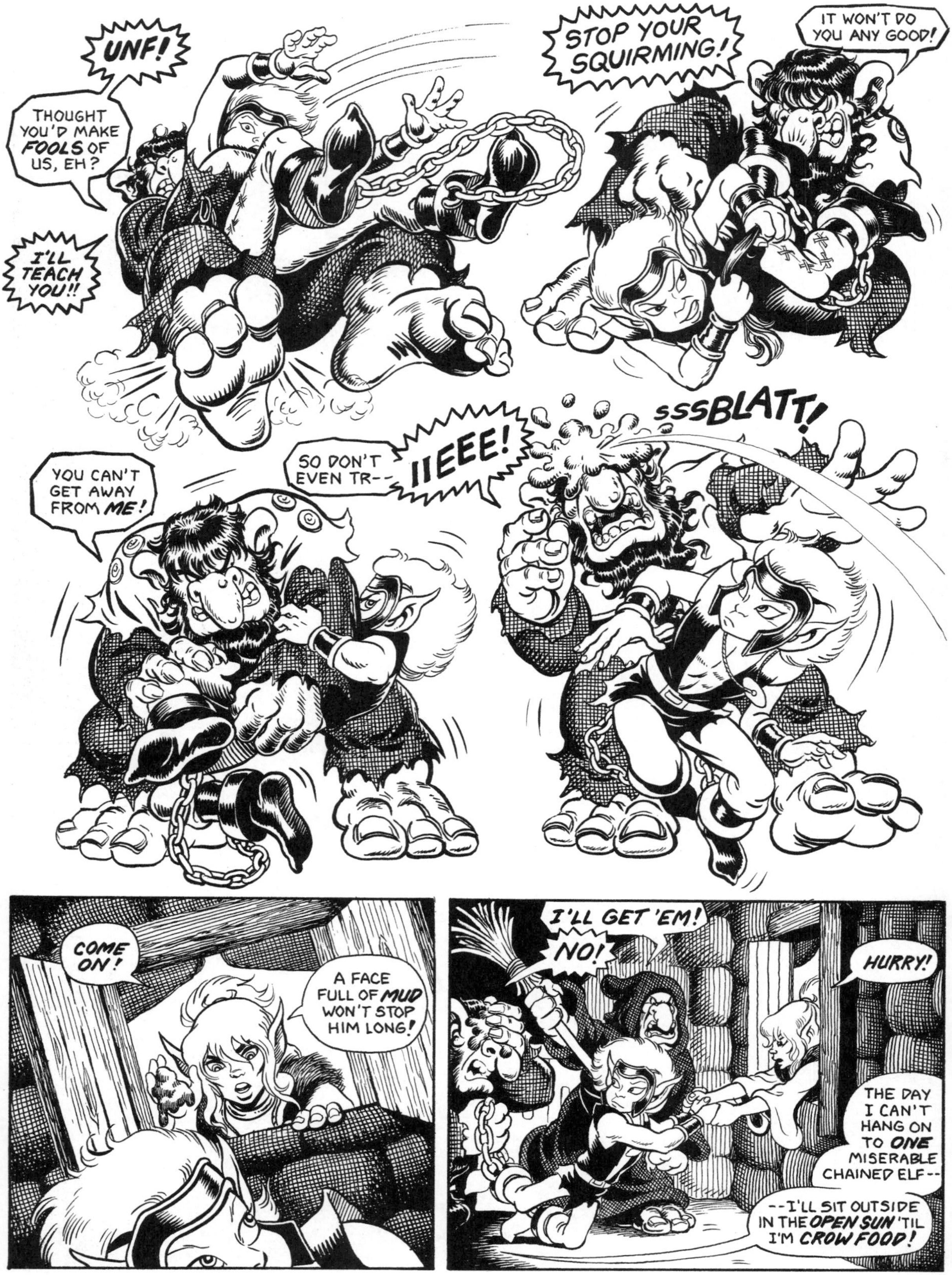
UNF!
THOUGHT YOU'D MAKE FOOLS OF US, EH?
I'LL TEACH YOU!!
STOP YOUR SQUIRMING!
IT WON'T DO YOU ANY GOOD!
YOU CAN'T GET AWAY FROM ME!
SO DON'T EVEN TR--
IIEEE!
SSSBLATT!
COME ON!
A FACE FULL OF MUD WON'T STOP HIM LONG!
I'LL GET 'EM!
NO!
HURRY!
THE DAY I CAN'T HANG ON TO ONE MISERABLE CHAINED ELF--
--I'LL SIT OUTSIDE IN THE OPEN SUN 'TIL I'M CROW FOOD!

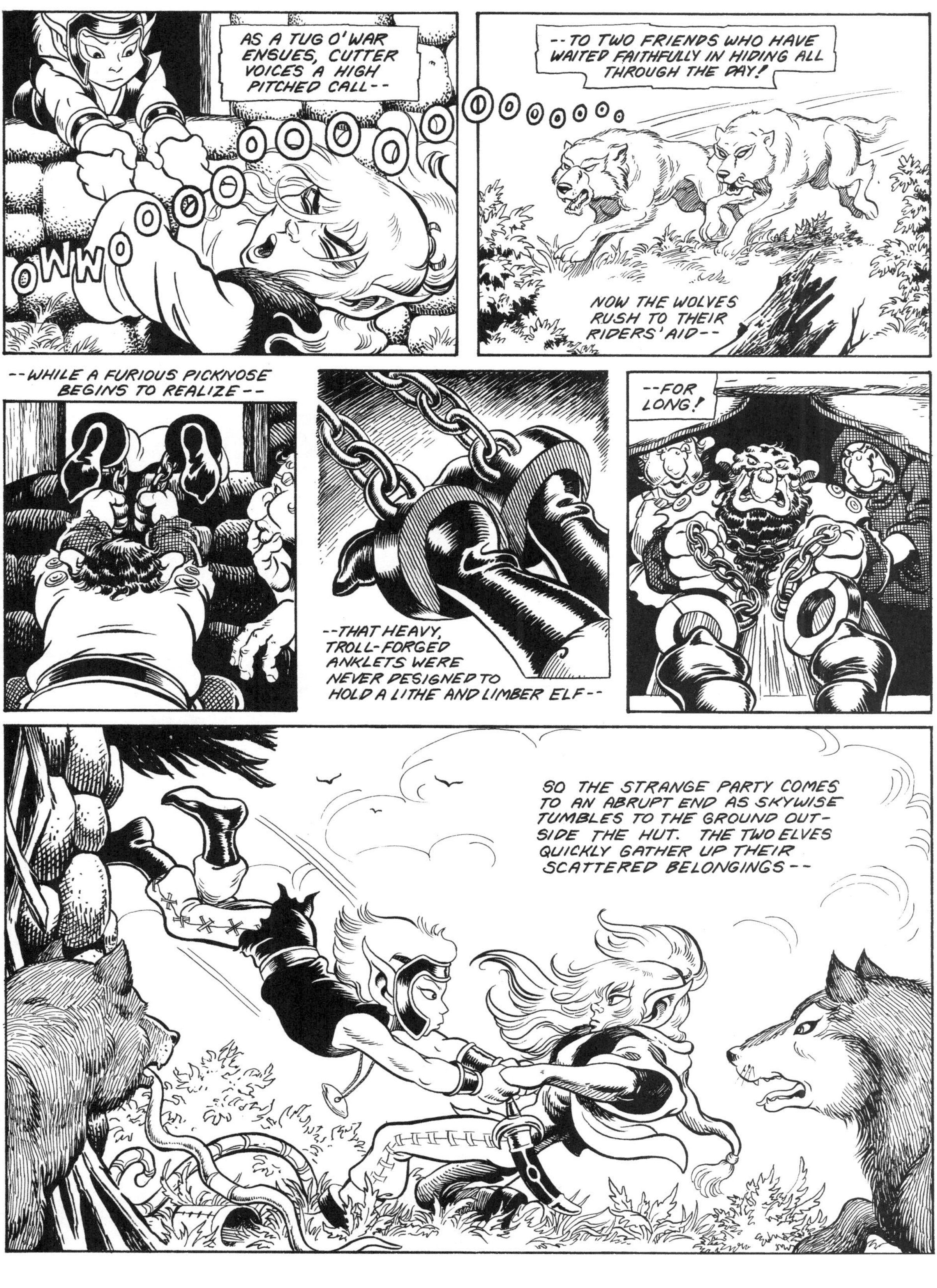
AS A TUG O' WAR ENSUES, CUTTER VOICES A HIGH PITCHED CALL--
OWWOOOOOOOOOOOOOOOOOO
--TO TWO FRIENDS WHO HAVE WAITED FAITHFULLY IN HIDING ALL THROUGH THE DAY!
NOW THE WOLVES RUSH TO THEIR RIDERS' AID--
--WHILE A FURIOUS PICKNOSE BEGINS TO REALIZE--
--THAT HEAVY, TROLL-FORGED ANKLETS WERE NEVER DESIGNED TO HOLD A LITHE AND LIMBER ELF--
--FOR LONG!
SO THE STRANGE PARTY COMES TO AN ABRUPT END AS SKYWISE TUMBLES TO THE GROUND OUTSIDE THE HUT. THE TWO ELVES QUICKLY GATHER UP THEIR SCATTERED BELONGINGS--

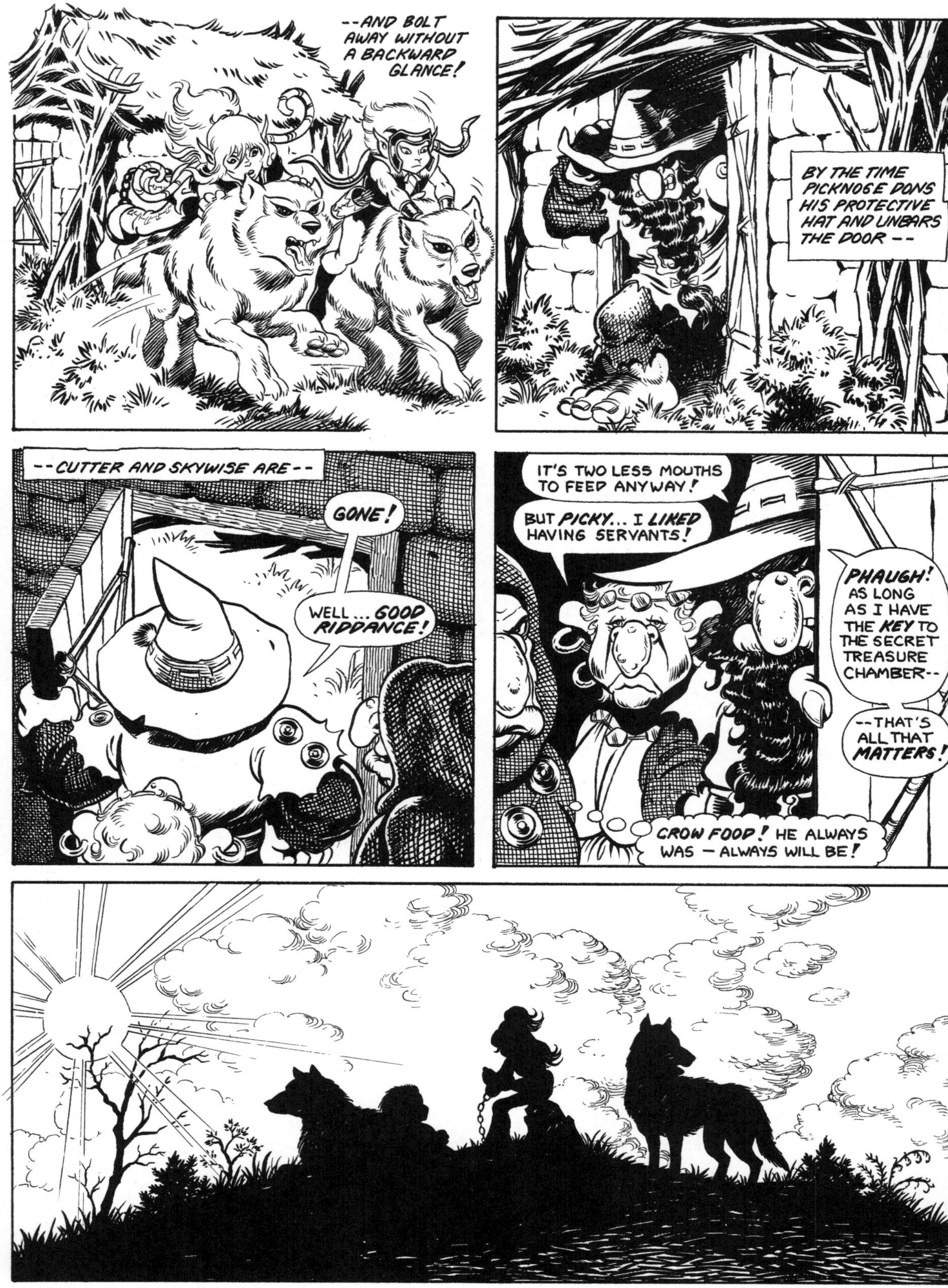
--AND BOLT AWAY WITHOUT A BACKWARD GLANCE!
BY THE TIME PICKNOSE DONS HIS PROTECTIVE HAT AND UNBARS THE DOOR --
--CUTTER AND SKYWISE ARE--
GONE!
WELL... GOOD RIDDANCE!
IT'S TWO LESS MOUTHS TO FEED ANYWAY!
BUT PICKY... I LIKED HAVING SERVANTS!
PHAUGH! AS LONG AS I HAVE THE KEY TO THE SECRET TREASURE CHAMBER--
--THAT'S ALL THAT MATTERS!
CROW FOOD! HE ALWAYS WAS — ALWAYS WILL BE!

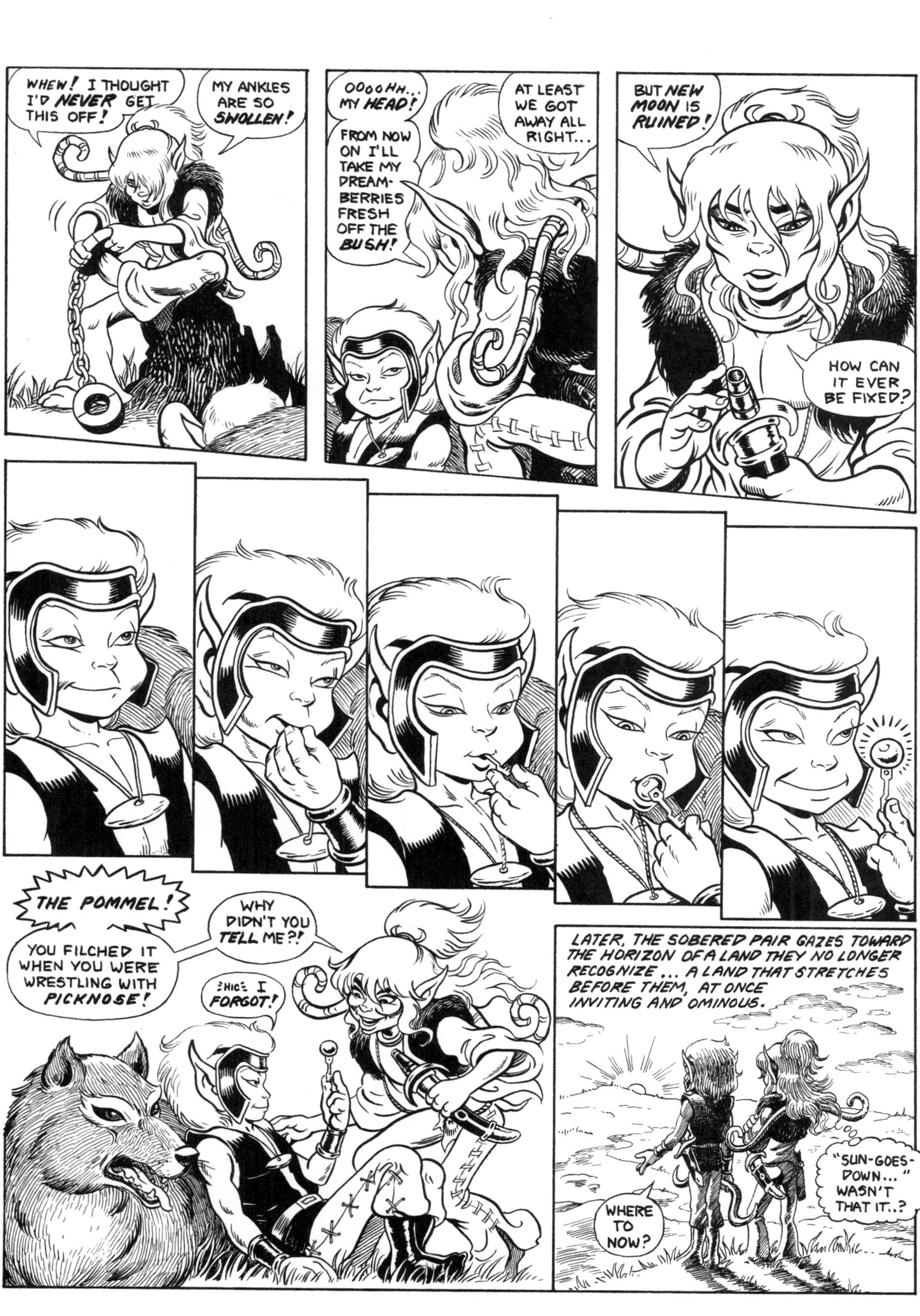

WHEW! I THOUGHT I'D NEVER GET THIS OFF!
MY ANKLES ARE SO SWOLLEN!
OOOOHH... MY HEAD!
AT LEAST WE GOT AWAY ALL RIGHT...
FROM NOW ON I'LL TAKE MY DREAM-BERRIES FRESH OFF THE BUSH!
BUT NEW MOON IS RUINED!
HOW CAN IT EVER BE FIXED?
THE POMMEL!
YOU FILCHED IT WHEN YOU WERE WRESTLING WITH PICKNOSE!
WHY DIDN'T YOU TELL ME?!
HIC I FORGOT!
LATER, THE SOBERED PAIR GAZES TOWARD THE HORIZON OF A LAND THEY NO LONGER RECOGNIZE ... A LAND THAT STRETCHES BEFORE THEM, AT ONCE INVITING AND OMINOUS.
"SUN-GOES-DOWN..." WASN'T THAT IT..?
WHERE TO NOW?

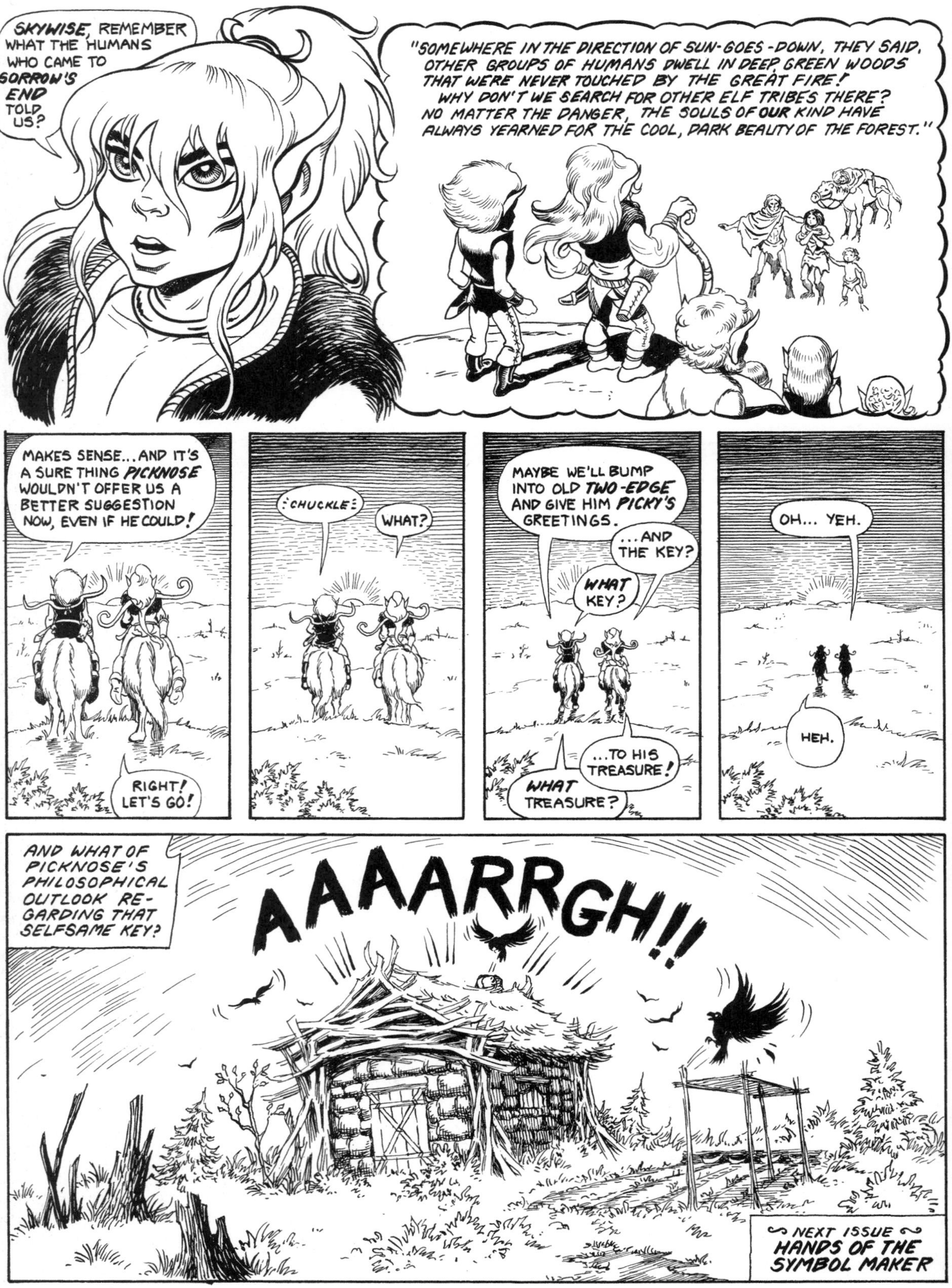
SKYWISE, REMEMBER WHAT THE HUMANS WHO CAME TO SORROW'S END TOLD US?
"SOMEWHERE IN THE DIRECTION OF SUN-GOES-DOWN, THEY SAID, OTHER GROUPS OF HUMANS DWELL IN DEEP GREEN WOODS THAT WERE NEVER TOUCHED BY THE GREAT FIRE!
WHY DON'T WE SEARCH FOR OTHER ELF TRIBES THERE? NO MATTER THE DANGER, THE SOULS OF OUR KIND HAVE ALWAYS YEARNED FOR THE COOL, DARK BEAUTY OF THE FOREST."
MAKES SENSE... AND IT'S A SURE THING PICKNOSE WOULDN'T OFFER US A BETTER SUGGESTION NOW, EVEN IF HE COULD!
RIGHT! LET'S GO!
:CHUCKLE:
WHAT?
MAYBE WE'LL BUMP INTO OLD TWO-EDGE AND GIVE HIM PICKY'S GREETINGS.
...AND THE KEY?
WHAT KEY?
...TO HIS TREASURE!
WHAT TREASURE?
OH... YEH.
HEH.
AND WHAT OF PICKNOSE'S PHILOSOPHICAL OUTLOOK RE-GARDING THAT SELFSAME KEY?
AAAARRGH!!
NEXT ISSUE
HANDS OF THE SYMBOL MAKER

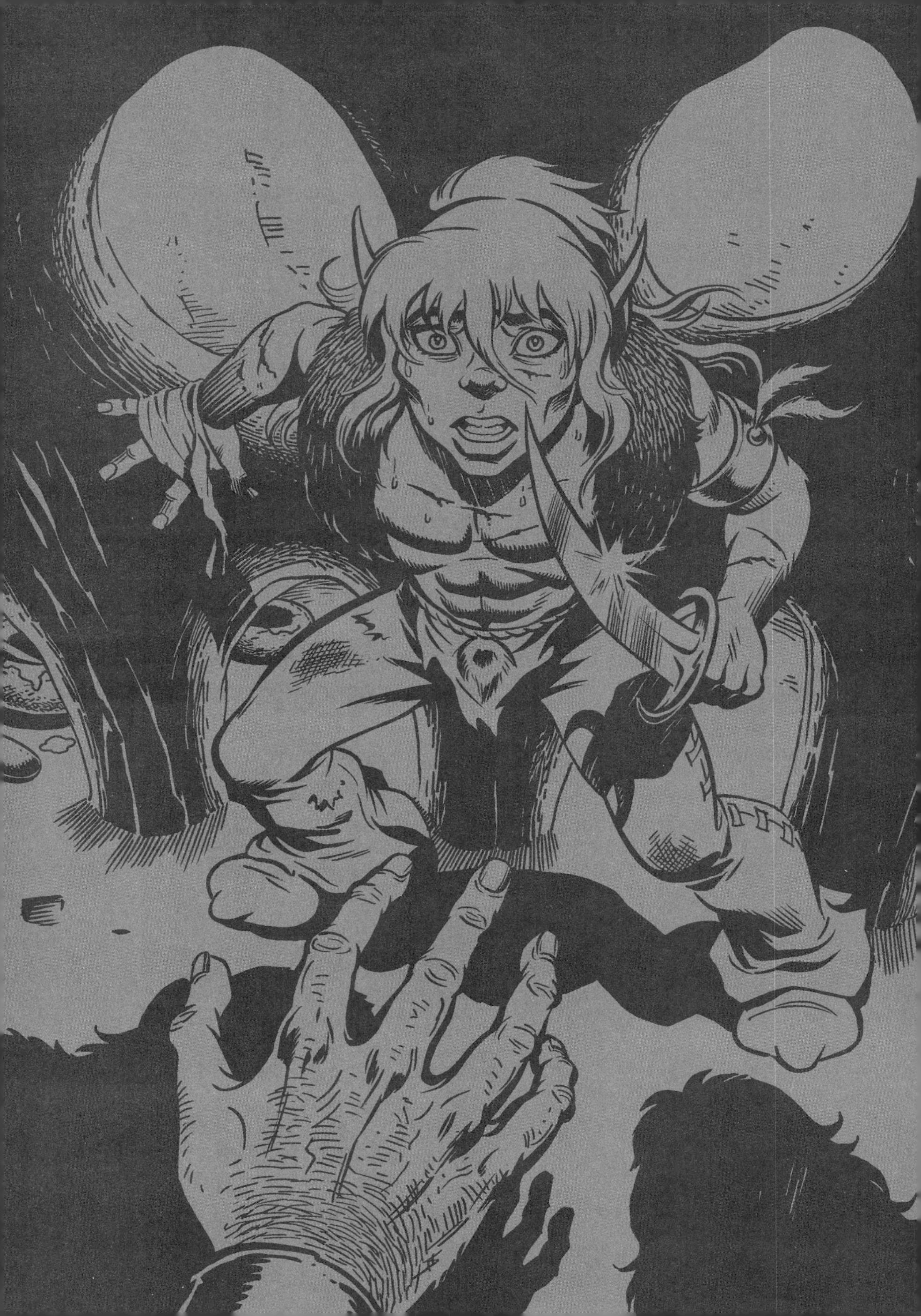

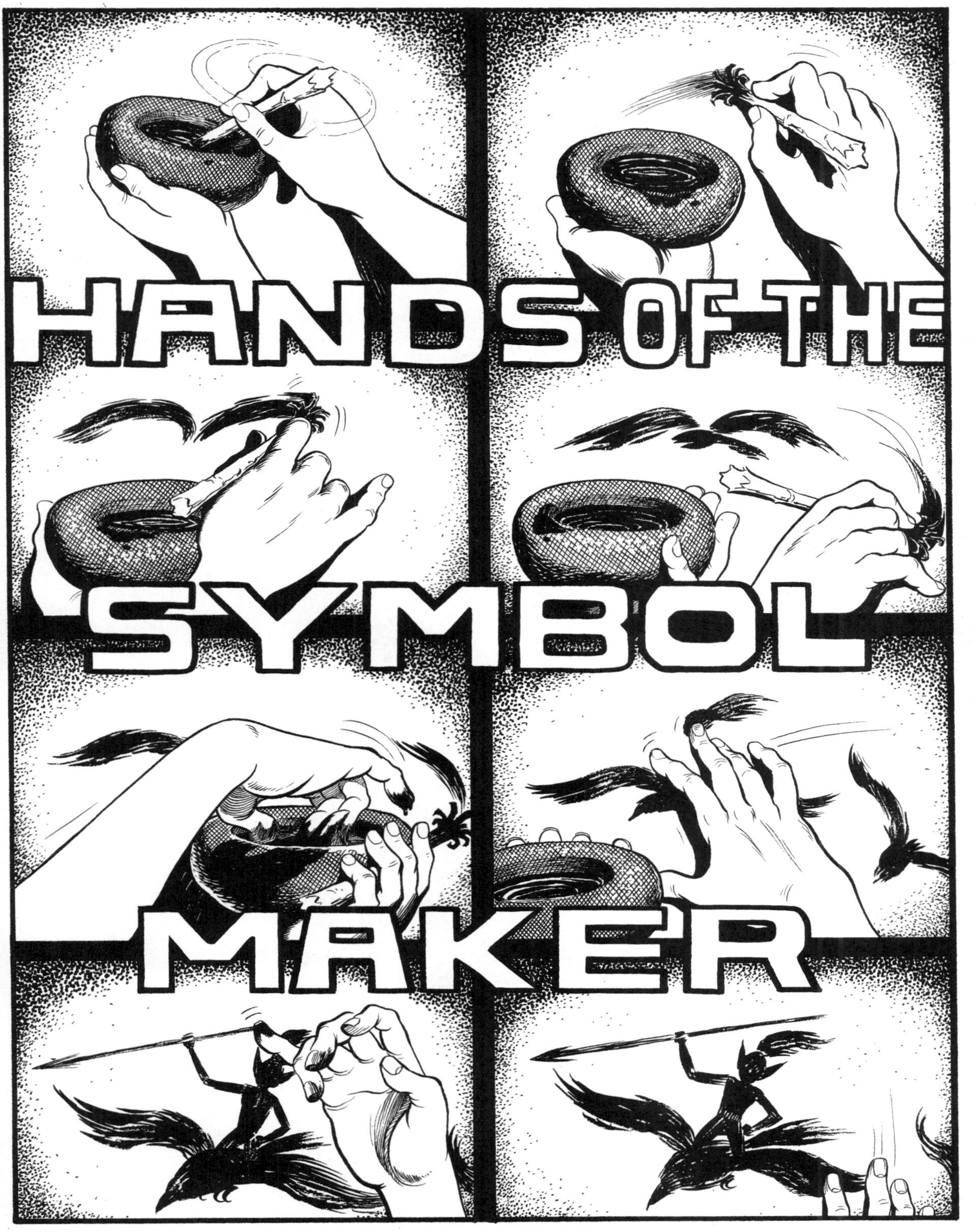
HANDS OF THE
SYMBOL
MAKER

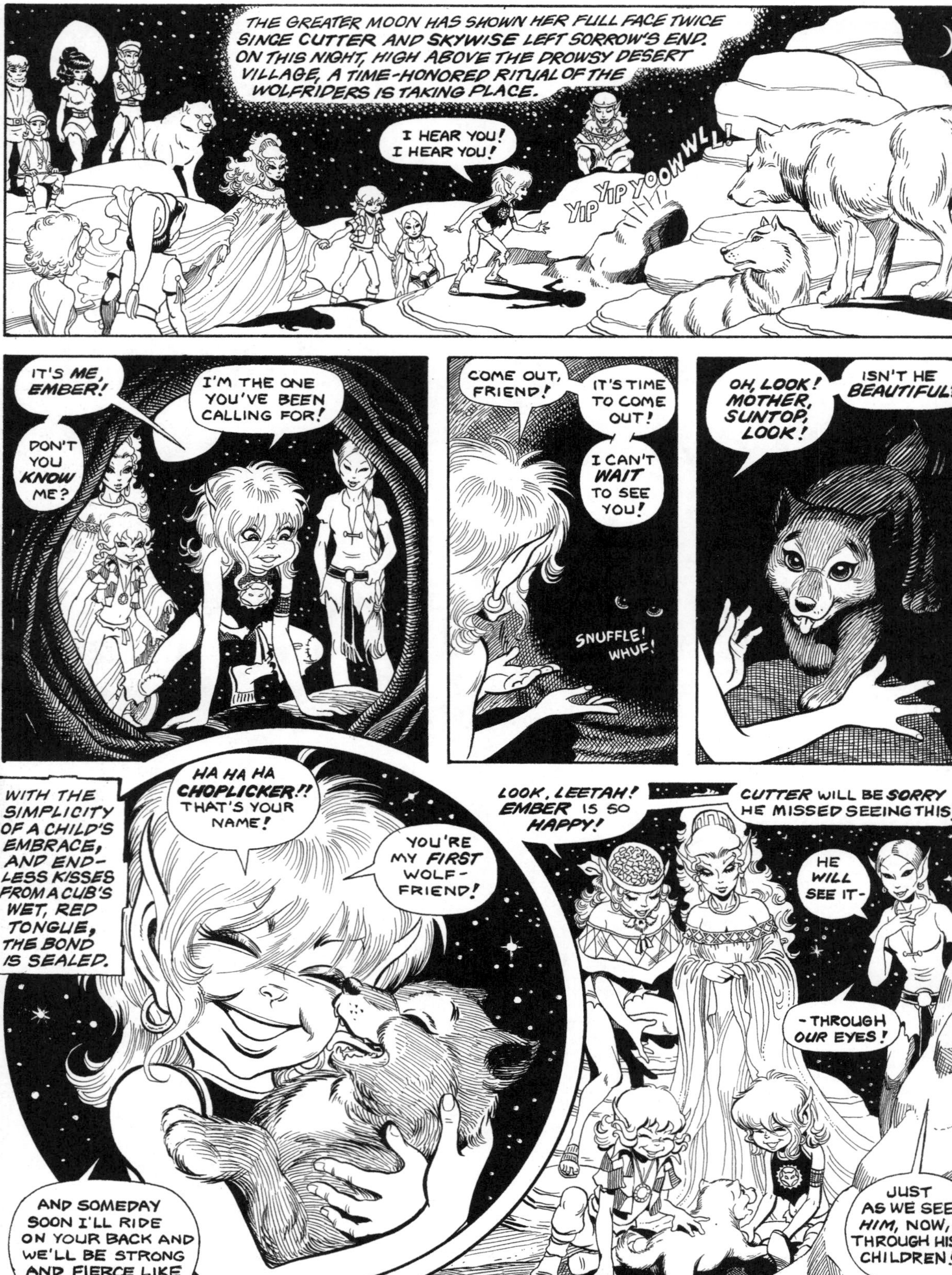

THE GREATER MOON HAS SHOWN HER FULL FACE TWICE SINCE CUTTER AND SKYWISE LEFT SORROW'S END. ON THIS NIGHT, HIGH ABOVE THE DROWSY DESERT VILLAGE, A TIME-HONORED RITUAL OF THE WOLFRIDERS IS TAKING PLACE.
I HEAR YOU! I HEAR YOU!
YIP YIP YOOWWLL!
IT'S ME, EMBER!
DON'T YOU KNOW ME?
I'M THE ONE YOU'VE BEEN CALLING FOR!
COME OUT, FRIEND!
IT'S TIME TO COME OUT!
I CAN'T WAIT TO SEE YOU!
SNUFFLE! WHUF!
OH, LOOK! MOTHER, SUNTOP, LOOK!
ISN'T HE BEAUTIFUL?!
WITH THE SIMPLICITY OF A CHILD'S EMBRACE, AND END-LESS KISSES FROM A CUB'S WET, RED TONGUE, THE BOND IS SEALED.
HA HA HA CHOPLICKER!! THAT'S YOUR NAME!
YOU'RE MY FIRST WOLF-FRIEND!
AND SOMEDAY SOON I'LL RIDE ON YOUR BACK AND WE'LL BE STRONG AND FIERCE LIKE MY FATHER!
LOOK, LEETAH! EMBER IS SO HAPPY!
CUTTER WILL BE SORRY HE MISSED SEEING THIS!
HE WILL SEE IT-
-THROUGH OUR EYES!
JUST AS WE SEE HIM, NOW, THROUGH HIS CHILDREN!

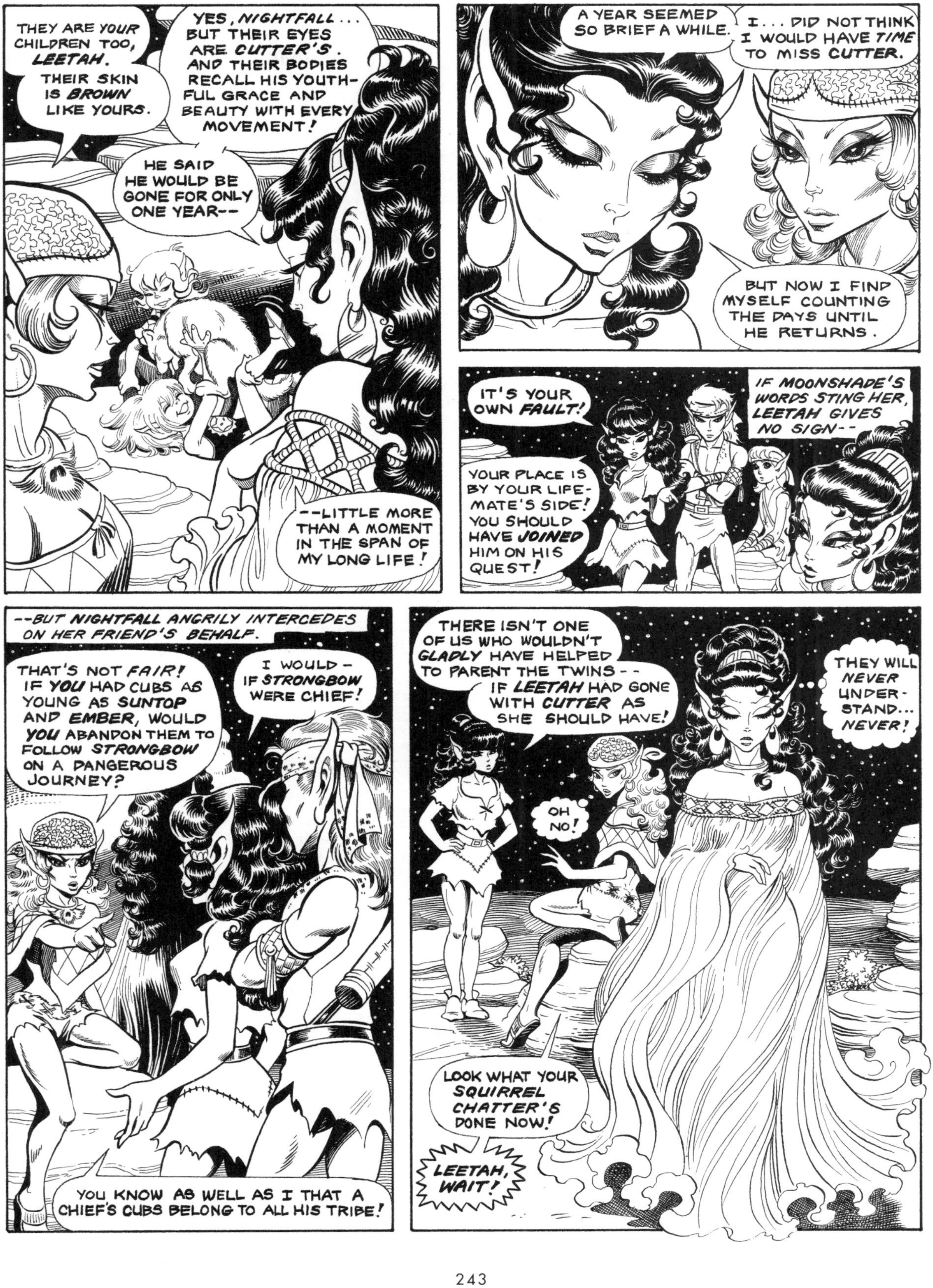
THEY ARE *YOUR* CHILDREN TOO, **LEETAH**.
THEIR SKIN IS **BROWN** LIKE YOURS.
YES, *NIGHTFALL*... BUT THEIR EYES ARE **CUTTER'S**. AND THEIR BODIES RECALL HIS YOUTHFUL GRACE AND BEAUTY WITH EVERY MOVEMENT!
HE SAID HE WOULD BE GONE FOR ONLY ONE YEAR--
--LITTLE MORE THAN A MOMENT IN THE SPAN OF MY LONG LIFE!
A YEAR SEEMED SO BRIEF A WHILE.
I... DID NOT THINK I WOULD HAVE *TIME* TO MISS **CUTTER**.
BUT NOW I FIND MYSELF COUNTING THE DAYS UNTIL HE RETURNS.
IT'S YOUR OWN ***FAULT!***
YOUR PLACE IS BY YOUR LIFEMATE'S SIDE! YOU SHOULD HAVE ***JOINED*** HIM ON HIS QUEST!
*IF **MOONSHADE'S** WORDS STING HER, **LEETAH** GIVES NO SIGN--*
*--BUT **NIGHTFALL** ANGRILY INTERCEDES ON HER FRIEND'S BEHALF.*
THAT'S NOT *FAIR!* IF ***YOU*** HAD CUBS AS YOUNG AS **SUNTOP** AND **EMBER**, WOULD ***YOU*** ABANDON THEM TO FOLLOW ***STRONGBOW*** ON A DANGEROUS JOURNEY?
I WOULD - IF ***STRONGBOW*** WERE CHIEF!
YOU KNOW **AS** WELL AS I THAT A CHIEF'S **CUBS** BELONG TO ALL HIS TRIBE!
THERE ISN'T ONE OF US WHO WOULDN'T ***GLADLY*** HAVE HELPED TO PARENT THE TWINS--
IF ***LEETAH*** HAD GONE WITH ***CUTTER*** AS SHE SHOULD HAVE!
THEY WILL *NEVER* UNDERSTAND... *NEVER!*
OH NO!
LOOK WHAT YOUR ***SQUIRREL CHATTER'S*** DONE NOW!
LEETAH, WAIT!

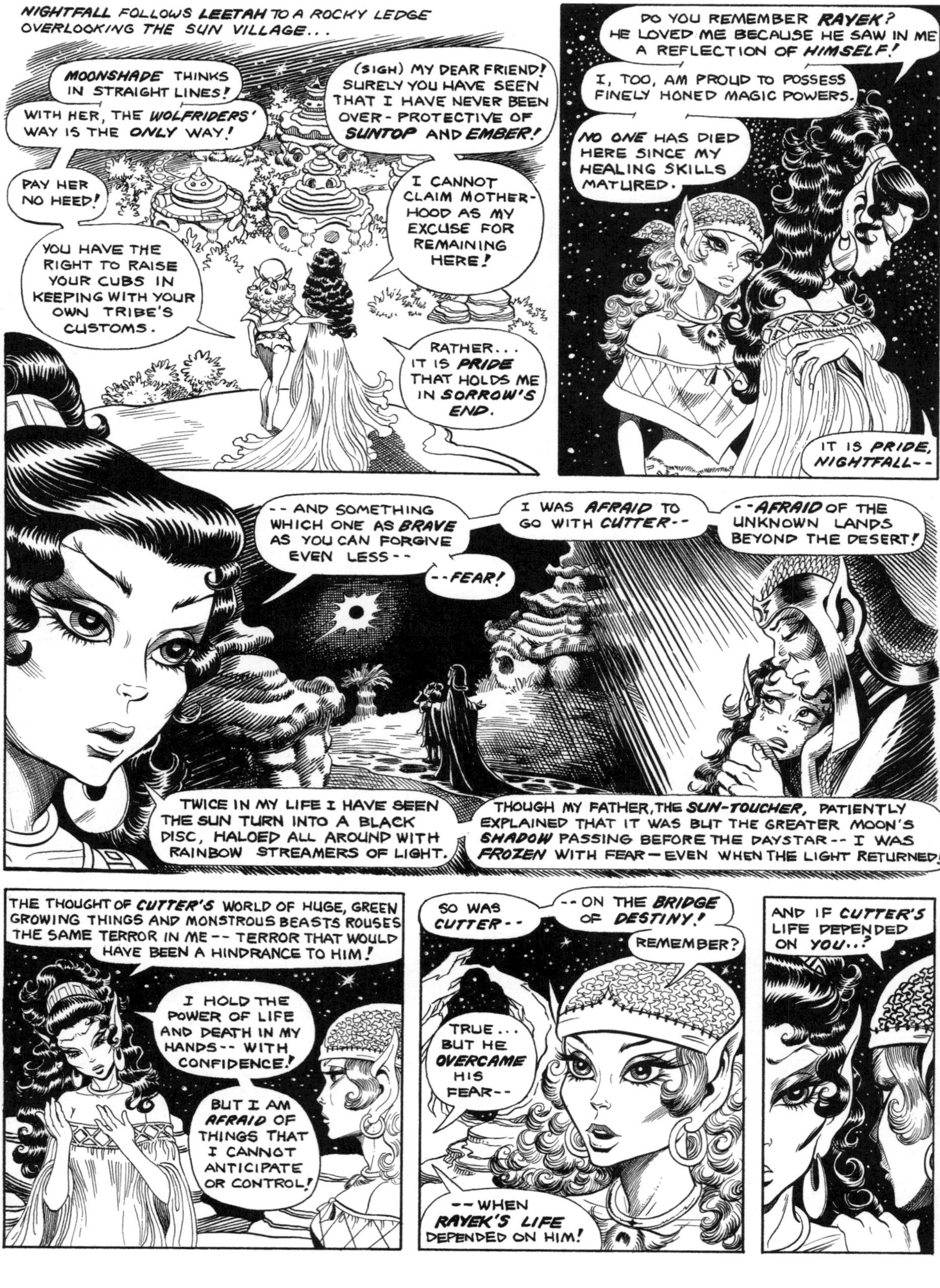

NIGHTFALL FOLLOWS LEETAH TO A ROCKY LEDGE OVERLOOKING THE SUN VILLAGE...
MOONSHADE THINKS IN STRAIGHT LINES!
WITH HER, THE WOLFRIDERS' WAY IS THE ONLY WAY!
PAY HER NO HEED!
YOU HAVE THE RIGHT TO RAISE YOUR CUBS IN KEEPING WITH YOUR OWN TRIBE'S CUSTOMS.
(SIGH) MY DEAR FRIEND! SURELY YOU HAVE SEEN THAT I HAVE NEVER BEEN OVER-PROTECTIVE OF SUNTOP AND EMBER!
I CANNOT CLAIM MOTHERHOOD AS MY EXCUSE FOR REMAINING HERE!
RATHER... IT IS PRIDE THAT HOLDS ME IN SORROW'S END.
DO YOU REMEMBER RAYEK? HE LOVED ME BECAUSE HE SAW IN ME A REFLECTION OF HIMSELF!
I, TOO, AM PROUD TO POSSESS FINELY HONED MAGIC POWERS.
NO ONE HAS DIED HERE SINCE MY HEALING SKILLS MATURED.
IT IS PRIDE, NIGHTFALL--
--AND SOMETHING WHICH ONE AS BRAVE AS YOU CAN FORGIVE EVEN LESS--
--FEAR!
I WAS AFRAID TO GO WITH CUTTER--
--AFRAID OF THE UNKNOWN LANDS BEYOND THE DESERT!
TWICE IN MY LIFE I HAVE SEEN THE SUN TURN INTO A BLACK DISC, HALOED ALL AROUND WITH RAINBOW STREAMERS OF LIGHT.
THOUGH MY FATHER, THE SUN-TOUCHER, PATIENTLY EXPLAINED THAT IT WAS BUT THE GREATER MOON'S SHADOW PASSING BEFORE THE DAYSTAR -- I WAS FROZEN WITH FEAR—EVEN WHEN THE LIGHT RETURNED!
THE THOUGHT OF CUTTER'S WORLD OF HUGE, GREEN GROWING THINGS AND MONSTROUS BEASTS ROUSES THE SAME TERROR IN ME -- TERROR THAT WOULD HAVE BEEN A HINDRANCE TO HIM!
I HOLD THE POWER OF LIFE AND DEATH IN MY HANDS -- WITH CONFIDENCE!
BUT I AM AFRAID OF THINGS THAT I CANNOT ANTICIPATE OR CONTROL!
SO WAS CUTTER--
--ON THE BRIDGE OF DESTINY!
REMEMBER?
TRUE... BUT HE OVERCAME HIS FEAR--
--WHEN RAYEK'S LIFE DEPENDED ON HIM!
AND IF CUTTER'S LIFE DEPENDED ON YOU..?

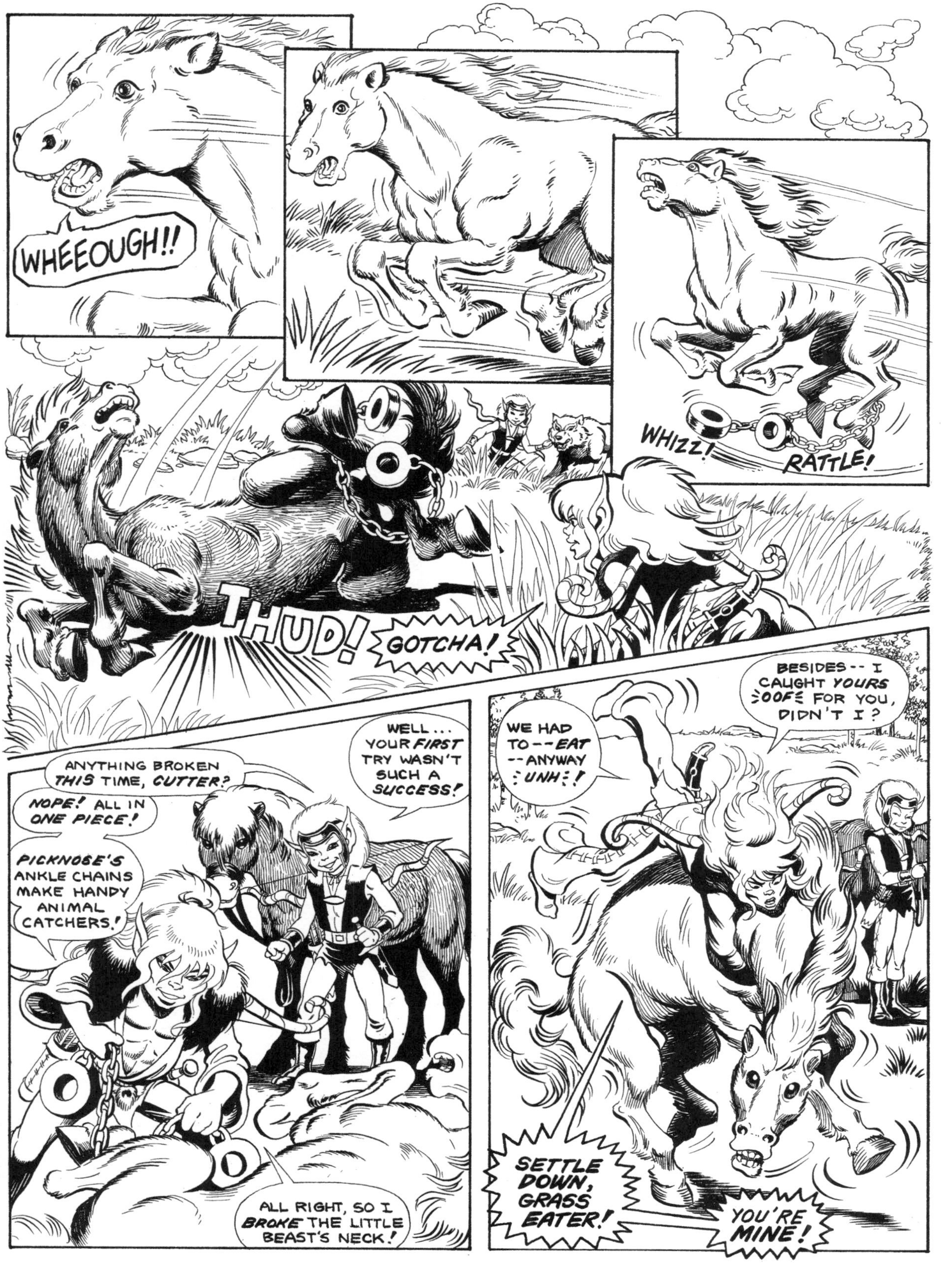
WHEEOUGH!!
WHIZZ!
RATTLE!
THUD!
GOTCHA!
ANYTHING BROKEN THIS TIME, CUTTER?
NOPE! ALL IN ONE PIECE!
PICKNOSE'S ANKLE CHAINS MAKE HANDY ANIMAL CATCHERS!
WELL... YOUR FIRST TRY WASN'T SUCH A SUCCESS!
ALL RIGHT, SO I BROKE THE LITTLE BEAST'S NECK!
WE HAD TO--EAT --ANYWAY UNH!
BESIDES--I CAUGHT YOURS OOF FOR YOU, DIDN'T I?
SETTLE DOWN, GRASS EATER!
YOU'RE MINE!

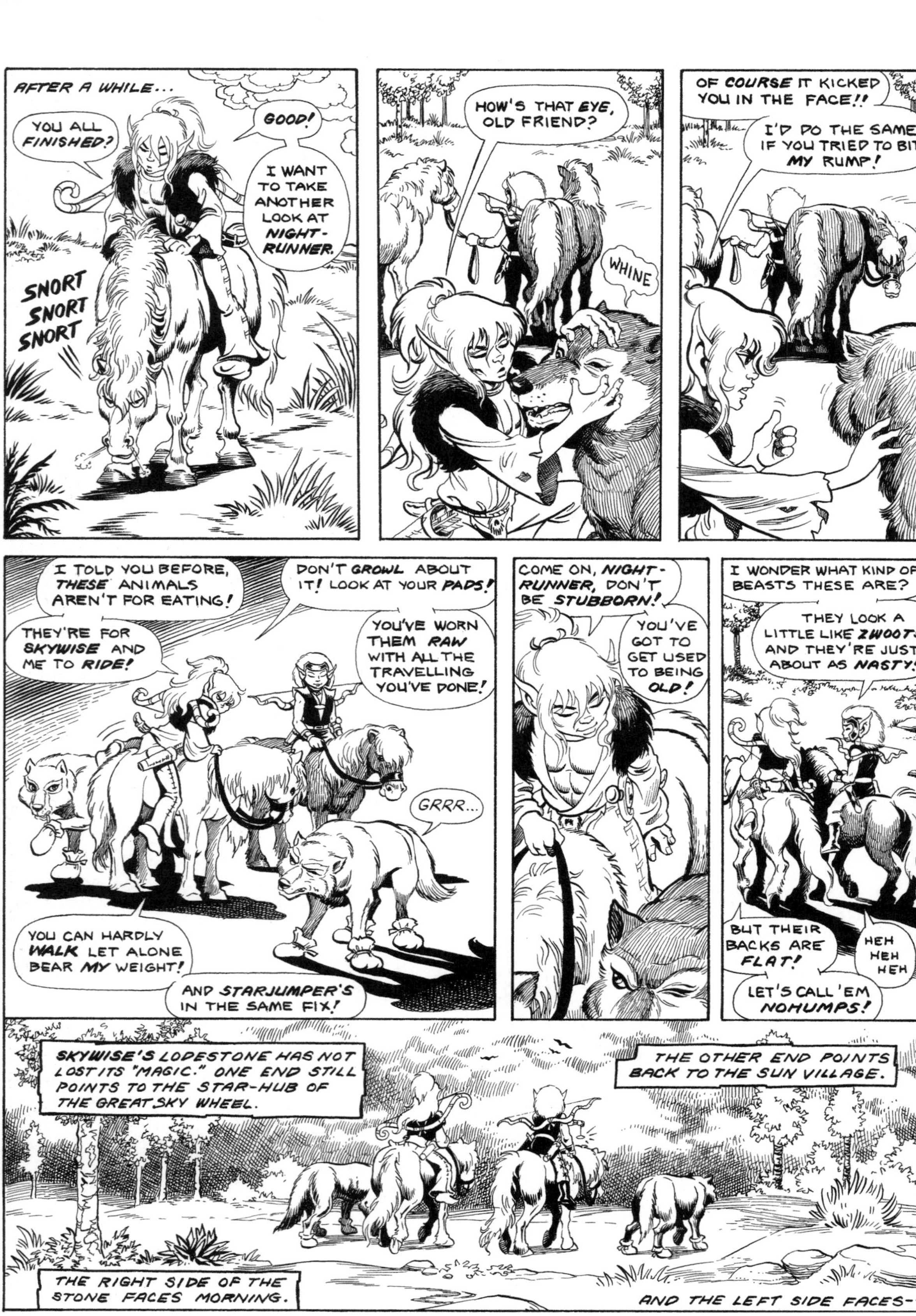

AFTER A WHILE...
YOU ALL FINISHED?
GOOD!
I WANT TO TAKE ANOTHER LOOK AT NIGHT-RUNNER.
SNORT SNORT SNORT
HOW'S THAT EYE, OLD FRIEND?
WHINE
OF COURSE IT KICKED YOU IN THE FACE!!
I'D DO THE SAME IF YOU TRIED TO BITE MY RUMP!
I TOLD YOU BEFORE, THESE ANIMALS AREN'T FOR EATING!
THEY'RE FOR SKYWISE AND ME TO RIDE!
DON'T GROWL ABOUT IT! LOOK AT YOUR PADS!
YOU'VE WORN THEM RAW WITH ALL THE TRAVELLING YOU'VE DONE!
GRRR...
YOU CAN HARDLY WALK LET ALONE BEAR MY WEIGHT!
AND STARJUMPER'S IN THE SAME FIX!
COME ON, NIGHT-RUNNER, DON'T BE STUBBORN!
YOU'VE GOT TO GET USED TO BEING OLD!
I WONDER WHAT KIND OF BEASTS THESE ARE?
THEY LOOK A LITTLE LIKE ZWOOTS AND THEY'RE JUST ABOUT AS NASTY!
BUT THEIR BACKS ARE FLAT!
HEH HEH HEH
LET'S CALL 'EM NOHUMPS!
SKYWISE'S LODESTONE HAS NOT LOST ITS "MAGIC." ONE END STILL POINTS TO THE STAR-HUB OF THE GREAT SKY WHEEL.
THE OTHER END POINTS BACK TO THE SUN VILLAGE.
THE RIGHT SIDE OF THE STONE FACES MORNING.
AND THE LEFT SIDE FACES--

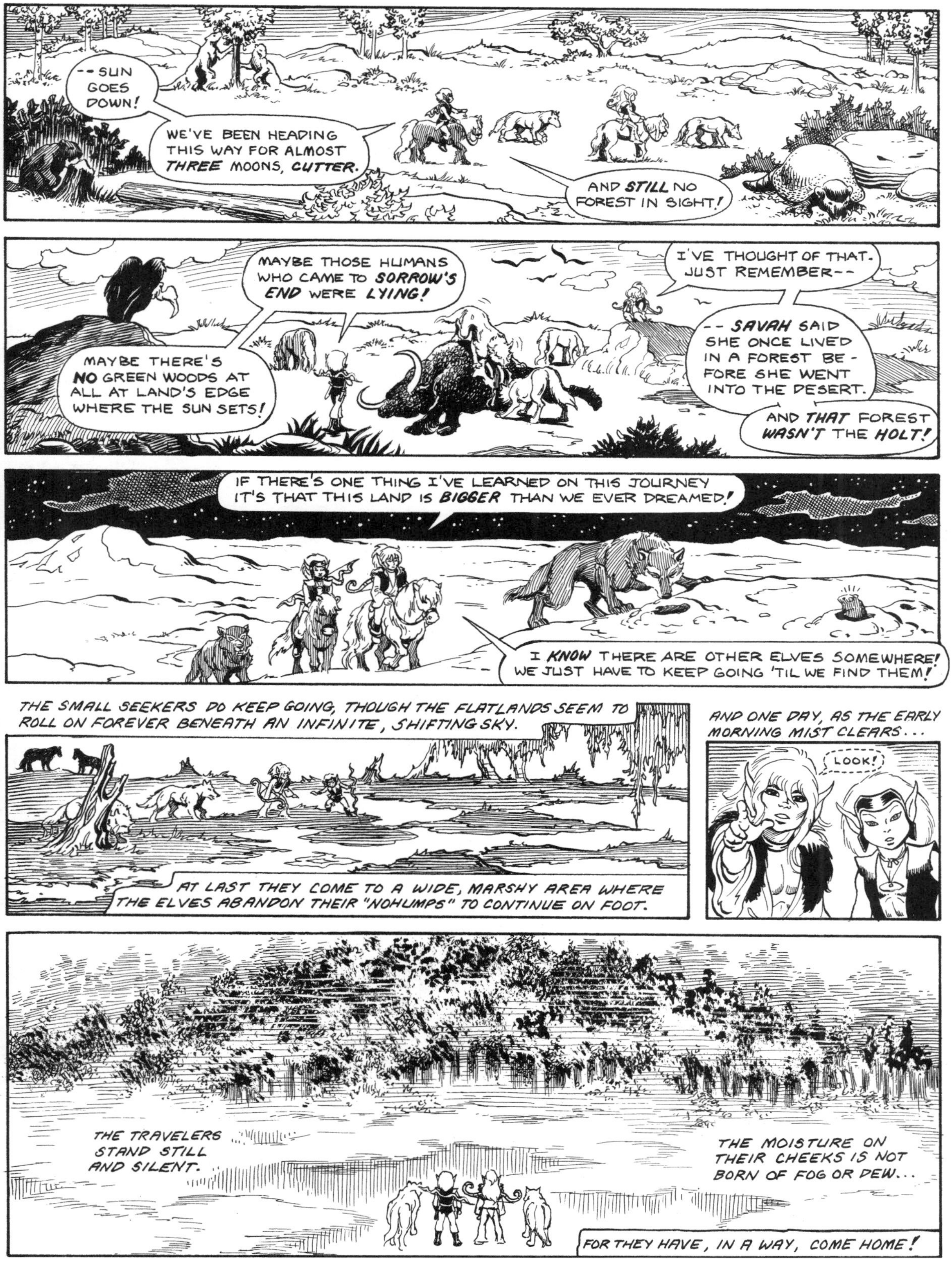

--SUN GOES DOWN!
WE'VE BEEN HEADING THIS WAY FOR ALMOST THREE MOONS, CUTTER.
AND STILL NO FOREST IN SIGHT!
MAYBE THOSE HUMANS WHO CAME TO SORROW'S END WERE LYING!
MAYBE THERE'S NO GREEN WOODS AT ALL AT LAND'S EDGE WHERE THE SUN SETS!
I'VE THOUGHT OF THAT. JUST REMEMBER--
--SAVAH SAID SHE ONCE LIVED IN A FOREST BE-FORE SHE WENT INTO THE DESERT.
AND THAT FOREST WASN'T THE HOLT!
IF THERE'S ONE THING I'VE LEARNED ON THIS JOURNEY IT'S THAT THIS LAND IS BIGGER THAN WE EVER DREAMED!
I KNOW THERE ARE OTHER ELVES SOMEWHERE! WE JUST HAVE TO KEEP GOING 'TIL WE FIND THEM!
THE SMALL SEEKERS DO KEEP GOING, THOUGH THE FLATLANDS SEEM TO ROLL ON FOREVER BENEATH AN INFINITE, SHIFTING SKY.
AT LAST THEY COME TO A WIDE, MARSHY AREA WHERE THE ELVES ABANDON THEIR "NOHUMPS" TO CONTINUE ON FOOT.
AND ONE DAY, AS THE EARLY MORNING MIST CLEARS...
LOOK!
THE TRAVELERS STAND STILL AND SILENT.
THE MOISTURE ON THEIR CHEEKS IS NOT BORN OF FOG OR DEW...
FOR THEY HAVE, IN A WAY, COME HOME!

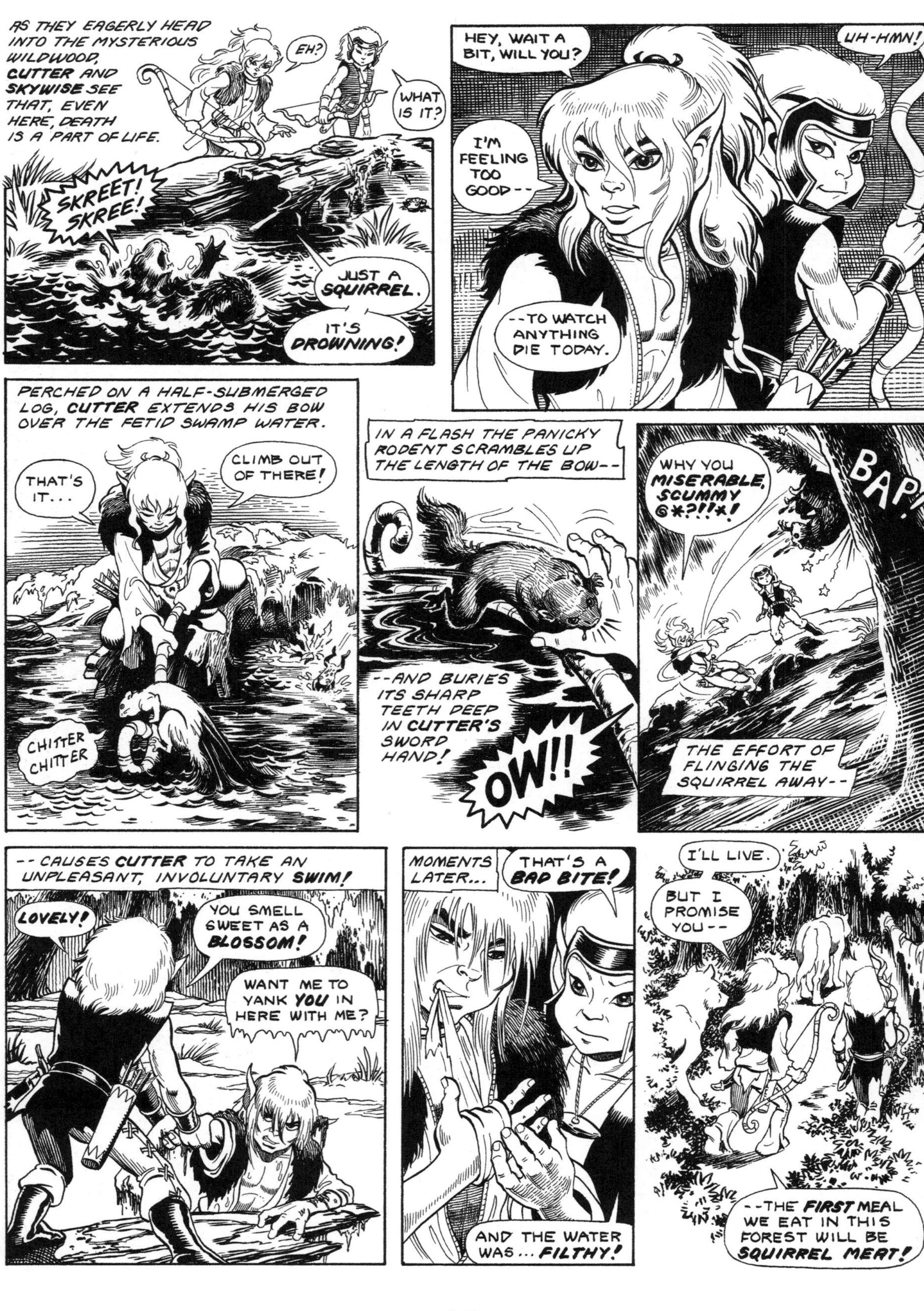
AS THEY EAGERLY HEAD INTO THE MYSTERIOUS WILDWOOD, CUTTER AND SKYWISE SEE THAT, EVEN HERE, DEATH IS A PART OF LIFE.
EH?
WHAT IS IT?
SKREET! SKREE!
JUST A SQUIRREL.
IT'S DROWNING!
HEY, WAIT A BIT, WILL YOU?
UH-HMN!
I'M FEELING TOO GOOD--
--TO WATCH ANYTHING DIE TODAY.
PERCHED ON A HALF-SUBMERGED LOG, CUTTER EXTENDS HIS BOW OVER THE FETID SWAMP WATER.
THAT'S IT...
CLIMB OUT OF THERE!
CHITTER CHITTER
IN A FLASH THE PANICKY RODENT SCRAMBLES UP THE LENGTH OF THE BOW--
--AND BURIES ITS SHARP TEETH DEEP IN CUTTER'S SWORD HAND!
OW!!
WHY YOU MISERABLE, SCUMMY @*?!!*!
BAP!
THE EFFORT OF FLINGING THE SQUIRREL AWAY--
--CAUSES CUTTER TO TAKE AN UNPLEASANT, INVOLUNTARY SWIM!
LOVELY!
YOU SMELL SWEET AS A BLOSSOM!
WANT ME TO YANK YOU IN HERE WITH ME?
MOMENTS LATER...
THAT'S A BAD BITE!
AND THE WATER WAS... FILTHY!
I'LL LIVE.
BUT I PROMISE YOU--
--THE FIRST MEAL WE EAT IN THIS FOREST WILL BE SQUIRREL MEAT!

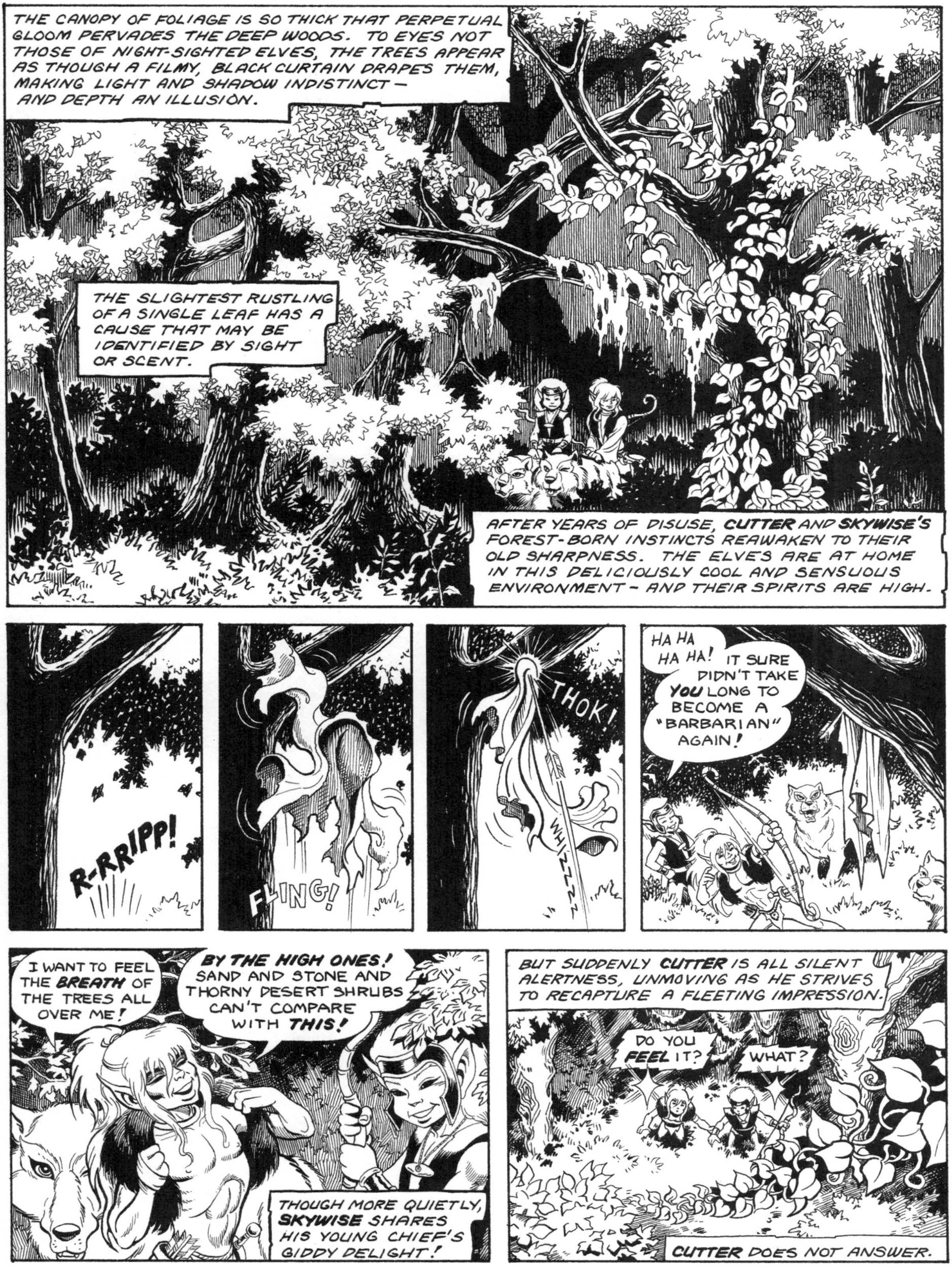

THE CANOPY OF FOLIAGE IS SO THICK THAT PERPETUAL GLOOM PERVADES THE DEEP WOODS. TO EYES NOT THOSE OF NIGHT-SIGHTED ELVES, THE TREES APPEAR AS THOUGH A FILMY, BLACK CURTAIN DRAPES THEM, MAKING LIGHT AND SHADOW INDISTINCT — AND DEPTH AN ILLUSION.
THE SLIGHTEST RUSTLING OF A SINGLE LEAF HAS A CAUSE THAT MAY BE IDENTIFIED BY SIGHT OR SCENT.
AFTER YEARS OF DISUSE, CUTTER AND SKYWISE'S FOREST-BORN INSTINCTS REAWAKEN TO THEIR OLD SHARPNESS. THE ELVES ARE AT HOME IN THIS DELICIOUSLY COOL AND SENSUOUS ENVIRONMENT — AND THEIR SPIRITS ARE HIGH.
R-RRIPP!
FLING!
THOK!
WHINNNN
HA HA HA HA!
IT SURE DIDN'T TAKE YOU LONG TO BECOME A "BARBARIAN" AGAIN!
I WANT TO FEEL THE BREATH OF THE TREES ALL OVER ME!
BY THE HIGH ONES! SAND AND STONE AND THORNY DESERT SHRUBS CAN'T COMPARE WITH THIS!
THOUGH MORE QUIETLY, SKYWISE SHARES HIS YOUNG CHIEF'S GIDDY DELIGHT!
BUT SUDDENLY CUTTER IS ALL SILENT ALERTNESS, UNMOVING AS HE STRIVES TO RECAPTURE A FLEETING IMPRESSION.
DO YOU FEEL IT?
WHAT?
CUTTER DOES NOT ANSWER.

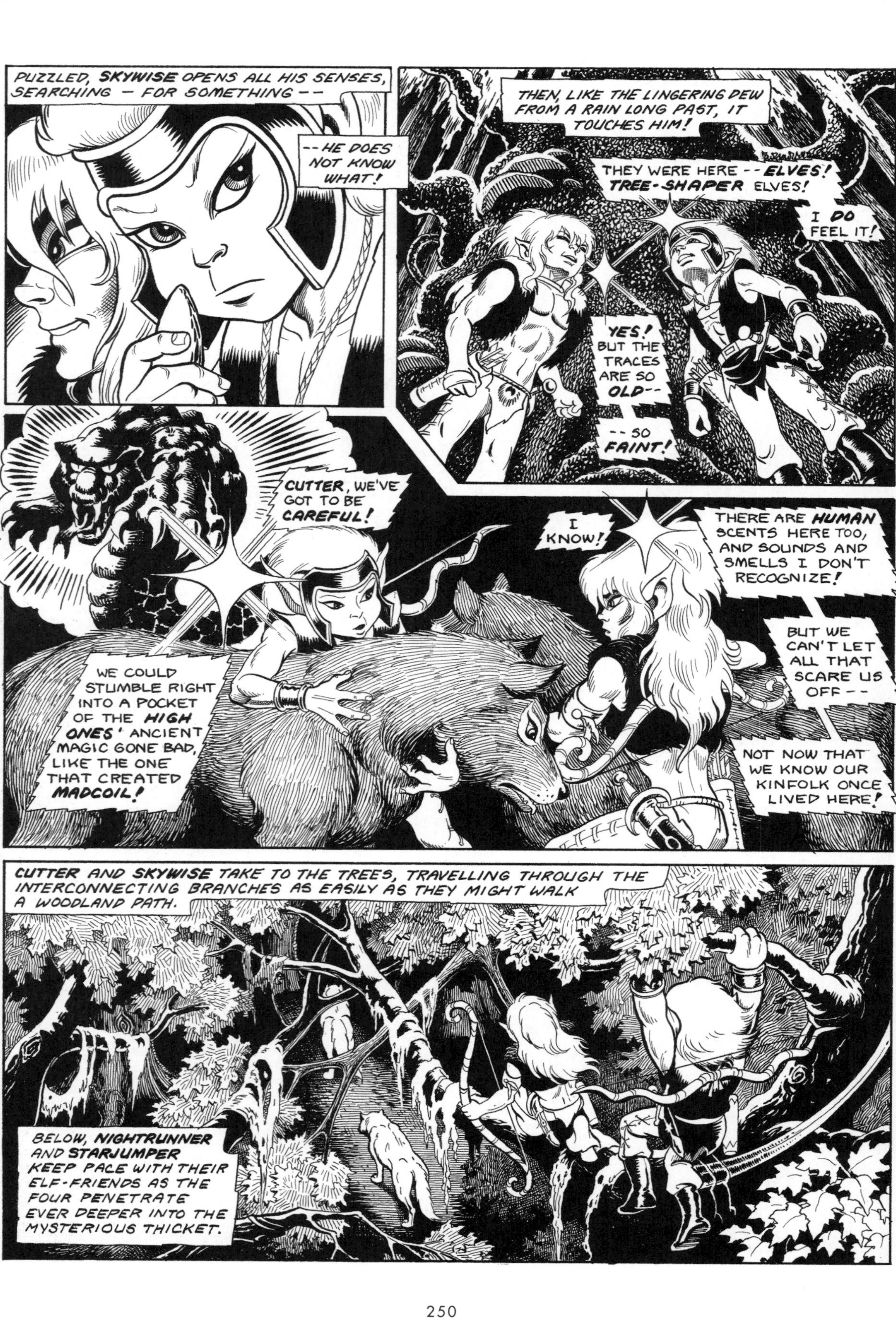
PUZZLED, SKYWISE OPENS ALL HIS SENSES, SEARCHING — FOR SOMETHING --
-- HE DOES NOT KNOW WHAT!
THEN, LIKE THE LINGERING DEW FROM A RAIN LONG PAST, IT TOUCHES HIM!
THEY WERE HERE -- ELVES! TREE-SHAPER ELVES!
I DO FEEL IT!
YES! BUT THE TRACES ARE SO OLD--
-- SO FAINT!
CUTTER, WE'VE GOT TO BE CAREFUL!
WE COULD STUMBLE RIGHT INTO A POCKET OF THE HIGH ONES' ANCIENT MAGIC GONE BAD, LIKE THE ONE THAT CREATED MADCOIL!
I KNOW!
THERE ARE HUMAN SCENTS HERE TOO, AND SOUNDS AND SMELLS I DON'T RECOGNIZE!
BUT WE CAN'T LET ALL THAT SCARE US OFF --
NOT NOW THAT WE KNOW OUR KINFOLK ONCE LIVED HERE!
CUTTER AND SKYWISE TAKE TO THE TREES, TRAVELLING THROUGH THE INTERCONNECTING BRANCHES AS EASILY AS THEY MIGHT WALK A WOODLAND PATH.
BELOW, NIGHTRUNNER AND STARJUMPER KEEP PACE WITH THEIR ELF-FRIENDS AS THE FOUR PENETRATE EVER DEEPER INTO THE MYSTERIOUS THICKET.

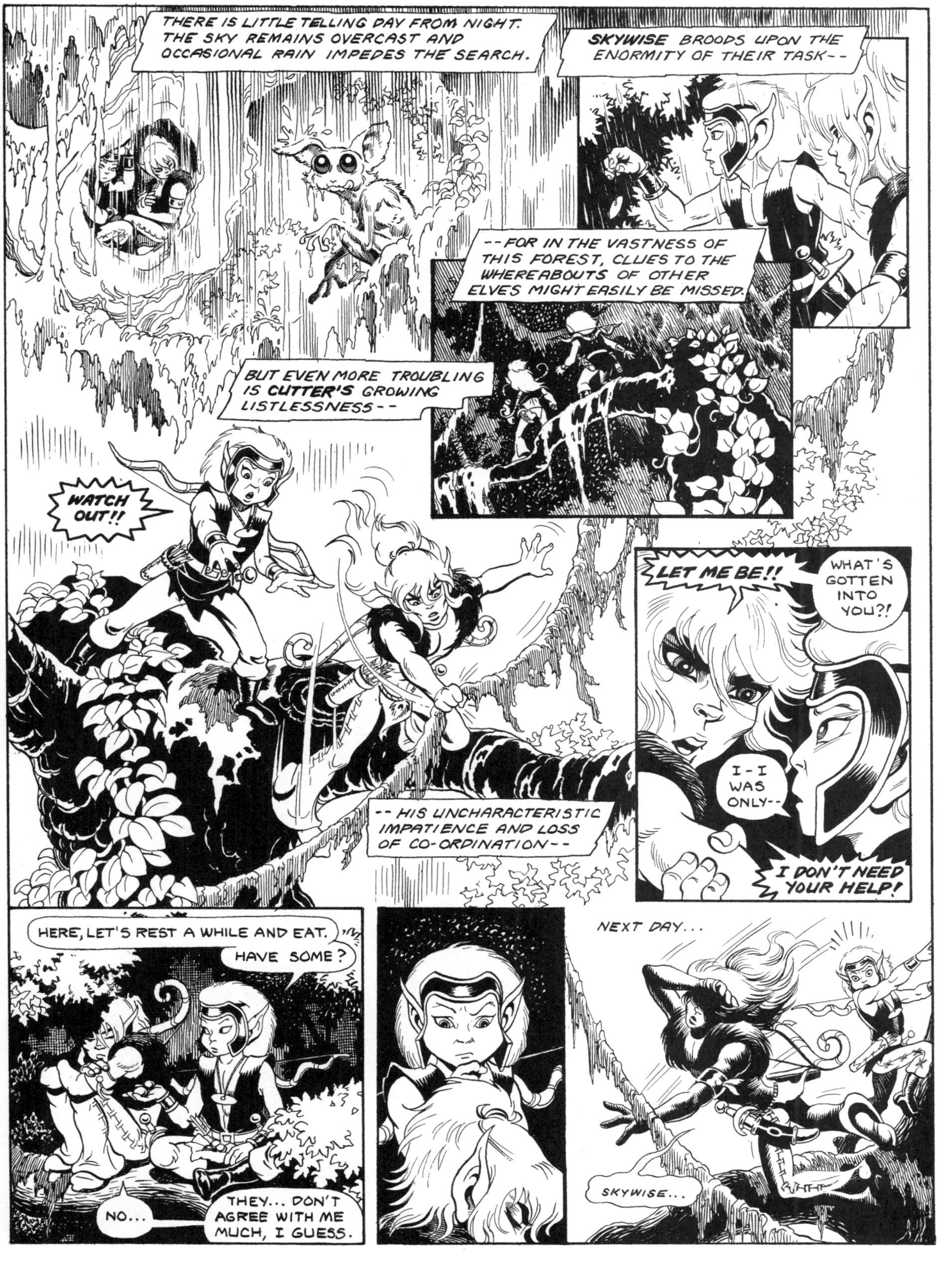

THERE IS LITTLE TELLING DAY FROM NIGHT. THE SKY REMAINS OVERCAST AND OCCASIONAL RAIN IMPEDES THE SEARCH.
SKYWISE BROODS UPON THE ENORMITY OF THEIR TASK--
--FOR IN THE VASTNESS OF THIS FOREST, CLUES TO THE WHEREABOUTS OF OTHER ELVES MIGHT EASILY BE MISSED.
BUT EVEN MORE TROUBLING IS CUTTER'S GROWING LISTLESSNESS--
WATCH OUT!!
--HIS UNCHARACTERISTIC IMPATIENCE AND LOSS OF CO-ORDINATION--
LET ME BE!!
WHAT'S GOTTEN INTO YOU?!
I-I WAS ONLY--
I DON'T NEED YOUR HELP!
HERE, LET'S REST A WHILE AND EAT.
HAVE SOME?
NO...
THEY... DON'T AGREE WITH ME MUCH, I GUESS.
NEXT DAY...
SKYWISE...

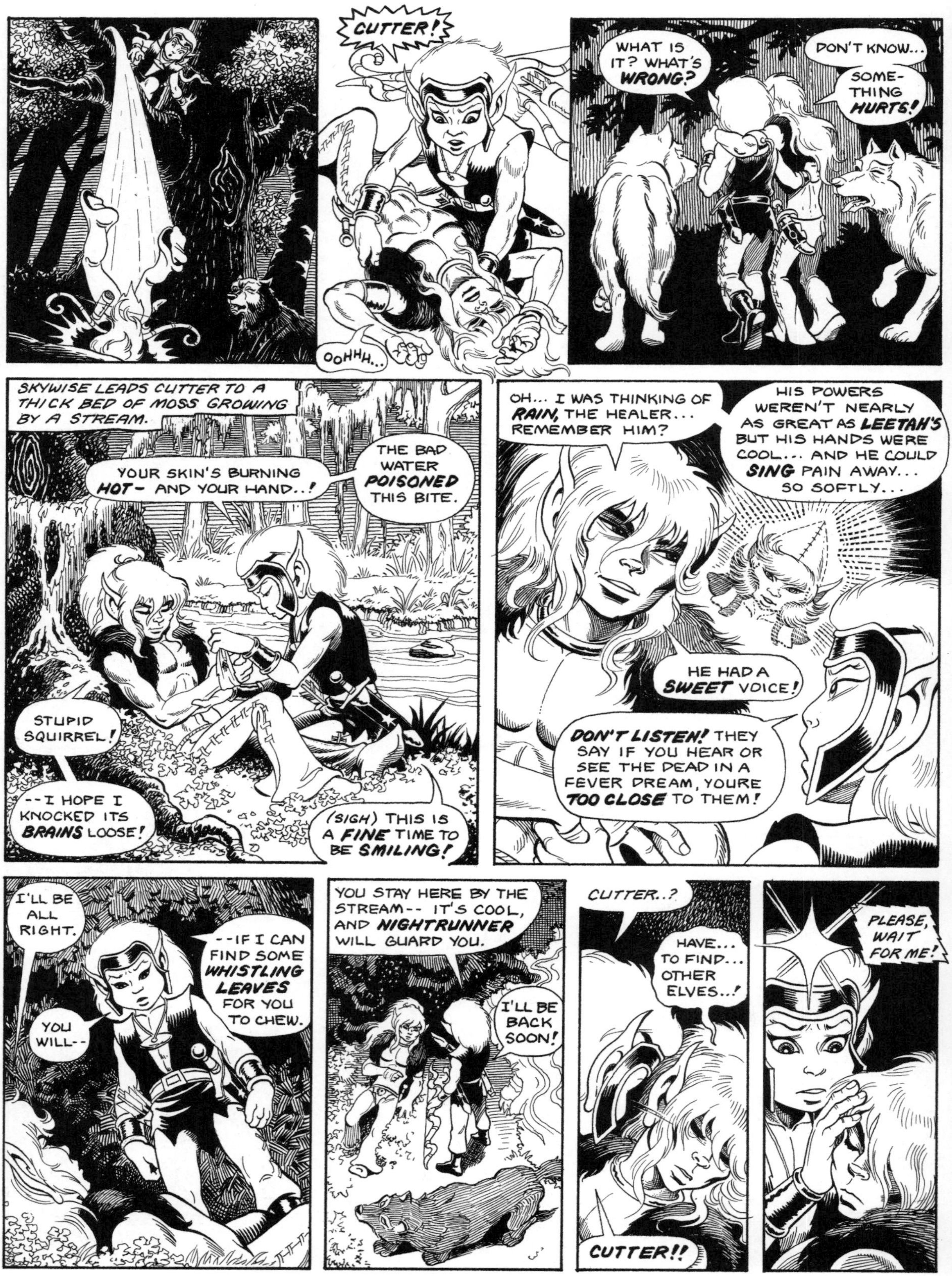
CUTTER!
OOHHH...
WHAT IS IT? WHAT'S WRONG?
DON'T KNOW...
SOME-THING HURTS!
SKYWISE LEADS CUTTER TO A THICK BED OF MOSS GROWING BY A STREAM.
YOUR SKIN'S BURNING HOT- AND YOUR HAND..!
THE BAD WATER POISONED THIS BITE.
STUPID SQUIRREL!
--I HOPE I KNOCKED ITS BRAINS LOOSE!
(SIGH) THIS IS A FINE TIME TO BE SMILING!
OH... I WAS THINKING OF RAIN, THE HEALER... REMEMBER HIM?
HIS POWERS WEREN'T NEARLY AS GREAT AS LEETAH'S BUT HIS HANDS WERE COOL... AND HE COULD SING PAIN AWAY... SO SOFTLY...
HE HAD A SWEET VOICE!
DON'T LISTEN! THEY SAY IF YOU HEAR OR SEE THE DEAD IN A FEVER DREAM, YOURE TOO CLOSE TO THEM!
I'LL BE ALL RIGHT.
YOU WILL--
--IF I CAN FIND SOME WHISTLING LEAVES FOR YOU TO CHEW.
YOU STAY HERE BY THE STREAM-- IT'S COOL, AND NIGHTRUNNER WILL GUARD YOU.
I'LL BE BACK SOON!
CUTTER..?
HAVE... TO FIND... OTHER ELVES..!
CUTTER!!
PLEASE, WAIT FOR ME!

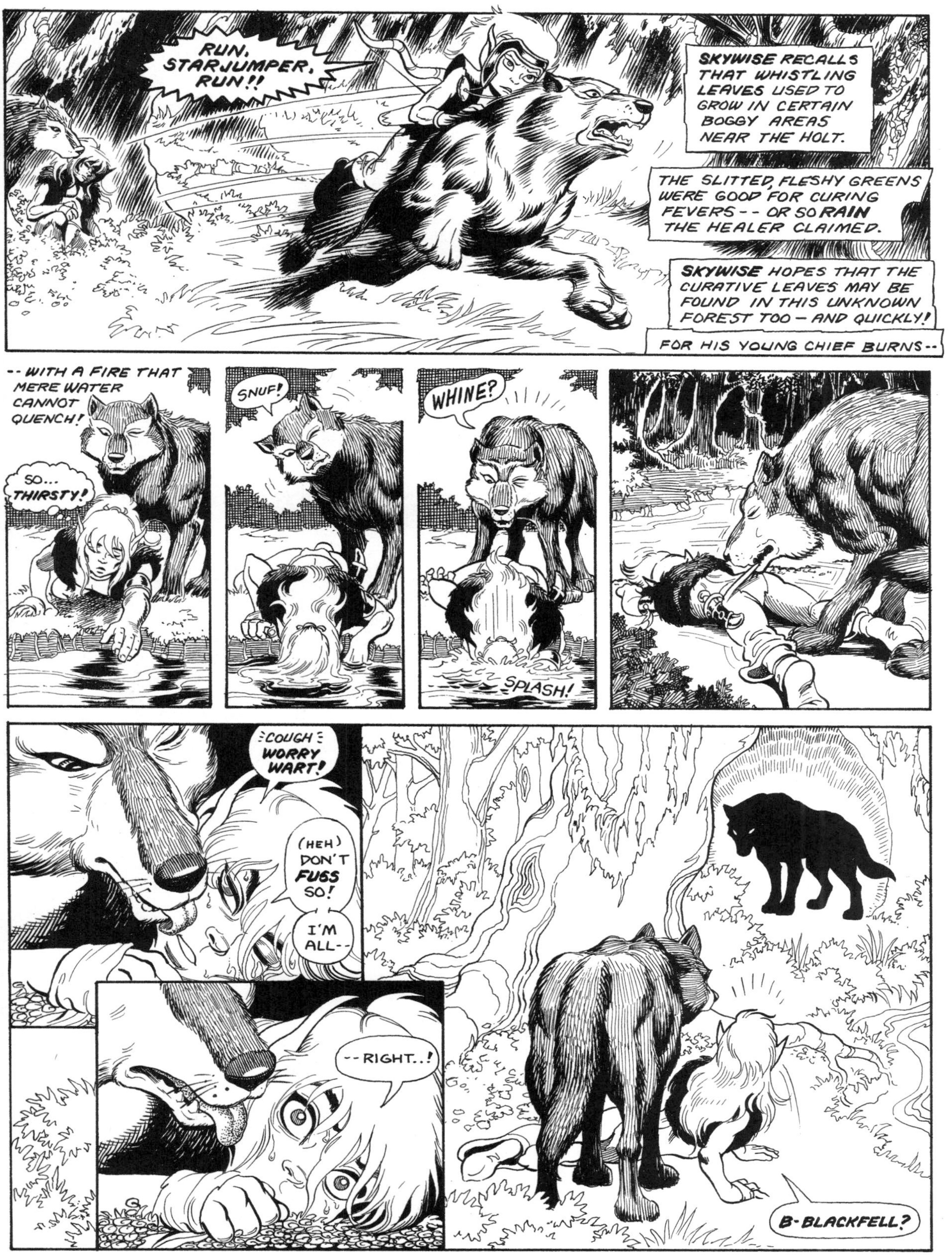
RUN, STARJUMPER, RUN!!
SKYWISE RECALLS THAT WHISTLING LEAVES USED TO GROW IN CERTAIN BOGGY AREAS NEAR THE HOLT.
THE SLITTED, FLESHY GREENS WERE GOOD FOR CURING FEVERS -- OR SO RAIN THE HEALER CLAIMED.
SKYWISE HOPES THAT THE CURATIVE LEAVES MAY BE FOUND IN THIS UNKNOWN FOREST TOO — AND QUICKLY!
FOR HIS YOUNG CHIEF BURNS--
-- WITH A FIRE THAT MERE WATER CANNOT QUENCH!
SO... THIRSTY!
SNUF!
WHINE?
SPLASH!
COUGH WORRY WART!
(HEH) DON'T FUSS SO!
I'M ALL--
--RIGHT..!
B-BLACKFELL?

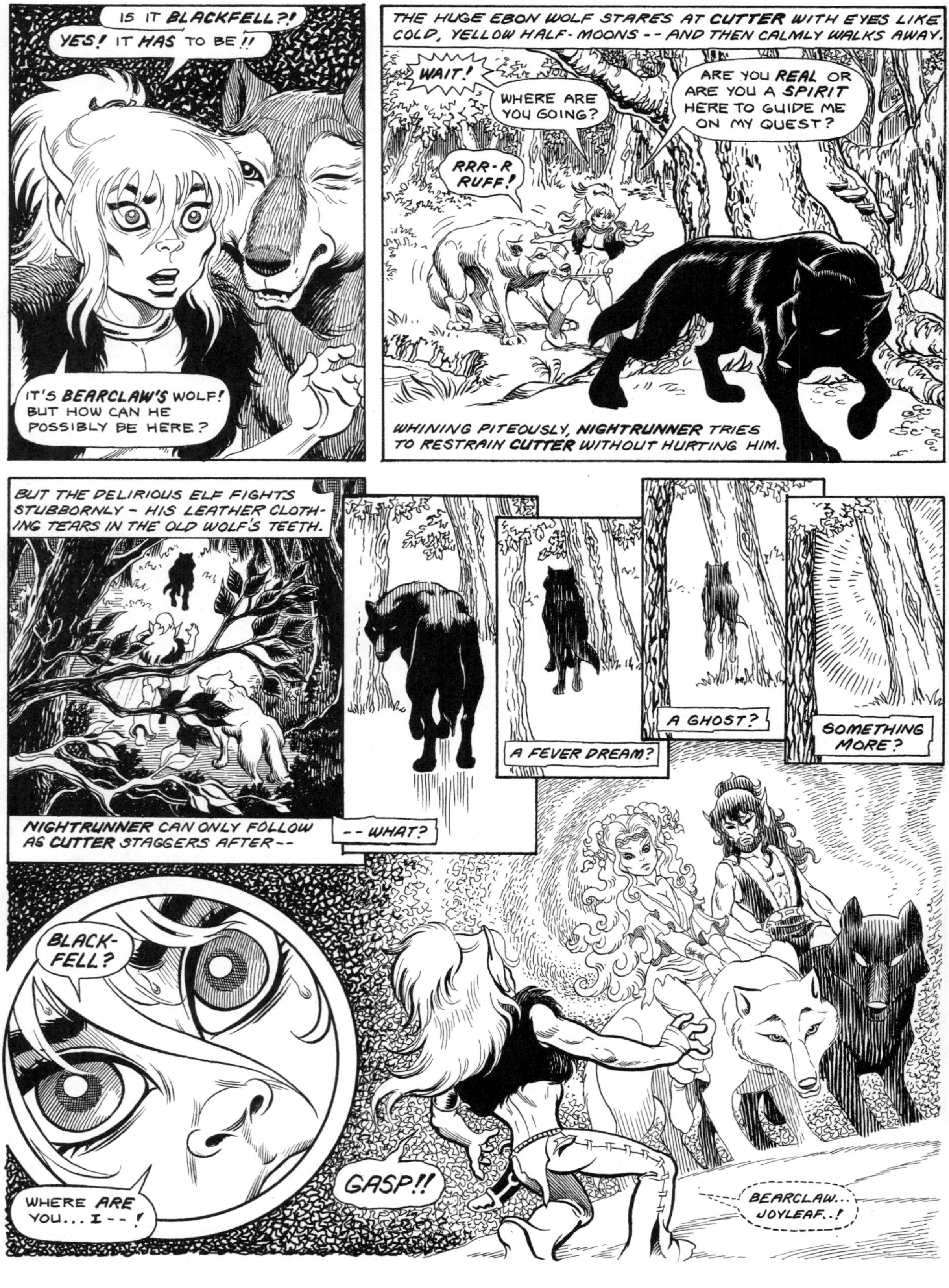

IS IT BLACKFELL?!
YES! IT HAS TO BE!!
IT'S BEARCLAW'S WOLF! BUT HOW CAN HE POSSIBLY BE HERE?
THE HUGE EBON WOLF STARES AT CUTTER WITH EYES LIKE COLD, YELLOW HALF-MOONS -- AND THEN CALMLY WALKS AWAY.
WAIT!
WHERE ARE YOU GOING?
ARE YOU REAL OR ARE YOU A SPIRIT HERE TO GUIDE ME ON MY QUEST?
RRR-R RUFF!
WHINING PITEOUSLY, NIGHTRUNNER TRIES TO RESTRAIN CUTTER WITHOUT HURTING HIM.
BUT THE DELIRIOUS ELF FIGHTS STUBBORNLY - HIS LEATHER CLOTHING TEARS IN THE OLD WOLF'S TEETH.
NIGHTRUNNER CAN ONLY FOLLOW AS CUTTER STAGGERS AFTER--
A FEVER DREAM?
A GHOST?
SOMETHING MORE?
-- WHAT?
BLACK-FELL?
WHERE ARE YOU... I--!
GASP!!
BEARCLAW... JOYLEAF..!

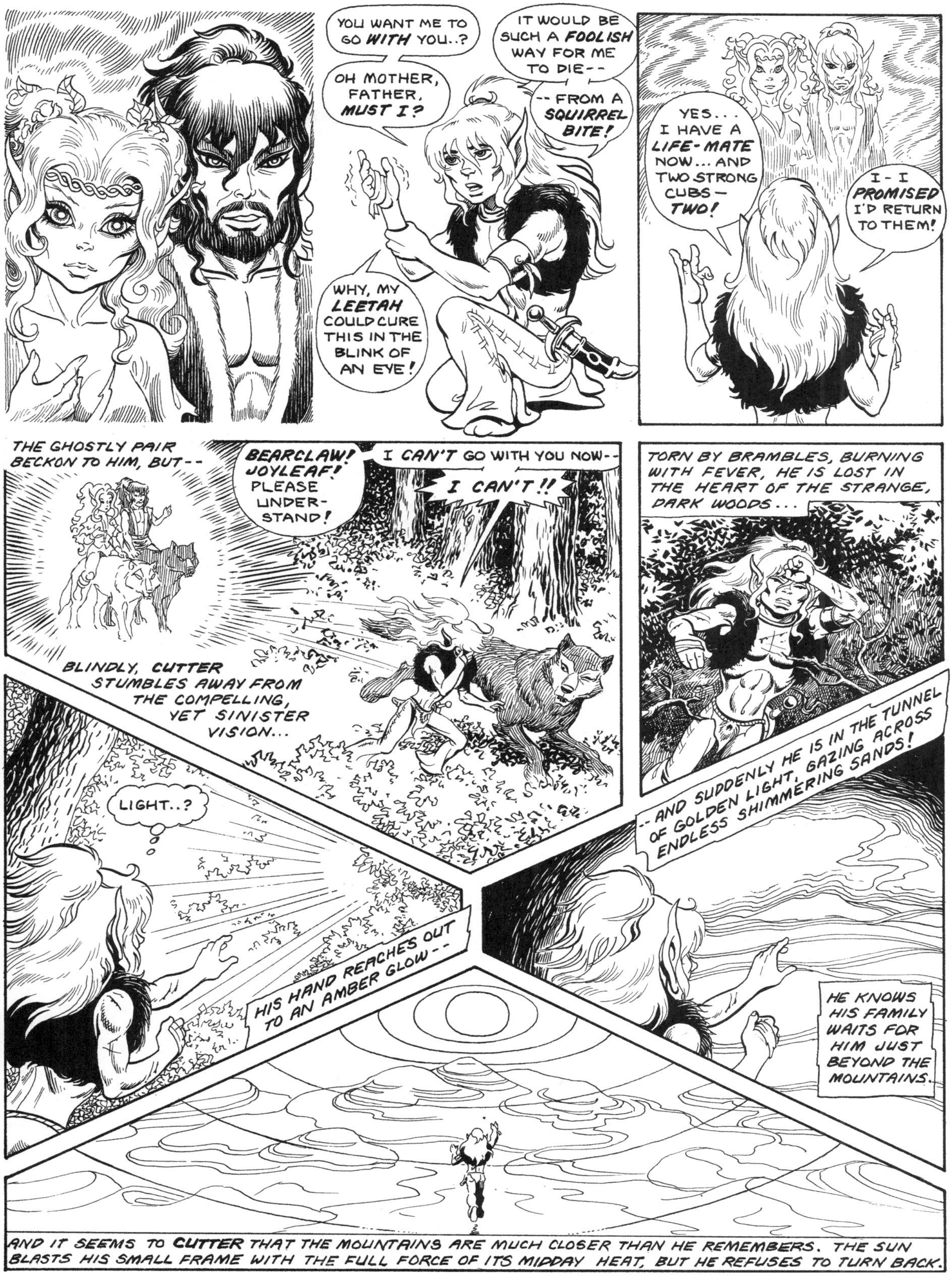
YOU WANT ME TO GO WITH YOU..?
OH MOTHER, FATHER, MUST I?
IT WOULD BE SUCH A FOOLISH WAY FOR ME TO DIE--
--FROM A SQUIRREL BITE!
WHY, MY LEETAH COULD CURE THIS IN THE BLINK OF AN EYE!
YES... I HAVE A LIFE-MATE NOW... AND TWO STRONG CUBS— TWO!
I- I PROMISED I'D RETURN TO THEM!
THE GHOSTLY PAIR BECKON TO HIM, BUT--
BEARCLAW! JOYLEAF! PLEASE UNDER-STAND!
I CAN'T GO WITH YOU NOW--
I CAN'T!!
BLINDLY, CUTTER STUMBLES AWAY FROM THE COMPELLING, YET SINISTER VISION...
TORN BY BRAMBLES, BURNING WITH FEVER, HE IS LOST IN THE HEART OF THE STRANGE, DARK WOODS...
LIGHT..?
HIS HAND REACHES OUT TO AN AMBER GLOW--
--AND SUDDENLY HE IS IN THE TUNNEL OF GOLDEN LIGHT, GAZING ACROSS ENDLESS SHIMMERING SANDS!
HE KNOWS HIS FAMILY WAITS FOR HIM JUST BEYOND THE MOUNTAINS.
AND IT SEEMS TO CUTTER THAT THE MOUNTAINS ARE MUCH CLOSER THAN HE REMEMBERS. THE SUN BLASTS HIS SMALL FRAME WITH THE FULL FORCE OF ITS MIDDAY HEAT, BUT HE REFUSES TO TURN BACK.

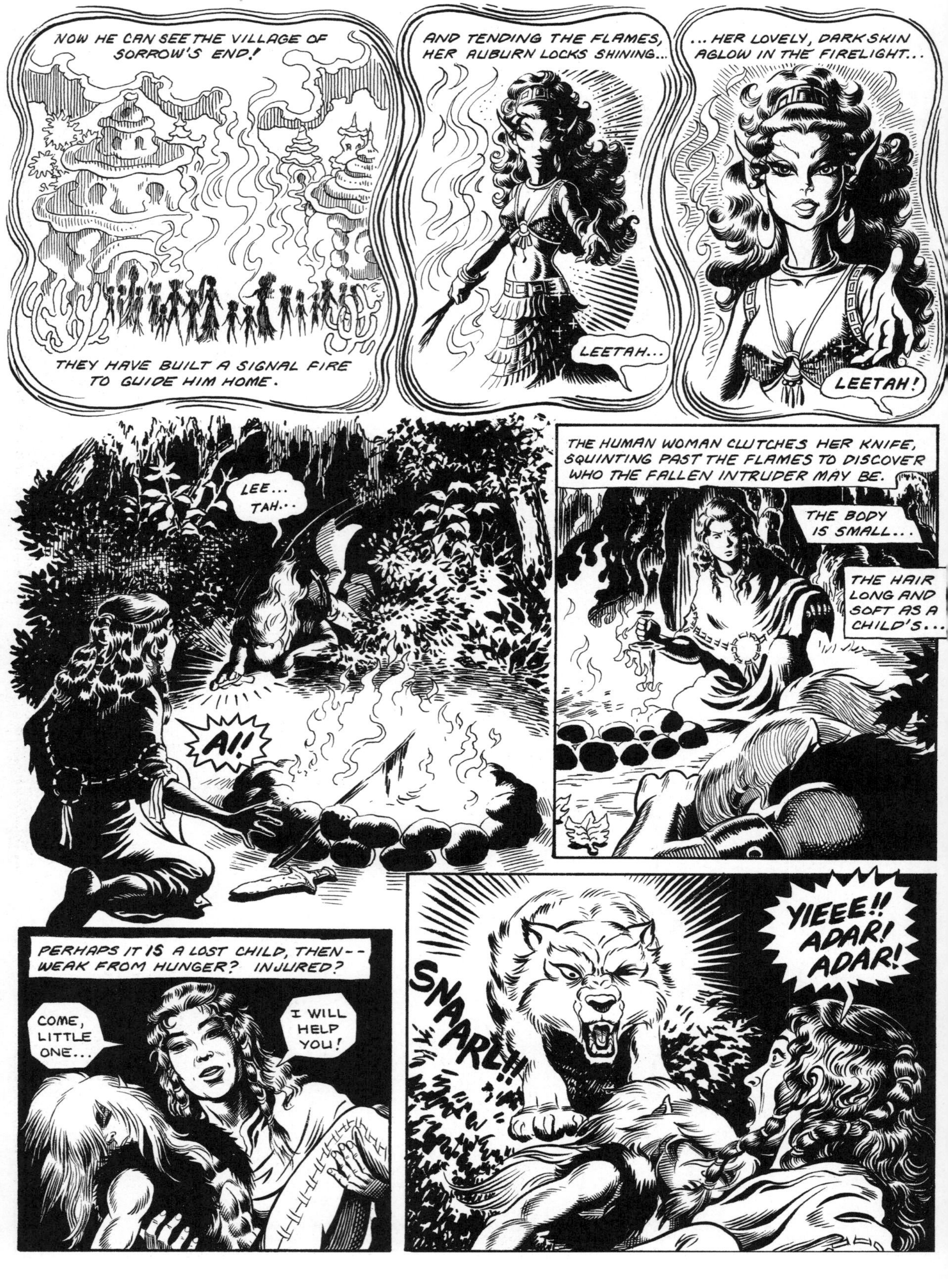
NOW HE CAN SEE THE VILLAGE OF SORROW'S END!
THEY HAVE BUILT A SIGNAL FIRE TO GUIDE HIM HOME.
AND TENDING THE FLAMES, HER AUBURN LOCKS SHINING...
LEETAH...
... HER LOVELY, DARKSKIN AGLOW IN THE FIRELIGHT...
LEETAH!
LEE... TAH...
AI!
THE HUMAN WOMAN CLUTCHES HER KNIFE, SQUINTING PAST THE FLAMES TO DISCOVER WHO THE FALLEN INTRUDER MAY BE.
THE BODY IS SMALL...
THE HAIR LONG AND SOFT AS A CHILD'S...
PERHAPS IT IS A LOST CHILD, THEN-- WEAK FROM HUNGER? INJURED?
COME, LITTLE ONE...
I WILL HELP YOU!
SNAARL!!
YIEEE!! ADAR! ADAR!

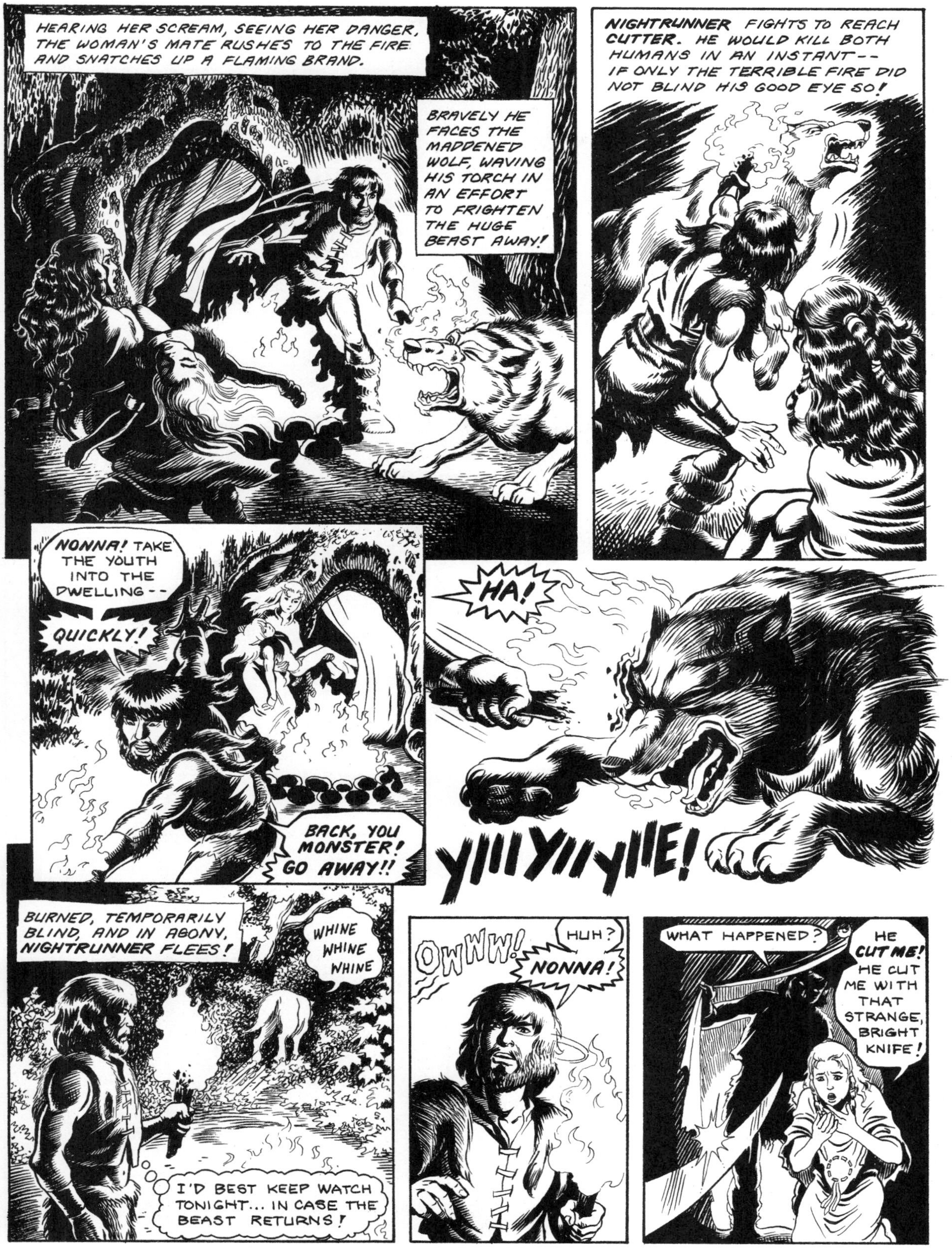
HEARING HER SCREAM, SEEING HER DANGER, THE WOMAN'S MATE RUSHES TO THE FIRE AND SNATCHES UP A FLAMING BRAND.
BRAVELY HE FACES THE MADDENED WOLF, WAVING HIS TORCH IN AN EFFORT TO FRIGHTEN THE HUGE BEAST AWAY!
NIGHTRUNNER FIGHTS TO REACH CUTTER. HE WOULD KILL BOTH HUMANS IN AN INSTANT-- IF ONLY THE TERRIBLE FIRE DID NOT BLIND HIS GOOD EYE SO!
NONNA! TAKE THE YOUTH INTO THE DWELLING--
QUICKLY!
BACK, YOU MONSTER! GO AWAY!!
HA!
YIIIYIIIYIIIE!
BURNED, TEMPORARILY BLIND, AND IN AGONY, NIGHTRUNNER FLEES!
WHINE WHINE WHINE
I'D BEST KEEP WATCH TONIGHT... IN CASE THE BEAST RETURNS!
OWWW!
HUH?
NONNA!
WHAT HAPPENED?
HE CUT ME! HE CUT ME WITH THAT STRANGE, BRIGHT KNIFE!

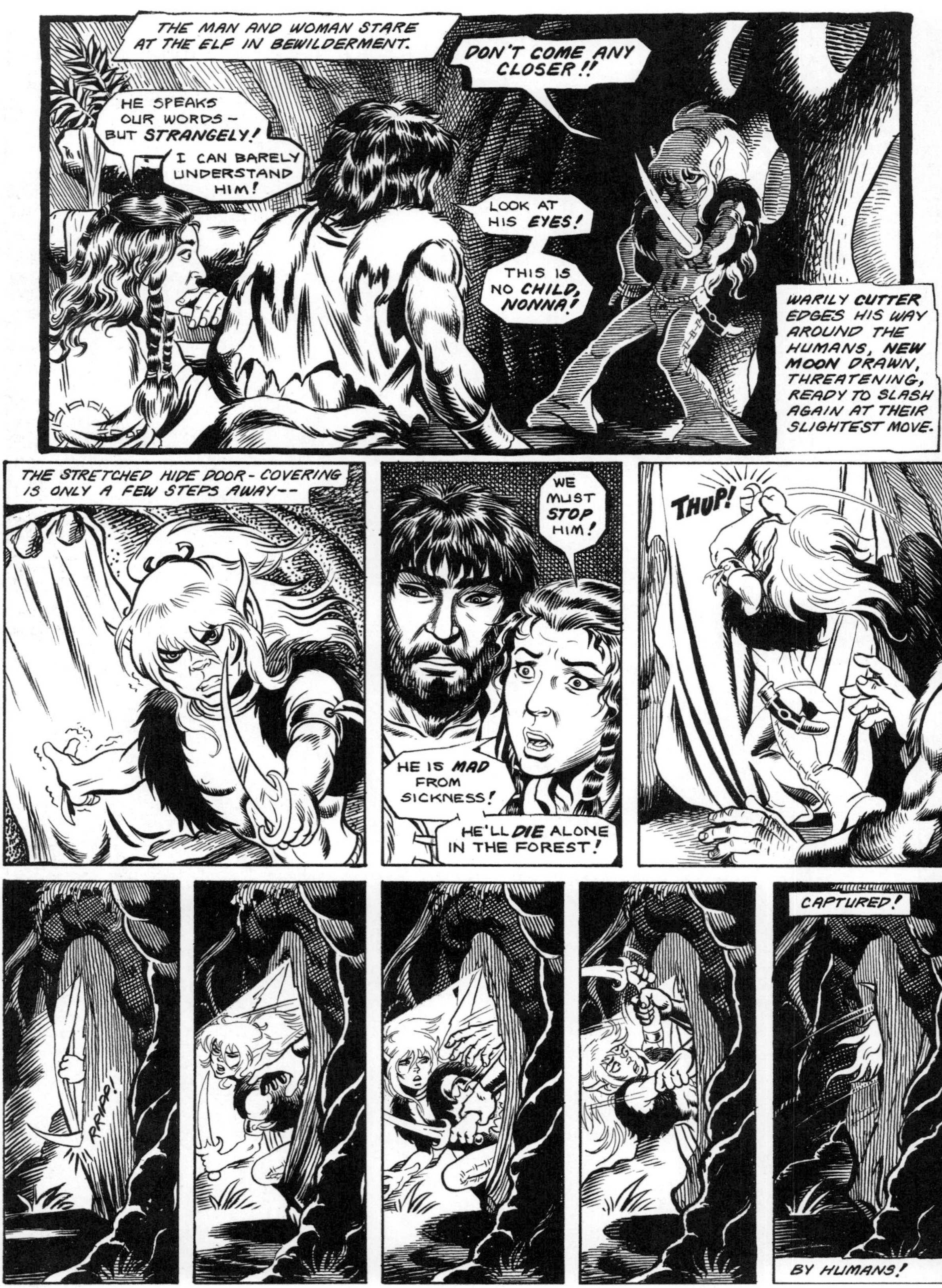
THE MAN AND WOMAN STARE AT THE ELF IN BEWILDERMENT.
DON'T COME ANY CLOSER!!
HE SPEAKS OUR WORDS -- BUT STRANGELY!
I CAN BARELY UNDERSTAND HIM!
LOOK AT HIS EYES!
THIS IS NO CHILD, NONNA!
WARILY CUTTER EDGES HIS WAY AROUND THE HUMANS, NEW MOON DRAWN, THREATENING, READY TO SLASH AGAIN AT THEIR SLIGHTEST MOVE.
THE STRETCHED HIDE DOOR-COVERING IS ONLY A FEW STEPS AWAY--
WE MUST STOP HIM!
HE IS MAD FROM SICKNESS!
HE'LL DIE ALONE IN THE FOREST!
THUP!
RRIPP!
CAPTURED!
BY HUMANS!

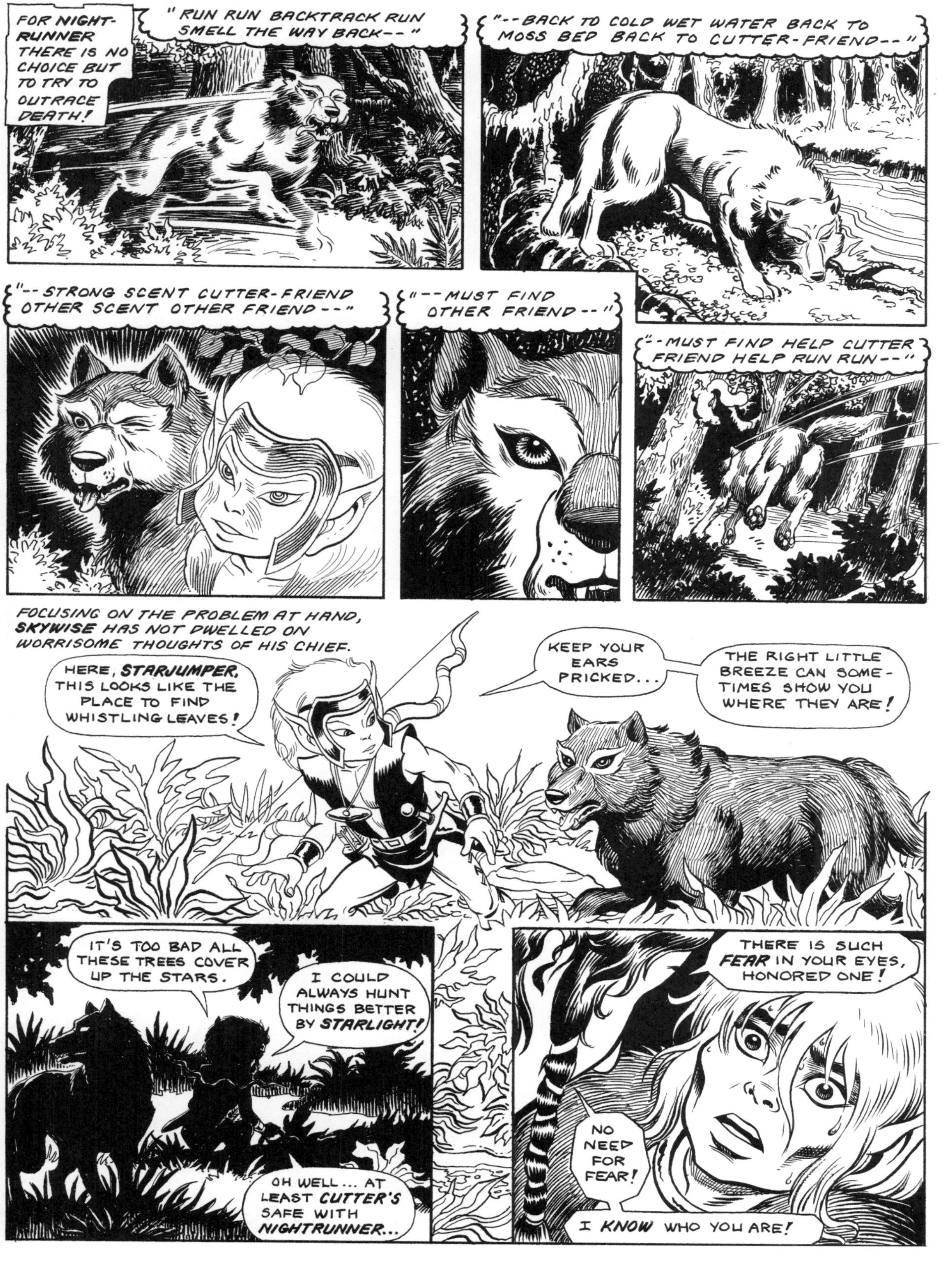

FOR NIGHT-RUNNER THERE IS NO CHOICE BUT TO TRY TO OUTRACE DEATH!
"RUN RUN BACKTRACK RUN SMELL THE WAY BACK--"
"--BACK TO COLD WET WATER BACK TO MOSS BED BACK TO CUTTER-FRIEND--"
"--STRONG SCENT CUTTER-FRIEND OTHER SCENT OTHER FRIEND--"
"--MUST FIND OTHER FRIEND--"
"--MUST FIND HELP CUTTER FRIEND HELP RUN RUN--"
FOCUSING ON THE PROBLEM AT HAND, SKYWISE HAS NOT DWELLED ON WORRISOME THOUGHTS OF HIS CHIEF.
HERE, STARJUMPER, THIS LOOKS LIKE THE PLACE TO FIND WHISTLING LEAVES!
KEEP YOUR EARS PRICKED...
THE RIGHT LITTLE BREEZE CAN SOME-TIMES SHOW YOU WHERE THEY ARE!
IT'S TOO BAD ALL THESE TREES COVER UP THE STARS.
I COULD ALWAYS HUNT THINGS BETTER BY STARLIGHT!
OH WELL... AT LEAST CUTTER'S SAFE WITH NIGHTRUNNER...
THERE IS SUCH FEAR IN YOUR EYES, HONORED ONE!
NO NEED FOR FEAR!
I KNOW WHO YOU ARE!

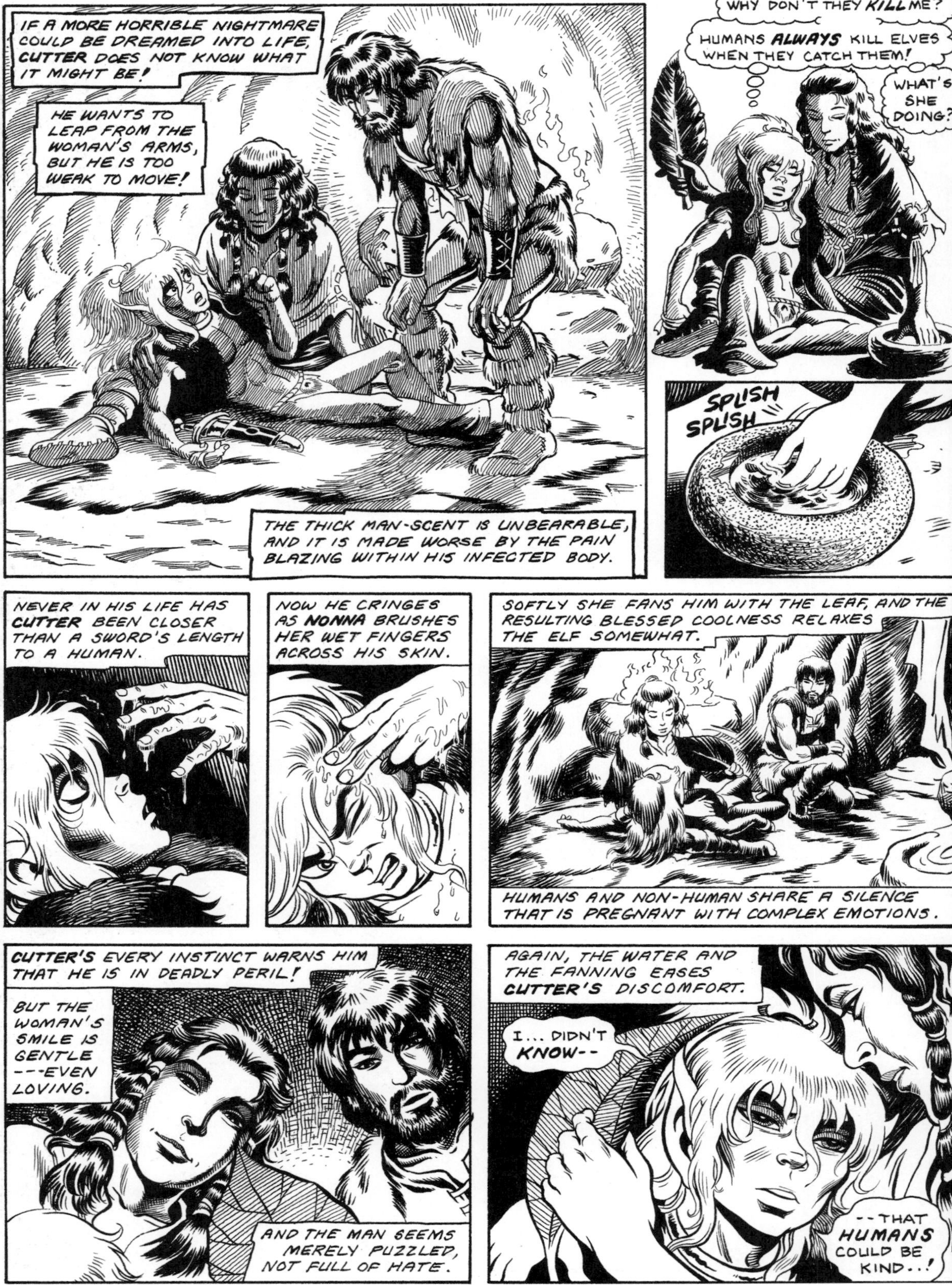
IF A MORE HORRIBLE NIGHTMARE COULD BE DREAMED INTO LIFE, CUTTER DOES NOT KNOW WHAT IT MIGHT BE!
HE WANTS TO LEAP FROM THE WOMAN'S ARMS, BUT HE IS TOO WEAK TO MOVE!
THE THICK MAN-SCENT IS UNBEARABLE, AND IT IS MADE WORSE BY THE PAIN BLAZING WITHIN HIS INFECTED BODY.
WHY DON'T THEY KILL ME?
HUMANS ALWAYS KILL ELVES WHEN THEY CATCH THEM!
WHAT'S SHE DOING?
SPLISH
SPLISH
NEVER IN HIS LIFE HAS CUTTER BEEN CLOSER THAN A SWORD'S LENGTH TO A HUMAN.
NOW HE CRINGES AS NONNA BRUSHES HER WET FINGERS ACROSS HIS SKIN.
SOFTLY SHE FANS HIM WITH THE LEAF, AND THE RESULTING BLESSED COOLNESS RELAXES THE ELF SOMEWHAT.
HUMANS AND NON-HUMAN SHARE A SILENCE THAT IS PREGNANT WITH COMPLEX EMOTIONS.
CUTTER'S EVERY INSTINCT WARNS HIM THAT HE IS IN DEADLY PERIL!
BUT THE WOMAN'S SMILE IS GENTLE ---EVEN LOVING.
AND THE MAN SEEMS MERELY PUZZLED, NOT FULL OF HATE.
AGAIN, THE WATER AND THE FANNING EASES CUTTER'S DISCOMFORT.
I... DIDN'T KNOW--
--THAT HUMANS COULD BE KIND..!

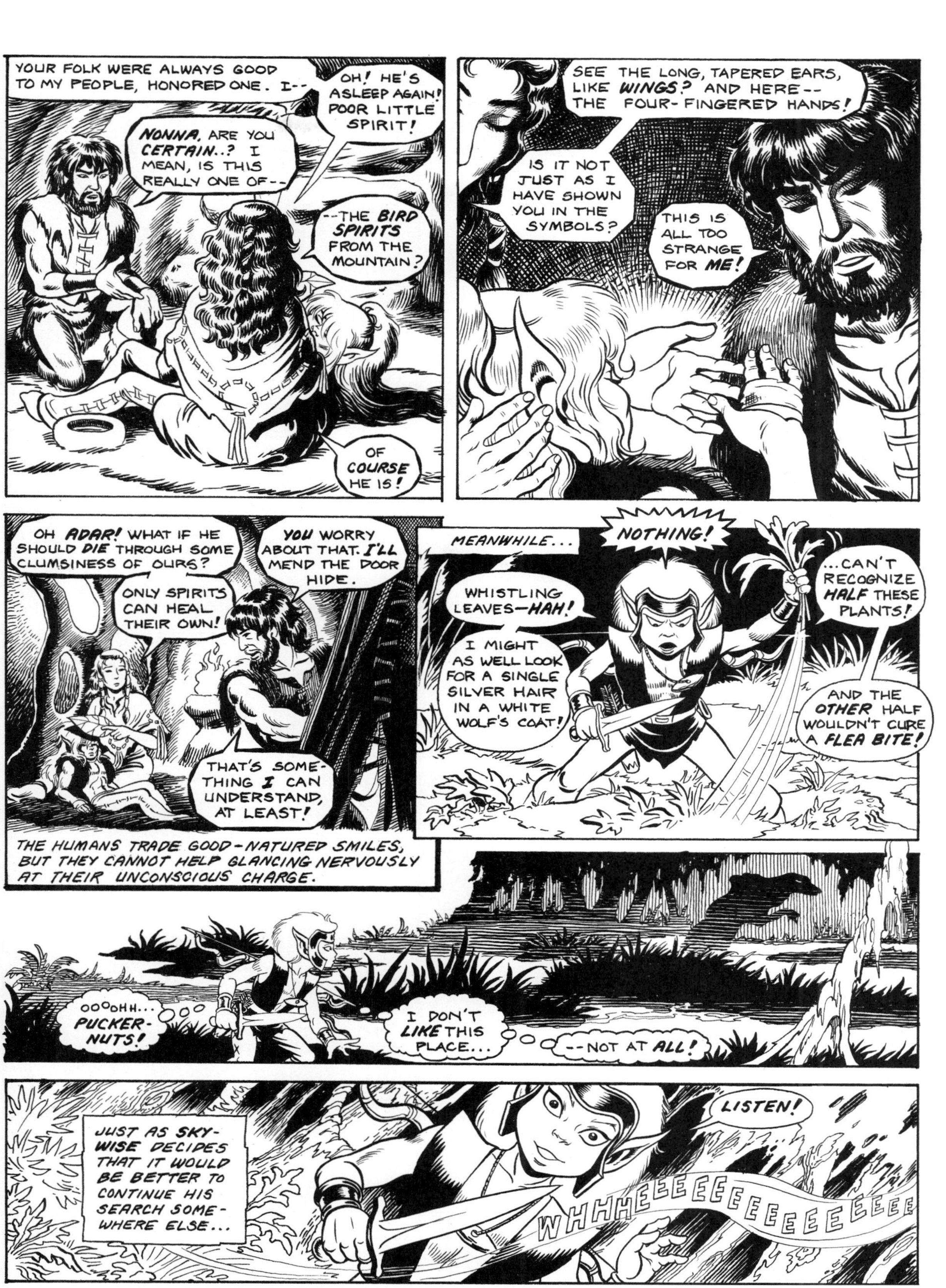
YOUR FOLK WERE ALWAYS GOOD TO MY PEOPLE, HONORED ONE. I--
OH! HE'S ASLEEP AGAIN! POOR LITTLE SPIRIT!
NONNA, ARE YOU CERTAIN..? I MEAN, IS THIS REALLY ONE OF--
--THE BIRD SPIRITS FROM THE MOUNTAIN?
OF COURSE HE IS!
SEE THE LONG, TAPERED EARS, LIKE WINGS? AND HERE-- THE FOUR-FINGERED HANDS!
IS IT NOT JUST AS I HAVE SHOWN YOU IN THE SYMBOLS?
THIS IS ALL TOO STRANGE FOR ME!
OH ADAR! WHAT IF HE SHOULD DIE THROUGH SOME CLUMSINESS OF OURS?
ONLY SPIRITS CAN HEAL THEIR OWN!
YOU WORRY ABOUT THAT. I'LL MEND THE DOOR HIDE.
THAT'S SOMETHING I CAN UNDERSTAND, AT LEAST!
THE HUMANS TRADE GOOD-NATURED SMILES, BUT THEY CANNOT HELP GLANCING NERVOUSLY AT THEIR UNCONSCIOUS CHARGE.
MEANWHILE...
NOTHING!
WHISTLING LEAVES—HAH!
I MIGHT AS WELL LOOK FOR A SINGLE SILVER HAIR IN A WHITE WOLF'S COAT!
...CAN'T RECOGNIZE HALF THESE PLANTS!
AND THE OTHER HALF WOULDN'T CURE A FLEA BITE!
OOOOHH... PUCKERNUTS!
I DON'T LIKE THIS PLACE...
--NOT AT ALL!
JUST AS SKYWISE DECIDES THAT IT WOULD BE BETTER TO CONTINUE HIS SEARCH SOMEWHERE ELSE...
LISTEN!
WHHHEEEEEEEEEEEEEEE

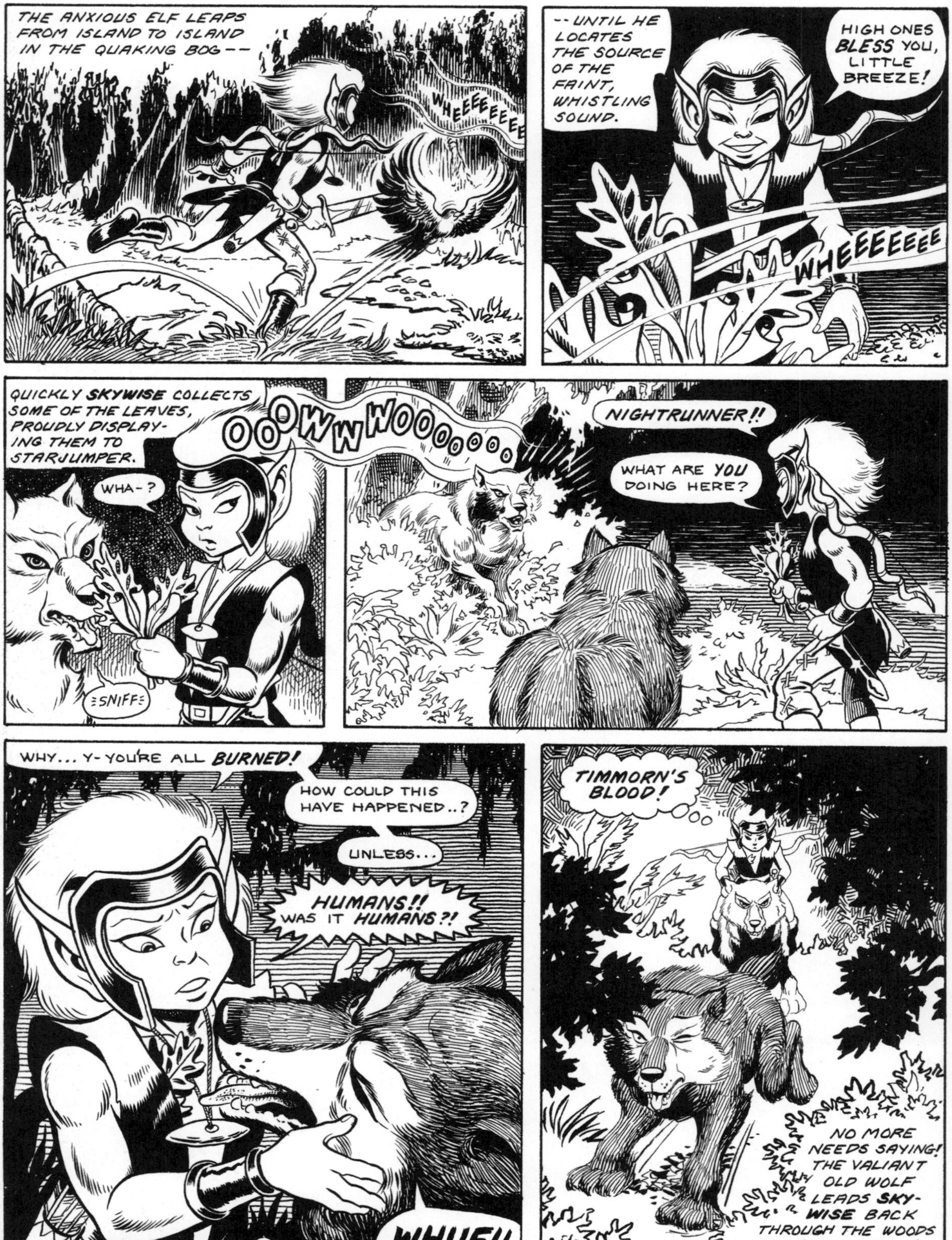
THE ANXIOUS ELF LEAPS FROM ISLAND TO ISLAND IN THE QUAKING BOG--
WHEEEEEEEE
--UNTIL HE LOCATES THE SOURCE OF THE FAINT, WHISTLING SOUND.
HIGH ONES BLESS YOU, LITTLE BREEZE!
WHEEEEEEEE
QUICKLY SKYWISE COLLECTS SOME OF THE LEAVES, PROUDLY DISPLAYING THEM TO STARJUMPER.
OOOWWWOOOOOOOO
WHA-?
SNIFF
NIGHTRUNNER!!
WHAT ARE YOU DOING HERE?
WHY... Y-YOU'RE ALL BURNED!
HOW COULD THIS HAVE HAPPENED..?
UNLESS...
HUMANS!! WAS IT HUMANS?!
WHUF!!
TIMMORN'S BLOOD!
NO MORE NEEDS SAYING! THE VALIANT OLD WOLF LEADS SKYWISE BACK THROUGH THE WOODS AT A DEAD RUN!

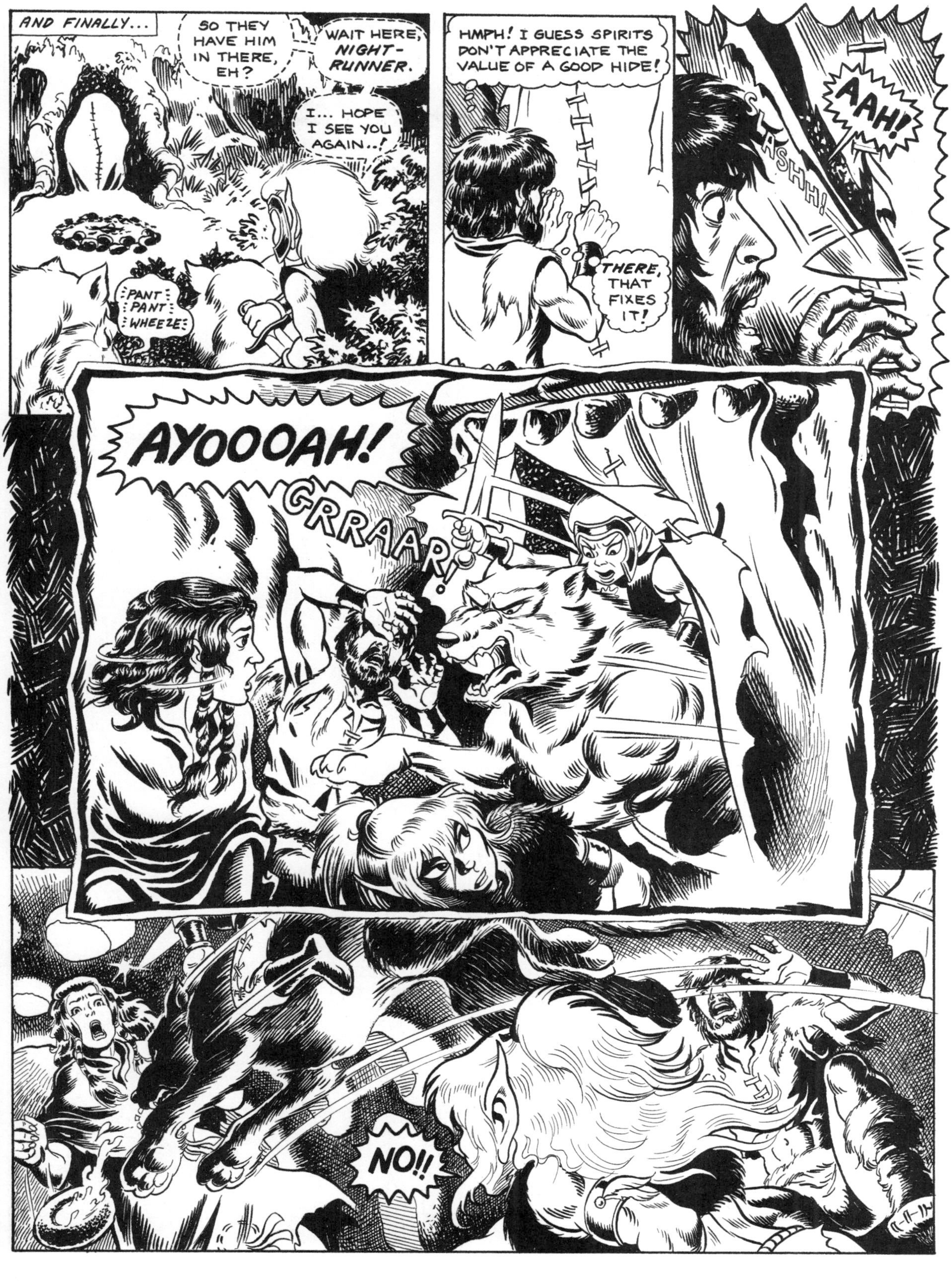

AND FINALLY...
SO THEY HAVE HIM IN THERE, EH?
WAIT HERE, NIGHT-RUNNER.
I... HOPE I SEE YOU AGAIN...!
PANT PANT WHEEZE
HMPH! I GUESS SPIRITS DON'T APPRECIATE THE VALUE OF A GOOD HIDE!
THERE, THAT FIXES IT!
SLASHH!
AAH!
AYOOOAH!
GRRRAAR!
NO!!

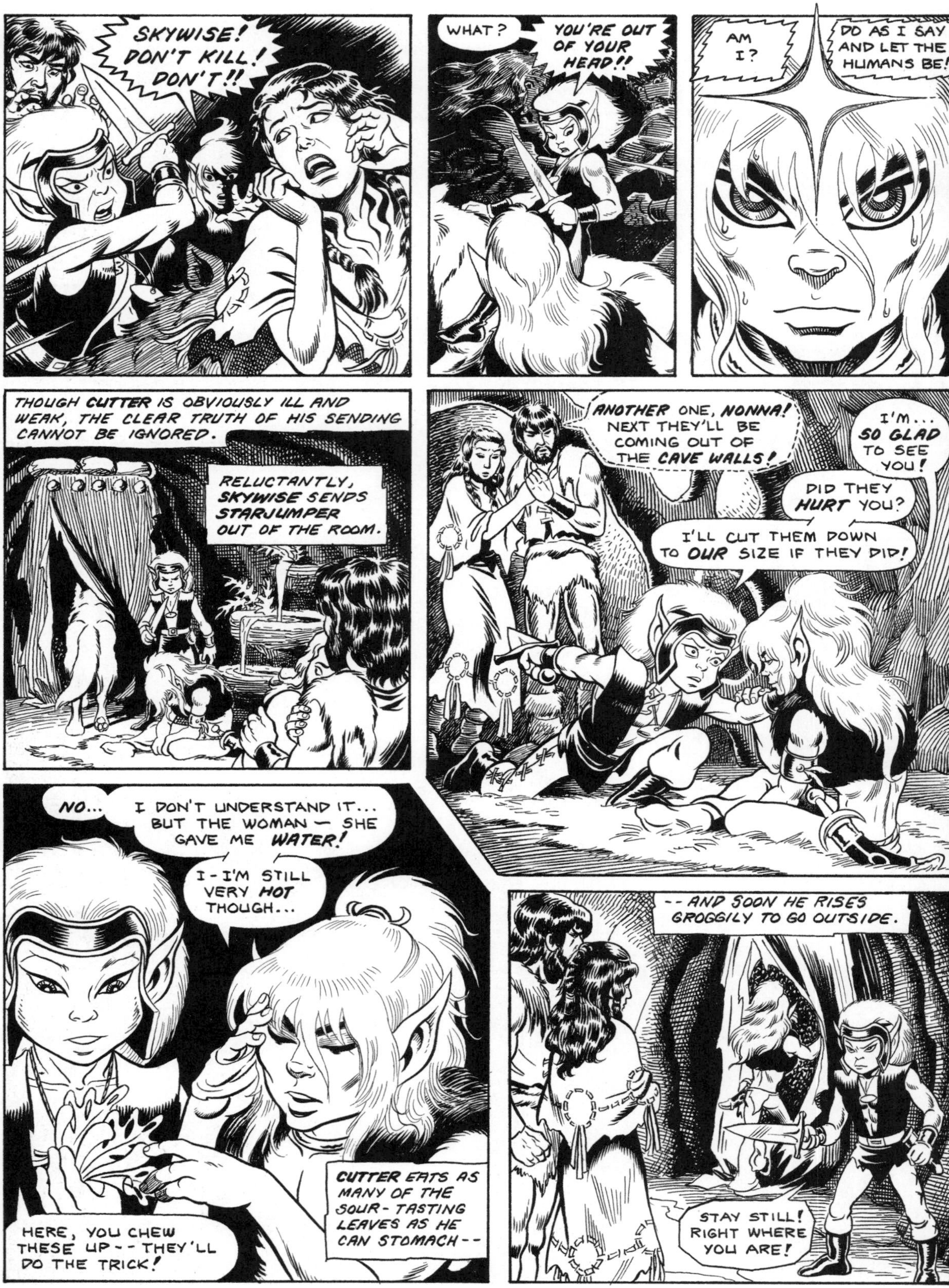
SKYWISE! DON'T KILL! DON'T!!
WHAT?
YOU'RE OUT OF YOUR HEAD!!
AM I?
DO AS I SAY AND LET THE HUMANS BE!
THOUGH CUTTER IS OBVIOUSLY ILL AND WEAK, THE CLEAR TRUTH OF HIS SENDING CANNOT BE IGNORED.
RELUCTANTLY, SKYWISE SENDS STARJUMPER OUT OF THE ROOM.
ANOTHER ONE, NONNA! NEXT THEY'LL BE COMING OUT OF THE CAVE WALLS!
I'M... SO GLAD TO SEE YOU!
DID THEY HURT YOU?
I'LL CUT THEM DOWN TO OUR SIZE IF THEY DID!
NO...
I DON'T UNDERSTAND IT... BUT THE WOMAN — SHE GAVE ME WATER!
I-I'M STILL VERY HOT THOUGH...
HERE, YOU CHEW THESE UP--THEY'LL DO THE TRICK!
CUTTER EATS AS MANY OF THE SOUR-TASTING LEAVES AS HE CAN STOMACH--
--AND SOON HE RISES GROGGILY TO GO OUTSIDE.
STAY STILL! RIGHT WHERE YOU ARE!

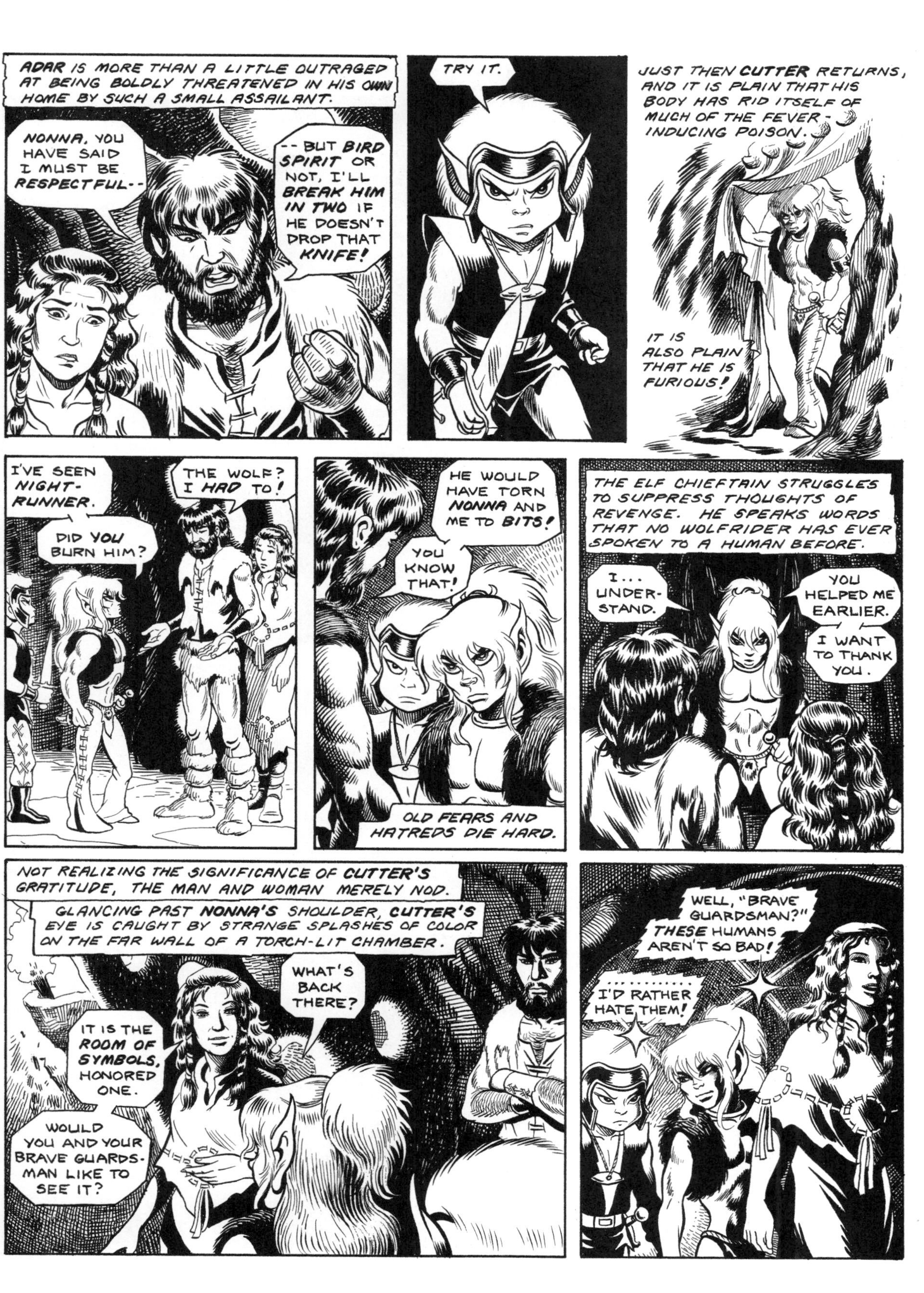
ADAR IS MORE THAN A LITTLE OUTRAGED AT BEING BOLDLY THREATENED IN HIS OWN HOME BY SUCH A SMALL ASSAILANT.
NONNA, YOU HAVE SAID I MUST BE RESPECTFUL--
--BUT BIRD SPIRIT OR NOT, I'LL BREAK HIM IN TWO IF HE DOESN'T DROP THAT KNIFE!
TRY IT.
JUST THEN CUTTER RETURNS, AND IT IS PLAIN THAT HIS BODY HAS RID ITSELF OF MUCH OF THE FEVER-INDUCING POISON.
IT IS ALSO PLAIN THAT HE IS FURIOUS!
I'VE SEEN NIGHT-RUNNER.
DID YOU BURN HIM?
THE WOLF? I HAD TO!
HE WOULD HAVE TORN NONNA AND ME TO BITS!
YOU KNOW THAT!
OLD FEARS AND HATREDS DIE HARD.
THE ELF CHIEFTAIN STRUGGLES TO SUPPRESS THOUGHTS OF REVENGE. HE SPEAKS WORDS THAT NO WOLFRIDER HAS EVER SPOKEN TO A HUMAN BEFORE.
I... UNDER-STAND.
YOU HELPED ME EARLIER.
I WANT TO THANK YOU.
NOT REALIZING THE SIGNIFICANCE OF CUTTER'S GRATITUDE, THE MAN AND WOMAN MERELY NOD.
GLANCING PAST NONNA'S SHOULDER, CUTTER'S EYE IS CAUGHT BY STRANGE SPLASHES OF COLOR ON THE FAR WALL OF A TORCH-LIT CHAMBER.
WHAT'S BACK THERE?
IT IS THE ROOM OF SYMBOLS, HONORED ONE.
WOULD YOU AND YOUR BRAVE GUARDS-MAN LIKE TO SEE IT?
WELL, "BRAVE GUARDSMAN?" THESE HUMANS AREN'T SO BAD!
I'D RATHER HATE THEM!

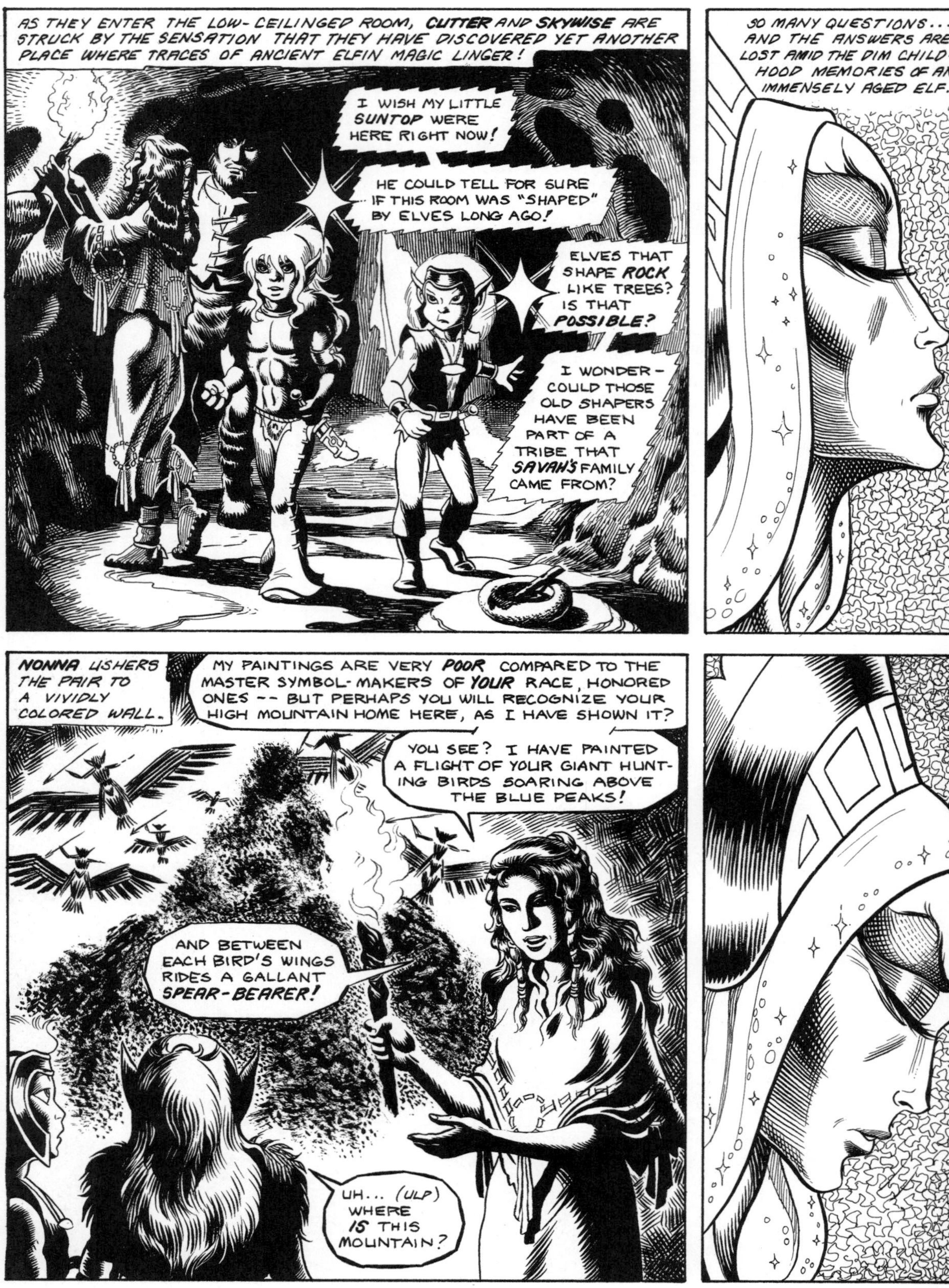
AS THEY ENTER THE LOW-CEILINGED ROOM, CUTTER AND SKYWISE ARE STRUCK BY THE SENSATION THAT THEY HAVE DISCOVERED YET ANOTHER PLACE WHERE TRACES OF ANCIENT ELFIN MAGIC LINGER!
I WISH MY LITTLE SUNTOP WERE HERE RIGHT NOW!
HE COULD TELL FOR SURE IF THIS ROOM WAS "SHAPED" BY ELVES LONG AGO!
ELVES THAT SHAPE ROCK LIKE TREES? IS THAT POSSIBLE?
I WONDER— COULD THOSE OLD SHAPERS HAVE BEEN PART OF A TRIBE THAT SAVAH'S FAMILY CAME FROM?
SO MANY QUESTIONS... AND THE ANSWERS ARE LOST AMID THE DIM CHILDHOOD MEMORIES OF AN IMMENSELY AGED ELF.
NONNA USHERS THE PAIR TO A VIVIDLY COLORED WALL.
MY PAINTINGS ARE VERY POOR COMPARED TO THE MASTER SYMBOL-MAKERS OF YOUR RACE, HONORED ONES -- BUT PERHAPS YOU WILL RECOGNIZE YOUR HIGH MOUNTAIN HOME HERE, AS I HAVE SHOWN IT?
YOU SEE? I HAVE PAINTED A FLIGHT OF YOUR GIANT HUNTING BIRDS SOARING ABOVE THE BLUE PEAKS!
AND BETWEEN EACH BIRD'S WINGS RIDES A GALLANT SPEAR-BEARER!
UH... (ULP) WHERE IS THIS MOUNTAIN?

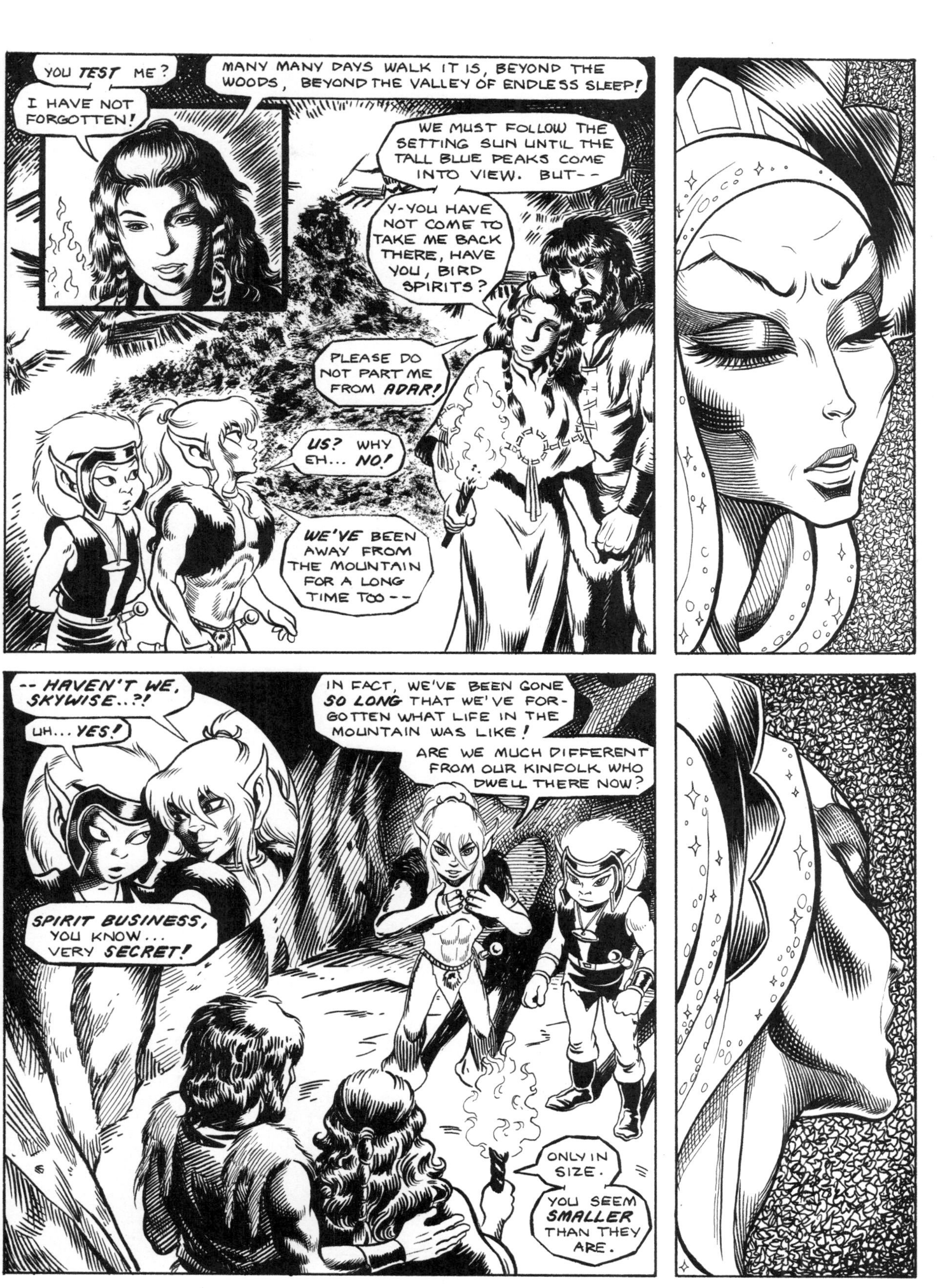
YOU TEST ME?
I HAVE NOT FORGOTTEN!
MANY MANY DAYS WALK IT IS, BEYOND THE WOODS, BEYOND THE VALLEY OF ENDLESS SLEEP!
WE MUST FOLLOW THE SETTING SUN UNTIL THE TALL BLUE PEAKS COME INTO VIEW. BUT--
Y-YOU HAVE NOT COME TO TAKE ME BACK THERE, HAVE YOU, BIRD SPIRITS?
PLEASE DO NOT PART ME FROM ADAR!
US? WHY EH... NO!
WE'VE BEEN AWAY FROM THE MOUNTAIN FOR A LONG TIME TOO--
--HAVEN'T WE, SKYWISE..?!
UH... YES!
SPIRIT BUSINESS, YOU KNOW... VERY SECRET!
IN FACT, WE'VE BEEN GONE SO LONG THAT WE'VE FOR-GOTTEN WHAT LIFE IN THE MOUNTAIN WAS LIKE!
ARE WE MUCH DIFFERENT FROM OUR KINFOLK WHO DWELL THERE NOW?
ONLY IN SIZE.
YOU SEEM SMALLER THAN THEY ARE.

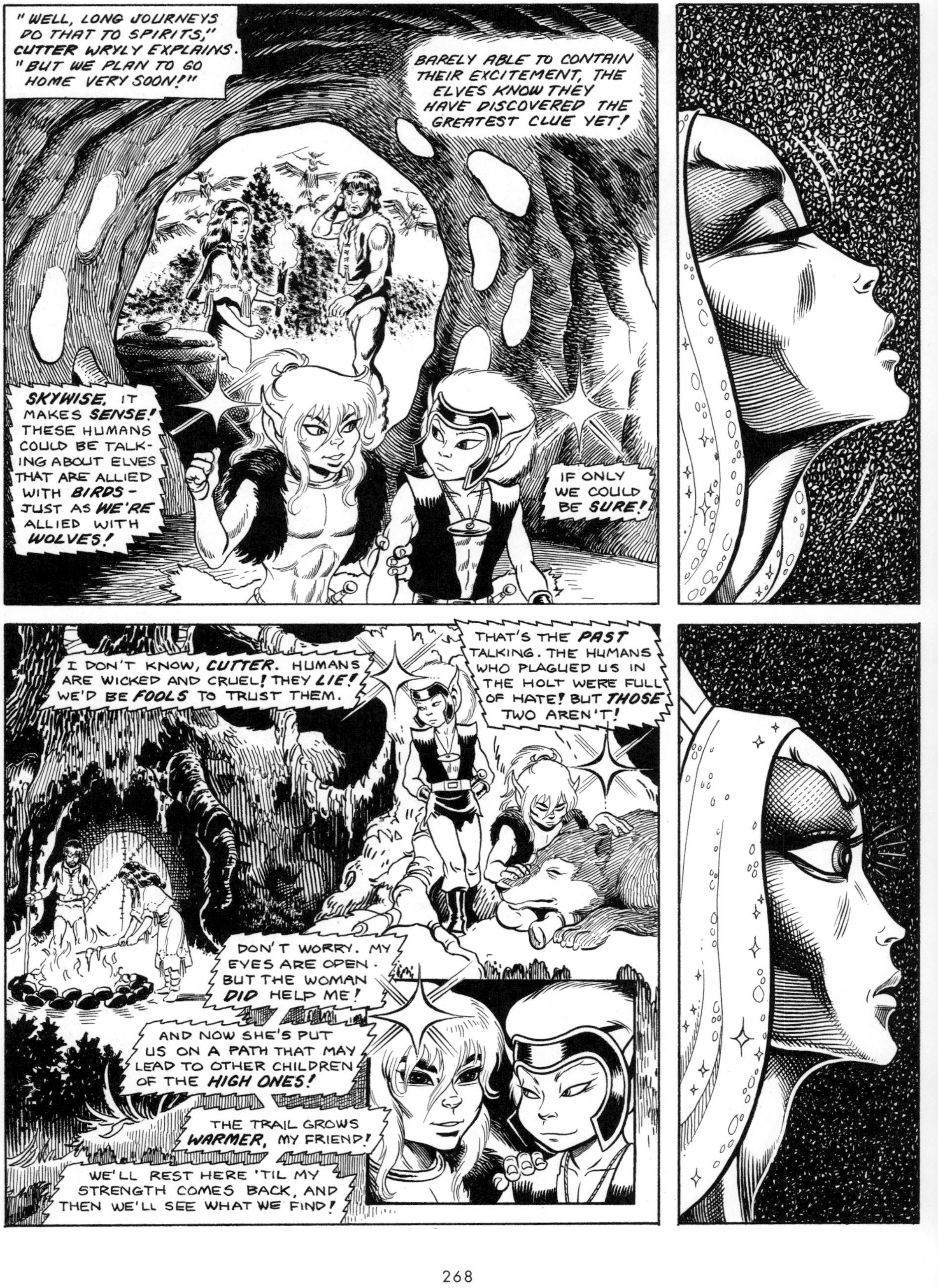
"WELL, LONG JOURNEYS DO THAT TO SPIRITS," CUTTER WRYLY EXPLAINS. "BUT WE PLAN TO GO HOME VERY SOON!"
BARELY ABLE TO CONTAIN THEIR EXCITEMENT, THE ELVES KNOW THEY HAVE DISCOVERED THE GREATEST CLUE YET!
SKYWISE, IT MAKES SENSE! THESE HUMANS COULD BE TALKING ABOUT ELVES THAT ARE ALLIED WITH BIRDS - JUST AS WE'RE ALLIED WITH WOLVES!
IF ONLY WE COULD BE SURE!
I DON'T KNOW, CUTTER. HUMANS ARE WICKED AND CRUEL! THEY LIE! WE'D BE FOOLS TO TRUST THEM.
THAT'S THE PAST TALKING. THE HUMANS WHO PLAGUED US IN THE HOLT WERE FULL OF HATE! BUT THOSE TWO AREN'T!
DON'T WORRY. MY EYES ARE OPEN. BUT THE WOMAN DID HELP ME!
AND NOW SHE'S PUT US ON A PATH THAT MAY LEAD TO OTHER CHILDREN OF THE HIGH ONES!
THE TRAIL GROWS WARMER, MY FRIEND!
WE'LL REST HERE 'TIL MY STRENGTH COMES BACK, AND THEN WE'LL SEE WHAT WE FIND!

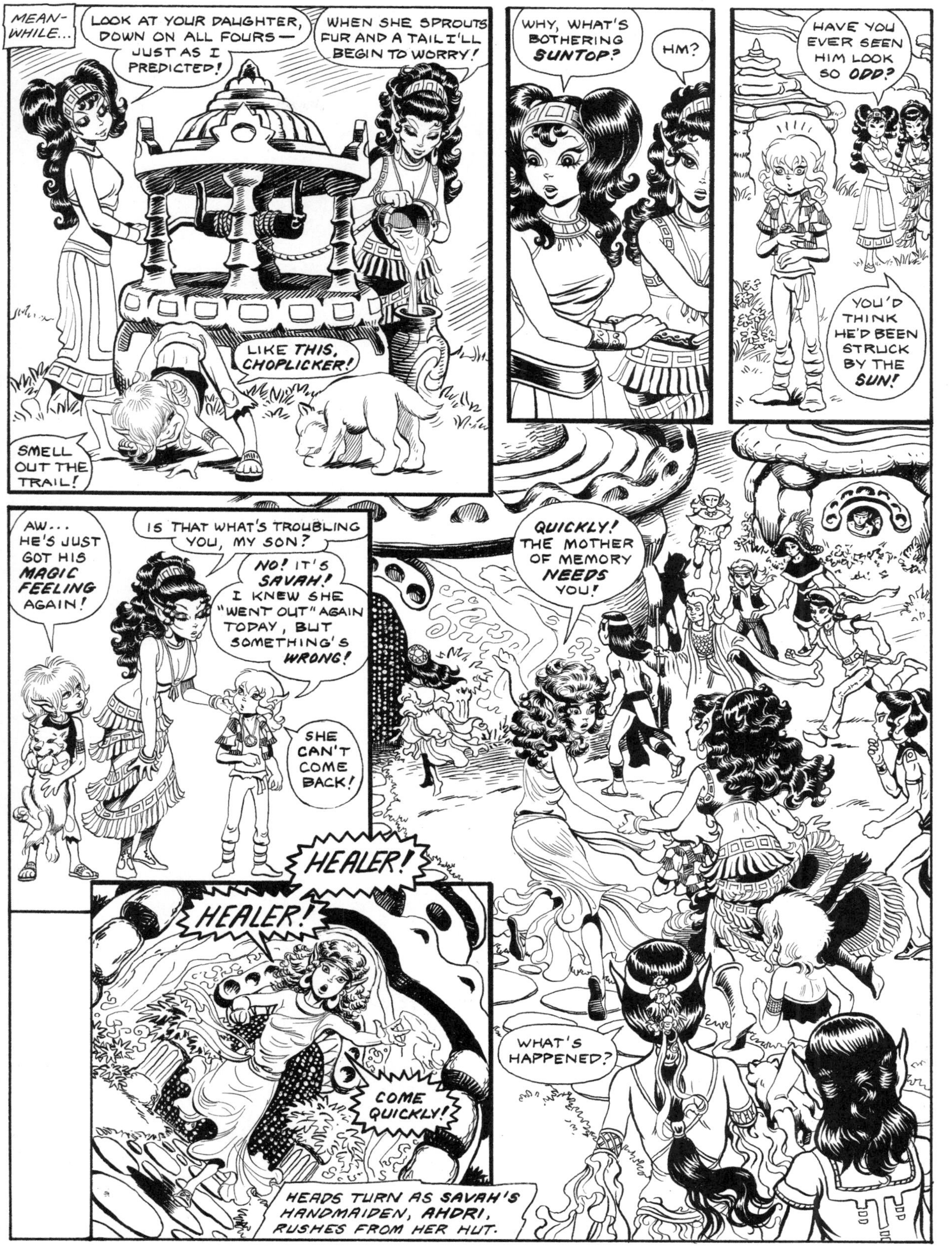

MEAN-WHILE...
LOOK AT YOUR DAUGHTER, DOWN ON ALL FOURS — JUST AS I PREDICTED!
WHEN SHE SPROUTS FUR AND A TAIL I'LL BEGIN TO WORRY!
LIKE THIS, CHOPLICKER!
SMELL OUT THE TRAIL!
WHY, WHAT'S BOTHERING SUNTOP?
HM?
HAVE YOU EVER SEEN HIM LOOK SO ODD?
YOU'D THINK HE'D BEEN STRUCK BY THE SUN!
AW... HE'S JUST GOT HIS MAGIC FEELING AGAIN!
IS THAT WHAT'S TROUBLING YOU, MY SON?
NO! IT'S SAVAH! I KNEW SHE "WENT OUT" AGAIN TODAY, BUT SOMETHING'S WRONG!
SHE CAN'T COME BACK!
HEALER!
HEALER!
COME QUICKLY!
HEADS TURN AS SAVAH'S HANDMAIDEN, AHDRI, RUSHES FROM HER HUT.
QUICKLY! THE MOTHER OF MEMORY NEEDS YOU!
WHAT'S HAPPENED?

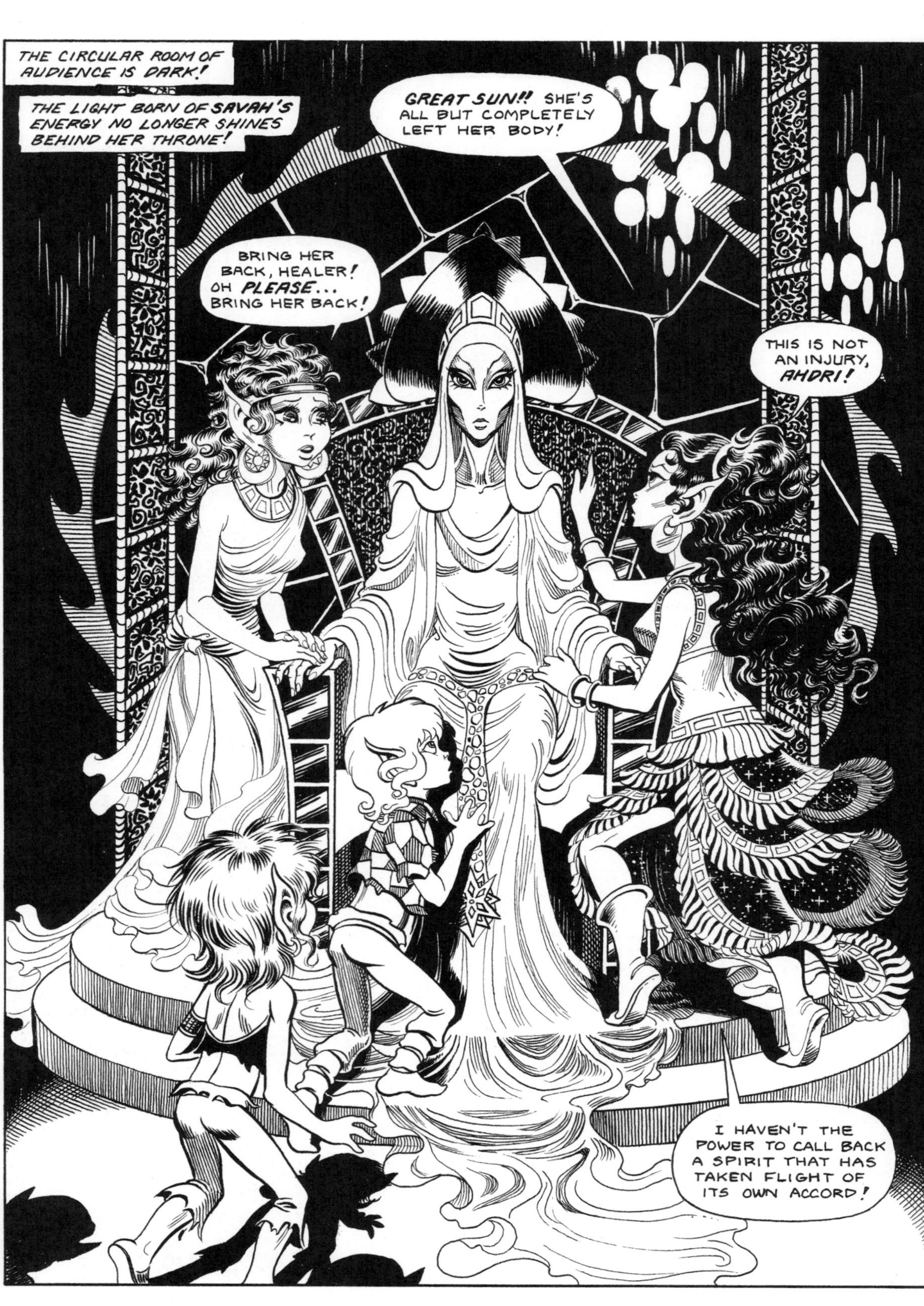
THE CIRCULAR ROOM OF AUDIENCE IS DARK!
THE LIGHT BORN OF SAVAH'S ENERGY NO LONGER SHINES BEHIND HER THRONE!
GREAT SUN!! SHE'S ALL BUT COMPLETELY LEFT HER BODY!
BRING HER BACK, HEALER! OH PLEASE... BRING HER BACK!
THIS IS NOT AN INJURY, AHDRI!
I HAVEN'T THE POWER TO CALL BACK A SPIRIT THAT HAS TAKEN FLIGHT OF ITS OWN ACCORD!

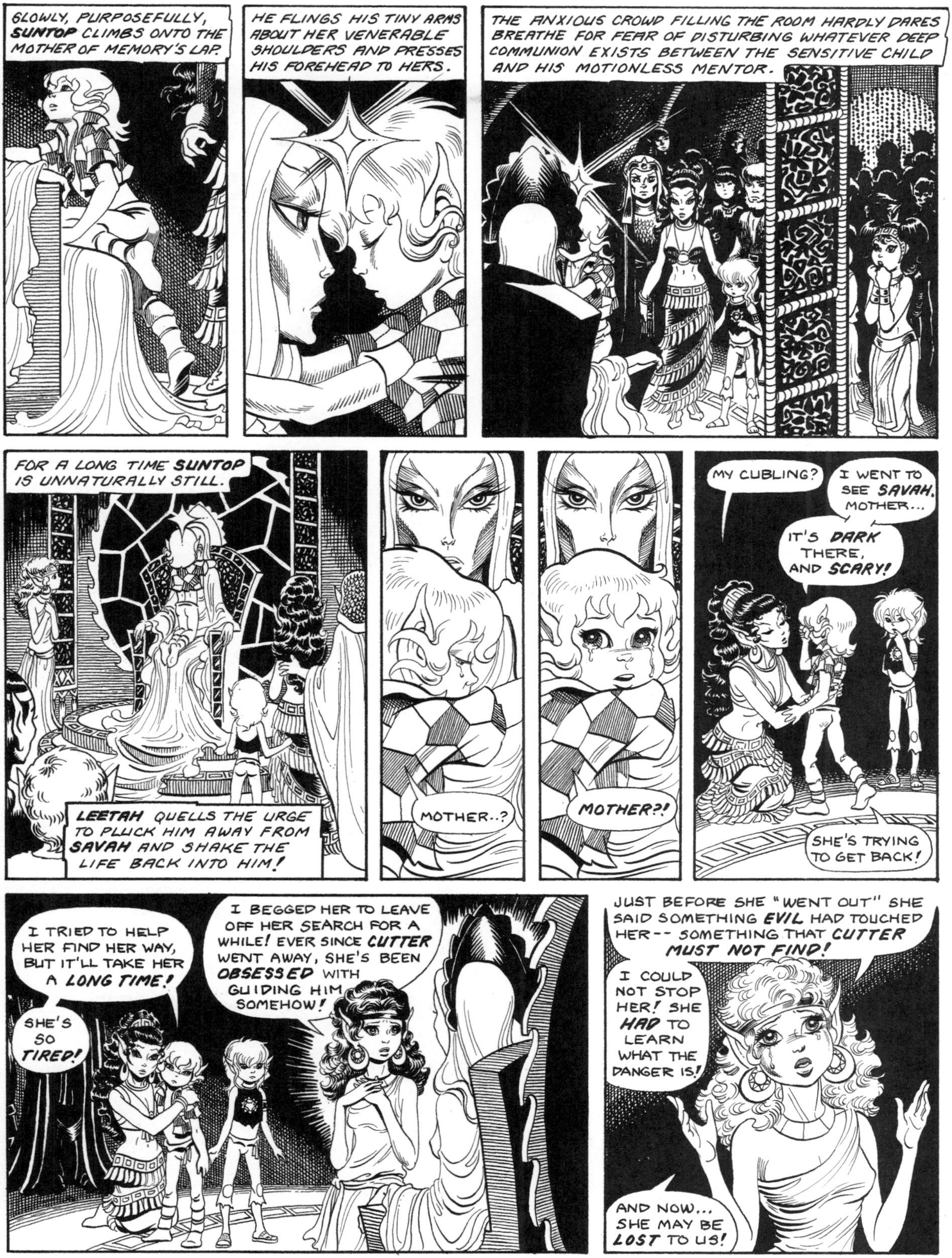
SLOWLY, PURPOSEFULLY, SUNTOP CLIMBS ONTO THE MOTHER OF MEMORY'S LAP.
HE FLINGS HIS TINY ARMS ABOUT HER VENERABLE SHOULDERS AND PRESSES HIS FOREHEAD TO HERS.
THE ANXIOUS CROWD FILLING THE ROOM HARDLY DARES BREATHE FOR FEAR OF DISTURBING WHATEVER DEEP COMMUNION EXISTS BETWEEN THE SENSITIVE CHILD AND HIS MOTIONLESS MENTOR.
FOR A LONG TIME SUNTOP IS UNNATURALLY STILL.
LEETAH QUELLS THE URGE TO PLUCK HIM AWAY FROM SAVAH AND SHAKE THE LIFE BACK INTO HIM!
MOTHER..?
MOTHER?!
MY CUBLING?
I WENT TO SEE SAVAH, MOTHER...
IT'S DARK THERE, AND SCARY!
SHE'S TRYING TO GET BACK!
I TRIED TO HELP HER FIND HER WAY, BUT IT'LL TAKE HER A LONG TIME!
SHE'S SO TIRED!
I BEGGED HER TO LEAVE OFF HER SEARCH FOR A WHILE! EVER SINCE CUTTER WENT AWAY, SHE'S BEEN OBSESSED WITH GUIDING HIM SOMEHOW!
JUST BEFORE SHE "WENT OUT" SHE SAID SOMETHING EVIL HAD TOUCHED HER-- SOMETHING THAT CUTTER MUST NOT FIND!
I COULD NOT STOP HER! SHE HAD TO LEARN WHAT THE DANGER IS!
AND NOW... SHE MAY BE LOST TO US!

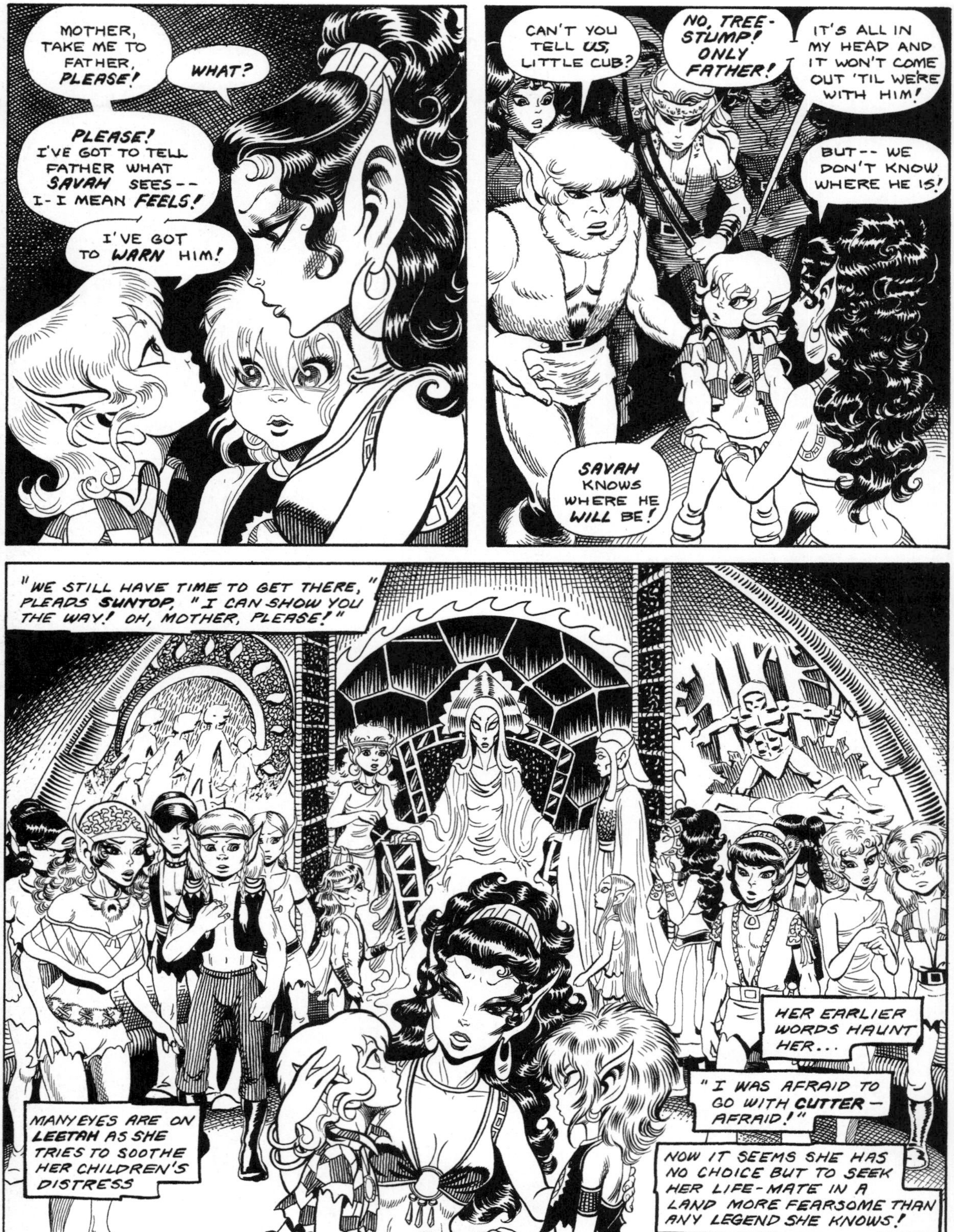
MOTHER, TAKE ME TO FATHER, PLEASE!
WHAT?
PLEASE! I'VE GOT TO TELL FATHER WHAT SAVAH SEES-- I- I MEAN FEELS!
I'VE GOT TO WARN HIM!
CAN'T YOU TELL US, LITTLE CUB?
NO, TREE-STUMP! ONLY FATHER!
IT'S ALL IN MY HEAD AND IT WON'T COME OUT 'TIL WE'RE WITH HIM!
BUT-- WE DON'T KNOW WHERE HE IS!
SAVAH KNOWS WHERE HE WILL BE!
"WE STILL HAVE TIME TO GET THERE," PLEADS SUNTOP. "I CAN SHOW YOU THE WAY! OH, MOTHER, PLEASE!"
MANY EYES ARE ON LEETAH AS SHE TRIES TO SOOTHE HER CHILDREN'S DISTRESS
HER EARLIER WORDS HAUNT HER...
"I WAS AFRAID TO GO WITH CUTTER — AFRAID!"
NOW IT SEEMS SHE HAS NO CHOICE BUT TO SEEK HER LIFE-MATE IN A LAND MORE FEARSOME THAN ANY LEGEND SHE KNOWS!
TO BE CONTINUED --

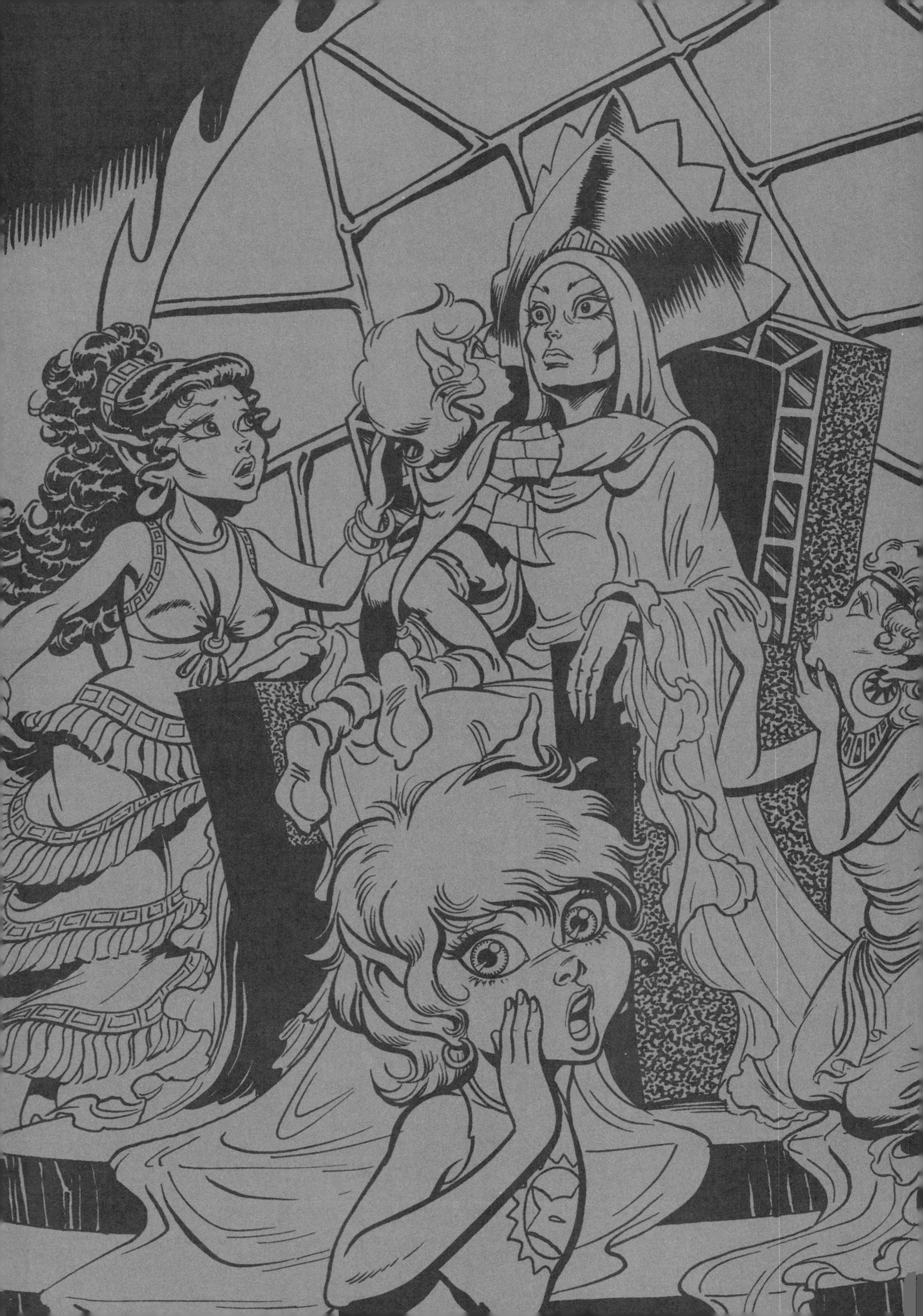

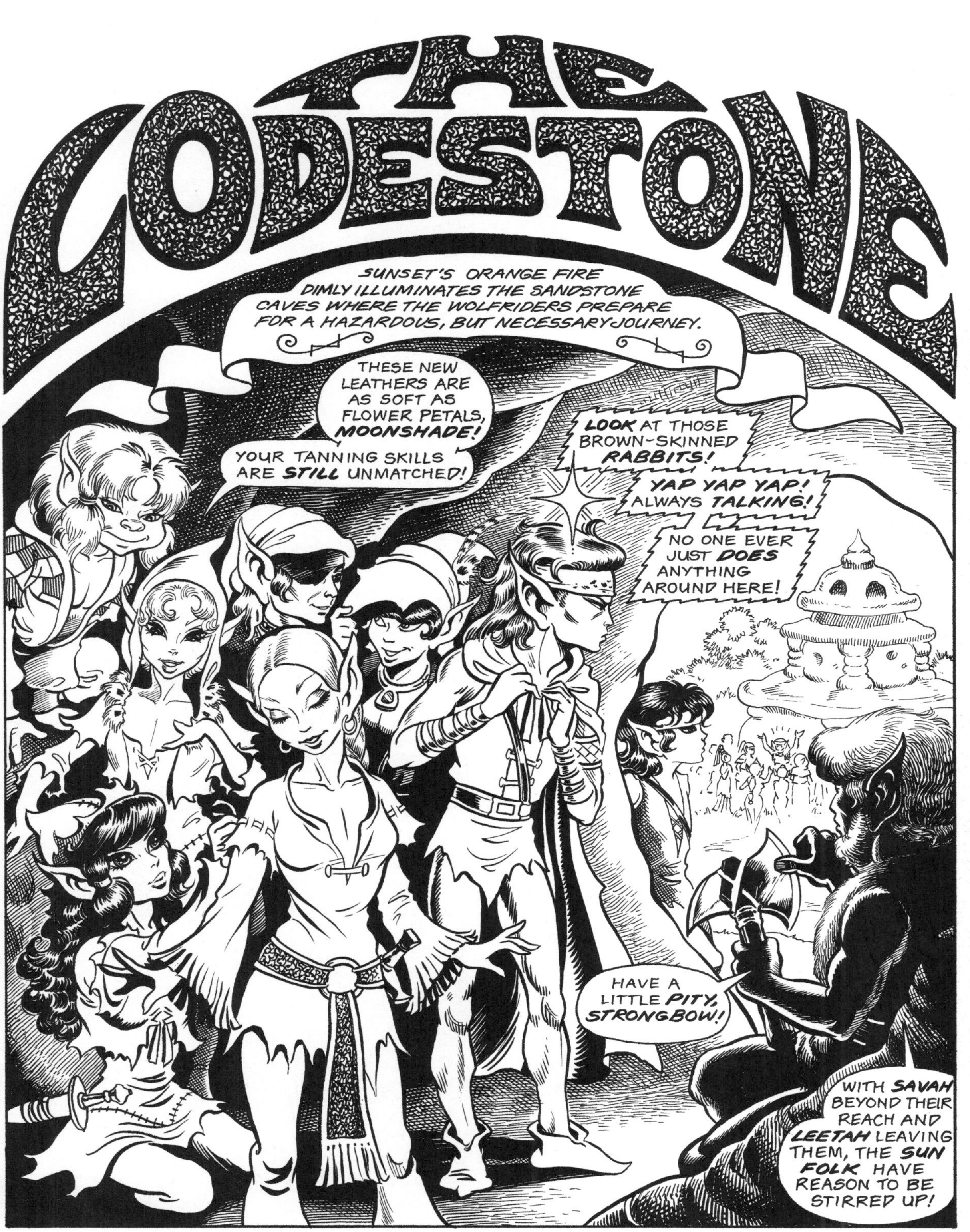
THE LODESTONE
SUNSET'S ORANGE FIRE DIMLY ILLUMINATES THE SANDSTONE CAVES WHERE THE WOLFRIDERS PREPARE FOR A HAZARDOUS, BUT NECESSARY JOURNEY.
THESE NEW LEATHERS ARE AS SOFT AS FLOWER PETALS, MOONSHADE!
YOUR TANNING SKILLS ARE STILL UNMATCHED!
LOOK AT THOSE BROWN-SKINNED RABBITS!
YAP YAP YAP! ALWAYS TALKING!
NO ONE EVER JUST DOES ANYTHING AROUND HERE!
HAVE A LITTLE PITY, STRONGBOW!
WITH SAVAH BEYOND THEIR REACH AND LEETAH LEAVING THEM, THE SUN FOLK HAVE REASON TO BE STIRRED UP!

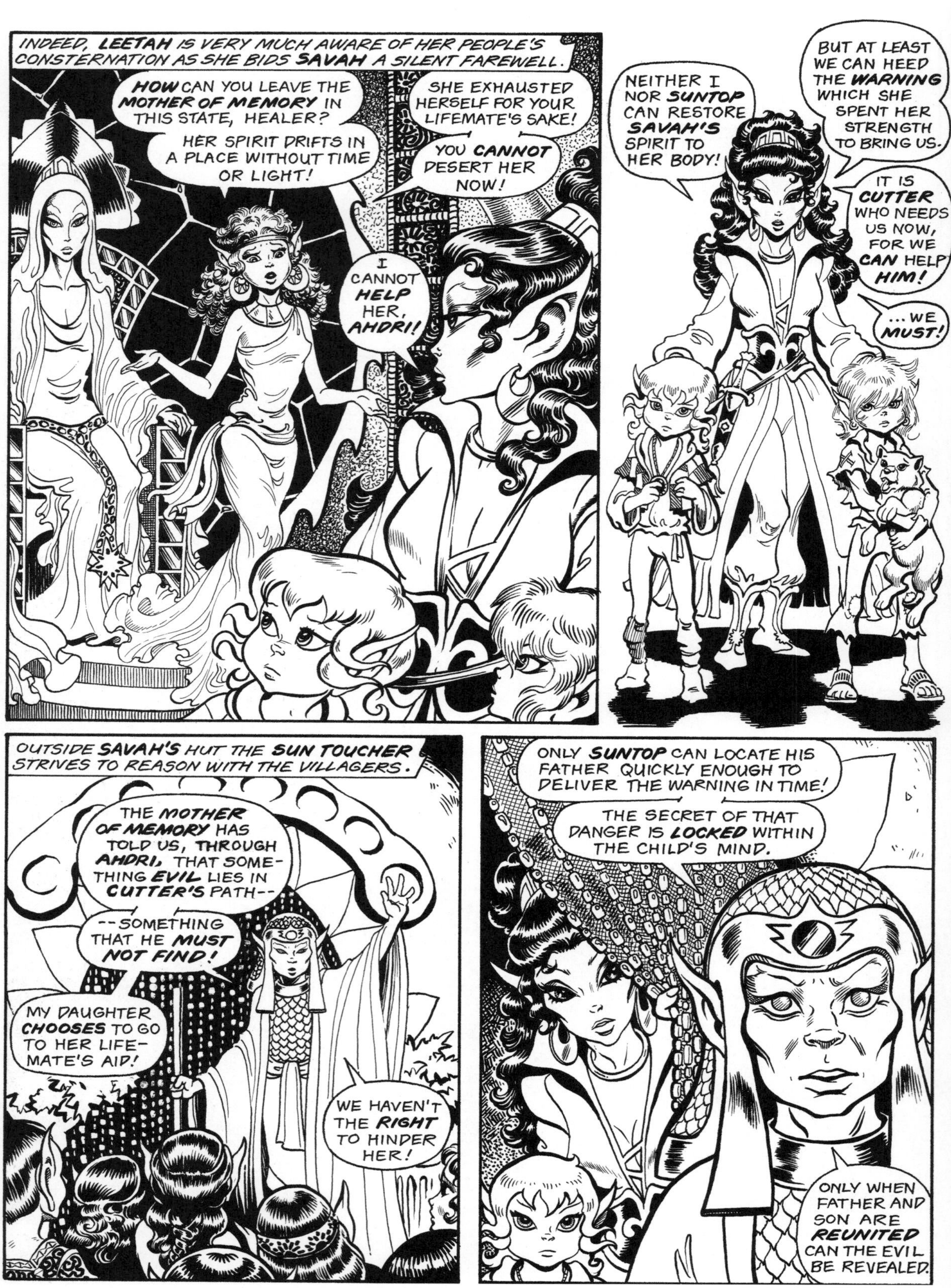
INDEED, LEETAH IS VERY MUCH AWARE OF HER PEOPLE'S CONSTERNATION AS SHE BIDS SAVAH A SILENT FAREWELL.
HOW CAN YOU LEAVE THE MOTHER OF MEMORY IN THIS STATE, HEALER?
HER SPIRIT DRIFTS IN A PLACE WITHOUT TIME OR LIGHT!
SHE EXHAUSTED HERSELF FOR YOUR LIFEMATE'S SAKE!
YOU CANNOT DESERT HER NOW!
I CANNOT HELP HER, AHDRI!
NEITHER I NOR SUNTOP CAN RESTORE SAVAH'S SPIRIT TO HER BODY!
BUT AT LEAST WE CAN HEED THE WARNING WHICH SHE SPENT HER STRENGTH TO BRING US.
IT IS CUTTER WHO NEEDS US NOW, FOR WE CAN HELP HIM!
...WE MUST!
OUTSIDE SAVAH'S HUT THE SUN TOUCHER STRIVES TO REASON WITH THE VILLAGERS.
THE MOTHER OF MEMORY HAS TOLD US, THROUGH AHDRI, THAT SOMETHING EVIL LIES IN CUTTER'S PATH--
--SOMETHING THAT HE MUST NOT FIND!
MY DAUGHTER CHOOSES TO GO TO HER LIFE-MATE'S AID!
WE HAVEN'T THE RIGHT TO HINDER HER!
ONLY SUNTOP CAN LOCATE HIS FATHER QUICKLY ENOUGH TO DELIVER THE WARNING IN TIME!
THE SECRET OF THAT DANGER IS LOCKED WITHIN THE CHILD'S MIND.
ONLY WHEN FATHER AND SON ARE REUNITED CAN THE EVIL BE REVEALED.

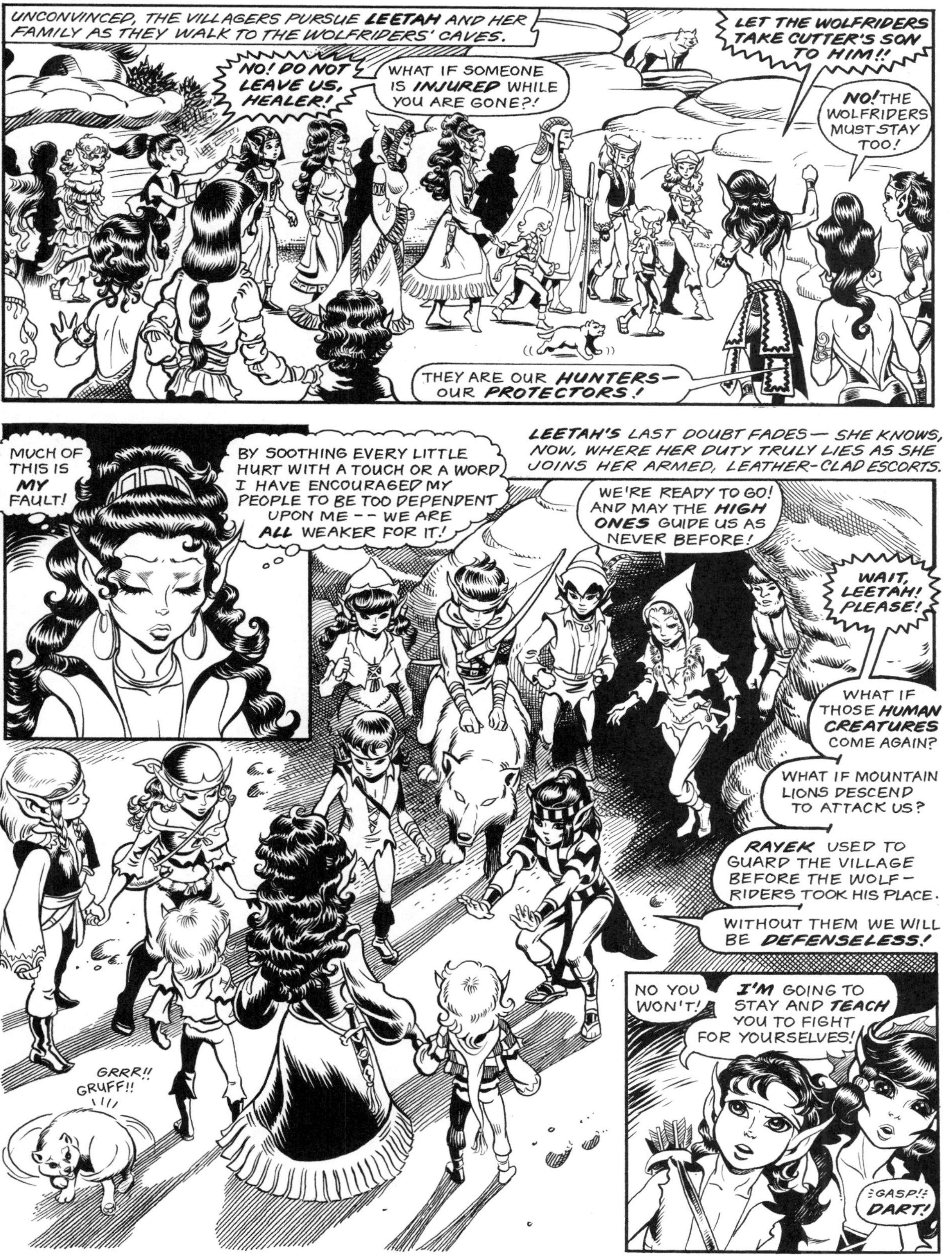
UNCONVINCED, THE VILLAGERS PURSUE LEETAH AND HER FAMILY AS THEY WALK TO THE WOLFRIDERS' CAVES.
NO! DO NOT LEAVE US, HEALER!
WHAT IF SOMEONE IS INJURED WHILE YOU ARE GONE?!
LET THE WOLFRIDERS TAKE CUTTER'S SON TO HIM!!
NO! THE WOLFRIDERS MUST STAY TOO!
THEY ARE OUR HUNTERS— OUR PROTECTORS!
MUCH OF THIS IS MY FAULT!
BY SOOTHING EVERY LITTLE HURT WITH A TOUCH OR A WORD I HAVE ENCOURAGED MY PEOPLE TO BE TOO DEPENDENT UPON ME -- WE ARE ALL WEAKER FOR IT!
LEETAH'S LAST DOUBT FADES — SHE KNOWS, NOW, WHERE HER DUTY TRULY LIES AS SHE JOINS HER ARMED, LEATHER-CLAD ESCORTS.
WE'RE READY TO GO! AND MAY THE HIGH ONES GUIDE US AS NEVER BEFORE!
WAIT, LEETAH! PLEASE!
WHAT IF THOSE HUMAN CREATURES COME AGAIN?
WHAT IF MOUNTAIN LIONS DESCEND TO ATTACK US?
RAYEK USED TO GUARD THE VILLAGE BEFORE THE WOLF-RIDERS TOOK HIS PLACE.
WITHOUT THEM WE WILL BE DEFENSELESS!
GRRR!! GRUFF!!
NO YOU WON'T!
I'M GOING TO STAY AND TEACH YOU TO FIGHT FOR YOURSELVES!
GASP! DART!

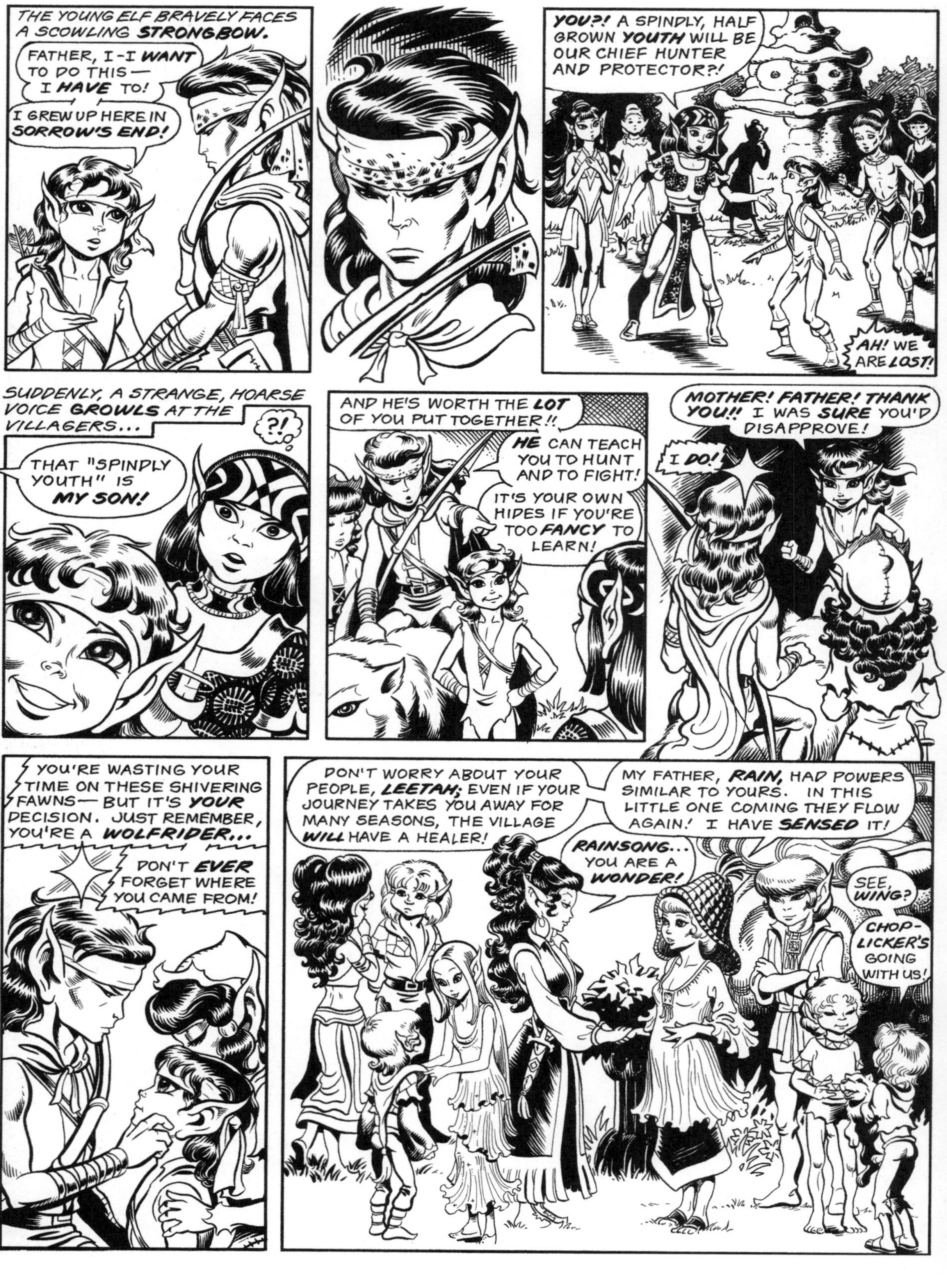

THE YOUNG ELF BRAVELY FACES A SCOWLING STRONGBOW.
FATHER, I-I WANT TO DO THIS— I HAVE TO!
I GREW UP HERE IN SORROW'S END!
YOU?! A SPINDLY, HALF GROWN YOUTH WILL BE OUR CHIEF HUNTER AND PROTECTOR?!
AH! WE ARE LOST!
SUDDENLY, A STRANGE, HOARSE VOICE GROWLS AT THE VILLAGERS...
?!
THAT "SPINDLY YOUTH" IS MY SON!
AND HE'S WORTH THE LOT OF YOU PUT TOGETHER!!
HE CAN TEACH YOU TO HUNT AND TO FIGHT!
IT'S YOUR OWN HIDES IF YOU'RE TOO FANCY TO LEARN!
MOTHER! FATHER! THANK YOU!! I WAS SURE YOU'D DISAPPROVE!
I DO!
YOU'RE WASTING YOUR TIME ON THESE SHIVERING FAWNS— BUT IT'S YOUR DECISION. JUST REMEMBER, YOU'RE A WOLFRIDER...
DON'T EVER FORGET WHERE YOU CAME FROM!
DON'T WORRY ABOUT YOUR PEOPLE, LEETAH; EVEN IF YOUR JOURNEY TAKES YOU AWAY FOR MANY SEASONS, THE VILLAGE WILL HAVE A HEALER!
MY FATHER, RAIN, HAD POWERS SIMILAR TO YOURS. IN THIS LITTLE ONE COMING THEY FLOW AGAIN! I HAVE SENSED IT!
RAINSONG... YOU ARE A WONDER!
SEE, WING?
CHOP-LICKER'S GOING WITH US!

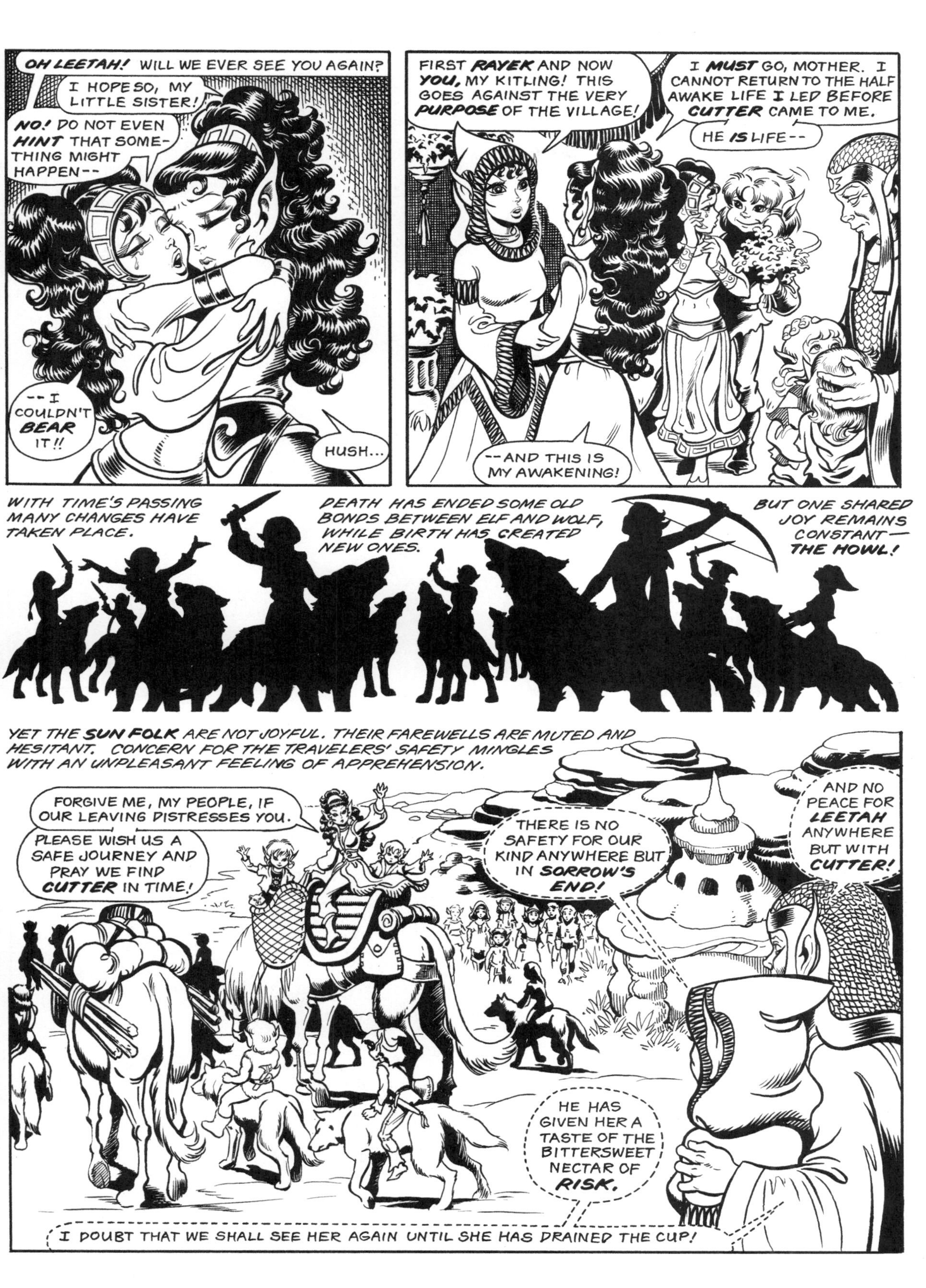

OH LEETAH! WILL WE EVER SEE YOU AGAIN?
I HOPE SO, MY LITTLE SISTER!
NO! DO NOT EVEN HINT THAT SOMETHING MIGHT HAPPEN--
--I COULDN'T BEAR IT!!
HUSH...
FIRST RAYEK AND NOW YOU, MY KITLING! THIS GOES AGAINST THE VERY PURPOSE OF THE VILLAGE!
I MUST GO, MOTHER. I CANNOT RETURN TO THE HALF AWAKE LIFE I LED BEFORE CUTTER CAME TO ME.
HE IS LIFE--
--AND THIS IS MY AWAKENING!
WITH TIME'S PASSING MANY CHANGES HAVE TAKEN PLACE.
DEATH HAS ENDED SOME OLD BONDS BETWEEN ELF AND WOLF, WHILE BIRTH HAS CREATED NEW ONES.
BUT ONE SHARED JOY REMAINS CONSTANT— THE HOWL!
YET THE SUN FOLK ARE NOT JOYFUL. THEIR FAREWELLS ARE MUTED AND HESITANT. CONCERN FOR THE TRAVELERS' SAFETY MINGLES WITH AN UNPLEASANT FEELING OF APPREHENSION.
FORGIVE ME, MY PEOPLE, IF OUR LEAVING DISTRESSES YOU.
PLEASE WISH US A SAFE JOURNEY AND PRAY WE FIND CUTTER IN TIME!
THERE IS NO SAFETY FOR OUR KIND ANYWHERE BUT IN SORROW'S END!
AND NO PEACE FOR LEETAH ANYWHERE BUT WITH CUTTER!
HE HAS GIVEN HER A TASTE OF THE BITTERSWEET NECTAR OF RISK.
I DOUBT THAT WE SHALL SEE HER AGAIN UNTIL SHE HAS DRAINED THE CUP!

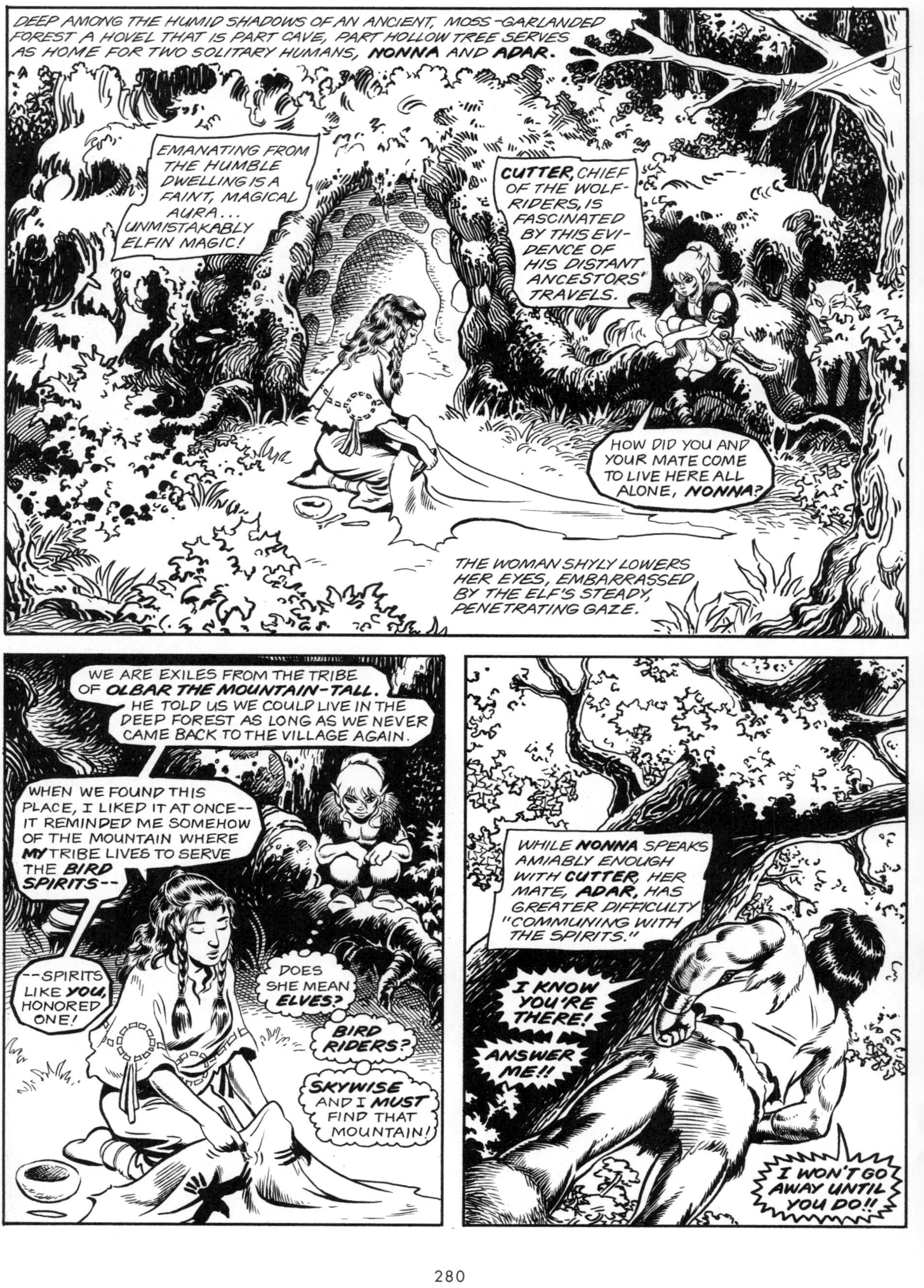
DEEP AMONG THE HUMID SHADOWS OF AN ANCIENT, MOSS-GARLANDED FOREST A HOVEL THAT IS PART CAVE, PART HOLLOW TREE SERVES AS HOME FOR TWO SOLITARY HUMANS, NONNA AND ADAR.
EMANATING FROM THE HUMBLE DWELLING IS A FAINT, MAGICAL AURA... UNMISTAKABLY ELFIN MAGIC!
CUTTER, CHIEF OF THE WOLF-RIDERS, IS FASCINATED BY THIS EVIDENCE OF HIS DISTANT ANCESTORS' TRAVELS.
HOW DID YOU AND YOUR MATE COME TO LIVE HERE ALL ALONE, NONNA?
THE WOMAN SHYLY LOWERS HER EYES, EMBARRASSED BY THE ELF'S STEADY, PENETRATING GAZE.
WE ARE EXILES FROM THE TRIBE OF OLBAR THE MOUNTAIN-TALL. HE TOLD US WE COULD LIVE IN THE DEEP FOREST AS LONG AS WE NEVER CAME BACK TO THE VILLAGE AGAIN.
WHEN WE FOUND THIS PLACE, I LIKED IT AT ONCE-- IT REMINDED ME SOMEHOW OF THE MOUNTAIN WHERE MY TRIBE LIVES TO SERVE THE BIRD SPIRITS--
--SPIRITS LIKE YOU, HONORED ONE!
DOES SHE MEAN ELVES?
BIRD RIDERS?
SKYWISE AND I MUST FIND THAT MOUNTAIN!
WHILE NONNA SPEAKS AMIABLY ENOUGH WITH CUTTER, HER MATE, ADAR, HAS GREATER DIFFICULTY "COMMUNING WITH THE SPIRITS."
I KNOW YOU'RE THERE!
ANSWER ME!!
I WON'T GO AWAY UNTIL YOU DO!!

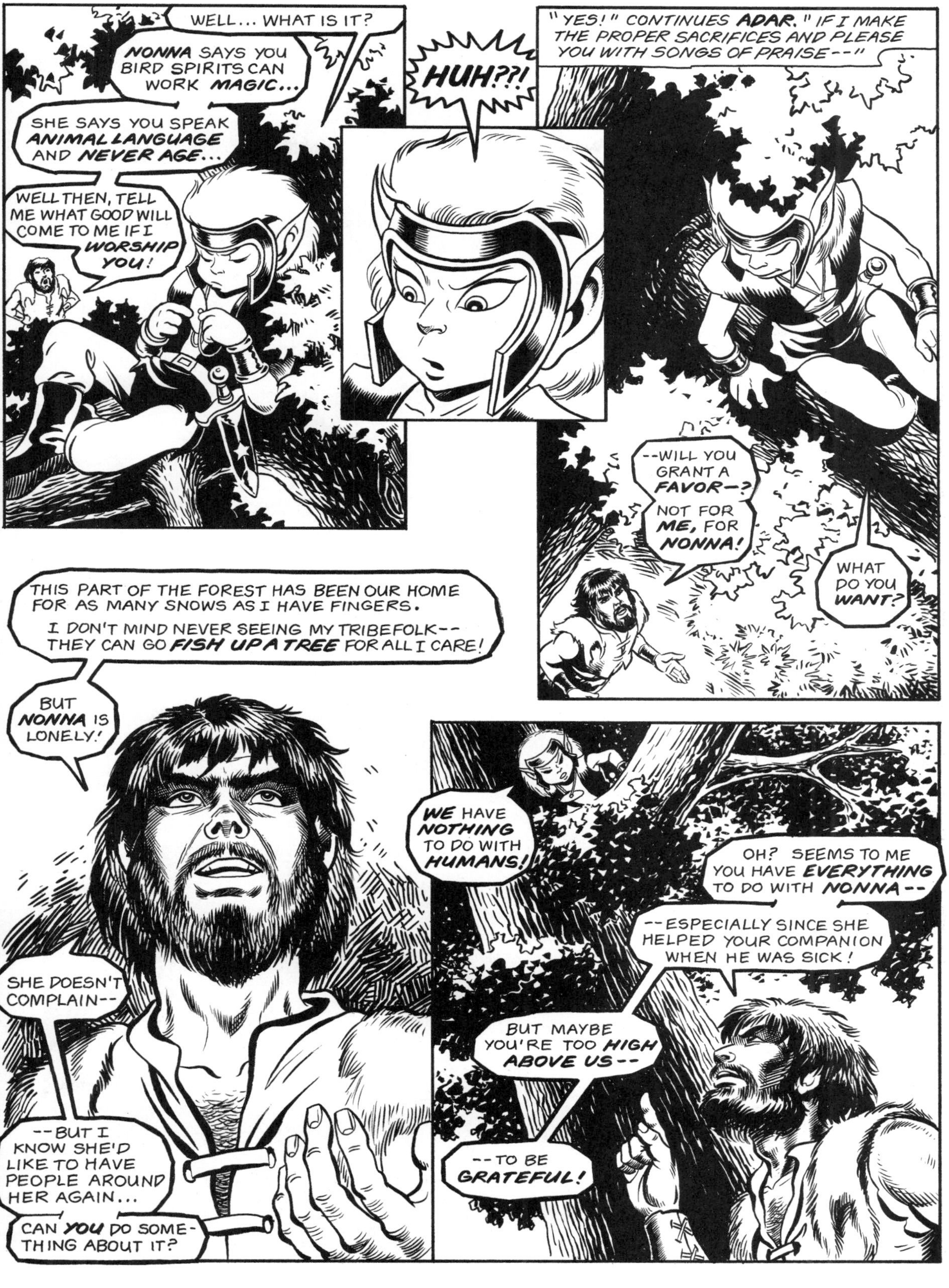

WELL... WHAT IS IT?
NONNA SAYS YOU BIRD SPIRITS CAN WORK MAGIC...
SHE SAYS YOU SPEAK ANIMAL LANGUAGE AND NEVER AGE...
WELL THEN, TELL ME WHAT GOOD WILL COME TO ME IF I WORSHIP YOU!
HUH??!
"YES!" CONTINUES ADAR. "IF I MAKE THE PROPER SACRIFICES AND PLEASE YOU WITH SONGS OF PRAISE--"
--WILL YOU GRANT A FAVOR--?
NOT FOR ME, FOR NONNA!
WHAT DO YOU WANT?
THIS PART OF THE FOREST HAS BEEN OUR HOME FOR AS MANY SNOWS AS I HAVE FINGERS.
I DON'T MIND NEVER SEEING MY TRIBEFOLK-- THEY CAN GO FISH UP A TREE FOR ALL I CARE!
BUT NONNA IS LONELY!
SHE DOESN'T COMPLAIN--
--BUT I KNOW SHE'D LIKE TO HAVE PEOPLE AROUND HER AGAIN...
CAN YOU DO SOMETHING ABOUT IT?
WE HAVE NOTHING TO DO WITH HUMANS!
OH? SEEMS TO ME YOU HAVE EVERYTHING TO DO WITH NONNA--
--ESPECIALLY SINCE SHE HELPED YOUR COMPANION WHEN HE WAS SICK!
BUT MAYBE YOU'RE TOO HIGH ABOVE US--
--TO BE GRATEFUL!

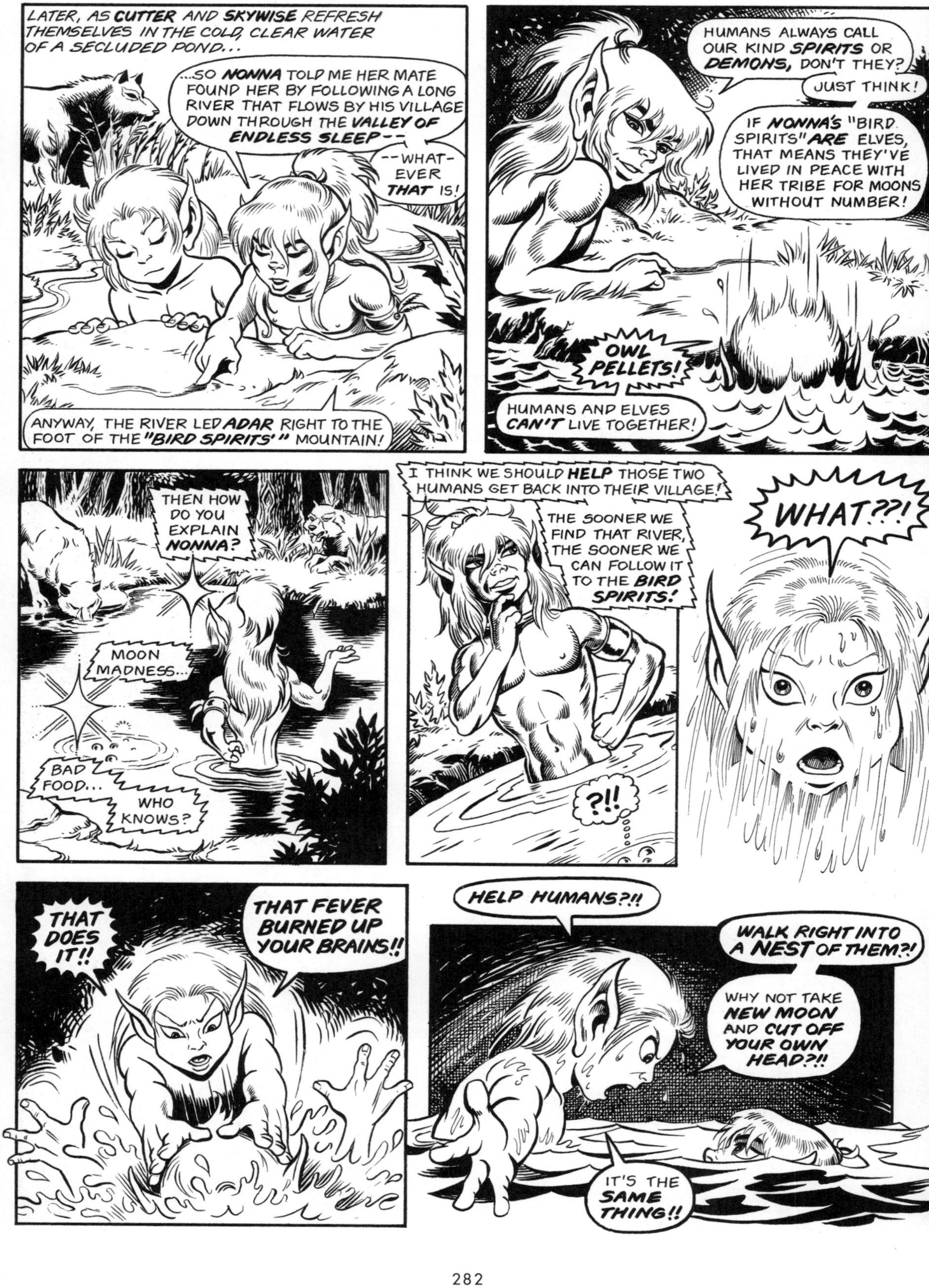
LATER, AS CUTTER AND SKYWISE REFRESH THEMSELVES IN THE COLD, CLEAR WATER OF A SECLUDED POND...
...SO NONNA TOLD ME HER MATE FOUND HER BY FOLLOWING A LONG RIVER THAT FLOWS BY HIS VILLAGE DOWN THROUGH THE VALLEY OF ENDLESS SLEEP--
--WHAT-EVER THAT IS!
ANYWAY, THE RIVER LED ADAR RIGHT TO THE FOOT OF THE "BIRD SPIRITS'" MOUNTAIN!
HUMANS ALWAYS CALL OUR KIND SPIRITS OR DEMONS, DON'T THEY?
JUST THINK!
IF NONNA'S "BIRD SPIRITS" ARE ELVES, THAT MEANS THEY'VE LIVED IN PEACE WITH HER TRIBE FOR MOONS WITHOUT NUMBER!
OWL PELLETS!
HUMANS AND ELVES CAN'T LIVE TOGETHER!
THEN HOW DO YOU EXPLAIN NONNA?
MOON MADNESS...
BAD FOOD...
WHO KNOWS?
I THINK WE SHOULD HELP THOSE TWO HUMANS GET BACK INTO THEIR VILLAGE!
THE SOONER WE FIND THAT RIVER, THE SOONER WE CAN FOLLOW IT TO THE BIRD SPIRITS!
?!!
WHAT??!
THAT DOES IT!!
THAT FEVER BURNED UP YOUR BRAINS!!
HELP HUMANS?!!
WALK RIGHT INTO A NEST OF THEM?!
WHY NOT TAKE NEW MOON AND CUT OFF YOUR OWN HEAD?!!
IT'S THE SAME THING!!

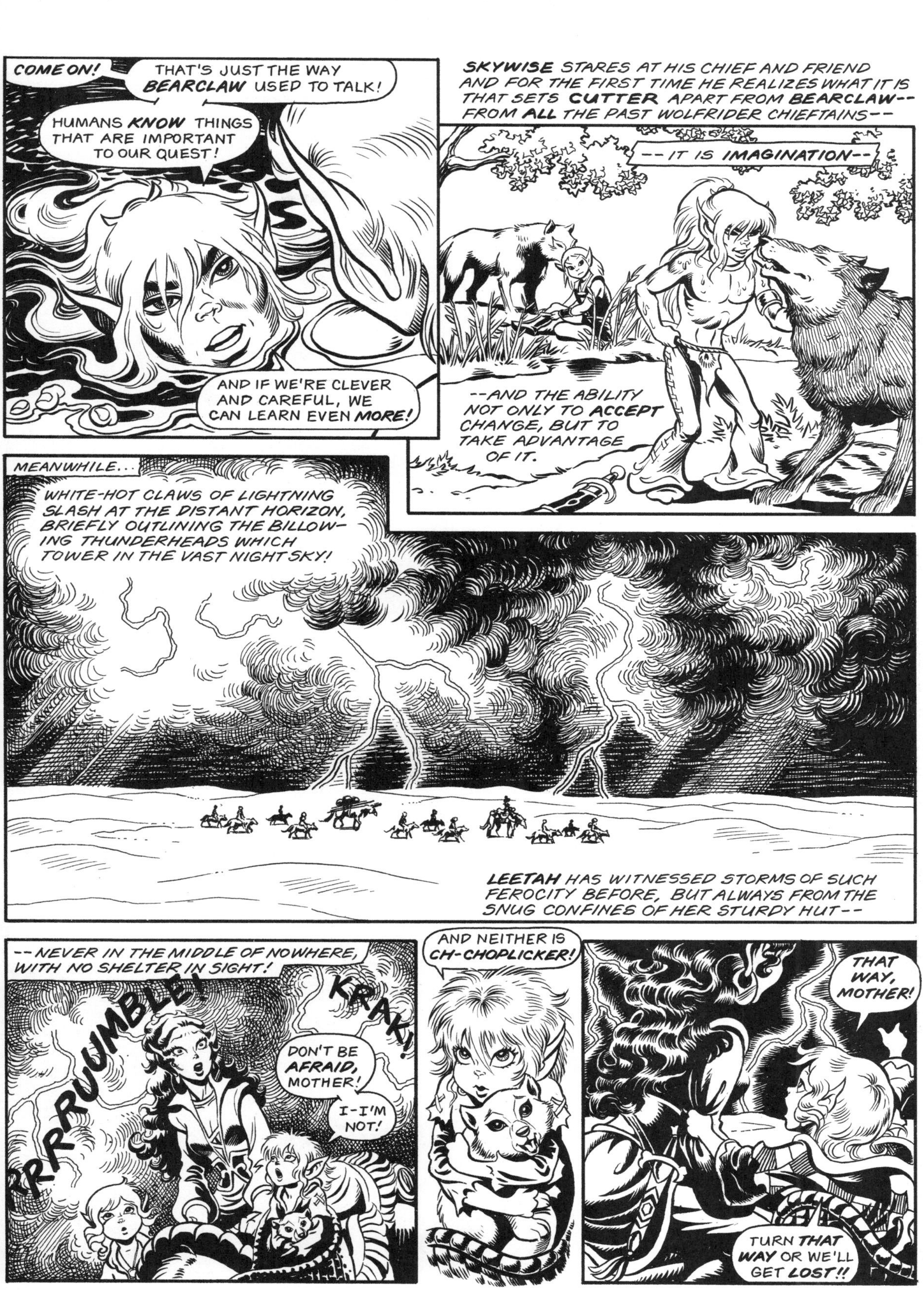

COME ON!
THAT'S JUST THE WAY BEARCLAW USED TO TALK!
HUMANS KNOW THINGS THAT ARE IMPORTANT TO OUR QUEST!
AND IF WE'RE CLEVER AND CAREFUL, WE CAN LEARN EVEN MORE!
SKYWISE STARES AT HIS CHIEF AND FRIEND AND FOR THE FIRST TIME HE REALIZES WHAT IT IS THAT SETS CUTTER APART FROM BEARCLAW-- FROM ALL THE PAST WOLFRIDER CHIEFTAINS--
--IT IS IMAGINATION--
--AND THE ABILITY NOT ONLY TO ACCEPT CHANGE, BUT TO TAKE ADVANTAGE OF IT.
MEANWHILE...
WHITE-HOT CLAWS OF LIGHTNING SLASH AT THE DISTANT HORIZON, BRIEFLY OUTLINING THE BILLOWING THUNDERHEADS WHICH TOWER IN THE VAST NIGHT SKY!
LEETAH HAS WITNESSED STORMS OF SUCH FEROCITY BEFORE, BUT ALWAYS FROM THE SNUG CONFINES OF HER STURDY HUT--
--NEVER IN THE MIDDLE OF NOWHERE, WITH NO SHELTER IN SIGHT!
RRRUUMBLE!
KRAK!
DON'T BE AFRAID, MOTHER!
I-I'M NOT!
AND NEITHER IS CH-CHOPLICKER!
THAT WAY, MOTHER!
TURN THAT WAY OR WE'LL GET LOST!!

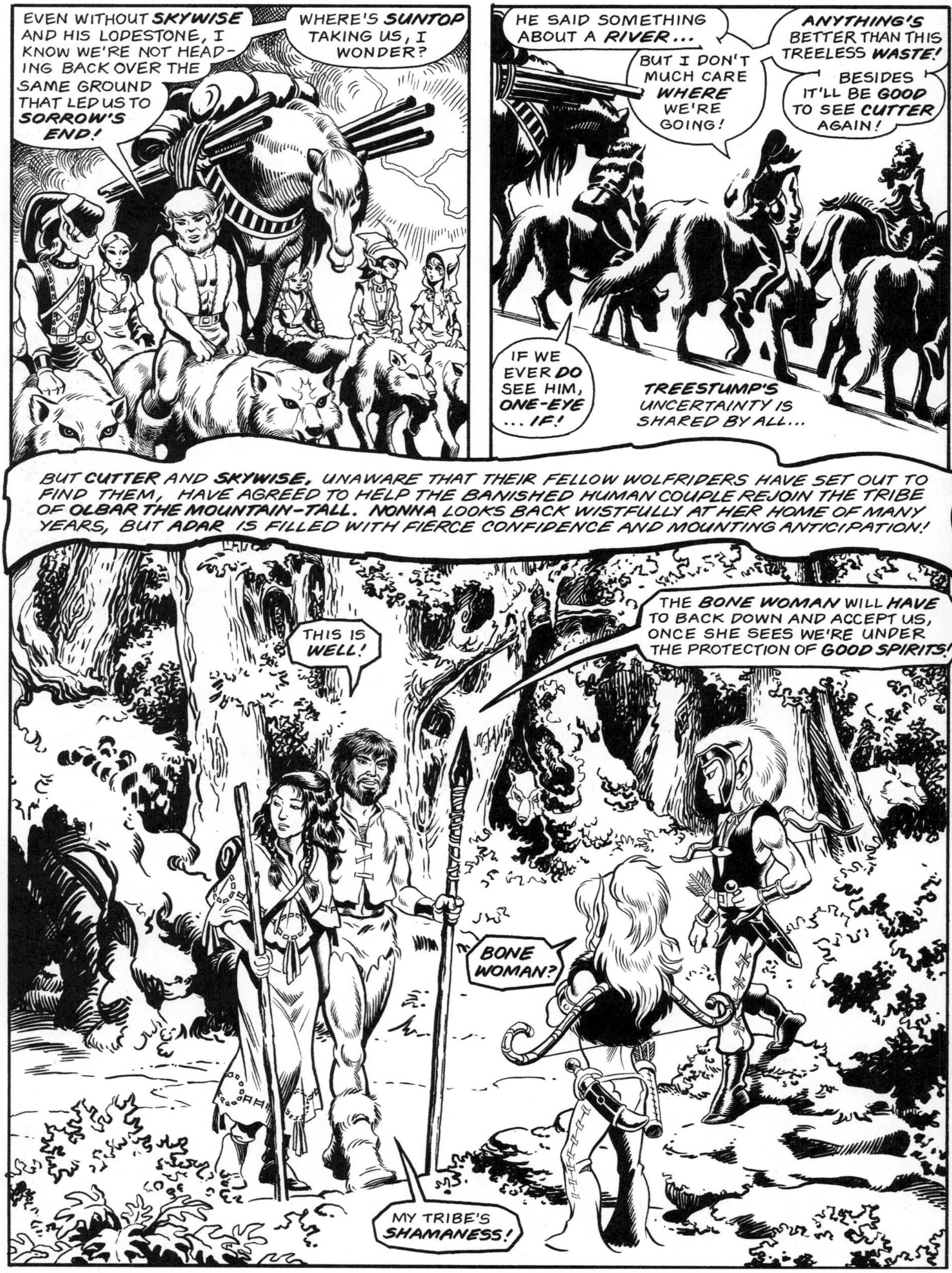
EVEN WITHOUT SKYWISE AND HIS LODESTONE, I KNOW WE'RE NOT HEADING BACK OVER THE SAME GROUND THAT LED US TO SORROW'S END!
WHERE'S SUNTOP TAKING US, I WONDER?
HE SAID SOMETHING ABOUT A RIVER...
BUT I DON'T MUCH CARE WHERE WE'RE GOING!
ANYTHING'S BETTER THAN THIS TREELESS WASTE!
BESIDES IT'LL BE GOOD TO SEE CUTTER AGAIN!
IF WE EVER DO SEE HIM, ONE-EYE ... IF!
TREESTUMP'S UNCERTAINTY IS SHARED BY ALL...
BUT CUTTER AND SKYWISE, UNAWARE THAT THEIR FELLOW WOLFRIDERS HAVE SET OUT TO FIND THEM, HAVE AGREED TO HELP THE BANISHED HUMAN COUPLE REJOIN THE TRIBE OF OLBAR THE MOUNTAIN-TALL. NONNA LOOKS BACK WISTFULLY AT HER HOME OF MANY YEARS, BUT ADAR IS FILLED WITH FIERCE CONFIDENCE AND MOUNTING ANTICIPATION!
THIS IS WELL!
THE BONE WOMAN WILL HAVE TO BACK DOWN AND ACCEPT US, ONCE SHE SEES WE'RE UNDER THE PROTECTION OF GOOD SPIRITS!
BONE WOMAN?
MY TRIBE'S SHAMANESS!

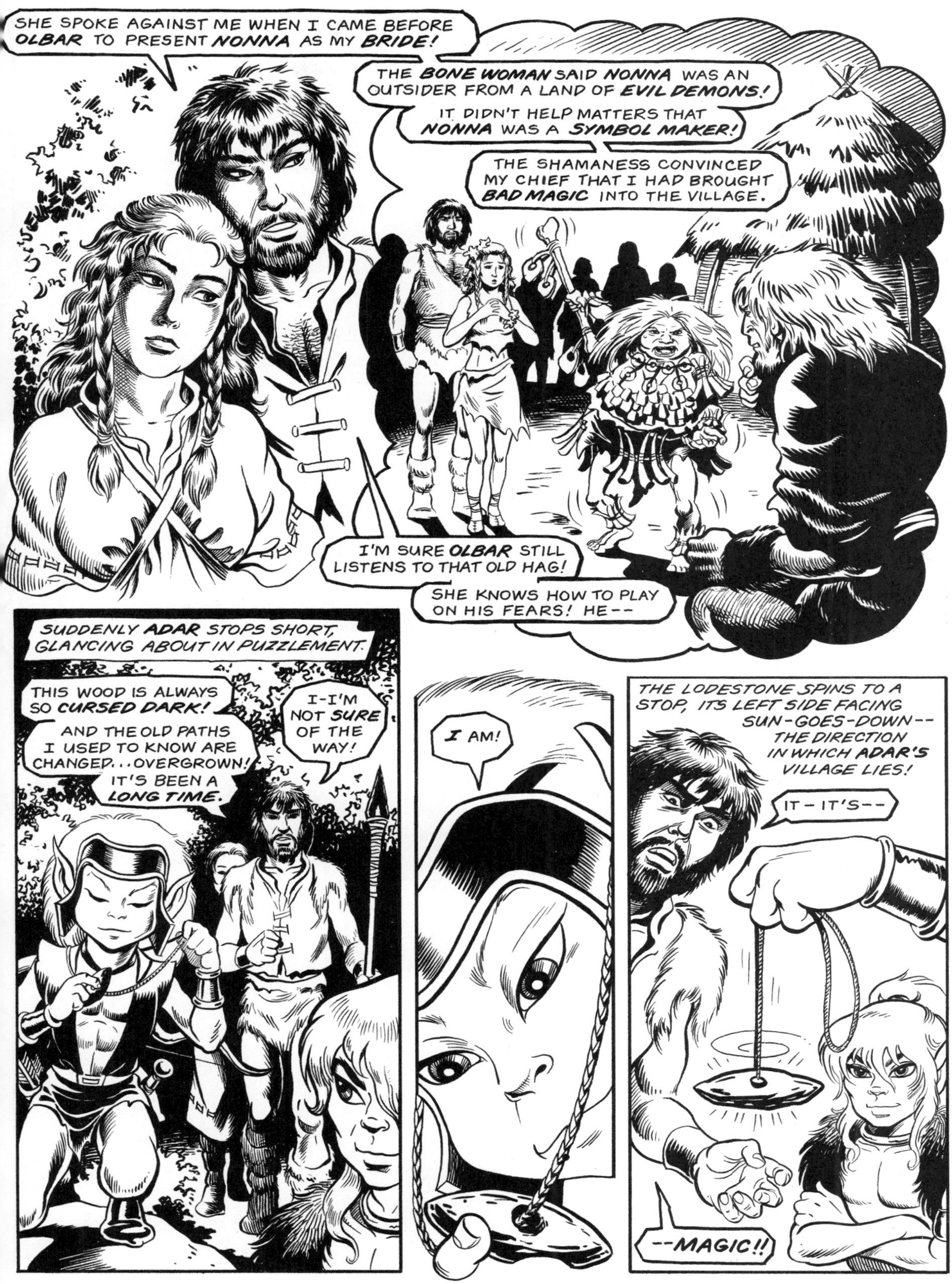
SHE SPOKE AGAINST ME WHEN I CAME BEFORE OLBAR TO PRESENT NONNA AS MY BRIDE!
THE BONE WOMAN SAID NONNA WAS AN OUTSIDER FROM A LAND OF EVIL DEMONS!
IT DIDN'T HELP MATTERS THAT NONNA WAS A SYMBOL MAKER!
THE SHAMANESS CONVINCED MY CHIEF THAT I HAD BROUGHT BAD MAGIC INTO THE VILLAGE.
I'M SURE OLBAR STILL LISTENS TO THAT OLD HAG!
SHE KNOWS HOW TO PLAY ON HIS FEARS! HE--
SUDDENLY ADAR STOPS SHORT, GLANCING ABOUT IN PUZZLEMENT.
THIS WOOD IS ALWAYS SO CURSED DARK!
AND THE OLD PATHS I USED TO KNOW ARE CHANGED... OVERGROWN!
IT'S BEEN A LONG TIME.
I-I'M NOT SURE OF THE WAY!
I AM!
THE LODESTONE SPINS TO A STOP, ITS LEFT SIDE FACING SUN-GOES-DOWN-- THE DIRECTION IN WHICH ADAR'S VILLAGE LIES!
IT - IT'S--
--MAGIC!!

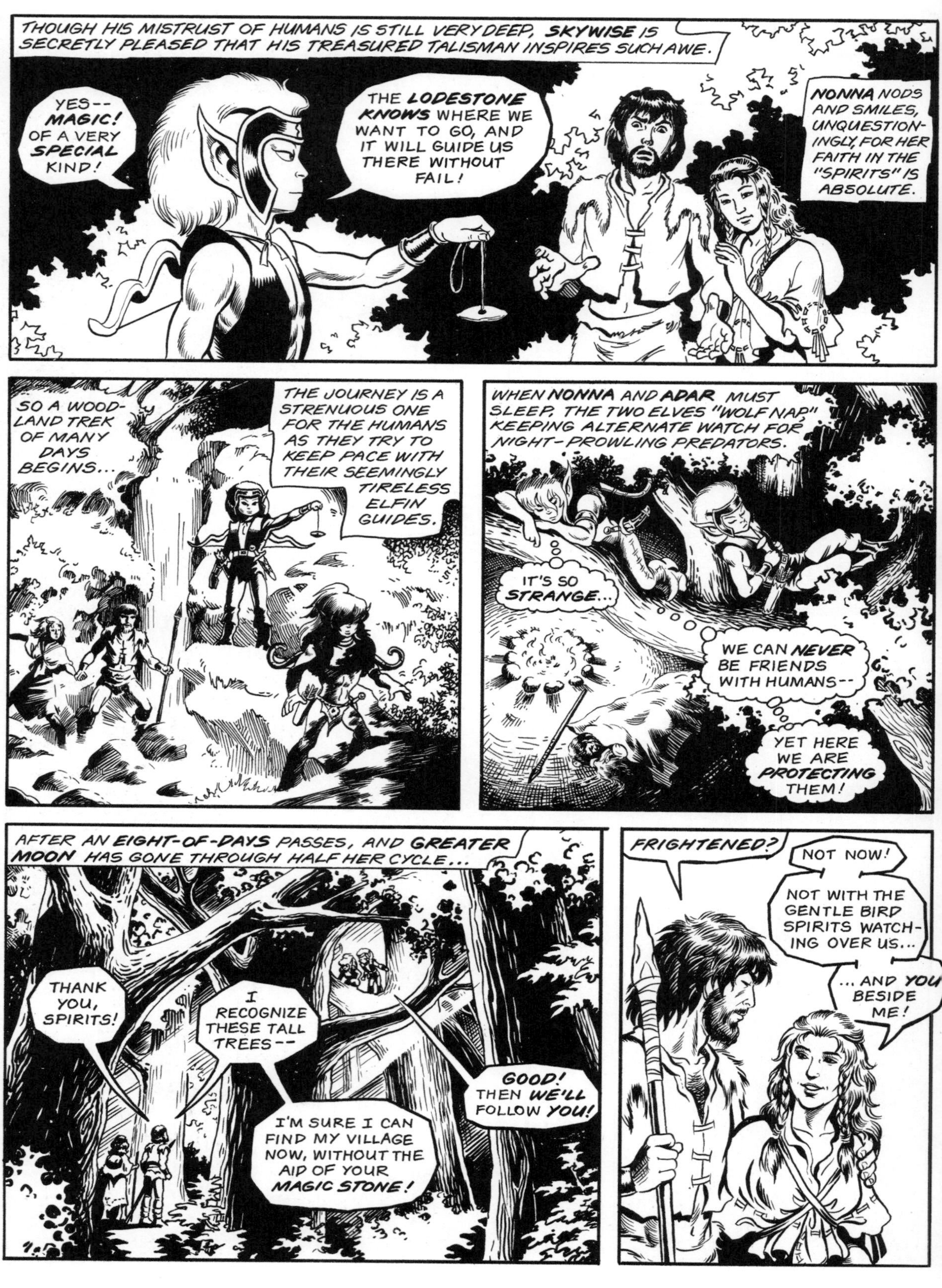
THOUGH HIS MISTRUST OF HUMANS IS STILL VERY DEEP, SKYWISE IS SECRETLY PLEASED THAT HIS TREASURED TALISMAN INSPIRES SUCH AWE.
YES-- MAGIC! OF A VERY SPECIAL KIND!
THE LODESTONE KNOWS WHERE WE WANT TO GO, AND IT WILL GUIDE US THERE WITHOUT FAIL!
NONNA NODS AND SMILES, UNQUESTIONINGLY, FOR HER FAITH IN THE "SPIRITS" IS ABSOLUTE.
SO A WOODLAND TREK OF MANY DAYS BEGINS...
THE JOURNEY IS A STRENUOUS ONE FOR THE HUMANS AS THEY TRY TO KEEP PACE WITH THEIR SEEMINGLY TIRELESS ELFIN GUIDES.
WHEN NONNA AND ADAR MUST SLEEP, THE TWO ELVES "WOLF NAP" KEEPING ALTERNATE WATCH FOR NIGHT-PROWLING PREDATORS.
IT'S SO STRANGE...
WE CAN NEVER BE FRIENDS WITH HUMANS--
YET HERE WE ARE PROTECTING THEM!
AFTER AN EIGHT-OF-DAYS PASSES, AND GREATER MOON HAS GONE THROUGH HALF HER CYCLE...
THANK YOU, SPIRITS!
I RECOGNIZE THESE TALL TREES--
I'M SURE I CAN FIND MY VILLAGE NOW, WITHOUT THE AID OF YOUR MAGIC STONE!
GOOD! THEN WE'LL FOLLOW YOU!
FRIGHTENED?
NOT NOW!
NOT WITH THE GENTLE BIRD SPIRITS WATCHING OVER US...
... AND YOU BESIDE ME!

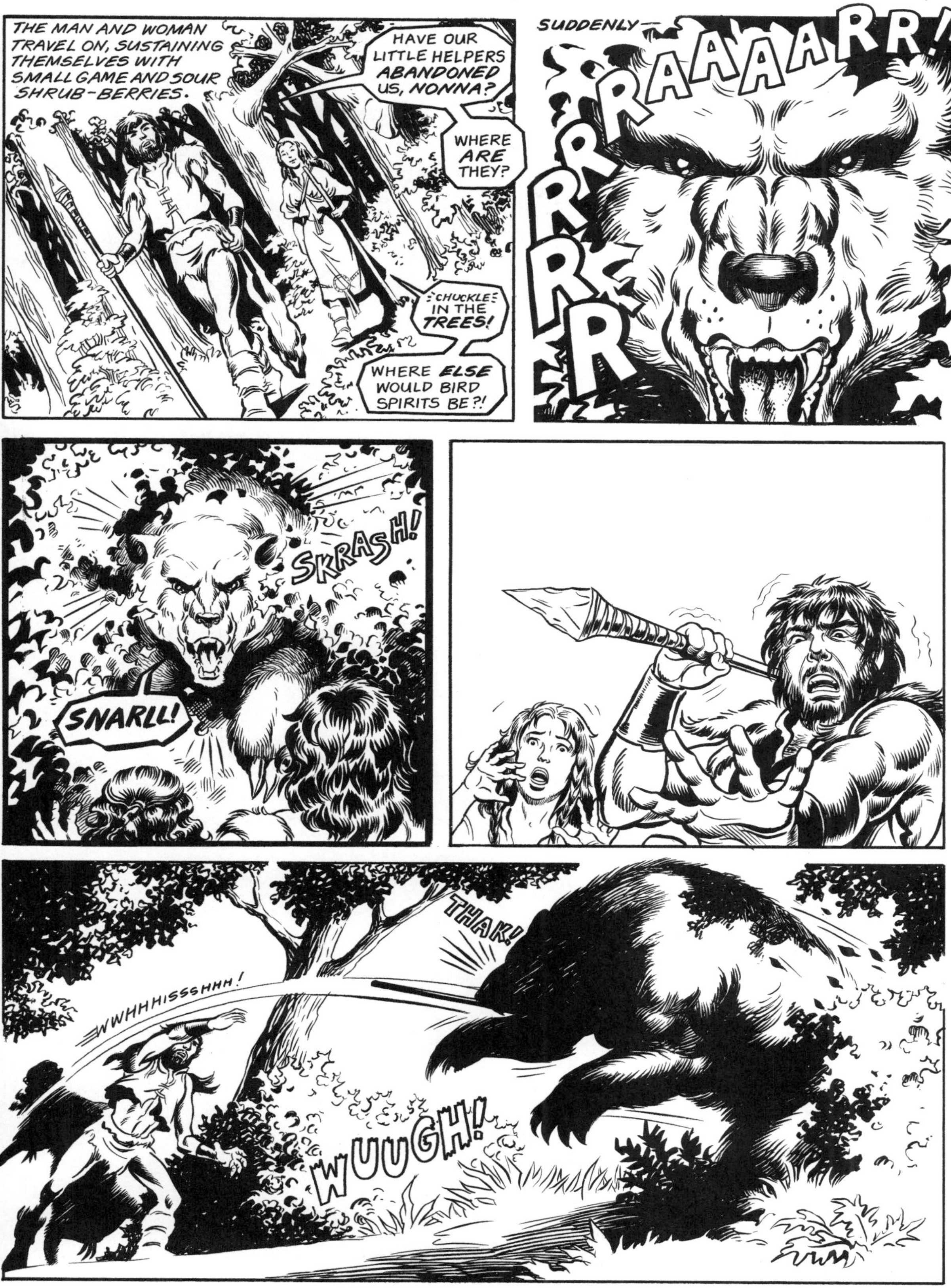

THE MAN AND WOMAN TRAVEL ON, SUSTAINING THEMSELVES WITH SMALL GAME AND SOUR SHRUB-BERRIES.
HAVE OUR LITTLE HELPERS ABANDONED US, NONNA?
WHERE ARE THEY?
CHUCKLE IN THE TREES!
WHERE ELSE WOULD BIRD SPIRITS BE?!
SUDDENLY—
RRRRRRAAAAARR!
SKRASH!
SNARLL!
THAK!
WWHHHISSSHHH!
WUUGH!

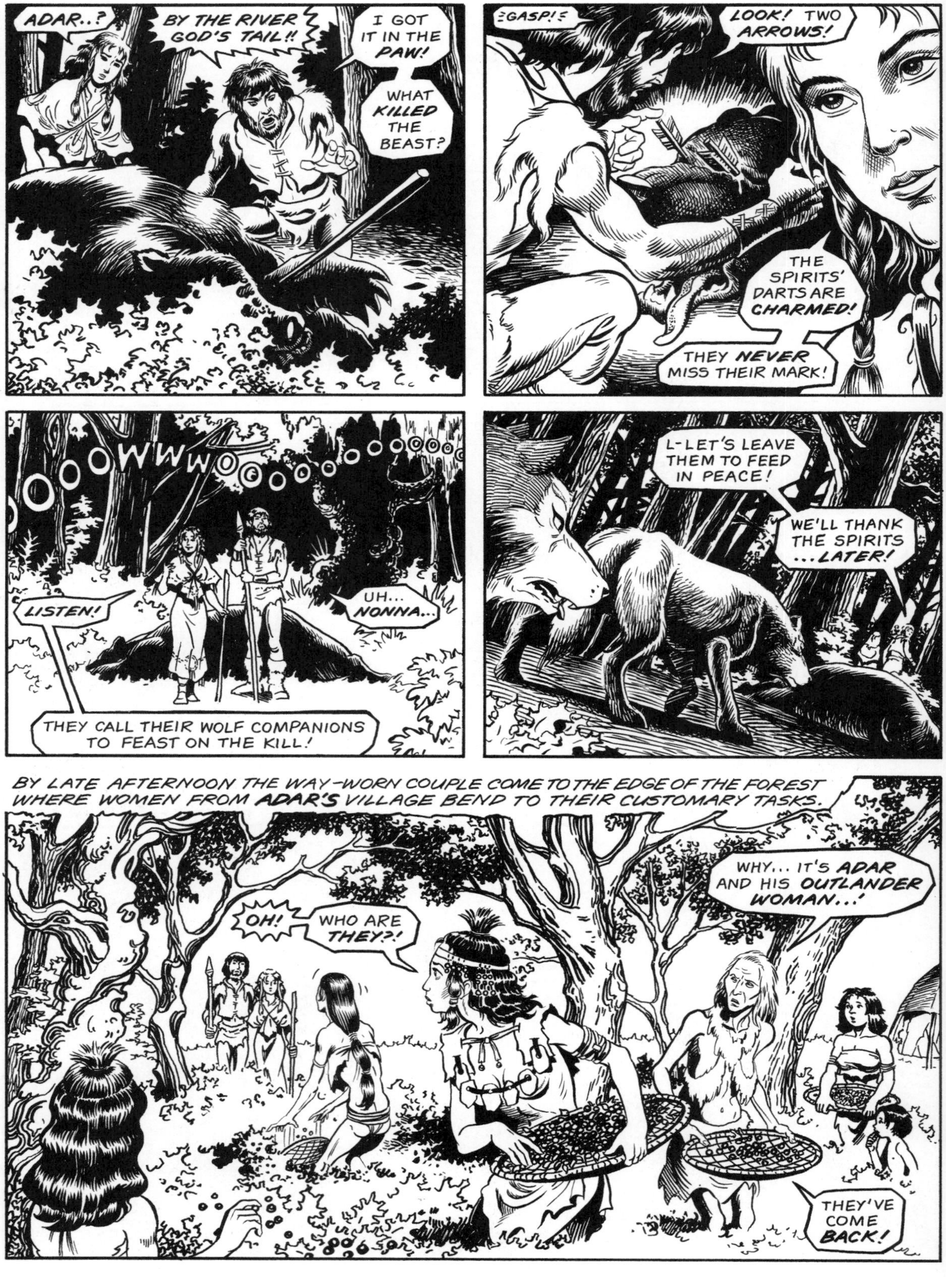
ADAR..?
BY THE RIVER GOD'S TAIL!!
I GOT IT IN THE PAW!
WHAT KILLED THE BEAST?
GASP!
LOOK! TWO ARROWS!
THE SPIRITS' DARTS ARE CHARMED!
THEY NEVER MISS THEIR MARK!
OOOOWWWWOOOOOOOOOOO
LISTEN!
UH... NONNA...
THEY CALL THEIR WOLF COMPANIONS TO FEAST ON THE KILL!
L-LET'S LEAVE THEM TO FEED IN PEACE!
WE'LL THANK THE SPIRITS ...LATER!
BY LATE AFTERNOON THE WAY-WORN COUPLE COME TO THE EDGE OF THE FOREST WHERE WOMEN FROM ADAR'S VILLAGE BEND TO THEIR CUSTOMARY TASKS.
OH!
WHO ARE THEY?!
WHY... IT'S ADAR AND HIS OUTLANDER WOMAN...!
THEY'VE COME BACK!

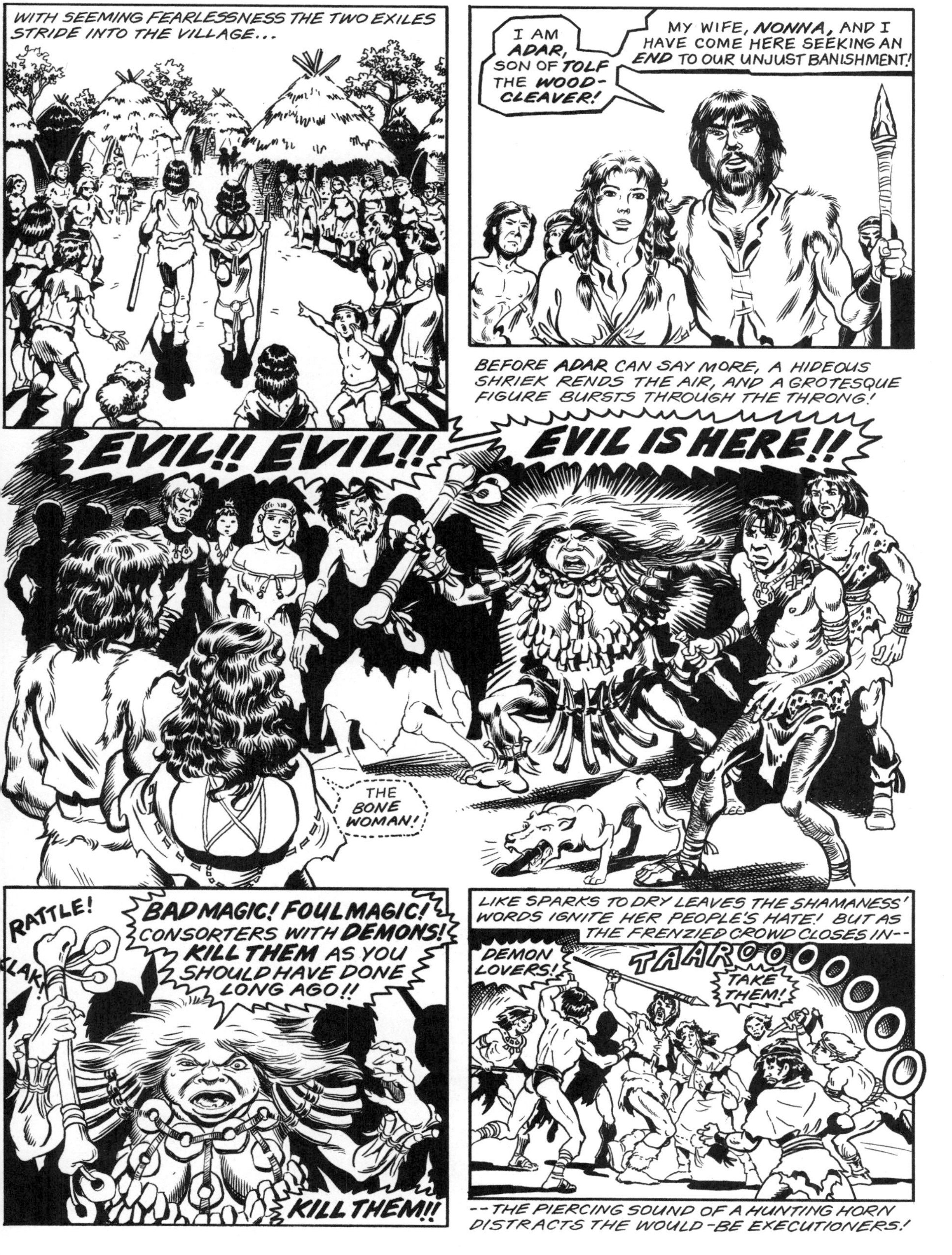
WITH SEEMING FEARLESSNESS THE TWO EXILES STRIDE INTO THE VILLAGE...
I AM ADAR, SON OF TOLF THE WOOD-CLEAVER!
MY WIFE, NONNA, AND I HAVE COME HERE SEEKING AN END TO OUR UNJUST BANISHMENT!
BEFORE ADAR CAN SAY MORE, A HIDEOUS SHRIEK RENDS THE AIR, AND A GROTESQUE FIGURE BURSTS THROUGH THE THRONG!
EVIL!! EVIL!!
EVIL IS HERE!!
THE BONE WOMAN!
RATTLE!
BAD MAGIC! FOUL MAGIC! CONSORTERS WITH DEMONS! KILL THEM AS YOU SHOULD HAVE DONE LONG AGO!!
KILL THEM!!
LIKE SPARKS TO DRY LEAVES THE SHAMANESS' WORDS IGNITE HER PEOPLE'S HATE! BUT AS THE FRENZIED CROWD CLOSES IN--
DEMON LOVERS!
TAAROOOOOOOOO
TAKE THEM!
--THE PIERCING SOUND OF A HUNTING HORN DISTRACTS THE WOULD-BE EXECUTIONERS!

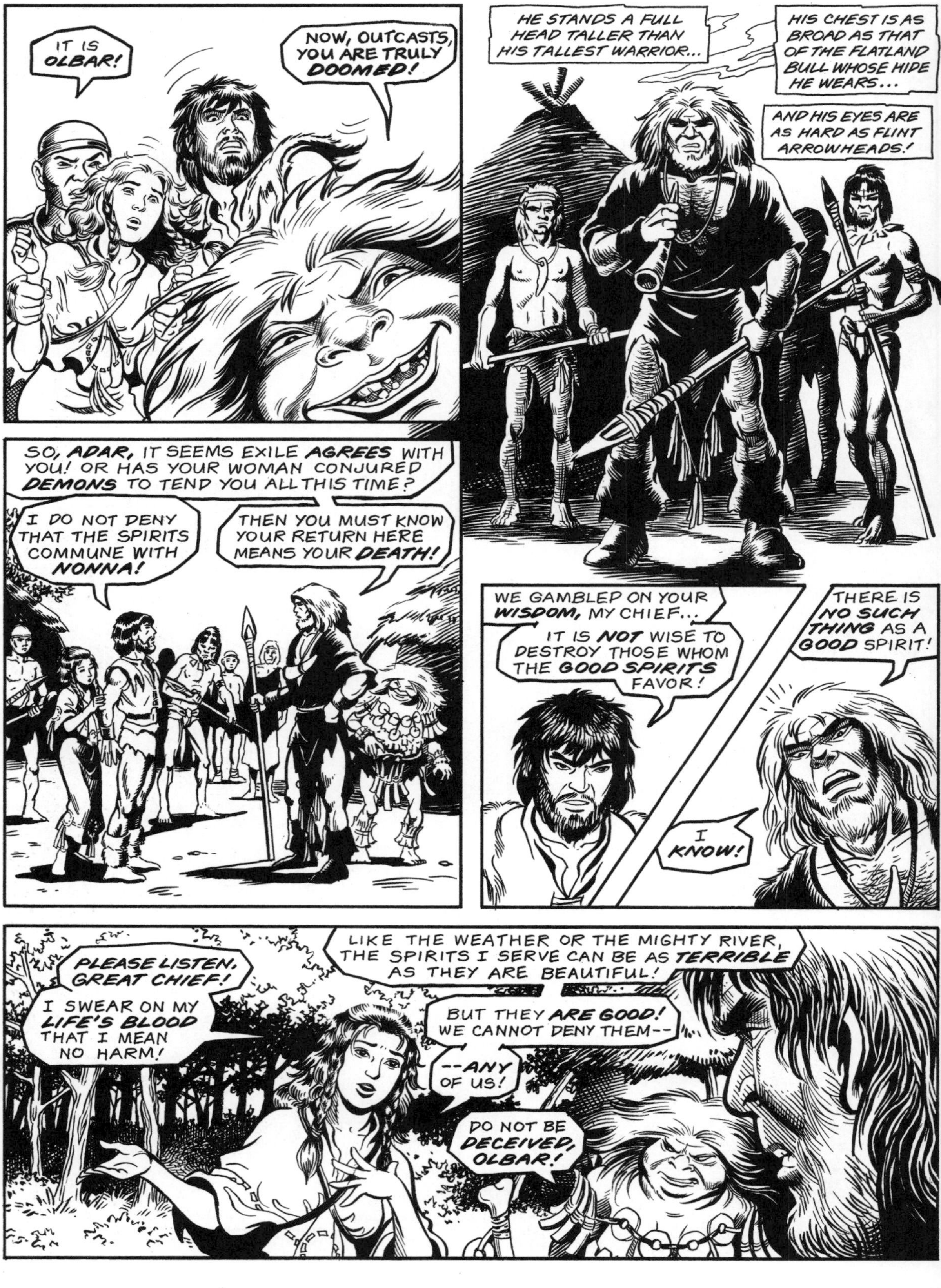

IT IS OLBAR!
NOW, OUTCASTS, YOU ARE TRULY DOOMED!
HE STANDS A FULL HEAD TALLER THAN HIS TALLEST WARRIOR...
HIS CHEST IS AS BROAD AS THAT OF THE FLATLAND BULL WHOSE HIDE HE WEARS...
AND HIS EYES ARE AS HARD AS FLINT ARROWHEADS!
SO, ADAR, IT SEEMS EXILE AGREES WITH YOU! OR HAS YOUR WOMAN CONJURED DEMONS TO TEND YOU ALL THIS TIME?
I DO NOT DENY THAT THE SPIRITS COMMUNE WITH NONNA!
THEN YOU MUST KNOW YOUR RETURN HERE MEANS YOUR DEATH!
WE GAMBLED ON YOUR WISDOM, MY CHIEF...
IT IS NOT WISE TO DESTROY THOSE WHOM THE GOOD SPIRITS FAVOR!
THERE IS NO SUCH THING AS A GOOD SPIRIT!
I KNOW!
PLEASE LISTEN, GREAT CHIEF!
I SWEAR ON MY LIFE'S BLOOD THAT I MEAN NO HARM!
LIKE THE WEATHER OR THE MIGHTY RIVER, THE SPIRITS I SERVE CAN BE AS TERRIBLE AS THEY ARE BEAUTIFUL!
BUT THEY ARE GOOD! WE CANNOT DENY THEM--
--ANY OF US!
DO NOT BE DECEIVED, OLBAR!

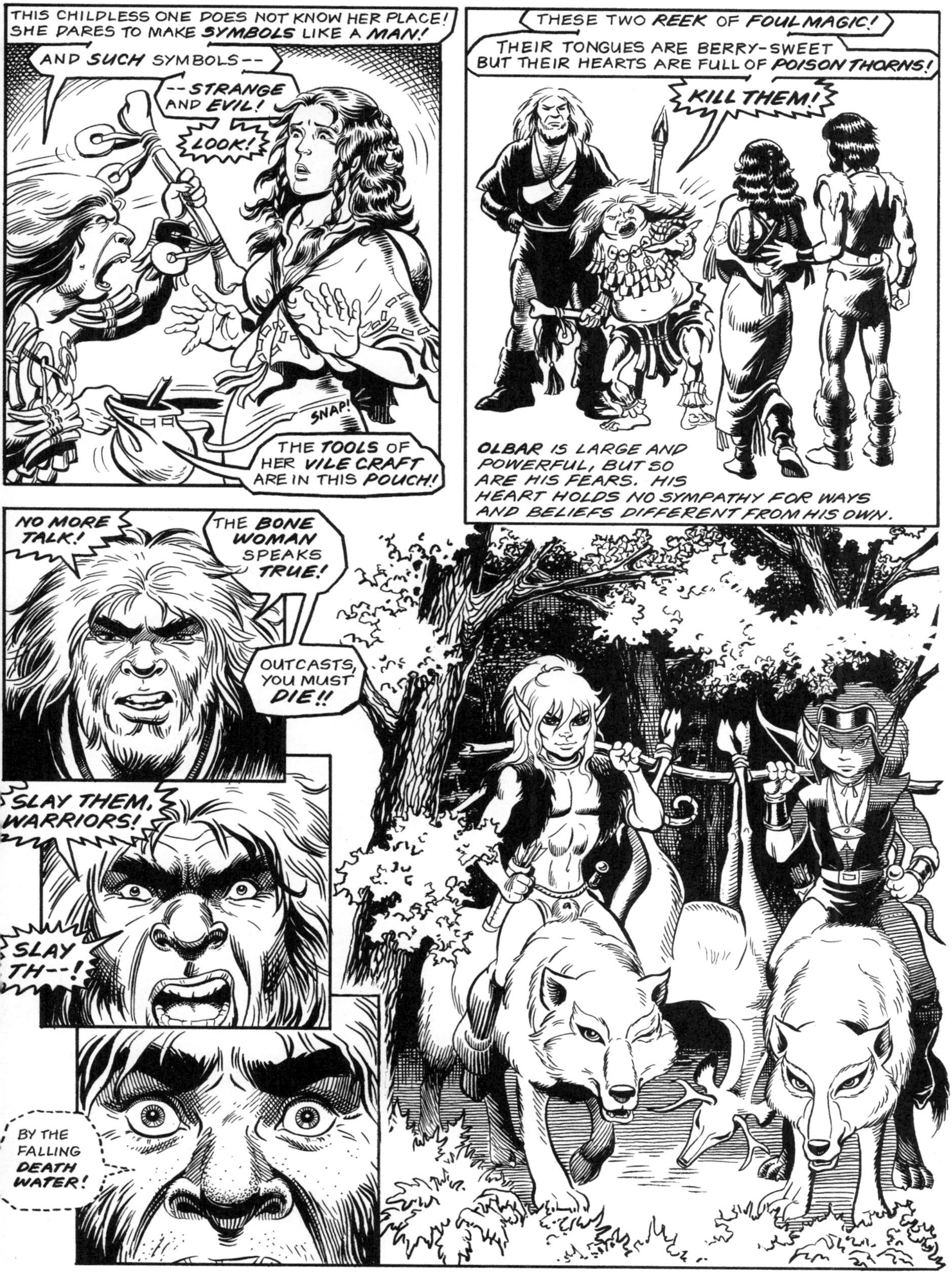
THIS CHILDLESS ONE DOES NOT KNOW HER PLACE! SHE DARES TO MAKE SYMBOLS LIKE A MAN!
AND SUCH SYMBOLS--
--STRANGE AND EVIL!
LOOK!
SNAP!
THE TOOLS OF HER VILE CRAFT ARE IN THIS POUCH!
THESE TWO REEK OF FOUL MAGIC!
THEIR TONGUES ARE BERRY-SWEET BUT THEIR HEARTS ARE FULL OF POISON THORNS!
KILL THEM!
OLBAR IS LARGE AND POWERFUL, BUT SO ARE HIS FEARS. HIS HEART HOLDS NO SYMPATHY FOR WAYS AND BELIEFS DIFFERENT FROM HIS OWN.
NO MORE TALK!
THE BONE WOMAN SPEAKS TRUE!
OUTCASTS, YOU MUST DIE!!
SLAY THEM, WARRIORS!
SLAY TH--!
BY THE FALLING DEATH WATER!

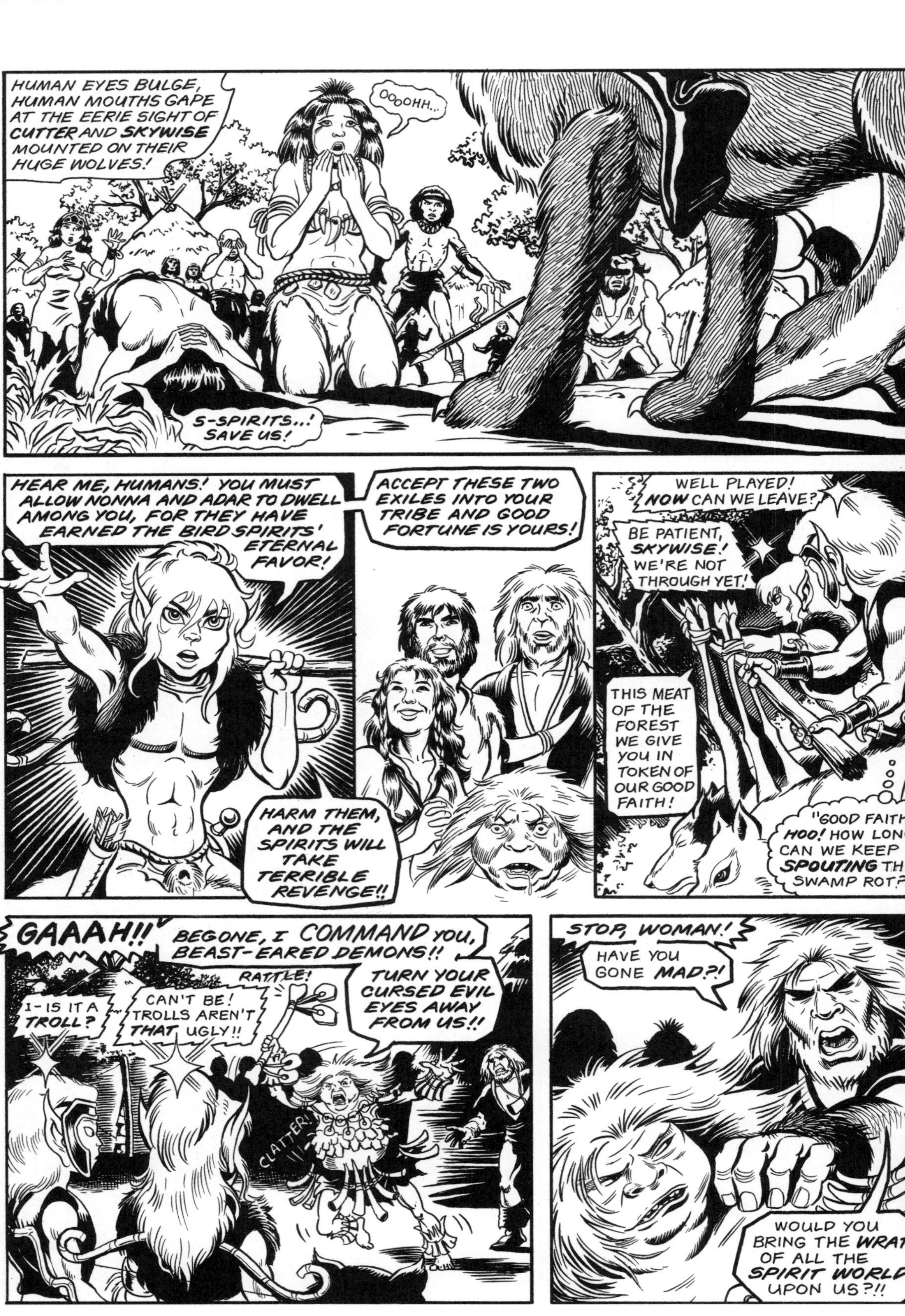
HUMAN EYES BULGE, HUMAN MOUTHS GAPE AT THE EERIE SIGHT OF CUTTER AND SKYWISE MOUNTED ON THEIR HUGE WOLVES!
OOOOHH...
S-SPIRITS...! SAVE US!
HEAR ME, HUMANS! YOU MUST ALLOW NONNA AND ADAR TO DWELL AMONG YOU, FOR THEY HAVE EARNED THE BIRD SPIRITS' ETERNAL FAVOR!
ACCEPT THESE TWO EXILES INTO YOUR TRIBE AND GOOD FORTUNE IS YOURS!
HARM THEM, AND THE SPIRITS WILL TAKE TERRIBLE REVENGE!!
WELL PLAYED! NOW CAN WE LEAVE?
BE PATIENT, SKYWISE! WE'RE NOT THROUGH YET!
THIS MEAT OF THE FOREST WE GIVE YOU IN TOKEN OF OUR GOOD FAITH!
"GOOD FAITH," HOO! HOW LONG CAN WE KEEP SPOUTING THIS SWAMP ROT?!
GAAAH!!
BEGONE, I COMMAND YOU, BEAST-EARED DEMONS!!
RATTLE!
TURN YOUR CURSED EVIL EYES AWAY FROM US!!
I-IS IT A TROLL?
CAN'T BE! TROLLS AREN'T THAT UGLY!!
CLATTER!
STOP, WOMAN!
HAVE YOU GONE MAD?!
WOULD YOU BRING THE WRATH OF ALL THE SPIRIT WORLD UPON US?!!

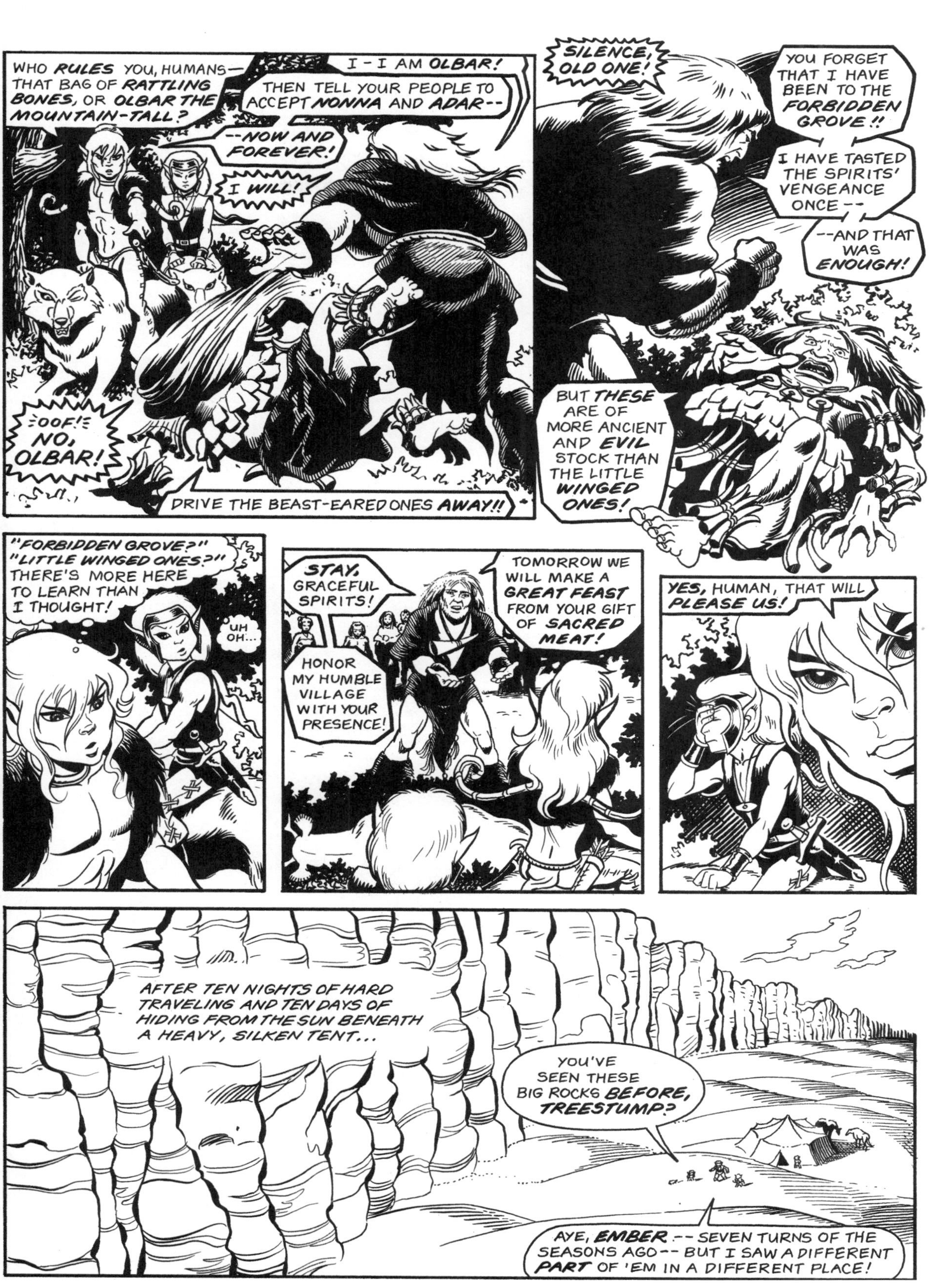
WHO RULES YOU, HUMANS— THAT BAG OF RATTLING BONES, OR OLBAR THE MOUNTAIN-TALL?
I-I AM OLBAR!
THEN TELL YOUR PEOPLE TO ACCEPT NONNA AND ADAR--
--NOW AND FOREVER!
I WILL!
OOF! NO, OLBAR!
DRIVE THE BEAST-EARED ONES AWAY!!
SILENCE, OLD ONE!
YOU FORGET THAT I HAVE BEEN TO THE FORBIDDEN GROVE!!
I HAVE TASTED THE SPIRITS' VENGEANCE ONCE--
--AND THAT WAS ENOUGH!
BUT THESE ARE OF MORE ANCIENT AND EVIL STOCK THAN THE LITTLE WINGED ONES!
"FORBIDDEN GROVE?" "LITTLE WINGED ONES?" THERE'S MORE HERE TO LEARN THAN I THOUGHT!
UH OH...
STAY, GRACEFUL SPIRITS!
HONOR MY HUMBLE VILLAGE WITH YOUR PRESENCE!
TOMORROW WE WILL MAKE A GREAT FEAST FROM YOUR GIFT OF SACRED MEAT!
YES, HUMAN, THAT WILL PLEASE US!
AFTER TEN NIGHTS OF HARD TRAVELING AND TEN DAYS OF HIDING FROM THE SUN BENEATH A HEAVY, SILKEN TENT...
YOU'VE SEEN THESE BIG ROCKS BEFORE, TREESTUMP?
AYE, EMBER -- SEVEN TURNS OF THE SEASONS AGO-- BUT I SAW A DIFFERENT PART OF 'EM IN A DIFFERENT PLACE!

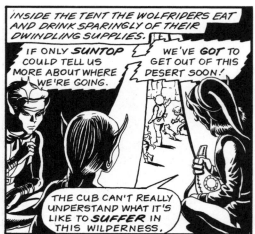

INSIDE THE TENT THE WOLFRIDERS EAT AND DRINK SPARINGLY OF THEIR DWINDLING SUPPLIES.

IF ONLY *SUNTOP* COULD TELL US MORE ABOUT WHERE WE'RE GOING.

WE'VE *GOT* TO GET OUT OF THIS DESERT SOON!

THE CUB CAN'T REALLY UNDERSTAND WHAT IT'S LIKE TO *SUFFER* IN THIS WILDERNESS.

SO WE LEFT THE TUNNEL OF *GOLDEN LIGHT* AND STARTED ACROSS THE SANDS...

MIND YOU, WE HAD NO *FOOD*, NO *TENT*, AND PRECIOUS LITTLE *WATER*!

YOUR FATHER LED US FOR *THREE DAYS* THROUGH HEAT AND THIRST-- HE WOULDN'T GIVE UP--

--EVEN WHEN MOST OF US WERE READY TO!

OH!

LOOK! OVER *THERE*!

"THERE'S A LITTLE *CAVE* IN THE CLIFF SIDE!" CRIES *EMBER*.

CAREFUL, SHE-CUB!

WATCH OUT FOR *SNAKES*!

OOO!

THERE'S NO SNAKES IN HERE, *TREESTUMP*--

BUT I SURE SMELL *SOME-THING*!

TREESTUMP SENDS FOR THE OTHERS TO SHARE IN *EMBER'S* DISCOVERY...

SUNTOP!

LOOK WHAT I FOUND!!

BONES!!

HERE'S A *FUNNY* LOOKING ONE!

SEE?

R-RRUFF! YAP!

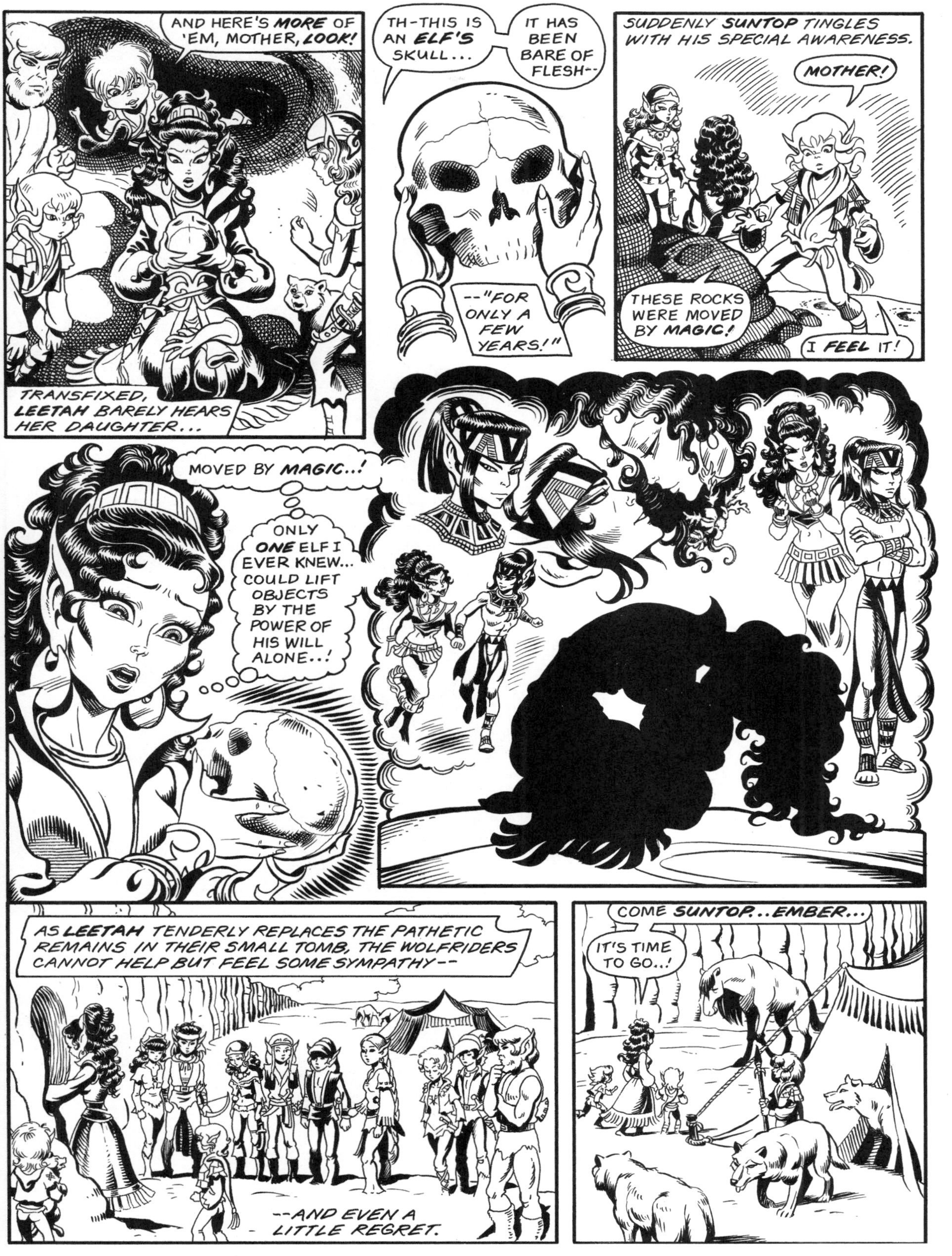
AND HERE'S MORE OF 'EM, MOTHER, LOOK!
TRANSFIXED, LEETAH BARELY HEARS HER DAUGHTER...
TH-THIS IS AN ELF'S SKULL...
IT HAS BEEN BARE OF FLESH--
--"FOR ONLY A FEW YEARS!"
SUDDENLY SUNTOP TINGLES WITH HIS SPECIAL AWARENESS.
MOTHER!
THESE ROCKS WERE MOVED BY MAGIC!
I FEEL IT!
MOVED BY MAGIC..!
ONLY ONE ELF I EVER KNEW... COULD LIFT OBJECTS BY THE POWER OF HIS WILL ALONE..!
AS LEETAH TENDERLY REPLACES THE PATHETIC REMAINS IN THEIR SMALL TOMB, THE WOLFRIDERS CANNOT HELP BUT FEEL SOME SYMPATHY--
--AND EVEN A LITTLE REGRET.
COME SUNTOP...EMBER...
IT'S TIME TO GO..!

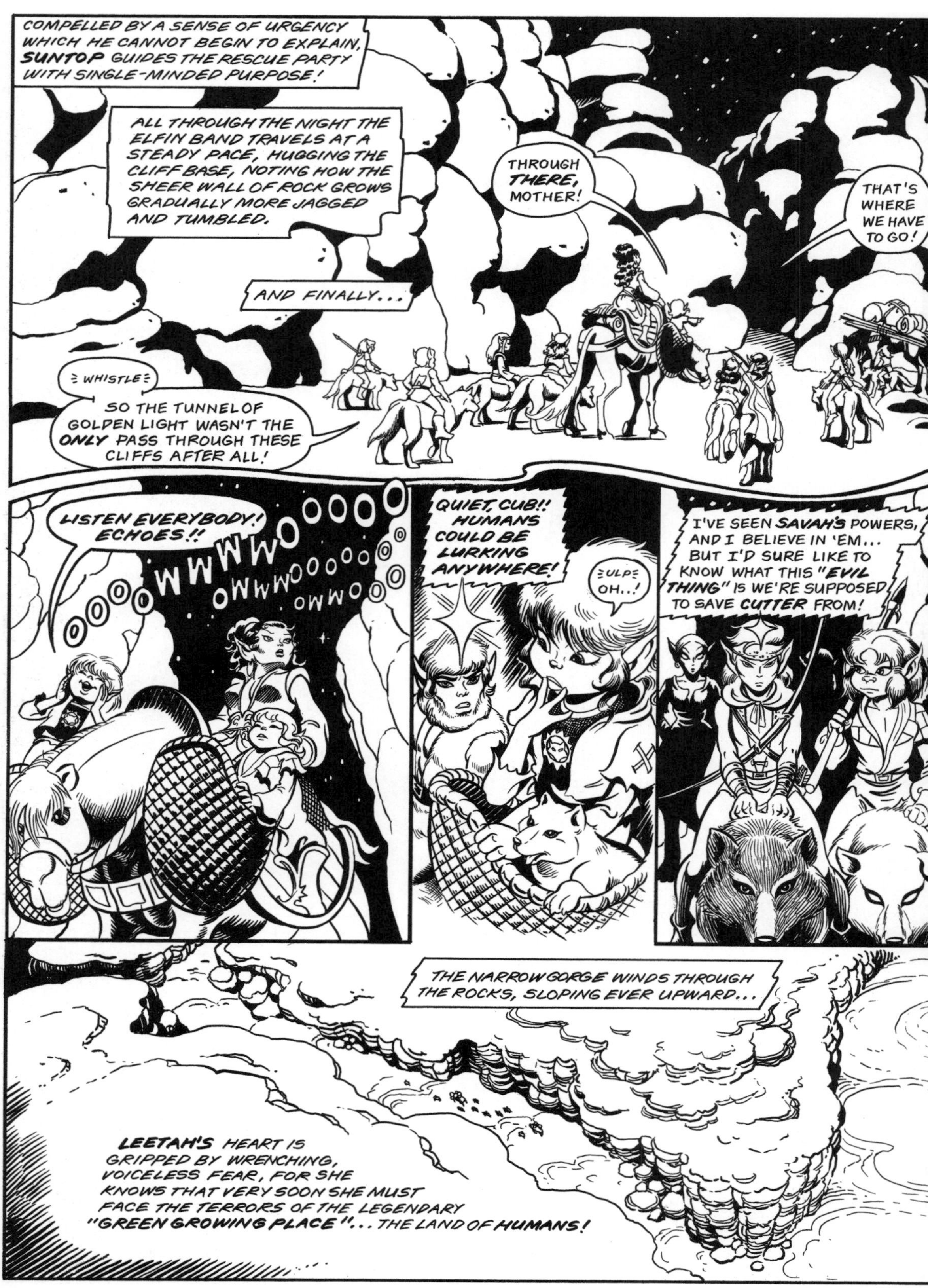

COMPELLED BY A SENSE OF URGENCY WHICH HE CANNOT BEGIN TO EXPLAIN, SUNTOP GUIDES THE RESCUE PARTY WITH SINGLE-MINDED PURPOSE!
ALL THROUGH THE NIGHT THE ELFIN BAND TRAVELS AT A STEADY PACE, HUGGING THE CLIFF BASE, NOTING HOW THE SHEER WALL OF ROCK GROWS GRADUALLY MORE JAGGED AND TUMBLED.
AND FINALLY...
THROUGH THERE, MOTHER!
THAT'S WHERE WE HAVE TO GO!
WHISTLE
SO THE TUNNEL OF GOLDEN LIGHT WASN'T THE ONLY PASS THROUGH THESE CLIFFS AFTER ALL!
LISTEN EVERYBODY! ECHOES!!
OOOOWWWWOOOOO
OWWWOOOOOO
OWWOOO
QUIET, CUB!! HUMANS COULD BE LURKING ANYWHERE!
ULP
OH..!
I'VE SEEN SAVAH'S POWERS, AND I BELIEVE IN 'EM... BUT I'D SURE LIKE TO KNOW WHAT THIS "EVIL THING" IS WE'RE SUPPOSED TO SAVE CUTTER FROM!
THE NARROW GORGE WINDS THROUGH THE ROCKS, SLOPING EVER UPWARD...
LEETAH'S HEART IS GRIPPED BY WRENCHING, VOICELESS FEAR, FOR SHE KNOWS THAT VERY SOON SHE MUST FACE THE TERRORS OF THE LEGENDARY "GREEN GROWING PLACE"... THE LAND OF HUMANS!

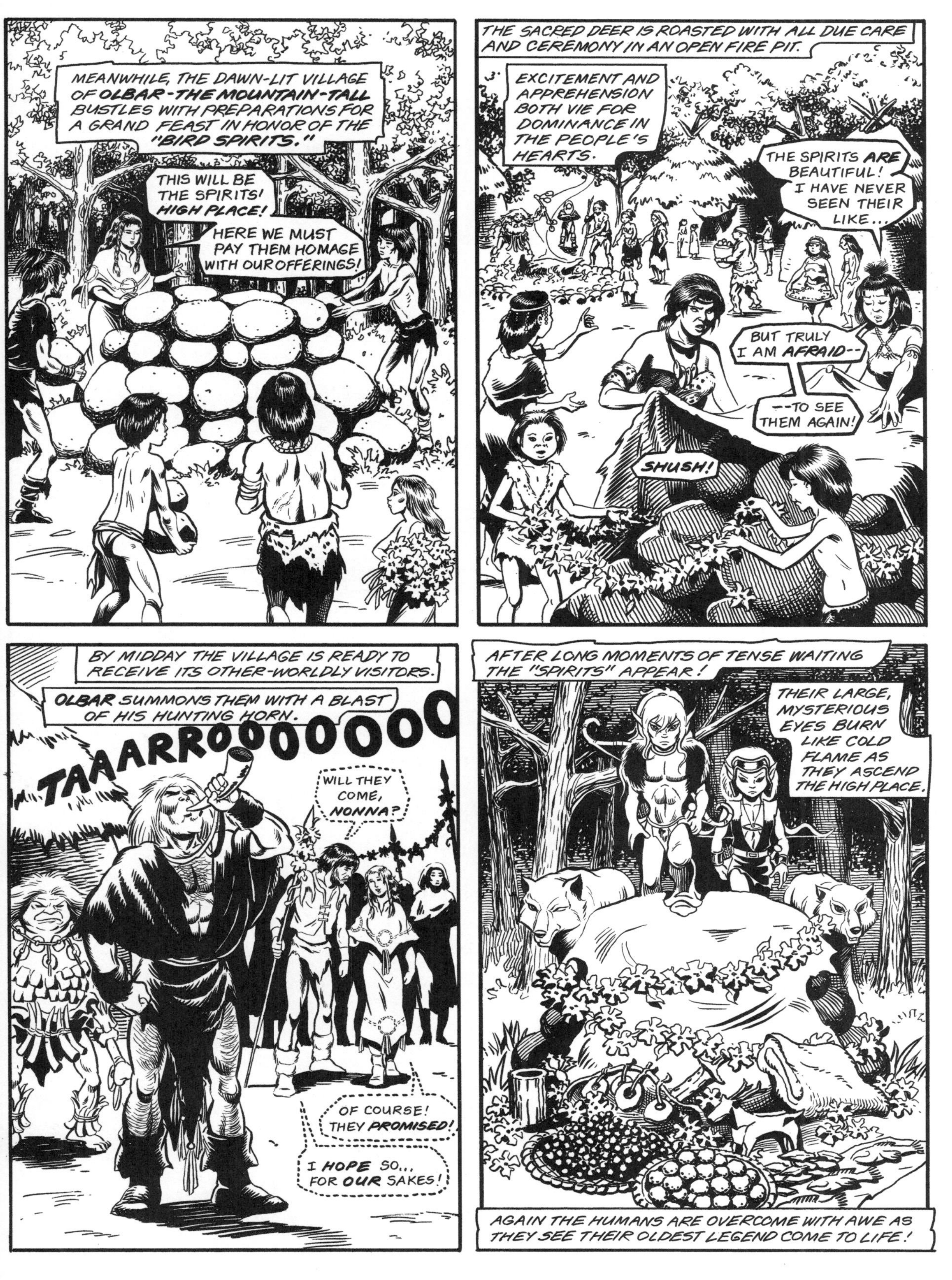

MEANWHILE, THE DAWN-LIT VILLAGE OF OLBAR-THE MOUNTAIN-TALL BUSTLES WITH PREPARATIONS FOR A GRAND FEAST IN HONOR OF THE "BIRD SPIRITS."
THIS WILL BE THE SPIRITS' HIGH PLACE!
HERE WE MUST PAY THEM HOMAGE WITH OUR OFFERINGS!
THE SACRED DEER IS ROASTED WITH ALL DUE CARE AND CEREMONY IN AN OPEN FIRE PIT.
EXCITEMENT AND APPREHENSION BOTH VIE FOR DOMINANCE IN THE PEOPLE'S HEARTS.
THE SPIRITS ARE BEAUTIFUL! I HAVE NEVER SEEN THEIR LIKE...
BUT TRULY I AM AFRAID--
--TO SEE THEM AGAIN!
SHUSH!
BY MIDDAY THE VILLAGE IS READY TO RECEIVE ITS OTHER-WORLDLY VISITORS.
OLBAR SUMMONS THEM WITH A BLAST OF HIS HUNTING HORN.
TAAARROOOOOOOO
WILL THEY COME, NONNA?
OF COURSE! THEY PROMISED!
I HOPE SO... FOR OUR SAKES!
AFTER LONG MOMENTS OF TENSE WAITING THE "SPIRITS" APPEAR!
THEIR LARGE, MYSTERIOUS EYES BURN LIKE COLD FLAME AS THEY ASCEND THE HIGH PLACE.
AGAIN THE HUMANS ARE OVERCOME WITH AWE AS THEY SEE THEIR OLDEST LEGEND COME TO LIFE!

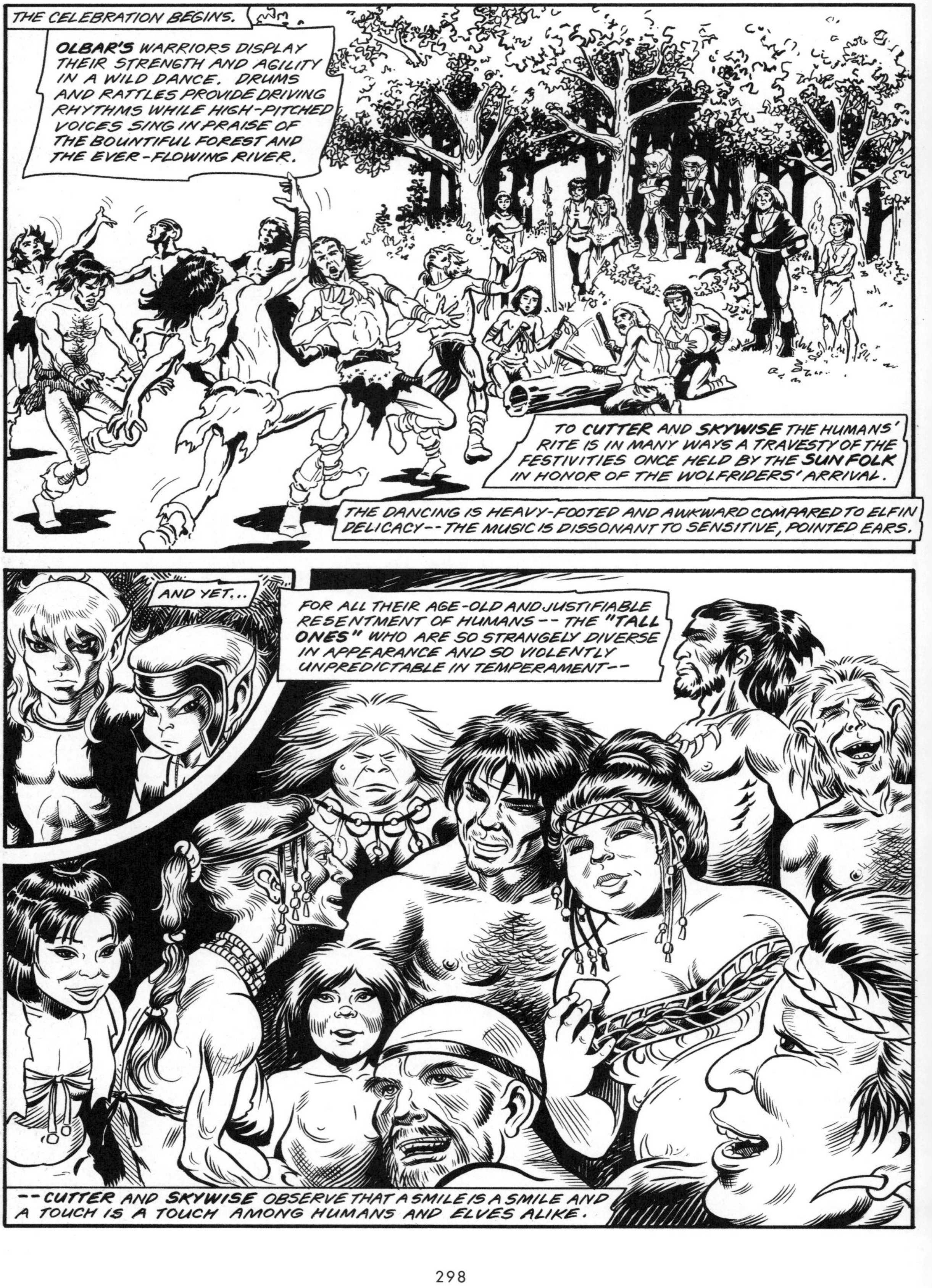
THE CELEBRATION BEGINS.
OLBAR'S WARRIORS DISPLAY THEIR STRENGTH AND AGILITY IN A WILD DANCE. DRUMS AND RATTLES PROVIDE DRIVING RHYTHMS WHILE HIGH-PITCHED VOICES SING IN PRAISE OF THE BOUNTIFUL FOREST AND THE EVER-FLOWING RIVER.
TO CUTTER AND SKYWISE THE HUMANS' RITE IS IN MANY WAYS A TRAVESTY OF THE FESTIVITIES ONCE HELD BY THE SUN FOLK IN HONOR OF THE WOLFRIDERS' ARRIVAL.
THE DANCING IS HEAVY-FOOTED AND AWKWARD COMPARED TO ELFIN DELICACY--THE MUSIC IS DISSONANT TO SENSITIVE, POINTED EARS.
AND YET...
FOR ALL THEIR AGE-OLD AND JUSTIFIABLE RESENTMENT OF HUMANS--THE "TALL ONES" WHO ARE SO STRANGELY DIVERSE IN APPEARANCE AND SO VIOLENTLY UNPREDICTABLE IN TEMPERAMENT--
--CUTTER AND SKYWISE OBSERVE THAT A SMILE IS A SMILE AND A TOUCH IS A TOUCH AMONG HUMANS AND ELVES ALIKE.

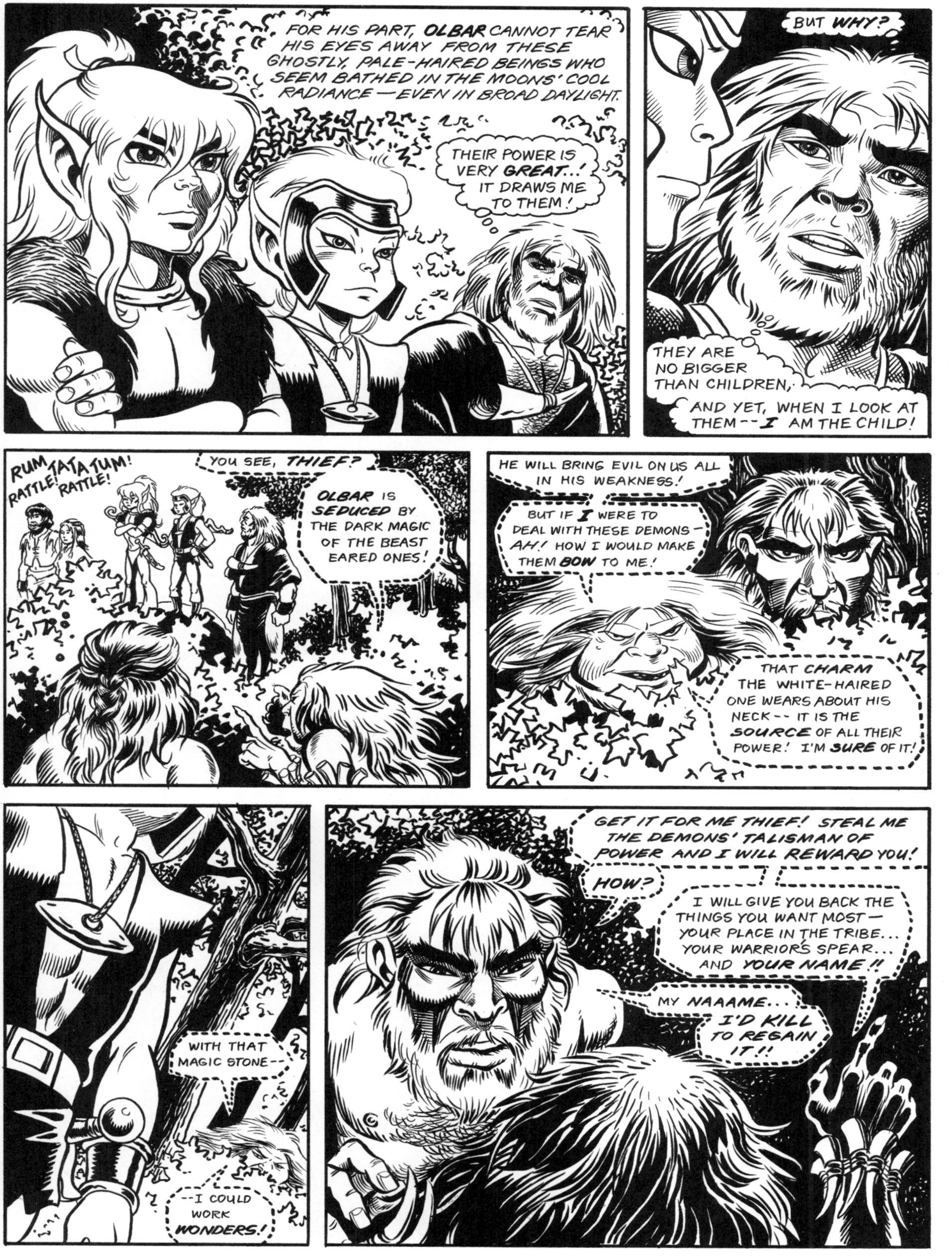
FOR HIS PART, OLBAR CANNOT TEAR HIS EYES AWAY FROM THESE GHOSTLY, PALE-HAIRED BEINGS WHO SEEM BATHED IN THE MOONS' COOL RADIANCE — EVEN IN BROAD DAYLIGHT.
THEIR POWER IS VERY GREAT..! IT DRAWS ME TO THEM!
BUT WHY?
THEY ARE NO BIGGER THAN CHILDREN,
AND YET, WHEN I LOOK AT THEM -- I AM THE CHILD!
RUM TA TA TUM!
RATTLE! RATTLE!
YOU SEE, THIEF?
OLBAR IS SEDUCED BY THE DARK MAGIC OF THE BEAST EARED ONES!
HE WILL BRING EVIL ON US ALL IN HIS WEAKNESS!
BUT IF I WERE TO DEAL WITH THESE DEMONS — AH! HOW I WOULD MAKE THEM BOW TO ME!
THAT CHARM THE WHITE-HAIRED ONE WEARS ABOUT HIS NECK -- IT IS THE SOURCE OF ALL THEIR POWER! I'M SURE OF IT!
WITH THAT MAGIC STONE--
--I COULD WORK WONDERS!
GET IT FOR ME THIEF! STEAL ME THE DEMONS' TALISMAN OF POWER AND I WILL REWARD YOU!
HOW?
I WILL GIVE YOU BACK THE THINGS YOU WANT MOST — YOUR PLACE IN THE TRIBE... YOUR WARRIOR'S SPEAR... AND YOUR NAME!!
MY NAAAME...
I'D KILL TO REGAIN IT!!

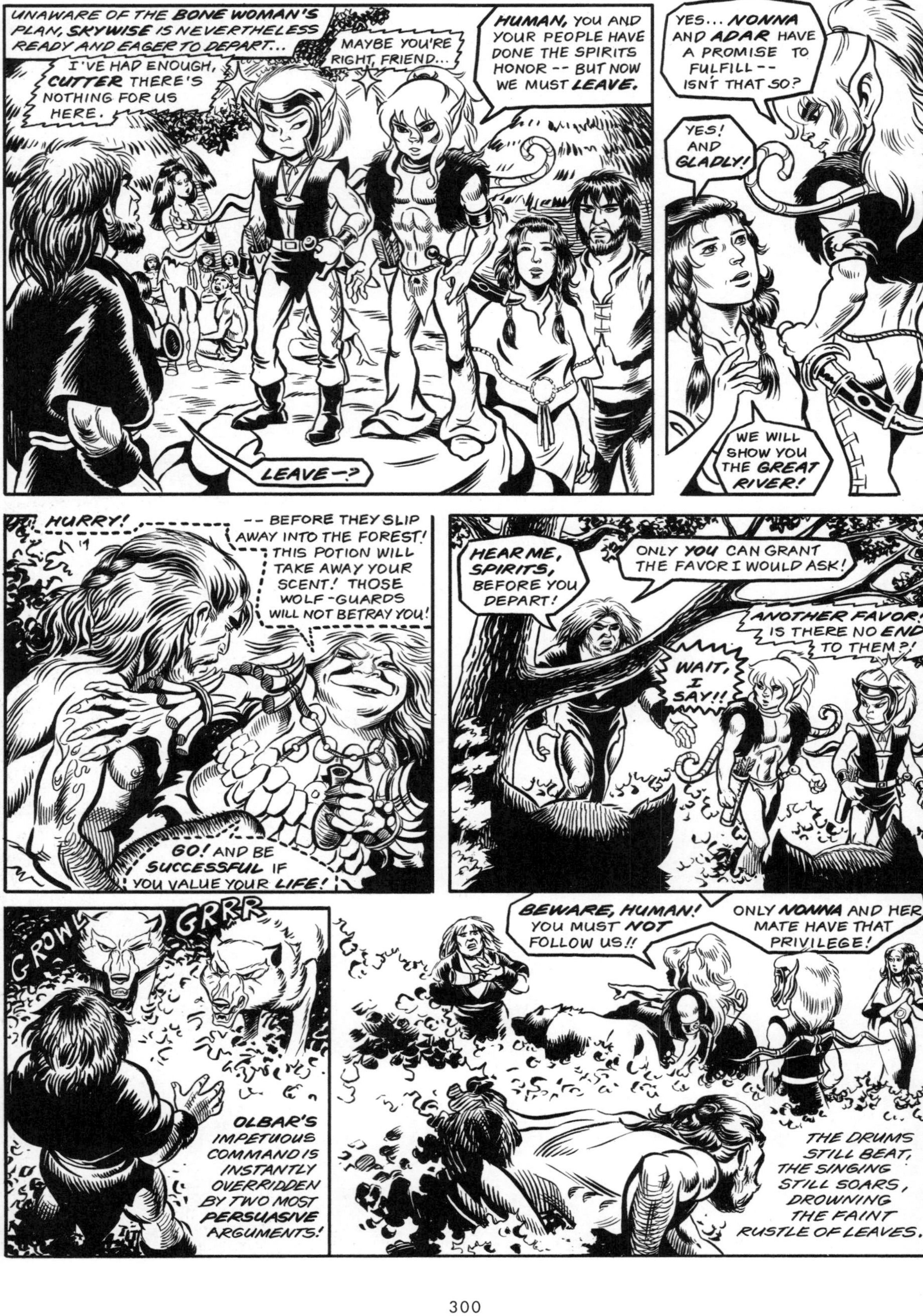
UNAWARE OF THE BONE WOMAN'S PLAN, SKYWISE IS NEVERTHELESS READY AND EAGER TO DEPART...
I'VE HAD ENOUGH, CUTTER THERE'S NOTHING FOR US HERE.
MAYBE YOU'RE RIGHT, FRIEND...
HUMAN, YOU AND YOUR PEOPLE HAVE DONE THE SPIRITS HONOR -- BUT NOW WE MUST LEAVE.
LEAVE--?
YES... NONNA AND ADAR HAVE A PROMISE TO FULFILL -- ISN'T THAT SO?
YES! AND GLADLY!
WE WILL SHOW YOU THE GREAT RIVER!
HURRY!
-- BEFORE THEY SLIP AWAY INTO THE FOREST! THIS POTION WILL TAKE AWAY YOUR SCENT! THOSE WOLF-GUARDS WILL NOT BETRAY YOU!
GO! AND BE SUCCESSFUL IF YOU VALUE YOUR LIFE!
HEAR ME, SPIRITS, BEFORE YOU DEPART!
ONLY YOU CAN GRANT THE FAVOR I WOULD ASK!
ANOTHER FAVOR! IS THERE NO END TO THEM?!
WAIT, I SAY!!
GROWL
GRRR
OLBAR'S IMPETUOUS COMMAND IS INSTANTLY OVERRIDDEN BY TWO MOST PERSUASIVE ARGUMENTS!
BEWARE, HUMAN! YOU MUST NOT FOLLOW US!!
ONLY NONNA AND HER MATE HAVE THAT PRIVILEGE!
THE DRUMS STILL BEAT, THE SINGING STILL SOARS, DROWNING THE FAINT RUSTLE OF LEAVES.

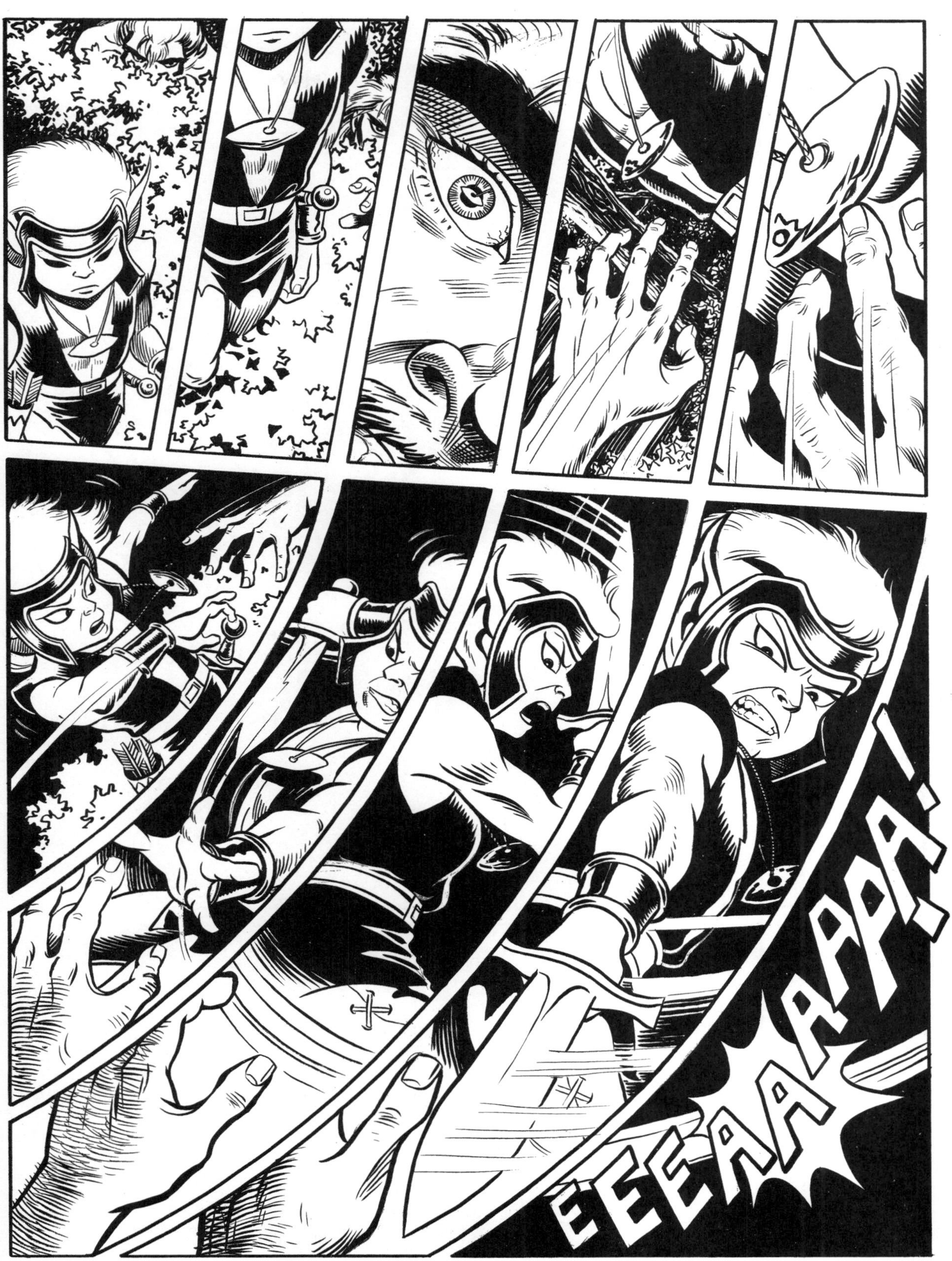
EEEAAAAAPPA!

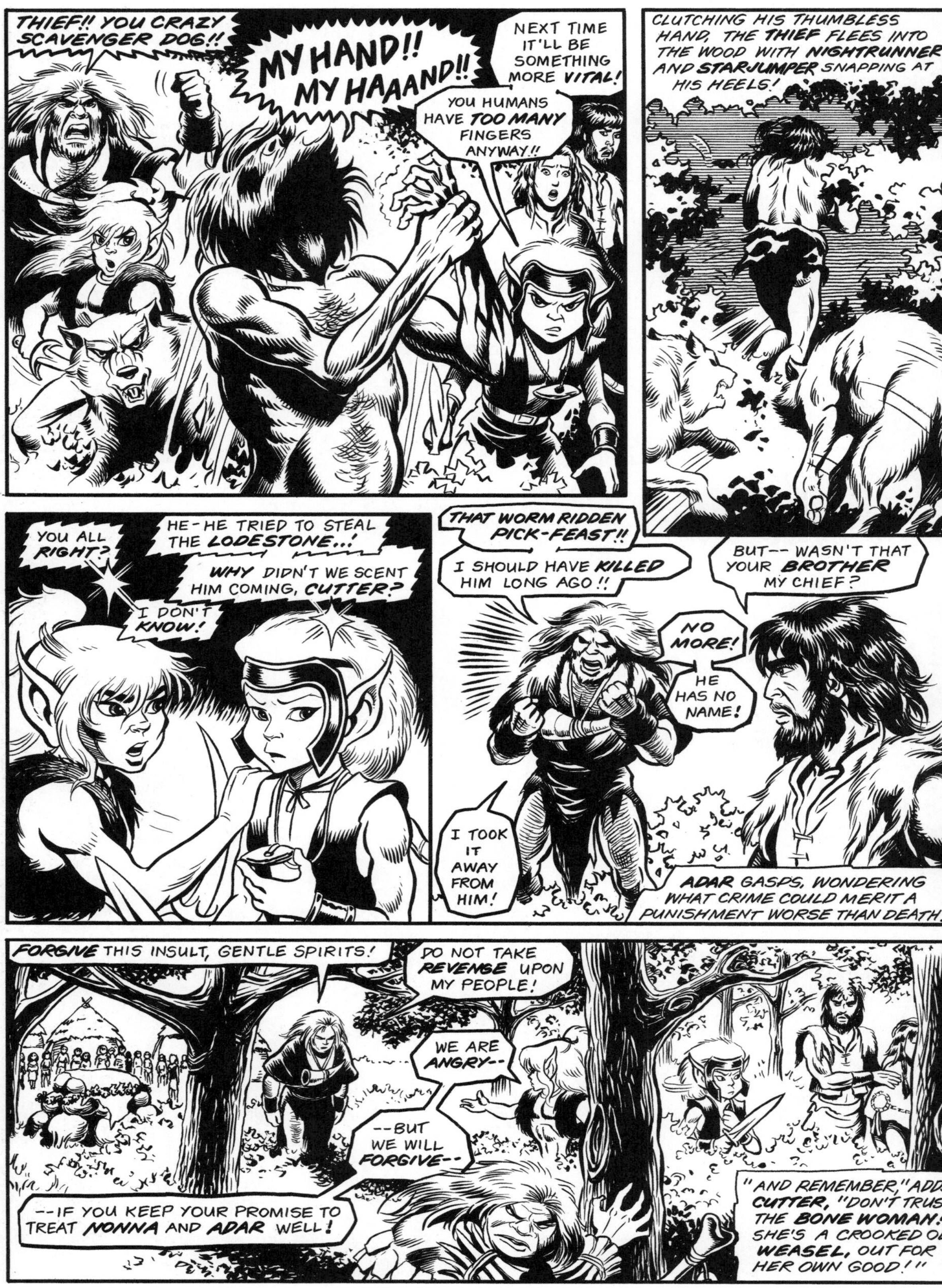

THIEF!! YOU CRAZY SCAVENGER DOG!!
MY HAND!! MY HAAAND!!
NEXT TIME IT'LL BE SOMETHING MORE VITAL!
YOU HUMANS HAVE TOO MANY FINGERS ANYWAY!!
CLUTCHING HIS THUMBLESS HAND, THE THIEF FLEES INTO THE WOOD WITH NIGHTRUNNER AND STARJUMPER SNAPPING AT HIS HEELS!
YOU ALL RIGHT?
HE-HE TRIED TO STEAL THE LODESTONE...!
WHY DIDN'T WE SCENT HIM COMING, CUTTER?
I DON'T KNOW!
THAT WORM RIDDEN PICK-FEAST!!
I SHOULD HAVE KILLED HIM LONG AGO!!
BUT-- WASN'T THAT YOUR BROTHER MY CHIEF?
NO MORE!
HE HAS NO NAME!
I TOOK IT AWAY FROM HIM!
ADAR GASPS, WONDERING WHAT CRIME COULD MERIT A PUNISHMENT WORSE THAN DEATH!
FORGIVE THIS INSULT, GENTLE SPIRITS!
DO NOT TAKE REVENGE UPON MY PEOPLE!
WE ARE ANGRY--
--BUT WE WILL FORGIVE--
--IF YOU KEEP YOUR PROMISE TO TREAT NONNA AND ADAR WELL!
"AND REMEMBER," ADDS CUTTER, "DON'T TRUST THE BONE WOMAN! SHE'S A CROOKED OLD WEASEL, OUT FOR HER OWN GOOD!"

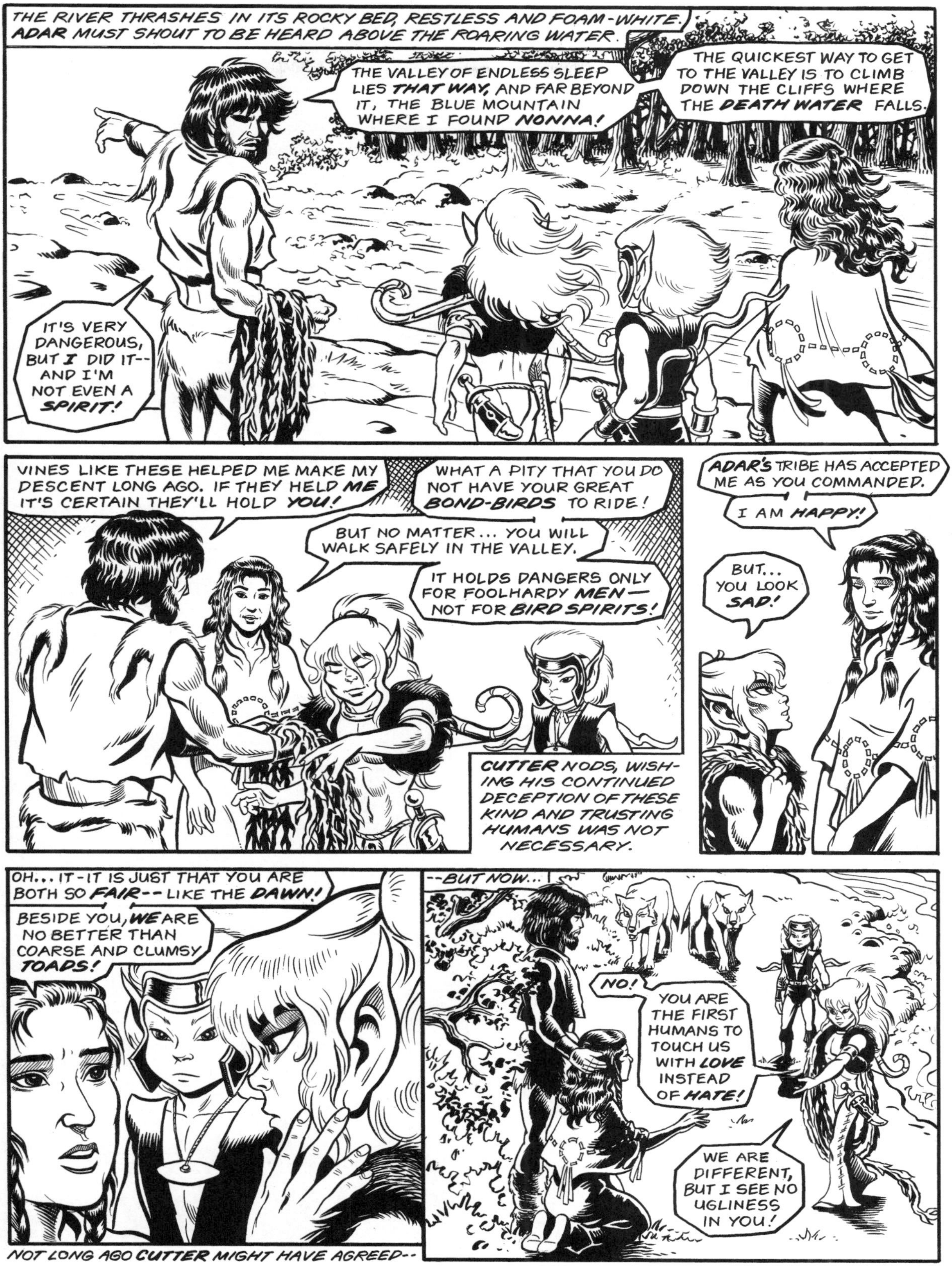
THE RIVER THRASHES IN ITS ROCKY BED, RESTLESS AND FOAM-WHITE. ADAR MUST SHOUT TO BE HEARD ABOVE THE ROARING WATER.
THE VALLEY OF ENDLESS SLEEP LIES THAT WAY, AND FAR BEYOND IT, THE BLUE MOUNTAIN WHERE I FOUND NONNA!
THE QUICKEST WAY TO GET TO THE VALLEY IS TO CLIMB DOWN THE CLIFFS WHERE THE DEATH WATER FALLS.
IT'S VERY DANGEROUS, BUT I DID IT-- AND I'M NOT EVEN A SPIRIT!
VINES LIKE THESE HELPED ME MAKE MY DESCENT LONG AGO. IF THEY HELD ME IT'S CERTAIN THEY'LL HOLD YOU!
WHAT A PITY THAT YOU DO NOT HAVE YOUR GREAT BOND-BIRDS TO RIDE!
BUT NO MATTER... YOU WILL WALK SAFELY IN THE VALLEY.
IT HOLDS DANGERS ONLY FOR FOOLHARDY MEN— NOT FOR BIRD SPIRITS!
CUTTER NODS, WISHING HIS CONTINUED DECEPTION OF THESE KIND AND TRUSTING HUMANS WAS NOT NECESSARY.
ADAR'S TRIBE HAS ACCEPTED ME AS YOU COMMANDED.
I AM HAPPY!
BUT... YOU LOOK SAD!
OH... IT-IT IS JUST THAT YOU ARE BOTH SO FAIR-- LIKE THE DAWN!
BESIDE YOU, WE ARE NO BETTER THAN COARSE AND CLUMSY TOADS!
NOT LONG AGO CUTTER MIGHT HAVE AGREED--
--BUT NOW...
NO!
YOU ARE THE FIRST HUMANS TO TOUCH US WITH LOVE INSTEAD OF HATE!
WE ARE DIFFERENT, BUT I SEE NO UGLINESS IN YOU!

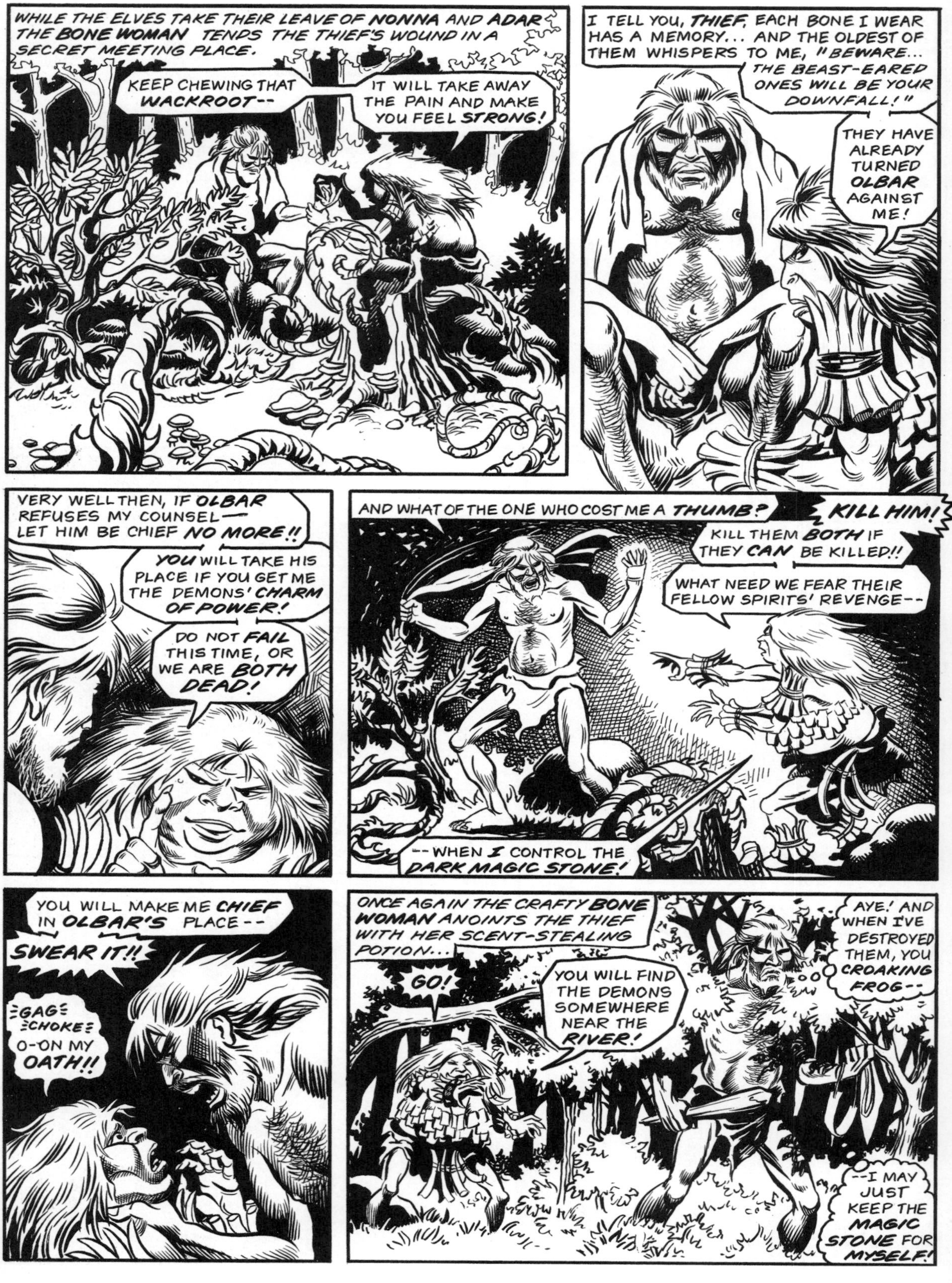
WHILE THE ELVES TAKE THEIR LEAVE OF NONNA AND ADAR THE BONE WOMAN TENDS THE THIEF'S WOUND IN A SECRET MEETING PLACE.
KEEP CHEWING THAT WACKROOT--
IT WILL TAKE AWAY THE PAIN AND MAKE YOU FEEL STRONG!
I TELL YOU, THIEF, EACH BONE I WEAR HAS A MEMORY... AND THE OLDEST OF THEM WHISPERS TO ME, "BEWARE... THE BEAST-EARED ONES WILL BE YOUR DOWNFALL!"
THEY HAVE ALREADY TURNED OLBAR AGAINST ME!
VERY WELL THEN, IF OLBAR REFUSES MY COUNSEL-- LET HIM BE CHIEF NO MORE!!
YOU WILL TAKE HIS PLACE IF YOU GET ME THE DEMONS' CHARM OF POWER!
DO NOT FAIL THIS TIME, OR WE ARE BOTH DEAD!
AND WHAT OF THE ONE WHO COST ME A THUMB?
KILL HIM!
KILL THEM BOTH IF THEY CAN BE KILLED!!
WHAT NEED WE FEAR THEIR FELLOW SPIRITS' REVENGE--
--WHEN I CONTROL THE DARK MAGIC STONE!
YOU WILL MAKE ME CHIEF IN OLBAR'S PLACE--
SWEAR IT!!
GAG CHOKE
O-ON MY OATH!!
ONCE AGAIN THE CRAFTY BONE WOMAN ANOINTS THE THIEF WITH HER SCENT-STEALING POTION...
GO!
YOU WILL FIND THE DEMONS SOMEWHERE NEAR THE RIVER!
AYE! AND WHEN I'VE DESTROYED THEM, YOU CROAKING FROG--
--I MAY JUST KEEP THE MAGIC STONE FOR MYSELF!

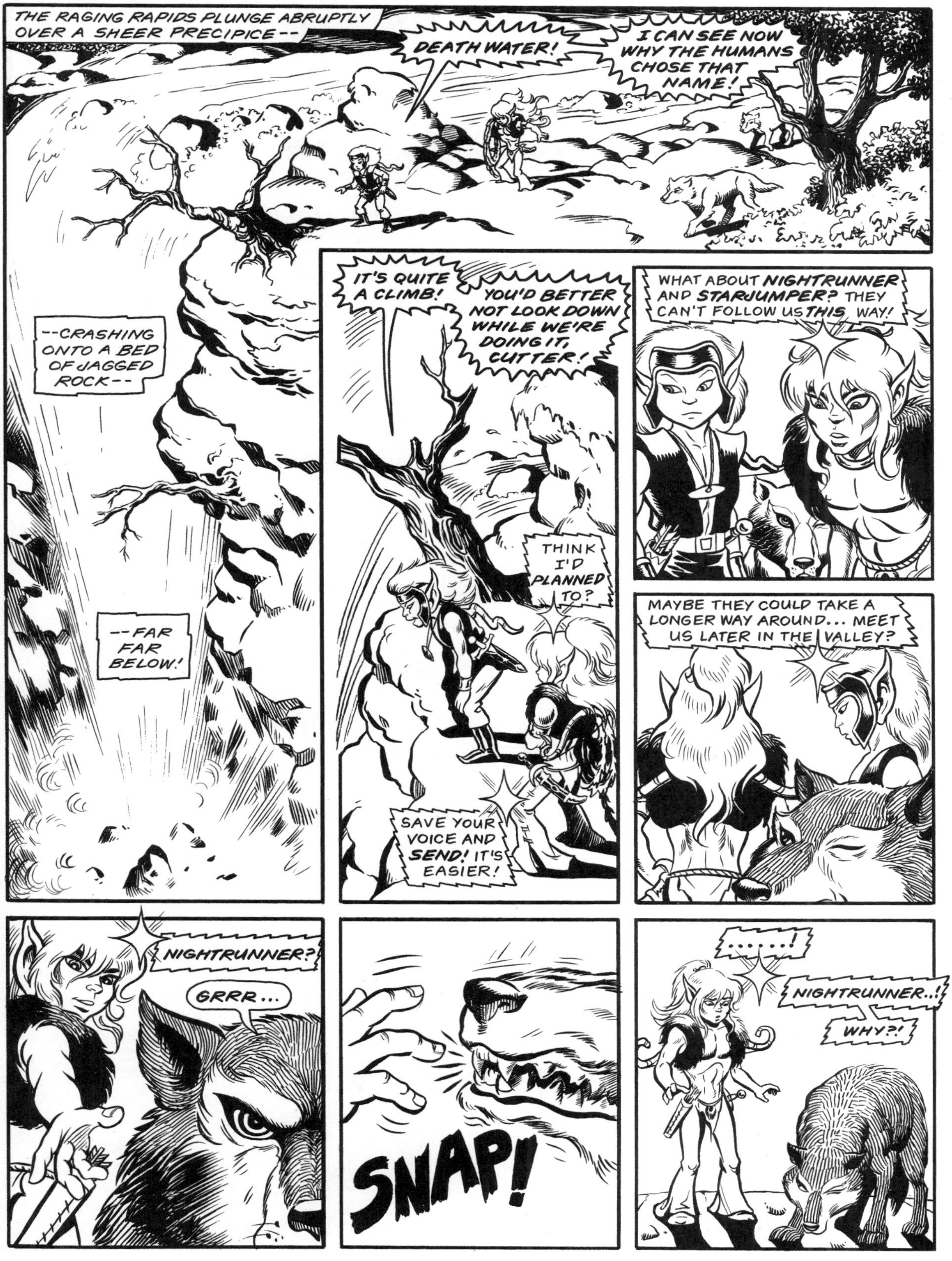

THE RAGING RAPIDS PLUNGE ABRUPTLY OVER A SHEER PRECIPICE--
DEATH WATER!
I CAN SEE NOW WHY THE HUMANS CHOSE THAT NAME!
--CRASHING ONTO A BED OF JAGGED ROCK--
--FAR FAR BELOW!
IT'S QUITE A CLIMB!
YOU'D BETTER NOT LOOK DOWN WHILE WE'RE DOING IT, CUTTER!
THINK I'D PLANNED TO?
SAVE YOUR VOICE AND SEND! IT'S EASIER!
WHAT ABOUT NIGHTRUNNER AND STARJUMPER? THEY CAN'T FOLLOW US THIS WAY!
MAYBE THEY COULD TAKE A LONGER WAY AROUND... MEET US LATER IN THE VALLEY?
NIGHTRUNNER?
GRRR...
SNAP!
......!
NIGHTRUNNER..!
WHY?!

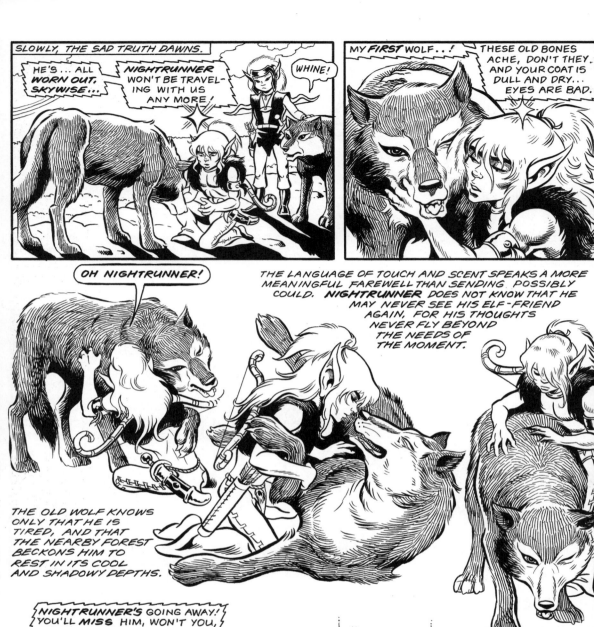

SLOWLY, THE SAD TRUTH DAWNS.

HE'S ... ALL *WORN OUT*, SKYWISE...

NIGHTRUNNER WON'T BE TRAVEL-ING WITH US ANY MORE!

WHINE!

MY *FIRST* WOLF..!

THESE OLD BONES ACHE, DON'T THEY. AND YOUR COAT IS DULL AND DRY... EYES ARE BAD...

OH *NIGHTRUNNER!*

THE LANGUAGE OF TOUCH AND SCENT SPEAKS A MORE MEANINGFUL FAREWELL THAN SENDING, POSSIBLY COULD. *NIGHTRUNNER* DOES NOT KNOW THAT HE MAY NEVER SEE HIS ELF-FRIEND AGAIN, FOR HIS THOUGHTS NEVER FLY BEYOND THE NEEDS OF THE MOMENT.

THE OLD WOLF KNOWS ONLY THAT HE IS TIRED, AND THAT THE NEARBY FOREST BECKONS HIM TO REST IN ITS COOL AND SHADOWY DEPTHS.

NIGHTRUNNER'S GOING AWAY! YOU'LL *MISS* HIM, WON'T YOU, *STARJUMPER* -- AS MUCH AS I'D MISS *CUTTER*...IF.....

GO ON ... I UNDERSTAND!

WHUF!

THEY-- THEY'RE *BOTH* GOING!

YES...

STARJUMPER'S STILL STRONG.

HE CAN LOOK AFTER *NIGHTRUNNER*... HUNT FOR HIM UNTIL--

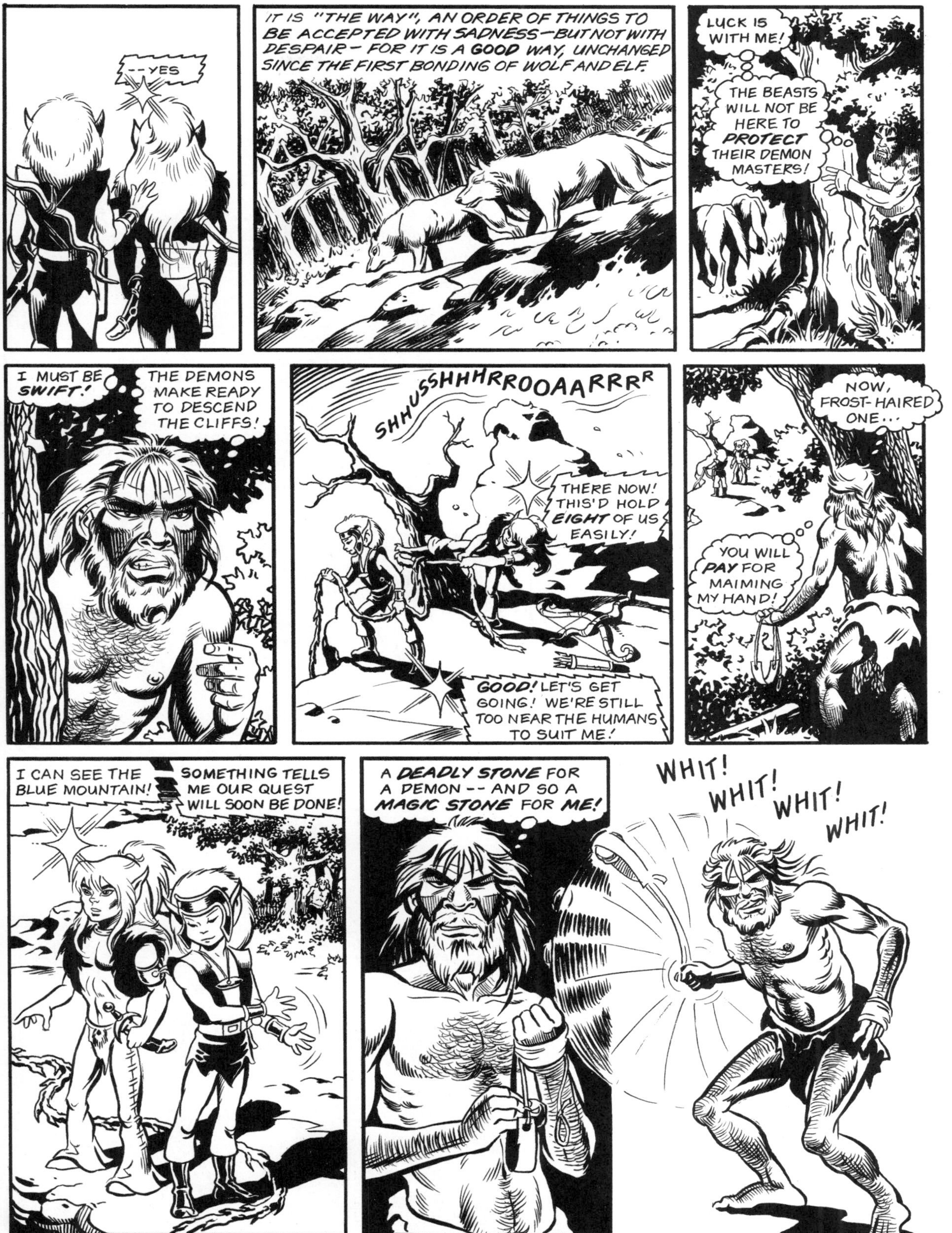

--YES
IT IS "THE WAY", AN ORDER OF THINGS TO BE ACCEPTED WITH SADNESS--BUT NOT WITH DESPAIR--FOR IT IS A GOOD WAY, UNCHANGED SINCE THE FIRST BONDING OF WOLF AND ELF.
LUCK IS WITH ME!
THE BEASTS WILL NOT BE HERE TO PROTECT THEIR DEMON MASTERS!
I MUST BE SWIFT!
THE DEMONS MAKE READY TO DESCEND THE CLIFFS!
SHHUSSHHHRROOAARRRR
THERE NOW! THIS'D HOLD EIGHT OF US EASILY!
GOOD! LET'S GET GOING! WE'RE STILL TOO NEAR THE HUMANS TO SUIT ME!
NOW, FROST-HAIRED ONE...
YOU WILL PAY FOR MAIMING MY HAND!
I CAN SEE THE BLUE MOUNTAIN!
SOMETHING TELLS ME OUR QUEST WILL SOON BE DONE!
A DEADLY STONE FOR A DEMON--AND SO A MAGIC STONE FOR ME!
WHIT!
WHIT!
WHIT!
WHIT!

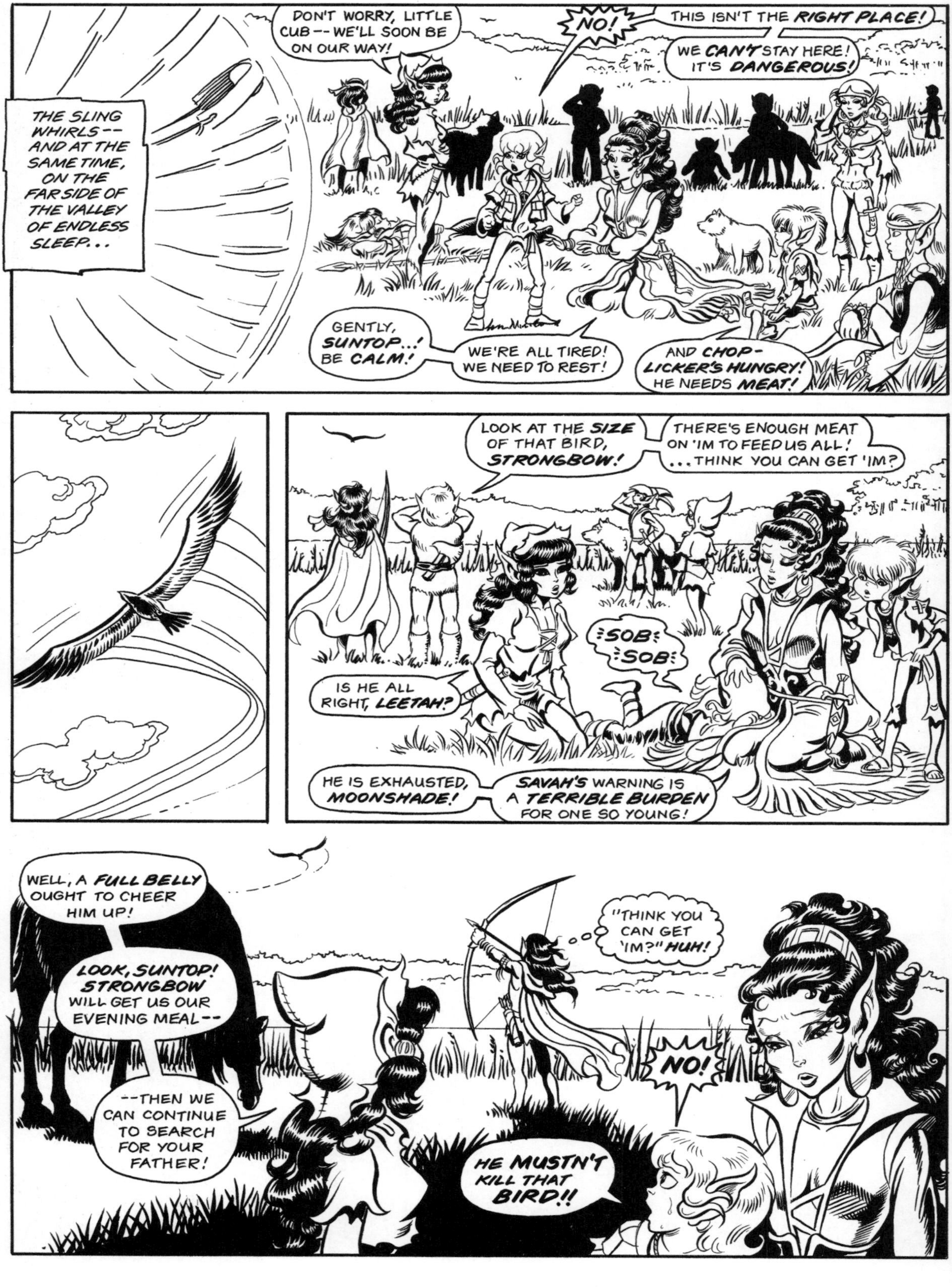
THE SLING WHIRLS-- AND AT THE SAME TIME, ON THE FAR SIDE OF THE VALLEY OF ENDLESS SLEEP...
DON'T WORRY, LITTLE CUB -- WE'LL SOON BE ON OUR WAY!
NO!
THIS ISN'T THE RIGHT PLACE!
WE CAN'T STAY HERE! IT'S DANGEROUS!
GENTLY, SUNTOP...! BE CALM!
WE'RE ALL TIRED! WE NEED TO REST!
AND CHOP-LICKER'S HUNGRY! HE NEEDS MEAT!
LOOK AT THE SIZE OF THAT BIRD, STRONGBOW!
THERE'S ENOUGH MEAT ON 'IM TO FEED US ALL! ...THINK YOU CAN GET 'IM?
SOB SOB
IS HE ALL RIGHT, LEETAH?
HE IS EXHAUSTED, MOONSHADE!
SAVAH'S WARNING IS A TERRIBLE BURDEN FOR ONE SO YOUNG!
WELL, A FULL BELLY OUGHT TO CHEER HIM UP!
LOOK, SUNTOP! STRONGBOW WILL GET US OUR EVENING MEAL--
--THEN WE CAN CONTINUE TO SEARCH FOR YOUR FATHER!
"THINK YOU CAN GET 'IM?" HUH!
NO!
HE MUSTN'T KILL THAT BIRD!!

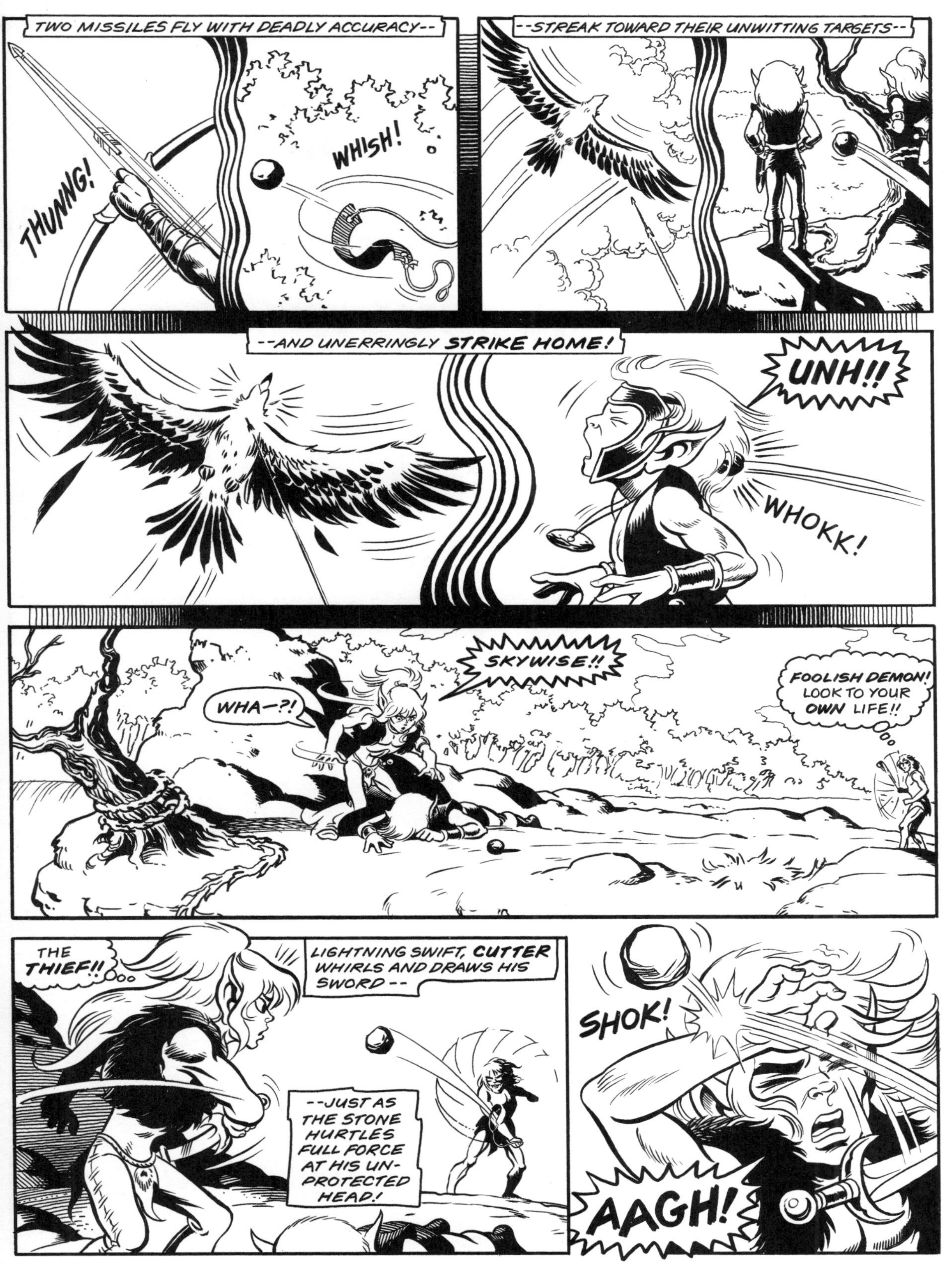
TWO MISSILES FLY WITH DEADLY ACCURACY--
THUNNG!
WHISH!
--STREAK TOWARD THEIR UNWITTING TARGETS--
--AND UNERRINGLY STRIKE HOME!
UNH!!
WHOKK!
SKYWISE!!
WHA--?!
FOOLISH DEMON! LOOK TO YOUR OWN LIFE!!
THE THIEF!!
LIGHTNING SWIFT, CUTTER WHIRLS AND DRAWS HIS SWORD --
--JUST AS THE STONE HURTLES FULL FORCE AT HIS UN-PROTECTED HEAD!
SHOK!
AAGH!

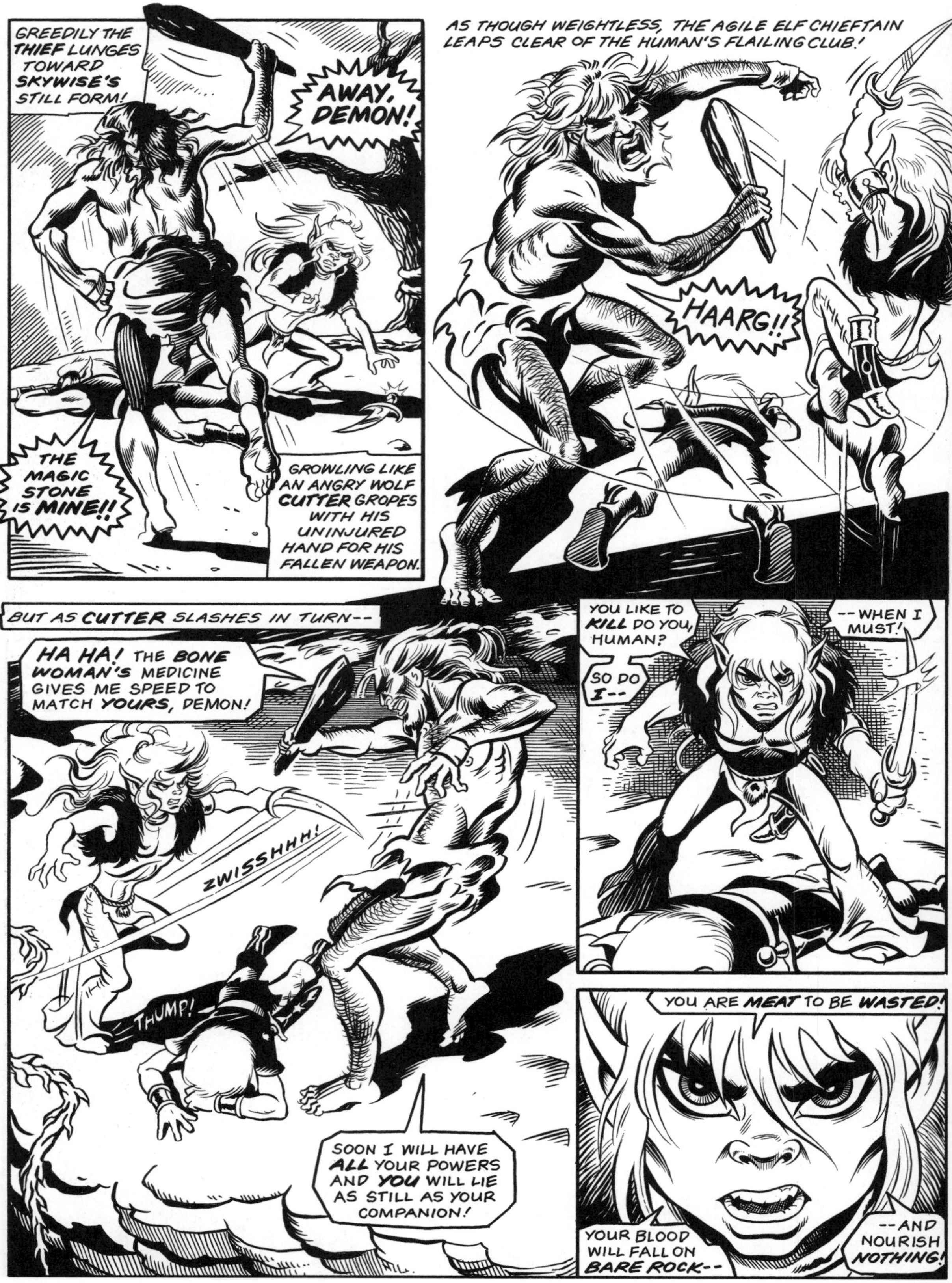
GREEDILY THE THIEF LUNGES TOWARD SKYWISE'S STILL FORM!
AWAY, DEMON!
THE MAGIC STONE IS MINE!!
GROWLING LIKE AN ANGRY WOLF CUTTER GROPES WITH HIS UNINJURED HAND FOR HIS FALLEN WEAPON.
AS THOUGH WEIGHTLESS, THE AGILE ELF CHIEFTAIN LEAPS CLEAR OF THE HUMAN'S FLAILING CLUB!
HAARG!!
BUT AS CUTTER SLASHES IN TURN--
HA HA! THE BONE WOMAN'S MEDICINE GIVES ME SPEED TO MATCH YOURS, DEMON!
ZWISSHHH!
THUMP!
SOON I WILL HAVE ALL YOUR POWERS AND YOU WILL LIE AS STILL AS YOUR COMPANION!
YOU LIKE TO KILL DO YOU, HUMAN?
--WHEN I MUST!
SO DO I--
YOU ARE MEAT TO BE WASTED!
YOUR BLOOD WILL FALL ON BARE ROCK--
--AND NOURISH NOTHING!

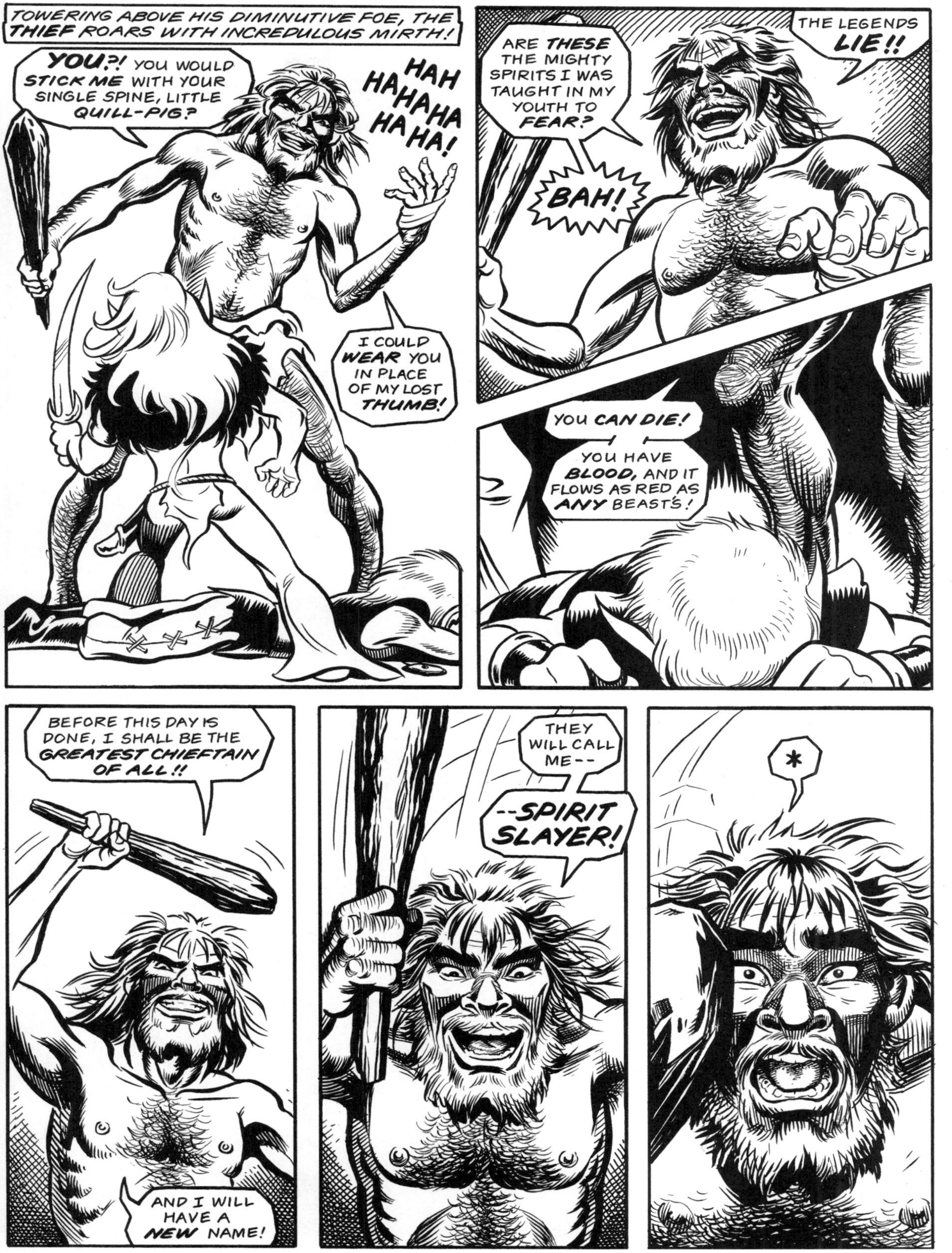

TOWERING ABOVE HIS DIMINUTIVE FOE, THE THIEF ROARS WITH INCREDULOUS MIRTH!
YOU?! YOU WOULD STICK ME WITH YOUR SINGLE SPINE, LITTLE QUILL-PIG?
HAH HA HA HA HA HA HA!
I COULD WEAR YOU IN PLACE OF MY LOST THUMB!
ARE THESE THE MIGHTY SPIRITS I WAS TAUGHT IN MY YOUTH TO FEAR?
THE LEGENDS LIE!!
BAH!
YOU CAN DIE!
YOU HAVE BLOOD, AND IT FLOWS AS RED AS ANY BEAST'S!
BEFORE THIS DAY IS DONE, I SHALL BE THE GREATEST CHIEFTAIN OF ALL!!
AND I WILL HAVE A NEW NAME!
THEY WILL CALL ME--
--SPIRIT SLAYER!
*

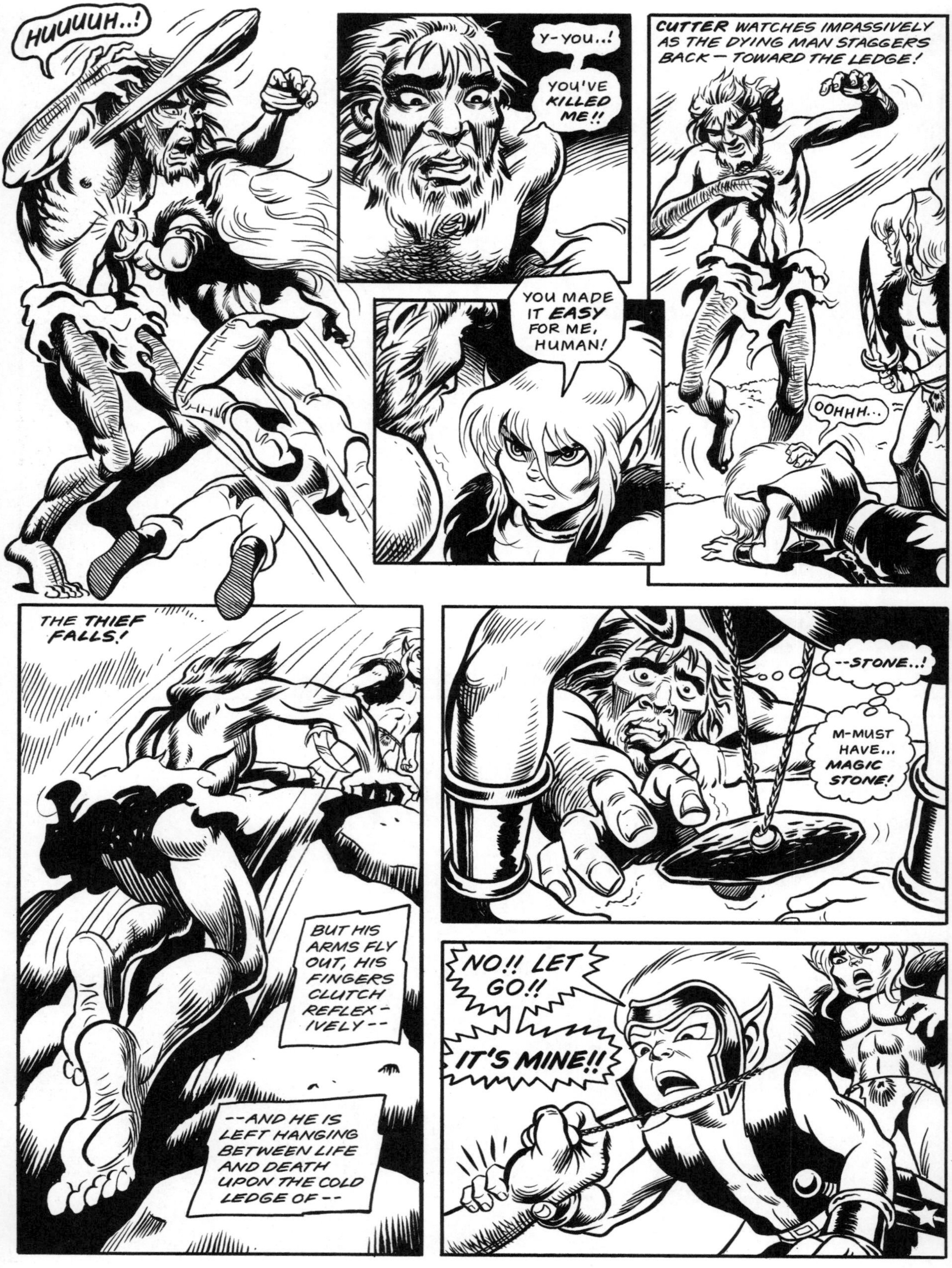
HUUUUH..!
Y-YOU..!
YOU'VE KILLED ME!!
YOU MADE IT EASY FOR ME, HUMAN!
CUTTER WATCHES IMPASSIVELY AS THE DYING MAN STAGGERS BACK — TOWARD THE LEDGE!
OOHHH...
THE THIEF FALLS!
BUT HIS ARMS FLY OUT, HIS FINGERS CLUTCH REFLEX-IVELY--
--AND HE IS LEFT HANGING BETWEEN LIFE AND DEATH UPON THE COLD LEDGE OF--
--STONE..!
M-MUST HAVE... MAGIC STONE!
NO!! LET GO!!
IT'S MINE!!

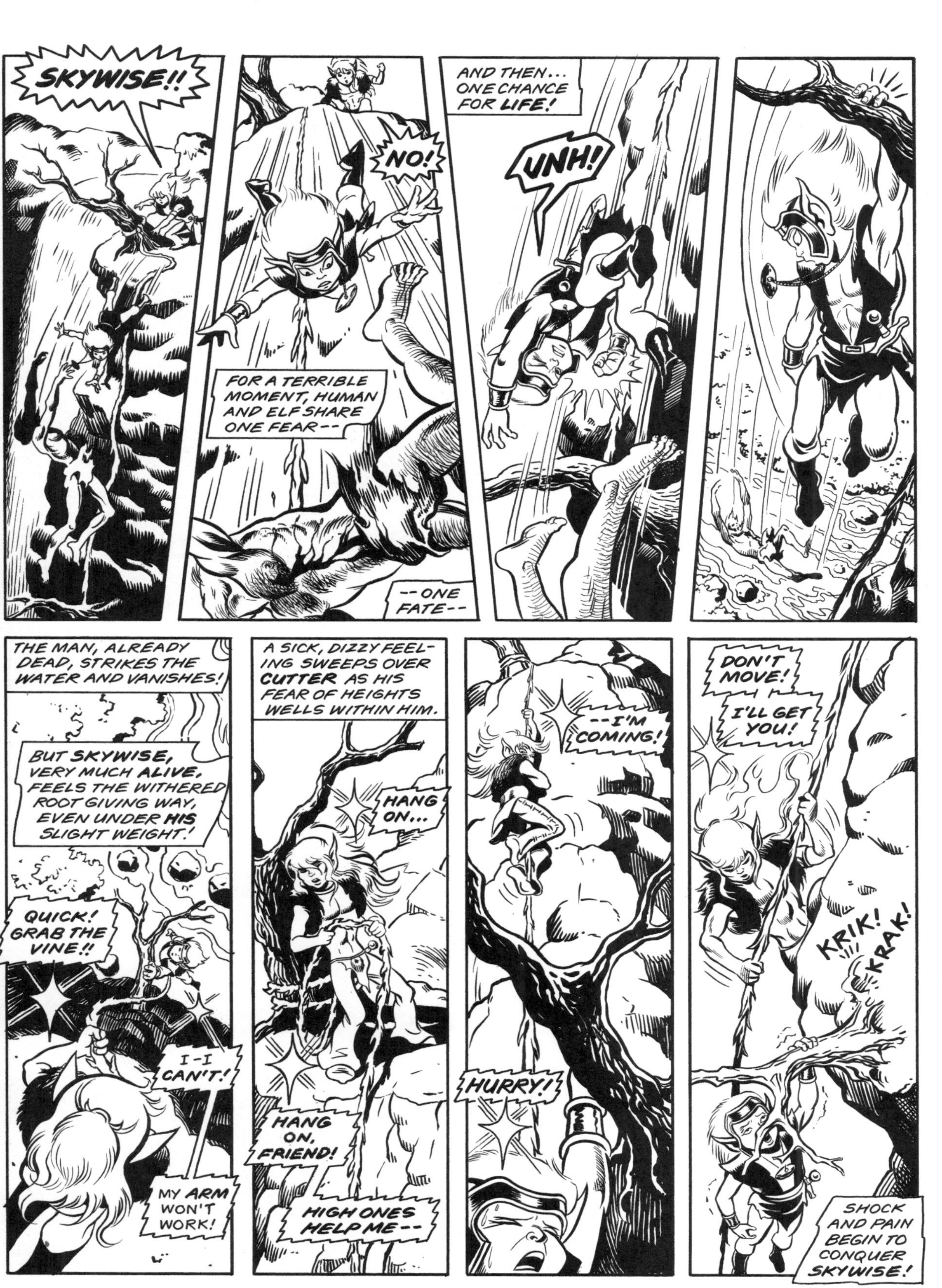
SKYWISE!!
NO!
FOR A TERRIBLE MOMENT, HUMAN AND ELF SHARE ONE FEAR--
--ONE FATE--
AND THEN... ONE CHANCE FOR LIFE!
UNH!
THE MAN, ALREADY DEAD, STRIKES THE WATER AND VANISHES!
BUT SKYWISE, VERY MUCH ALIVE, FEELS THE WITHERED ROOT GIVING WAY, EVEN UNDER HIS SLIGHT WEIGHT!
QUICK! GRAB THE VINE!!
I-I CAN'T!
MY ARM WON'T WORK!
A SICK, DIZZY FEELING SWEEPS OVER CUTTER AS HIS FEAR OF HEIGHTS WELLS WITHIN HIM.
HANG ON...
HANG ON, FRIEND!
HIGH ONES HELP ME--
--I'M COMING!
HURRY!
DON'T MOVE!
I'LL GET YOU!
KRIK! KRAK!
SHOCK AND PAIN BEGIN TO CONQUER SKYWISE!

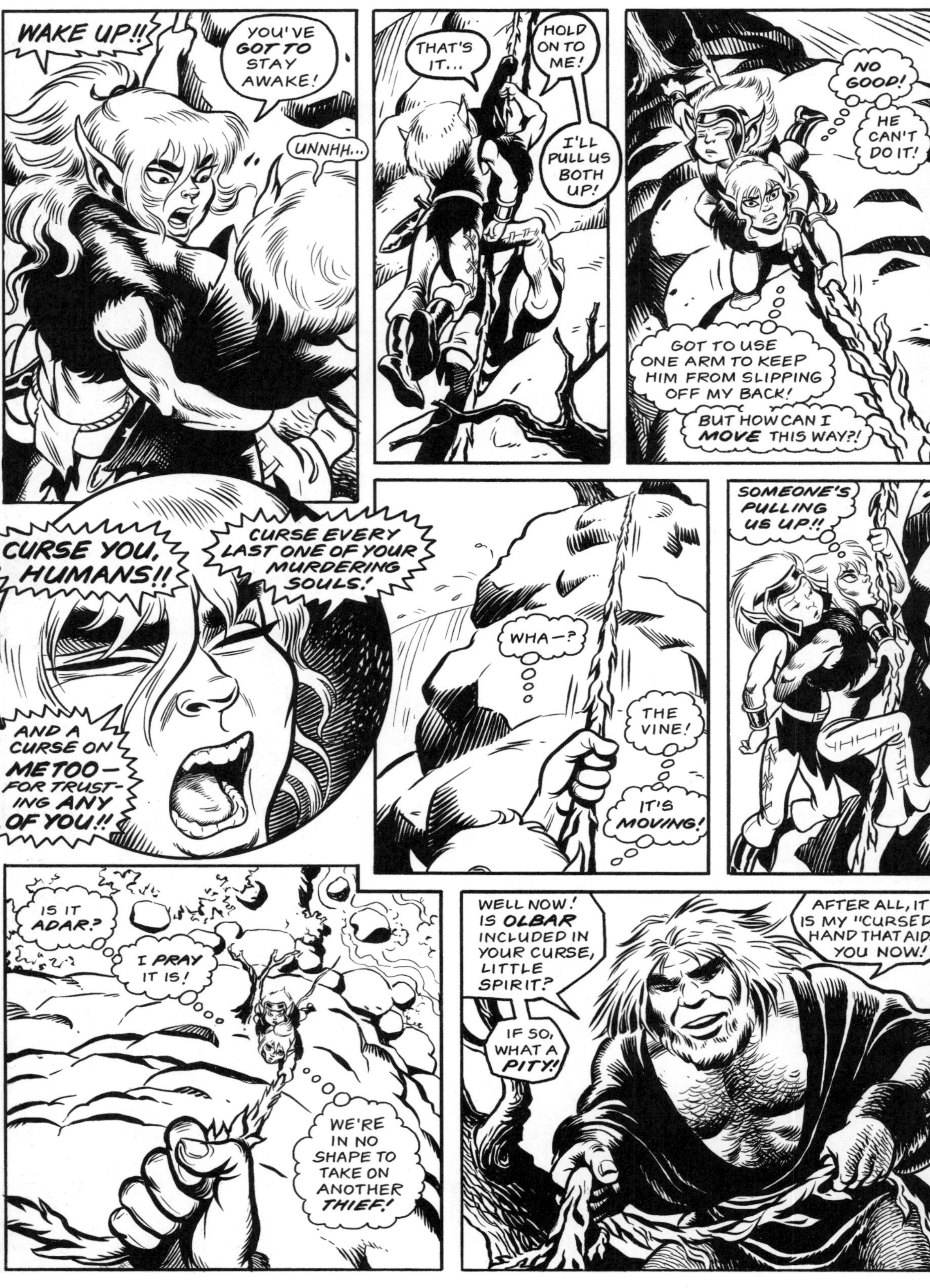
WAKE UP!!
YOU'VE GOT TO STAY AWAKE!
UNNHH...
THAT'S IT...
HOLD ON TO ME!
I'LL PULL US BOTH UP!
NO GOOD!
HE CAN'T DO IT!
GOT TO USE ONE ARM TO KEEP HIM FROM SLIPPING OFF MY BACK!
BUT HOW CAN I MOVE THIS WAY?!
CURSE YOU, HUMANS!!
CURSE EVERY LAST ONE OF YOUR MURDERING SOULS!
AND A CURSE ON METOO— FOR TRUSTING ANY OF YOU!!
WHA—?
THE VINE!
IT'S MOVING!
SOMEONE'S PULLING US UP!!
IS IT ADAR?
I PRAY IT IS!
WE'RE IN NO SHAPE TO TAKE ON ANOTHER THIEF!
WELL NOW! IS OLBAR INCLUDED IN YOUR CURSE, LITTLE SPIRIT?
IF SO, WHAT A PITY!
AFTER ALL, IT IS MY "CURSED" HAND THAT AIDS YOU NOW!

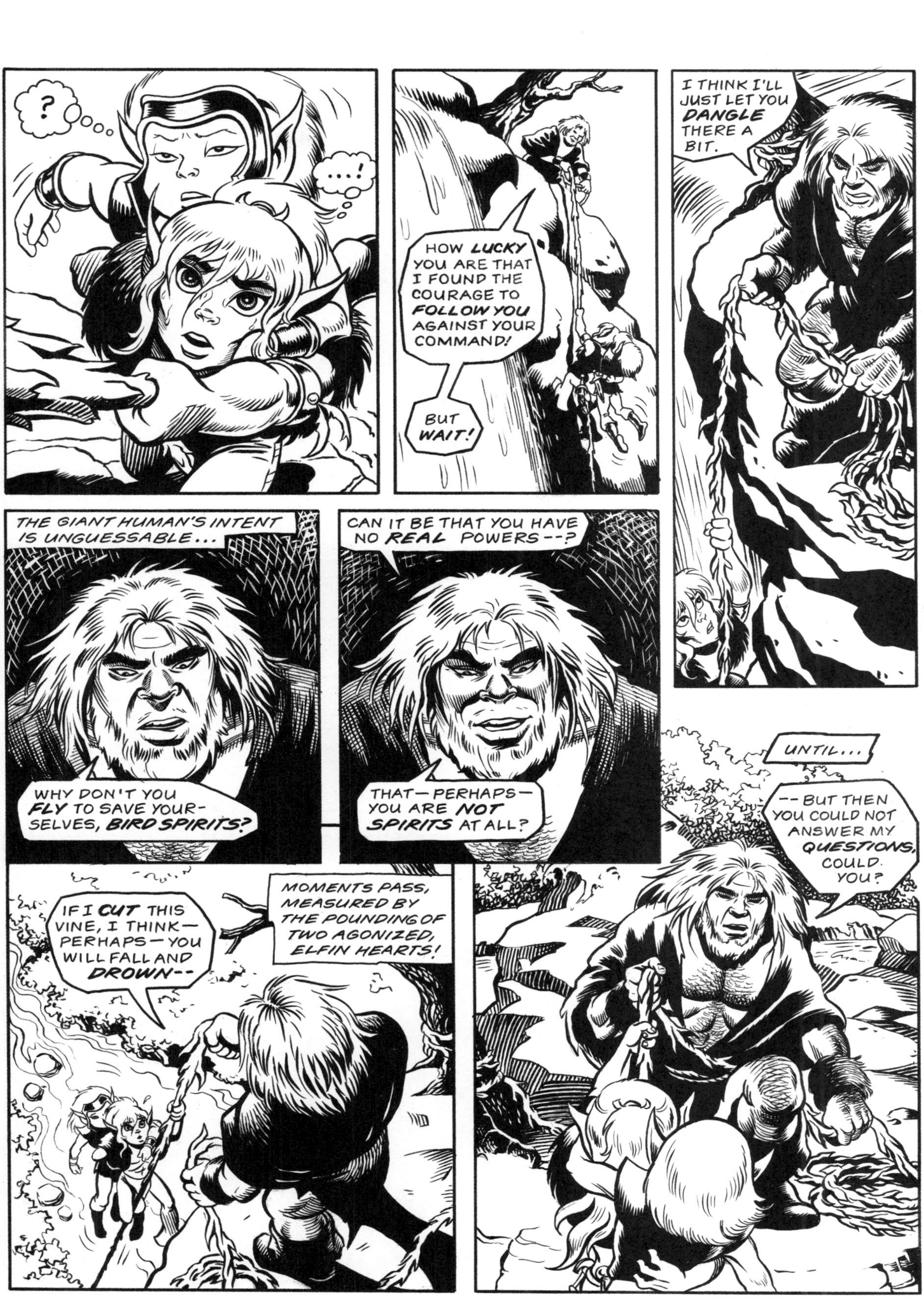
?
...!
HOW LUCKY YOU ARE THAT I FOUND THE COURAGE TO FOLLOW YOU AGAINST YOUR COMMAND!
BUT WAIT!
I THINK I'LL JUST LET YOU DANGLE THERE A BIT.
THE GIANT HUMAN'S INTENT IS UNGUESSABLE...
WHY DON'T YOU FLY TO SAVE YOURSELVES, BIRD SPIRITS?
CAN IT BE THAT YOU HAVE NO REAL POWERS--?
THAT—PERHAPS—YOU ARE NOT SPIRITS AT ALL?
IF I CUT THIS VINE, I THINK—PERHAPS—YOU WILL FALL AND DROWN--
MOMENTS PASS, MEASURED BY THE POUNDING OF TWO AGONIZED, ELFIN HEARTS!
UNTIL...
--BUT THEN YOU COULD NOT ANSWER MY QUESTIONS, COULD YOU?

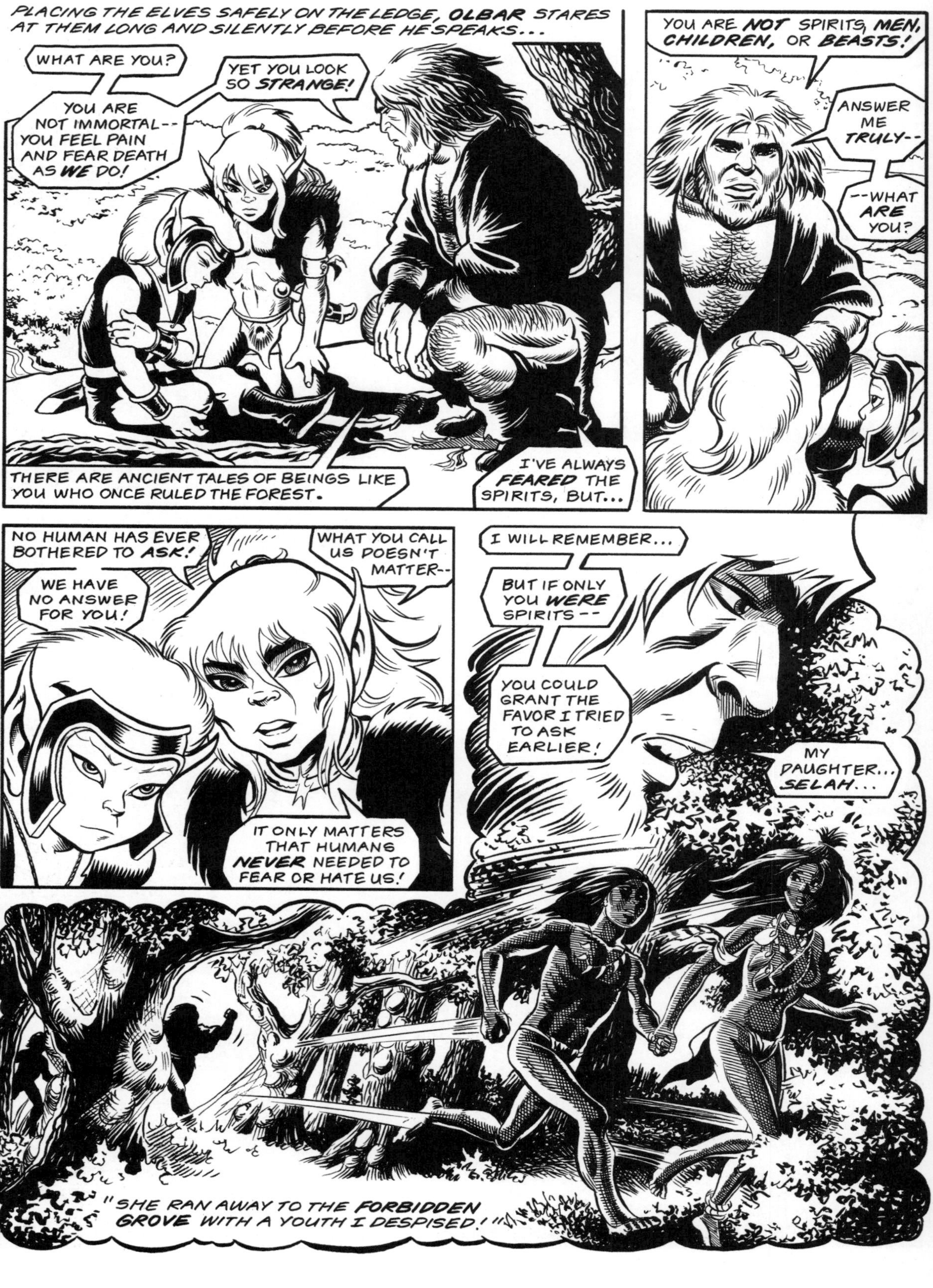

PLACING THE ELVES SAFELY ON THE LEDGE, OLBAR STARES AT THEM LONG AND SILENTLY BEFORE HE SPEAKS...
WHAT ARE YOU?
YOU ARE NOT IMMORTAL-- YOU FEEL PAIN AND FEAR DEATH AS WE DO!
YET YOU LOOK SO STRANGE!
THERE ARE ANCIENT TALES OF BEINGS LIKE YOU WHO ONCE RULED THE FOREST.
I'VE ALWAYS FEARED THE SPIRITS, BUT...
YOU ARE NOT SPIRITS, MEN, CHILDREN, OR BEASTS!
ANSWER ME TRULY--
--WHAT ARE YOU?
NO HUMAN HAS EVER BOTHERED TO ASK!
WE HAVE NO ANSWER FOR YOU!
WHAT YOU CALL US DOESN'T MATTER--
IT ONLY MATTERS THAT HUMANS NEVER NEEDED TO FEAR OR HATE US!
I WILL REMEMBER...
BUT IF ONLY YOU WERE SPIRITS--
YOU COULD GRANT THE FAVOR I TRIED TO ASK EARLIER!
MY DAUGHTER... SELAH...
"SHE RAN AWAY TO THE FORBIDDEN GROVE WITH A YOUTH I DESPISED!"

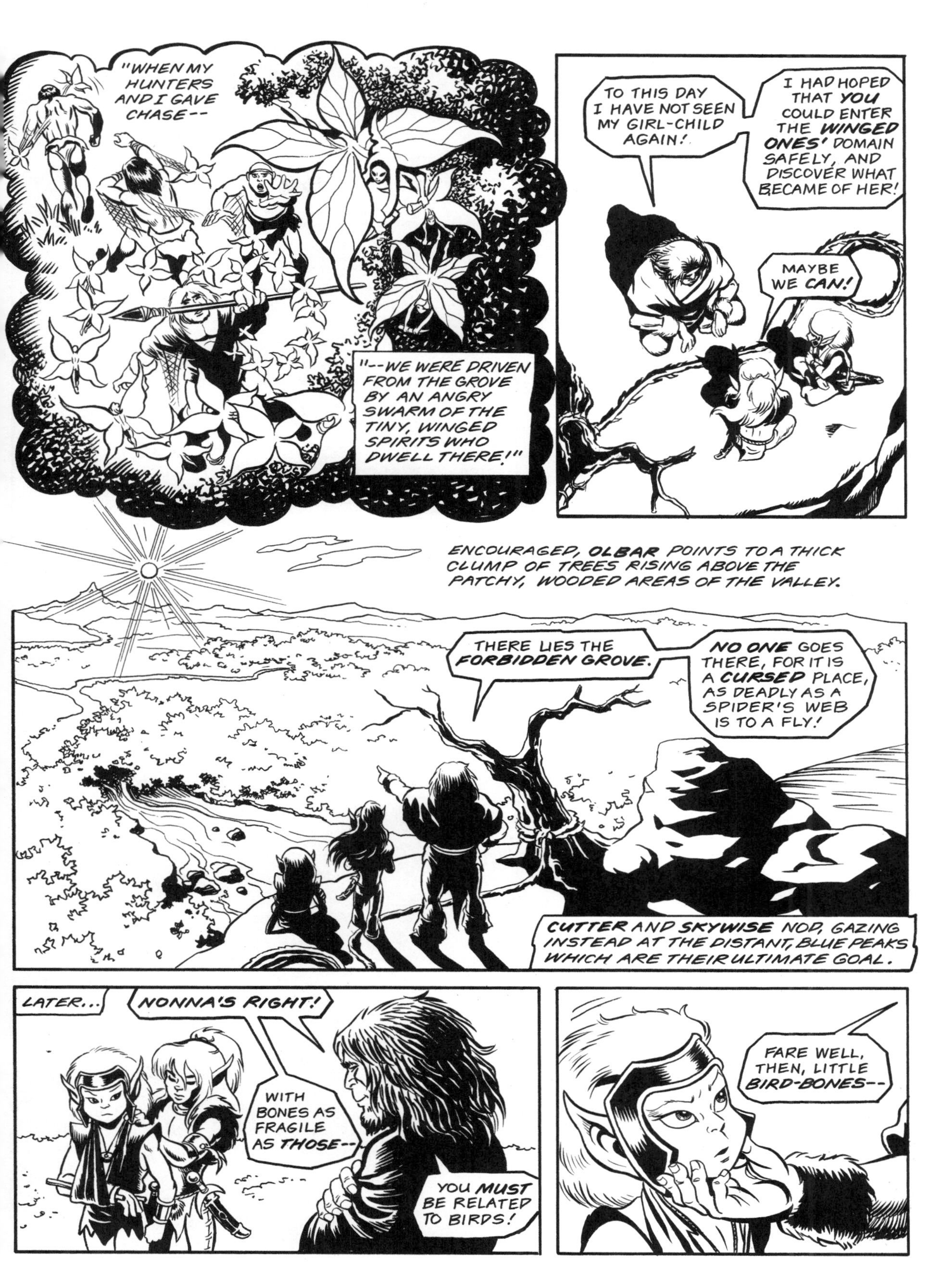
"WHEN MY HUNTERS AND I GAVE CHASE--
"--WE WERE DRIVEN FROM THE GROVE BY AN ANGRY SWARM OF THE TINY, WINGED SPIRITS WHO DWELL THERE!"
TO THIS DAY I HAVE NOT SEEN MY GIRL-CHILD AGAIN!
I HAD HOPED THAT YOU COULD ENTER THE WINGED ONES' DOMAIN SAFELY, AND DISCOVER WHAT BECAME OF HER!
MAYBE WE CAN!
ENCOURAGED, OLBAR POINTS TO A THICK CLUMP OF TREES RISING ABOVE THE PATCHY, WOODED AREAS OF THE VALLEY.
THERE LIES THE FORBIDDEN GROVE.
NO ONE GOES THERE, FOR IT IS A CURSED PLACE, AS DEADLY AS A SPIDER'S WEB IS TO A FLY!
CUTTER AND SKYWISE NOD, GAZING INSTEAD AT THE DISTANT, BLUE PEAKS WHICH ARE THEIR ULTIMATE GOAL.
LATER...
NONNA'S RIGHT!
WITH BONES AS FRAGILE AS THOSE--
YOU MUST BE RELATED TO BIRDS!
FARE WELL, THEN, LITTLE BIRD-BONES--

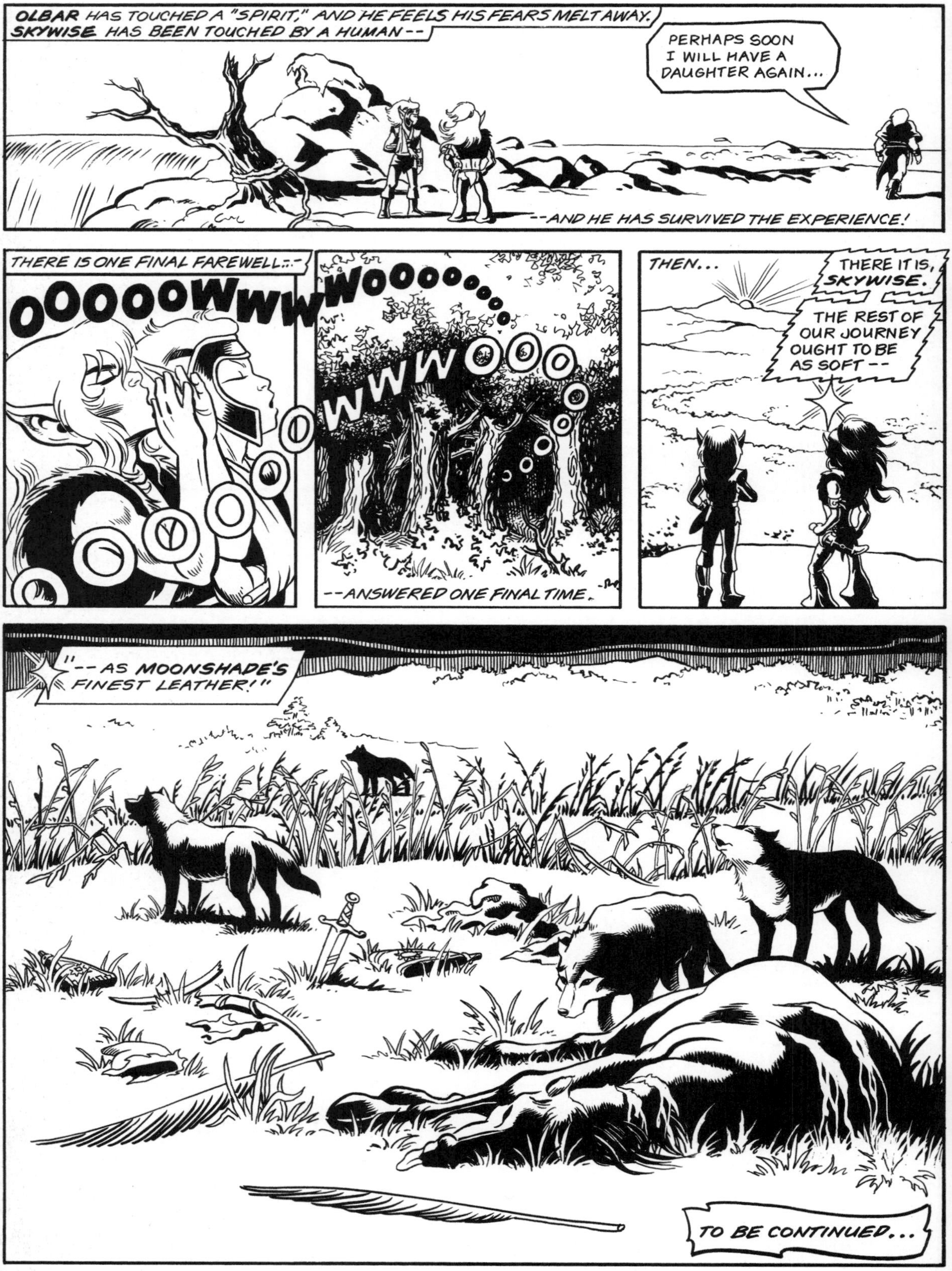
OLBAR HAS TOUCHED A "SPIRIT," AND HE FEELS HIS FEARS MELT AWAY.
SKYWISE HAS BEEN TOUCHED BY A HUMAN--
PERHAPS SOON I WILL HAVE A DAUGHTER AGAIN...
--AND HE HAS SURVIVED THE EXPERIENCE!
THERE IS ONE FINAL FAREWELL...-
OOOOOOWWWWWOOOOOOOOO
WWWOOOO
--ANSWERED ONE FINAL TIME.
THEN...
THERE IT IS, SKYWISE.
THE REST OF OUR JOURNEY OUGHT TO BE AS SOFT --
"--AS MOONSHADE'S FINEST LEATHER!"
TO BE CONTINUED...

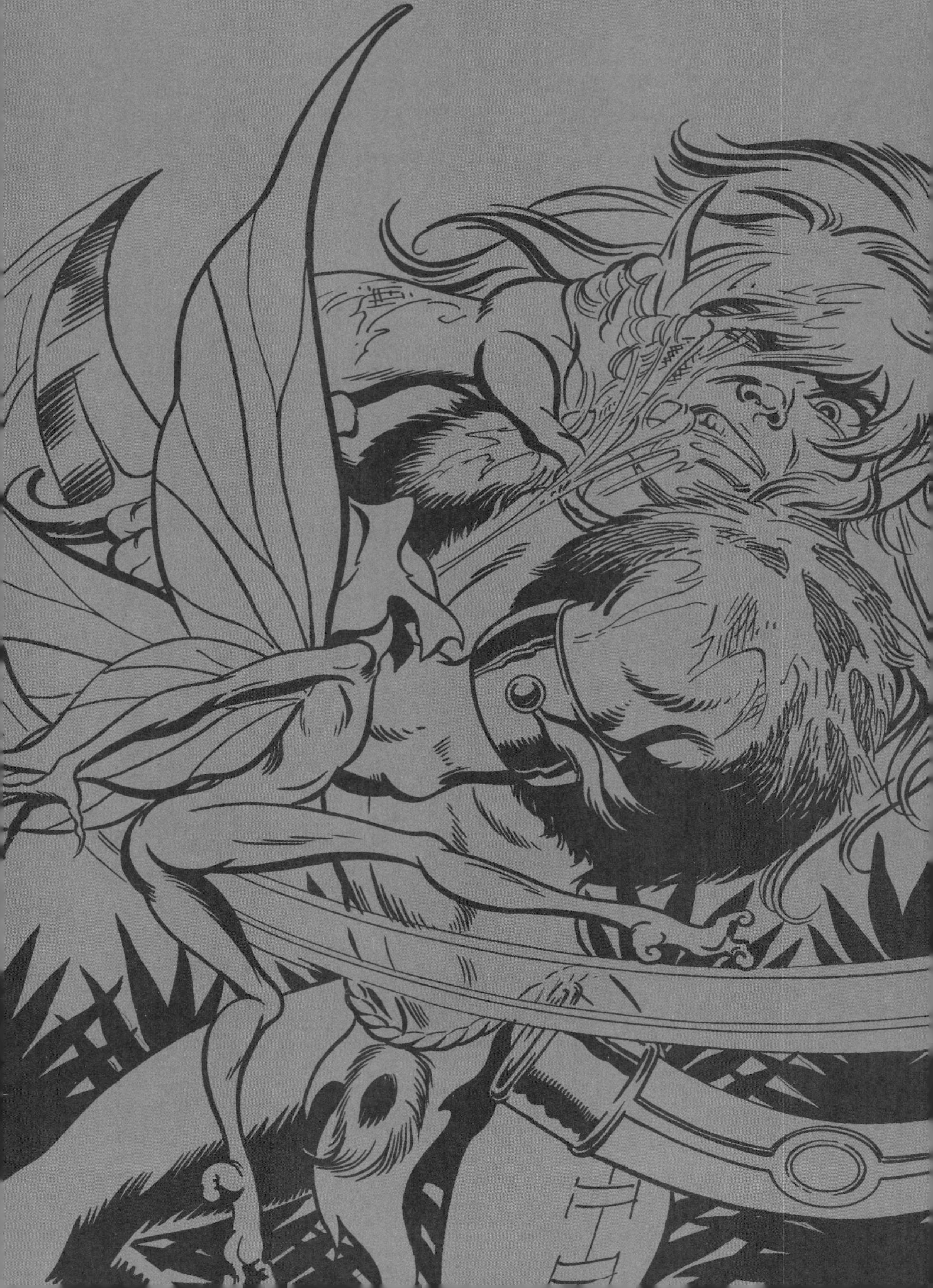

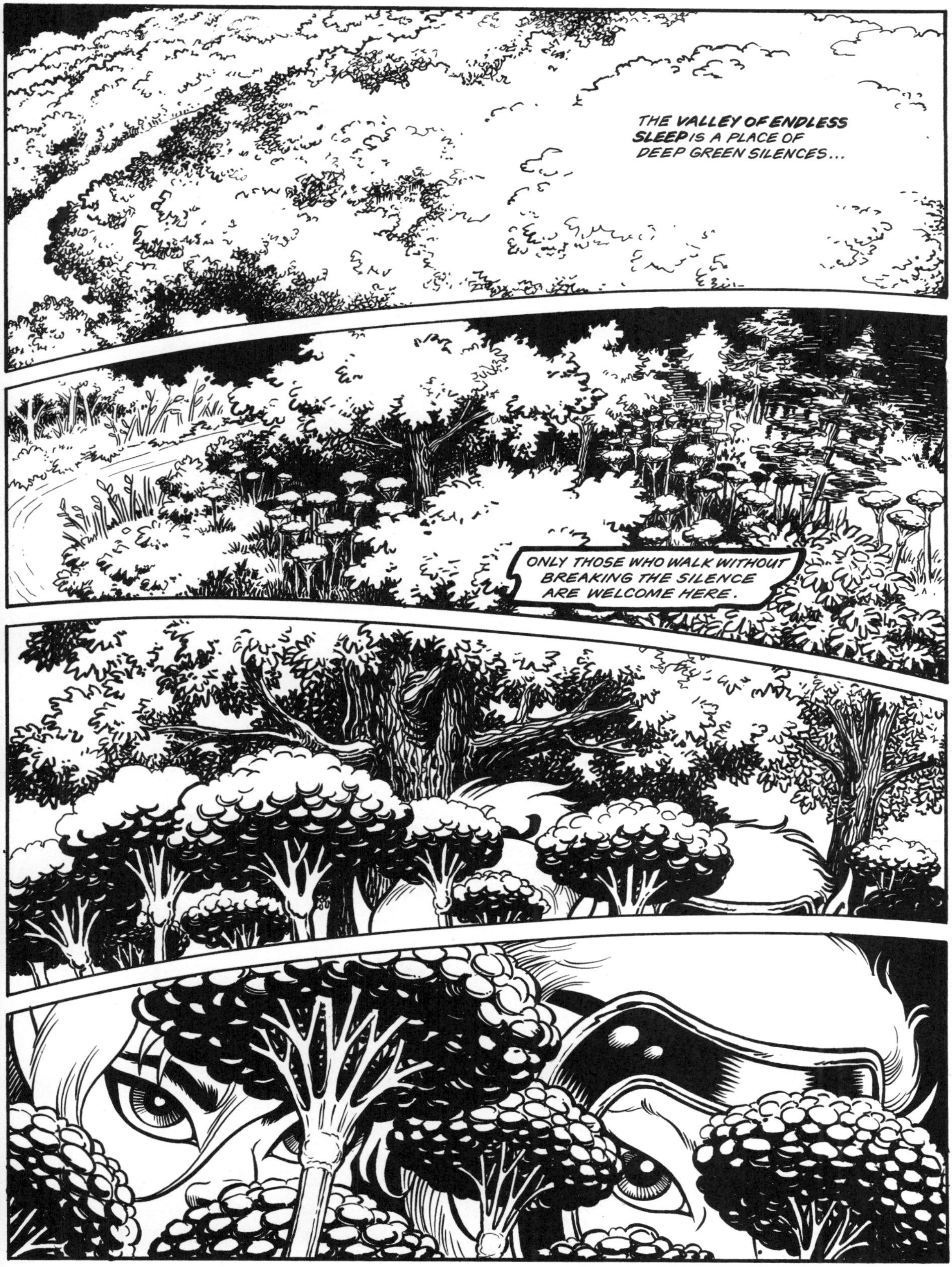
THE VALLEY OF ENDLESS SLEEP IS A PLACE OF DEEP GREEN SILENCES...
ONLY THOSE WHO WALK WITHOUT BREAKING THE SILENCE ARE WELCOME HERE.

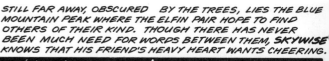

STILL FAR AWAY, OBSCURED BY THE TREES, LIES THE BLUE MOUNTAIN PEAK WHERE THE ELFIN PAIR HOPE TO FIND OTHERS OF THEIR KIND. THOUGH THERE HAS NEVER BEEN MUCH NEED FOR WORDS BETWEEN THEM, SKYWISE KNOWS THAT HIS FRIEND'S HEAVY HEART WANTS CHEERING.

WE'RE TWO NIGHTS CLOSER TO *BLUE MOUNTAIN*, BUT THE NEARER WE GET-- THE LESS *CUTTER* SEEMS TO CARE!

HE MISSES *NIGHTRUNNER* --BUT IT'S MORE THAN THAT.

LOOK! THE TWO STARS I GAVE YOU AND *LEETAH* ON YOUR JOIN-ING NIGHT...

THEY'RE RIGHT OVERHEAD!

HMM... THEY SEEM FAR APART.

BUT ALWAYS TOGETHER!

YES... IT'S GOOD TO KNOW THAT *LEETAH* AND THE CUBS ARE SAFE IN *SORROW'S END.*

SHE WAS *WISE* NOT TO COME WITH ME ON THIS QUEST.

AND I SUPPOSE THAT MAKES *ME* A *FOOL!*

IF YOU HADN'T GRABBED THAT *ROOT* WHEN YOU FELL... IF YOU HAD *DROWNED* IN THE DEATHWATER...

I-I DON'T KNOW WHAT I--

YOU... WOULD HAVE MARCHED RIGHT UP TO THE *BIRD SPIRITS* AND ANNOUNCED YOURSELF WITH YOUR *SWORD!*

LUCKILY *I'M* STILL HERE TO MAKE APOLOGIES FOR MY CHIEF--

--WHO *STILL* HAS A FOUL DISPOSITION AND THE MANNERS OF A *TROLL!*

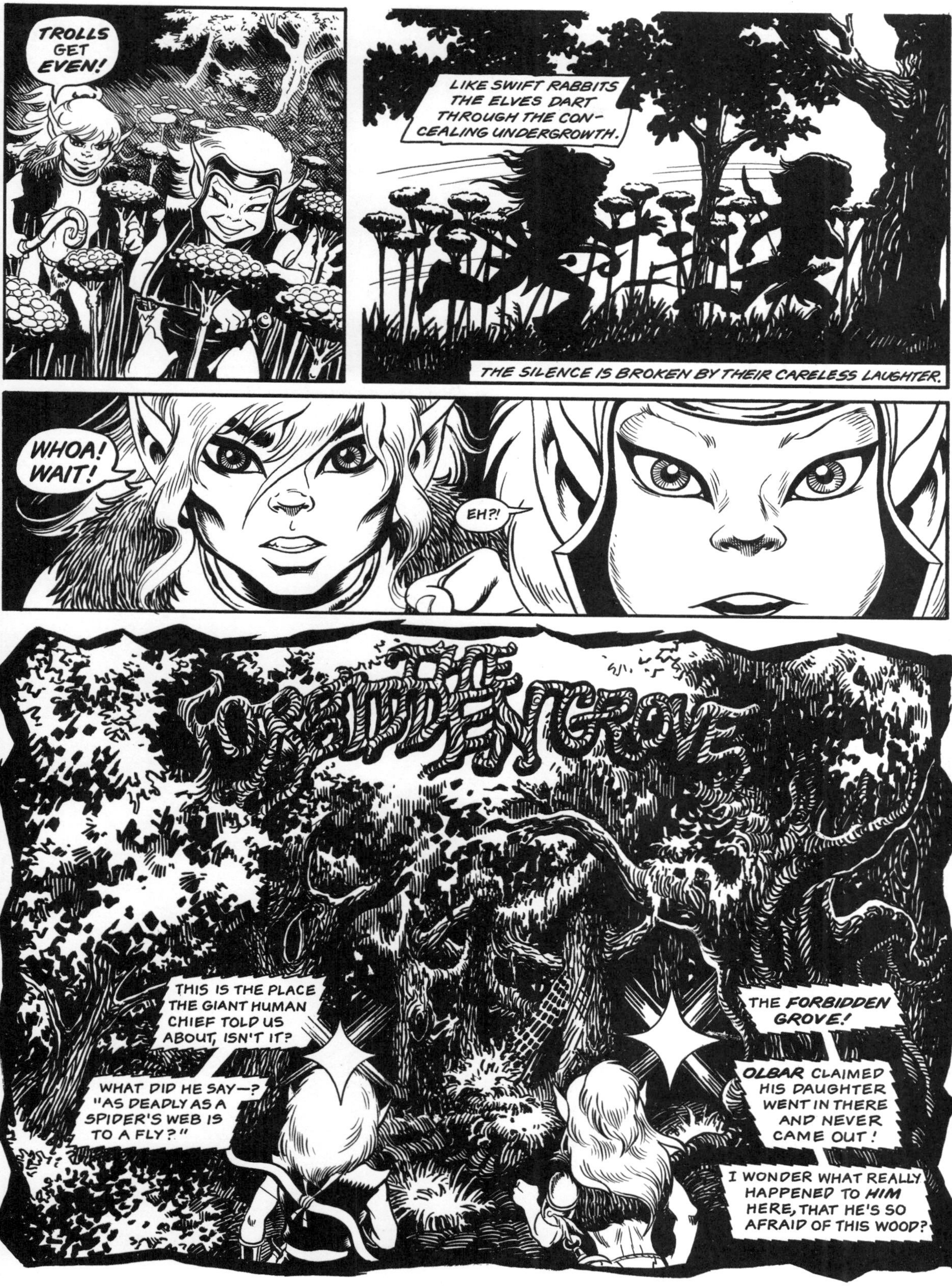
TROLLS GET EVEN!
LIKE SWIFT RABBITS THE ELVES DART THROUGH THE CON-CEALING UNDERGROWTH.
THE SILENCE IS BROKEN BY THEIR CARELESS LAUGHTER.
WHOA! WAIT!
EH?!
THE FORBIDDEN GROVE
THIS IS THE PLACE THE GIANT HUMAN CHIEF TOLD US ABOUT, ISN'T IT?
WHAT DID HE SAY—? "AS DEADLY AS A SPIDER'S WEB IS TO A FLY?"
THE FORBIDDEN GROVE!
OLBAR CLAIMED HIS DAUGHTER WENT IN THERE AND NEVER CAME OUT!
I WONDER WHAT REALLY HAPPENED TO HIM HERE, THAT HE'S SO AFRAID OF THIS WOOD?

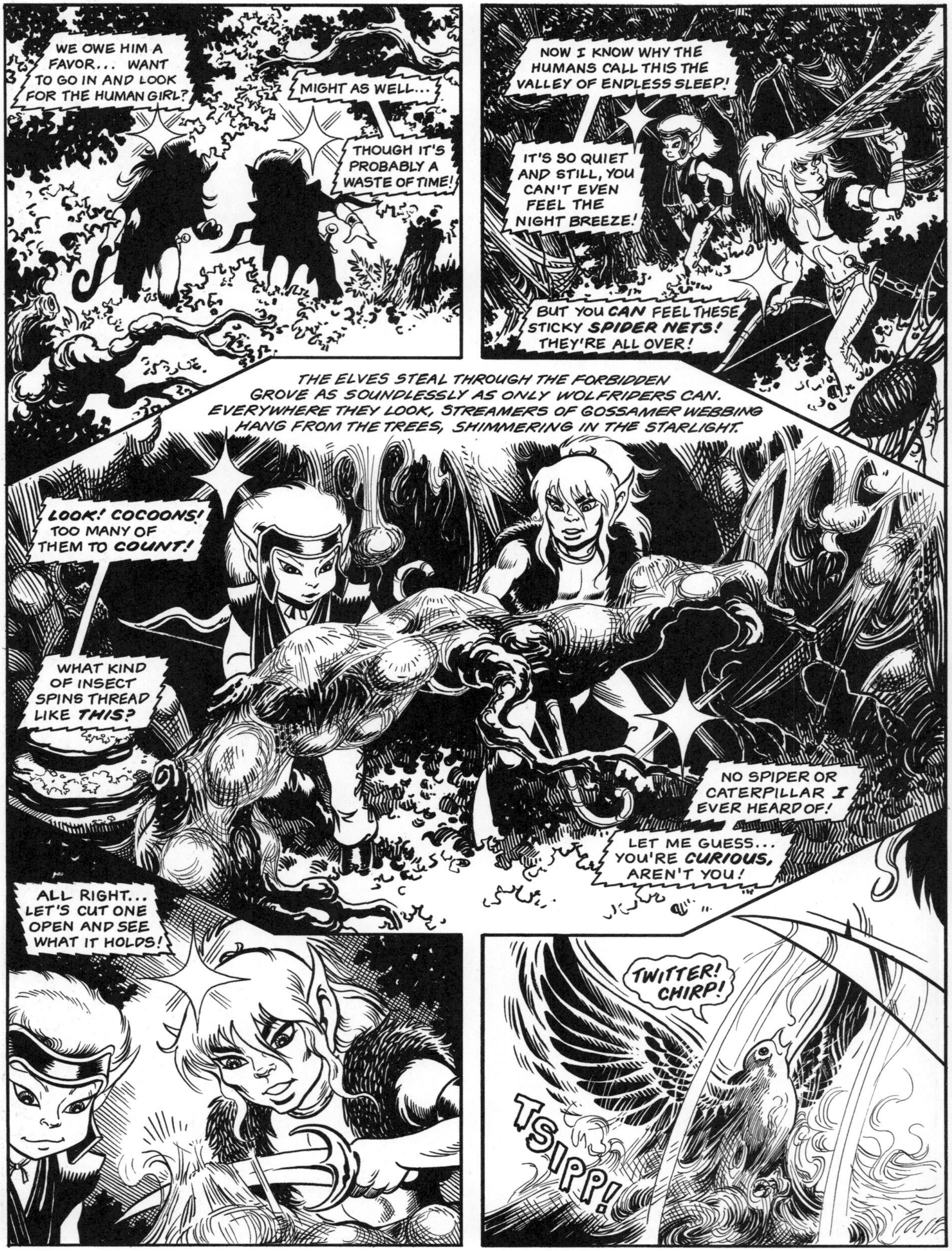
WE OWE HIM A FAVOR... WANT TO GO IN AND LOOK FOR THE HUMAN GIRL?
MIGHT AS WELL...
THOUGH IT'S PROBABLY A WASTE OF TIME!
NOW I KNOW WHY THE HUMANS CALL THIS THE VALLEY OF ENDLESS SLEEP!
IT'S SO QUIET AND STILL, YOU CAN'T EVEN FEEL THE NIGHT BREEZE!
BUT YOU CAN FEEL THESE STICKY SPIDER NETS! THEY'RE ALL OVER!
THE ELVES STEAL THROUGH THE FORBIDDEN GROVE AS SOUNDLESSLY AS ONLY WOLFRIDERS CAN. EVERYWHERE THEY LOOK, STREAMERS OF GOSSAMER WEBBING HANG FROM THE TREES, SHIMMERING IN THE STARLIGHT.
LOOK! COCOONS! TOO MANY OF THEM TO COUNT!
WHAT KIND OF INSECT SPINS THREAD LIKE THIS?
NO SPIDER OR CATERPILLAR I EVER HEARD OF!
LET ME GUESS... YOU'RE CURIOUS, AREN'T YOU!
ALL RIGHT... LET'S CUT ONE OPEN AND SEE WHAT IT HOLDS!
TWITTER! CHIRP!
TSIPP!

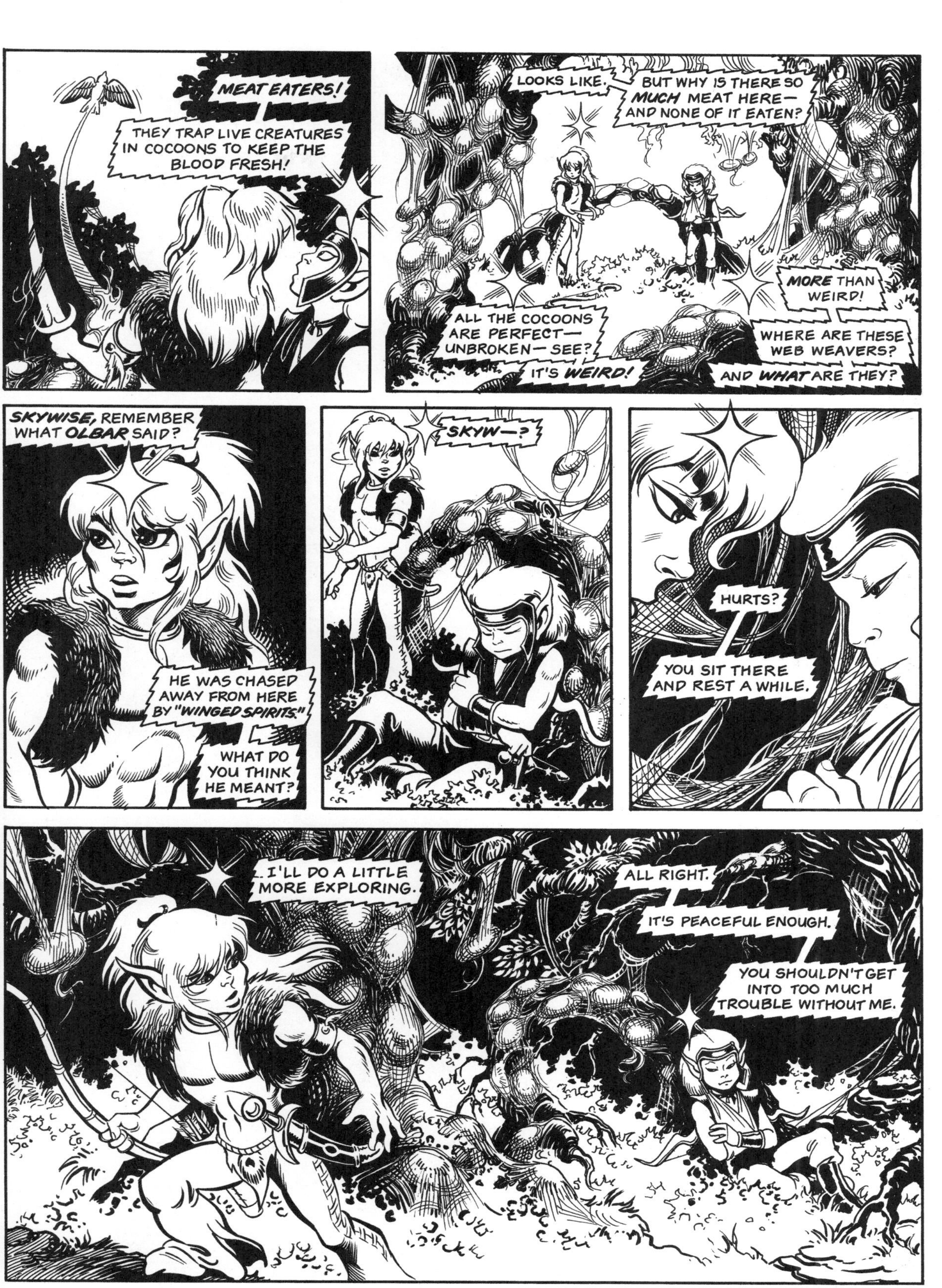

MEAT EATERS!
THEY TRAP LIVE CREATURES IN COCOONS TO KEEP THE BLOOD FRESH!
LOOKS LIKE.
BUT WHY IS THERE SO MUCH MEAT HERE— AND NONE OF IT EATEN?
ALL THE COCOONS ARE PERFECT— UNBROKEN— SEE?
IT'S WEIRD!
MORE THAN WEIRD!
WHERE ARE THESE WEB WEAVERS?
AND WHAT ARE THEY?
SKYWISE, REMEMBER WHAT OLBAR SAID?
HE WAS CHASED AWAY FROM HERE BY "WINGED SPIRITS."
WHAT DO YOU THINK HE MEANT?
SKYW—?
HURTS?
YOU SIT THERE AND REST A WHILE.
I'LL DO A LITTLE MORE EXPLORING.
ALL RIGHT.
IT'S PEACEFUL ENOUGH.
YOU SHOULDN'T GET INTO TOO MUCH TROUBLE WITHOUT ME.

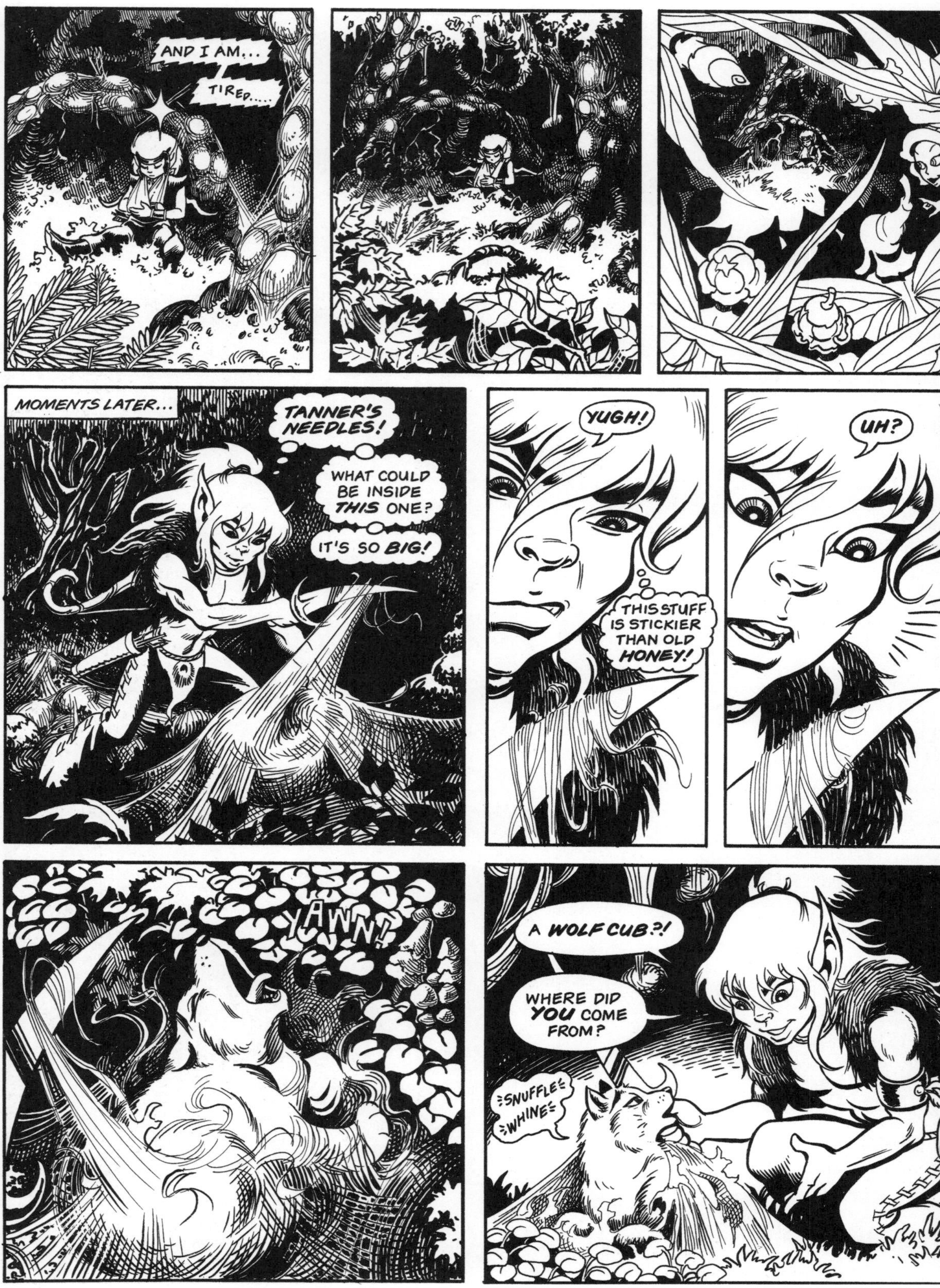
AND I AM...
TIRED.....
MOMENTS LATER...
TANNER'S NEEDLES!
WHAT COULD BE INSIDE THIS ONE?
IT'S SO BIG!
YUGH!
THIS STUFF IS STICKIER THAN OLD HONEY!
UH?
YAWN!
A WOLF CUB?!
WHERE DID YOU COME FROM?
SNUFFLE
WHINE

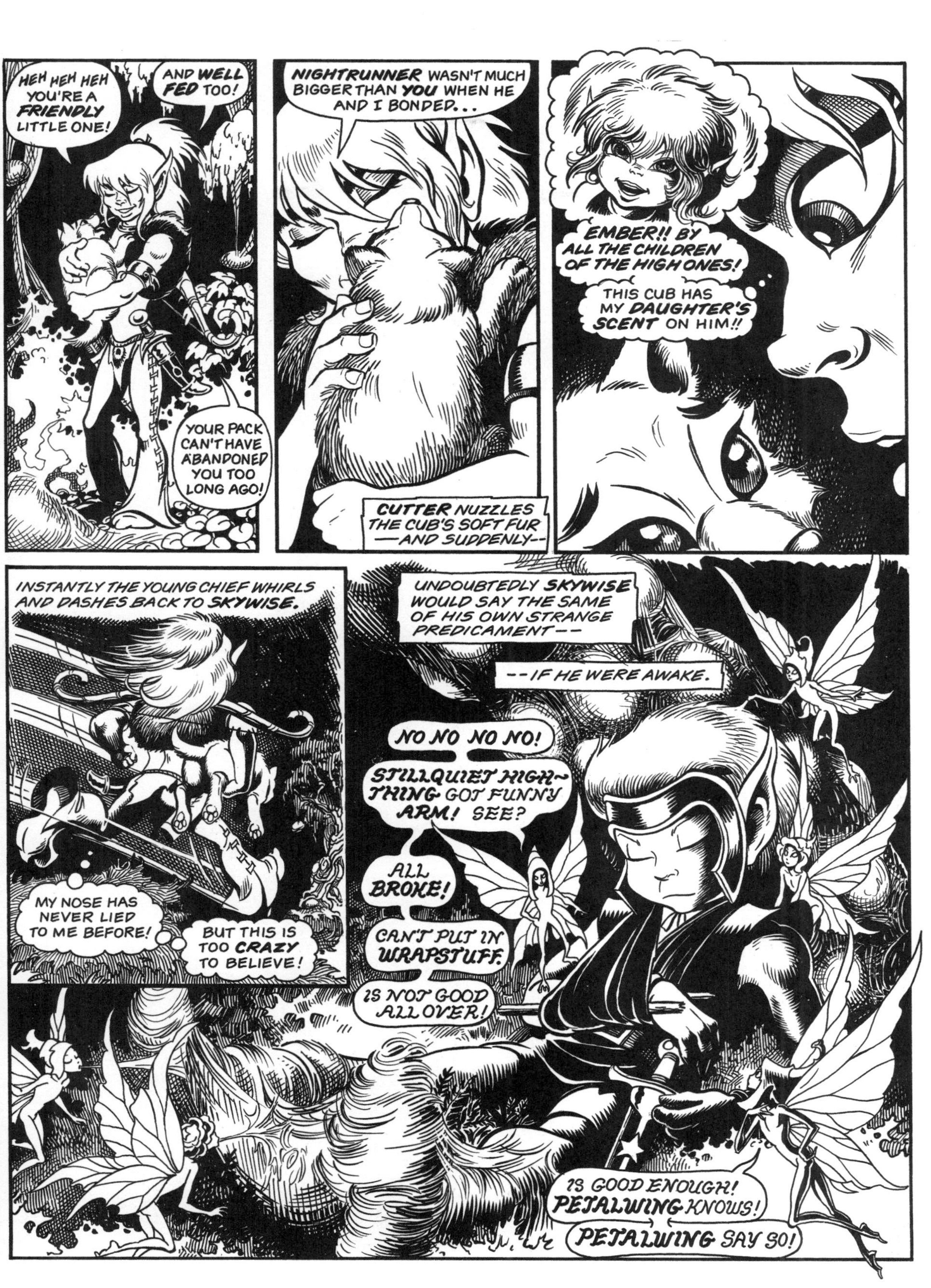
HEH HEH HEH YOU'RE A FRIENDLY LITTLE ONE!
AND WELL FED TOO!
YOUR PACK CAN'T HAVE ABANDONED YOU TOO LONG AGO!
NIGHTRUNNER WASN'T MUCH BIGGER THAN YOU WHEN HE AND I BONDED...
CUTTER NUZZLES THE CUB'S SOFT FUR —AND SUDDENLY—
EMBER!! BY ALL THE CHILDREN OF THE HIGH ONES!
THIS CUB HAS MY DAUGHTER'S SCENT ON HIM!!
INSTANTLY THE YOUNG CHIEF WHIRLS AND DASHES BACK TO SKYWISE.
MY NOSE HAS NEVER LIED TO ME BEFORE!
BUT THIS IS TOO CRAZY TO BELIEVE!
UNDOUBTEDLY SKYWISE WOULD SAY THE SAME OF HIS OWN STRANGE PREDICAMENT --
--IF HE WERE AWAKE.
NO NO NO NO!
STILLQUIET HIGH-THING GOT FUNNY ARM! SEE?
ALL BROKE!
CAN'T PUT IN WRAPSTUFF.
IS NOT GOOD ALL OVER!
IS GOOD ENOUGH! PETALWING KNOWS!
PETALWING SAY SO!

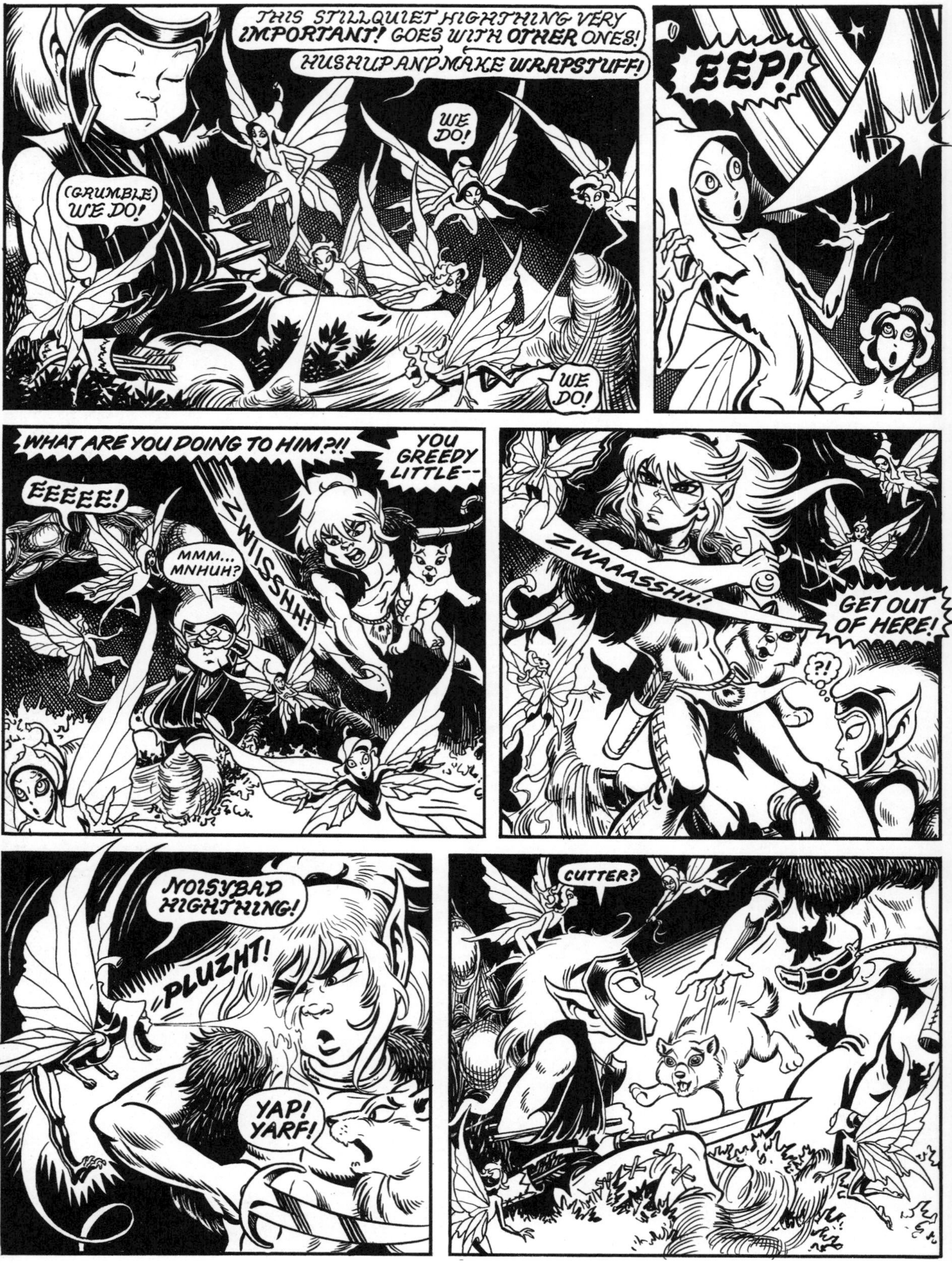
THIS STILLQUIET HIGHTHING VERY IMPORTANT! GOES WITH OTHER ONES!
HUSHUP AND MAKE WRAPSTUFF!
WE DO!
(GRUMBLE) WE DO!
WE DO!
EEP!
WHAT ARE YOU DOING TO HIM?!!
YOU GREEDY LITTLE--
EEEEE!
ZWIISSHH!
MMM... MNHUH?
ZWAAAASSHH!
GET OUT OF HERE!
?!
NOISYBAD HIGHTHING!
PLUZHT!
YAP! YARF!
CUTTER?

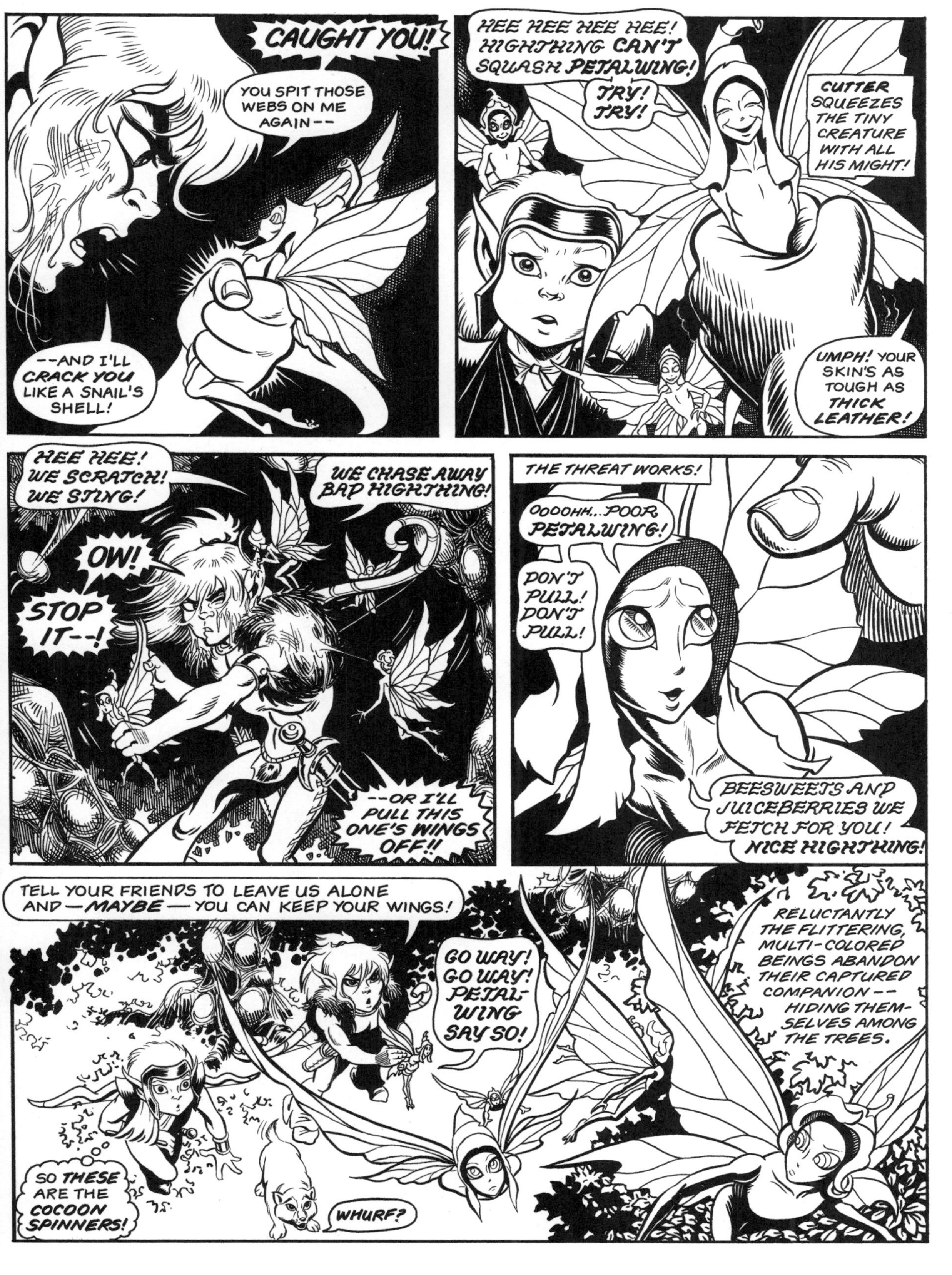

CAUGHT YOU!
YOU SPIT THOSE WEBS ON ME AGAIN--
--AND I'LL CRACK YOU LIKE A SNAIL'S SHELL!
HEE HEE HEE HEE! HIGHTHING CAN'T SQUASH PETALWING!
TRY! TRY!
CUTTER SQUEEZES THE TINY CREATURE WITH ALL HIS MIGHT!
UMPH! YOUR SKIN'S AS TOUGH AS THICK LEATHER!
HEE HEE! WE SCRATCH! WE STING!
WE CHASE AWAY BAD HIGHTHING!
OW!
STOP IT--!
--OR I'LL PULL THIS ONE'S WINGS OFF!!
THE THREAT WORKS!
OOOOHH... POOR PETALWING!
DON'T PULL! DON'T PULL!
BEESWEETS AND JUICEBERRIES WE FETCH FOR YOU! NICE HIGHTHING!
TELL YOUR FRIENDS TO LEAVE US ALONE AND — MAYBE — YOU CAN KEEP YOUR WINGS!
GO WAY! GO WAY! PETAL-WING SAY SO!
RELUCTANTLY THE FLITTERING, MULTI-COLORED BEINGS ABANDON THEIR CAPTURED COMPANION -- HIDING THEM-SELVES AMONG THE TREES.
SO THESE ARE THE COCOON SPINNERS!
WHURF?

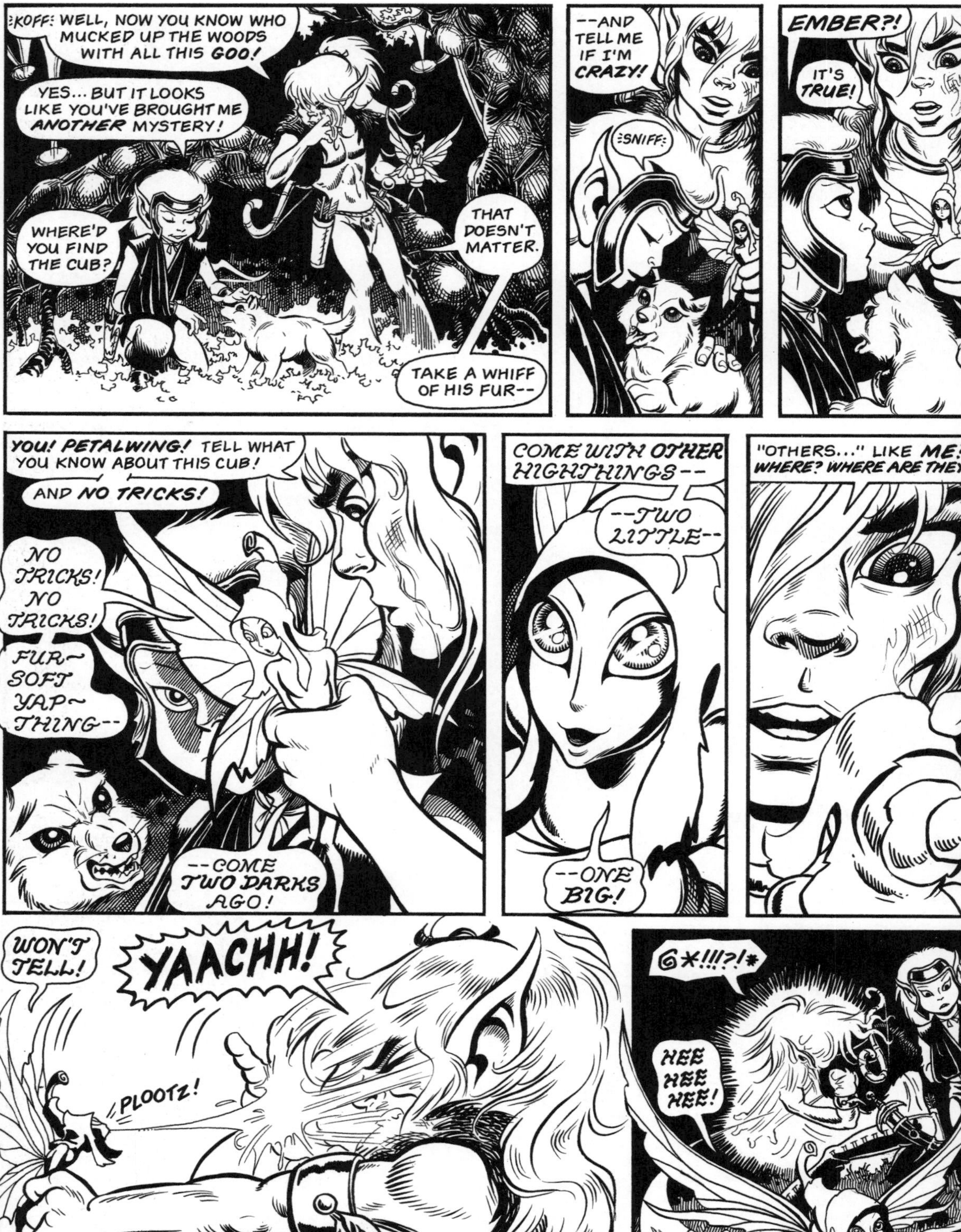
KOFF: WELL, NOW YOU KNOW WHO MUCKED UP THE WOODS WITH ALL THIS GOO!
YES... BUT IT LOOKS LIKE YOU'VE BROUGHT ME ANOTHER MYSTERY!
WHERE'D YOU FIND THE CUB?
THAT DOESN'T MATTER.
TAKE A WHIFF OF HIS FUR--
--AND TELL ME IF I'M CRAZY!
SNIFF
EMBER?!
IT'S TRUE!
YOU! PETALWING! TELL WHAT YOU KNOW ABOUT THIS CUB!
AND NO TRICKS!
NO TRICKS! NO TRICKS!
FUR-SOFT YAP-THING--
--COME TWO DARKS AGO!
COME WITH OTHER HIGHTHINGS--
--TWO LITTLE--
--ONE BIG!
"OTHERS..." LIKE ME? WHERE? WHERE ARE THEY?
WON'T TELL!
YAACHH!
PLOOTZ!
6*!!!?!*
HEE HEE HEE!

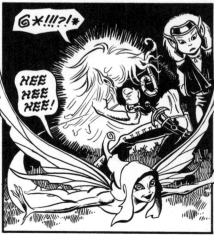

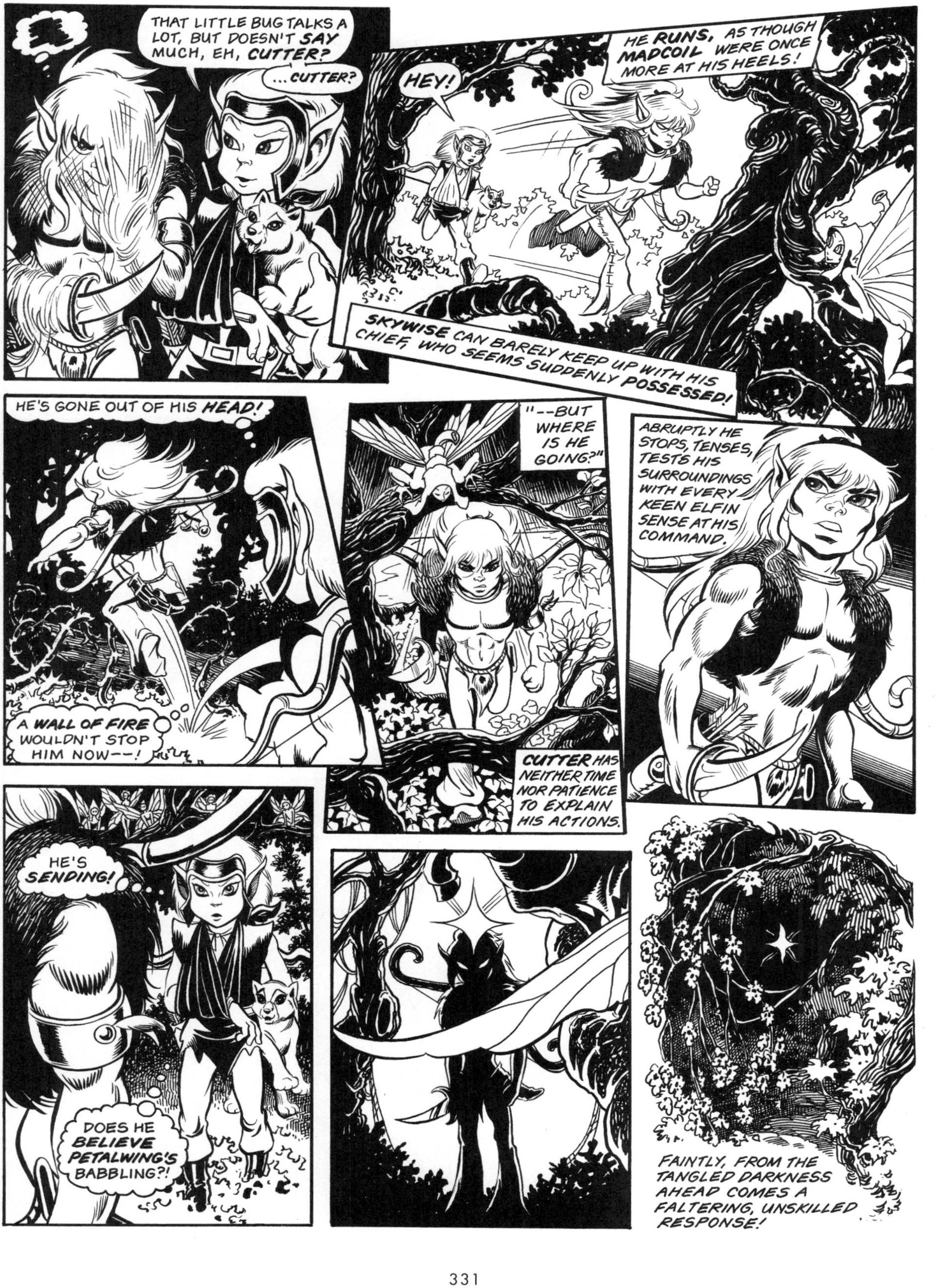
THAT LITTLE BUG TALKS A LOT, BUT DOESN'T SAY MUCH, EH, CUTTER?
...CUTTER?
HEY!
HE RUNS, AS THOUGH MADCOIL WERE ONCE MORE AT HIS HEELS!
SKYWISE CAN BARELY KEEP UP WITH HIS CHIEF, WHO SEEMS SUDDENLY POSSESSED!
HE'S GONE OUT OF HIS HEAD!
A WALL OF FIRE WOULDN'T STOP HIM NOW--!
"--BUT WHERE IS HE GOING?"
CUTTER HAS NEITHER TIME NOR PATIENCE TO EXPLAIN HIS ACTIONS.
ABRUPTLY HE STOPS, TENSES, TESTS HIS SURROUNDINGS WITH EVERY KEEN ELFIN SENSE AT HIS COMMAND.
HE'S SENDING!
DOES HE BELIEVE PETALWING'S BABBLING?!
FAINTLY, FROM THE TANGLED DARKNESS AHEAD COMES A FALTERING, UNSKILLED RESPONSE!

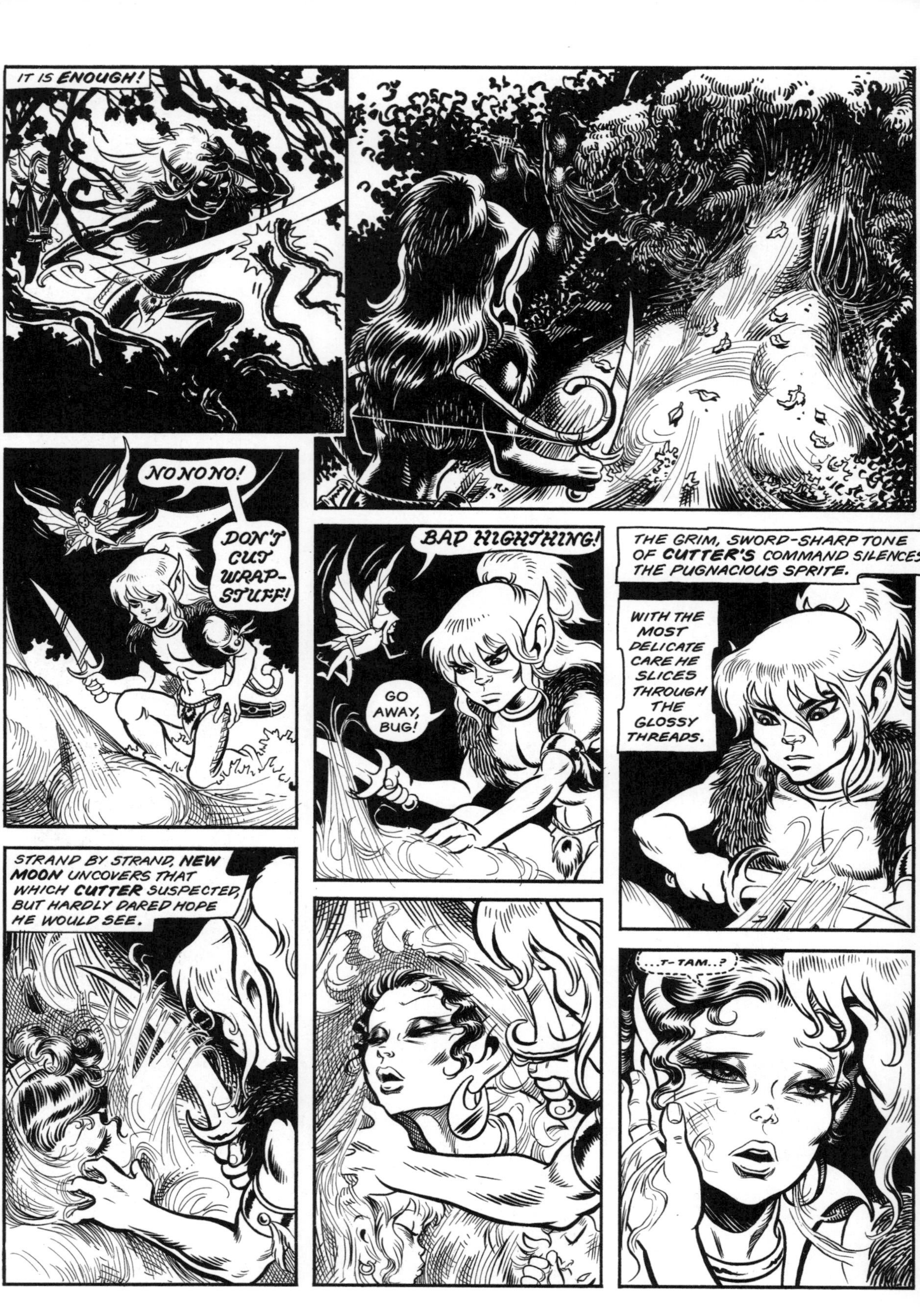

IT IS ENOUGH!
NONONO!
DON'T CUT WRAP-STUFF!
BAP HIGHTHING!
GO AWAY, BUG!
THE GRIM, SWORD-SHARP TONE OF CUTTER'S COMMAND SILENCES THE PUGNACIOUS SPRITE.
WITH THE MOST DELICATE CARE HE SLICES THROUGH THE GLOSSY THREADS.
STRAND BY STRAND, NEW MOON UNCOVERS THAT WHICH CUTTER SUSPECTED, BUT HARDLY DARED HOPE HE WOULD SEE.
...T-TAM...?

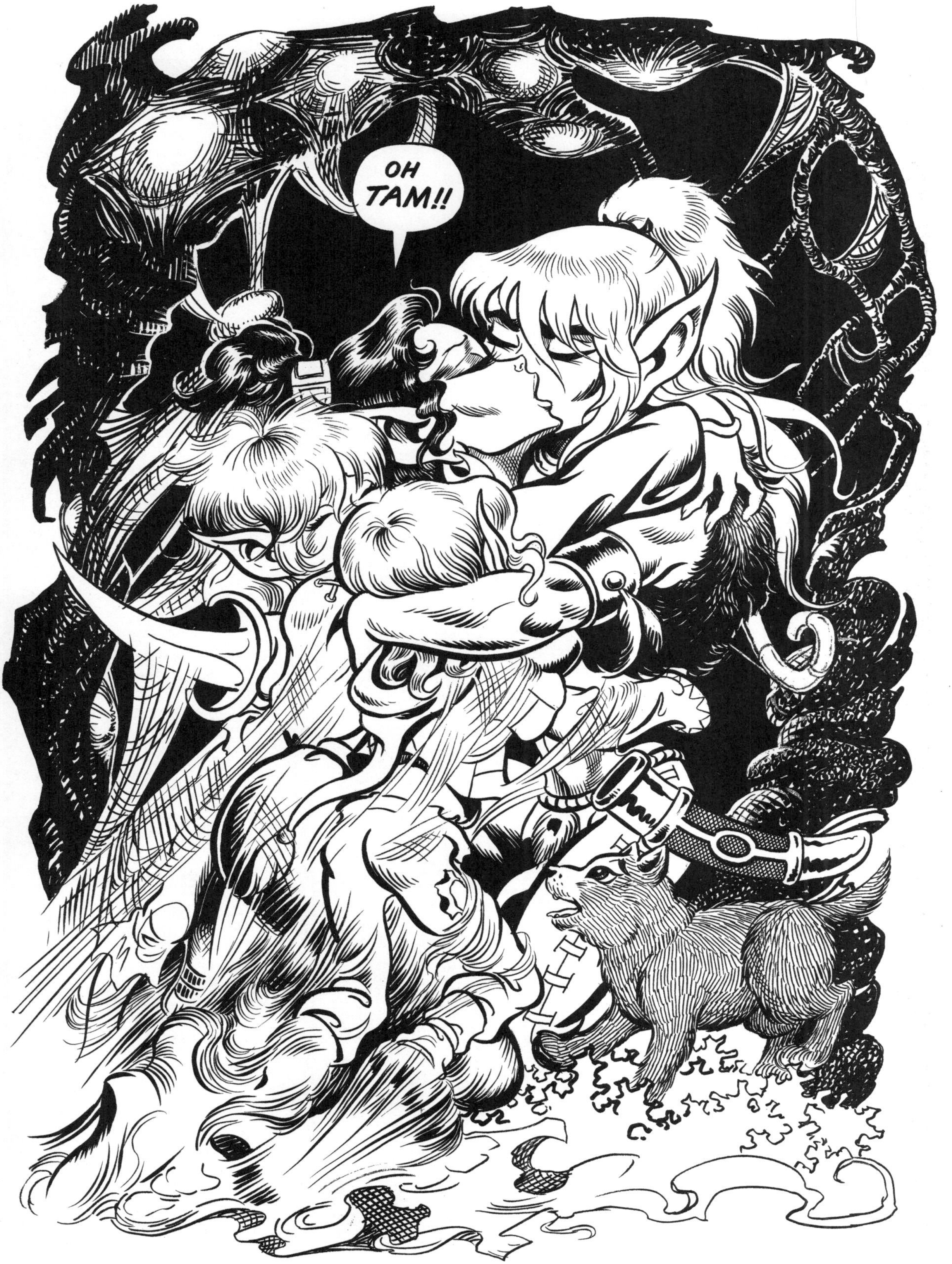
OH TAM!!

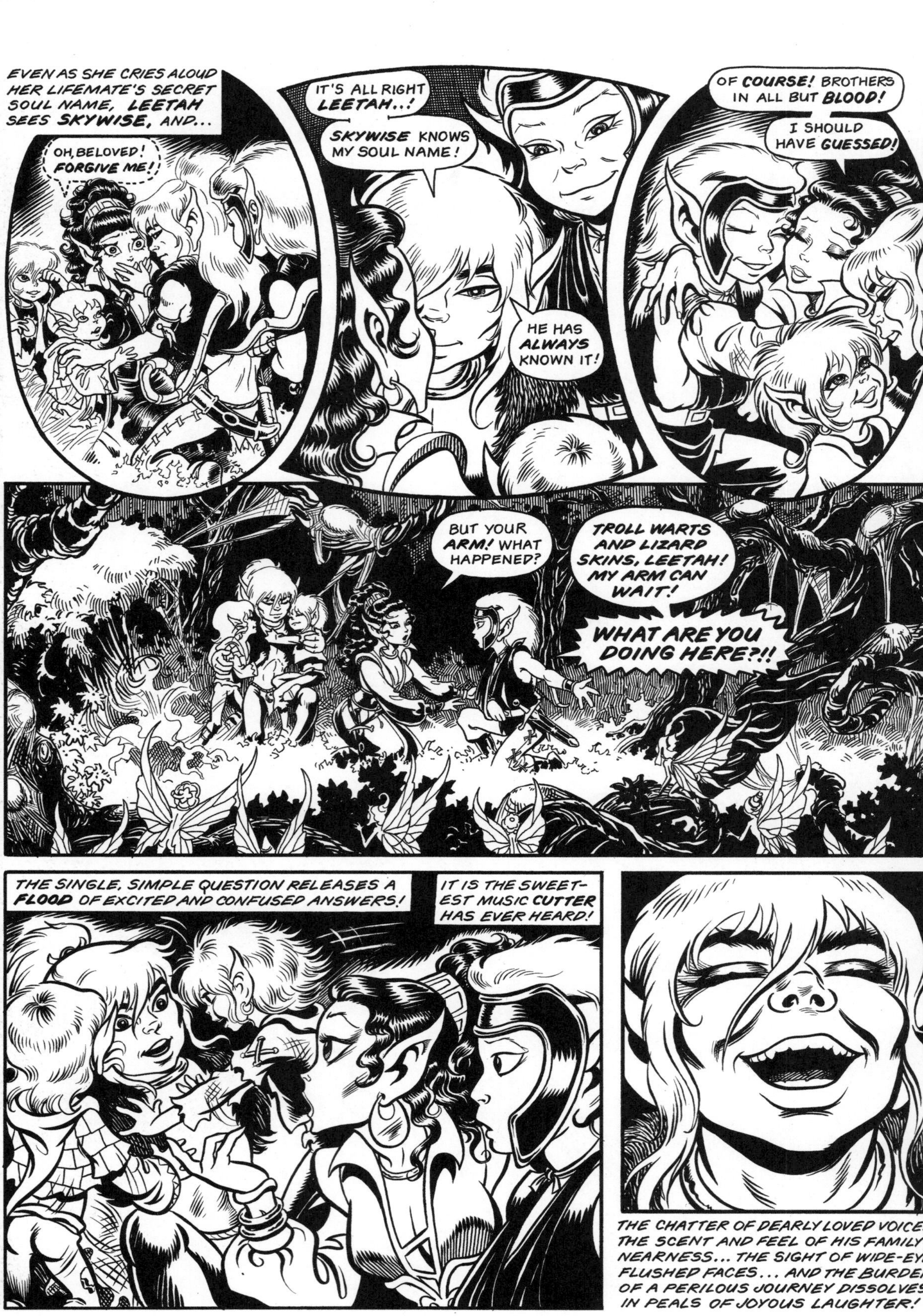
EVEN AS SHE CRIES ALOUD HER LIFEMATE'S SECRET SOUL NAME, LEETAH SEES SKYWISE, AND...
OH, BELOVED! FORGIVE ME!
IT'S ALL RIGHT LEETAH..!
SKYWISE KNOWS MY SOUL NAME!
HE HAS ALWAYS KNOWN IT!
OF COURSE! BROTHERS IN ALL BUT BLOOD!
I SHOULD HAVE GUESSED!
BUT YOUR ARM! WHAT HAPPENED?
TROLL WARTS AND LIZARD SKINS, LEETAH! MY ARM CAN WAIT!
WHAT ARE YOU DOING HERE?!!
THE SINGLE, SIMPLE QUESTION RELEASES A FLOOD OF EXCITED AND CONFUSED ANSWERS!
IT IS THE SWEETEST MUSIC CUTTER HAS EVER HEARD!
THE CHATTER OF DEARLY LOVED VOICES... THE SCENT AND FEEL OF HIS FAMILY'S NEARNESS... THE SIGHT OF WIDE-EYED, FLUSHED FACES... AND THE BURDEN OF A PERILOUS JOURNEY DISSOLVES IN PEALS OF JOYOUS LAUGHTER!

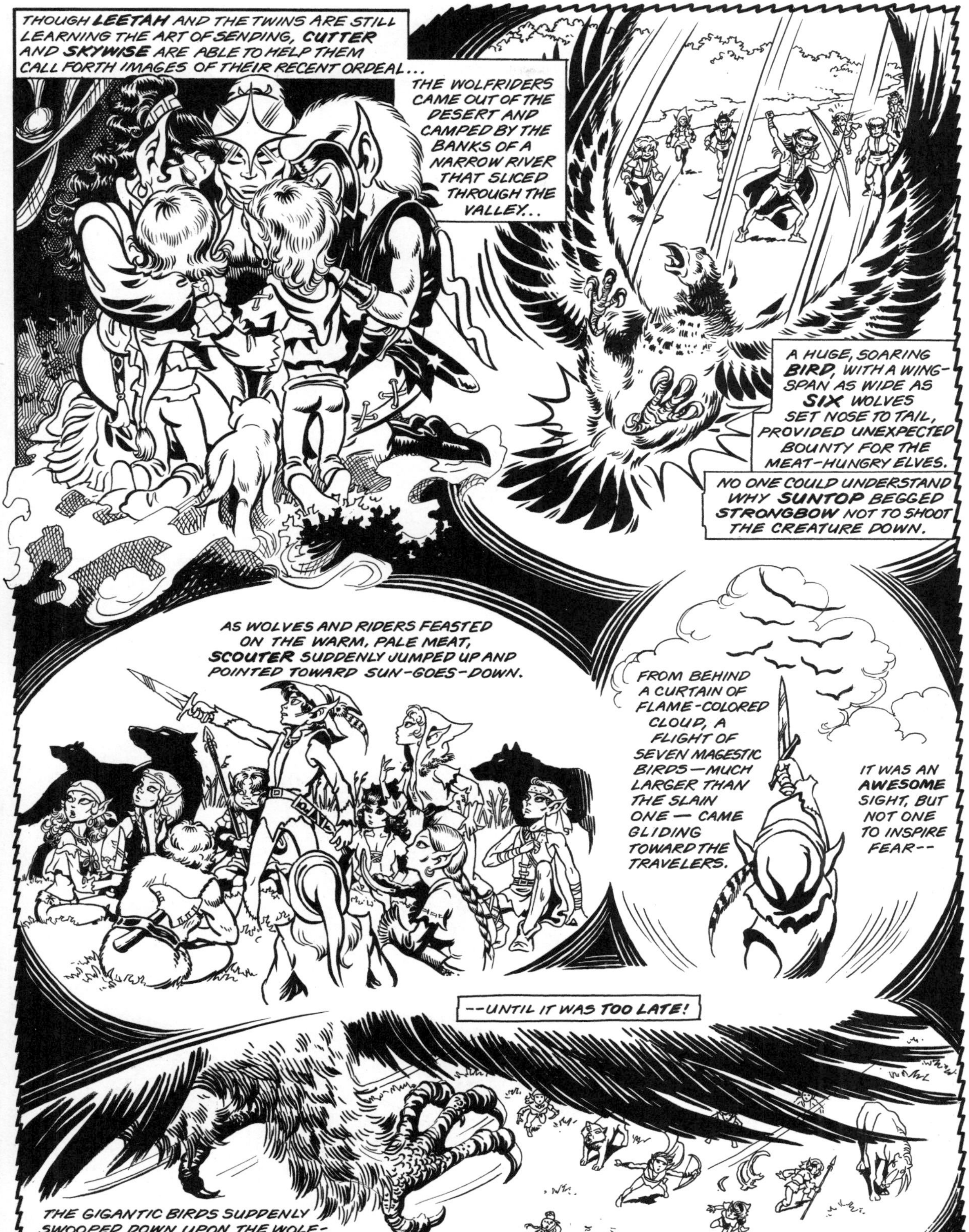
THOUGH LEETAH AND THE TWINS ARE STILL LEARNING THE ART OF SENDING, CUTTER AND SKYWISE ARE ABLE TO HELP THEM CALL FORTH IMAGES OF THEIR RECENT ORDEAL...
THE WOLFRIDERS CAME OUT OF THE DESERT AND CAMPED BY THE BANKS OF A NARROW RIVER THAT SLICED THROUGH THE VALLEY...
A HUGE, SOARING BIRD, WITH A WING-SPAN AS WIDE AS SIX WOLVES SET NOSE TO TAIL, PROVIDED UNEXPECTED BOUNTY FOR THE MEAT-HUNGRY ELVES.
NO ONE COULD UNDERSTAND WHY SUNTOP BEGGED STRONGBOW NOT TO SHOOT THE CREATURE DOWN.
AS WOLVES AND RIDERS FEASTED ON THE WARM, PALE MEAT, SCOUTER SUDDENLY JUMPED UP AND POINTED TOWARD SUN-GOES-DOWN.
FROM BEHIND A CURTAIN OF FLAME-COLORED CLOUD, A FLIGHT OF SEVEN MAGESTIC BIRDS—MUCH LARGER THAN THE SLAIN ONE — CAME GLIDING TOWARD THE TRAVELERS.
IT WAS AN AWESOME SIGHT, BUT NOT ONE TO INSPIRE FEAR--
--UNTIL IT WAS TOO LATE!
THE GIGANTIC BIRDS SUDDENLY SWOOPED DOWN UPON THE WOLF-RIDERS WITH CLAWS EXTENDED FOR THE ATTACK!

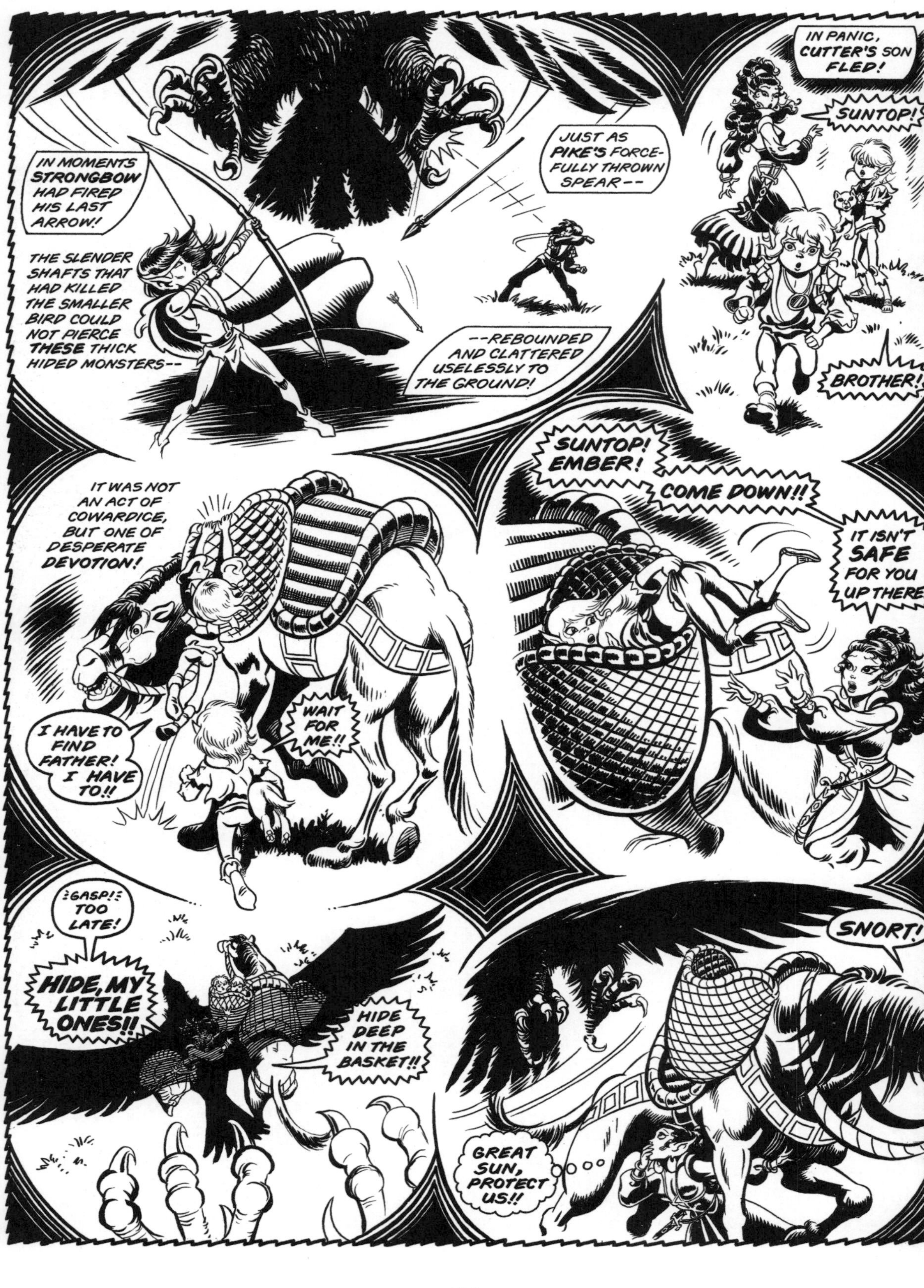
IN MOMENTS STRONGBOW HAD FIRED HIS LAST ARROW!
THE SLENDER SHAFTS THAT HAD KILLED THE SMALLER BIRD COULD NOT PIERCE THESE THICK HIDED MONSTERS--
JUST AS PIKE'S FORCE-FULLY THROWN SPEAR--
--REBOUNDED AND CLATTERED USELESSLY TO THE GROUND!
IN PANIC, CUTTER'S SON FLED!
SUNTOP!
BROTHER!
IT WAS NOT AN ACT OF COWARDICE, BUT ONE OF DESPERATE DEVOTION!
I HAVE TO FIND FATHER! I HAVE TO!!
WAIT FOR ME!!
SUNTOP! EMBER!
COME DOWN!!
IT ISN'T SAFE FOR YOU UP THERE!
GASP! TOO LATE!
HIDE, MY LITTLE ONES!!
HIDE DEEP IN THE BASKET!!
SNORT!
GREAT SUN, PROTECT US!!

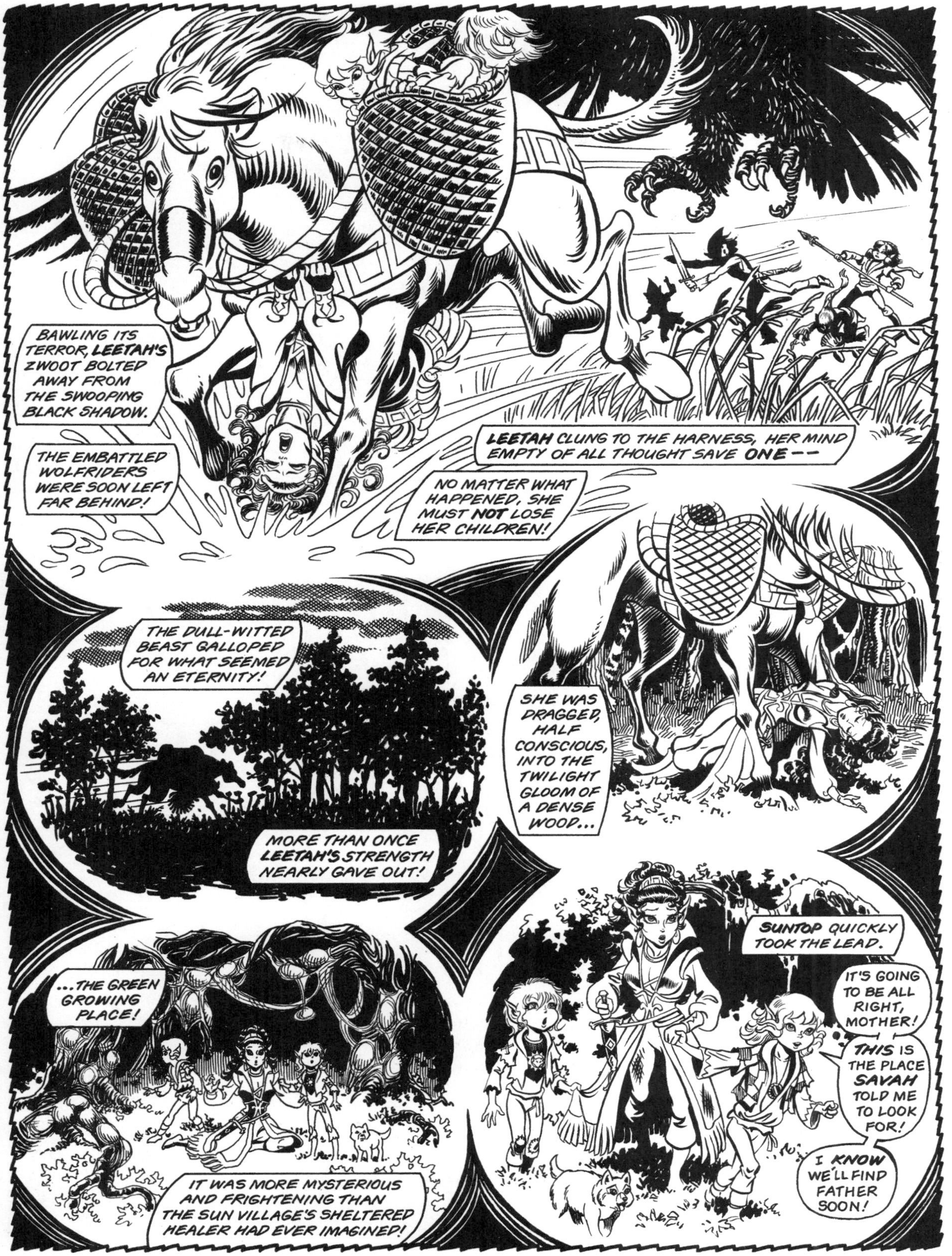

BAWLING ITS TERROR, LEETAH'S ZWOOT BOLTED AWAY FROM THE SWOOPING BLACK SHADOW.
THE EMBATTLED WOLFRIDERS WERE SOON LEFT FAR BEHIND!
LEETAH CLUNG TO THE HARNESS, HER MIND EMPTY OF ALL THOUGHT SAVE ONE--
NO MATTER WHAT HAPPENED, SHE MUST NOT LOSE HER CHILDREN!
THE DULL-WITTED BEAST GALLOPED FOR WHAT SEEMED AN ETERNITY!
MORE THAN ONCE LEETAH'S STRENGTH NEARLY GAVE OUT!
SHE WAS DRAGGED, HALF CONSCIOUS, INTO THE TWILIGHT GLOOM OF A DENSE WOOD...
...THE GREEN GROWING PLACE!
IT WAS MORE MYSTERIOUS AND FRIGHTENING THAN THE SUN VILLAGE'S SHELTERED HEALER HAD EVER IMAGINED!
SUNTOP QUICKLY TOOK THE LEAD.
IT'S GOING TO BE ALL RIGHT, MOTHER!
THIS IS THE PLACE SAVAH TOLD ME TO LOOK FOR!
I KNOW WE'LL FIND FATHER SOON!

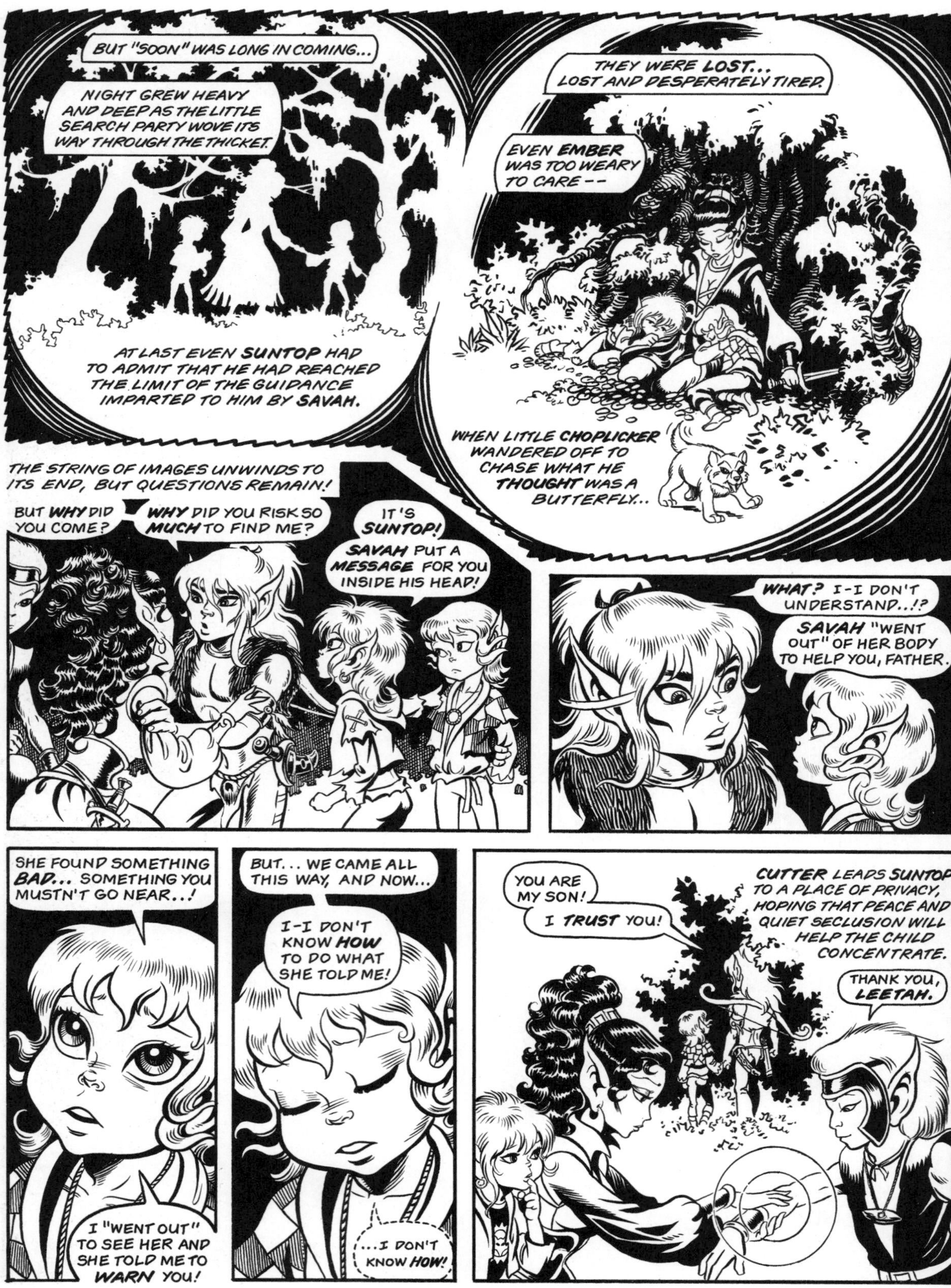
BUT "SOON" WAS LONG IN COMING...
NIGHT GREW HEAVY AND DEEP AS THE LITTLE SEARCH PARTY WOVE ITS WAY THROUGH THE THICKET.
AT LAST EVEN SUNTOP HAD TO ADMIT THAT HE HAD REACHED THE LIMIT OF THE GUIDANCE IMPARTED TO HIM BY SAVAH.
THEY WERE LOST... LOST AND DESPERATELY TIRED.
EVEN EMBER WAS TOO WEARY TO CARE --
WHEN LITTLE CHOPLICKER WANDERED OFF TO CHASE WHAT HE THOUGHT WAS A BUTTERFLY...
THE STRING OF IMAGES UNWINDS TO ITS END, BUT QUESTIONS REMAIN!
BUT WHY DID YOU COME?
WHY DID YOU RISK SO MUCH TO FIND ME?
IT'S SUNTOP! SAVAH PUT A MESSAGE FOR YOU INSIDE HIS HEAD!
WHAT? I-I DON'T UNDERSTAND..!?
SAVAH "WENT OUT" OF HER BODY TO HELP YOU, FATHER.
SHE FOUND SOMETHING BAD... SOMETHING YOU MUSTN'T GO NEAR..!
I "WENT OUT" TO SEE HER AND SHE TOLD ME TO WARN YOU!
BUT... WE CAME ALL THIS WAY, AND NOW...
I-I DON'T KNOW HOW TO DO WHAT SHE TOLD ME!
...I DON'T KNOW HOW!
YOU ARE MY SON!
I TRUST YOU!
CUTTER LEADS SUNTOP TO A PLACE OF PRIVACY, HOPING THAT PEACE AND QUIET SECLUSION WILL HELP THE CHILD CONCENTRATE.
THANK YOU, LEETAH.

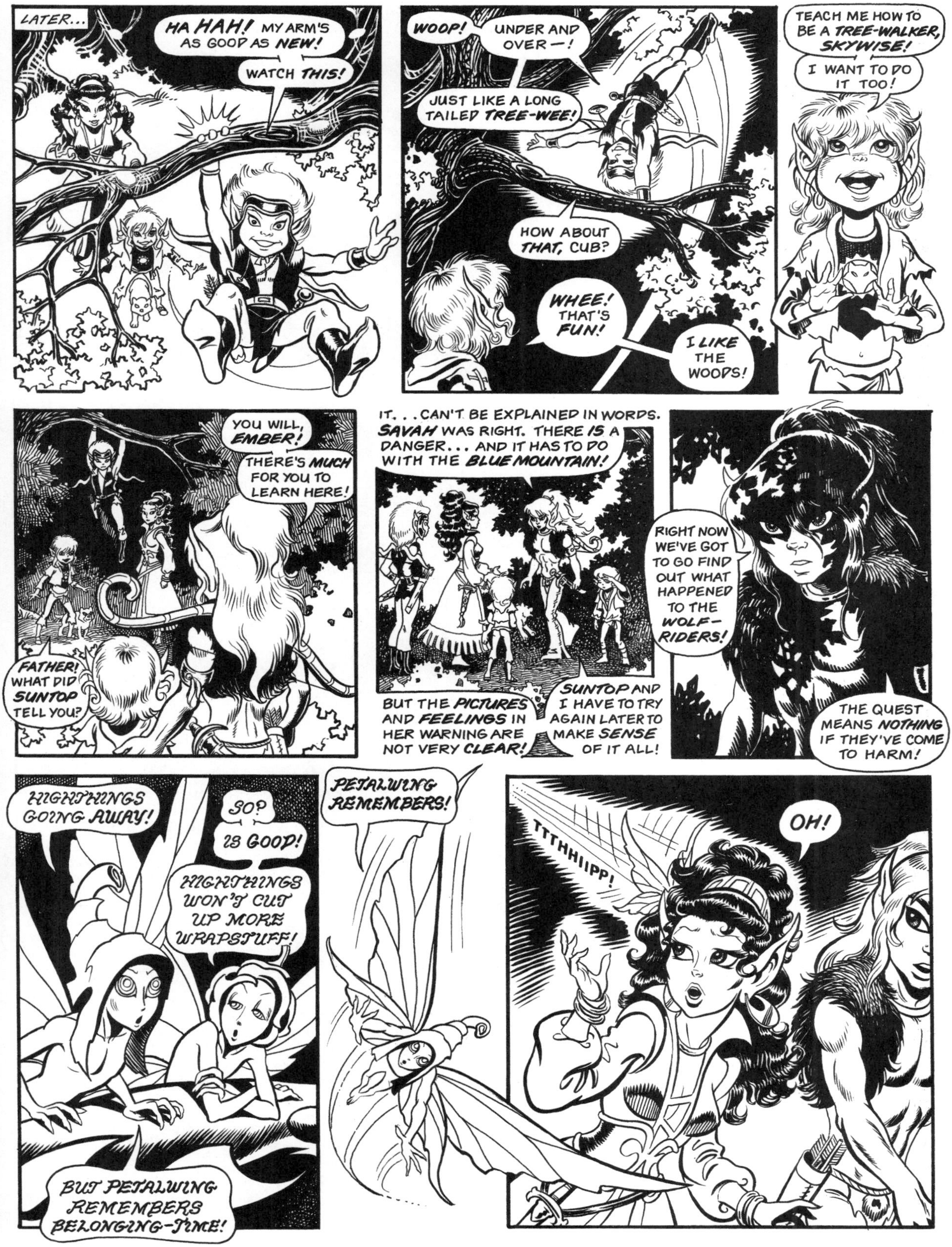
LATER...
HA HAH! MY ARM'S AS GOOD AS NEW!
WATCH THIS!
WOOP!
UNDER AND OVER—!
JUST LIKE A LONG TAILED TREE-WEE!
HOW ABOUT THAT, CUB?
WHEE! THAT'S FUN!
I LIKE THE WOODS!
TEACH ME HOW TO BE A TREE-WALKER, SKYWISE!
I WANT TO DO IT TOO!
YOU WILL, EMBER!
THERE'S MUCH FOR YOU TO LEARN HERE!
FATHER! WHAT DID SUNTOP TELL YOU?
IT. . . CAN'T BE EXPLAINED IN WORDS. SAVAH WAS RIGHT. THERE IS A DANGER... AND IT HAS TO DO WITH THE BLUE MOUNTAIN!
BUT THE PICTURES AND FEELINGS IN HER WARNING ARE NOT VERY CLEAR!
SUNTOP AND I HAVE TO TRY AGAIN LATER TO MAKE SENSE OF IT ALL!
RIGHT NOW WE'VE GOT TO GO FIND OUT WHAT HAPPENED TO THE WOLF-RIDERS!
THE QUEST MEANS NOTHING IF THEY'VE COME TO HARM!
HIGHTHINGS GOING AWAY!
SO?
IS GOOD!
HIGHTHINGS WON'T CUT UP MORE WRAPSTUFF!
BUT PETALWING REMEMBERS BELONGING-TIME!
PETALWING REMEMBERS!
TTTHHIIPP!
OH!

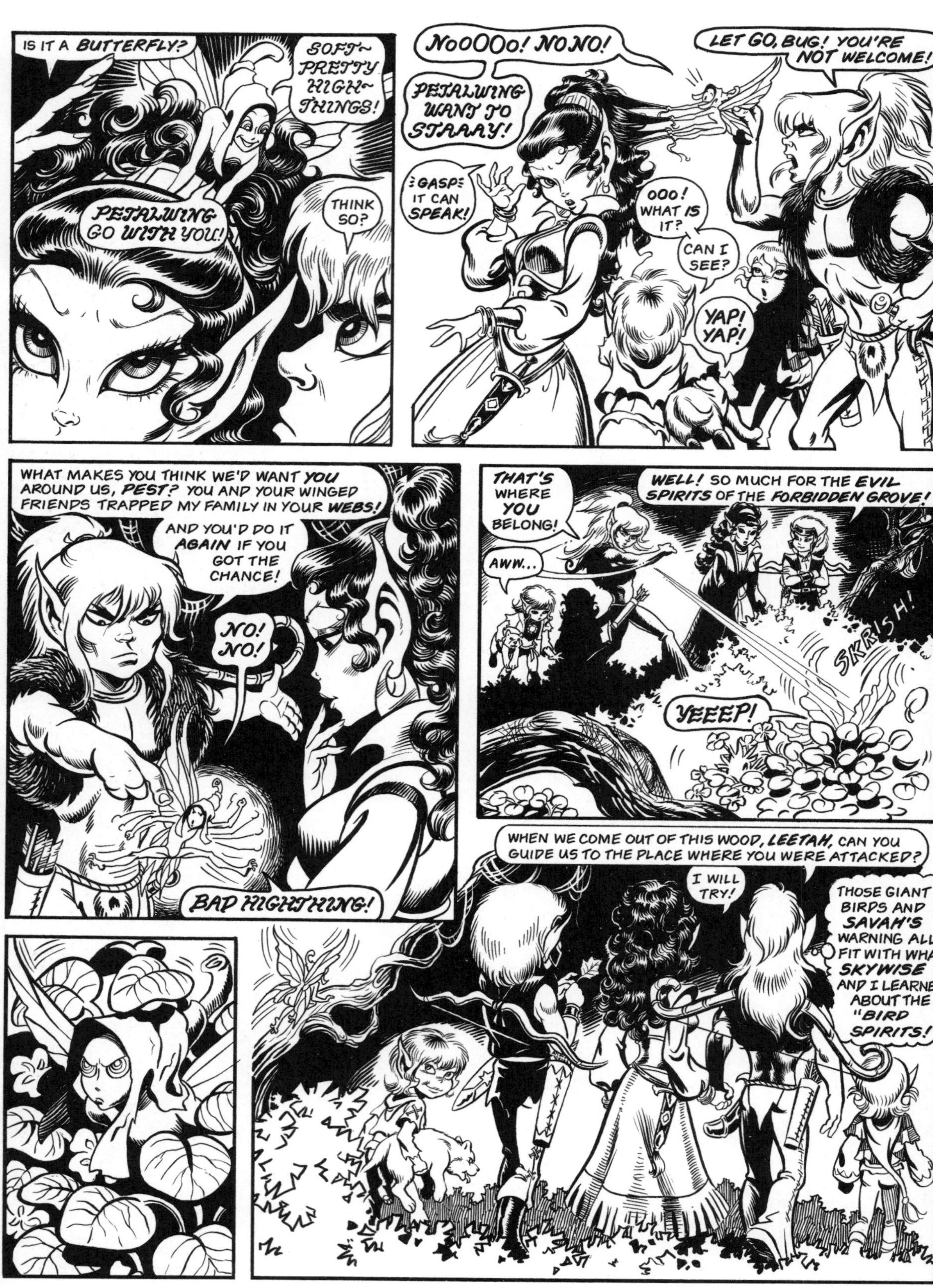
IS IT A BUTTERFLY?
SOFT~ PRETTY HIGH~ THINGS!
PETALWING GO WITH YOU!
THINK SO?
NoOOOo! NO NO!
PETALWING WANT TO STAAAAY!
LET GO, BUG! YOU'RE NOT WELCOME!
GASP IT CAN SPEAK!
OOO! WHAT IS IT?
CAN I SEE?
YAP! YAP!
WHAT MAKES YOU THINK WE'D WANT YOU AROUND US, PEST? YOU AND YOUR WINGED FRIENDS TRAPPED MY FAMILY IN YOUR WEBS!
AND YOU'D DO IT AGAIN IF YOU GOT THE CHANCE!
NO! NO!
BAD HIGHTHING!
THAT'S WHERE YOU BELONG!
WELL! SO MUCH FOR THE EVIL SPIRITS OF THE FORBIDDEN GROVE!
AWW...
SKRISH!
YEEEP!
WHEN WE COME OUT OF THIS WOOD, LEETAH, CAN YOU GUIDE US TO THE PLACE WHERE YOU WERE ATTACKED?
I WILL TRY!
THOSE GIANT BIRDS AND SAVAH'S WARNING ALL FIT WITH WHAT SKYWISE AND I LEARNED ABOUT THE "BIRD SPIRITS!"

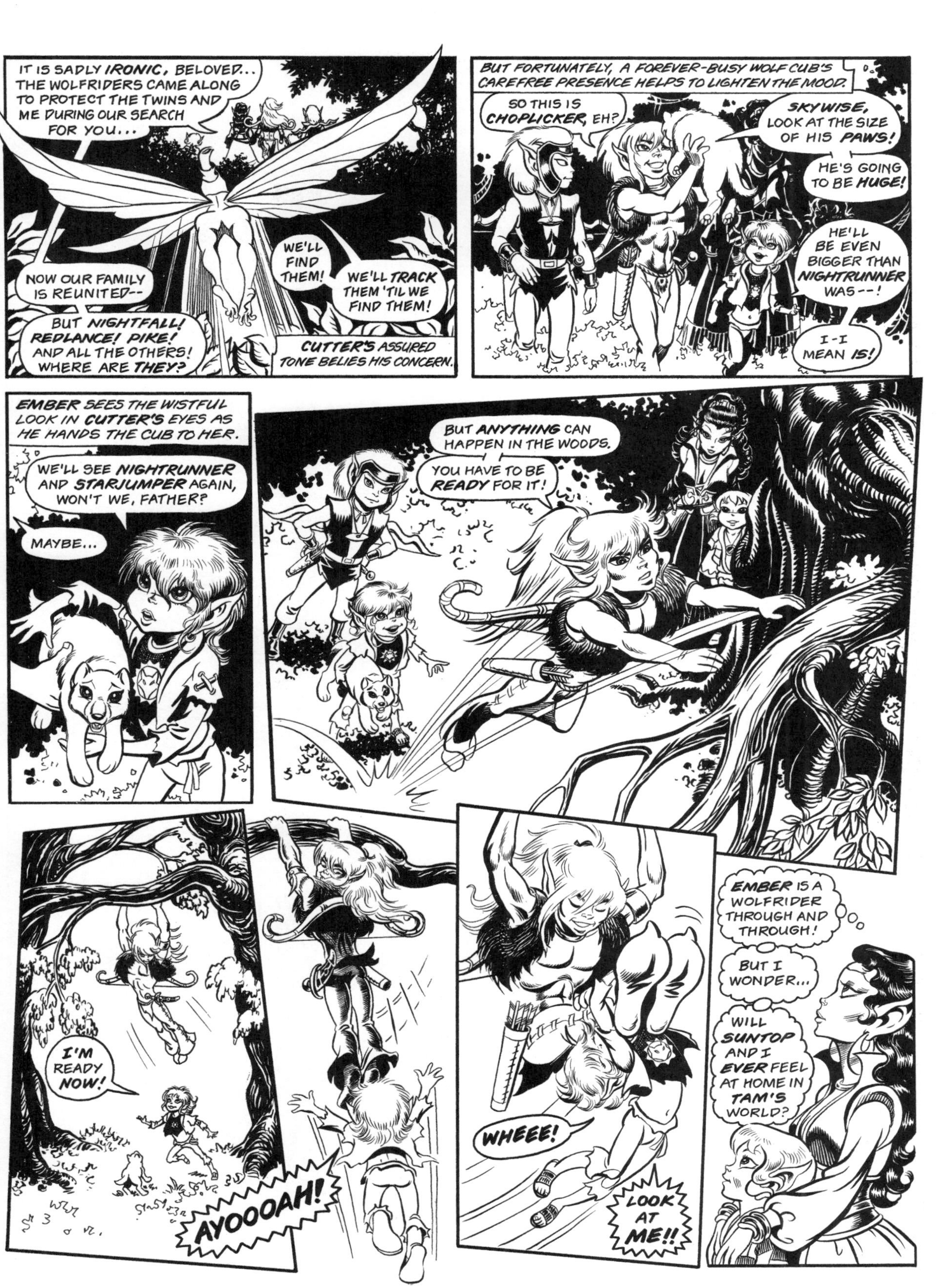
IT IS SADLY IRONIC, BELOVED... THE WOLFRIDERS CAME ALONG TO PROTECT THE TWINS AND ME DURING OUR SEARCH FOR YOU...
NOW OUR FAMILY IS REUNITED--
BUT NIGHTFALL! REDLANCE! PIKE! AND ALL THE OTHERS! WHERE ARE THEY?
WE'LL FIND THEM!
WE'LL TRACK THEM 'TIL WE FIND THEM!
CUTTER'S ASSURED TONE BELIES HIS CONCERN.
BUT FORTUNATELY, A FOREVER-BUSY WOLF CUB'S CAREFREE PRESENCE HELPS TO LIGHTEN THE MOOD.
SO THIS IS CHOPLICKER, EH?
SKYWISE, LOOK AT THE SIZE OF HIS PAWS!
HE'S GOING TO BE HUGE!
HE'LL BE EVEN BIGGER THAN NIGHTRUNNER WAS--!
I-I MEAN IS!
EMBER SEES THE WISTFUL LOOK IN CUTTER'S EYES AS HE HANDS THE CUB TO HER.
WE'LL SEE NIGHTRUNNER AND STARJUMPER AGAIN, WON'T WE, FATHER?
MAYBE...
BUT ANYTHING CAN HAPPEN IN THE WOODS.
YOU HAVE TO BE READY FOR IT!
I'M READY NOW!
AYOOOAH!
WHEEE!
LOOK AT ME!!
EMBER IS A WOLFRIDER THROUGH AND THROUGH!
BUT I WONDER...
WILL SUNTOP AND I EVER FEEL AT HOME IN TAM'S WORLD?

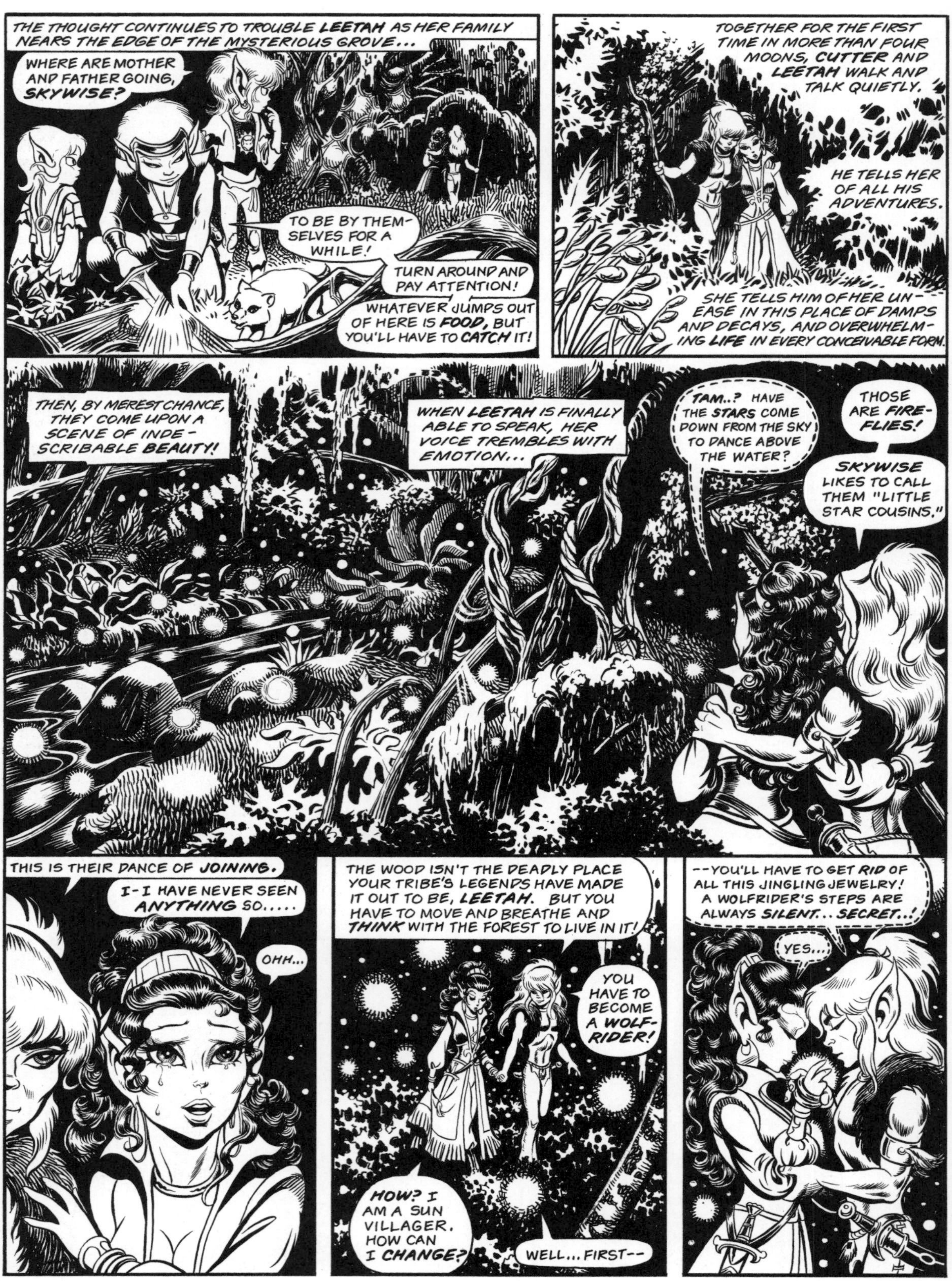
THE THOUGHT CONTINUES TO TROUBLE LEETAH AS HER FAMILY NEARS THE EDGE OF THE MYSTERIOUS GROVE...
WHERE ARE MOTHER AND FATHER GOING, SKYWISE?
TO BE BY THEMSELVES FOR A WHILE!
TURN AROUND AND PAY ATTENTION!
WHATEVER JUMPS OUT OF HERE IS FOOD, BUT YOU'LL HAVE TO CATCH IT!
TOGETHER FOR THE FIRST TIME IN MORE THAN FOUR MOONS, CUTTER AND LEETAH WALK AND TALK QUIETLY.
HE TELLS HER OF ALL HIS ADVENTURES.
SHE TELLS HIM OF HER UNEASE IN THIS PLACE OF DAMPS AND DECAYS, AND OVERWHELMING LIFE IN EVERY CONCEIVABLE FORM.
THEN, BY MEREST CHANCE, THEY COME UPON A SCENE OF INDESCRIBABLE BEAUTY!
WHEN LEETAH IS FINALLY ABLE TO SPEAK, HER VOICE TREMBLES WITH EMOTION...
TAM..? HAVE THE STARS COME DOWN FROM THE SKY TO DANCE ABOVE THE WATER?
THOSE ARE FIREFLIES!
SKYWISE LIKES TO CALL THEM "LITTLE STAR COUSINS."
THIS IS THEIR DANCE OF JOINING.
I-I HAVE NEVER SEEN ANYTHING SO.....
OHH...
THE WOOD ISN'T THE DEADLY PLACE YOUR TRIBE'S LEGENDS HAVE MADE IT OUT TO BE, LEETAH. BUT YOU HAVE TO MOVE AND BREATHE AND THINK WITH THE FOREST TO LIVE IN IT!
YOU HAVE TO BECOME A WOLFRIDER!
HOW? I AM A SUN VILLAGER. HOW CAN I CHANGE?
WELL... FIRST--
--YOU'LL HAVE TO GET RID OF ALL THIS JINGLING JEWELRY! A WOLFRIDER'S STEPS ARE ALWAYS SILENT... SECRET..!
YES...

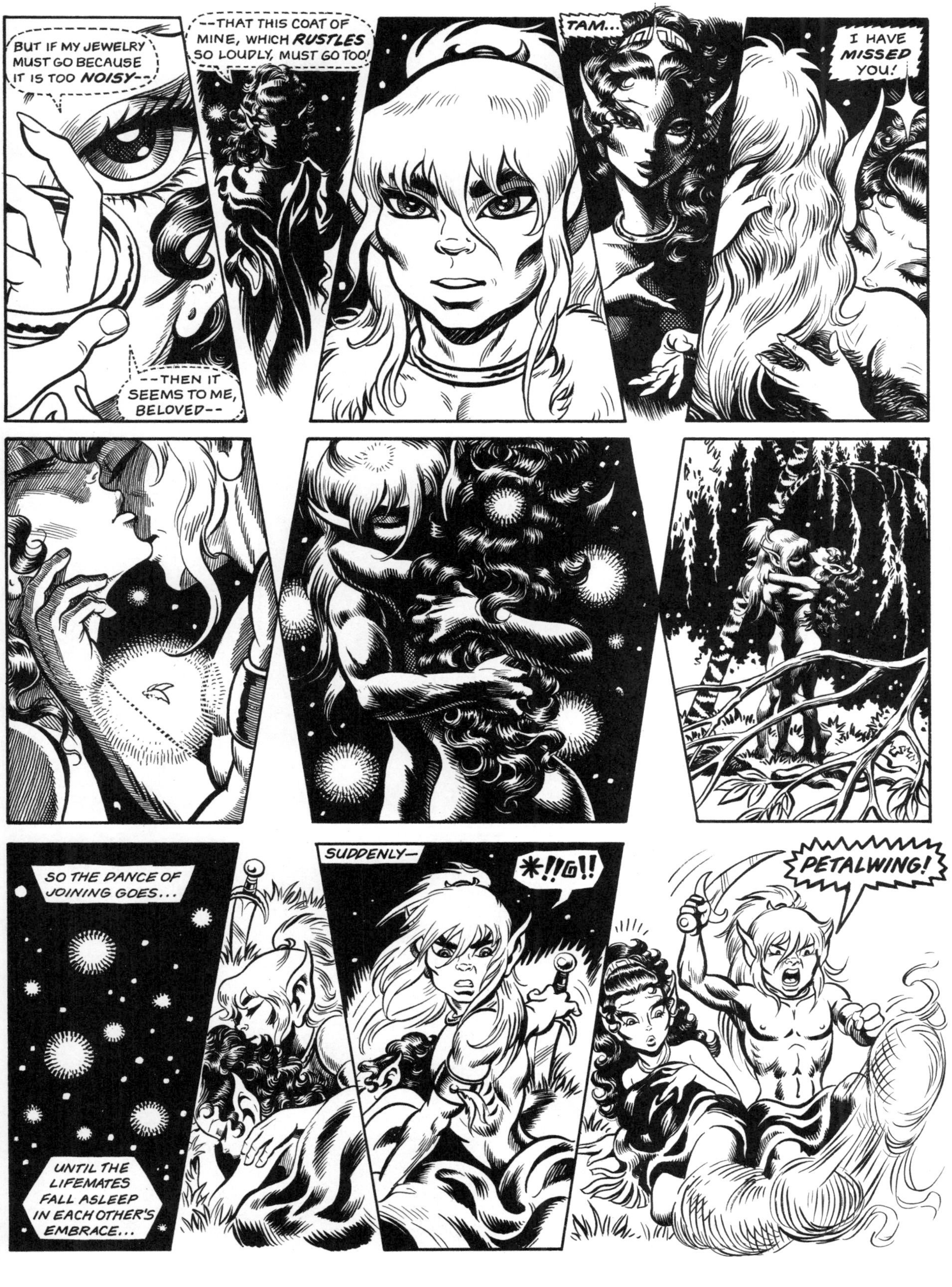

BUT IF MY JEWELRY MUST GO BECAUSE IT IS TOO NOISY--
--THEN IT SEEMS TO ME, BELOVED--
--THAT THIS COAT OF MINE, WHICH RUSTLES SO LOUDLY, MUST GO TOO!
TAM...
I HAVE MISSED YOU!
SO THE DANCE OF JOINING GOES...
UNTIL THE LIFEMATES FALL ASLEEP IN EACH OTHER'S EMBRACE...
SUDDENLY—
*!!G!!
PETALWING!

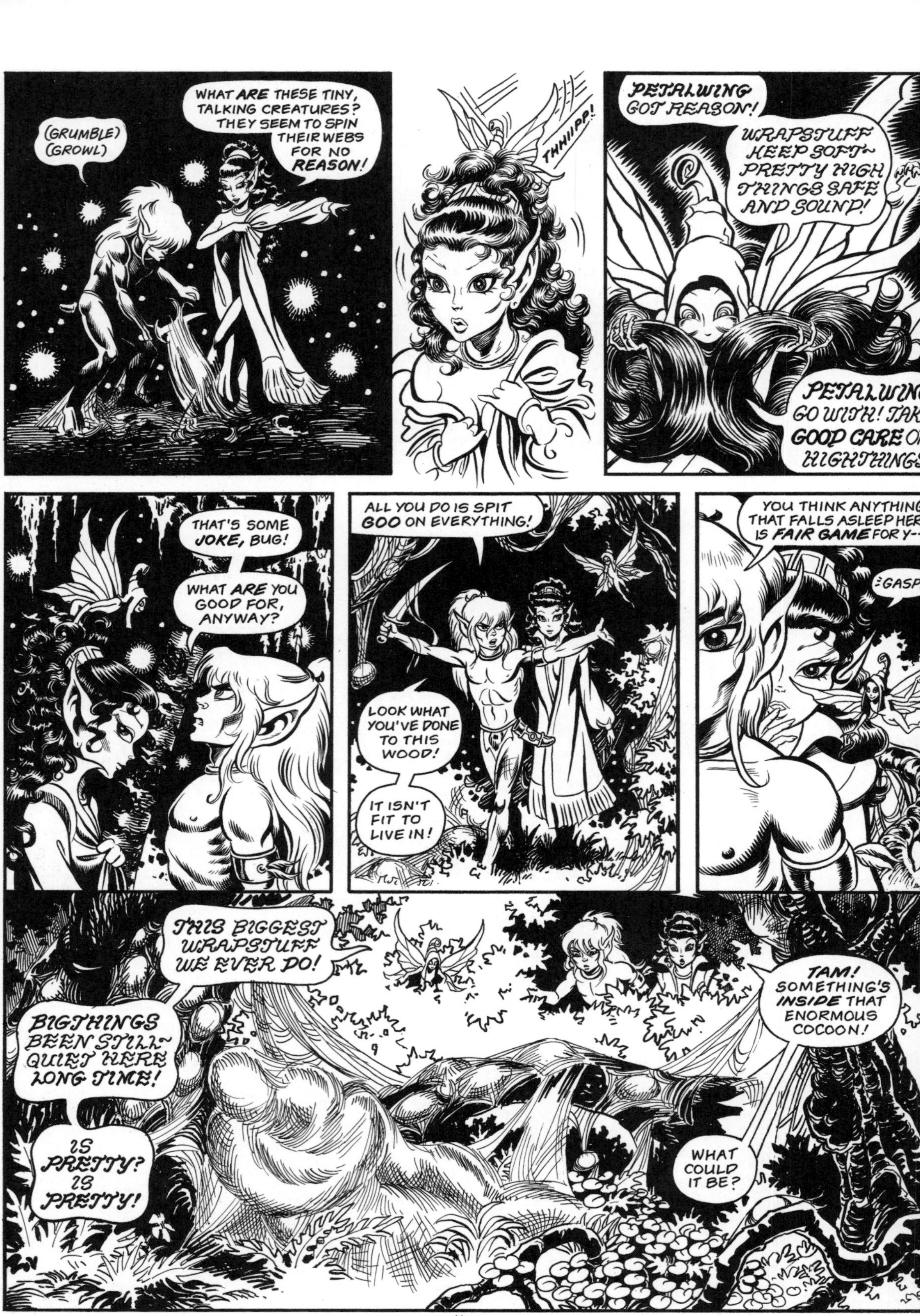
(GRUMBLE) (GROWL)
WHAT ARE THESE TINY, TALKING CREATURES? THEY SEEM TO SPIN THEIR WEBS FOR NO REASON!
THHIIPP!
PETALWING GOT REASON!
WRAPSTUFF KEEP SOFT-PRETTY HIGH THINGS SAFE AND SOUND!
PETALWING GO WITH! TAKE GOOD CARE OF HIGHTHINGS!
THAT'S SOME JOKE, BUG!
WHAT ARE YOU GOOD FOR, ANYWAY?
ALL YOU DO IS SPIT GOO ON EVERYTHING!
LOOK WHAT YOU'VE DONE TO THIS WOOD!
IT ISN'T FIT TO LIVE IN!
YOU THINK ANYTHING THAT FALLS ASLEEP HERE IS FAIR GAME FOR Y--!
GASP!
THIS BIGGEST WRAPSTUFF WE EVER DO!
BIGTHINGS BEEN STILL-QUIET HERE LONG TIME!
IS PRETTY? IS PRETTY!
TAM! SOMETHING'S INSIDE THAT ENORMOUS COCOON!
WHAT COULD IT BE?

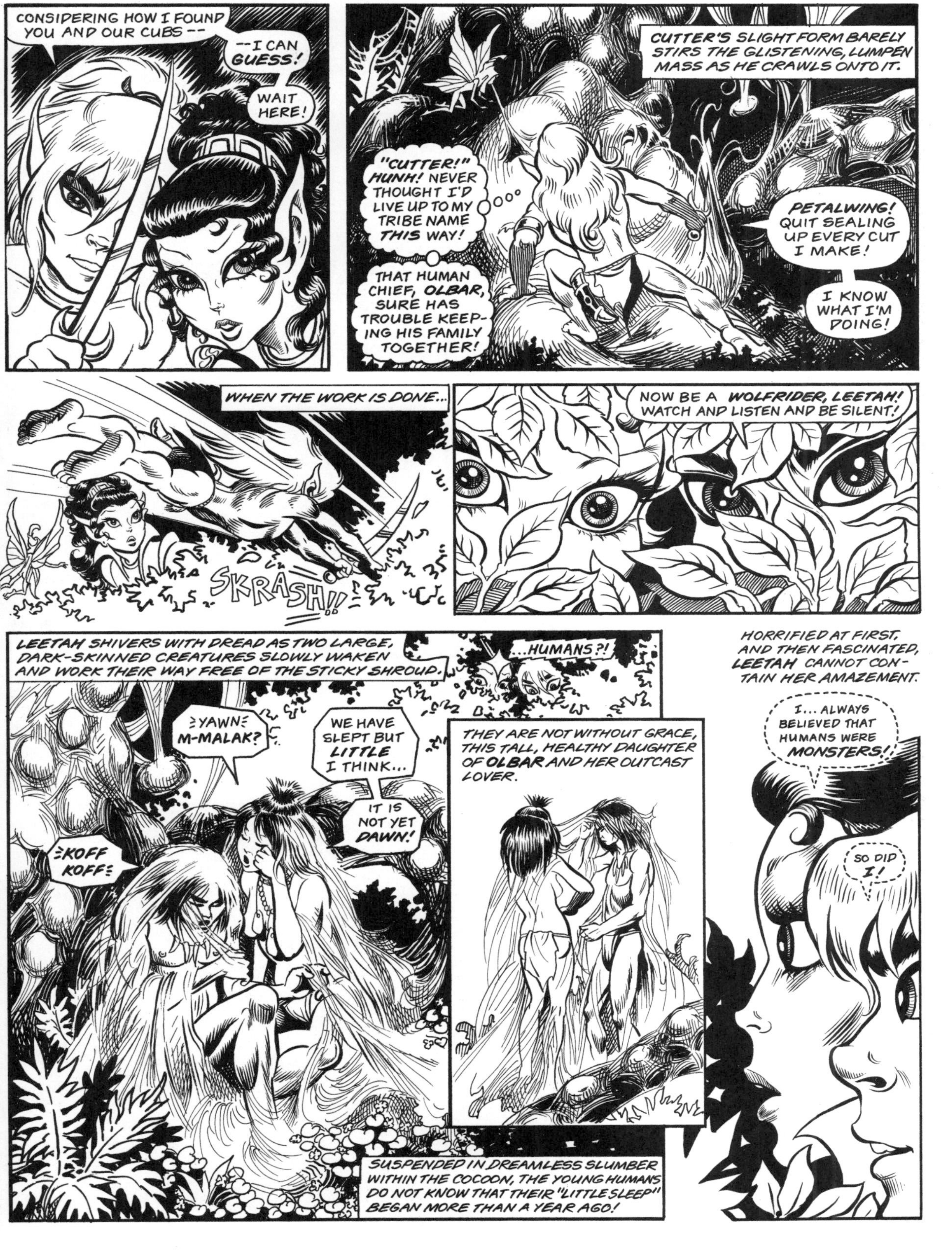

CONSIDERING HOW I FOUND YOU AND OUR CUBS --
--I CAN GUESS!
WAIT HERE!
CUTTER'S SLIGHT FORM BARELY STIRS THE GLISTENING, LUMPEN MASS AS HE CRAWLS ONTO IT.
"CUTTER!" HUNH! NEVER THOUGHT I'D LIVE UP TO MY TRIBE NAME THIS WAY!
THAT HUMAN CHIEF, OLBAR, SURE HAS TROUBLE KEEPING HIS FAMILY TOGETHER!
PETALWING! QUIT SEALING UP EVERY CUT I MAKE!
I KNOW WHAT I'M DOING!
WHEN THE WORK IS DONE...
SKRASH!!
NOW BE A WOLFRIDER, LEETAH! WATCH AND LISTEN AND BE SILENT!
LEETAH SHIVERS WITH DREAD AS TWO LARGE, DARK-SKINNED CREATURES SLOWLY WAKEN AND WORK THEIR WAY FREE OF THE STICKY SHROUD.
...HUMANS?!
YAWN M-MALAK?
WE HAVE SLEPT BUT LITTLE I THINK...
IT IS NOT YET DAWN!
KOFF KOFF
THEY ARE NOT WITHOUT GRACE, THIS TALL, HEALTHY DAUGHTER OF OLBAR AND HER OUTCAST LOVER.
SUSPENDED IN DREAMLESS SLUMBER WITHIN THE COCOON, THE YOUNG HUMANS DO NOT KNOW THAT THEIR "LITTLE SLEEP" BEGAN MORE THAN A YEAR AGO!
HORRIFIED AT FIRST, AND THEN FASCINATED, LEETAH CANNOT CONTAIN HER AMAZEMENT.
I... ALWAYS BELIEVED THAT HUMANS WERE MONSTERS!
SO DID I!

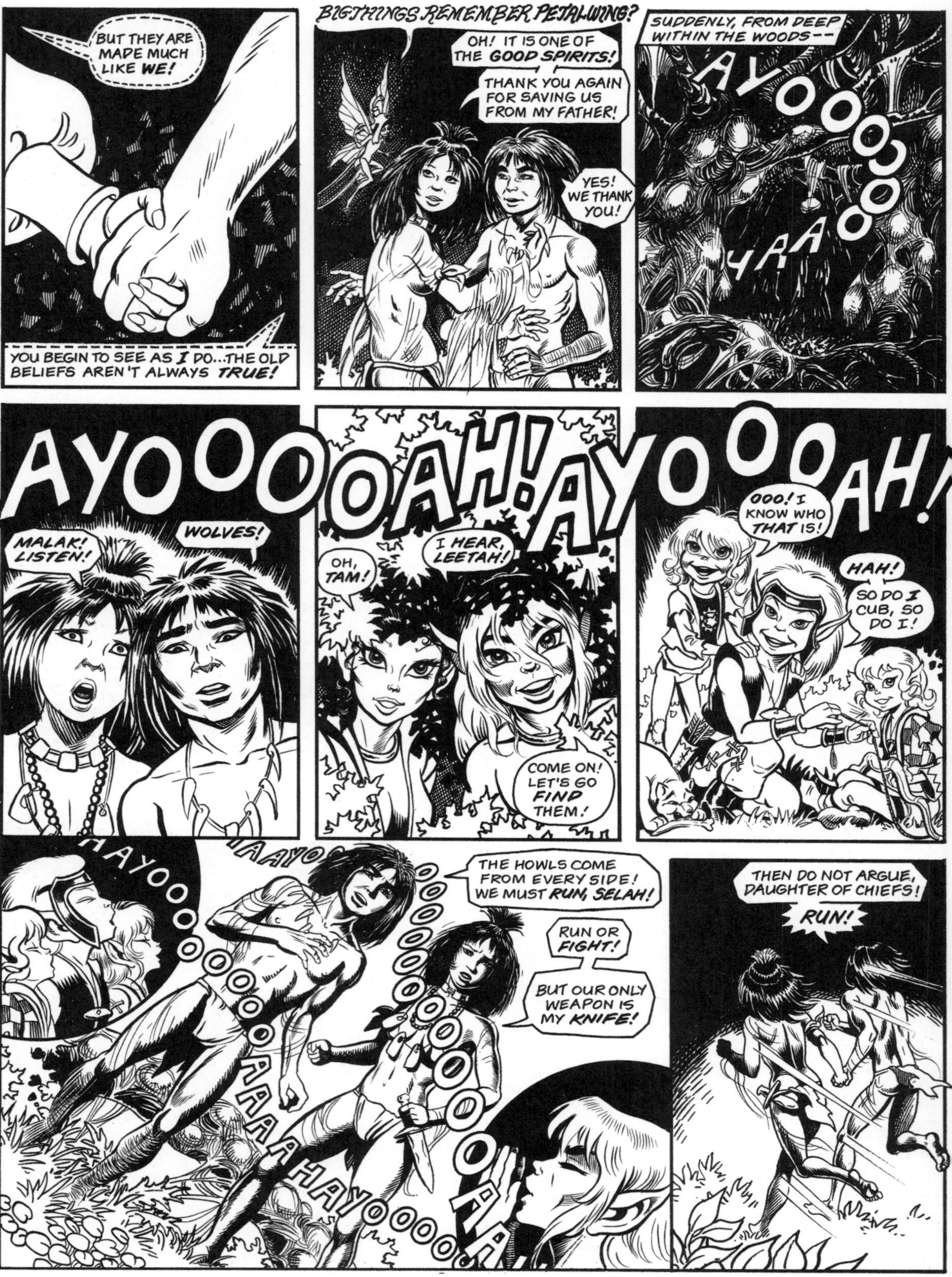

BUT THEY ARE MADE MUCH LIKE WE!
YOU BEGIN TO SEE AS I DO...THE OLD BELIEFS AREN'T ALWAYS TRUE!
BIGTHINGS REMEMBER PETALWING?
OH! IT IS ONE OF THE GOOD SPIRITS!
THANK YOU AGAIN FOR SAVING US FROM MY FATHER!
YES! WE THANK YOU!
SUDDENLY, FROM DEEP WITHIN THE WOODS--
AYOOOOOOYRAA
AYOOOOAH! AYOOOAH!
MALAK! LISTEN!
WOLVES!
OH, TAM!
I HEAR, LEETAH!
COME ON! LET'S GO FIND THEM!
OOO! I KNOW WHO THAT IS!
HAH! SO DO I CUB, SO DO I!
THE HOWLS COME FROM EVERY SIDE! WE MUST RUN, SELAH!
RUN OR FIGHT!
BUT OUR ONLY WEAPON IS MY KNIFE!
THEN DO NOT ARGUE, DAUGHTER OF CHIEFS!
RUN!

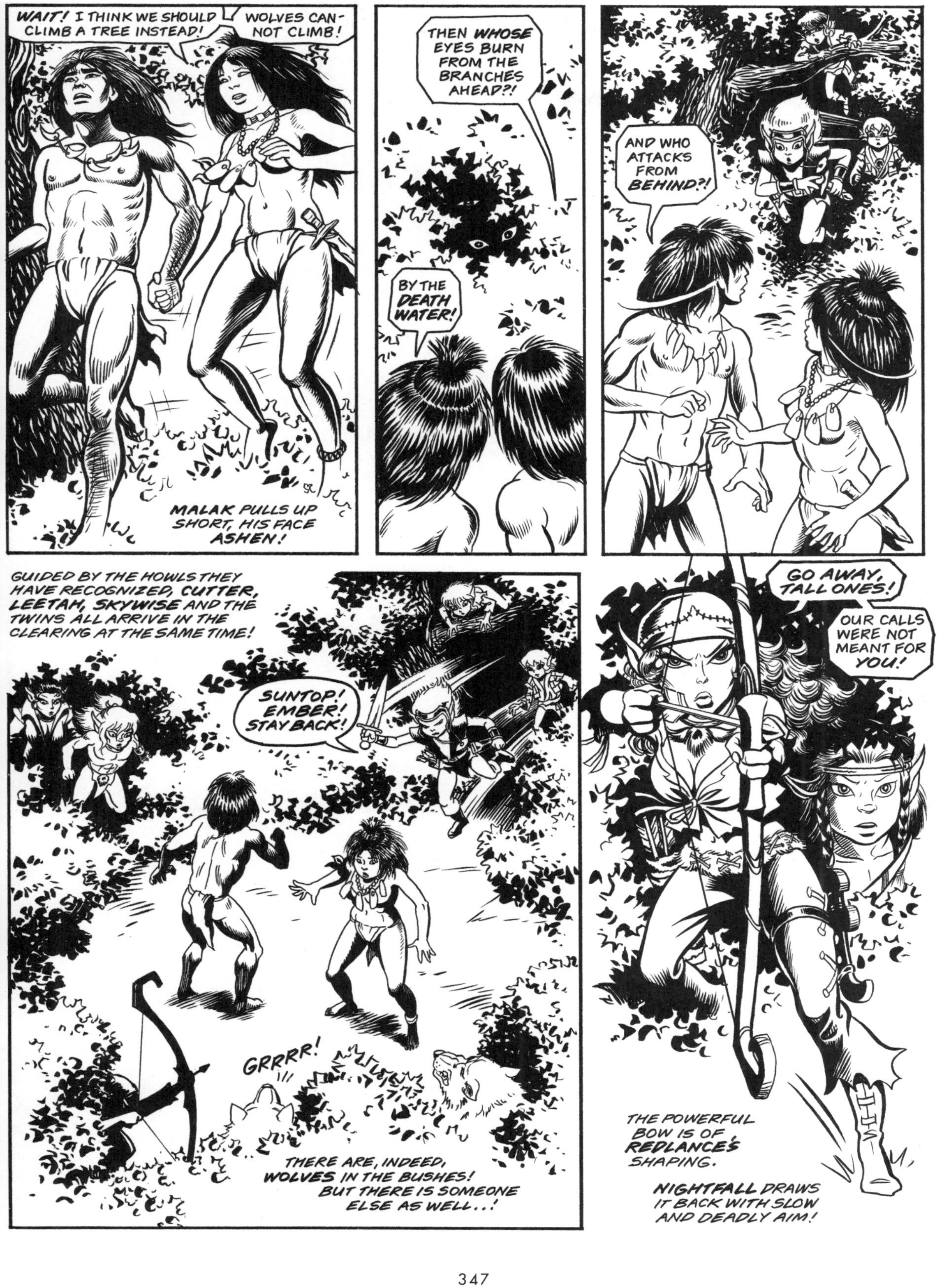

WAIT! I THINK WE SHOULD CLIMB A TREE INSTEAD!
WOLVES CAN-NOT CLIMB!
MALAK PULLS UP SHORT, HIS FACE ASHEN!
THEN WHOSE EYES BURN FROM THE BRANCHES AHEAD?!
BY THE DEATH WATER!
AND WHO ATTACKS FROM BEHIND?!
GUIDED BY THE HOWLS THEY HAVE RECOGNIZED, CUTTER, LEETAH, SKYWISE AND THE TWINS ALL ARRIVE IN THE CLEARING AT THE SAME TIME!
SUNTOP! EMBER! STAY BACK!
GRRRR!
THERE ARE, INDEED, WOLVES IN THE BUSHES! BUT THERE IS SOMEONE ELSE AS WELL..!
GO AWAY, TALL ONES!
OUR CALLS WERE NOT MEANT FOR YOU!
THE POWERFUL BOW IS OF REDLANCE'S SHAPING.
NIGHTFALL DRAWS IT BACK WITH SLOW AND DEADLY AIM!

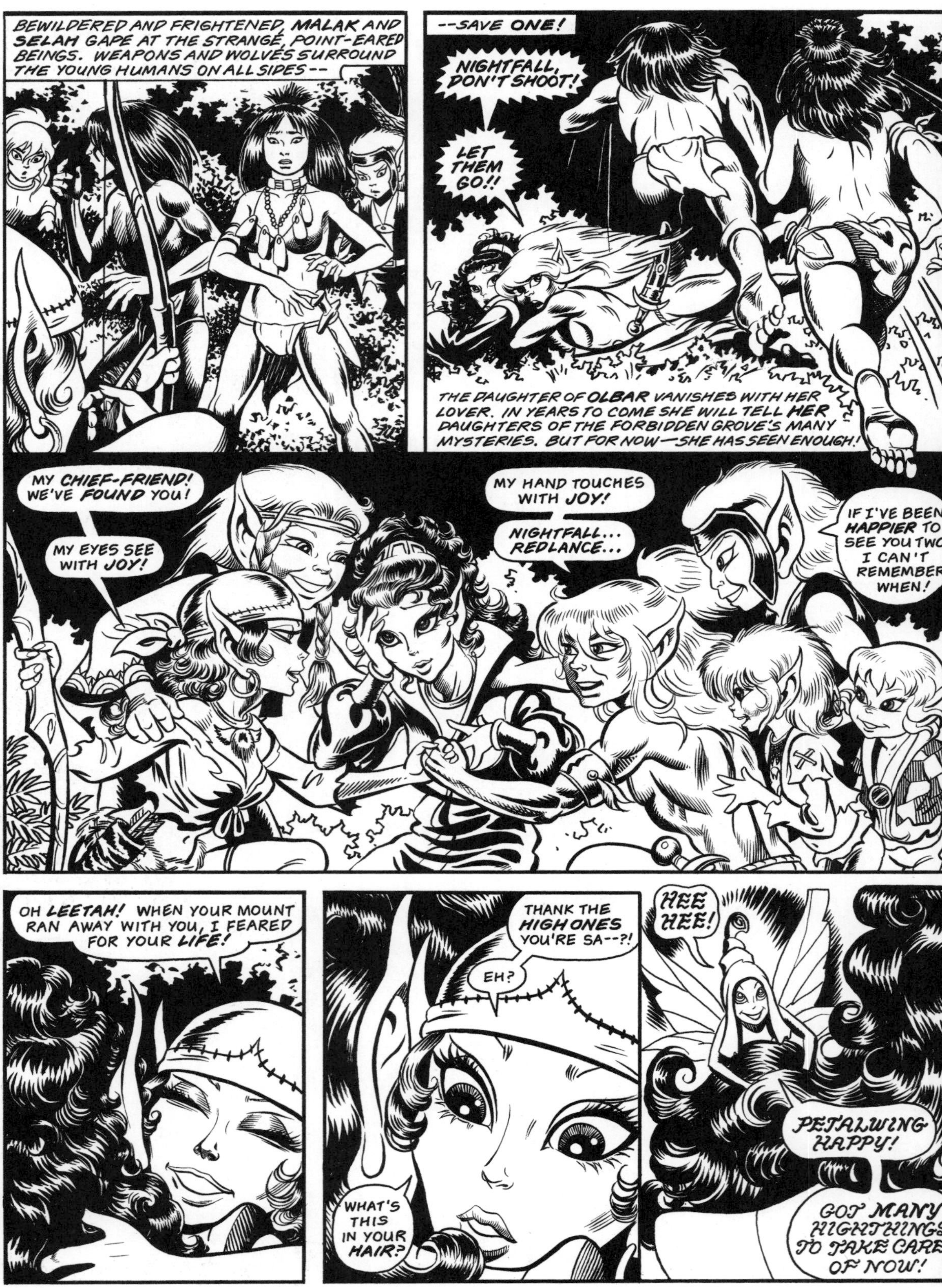
BEWILDERED AND FRIGHTENED, MALAK AND SELAH GAPE AT THE STRANGE, POINT-EARED BEINGS. WEAPONS AND WOLVES SURROUND THE YOUNG HUMANS ON ALL SIDES--
--SAVE ONE!
NIGHTFALL, DON'T SHOOT!
LET THEM GO!!
THE DAUGHTER OF OLBAR VANISHES WITH HER LOVER. IN YEARS TO COME SHE WILL TELL HER DAUGHTERS OF THE FORBIDDEN GROVE'S MANY MYSTERIES. BUT FOR NOW—SHE HAS SEEN ENOUGH!
MY CHIEF-FRIEND! WE'VE FOUND YOU!
MY EYES SEE WITH JOY!
MY HAND TOUCHES WITH JOY!
NIGHTFALL... REDLANCE...
IF I'VE BEEN HAPPIER TO SEE YOU TWO, I CAN'T REMEMBER WHEN!
OH LEETAH! WHEN YOUR MOUNT RAN AWAY WITH YOU, I FEARED FOR YOUR LIFE!
THANK THE HIGH ONES YOU'RE SA--?!
EH?
WHAT'S THIS IN YOUR HAIR?
HEE HEE!
PETALWING HAPPY!
GOT MANY HIGHTHINGS TO TAKE CARE OF NOW!

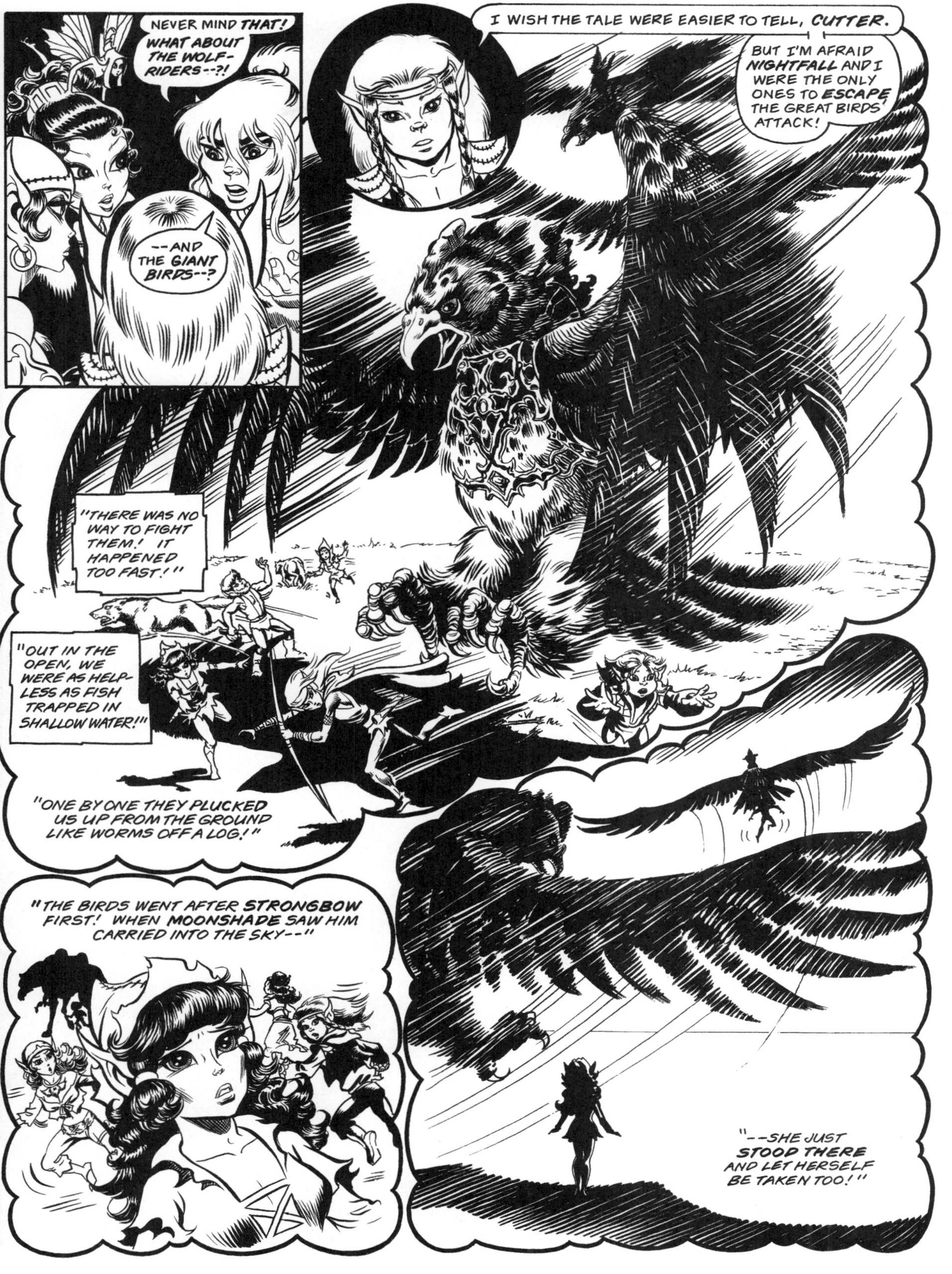
NEVER MIND THAT! WHAT ABOUT THE WOLF-RIDERS--?!
--AND THE GIANT BIRDS--?
I WISH THE TALE WERE EASIER TO TELL, CUTTER.
BUT I'M AFRAID NIGHTFALL AND I WERE THE ONLY ONES TO ESCAPE THE GREAT BIRDS' ATTACK!
"THERE WAS NO WAY TO FIGHT THEM! IT HAPPENED TOO FAST!"
"OUT IN THE OPEN, WE WERE AS HELP-LESS AS FISH TRAPPED IN SHALLOW WATER!"
"ONE BY ONE THEY PLUCKED US UP FROM THE GROUND LIKE WORMS OFF A LOG!"
"THE BIRDS WENT AFTER STRONGBOW FIRST! WHEN MOONSHADE SAW HIM CARRIED INTO THE SKY--"
"--SHE JUST STOOD THERE AND LET HERSELF BE TAKEN TOO!"

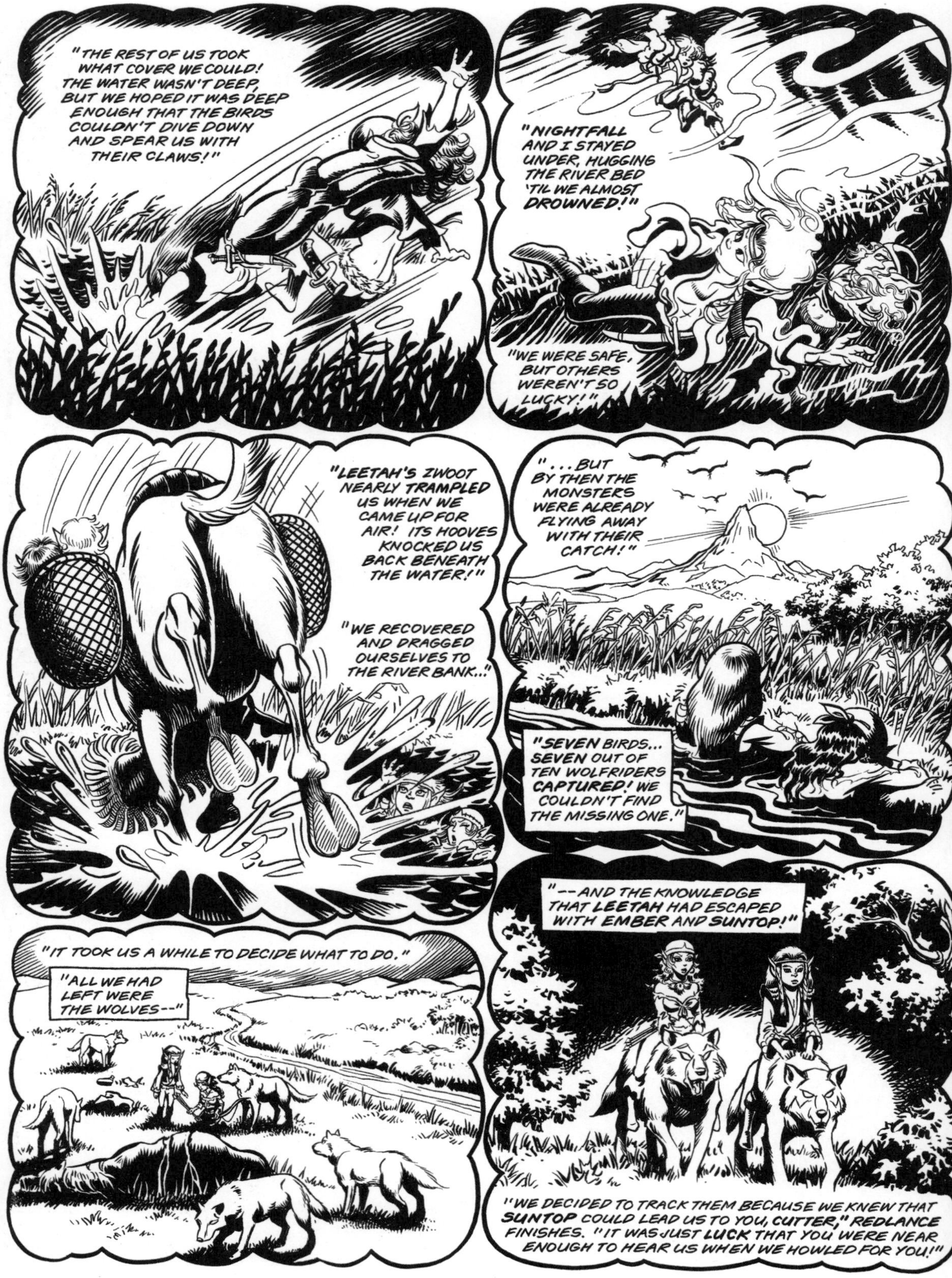
"THE REST OF US TOOK WHAT COVER WE COULD! THE WATER WASN'T DEEP, BUT WE HOPED IT WAS DEEP ENOUGH THAT THE BIRDS COULDN'T DIVE DOWN AND SPEAR US WITH THEIR CLAWS!"
"NIGHTFALL AND I STAYED UNDER, HUGGING THE RIVER BED 'TIL WE ALMOST DROWNED!"
"WE WERE SAFE, BUT OTHERS WEREN'T SO LUCKY!"
"LEETAH'S ZWOOT NEARLY TRAMPLED US WHEN WE CAME UP FOR AIR! ITS HOOVES KNOCKED US BACK BENEATH THE WATER!"
"WE RECOVERED AND DRAGGED OURSELVES TO THE RIVER BANK..."
"...BUT BY THEN THE MONSTERS WERE ALREADY FLYING AWAY WITH THEIR CATCH!"
"SEVEN BIRDS... SEVEN OUT OF TEN WOLFRIDERS CAPTURED! WE COULDN'T FIND THE MISSING ONE."
"IT TOOK US A WHILE TO DECIDE WHAT TO DO."
"ALL WE HAD LEFT WERE THE WOLVES--"
"--AND THE KNOWLEDGE THAT LEETAH HAD ESCAPED WITH EMBER AND SUNTOP!"
"WE DECIDED TO TRACK THEM BECAUSE WE KNEW THAT SUNTOP COULD LEAD US TO YOU, CUTTER," REDLANCE FINISHES. "IT WAS JUST LUCK THAT YOU WERE NEAR ENOUGH TO HEAR US WHEN WE HOWLED FOR YOU!"

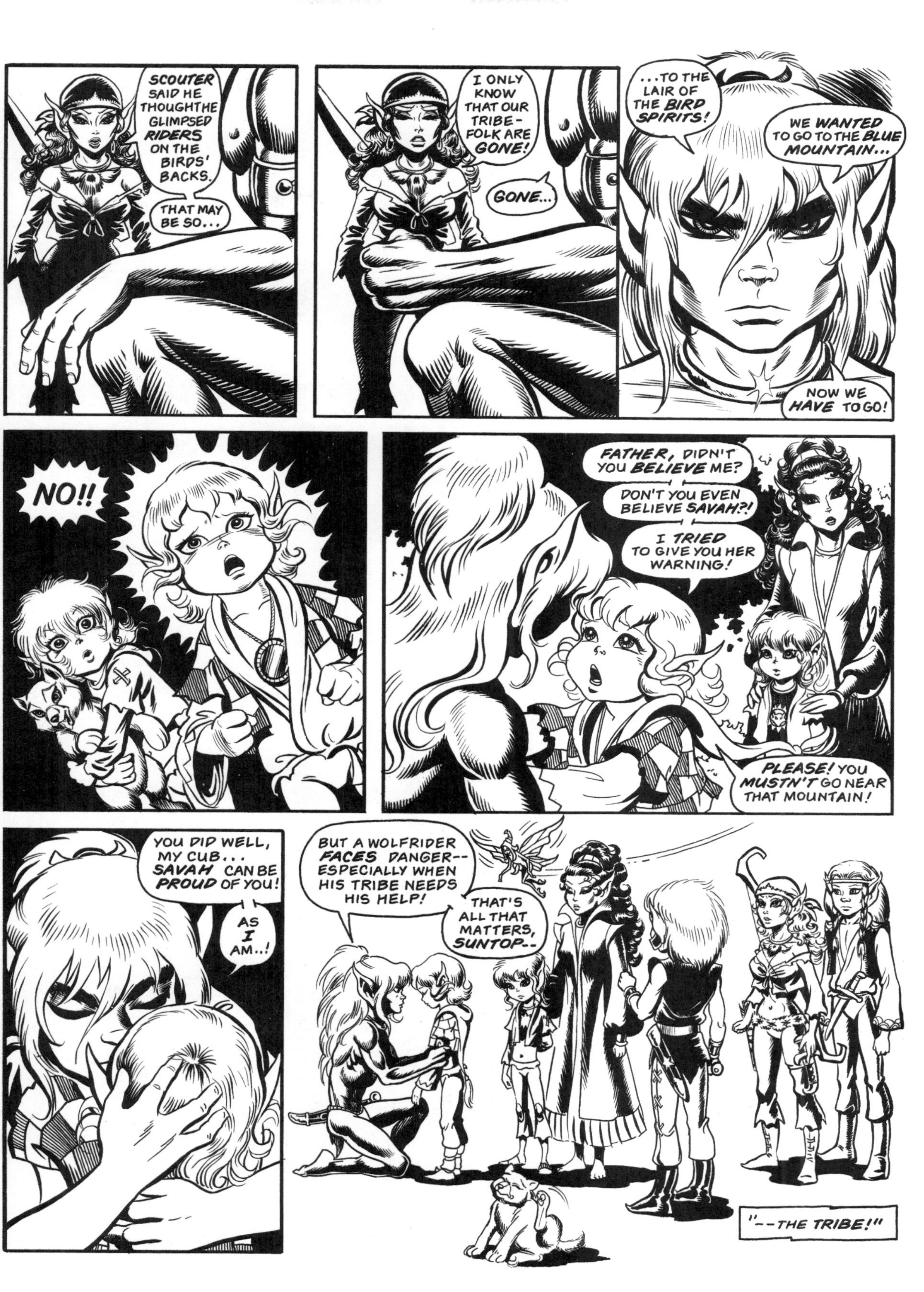
SCOUTER SAID HE THOUGHT HE GLIMPSED RIDERS ON THE BIRDS' BACKS.
THAT MAY BE SO...
I ONLY KNOW THAT OUR TRIBE-FOLK ARE GONE!
GONE...
...TO THE LAIR OF THE BIRD SPIRITS!
WE WANTED TO GO TO THE BLUE MOUNTAIN...
NOW WE HAVE TO GO!
NO!!
FATHER, DIDN'T YOU BELIEVE ME?
DON'T YOU EVEN BELIEVE SAVAH?!
I TRIED TO GIVE YOU HER WARNING!
PLEASE! YOU MUSTN'T GO NEAR THAT MOUNTAIN!
YOU DID WELL, MY CUB... SAVAH CAN BE PROUD OF YOU!
AS I AM..!
BUT A WOLFRIDER FACES DANGER-- ESPECIALLY WHEN HIS TRIBE NEEDS HIS HELP!
THAT'S ALL THAT MATTERS, SUNTOP--
"--THE TRIBE!"

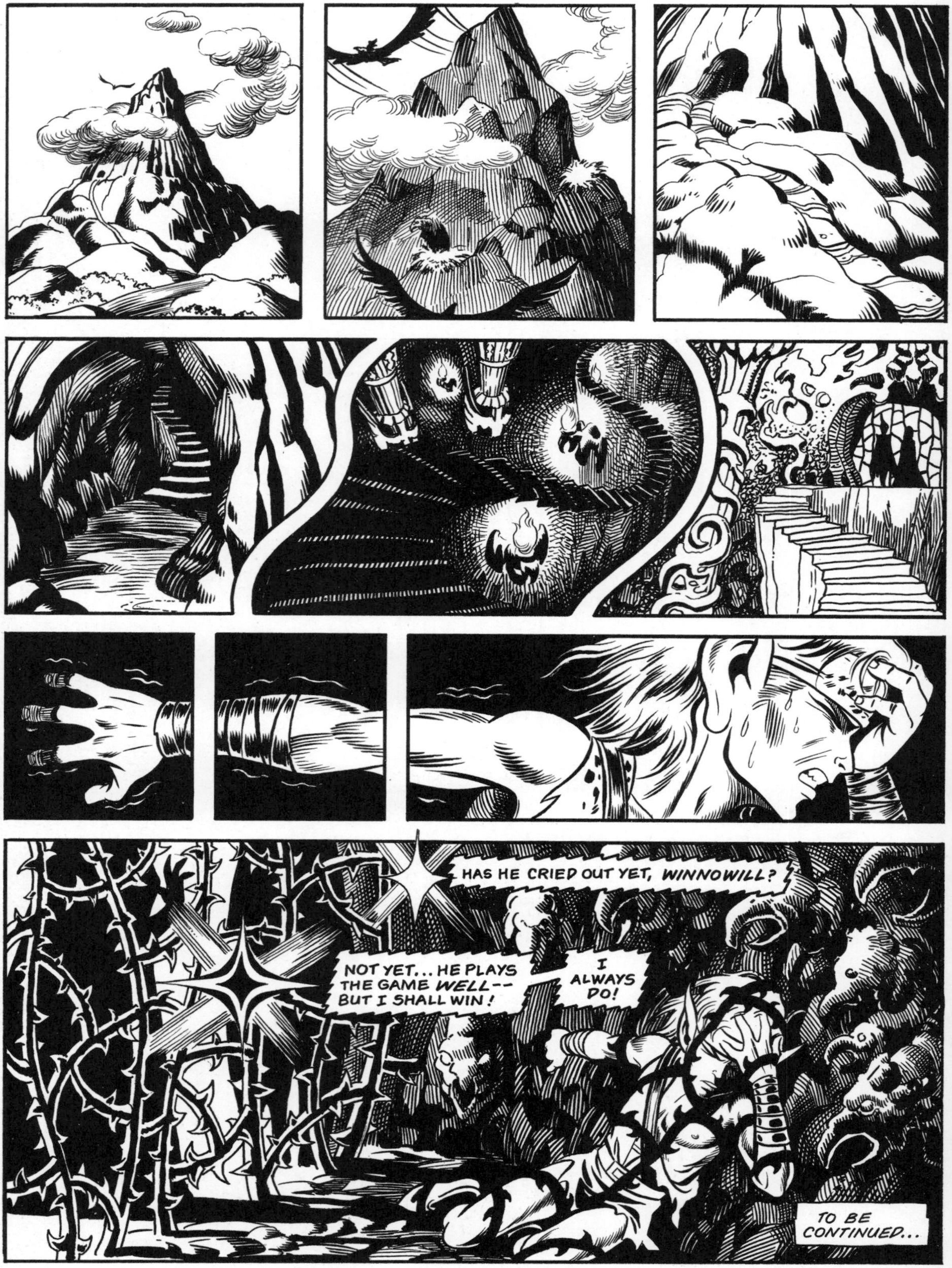

HAS HE CRIED OUT YET, WINNOWILL?
NOT YET... HE PLAYS THE GAME WELL-- BUT I SHALL WIN!
I ALWAYS DO!
TO BE CONTINUED...

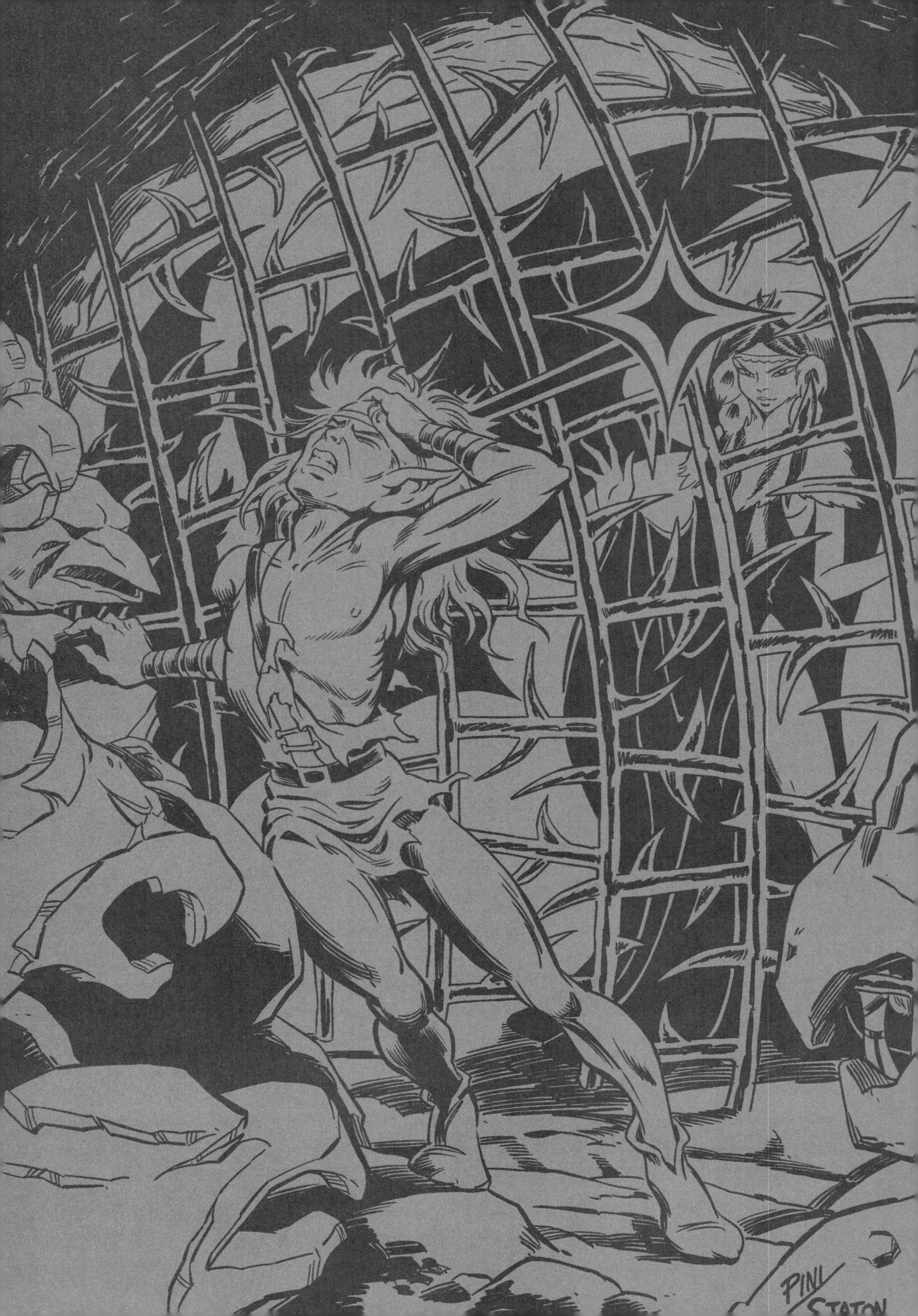
PINI
STATON

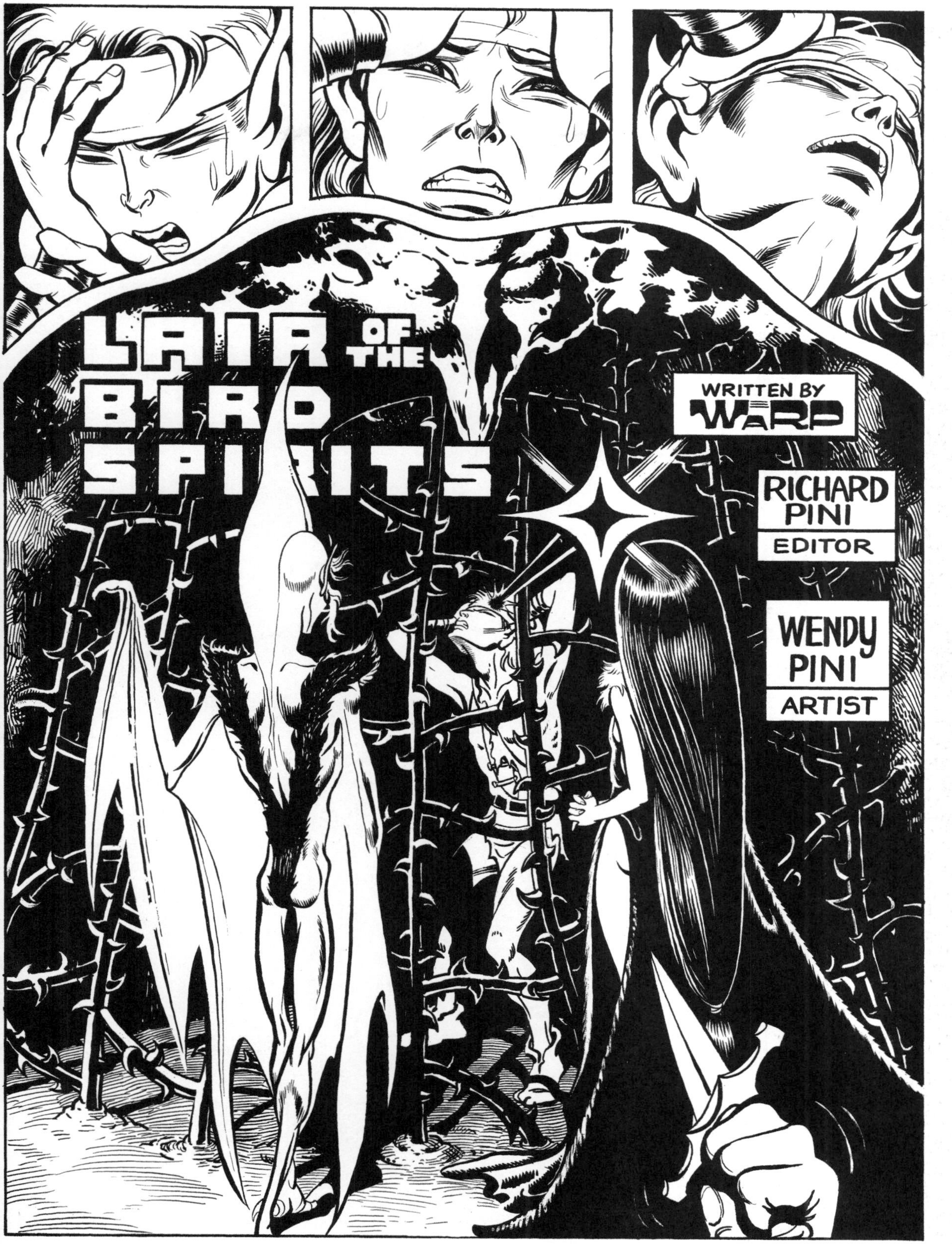
LAIR OF THE BIRD SPIRITS
WRITTEN BY WARP
RICHARD PINI
EDITOR
WENDY PINI
ARTIST

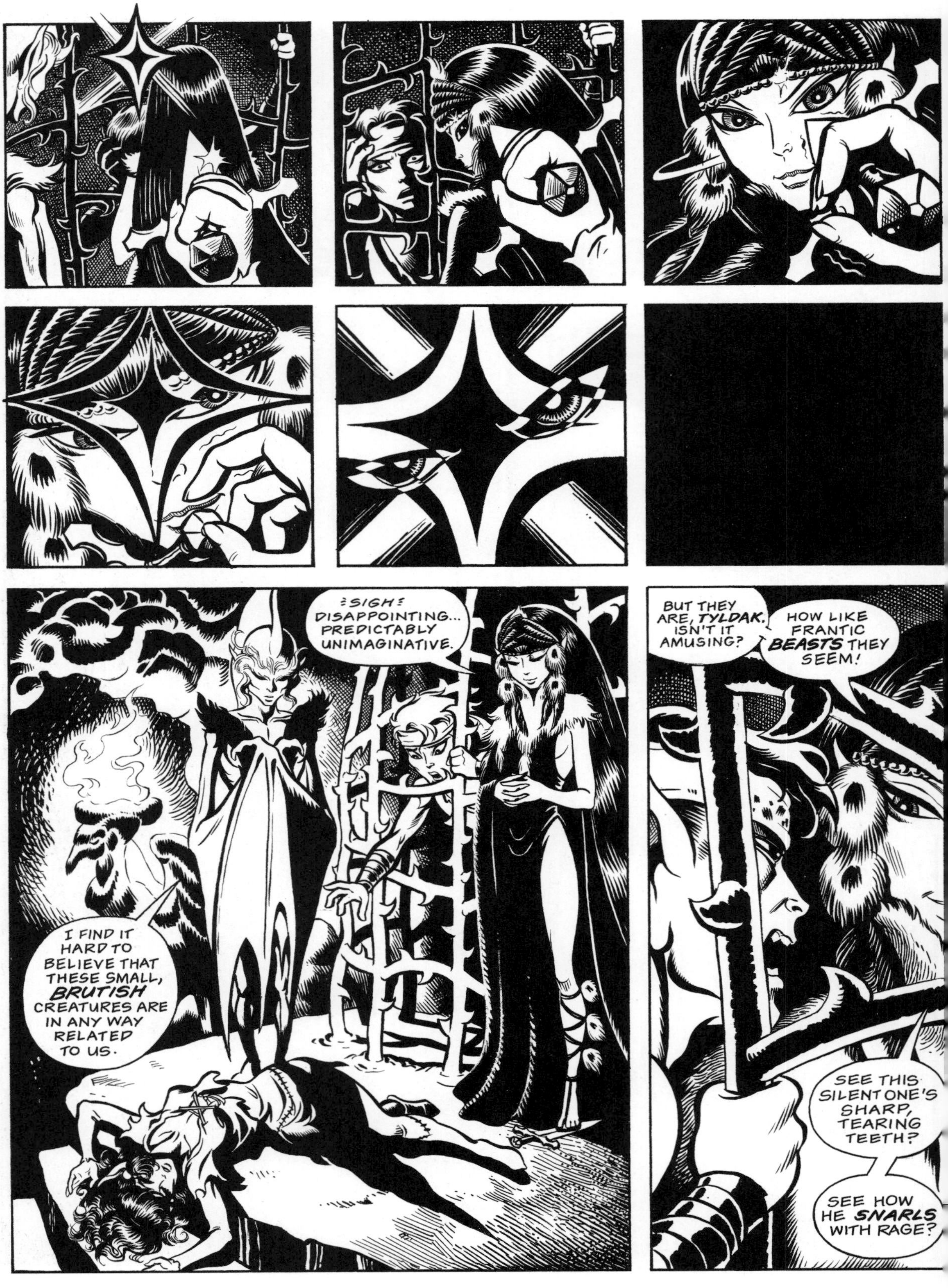

:SIGH:
DISAPPOINTING... PREDICTABLY UNIMAGINATIVE.
I FIND IT HARD TO BELIEVE THAT THESE SMALL, BRUTISH CREATURES ARE IN ANY WAY RELATED TO US.
BUT THEY ARE, TYLDAK. ISN'T IT AMUSING?
HOW LIKE FRANTIC BEASTS THEY SEEM!
SEE THIS SILENT ONE'S SHARP, TEARING TEETH?
SEE HOW HE SNARLS WITH RAGE?

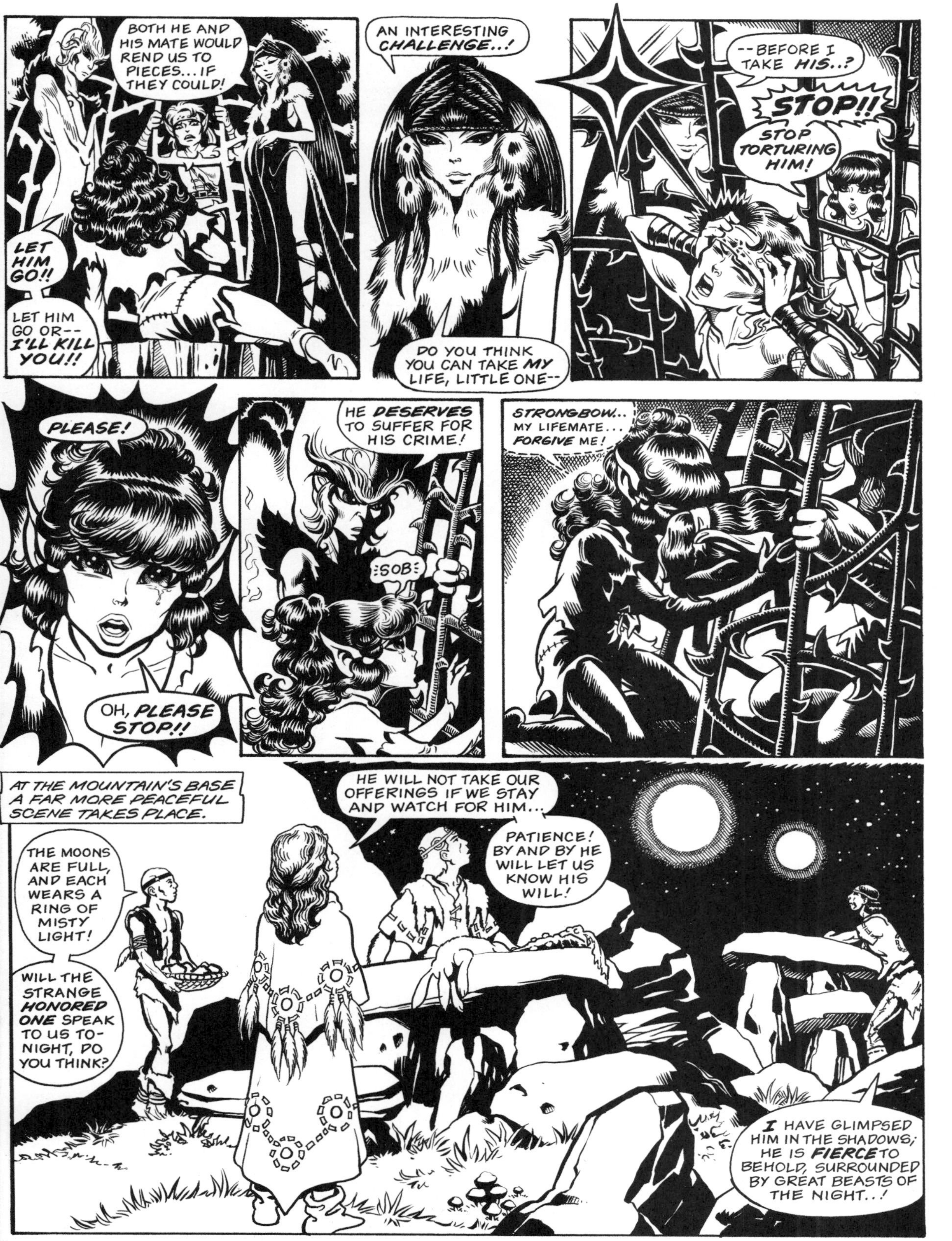

BOTH HE AND HIS MATE WOULD REND US TO PIECES... IF THEY COULD!
LET HIM GO!!
LET HIM GO OR-- I'LL KILL YOU!!
AN INTERESTING CHALLENGE..!
DO YOU THINK YOU CAN TAKE MY LIFE, LITTLE ONE--
--BEFORE I TAKE HIS..?
STOP!!
STOP TORTURING HIM!
PLEASE!
OH, PLEASE STOP!!
HE DESERVES TO SUFFER FOR HIS CRIME!
SOB
STRONGBOW... MY LIFEMATE... FORGIVE ME!
AT THE MOUNTAIN'S BASE A FAR MORE PEACEFUL SCENE TAKES PLACE.
THE MOONS ARE FULL, AND EACH WEARS A RING OF MISTY LIGHT!
WILL THE STRANGE HONORED ONE SPEAK TO US TO-NIGHT, DO YOU THINK?
HE WILL NOT TAKE OUR OFFERINGS IF WE STAY AND WATCH FOR HIM...
PATIENCE! BY AND BY HE WILL LET US KNOW HIS WILL!
I HAVE GLIMPSED HIM IN THE SHADOWS; HE IS FIERCE TO BEHOLD, SURROUNDED BY GREAT BEASTS OF THE NIGHT..!

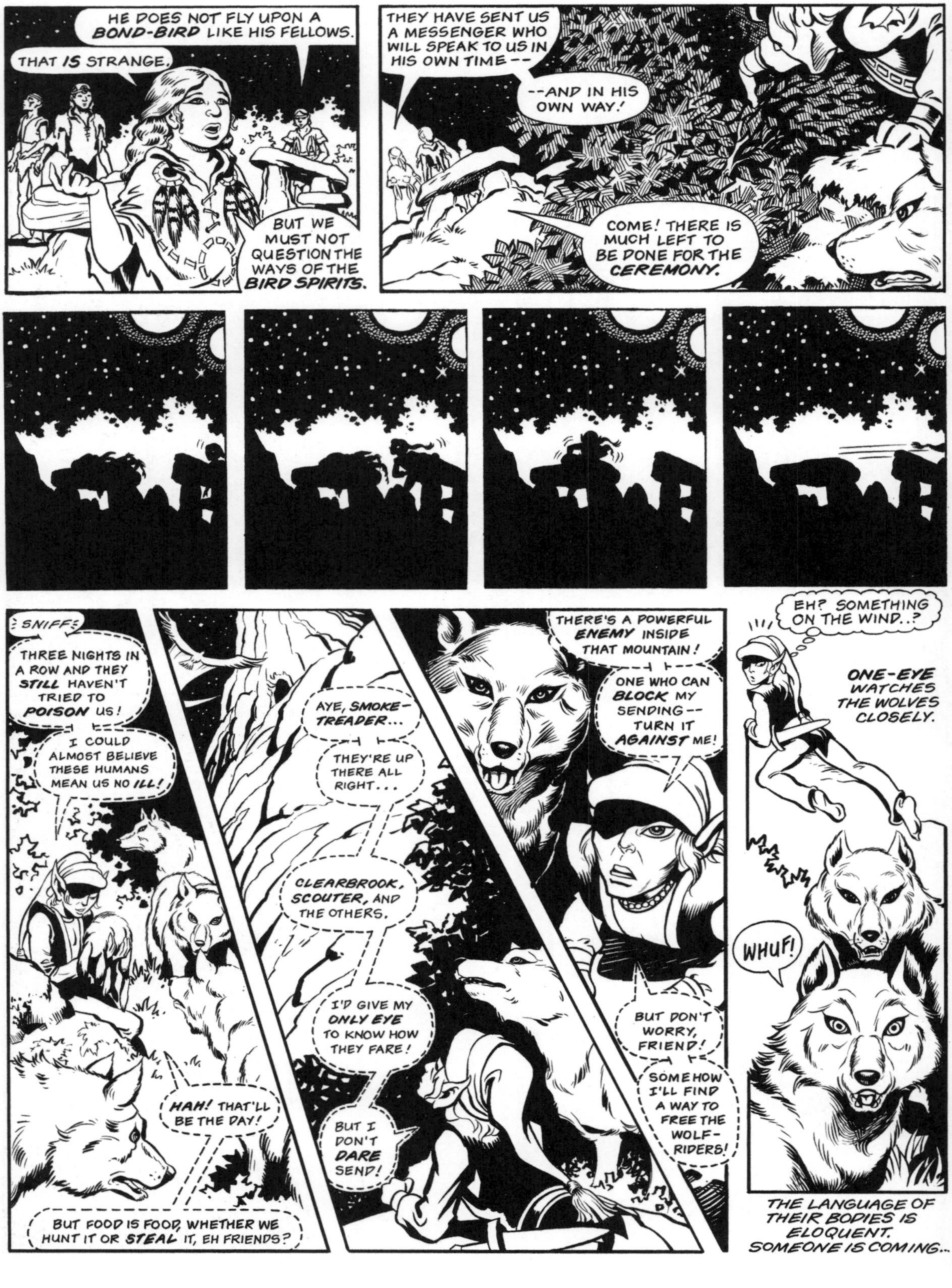

HE DOES NOT FLY UPON A BOND-BIRD LIKE HIS FELLOWS.
THAT IS STRANGE.
BUT WE MUST NOT QUESTION THE WAYS OF THE BIRD SPIRITS.
THEY HAVE SENT US A MESSENGER WHO WILL SPEAK TO US IN HIS OWN TIME --
--AND IN HIS OWN WAY!
COME! THERE IS MUCH LEFT TO BE DONE FOR THE CEREMONY.
SNIFF
THREE NIGHTS IN A ROW AND THEY STILL HAVEN'T TRIED TO POISON US!
I COULD ALMOST BELIEVE THESE HUMANS MEAN US NO ILL!
HAH! THAT'LL BE THE DAY!
BUT FOOD IS FOOD, WHETHER WE HUNT IT OR STEAL IT, EH FRIENDS?
AYE, SMOKE-TREADER...
THEY'RE UP THERE ALL RIGHT...
CLEARBROOK, SCOUTER, AND THE OTHERS.
I'D GIVE MY ONLY EYE TO KNOW HOW THEY FARE!
BUT I DON'T DARE SEND!
THERE'S A POWERFUL ENEMY INSIDE THAT MOUNTAIN!
ONE WHO CAN BLOCK MY SENDING -- TURN IT AGAINST ME!
BUT DON'T WORRY, FRIEND!
SOMEHOW I'LL FIND A WAY TO FREE THE WOLF-RIDERS!
EH? SOMETHING ON THE WIND..?
ONE-EYE WATCHES THE WOLVES CLOSELY.
WHUF!
THE LANGUAGE OF THEIR BODIES IS ELOQUENT. SOMEONE IS COMING...

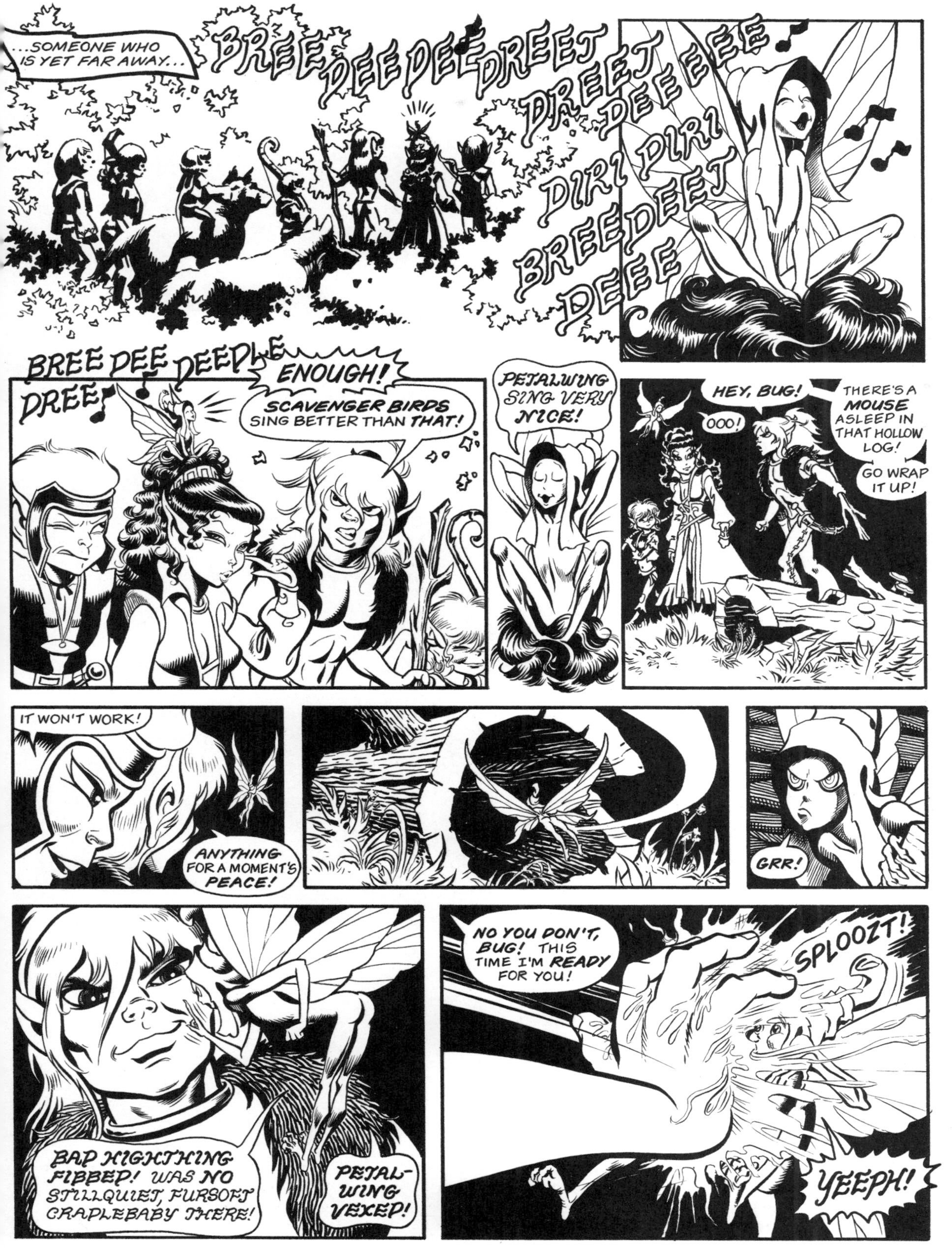

...SOMEONE WHO IS YET FAR AWAY...
BREE DEE DEE DREET DREET DEE EEEE DIRI DIRI BREEDEET DEEE
BREE DEE DEEPLE DREE
ENOUGH! SCAVENGER BIRDS SING BETTER THAN THAT!
PETALWING SING VERY NICE!
HEY, BUG!
OOO!
THERE'S A MOUSE ASLEEP IN THAT HOLLOW LOG!
GO WRAP IT UP!
IT WON'T WORK!
ANYTHING FOR A MOMENT'S PEACE!
GRR!
BAD HIGHTHING FIBBED! WAS NO STILLQUIET, FURSOFT CRADLEBABY THERE!
PETAL-WING VEXED!
NO YOU DON'T, BUG! THIS TIME I'M READY FOR YOU!
SPLOOZT!
YEEPH!

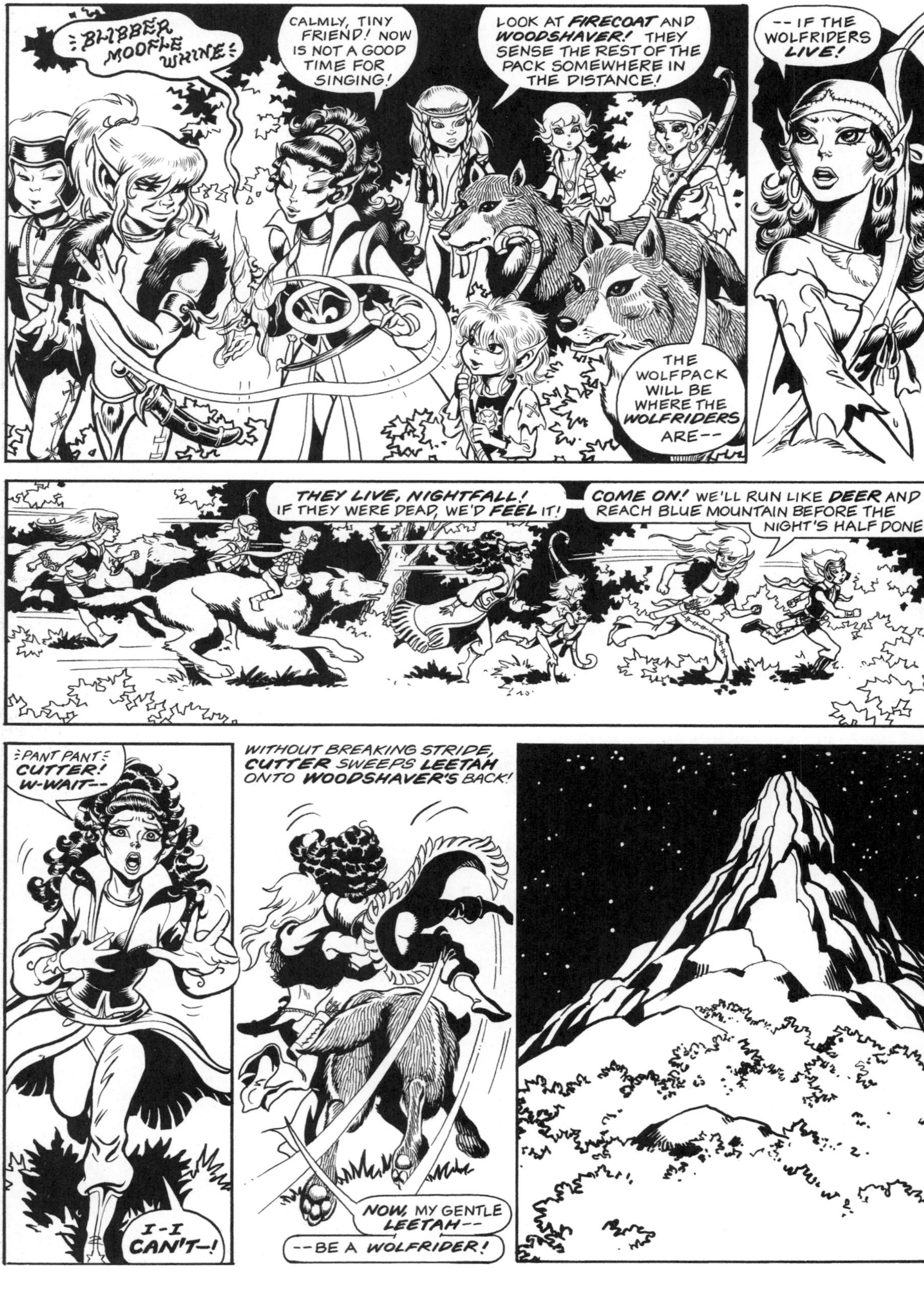
BLIBBER MOOFLE WHINE
CALMLY, TINY FRIEND! NOW IS NOT A GOOD TIME FOR SINGING!
LOOK AT FIRECOAT AND WOODSHAVER! THEY SENSE THE REST OF THE PACK SOMEWHERE IN THE DISTANCE!
THE WOLFPACK WILL BE WHERE THE WOLFRIDERS ARE--
--IF THE WOLFRIDERS LIVE!
THEY LIVE, NIGHTFALL! IF THEY WERE DEAD, WE'D FEEL IT!
COME ON! WE'LL RUN LIKE DEER AND REACH BLUE MOUNTAIN BEFORE THE NIGHT'S HALF DONE!
PANT PANT CUTTER! W-WAIT--
I-I CAN'T--!
WITHOUT BREAKING STRIDE, CUTTER SWEEPS LEETAH ONTO WOODSHAVER'S BACK!
NOW, MY GENTLE LEETAH--
--BE A WOLFRIDER!

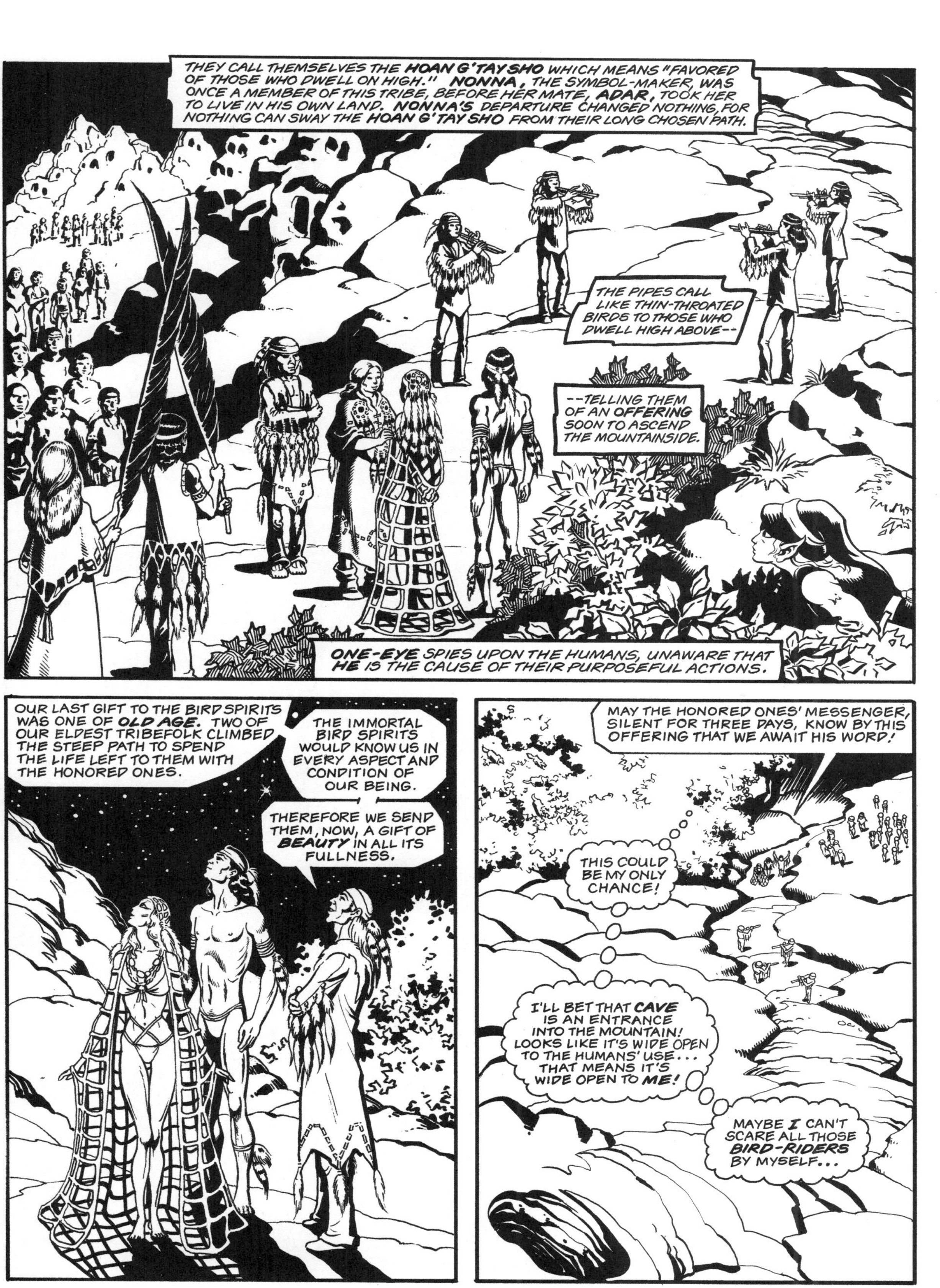
THEY CALL THEMSELVES THE **HOAN G'TAY SHO** WHICH MEANS "FAVORED OF THOSE WHO DWELL ON HIGH." **NONNA**, THE SYMBOL-MAKER, WAS ONCE A MEMBER OF THIS TRIBE, BEFORE HER MATE, **ADAR**, TOOK HER TO LIVE IN HIS OWN LAND. **NONNA'S** DEPARTURE CHANGED NOTHING, FOR NOTHING CAN SWAY THE **HOAN G'TAY SHO** FROM THEIR LONG CHOSEN PATH.
THE PIPES CALL LIKE THIN-THROATED BIRDS TO THOSE WHO DWELL HIGH ABOVE--
--TELLING THEM OF AN **OFFERING** SOON TO ASCEND THE MOUNTAINSIDE.
ONE-EYE SPIES UPON THE HUMANS, UNAWARE THAT **HE** IS THE CAUSE OF THEIR PURPOSEFUL ACTIONS.
OUR LAST GIFT TO THE BIRD SPIRITS WAS ONE OF **OLD AGE**. TWO OF OUR ELDEST TRIBEFOLK CLIMBED THE STEEP PATH TO SPEND THE LIFE LEFT TO THEM WITH THE HONORED ONES.
THE IMMORTAL BIRD SPIRITS WOULD KNOW US IN EVERY ASPECT AND CONDITION OF OUR BEING.
THEREFORE WE SEND THEM, NOW, A GIFT OF **BEAUTY** IN ALL ITS FULLNESS.
MAY THE HONORED ONES' MESSENGER, SILENT FOR THREE DAYS, KNOW BY THIS OFFERING THAT WE AWAIT HIS WORD!
THIS COULD BE MY ONLY CHANCE!
I'LL BET THAT **CAVE** IS AN ENTRANCE INTO THE MOUNTAIN! LOOKS LIKE IT'S WIDE OPEN TO THE HUMANS' USE... THAT MEANS IT'S WIDE OPEN TO **ME**!
MAYBE **I** CAN'T SCARE ALL THOSE **BIRD-RIDERS** BY MYSELF...

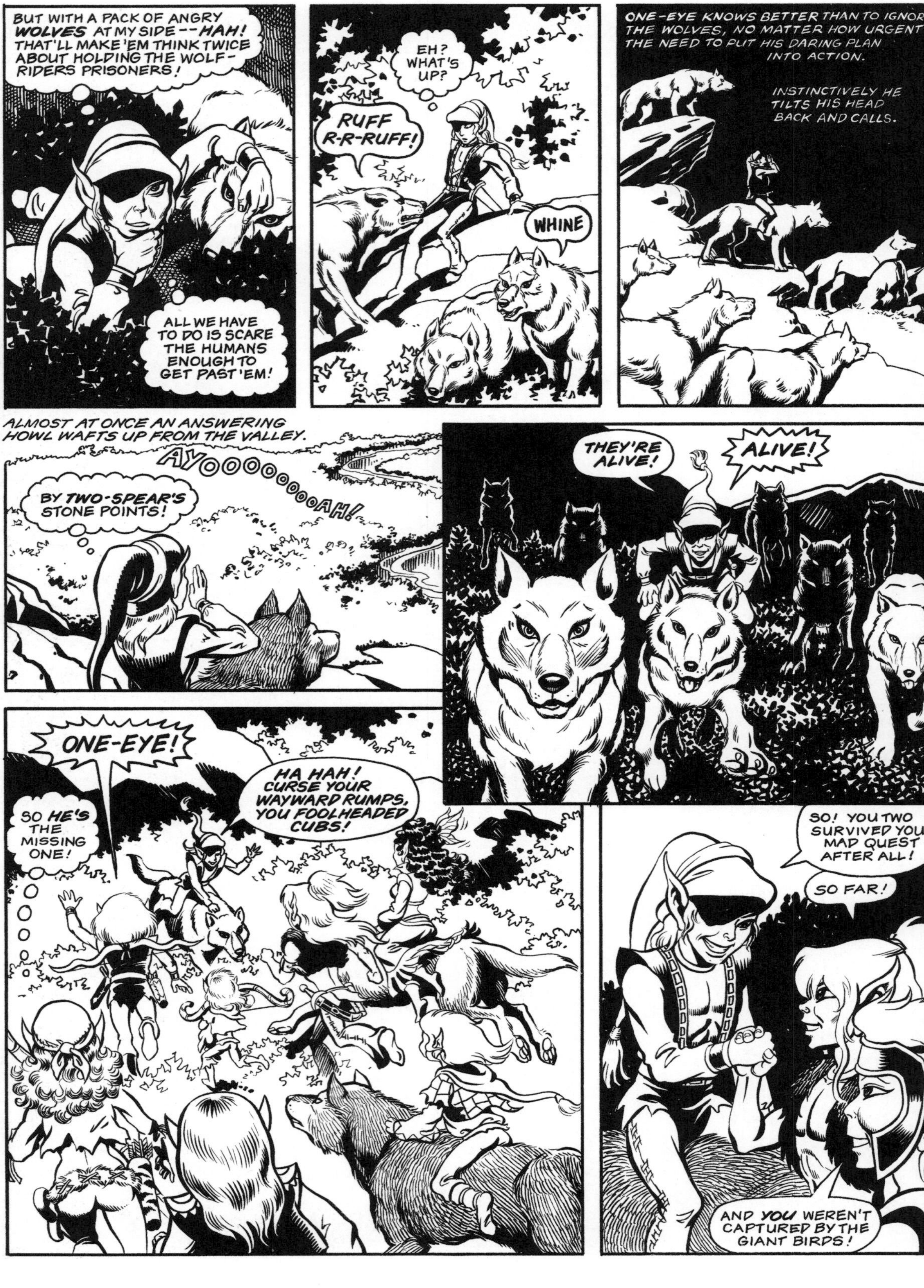

BUT WITH A PACK OF ANGRY WOLVES AT MY SIDE--HAH! THAT'LL MAKE 'EM THINK TWICE ABOUT HOLDING THE WOLF-RIDERS PRISONERS!
ALL WE HAVE TO DO IS SCARE THE HUMANS ENOUGH TO GET PAST 'EM!
EH? WHAT'S UP?
RUFF R-R-RUFF!
WHINE
ONE-EYE KNOWS BETTER THAN TO IGNORE THE WOLVES, NO MATTER HOW URGENT THE NEED TO PUT HIS DARING PLAN INTO ACTION.
INSTINCTIVELY HE TILTS HIS HEAD BACK AND CALLS.
ALMOST AT ONCE AN ANSWERING HOWL WAFTS UP FROM THE VALLEY.
AYOOOOOOOOOOAH!
BY TWO-SPEAR'S STONE POINTS!
THEY'RE ALIVE!
ALIVE!
ONE-EYE!
SO HE'S THE MISSING ONE!
HA HAH! CURSE YOUR WAYWARD RUMPS, YOU FOOLHEADED CUBS!
SO! YOU TWO SURVIVED YOUR MAD QUEST AFTER ALL!
SO FAR!
AND YOU WEREN'T CAPTURED BY THE GIANT BIRDS!

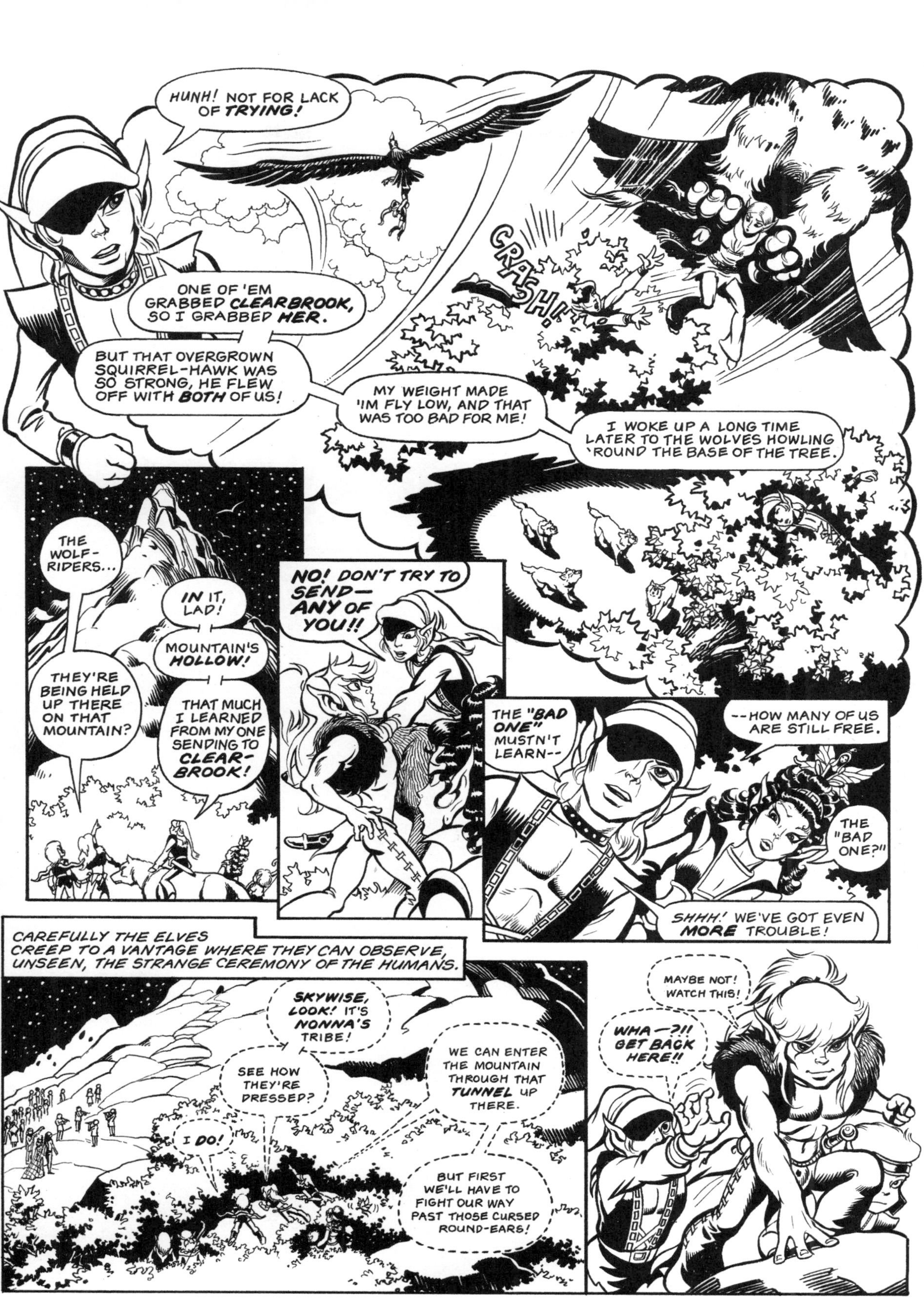

HUNH! NOT FOR LACK OF **TRYING!**
ONE OF 'EM GRABBED **CLEARBROOK,** SO I GRABBED **HER.**
BUT THAT OVERGROWN SQUIRREL-HAWK WAS SO STRONG, HE FLEW OFF WITH **BOTH** OF US!
CRASH!
MY WEIGHT MADE 'IM FLY LOW, AND THAT WAS TOO BAD FOR ME!
I WOKE UP A LONG TIME LATER TO THE WOLVES HOWLING 'ROUND THE BASE OF THE TREE.
THE WOLF-RIDERS...
THEY'RE BEING HELD UP THERE ON THAT MOUNTAIN?
IN IT, LAD!
MOUNTAIN'S **HOLLOW!**
THAT MUCH I LEARNED FROM MY ONE SENDING TO **CLEAR-BROOK!**
NO! DON'T TRY TO SEND— ANY OF YOU!!
THE **"BAD ONE"** MUSTN'T LEARN--
--HOW MANY OF US ARE STILL FREE.
THE "BAD ONE?"
SHHH! WE'VE GOT EVEN **MORE** TROUBLE!
CAREFULLY THE ELVES CREEP TO A VANTAGE WHERE THEY CAN OBSERVE, UNSEEN, THE STRANGE CEREMONY OF THE HUMANS.
SKYWISE, LOOK! IT'S **NONNA'S** TRIBE!
SEE HOW THEY'RE DRESSED?
I **DO!**
WE CAN ENTER THE MOUNTAIN THROUGH THAT **TUNNEL** UP THERE.
BUT FIRST WE'LL HAVE TO FIGHT OUR WAY PAST THOSE CURSED ROUND-EARS!
MAYBE NOT! WATCH THIS!
WHA—?!! GET BACK HERE!!

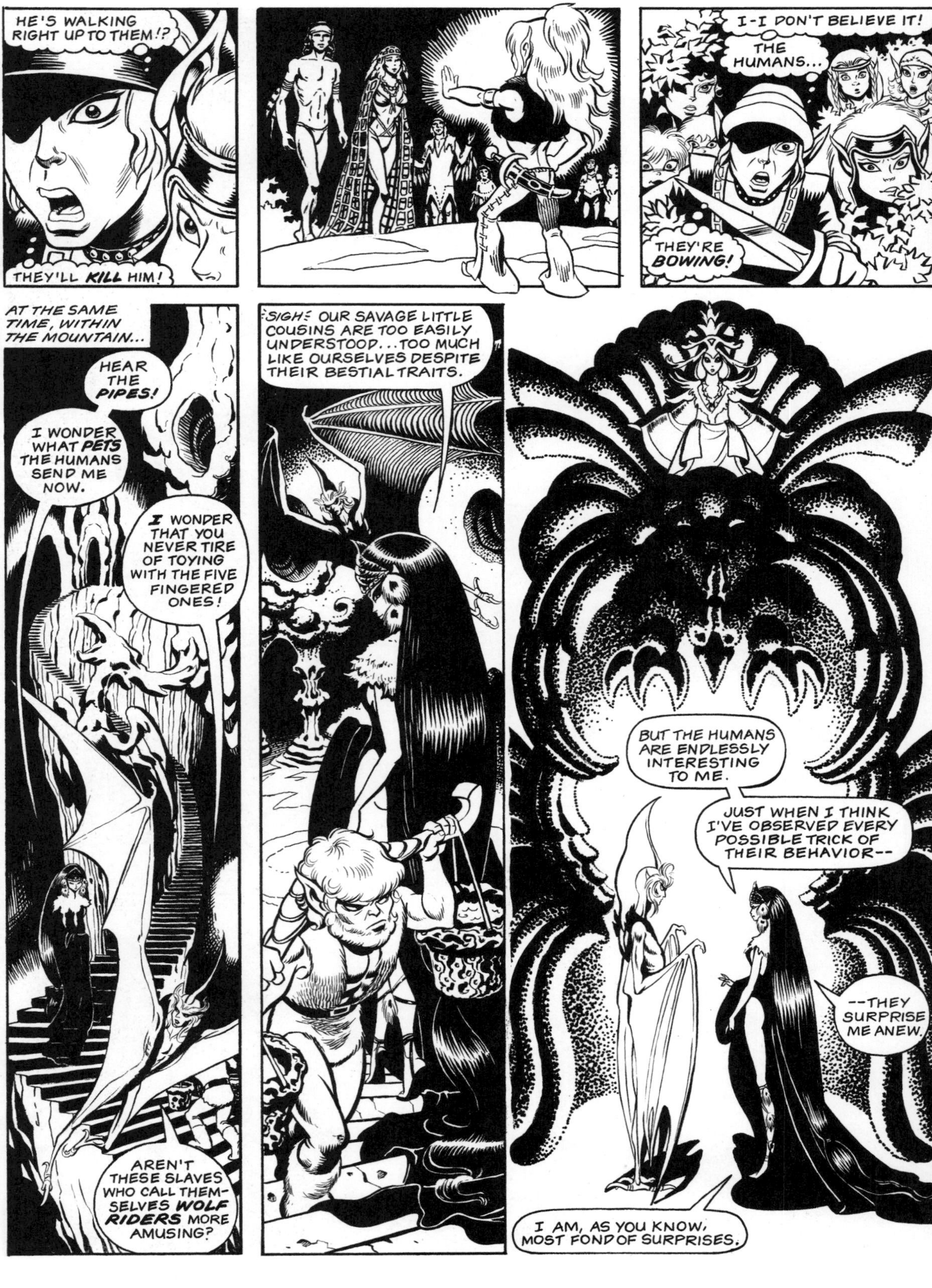
HE'S WALKING RIGHT UP TO THEM!?
THEY'LL KILL HIM!
I-I DON'T BELIEVE IT!
THE HUMANS...
THEY'RE BOWING!
AT THE SAME TIME, WITHIN THE MOUNTAIN...
HEAR THE PIPES!
I WONDER WHAT PETS THE HUMANS SEND ME NOW.
I WONDER THAT YOU NEVER TIRE OF TOYING WITH THE FIVE FINGERED ONES!
AREN'T THESE SLAVES WHO CALL THEMSELVES WOLF RIDERS MORE AMUSING?
SIGH OUR SAVAGE LITTLE COUSINS ARE TOO EASILY UNDERSTOOD... TOO MUCH LIKE OURSELVES DESPITE THEIR BESTIAL TRAITS.
BUT THE HUMANS ARE ENDLESSLY INTERESTING TO ME.
JUST WHEN I THINK I'VE OBSERVED EVERY POSSIBLE TRICK OF THEIR BEHAVIOR--
--THEY SURPRISE ME ANEW.
I AM, AS YOU KNOW, MOST FOND OF SURPRISES.

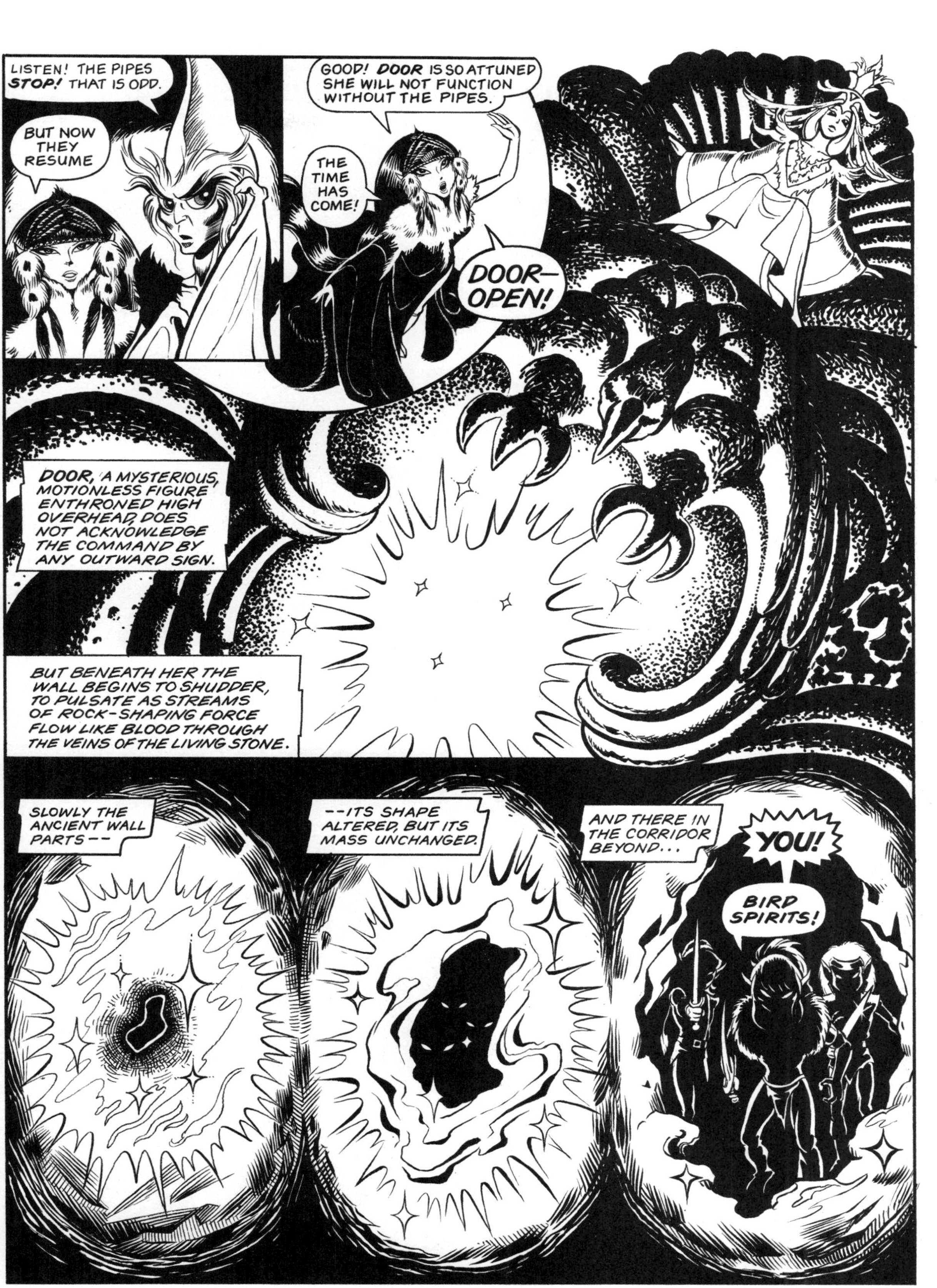

LISTEN! THE PIPES STOP! THAT IS ODD.
BUT NOW THEY RESUME
GOOD! DOOR IS SO ATTUNED SHE WILL NOT FUNCTION WITHOUT THE PIPES.
THE TIME HAS COME!
DOOR—OPEN!
DOOR, A MYSTERIOUS, MOTIONLESS FIGURE ENTHRONED HIGH OVERHEAD, DOES NOT ACKNOWLEDGE THE COMMAND BY ANY OUTWARD SIGN.
BUT BENEATH HER THE WALL BEGINS TO SHUDDER, TO PULSATE AS STREAMS OF ROCK-SHAPING FORCE FLOW LIKE BLOOD THROUGH THE VEINS OF THE LIVING STONE.
SLOWLY THE ANCIENT WALL PARTS--
--ITS SHAPE ALTERED, BUT ITS MASS UNCHANGED.
AND THERE IN THE CORRIDOR BEYOND...
YOU!
BIRD SPIRITS!

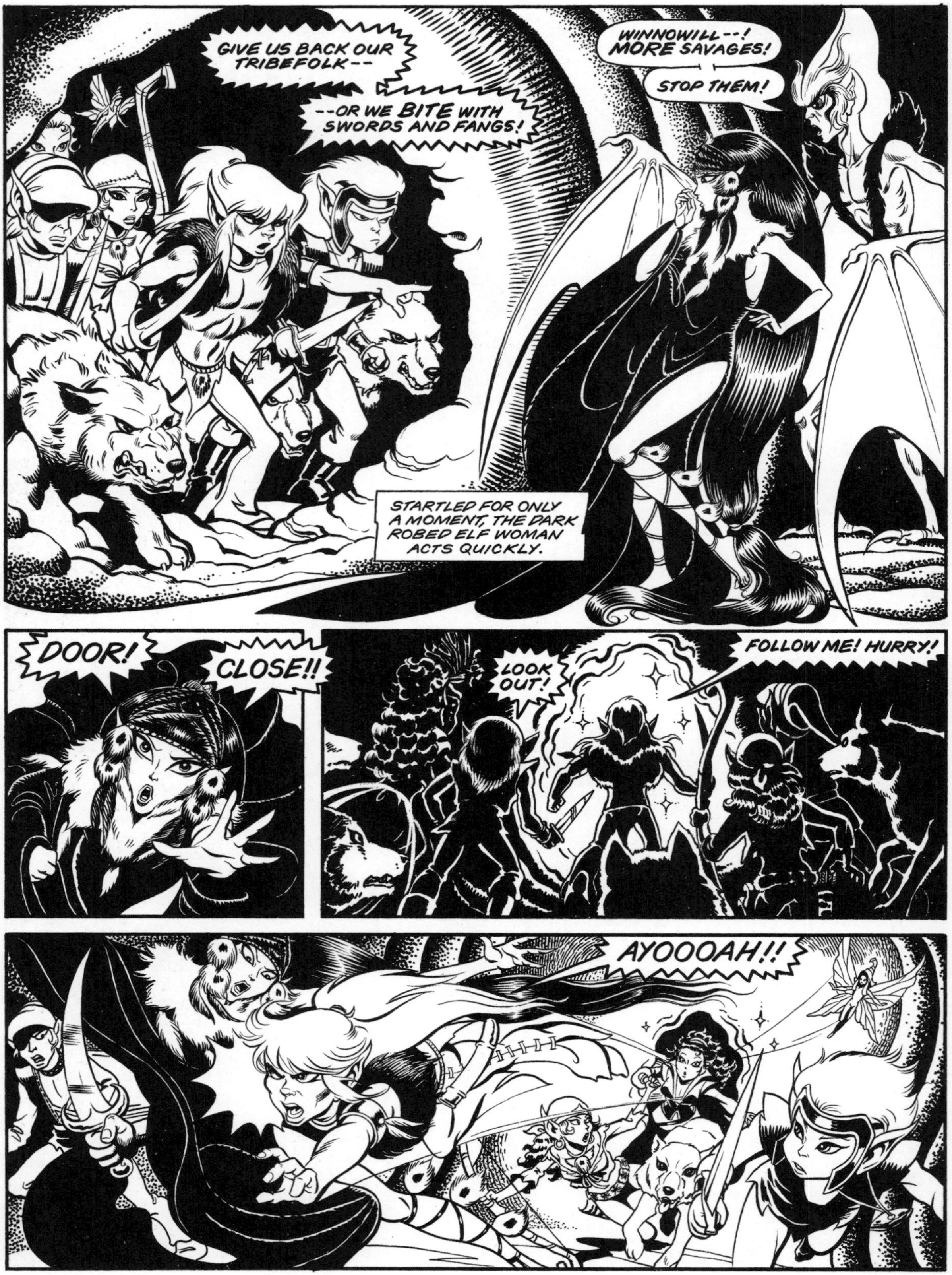

GIVE US BACK OUR TRIBEFOLK--
--OR WE BITE WITH SWORDS AND FANGS!
WINNOWILL--! MORE SAVAGES!
STOP THEM!
STARTLED FOR ONLY A MOMENT, THE DARK ROBED ELF WOMAN ACTS QUICKLY.
DOOR!
CLOSE!!
LOOK OUT!
FOLLOW ME! HURRY!
AYOOOAH!!

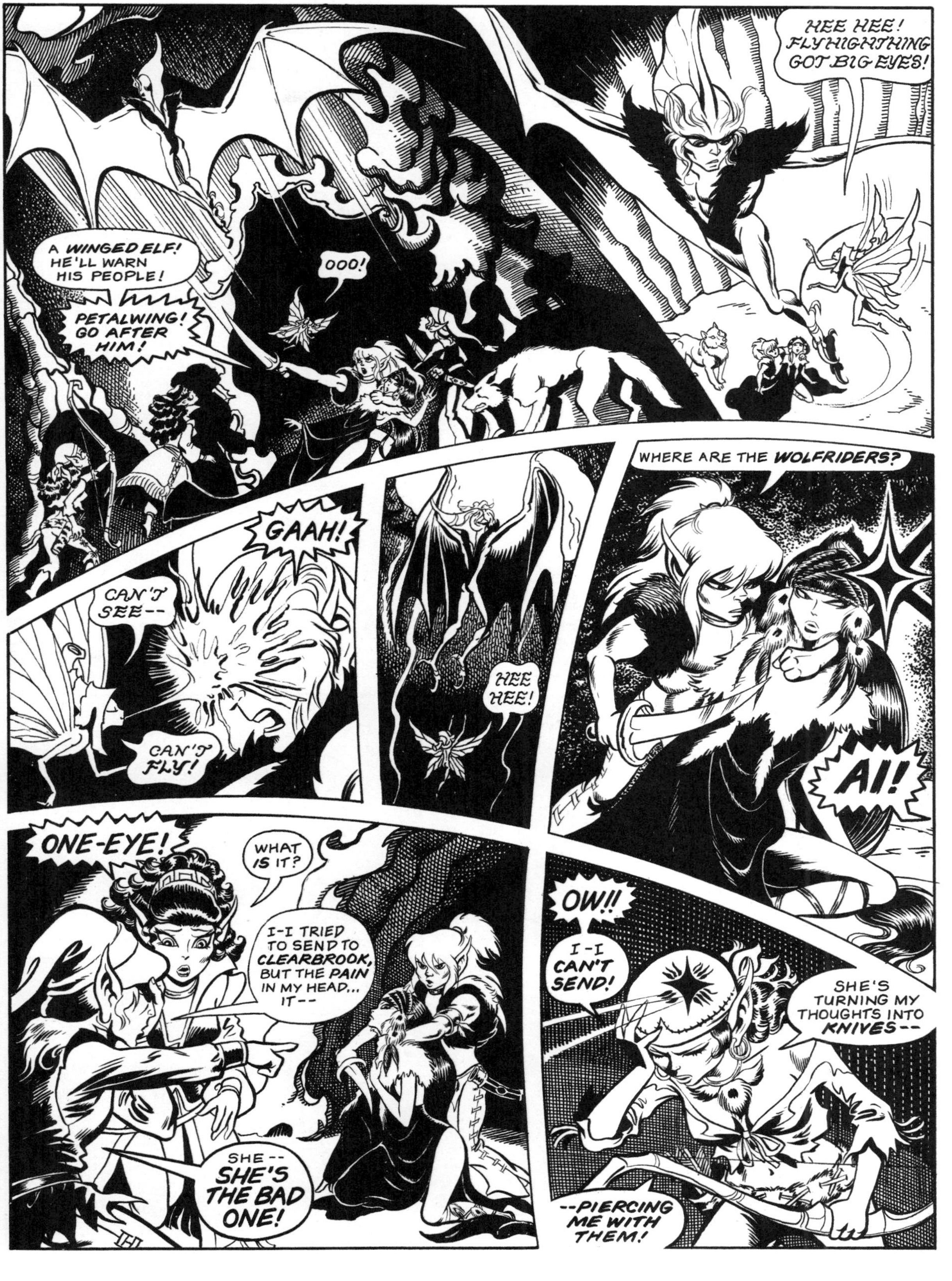
A WINGED ELF! HE'LL WARN HIS PEOPLE!
PETALWING! GO AFTER HIM!
OOO!
HEE HEE! FLYHIGHTHING GOT BIG-EYES!
GAAH!
CAN'T SEE--
CAN'T FLY!
HEE HEE!
WHERE ARE THE WOLFRIDERS?
AI!
ONE-EYE!
WHAT IS IT?
I-I TRIED TO SEND TO CLEARBROOK, BUT THE PAIN IN MY HEAD... IT--
SHE-- SHE'S THE BAD ONE!
OW!!
I-I CAN'T SEND!
SHE'S TURNING MY THOUGHTS INTO KNIVES--
--PIERCING ME WITH THEM!

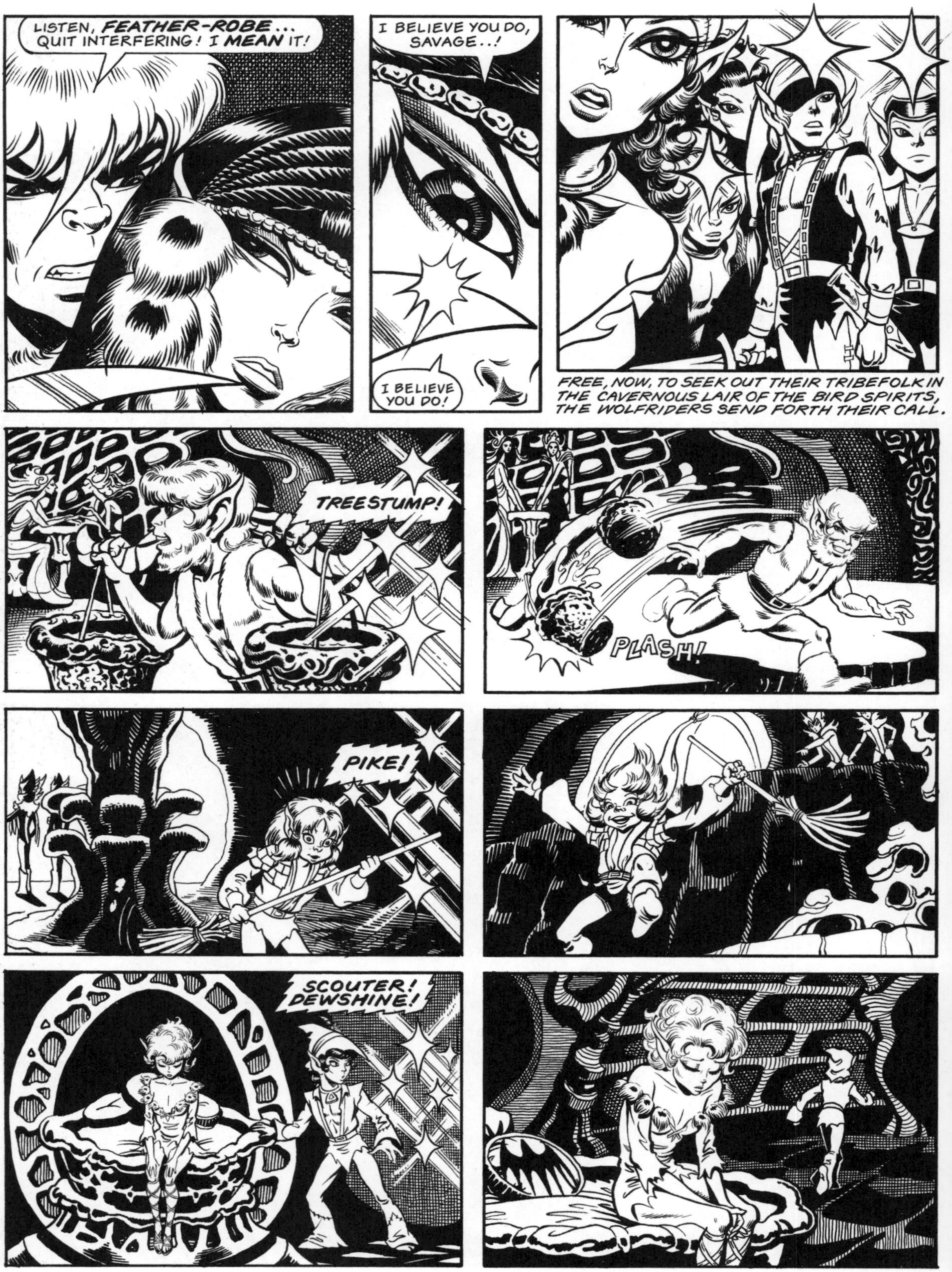
LISTEN, FEATHER-ROBE... QUIT INTERFERING! I MEAN IT!
I BELIEVE YOU DO, SAVAGE..!
I BELIEVE YOU DO!
FREE, NOW, TO SEEK OUT THEIR TRIBEFOLK IN THE CAVERNOUS LAIR OF THE BIRD SPIRITS, THE WOLFRIDERS SEND FORTH THEIR CALL.
TREESTUMP!
PLASH!
PIKE!
SCOUTER! DEWSHINE!

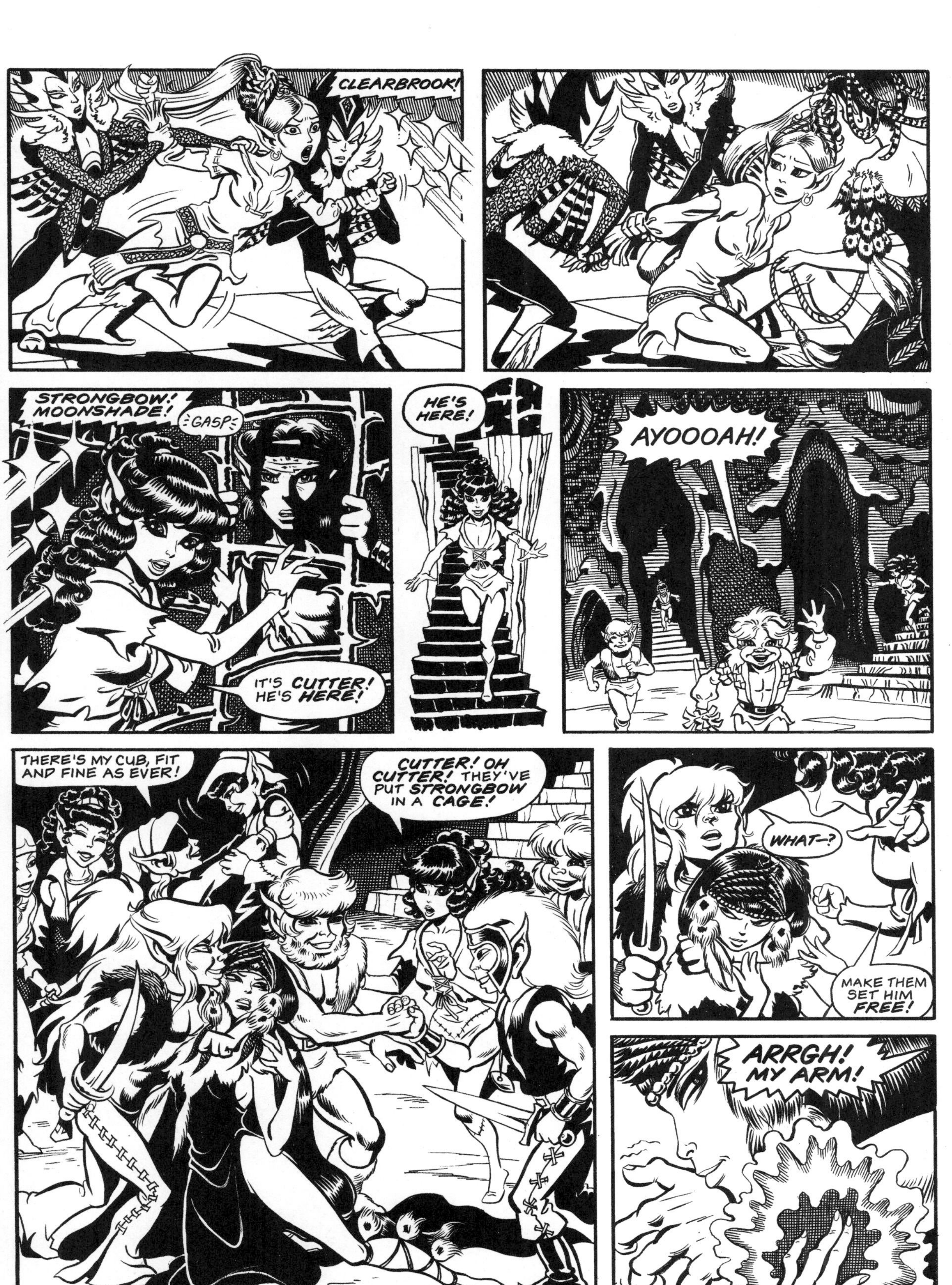
CLEARBROOK!
STRONGBOW! MOONSHADE!
GASP
IT'S CUTTER! HE'S HERE!
HE'S HERE!
AYOOOAH!
THERE'S MY CUB, FIT AND FINE AS EVER!
CUTTER! OH CUTTER! THEY'VE PUT STRONGBOW IN A CAGE!
WHAT--?
MAKE THEM SET HIM FREE!
ARRGH! MY ARM!

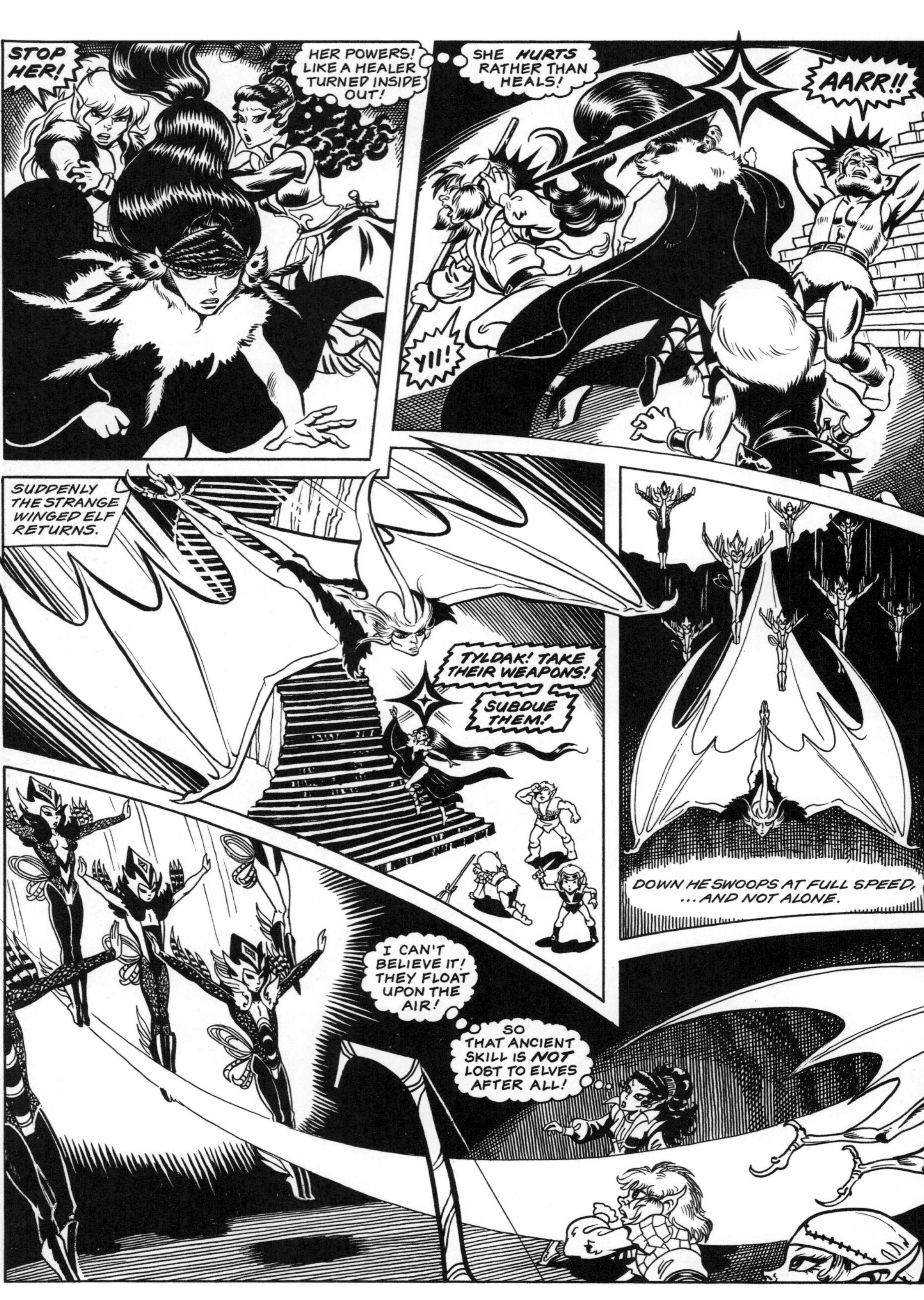
STOP HER!
HER POWERS! LIKE A HEALER TURNED INSIDE OUT!
SHE HURTS RATHER THAN HEALS!
AARR!!
YII!
SUDDENLY THE STRANGE WINGED ELF RETURNS.
TYLDAK! TAKE THEIR WEAPONS!
SUBDUE THEM!
DOWN HE SWOOPS AT FULL SPEED, ...AND NOT ALONE.
I CAN'T BELIEVE IT! THEY FLOAT UPON THE AIR!
SO THAT ANCIENT SKILL IS NOT LOST TO ELVES AFTER ALL!

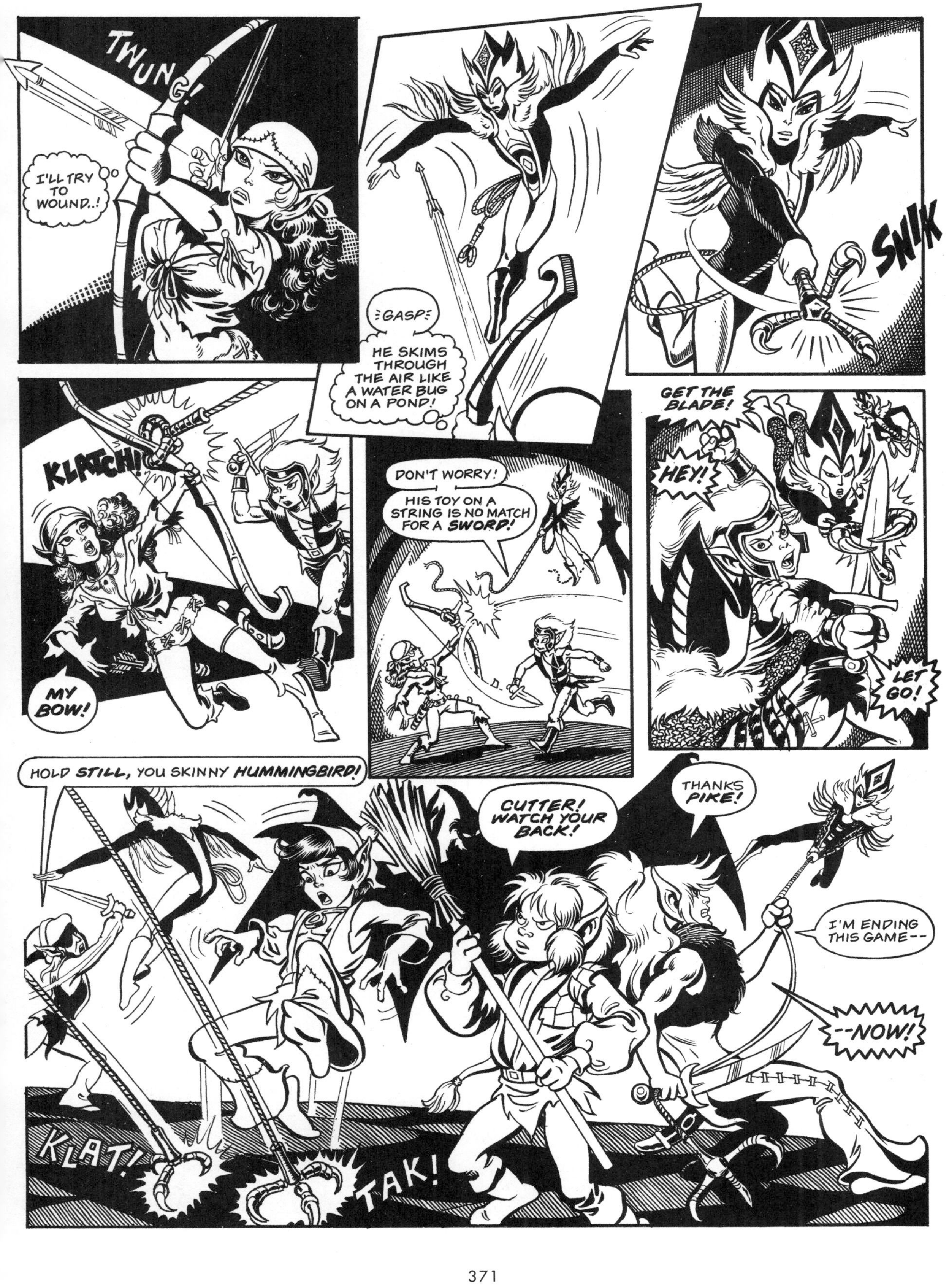

TWUNG!
I'LL TRY TO WOUND..!
GASP
HE SKIMS THROUGH THE AIR LIKE A WATER BUG ON A POND!
SNIK
KLATCH!
MY BOW!
DON'T WORRY!
HIS TOY ON A STRING IS NO MATCH FOR A SWORD!
GET THE BLADE!
HEY!
LET GO!
HOLD STILL, YOU SKINNY HUMMINGBIRD!
CUTTER! WATCH YOUR BACK!
THANKS PIKE!
I'M ENDING THIS GAME--
--NOW!
KLAT!
TAK!

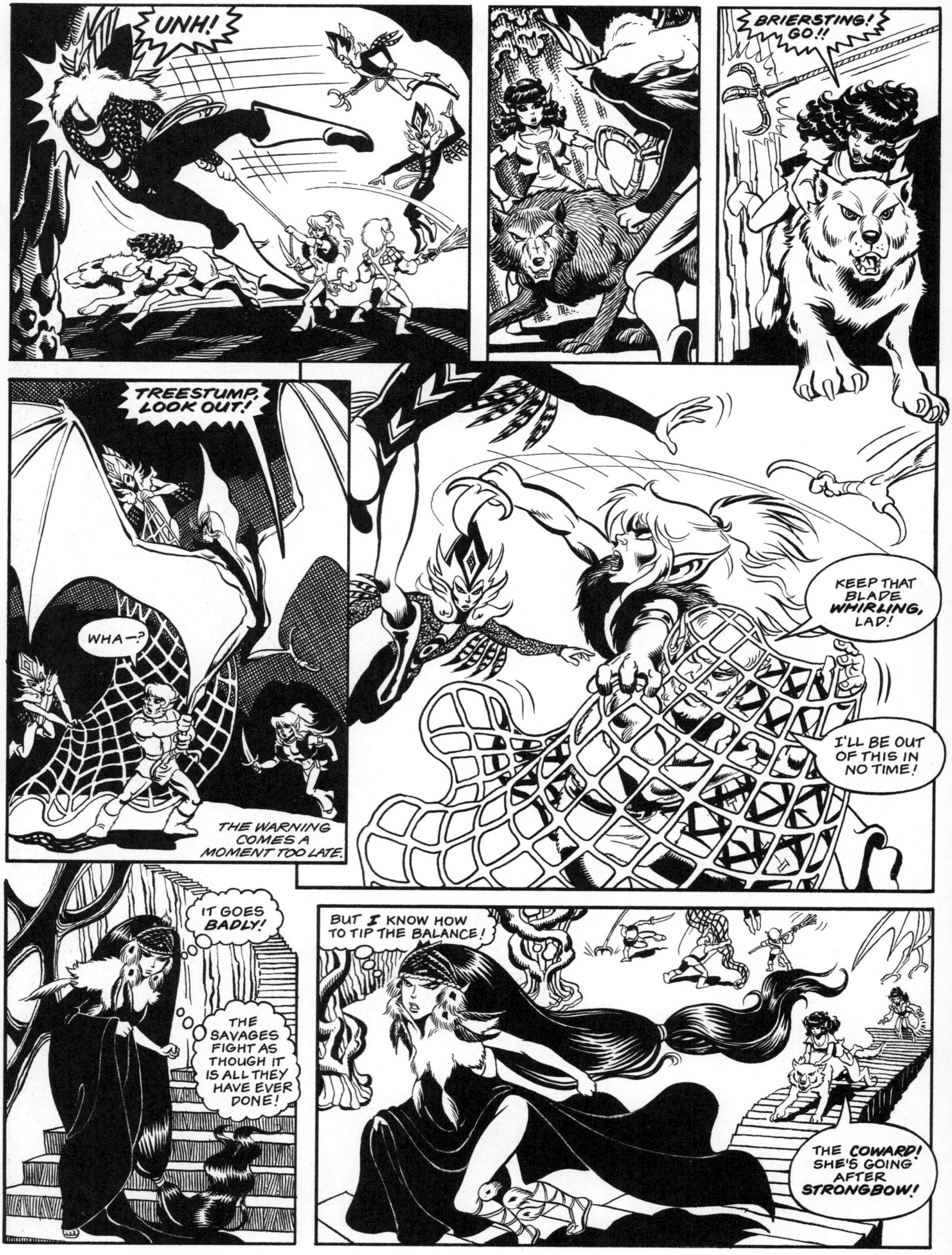
UNH!
BRIERSTING! GO!!
TREESTUMP, LOOK OUT!
WHA--?
THE WARNING COMES A MOMENT TOO LATE.
KEEP THAT BLADE WHIRLING, LAD!
I'LL BE OUT OF THIS IN NO TIME!
IT GOES BADLY!
THE SAVAGES FIGHT AS THOUGH IT IS ALL THEY HAVE EVER DONE!
BUT I KNOW HOW TO TIP THE BALANCE!
THE COWARD! SHE'S GOING AFTER STRONGBOW!

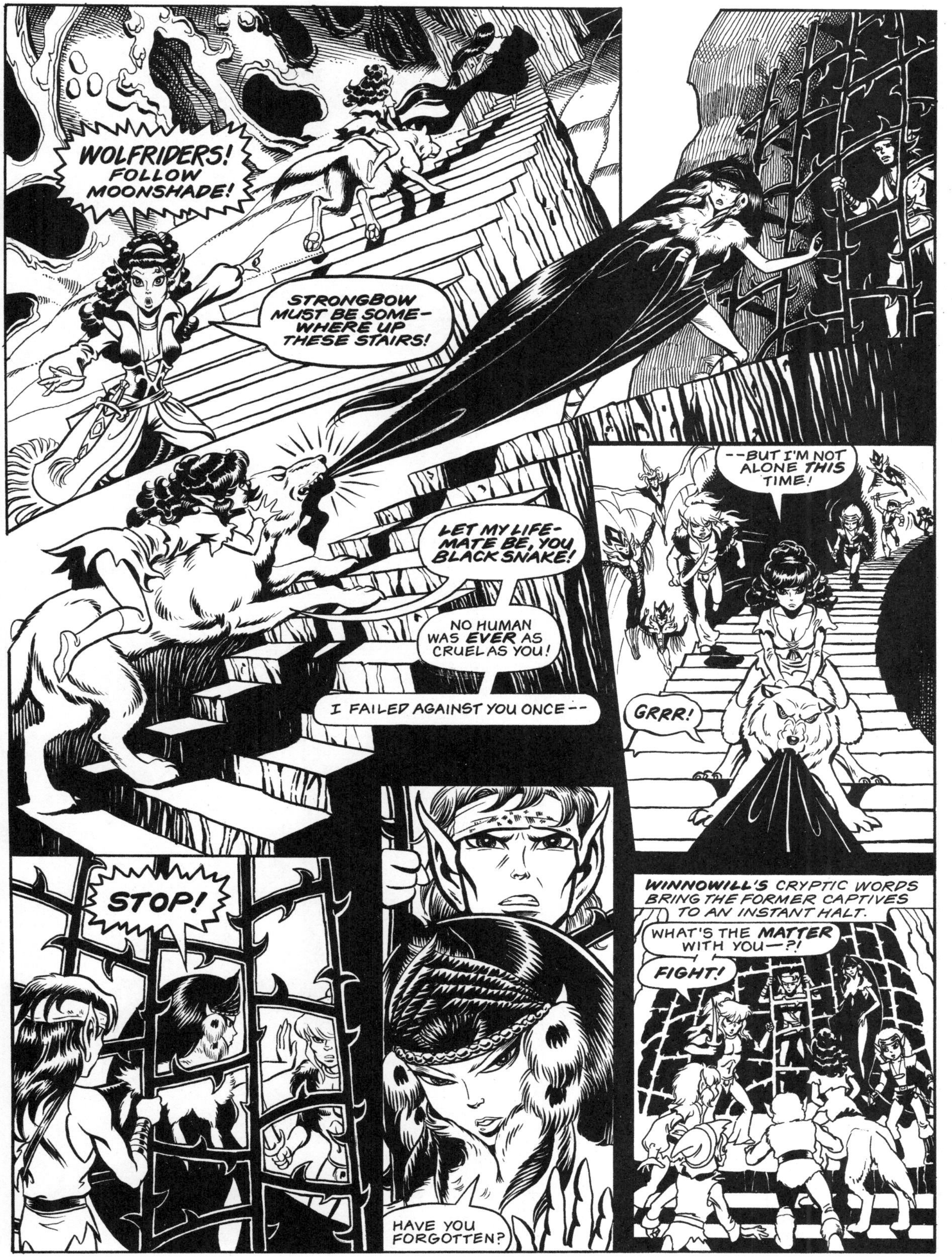
WOLFRIDERS! FOLLOW MOONSHADE!
STRONGBOW MUST BE SOME-WHERE UP THESE STAIRS!
LET MY LIFE-MATE BE, YOU BLACK SNAKE!
NO HUMAN WAS EVER AS CRUEL AS YOU!
I FAILED AGAINST YOU ONCE--
--BUT I'M NOT ALONE THIS TIME!
GRRR!
STOP!
HAVE YOU FORGOTTEN?
WINNOWILL'S CRYPTIC WORDS BRING THE FORMER CAPTIVES TO AN INSTANT HALT.
WHAT'S THE MATTER WITH YOU—?!
FIGHT!

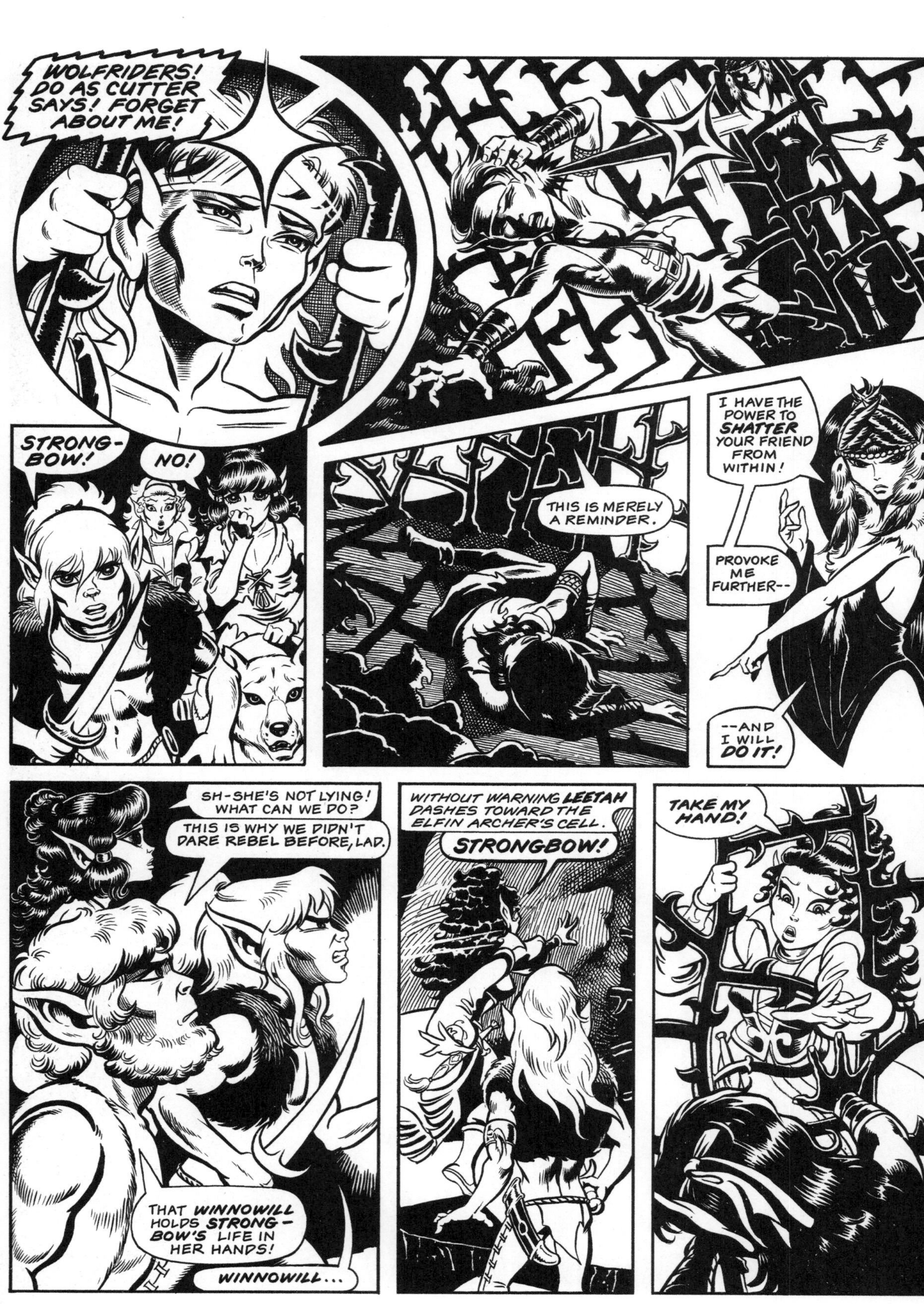
WOLFRIDERS! DO AS CUTTER SAYS! FORGET ABOUT ME!
STRONG-BOW!
NO!
THIS IS MERELY A REMINDER.
I HAVE THE POWER TO SHATTER YOUR FRIEND FROM WITHIN!
PROVOKE ME FURTHER--
--AND I WILL DO IT!
SH-SHE'S NOT LYING! WHAT CAN WE DO?
THIS IS WHY WE DIDN'T DARE REBEL BEFORE, LAD.
THAT WINNOWILL HOLDS STRONG-BOW'S LIFE IN HER HANDS!
WINNOWILL...
WITHOUT WARNING LEETAH DASHES TOWARD THE ELFIN ARCHER'S CELL.
STRONGBOW!
TAKE MY HAND!

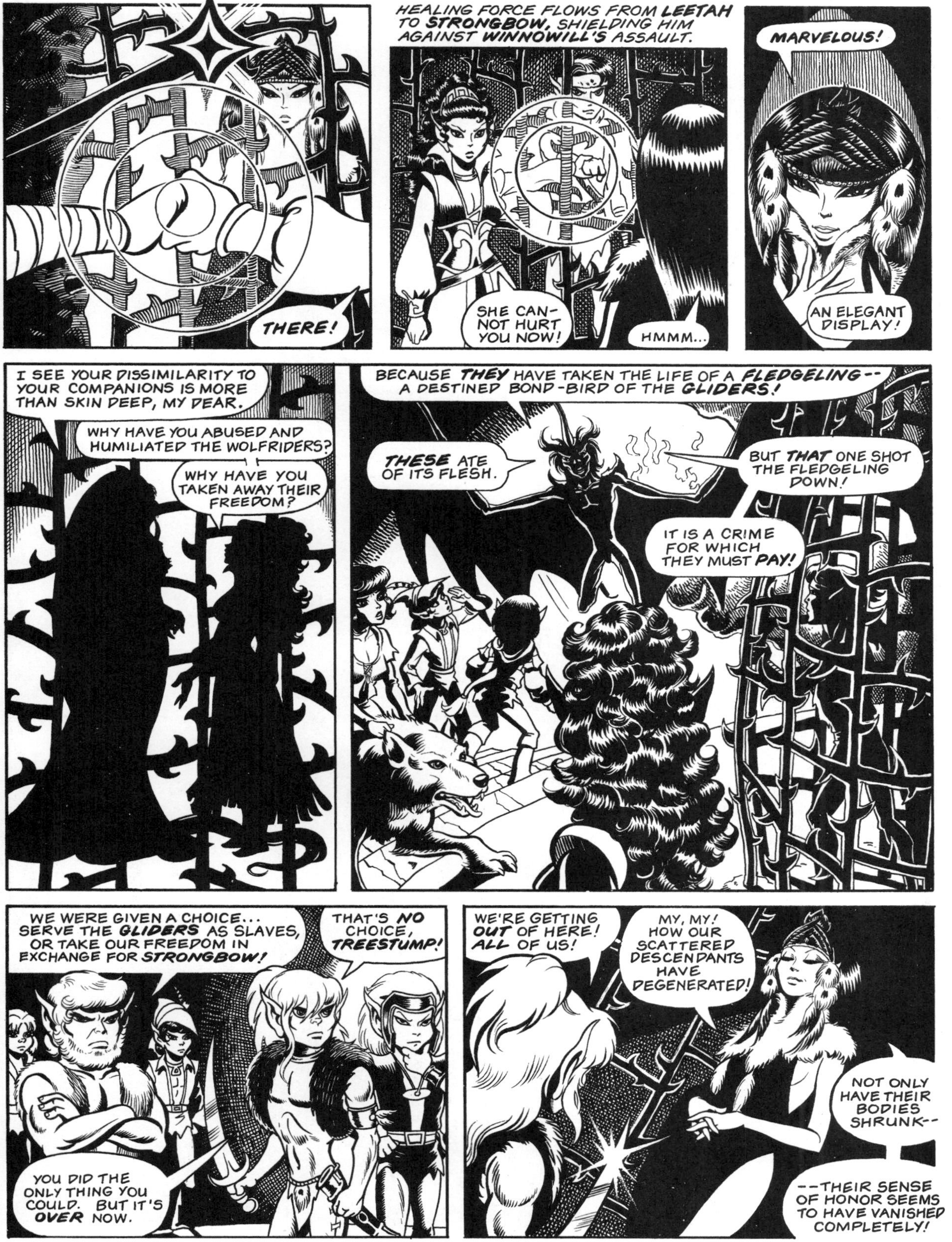
THERE!
HEALING FORCE FLOWS FROM LEETAH TO STRONGBOW, SHIELDING HIM AGAINST WINNOWILL'S ASSAULT.
SHE CAN-NOT HURT YOU NOW!
HMMM...
MARVELOUS!
AN ELEGANT DISPLAY!
I SEE YOUR DISSIMILARITY TO YOUR COMPANIONS IS MORE THAN SKIN DEEP, MY DEAR.
WHY HAVE YOU ABUSED AND HUMILIATED THE WOLFRIDERS?
WHY HAVE YOU TAKEN AWAY THEIR FREEDOM?
BECAUSE THEY HAVE TAKEN THE LIFE OF A FLEDGELING-- A DESTINED BOND-BIRD OF THE GLIDERS!
THESE ATE OF ITS FLESH.
BUT THAT ONE SHOT THE FLEDGELING DOWN!
IT IS A CRIME FOR WHICH THEY MUST PAY!
WE WERE GIVEN A CHOICE... SERVE THE GLIDERS AS SLAVES, OR TAKE OUR FREEDOM IN EXCHANGE FOR STRONGBOW!
THAT'S NO CHOICE, TREESTUMP!
YOU DID THE ONLY THING YOU COULD. BUT IT'S OVER NOW.
WE'RE GETTING OUT OF HERE! ALL OF US!
MY, MY! HOW OUR SCATTERED DESCENDANTS HAVE DEGENERATED!
NOT ONLY HAVE THEIR BODIES SHRUNK--
--THEIR SENSE OF HONOR SEEMS TO HAVE VANISHED COMPLETELY!

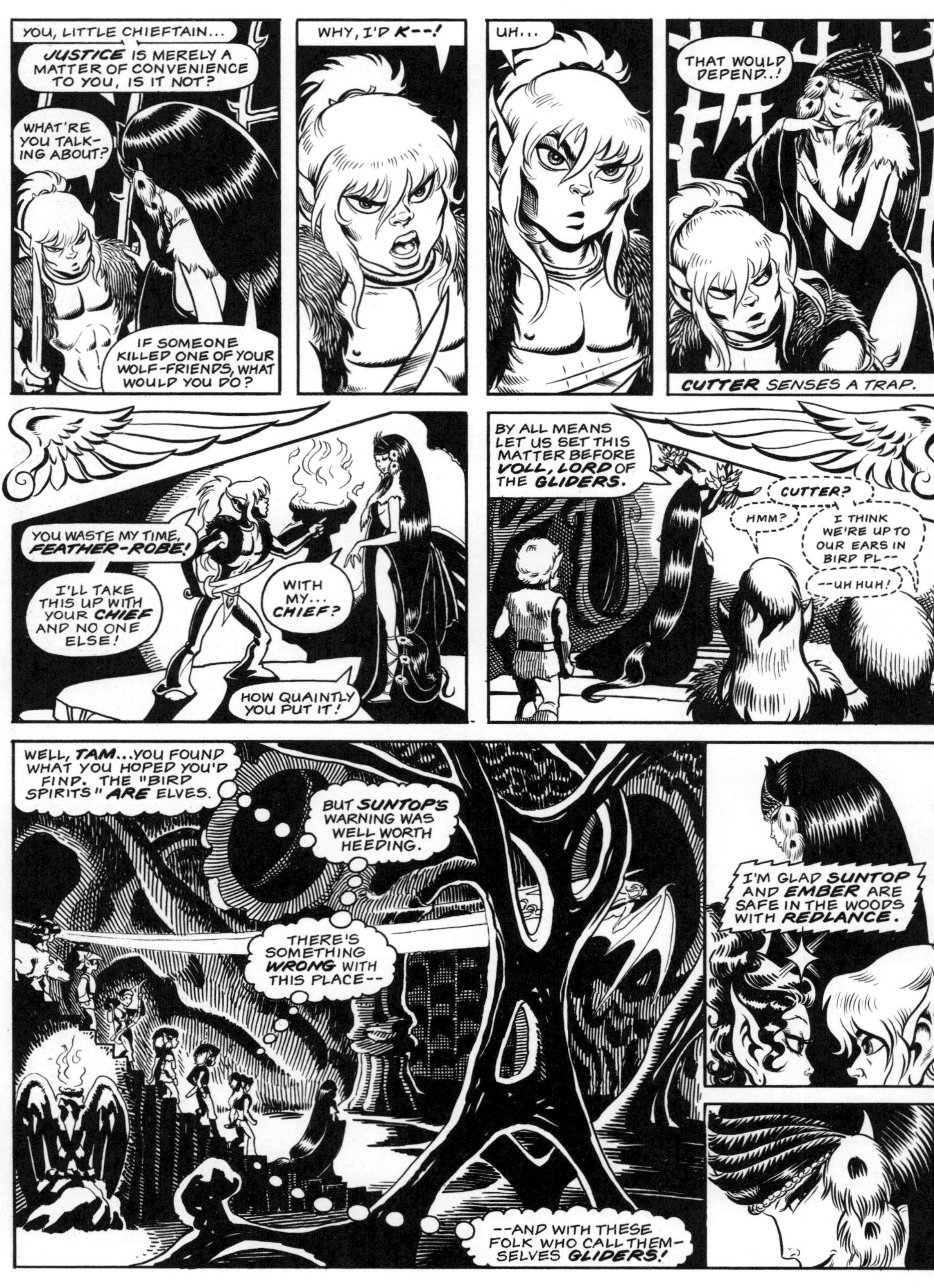
YOU, LITTLE CHIEFTAIN...
JUSTICE IS MERELY A MATTER OF CONVENIENCE TO YOU, IS IT NOT?
WHAT'RE YOU TALKING ABOUT?
IF SOMEONE KILLED ONE OF YOUR WOLF-FRIENDS, WHAT WOULD YOU DO?
WHY, I'D K--!
UH...
THAT WOULD DEPEND..!
CUTTER SENSES A TRAP.
YOU WASTE MY TIME, FEATHER-ROBE!
I'LL TAKE THIS UP WITH YOUR CHIEF AND NO ONE ELSE!
WITH MY... CHIEF?
HOW QUAINTLY YOU PUT IT!
BY ALL MEANS LET US SET THIS MATTER BEFORE VOLL, LORD OF THE GLIDERS.
CUTTER?
HMM?
I THINK WE'RE UP TO OUR EARS IN BIRD PL--
--UH HUH!
WELL, TAM...YOU FOUND WHAT YOU HOPED YOU'D FIND. THE "BIRD SPIRITS" ARE ELVES.
BUT SUNTOP'S WARNING WAS WELL WORTH HEEDING.
THERE'S SOMETHING WRONG WITH THIS PLACE--
--AND WITH THESE FOLK WHO CALL THEMSELVES GLIDERS!
I'M GLAD SUNTOP AND EMBER ARE SAFE IN THE WOODS WITH REDLANCE.

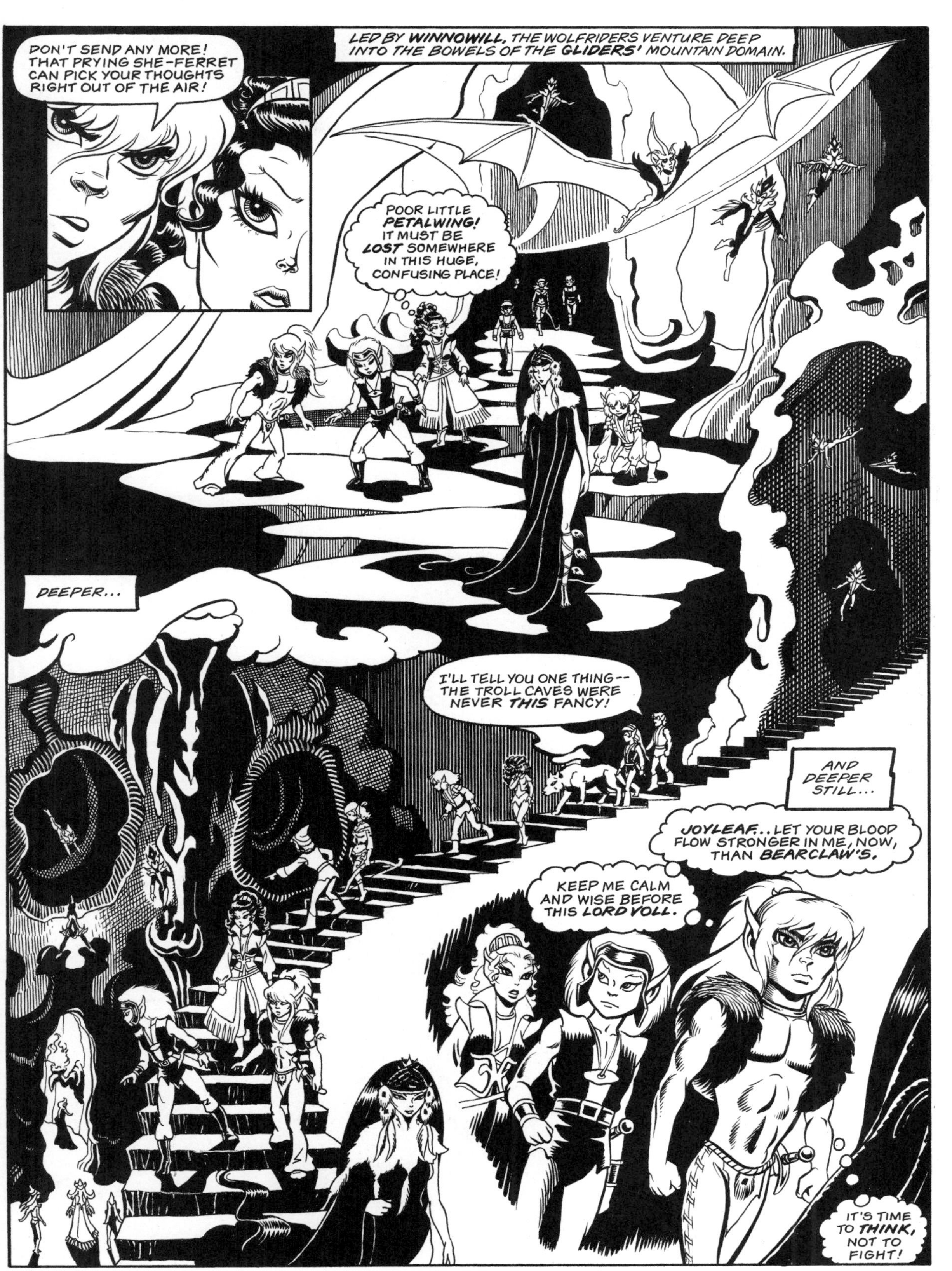
DON'T SEND ANY MORE! THAT PRYING SHE-FERRET CAN PICK YOUR THOUGHTS RIGHT OUT OF THE AIR!
LED BY WINNOWILL, THE WOLFRIDERS VENTURE DEEP INTO THE BOWELS OF THE GLIDERS' MOUNTAIN DOMAIN.
POOR LITTLE PETALWING! IT MUST BE LOST SOMEWHERE IN THIS HUGE, CONFUSING PLACE!
DEEPER...
I'LL TELL YOU ONE THING-- THE TROLL CAVES WERE NEVER THIS FANCY!
AND DEEPER STILL...
JOYLEAF... LET YOUR BLOOD FLOW STRONGER IN ME, NOW, THAN BEARCLAW'S.
KEEP ME CALM AND WISE BEFORE THIS LORD VOLL.
IT'S TIME TO THINK, NOT TO FIGHT!

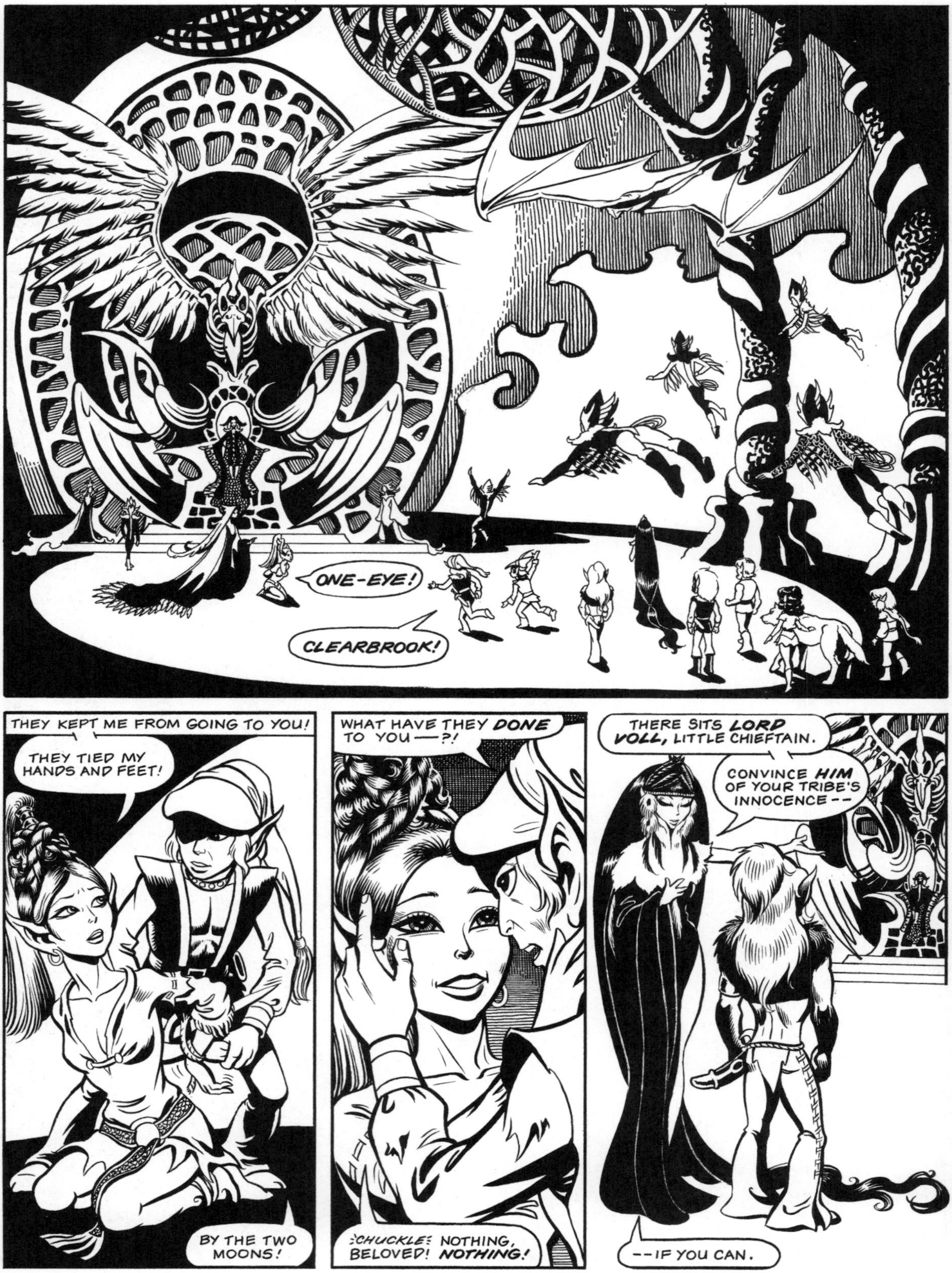

ONE-EYE!
CLEARBROOK!
THEY KEPT ME FROM GOING TO YOU!
THEY TIED MY HANDS AND FEET!
BY THE TWO MOONS!
WHAT HAVE THEY DONE TO YOU--?!
:CHUCKLE: NOTHING, BELOVED! NOTHING!
THERE SITS LORD VOLL, LITTLE CHIEFTAIN.
CONVINCE HIM OF YOUR TRIBE'S INNOCENCE--
--IF YOU CAN.

BOLDLY **CUTTER** STEPS TO THE FOOT OF **VOLL'S** ELABORATE PERCH. THE TWO LEADERS EYE EACH OTHER COOLLY.

I AM **CUTTER,** CHIEF OF THE WOLFRIDERS.

I DEMAND THAT YOU RELEASE **STRONG-BOW** AND LET ME AND MY TRIBE GO IN PEACE.

HE SEEMS EVEN OLDER THAN **SAVAH!**

A CLOAK MADE OF SO MANY YEARS MUST WEIGH HEAVILY ON HIM...

HE WEARS IT WITHOUT JOY!

VOLL SUMMONS ONE OF THE GLIDERS TO THE DAIS.

THIS IS **KUREEL.**

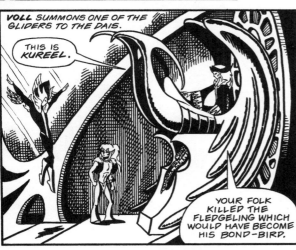

YOUR FOLK KILLED THE FLEDGELING WHICH WOULD HAVE BECOME HIS BOND-BIRD.

I'M SORRY FOR THAT. WE'RE **HUNTERS.**

STRONGBOW SHOT THE BIRD DOWN FOR FOOD.

HE DIDN'T KNOW.

THE **CHOSEN EIGHT** WHO RIDE THE GREAT BIRDS ARE HUNTERS TOO.

AND WAIT LONGER STILL, UNTIL HIS NEW MOUNT IS FULL-FLEDGED AND READY TO FLY THE HUNT.

BUT **KUREEL** MUST WAIT, NOW, FOR THE NEXT HATCHING.

THEN LET MY TRIBE GO--

AND **WE'LL** BRING YOU MEAT TO MAKE UP FOR THE BIRD'S DEATH.

THAT HARDLY SEEMS ADEQUATE ATONEMENT, **LORD VOLL...**

I WOULD SAY THAT A LIFE FOR A LIFE IS MORE IN ORDER!

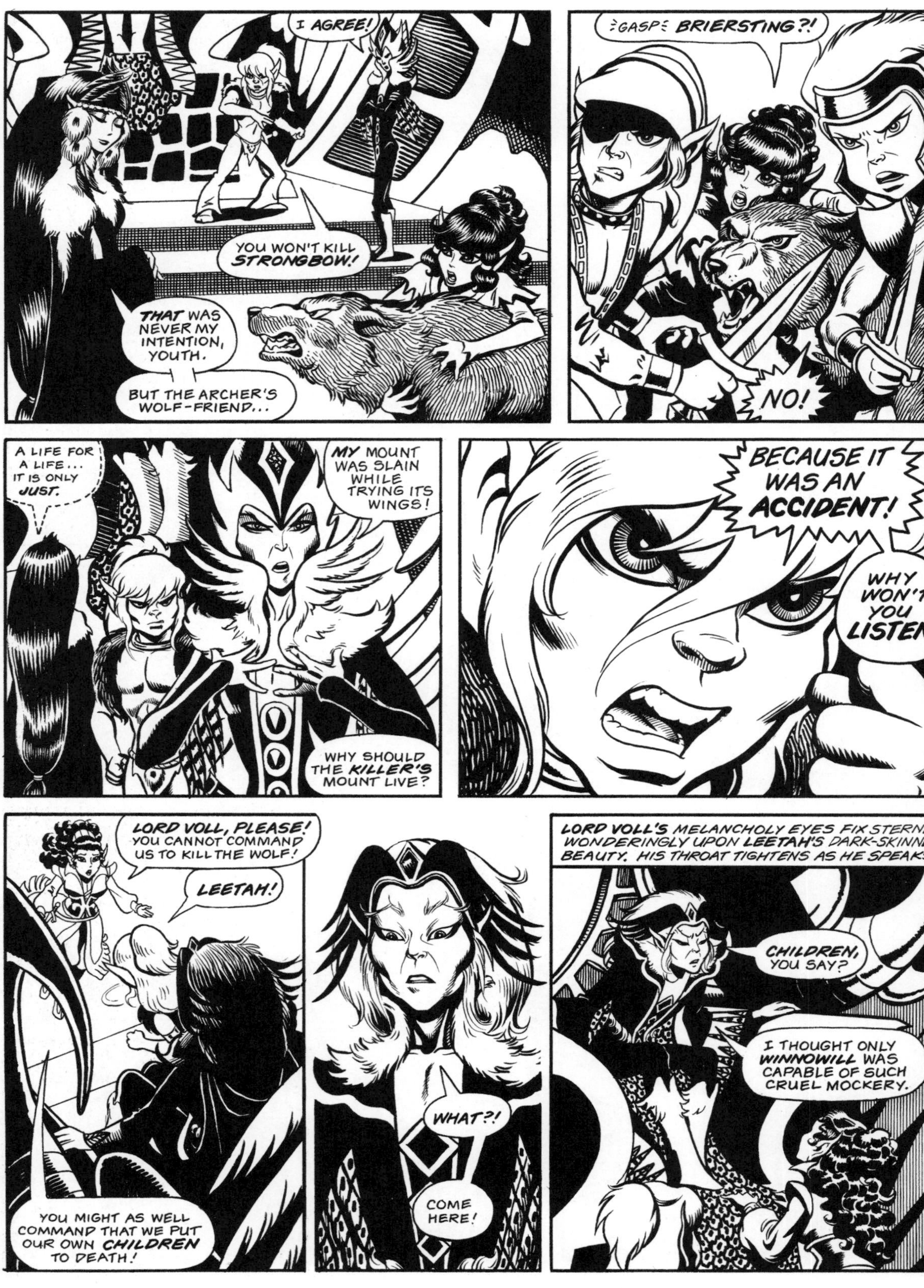
I AGREE!
YOU WON'T KILL STRONGBOW!
THAT WAS NEVER MY INTENTION, YOUTH.
BUT THE ARCHER'S WOLF-FRIEND...
GASP BRIERSTING?!
NO!
A LIFE FOR A LIFE... IT IS ONLY JUST.
MY MOUNT WAS SLAIN WHILE TRYING ITS WINGS!
WHY SHOULD THE KILLER'S MOUNT LIVE?
BECAUSE IT WAS AN ACCIDENT!
WHY WON'T YOU LISTEN?
LORD VOLL, PLEASE! YOU CANNOT COMMAND US TO KILL THE WOLF!
LEETAH!
YOU MIGHT AS WELL COMMAND THAT WE PUT OUR OWN CHILDREN TO DEATH!
WHAT?!
COME HERE!
LORD VOLL'S MELANCHOLY EYES FIX STERNLY, WONDERINGLY UPON LEETAH'S DARK-SKINNED BEAUTY. HIS THROAT TIGHTENS AS HE SPEAKS.
CHILDREN, YOU SAY?
I THOUGHT ONLY WINNOWILL WAS CAPABLE OF SUCH CRUEL MOCKERY.

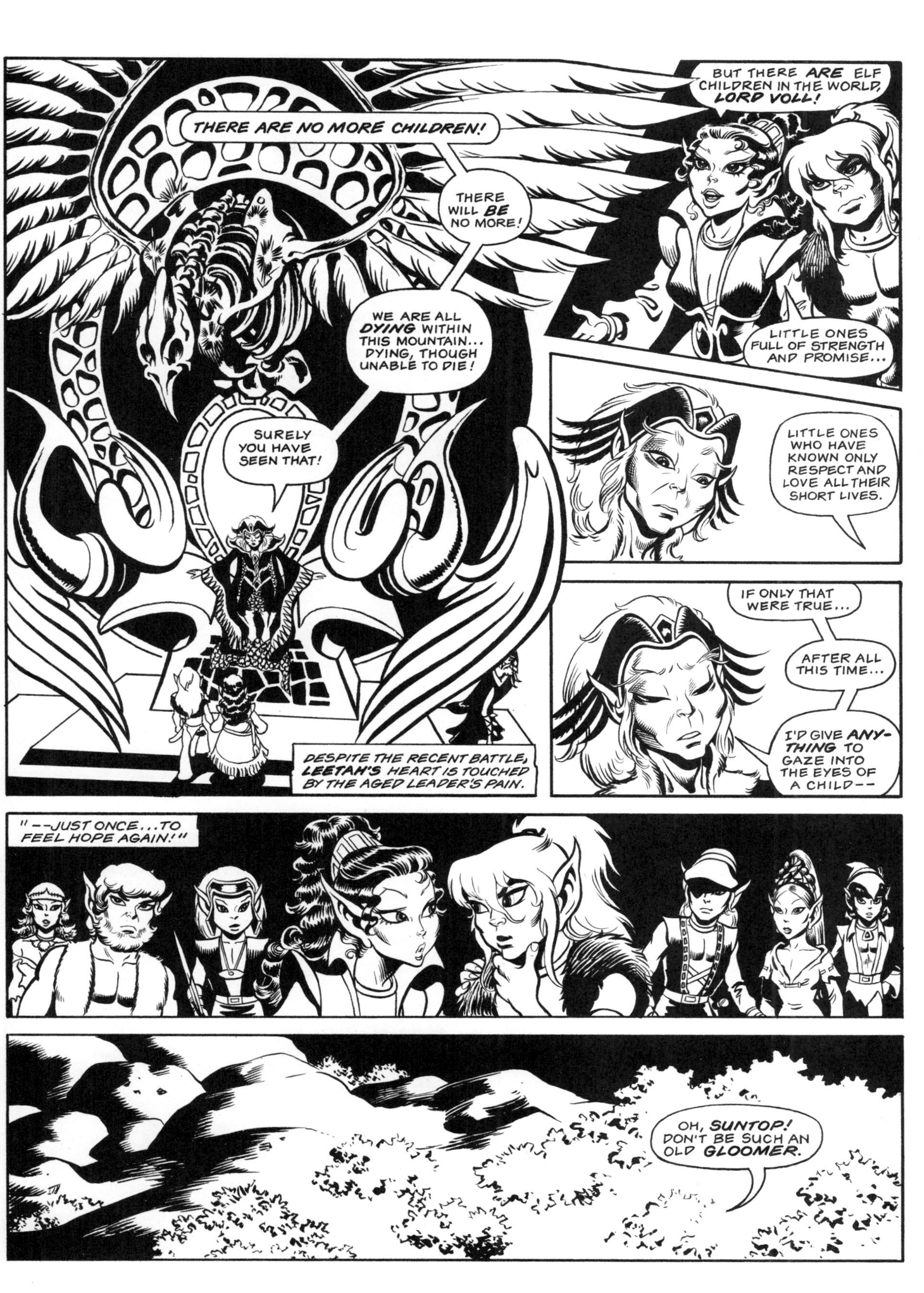
THERE ARE NO MORE CHILDREN!
THERE WILL BE NO MORE!
WE ARE ALL DYING WITHIN THIS MOUNTAIN... DYING, THOUGH UNABLE TO DIE!
SURELY YOU HAVE SEEN THAT!
DESPITE THE RECENT BATTLE, LEETAH'S HEART IS TOUCHED BY THE AGED LEADER'S PAIN.
BUT THERE ARE ELF CHILDREN IN THE WORLD, LORD VOLL!
LITTLE ONES FULL OF STRENGTH AND PROMISE...
LITTLE ONES WHO HAVE KNOWN ONLY RESPECT AND LOVE ALL THEIR SHORT LIVES.
IF ONLY THAT WERE TRUE...
AFTER ALL THIS TIME...
I'D GIVE ANYTHING TO GAZE INTO THE EYES OF A CHILD--
"--JUST ONCE...TO FEEL HOPE AGAIN!"
OH, SUNTOP! DON'T BE SUCH AN OLD GLOOMER.

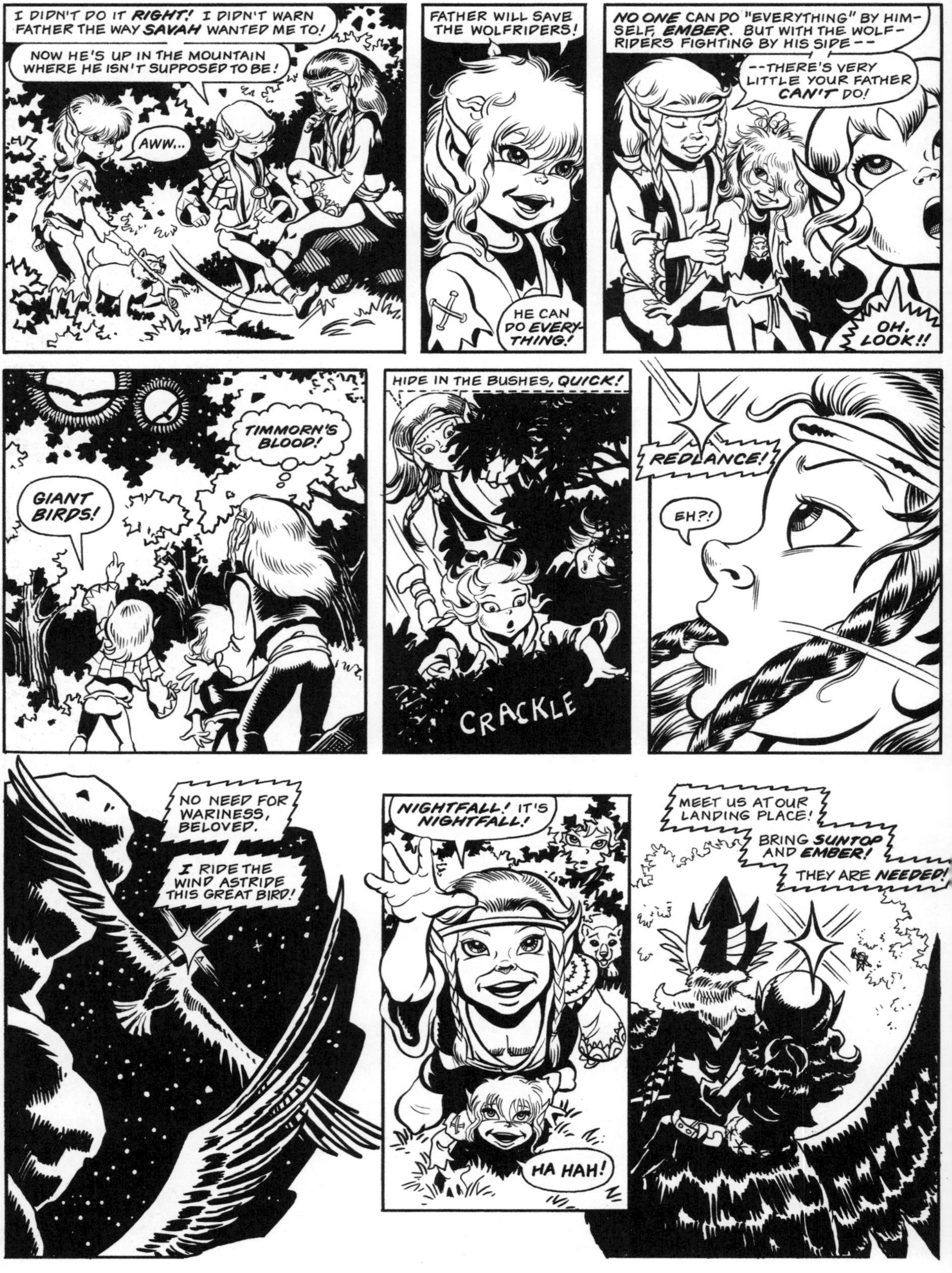

I DIDN'T DO IT RIGHT! I DIDN'T WARN FATHER THE WAY SAVAH WANTED ME TO!
NOW HE'S UP IN THE MOUNTAIN WHERE HE ISN'T SUPPOSED TO BE!
AWW...
FATHER WILL SAVE THE WOLFRIDERS!
HE CAN DO EVERYTHING!
NO ONE CAN DO "EVERYTHING" BY HIMSELF, EMBER. BUT WITH THE WOLFRIDERS FIGHTING BY HIS SIDE--
--THERE'S VERY LITTLE YOUR FATHER CAN'T DO!
OH. LOOK!!
TIMMORN'S BLOOD!
GIANT BIRDS!
HIDE IN THE BUSHES, QUICK!
CRACKLE
REDLANCE!
EH?!
NO NEED FOR WARINESS, BELOVED.
I RIDE THE WIND ASTRIDE THIS GREAT BIRD!
NIGHTFALL! IT'S NIGHTFALL!
HA HAH!
MEET US AT OUR LANDING PLACE!
BRING SUNTOP AND EMBER!
THEY ARE NEEDED!

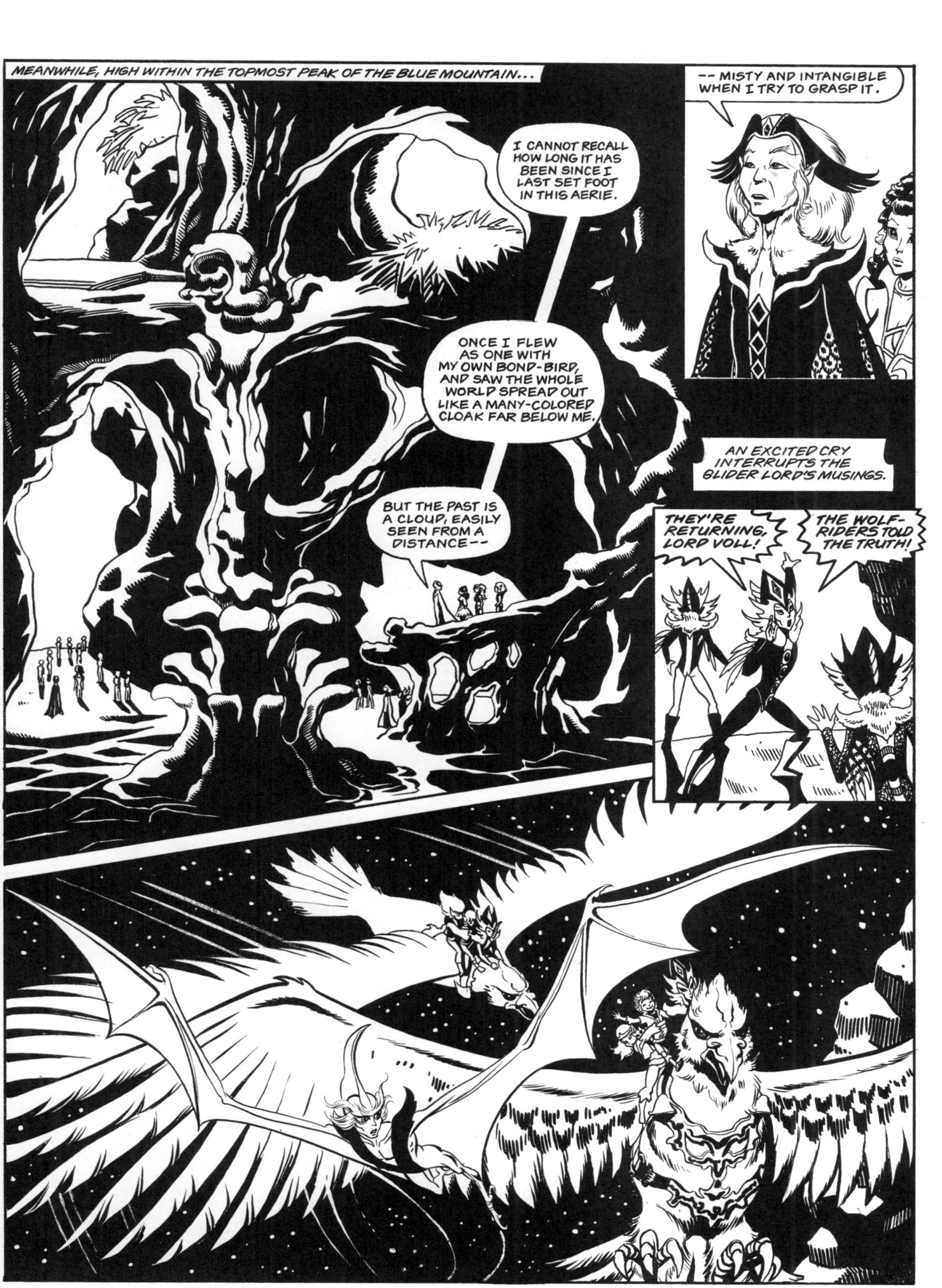

MEANWHILE, HIGH WITHIN THE TOPMOST PEAK OF THE BLUE MOUNTAIN...
I CANNOT RECALL HOW LONG IT HAS BEEN SINCE I LAST SET FOOT IN THIS AERIE.
ONCE I FLEW AS ONE WITH MY OWN BOND-BIRD, AND SAW THE WHOLE WORLD SPREAD OUT LIKE A MANY-COLORED CLOAK FAR BELOW ME.
BUT THE PAST IS A CLOUD, EASILY SEEN FROM A DISTANCE--
-- MISTY AND INTANGIBLE WHEN I TRY TO GRASP IT.
AN EXCITED CRY INTERRUPTS THE GLIDER LORD'S MUSINGS.
THEY'RE RETURNING, LORD VOLL!
THE WOLF-RIDERS TOLD THE TRUTH!

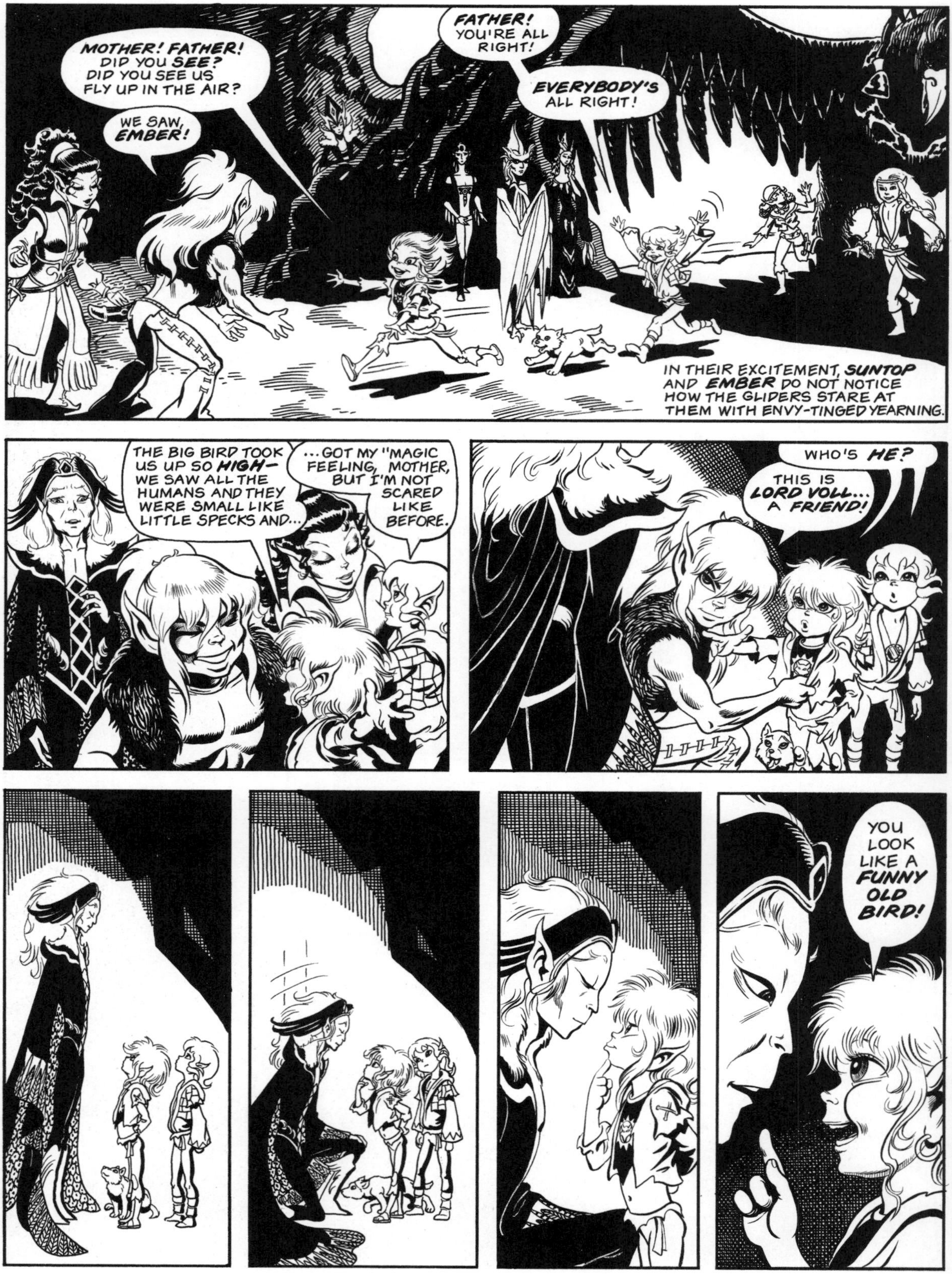

MOTHER! FATHER! DID YOU SEE? DID YOU SEE US FLY UP IN THE AIR?
WE SAW, EMBER!
FATHER! YOU'RE ALL RIGHT!
EVERYBODY'S ALL RIGHT!
IN THEIR EXCITEMENT, SUNTOP AND EMBER DO NOT NOTICE HOW THE GLIDERS STARE AT THEM WITH ENVY-TINGED YEARNING.
THE BIG BIRD TOOK US UP SO HIGH— WE SAW ALL THE HUMANS AND THEY WERE SMALL LIKE LITTLE SPECKS AND...
...GOT MY "MAGIC FEELING, MOTHER, BUT I'M NOT SCARED LIKE BEFORE.
WHO'S HE?
THIS IS LORD VOLL... A FRIEND!
YOU LOOK LIKE A FUNNY OLD BIRD!

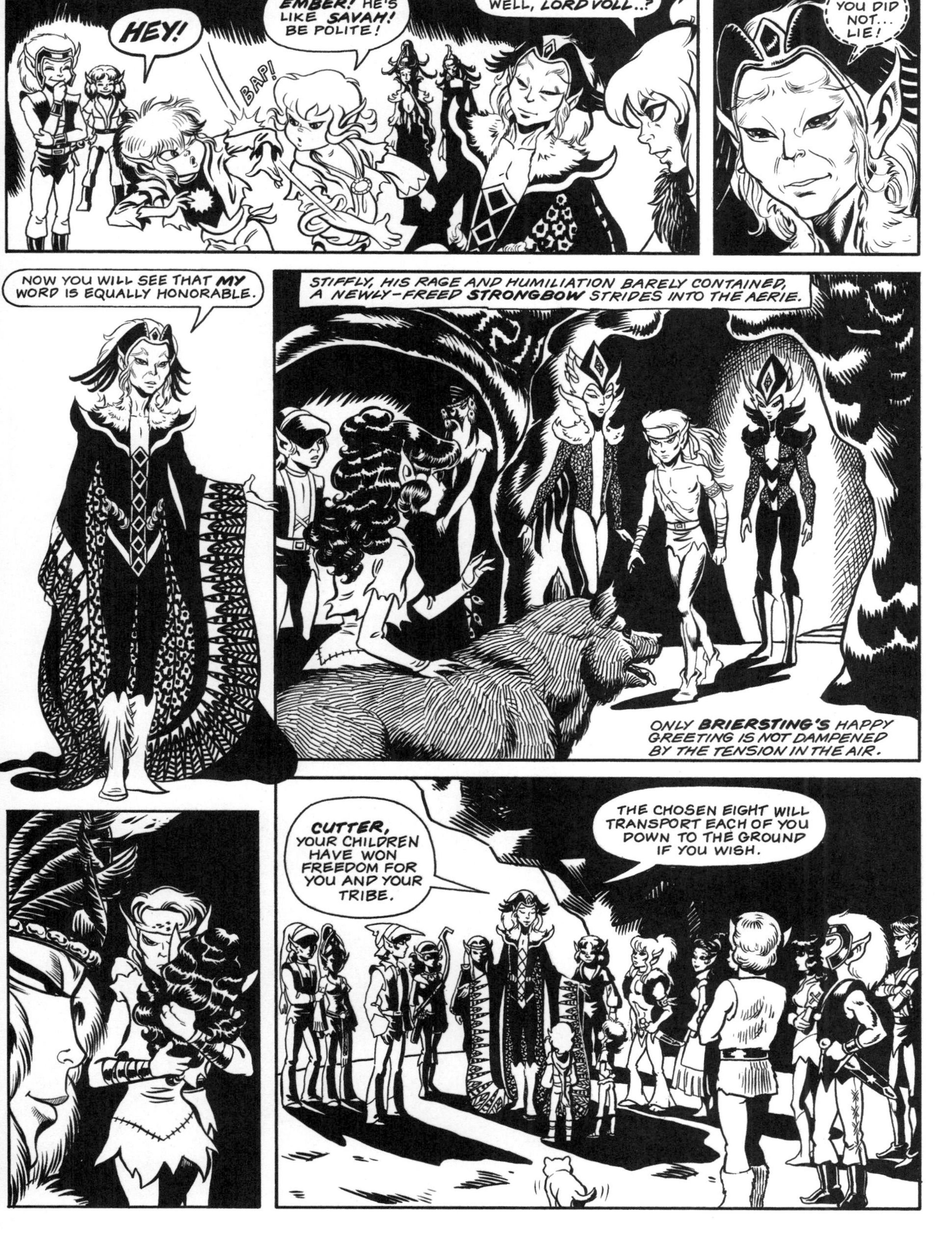
HEY!
EMBER! HE'S LIKE SAVAH! BE POLITE!
BAP!
WELL, LORD VOLL..?
YOU DID NOT... LIE!
NOW YOU WILL SEE THAT MY WORD IS EQUALLY HONORABLE.
STIFFLY, HIS RAGE AND HUMILIATION BARELY CONTAINED, A NEWLY-FREED STRONGBOW STRIDES INTO THE AERIE.
ONLY BRIERSTING'S HAPPY GREETING IS NOT DAMPENED BY THE TENSION IN THE AIR.
CUTTER, YOUR CHILDREN HAVE WON FREEDOM FOR YOU AND YOUR TRIBE.
THE CHOSEN EIGHT WILL TRANSPORT EACH OF YOU DOWN TO THE GROUND IF YOU WISH.

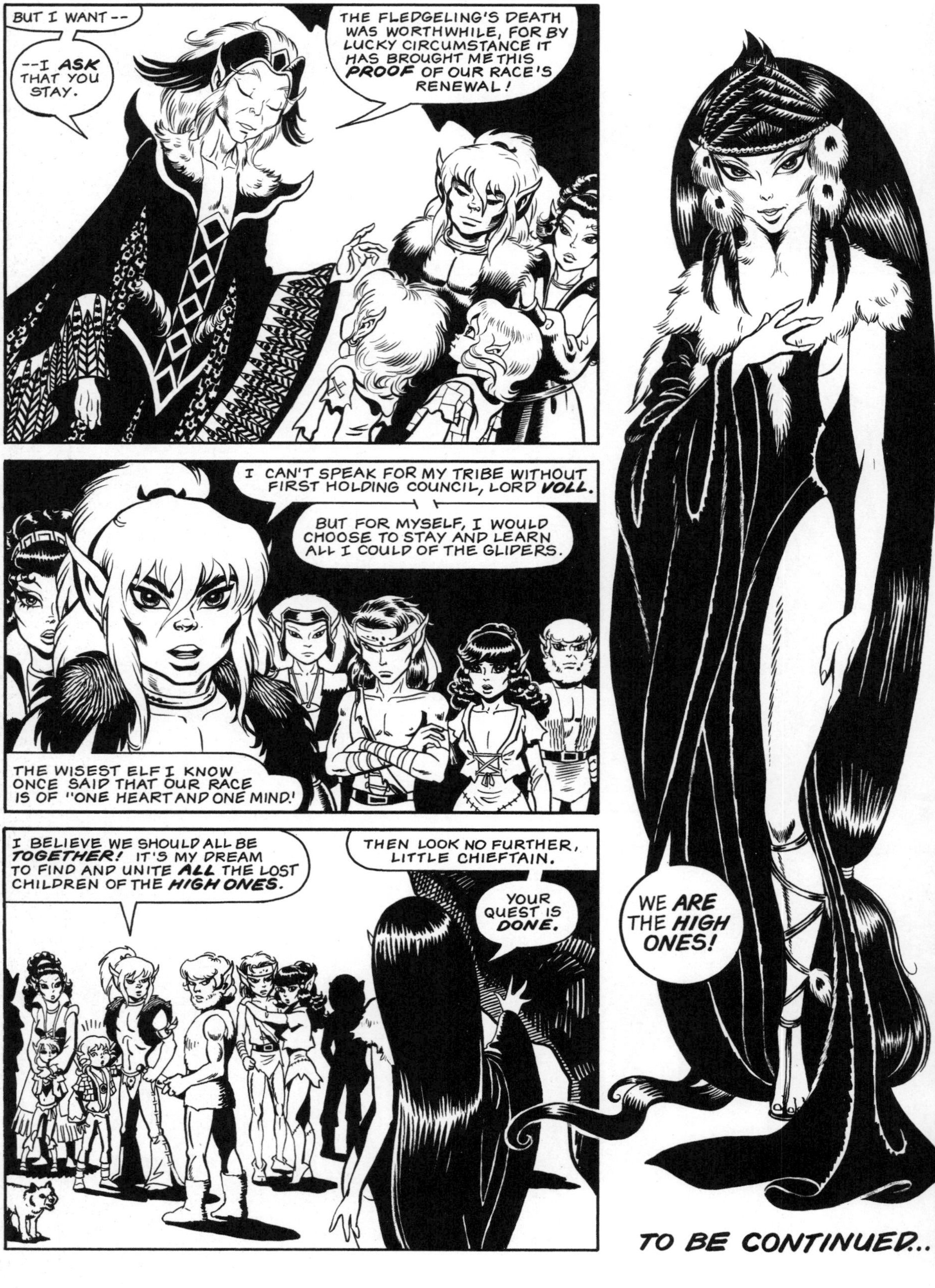

BUT I WANT --
--I ASK THAT YOU STAY.
THE FLEDGELING'S DEATH WAS WORTHWHILE, FOR BY LUCKY CIRCUMSTANCE IT HAS BROUGHT ME THIS PROOF OF OUR RACE'S RENEWAL!
I CAN'T SPEAK FOR MY TRIBE WITHOUT FIRST HOLDING COUNCIL, LORD VOLL.
BUT FOR MYSELF, I WOULD CHOOSE TO STAY AND LEARN ALL I COULD OF THE GLIDERS.
THE WISEST ELF I KNOW ONCE SAID THAT OUR RACE IS OF "ONE HEART AND ONE MIND!
I BELIEVE WE SHOULD ALL BE TOGETHER! IT'S MY DREAM TO FIND AND UNITE ALL THE LOST CHILDREN OF THE HIGH ONES.
THEN LOOK NO FURTHER, LITTLE CHIEFTAIN.
YOUR QUEST IS DONE.
WE ARE THE HIGH ONES!
TO BE CONTINUED...

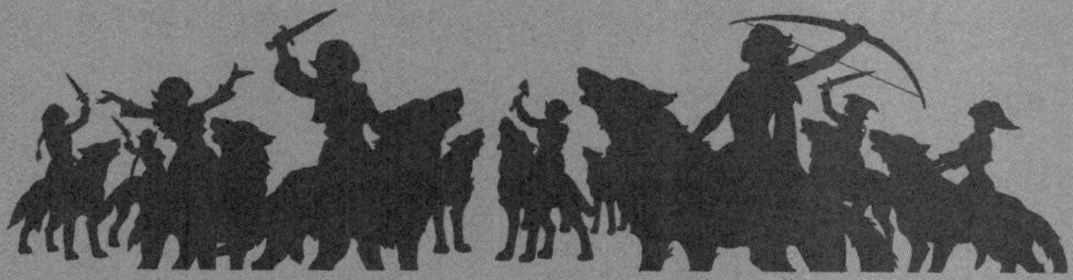

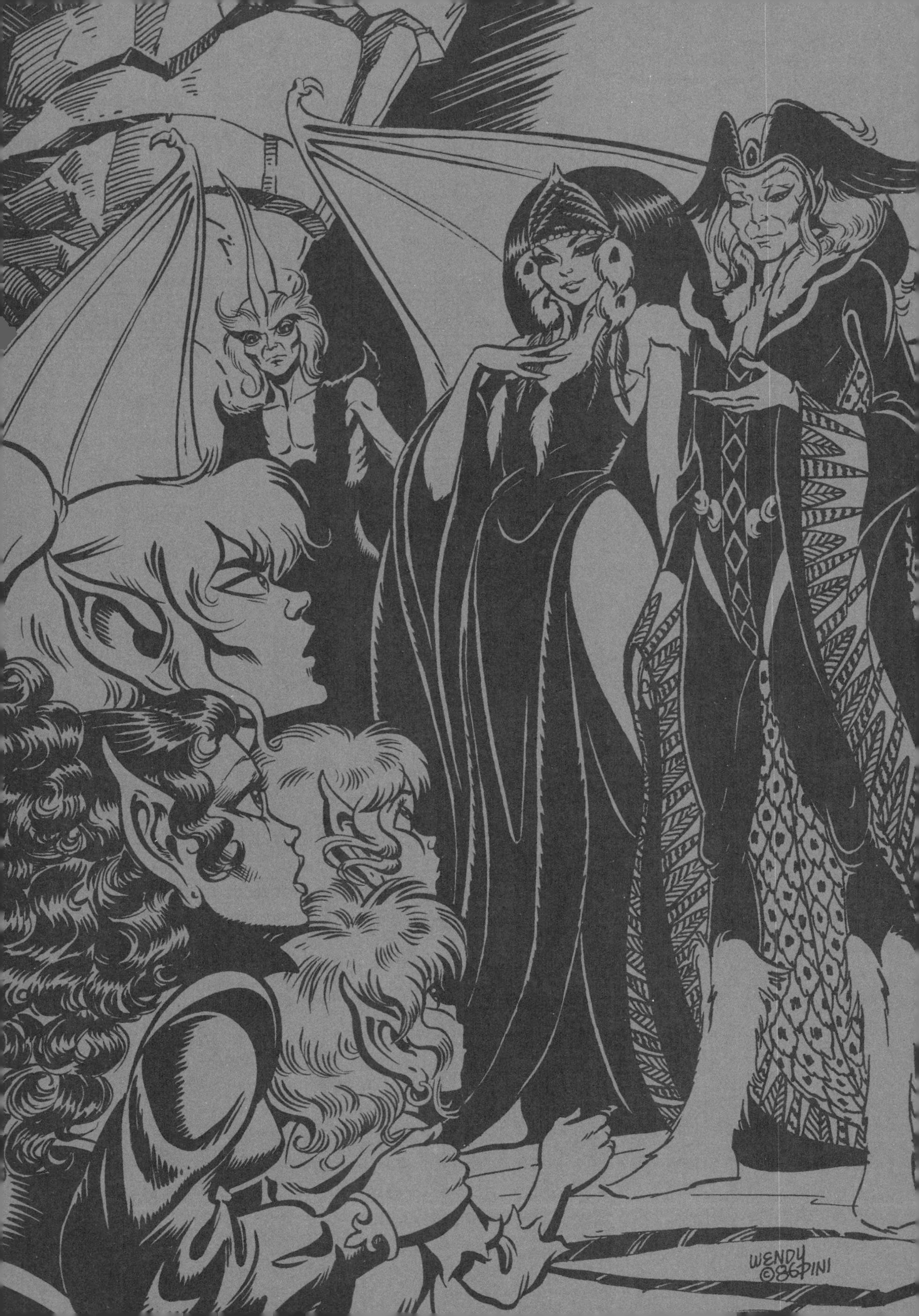
WENDY
©86 PINI

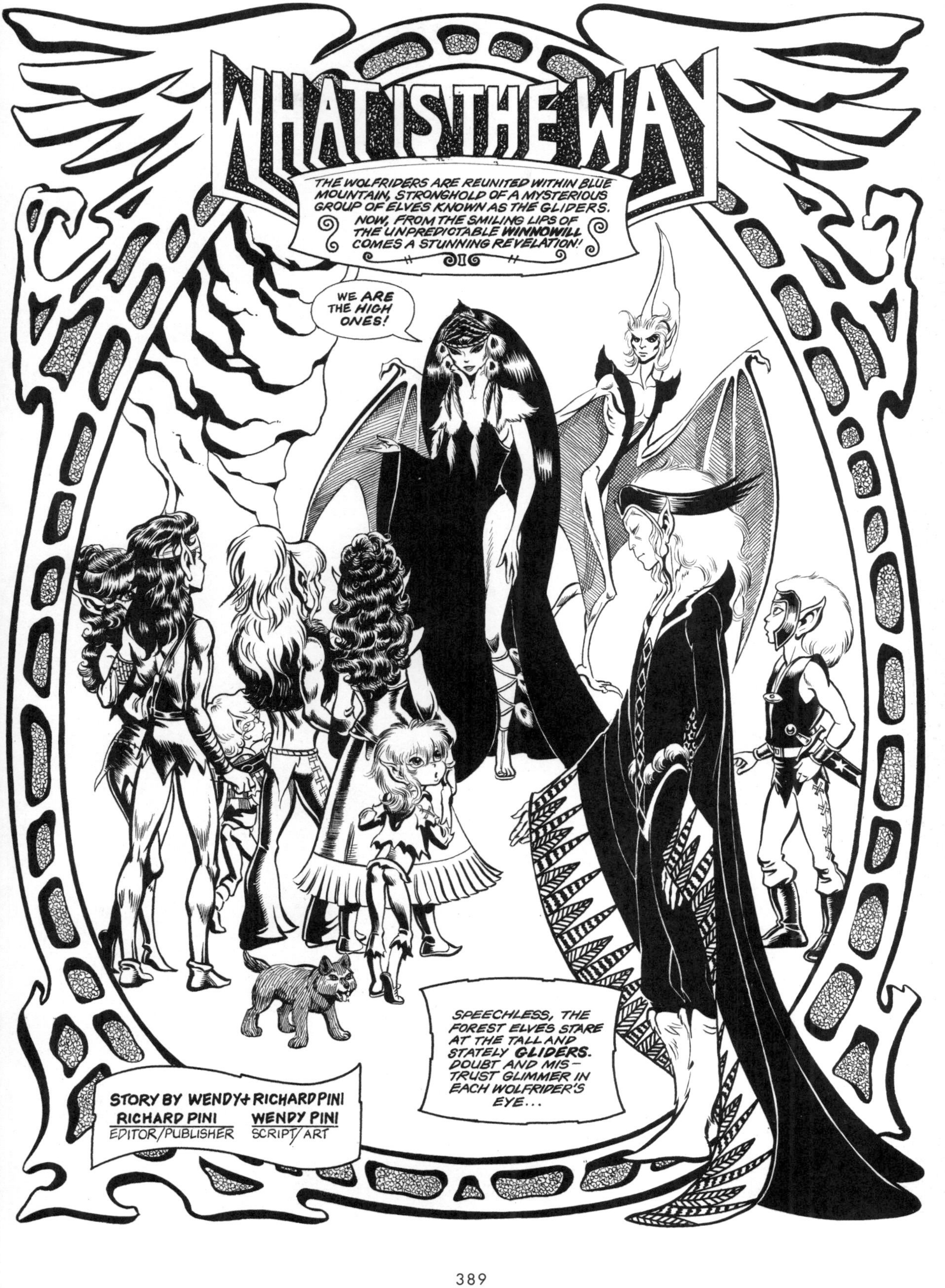
WHAT IS THE WAY
THE WOLFRIDERS ARE REUNITED WITHIN BLUE MOUNTAIN, STRONGHOLD OF A MYSTERIOUS GROUP OF ELVES KNOWN AS THE GLIDERS. NOW, FROM THE SMILING LIPS OF THE UNPREDICTABLE WINNOWILL COMES A STUNNING REVELATION!
WE ARE THE HIGH ONES!
SPEECHLESS, THE FOREST ELVES STARE AT THE TALL AND STATELY GLIDERS. DOUBT AND MIS-TRUST GLIMMER IN EACH WOLFRIDER'S EYE...
STORY BY WENDY & RICHARD PINI
RICHARD PINI EDITOR/PUBLISHER
WENDY PINI SCRIPT/ART

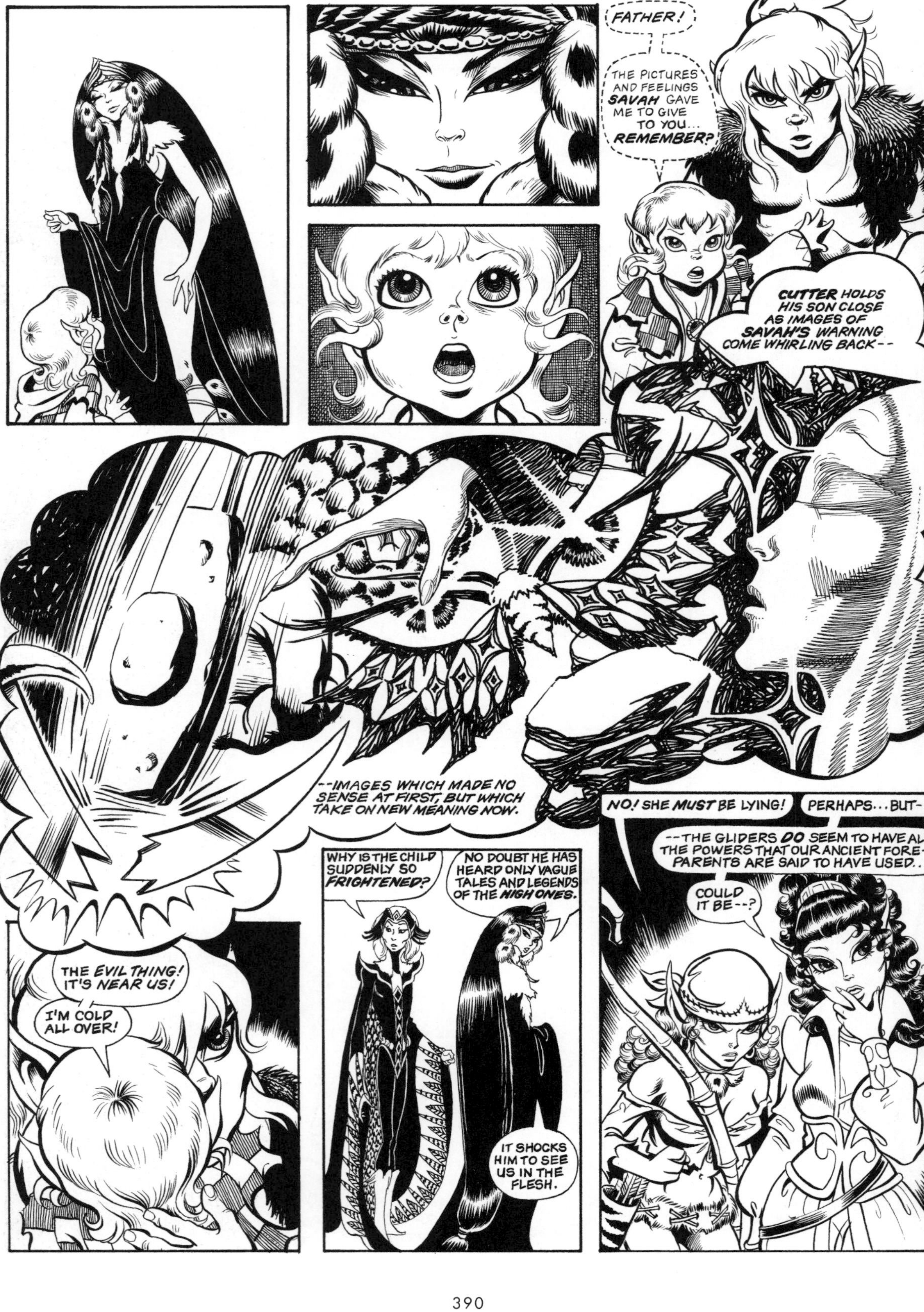
FATHER!
THE PICTURES AND FEELINGS SAVAH GAVE ME TO GIVE TO YOU... REMEMBER?
CUTTER HOLDS HIS SON CLOSE AS IMAGES OF SAVAH'S WARNING COME WHIRLING BACK--
--IMAGES WHICH MADE NO SENSE AT FIRST, BUT WHICH TAKE ON NEW MEANING NOW.
THE EVIL THING! IT'S NEAR US!
I'M COLD ALL OVER!
WHY IS THE CHILD SUDDENLY SO FRIGHTENED?
NO DOUBT HE HAS HEARD ONLY VAGUE TALES AND LEGENDS OF THE HIGH ONES.
IT SHOCKS HIM TO SEE US IN THE FLESH.
NO! SHE MUST BE LYING!
PERHAPS... BUT--
--THE GLIDERS DO SEEM TO HAVE ALL THE POWERS THAT OUR ANCIENT FORE-PARENTS ARE SAID TO HAVE USED...
COULD IT BE--?

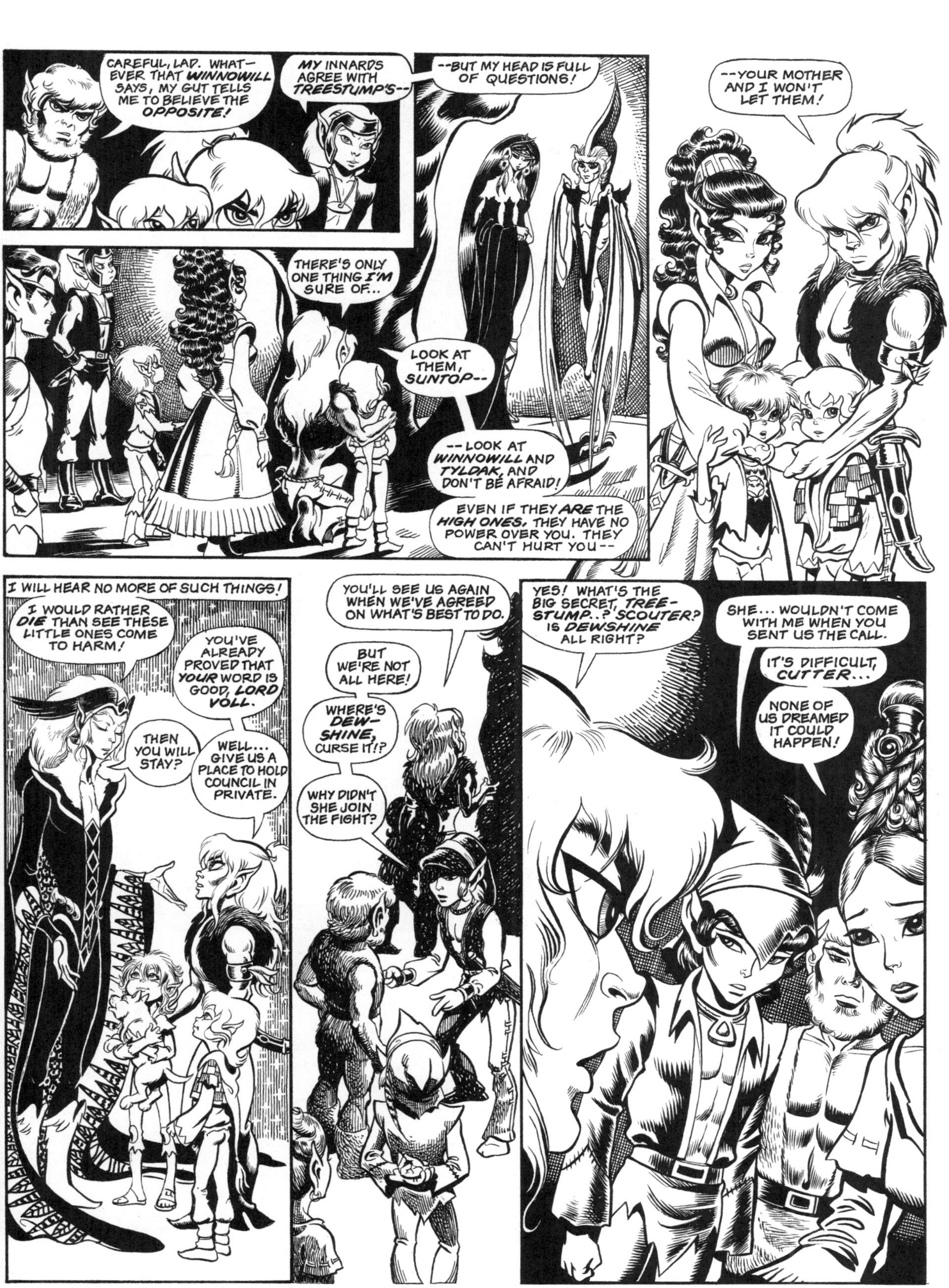
CAREFUL, LAD. WHATEVER THAT WINNOWILL SAYS, MY GUT TELLS ME TO BELIEVE THE OPPOSITE!
MY INNARDS AGREE WITH TREESTUMP'S--
--BUT MY HEAD IS FULL OF QUESTIONS!
THERE'S ONLY ONE THING I'M SURE OF...
LOOK AT THEM, SUNTOP--
--LOOK AT WINNOWILL AND TYLDAK, AND DON'T BE AFRAID!
EVEN IF THEY ARE THE HIGH ONES, THEY HAVE NO POWER OVER YOU. THEY CAN'T HURT YOU--
--YOUR MOTHER AND I WON'T LET THEM!
I WILL HEAR NO MORE OF SUCH THINGS!
I WOULD RATHER DIE THAN SEE THESE LITTLE ONES COME TO HARM!
YOU'VE ALREADY PROVED THAT YOUR WORD IS GOOD, LORD VOLL.
THEN YOU WILL STAY?
WELL... GIVE US A PLACE TO HOLD COUNCIL IN PRIVATE.
YOU'LL SEE US AGAIN WHEN WE'VE AGREED ON WHAT'S BEST TO DO.
BUT WE'RE NOT ALL HERE!
WHERE'S DEWSHINE, CURSE IT!?
WHY DIDN'T SHE JOIN THE FIGHT?
YES! WHAT'S THE BIG SECRET, TREESTUMP..? SCOUTER? IS DEWSHINE ALL RIGHT?
SHE... WOULDN'T COME WITH ME WHEN YOU SENT US THE CALL.
IT'S DIFFICULT, CUTTER...
NONE OF US DREAMED IT COULD HAPPEN!

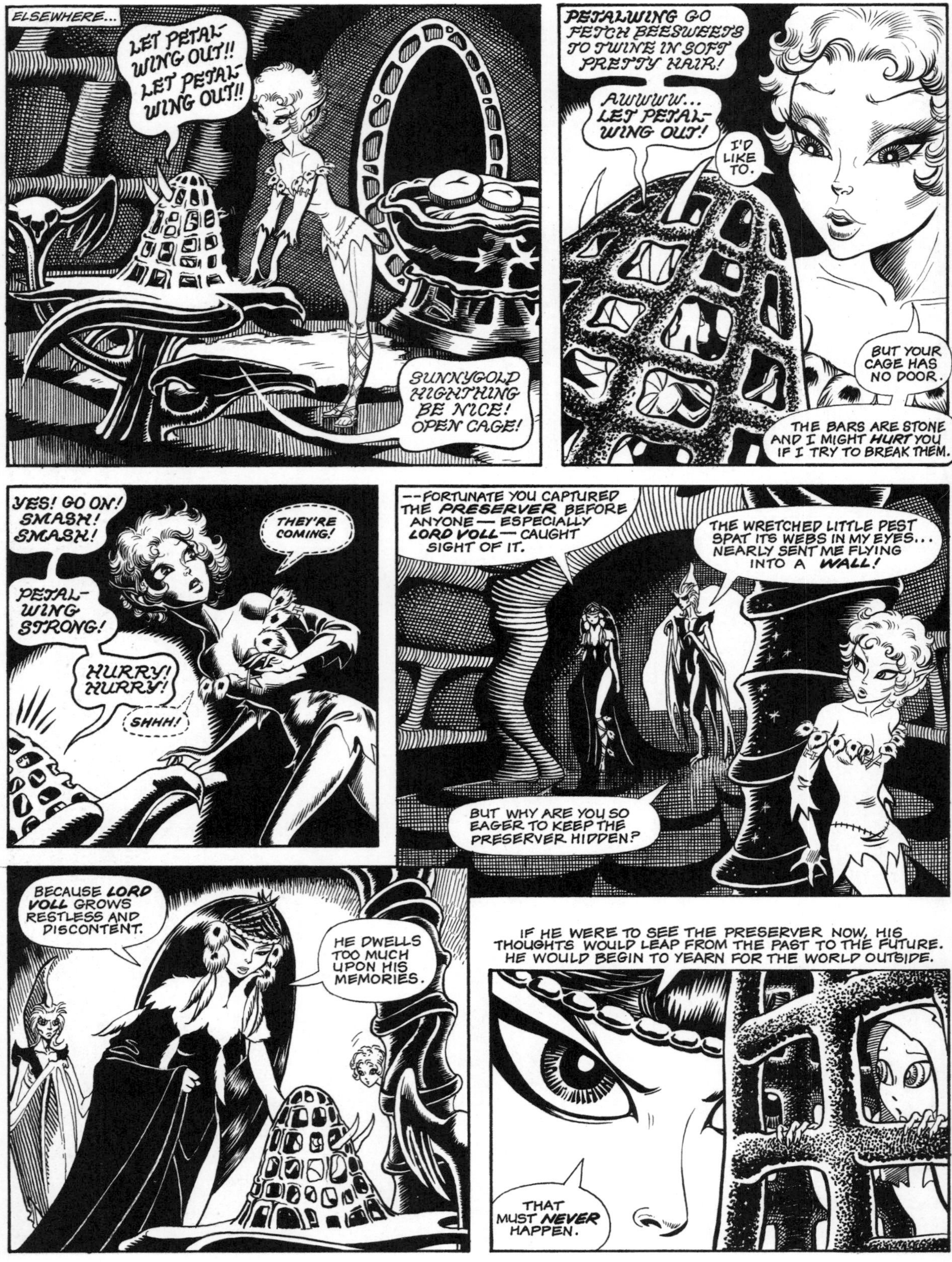

ELSEWHERE...
LET PETAL-WING OUT!! LET PETAL-WING OUT!!
SUNNYGOLD HIGHTHING BE NICE! OPEN CAGE!
PETALWING GO FETCH BEESWEETS TO TWINE IN SOFT PRETTY HAIR!
AWWWW... LET PETAL-WING OUT!
I'D LIKE TO.
BUT YOUR CAGE HAS NO DOOR.
THE BARS ARE STONE AND I MIGHT HURT YOU IF I TRY TO BREAK THEM.
YES! GO ON! SMASH! SMASH!
PETAL-WING STRONG!
THEY'RE COMING!
HURRY! HURRY!
SHHH!
--FORTUNATE YOU CAPTURED THE PRESERVER BEFORE ANYONE — ESPECIALLY LORD VOLL — CAUGHT SIGHT OF IT.
THE WRETCHED LITTLE PEST SPAT ITS WEBS IN MY EYES... NEARLY SENT ME FLYING INTO A WALL!
BUT WHY ARE YOU SO EAGER TO KEEP THE PRESERVER HIDDEN?
BECAUSE LORD VOLL GROWS RESTLESS AND DISCONTENT.
HE DWELLS TOO MUCH UPON HIS MEMORIES.
IF HE WERE TO SEE THE PRESERVER NOW, HIS THOUGHTS WOULD LEAP FROM THE PAST TO THE FUTURE. HE WOULD BEGIN TO YEARN FOR THE WORLD OUTSIDE.
THAT MUST NEVER HAPPEN.

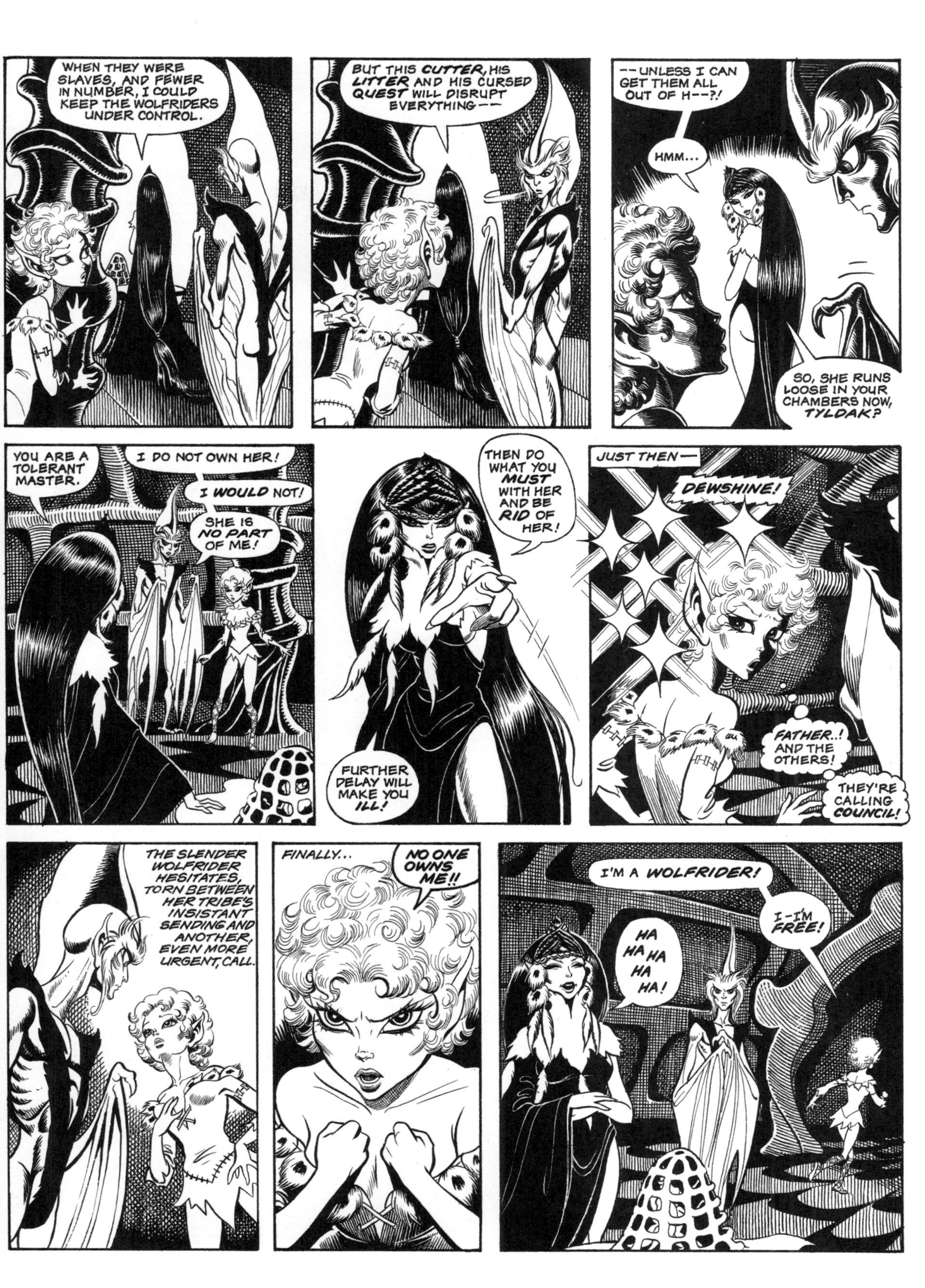
WHEN THEY WERE SLAVES, AND FEWER IN NUMBER, I COULD KEEP THE WOLFRIDERS UNDER CONTROL.
BUT THIS CUTTER, HIS LITTER AND HIS CURSED QUEST WILL DISRUPT EVERYTHING--
--UNLESS I CAN GET THEM ALL OUT OF H--?!
HMM...
SO, SHE RUNS LOOSE IN YOUR CHAMBERS NOW, TYLDAK?
YOU ARE A TOLERANT MASTER.
I DO NOT OWN HER!
I WOULD NOT!
SHE IS NO PART OF ME!
THEN DO WHAT YOU MUST WITH HER AND BE RID OF HER!
FURTHER DELAY WILL MAKE YOU ILL!
JUST THEN—
DEWSHINE!
FATHER..! AND THE OTHERS!
THEY'RE CALLING COUNCIL!
THE SLENDER WOLFRIDER HESITATES, TORN BETWEEN HER TRIBE'S INSISTANT SENDING AND ANOTHER, EVEN MORE URGENT, CALL.
FINALLY...
NO ONE OWNS ME!!
I'M A WOLFRIDER!
I-I'M FREE!
HA HA HA HA HA!

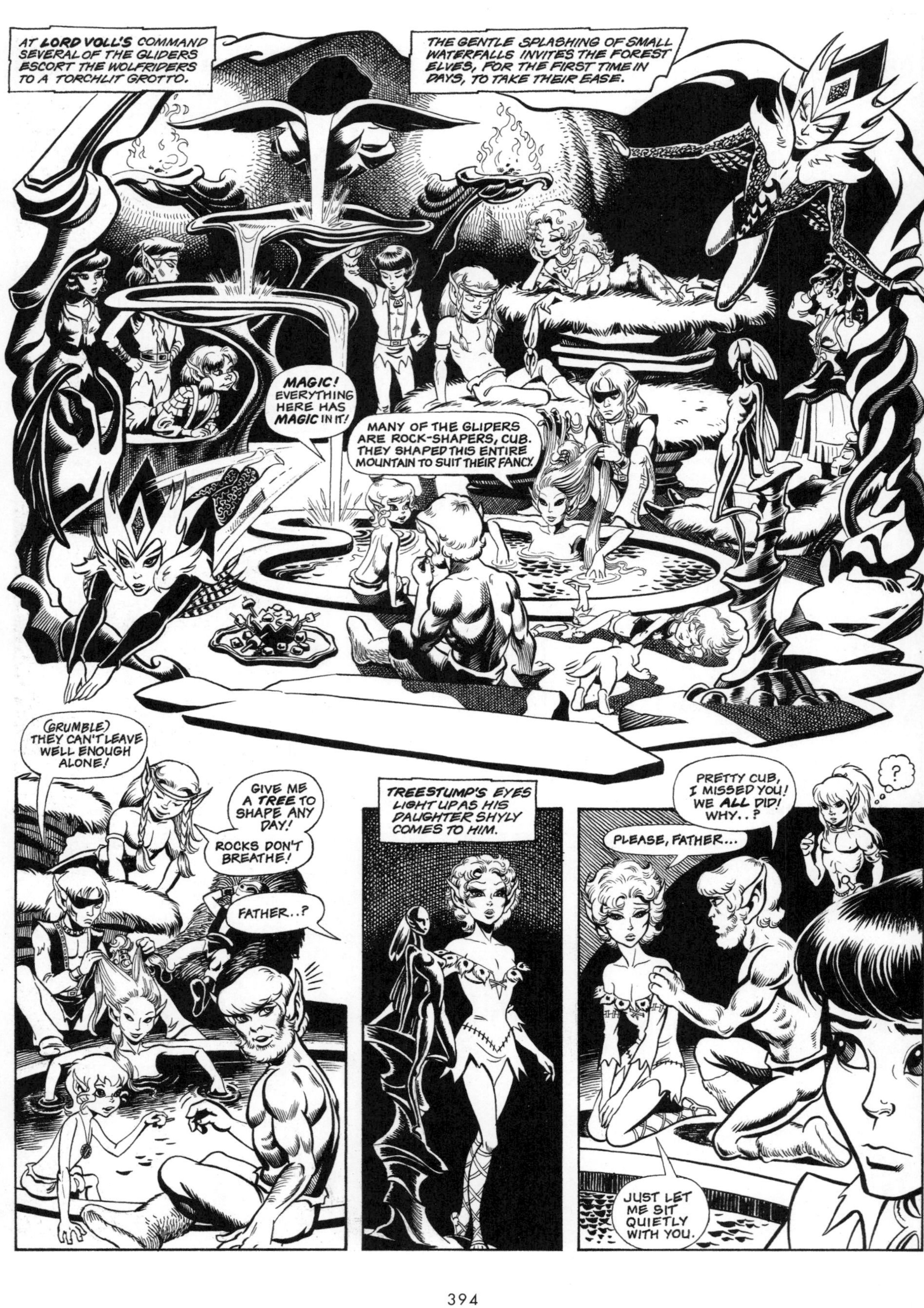

AT LORD VOLL'S COMMAND SEVERAL OF THE GLIDERS ESCORT THE WOLFRIDERS TO A TORCHLIT GROTTO.
THE GENTLE SPLASHING OF SMALL WATERFALLS INVITES THE FOREST ELVES, FOR THE FIRST TIME IN DAYS, TO TAKE THEIR EASE.
MAGIC! EVERYTHING HERE HAS MAGIC IN IT!
MANY OF THE GLIDERS ARE ROCK-SHAPERS, CUB. THEY SHAPED THIS ENTIRE MOUNTAIN TO SUIT THEIR FANCY.
(GRUMBLE) THEY CAN'T LEAVE WELL ENOUGH ALONE!
GIVE ME A TREE TO SHAPE ANY DAY!
ROCKS DON'T BREATHE!
FATHER..?
TREESTUMP'S EYES LIGHT UP AS HIS DAUGHTER SHYLY COMES TO HIM.
PRETTY CUB, I MISSED YOU! WE ALL DID! WHY..?
PLEASE, FATHER...
?
JUST LET ME SIT QUIETLY WITH YOU.

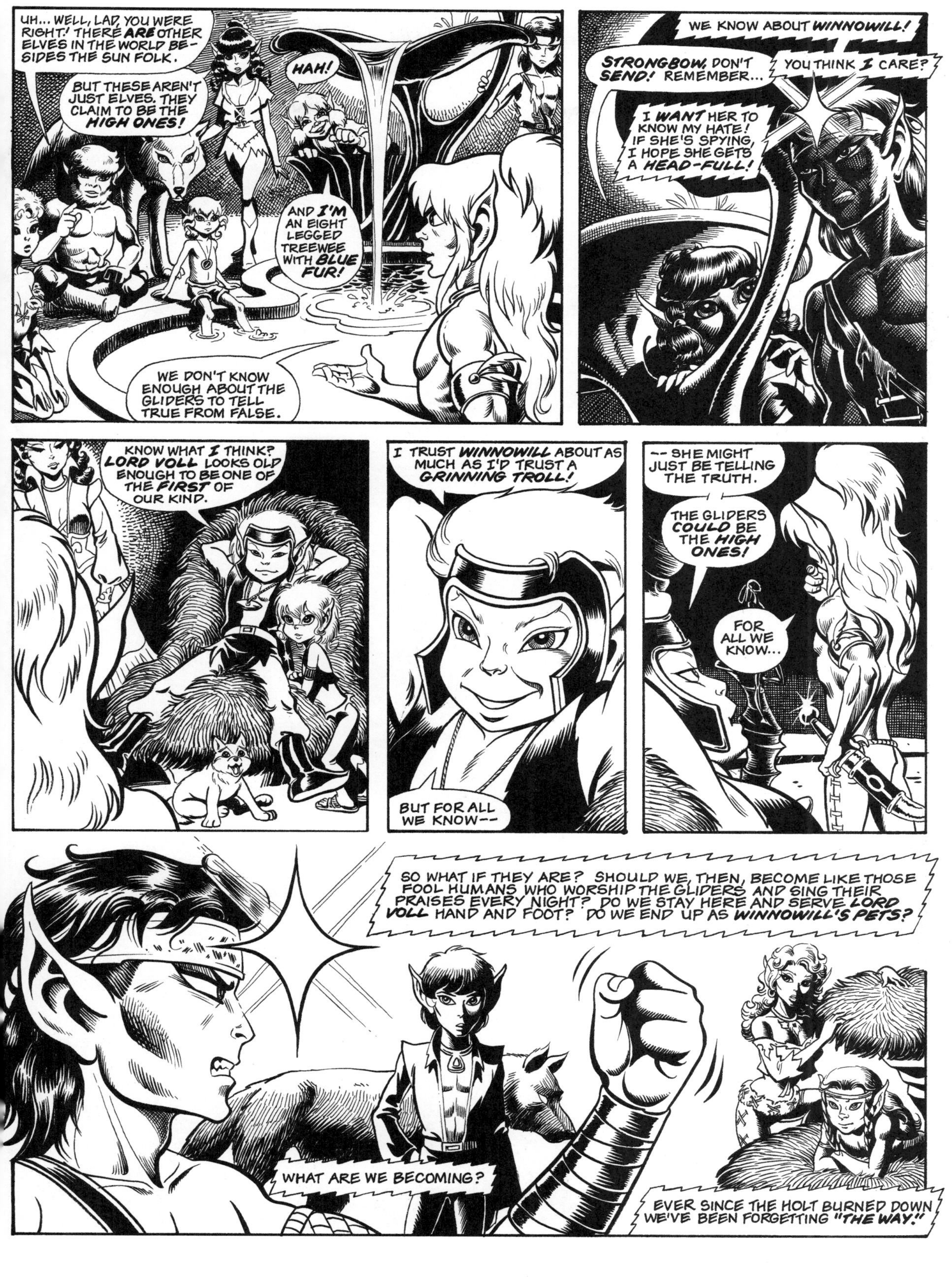
UH... WELL, LAD, YOU WERE RIGHT! THERE ARE OTHER ELVES IN THE WORLD BESIDES THE SUN FOLK.
BUT THESE AREN'T JUST ELVES. THEY CLAIM TO BE THE HIGH ONES!
HAH!
AND I'M AN EIGHT LEGGED TREEWEE WITH BLUE FUR!
WE DON'T KNOW ENOUGH ABOUT THE GLIDERS TO TELL TRUE FROM FALSE.
WE KNOW ABOUT WINNOWILL!
STRONGBOW, DON'T SEND! REMEMBER...
YOU THINK I CARE?
I WANT HER TO KNOW MY HATE! IF SHE'S SPYING, I HOPE SHE GETS A HEAD-FULL!
KNOW WHAT I THINK? LORD VOLL LOOKS OLD ENOUGH TO BE ONE OF THE FIRST OF OUR KIND.
I TRUST WINNOWILL ABOUT AS MUCH AS I'D TRUST A GRINNING TROLL!
BUT FOR ALL WE KNOW--
-- SHE MIGHT JUST BE TELLING THE TRUTH.
THE GLIDERS COULD BE THE HIGH ONES!
FOR ALL WE KNOW...
SO WHAT IF THEY ARE? SHOULD WE, THEN, BECOME LIKE THOSE FOOL HUMANS WHO WORSHIP THE GLIDERS AND SING THEIR PRAISES EVERY NIGHT? DO WE STAY HERE AND SERVE LORD VOLL HAND AND FOOT? DO WE END UP AS WINNOWILL'S PETS?
WHAT ARE WE BECOMING?
EVER SINCE THE HOLT BURNED DOWN WE'VE BEEN FORGETTING "THE WAY."

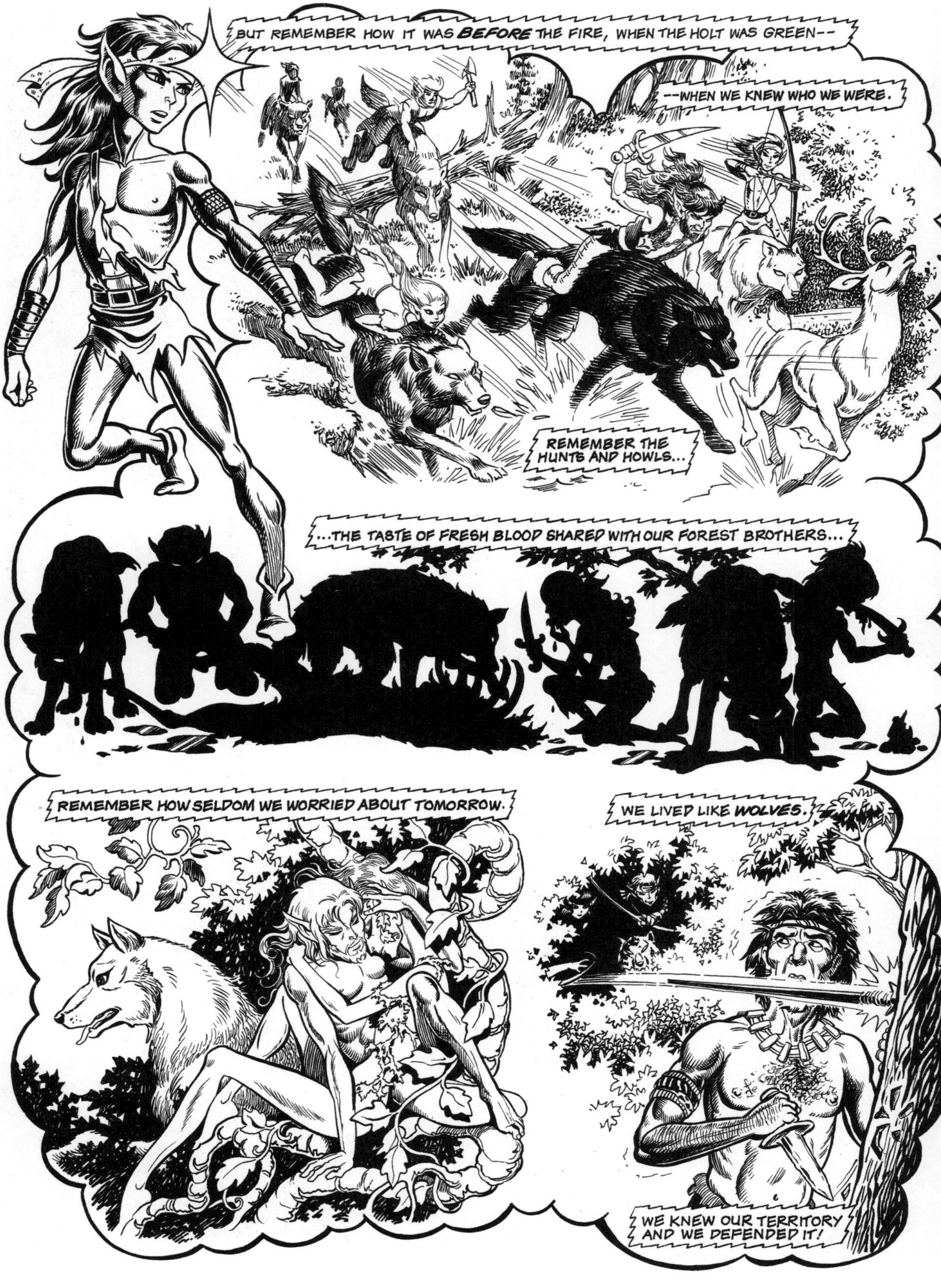
BUT REMEMBER HOW IT WAS BEFORE THE FIRE, WHEN THE HOLT WAS GREEN--
--WHEN WE KNEW WHO WE WERE.
REMEMBER THE HUNTS AND HOWLS...
...THE TASTE OF FRESH BLOOD SHARED WITH OUR FOREST BROTHERS...
REMEMBER HOW SELDOM WE WORRIED ABOUT TOMORROW.
WE LIVED LIKE WOLVES.
WE KNEW OUR TERRITORY AND WE DEFENDED IT!

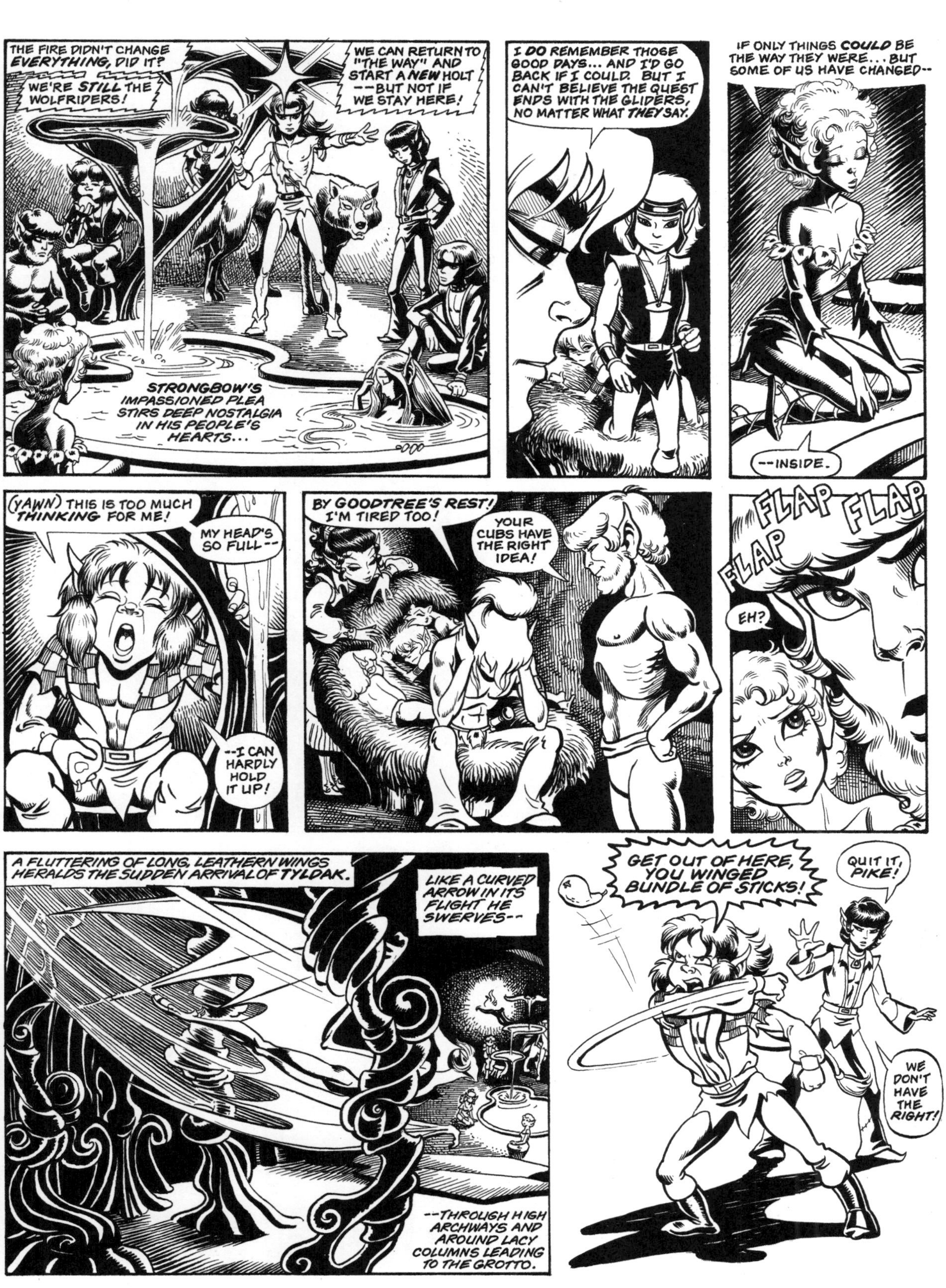
THE FIRE DIDN'T CHANGE EVERYTHING, DID IT?
WE'RE STILL THE WOLFRIDERS!
WE CAN RETURN TO "THE WAY" AND START A NEW HOLT --BUT NOT IF WE STAY HERE!
STRONGBOW'S IMPASSIONED PLEA STIRS DEEP NOSTALGIA IN HIS PEOPLE'S HEARTS...
I DO REMEMBER THOSE GOOD DAYS... AND I'D GO BACK IF I COULD. BUT I CAN'T BELIEVE THE QUEST ENDS WITH THE GLIDERS, NO MATTER WHAT THEY SAY.
IF ONLY THINGS COULD BE THE WAY THEY WERE... BUT SOME OF US HAVE CHANGED--
--INSIDE.
(YAWN) THIS IS TOO MUCH THINKING FOR ME!
MY HEAD'S SO FULL--
--I CAN HARDLY HOLD IT UP!
BY GOODTREE'S REST! I'M TIRED TOO!
YOUR CUBS HAVE THE RIGHT IDEA!
FLAP FLAP FLAP
EH?
A FLUTTERING OF LONG, LEATHERN WINGS HERALDS THE SUDDEN ARRIVAL OF TYLDAK.
LIKE A CURVED ARROW IN ITS FLIGHT HE SWERVES--
--THROUGH HIGH ARCHWAYS AND AROUND LACY COLUMNS LEADING TO THE GROTTO.
GET OUT OF HERE, YOU WINGED BUNDLE OF STICKS!
QUIT IT, PIKE!
WE DON'T HAVE THE RIGHT!

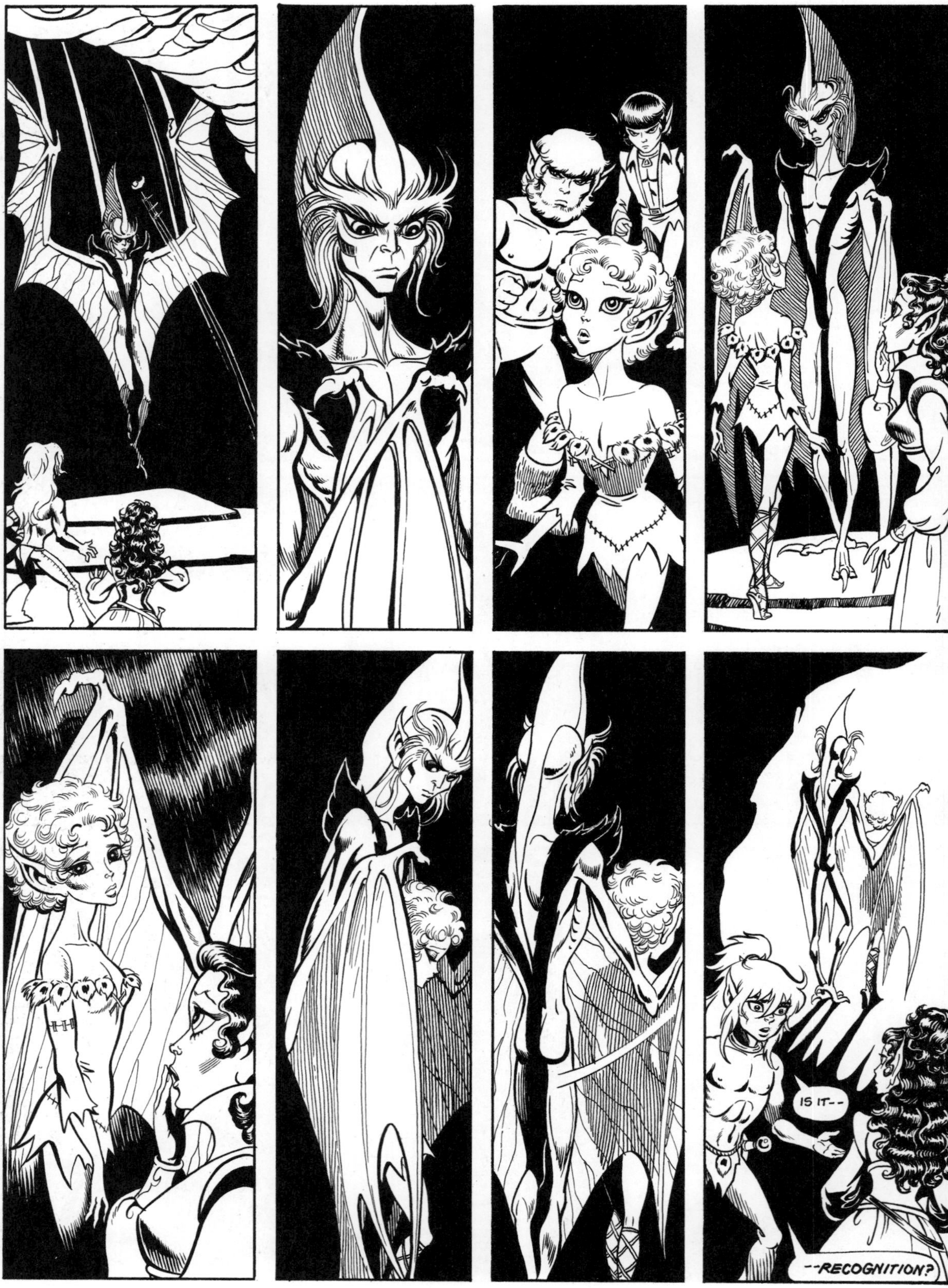
IS IT--
--RECOGNITION?

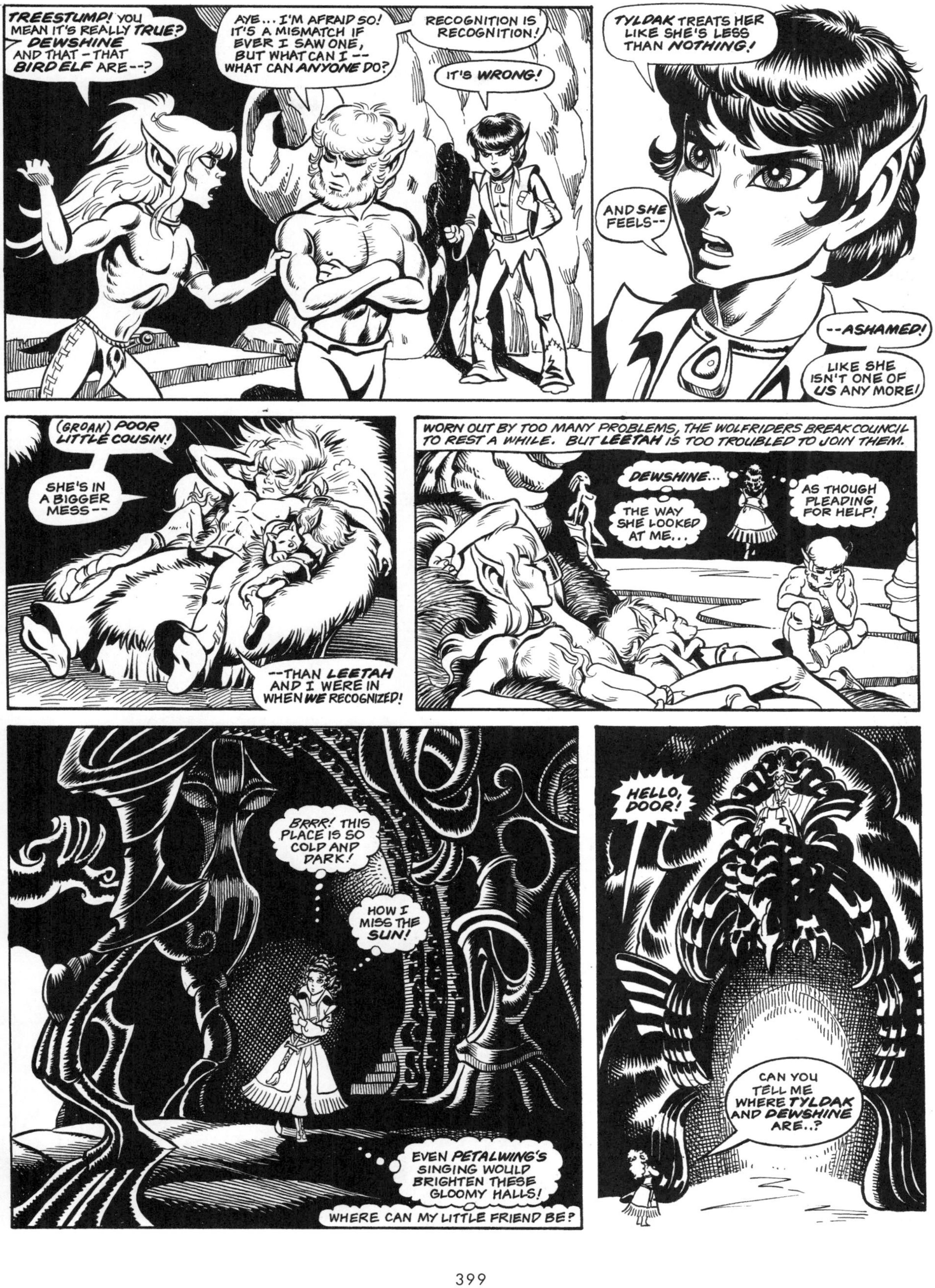
TREESTUMP! YOU MEAN IT'S REALLY TRUE? DEWSHINE AND THAT - THAT BIRDELF ARE--?
AYE... I'M AFRAID SO! IT'S A MISMATCH IF EVER I SAW ONE, BUT WHAT CAN I -- WHAT CAN ANYONE DO?
RECOGNITION IS RECOGNITION!
IT'S WRONG!
TYLDAK TREATS HER LIKE SHE'S LESS THAN NOTHING!
AND SHE FEELS--
--ASHAMED!
LIKE SHE ISN'T ONE OF US ANY MORE!
(GROAN) POOR LITTLE COUSIN!
SHE'S IN A BIGGER MESS--
--THAN LEETAH AND I WERE IN WHEN WE RECOGNIZED!
WORN OUT BY TOO MANY PROBLEMS, THE WOLFRIDERS BREAK COUNCIL TO REST A WHILE. BUT LEETAH IS TOO TROUBLED TO JOIN THEM.
DEWSHINE...
THE WAY SHE LOOKED AT ME...
AS THOUGH PLEADING FOR HELP!
BRRR! THIS PLACE IS SO COLD AND DARK!
HOW I MISS THE SUN!
EVEN PETALWING'S SINGING WOULD BRIGHTEN THESE GLOOMY HALLS!
WHERE CAN MY LITTLE FRIEND BE?
HELLO, DOOR!
CAN YOU TELL ME WHERE TYLDAK AND DEWSHINE ARE..?

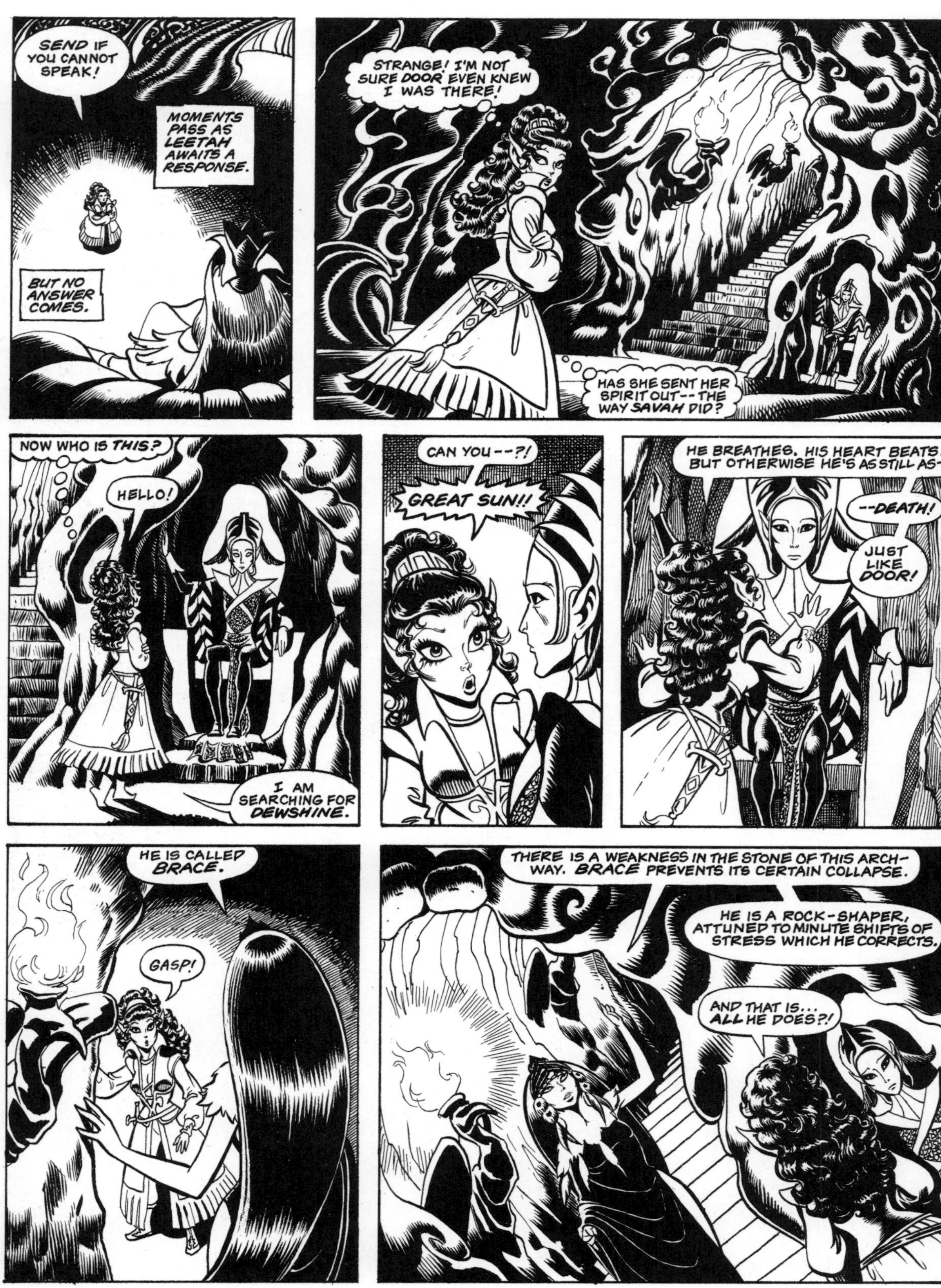

SEND IF YOU CANNOT SPEAK!
MOMENTS PASS AS LEETAH AWAITS A RESPONSE.
BUT NO ANSWER COMES.
STRANGE! I'M NOT SURE DOOR EVEN KNEW I WAS THERE!
HAS SHE SENT HER SPIRIT OUT--THE WAY SAVAH DID?
NOW WHO IS THIS?
HELLO!
I AM SEARCHING FOR DEWSHINE.
CAN YOU--?!
GREAT SUN!!
HE BREATHES. HIS HEART BEATS. BUT OTHERWISE HE'S AS STILL AS--
--DEATH!
JUST LIKE DOOR!
HE IS CALLED BRACE.
GASP!
THERE IS A WEAKNESS IN THE STONE OF THIS ARCHWAY. BRACE PREVENTS ITS CERTAIN COLLAPSE.
HE IS A ROCK-SHAPER, ATTUNED TO MINUTE SHIFTS OF STRESS WHICH HE CORRECTS.
AND THAT IS... ALL HE DOES?!

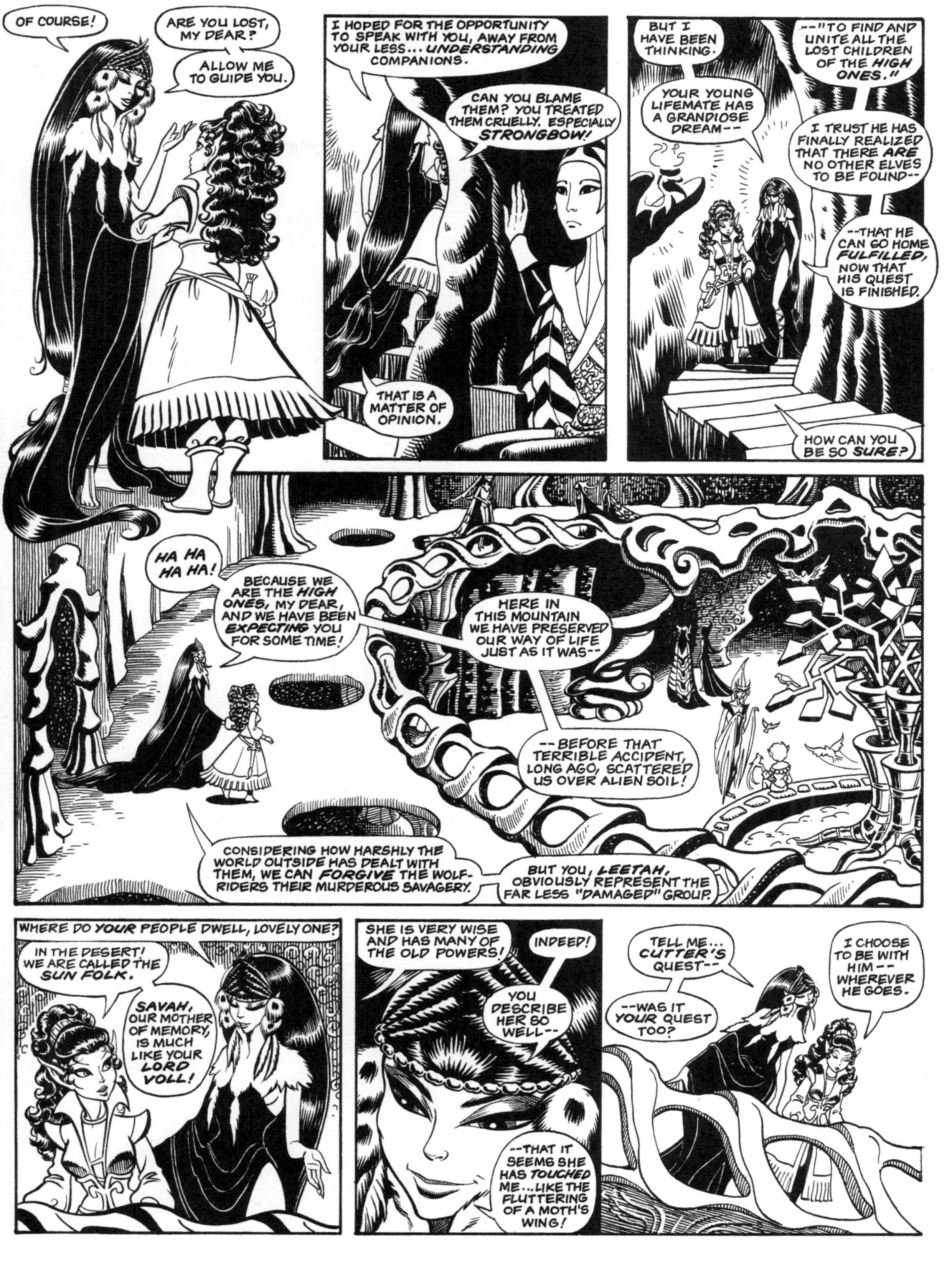

OF COURSE!
ARE YOU LOST, MY DEAR?
ALLOW ME TO GUIDE YOU.
I HOPED FOR THE OPPORTUNITY TO SPEAK WITH YOU, AWAY FROM YOUR LESS... UNDERSTANDING COMPANIONS.
CAN YOU BLAME THEM? YOU TREATED THEM CRUELLY. ESPECIALLY STRONGBOW!
THAT IS A MATTER OF OPINION.
BUT I HAVE BEEN THINKING.
YOUR YOUNG LIFEMATE HAS A GRANDIOSE DREAM--
--"TO FIND AND UNITE ALL THE LOST CHILDREN OF THE HIGH ONES."
I TRUST HE HAS FINALLY REALIZED THAT THERE ARE NO OTHER ELVES TO BE FOUND--
--THAT HE CAN GO HOME FULFILLED, NOW THAT HIS QUEST IS FINISHED.
HOW CAN YOU BE SO SURE?
HA HA HA HA!
BECAUSE WE ARE THE HIGH ONES, MY DEAR, AND WE HAVE BEEN EXPECTING YOU FOR SOME TIME!
HERE IN THIS MOUNTAIN WE HAVE PRESERVED OUR WAY OF LIFE JUST AS IT WAS--
--BEFORE THAT TERRIBLE ACCIDENT, LONG AGO, SCATTERED US OVER ALIEN SOIL!
CONSIDERING HOW HARSHLY THE WORLD OUTSIDE HAS DEALT WITH THEM, WE CAN FORGIVE THE WOLF-RIDERS THEIR MURDEROUS SAVAGERY.
BUT YOU, LEETAH, OBVIOUSLY REPRESENT THE FAR LESS "DAMAGED" GROUP.
WHERE DO YOUR PEOPLE DWELL, LOVELY ONE?
IN THE DESERT! WE ARE CALLED THE SUN FOLK.
SAVAH, OUR MOTHER OF MEMORY, IS MUCH LIKE YOUR LORD VOLL!
SHE IS VERY WISE AND HAS MANY OF THE OLD POWERS!
INDEED!
YOU DESCRIBE HER SO WELL--
--THAT IT SEEMS SHE HAS TOUCHED ME... LIKE THE FLUTTERING OF A MOTH'S WING!
TELL ME... CUTTER'S QUEST--
--WAS IT YOUR QUEST TOO?
I CHOOSE TO BE WITH HIM-- WHEREVER HE GOES.

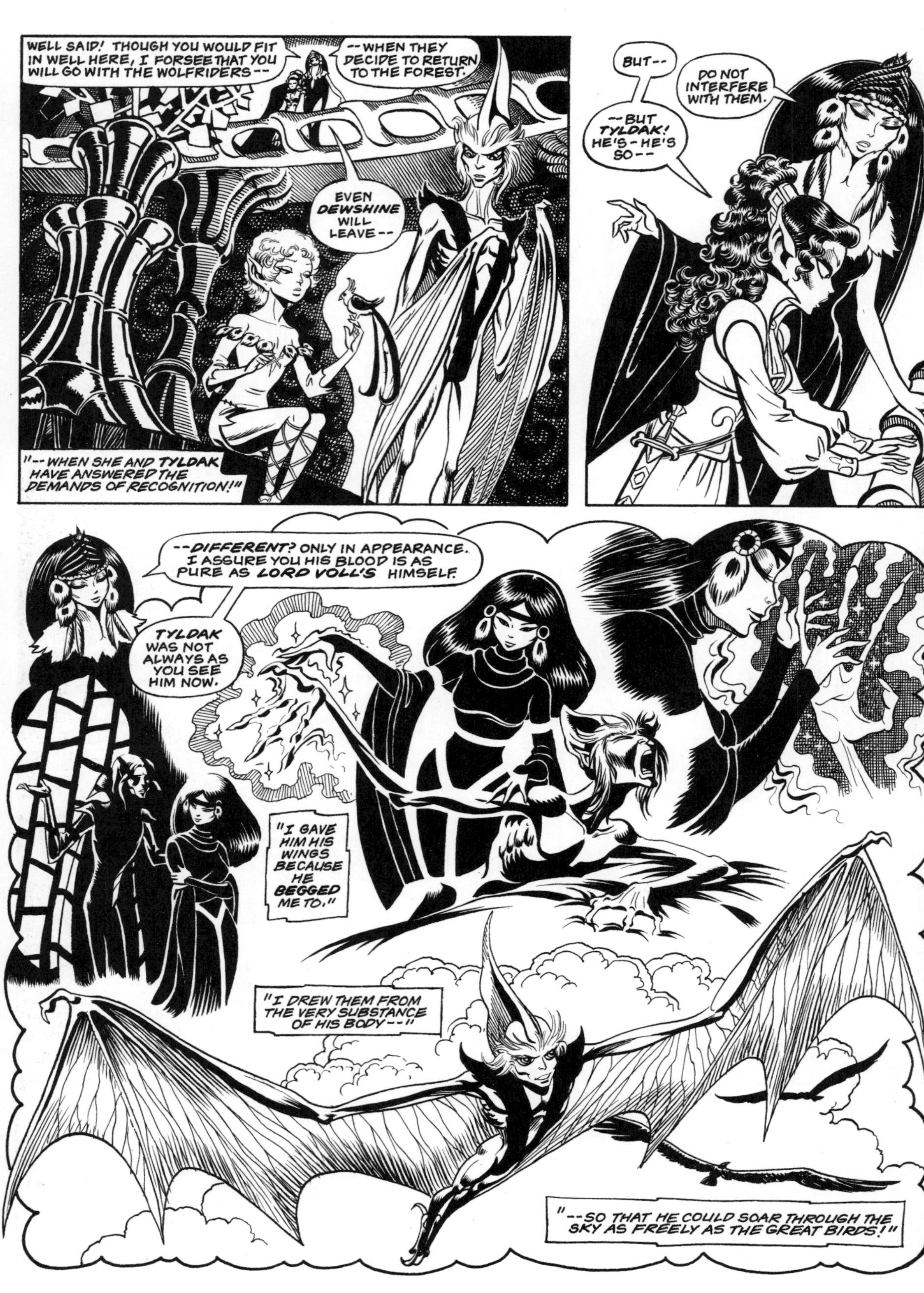
WELL SAID! THOUGH YOU WOULD FIT IN WELL HERE, I FORSEE THAT YOU WILL GO WITH THE WOLFRIDERS --
-- WHEN THEY DECIDE TO RETURN TO THE FOREST.
EVEN DEWSHINE WILL LEAVE --
"-- WHEN SHE AND TYLDAK HAVE ANSWERED THE DEMANDS OF RECOGNITION!"
BUT --
DO NOT INTERFERE WITH THEM.
-- BUT TYLDAK! HE'S - HE'S SO --
-- DIFFERENT? ONLY IN APPEARANCE. I ASSURE YOU HIS BLOOD IS AS PURE AS LORD VOLL'S HIMSELF.
TYLDAK WAS NOT ALWAYS AS YOU SEE HIM NOW.
"I GAVE HIM HIS WINGS BECAUSE HE BEGGED ME TO."
"I DREW THEM FROM THE VERY SUBSTANCE OF HIS BODY --"
"-- SO THAT HE COULD SOAR THROUGH THE SKY AS FREELY AS THE GREAT BIRDS!"

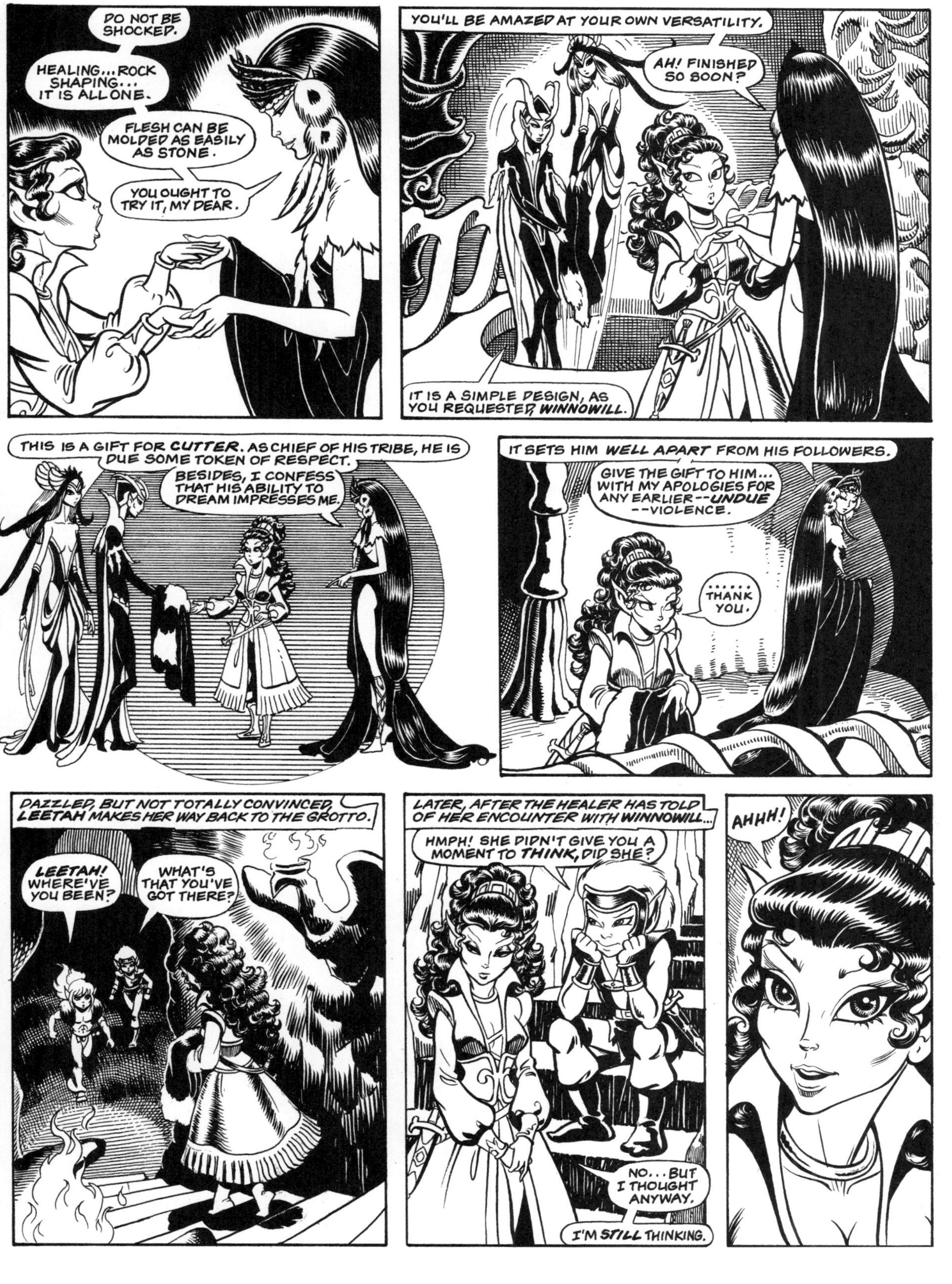

DO NOT BE SHOCKED.
HEALING... ROCK SHAPING... IT IS ALL ONE.
FLESH CAN BE MOLDED AS EASILY AS STONE.
YOU OUGHT TO TRY IT, MY DEAR.
YOU'LL BE AMAZED AT YOUR OWN VERSATILITY.
AH! FINISHED SO SOON?
IT IS A SIMPLE DESIGN, AS YOU REQUESTED, WINNOWILL.
THIS IS A GIFT FOR CUTTER. AS CHIEF OF HIS TRIBE, HE IS DUE SOME TOKEN OF RESPECT.
BESIDES, I CONFESS THAT HIS ABILITY TO DREAM IMPRESSES ME.
IT SETS HIM WELL APART FROM HIS FOLLOWERS.
GIVE THE GIFT TO HIM... WITH MY APOLOGIES FOR ANY EARLIER--UNDUE--VIOLENCE.
...... THANK YOU.
DAZZLED, BUT NOT TOTALLY CONVINCED, LEETAH MAKES HER WAY BACK TO THE GROTTO.
LEETAH! WHERE'VE YOU BEEN?
WHAT'S THAT YOU'VE GOT THERE?
LATER, AFTER THE HEALER HAS TOLD OF HER ENCOUNTER WITH WINNOWILL...
HMPH! SHE DIDN'T GIVE YOU A MOMENT TO THINK, DID SHE?
NO... BUT I THOUGHT ANYWAY.
I'M STILL THINKING.
AHHH!

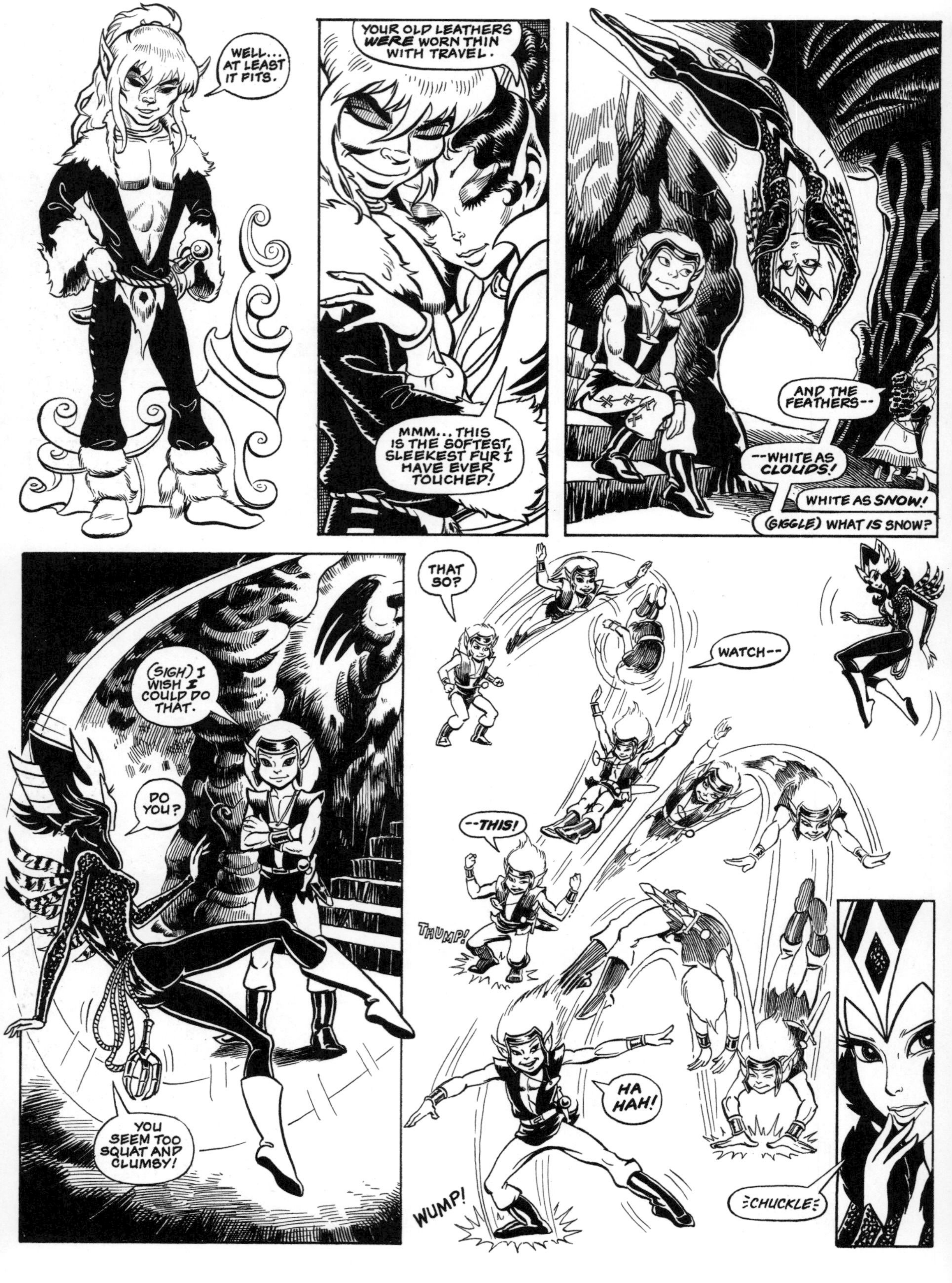
WELL... AT LEAST IT FITS.
YOUR OLD LEATHERS WERE WORN THIN WITH TRAVEL.
MMM... THIS IS THE SOFTEST, SLEEKEST FUR I HAVE EVER TOUCHED!
AND THE FEATHERS--
--WHITE AS CLOUDS!
WHITE AS SNOW!
(GIGGLE) WHAT IS SNOW?
(SIGH) I WISH I COULD DO THAT.
DO YOU?
YOU SEEM TOO SQUAT AND CLUMSY!
THAT SO?
WATCH--
--THIS!
THUMP!
HA HAH!
WUMP!
CHUCKLE

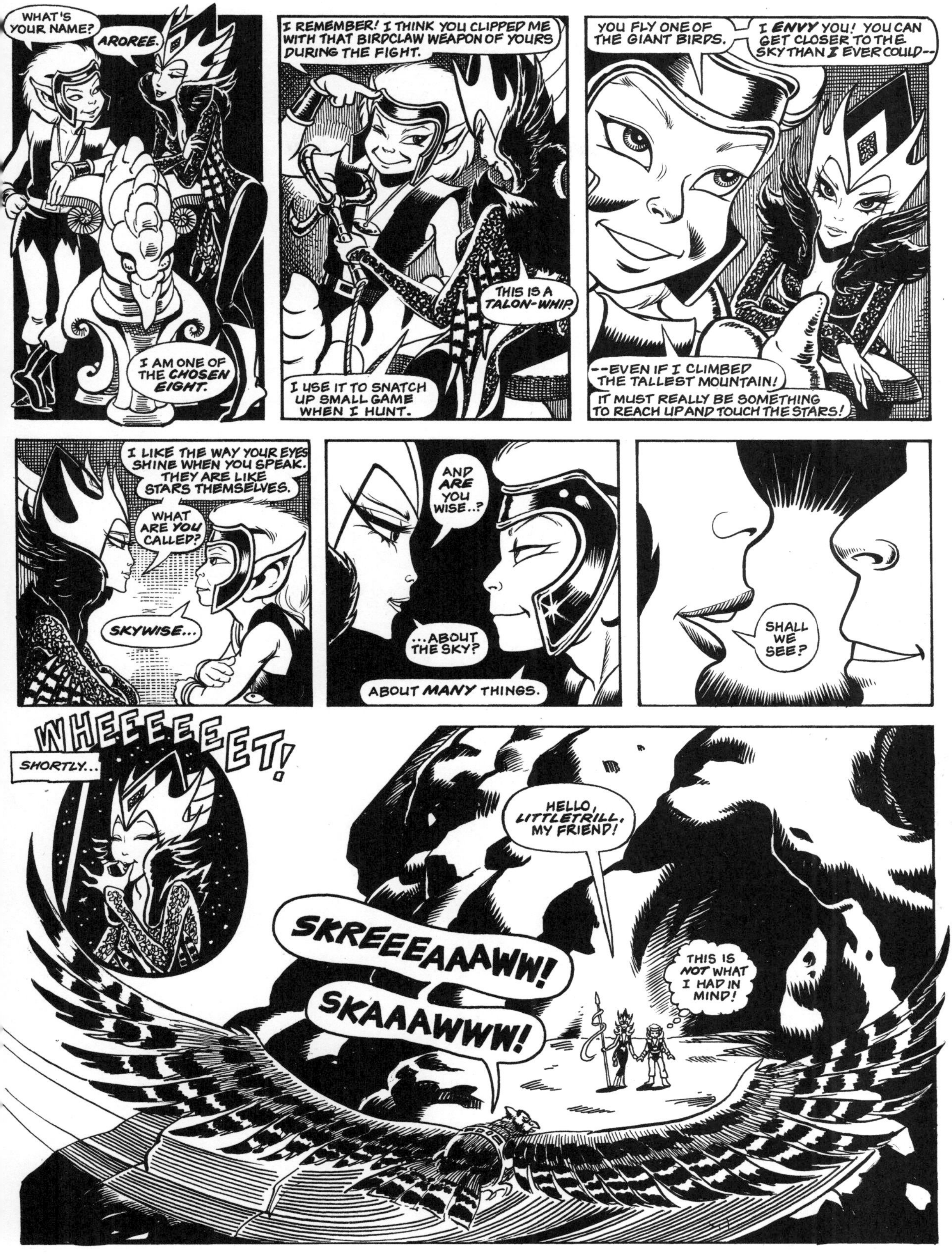
WHAT'S YOUR NAME?
AROREE.
I AM ONE OF THE CHOSEN EIGHT.
I REMEMBER! I THINK YOU CLIPPED ME WITH THAT BIRDCLAW WEAPON OF YOURS DURING THE FIGHT.
THIS IS A TALON-WHIP.
I USE IT TO SNATCH UP SMALL GAME WHEN I HUNT.
YOU FLY ONE OF THE GIANT BIRDS.
I ENVY YOU! YOU CAN GET CLOSER TO THE SKY THAN I EVER COULD--
--EVEN IF I CLIMBED THE TALLEST MOUNTAIN!
IT MUST REALLY BE SOMETHING TO REACH UP AND TOUCH THE STARS!
I LIKE THE WAY YOUR EYES SHINE WHEN YOU SPEAK. THEY ARE LIKE STARS THEMSELVES.
WHAT ARE YOU CALLED?
SKYWISE...
AND ARE YOU WISE..?
...ABOUT THE SKY?
ABOUT MANY THINGS.
SHALL WE SEE?
WHEEEEEEET!
SHORTLY...
HELLO, LITTLETRILL, MY FRIEND!
SKREEEAAAWW!
SKAAAWWW!
THIS IS NOT WHAT I HAD IN MIND!

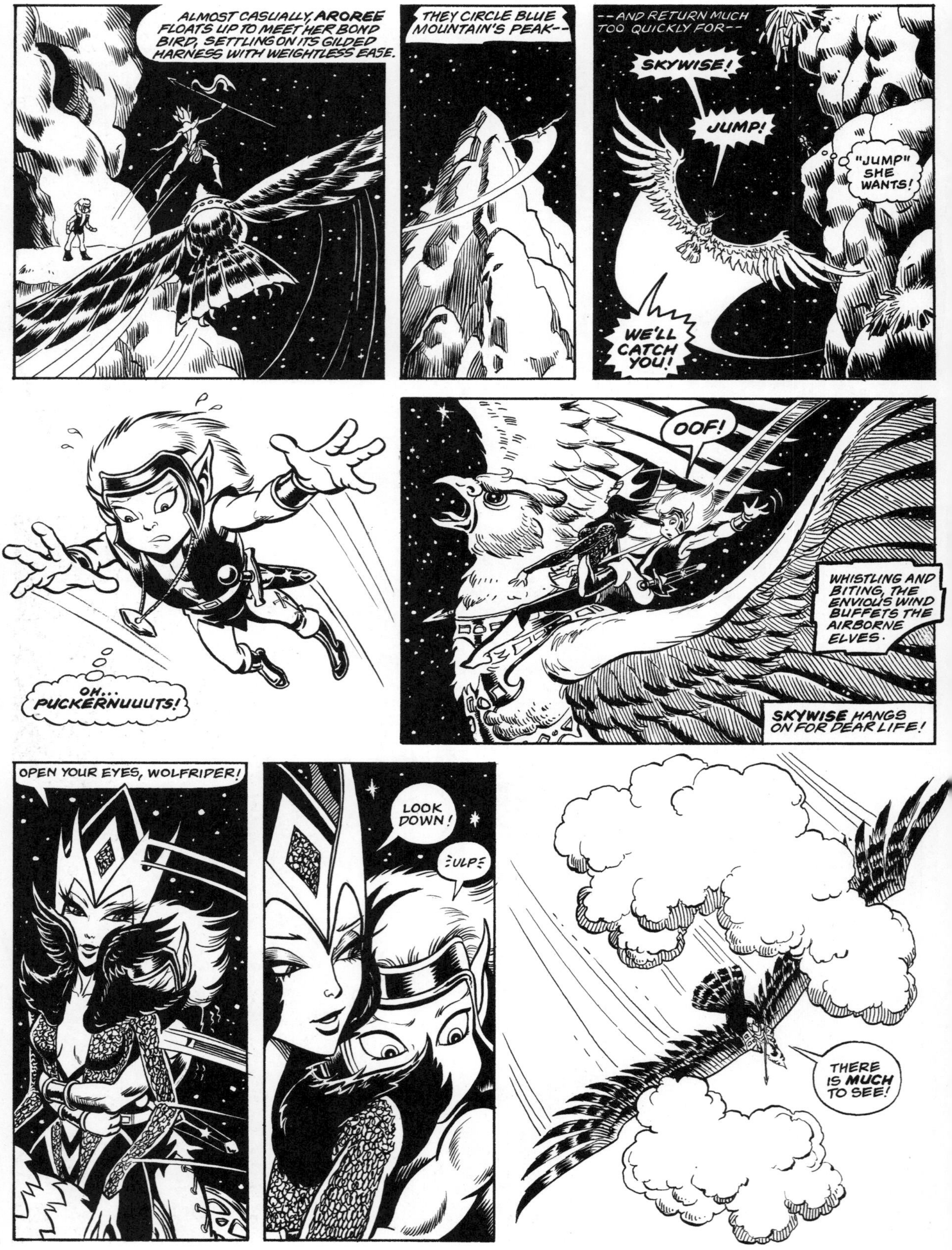
ALMOST CASUALLY, AROREE FLOATS UP TO MEET HER BOND BIRD, SETTLING ON ITS GILDED HARNESS WITH WEIGHTLESS EASE.
THEY CIRCLE BLUE MOUNTAIN'S PEAK--
--AND RETURN MUCH TOO QUICKLY FOR--
SKYWISE!
JUMP!
"JUMP" SHE WANTS!
WE'LL CATCH YOU!
OH... PUCKERNUUUTS!
OOF!
WHISTLING AND BITING, THE ENVIOUS WIND BUFFETS THE AIRBORNE ELVES.
SKYWISE HANGS ON FOR DEAR LIFE!
OPEN YOUR EYES, WOLFRIDER!
LOOK DOWN!
ULP
THERE IS MUCH TO SEE!

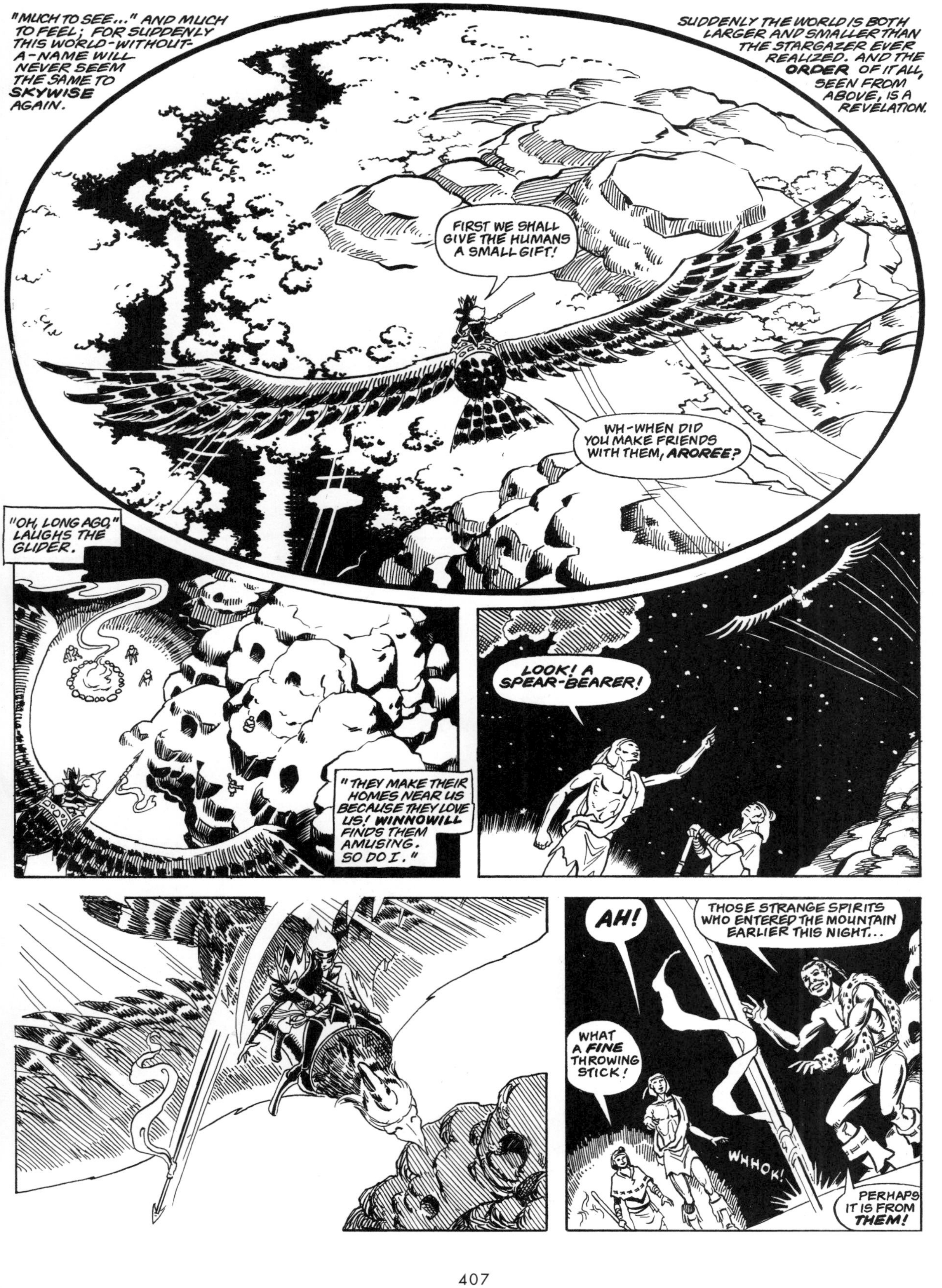
"MUCH TO SEE..." AND MUCH TO FEEL; FOR SUDDENLY THIS WORLD-WITHOUT-A-NAME WILL NEVER SEEM THE SAME TO SKYWISE AGAIN.
SUDDENLY THE WORLD IS BOTH LARGER AND SMALLER THAN THE STARGAZER EVER REALIZED. AND THE ORDER OF IT ALL, SEEN FROM ABOVE, IS A REVELATION.
FIRST WE SHALL GIVE THE HUMANS A SMALL GIFT!
WH-WHEN DID YOU MAKE FRIENDS WITH THEM, AROREE?
"OH, LONG AGO," LAUGHS THE GLIDER.
"THEY MAKE THEIR HOMES NEAR US BECAUSE THEY LOVE US! WINNOWILL FINDS THEM AMUSING. SO DO I."
LOOK! A SPEAR-BEARER!
AH!
THOSE STRANGE SPIRITS WHO ENTERED THE MOUNTAIN EARLIER THIS NIGHT...
WHAT A FINE THROWING STICK!
WHHOK!
PERHAPS IT IS FROM THEM!

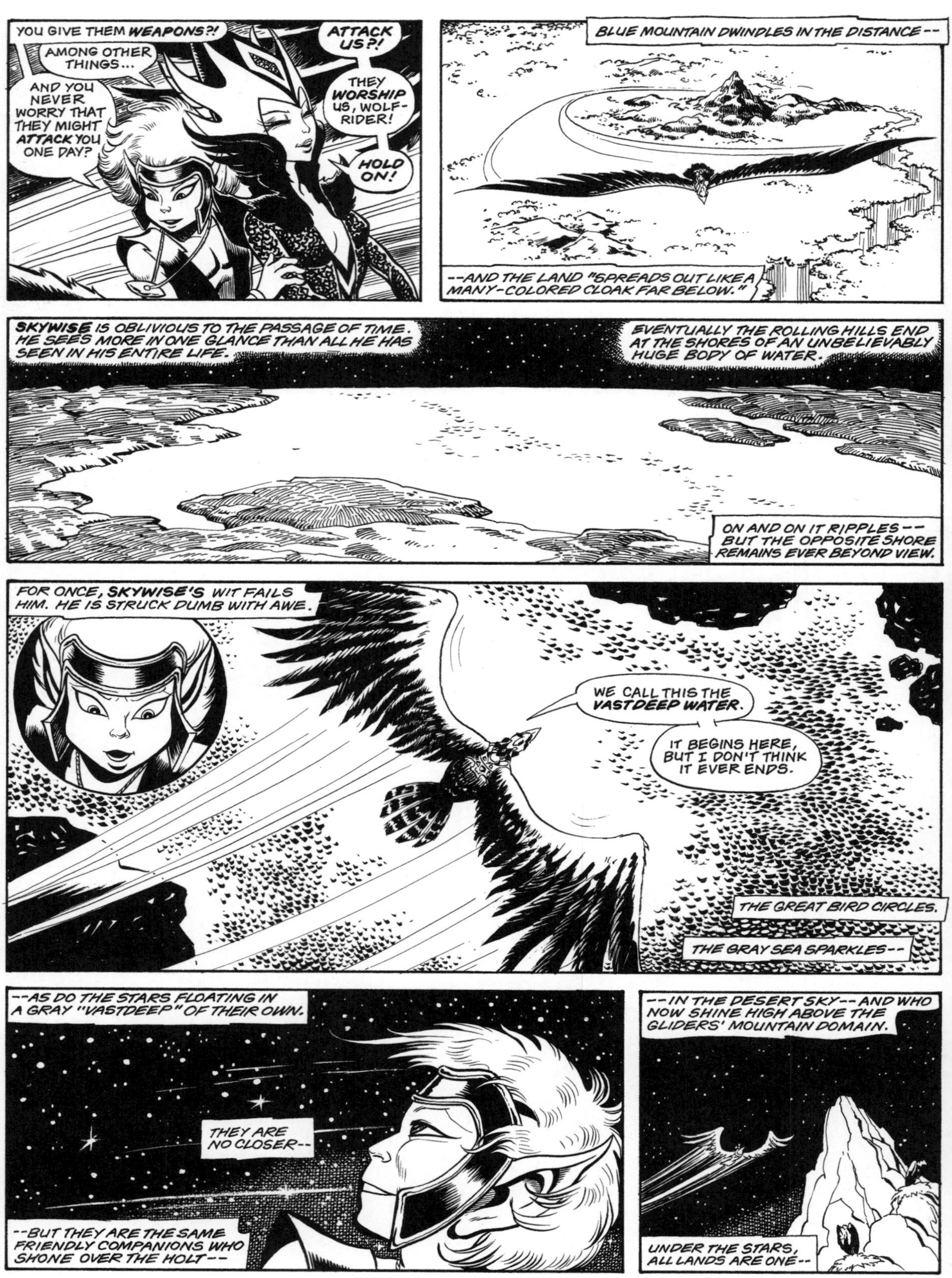
YOU GIVE THEM **WEAPONS**?!
AMONG OTHER THINGS...
AND YOU NEVER WORRY THAT THEY MIGHT **ATTACK** YOU ONE DAY?
ATTACK US?!
THEY **WORSHIP** US, WOLF-RIDER!
HOLD ON!
BLUE MOUNTAIN DWINDLES IN THE DISTANCE--
--AND THE LAND "SPREADS OUT LIKE A MANY-COLORED CLOAK FAR BELOW."
SKYWISE IS OBLIVIOUS TO THE PASSAGE OF TIME. HE SEES MORE IN ONE GLANCE THAN ALL HE HAS SEEN IN HIS ENTIRE LIFE.
EVENTUALLY THE ROLLING HILLS END AT THE SHORES OF AN UNBELIEVABLY HUGE BODY OF WATER.
ON AND ON IT RIPPLES-- BUT THE OPPOSITE SHORE REMAINS EVER BEYOND VIEW.
FOR ONCE, **SKYWISE'S** WIT FAILS HIM. HE IS STRUCK DUMB WITH AWE.
WE CALL THIS THE **VASTDEEP WATER**.
IT BEGINS HERE, BUT I DON'T THINK IT EVER ENDS.
THE GREAT BIRD CIRCLES.
THE GRAY SEA SPARKLES--
--AS DO THE STARS FLOATING IN A GRAY "VASTDEEP" OF THEIR OWN.
THEY ARE NO CLOSER--
--BUT THEY ARE THE SAME FRIENDLY COMPANIONS WHO SHONE OVER THE HOLT--
--IN THE DESERT SKY--AND WHO NOW SHINE HIGH ABOVE THE GLIDERS' MOUNTAIN DOMAIN.
UNDER THE STARS, ALL LANDS ARE ONE--

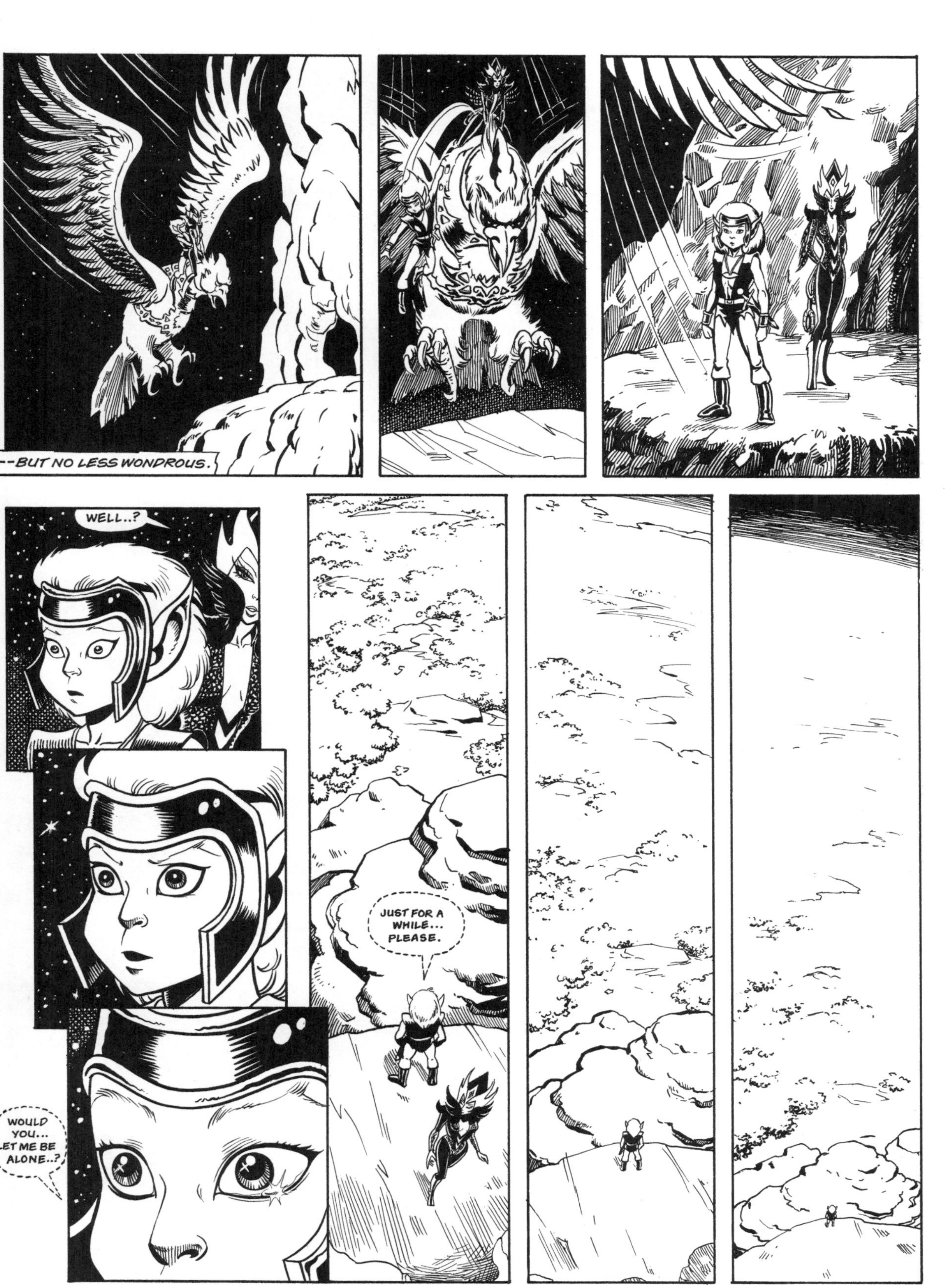
--BUT NO LESS WONDROUS.
WELL..?
WOULD YOU... LET ME BE ALONE..?
JUST FOR A WHILE... PLEASE.

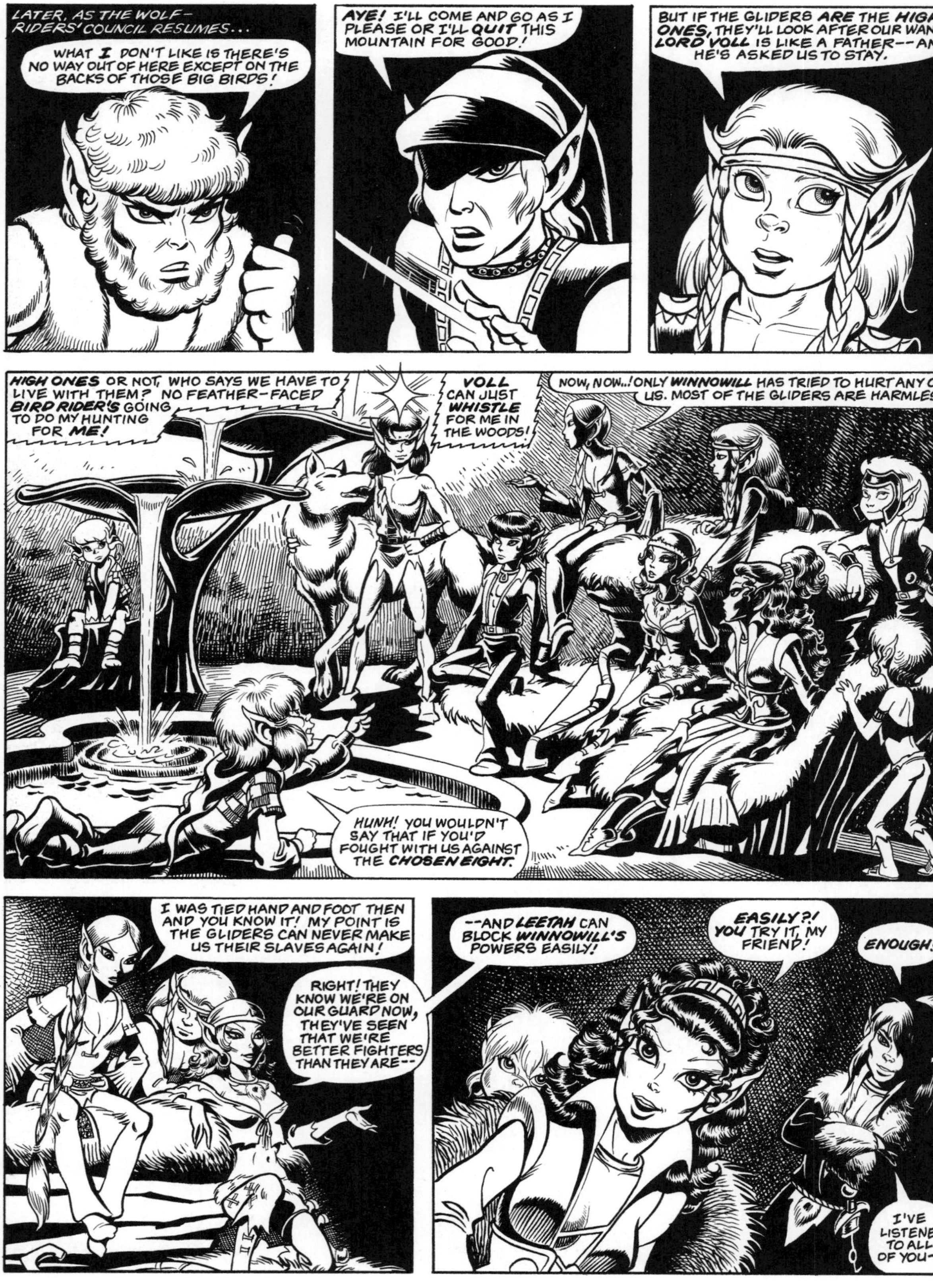
LATER, AS THE WOLF-RIDERS' COUNCIL RESUMES...
WHAT I DON'T LIKE IS THERE'S NO WAY OUT OF HERE EXCEPT ON THE BACKS OF THOSE BIG BIRDS!
AYE! I'LL COME AND GO AS I PLEASE OR I'LL QUIT THIS MOUNTAIN FOR GOOD!
BUT IF THE GLIDERS ARE THE HIGH ONES, THEY'LL LOOK AFTER OUR WANTS. LORD VOLL IS LIKE A FATHER--AND HE'S ASKED US TO STAY.
HIGH ONES OR NOT, WHO SAYS WE HAVE TO LIVE WITH THEM? NO FEATHER-FACED BIRD RIDER'S GOING TO DO MY HUNTING FOR ME!
VOLL CAN JUST WHISTLE FOR ME IN THE WOODS!
NOW, NOW..! ONLY WINNOWILL HAS TRIED TO HURT ANY OF US. MOST OF THE GLIDERS ARE HARMLESS.
HUNH! YOU WOULDN'T SAY THAT IF YOU'D FOUGHT WITH US AGAINST THE CHOSEN EIGHT.
I WAS TIED HAND AND FOOT THEN AND YOU KNOW IT! MY POINT IS THE GLIDERS CAN NEVER MAKE US THEIR SLAVES AGAIN!
RIGHT! THEY KNOW WE'RE ON OUR GUARD NOW, THEY'VE SEEN THAT WE'RE BETTER FIGHTERS THAN THEY ARE--
--AND LEETAH CAN BLOCK WINNOWILL'S POWERS EASILY!
EASILY?! YOU TRY IT, MY FRIEND!
ENOUGH!
I'VE LISTENED TO ALL OF YOU--

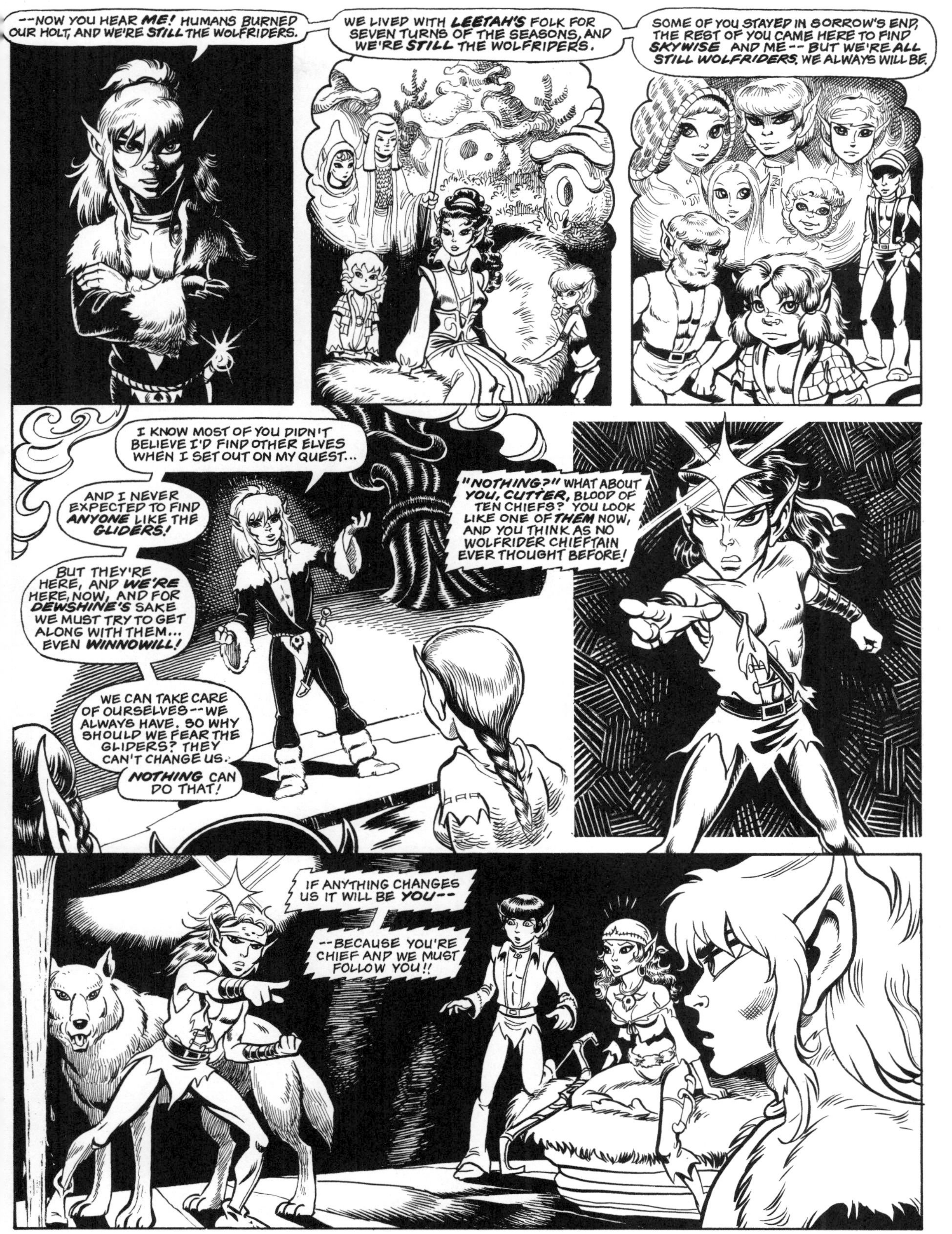
--NOW YOU HEAR ME! HUMANS BURNED OUR HOLT, AND WE'RE STILL THE WOLFRIDERS.
WE LIVED WITH LEETAH'S FOLK FOR SEVEN TURNS OF THE SEASONS, AND WE'RE STILL THE WOLFRIDERS.
SOME OF YOU STAYED IN SORROW'S END, THE REST OF YOU CAME HERE TO FIND SKYWISE AND ME-- BUT WE'RE ALL STILL WOLFRIDERS. WE ALWAYS WILL BE.
I KNOW MOST OF YOU DIDN'T BELIEVE I'D FIND OTHER ELVES WHEN I SET OUT ON MY QUEST...
AND I NEVER EXPECTED TO FIND ANYONE LIKE THE GLIDERS!
BUT THEY'RE HERE, AND WE'RE HERE NOW, AND FOR DEWSHINE'S SAKE WE MUST TRY TO GET ALONG WITH THEM... EVEN WINNOWILL!
WE CAN TAKE CARE OF OURSELVES--WE ALWAYS HAVE. SO WHY SHOULD WE FEAR THE GLIDERS? THEY CAN'T CHANGE US.
NOTHING CAN DO THAT!
"NOTHING?" WHAT ABOUT YOU, CUTTER, BLOOD OF TEN CHIEFS? YOU LOOK LIKE ONE OF THEM NOW, AND YOU THINK AS NO WOLFRIDER CHIEFTAIN EVER THOUGHT BEFORE!
IF ANYTHING CHANGES US IT WILL BE YOU--
--BECAUSE YOU'RE CHIEF AND WE MUST FOLLOW YOU!!

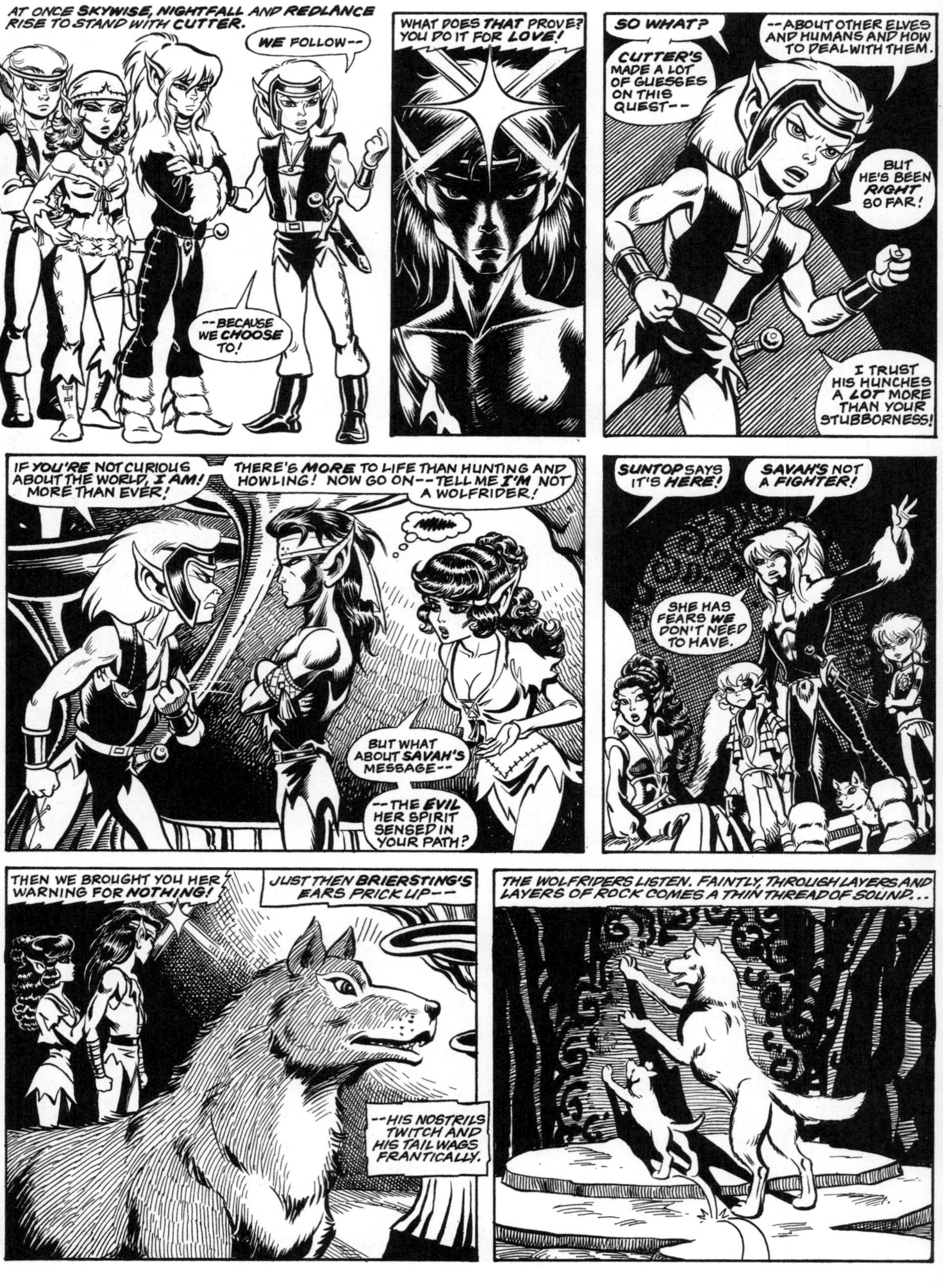

AT ONCE SKYWISE, NIGHTFALL AND REDLANCE RISE TO STAND WITH CUTTER.
WE FOLLOW--
--BECAUSE WE CHOOSE TO!
WHAT DOES THAT PROVE? YOU DO IT FOR LOVE!
SO WHAT?
CUTTER'S MADE A LOT OF GUESSES ON THIS QUEST--
--ABOUT OTHER ELVES AND HUMANS AND HOW TO DEAL WITH THEM.
BUT HE'S BEEN RIGHT SO FAR!
I TRUST HIS HUNCHES A LOT MORE THAN YOUR STUBBORNESS!
IF YOU'RE NOT CURIOUS ABOUT THE WORLD, I AM! MORE THAN EVER!
THERE'S MORE TO LIFE THAN HUNTING AND HOWLING! NOW GO ON--TELL ME I'M NOT A WOLFRIDER!
BUT WHAT ABOUT SAVAH'S MESSAGE--
--THE EVIL HER SPIRIT SENSED IN YOUR PATH?
SUNTOP SAYS IT'S HERE!
SAVAH'S NOT A FIGHTER!
SHE HAS FEARS WE DON'T NEED TO HAVE.
THEN WE BROUGHT YOU HER WARNING FOR NOTHING!
JUST THEN BRIERSTING'S EARS PRICK UP--
--HIS NOSTRILS TWITCH AND HIS TAIL WAGS FRANTICALLY.
THE WOLFRIDERS LISTEN. FAINTLY, THROUGH LAYERS AND LAYERS OF ROCK COMES A THIN THREAD OF SOUND...

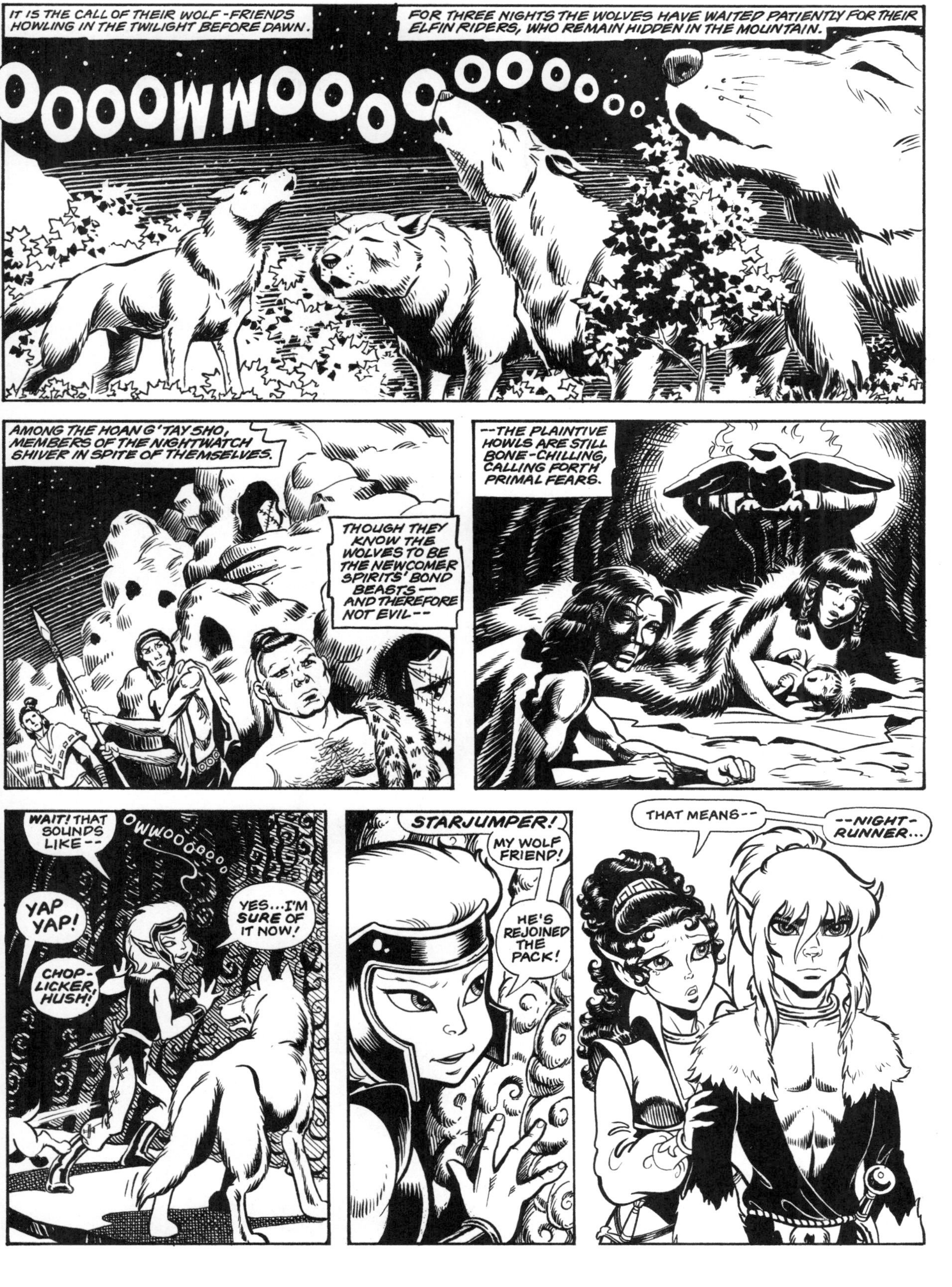
IT IS THE CALL OF THEIR WOLF-FRIENDS HOWLING IN THE TWILIGHT BEFORE DAWN.
FOR THREE NIGHTS THE WOLVES HAVE WAITED PATIENTLY FOR THEIR ELFIN RIDERS, WHO REMAIN HIDDEN IN THE MOUNTAIN.
OOOOWWOOOOOOOOOO...
AMONG THE HOAN G'TAY SHO, MEMBERS OF THE NIGHTWATCH SHIVER IN SPITE OF THEMSELVES.
THOUGH THEY KNOW THE WOLVES TO BE THE NEWCOMER SPIRITS' BOND BEASTS — AND THEREFORE NOT EVIL--
--THE PLAINTIVE HOWLS ARE STILL BONE-CHILLING, CALLING FORTH PRIMAL FEARS.
WAIT! THAT SOUNDS LIKE--
OWWOOOOOOOO
YAP YAP!
CHOP-LICKER, HUSH!
YES...I'M SURE OF IT NOW!
STARJUMPER!
MY WOLF FRIEND!
HE'S REJOINED THE PACK!
THAT MEANS--
--NIGHT-RUNNER...

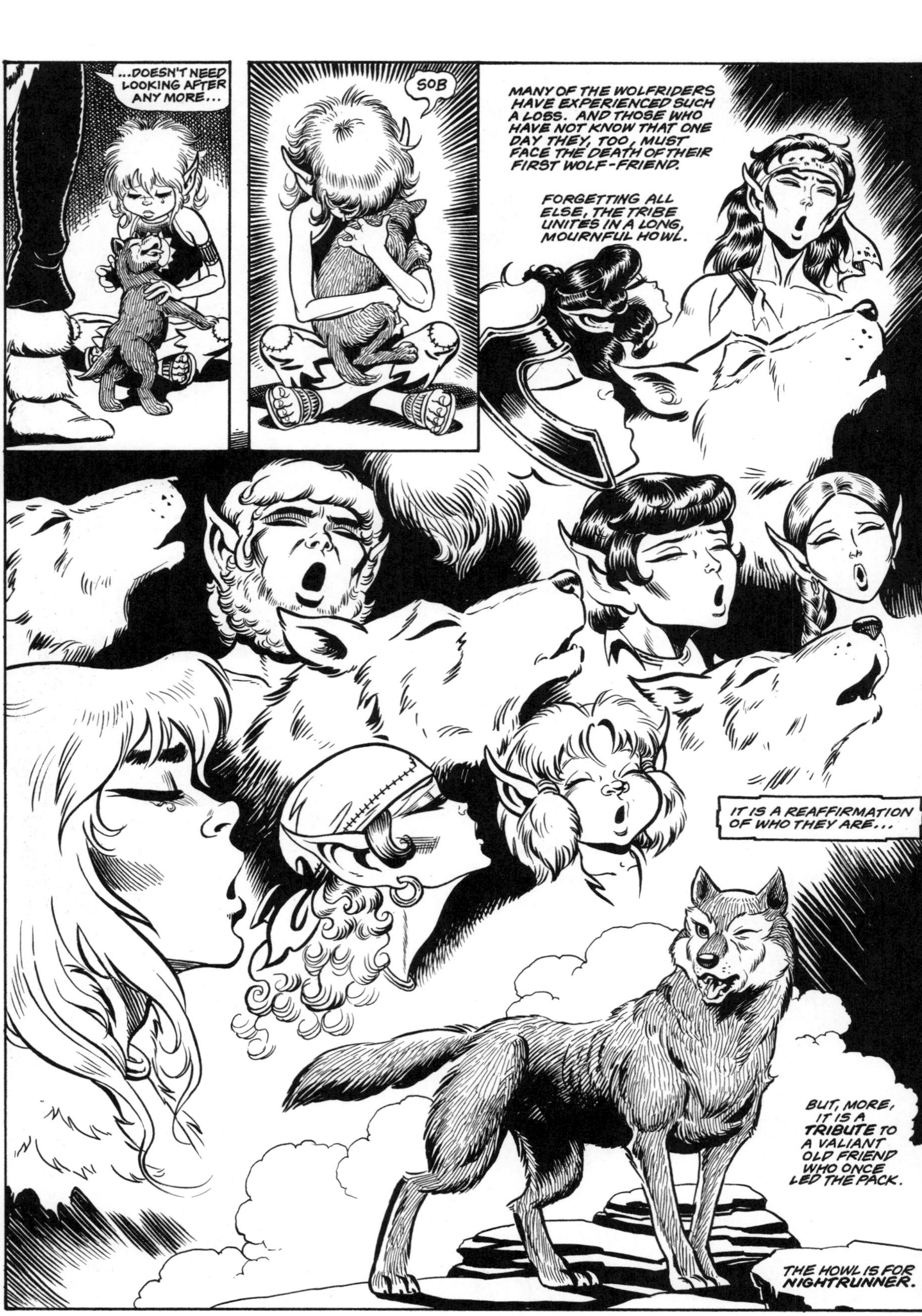

...DOESN'T NEED LOOKING AFTER ANY MORE...
SOB
MANY OF THE WOLFRIDERS HAVE EXPERIENCED SUCH A LOSS. AND THOSE WHO HAVE NOT KNOW THAT ONE DAY THEY, TOO, MUST FACE THE DEATH OF THEIR FIRST WOLF-FRIEND.
FORGETTING ALL ELSE, THE TRIBE UNITES IN A LONG, MOURNFUL HOWL.
IT IS A REAFFIRMATION OF WHO THEY ARE...
BUT, MORE, IT IS A TRIBUTE TO A VALIANT OLD FRIEND WHO ONCE LED THE PACK.
THE HOWL IS FOR NIGHTRUNNER.

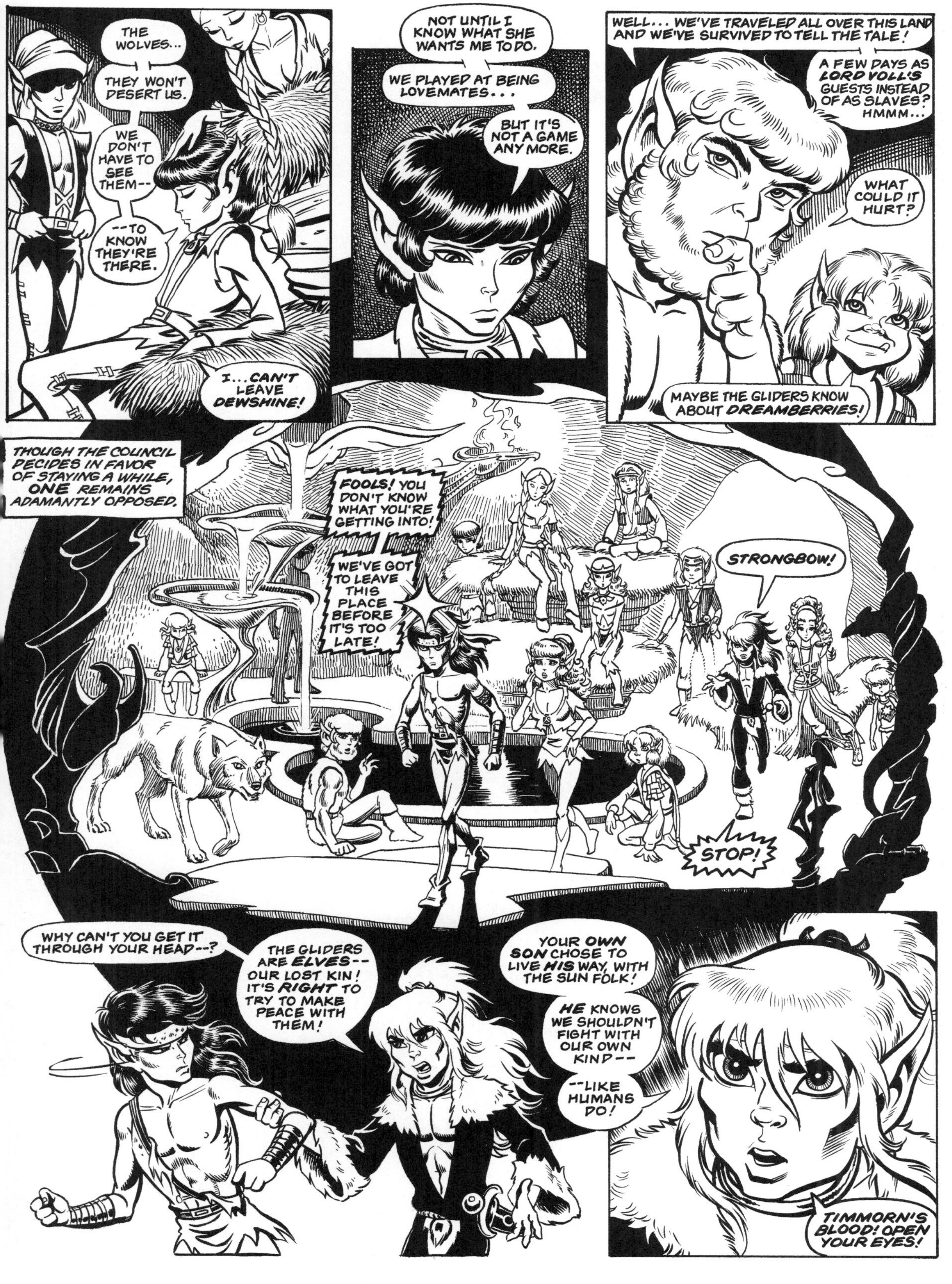

THE WOLVES...
THEY WON'T DESERT US.
WE DON'T HAVE TO SEE THEM--
--TO KNOW THEY'RE THERE.
I...CAN'T LEAVE DEWSHINE!
NOT UNTIL I KNOW WHAT SHE WANTS ME TO DO.
WE PLAYED AT BEING LOVEMATES...
BUT IT'S NOT A GAME ANY MORE.
WELL... WE'VE TRAVELED ALL OVER THIS LAND AND WE'VE SURVIVED TO TELL THE TALE!
A FEW DAYS AS LORD VOLL'S GUESTS INSTEAD OF AS SLAVES? HMMM...
WHAT COULD IT HURT?
MAYBE THE GLIDERS KNOW ABOUT DREAMBERRIES!
THOUGH THE COUNCIL DECIDES IN FAVOR OF STAYING A WHILE, ONE REMAINS ADAMANTLY OPPOSED.
FOOLS! YOU DON'T KNOW WHAT YOU'RE GETTING INTO!
WE'VE GOT TO LEAVE THIS PLACE BEFORE IT'S TOO LATE!
STRONGBOW!
STOP!
WHY CAN'T YOU GET IT THROUGH YOUR HEAD--?
THE GLIDERS ARE ELVES-- OUR LOST KIN! IT'S RIGHT TO TRY TO MAKE PEACE WITH THEM!
YOUR OWN SON CHOSE TO LIVE HIS WAY, WITH THE SUN FOLK!
HE KNOWS WE SHOULDN'T FIGHT WITH OUR OWN KIND--
--LIKE HUMANS DO!
TIMMORN'S BLOOD! OPEN YOUR EYES!

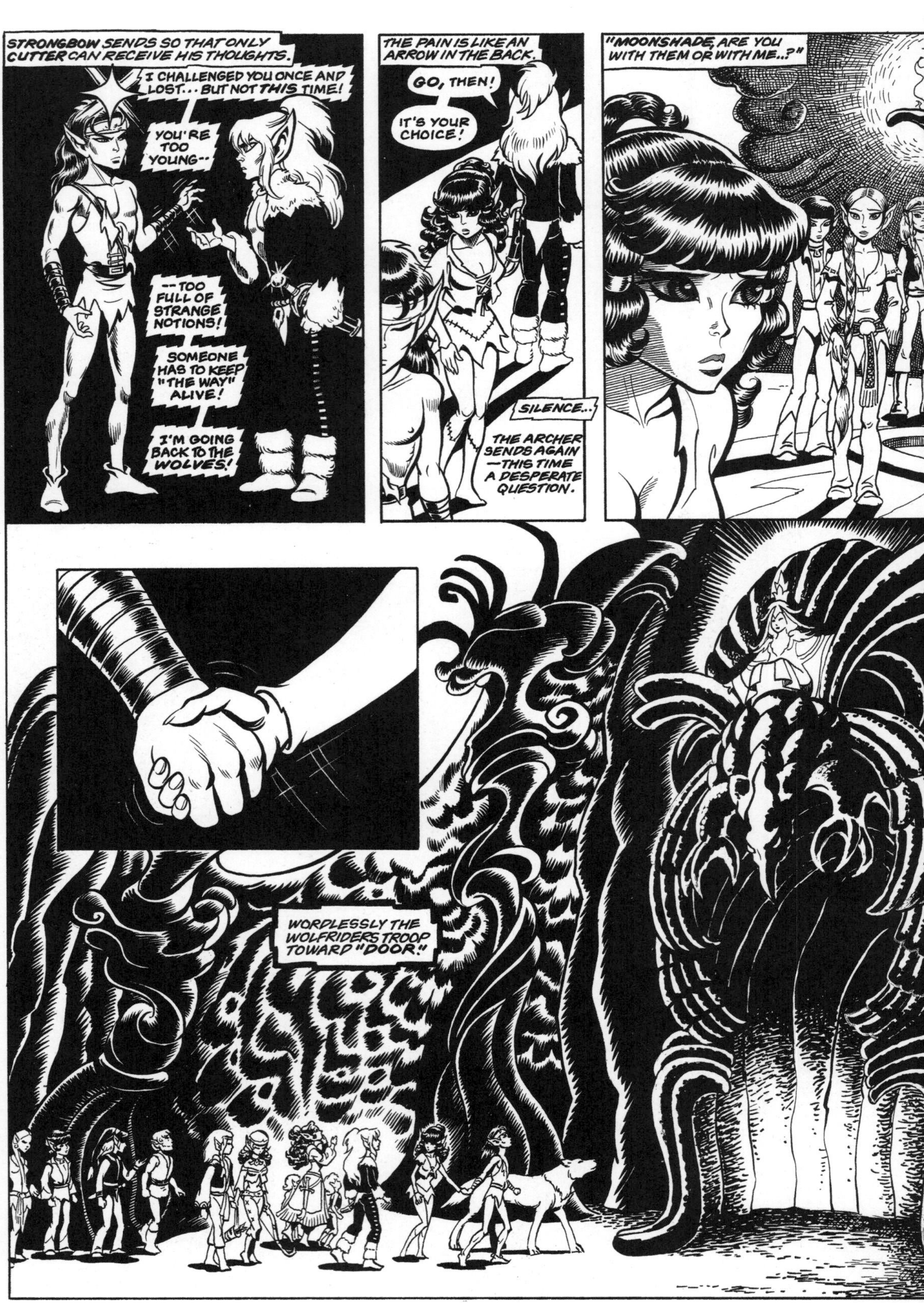
STRONGBOW SENDS SO THAT ONLY CUTTER CAN RECEIVE HIS THOUGHTS.
I CHALLENGED YOU ONCE AND LOST... BUT NOT THIS TIME!
YOU'RE TOO YOUNG--
--TOO FULL OF STRANGE NOTIONS!
SOMEONE HAS TO KEEP "THE WAY" ALIVE!
I'M GOING BACK TO THE WOLVES!
THE PAIN IS LIKE AN ARROW IN THE BACK.
GO, THEN!
IT'S YOUR CHOICE!
SILENCE...
THE ARCHER SENDS AGAIN —THIS TIME A DESPERATE QUESTION.
"MOONSHADE, ARE YOU WITH THEM OR WITH ME..?"
WORDLESSLY THE WOLFRIDERS TROOP TOWARD "DOOR."

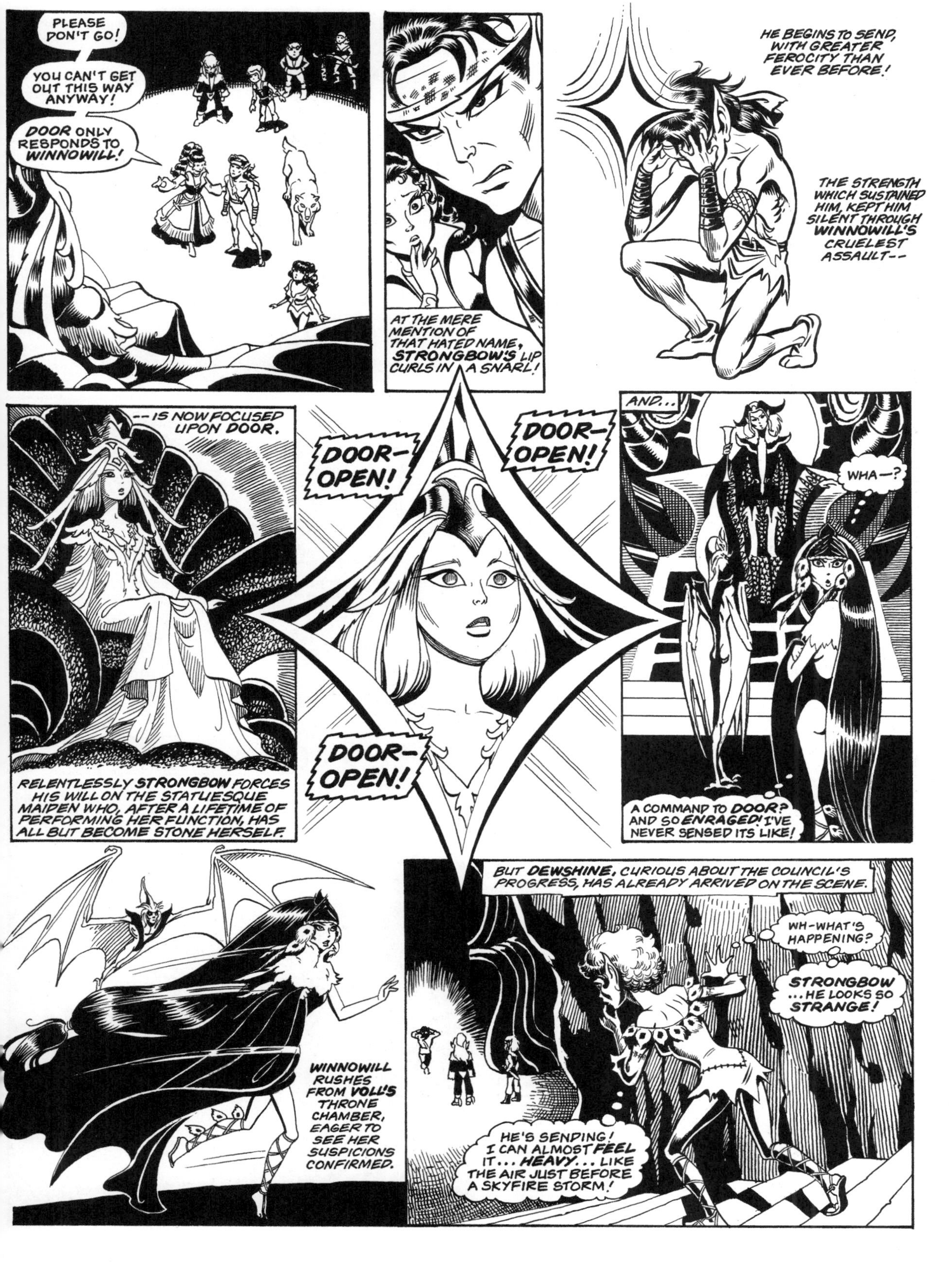

PLEASE DON'T GO!
YOU CAN'T GET OUT THIS WAY ANYWAY!
DOOR ONLY RESPONDS TO WINNOWILL!
AT THE MERE MENTION OF THAT HATED NAME, STRONGBOW'S LIP CURLS IN A SNARL!
HE BEGINS TO SEND, WITH GREATER FEROCITY THAN EVER BEFORE!
THE STRENGTH WHICH SUSTAINED HIM, KEPT HIM SILENT THROUGH WINNOWILL'S CRUELEST ASSAULT--
--IS NOW FOCUSED UPON DOOR.
RELENTLESSLY STRONGBOW FORCES HIS WILL ON THE STATUESQUE MAIDEN WHO, AFTER A LIFETIME OF PERFORMING HER FUNCTION, HAS ALL BUT BECOME STONE HERSELF.
DOOR-OPEN!
DOOR-OPEN!
DOOR-OPEN!
AND...
WHA—?
A COMMAND TO DOOR? AND SO ENRAGED! I'VE NEVER SENSED ITS LIKE!
WINNOWILL RUSHES FROM VOLL'S THRONE CHAMBER, EAGER TO SEE HER SUSPICIONS CONFIRMED.
BUT DEWSHINE, CURIOUS ABOUT THE COUNCIL'S PROGRESS, HAS ALREADY ARRIVED ON THE SCENE.
WH-WHAT'S HAPPENING?
STRONGBOW ...HE LOOKS SO STRANGE!
HE'S SENDING! I CAN ALMOST FEEL IT... HEAVY... LIKE THE AIR JUST BEFORE A SKYFIRE STORM!

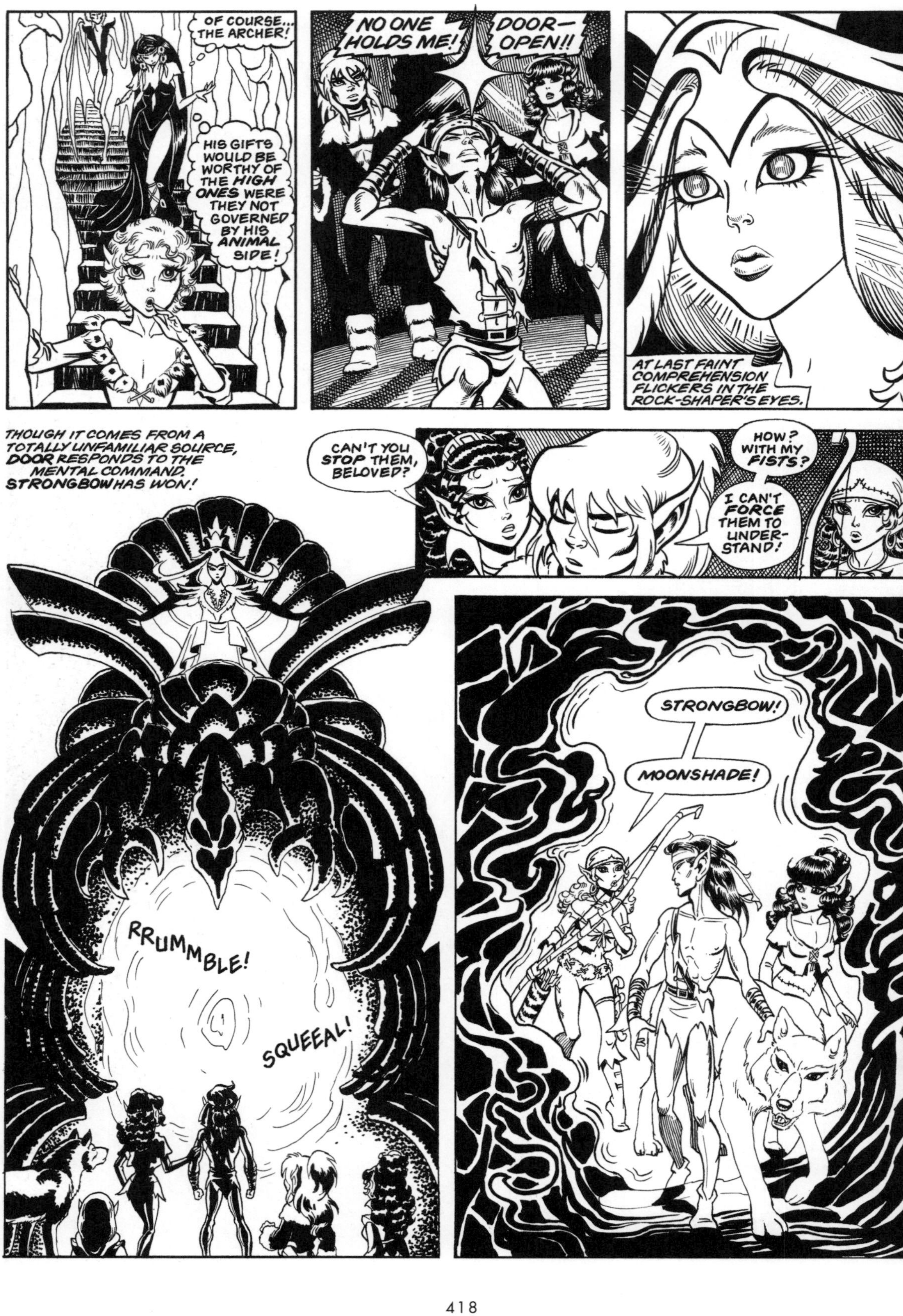

OF COURSE... THE ARCHER!
HIS GIFTS WOULD BE WORTHY OF THE HIGH ONES WERE THEY NOT GOVERNED BY HIS ANIMAL SIDE!
NO ONE HOLDS ME!
DOOR— OPEN!!
AT LAST FAINT COMPREHENSION FLICKERS IN THE ROCK-SHAPER'S EYES.
THOUGH IT COMES FROM A TOTALLY UNFAMILIAR SOURCE, DOOR RESPONDS TO THE MENTAL COMMAND. STRONGBOW HAS WON!
CAN'T YOU STOP THEM, BELOVED?
HOW? WITH MY FISTS?
I CAN'T FORCE THEM TO UNDERSTAND!
RRUMMBLE!
SQUEEAL!
STRONGBOW!
MOONSHADE!

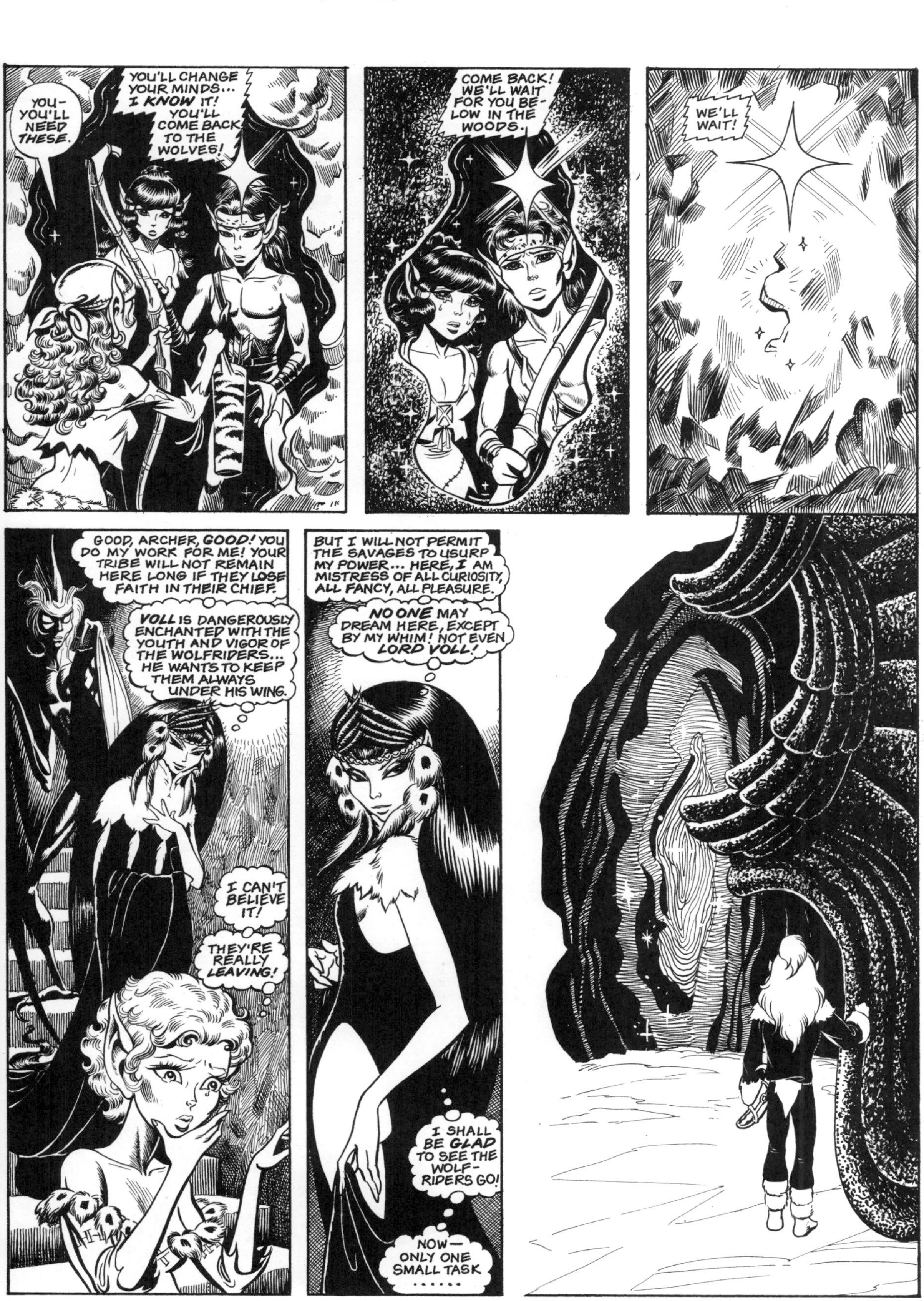
YOU—YOU'LL NEED THESE.
YOU'LL CHANGE YOUR MINDS... I KNOW IT! YOU'LL COME BACK TO THE WOLVES!
COME BACK! WE'LL WAIT FOR YOU BELOW IN THE WOODS.
WE'LL WAIT!
GOOD, ARCHER, GOOD! YOU DO MY WORK FOR ME! YOUR TRIBE WILL NOT REMAIN HERE LONG IF THEY LOSE FAITH IN THEIR CHIEF.
VOLL IS DANGEROUSLY ENCHANTED WITH THE YOUTH AND VIGOR OF THE WOLFRIDERS... HE WANTS TO KEEP THEM ALWAYS UNDER HIS WING.
I CAN'T BELIEVE IT!
THEY'RE REALLY LEAVING!
BUT I WILL NOT PERMIT THE SAVAGES TO USURP MY POWER... HERE, I AM MISTRESS OF ALL CURIOSITY, ALL FANCY, ALL PLEASURE.
NO ONE MAY DREAM HERE, EXCEPT BY MY WHIM! NOT EVEN LORD VOLL!
I SHALL BE GLAD TO SEE THE WOLFRIDERS GO!
NOW—ONLY ONE SMALL TASK ......

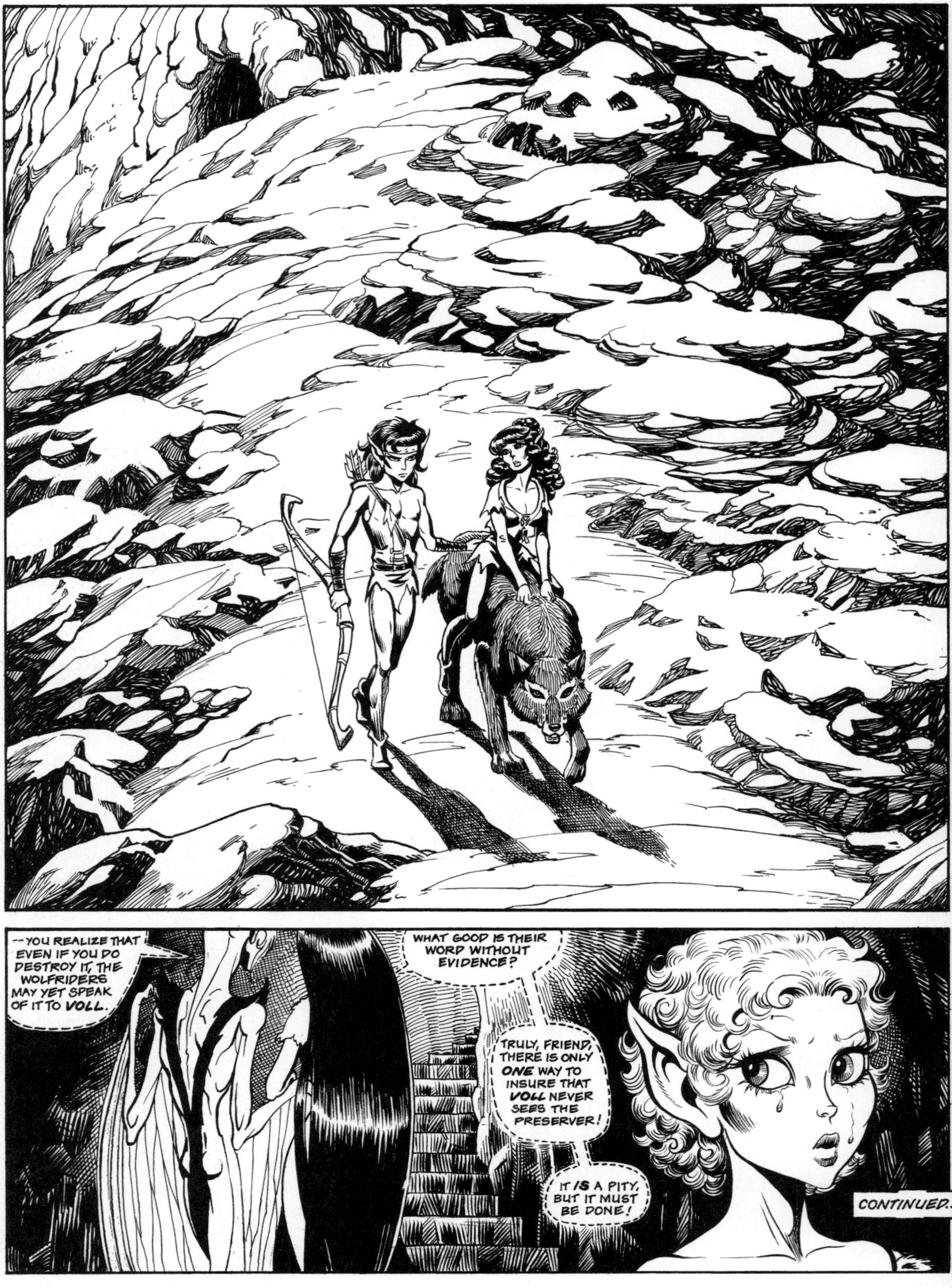
--YOU REALIZE THAT EVEN IF YOU DO DESTROY IT, THE WOLFRIDERS MAY YET SPEAK OF IT TO VOLL.
WHAT GOOD IS THEIR WORD WITHOUT EVIDENCE?
TRULY, FRIEND, THERE IS ONLY ONE WAY TO INSURE THAT VOLL NEVER SEES THE PRESERVER!
IT IS A PITY, BUT IT MUST BE DONE!
CONTINUED...

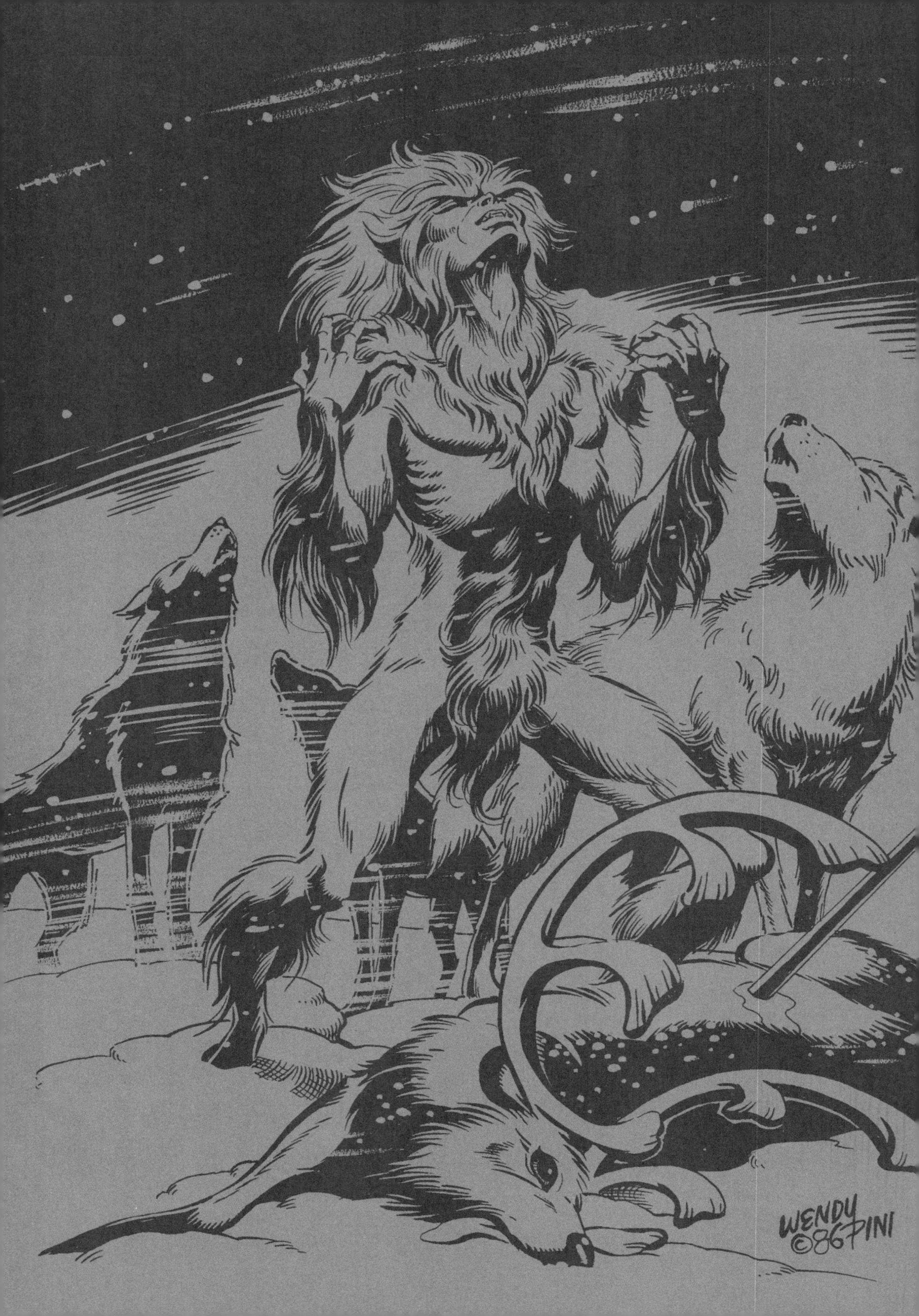
WENDY PINI
©86

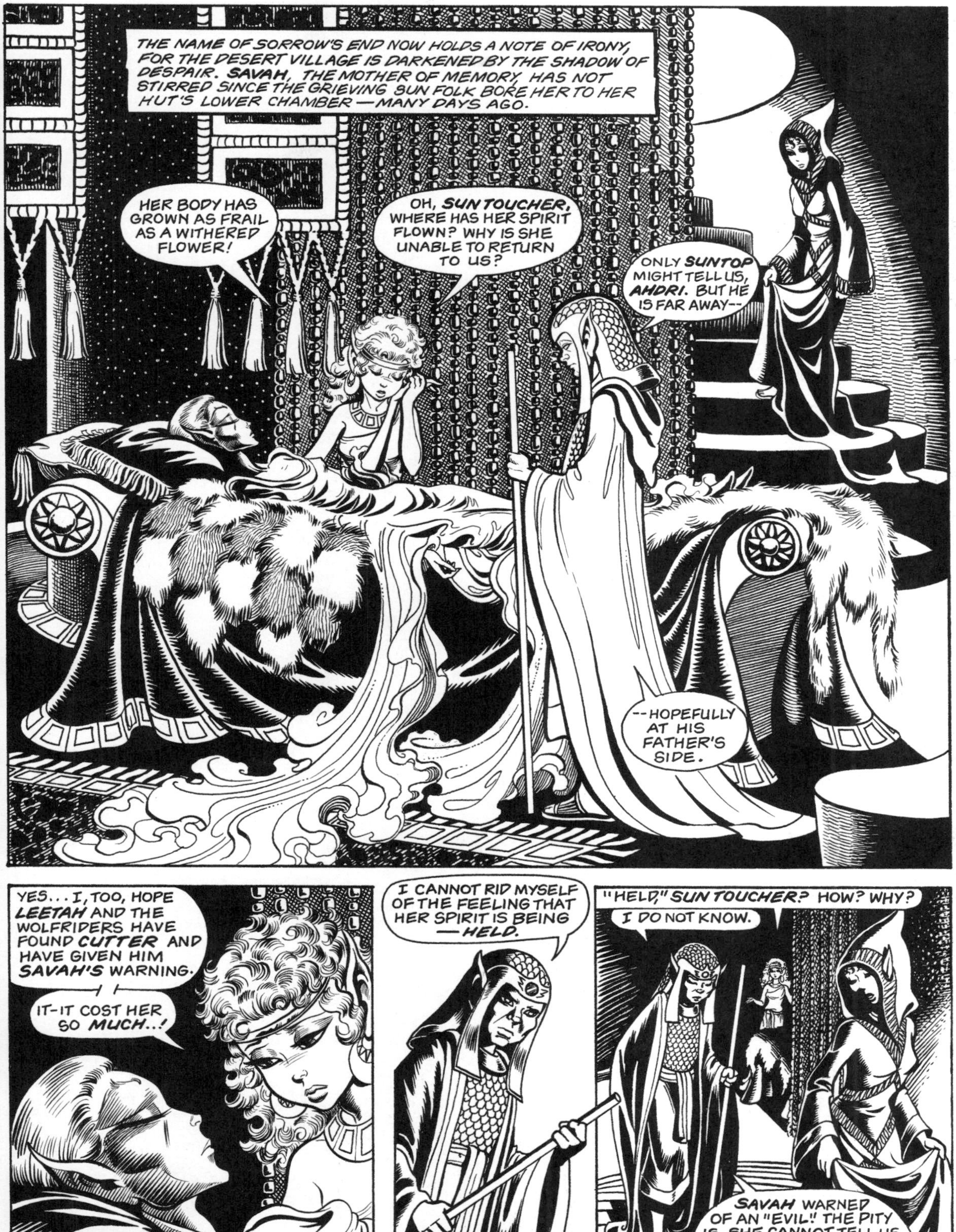
THE NAME OF SORROW'S END NOW HOLDS A NOTE OF IRONY, FOR THE DESERT VILLAGE IS DARKENED BY THE SHADOW OF DESPAIR. SAVAH, THE MOTHER OF MEMORY, HAS NOT STIRRED SINCE THE GRIEVING SUN FOLK BORE HER TO HER HUT'S LOWER CHAMBER — MANY DAYS AGO.
HER BODY HAS GROWN AS FRAIL AS A WITHERED FLOWER!
OH, SUNTOUCHER, WHERE HAS HER SPIRIT FLOWN? WHY IS SHE UNABLE TO RETURN TO US?
ONLY SUNTOP MIGHT TELL US, AHDRI. BUT HE IS FAR AWAY--
--HOPEFULLY AT HIS FATHER'S SIDE.
YES... I, TOO, HOPE LEETAH AND THE WOLFRIDERS HAVE FOUND CUTTER AND HAVE GIVEN HIM SAVAH'S WARNING.
IT-IT COST HER SO MUCH..!
I CANNOT RID MYSELF OF THE FEELING THAT HER SPIRIT IS BEING —HELD.
"HELD," SUN TOUCHER? HOW? WHY?
I DO NOT KNOW.
SAVAH WARNED OF AN "EVIL." THE PITY IS, SHE CANNOT TELL US WHAT SHAPE IT HAS — OR HOW IT HAS TOUCHED HER.

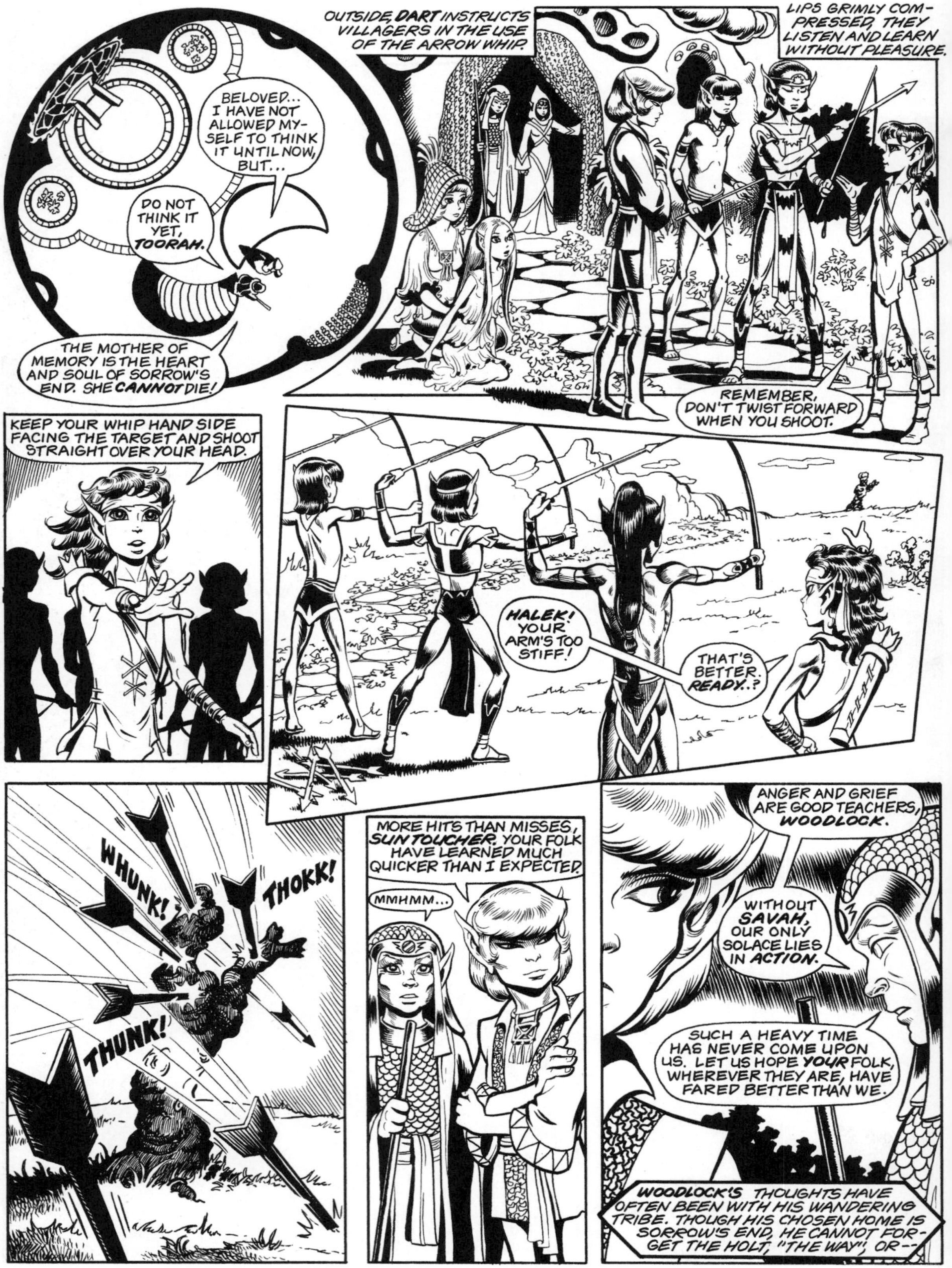
BELOVED... I HAVE NOT ALLOWED MYSELF TO THINK IT UNTIL NOW, BUT...
DO NOT THINK IT YET, TOORAH.
THE MOTHER OF MEMORY IS THE HEART AND SOUL OF SORROW'S END. SHE CANNOT DIE!
OUTSIDE, DART INSTRUCTS VILLAGERS IN THE USE OF THE ARROW WHIP.
LIPS GRIMLY COMPRESSED, THEY LISTEN AND LEARN WITHOUT PLEASURE.
REMEMBER, DON'T TWIST FORWARD WHEN YOU SHOOT.
KEEP YOUR WHIP HAND SIDE FACING THE TARGET AND SHOOT STRAIGHT OVER YOUR HEAD.
HALEK! YOUR ARM'S TOO STIFF!
THAT'S BETTER. READY..?
WHUNK!
THOKK!
THUNK!
MORE HITS THAN MISSES, SUNTOUCHER. YOUR FOLK HAVE LEARNED MUCH QUICKER THAN I EXPECTED.
MMHMM...
ANGER AND GRIEF ARE GOOD TEACHERS, WOODLOCK.
WITHOUT SAVAH, OUR ONLY SOLACE LIES IN ACTION.
SUCH A HEAVY TIME HAS NEVER COME UPON US. LET US HOPE YOUR FOLK, WHEREVER THEY ARE, HAVE FARED BETTER THAN WE.
WOODLOCK'S THOUGHTS HAVE OFTEN BEEN WITH HIS WANDERING TRIBE. THOUGH HIS CHOSEN HOME IS SORROW'S END, HE CANNOT FORGET THE HOLT, "THE WAY", OR--

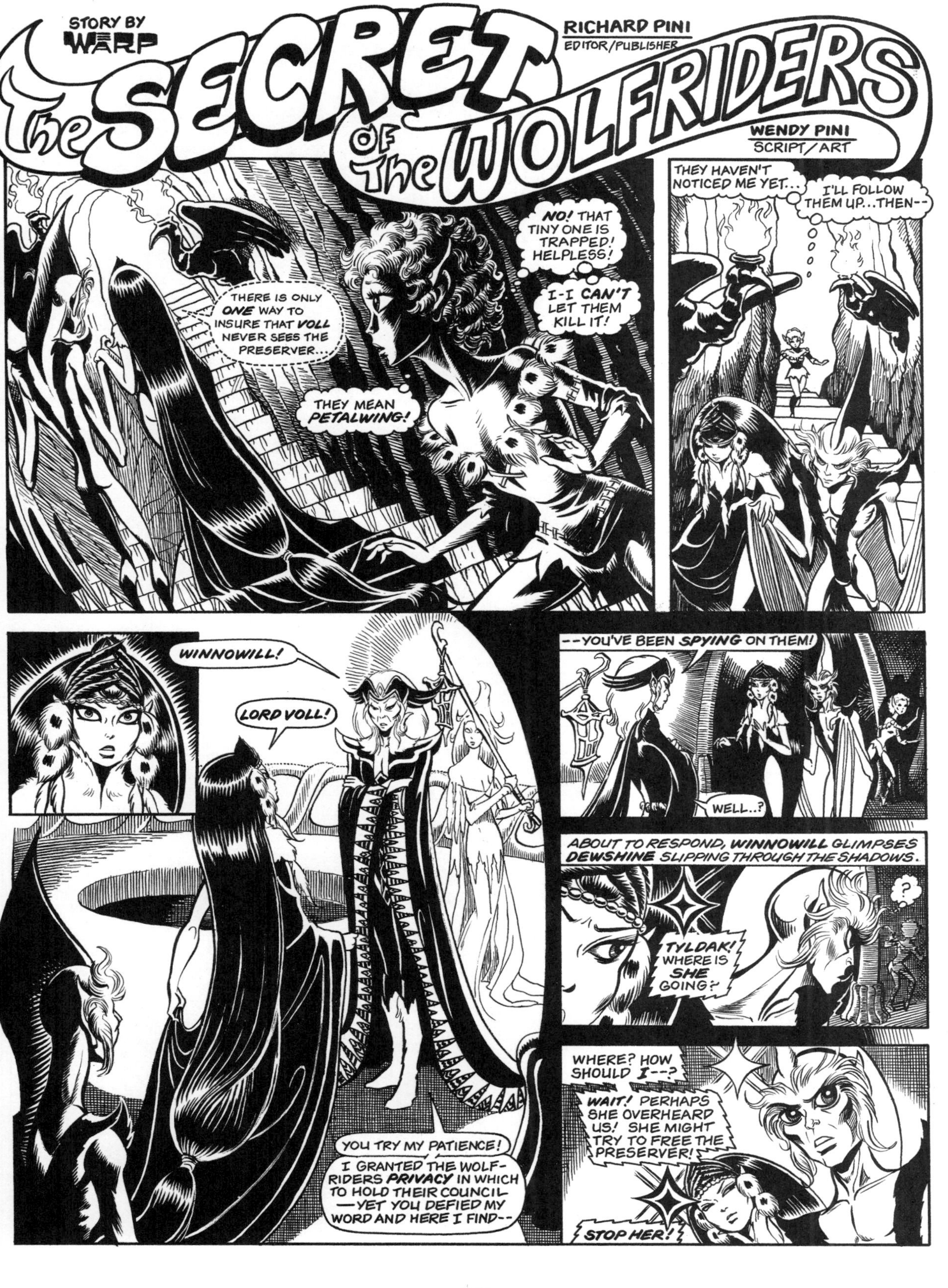
STORY BY WARP
The SECRET of The WOLFRIDERS
RICHARD PINI EDITOR/PUBLISHER
WENDY PINI SCRIPT/ART
THERE IS ONLY ONE WAY TO INSURE THAT VOLL NEVER SEES THE PRESERVER...
THEY MEAN PETALWING!
NO! THAT TINY ONE IS TRAPPED! HELPLESS!
I-I CAN'T LET THEM KILL IT!
THEY HAVEN'T NOTICED ME YET...
I'LL FOLLOW THEM UP...THEN--
WINNOWILL!
LORD VOLL!
YOU TRY MY PATIENCE!
I GRANTED THE WOLF-RIDERS PRIVACY IN WHICH TO HOLD THEIR COUNCIL —YET YOU DEFIED MY WORD AND HERE I FIND--
--YOU'VE BEEN SPYING ON THEM!
WELL..?
ABOUT TO RESPOND, WINNOWILL GLIMPSES DEWSHINE SLIPPING THROUGH THE SHADOWS.
TYLDAK! WHERE IS SHE GOING?
?
WHERE? HOW SHOULD I--?
WAIT! PERHAPS SHE OVERHEARD US! SHE MIGHT TRY TO FREE THE PRESERVER!
STOP HER!

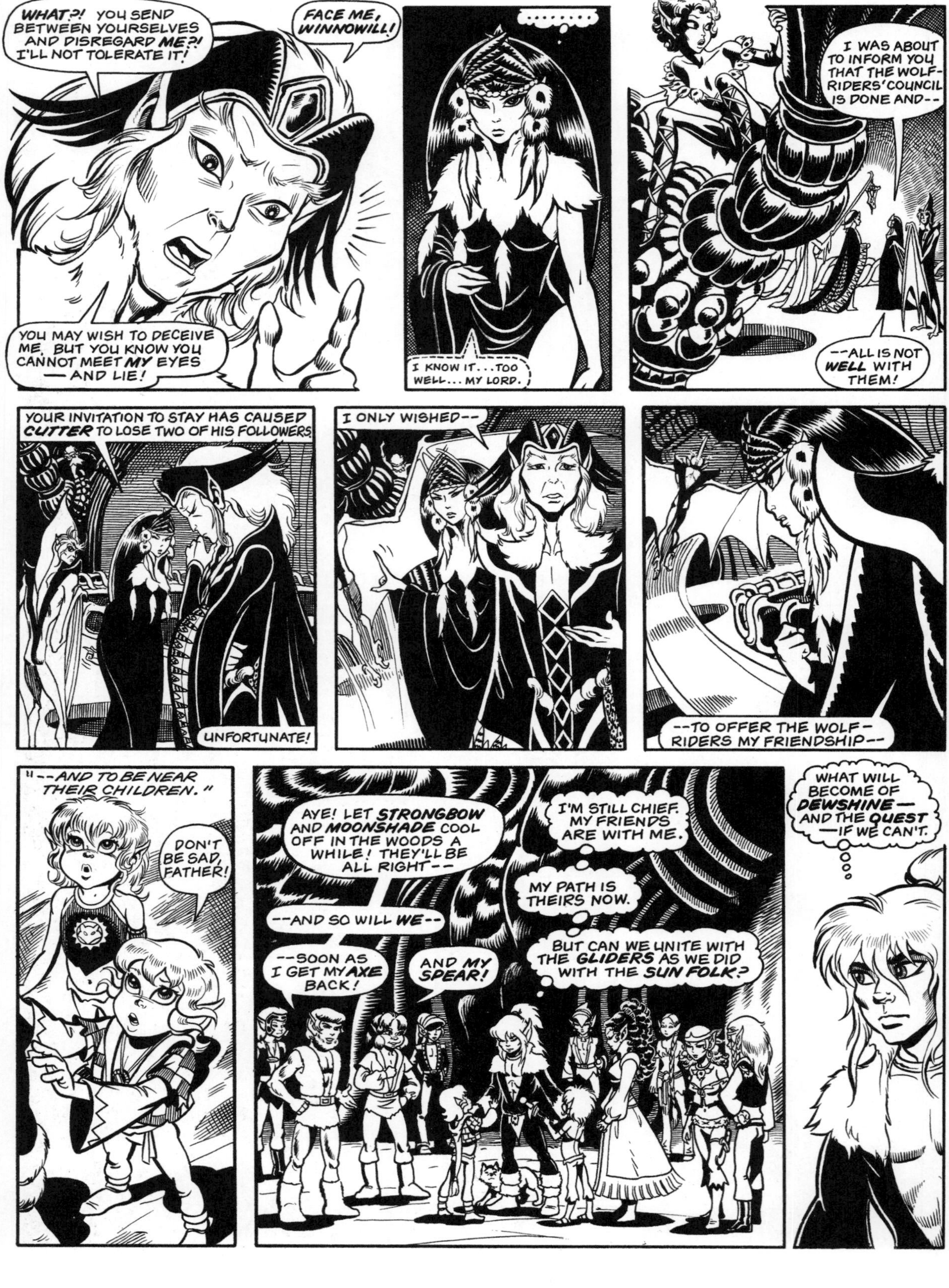
WHAT?! YOU SEND BETWEEN YOURSELVES AND DISREGARD ME?! I'LL NOT TOLERATE IT!
FACE ME, WINNOWILL!
YOU MAY WISH TO DECEIVE ME, BUT YOU KNOW YOU CANNOT MEET MY EYES —AND LIE!
....
I KNOW IT... TOO WELL... MY LORD.
I WAS ABOUT TO INFORM YOU THAT THE WOLF-RIDERS' COUNCIL IS DONE AND--
--ALL IS NOT WELL WITH THEM!
YOUR INVITATION TO STAY HAS CAUSED CUTTER TO LOSE TWO OF HIS FOLLOWERS.
UNFORTUNATE!
I ONLY WISHED--
--TO OFFER THE WOLF-RIDERS MY FRIENDSHIP--
"--AND TO BE NEAR THEIR CHILDREN."
DON'T BE SAD, FATHER!
AYE! LET STRONGBOW AND MOONSHADE COOL OFF IN THE WOODS A WHILE! THEY'LL BE ALL RIGHT--
--AND SO WILL WE--
--SOON AS I GET MY AXE BACK!
AND MY SPEAR!
I'M STILL CHIEF. MY FRIENDS ARE WITH ME.
MY PATH IS THEIRS NOW.
BUT CAN WE UNITE WITH THE GLIDERS AS WE DID WITH THE SUN FOLK?
WHAT WILL BECOME OF DEWSHINE— AND THE QUEST —IF WE CAN'T.

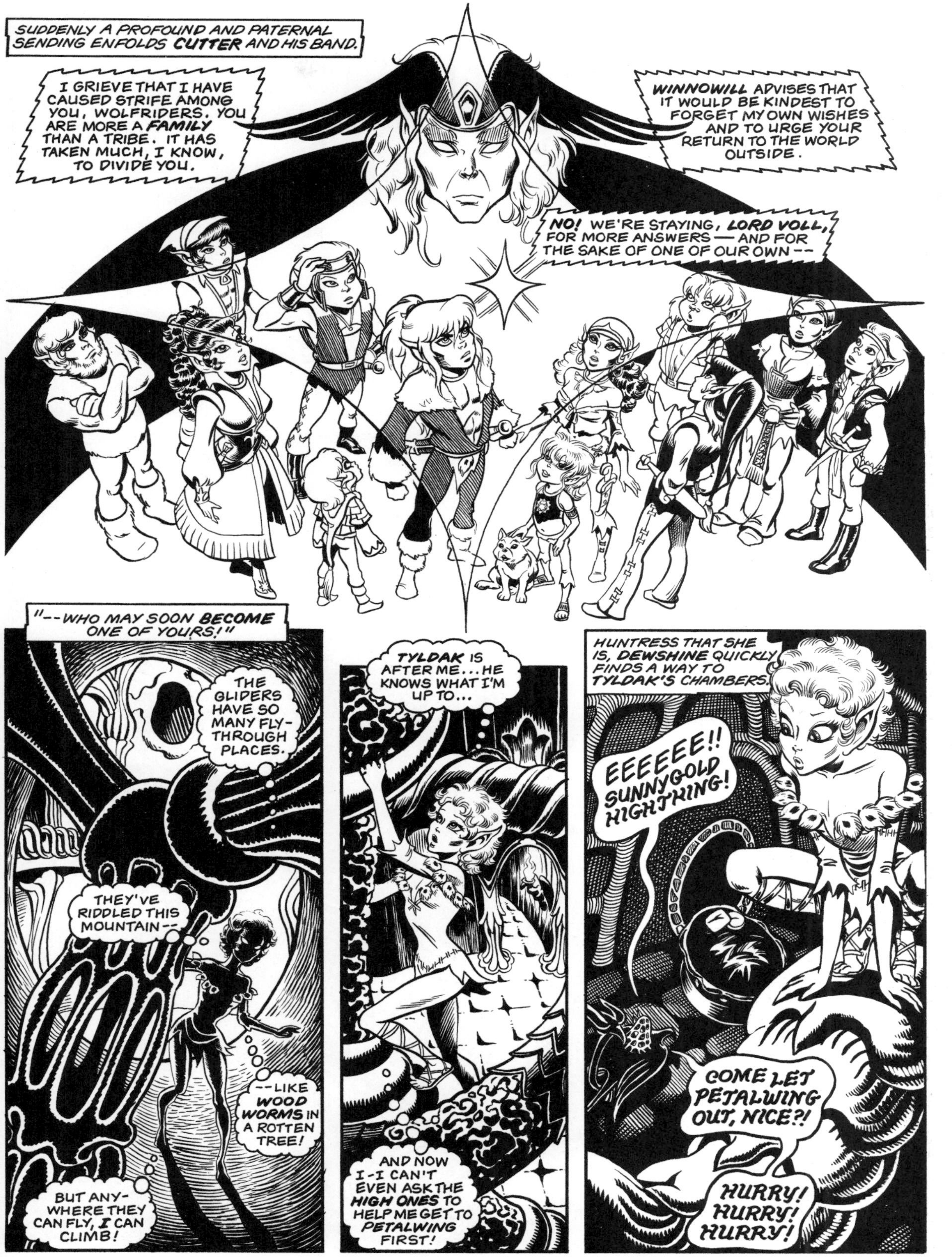
SUDDENLY A PROFOUND AND PATERNAL SENDING ENFOLDS CUTTER AND HIS BAND.
I GRIEVE THAT I HAVE CAUSED STRIFE AMONG YOU, WOLFRIDERS. YOU ARE MORE A FAMILY THAN A TRIBE. IT HAS TAKEN MUCH, I KNOW, TO DIVIDE YOU.
WINNOWILL ADVISES THAT IT WOULD BE KINDEST TO FORGET MY OWN WISHES AND TO URGE YOUR RETURN TO THE WORLD OUTSIDE.
NO! WE'RE STAYING, LORD VOLL, FOR MORE ANSWERS — AND FOR THE SAKE OF ONE OF OUR OWN --
"--WHO MAY SOON BECOME ONE OF YOURS!"
THE GLIDERS HAVE SO MANY FLY-THROUGH PLACES.
THEY'VE RIDDLED THIS MOUNTAIN --
--LIKE WOOD WORMS IN A ROTTEN TREE!
BUT ANYWHERE THEY CAN FLY, I CAN CLIMB!
TYLDAK IS AFTER ME... HE KNOWS WHAT I'M UP TO...
AND NOW I-I CAN'T EVEN ASK THE HIGH ONES TO HELP ME GET TO PETALWING FIRST!
HUNTRESS THAT SHE IS, DEWSHINE QUICKLY FINDS A WAY TO TYLDAK'S CHAMBERS.
EEEEEEE!! SUNNYGOLD HIGHTHING!
COME LET PETALWING OUT, NICE?!
HURRY! HURRY! HURRY!

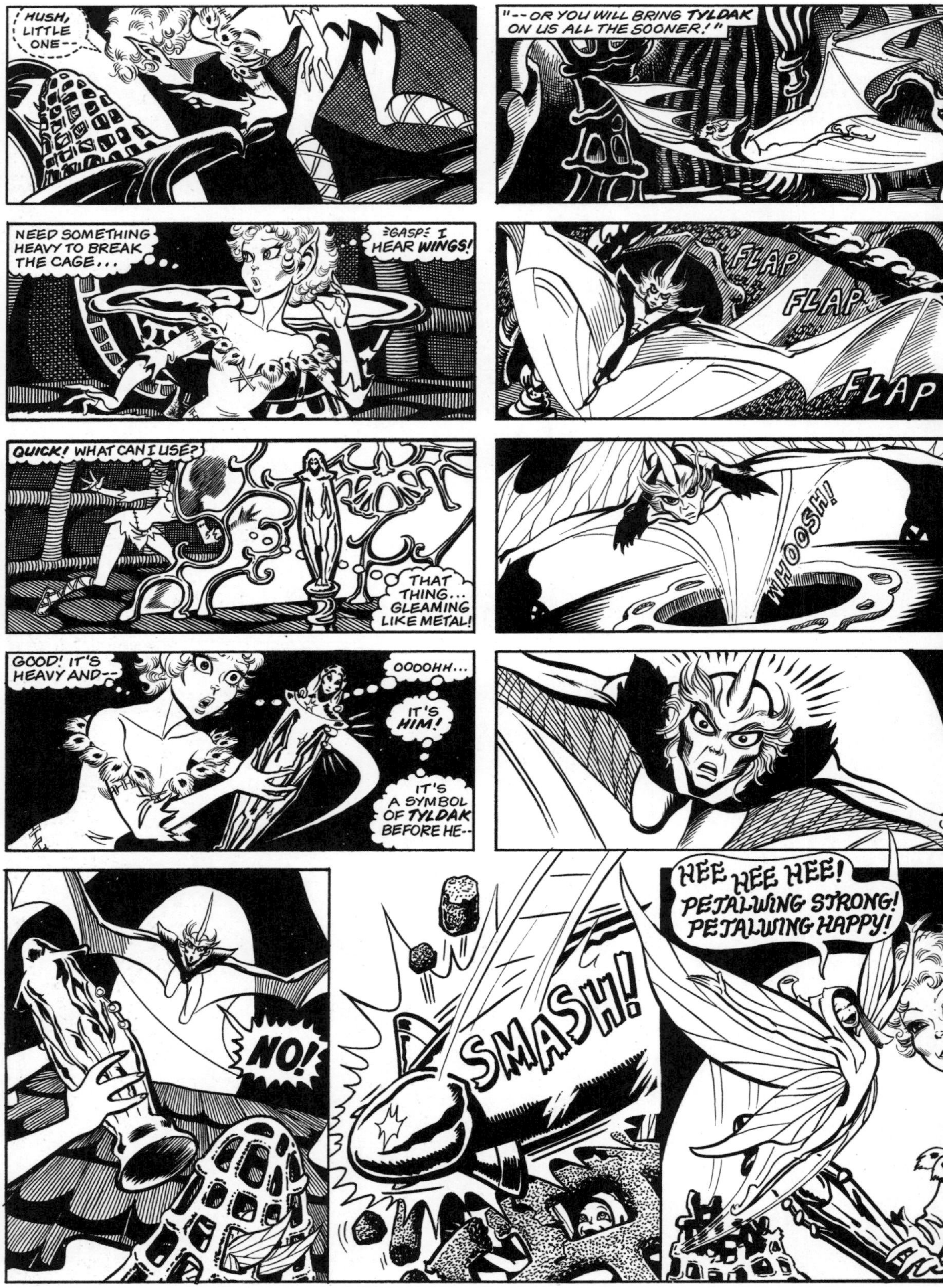

HUSH, LITTLE ONE--
"--OR YOU WILL BRING TYLDAK ON US ALL THE SOONER!"
NEED SOMETHING HEAVY TO BREAK THE CAGE...
GASP I HEAR WINGS!
FLAP
FLAP
FLAP
QUICK! WHAT CAN I USE?
THAT THING... GLEAMING LIKE METAL!
WHOOSH!
GOOD! IT'S HEAVY AND--
OOOOHH...
IT'S HIM!
IT'S A SYMBOL OF TYLDAK BEFORE HE--
NO!
SMASH!
HEE HEE HEE! PETALWING STRONG! PETALWING HAPPY!

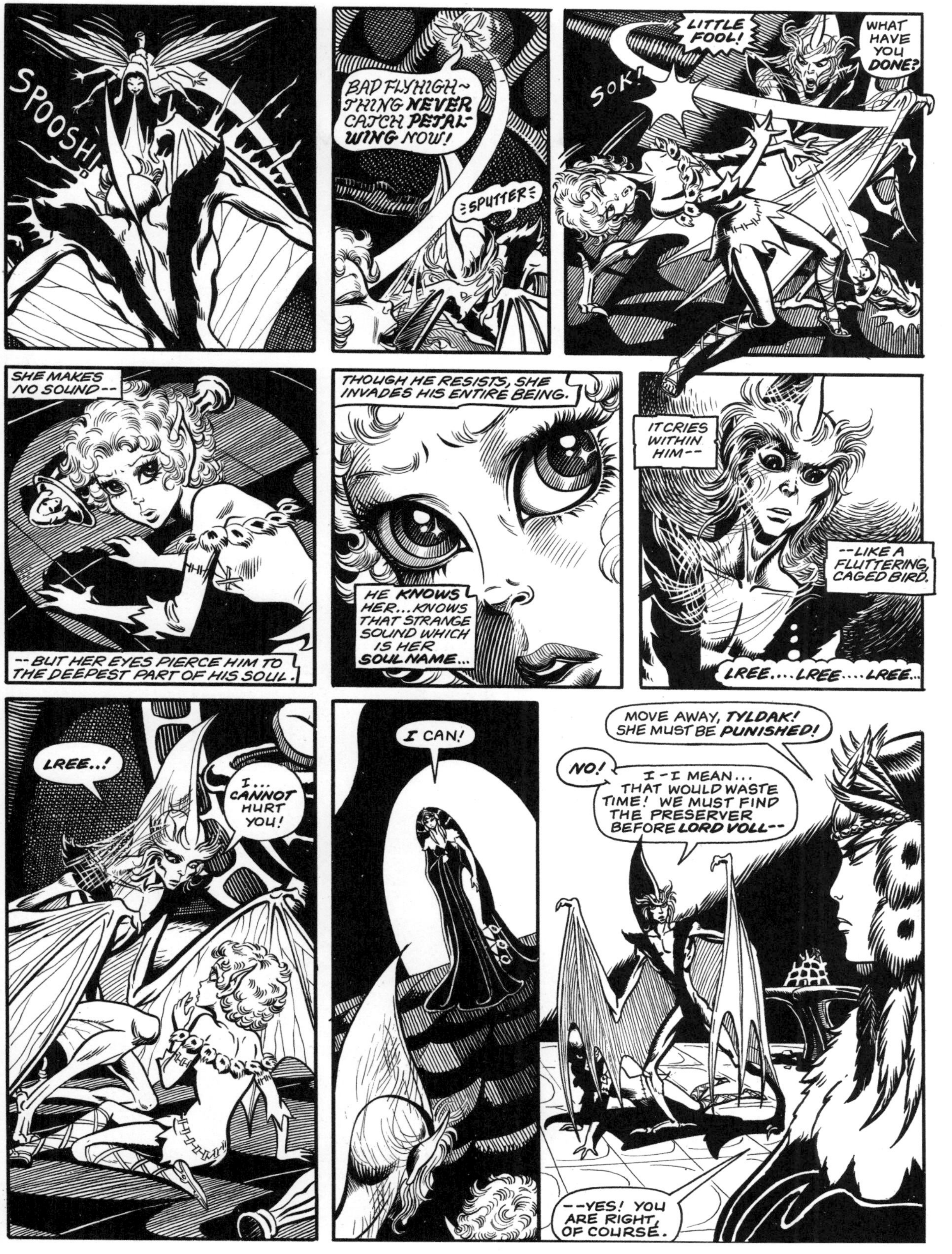
SPOOSH!
BAD FLYHIGH-THING NEVER CATCH PETALWING NOW!
SPUTTER
LITTLE FOOL!
WHAT HAVE YOU DONE?
SOK!
SHE MAKES NO SOUND--
--BUT HER EYES PIERCE HIM TO THE DEEPEST PART OF HIS SOUL.
THOUGH HE RESISTS, SHE INVADES HIS ENTIRE BEING.
HE KNOWS HER... KNOWS THAT STRANGE SOUND WHICH IS HER SOUL NAME...
IT CRIES WITHIN HIM--
--LIKE A FLUTTERING, CAGED BIRD.
LREE.... LREE.... LREE...
LREE...!
I... CANNOT HURT YOU!
I CAN!
MOVE AWAY, TYLDAK! SHE MUST BE PUNISHED!
NO!
I-I MEAN... THAT WOULD WASTE TIME! WE MUST FIND THE PRESERVER BEFORE LORD VOLL--
--YES! YOU ARE RIGHT, OF COURSE.

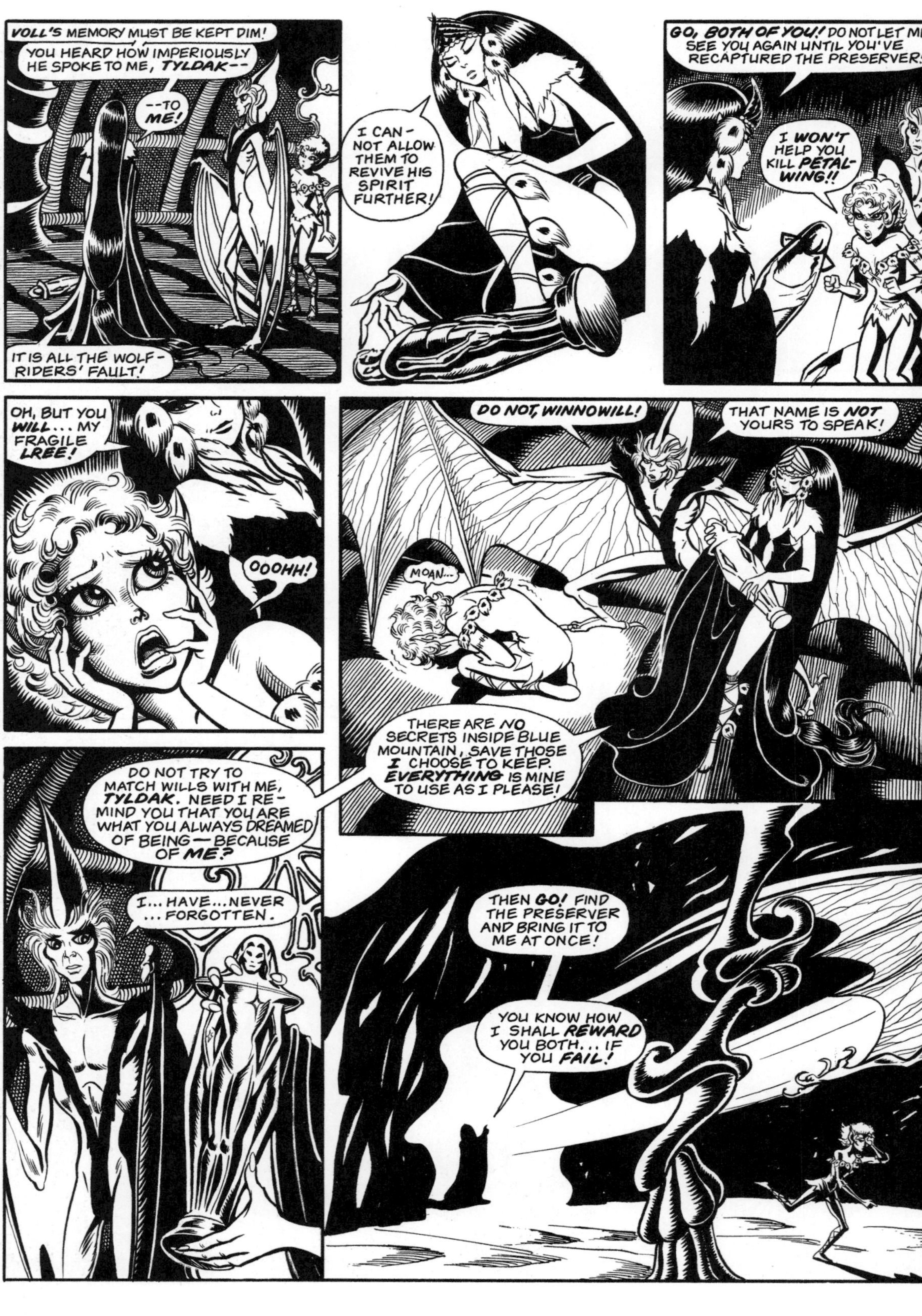
VOLL'S MEMORY MUST BE KEPT DIM!
YOU HEARD HOW IMPERIOUSLY HE SPOKE TO ME, TYLDAK--
--TO ME!
IT IS ALL THE WOLF-RIDERS' FAULT!
I CAN-NOT ALLOW THEM TO REVIVE HIS SPIRIT FURTHER!
GO, BOTH OF YOU! DO NOT LET ME SEE YOU AGAIN UNTIL YOU'VE RECAPTURED THE PRESERVER!
I WON'T HELP YOU KILL PETAL-WING!!
OH, BUT YOU WILL... MY FRAGILE LREE!
OOOHH!
DO NOT, WINNOWILL!
THAT NAME IS NOT YOURS TO SPEAK!
MOAN...
THERE ARE NO SECRETS INSIDE BLUE MOUNTAIN, SAVE THOSE I CHOOSE TO KEEP. EVERYTHING IS MINE TO USE AS I PLEASE!
DO NOT TRY TO MATCH WILLS WITH ME, TYLDAK. NEED I RE-MIND YOU THAT YOU ARE WHAT YOU ALWAYS DREAMED OF BEING — BECAUSE OF ME?
I... HAVE... NEVER ... FORGOTTEN.
THEN GO! FIND THE PRESERVER AND BRING IT TO ME AT ONCE!
YOU KNOW HOW I SHALL REWARD YOU BOTH... IF YOU FAIL!

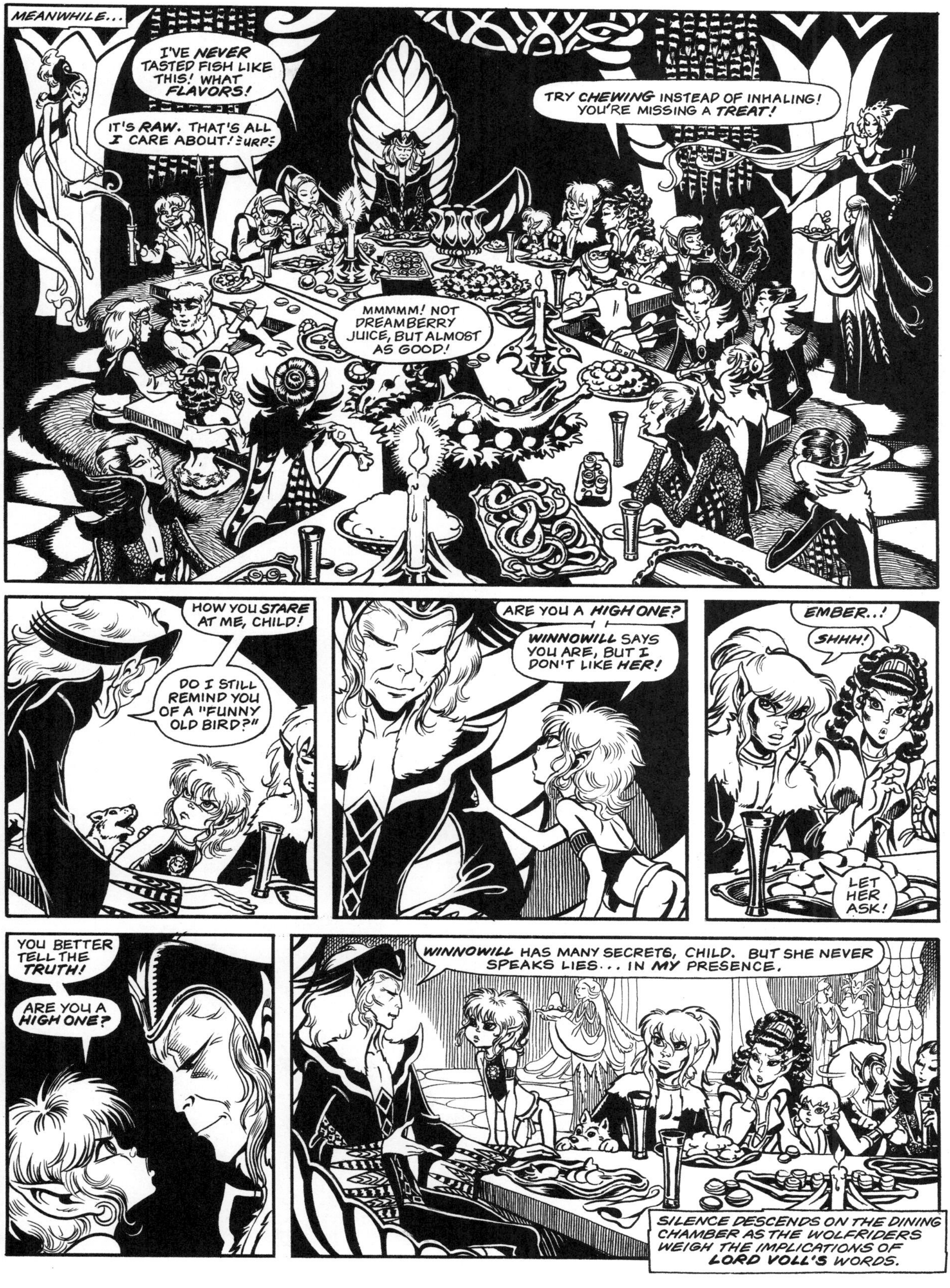

MEANWHILE...
I'VE NEVER TASTED FISH LIKE THIS! WHAT FLAVORS!
IT'S RAW. THAT'S ALL I CARE ABOUT! *URP*
TRY CHEWING INSTEAD OF INHALING! YOU'RE MISSING A TREAT!
MMMMM! NOT DREAMBERRY JUICE, BUT ALMOST AS GOOD!
HOW YOU STARE AT ME, CHILD!
DO I STILL REMIND YOU OF A "FUNNY OLD BIRD?"
ARE YOU A HIGH ONE?
WINNOWILL SAYS YOU ARE, BUT I DON'T LIKE HER!
EMBER..!
SHHH!
LET HER ASK!
YOU BETTER TELL THE TRUTH!
ARE YOU A HIGH ONE?
WINNOWILL HAS MANY SECRETS, CHILD. BUT SHE NEVER SPEAKS LIES... IN MY PRESENCE.
SILENCE DESCENDS ON THE DINING CHAMBER AS THE WOLFRIDERS WEIGH THE IMPLICATIONS OF LORD VOLL'S WORDS.

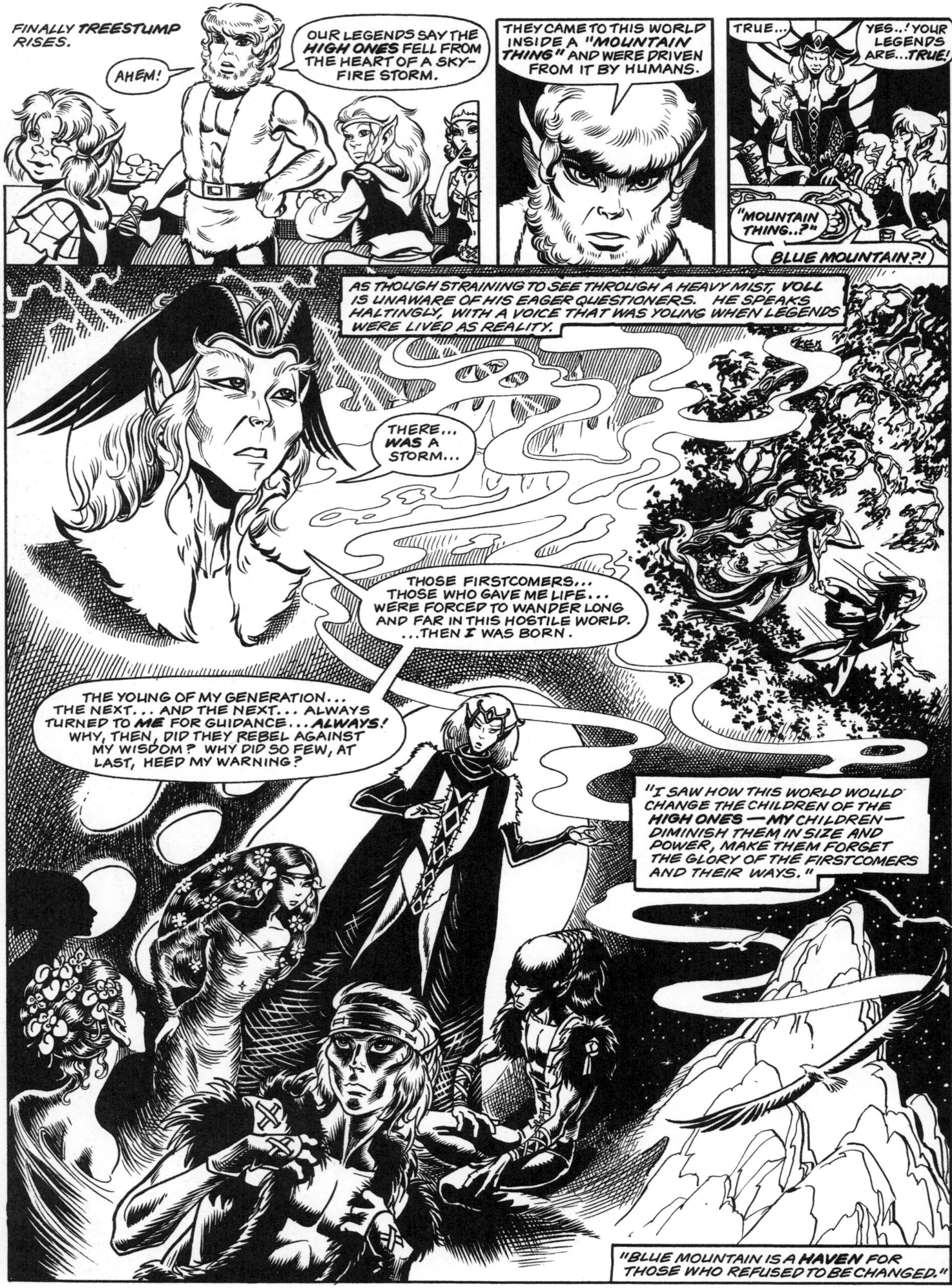
FINALLY TREESTUMP RISES.
AHEM!
OUR LEGENDS SAY THE HIGH ONES FELL FROM THE HEART OF A SKY-FIRE STORM.
THEY CAME TO THIS WORLD INSIDE A "MOUNTAIN THING" AND WERE DRIVEN FROM IT BY HUMANS.
TRUE...
YES..! YOUR LEGENDS ARE...TRUE!
"MOUNTAIN THING..?"
BLUE MOUNTAIN?!
AS THOUGH STRAINING TO SEE THROUGH A HEAVY MIST, VOLL IS UNAWARE OF HIS EAGER QUESTIONERS. HE SPEAKS HALTINGLY, WITH A VOICE THAT WAS YOUNG WHEN LEGENDS WERE LIVED AS REALITY.
THERE... WAS A STORM...
THOSE FIRSTCOMERS... THOSE WHO GAVE ME LIFE... WERE FORCED TO WANDER LONG AND FAR IN THIS HOSTILE WORLD. ...THEN I WAS BORN.
THE YOUNG OF MY GENERATION... THE NEXT... AND THE NEXT... ALWAYS TURNED TO ME FOR GUIDANCE... ALWAYS! WHY, THEN, DID THEY REBEL AGAINST MY WISDOM? WHY DID SO FEW, AT LAST, HEED MY WARNING?
"I SAW HOW THIS WORLD WOULD CHANGE THE CHILDREN OF THE HIGH ONES — MY CHILDREN — DIMINISH THEM IN SIZE AND POWER, MAKE THEM FORGET THE GLORY OF THE FIRSTCOMERS AND THEIR WAYS."
"BLUE MOUNTAIN IS A HAVEN FOR THOSE WHO REFUSED TO BE CHANGED."

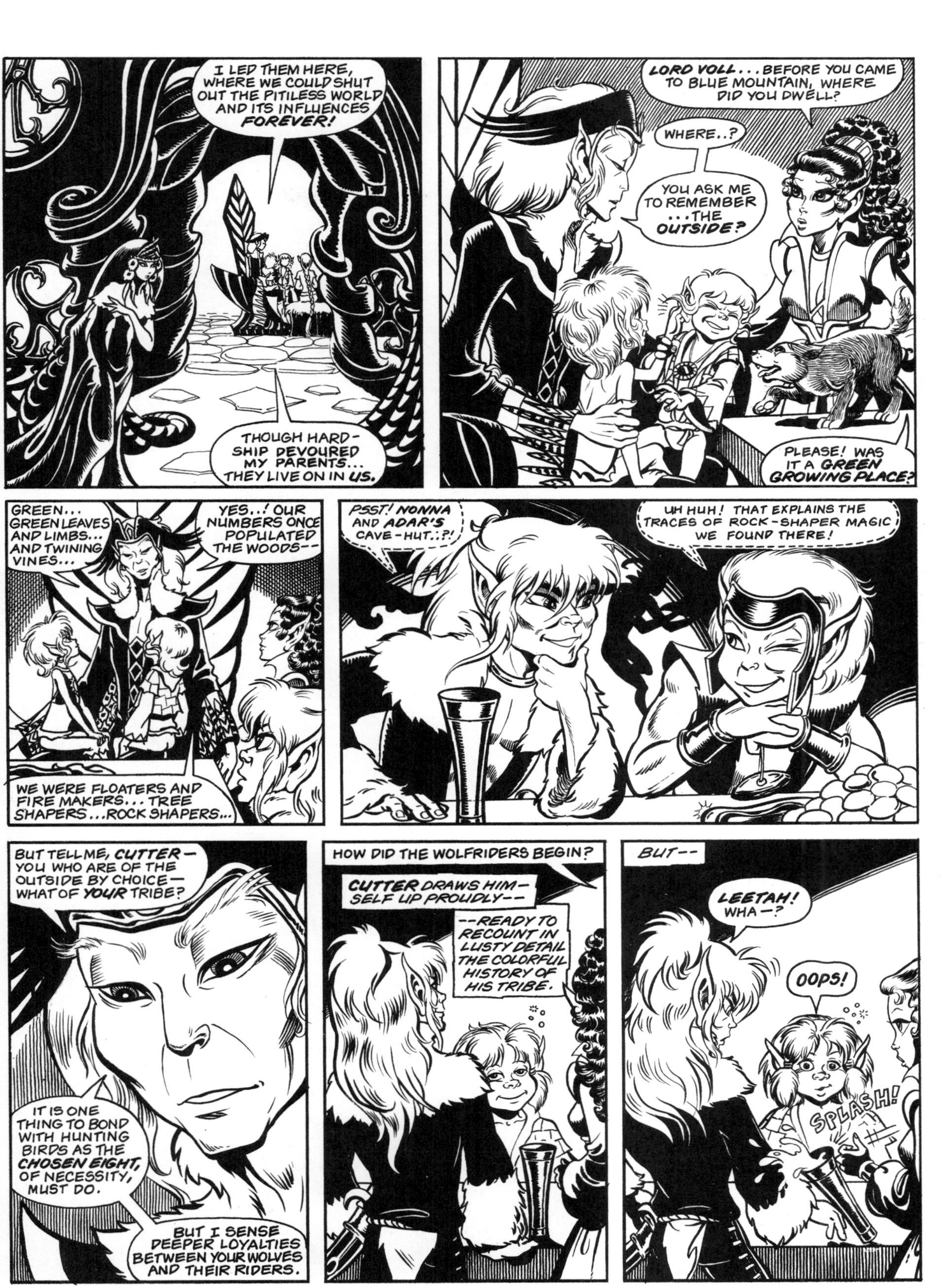

I LED THEM HERE, WHERE WE COULD SHUT OUT THE PITILESS WORLD AND ITS INFLUENCES FOREVER!
THOUGH HARD-SHIP DEVOURED MY PARENTS... THEY LIVE ON IN US.
LORD VOLL... BEFORE YOU CAME TO BLUE MOUNTAIN, WHERE DID YOU DWELL?
WHERE..?
YOU ASK ME TO REMEMBER ...THE OUTSIDE?
PLEASE! WAS IT A GREEN GROWING PLACE?
GREEN... GREEN LEAVES AND LIMBS... AND TWINING VINES...
YES..! OUR NUMBERS ONCE POPULATED THE WOODS--
WE WERE FLOATERS AND FIRE MAKERS... TREE SHAPERS...ROCK SHAPERS...
PSST! NONNA AND ADAR'S CAVE-HUT..?!
UH HUH! THAT EXPLAINS THE TRACES OF ROCK-SHAPER MAGIC WE FOUND THERE!
BUT TELL ME, CUTTER — YOU WHO ARE OF THE OUTSIDE BY CHOICE — WHAT OF YOUR TRIBE?
IT IS ONE THING TO BOND WITH HUNTING BIRDS AS THE CHOSEN EIGHT, OF NECESSITY, MUST DO.
BUT I SENSE DEEPER LOYALTIES BETWEEN YOUR WOLVES AND THEIR RIDERS.
HOW DID THE WOLFRIDERS BEGIN?
CUTTER DRAWS HIMSELF UP PROUDLY--
--READY TO RECOUNT IN LUSTY DETAIL THE COLORFUL HISTORY OF HIS TRIBE.
BUT--
LEETAH! WHA—?
OOPS!
SPLASH!

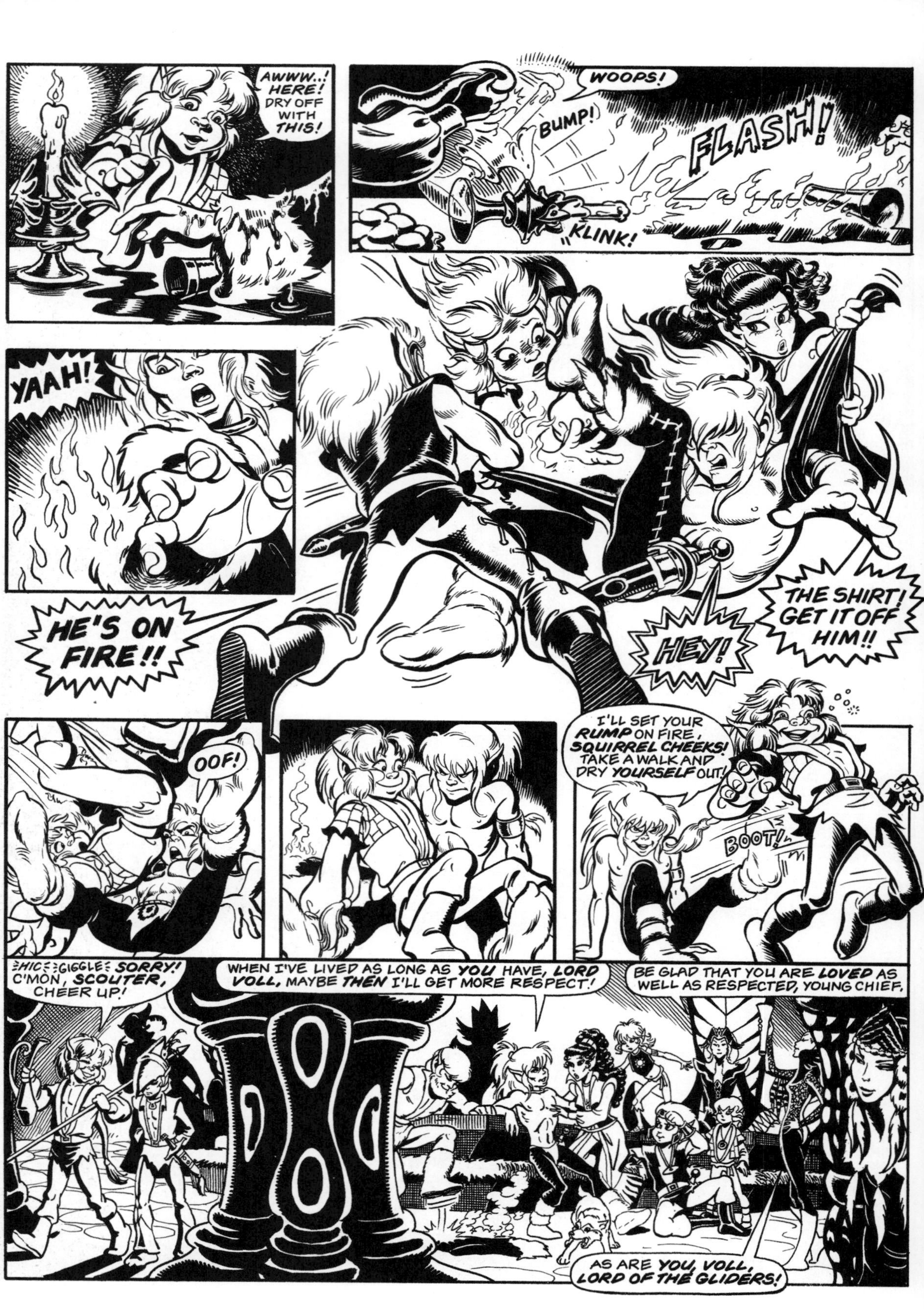
AWWW..! HERE! DRY OFF WITH THIS!
WOOPS!
BUMP!
FLASH!
KLINK!
YAAH!
HE'S ON FIRE!!
HEY!
THE SHIRT! GET IT OFF HIM!!
OOF!
I'LL SET YOUR RUMP ON FIRE, SQUIRREL CHEEKS! TAKE A WALK AND DRY YOURSELF OUT!
BOOT!
HIC GIGGLE SORRY! C'MON, SCOUTER, CHEER UP!
WHEN I'VE LIVED AS LONG AS YOU HAVE, LORD VOLL, MAYBE THEN I'LL GET MORE RESPECT!
BE GLAD THAT YOU ARE LOVED AS WELL AS RESPECTED, YOUNG CHIEF.
AS ARE YOU, VOLL, LORD OF THE GLIDERS!

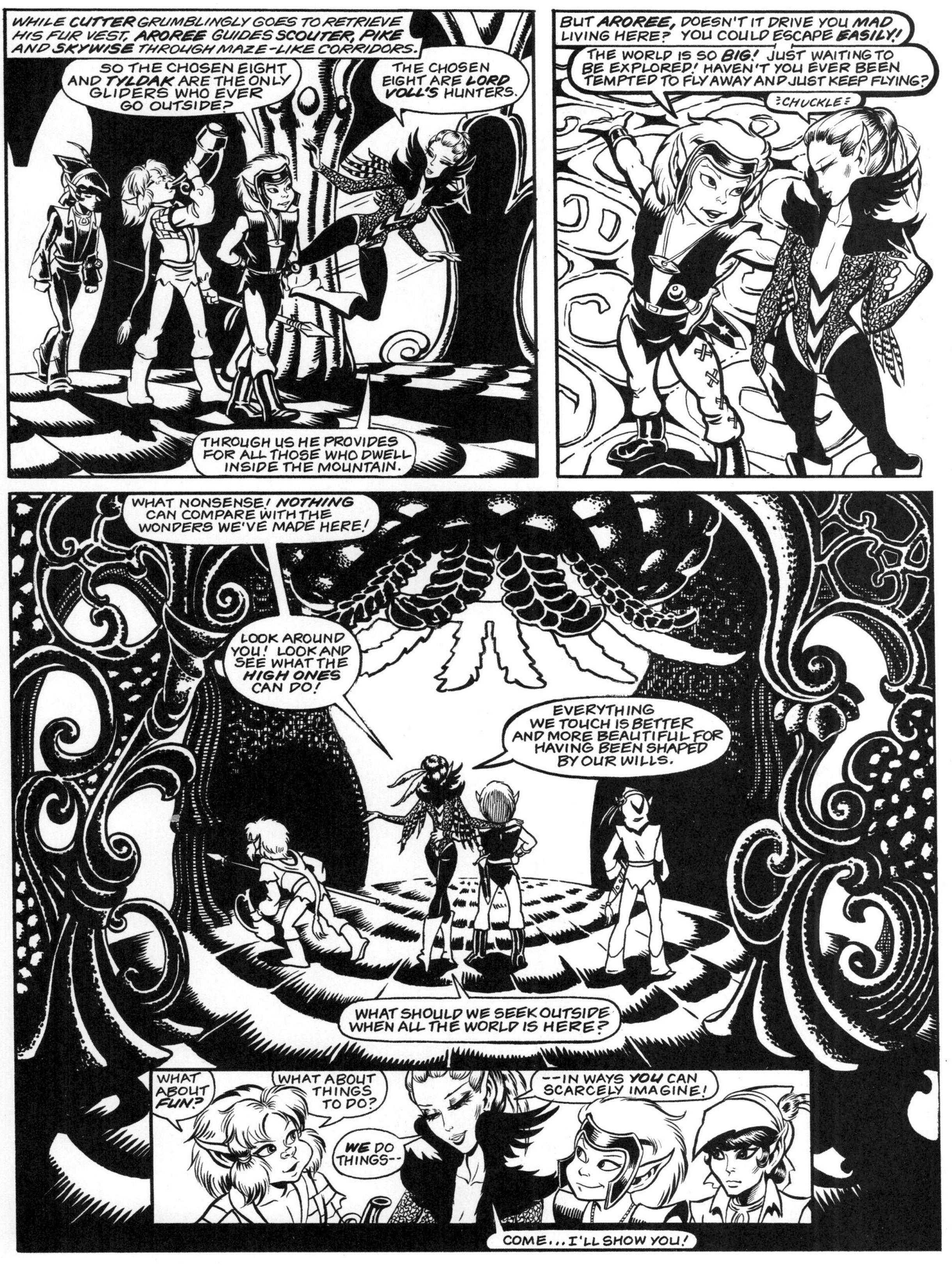
WHILE CUTTER GRUMBLINGLY GOES TO RETRIEVE HIS FUR VEST, AROREE GUIDES SCOUTER, PIKE AND SKYWISE THROUGH MAZE-LIKE CORRIDORS.
SO THE CHOSEN EIGHT AND TYLDAK ARE THE ONLY GLIDERS WHO EVER GO OUTSIDE?
THE CHOSEN EIGHT ARE LORD VOLL'S HUNTERS.
THROUGH US HE PROVIDES FOR ALL THOSE WHO DWELL INSIDE THE MOUNTAIN.
BUT AROREE, DOESN'T IT DRIVE YOU MAD LIVING HERE? YOU COULD ESCAPE EASILY!
THE WORLD IS SO BIG! JUST WAITING TO BE EXPLORED! HAVEN'T YOU EVER BEEN TEMPTED TO FLY AWAY AND JUST KEEP FLYING?
CHUCKLE
WHAT NONSENSE! NOTHING CAN COMPARE WITH THE WONDERS WE'VE MADE HERE!
LOOK AROUND YOU! LOOK AND SEE WHAT THE HIGH ONES CAN DO!
EVERYTHING WE TOUCH IS BETTER AND MORE BEAUTIFUL FOR HAVING BEEN SHAPED BY OUR WILLS.
WHAT SHOULD WE SEEK OUTSIDE WHEN ALL THE WORLD IS HERE?
WHAT ABOUT FUN?
WHAT ABOUT THINGS TO DO?
WE DO THINGS--
--IN WAYS YOU CAN SCARCELY IMAGINE!
COME... I'LL SHOW YOU!

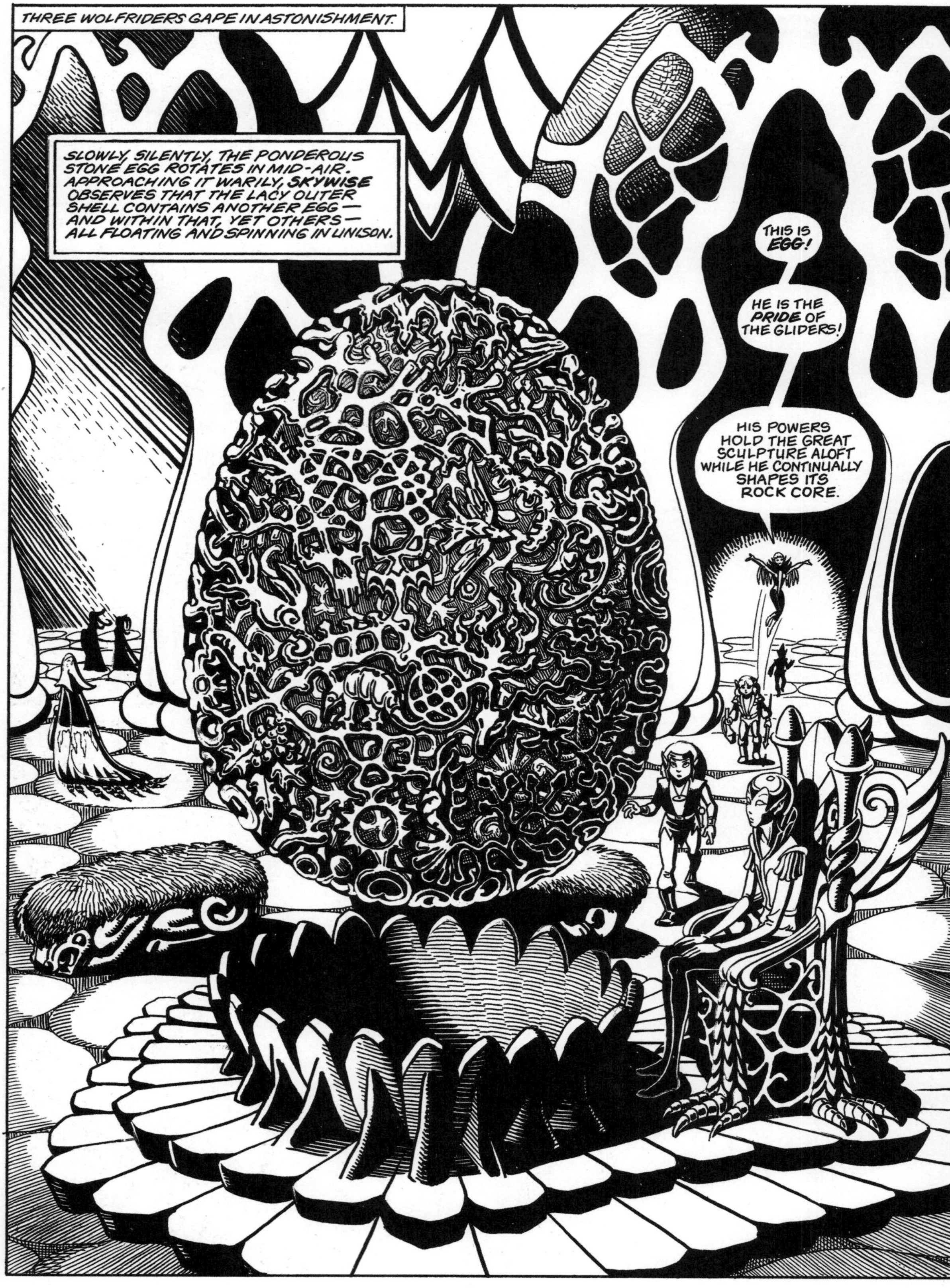
THREE WOLFRIDERS GAPE IN ASTONISHMENT.
SLOWLY, SILENTLY, THE PONDEROUS STONE EGG ROTATES IN MID-AIR. APPROACHING IT WARILY, SKYWISE OBSERVES THAT THE LACY OUTER SHELL CONTAINS ANOTHER EGG— AND WITHIN THAT, YET OTHERS— ALL FLOATING AND SPINNING IN UNISON.
THIS IS EGG!
HE IS THE PRIDE OF THE GLIDERS!
HIS POWERS HOLD THE GREAT SCULPTURE ALOFT WHILE HE CONTINUALLY SHAPES ITS ROCK CORE.

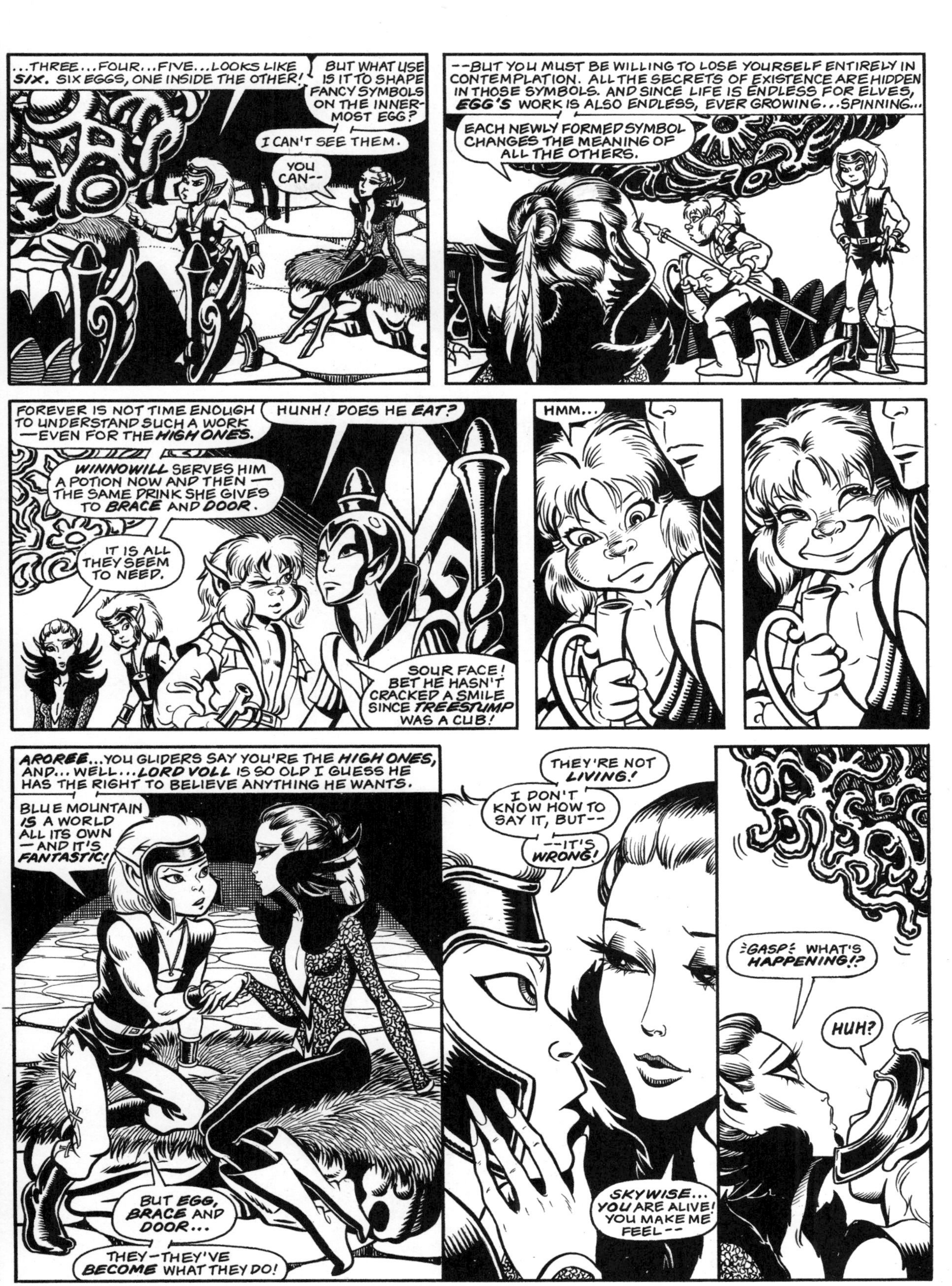
...THREE...FOUR...FIVE...LOOKS LIKE SIX. SIX EGGS, ONE INSIDE THE OTHER!
BUT WHAT USE IS IT TO SHAPE FANCY SYMBOLS ON THE INNERMOST EGG?
I CAN'T SEE THEM.
YOU CAN--
--BUT YOU MUST BE WILLING TO LOSE YOURSELF ENTIRELY IN CONTEMPLATION. ALL THE SECRETS OF EXISTENCE ARE HIDDEN IN THOSE SYMBOLS. AND SINCE LIFE IS ENDLESS FOR ELVES, EGG'S WORK IS ALSO ENDLESS, EVER GROWING...SPINNING...
EACH NEWLY FORMED SYMBOL CHANGES THE MEANING OF ALL THE OTHERS.
FOREVER IS NOT TIME ENOUGH TO UNDERSTAND SUCH A WORK —EVEN FOR THE HIGH ONES.
HUNH! DOES HE EAT?
WINNOWILL SERVES HIM A POTION NOW AND THEN — THE SAME DRINK SHE GIVES TO BRACE AND DOOR.
IT IS ALL THEY SEEM TO NEED.
SOUR FACE! BET HE HASN'T CRACKED A SMILE SINCE TREESTUMP WAS A CUB!
HMM...
AROREE...YOU GLIDERS SAY YOU'RE THE HIGH ONES, AND...WELL...LORD VOLL IS SO OLD I GUESS HE HAS THE RIGHT TO BELIEVE ANYTHING HE WANTS.
BLUE MOUNTAIN IS A WORLD ALL ITS OWN — AND IT'S FANTASTIC!
BUT EGG, BRACE AND DOOR...
THEY—THEY'VE BECOME WHAT THEY DO!
THEY'RE NOT LIVING!
I DON'T KNOW HOW TO SAY IT, BUT--
--IT'S WRONG!
SKYWISE... YOU ARE ALIVE! YOU MAKE ME FEEL--
:GASP: WHAT'S HAPPENING!?
HUH?

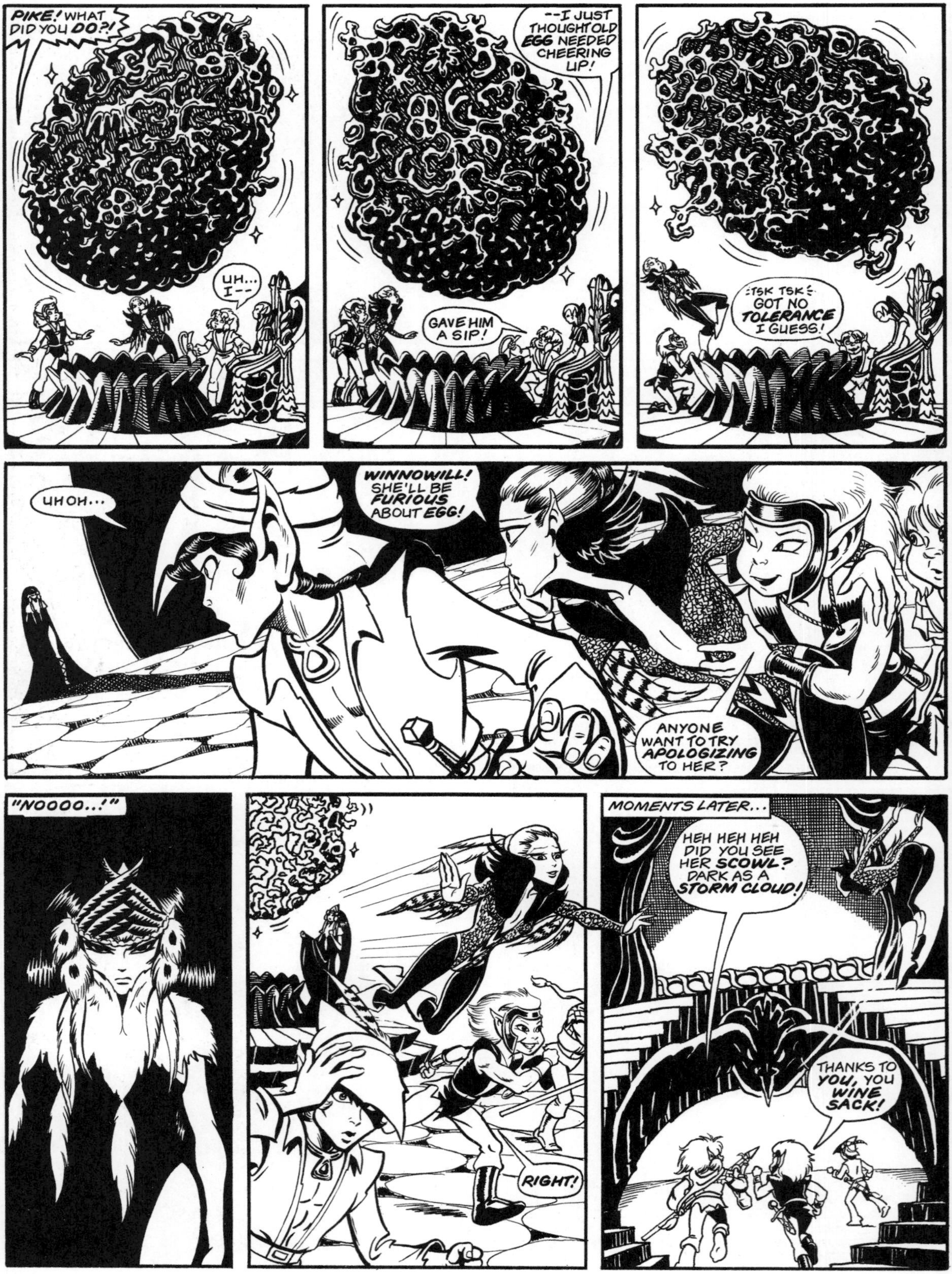
PIKE! WHAT DID YOU DO?!
UH... I--
--I JUST THOUGHT OLD EGG NEEDED CHEERING UP!
GAVE HIM A SIP!
TSK TSK GOT NO TOLERANCE I GUESS!
UHOH...
WINNOWILL! SHE'LL BE FURIOUS ABOUT EGG!
ANYONE WANT TO TRY APOLOGIZING TO HER?
"NOOOO...!"
RIGHT!
MOMENTS LATER...
HEH HEH HEH DID YOU SEE HER SCOWL? DARK AS A STORM CLOUD!
THANKS TO YOU, YOU WINE SACK!

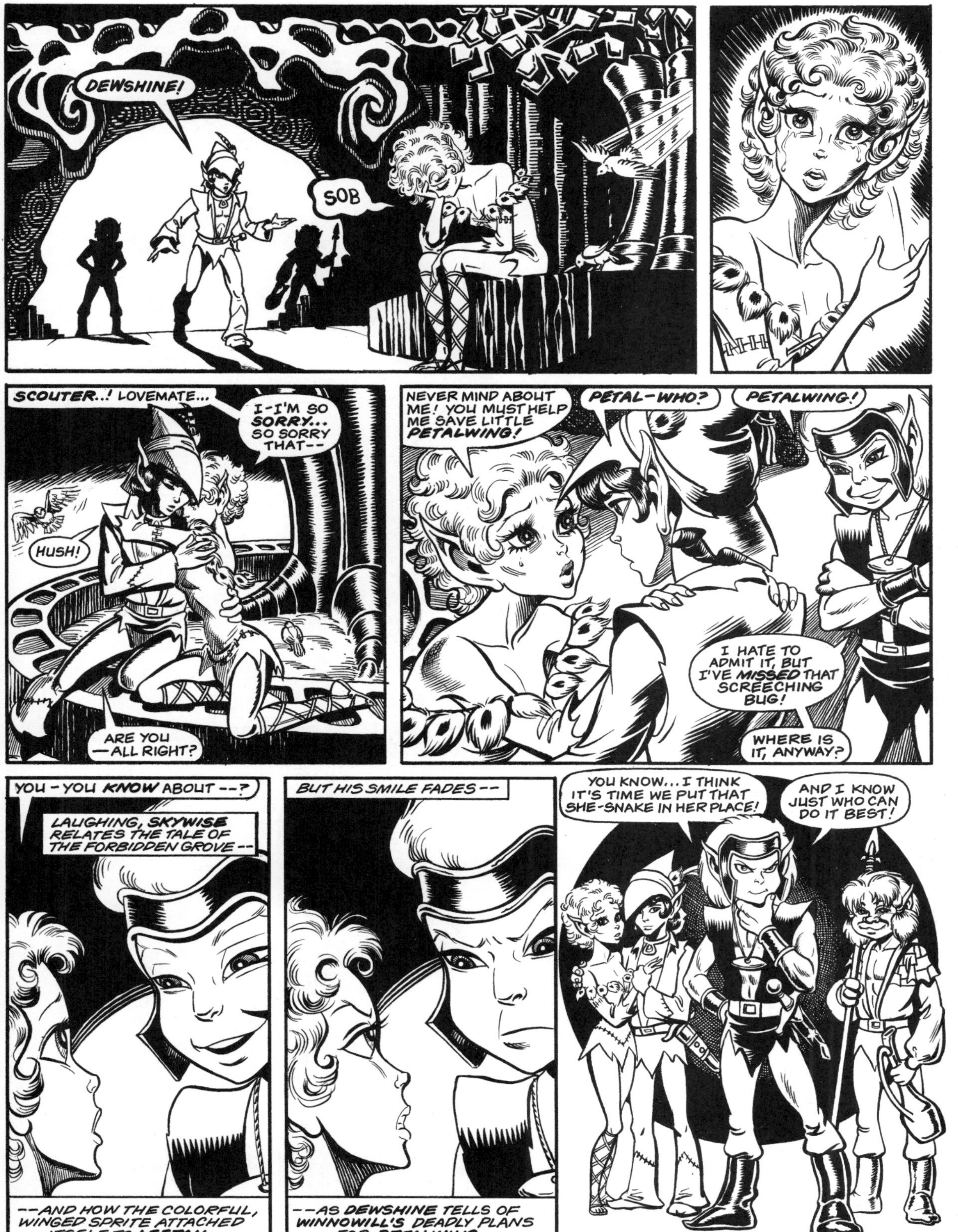

DEWSHINE!
SOB
SCOUTER..! LOVEMATE...
I-I'M SO SORRY... SO SORRY THAT--
HUSH!
ARE YOU —ALL RIGHT?
NEVER MIND ABOUT ME! YOU MUST HELP ME SAVE LITTLE PETALWING!
PETAL-WHO?
PETALWING!
I HATE TO ADMIT IT, BUT I'VE MISSED THAT SCREECHING BUG!
WHERE IS IT, ANYWAY?
YOU - YOU KNOW ABOUT --?
LAUGHING, SKYWISE RELATES THE TALE OF THE FORBIDDEN GROVE --
--AND HOW THE COLORFUL, WINGED SPRITE ATTACHED ITSELF TO LEETAH.
BUT HIS SMILE FADES --
--AS DEWSHINE TELLS OF WINNOWILL'S DEADLY PLANS FOR PETALWING.
YOU KNOW... I THINK IT'S TIME WE PUT THAT SHE-SNAKE IN HER PLACE!
AND I KNOW JUST WHO CAN DO IT BEST!

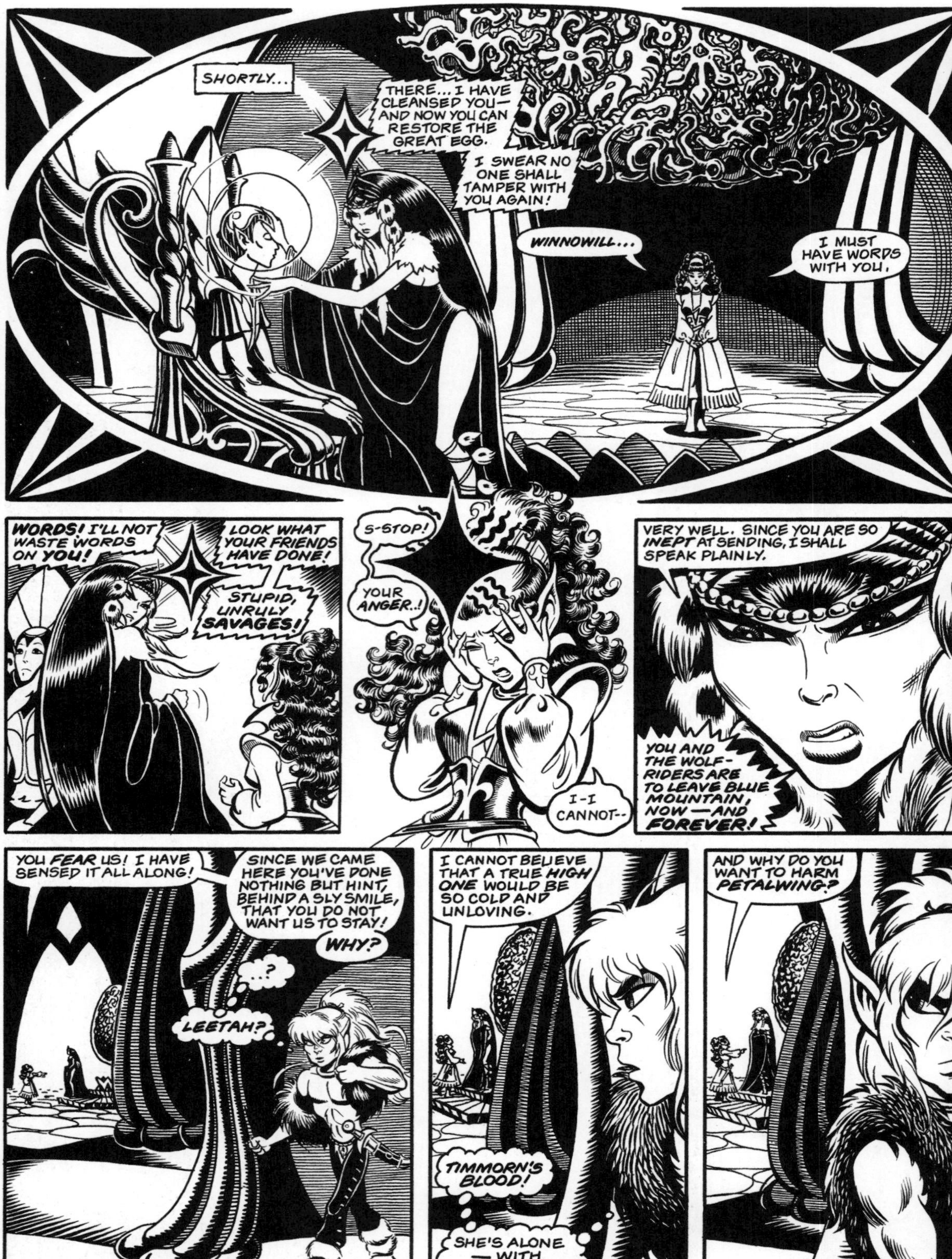
SHORTLY...
THERE... I HAVE CLEANSED YOU— AND NOW YOU CAN RESTORE THE GREAT EGG.
I SWEAR NO ONE SHALL TAMPER WITH YOU AGAIN!
WINNOWILL...
I MUST HAVE WORDS WITH YOU.
WORDS! I'LL NOT WASTE WORDS ON YOU!
LOOK WHAT YOUR FRIENDS HAVE DONE!
STUPID, UNRULY SAVAGES!
S-STOP!
YOUR ANGER..!
I-I CANNOT--
VERY WELL. SINCE YOU ARE SO INEPT AT SENDING, I SHALL SPEAK PLAINLY.
YOU AND THE WOLF-RIDERS ARE TO LEAVE BLUE MOUNTAIN, NOW — AND FOREVER!
YOU FEAR US! I HAVE SENSED IT ALL ALONG!
SINCE WE CAME HERE YOU'VE DONE NOTHING BUT HINT, BEHIND A SLY SMILE, THAT YOU DO NOT WANT US TO STAY!
WHY?
...?
LEETAH?
I CANNOT BELIEVE THAT A TRUE HIGH ONE WOULD BE SO COLD AND UNLOVING.
TIMMORN'S BLOOD!
SHE'S ALONE — WITH WINNOWILL!
AND WHY DO YOU WANT TO HARM PETALWING?

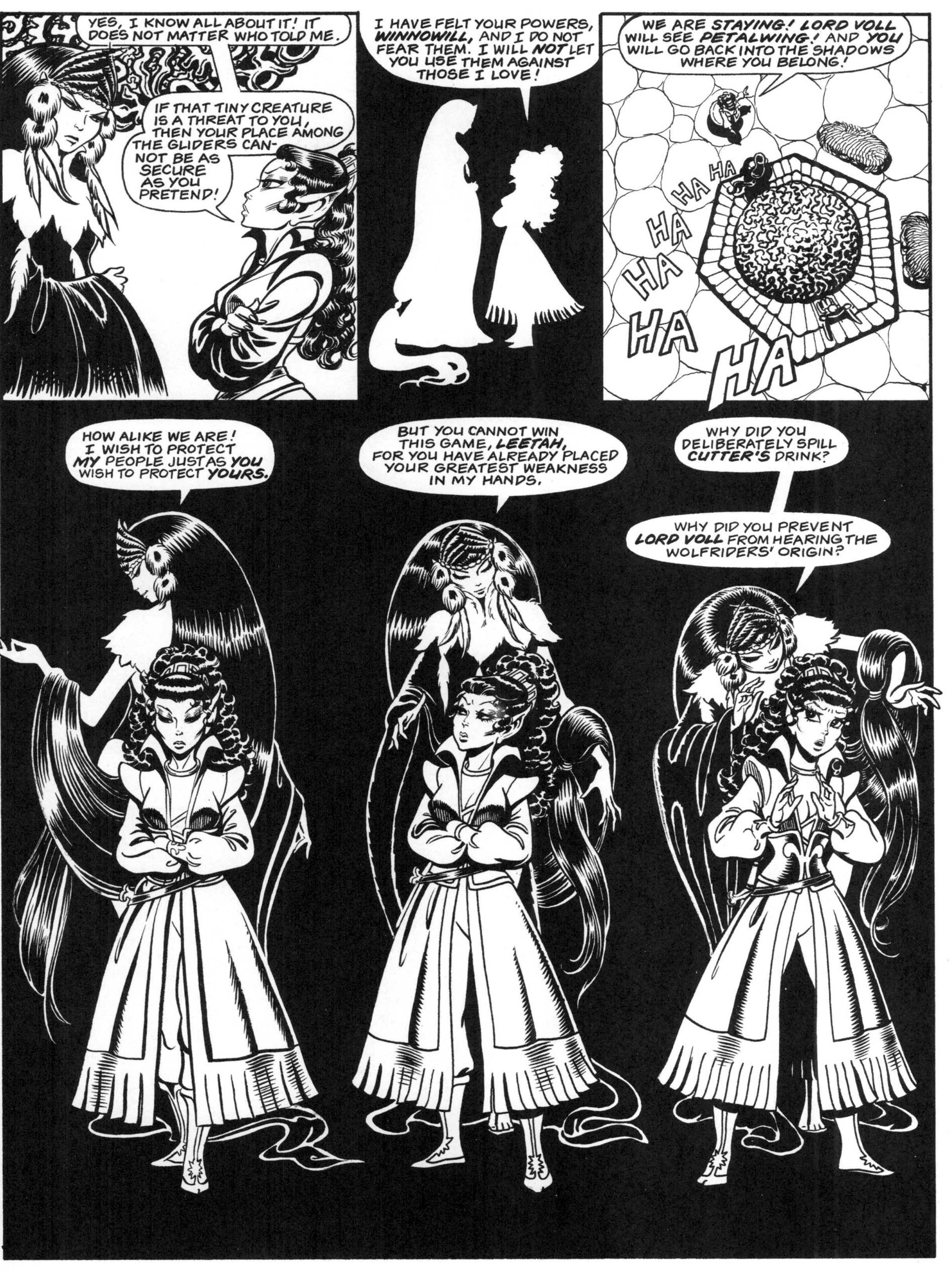
YES, I KNOW ALL ABOUT IT! IT DOES NOT MATTER WHO TOLD ME.
IF THAT TINY CREATURE IS A THREAT TO YOU, THEN YOUR PLACE AMONG THE GLIDERS CANNOT BE AS SECURE AS YOU PRETEND!
I HAVE FELT YOUR POWERS, WINNOWILL, AND I DO NOT FEAR THEM. I WILL NOT LET YOU USE THEM AGAINST THOSE I LOVE!
WE ARE STAYING! LORD VOLL WILL SEE PETALWING! AND YOU WILL GO BACK INTO THE SHADOWS WHERE YOU BELONG!
HA HA HA HA HA HA HA
HOW ALIKE WE ARE! I WISH TO PROTECT MY PEOPLE JUST AS YOU WISH TO PROTECT YOURS.
BUT YOU CANNOT WIN THIS GAME, LEETAH, FOR YOU HAVE ALREADY PLACED YOUR GREATEST WEAKNESS IN MY HANDS.
WHY DID YOU DELIBERATELY SPILL CUTTER'S DRINK?
WHY DID YOU PREVENT LORD VOLL FROM HEARING THE WOLFRIDERS' ORIGIN?

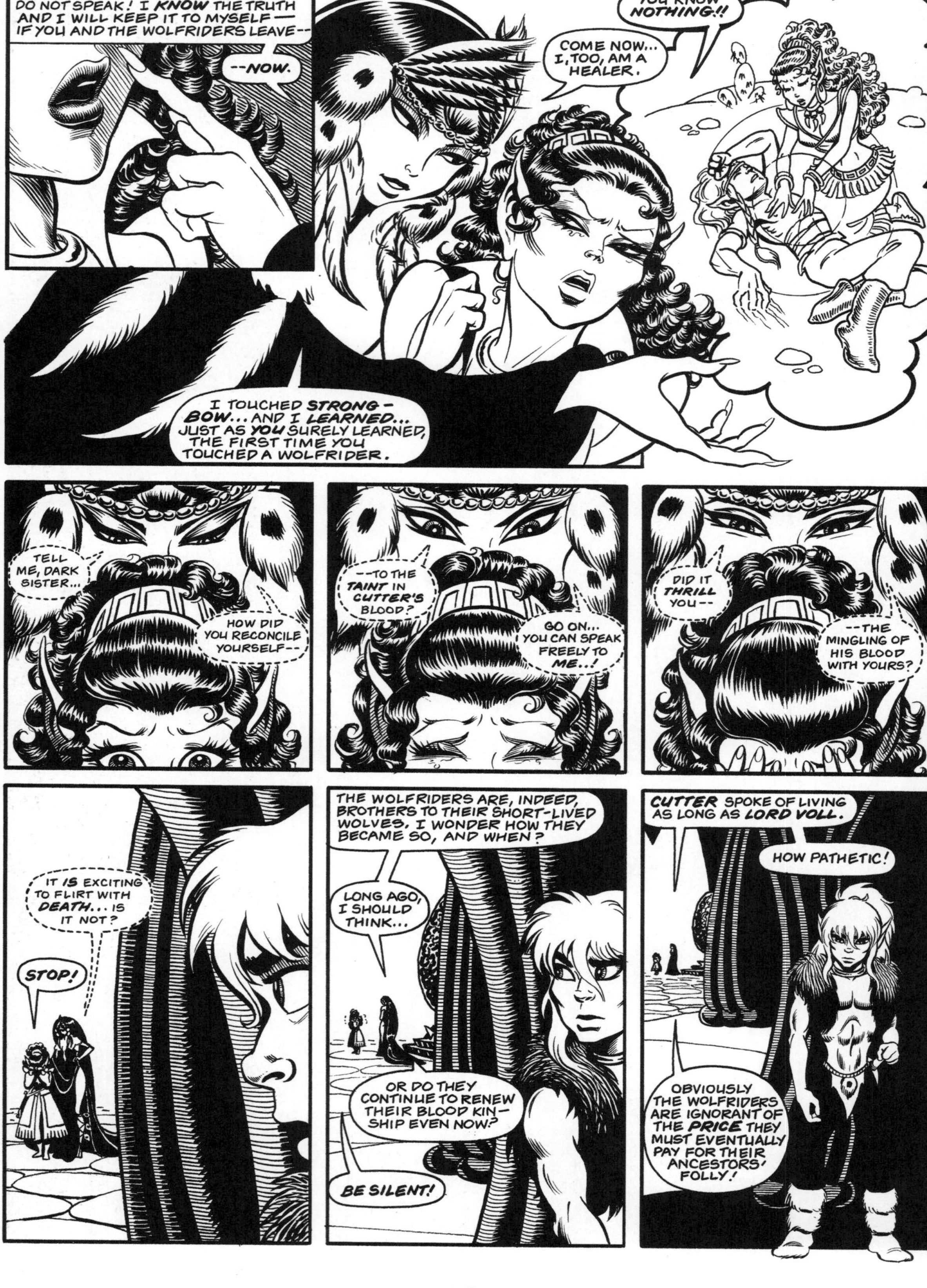
DO NOT SPEAK! I KNOW THE TRUTH AND I WILL KEEP IT TO MYSELF — IF YOU AND THE WOLFRIDERS LEAVE--
--NOW.
COME NOW... I, TOO, AM A HEALER.
YOU KNOW NOTHING!!
I TOUCHED STRONG-BOW... AND I LEARNED... JUST AS YOU SURELY LEARNED, THE FIRST TIME YOU TOUCHED A WOLFRIDER.
TELL ME, DARK SISTER...
HOW DID YOU RECONCILE YOURSELF--
--TO THE TAINT IN CUTTER'S BLOOD?
GO ON... YOU CAN SPEAK FREELY TO ME...!
DID IT THRILL YOU--
--THE MINGLING OF HIS BLOOD WITH YOURS?
IT IS EXCITING TO FLIRT WITH DEATH... IS IT NOT?
STOP!
THE WOLFRIDERS ARE, INDEED, BROTHERS TO THEIR SHORT-LIVED WOLVES. I WONDER HOW THEY BECAME SO, AND WHEN?
LONG AGO, I SHOULD THINK...
OR DO THEY CONTINUE TO RENEW THEIR BLOOD KIN-SHIP EVEN NOW?
BE SILENT!
CUTTER SPOKE OF LIVING AS LONG AS LORD VOLL.
HOW PATHETIC!
OBVIOUSLY THE WOLFRIDERS ARE IGNORANT OF THE PRICE THEY MUST EVENTUALLY PAY FOR THEIR ANCESTORS' FOLLY!

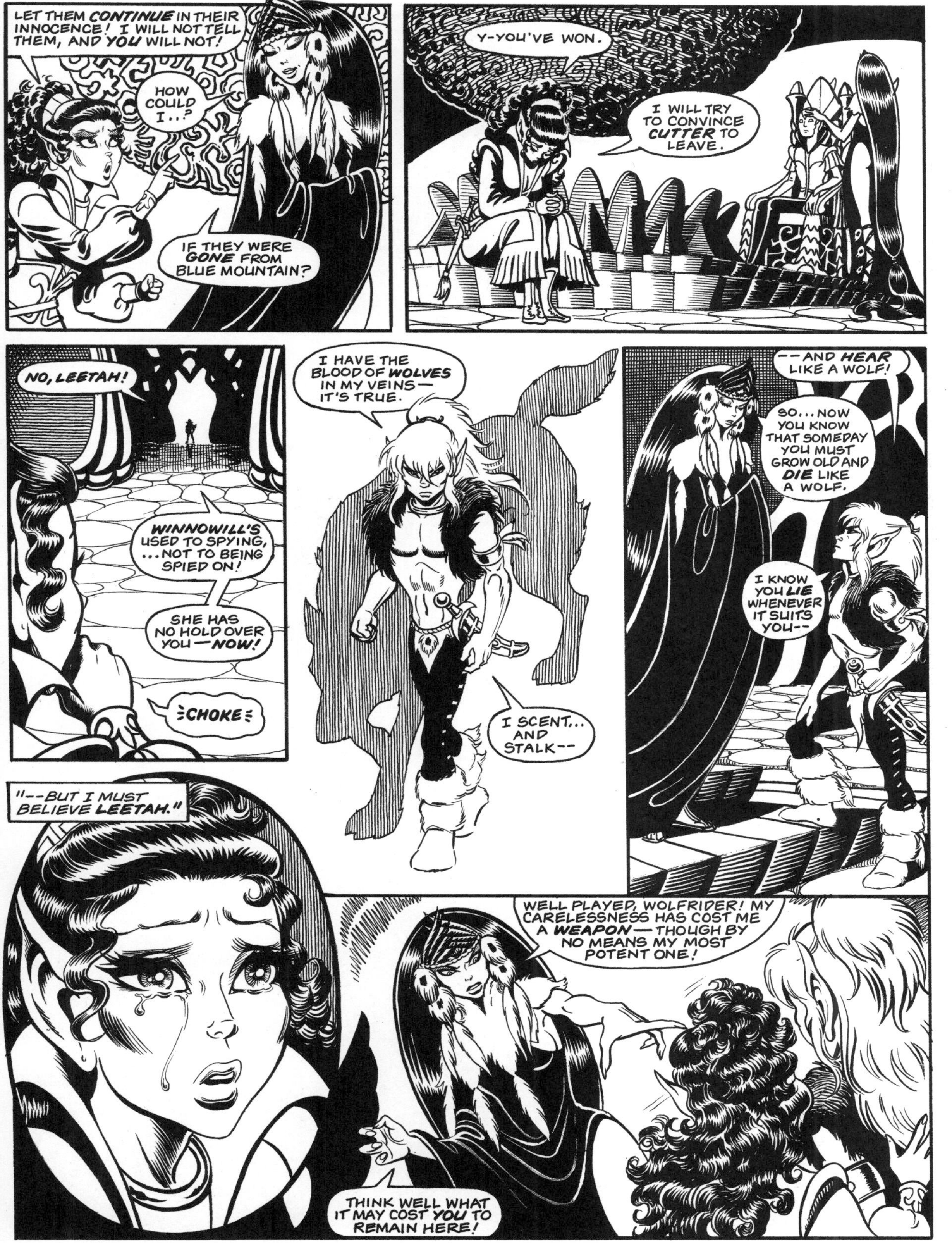
LET THEM CONTINUE IN THEIR INNOCENCE! I WILL NOT TELL THEM, AND YOU WILL NOT!
HOW COULD I...?
IF THEY WERE GONE FROM BLUE MOUNTAIN?
Y-YOU'VE WON.
I WILL TRY TO CONVINCE CUTTER TO LEAVE.
NO, LEETAH!
WINNOWILL'S USED TO SPYING, ...NOT TO BEING SPIED ON!
SHE HAS NO HOLD OVER YOU—NOW!
CHOKE
I HAVE THE BLOOD OF WOLVES IN MY VEINS— IT'S TRUE.
I SCENT... AND STALK--
--AND HEAR LIKE A WOLF!
SO... NOW YOU KNOW THAT SOMEDAY YOU MUST GROW OLD AND DIE LIKE A WOLF.
I KNOW YOU LIE WHENEVER IT SUITS YOU--
"--BUT I MUST BELIEVE LEETAH."
WELL PLAYED, WOLFRIDER! MY CARELESSNESS HAS COST ME A WEAPON—THOUGH BY NO MEANS MY MOST POTENT ONE!
THINK WELL WHAT IT MAY COST YOU TO REMAIN HERE!

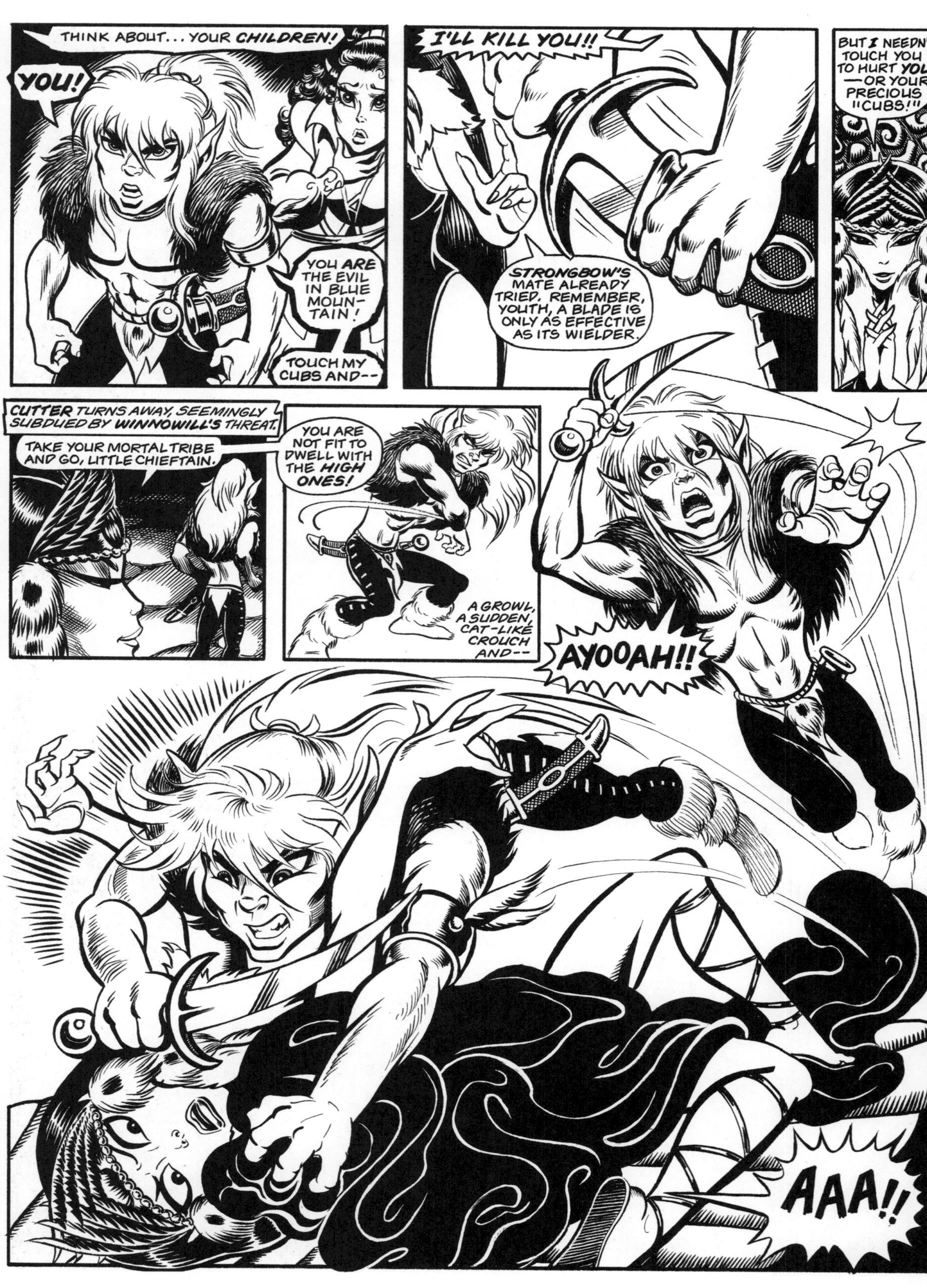
THINK ABOUT... YOUR CHILDREN!
YOU!
YOU ARE THE EVIL IN BLUE MOUNTAIN!
TOUCH MY CUBS AND--
I'LL KILL YOU!!
STRONGBOW'S MATE ALREADY TRIED. REMEMBER, YOUTH, A BLADE IS ONLY AS EFFECTIVE AS ITS WIELDER.
BUT I NEEDN'T TOUCH YOU TO HURT YOU—OR YOUR PRECIOUS "CUBS!"
CUTTER TURNS AWAY, SEEMINGLY SUBDUED BY WINNOWILL'S THREAT.
TAKE YOUR MORTAL TRIBE AND GO, LITTLE CHIEFTAIN.
YOU ARE NOT FIT TO DWELL WITH THE HIGH ONES!
A GROWL, A SUDDEN, CAT-LIKE CROUCH AND--
AYOOAH!!
AAA!!

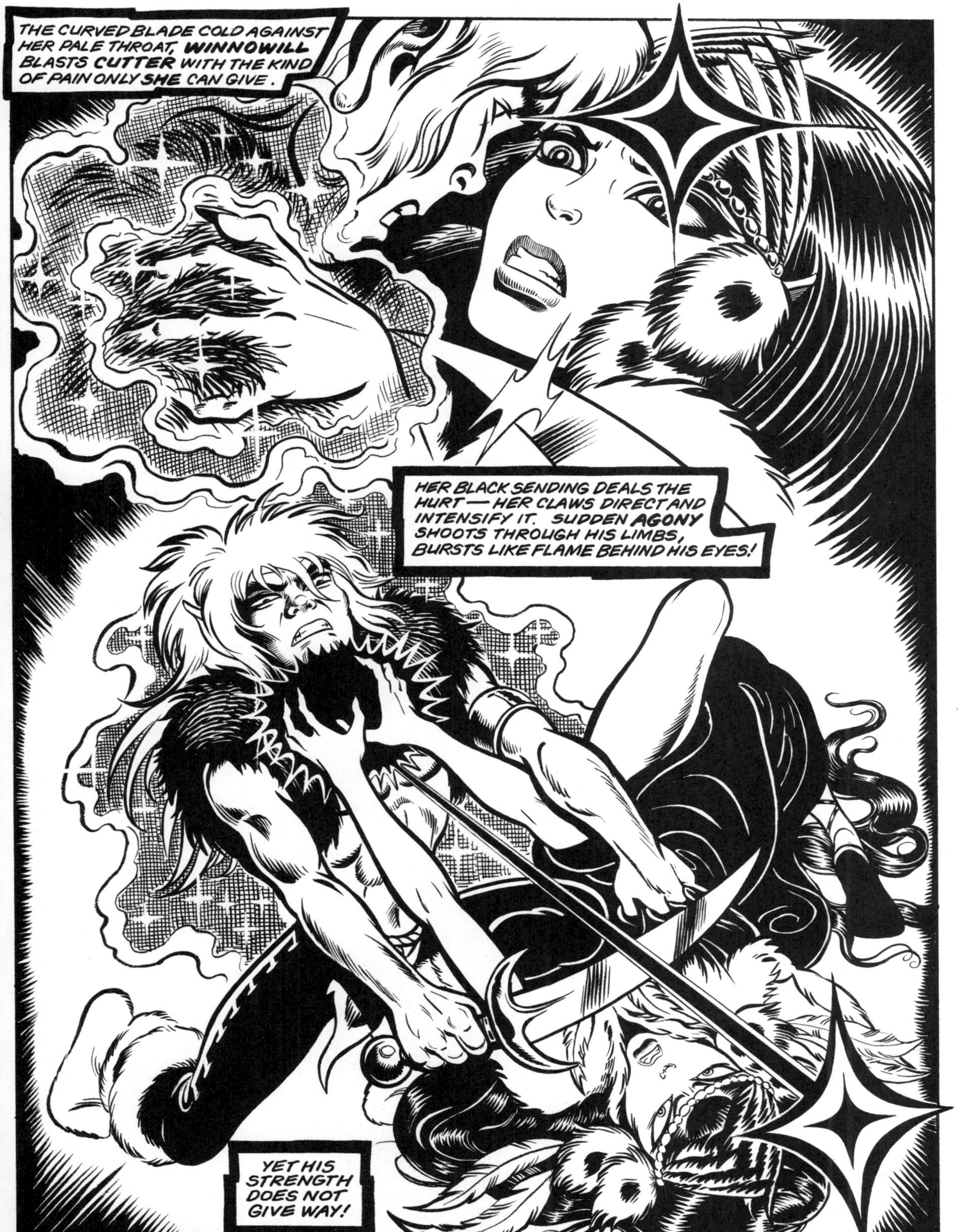
THE CURVED BLADE COLD AGAINST HER PALE THROAT, WINNOWILL BLASTS CUTTER WITH THE KIND OF PAIN ONLY SHE CAN GIVE.
HER BLACK SENDING DEALS THE HURT — HER CLAWS DIRECT AND INTENSIFY IT. SUDDEN AGONY SHOOTS THROUGH HIS LIMBS, BURSTS LIKE FLAME BEHIND HIS EYES!
YET HIS STRENGTH DOES NOT GIVE WAY!

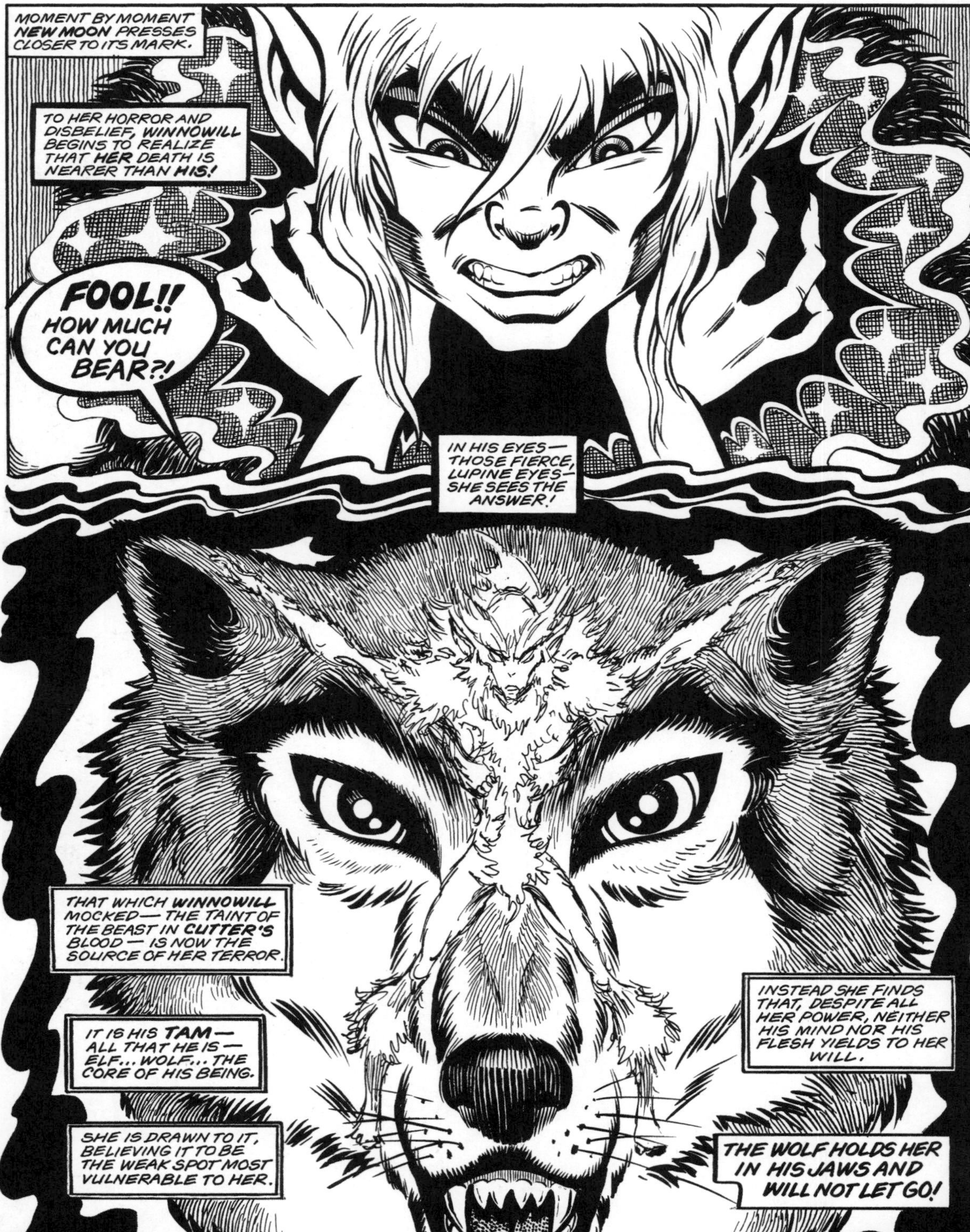

MOMENT BY MOMENT NEW MOON PRESSES CLOSER TO ITS MARK.
TO HER HORROR AND DISBELIEF, WINNOWILL BEGINS TO REALIZE THAT HER DEATH IS NEARER THAN HIS!
FOOL!! HOW MUCH CAN YOU BEAR?!
IN HIS EYES— THOSE FIERCE, LUPINE EYES— SHE SEES THE ANSWER!
THAT WHICH WINNOWILL MOCKED— THE TAINT OF THE BEAST IN CUTTER'S BLOOD — IS NOW THE SOURCE OF HER TERROR.
IT IS HIS TAM— ALL THAT HE IS— ELF... WOLF... THE CORE OF HIS BEING.
SHE IS DRAWN TO IT, BELIEVING IT TO BE THE WEAK SPOT MOST VULNERABLE TO HER.
INSTEAD SHE FINDS THAT, DESPITE ALL HER POWER, NEITHER HIS MIND NOR HIS FLESH YIELDS TO HER WILL.
THE WOLF HOLDS HER IN HIS JAWS AND WILL NOT LET GO!

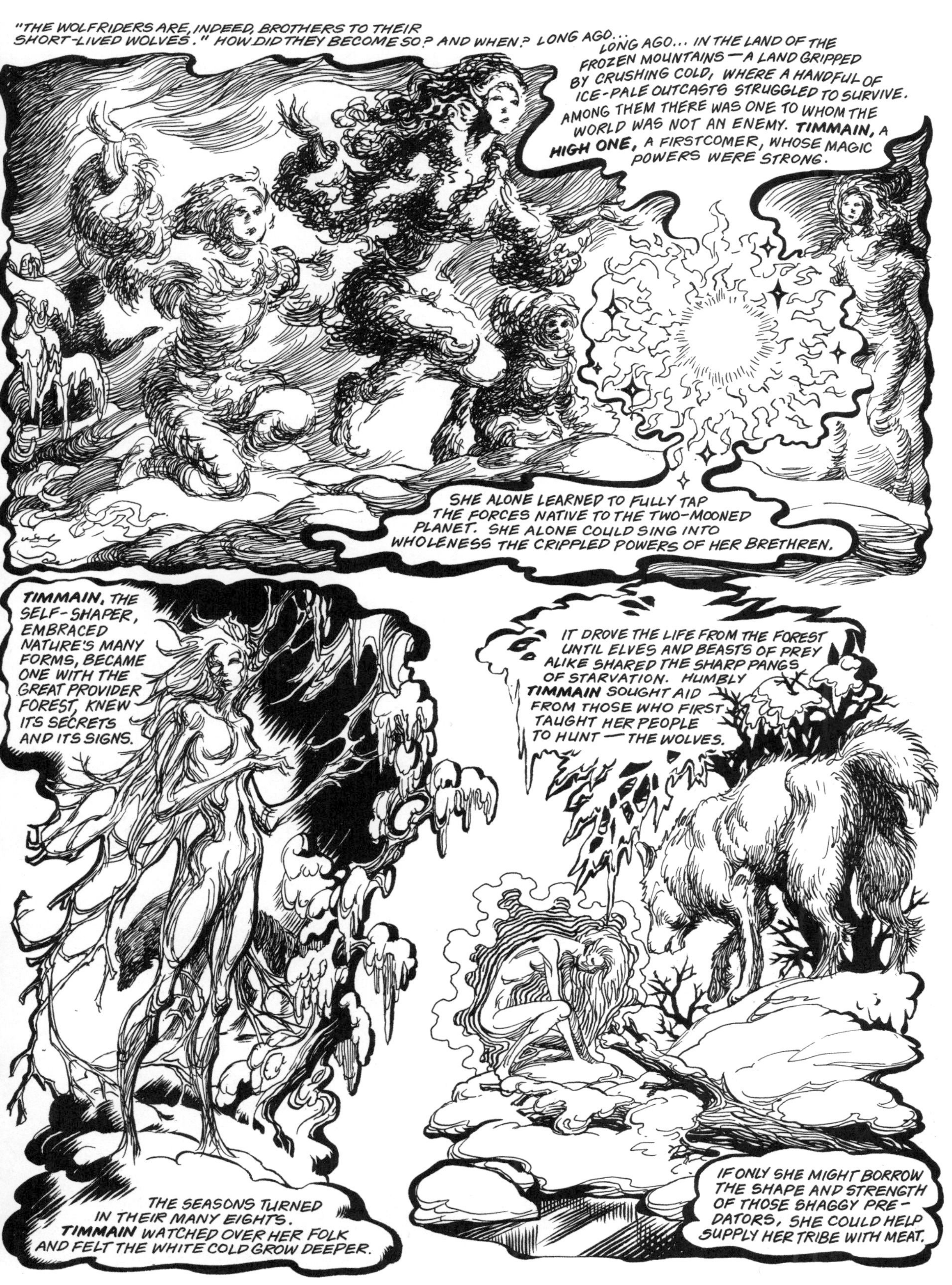
"THE WOLFRIDERS ARE, INDEED, BROTHERS TO THEIR SHORT-LIVED WOLVES." HOW DID THEY BECOME SO? AND WHEN? LONG AGO...
LONG AGO... IN THE LAND OF THE FROZEN MOUNTAINS — A LAND GRIPPED BY CRUSHING COLD, WHERE A HANDFUL OF ICE-PALE OUTCASTS STRUGGLED TO SURVIVE. AMONG THEM THERE WAS ONE TO WHOM THE WORLD WAS NOT AN ENEMY. TIMMAIN, A HIGH ONE, A FIRSTCOMER, WHOSE MAGIC POWERS WERE STRONG.
SHE ALONE LEARNED TO FULLY TAP THE FORCES NATIVE TO THE TWO-MOONED PLANET. SHE ALONE COULD SING INTO WHOLENESS THE CRIPPLED POWERS OF HER BRETHREN.
TIMMAIN, THE SELF-SHAPER, EMBRACED NATURE'S MANY FORMS, BECAME ONE WITH THE GREAT PROVIDER FOREST, KNEW ITS SECRETS AND ITS SIGNS.
THE SEASONS TURNED IN THEIR MANY EIGHTS. TIMMAIN WATCHED OVER HER FOLK AND FELT THE WHITE COLD GROW DEEPER.
IT DROVE THE LIFE FROM THE FOREST UNTIL ELVES AND BEASTS OF PREY ALIKE SHARED THE SHARP PANGS OF STARVATION. HUMBLY TIMMAIN SOUGHT AID FROM THOSE WHO FIRST TAUGHT HER PEOPLE TO HUNT — THE WOLVES.
IF ONLY SHE MIGHT BORROW THE SHAPE AND STRENGTH OF THOSE SHAGGY PREDATORS, SHE COULD HELP SUPPLY HER TRIBE WITH MEAT.

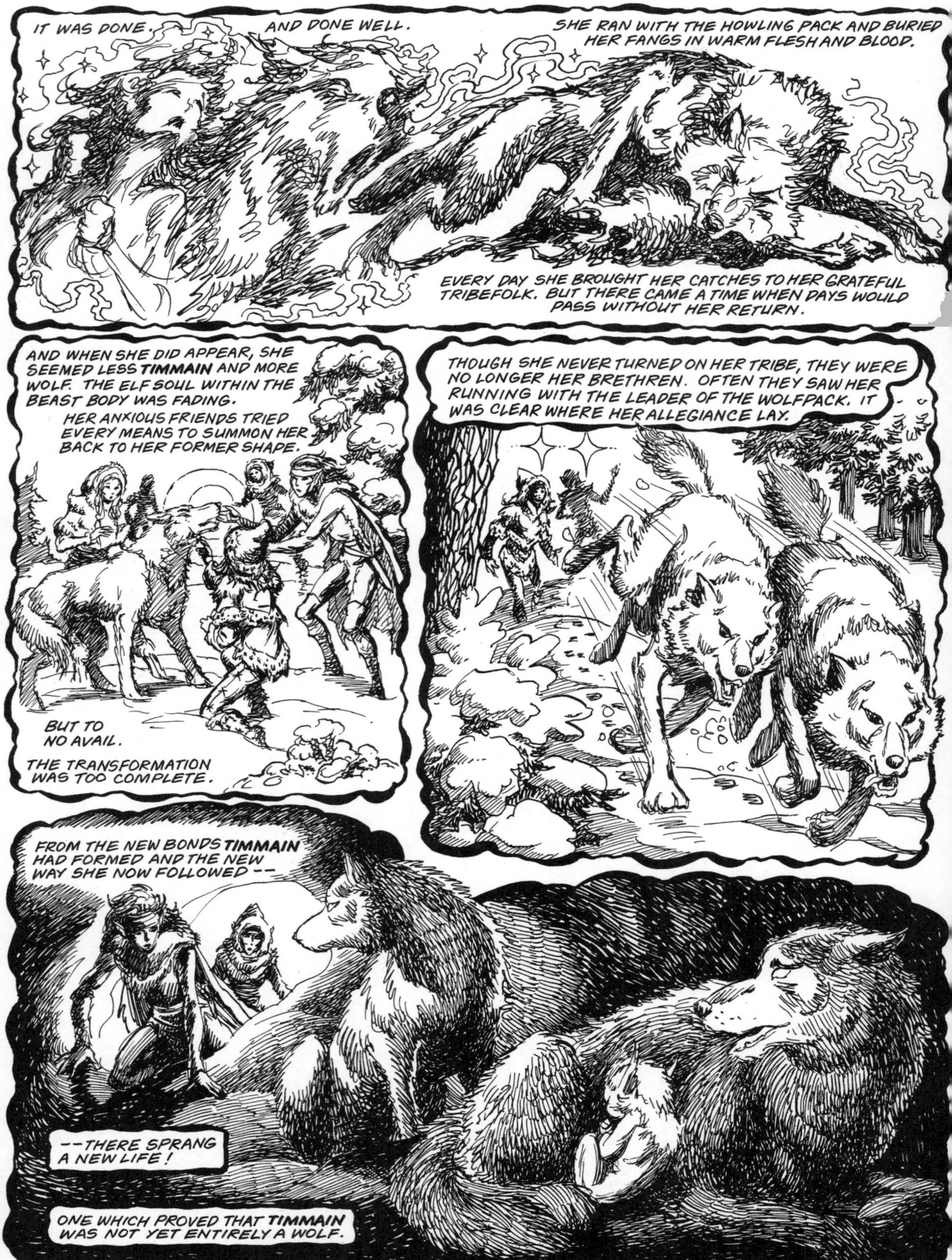

IT WAS DONE.
AND DONE WELL.
SHE RAN WITH THE HOWLING PACK AND BURIED HER FANGS IN WARM FLESH AND BLOOD.
EVERY DAY SHE BROUGHT HER CATCHES TO HER GRATEFUL TRIBEFOLK. BUT THERE CAME A TIME WHEN DAYS WOULD PASS WITHOUT HER RETURN.
AND WHEN SHE DID APPEAR, SHE SEEMED LESS TIMMAIN AND MORE WOLF. THE ELF SOUL WITHIN THE BEAST BODY WAS FADING.
HER ANXIOUS FRIENDS TRIED EVERY MEANS TO SUMMON HER BACK TO HER FORMER SHAPE.
BUT TO NO AVAIL.
THE TRANSFORMATION WAS TOO COMPLETE.
THOUGH SHE NEVER TURNED ON HER TRIBE, THEY WERE NO LONGER HER BRETHREN. OFTEN THEY SAW HER RUNNING WITH THE LEADER OF THE WOLFPACK. IT WAS CLEAR WHERE HER ALLEGIANCE LAY.
FROM THE NEW BONDS TIMMAIN HAD FORMED AND THE NEW WAY SHE NOW FOLLOWED --
--THERE SPRANG A NEW LIFE!
ONE WHICH PROVED THAT TIMMAIN WAS NOT YET ENTIRELY A WOLF.

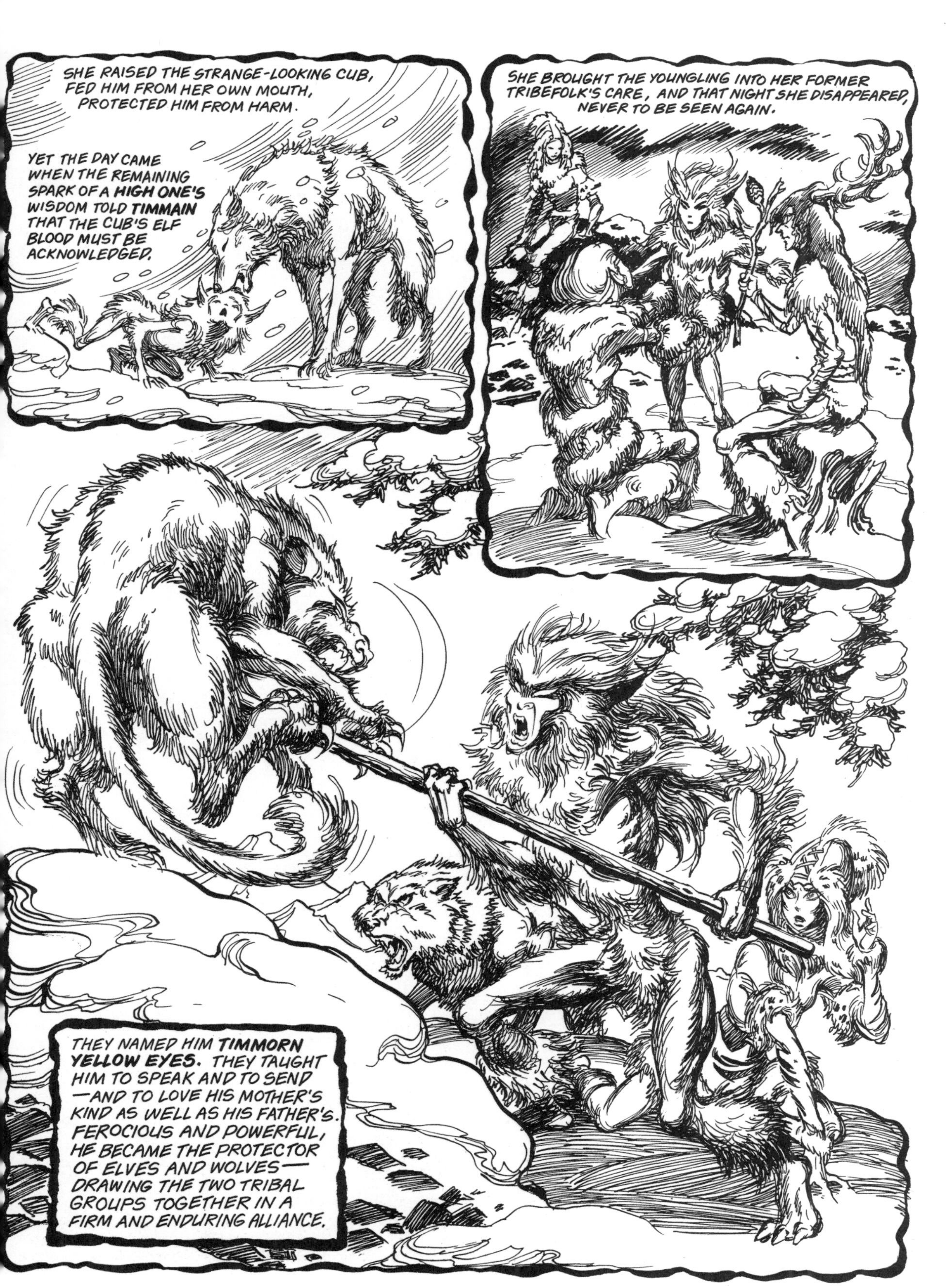
SHE RAISED THE STRANGE-LOOKING CUB, FED HIM FROM HER OWN MOUTH, PROTECTED HIM FROM HARM.
YET THE DAY CAME WHEN THE REMAINING SPARK OF A **HIGH ONE'S** WISDOM TOLD **TIMMAIN** THAT THE CUB'S ELF BLOOD MUST BE ACKNOWLEDGED.
SHE BROUGHT THE YOUNGLING INTO HER FORMER TRIBEFOLK'S CARE, AND THAT NIGHT SHE DISAPPEARED, NEVER TO BE SEEN AGAIN.
THEY NAMED HIM **TIMMORN YELLOW EYES.** THEY TAUGHT HIM TO SPEAK AND TO SEND —AND TO LOVE HIS MOTHER'S KIND AS WELL AS HIS FATHER'S. FEROCIOUS AND POWERFUL, HE BECAME THE PROTECTOR OF ELVES AND WOLVES— DRAWING THE TWO TRIBAL GROUPS TOGETHER IN A FIRM AND ENDURING ALLIANCE.

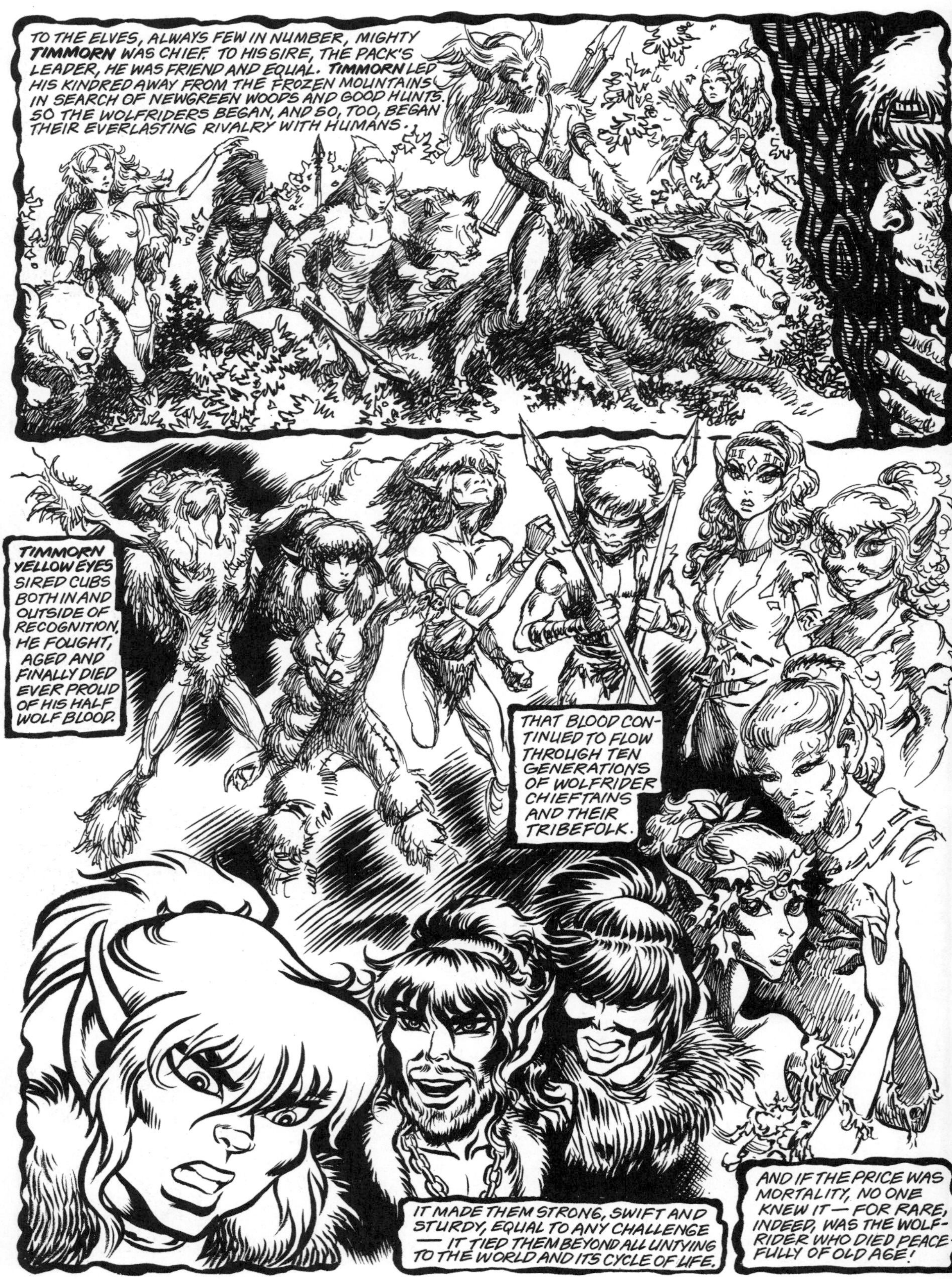
TO THE ELVES, ALWAYS FEW IN NUMBER, MIGHTY TIMMORN WAS CHIEF. TO HIS SIRE, THE PACK'S LEADER, HE WAS FRIEND AND EQUAL. TIMMORN LED HIS KINDRED AWAY FROM THE FROZEN MOUNTAINS IN SEARCH OF NEWGREEN WOODS AND GOOD HUNTS. SO THE WOLFRIDERS BEGAN, AND SO, TOO, BEGAN THEIR EVERLASTING RIVALRY WITH HUMANS.
TIMMORN YELLOW EYES SIRED CUBS BOTH IN AND OUTSIDE OF RECOGNITION. HE FOUGHT, AGED AND FINALLY DIED EVER PROUD OF HIS HALF WOLF BLOOD.
THAT BLOOD CONTINUED TO FLOW THROUGH TEN GENERATIONS OF WOLFRIDER CHIEFTAINS AND THEIR TRIBEFOLK.
IT MADE THEM STRONG, SWIFT AND STURDY, EQUAL TO ANY CHALLENGE — IT TIED THEM BEYOND ALL UNTYING TO THE WORLD AND ITS CYCLE OF LIFE.
AND IF THE PRICE WAS MORTALITY, NO ONE KNEW IT — FOR RARE, INDEED, WAS THE WOLF-RIDER WHO DIED PEACEFULLY OF OLD AGE!

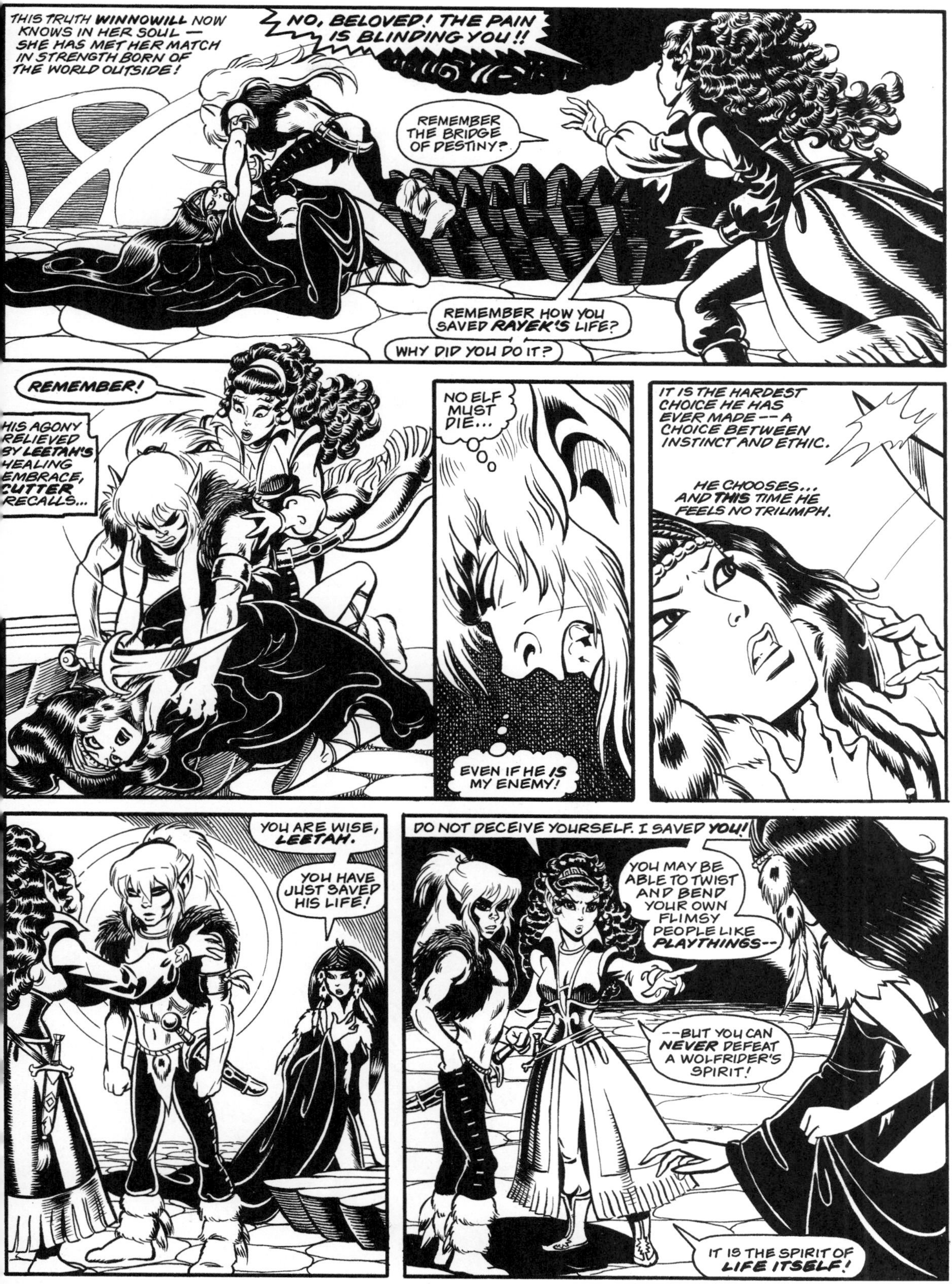
THIS TRUTH WINNOWILL NOW KNOWS IN HER SOUL — SHE HAS MET HER MATCH IN STRENGTH BORN OF THE WORLD OUTSIDE!
NO, BELOVED! THE PAIN IS BLINDING YOU!!
REMEMBER THE BRIDGE OF DESTINY?
REMEMBER HOW YOU SAVED RAYEK'S LIFE?
WHY DID YOU DO IT?
REMEMBER!
HIS AGONY RELIEVED BY LEETAH'S HEALING EMBRACE, CUTTER RECALLS...
NO ELF MUST DIE...
EVEN IF HE IS MY ENEMY!
IT IS THE HARDEST CHOICE HE HAS EVER MADE -- A CHOICE BETWEEN INSTINCT AND ETHIC.
HE CHOOSES... AND THIS TIME HE FEELS NO TRIUMPH.
YOU ARE WISE, LEETAH.
YOU HAVE JUST SAVED HIS LIFE!
DO NOT DECEIVE YOURSELF. I SAVED YOU!
YOU MAY BE ABLE TO TWIST AND BEND YOUR OWN FLIMSY PEOPLE LIKE PLAYTHINGS--
--BUT YOU CAN NEVER DEFEAT A WOLFRIDER'S SPIRIT!
IT IS THE SPIRIT OF LIFE ITSELF!

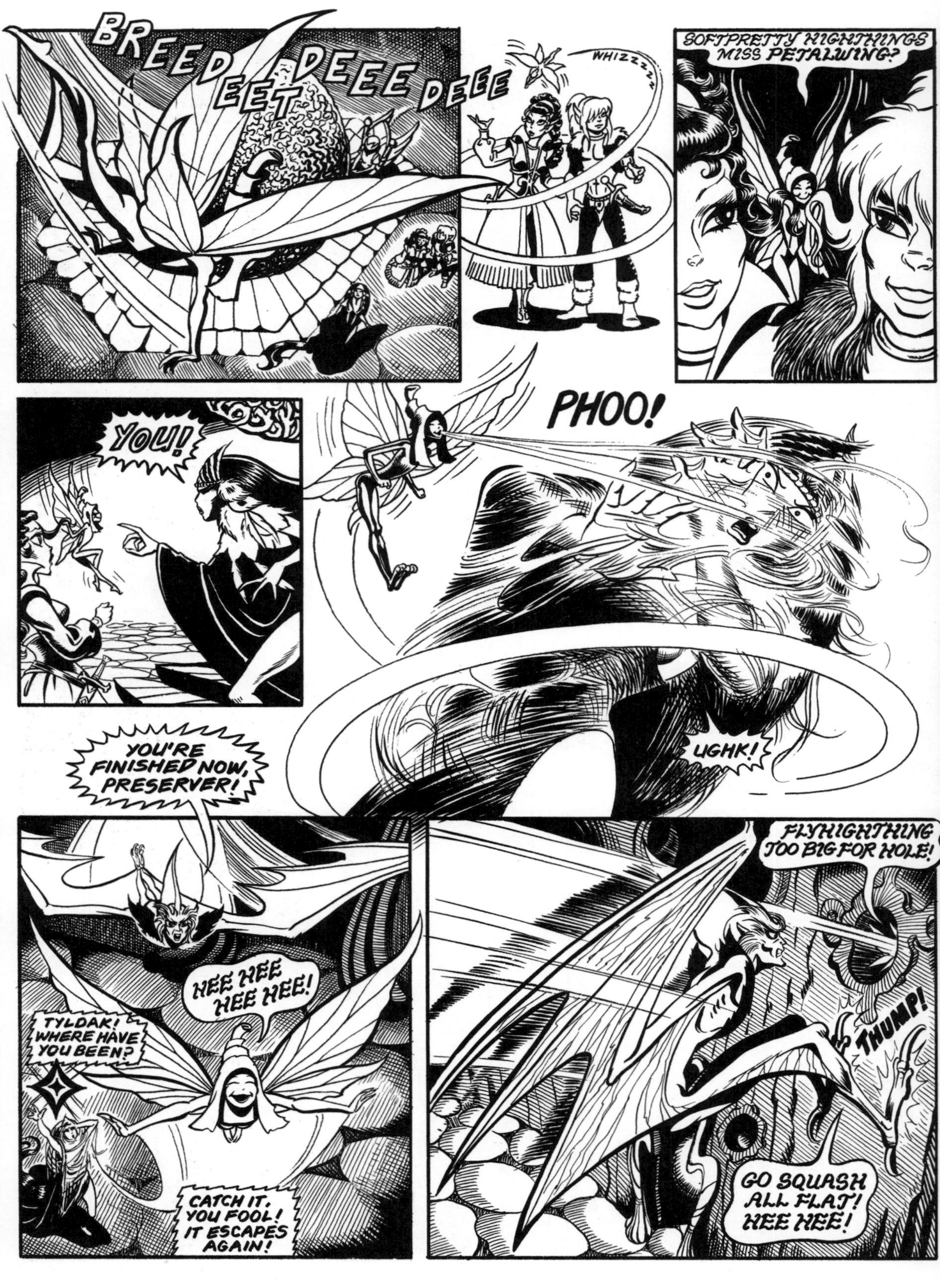
BREEDEET DEEEE DEEE
WHIZZZZZ
SOFTPRETTY HIGHTHINGS MISS PETALWING?
YOU!
PHOO!
UGHK!
YOU'RE FINISHED NOW, PRESERVER!
HEE HEE HEE HEE!
TYLDAK! WHERE HAVE YOU BEEN?
CATCH IT, YOU FOOL! IT ESCAPES AGAIN!
FLYHIGHTHING TOO BIG FOR HOLE!
THUMP!
GO SQUASH ALL FLAT! HEE HEE!

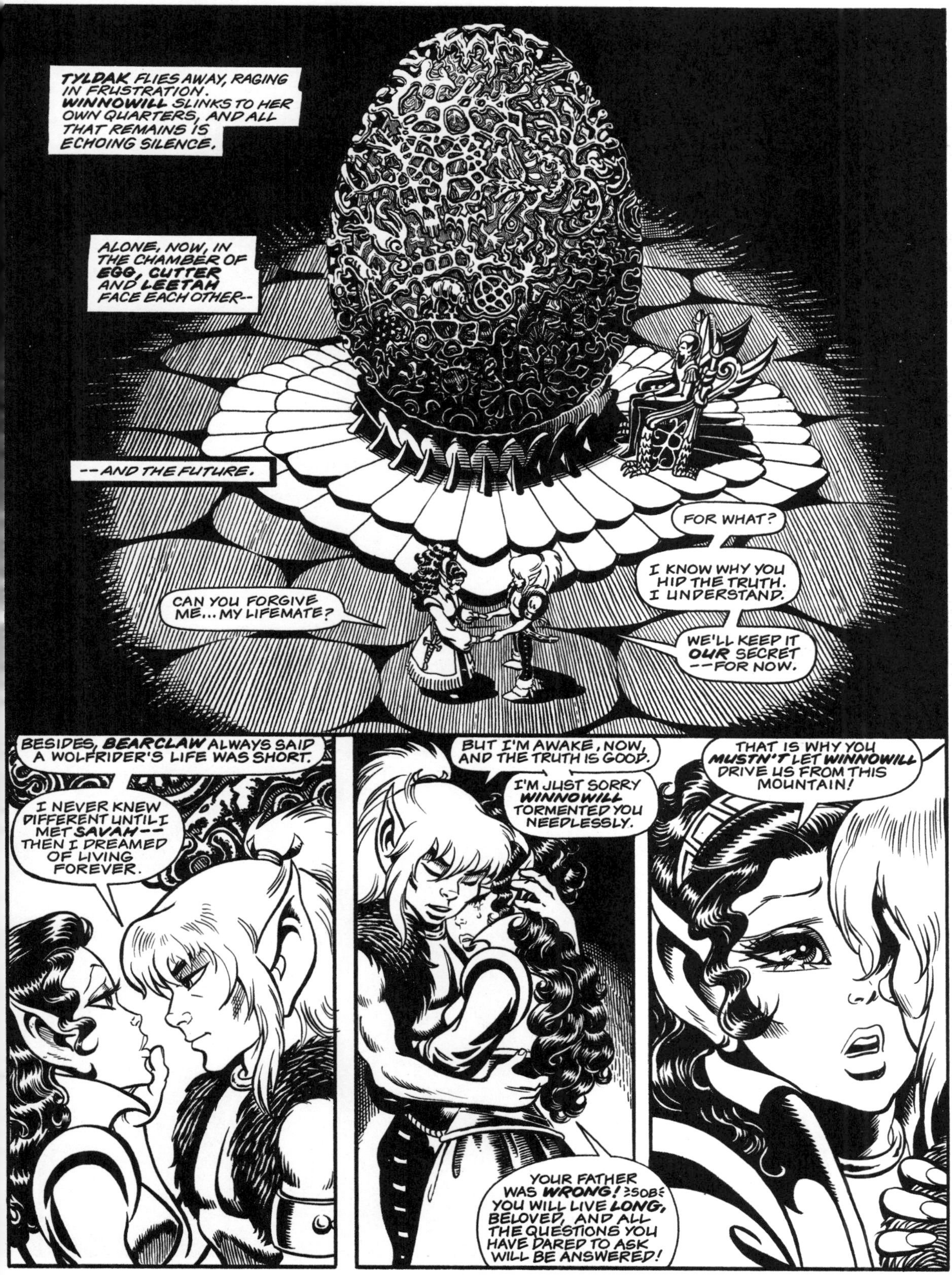
TYLDAK FLIES AWAY, RAGING IN FRUSTRATION. WINNOWILL SLINKS TO HER OWN QUARTERS, AND ALL THAT REMAINS IS ECHOING SILENCE.
ALONE, NOW, IN THE CHAMBER OF EGG, CUTTER AND LEETAH FACE EACH OTHER--
--AND THE FUTURE.
CAN YOU FORGIVE ME... MY LIFEMATE?
FOR WHAT?
I KNOW WHY YOU HID THE TRUTH. I UNDERSTAND.
WE'LL KEEP IT OUR SECRET --FOR NOW.
BESIDES, BEARCLAW ALWAYS SAID A WOLFRIDER'S LIFE WAS SHORT.
I NEVER KNEW DIFFERENT UNTIL I MET SAVAH-- THEN I DREAMED OF LIVING FOREVER.
BUT I'M AWAKE, NOW, AND THE TRUTH IS GOOD.
I'M JUST SORRY WINNOWILL TORMENTED YOU NEEDLESSLY.
YOUR FATHER WAS WRONG! >SOB< YOU WILL LIVE LONG, BELOVED, AND ALL THE QUESTIONS YOU HAVE DARED TO ASK WILL BE ANSWERED!
THAT IS WHY YOU MUSTN'T LET WINNOWILL DRIVE US FROM THIS MOUNTAIN!

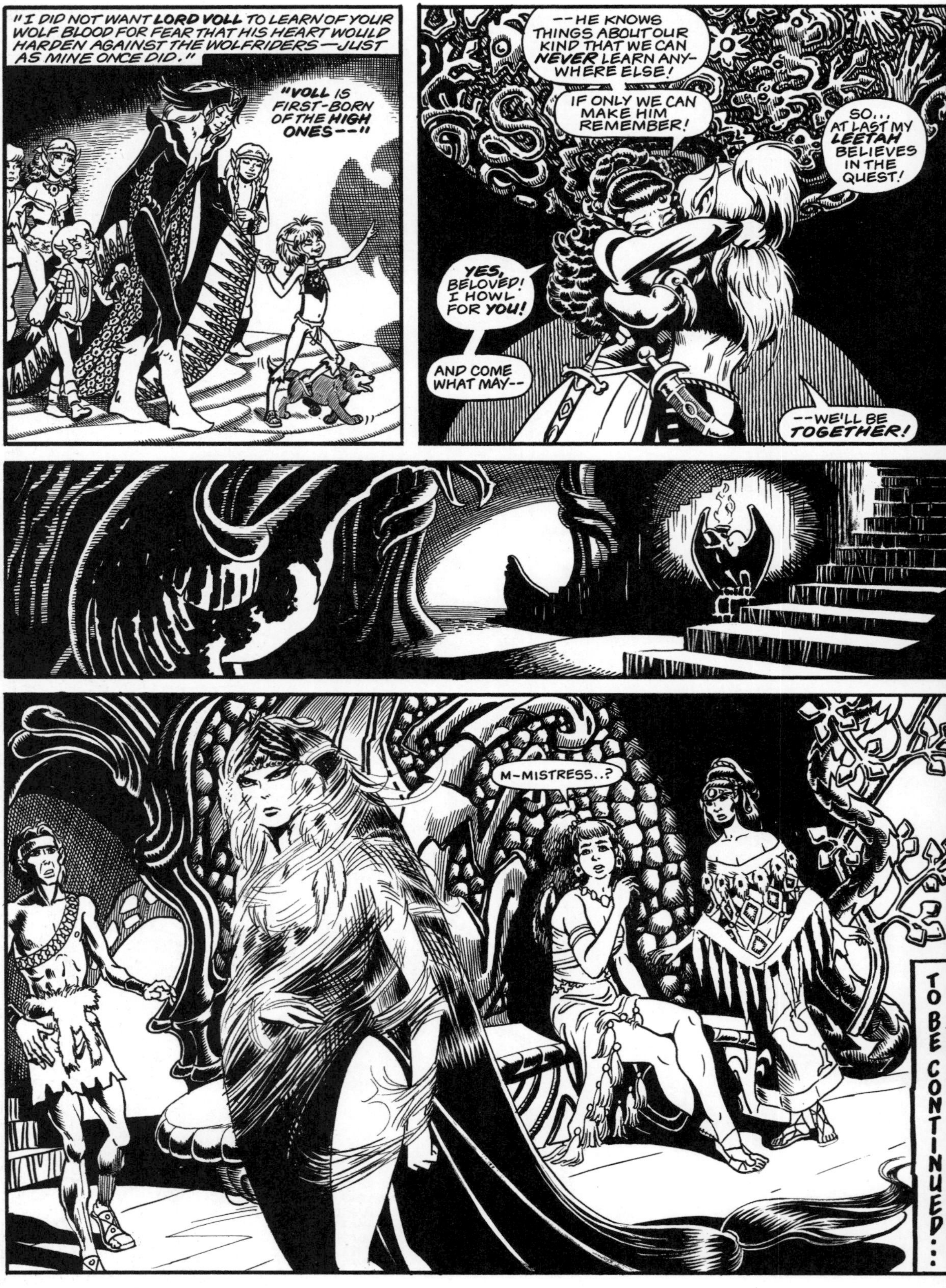
"I DID NOT WANT LORD VOLL TO LEARN OF YOUR WOLF BLOOD FOR FEAR THAT HIS HEART WOULD HARDEN AGAINST THE WOLFRIDERS—JUST AS MINE ONCE DID."
"VOLL IS FIRST-BORN OF THE HIGH ONES--"
--HE KNOWS THINGS ABOUT OUR KIND THAT WE CAN NEVER LEARN ANYWHERE ELSE!
IF ONLY WE CAN MAKE HIM REMEMBER!
SO... AT LAST MY LEETAH BELIEVES IN THE QUEST!
YES, BELOVED! I HOWL FOR YOU!
AND COME WHAT MAY--
--WE'LL BE TOGETHER!
M-MISTRESS..?
TO BE CONTINUED...

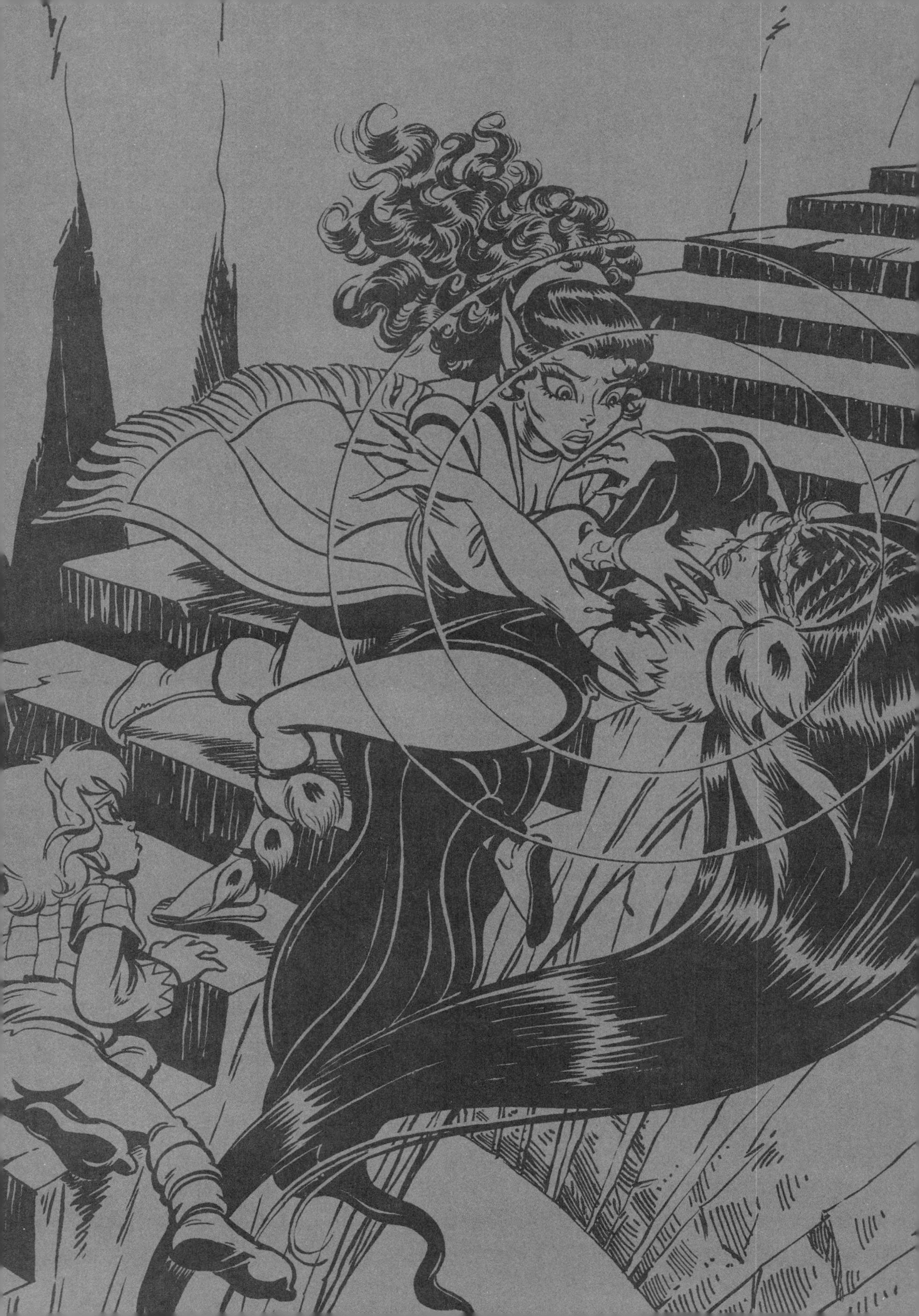

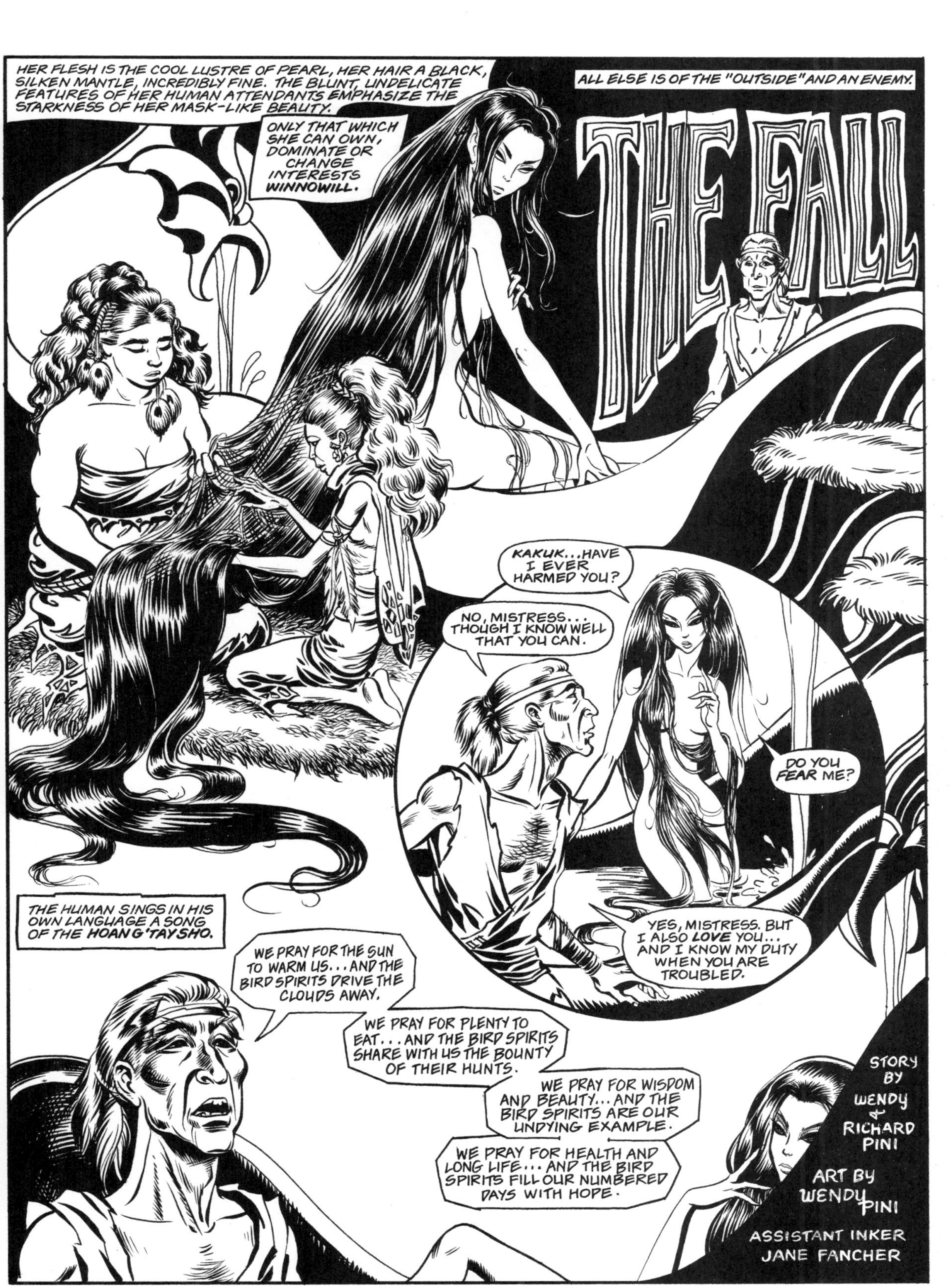
HER FLESH IS THE COOL LUSTRE OF PEARL, HER HAIR A BLACK, SILKEN MANTLE, INCREDIBLY FINE. THE BLUNT, UNDELICATE FEATURES OF HER HUMAN ATTENDANTS EMPHASIZE THE STARKNESS OF HER MASK-LIKE BEAUTY.
ONLY THAT WHICH SHE CAN OWN, DOMINATE OR CHANGE INTERESTS WINNOWILL.
ALL ELSE IS OF THE "OUTSIDE" AND AN ENEMY.
THE FALL
KAKUK... HAVE I EVER HARMED YOU?
NO, MISTRESS... THOUGH I KNOW WELL THAT YOU CAN.
DO YOU FEAR ME?
YES, MISTRESS. BUT I ALSO LOVE YOU... AND I KNOW MY DUTY WHEN YOU ARE TROUBLED.
THE HUMAN SINGS IN HIS OWN LANGUAGE A SONG OF THE HOANG'TAYSHO.
WE PRAY FOR THE SUN TO WARM US... AND THE BIRD SPIRITS DRIVE THE CLOUDS AWAY.
WE PRAY FOR PLENTY TO EAT... AND THE BIRD SPIRITS SHARE WITH US THE BOUNTY OF THEIR HUNTS.
WE PRAY FOR WISDOM AND BEAUTY... AND THE BIRD SPIRITS ARE OUR UNDYING EXAMPLE.
WE PRAY FOR HEALTH AND LONG LIFE... AND THE BIRD SPIRITS FILL OUR NUMBERED DAYS WITH HOPE.
STORY BY WENDY & RICHARD PINI
ART BY WENDY PINI
ASSISTANT INKER JANE FANCHER

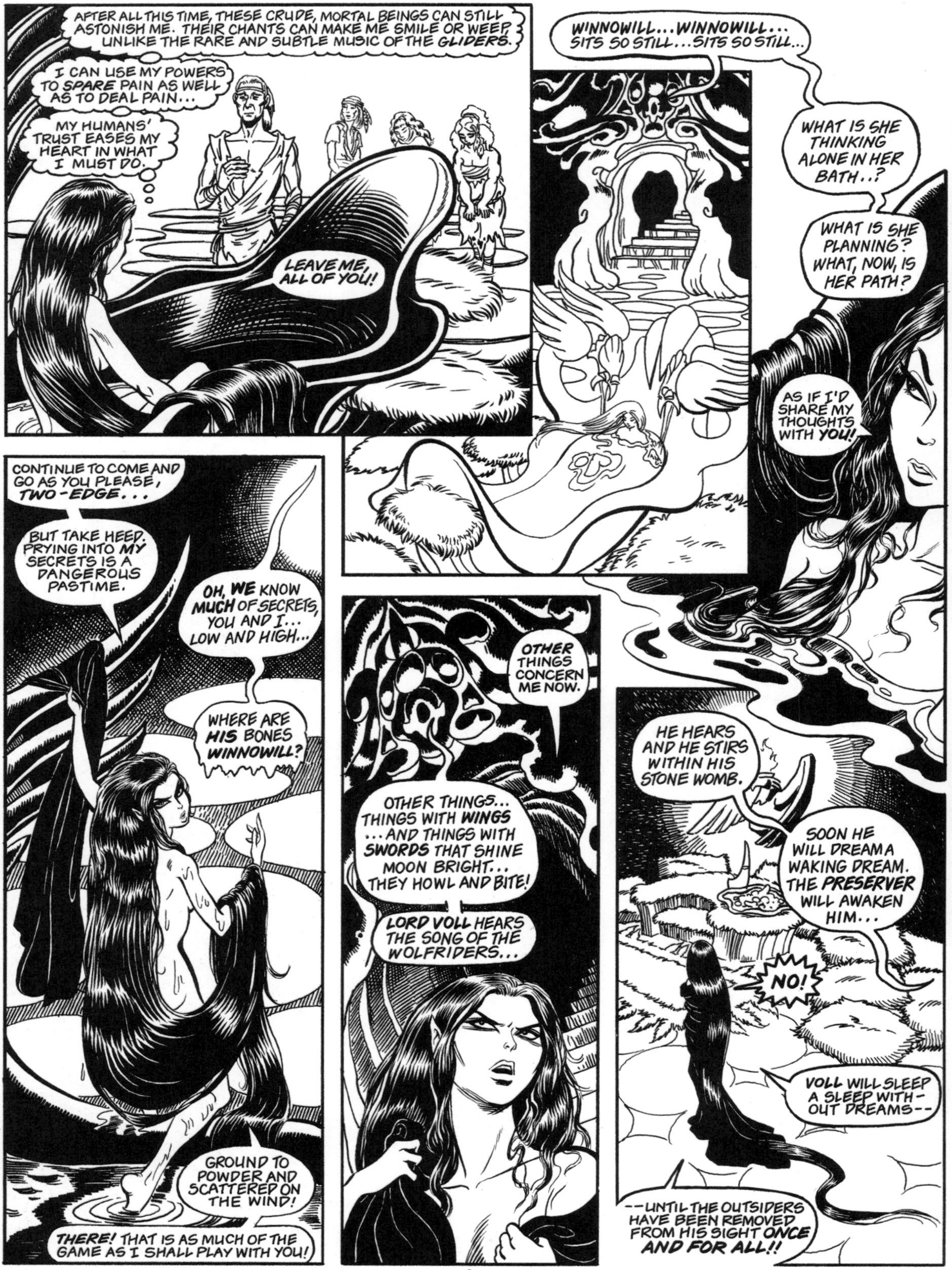

AFTER ALL THIS TIME, THESE CRUDE, MORTAL BEINGS CAN STILL ASTONISH ME. THEIR CHANTS CAN MAKE ME SMILE OR WEEP, UNLIKE THE RARE AND SUBTLE MUSIC OF THE GLIDERS.
I CAN USE MY POWERS TO SPARE PAIN AS WELL AS TO DEAL PAIN...
MY HUMANS' TRUST EASES MY HEART IN WHAT I MUST DO.
LEAVE ME, ALL OF YOU!
WINNOWILL... WINNOWILL... SITS SO STILL... SITS SO STILL...
WHAT IS SHE THINKING ALONE IN HER BATH..?
WHAT IS SHE PLANNING? WHAT, NOW, IS HER PATH?
AS IF I'D SHARE MY THOUGHTS WITH YOU!
CONTINUE TO COME AND GO AS YOU PLEASE, TWO-EDGE...
BUT TAKE HEED. PRYING INTO MY SECRETS IS A DANGEROUS PASTIME.
OH, WE KNOW MUCH OF SECRETS, YOU AND I... LOW AND HIGH...
WHERE ARE HIS BONES WINNOWILL?
GROUND TO POWDER AND SCATTERED ON THE WIND!
THERE! THAT IS AS MUCH OF THE GAME AS I SHALL PLAY WITH YOU!
OTHER THINGS CONCERN ME NOW.
OTHER THINGS... THINGS WITH WINGS ...AND THINGS WITH SWORDS THAT SHINE MOON BRIGHT... THEY HOWL AND BITE!
LORD VOLL HEARS THE SONG OF THE WOLFRIDERS...
HE HEARS AND HE STIRS WITHIN HIS STONE WOMB.
SOON HE WILL DREAM A WAKING DREAM. THE PRESERVER WILL AWAKEN HIM...
NO!
VOLL WILL SLEEP A SLEEP WITH-OUT DREAMS--
--UNTIL THE OUTSIDERS HAVE BEEN REMOVED FROM HIS SIGHT ONCE AND FOR ALL!!

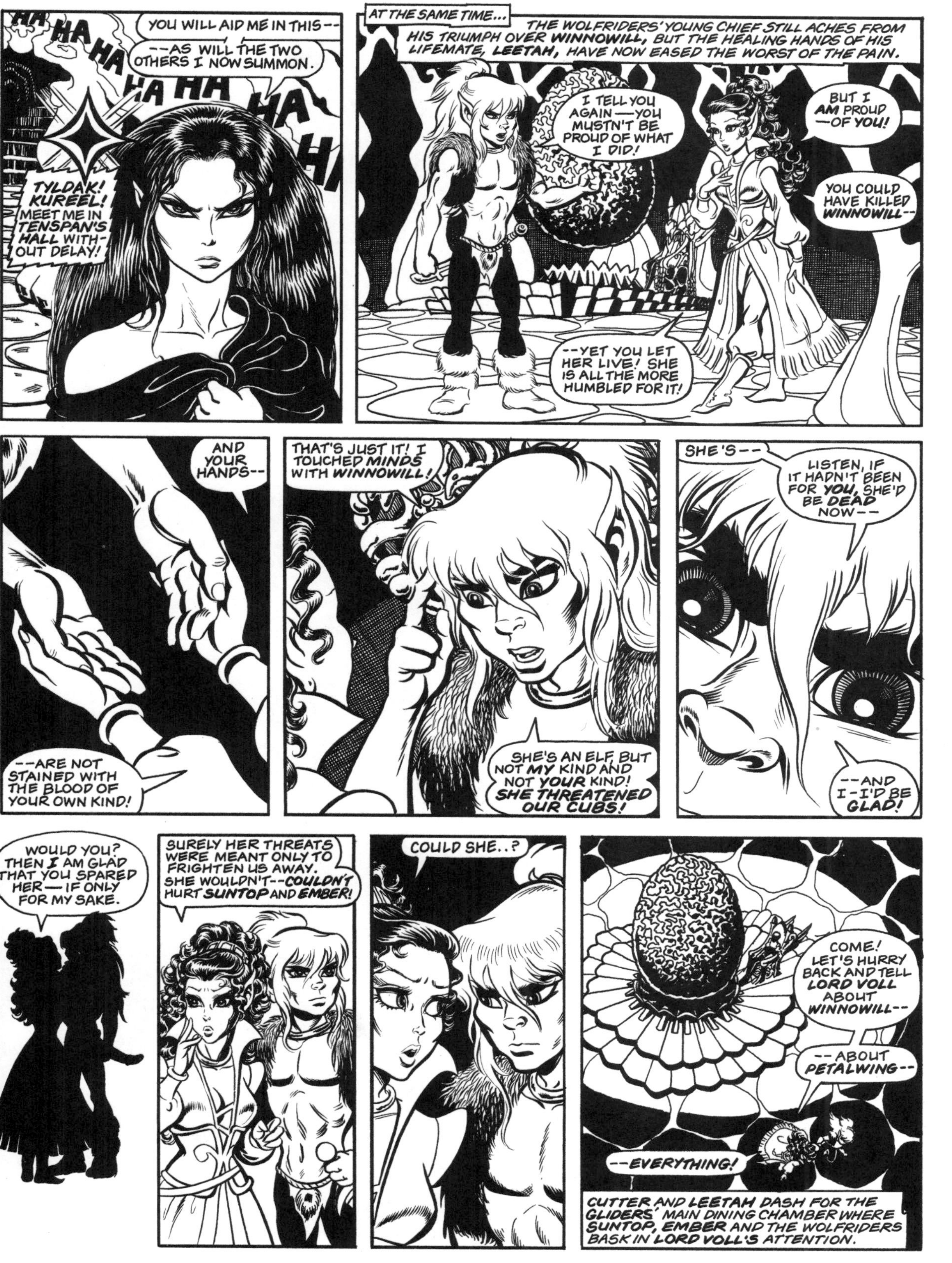
HA HA HA HA HA HA HA HA
YOU WILL AID ME IN THIS--
--AS WILL THE TWO OTHERS I NOW SUMMON.
TYLDAK! KUREEL! MEET ME IN TENSPAN'S HALL WITHOUT DELAY!
AT THE SAME TIME...
THE WOLFRIDERS' YOUNG CHIEF STILL ACHES FROM HIS TRIUMPH OVER WINNOWILL, BUT THE HEALING HANDS OF HIS LIFEMATE, LEETAH, HAVE NOW EASED THE WORST OF THE PAIN.
I TELL YOU AGAIN — YOU MUSTN'T BE PROUD OF WHAT I DID!
BUT I AM PROUD —OF YOU!
YOU COULD HAVE KILLED WINNOWILL--
--YET YOU LET HER LIVE! SHE IS ALL THE MORE HUMBLED FOR IT!
AND YOUR HANDS--
--ARE NOT STAINED WITH THE BLOOD OF YOUR OWN KIND!
THAT'S JUST IT! I TOUCHED MINDS WITH WINNOWILL!
SHE'S AN ELF, BUT NOT MY KIND AND NOT YOUR KIND! SHE THREATENED OUR CUBS!
SHE'S--
LISTEN, IF IT HADN'T BEEN FOR YOU, SHE'D BE DEAD NOW--
--AND I-I'D BE GLAD!
WOULD YOU? THEN I AM GLAD THAT YOU SPARED HER — IF ONLY FOR MY SAKE.
SURELY HER THREATS WERE MEANT ONLY TO FRIGHTEN US AWAY. SHE WOULDN'T--COULDN'T HURT SUNTOP AND EMBER!
COULD SHE..?
COME! LET'S HURRY BACK AND TELL LORD VOLL ABOUT WINNOWILL--
--ABOUT PETALWING--
--EVERYTHING!
CUTTER AND LEETAH DASH FOR THE GLIDERS' MAIN DINING CHAMBER WHERE SUNTOP, EMBER AND THE WOLFRIDERS BASK IN LORD VOLL'S ATTENTION.

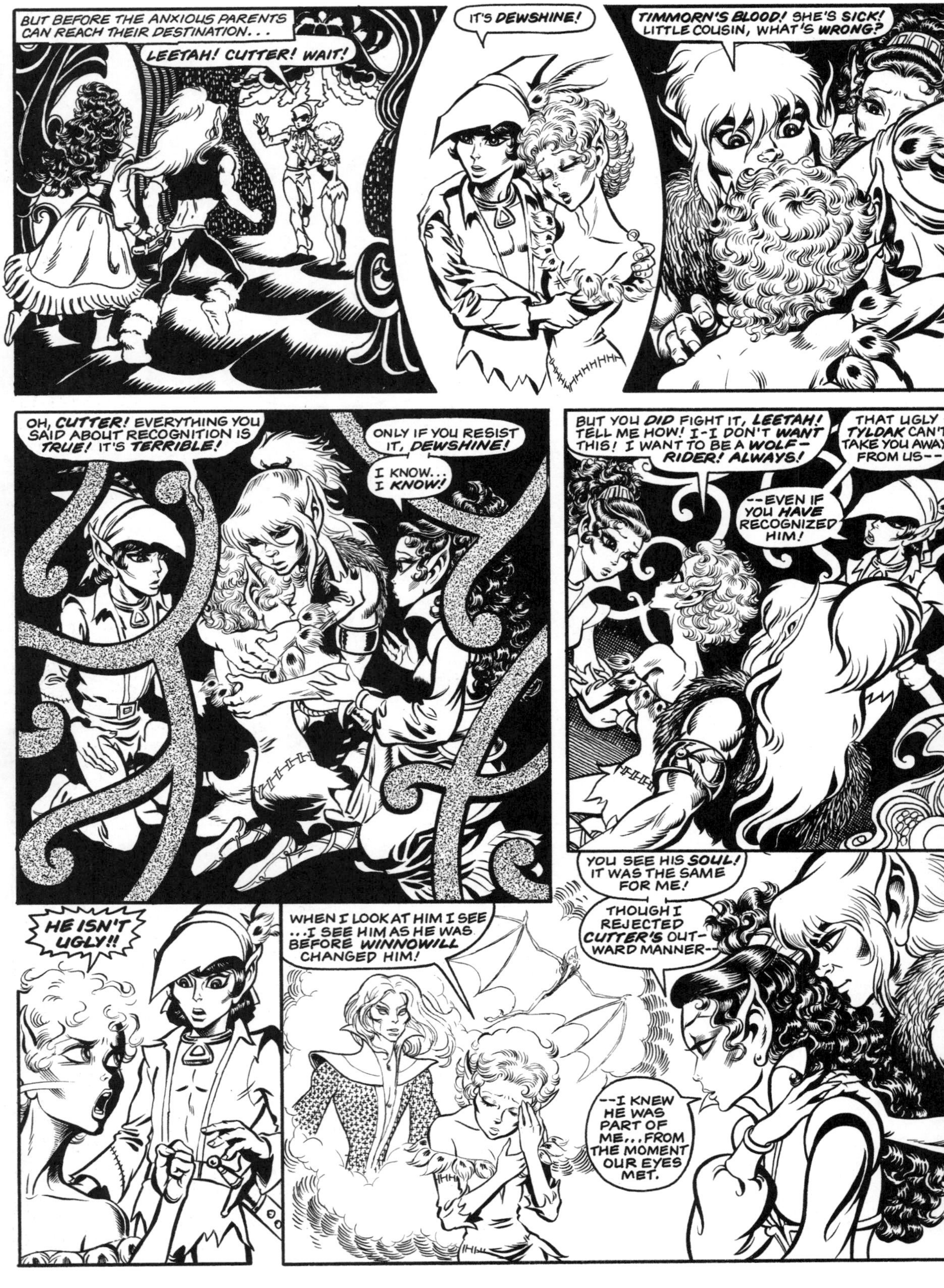

BUT BEFORE THE ANXIOUS PARENTS CAN REACH THEIR DESTINATION...
LEETAH! CUTTER! WAIT!
IT'S DEWSHINE!
TIMMORN'S BLOOD! SHE'S SICK! LITTLE COUSIN, WHAT'S WRONG?
OH, CUTTER! EVERYTHING YOU SAID ABOUT RECOGNITION IS TRUE! IT'S TERRIBLE!
ONLY IF YOU RESIST IT, DEWSHINE!
I KNOW... I KNOW!
BUT YOU DID FIGHT IT, LEETAH! TELL ME HOW! I-I DON'T WANT THIS! I WANT TO BE A WOLF-RIDER! ALWAYS!
THAT UGLY TYLDAK CAN'T TAKE YOU AWAY FROM US--
--EVEN IF YOU HAVE RECOGNIZED HIM!
HE ISN'T UGLY!!
WHEN I LOOK AT HIM I SEE ...I SEE HIM AS HE WAS BEFORE WINNOWILL CHANGED HIM!
YOU SEE HIS SOUL! IT WAS THE SAME FOR ME!
THOUGH I REJECTED CUTTER'S OUTWARD MANNER--
--I KNEW HE WAS PART OF ME... FROM THE MOMENT OUR EYES MET.

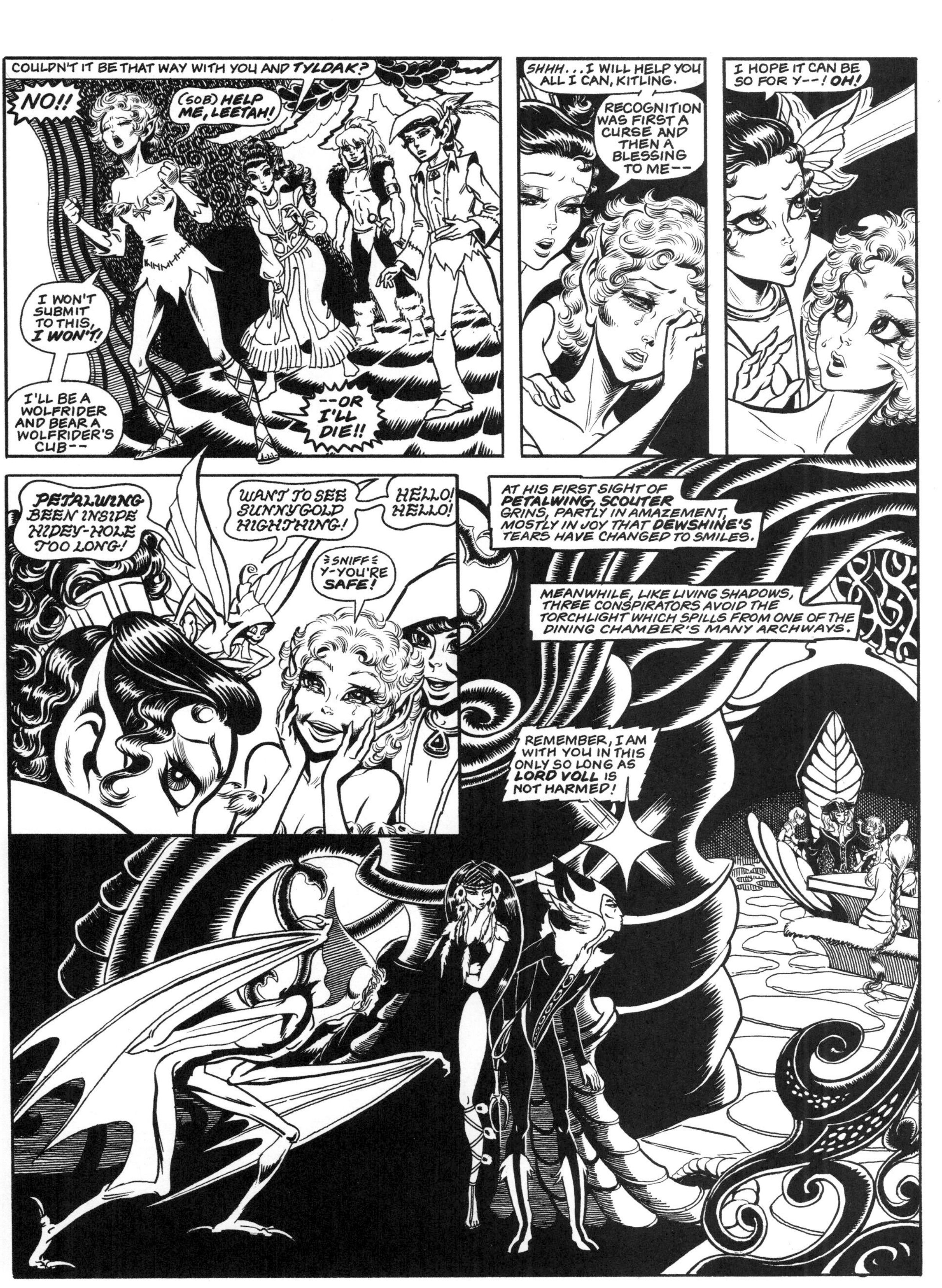

COULDN'T IT BE THAT WAY WITH YOU AND TYLDAK?
NO!!
(SOB) HELP ME, LEETAH!
I WON'T SUBMIT TO THIS, I WON'T!
I'LL BE A WOLFRIDER AND BEAR A WOLFRIDER'S CUB--
--OR I'LL DIE!!
SHHH...I WILL HELP YOU ALL I CAN, KITLING.
RECOGNITION WAS FIRST A CURSE AND THEN A BLESSING TO ME--
I HOPE IT CAN BE SO FOR Y--! OH!
PETALWING BEEN INSIDE HIDEY-HOLE TOO LONG!
WANT TO SEE SUNNYGOLD HIGHTHING!
HELLO! HELLO!
SNIFF Y-YOU'RE SAFE!
AT HIS FIRST SIGHT OF PETALWING, SCOUTER GRINS, PARTLY IN AMAZEMENT, MOSTLY IN JOY THAT DEWSHINE'S TEARS HAVE CHANGED TO SMILES.
MEANWHILE, LIKE LIVING SHADOWS, THREE CONSPIRATORS AVOID THE TORCHLIGHT WHICH SPILLS FROM ONE OF THE DINING CHAMBER'S MANY ARCHWAYS.
REMEMBER, I AM WITH YOU IN THIS ONLY SO LONG AS LORD VOLL IS NOT HARMED!

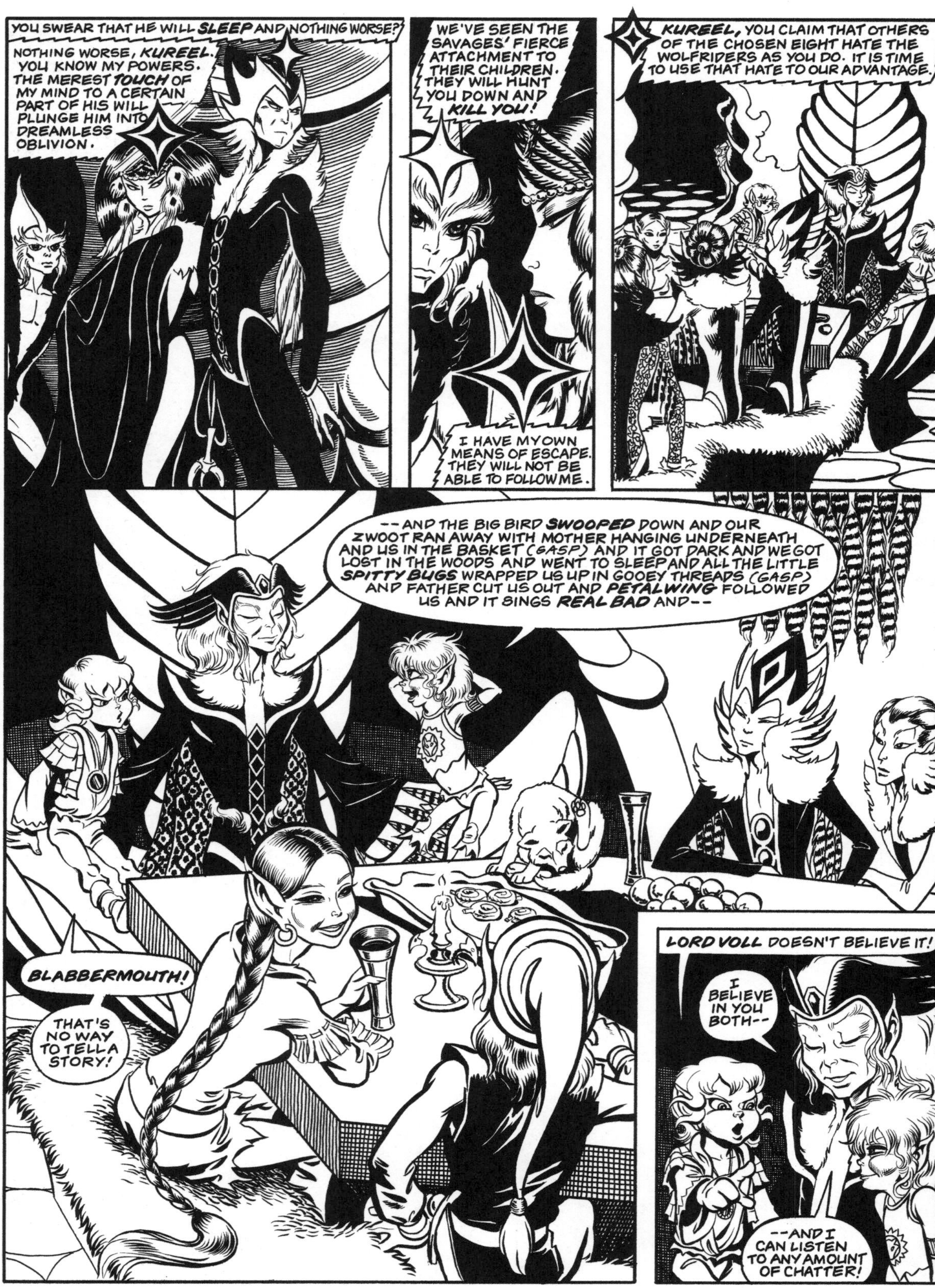
YOU SWEAR THAT HE WILL SLEEP AND NOTHING WORSE?
NOTHING WORSE, KUREEL. YOU KNOW MY POWERS. THE MEREST TOUCH OF MY MIND TO A CERTAIN PART OF HIS WILL PLUNGE HIM INTO DREAMLESS OBLIVION.
WE'VE SEEN THE SAVAGES' FIERCE ATTACHMENT TO THEIR CHILDREN. THEY WILL HUNT YOU DOWN AND KILL YOU!
I HAVE MY OWN MEANS OF ESCAPE. THEY WILL NOT BE ABLE TO FOLLOW ME.
KUREEL, YOU CLAIM THAT OTHERS OF THE CHOSEN EIGHT HATE THE WOLFRIDERS AS YOU DO. IT IS TIME TO USE THAT HATE TO OUR ADVANTAGE.
--AND THE BIG BIRD SWOOPED DOWN AND OUR ZWOOT RAN AWAY WITH MOTHER HANGING UNDERNEATH AND US IN THE BASKET (GASP) AND IT GOT DARK AND WE GOT LOST IN THE WOODS AND WENT TO SLEEP AND ALL THE LITTLE SPITTY BUGS WRAPPED US UP IN GOOEY THREADS (GASP) AND FATHER CUT US OUT AND PETALWING FOLLOWED US AND IT SINGS REAL BAD AND--
BLABBERMOUTH!
THAT'S NO WAY TO TELL A STORY!
LORD VOLL DOESN'T BELIEVE IT!
I BELIEVE IN YOU BOTH--
--AND I CAN LISTEN TO ANY AMOUNT OF CHATTER!

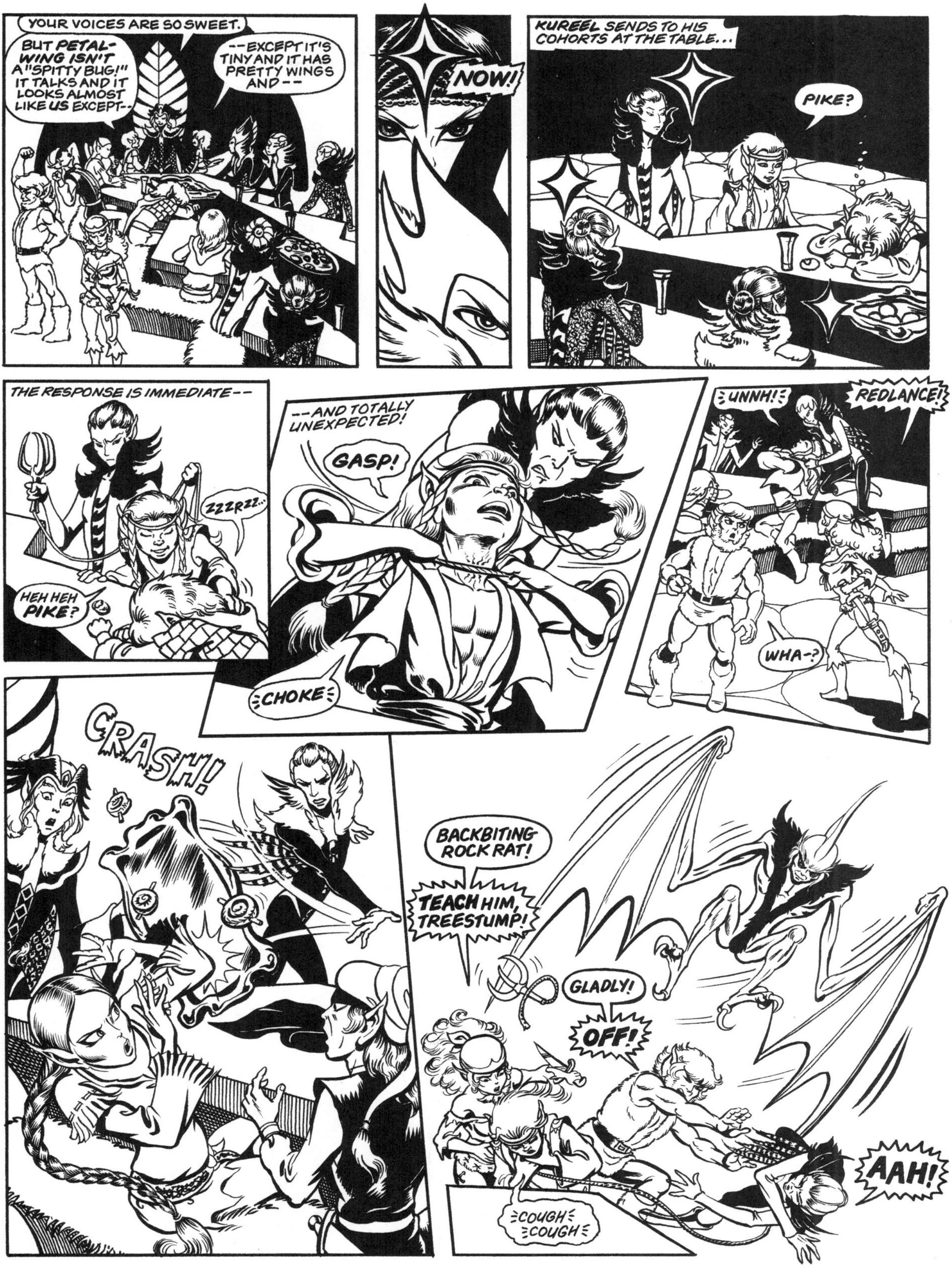
YOUR VOICES ARE SO SWEET.
BUT PETAL-WING ISN'T A "SPITTY BUG!" IT TALKS AND IT LOOKS ALMOST LIKE US EXCEPT--
--EXCEPT IT'S TINY AND IT HAS PRETTY WINGS AND--
NOW!
KUREEL SENDS TO HIS COHORTS AT THE TABLE...
PIKE?
THE RESPONSE IS IMMEDIATE--
ZZZRZZ...
HEH HEH PIKE?
--AND TOTALLY UNEXPECTED!
GASP!
CHOKE
UNNH!
REDLANCE!
WHA-?
CRASH!
BACKBITING ROCK RAT!
TEACH HIM, TREESTUMP!
GLADLY!
OFF!
AAH!
COUGH COUGH

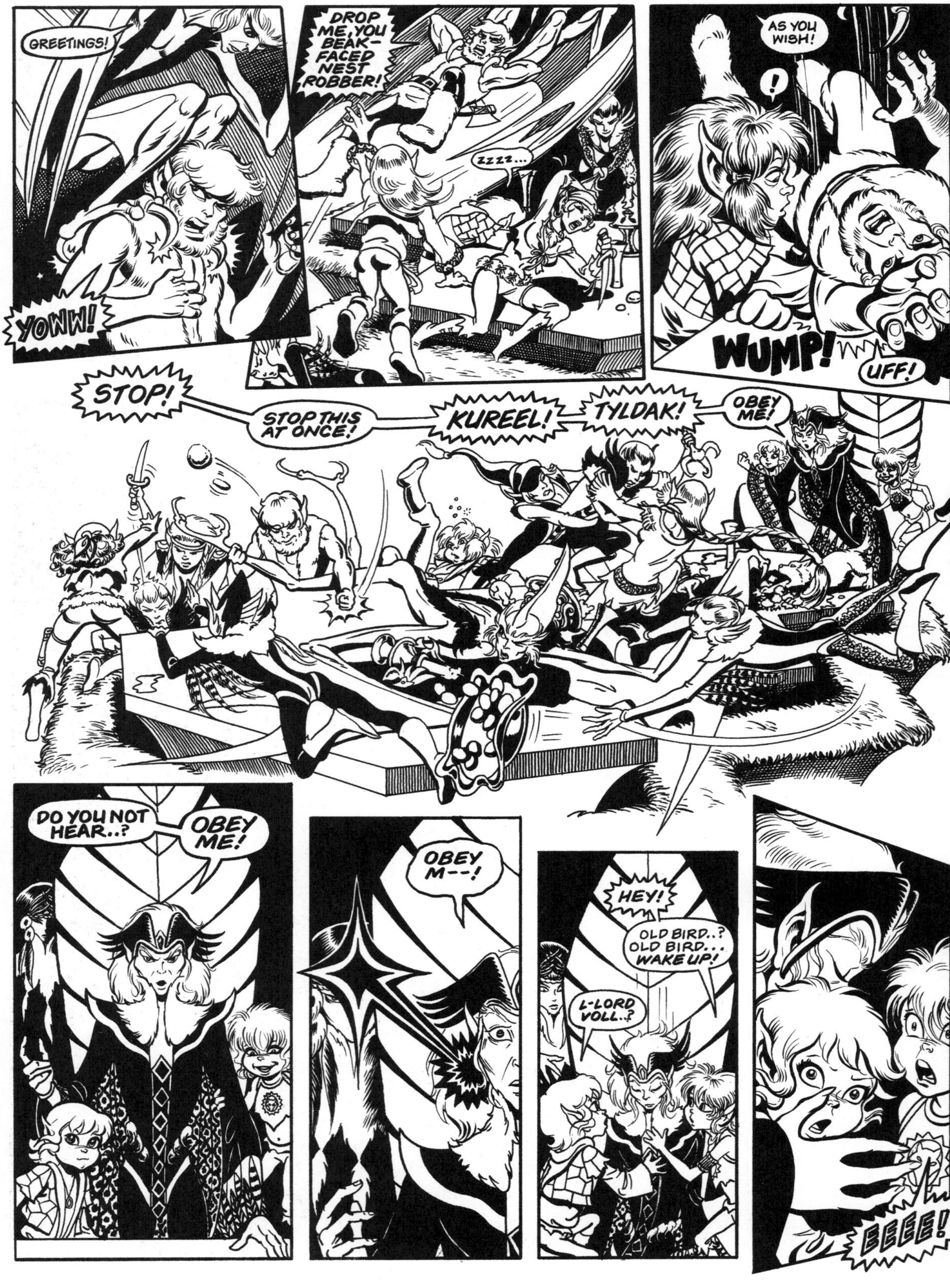

GREETINGS!
YOWW!
DROP ME, YOU BEAK-FACED NEST ROBBER!
ZZZZ...
AS YOU WISH!
!
WUMP!
UFF!
STOP!
STOP THIS AT ONCE!
KUREEL!
TYLDAK!
OBEY ME!
DO YOU NOT HEAR..?
OBEY ME!
OBEY M--!
HEY!
OLD BIRD..? OLD BIRD... WAKE UP!
L-LORD VOLL..?
BEEE!

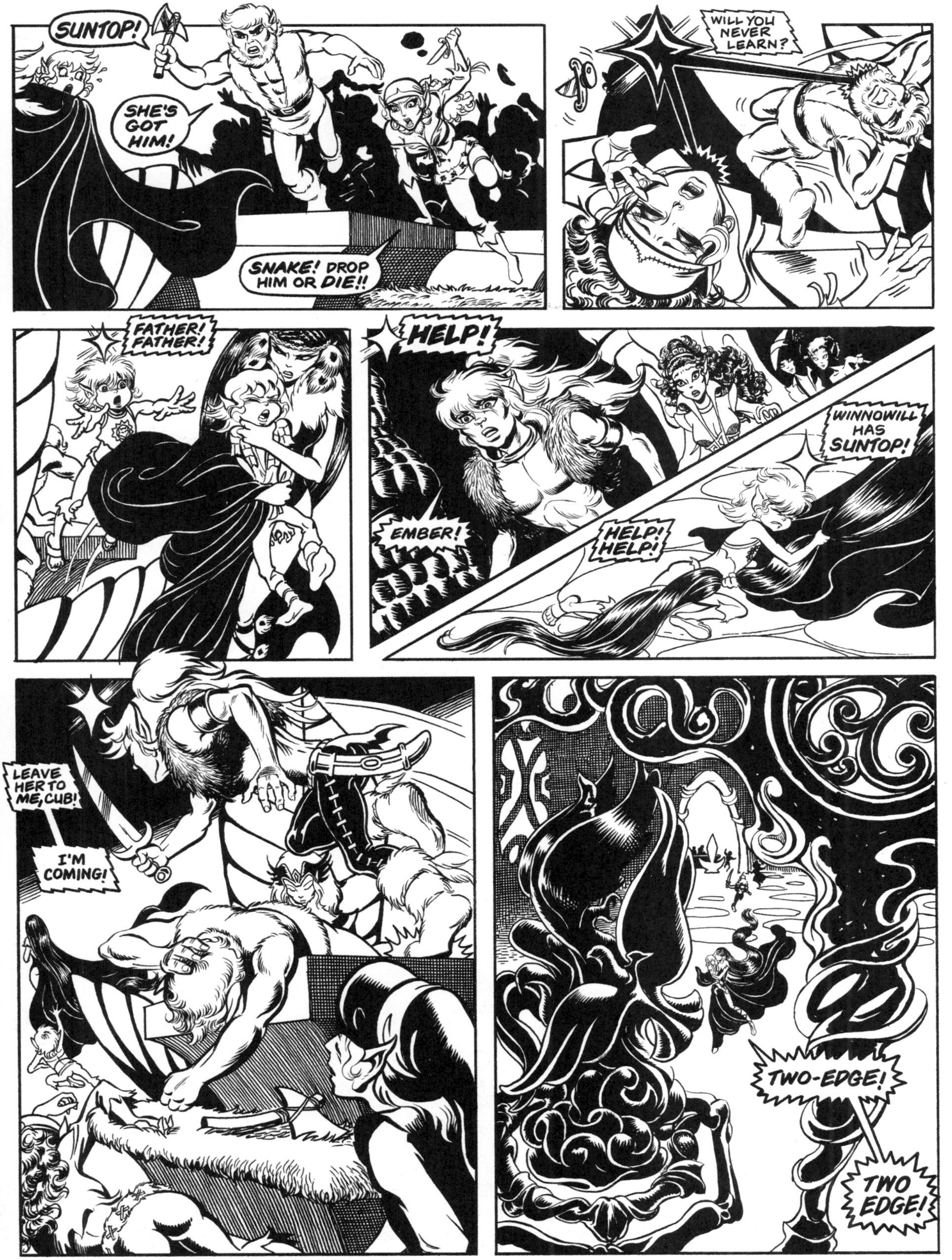
SUNTOP!
SHE'S GOT HIM!
SNAKE! DROP HIM OR DIE!!
WILL YOU NEVER LEARN?
FATHER! FATHER!
HELP!
EMBER!
WINNOWILL HAS SUNTOP!
HELP! HELP!
LEAVE HER TO ME, CUB!
I'M COMING!
TWO-EDGE!
TWO EDGE!

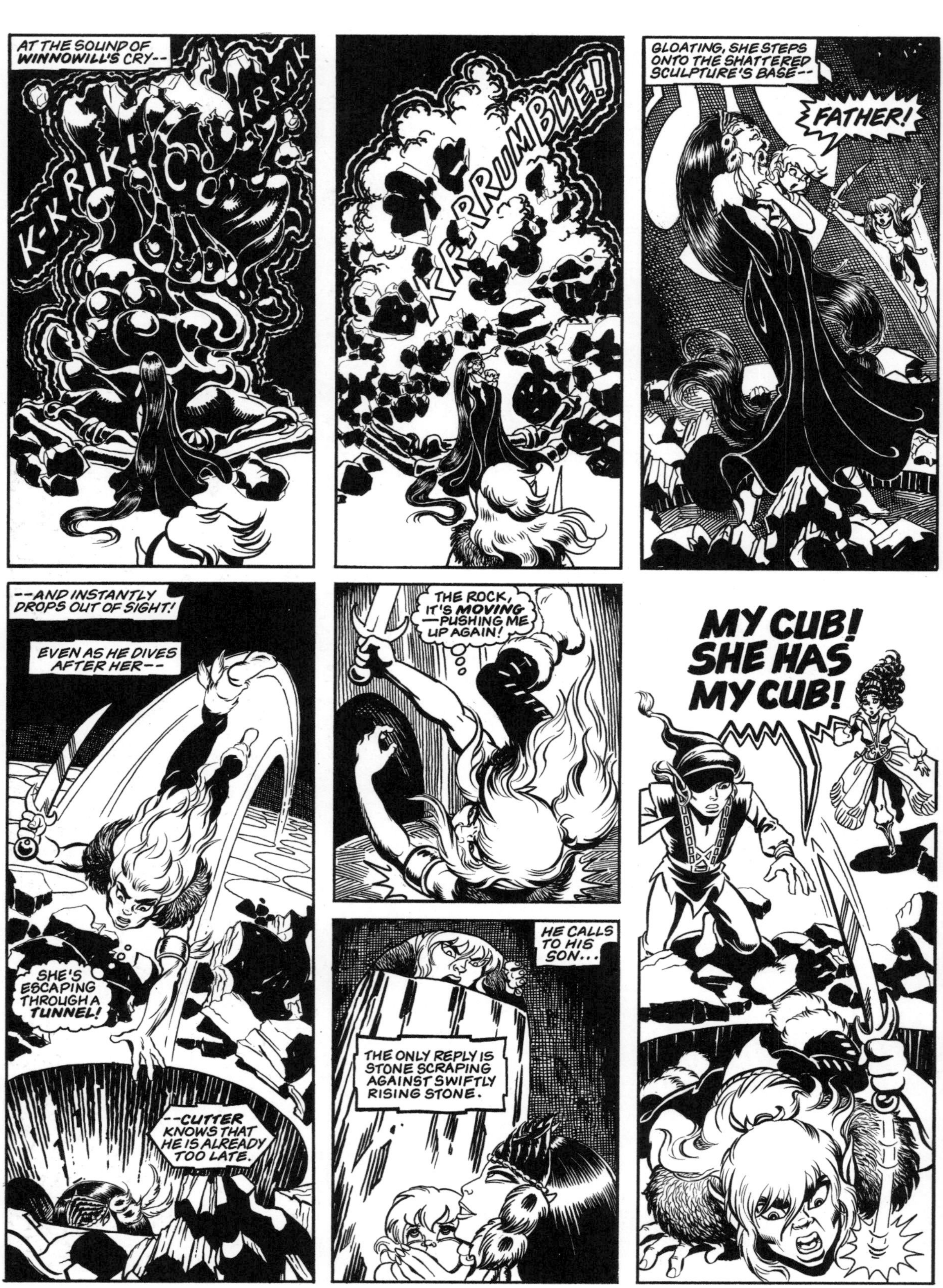
AT THE SOUND OF WINNOWILL'S CRY--
K-KRIK!
KRRAK
K-RRRUMBLE!
GLOATING, SHE STEPS ONTO THE SHATTERED SCULPTURE'S BASE--
FATHER!
--AND INSTANTLY DROPS OUT OF SIGHT!
EVEN AS HE DIVES AFTER HER--
SHE'S ESCAPING THROUGH A TUNNEL!
--CUTTER KNOWS THAT HE IS ALREADY TOO LATE.
THE ROCK, IT'S MOVING --PUSHING ME UP AGAIN!
HE CALLS TO HIS SON...
THE ONLY REPLY IS STONE SCRAPING AGAINST SWIFTLY RISING STONE.
MY CUB! SHE HAS MY CUB!

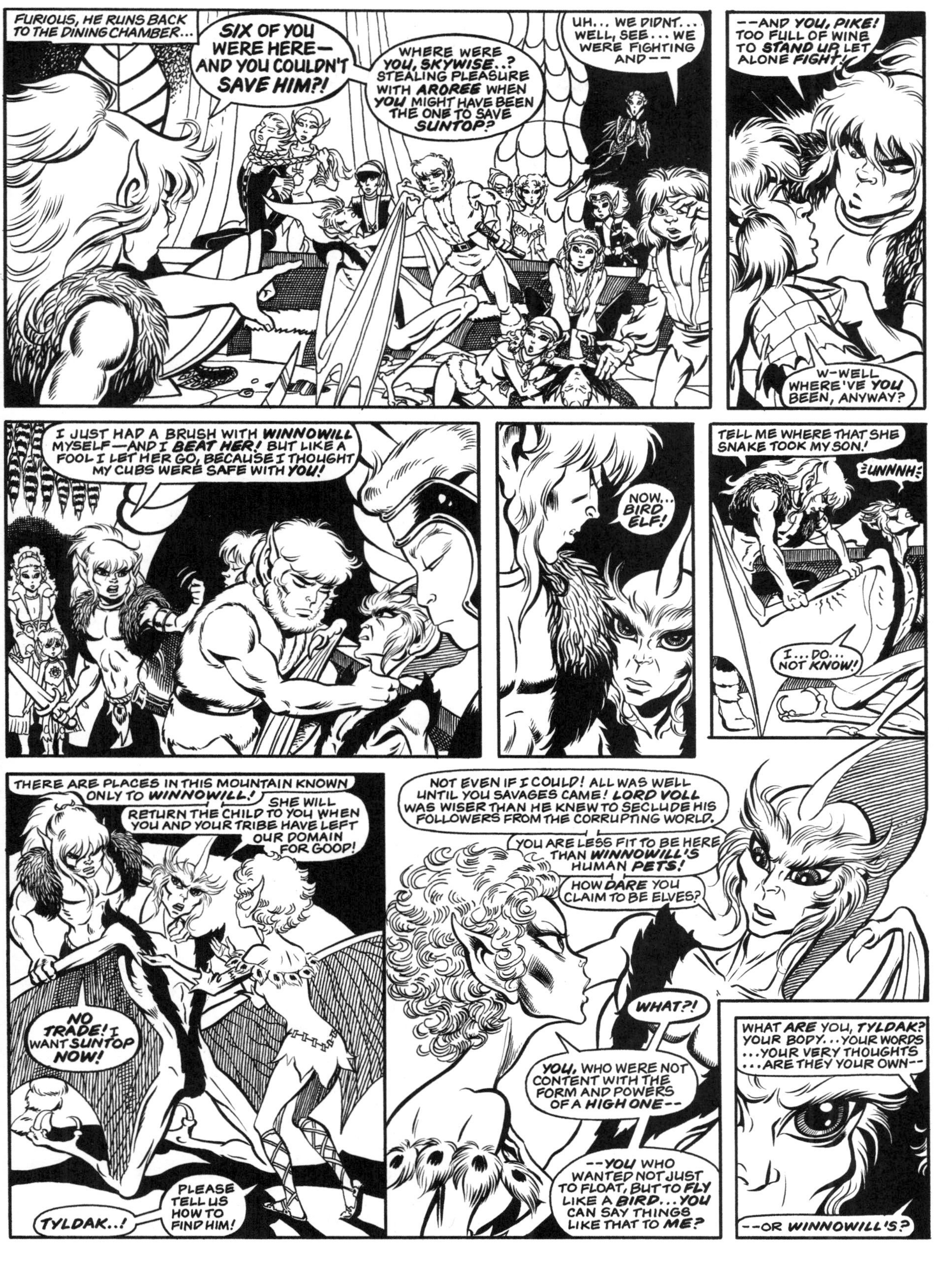

FURIOUS, HE RUNS BACK TO THE DINING CHAMBER...
SIX OF YOU WERE HERE— AND YOU COULDN'T SAVE HIM?!
WHERE WERE YOU, SKYWISE..? STEALING PLEASURE WITH AROREE WHEN YOU MIGHT HAVE BEEN THE ONE TO SAVE SUNTOP?
UH... WE DIDNT... WELL, SEE... WE WERE FIGHTING AND--
--AND YOU, PIKE! TOO FULL OF WINE TO STAND UP, LET ALONE FIGHT!
W-WELL WHERE'VE YOU BEEN, ANYWAY?
I JUST HAD A BRUSH WITH WINNOWILL MYSELF—AND I BEAT HER! BUT LIKE A FOOL I LET HER GO, BECAUSE I THOUGHT MY CUBS WERE SAFE WITH YOU!
NOW... BIRD ELF!
TELL ME WHERE THAT SHE SNAKE TOOK MY SON!
UNNNH!
I... DO... NOT KNOW!
THERE ARE PLACES IN THIS MOUNTAIN KNOWN ONLY TO WINNOWILL!
SHE WILL RETURN THE CHILD TO YOU WHEN YOU AND YOUR TRIBE HAVE LEFT OUR DOMAIN FOR GOOD!
NO TRADE! I WANT SUNTOP NOW!
TYLDAK..!
PLEASE TELL US HOW TO FIND HIM!
NOT EVEN IF I COULD! ALL WAS WELL UNTIL YOU SAVAGES CAME! LORD VOLL WAS WISER THAN HE KNEW TO SECLUDE HIS FOLLOWERS FROM THE CORRUPTING WORLD.
YOU ARE LESS FIT TO BE HERE THAN WINNOWILL'S HUMAN PETS!
HOW DARE YOU CLAIM TO BE ELVES?
WHAT?!
YOU, WHO WERE NOT CONTENT WITH THE FORM AND POWERS OF A HIGH ONE--
--YOU WHO WANTED NOT JUST TO FLOAT, BUT TO FLY LIKE A BIRD... YOU CAN SAY THINGS LIKE THAT TO ME?
WHAT ARE YOU, TYLDAK? YOUR BODY... YOUR WORDS ...YOUR VERY THOUGHTS ...ARE THEY YOUR OWN--
--OR WINNOWILL'S?

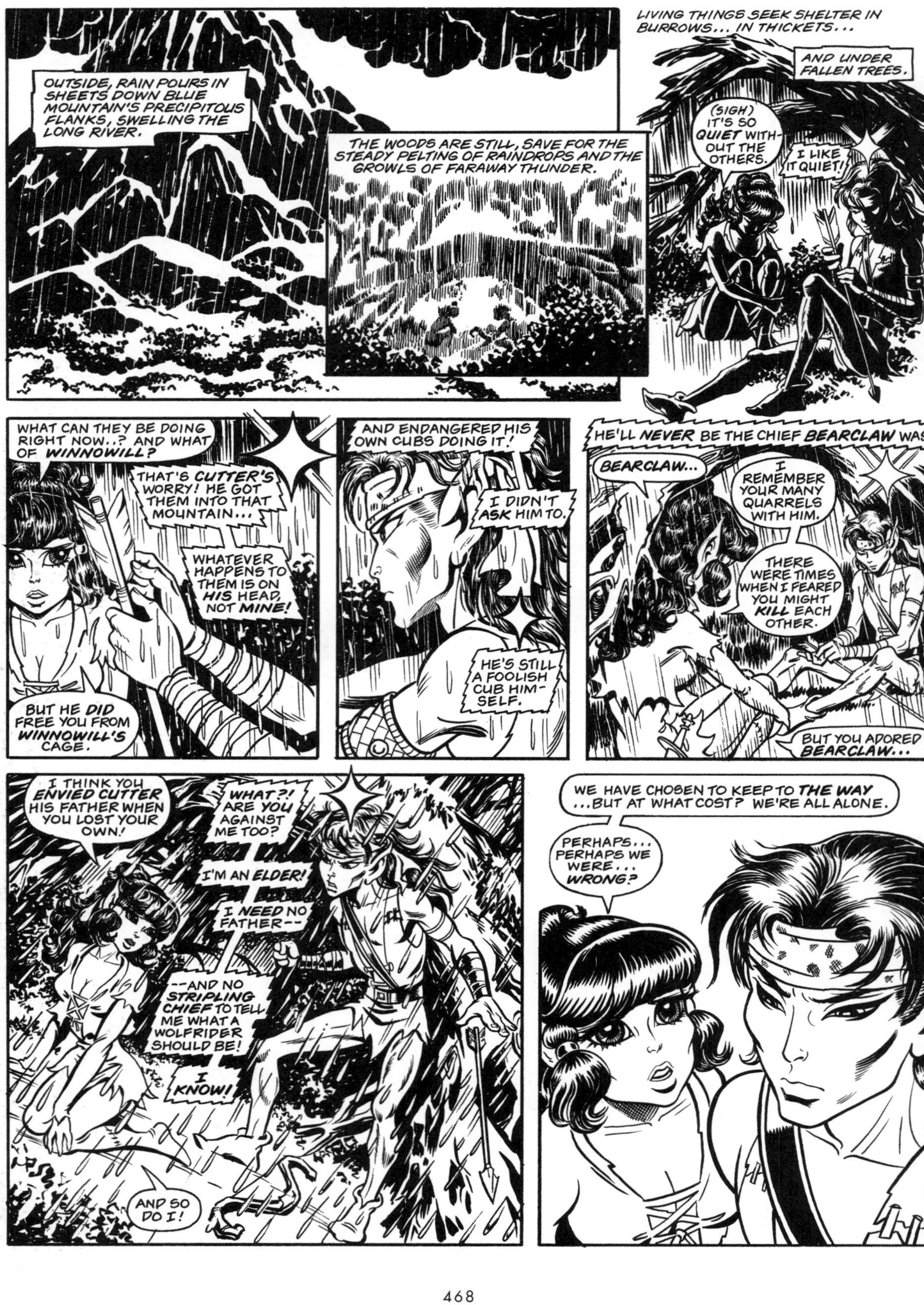
OUTSIDE, RAIN POURS IN SHEETS DOWN BLUE MOUNTAIN'S PRECIPITOUS FLANKS, SWELLING THE LONG RIVER.
THE WOODS ARE STILL, SAVE FOR THE STEADY PELTING OF RAINDROPS AND THE GROWLS OF FARAWAY THUNDER.
LIVING THINGS SEEK SHELTER IN BURROWS... IN THICKETS...
AND UNDER FALLEN TREES.
(SIGH) IT'S SO QUIET WITHOUT THE OTHERS.
I LIKE IT QUIET!
WHAT CAN THEY BE DOING RIGHT NOW..? AND WHAT OF WINNOWILL?
THAT'S CUTTER'S WORRY! HE GOT THEM INTO THAT MOUNTAIN...
WHATEVER HAPPENS TO THEM IS ON HIS HEAD, NOT MINE!
BUT HE DID FREE YOU FROM WINNOWILL'S CAGE.
AND ENDANGERED HIS OWN CUBS DOING IT!
I DIDN'T ASK HIM TO.
HE'S STILL A FOOLISH CUB HIMSELF.
HE'LL NEVER BE THE CHIEF BEARCLAW WAS.
BEARCLAW...
I REMEMBER YOUR MANY QUARRELS WITH HIM.
THERE WERE TIMES WHEN I FEARED YOU MIGHT KILL EACH OTHER.
BUT YOU ADORED BEARCLAW...
I THINK YOU ENVIED CUTTER HIS FATHER WHEN YOU LOST YOUR OWN!
WHAT?! ARE YOU AGAINST ME TOO?
I'M AN ELDER!
I NEED NO FATHER--
--AND NO STRIPLING CHIEF TO TELL ME WHAT A WOLFRIDER SHOULD BE!
I KNOW!
AND SO DO I!
WE HAVE CHOSEN TO KEEP TO THE WAY ...BUT AT WHAT COST? WE'RE ALL ALONE.
PERHAPS... PERHAPS WE WERE... WRONG?

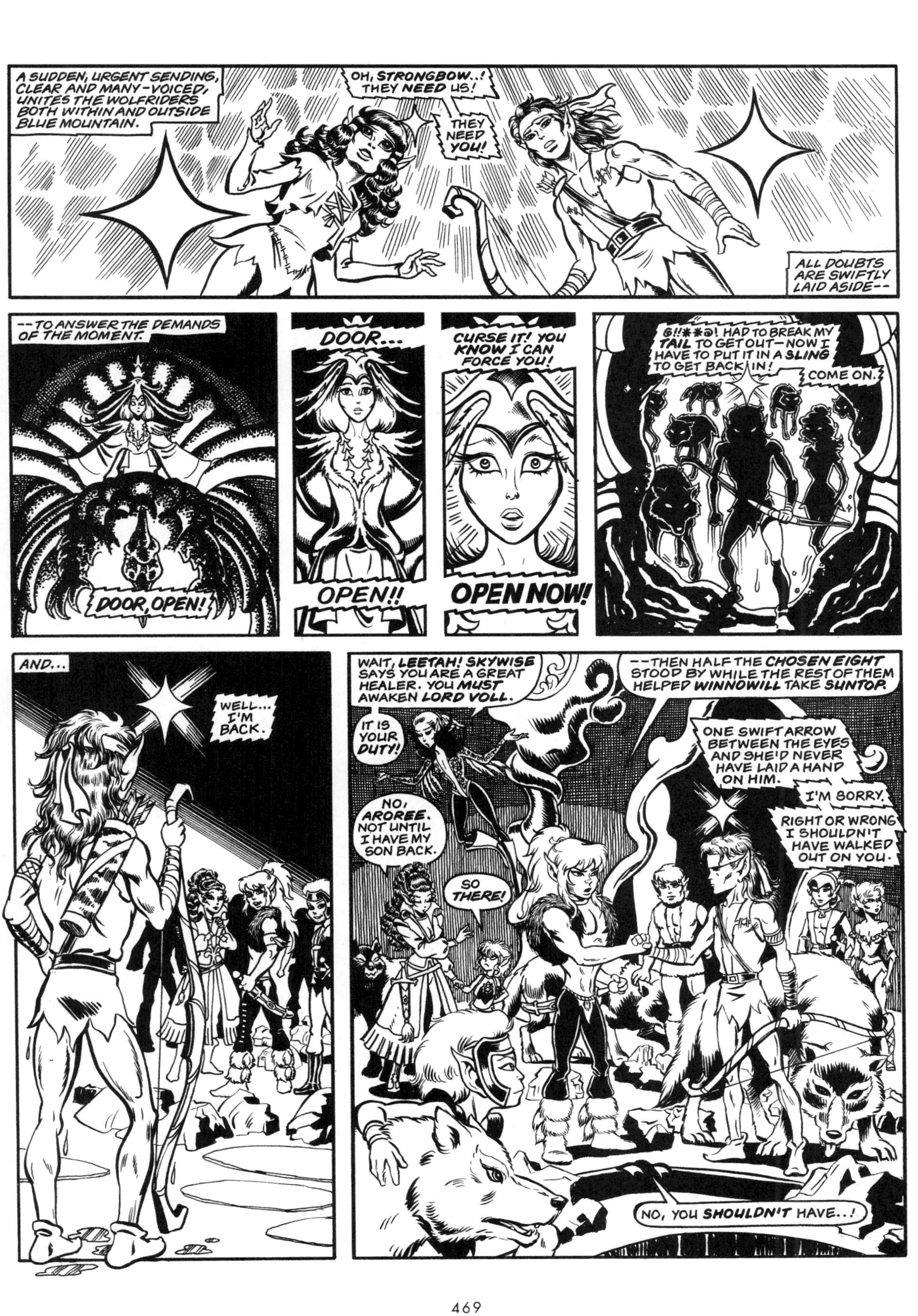

A SUDDEN, URGENT SENDING, CLEAR AND MANY-VOICED, UNITES THE WOLFRIDERS BOTH WITHIN AND OUTSIDE BLUE MOUNTAIN.
OH, STRONGBOW..! THEY NEED US!
THEY NEED YOU!
ALL DOUBTS ARE SWIFTLY LAID ASIDE--
--TO ANSWER THE DEMANDS OF THE MOMENT.
DOOR, OPEN!
DOOR...
OPEN!!
CURSE IT! YOU KNOW I CAN FORCE YOU!
OPEN NOW!
G!!✱✱∂! HAD TO BREAK MY TAIL TO GET OUT—NOW I HAVE TO PUT IT IN A SLING TO GET BACK IN!
COME ON.
AND...
WELL... I'M BACK.
WAIT, LEETAH! SKYWISE SAYS YOU ARE A GREAT HEALER. YOU MUST AWAKEN LORD VOLL.
IT IS YOUR DUTY!
NO, AROREE. NOT UNTIL I HAVE MY SON BACK.
SO THERE!
--THEN HALF THE CHOSEN EIGHT STOOD BY WHILE THE REST OF THEM HELPED WINNOWILL TAKE SUNTOP.
ONE SWIFT ARROW BETWEEN THE EYES AND SHE'D NEVER HAVE LAID A HAND ON HIM.
I'M SORRY.
RIGHT OR WRONG I SHOULDN'T HAVE WALKED OUT ON YOU.
NO, YOU SHOULDN'T HAVE..!

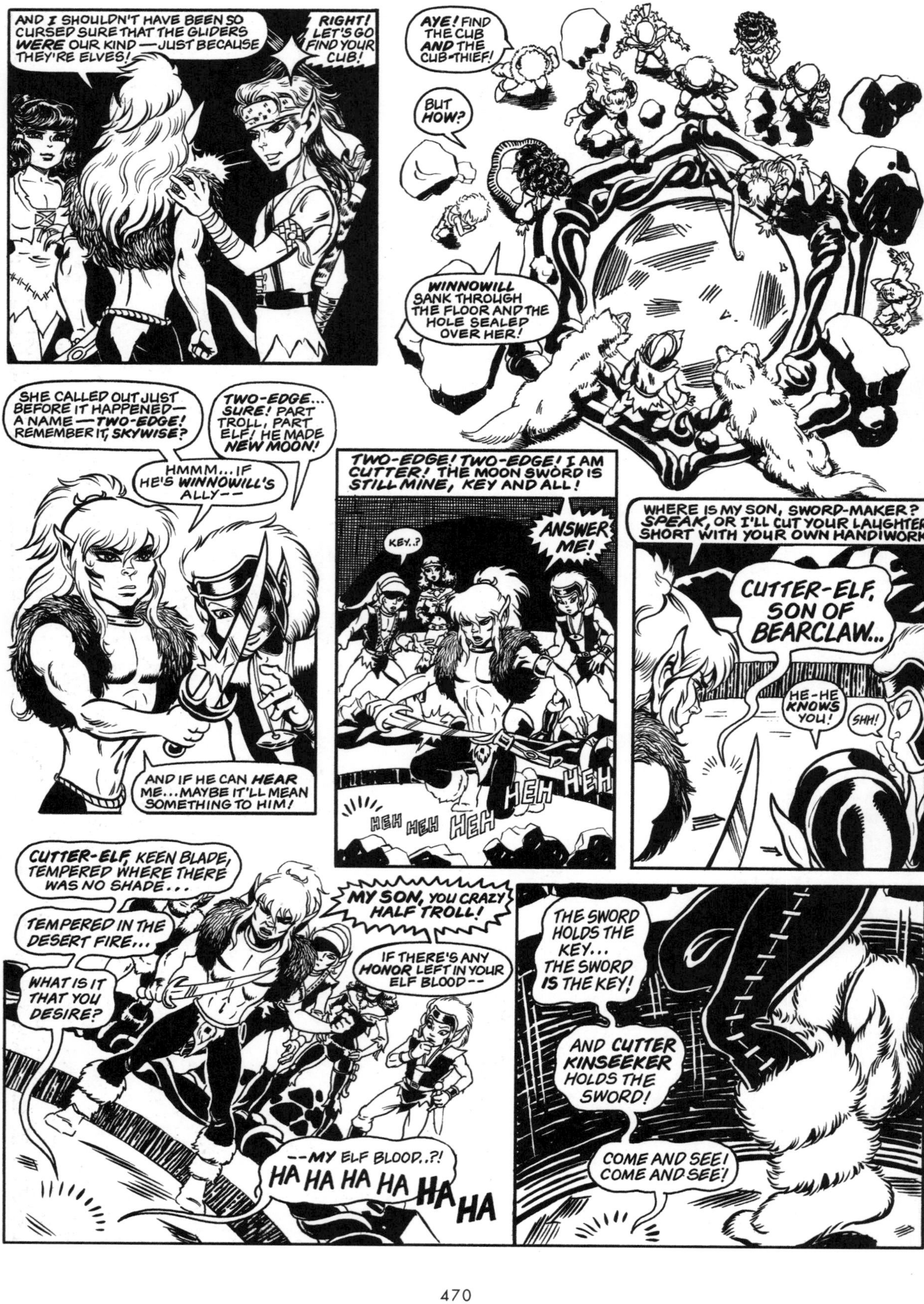
AND I SHOULDN'T HAVE BEEN SO CURSED SURE THAT THE GLIDERS WERE OUR KIND — JUST BECAUSE THEY'RE ELVES!
RIGHT! LET'S GO FIND YOUR CUB!
AYE! FIND THE CUB AND THE CUB-THIEF!
BUT HOW?
WINNOWILL SANK THROUGH THE FLOOR AND THE HOLE SEALED OVER HER!
SHE CALLED OUT JUST BEFORE IT HAPPENED— A NAME—TWO-EDGE! REMEMBER IT, SKYWISE?
TWO-EDGE... SURE! PART TROLL, PART ELF! HE MADE NEW MOON!
HMMM... IF HE'S WINNOWILL'S ALLY--
AND IF HE CAN HEAR ME... MAYBE IT'LL MEAN SOMETHING TO HIM!
TWO-EDGE! TWO-EDGE! I AM CUTTER! THE MOON SWORD IS STILL MINE, KEY AND ALL!
KEY..?
ANSWER ME!
HEH HEH HEH HEH HEH
WHERE IS MY SON, SWORD-MAKER? SPEAK, OR I'LL CUT YOUR LAUGHTER SHORT WITH YOUR OWN HANDIWORK!
CUTTER-ELF, SON OF BEARCLAW...
HE-HE KNOWS YOU!
SHH!
CUTTER-ELF, KEEN BLADE, TEMPERED WHERE THERE WAS NO SHADE...
TEMPERED IN THE DESERT FIRE...
WHAT IS IT THAT YOU DESIRE?
MY SON, YOU CRAZY HALF TROLL!
IF THERE'S ANY HONOR LEFT IN YOUR ELF BLOOD--
--MY ELF BLOOD..?!
HA HA HA HA HA HA
THE SWORD HOLDS THE KEY... THE SWORD IS THE KEY!
AND CUTTER KINSEEKER HOLDS THE SWORD!
COME AND SEE! COME AND SEE!

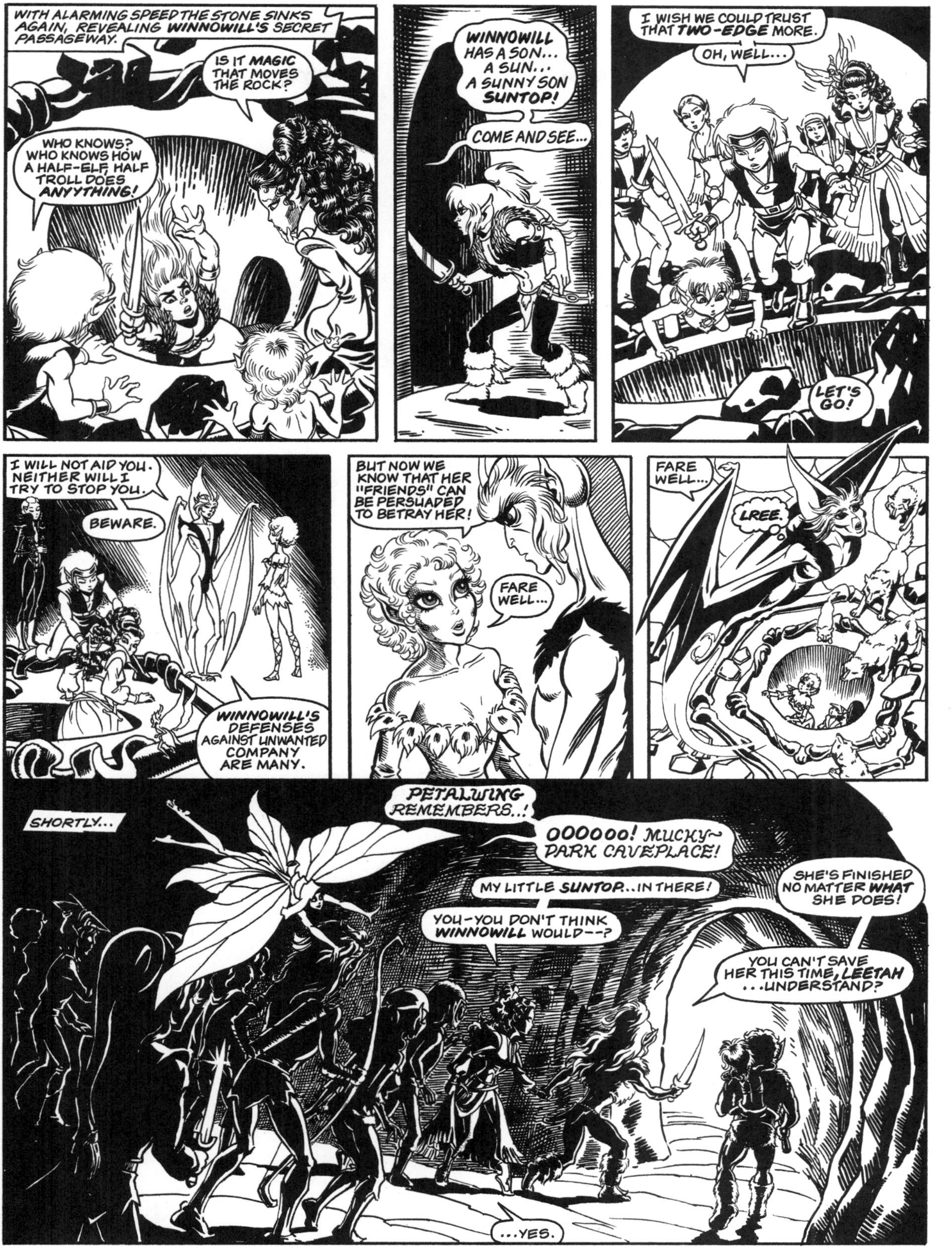
WITH ALARMING SPEED THE STONE SINKS AGAIN, REVEALING WINNOWILL'S SECRET PASSAGEWAY.
IS IT MAGIC THAT MOVES THE ROCK?
WHO KNOWS? WHO KNOWS HOW A HALF-ELF, HALF TROLL DOES ANYTHING!
WINNOWILL HAS A SON... A SUN... A SUNNY SON SUNTOP!
COME AND SEE...
I WISH WE COULD TRUST THAT TWO-EDGE MORE.
OH, WELL...
LET'S GO!
I WILL NOT AID YOU. NEITHER WILL I TRY TO STOP YOU.
BEWARE.
WINNOWILL'S DEFENSES AGAINST UNWANTED COMPANY ARE MANY.
BUT NOW WE KNOW THAT HER "FRIENDS" CAN BE PERSUADED TO BETRAY HER!
FARE WELL...
FARE WELL...
LREE.
SHORTLY...
PETALWING REMEMBERS..!
OOOOOO! MUCKY-DARK CAVEPLACE!
MY LITTLE SUNTOP...IN THERE!
YOU-YOU DON'T THINK WINNOWILL WOULD--?
SHE'S FINISHED NO MATTER WHAT SHE DOES!
YOU CAN'T SAVE HER THIS TIME, LEETAH ...UNDERSTAND?
...YES.

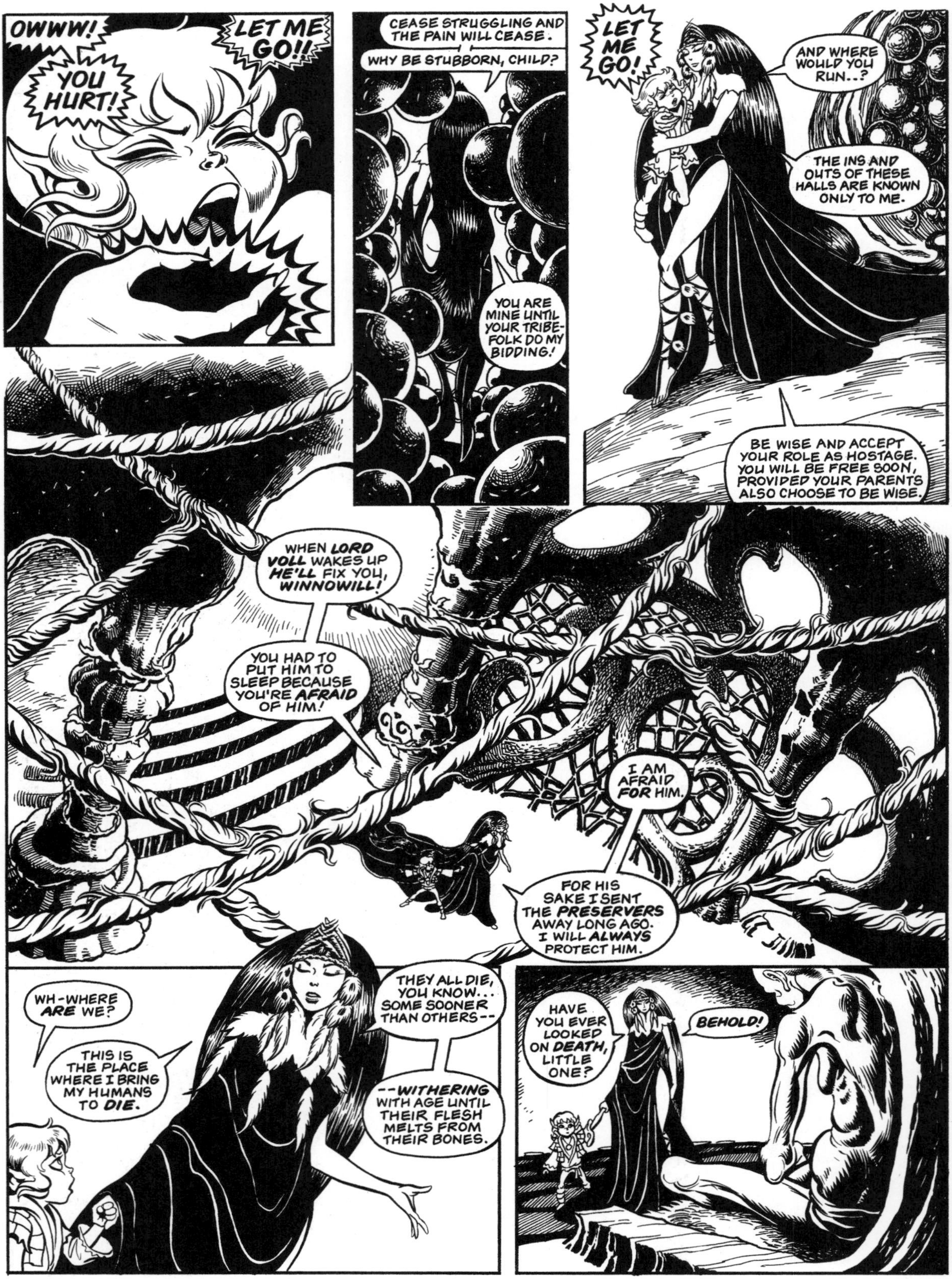

OWWW!
YOU HURT!
LET ME GO!!
CEASE STRUGGLING AND THE PAIN WILL CEASE.
WHY BE STUBBORN, CHILD?
YOU ARE MINE UNTIL YOUR TRIBE-FOLK DO MY BIDDING!
LET ME GO!
AND WHERE WOULD YOU RUN..?
THE INS AND OUTS OF THESE HALLS ARE KNOWN ONLY TO ME.
BE WISE AND ACCEPT YOUR ROLE AS HOSTAGE. YOU WILL BE FREE SOON, PROVIDED YOUR PARENTS ALSO CHOOSE TO BE WISE.
WHEN LORD VOLL WAKES UP HE'LL FIX YOU, WINNOWILL!
YOU HAD TO PUT HIM TO SLEEP BECAUSE YOU'RE AFRAID OF HIM!
I AM AFRAID FOR HIM.
FOR HIS SAKE I SENT THE PRESERVERS AWAY LONG AGO. I WILL ALWAYS PROTECT HIM.
WH-WHERE ARE WE?
THIS IS THE PLACE WHERE I BRING MY HUMANS TO DIE.
THEY ALL DIE, YOU KNOW... SOME SOONER THAN OTHERS--
--WITHERING WITH AGE UNTIL THEIR FLESH MELTS FROM THEIR BONES.
HAVE YOU EVER LOOKED ON DEATH, LITTLE ONE?
BEHOLD!

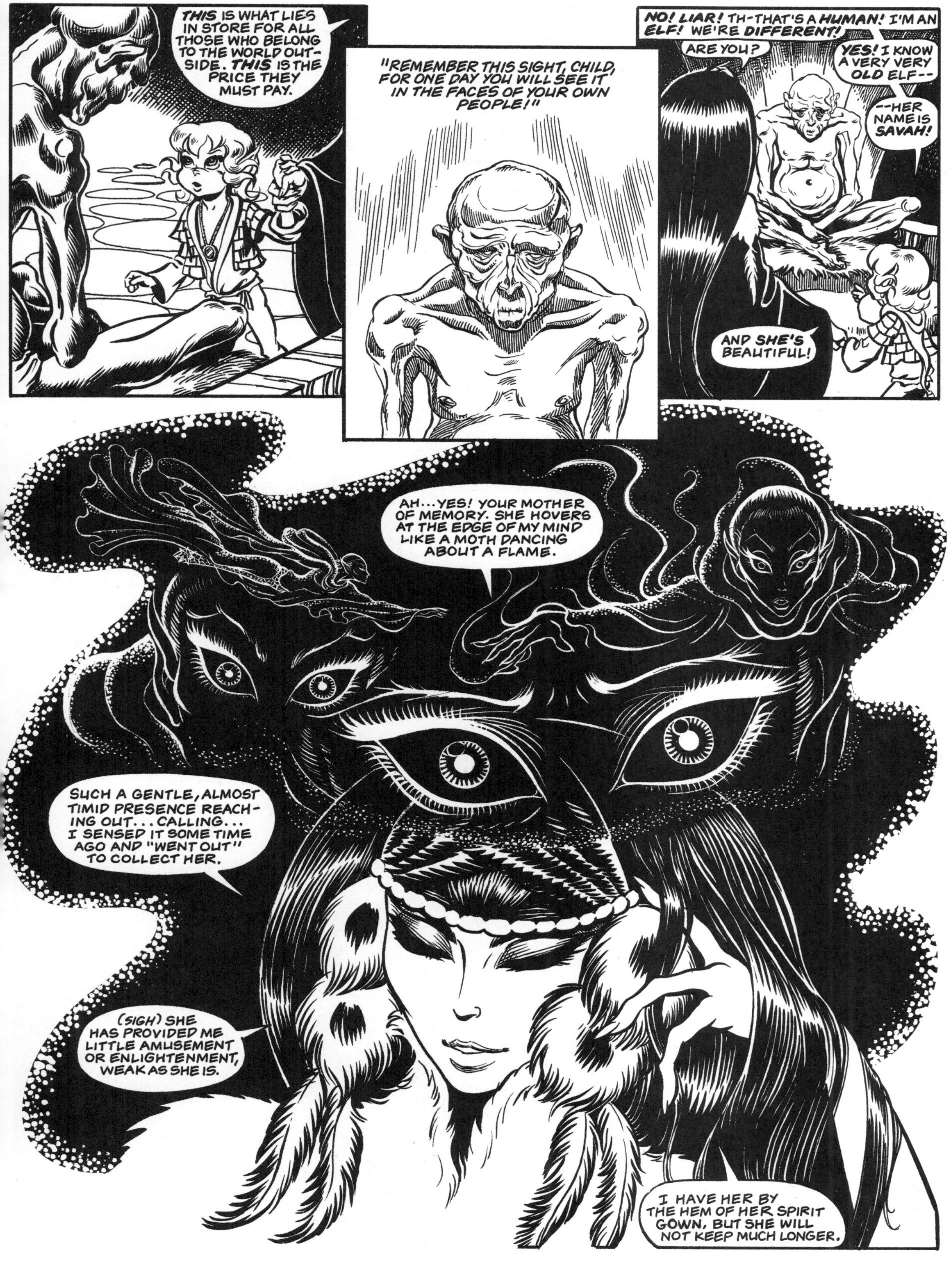
THIS IS WHAT LIES IN STORE FOR ALL THOSE WHO BELONG TO THE WORLD OUT-SIDE. THIS IS THE PRICE THEY MUST PAY.
"REMEMBER THIS SIGHT, CHILD, FOR ONE DAY YOU WILL SEE IT IN THE FACES OF YOUR OWN PEOPLE!"
NO! LIAR! TH-THAT'S A HUMAN! I'M AN ELF! WE'RE DIFFERENT!
ARE YOU?
YES! I KNOW A VERY VERY OLD ELF--
--HER NAME IS SAVAH!
AND SHE'S BEAUTIFUL!
AH...YES! YOUR MOTHER OF MEMORY. SHE HOVERS AT THE EDGE OF MY MIND LIKE A MOTH DANCING ABOUT A FLAME.
SUCH A GENTLE, ALMOST TIMID PRESENCE REACH-ING OUT... CALLING... I SENSED IT SOME TIME AGO AND "WENT OUT" TO COLLECT HER.
(SIGH) SHE HAS PROVIDED ME LITTLE AMUSEMENT OR ENLIGHTENMENT, WEAK AS SHE IS.
I HAVE HER BY THE HEM OF HER SPIRIT GOWN, BUT SHE WILL NOT KEEP MUCH LONGER.

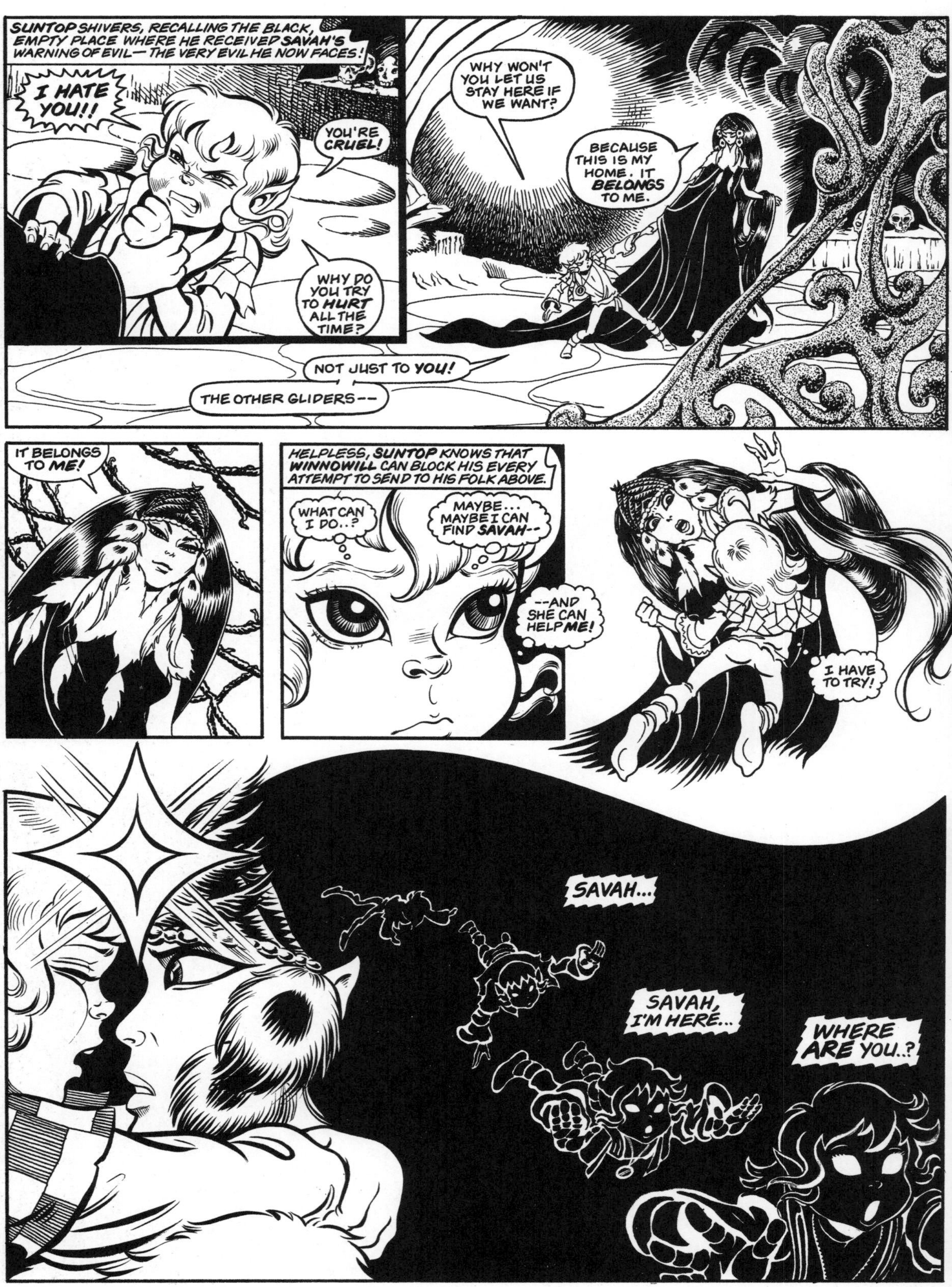
SUNTOP SHIVERS, RECALLING THE BLACK, EMPTY PLACE WHERE HE RECEIVED SAVAH'S WARNING OF EVIL— THE VERY EVIL HE NOW FACES!
I HATE YOU!!
YOU'RE CRUEL!
WHY DO YOU TRY TO HURT ALL THE TIME?
WHY WON'T YOU LET US STAY HERE IF WE WANT?
BECAUSE THIS IS MY HOME. IT BELONGS TO ME.
NOT JUST TO YOU!
THE OTHER GLIDERS--
IT BELONGS TO ME!
HELPLESS, SUNTOP KNOWS THAT WINNOWILL CAN BLOCK HIS EVERY ATTEMPT TO SEND TO HIS FOLK ABOVE.
WHAT CAN I DO..?
MAYBE... MAYBE I CAN FIND SAVAH--
--AND SHE CAN HELP ME!
I HAVE TO TRY!
SAVAH...
SAVAH, I'M HERE...
WHERE ARE YOU..?

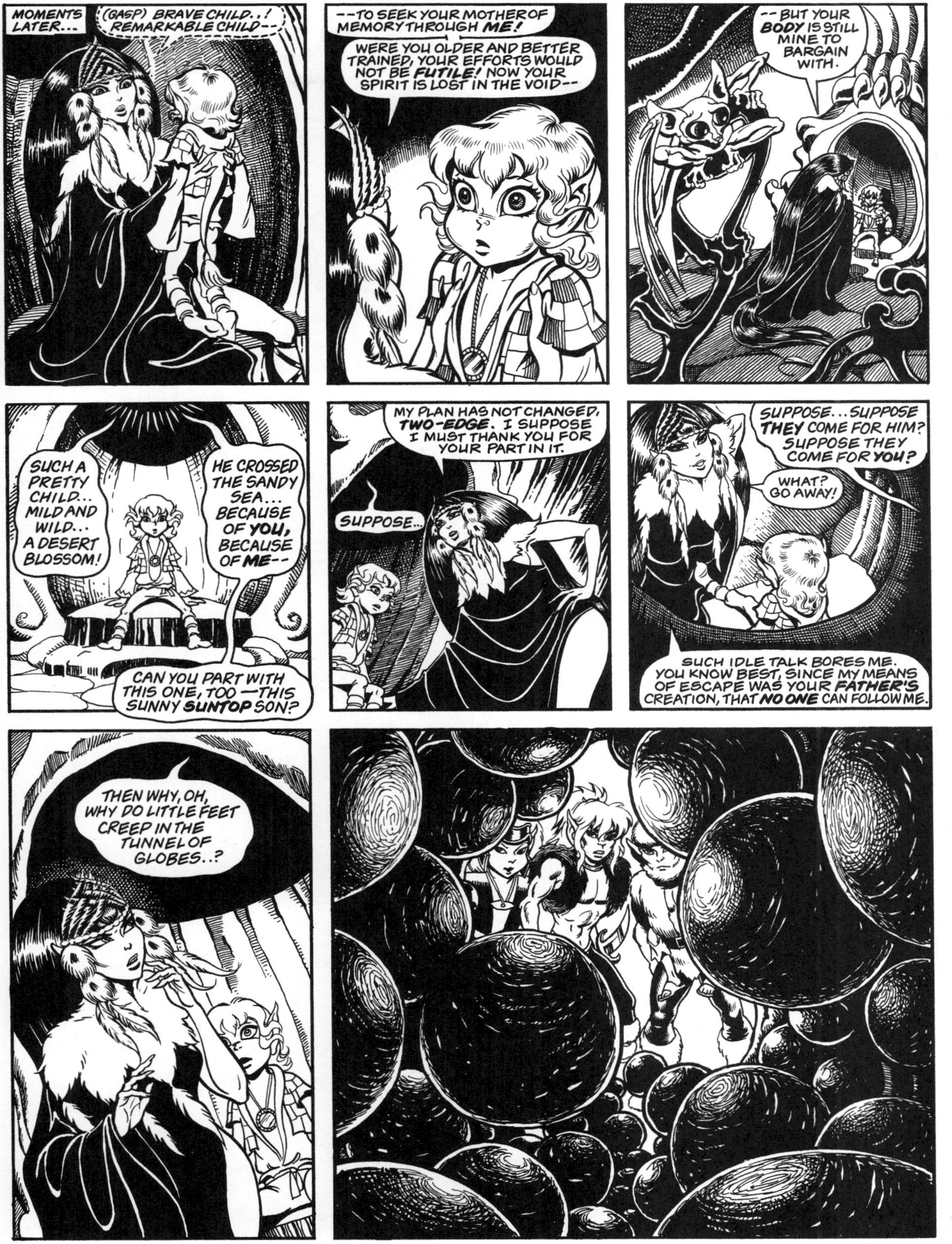
MOMENTS LATER...
(GASP) BRAVE CHILD..! REMARKABLE CHILD--
--TO SEEK YOUR MOTHER OF MEMORY THROUGH ME!
WERE YOU OLDER AND BETTER TRAINED, YOUR EFFORTS WOULD NOT BE FUTILE! NOW YOUR SPIRIT IS LOST IN THE VOID--
--BUT YOUR BODY IS STILL MINE TO BARGAIN WITH.
SUCH A PRETTY CHILD... MILD AND WILD... A DESERT BLOSSOM!
HE CROSSED THE SANDY SEA... BECAUSE OF YOU, BECAUSE OF ME--
CAN YOU PART WITH THIS ONE, TOO—THIS SUNNY SUNTOP SON?
MY PLAN HAS NOT CHANGED, TWO-EDGE. I SUPPOSE I MUST THANK YOU FOR YOUR PART IN IT.
SUPPOSE...
SUPPOSE... SUPPOSE THEY COME FOR HIM? SUPPOSE THEY COME FOR YOU?
WHAT? GO AWAY!
SUCH IDLE TALK BORES ME. YOU KNOW BEST, SINCE MY MEANS OF ESCAPE WAS YOUR FATHER'S CREATION, THAT NO ONE CAN FOLLOW ME.
THEN WHY, OH, WHY DO LITTLE FEET CREEP IN THE TUNNEL OF GLOBES..?

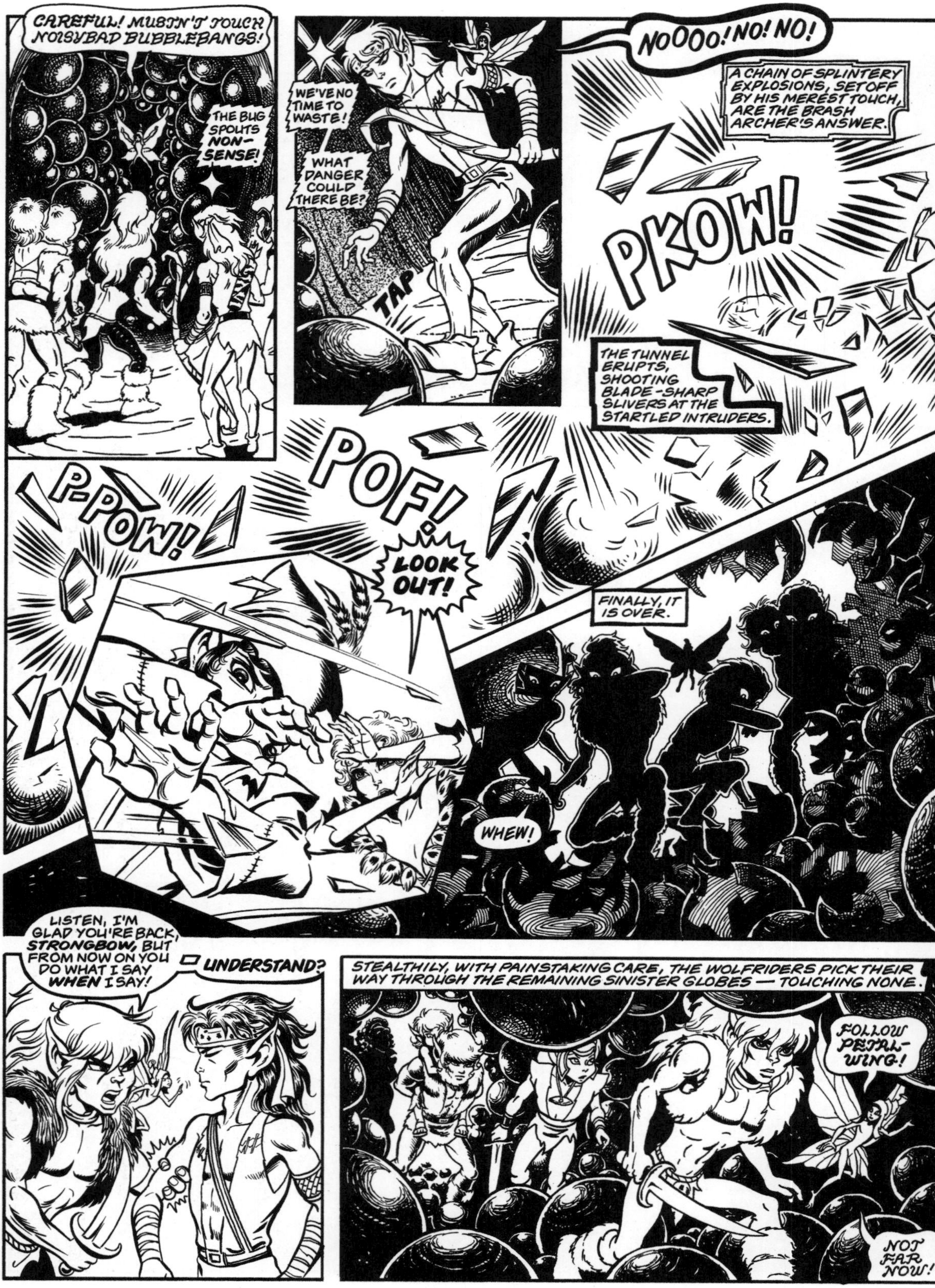
CAREFUL! MUSTN'T TOUCH NOISYBAD BUBBLEBANGS!
THE BUG SPOUTS NON-SENSE!
WE'VE NO TIME TO WASTE!
WHAT DANGER COULD THERE BE?
TAP
NOOOO! NO! NO!
A CHAIN OF SPLINTERY EXPLOSIONS, SET OFF BY HIS MEREST TOUCH, ARE THE BRASH ARCHER'S ANSWER.
PKOW!
THE TUNNEL ERUPTS, SHOOTING BLADE-SHARP SLIVERS AT THE STARTLED INTRUDERS.
P-POW!
POF!
LOOK OUT!
FINALLY, IT IS OVER.
WHEW!
LISTEN, I'M GLAD YOU'RE BACK, STRONGBOW, BUT FROM NOW ON YOU DO WHAT I SAY WHEN I SAY!
UNDERSTAND?
STEALTHILY, WITH PAINSTAKING CARE, THE WOLFRIDERS PICK THEIR WAY THROUGH THE REMAINING SINISTER GLOBES — TOUCHING NONE.
FOLLOW PETAL-WING!
NOT FAR NOW!

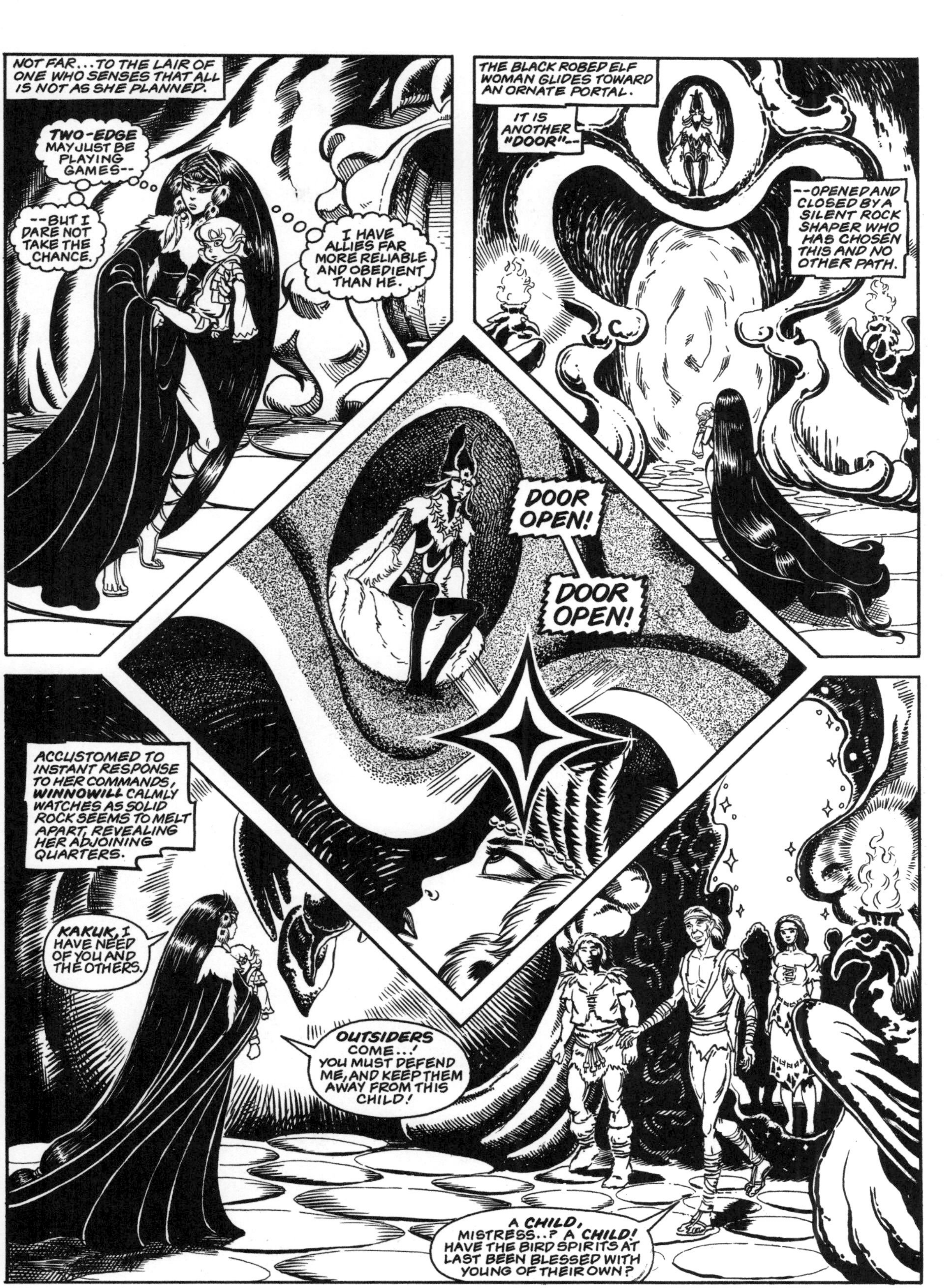
NOT FAR...TO THE LAIR OF ONE WHO SENSES THAT ALL IS NOT AS SHE PLANNED.
TWO-EDGE MAY JUST BE PLAYING GAMES--
--BUT I DARE NOT TAKE THE CHANCE.
I HAVE ALLIES FAR MORE RELIABLE AND OBEDIENT THAN HE.
THE BLACK ROBED ELF WOMAN GLIDES TOWARD AN ORNATE PORTAL.
IT IS ANOTHER "DOOR"--
--OPENED AND CLOSED BY A SILENT ROCK SHAPER WHO HAS CHOSEN THIS AND NO OTHER PATH.
DOOR OPEN!
DOOR OPEN!
ACCUSTOMED TO INSTANT RESPONSE TO HER COMMANDS, WINNOWILL CALMLY WATCHES AS SOLID ROCK SEEMS TO MELT APART, REVEALING HER ADJOINING QUARTERS.
KAKUK, I HAVE NEED OF YOU AND THE OTHERS.
OUTSIDERS COME...! YOU MUST DEFEND ME, AND KEEP THEM AWAY FROM THIS CHILD!
A CHILD, MISTRESS..? A CHILD! HAVE THE BIRD SPIRITS AT LAST BEEN BLESSED WITH YOUNG OF THEIR OWN?

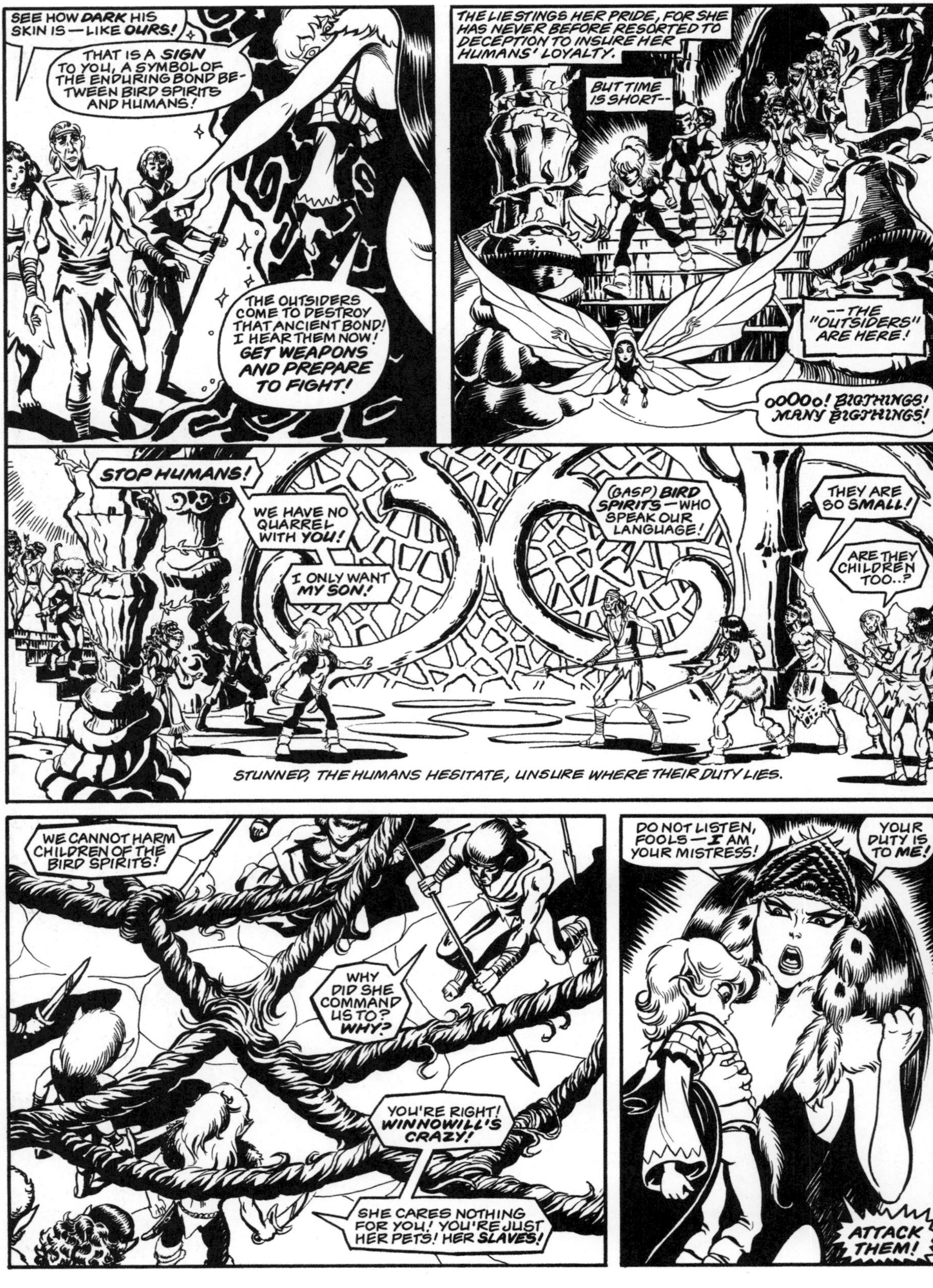
SEE HOW DARK HIS SKIN IS—LIKE OURS!
THAT IS A SIGN TO YOU, A SYMBOL OF THE ENDURING BOND BETWEEN BIRD SPIRITS AND HUMANS!
THE OUTSIDERS COME TO DESTROY THAT ANCIENT BOND! I HEAR THEM NOW! GET WEAPONS AND PREPARE TO FIGHT!
THE LIE STINGS HER PRIDE, FOR SHE HAS NEVER BEFORE RESORTED TO DECEPTION TO INSURE HER HUMANS' LOYALTY.
BUT TIME IS SHORT--
--THE "OUTSIDERS" ARE HERE!
OOOOo! BIGTHINGS! MANY BIGTHINGS!
STOP HUMANS!
WE HAVE NO QUARREL WITH YOU!
I ONLY WANT MY SON!
(GASP) BIRD SPIRITS—WHO SPEAK OUR LANGUAGE!
THEY ARE SO SMALL!
ARE THEY CHILDREN TOO..?
STUNNED, THE HUMANS HESITATE, UNSURE WHERE THEIR DUTY LIES.
WE CANNOT HARM CHILDREN OF THE BIRD SPIRITS!
WHY DID SHE COMMAND US TO? WHY?
YOU'RE RIGHT! WINNOWILL'S CRAZY!
SHE CARES NOTHING FOR YOU! YOU'RE JUST HER PETS! HER SLAVES!
DO NOT LISTEN, FOOLS—I AM YOUR MISTRESS!
YOUR DUTY IS TO ME!
ATTACK THEM!

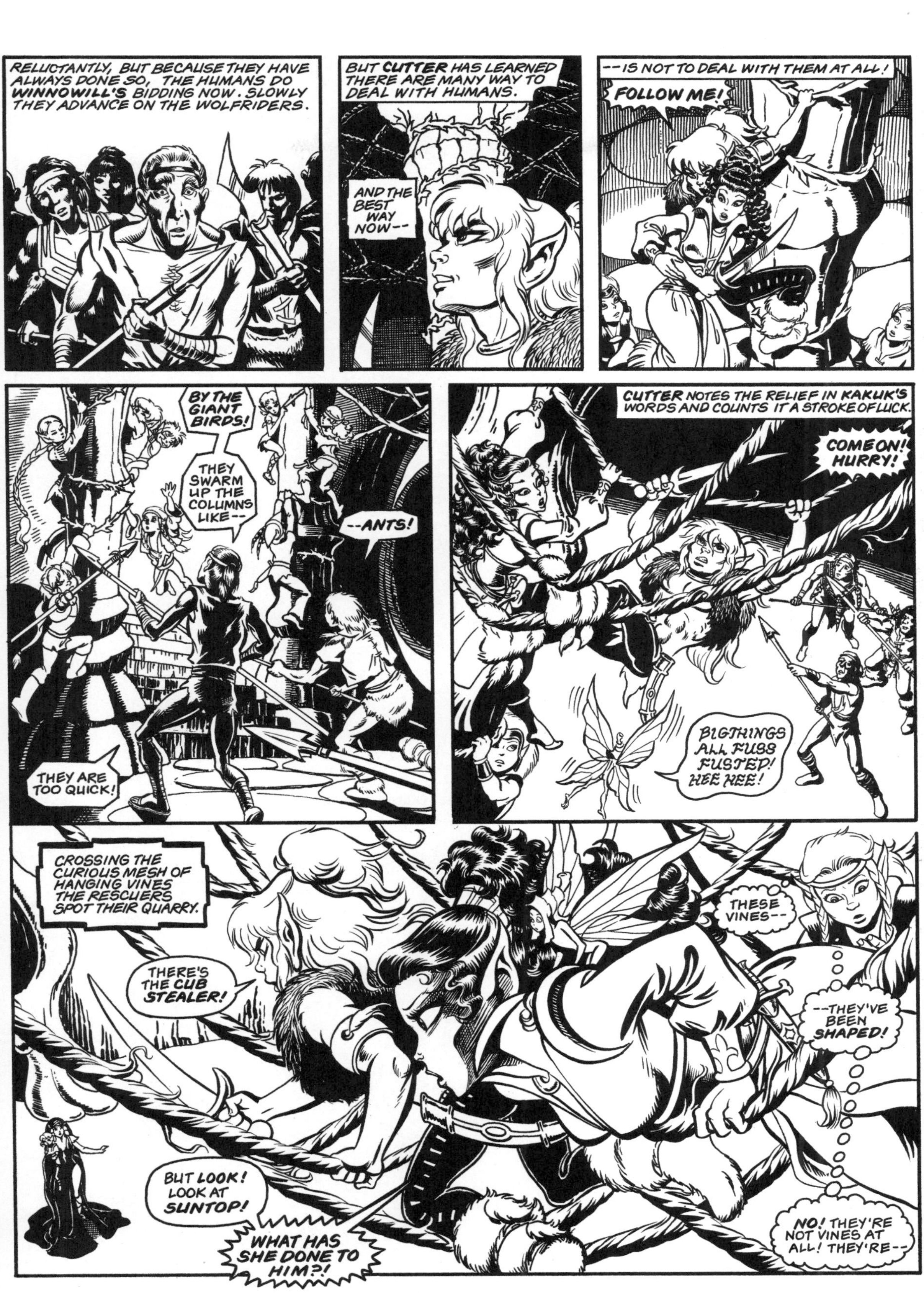

RELUCTANTLY, BUT BECAUSE THEY HAVE ALWAYS DONE SO, THE HUMANS DO WINNOWILL'S BIDDING NOW. SLOWLY THEY ADVANCE ON THE WOLFRIDERS.
BUT CUTTER HAS LEARNED THERE ARE MANY WAY TO DEAL WITH HUMANS.
AND THE BEST WAY NOW--
--IS NOT TO DEAL WITH THEM AT ALL!
FOLLOW ME!
BY THE GIANT BIRDS!
THEY SWARM UP THE COLUMNS LIKE--
--ANTS!
THEY ARE TOO QUICK!
CUTTER NOTES THE RELIEF IN KAKUK'S WORDS AND COUNTS IT A STROKE OF LUCK.
COME ON! HURRY!
BIGTHINGS ALL FUSS FUSTED! HEE HEE!
CROSSING THE CURIOUS MESH OF HANGING VINES THE RESCUERS SPOT THEIR QUARRY.
THERE'S THE CUB STEALER!
THESE VINES--
--THEY'VE BEEN SHAPED!
BUT LOOK! LOOK AT SUNTOP!
WHAT HAS SHE DONE TO HIM?!
NO! THEY'RE NOT VINES AT ALL! THEY'RE--

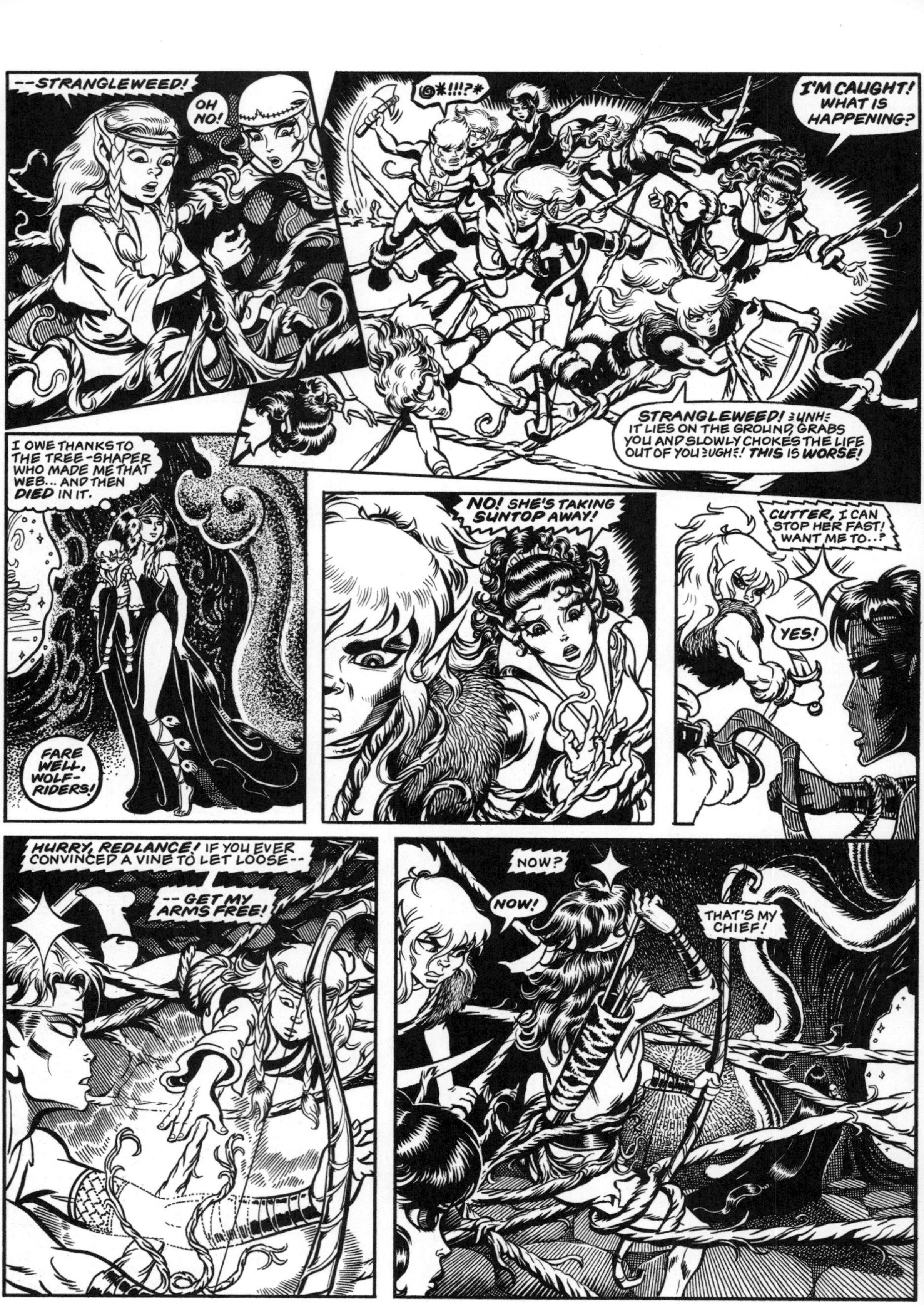
--STRANGLEWEED!
OH NO!
@*!!!?*
I'M CAUGHT! WHAT IS HAPPENING?
STRANGLEWEED! UNH! IT LIES ON THE GROUND, GRABS YOU AND SLOWLY CHOKES THE LIFE OUT OF YOU! UGH! THIS IS WORSE!
I OWE THANKS TO THE TREE-SHAPER WHO MADE ME THAT WEB... AND THEN DIED IN IT.
FARE WELL, WOLF-RIDERS!
NO! SHE'S TAKING SUNTOP AWAY!
CUTTER, I CAN STOP HER FAST! WANT ME TO..?
YES!
HURRY, REDLANCE! IF YOU EVER CONVINCED A VINE TO LET LOOSE--
--GET MY ARMS FREE!
NOW?
NOW!
THAT'S MY CHIEF!

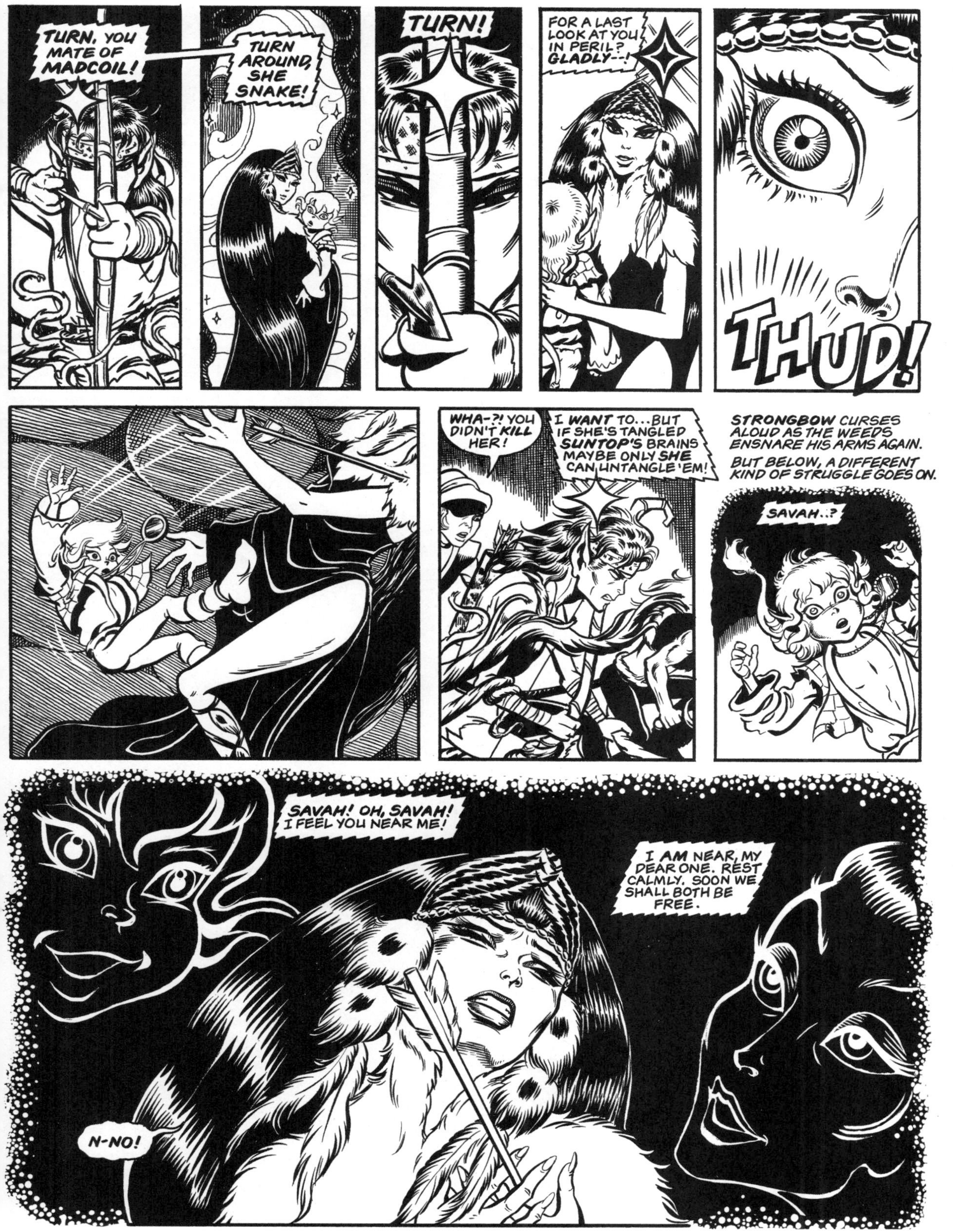
TURN, YOU MATE OF MADCOIL!
TURN AROUND, SHE SNAKE!
TURN!
FOR A LAST LOOK AT YOU IN PERIL? GLADLY--!
THUD!
WHA-?! YOU DIDN'T KILL HER!
I WANT TO... BUT IF SHE'S TANGLED SUNTOP'S BRAINS MAYBE ONLY SHE CAN UNTANGLE 'EM!
STRONGBOW CURSES ALOUD AS THE WEEDS ENSNARE HIS ARMS AGAIN.
BUT BELOW, A DIFFERENT KIND OF STRUGGLE GOES ON.
SAVAH..?
SAVAH! OH, SAVAH! I FEEL YOU NEAR ME!
I AM NEAR, MY DEAR ONE. REST CALMLY. SOON WE SHALL BOTH BE FREE.
N-NO!

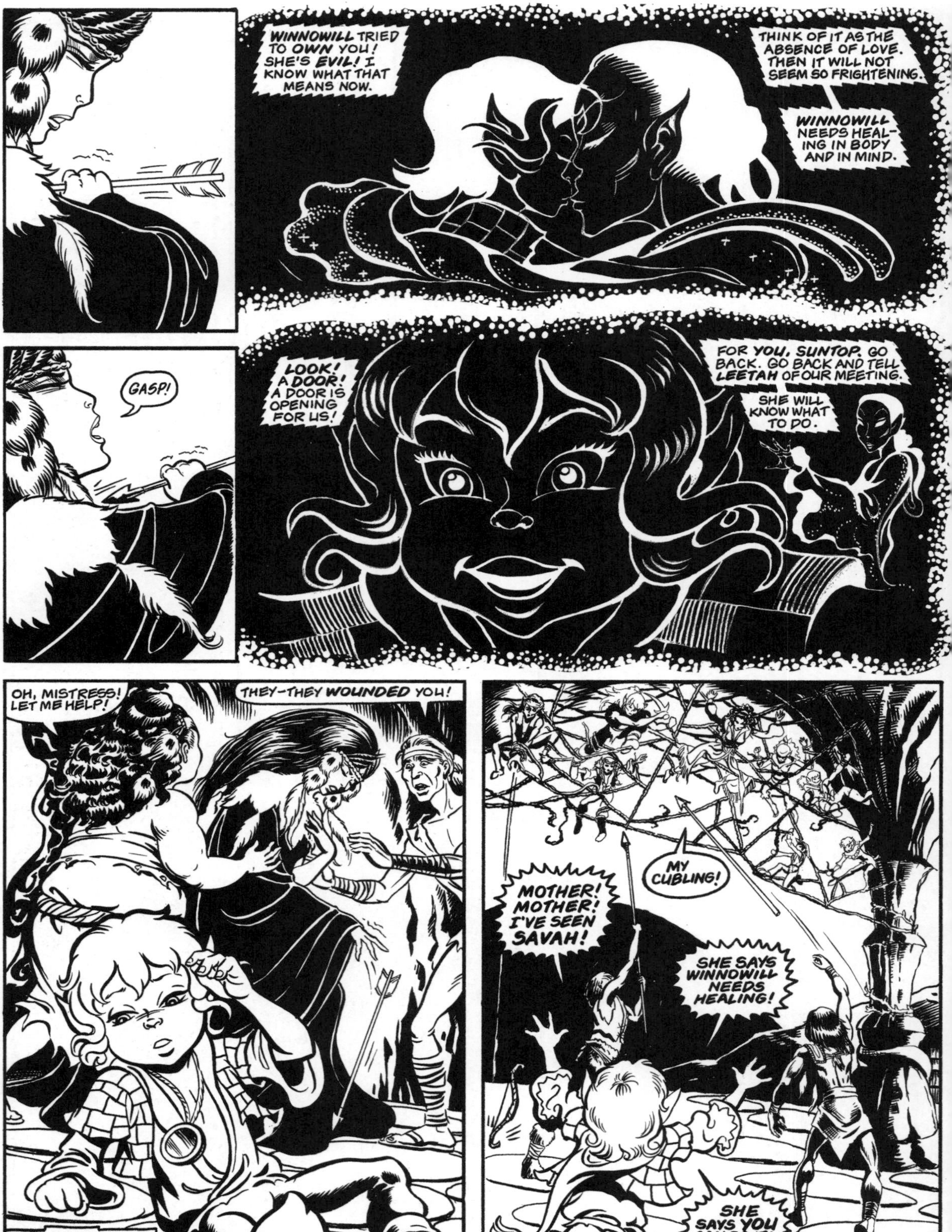
WINNOWILL TRIED TO OWN YOU! SHE'S EVIL! I KNOW WHAT THAT MEANS NOW.
THINK OF IT AS THE ABSENCE OF LOVE. THEN IT WILL NOT SEEM SO FRIGHTENING.
WINNOWILL NEEDS HEALING IN BODY AND IN MIND.
GASP!
LOOK! A DOOR! A DOOR IS OPENING FOR US!
FOR YOU, SUNTOP. GO BACK. GO BACK AND TELL LEETAH OF OUR MEETING.
SHE WILL KNOW WHAT TO DO.
OH, MISTRESS! LET ME HELP!
THEY—THEY WOUNDED YOU!
UNNOTICED, SUNTOP AWAKENS.
MOTHER! MOTHER! I'VE SEEN SAVAH!
MY CUBLING!
SHE SAYS WINNOWILL NEEDS HEALING!
SHE SAYS YOU CAN DO IT!

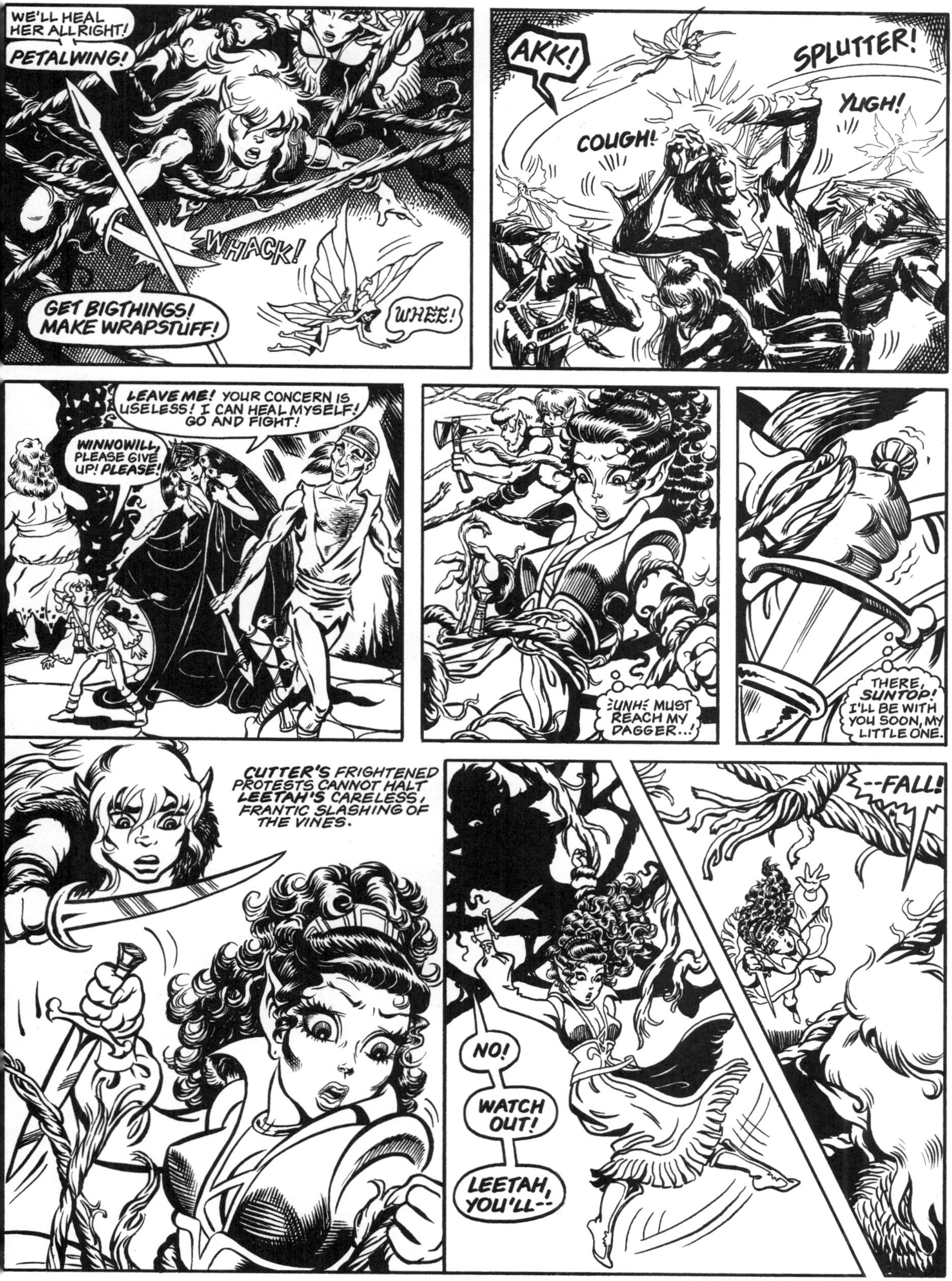
WE'LL HEAL HER ALL RIGHT!
PETALWING!
WHACK!
GET BIGTHINGS! MAKE WRAPSTUFF!
WHEE!
AKK!
SPLUTTER!
YUGH!
COUGH!
LEAVE ME! YOUR CONCERN IS USELESS! I CAN HEAL MYSELF! GO AND FIGHT!
WINNOWILL, PLEASE GIVE UP! PLEASE!
UNH MUST REACH MY DAGGER...!
THERE, SUNTOP! I'LL BE WITH YOU SOON, MY LITTLE ONE.
CUTTER'S FRIGHTENED PROTESTS CANNOT HALT LEETAH'S CARELESS, FRANTIC SLASHING OF THE VINES.
NO!
WATCH OUT!
LEETAH, YOU'LL--
--FALL!

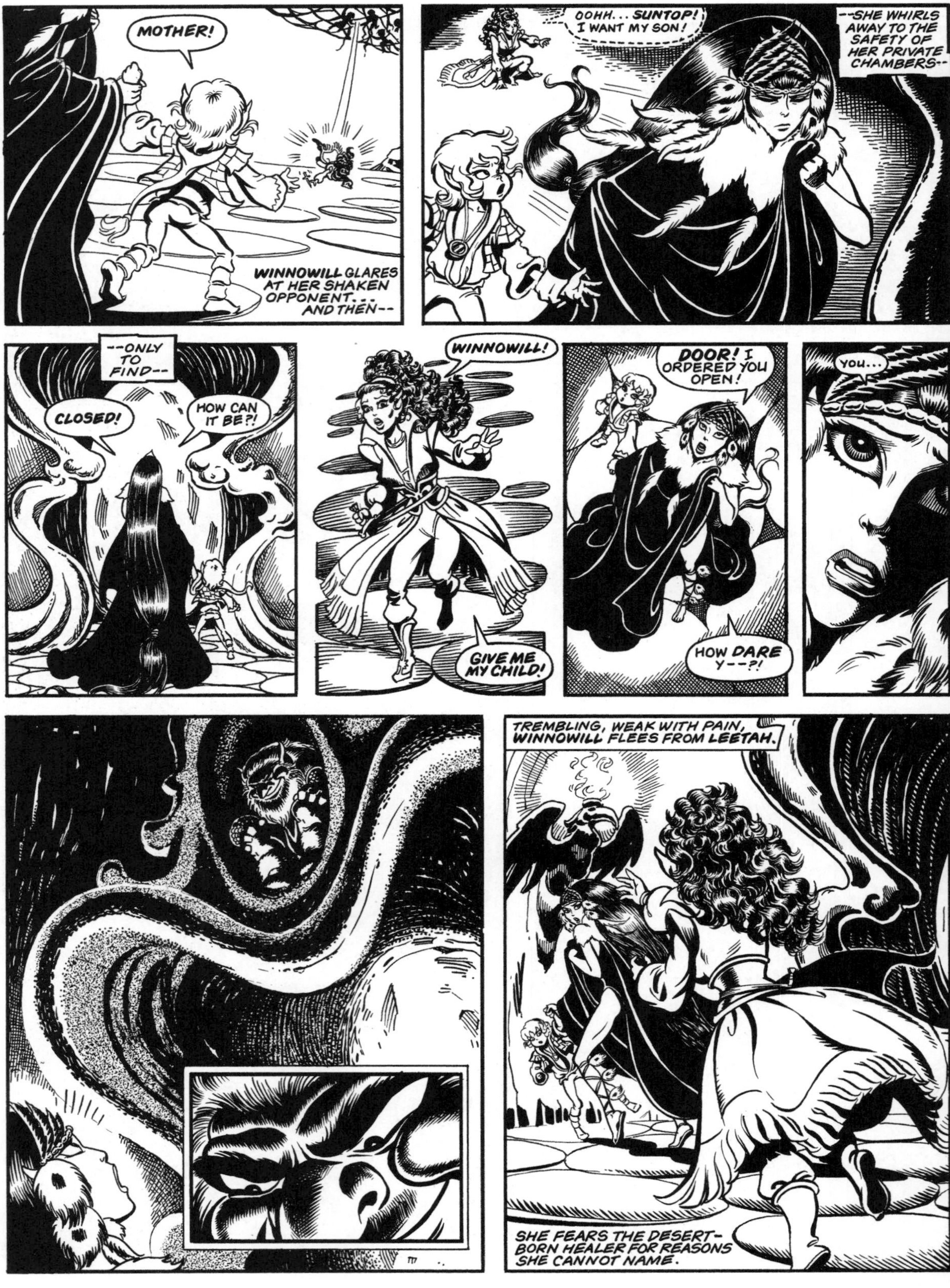

MOTHER!
WINNOWILL GLARES AT HER SHAKEN OPPONENT... AND THEN--
OOHH... SUNTOP! I WANT MY SON!
--SHE WHIRLS AWAY TO THE SAFETY OF HER PRIVATE CHAMBERS--
--ONLY TO FIND--
CLOSED!
HOW CAN IT BE?!
WINNOWILL!
GIVE ME MY CHILD!
DOOR! I ORDERED YOU OPEN!
HOW DARE Y--?!
YOU...
TREMBLING, WEAK WITH PAIN, WINNOWILL FLEES FROM LEETAH.
SHE FEARS THE DESERT-BORN HEALER FOR REASONS SHE CANNOT NAME.

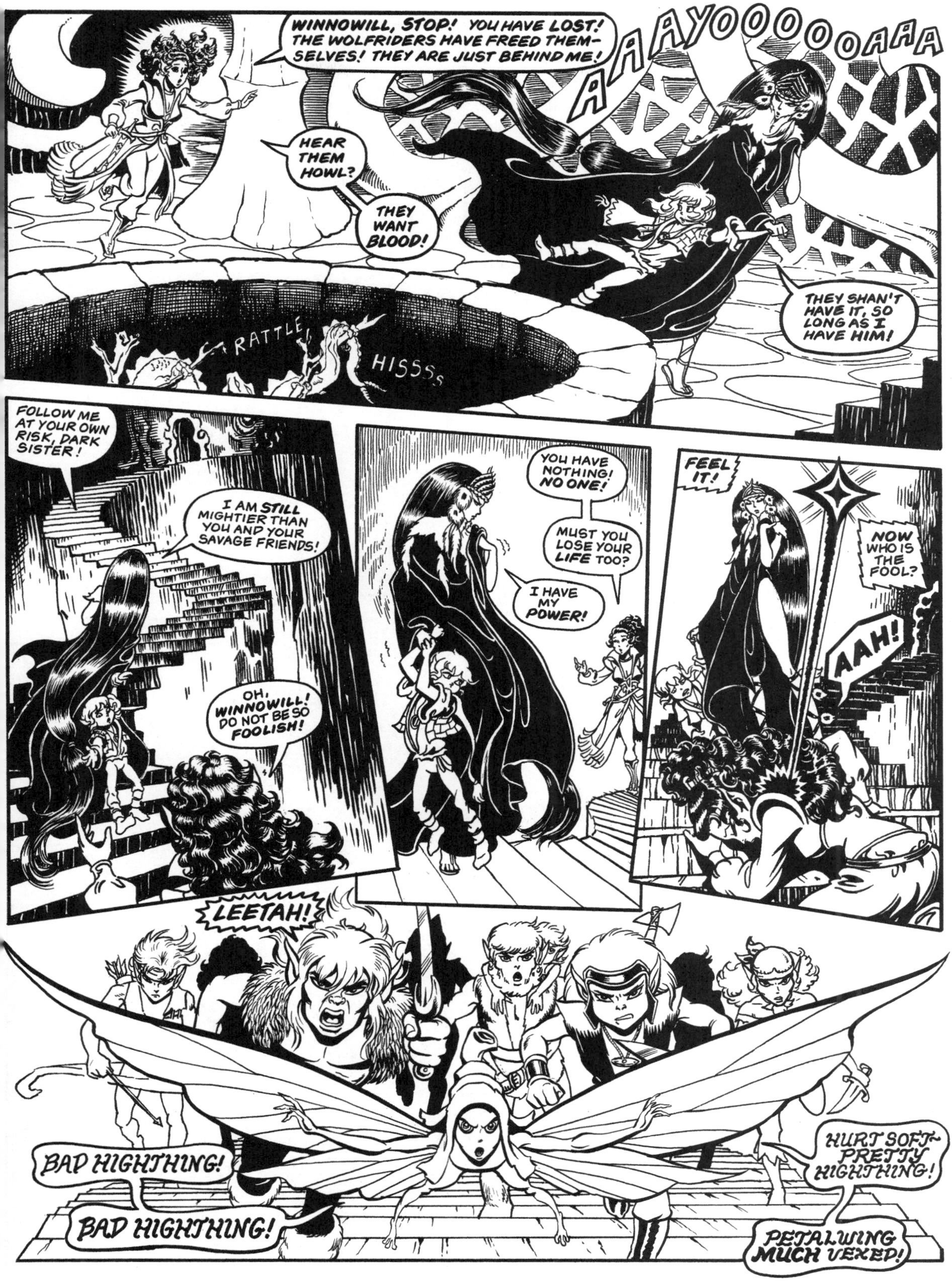
WINNOWILL, STOP! YOU HAVE LOST! THE WOLFRIDERS HAVE FREED THEMSELVES! THEY ARE JUST BEHIND ME!
AAAYOOOOOOAAA
HEAR THEM HOWL?
THEY WANT BLOOD!
THEY SHAN'T HAVE IT, SO LONG AS I HAVE HIM!
RATTLE
HISSSS
FOLLOW ME AT YOUR OWN RISK, DARK SISTER!
I AM STILL MIGHTIER THAN YOU AND YOUR SAVAGE FRIENDS!
OH, WINNOWILL! DO NOT BE SO FOOLISH!
YOU HAVE NOTHING! NO ONE!
MUST YOU LOSE YOUR LIFE TOO?
I HAVE MY POWER!
FEEL IT!
NOW WHO IS THE FOOL?
AAH!
LEETAH!
BAD HIGHTHING!
BAD HIGHTHING!
HURT SOFT-PRETTY HIGHTHING!
PETALWING MUCH VEXED!

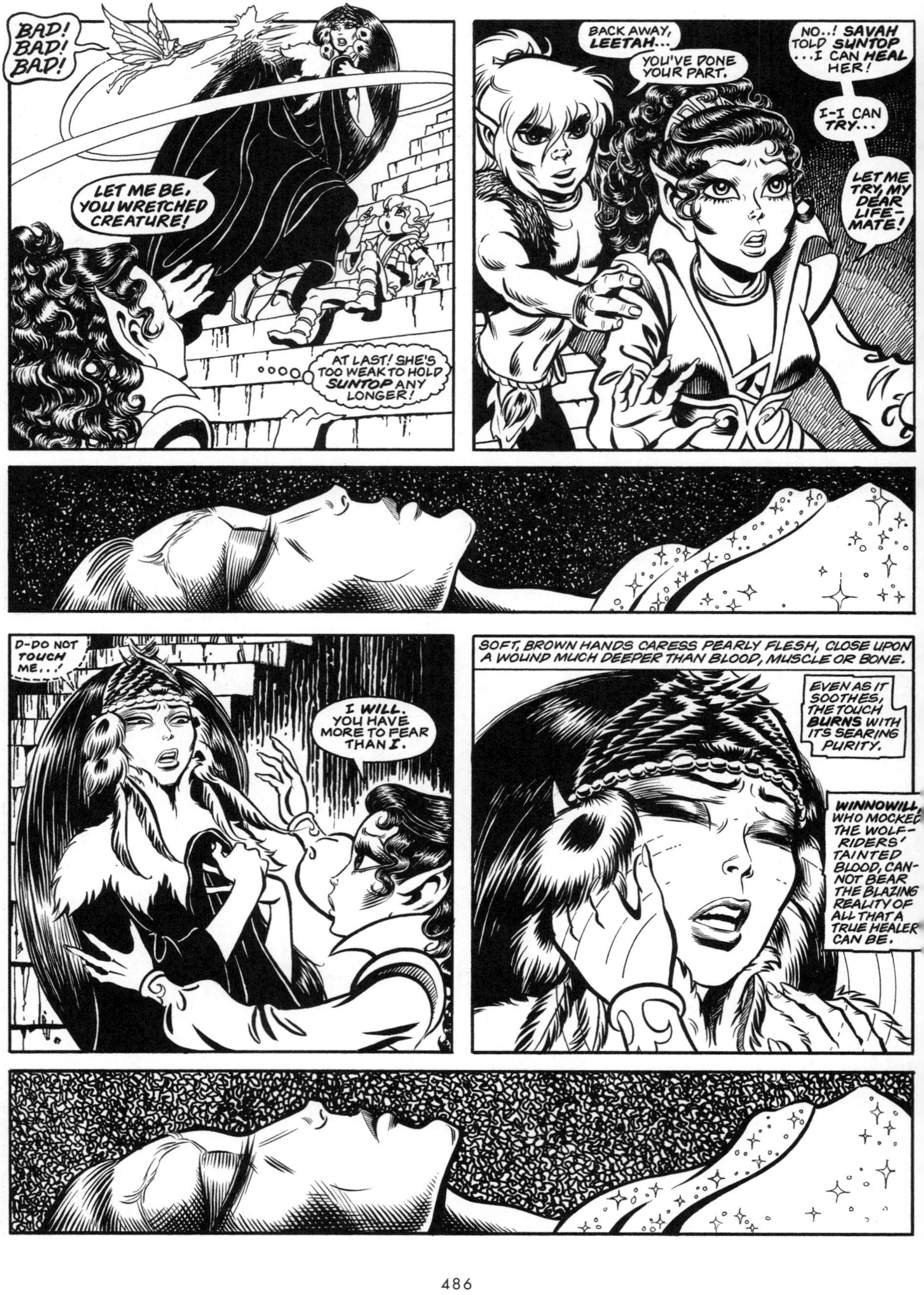

BAD! BAD! BAD!
LET ME BE, YOU WRETCHED CREATURE!
AT LAST! SHE'S TOO WEAK TO HOLD SUNTOP ANY LONGER!
BACK AWAY, LEETAH...
YOU'VE DONE YOUR PART.
NO..! SAVAH TOLD SUNTOP ...I CAN HEAL HER!
I-I CAN TRY...
LET ME TRY, MY DEAR LIFE-MATE!
D-DO NOT TOUCH ME...!
I WILL. YOU HAVE MORE TO FEAR THAN I.
SOFT, BROWN HANDS CARESS PEARLY FLESH, CLOSE UPON A WOUND MUCH DEEPER THAN BLOOD, MUSCLE OR BONE.
EVEN AS IT SOOTHES, THE TOUCH BURNS WITH ITS SEARING PURITY.
WINNOWILL, WHO MOCKED THE WOLF-RIDERS' TAINTED BLOOD, CANNOT BEAR THE BLAZING REALITY OF ALL THAT A TRUE HEALER CAN BE.

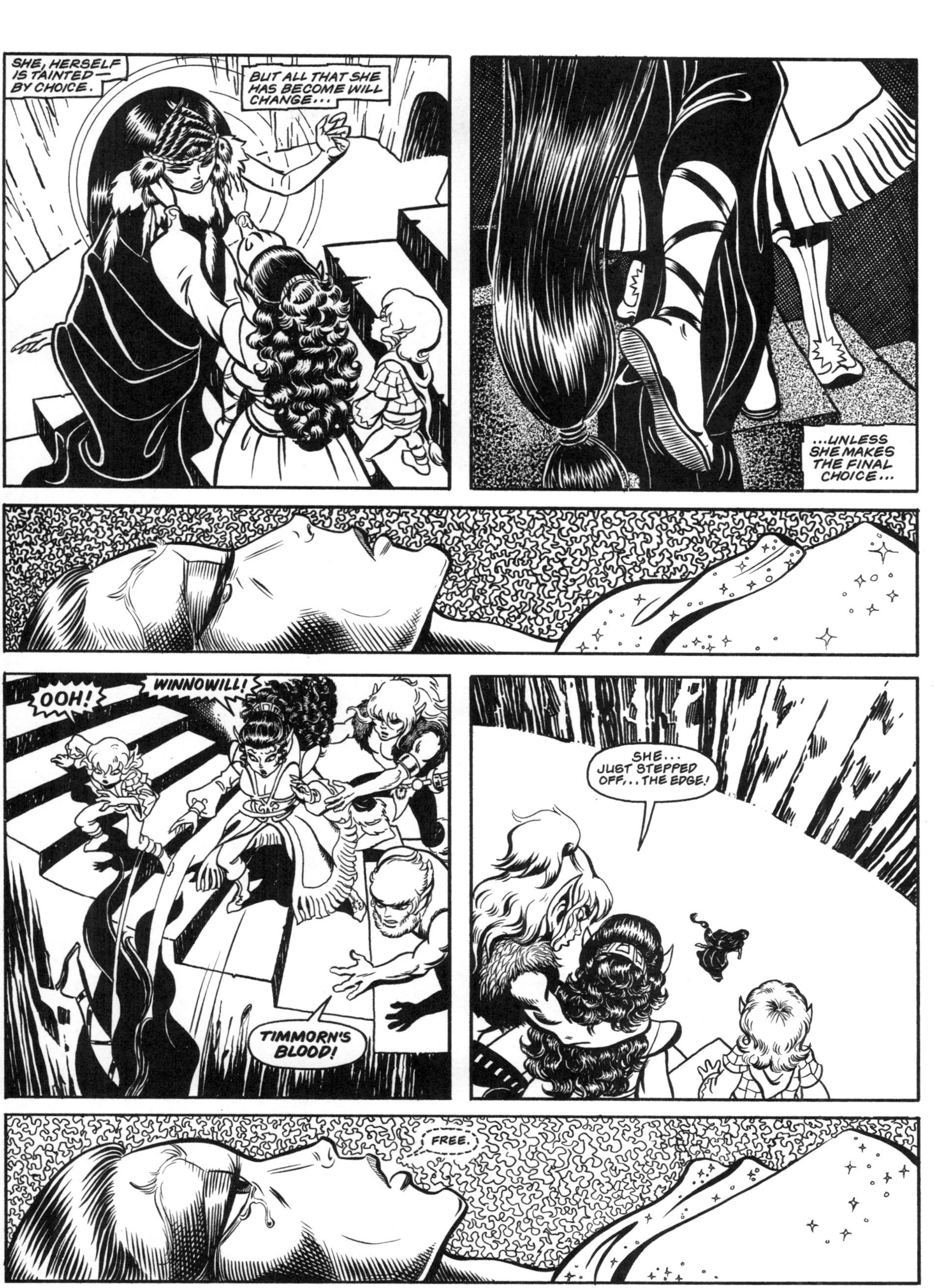
SHE, HERSELF IS TAINTED— BY CHOICE.
BUT ALL THAT SHE HAS BECOME WILL CHANGE...
...UNLESS SHE MAKES THE FINAL CHOICE...
OOH!
WINNOWILL!
TIMMORN'S BLOOD!
SHE... JUST STEPPED OFF... THE EDGE!
FREE.

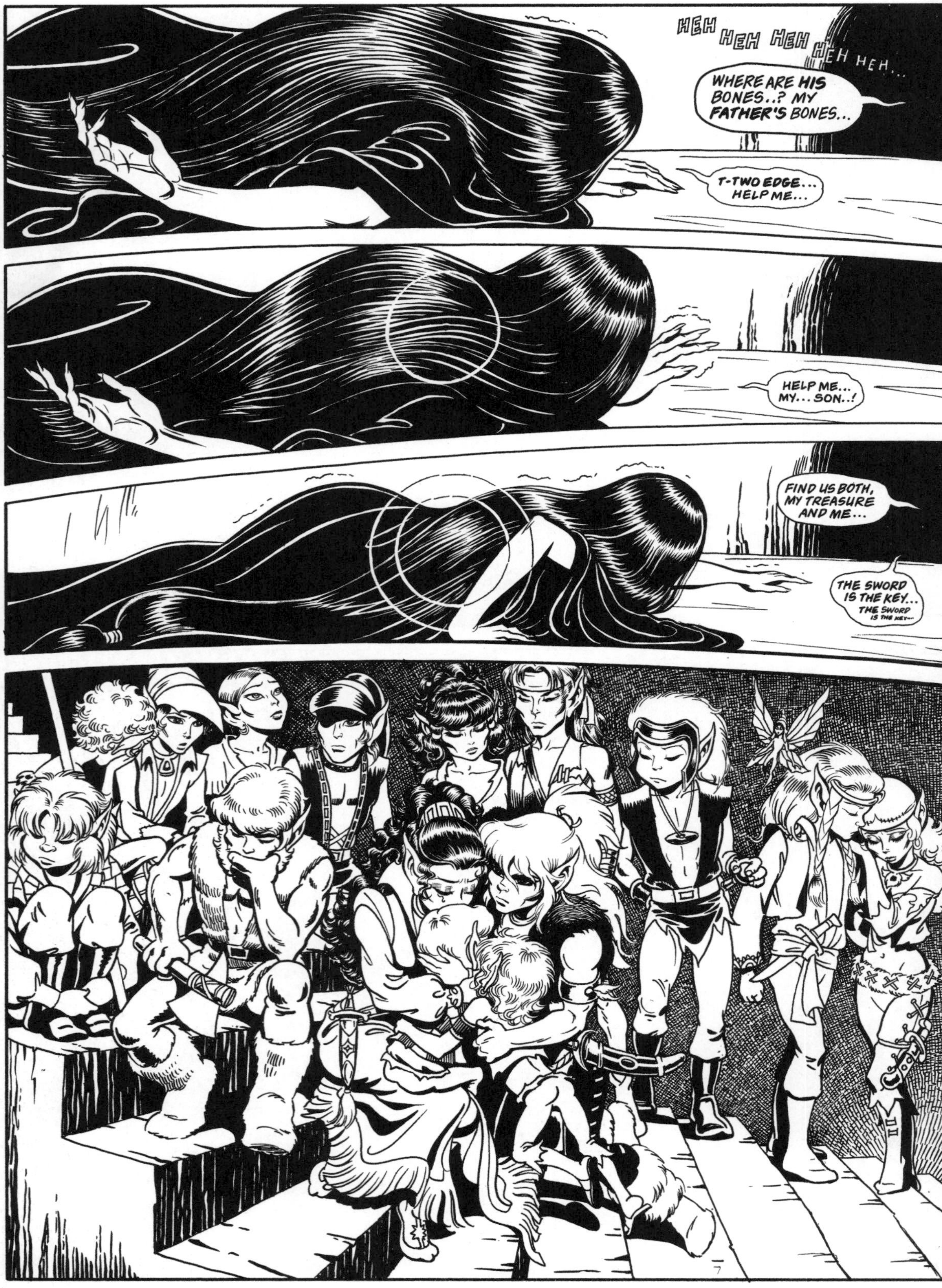
HEH HEH HEH HEH HEH HEH...
WHERE ARE HIS BONES..? MY FATHER'S BONES...
T-TWO EDGE... HELP ME...
HELP ME... MY... SON..!
FIND US BOTH, MY TREASURE AND ME...
THE SWORD IS THE KEY...
THE SWORD IS THE KEY...

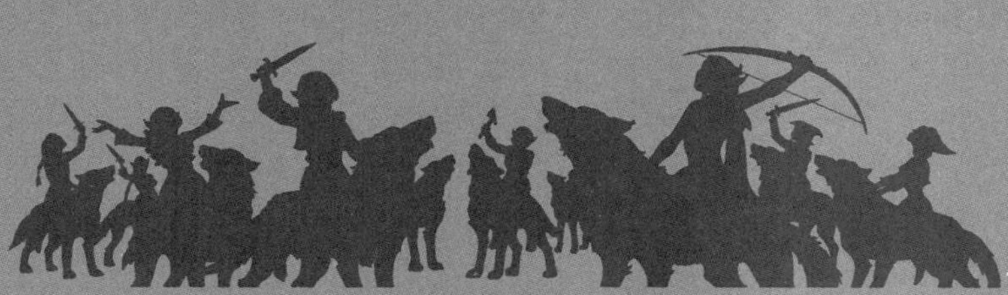

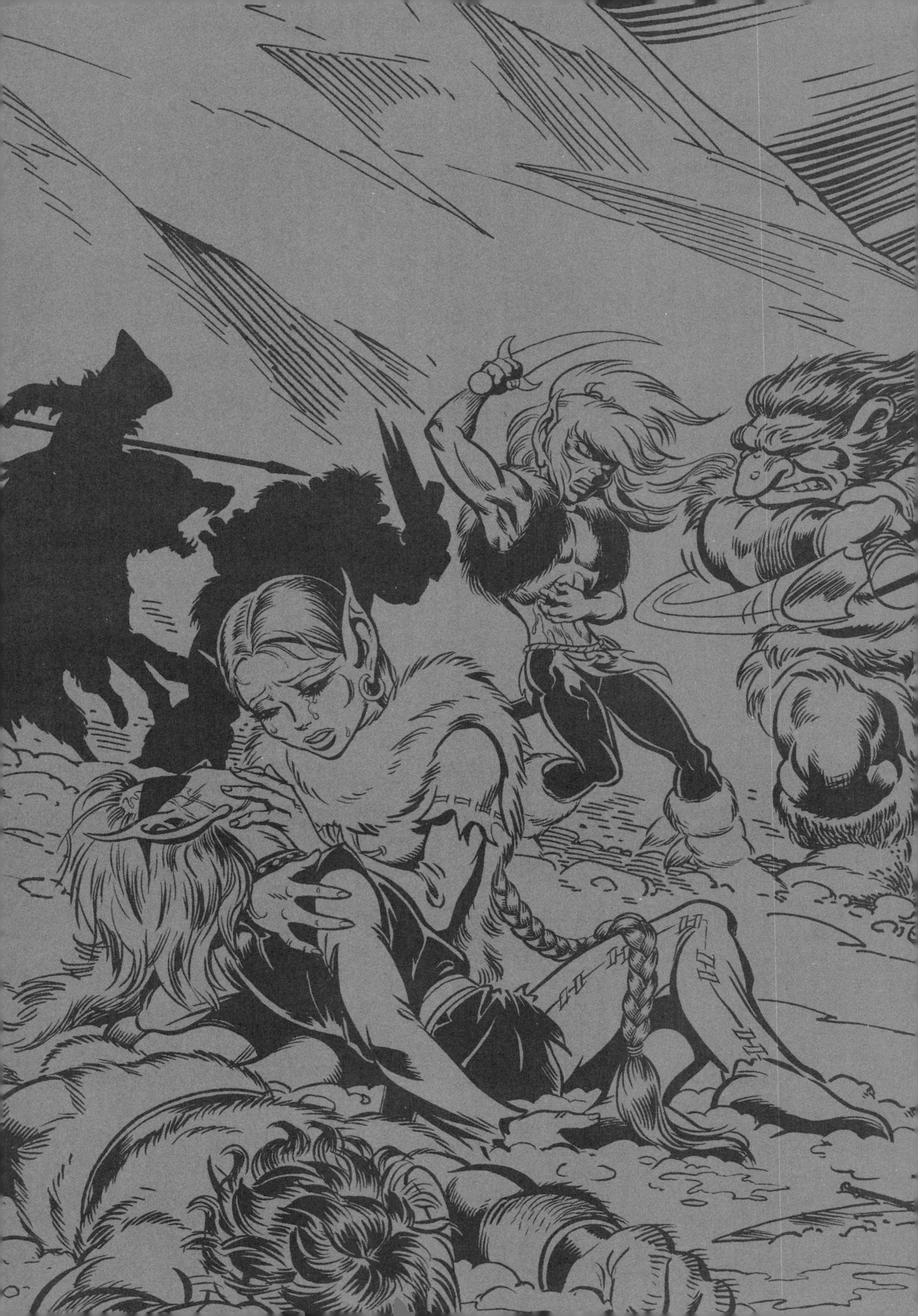

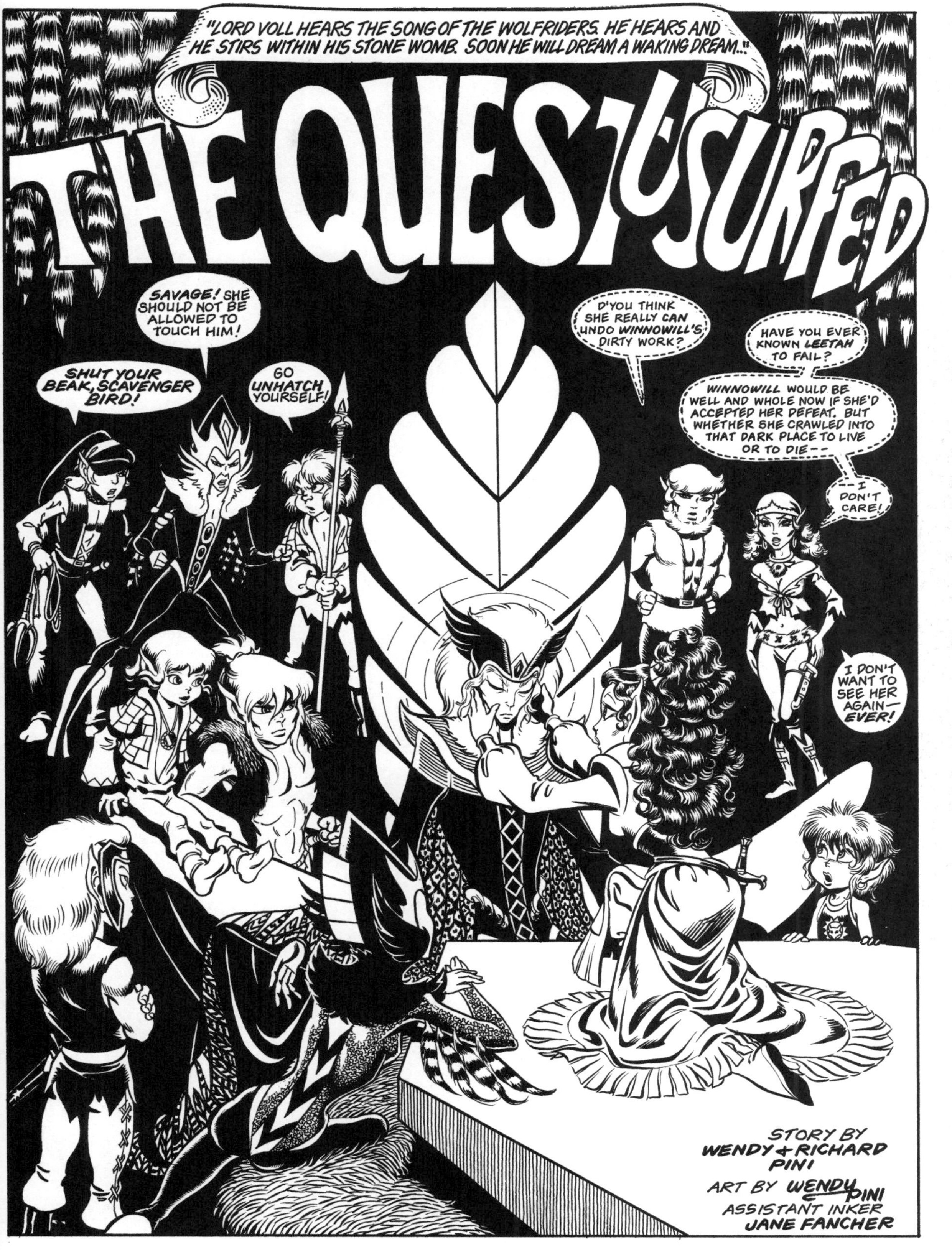
"LORD VOLL HEARS THE SONG OF THE WOLFRIDERS. HE HEARS AND HE STIRS WITHIN HIS STONE WOMB. SOON HE WILL DREAM A WAKING DREAM..."
THE QUEST USURPED
SAVAGE! SHE SHOULD NOT BE ALLOWED TO TOUCH HIM!
SHUT YOUR BEAK, SCAVENGER BIRD!
GO UNHATCH YOURSELF!
D'YOU THINK SHE REALLY CAN UNDO WINNOWILL'S DIRTY WORK?
HAVE YOU EVER KNOWN LEETAH TO FAIL?
WINNOWILL WOULD BE WELL AND WHOLE NOW IF SHE'D ACCEPTED HER DEFEAT. BUT WHETHER SHE CRAWLED INTO THAT DARK PLACE TO LIVE OR TO DIE--
--I DON'T CARE!
I DON'T WANT TO SEE HER AGAIN— EVER!
STORY BY WENDY & RICHARD PINI
ART BY WENDY PINI
ASSISTANT INKER JANE FANCHER

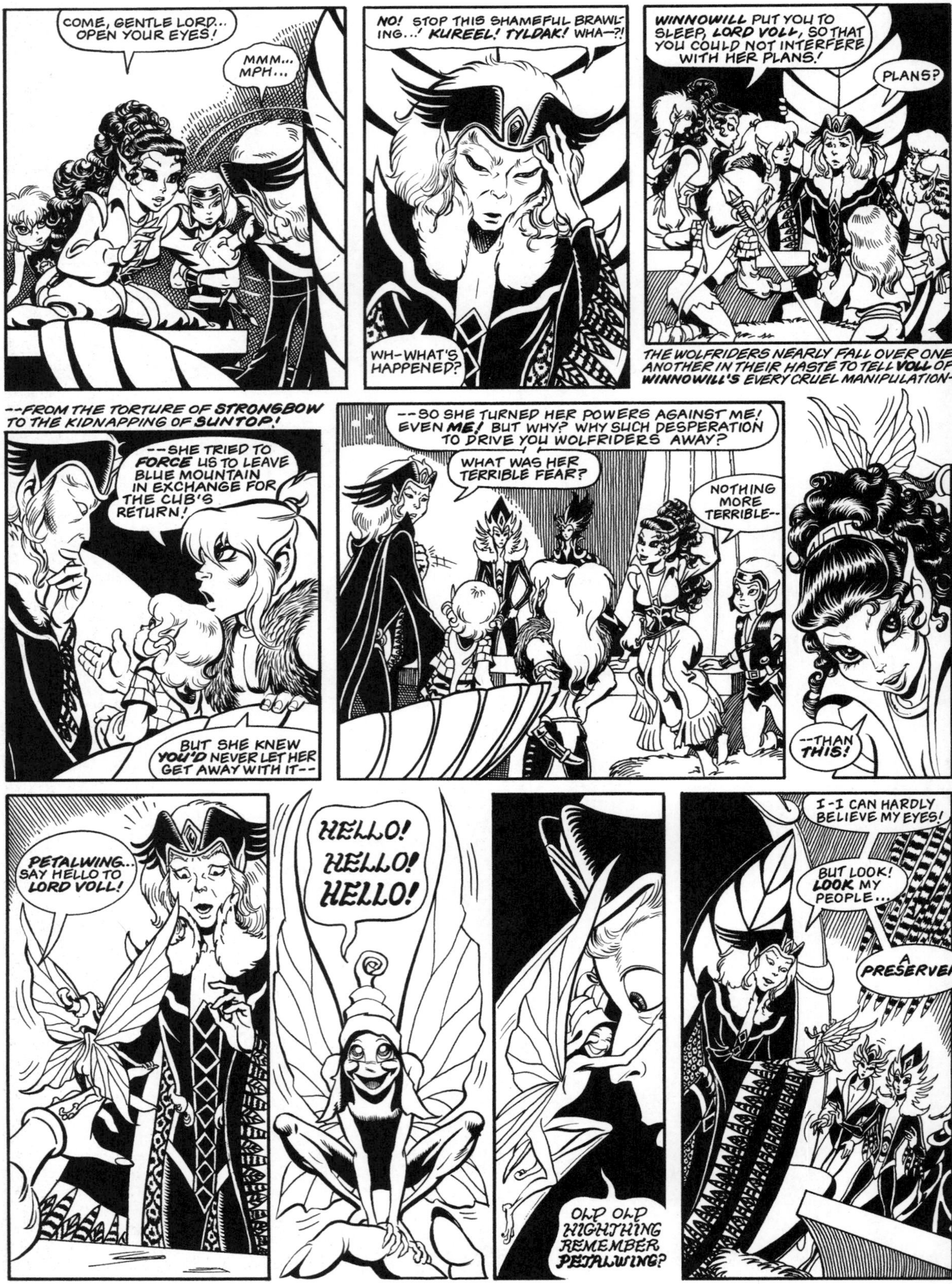
COME, GENTLE LORD... OPEN YOUR EYES!
MMM... MPH...
NO! STOP THIS SHAMEFUL BRAWLING...! KUREEL! TYLDAK! WHA--?!
WH-WHAT'S HAPPENED?
WINNOWILL PUT YOU TO SLEEP, LORD VOLL, SO THAT YOU COULD NOT INTERFERE WITH HER PLANS!
PLANS?
THE WOLFRIDERS NEARLY FALL OVER ONE ANOTHER IN THEIR HASTE TO TELL VOLL OF WINNOWILL'S EVERY CRUEL MANIPULATION--
--FROM THE TORTURE OF STRONGBOW TO THE KIDNAPPING OF SUNTOP!
--SHE TRIED TO FORCE US TO LEAVE BLUE MOUNTAIN IN EXCHANGE FOR THE CUB'S RETURN!
BUT SHE KNEW YOU'D NEVER LET HER GET AWAY WITH IT--
--SO SHE TURNED HER POWERS AGAINST ME! EVEN ME! BUT WHY? WHY SUCH DESPERATION TO DRIVE YOU WOLFRIDERS AWAY?
WHAT WAS HER TERRIBLE FEAR?
NOTHING MORE TERRIBLE--
--THAN THIS!
PETALWING... SAY HELLO TO LORD VOLL!
HELLO! HELLO! HELLO!
OLD OLD HIGHTHING REMEMBER PETALWING?
I-I CAN HARDLY BELIEVE MY EYES!
BUT LOOK! LOOK MY PEOPLE...
A PRESERVER

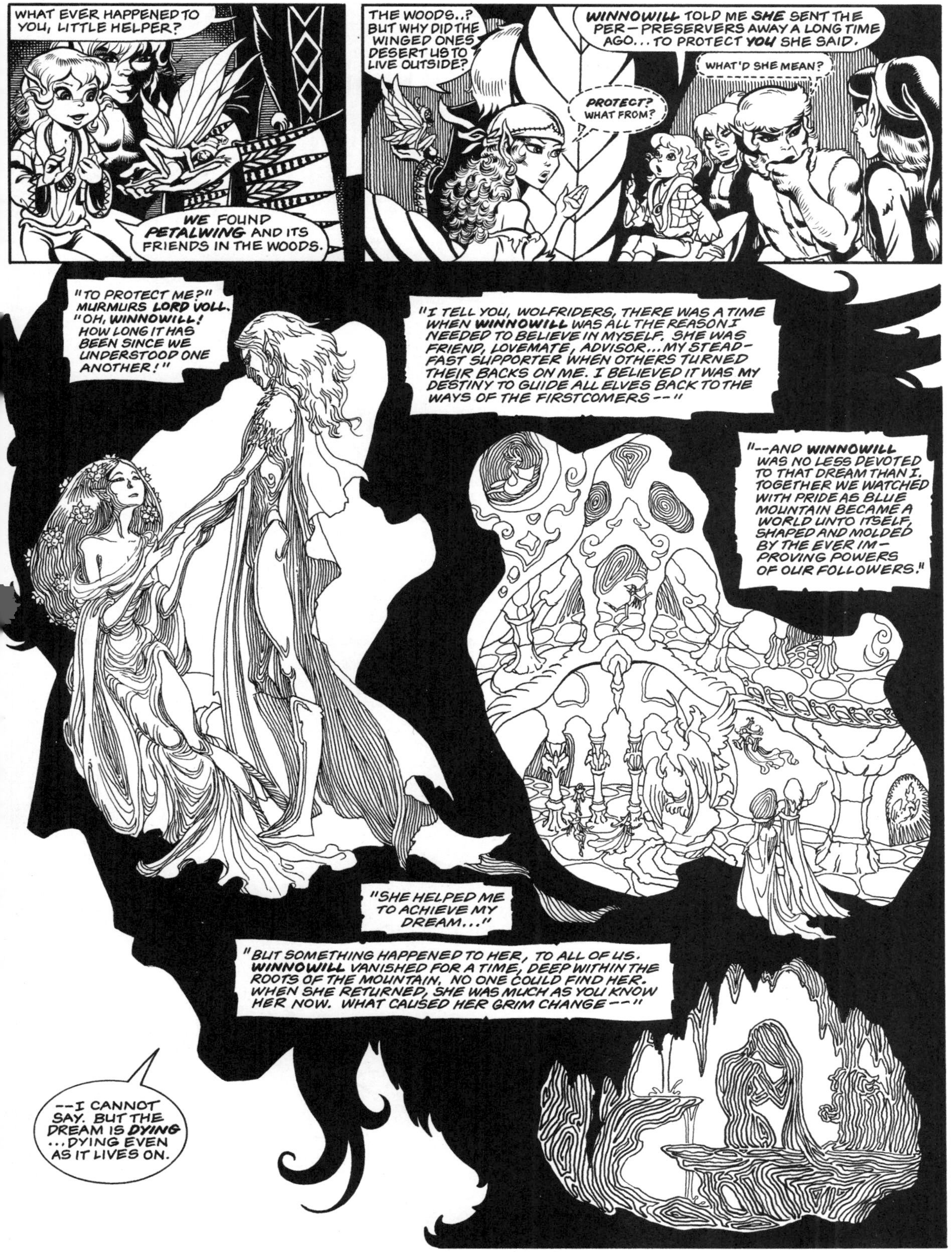
WHAT EVER HAPPENED TO YOU, LITTLE HELPER?
WE FOUND PETALWING AND ITS FRIENDS IN THE WOODS.
THE WOODS..? BUT WHY DID THE WINGED ONES DESERT US TO LIVE OUTSIDE?
WINNOWILL TOLD ME SHE SENT THE PER—PRESERVERS AWAY A LONG TIME AGO... TO PROTECT YOU SHE SAID.
WHAT'D SHE MEAN?
PROTECT? WHAT FROM?
"TO PROTECT ME?" MURMURS LORD VOLL. "OH, WINNOWILL! HOW LONG IT HAS BEEN SINCE WE UNDERSTOOD ONE ANOTHER!"
"I TELL YOU, WOLFRIDERS, THERE WAS A TIME WHEN WINNOWILL WAS ALL THE REASON I NEEDED TO BELIEVE IN MYSELF. SHE WAS FRIEND, LOVEMATE, ADVISOR... MY STEADFAST SUPPORTER WHEN OTHERS TURNED THEIR BACKS ON ME. I BELIEVED IT WAS MY DESTINY TO GUIDE ALL ELVES BACK TO THE WAYS OF THE FIRSTCOMERS--"
"--AND WINNOWILL WAS NO LESS DEVOTED TO THAT DREAM THAN I. TOGETHER WE WATCHED WITH PRIDE AS BLUE MOUNTAIN BECAME A WORLD UNTO ITSELF, SHAPED AND MOLDED BY THE EVER IM-PROVING POWERS OF OUR FOLLOWERS."
"SHE HELPED ME TO ACHIEVE MY DREAM..."
"BUT SOMETHING HAPPENED TO HER, TO ALL OF US. WINNOWILL VANISHED FOR A TIME, DEEP WITHIN THE ROOTS OF THE MOUNTAIN. NO ONE COULD FIND HER. WHEN SHE RETURNED, SHE WAS MUCH AS YOU KNOW HER NOW. WHAT CAUSED HER GRIM CHANGE--"
--I CANNOT SAY. BUT THE DREAM IS DYING ...DYING EVEN AS IT LIVES ON.

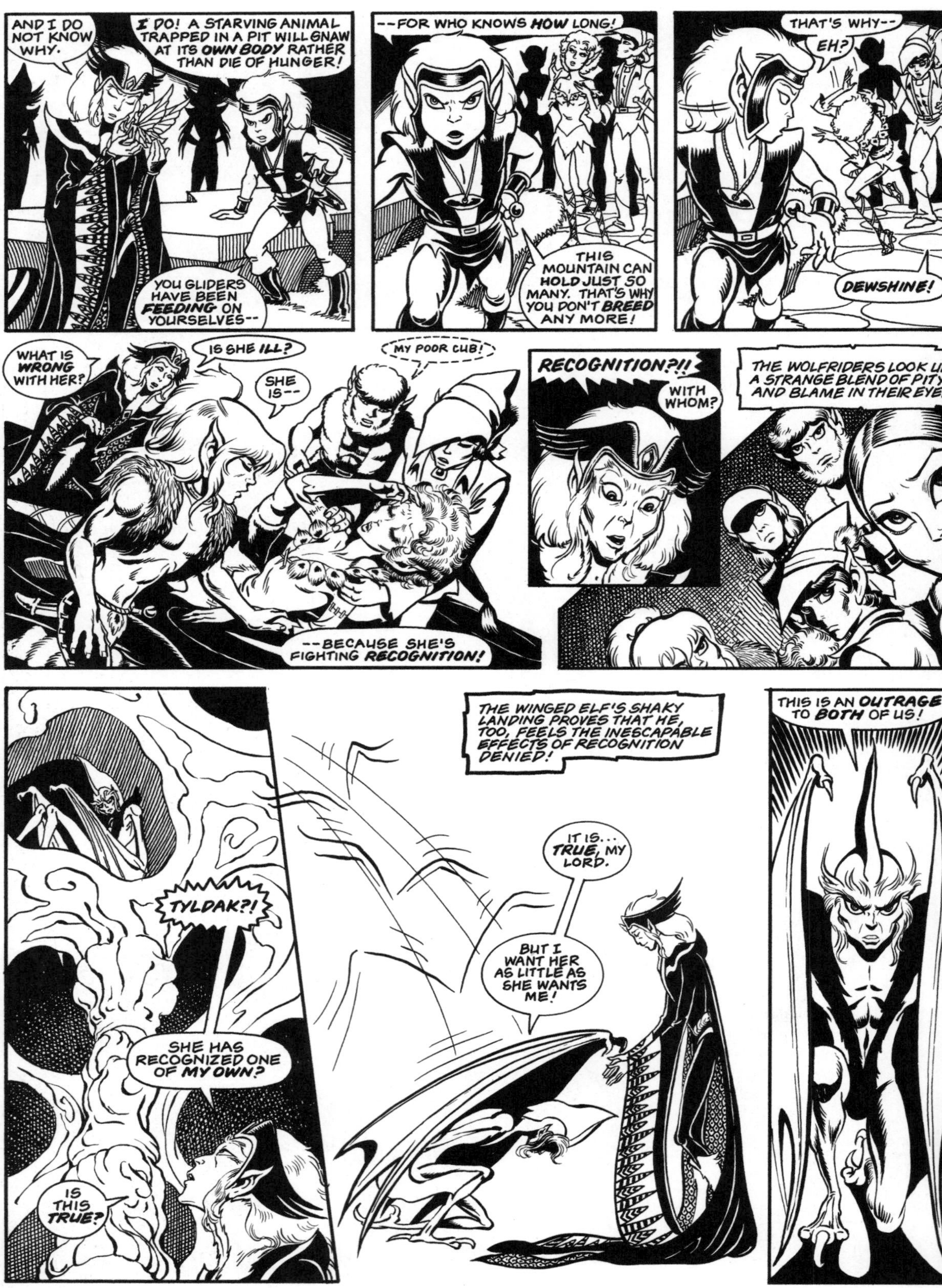
AND I DO NOT KNOW WHY.
I DO! A STARVING ANIMAL TRAPPED IN A PIT WILL GNAW AT ITS OWN BODY RATHER THAN DIE OF HUNGER!
YOU GLIDERS HAVE BEEN FEEDING ON YOURSELVES--
--FOR WHO KNOWS HOW LONG!
THIS MOUNTAIN CAN HOLD JUST SO MANY. THAT'S WHY YOU DON'T BREED ANY MORE!
THAT'S WHY--
EH?
DEWSHINE!
WHAT IS WRONG WITH HER?
IS SHE ILL?
SHE IS--
MY POOR CUB!
--BECAUSE SHE'S FIGHTING RECOGNITION!
RECOGNITION?!!
WITH WHOM?
THE WOLFRIDERS LOOK UP, A STRANGE BLEND OF PITY AND BLAME IN THEIR EYES.
TYLDAK?!
SHE HAS RECOGNIZED ONE OF MY OWN?
IS THIS TRUE?
THE WINGED ELF'S SHAKY LANDING PROVES THAT HE, TOO, FEELS THE INESCAPABLE EFFECTS OF RECOGNITION DENIED!
IT IS... TRUE, MY LORD.
BUT I WANT HER AS LITTLE AS SHE WANTS ME!
THIS IS AN OUTRAGE TO BOTH OF US!

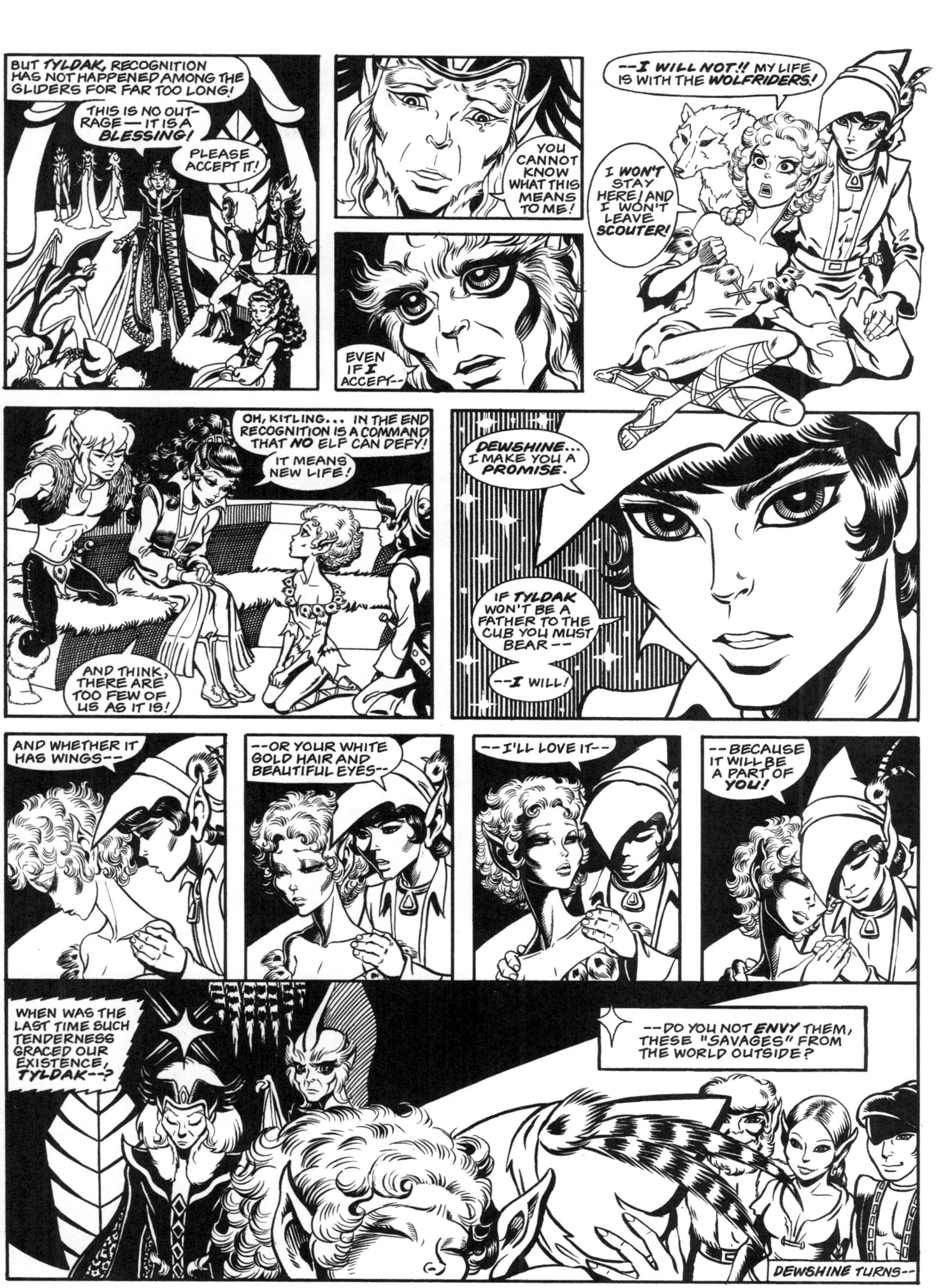

BUT TYLDAK, RECOGNITION HAS NOT HAPPENED AMONG THE GLIDERS FOR FAR TOO LONG!
THIS IS NO OUTRAGE — IT IS A BLESSING!
PLEASE ACCEPT IT!
YOU CANNOT KNOW WHAT THIS MEANS TO ME!
EVEN IF I ACCEPT--
--I WILL NOT!! MY LIFE IS WITH THE WOLFRIDERS!
I WON'T STAY HERE! AND I WON'T LEAVE SCOUTER!
OH, KITLING... IN THE END RECOGNITION IS A COMMAND THAT NO ELF CAN DEFY!
IT MEANS NEW LIFE!
AND THINK, THERE ARE TOO FEW OF US AS IT IS!
DEWSHINE... I MAKE YOU A PROMISE.
IF TYLDAK WON'T BE A FATHER TO THE CUB YOU MUST BEAR --
--I WILL!
AND WHETHER IT HAS WINGS--
--OR YOUR WHITE GOLD HAIR AND BEAUTIFUL EYES--
--I'LL LOVE IT--
--BECAUSE IT WILL BE A PART OF YOU!
WHEN WAS THE LAST TIME SUCH TENDERNESS GRACED OUR EXISTENCE, TYLDAK--?
--DO YOU NOT ENVY THEM, THESE "SAVAGES" FROM THE WORLD OUTSIDE?
DEWSHINE TURNS--

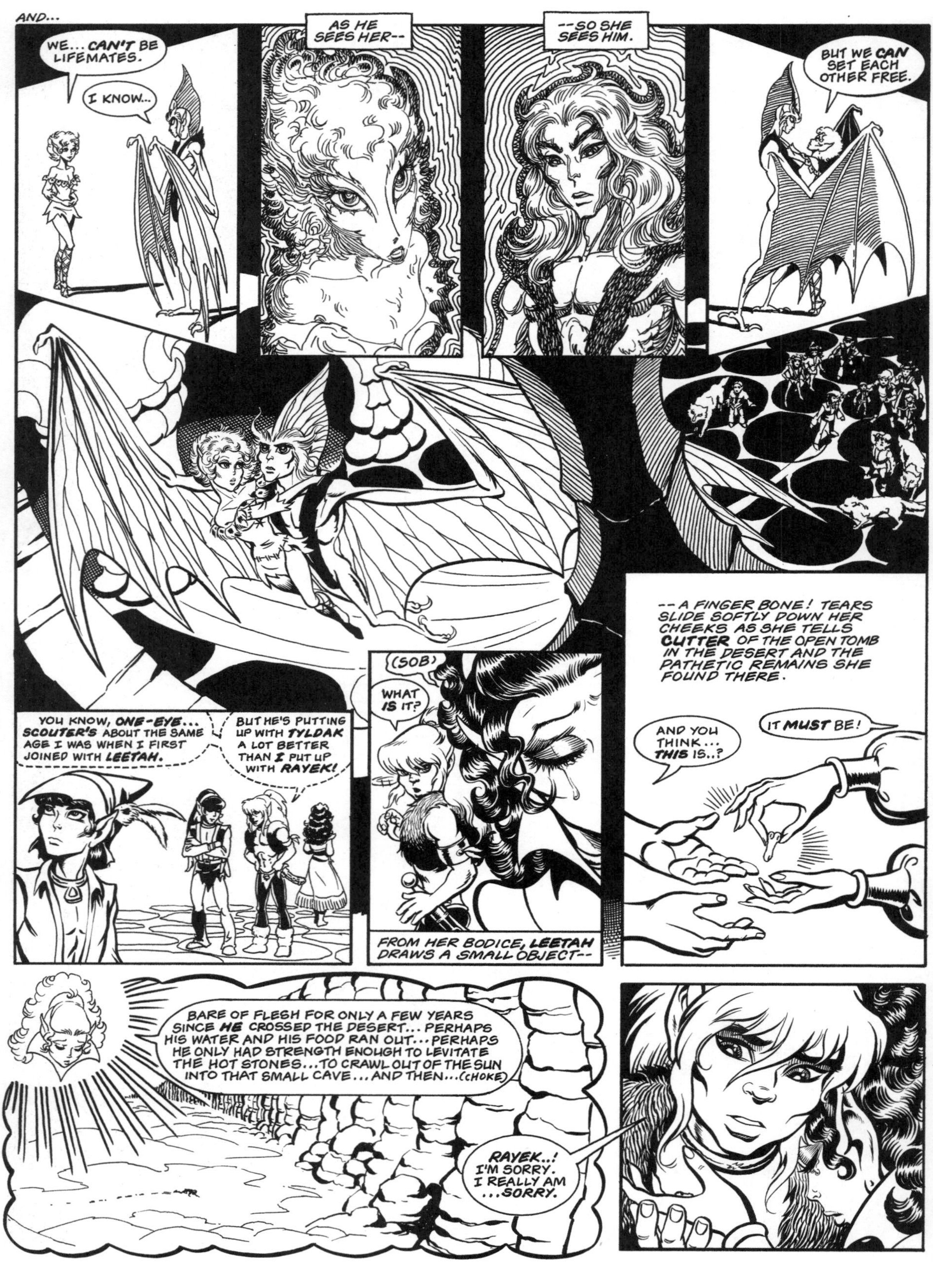
AND...
WE... CAN'T BE LIFEMATES.
I KNOW...
AS HE SEES HER--
--SO SHE SEES HIM.
BUT WE CAN SET EACH OTHER FREE.
--A FINGER BONE! TEARS SLIDE SOFTLY DOWN HER CHEEKS AS SHE TELLS CUTTER OF THE OPEN TOMB IN THE DESERT AND THE PATHETIC REMAINS SHE FOUND THERE.
YOU KNOW, ONE-EYE... SCOUTER'S ABOUT THE SAME AGE I WAS WHEN I FIRST JOINED WITH LEETAH.
BUT HE'S PUTTING UP WITH TYLDAK A LOT BETTER THAN I PUT UP WITH RAYEK!
(SOB)
WHAT IS IT?
FROM HER BODICE, LEETAH DRAWS A SMALL OBJECT--
AND YOU THINK... THIS IS..?
IT MUST BE!
BARE OF FLESH FOR ONLY A FEW YEARS SINCE HE CROSSED THE DESERT... PERHAPS HIS WATER AND HIS FOOD RAN OUT... PERHAPS HE ONLY HAD STRENGTH ENOUGH TO LEVITATE THE HOT STONES... TO CRAWL OUT OF THE SUN INTO THAT SMALL CAVE... AND THEN... (CHOKE)
RAYEK..! I'M SORRY. I REALLY AM ...SORRY.

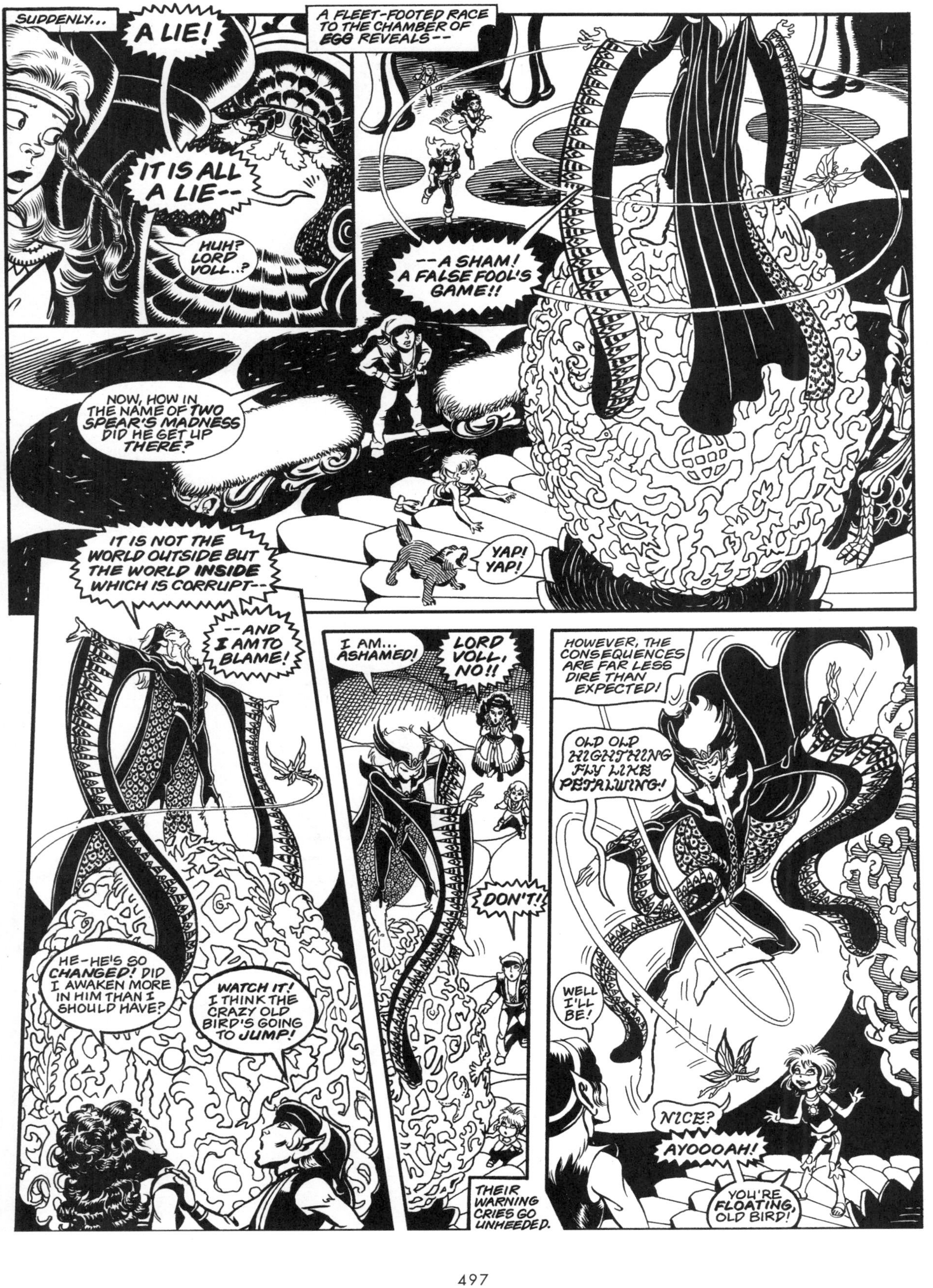

SUDDENLY...
A LIE!
IT IS ALL A LIE--
HUH? LORD VOLL..?
A FLEET-FOOTED RACE TO THE CHAMBER OF EGG REVEALS--
--A SHAM! A FALSE FOOL'S GAME!!
NOW, HOW IN THE NAME OF TWO SPEAR'S MADNESS DID HE GET UP THERE?
YAP! YAP!
IT IS NOT THE WORLD OUTSIDE BUT THE WORLD INSIDE WHICH IS CORRUPT--
--AND I AM TO BLAME!
HE-HE'S SO CHANGED! DID I AWAKEN MORE IN HIM THAN I SHOULD HAVE?
WATCH IT! I THINK THE CRAZY OLD BIRD'S GOING TO JUMP!
I AM... ASHAMED!
LORD VOLL, NO!!
DON'T!!
THEIR WARNING CRIES GO UNHEEDED.
HOWEVER, THE CONSEQUENCES ARE FAR LESS DIRE THAN EXPECTED!
OLD OLD HIGHTHING FLY LIKE PETALWING!
WELL I'LL BE!
NICE?
AYOOOAH!
YOU'RE FLOATING, OLD BIRD!

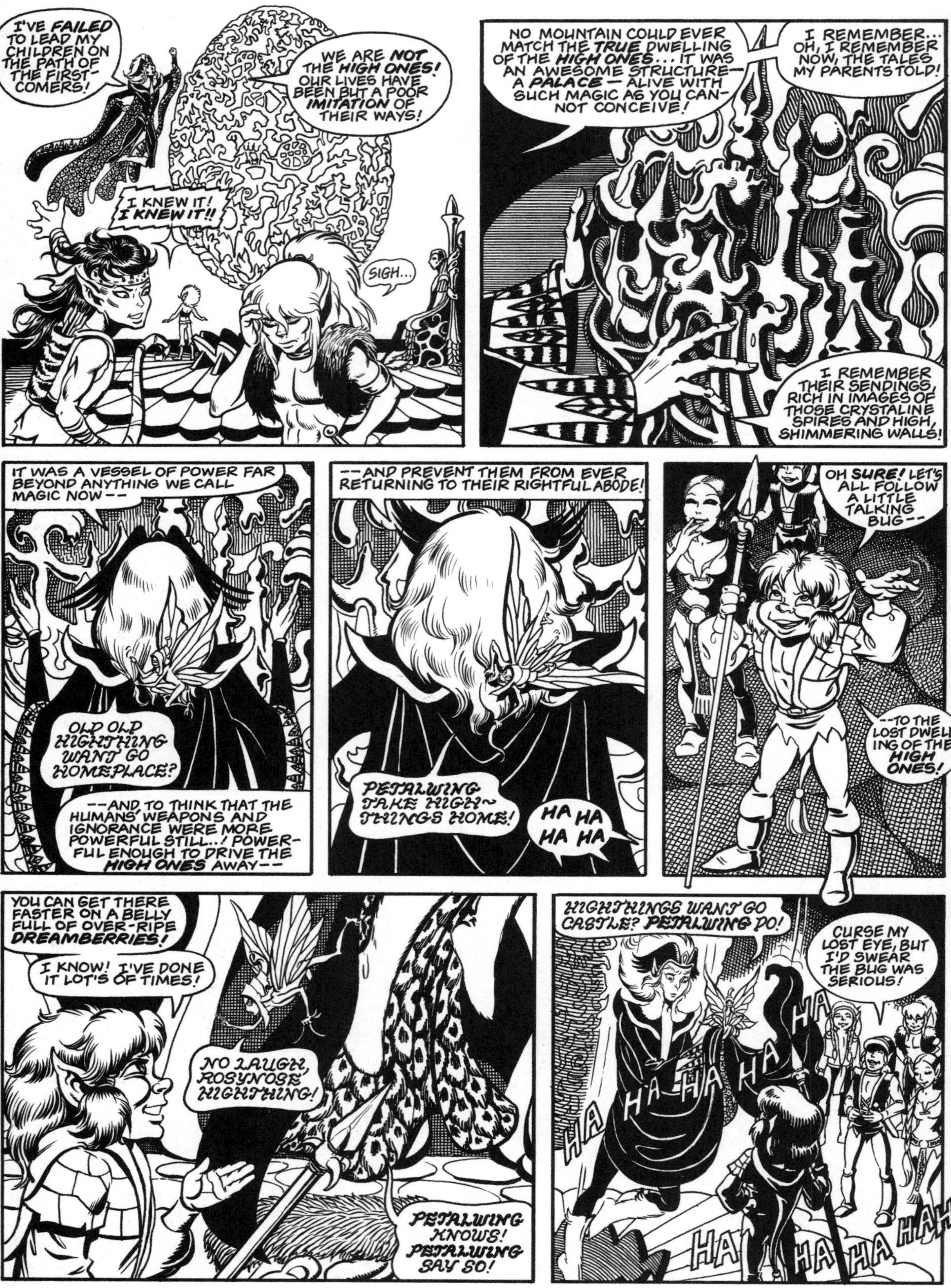
I'VE FAILED TO LEAD MY CHILDREN ON THE PATH OF THE FIRST-COMERS!
WE ARE NOT THE HIGH ONES! OUR LIVES HAVE BEEN BUT A POOR IMITATION OF THEIR WAYS!
I KNEW IT! I KNEW IT!!
SIGH...
NO MOUNTAIN COULD EVER MATCH THE TRUE DWELLING OF THE HIGH ONES... IT WAS AN AWESOME STRUCTURE-- A PALACE -- ALIVE WITH SUCH MAGIC AS YOU CANNOT CONCEIVE!
I REMEMBER... OH, I REMEMBER NOW, THE TALES MY PARENTS TOLD!
I REMEMBER THEIR SENDINGS, RICH IN IMAGES OF THOSE CRYSTALINE SPIRES AND HIGH, SHIMMERING WALLS!
IT WAS A VESSEL OF POWER FAR BEYOND ANYTHING WE CALL MAGIC NOW--
OLD OLD HIGHTHING WANT GO HOMEPLACE?
--AND TO THINK THAT THE HUMANS' WEAPONS AND IGNORANCE WERE MORE POWERFUL STILL...! POWERFUL ENOUGH TO DRIVE THE HIGH ONES AWAY--
--AND PREVENT THEM FROM EVER RETURNING TO THEIR RIGHTFUL ABODE!
PETALWING TAKE HIGHTHINGS HOME!
HA HA HA HA
OH SURE! LET'S ALL FOLLOW A LITTLE TALKING BUG--
--TO THE LOST DWELLING OF THE HIGH ONES!
YOU CAN GET THERE FASTER ON A BELLY FULL OF OVER-RIPE DREAMBERRIES!
I KNOW! I'VE DONE IT LOT'S OF TIMES!
NO LAUGH, ROSYNOSE HIGHTHING!
PETALWING KNOWS! PETALWING SAY SO!
HIGHTHINGS WANT GO CASTLE? PETALWING DO!
CURSE MY LOST EYE, BUT I'D SWEAR THE BUG WAS SERIOUS!
HA HA HA HA HA HA HA
HA HA HA HA HAH

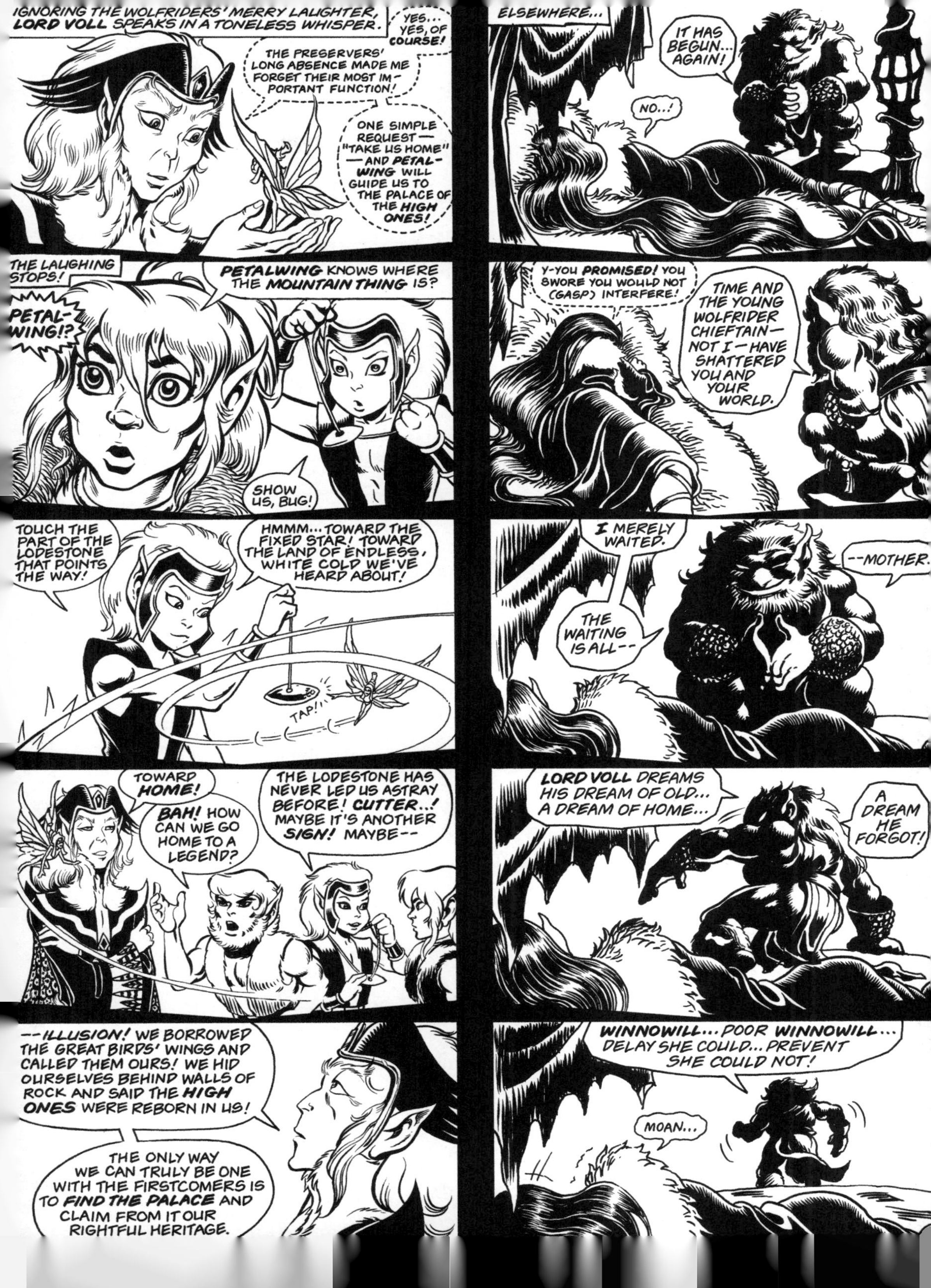
IGNORING THE WOLFRIDERS' MERRY LAUGHTER, LORD VOLL SPEAKS IN A TONELESS WHISPER.
YES... YES, OF COURSE!
THE PRESERVERS' LONG ABSENCE MADE ME FORGET THEIR MOST IMPORTANT FUNCTION!
ONE SIMPLE REQUEST — "TAKE US HOME" — AND PETALWING WILL GUIDE US TO THE PALACE OF THE HIGH ONES!
THE LAUGHING STOPS!
PETALWING!?
PETALWING KNOWS WHERE THE MOUNTAIN THING IS?
SHOW US, BUG!
TOUCH THE PART OF THE LODESTONE THAT POINTS THE WAY!
HMMM... TOWARD THE FIXED STAR! TOWARD THE LAND OF ENDLESS, WHITE COLD WE'VE HEARD ABOUT!
TAP!
TOWARD HOME!
BAH! HOW CAN WE GO HOME TO A LEGEND?
THE LODESTONE HAS NEVER LED US ASTRAY BEFORE! CUTTER..! MAYBE IT'S ANOTHER SIGN! MAYBE--
--ILLUSION! WE BORROWED THE GREAT BIRDS' WINGS AND CALLED THEM OURS! WE HID OURSELVES BEHIND WALLS OF ROCK AND SAID THE HIGH ONES WERE REBORN IN US!
THE ONLY WAY WE CAN TRULY BE ONE WITH THE FIRSTCOMERS IS TO FIND THE PALACE AND CLAIM FROM IT OUR RIGHTFUL HERITAGE.
ELSEWHERE...
IT HAS BEGUN... AGAIN!
NO...!
Y-YOU PROMISED! YOU SWORE YOU WOULD NOT (GASP) INTERFERE!
TIME AND THE YOUNG WOLFRIDER CHIEFTAIN— NOT I—HAVE SHATTERED YOU AND YOUR WORLD.
I MERELY WAITED.
THE WAITING IS ALL--
--MOTHER.
LORD VOLL DREAMS HIS DREAM OF OLD... A DREAM OF HOME...
A DREAM HE FORGOT!
WINNOWILL... POOR WINNOWILL... DELAY SHE COULD... PREVENT SHE COULD NOT!
MOAN...

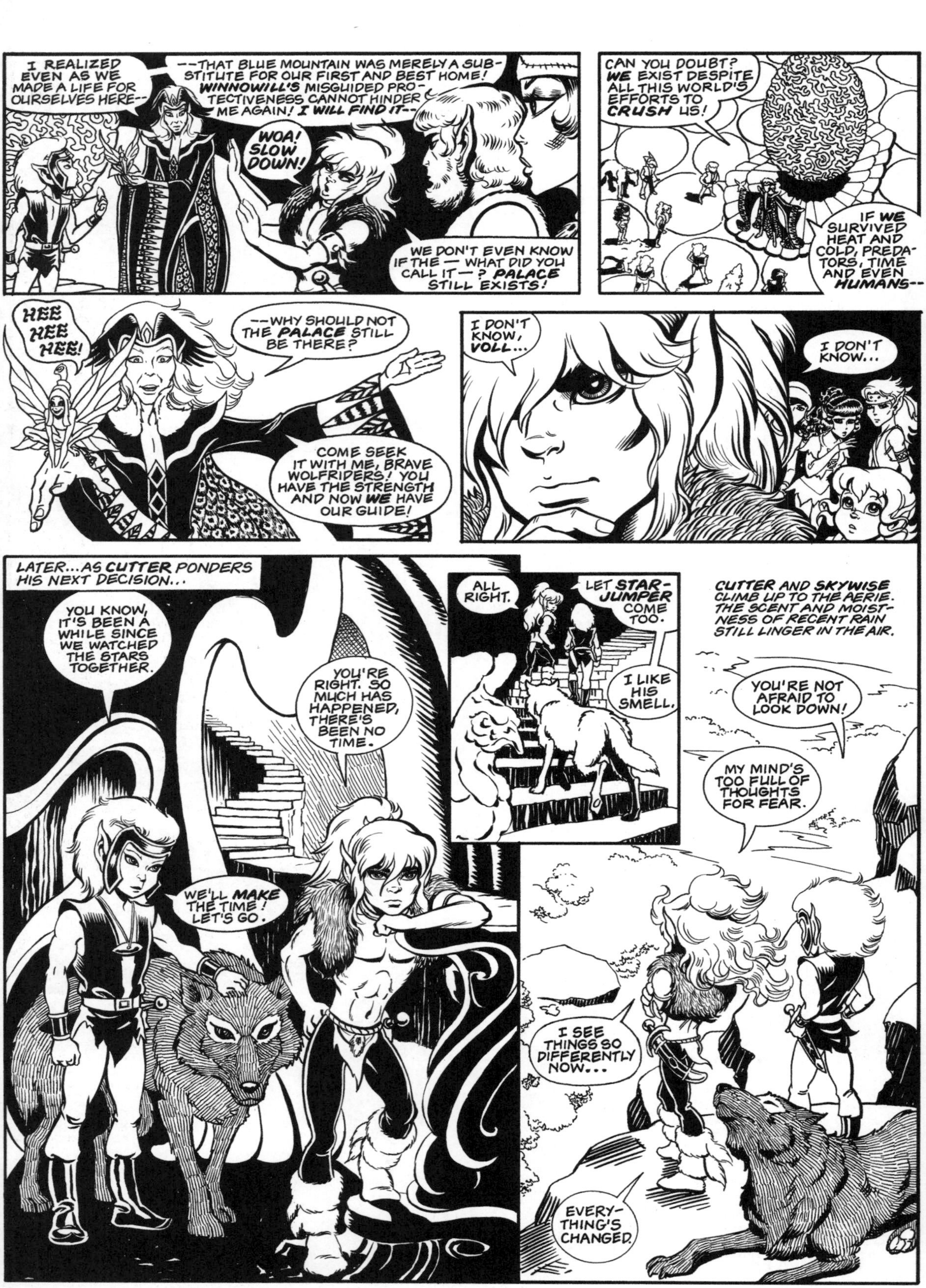

I REALIZED EVEN AS WE MADE A LIFE FOR OURSELVES HERE--
--THAT BLUE MOUNTAIN WAS MERELY A SUBSTITUTE FOR OUR FIRST AND BEST HOME! WINNOWILL'S MISGUIDED PROTECTIVENESS CANNOT HINDER ME AGAIN! I WILL FIND IT--
WOA! SLOW DOWN!
WE DON'T EVEN KNOW IF THE — WHAT DID YOU CALL IT — ? PALACE STILL EXISTS!
CAN YOU DOUBT? WE EXIST DESPITE ALL THIS WORLD'S EFFORTS TO CRUSH US!
IF WE SURVIVED HEAT AND COLD, PREDATORS, TIME AND EVEN HUMANS--
HEE HEE HEE!
--WHY SHOULD NOT THE PALACE STILL BE THERE?
COME SEEK IT WITH ME, BRAVE WOLFRIDERS! YOU HAVE THE STRENGTH AND NOW WE HAVE OUR GUIDE!
I DON'T KNOW, VOLL...
I DON'T KNOW...
LATER... AS CUTTER PONDERS HIS NEXT DECISION...
YOU KNOW, IT'S BEEN A WHILE SINCE WE WATCHED THE STARS TOGETHER.
YOU'RE RIGHT. SO MUCH HAS HAPPENED, THERE'S BEEN NO TIME.
WE'LL MAKE THE TIME! LET'S GO.
ALL RIGHT.
LET STARJUMPER COME TOO.
I LIKE HIS SMELL.
CUTTER AND SKYWISE CLIMB UP TO THE AERIE. THE SCENT AND MOISTNESS OF RECENT RAIN STILL LINGER IN THE AIR.
YOU'RE NOT AFRAID TO LOOK DOWN!
MY MIND'S TOO FULL OF THOUGHTS FOR FEAR.
I SEE THINGS SO DIFFERENTLY NOW...
EVERYTHING'S CHANGED.

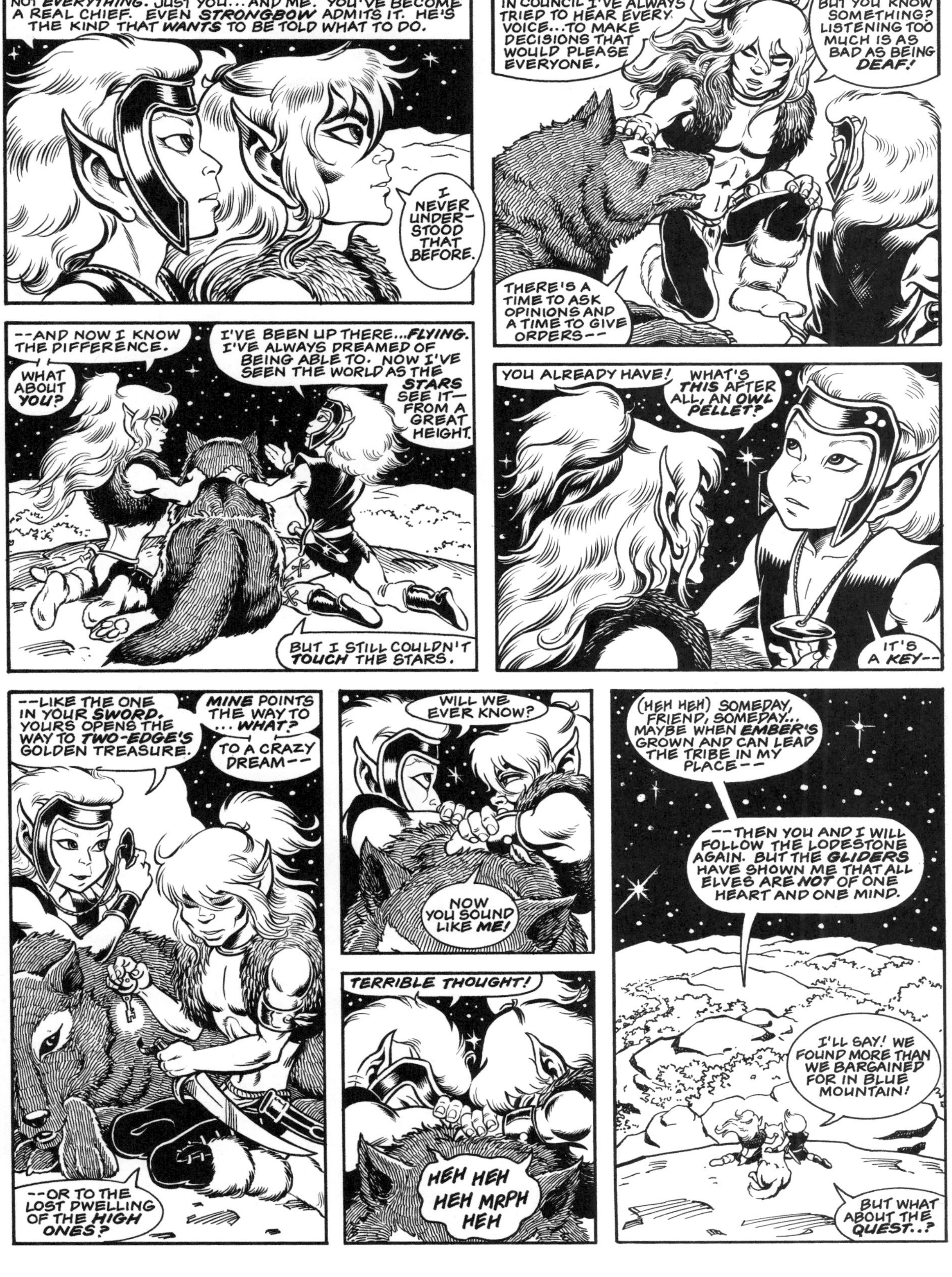
NOT EVERYTHING. JUST YOU... AND ME. YOU'VE BECOME A REAL CHIEF. EVEN STRONGBOW ADMITS IT. HE'S THE KIND THAT WANTS TO BE TOLD WHAT TO DO.
I NEVER UNDER-STOOD THAT BEFORE.
IN COUNCIL I'VE ALWAYS TRIED TO HEAR EVERY VOICE... TO MAKE DECISIONS THAT WOULD PLEASE EVERYONE.
BUT YOU KNOW SOMETHING? LISTENING TOO MUCH IS AS BAD AS BEING DEAF!
THERE'S A TIME TO ASK OPINIONS AND A TIME TO GIVE ORDERS--
--AND NOW I KNOW THE DIFFERENCE.
WHAT ABOUT YOU?
I'VE BEEN UP THERE... FLYING. I'VE ALWAYS DREAMED OF BEING ABLE TO. NOW I'VE SEEN THE WORLD AS THE STARS SEE IT— FROM A GREAT HEIGHT.
BUT I STILL COULDN'T TOUCH THE STARS.
YOU ALREADY HAVE!
WHAT'S THIS AFTER ALL, AN OWL PELLET?
IT'S A KEY--
--LIKE THE ONE IN YOUR SWORD. YOURS OPENS THE WAY TO TWO-EDGE'S GOLDEN TREASURE.
MINE POINTS THE WAY TO ... WHAT?
TO A CRAZY DREAM--
--OR TO THE LOST DWELLING OF THE HIGH ONES?
WILL WE EVER KNOW?
NOW YOU SOUND LIKE ME!
TERRIBLE THOUGHT!
HEH HEH HEH MRPH HEH
(HEH HEH) SOMEDAY, FRIEND, SOMEDAY... MAYBE WHEN EMBER'S GROWN AND CAN LEAD THE TRIBE IN MY PLACE--
--THEN YOU AND I WILL FOLLOW THE LODESTONE AGAIN. BUT THE GLIDERS HAVE SHOWN ME THAT ALL ELVES ARE NOT OF ONE HEART AND ONE MIND.
I'LL SAY! WE FOUND MORE THAN WE BARGAINED FOR IN BLUE MOUNTAIN!
BUT WHAT ABOUT THE QUEST..?

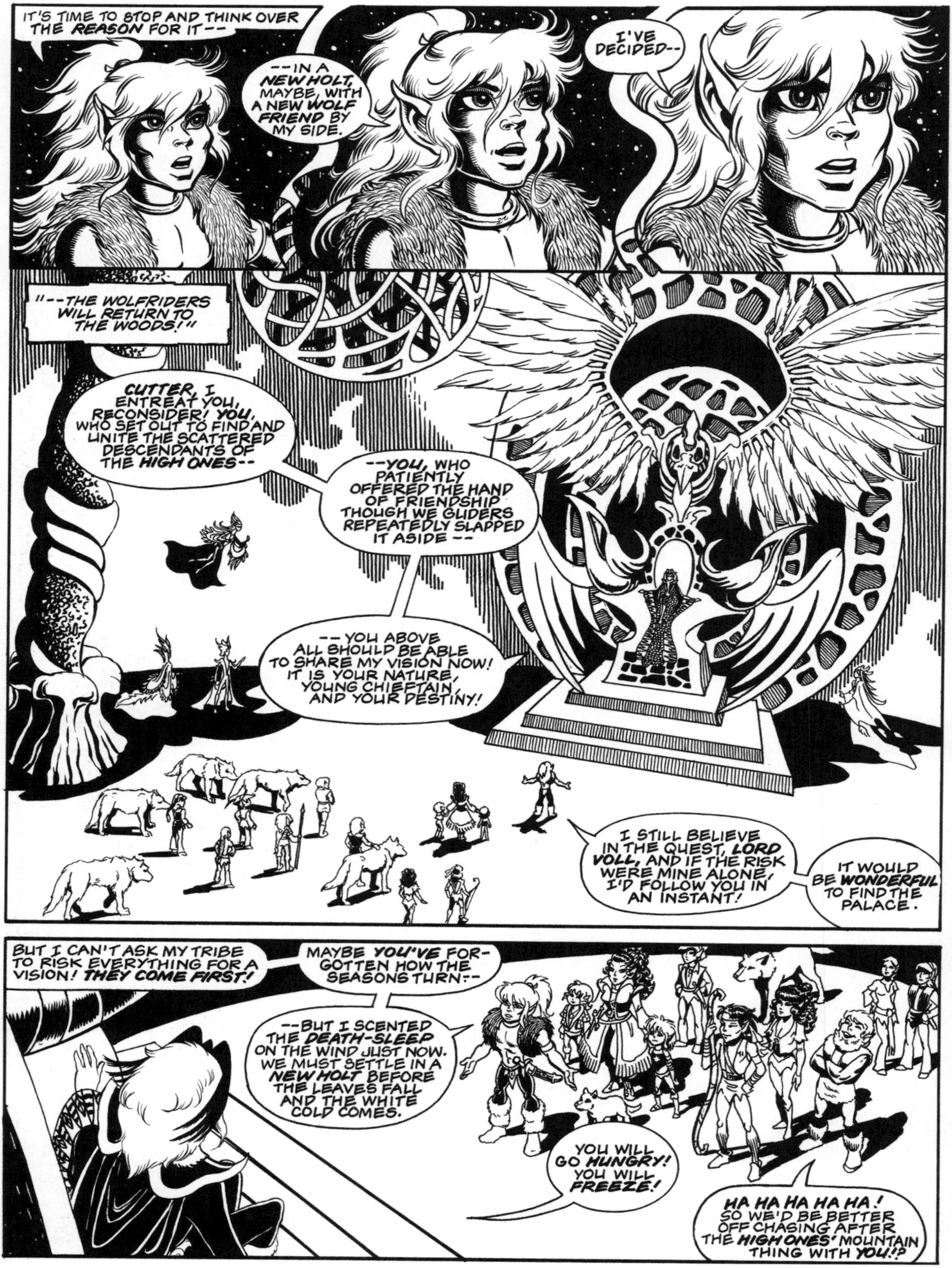
IT'S TIME TO STOP AND THINK OVER THE REASON FOR IT--
--IN A NEW HOLT, MAYBE, WITH A NEW WOLF FRIEND BY MY SIDE.
I'VE DECIDED--
"--THE WOLFRIDERS WILL RETURN TO THE WOODS!"
CUTTER, I ENTREAT YOU, RECONSIDER! YOU, WHO SET OUT TO FIND AND UNITE THE SCATTERED DESCENDANTS OF THE HIGH ONES--
--YOU, WHO PATIENTLY OFFERED THE HAND OF FRIENDSHIP THOUGH WE GLIDERS REPEATEDLY SLAPPED IT ASIDE--
--YOU ABOVE ALL SHOULD BE ABLE TO SHARE MY VISION NOW! IT IS YOUR NATURE, YOUNG CHIEFTAIN, AND YOUR DESTINY!
I STILL BELIEVE IN THE QUEST, LORD VOLL, AND IF THE RISK WERE MINE ALONE, I'D FOLLOW YOU IN AN INSTANT!
IT WOULD BE WONDERFUL TO FIND THE PALACE.
BUT I CAN'T ASK MY TRIBE TO RISK EVERYTHING FOR A VISION! THEY COME FIRST!
MAYBE YOU'VE FORGOTTEN HOW THE SEASONS TURN--
--BUT I SCENTED THE DEATH-SLEEP ON THE WIND JUST NOW. WE MUST SETTLE IN A NEW HOLT BEFORE THE LEAVES FALL AND THE WHITE COLD COMES.
YOU WILL GO HUNGRY! YOU WILL FREEZE!
HA HA HA HA HA! SO WE'D BE BETTER OFF CHASING AFTER THE HIGH ONES' MOUNTAIN THING WITH YOU!?

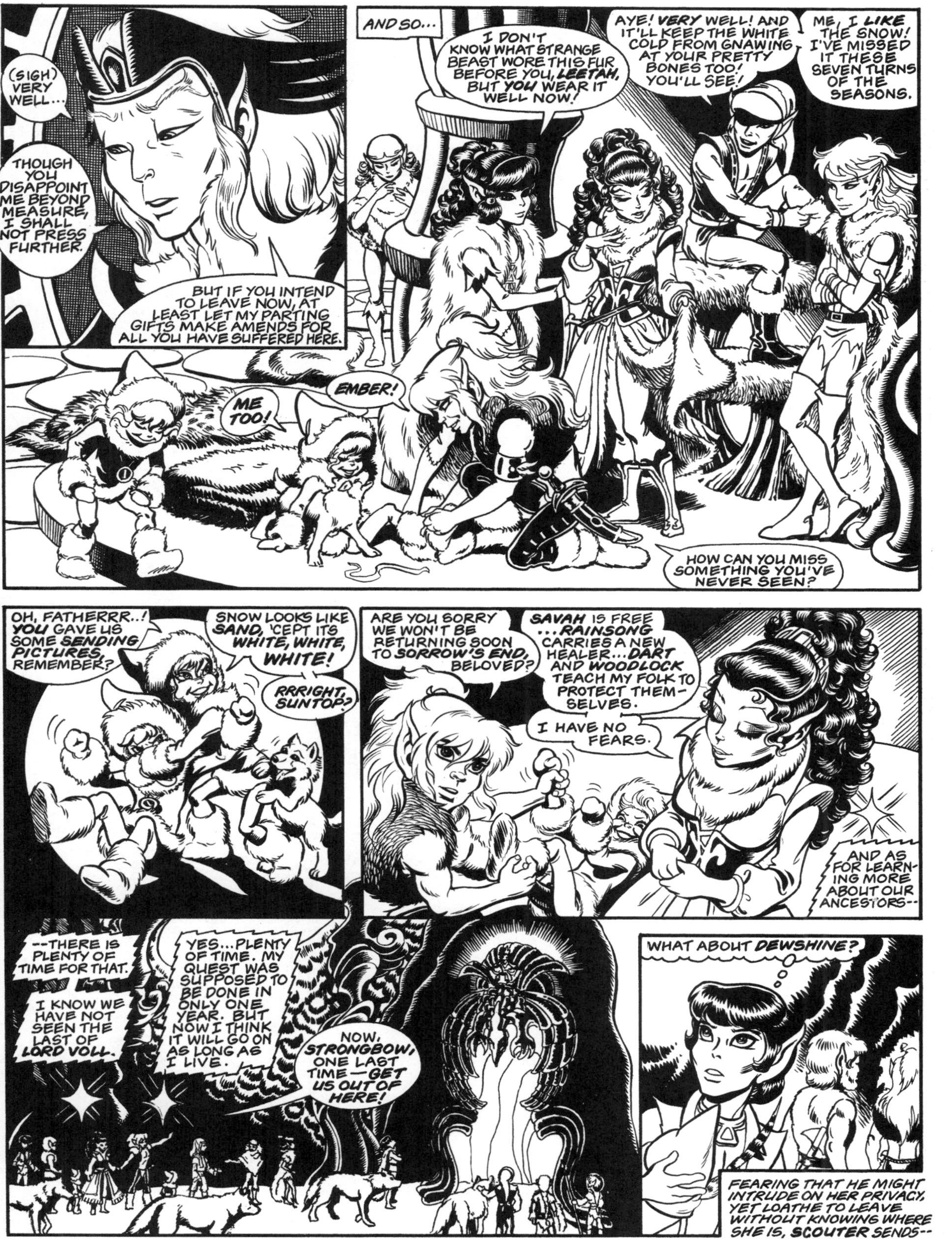
(SIGH) VERY WELL...
THOUGH YOU DISAPPOINT ME BEYOND MEASURE, I SHALL NOT PRESS FURTHER.
BUT IF YOU INTEND TO LEAVE NOW, AT LEAST LET MY PARTING GIFTS MAKE AMENDS FOR ALL YOU HAVE SUFFERED HERE.
AND SO...
I DON'T KNOW WHAT STRANGE BEAST WORE THIS FUR BEFORE YOU, LEETAH, BUT YOU WEAR IT WELL NOW!
AYE! VERY WELL! AND IT'LL KEEP THE WHITE COLD FROM GNAWING AT YOUR PRETTY BONES TOO! YOU'LL SEE!
ME, I LIKE THE SNOW! I'VE MISSED IT THESE SEVEN TURNS OF THE SEASONS.
EMBER!
ME TOO!
HOW CAN YOU MISS SOMETHING YOU'VE NEVER SEEN?
OH, FATHERRR..! YOU GAVE US SOME SENDING PICTURES, REMEMBER?
SNOW LOOKS LIKE SAND, 'CEPT ITS WHITE, WHITE, WHITE!
RRRIGHT, SUNTOP?
ARE YOU SORRY WE WON'T BE RETURNING SOON TO SORROW'S END, BELOVED?
SAVAH IS FREE ...RAINSONG CARRIES A NEW HEALER...DART AND WOODLOCK TEACH MY FOLK TO PROTECT THEMSELVES.
I HAVE NO FEARS.
AND AS FOR LEARNING MORE ABOUT OUR ANCESTORS--
--THERE IS PLENTY OF TIME FOR THAT.
I KNOW WE HAVE NOT SEEN THE LAST OF LORD VOLL.
YES...PLENTY OF TIME. MY QUEST WAS SUPPOSED TO BE DONE IN ONLY ONE YEAR. BUT NOW I THINK IT WILL GO ON AS LONG AS I LIVE.
NOW, STRONGBOW, ONE LAST TIME—GET US OUT OF HERE!
WHAT ABOUT DEWSHINE?
FEARING THAT HE MIGHT INTRUDE ON HER PRIVACY, YET LOATHE TO LEAVE WITHOUT KNOWING WHERE SHE IS, SCOUTER SENDS--

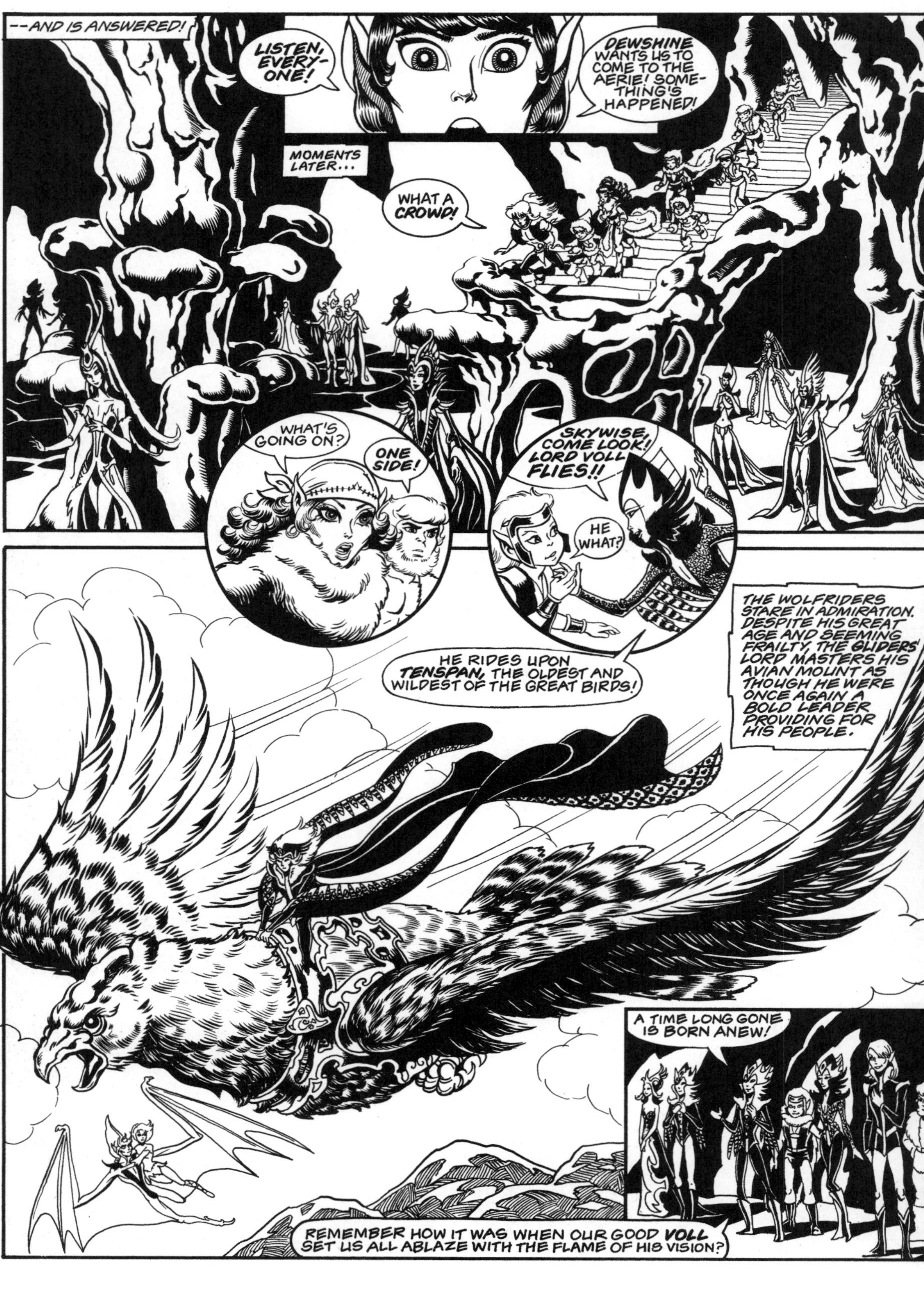
--AND IS ANSWERED!
LISTEN, EVERY-ONE!
DEWSHINE WANTS US TO COME TO THE AERIE! SOME-THING'S HAPPENED!
MOMENTS LATER...
WHAT A CROWD!
WHAT'S GOING ON?
ONE SIDE!
SKYWISE, COME LOOK! LORD VOLL FLIES!!
HE WHAT?
THE WOLFRIDERS STARE IN ADMIRATION. DESPITE HIS GREAT AGE AND SEEMING FRAILTY, THE GLIDERS' LORD MASTERS HIS AVIAN MOUNT AS THOUGH HE WERE ONCE AGAIN A BOLD LEADER PROVIDING FOR HIS PEOPLE.
HE RIDES UPON TENSPAN, THE OLDEST AND WILDEST OF THE GREAT BIRDS!
A TIME LONG GONE IS BORN ANEW!
REMEMBER HOW IT WAS WHEN OUR GOOD VOLL SET US ALL ABLAZE WITH THE FLAME OF HIS VISION?

YOU MUST LET ME GO NOW, *TYLDAK.*

I BELONG WITH MY OWN PEOPLE.

YES... BUT I SHALL NOT FORGET...*LREE.*

NEITHER WILL I.

OH...I *WISH* WE COULD RIDE ON THE BIG BIRDS AGAIN, DON'T YOU, *SUNTOP?*

IT WAS FUN!

YOU MAY FLY WITH *ME* IF YOU LIKE, CHILD.

WE *CAN?!*

PLEASE, MOTHER? FATHER? *PLEEEEEEZE?*

COME, CUTTER! LET YOUR CHILDREN RIDE THE WIND ONCE MORE! OR BETTER STILL—*YOU* RIDE WITH THEM!

DO IT! WHO KNOWS WHEN YOU'LL GET ANOTHER CHANCE?

IT'S REALLY SOMETHING, FRIEND—

—SOMETHING YOU SHOULDN'T MISS!

COME! ONE LAST UNFORGET-TABLE FLIGHT—

—TO PLEASE YOUR YOUNG ONES AND ME!

YOU COME TOO, MOTHER! JUST WAIT TILL YOU SEE HOW HIGH WE CAN GO!

PLEASE!

WELL...

GO ON! *ARORÉE* WON'T LET ANYTHING HAPPEN TO YOU. SHE'S *WONDERFUL!*

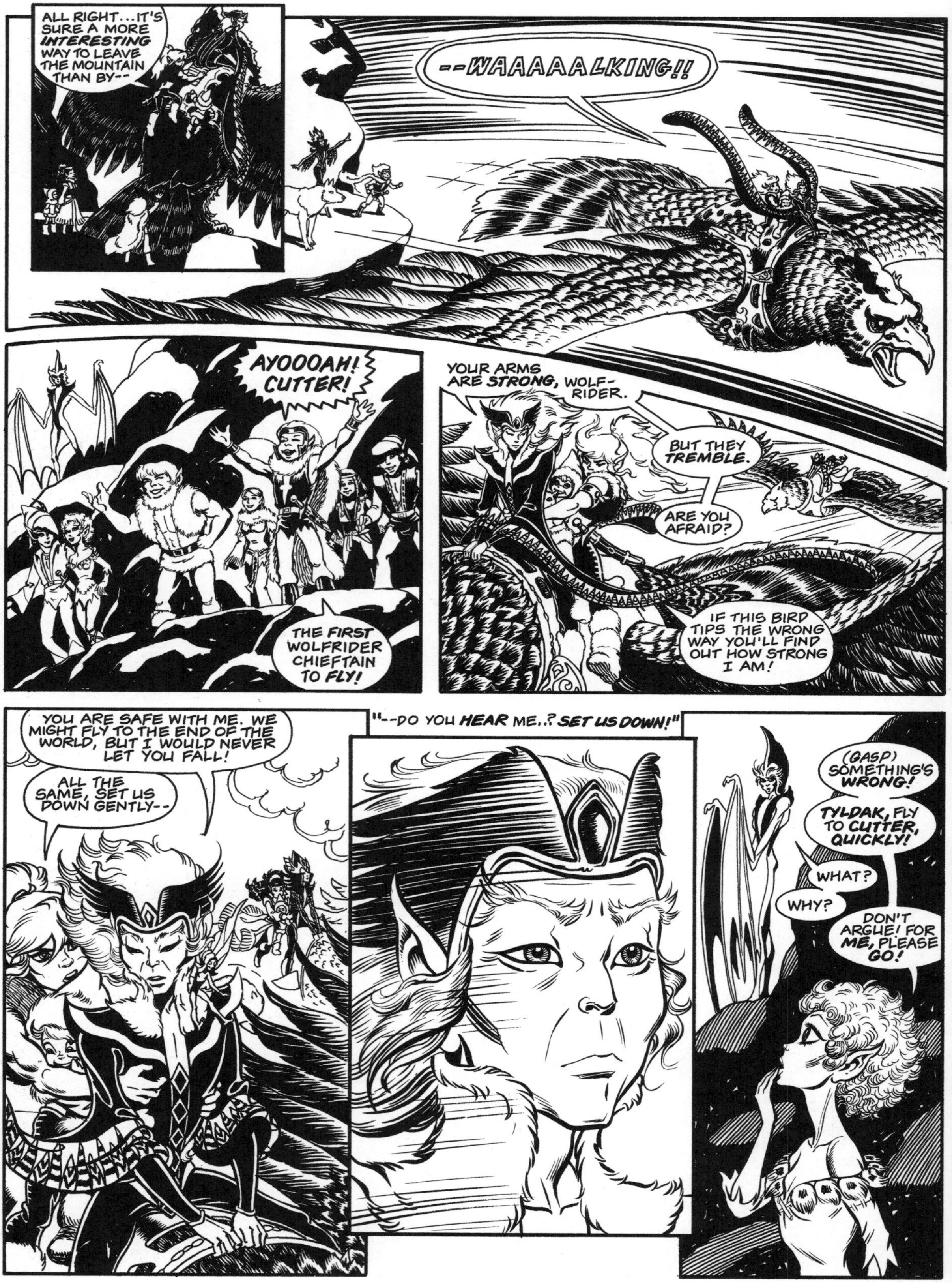
ALL RIGHT... IT'S SURE A MORE INTERESTING WAY TO LEAVE THE MOUNTAIN THAN BY--
--WAAAAALKING!!
AYOOOAH! CUTTER!
THE FIRST WOLFRIDER CHIEFTAIN TO FLY!
YOUR ARMS ARE STRONG, WOLF-RIDER.
BUT THEY TREMBLE.
ARE YOU AFRAID?
IF THIS BIRD TIPS THE WRONG WAY YOU'LL FIND OUT HOW STRONG I AM!
YOU ARE SAFE WITH ME. WE MIGHT FLY TO THE END OF THE WORLD, BUT I WOULD NEVER LET YOU FALL!
ALL THE SAME, SET US DOWN GENTLY--
"--DO YOU HEAR ME..? SET US DOWN!"
(GASP) SOMETHING'S WRONG!
TYLDAK, FLY TO CUTTER, QUICKLY!
WHAT?
WHY?
DON'T ARGUE! FOR ME, PLEASE GO!

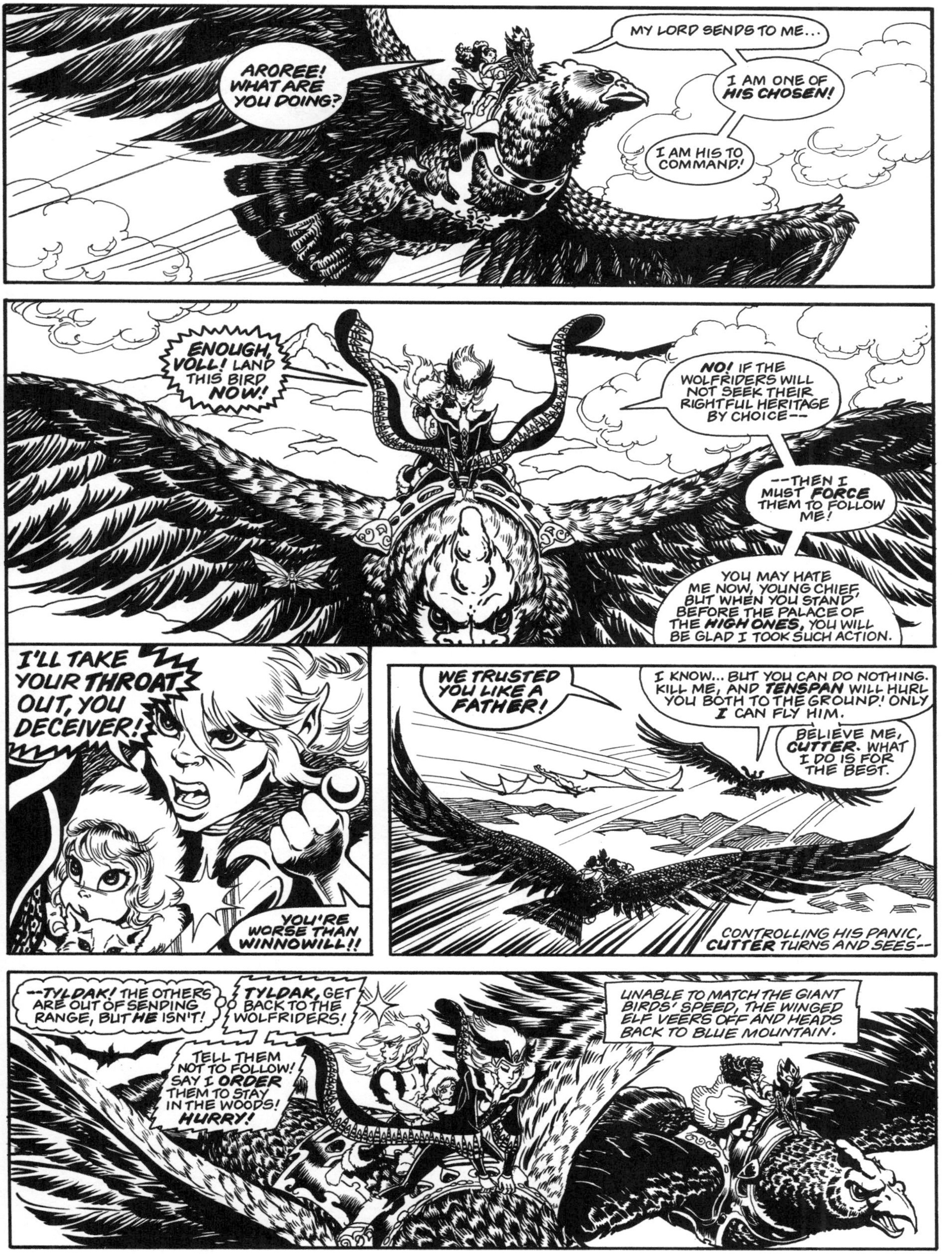
AROREE! WHAT ARE YOU DOING?
MY LORD SENDS TO ME...
I AM ONE OF HIS CHOSEN!
I AM HIS TO COMMAND!
ENOUGH, VOLL! LAND THIS BIRD NOW!
NO! IF THE WOLFRIDERS WILL NOT SEEK THEIR RIGHTFUL HERITAGE BY CHOICE--
--THEN I MUST FORCE THEM TO FOLLOW ME!
YOU MAY HATE ME NOW, YOUNG CHIEF, BUT WHEN YOU STAND BEFORE THE PALACE OF THE HIGH ONES, YOU WILL BE GLAD I TOOK SUCH ACTION.
I'LL TAKE YOUR THROAT OUT, YOU DECEIVER!
YOU'RE WORSE THAN WINNOWILL!!
WE TRUSTED YOU LIKE A FATHER!
I KNOW... BUT YOU CAN DO NOTHING. KILL ME, AND TENSPAN WILL HURL YOU BOTH TO THE GROUND! ONLY I CAN FLY HIM.
BELIEVE ME, CUTTER. WHAT I DO IS FOR THE BEST.
CONTROLLING HIS PANIC, CUTTER TURNS AND SEES--
--TYLDAK! THE OTHERS ARE OUT OF SENDING RANGE, BUT HE ISN'T!
TYLDAK, GET BACK TO THE WOLFRIDERS!
TELL THEM NOT TO FOLLOW! SAY I ORDER THEM TO STAY IN THE WOODS! HURRY!
UNABLE TO MATCH THE GIANT BIRDS' SPEED, THE WINGED ELF VEERS OFF AND HEADS BACK TO BLUE MOUNTAIN.

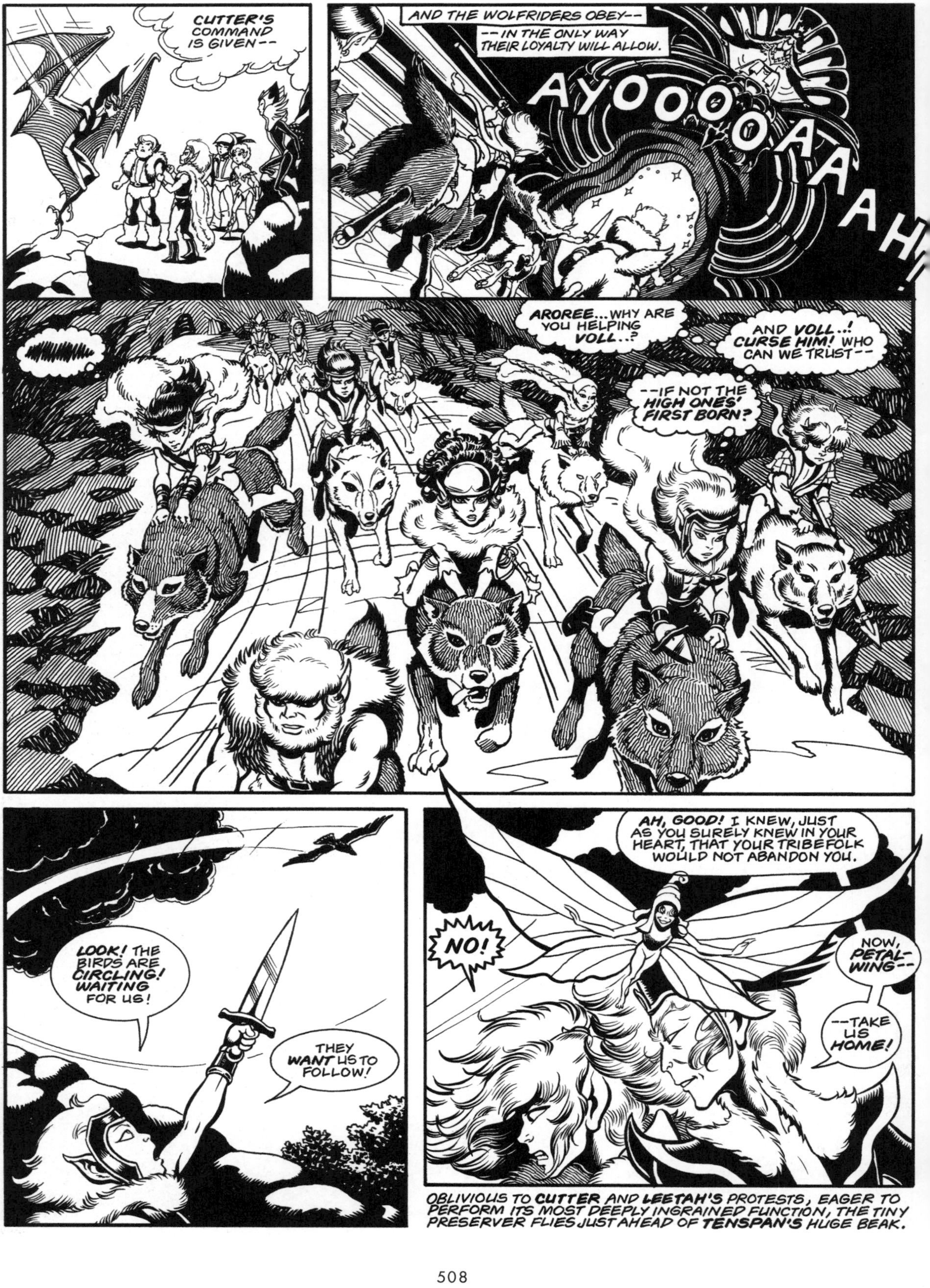
CUTTER'S COMMAND IS GIVEN--
AND THE WOLFRIDERS OBEY--
--IN THE ONLY WAY THEIR LOYALTY WILL ALLOW.
AYOOOOAAAAH!
AROREE... WHY ARE YOU HELPING VOLL...?
AND VOLL..! CURSE HIM! WHO CAN WE TRUST--
--IF NOT THE HIGH ONES' FIRST BORN?
LOOK! THE BIRDS ARE CIRCLING! WAITING FOR US!
THEY WANT US TO FOLLOW!
AH, GOOD! I KNEW, JUST AS YOU SURELY KNEW IN YOUR HEART, THAT YOUR TRIBEFOLK WOULD NOT ABANDON YOU.
NO!
NOW, PETALWING--
--TAKE US HOME!
OBLIVIOUS TO CUTTER AND LEETAH'S PROTESTS, EAGER TO PERFORM ITS MOST DEEPLY INGRAINED FUNCTION, THE TINY PRESERVER FLIES JUST AHEAD OF TENSPAN'S HUGE BEAK.

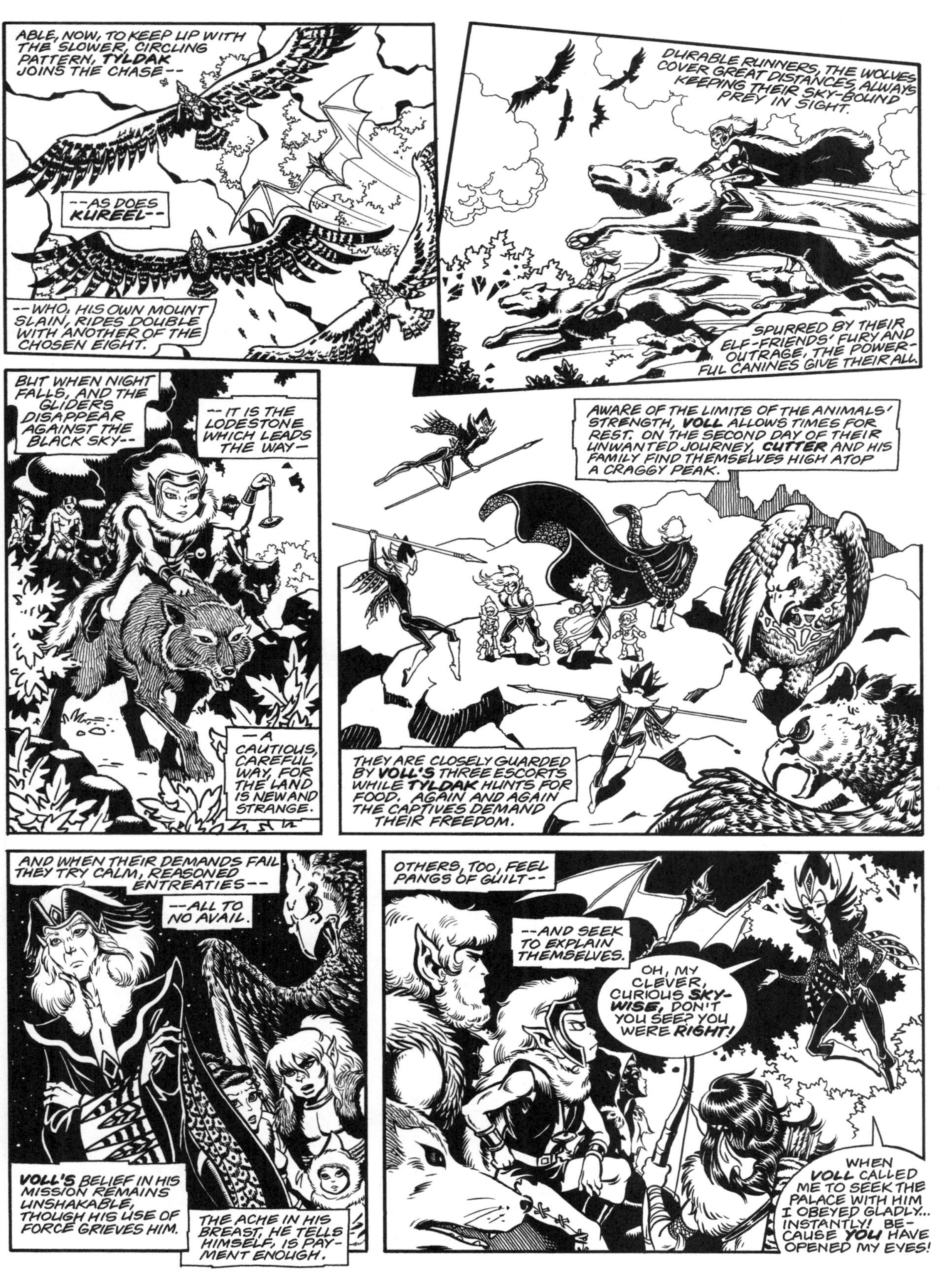

ABLE, NOW, TO KEEP UP WITH THE SLOWER, CIRCLING PATTERN, TYLDAK JOINS THE CHASE--
--AS DOES KUREEL--
--WHO, HIS OWN MOUNT SLAIN, RIDES DOUBLE WITH ANOTHER OF THE CHOSEN EIGHT.
DURABLE RUNNERS, THE WOLVES COVER GREAT DISTANCES, ALWAYS KEEPING THEIR SKY-BOUND PREY IN SIGHT.
SPURRED BY THEIR ELF-FRIENDS' FURY AND OUTRAGE, THE POWERFUL CANINES GIVE THEIR ALL.
BUT WHEN NIGHT FALLS, AND THE GLIDERS DISAPPEAR AGAINST THE BLACK SKY--
--IT IS THE LODESTONE WHICH LEADS THE WAY--
--A CAUTIOUS, CAREFUL WAY, FOR THE LAND IS NEW AND STRANGE.
AWARE OF THE LIMITS OF THE ANIMALS' STRENGTH, VOLL ALLOWS TIMES FOR REST. ON THE SECOND DAY OF THEIR UNWANTED JOURNEY, CUTTER AND HIS FAMILY FIND THEMSELVES HIGH ATOP A CRAGGY PEAK.
THEY ARE CLOSELY GUARDED BY VOLL'S THREE ESCORTS WHILE TYLDAK HUNTS FOR FOOD. AGAIN AND AGAIN THE CAPTIVES DEMAND THEIR FREEDOM.
AND WHEN THEIR DEMANDS FAIL THEY TRY CALM, REASONED ENTREATIES--
--ALL TO NO AVAIL.
VOLL'S BELIEF IN HIS MISSION REMAINS UNSHAKABLE, THOUGH HIS USE OF FORCE GRIEVES HIM.
THE ACHE IN HIS BREAST, HE TELLS HIMSELF, IS PAYMENT ENOUGH.
OTHERS, TOO, FEEL PANGS OF GUILT--
--AND SEEK TO EXPLAIN THEMSELVES.
OH, MY CLEVER, CURIOUS SKYWISE, DON'T YOU SEE? YOU WERE RIGHT!
WHEN VOLL CALLED ME TO SEEK THE PALACE WITH HIM I OBEYED GLADLY... INSTANTLY! BECAUSE YOU HAVE OPENED MY EYES!

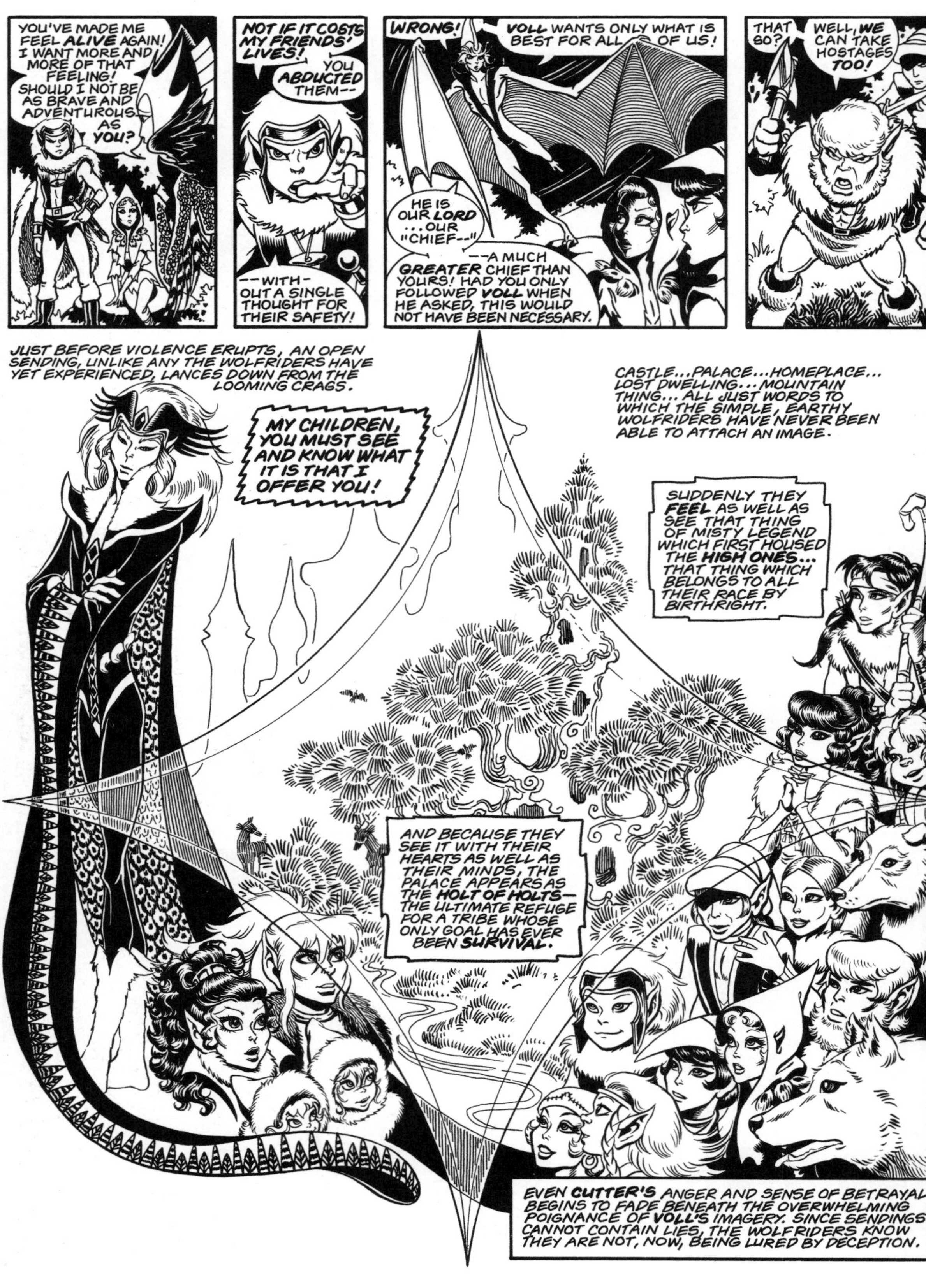

YOU'VE MADE ME FEEL ALIVE AGAIN! I WANT MORE AND MORE OF THAT FEELING! SHOULD I NOT BE AS BRAVE AND ADVENTUROUS AS YOU?
NOT IF IT COSTS MY FRIENDS' LIVES!
YOU ABDUCTED THEM--
--WITHOUT A SINGLE THOUGHT FOR THEIR SAFETY!
WRONG!
VOLL WANTS ONLY WHAT IS BEST FOR ALL OF US!
HE IS OUR LORD ...OUR "CHIEF--"
--A MUCH GREATER CHIEF THAN YOURS! HAD YOU ONLY FOLLOWED VOLL WHEN HE ASKED, THIS WOULD NOT HAVE BEEN NECESSARY.
THAT SO?
WELL, WE CAN TAKE HOSTAGES TOO!
JUST BEFORE VIOLENCE ERUPTS, AN OPEN SENDING, UNLIKE ANY THE WOLFRIDERS HAVE YET EXPERIENCED, LANCES DOWN FROM THE LOOMING CRAGS.
MY CHILDREN, YOU MUST SEE AND KNOW WHAT IT IS THAT I OFFER YOU!
CASTLE...PALACE...HOMEPLACE... LOST DWELLING... MOUNTAIN THING... ALL JUST WORDS TO WHICH THE SIMPLE, EARTHY WOLFRIDERS HAVE NEVER BEEN ABLE TO ATTACH AN IMAGE.
SUDDENLY THEY FEEL AS WELL AS SEE THAT THING OF MISTY LEGEND WHICH FIRST HOUSED THE HIGH ONES... THAT THING WHICH BELONGS TO ALL THEIR RACE BY BIRTHRIGHT.
AND BECAUSE THEY SEE IT WITH THEIR HEARTS AS WELL AS THEIR MINDS, THE PALACE APPEARS AS THE HOLT OF HOLTS— THE ULTIMATE REFUGE FOR A TRIBE WHOSE ONLY GOAL HAS EVER BEEN SURVIVAL.
EVEN CUTTER'S ANGER AND SENSE OF BETRAYAL BEGINS TO FADE BENEATH THE OVERWHELMING POIGNANCE OF VOLL'S IMAGERY. SINCE SENDINGS CANNOT CONTAIN LIES, THE WOLFRIDERS KNOW THEY ARE NOT, NOW, BEING LURED BY DECEPTION.

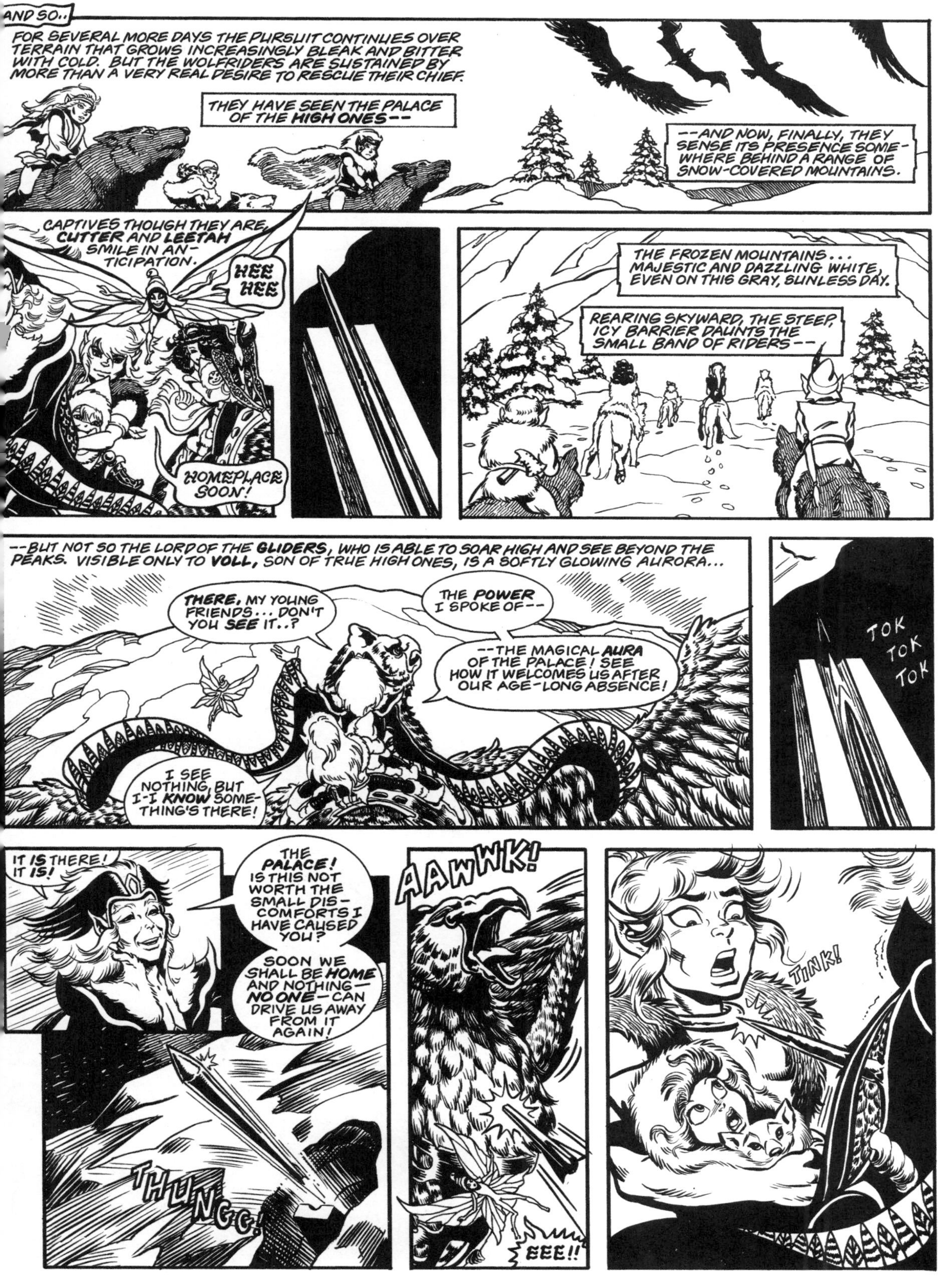
AND SO..
FOR SEVERAL MORE DAYS THE PURSUIT CONTINUES OVER TERRAIN THAT GROWS INCREASINGLY BLEAK AND BITTER WITH COLD. BUT THE WOLFRIDERS ARE SUSTAINED BY MORE THAN A VERY REAL DESIRE TO RESCUE THEIR CHIEF.
THEY HAVE SEEN THE PALACE OF THE HIGH ONES--
--AND NOW, FINALLY, THEY SENSE ITS PRESENCE SOMEWHERE BEHIND A RANGE OF SNOW-COVERED MOUNTAINS.
CAPTIVES THOUGH THEY ARE, CUTTER AND LEETAH SMILE IN ANTICIPATION.
HEE HEE
HOMEPLACE SOON!
THE FROZEN MOUNTAINS... MAJESTIC AND DAZZLING WHITE, EVEN ON THIS GRAY, SUNLESS DAY.
REARING SKYWARD, THE STEEP, ICY BARRIER DAUNTS THE SMALL BAND OF RIDERS--
--BUT NOT SO THE LORD OF THE GLIDERS, WHO IS ABLE TO SOAR HIGH AND SEE BEYOND THE PEAKS. VISIBLE ONLY TO VOLL, SON OF TRUE HIGH ONES, IS A SOFTLY GLOWING AURORA...
THERE, MY YOUNG FRIENDS... DON'T YOU SEE IT..?
THE POWER I SPOKE OF--
--THE MAGICAL AURA OF THE PALACE! SEE HOW IT WELCOMES US AFTER OUR AGE-LONG ABSENCE!
I SEE NOTHING, BUT I-I KNOW SOMETHING'S THERE!
TOK TOK TOK
IT IS THERE! IT IS!
THE PALACE! IS THIS NOT WORTH THE SMALL DISCOMFORTS I HAVE CAUSED YOU?
SOON WE SHALL BE HOME AND NOTHING--NO ONE--CAN DRIVE US AWAY FROM IT AGAIN!
THUNGG!
AAWWK!
EEE!!
TINK!

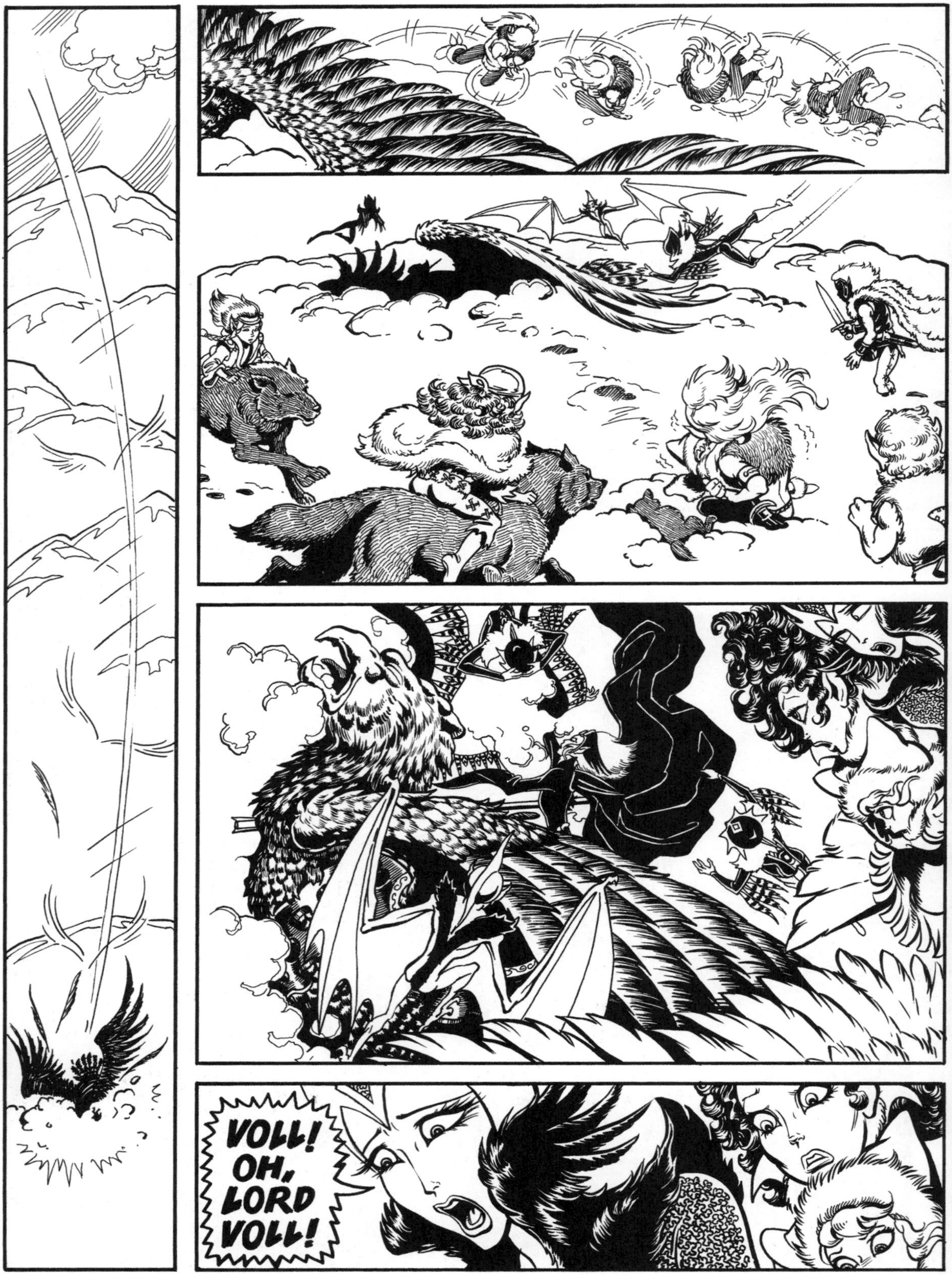
VOLL! OH, LORD VOLL!

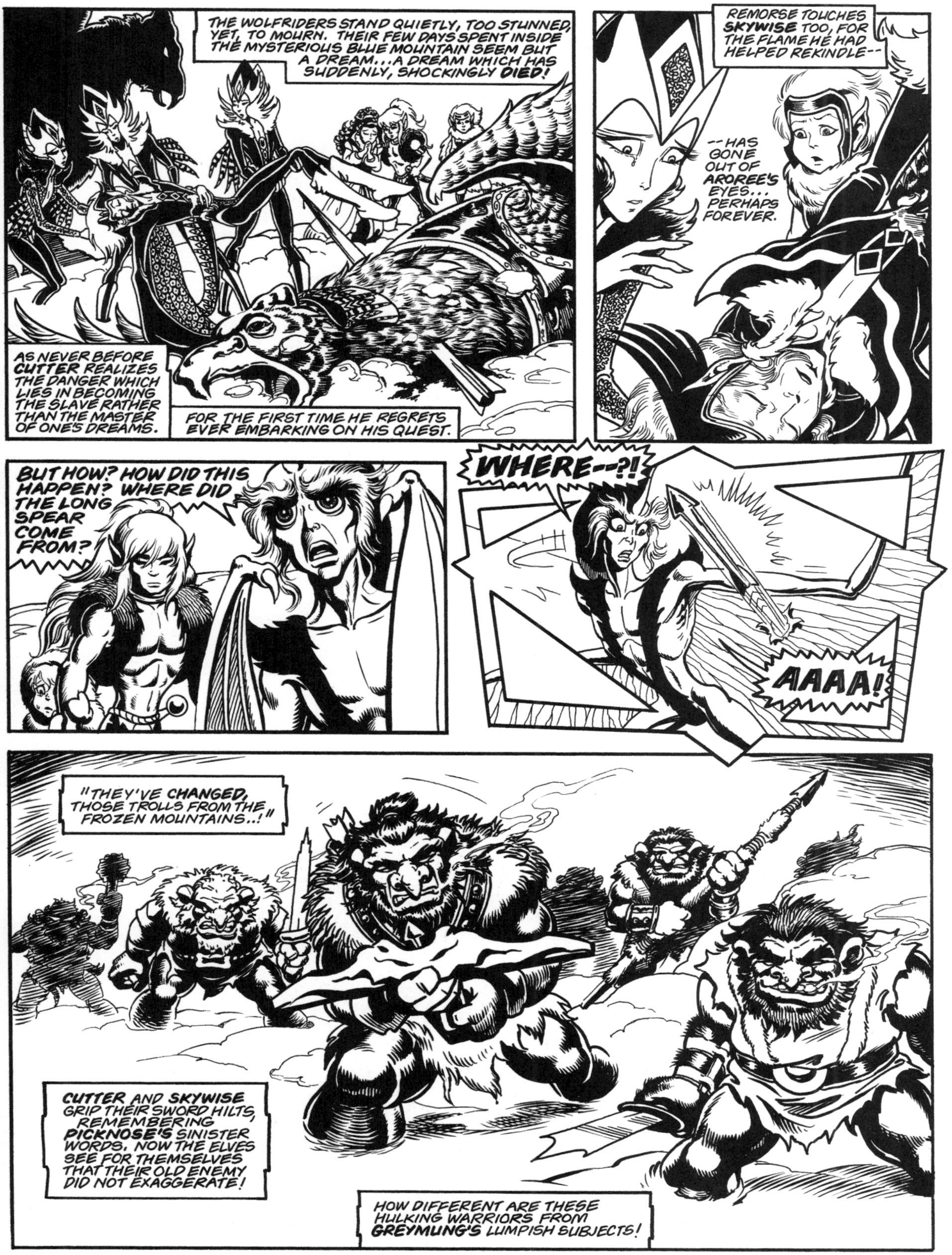
THE WOLFRIDERS STAND QUIETLY, TOO STUNNED, YET, TO MOURN. THEIR FEW DAYS SPENT INSIDE THE MYSTERIOUS BLUE MOUNTAIN SEEM BUT A DREAM... A DREAM WHICH HAS SUDDENLY, SHOCKINGLY DIED!
AS NEVER BEFORE CUTTER REALIZES THE DANGER WHICH LIES IN BECOMING THE SLAVE RATHER THAN THE MASTER OF ONE'S DREAMS.
FOR THE FIRST TIME HE REGRETS EVER EMBARKING ON HIS QUEST.
REMORSE TOUCHES SKYWISE TOO, FOR THE FLAME HE HAD HELPED REKINDLE--
--HAS GONE OUT OF AROREE'S EYES... PERHAPS FOREVER.
BUT HOW? HOW DID THIS HAPPEN? WHERE DID THE LONG SPEAR COME FROM?
WHERE--?!
AAAA!
"THEY'VE CHANGED, THOSE TROLLS FROM THE FROZEN MOUNTAINS..!"
CUTTER AND SKYWISE GRIP THEIR SWORD HILTS, REMEMBERING PICKNOSE'S SINISTER WORDS. NOW THE ELVES SEE FOR THEMSELVES THAT THEIR OLD ENEMY DID NOT EXAGGERATE!
HOW DIFFERENT ARE THESE HULKING WARRIORS FROM GREYMUNG'S LUMPISH SUBJECTS!

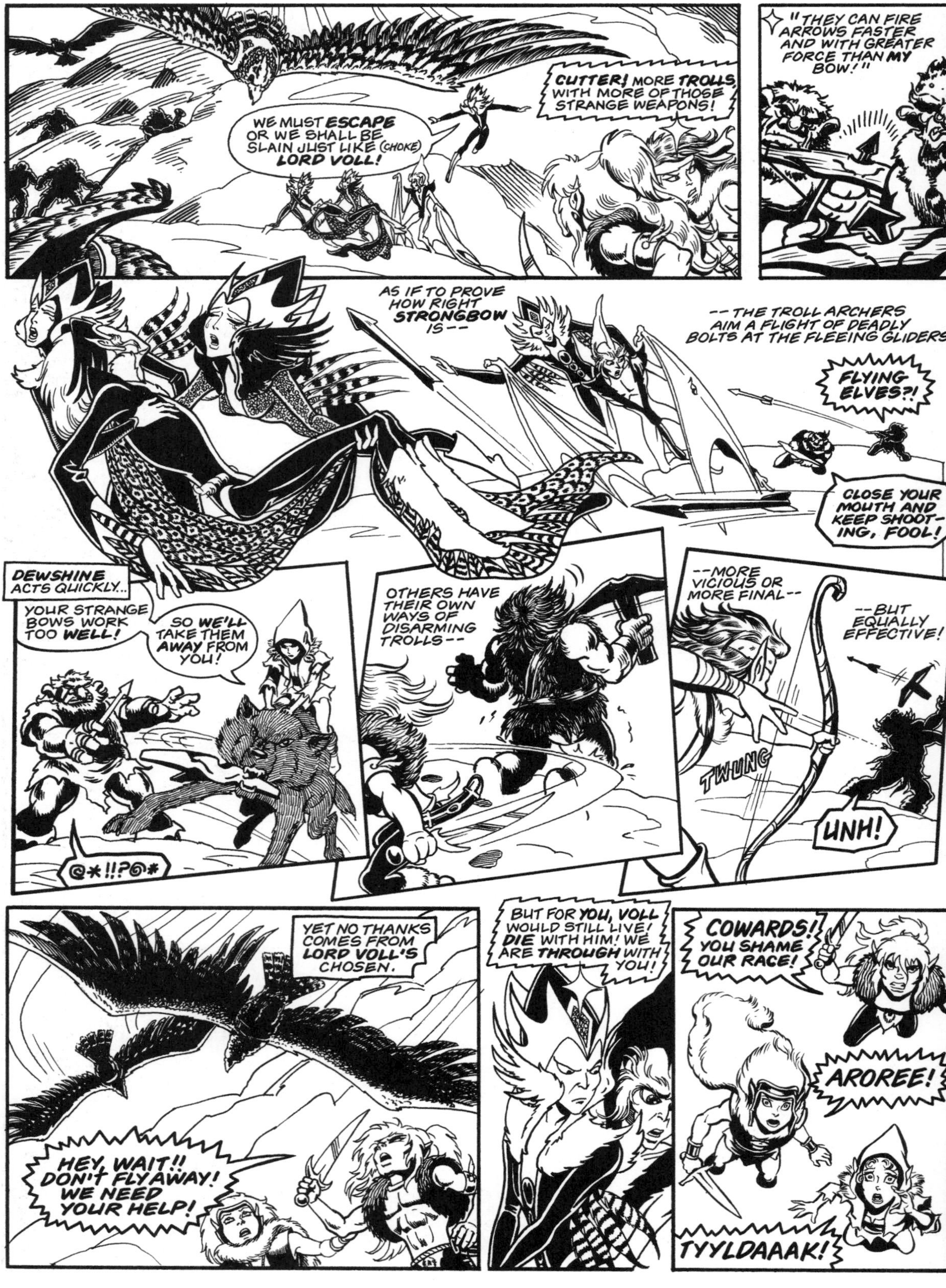
WE MUST ESCAPE OR WE SHALL BE SLAIN JUST LIKE (CHOKE) LORD VOLL!
CUTTER! MORE TROLLS, WITH MORE OF THOSE STRANGE WEAPONS!
"THEY CAN FIRE ARROWS FASTER AND WITH GREATER FORCE THAN MY BOW!"
AS IF TO PROVE HOW RIGHT STRONGBOW IS --
-- THE TROLL ARCHERS AIM A FLIGHT OF DEADLY BOLTS AT THE FLEEING GLIDERS.
FLYING ELVES?!
CLOSE YOUR MOUTH AND KEEP SHOOTING, FOOL!
DEWSHINE ACTS QUICKLY...
YOUR STRANGE BOWS WORK TOO WELL!
SO WE'LL TAKE THEM AWAY FROM YOU!
@*!!?@*
OTHERS HAVE THEIR OWN WAYS OF DISARMING TROLLS --
-- MORE VICIOUS OR MORE FINAL --
-- BUT EQUALLY EFFECTIVE!
TWUNG
UNH!
YET NO THANKS COMES FROM LORD VOLL'S CHOSEN.
HEY, WAIT!! DON'T FLY AWAY! WE NEED YOUR HELP!
BUT FOR YOU, VOLL WOULD STILL LIVE! DIE WITH HIM! WE ARE THROUGH WITH YOU!
COWARDS! YOU SHAME OUR RACE!
AROREE!
TYYLDAAAK!

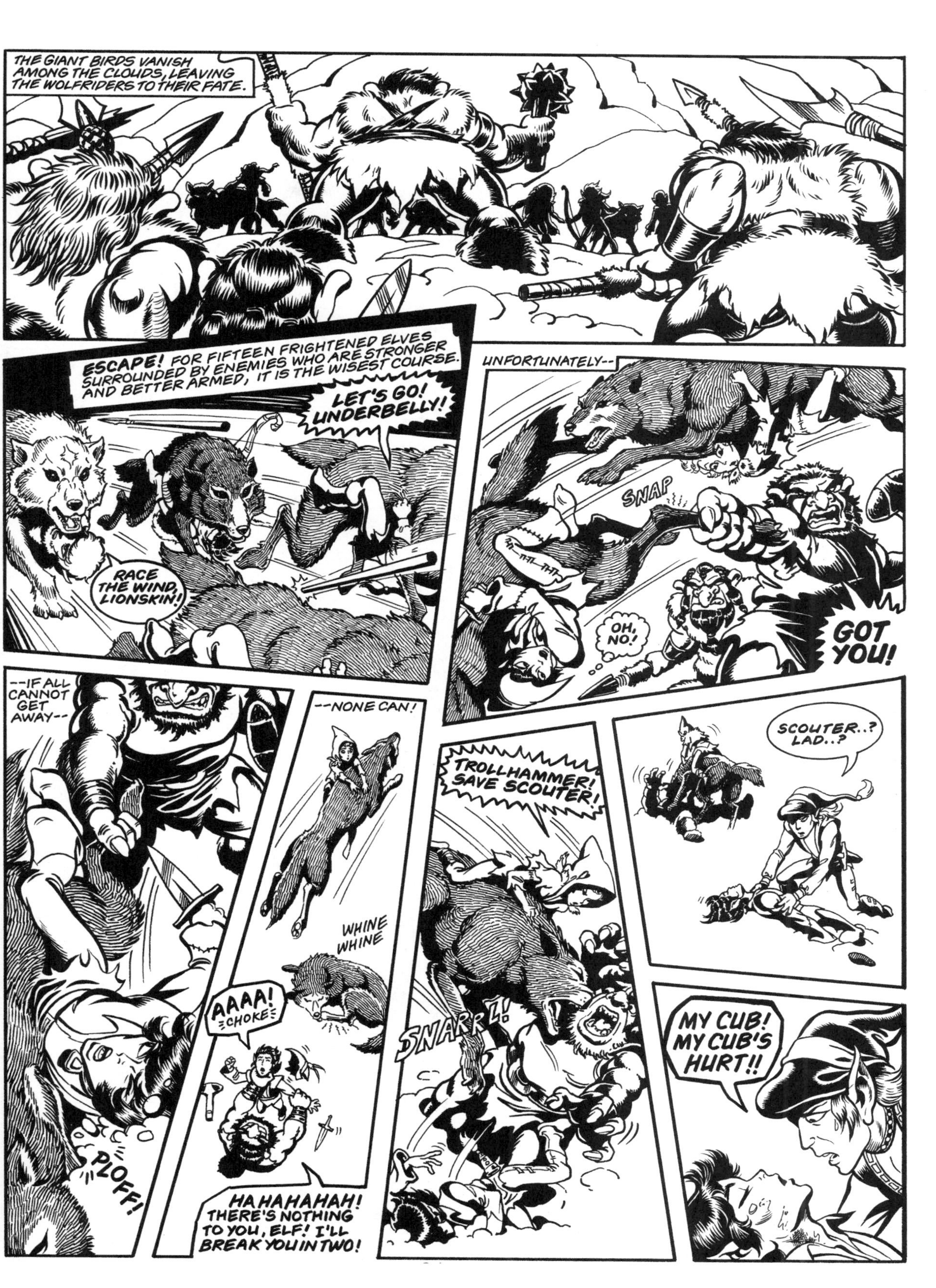

THE GIANT BIRDS VANISH AMONG THE CLOUDS, LEAVING THE WOLFRIDERS TO THEIR FATE.
ESCAPE! FOR FIFTEEN FRIGHTENED ELVES SURROUNDED BY ENEMIES WHO ARE STRONGER AND BETTER ARMED, IT IS THE WISEST COURSE.
LET'S GO! UNDERBELLY!
RACE THE WIND, LIONSKIN!
UNFORTUNATELY--
SNAP
OH, NO!
GOT YOU!
--IF ALL CANNOT GET AWAY--
PLOFF!
--NONE CAN!
WHINE WHINE
AAAA! CHOKE
HAHAHAHAH! THERE'S NOTHING TO YOU, ELF! I'LL BREAK YOU IN TWO!
TROLLHAMMER! SAVE SCOUTER!
SNARRL!
SCOUTER..? LAD..?
MY CUB! MY CUB'S HURT!!

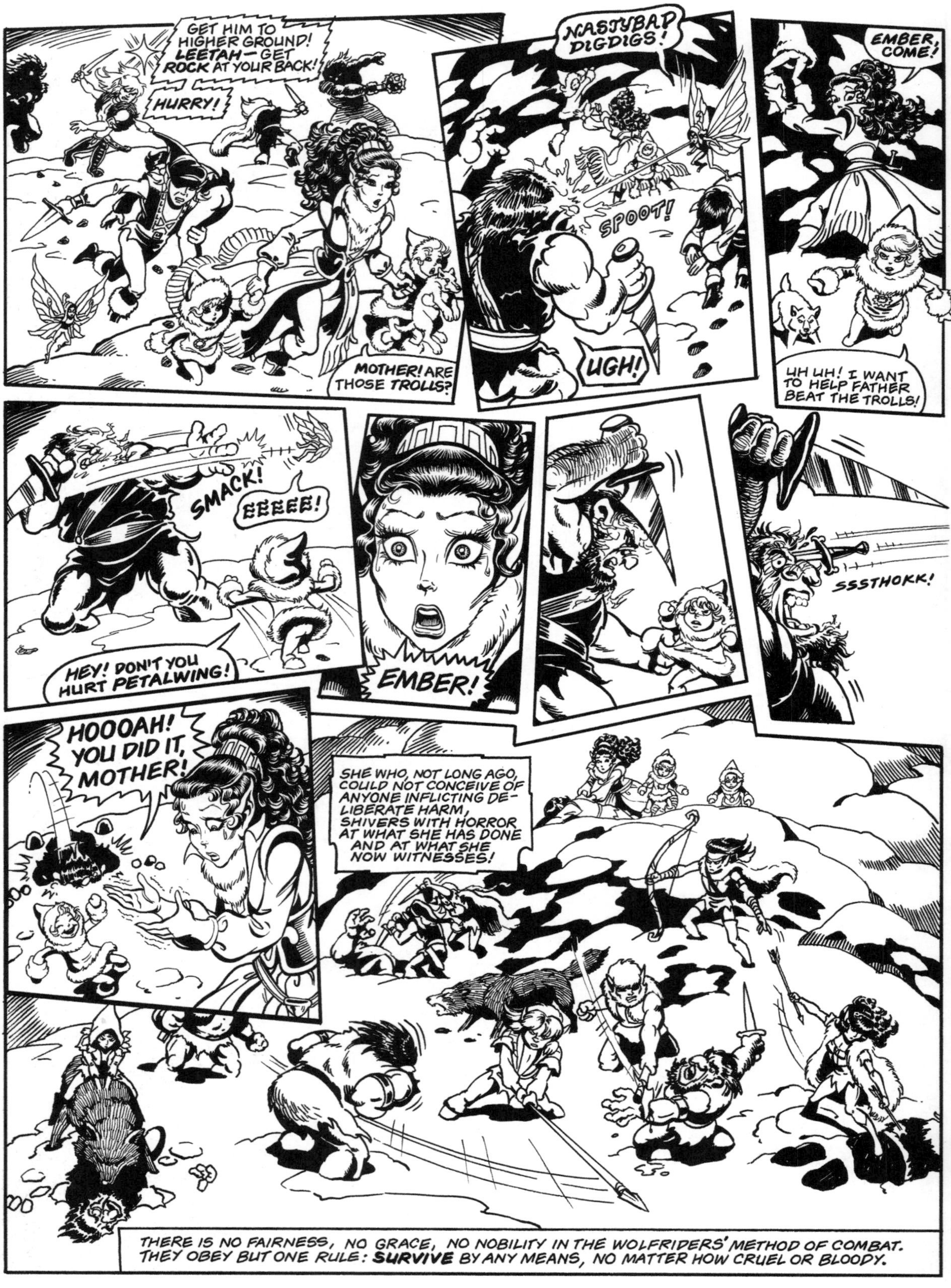
GET HIM TO HIGHER GROUND! LEETAH — GET ROCK AT YOUR BACK!
HURRY!
MOTHER! ARE THOSE TROLLS?
NASTYBAD DIGDIGS!
SPOOT!
UGH!
EMBER, COME!
UH UH! I WANT TO HELP FATHER BEAT THE TROLLS!
SMACK!
EEEEE!
HEY! DON'T YOU HURT PETALWING!
EMBER!
SSSTHOKK!
HOOOAH! YOU DID IT, MOTHER!
SHE WHO, NOT LONG AGO, COULD NOT CONCEIVE OF ANYONE INFLICTING DELIBERATE HARM, SHIVERS WITH HORROR AT WHAT SHE HAS DONE AND AT WHAT SHE NOW WITNESSES!
THERE IS NO FAIRNESS, NO GRACE, NO NOBILITY IN THE WOLFRIDERS' METHOD OF COMBAT. THEY OBEY BUT ONE RULE: SURVIVE BY ANY MEANS, NO MATTER HOW CRUEL OR BLOODY.

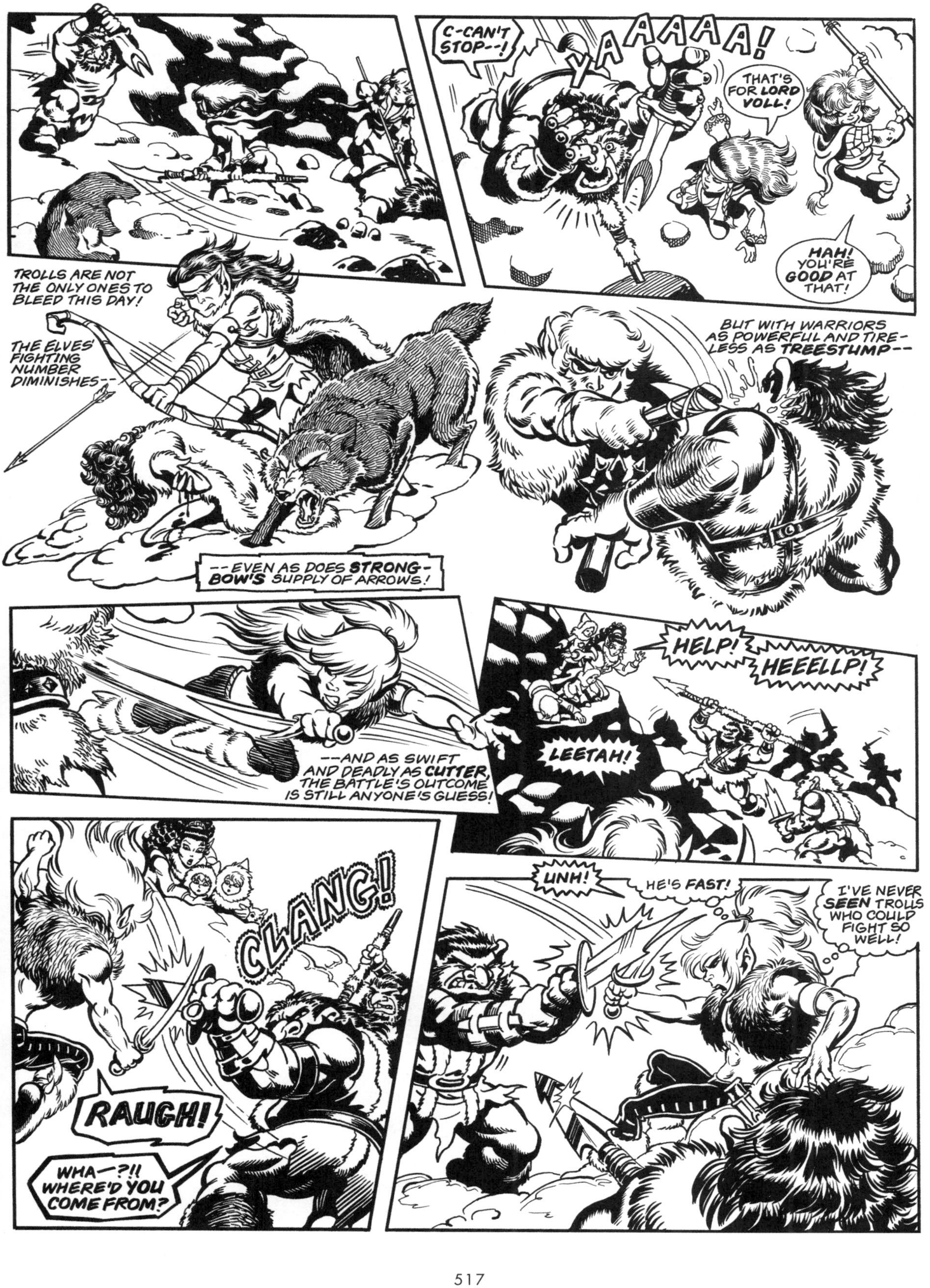
C-CAN'T STOP--!
YAAAAAA!
THAT'S FOR LORD VOLL!
HAH! YOU'RE GOOD AT THAT!
TROLLS ARE NOT THE ONLY ONES TO BLEED THIS DAY!
THE ELVES' FIGHTING NUMBER DIMINISHES--
--EVEN AS DOES STRONG-BOW'S SUPPLY OF ARROWS!
BUT WITH WARRIORS AS POWERFUL AND TIRE-LESS AS TREESTUMP--
--AND AS SWIFT AND DEADLY AS CUTTER, THE BATTLE'S OUTCOME IS STILL ANYONE'S GUESS!
HELP!
HEEELLP!
LEETAH!
CLANG!
RAUGH!
WHA--?!! WHERE'D YOU COME FROM?
UNH!
HE'S FAST!
I'VE NEVER SEEN TROLLS WHO COULD FIGHT SO WELL!

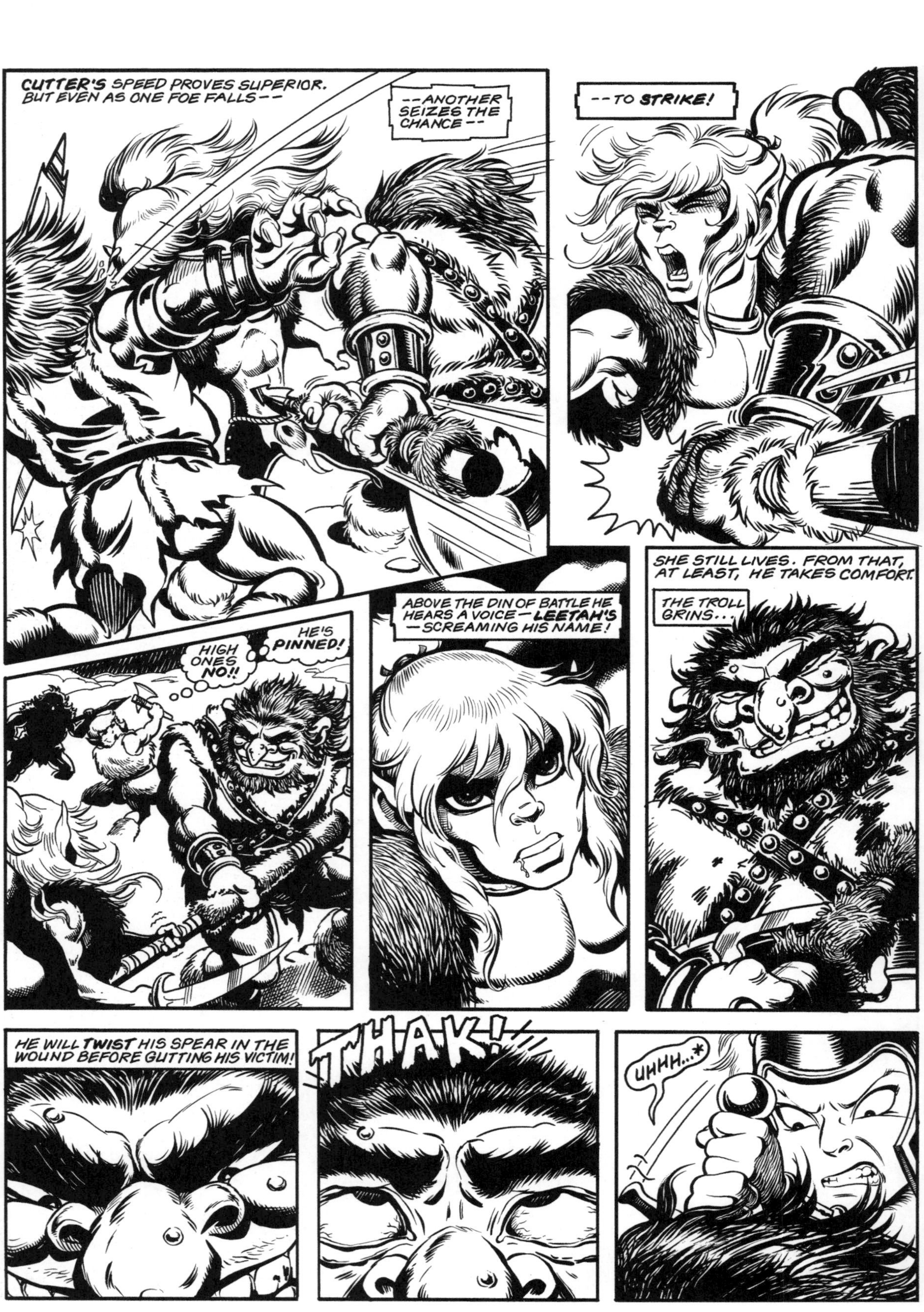
CUTTER'S SPEED PROVES SUPERIOR. BUT EVEN AS ONE FOE FALLS--
--ANOTHER SEIZES THE CHANCE--
--TO STRIKE!
HIGH ONES NO!!
HE'S PINNED!
ABOVE THE DIN OF BATTLE HE HEARS A VOICE—LEETAH'S—SCREAMING HIS NAME!
SHE STILL LIVES. FROM THAT, AT LEAST, HE TAKES COMFORT.
THE TROLL GRINS...
HE WILL TWIST HIS SPEAR IN THE WOUND BEFORE GUTTING HIS VICTIM!
THAK!
UHHH...*

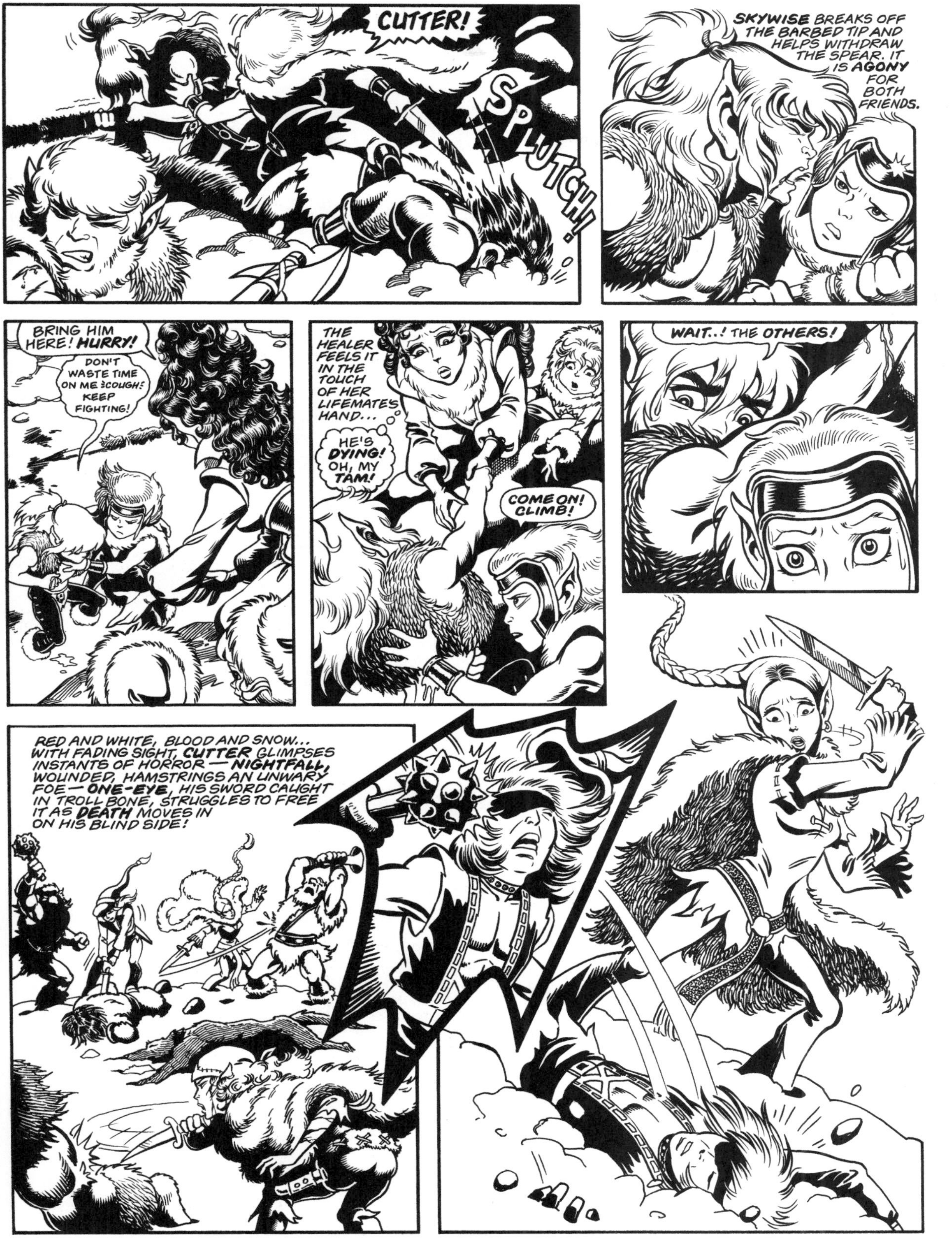

CUTTER!
SPLUTCH!
SKYWISE BREAKS OFF THE BARBED TIP AND HELPS WITHDRAW THE SPEAR. IT IS AGONY FOR BOTH FRIENDS.
BRING HIM HERE! HURRY!
DON'T WASTE TIME ON ME *COUGH* KEEP FIGHTING!
THE HEALER FEELS IT IN THE TOUCH OF HER LIFEMATE'S HAND...
HE'S DYING! OH, MY TAM!
COME ON! CLIMB!
WAIT..! THE OTHERS!
RED AND WHITE, BLOOD AND SNOW... WITH FADING SIGHT, CUTTER GLIMPSES INSTANTS OF HORROR — NIGHTFALL, WOUNDED, HAMSTRINGS AN UNWARY FOE — ONE-EYE, HIS SWORD CAUGHT IN TROLL BONE, STRUGGLES TO FREE IT AS DEATH MOVES IN ON HIS BLIND SIDE!

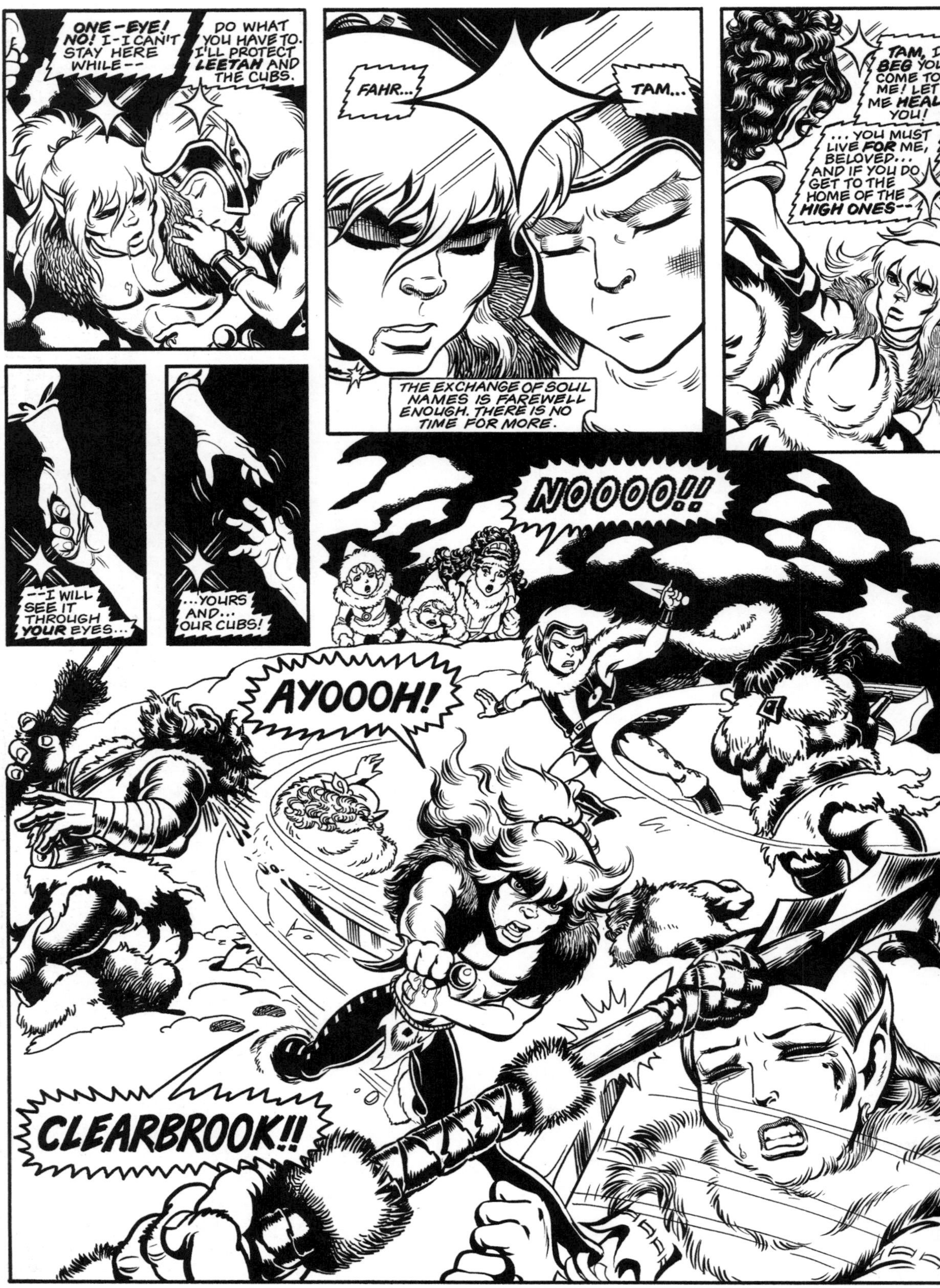
ONE-EYE! NO! I-I CAN'T STAY HERE WHILE--
DO WHAT YOU HAVE TO. I'LL PROTECT LEETAH AND THE CUBS.
FAHR...
TAM...
THE EXCHANGE OF SOUL NAMES IS FAREWELL ENOUGH. THERE IS NO TIME FOR MORE.
TAM, I BEG YOU, COME TO ME! LET ME HEAL YOU!
...YOU MUST LIVE FOR ME, BELOVED... AND IF YOU DO GET TO THE HOME OF THE HIGH ONES--
--I WILL SEE IT THROUGH YOUR EYES...
...YOURS AND... OUR CUBS!
NOOOO!!
AYOOOH!
CLEARBROOK!!

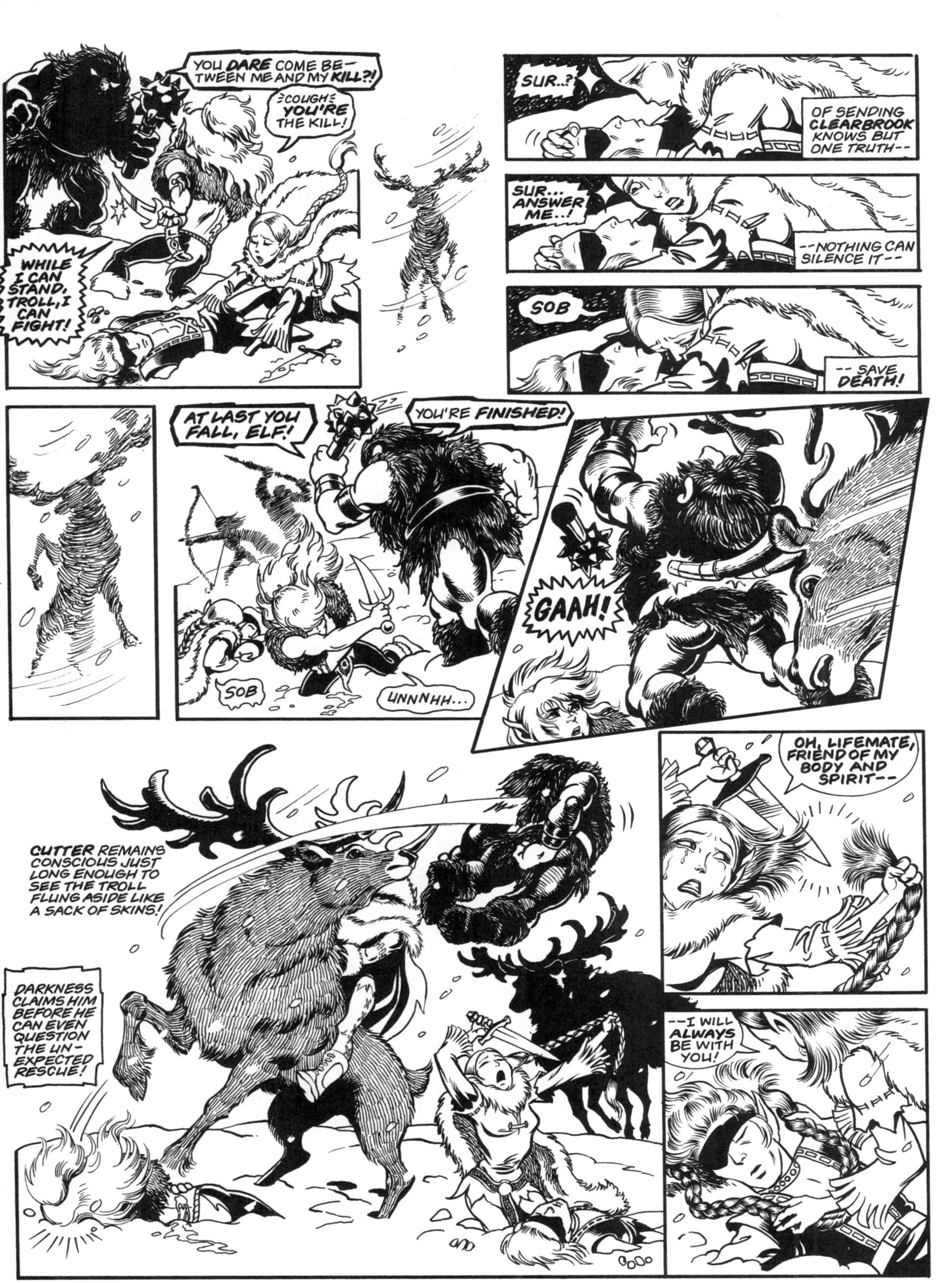

YOU DARE COME BETWEEN ME AND MY KILL?!
COUGH YOU'RE THE KILL!
WHILE I CAN STAND, TROLL, I CAN FIGHT!
SUR..?
OF SENDING CLEARBROOK KNOWS BUT ONE TRUTH--
SUR... ANSWER ME...!
--NOTHING CAN SILENCE IT--
SOB
--SAVE DEATH!
AT LAST YOU FALL, ELF!
YOU'RE FINISHED!
SOB
UNNNHH...
GAAH!
CUTTER REMAINS CONSCIOUS JUST LONG ENOUGH TO SEE THE TROLL FLUNG ASIDE LIKE A SACK OF SKINS!
DARKNESS CLAIMS HIM BEFORE HE CAN EVEN QUESTION THE UNEXPECTED RESCUE!
OH, LIFEMATE, FRIEND OF MY BODY AND SPIRIT--
--I WILL ALWAYS BE WITH YOU!

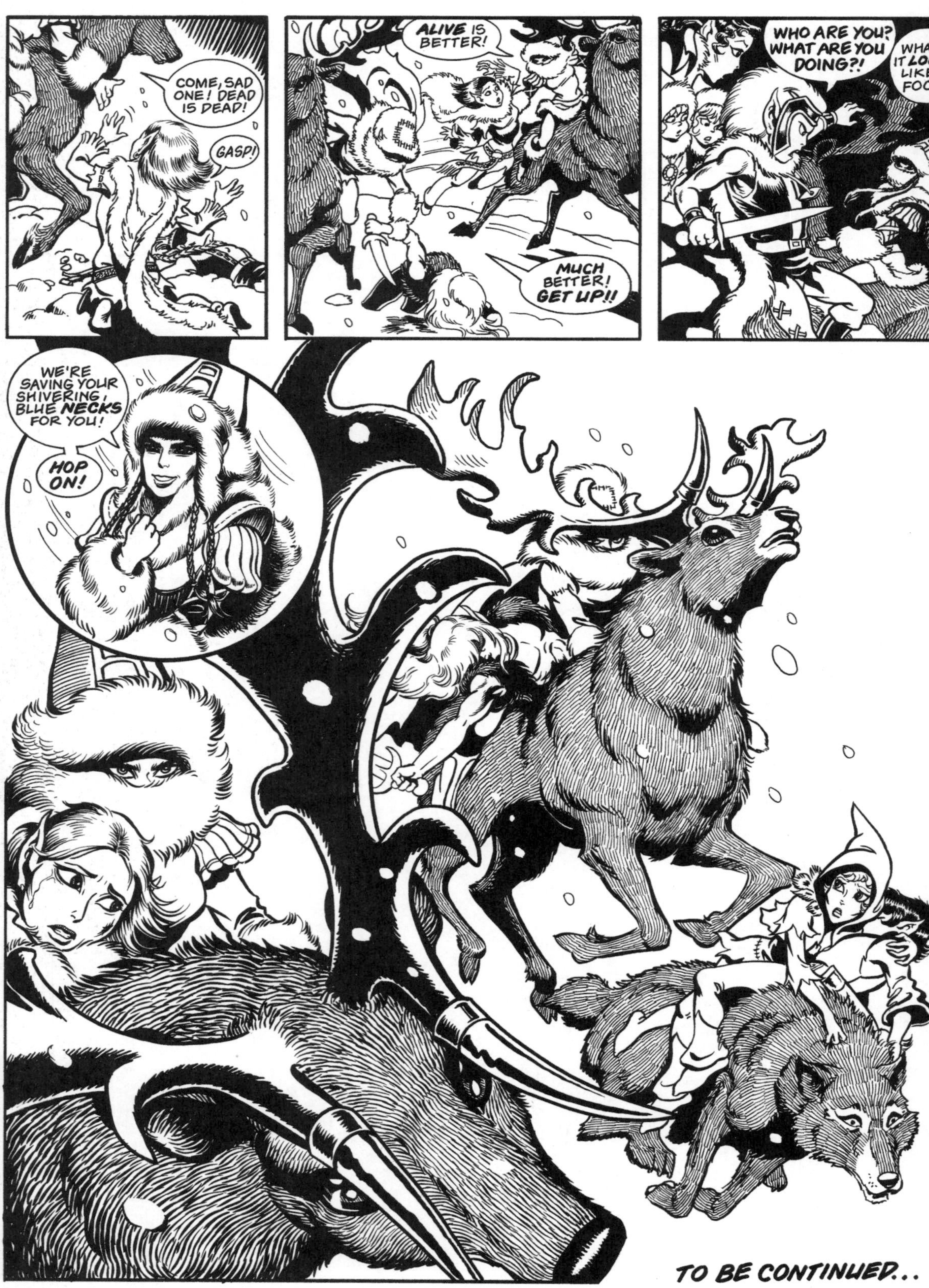
COME, SAD ONE! DEAD IS DEAD!
GASP!
ALIVE IS BETTER!
MUCH BETTER! GET UP!!
WHO ARE YOU? WHAT ARE YOU DOING?!
WHAT'S IT LOOK LIKE, FOOL?
WE'RE SAVING YOUR SHIVERING, BLUE NECKS FOR YOU!
HOP ON!
TO BE CONTINUED...

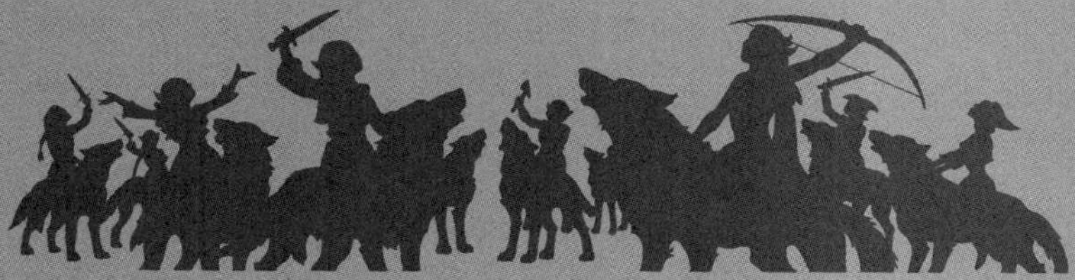

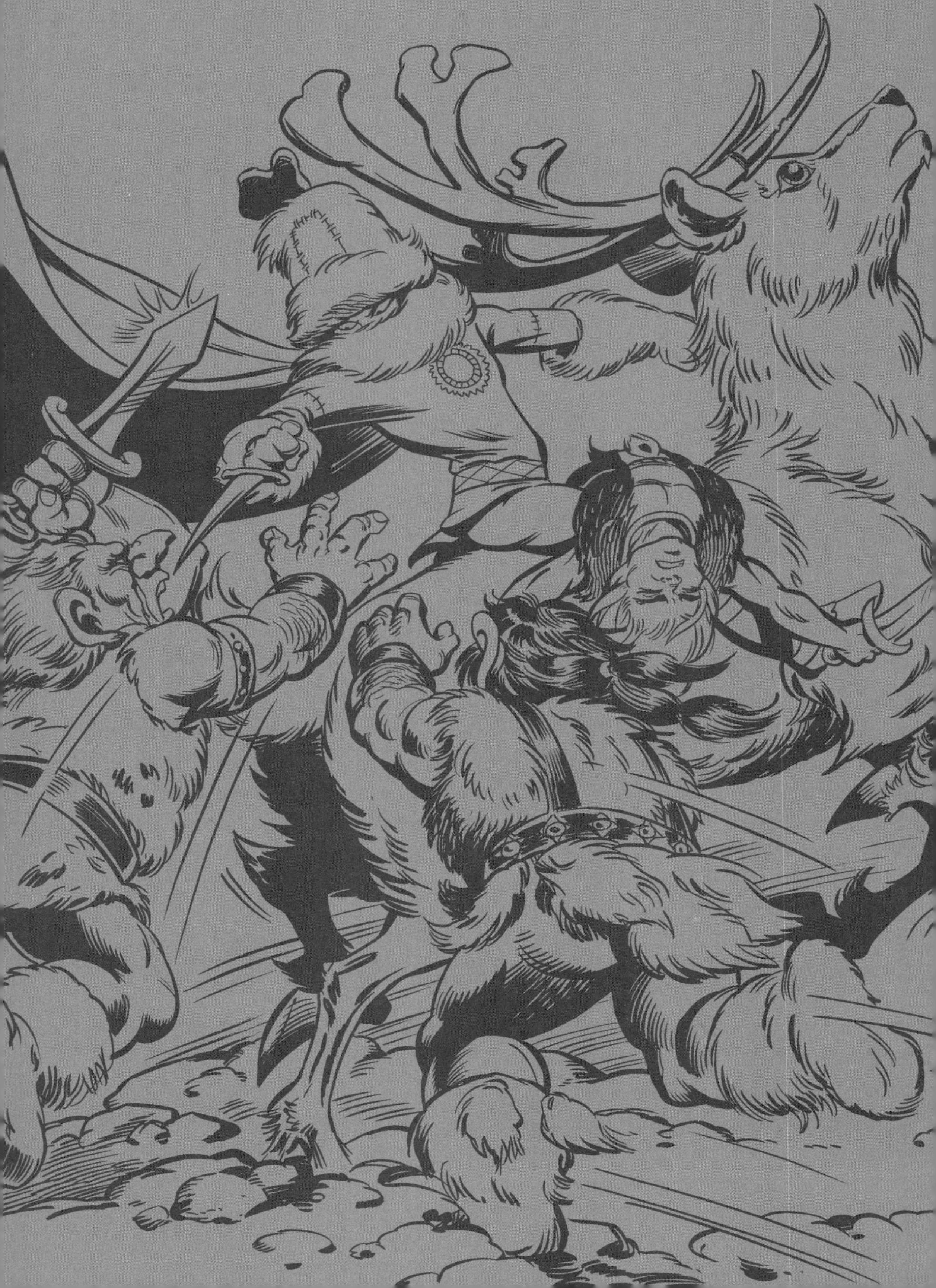

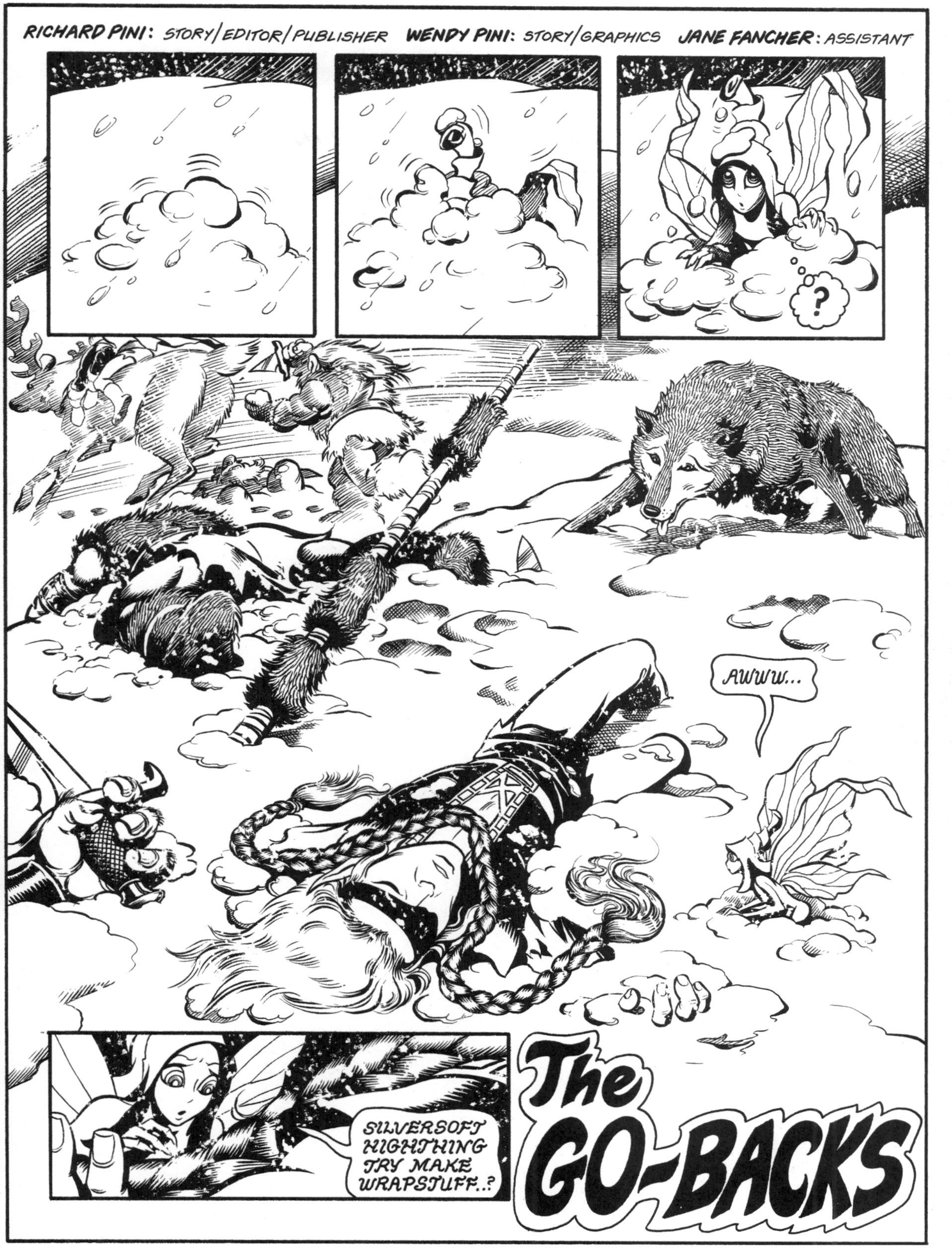
RICHARD PINI: STORY/EDITOR/PUBLISHER WENDY PINI: STORY/GRAPHICS JANE FANCHER: ASSISTANT
?
AWWW...
SILVERSOFT HIGHTHING TRY MAKE WRAPSTUFF..?
The GO-BACKS

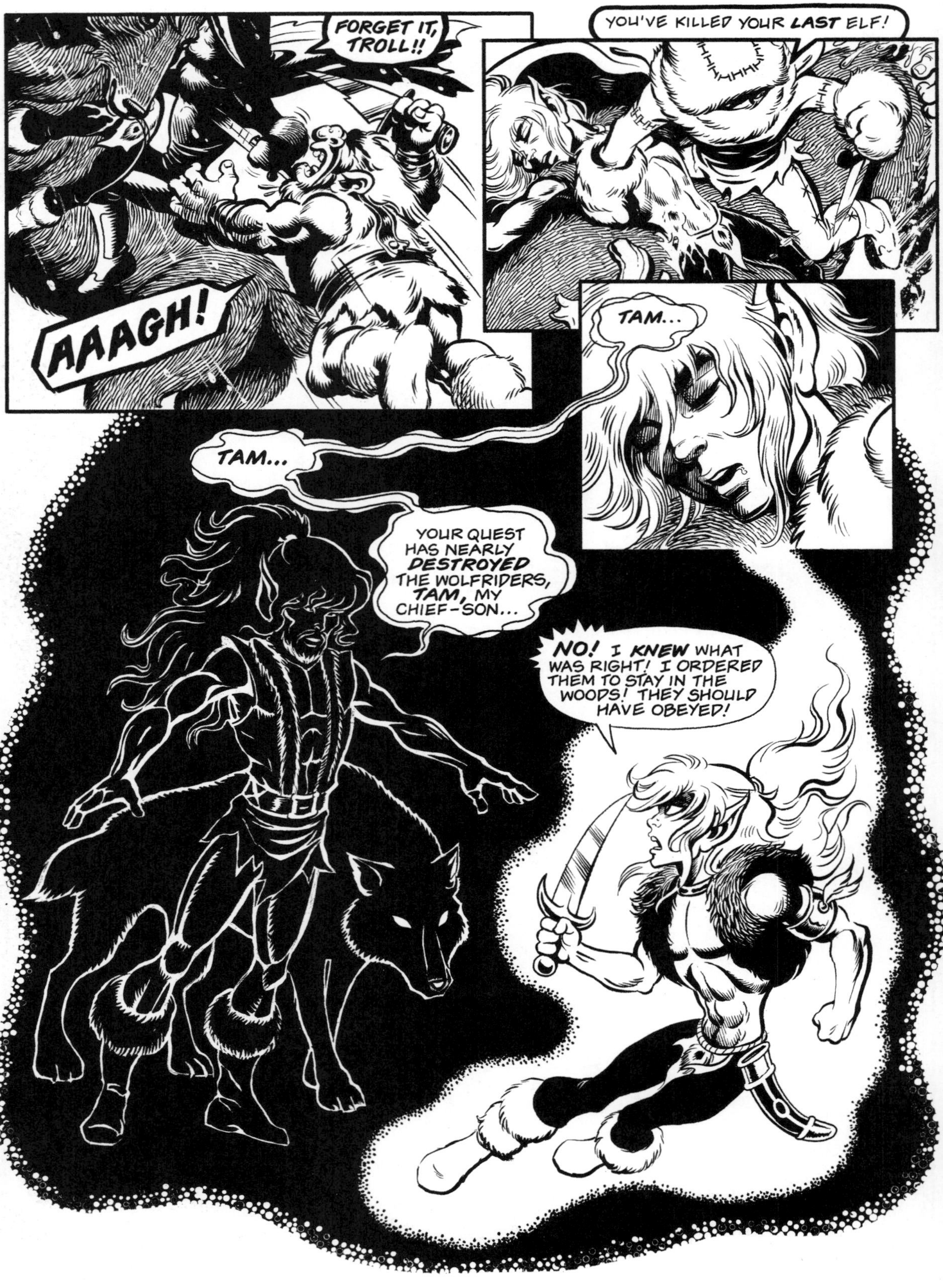
FORGET IT, TROLL!!
AAAGH!
YOU'VE KILLED YOUR LAST ELF!
TAM...
TAM...
YOUR QUEST HAS NEARLY DESTROYED THE WOLFRIDERS, TAM, MY CHIEF-SON...
NO! I KNEW WHAT WAS RIGHT! I ORDERED THEM TO STAY IN THE WOODS! THEY SHOULD HAVE OBEYED!

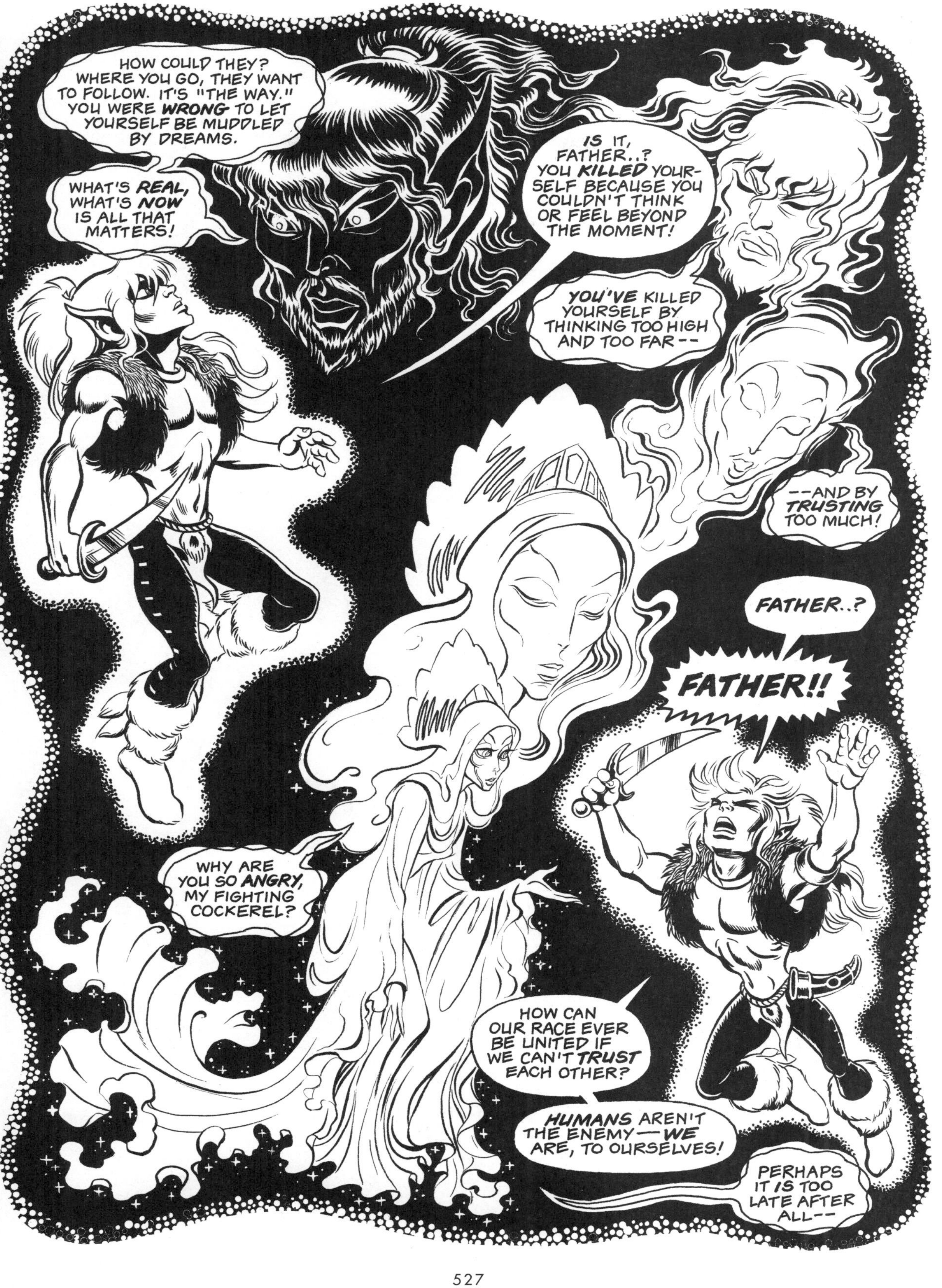
HOW COULD THEY? WHERE YOU GO, THEY WANT TO FOLLOW. IT'S "THE WAY." YOU WERE WRONG TO LET YOURSELF BE MUDDLED BY DREAMS.
WHAT'S REAL, WHAT'S NOW IS ALL THAT MATTERS!
IS IT, FATHER..? YOU KILLED YOURSELF BECAUSE YOU COULDN'T THINK OR FEEL BEYOND THE MOMENT!
YOU'VE KILLED YOURSELF BY THINKING TOO HIGH AND TOO FAR --
--AND BY TRUSTING TOO MUCH!
FATHER..?
FATHER!!
WHY ARE YOU SO ANGRY, MY FIGHTING COCKEREL?
HOW CAN OUR RACE EVER BE UNITED IF WE CAN'T TRUST EACH OTHER?
HUMANS AREN'T THE ENEMY—WE ARE, TO OURSELVES!
PERHAPS IT IS TOO LATE AFTER ALL--

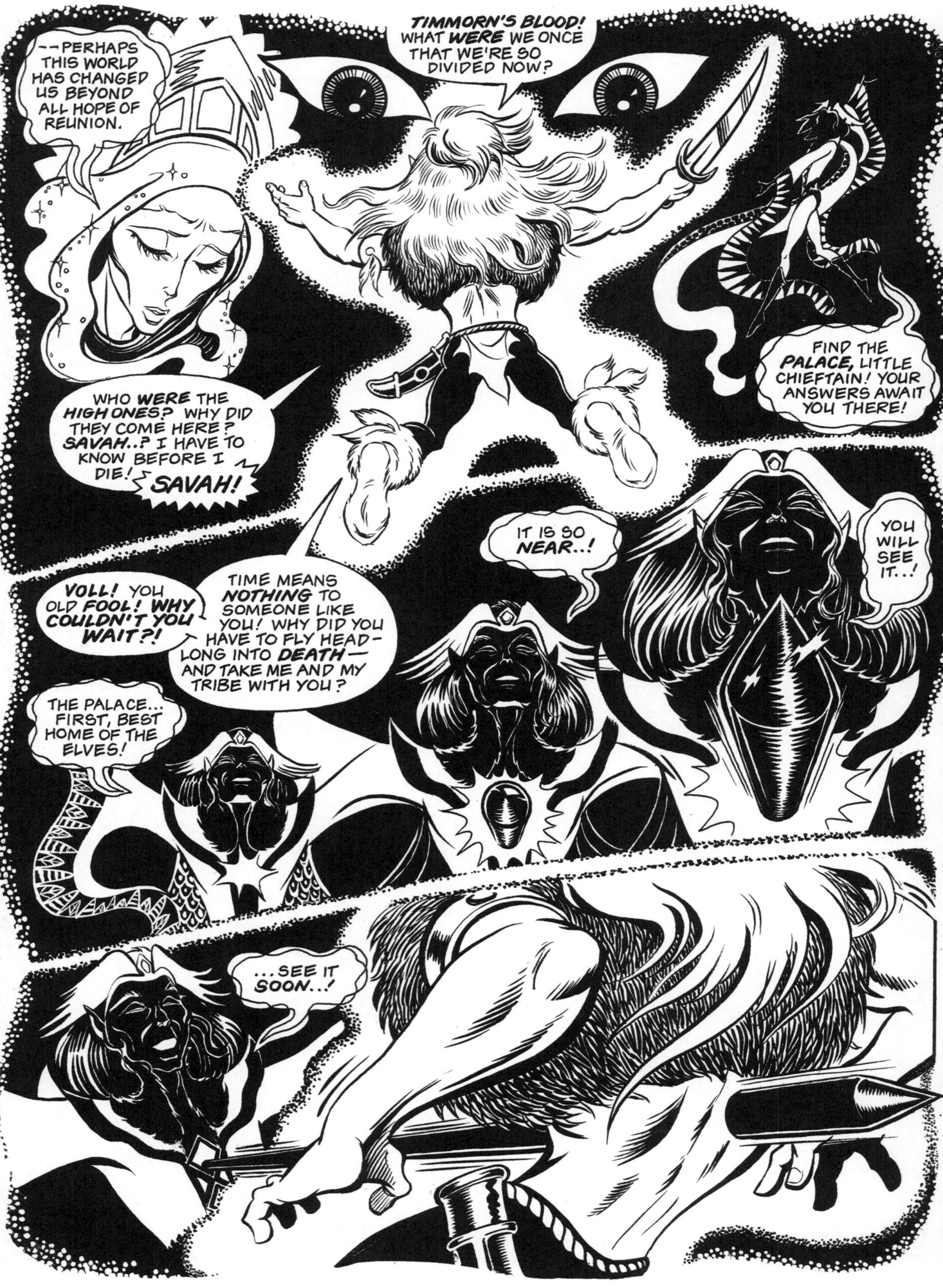
--PERHAPS THIS WORLD HAS CHANGED US BEYOND ALL HOPE OF REUNION.
TIMMORN'S BLOOD! WHAT WERE WE ONCE THAT WE'RE SO DIVIDED NOW?
WHO WERE THE HIGH ONES? WHY DID THEY COME HERE? SAVAH..? I HAVE TO KNOW BEFORE I DIE!
SAVAH!
FIND THE PALACE, LITTLE CHIEFTAIN! YOUR ANSWERS AWAIT YOU THERE!
VOLL! YOU OLD FOOL! WHY COULDN'T YOU WAIT?!
TIME MEANS NOTHING TO SOMEONE LIKE YOU! WHY DID YOU HAVE TO FLY HEAD-LONG INTO DEATH— AND TAKE ME AND MY TRIBE WITH YOU?
IT IS SO NEAR..!
YOU WILL SEE IT..!
THE PALACE... FIRST, BEST HOME OF THE ELVES!
...SEE IT SOON..!

HUUHNNH!?
THE SCENT OF EVERGREEN AND BURNING WOOD... THE SOUND OF SHARP HOOVES PUNCHING THROUGH CRUSTED SNOW... A HUSKY VOICE BARKS TERSE COMMANDS...
TAKE YOUR WOUNDED INSIDE!
VAYA! GET YOUR SCOUTS TO THEIR PERCHES!
GIVE HIM TO ME, QUICKLY!
LEETAH!! WHERE ARE YOU?
I'M COMING!
YIF! SKOT! KRIM! SNIFF AROUND FOR NEW TUNNELS! IT'D BE JUST LIKE THOSE REEKING TROLLS--
--TO WORM THEIR WAY UNDER OUR FLOORS WHILE WE WERE OUT KILLING THEIR KIN!
HMPH! THAT ONE'S BLED WHITE! BETTER DUMP HIM!
HE'LL BE DEAD BEFORE YOU GET INSIDE, ANYWAY!
HE'S OUR CHIEF AND MY FRIEND, YOU COLD-HEARTED--
--HE IS MY LIFEMATE!

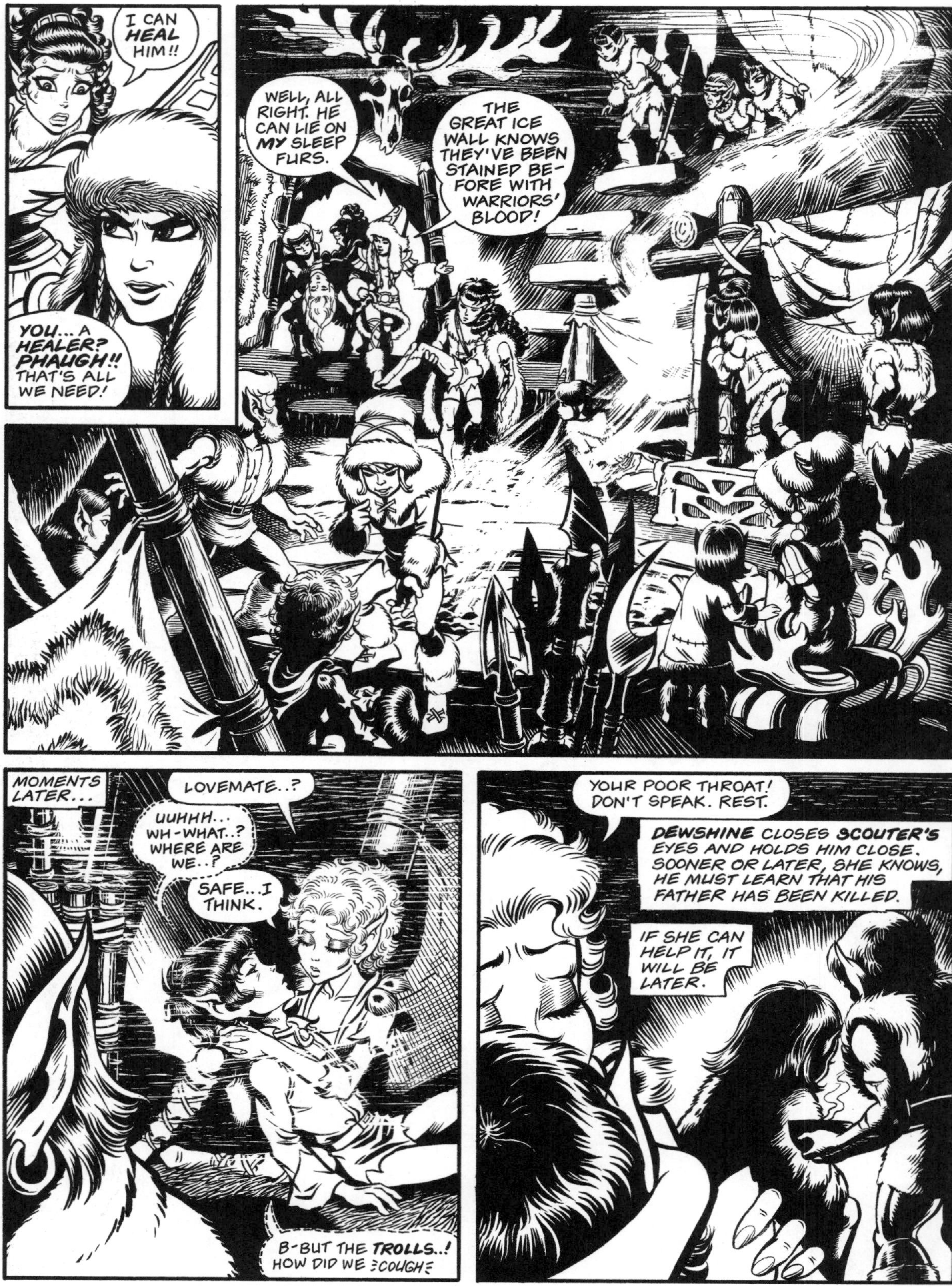
I CAN **HEAL** HIM!!
YOU... A **HEALER**? **PHAUGH!!** THAT'S ALL WE NEED!
WELL, ALL RIGHT. HE CAN LIE ON **MY** SLEEP FURS.
THE GREAT ICE WALL KNOWS THEY'VE BEEN STAINED BE-FORE WITH WARRIORS' BLOOD!
MOMENTS LATER...
LOVEMATE..?
UUHHH... WH-WHAT..? WHERE ARE WE..?
SAFE...I THINK.
B-BUT THE **TROLLS**..! HOW DID WE COUGH
YOUR POOR THROAT! DON'T SPEAK. REST.
DEWSHINE CLOSES **SCOUTER'S** EYES AND HOLDS HIM CLOSE. SOONER OR LATER, SHE KNOWS, HE MUST LEARN THAT HIS FATHER HAS BEEN KILLED.
IF SHE CAN HELP IT, IT WILL BE LATER.

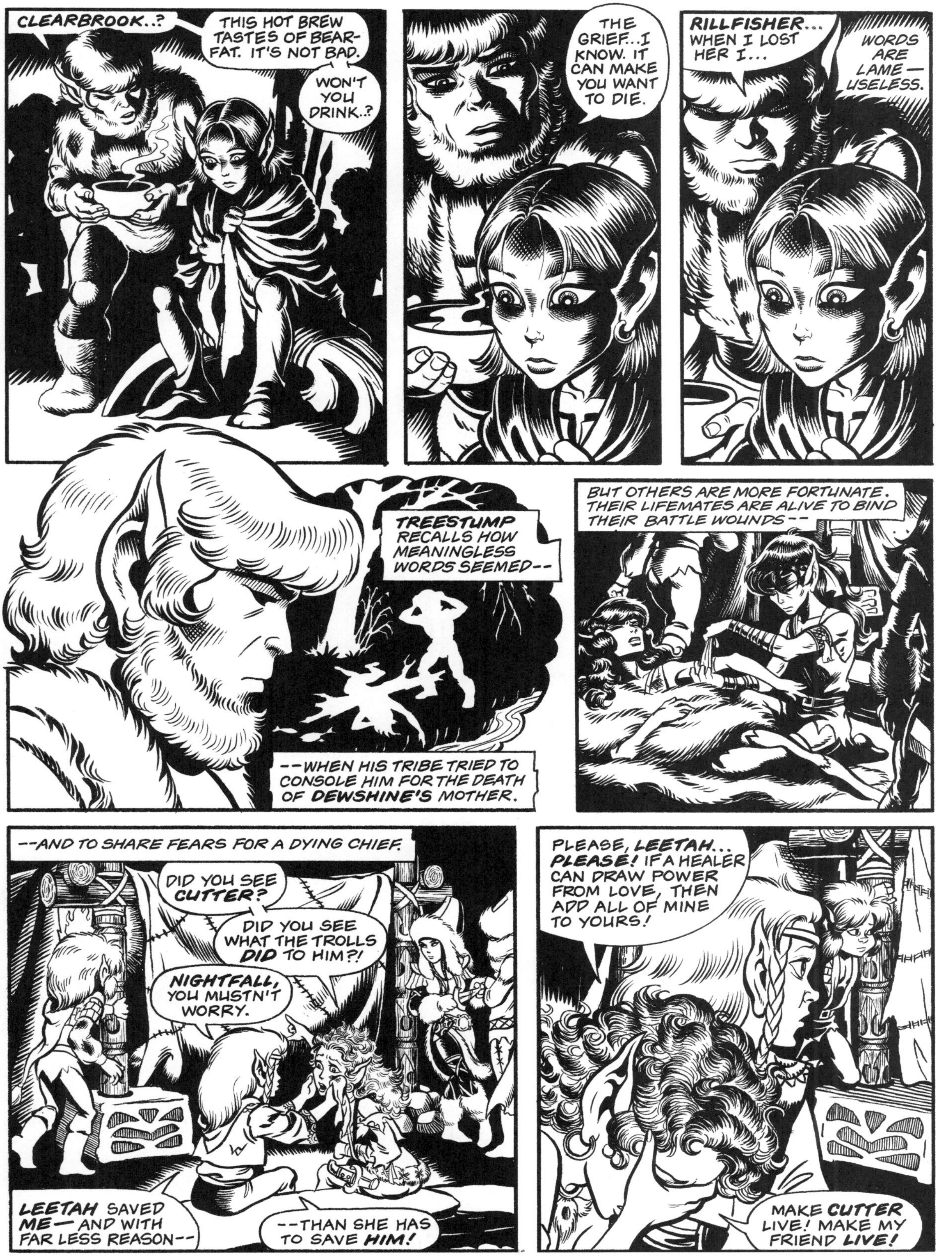

CLEARBROOK..?
THIS HOT BREW TASTES OF BEAR-FAT. IT'S NOT BAD.
WON'T YOU DRINK..?
THE GRIEF...I KNOW. IT CAN MAKE YOU WANT TO DIE.
RILLFISHER... WHEN I LOST HER I...
WORDS ARE LAME — USELESS.
TREESTUMP RECALLS HOW MEANINGLESS WORDS SEEMED--
--WHEN HIS TRIBE TRIED TO CONSOLE HIM FOR THE DEATH OF DEWSHINE'S MOTHER.
BUT OTHERS ARE MORE FORTUNATE. THEIR LIFEMATES ARE ALIVE TO BIND THEIR BATTLE WOUNDS--
--AND TO SHARE FEARS FOR A DYING CHIEF.
DID YOU SEE CUTTER?
DID YOU SEE WHAT THE TROLLS DID TO HIM?!
NIGHTFALL, YOU MUSTN'T WORRY.
LEETAH SAVED ME— AND WITH FAR LESS REASON--
--THAN SHE HAS TO SAVE HIM!
PLEASE, LEETAH... PLEASE! IF A HEALER CAN DRAW POWER FROM LOVE, THEN ADD ALL OF MINE TO YOURS!
MAKE CUTTER LIVE! MAKE MY FRIEND LIVE!

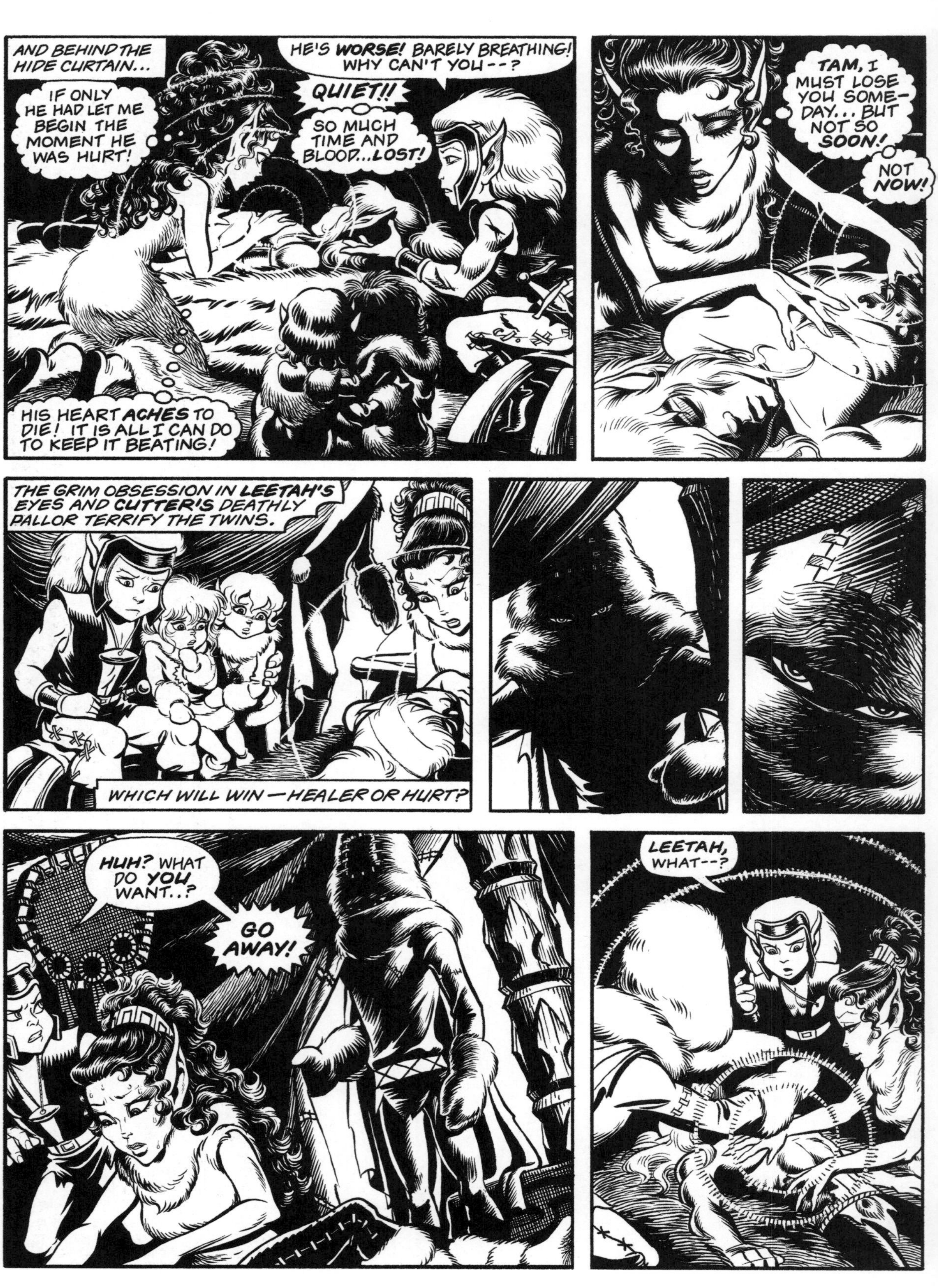
AND BEHIND THE HIDE CURTAIN...
HE'S **WORSE!** BARELY BREATHING! WHY CAN'T YOU--?
IF ONLY HE HAD LET ME BEGIN THE MOMENT HE WAS HURT!
QUIET!!
SO MUCH TIME AND BLOOD...**LOST!**
HIS HEART **ACHES** TO DIE! IT IS ALL I CAN DO TO KEEP IT BEATING!
TAM, I MUST LOSE YOU SOMEDAY... BUT NOT SO **SOON!**
NOT **NOW!**
THE GRIM OBSESSION IN **LEETAH'S** EYES AND **CUTTER'S** DEATHLY PALLOR TERRIFY THE TWINS.
WHICH WILL WIN — HEALER OR HURT?
HUH? WHAT DO **YOU** WANT..?
GO AWAY!
LEETAH, WHAT--?

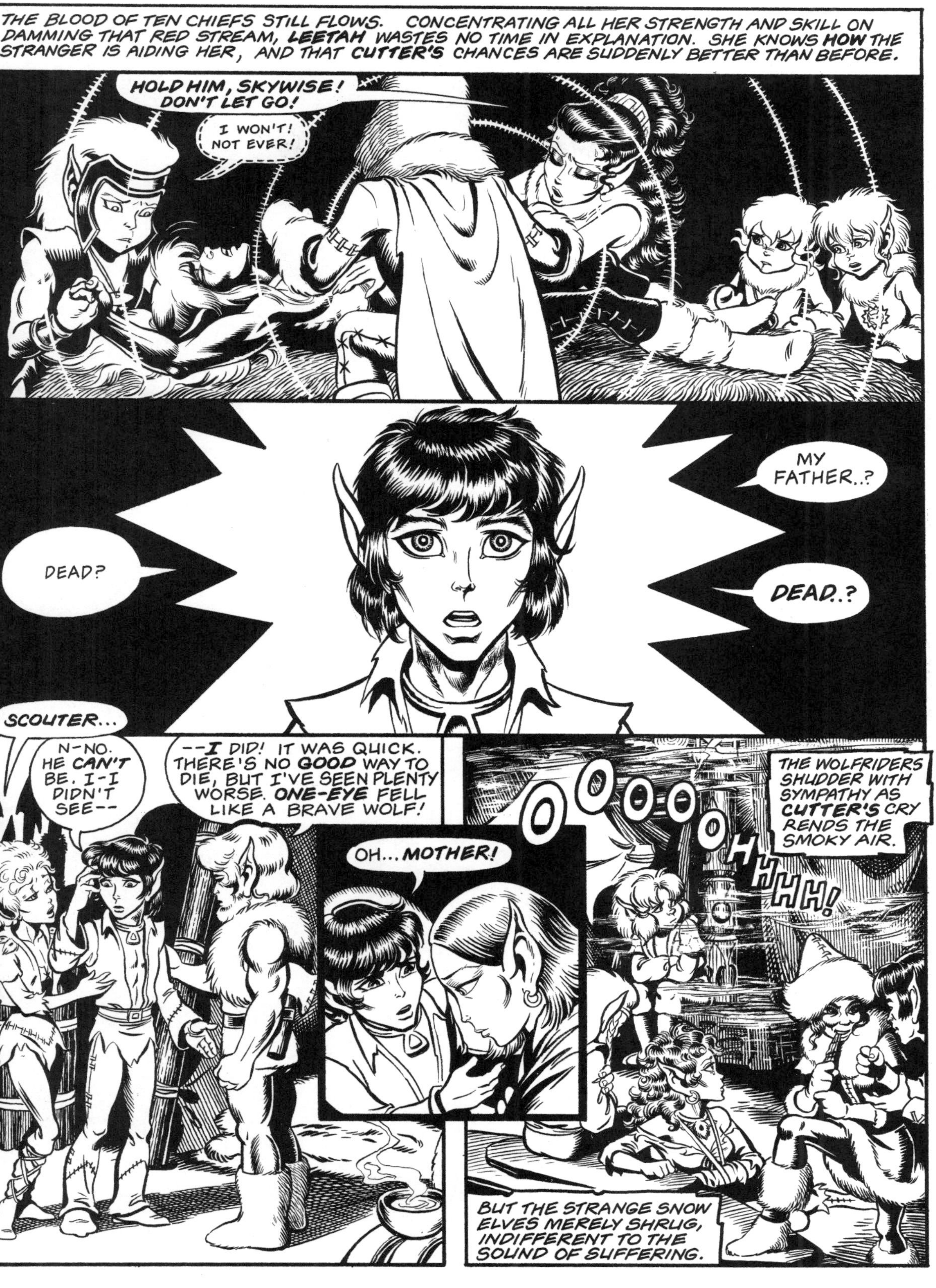

THE BLOOD OF TEN CHIEFS STILL FLOWS. CONCENTRATING ALL HER STRENGTH AND SKILL ON DAMMING THAT RED STREAM, LEETAH WASTES NO TIME IN EXPLANATION. SHE KNOWS HOW THE STRANGER IS AIDING HER, AND THAT CUTTER'S CHANCES ARE SUDDENLY BETTER THAN BEFORE.
HOLD HIM, SKYWISE! DON'T LET GO!
I WON'T! NOT EVER!
MY FATHER..?
DEAD?
DEAD..?
SCOUTER...
N-NO. HE CAN'T BE. I-I DIDN'T SEE--
--I DID! IT WAS QUICK. THERE'S NO GOOD WAY TO DIE, BUT I'VE SEEN PLENTY WORSE. ONE-EYE FELL LIKE A BRAVE WOLF!
OH... MOTHER!
OOOOOOHHHHH!
THE WOLFRIDERS SHUDDER WITH SYMPATHY AS CUTTER'S CRY RENDS THE SMOKY AIR.
BUT THE STRANGE SNOW ELVES MERELY SHRUG, INDIFFERENT TO THE SOUND OF SUFFERING.

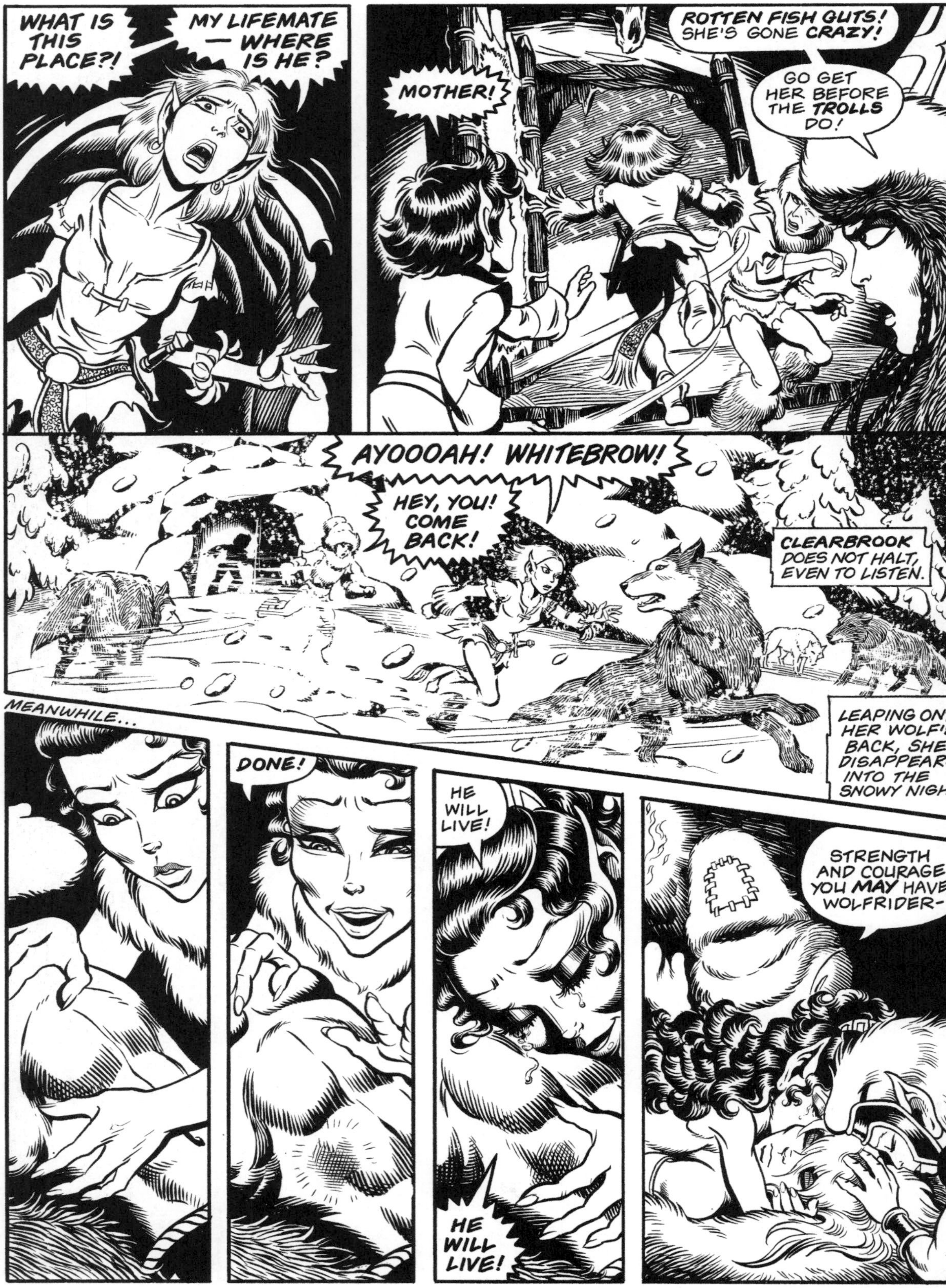
WHAT IS THIS PLACE?!
MY LIFEMATE — WHERE IS HE?
MOTHER!
ROTTEN FISH GUTS! SHE'S GONE CRAZY!
GO GET HER BEFORE THE TROLLS DO!
AYOOOAH! WHITEBROW!
HEY, YOU! COME BACK!
CLEARBROOK DOES NOT HALT, EVEN TO LISTEN.
LEAPING ONTO HER WOLF'S BACK, SHE DISAPPEARS INTO THE SNOWY NIGHT.
MEANWHILE...
DONE!
HE WILL LIVE!
HE WILL LIVE!
STRENGTH AND COURAGE YOU MAY HAVE, WOLFRIDER--

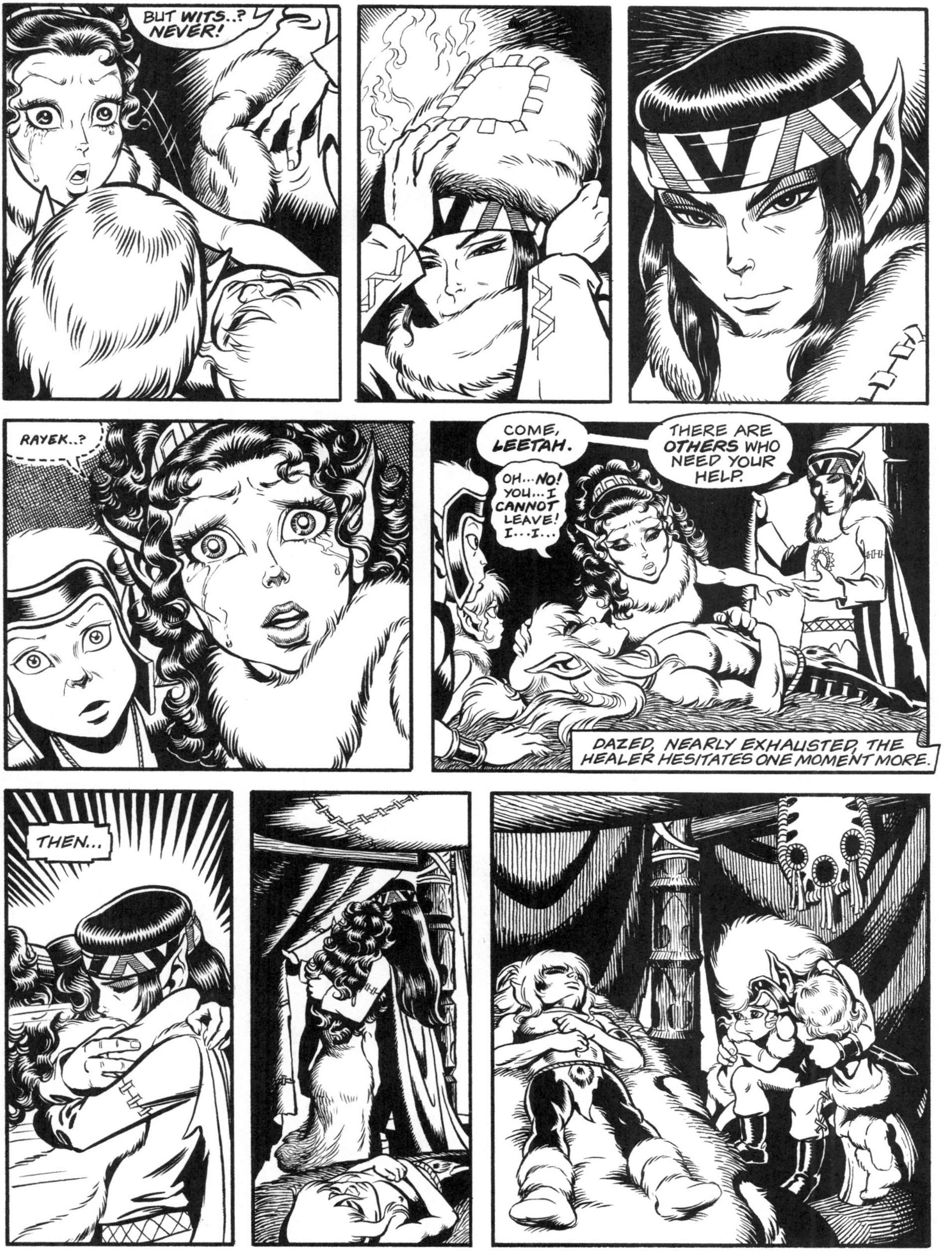
BUT WITS..? NEVER!
RAYEK..?
COME, LEETAH.
THERE ARE OTHERS WHO NEED YOUR HELP.
OH...NO! YOU...I CANNOT LEAVE! I...I...
DAZED, NEARLY EXHAUSTED, THE HEALER HESITATES ONE MOMENT MORE.
THEN...

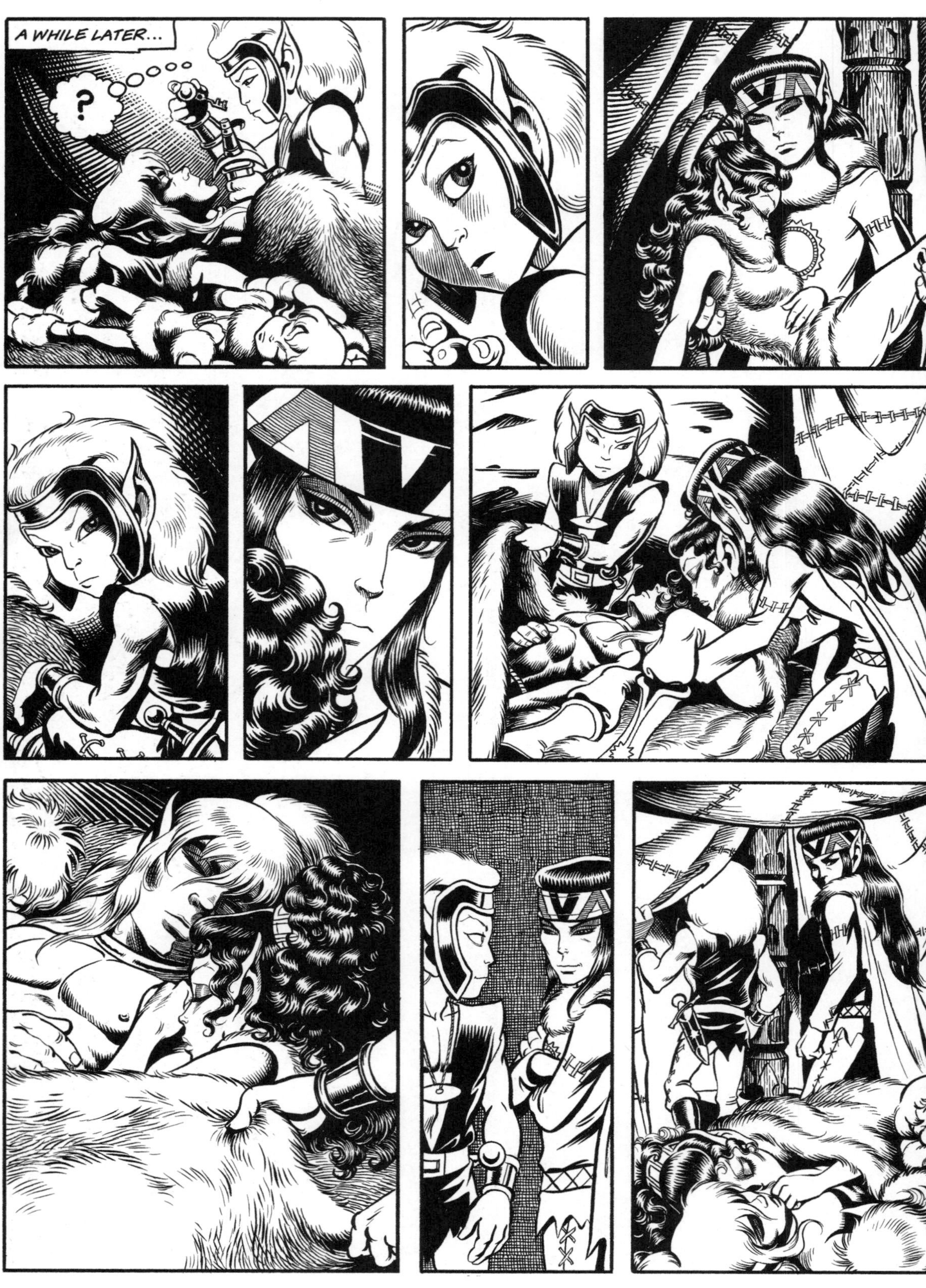
A WHILE LATER...
?

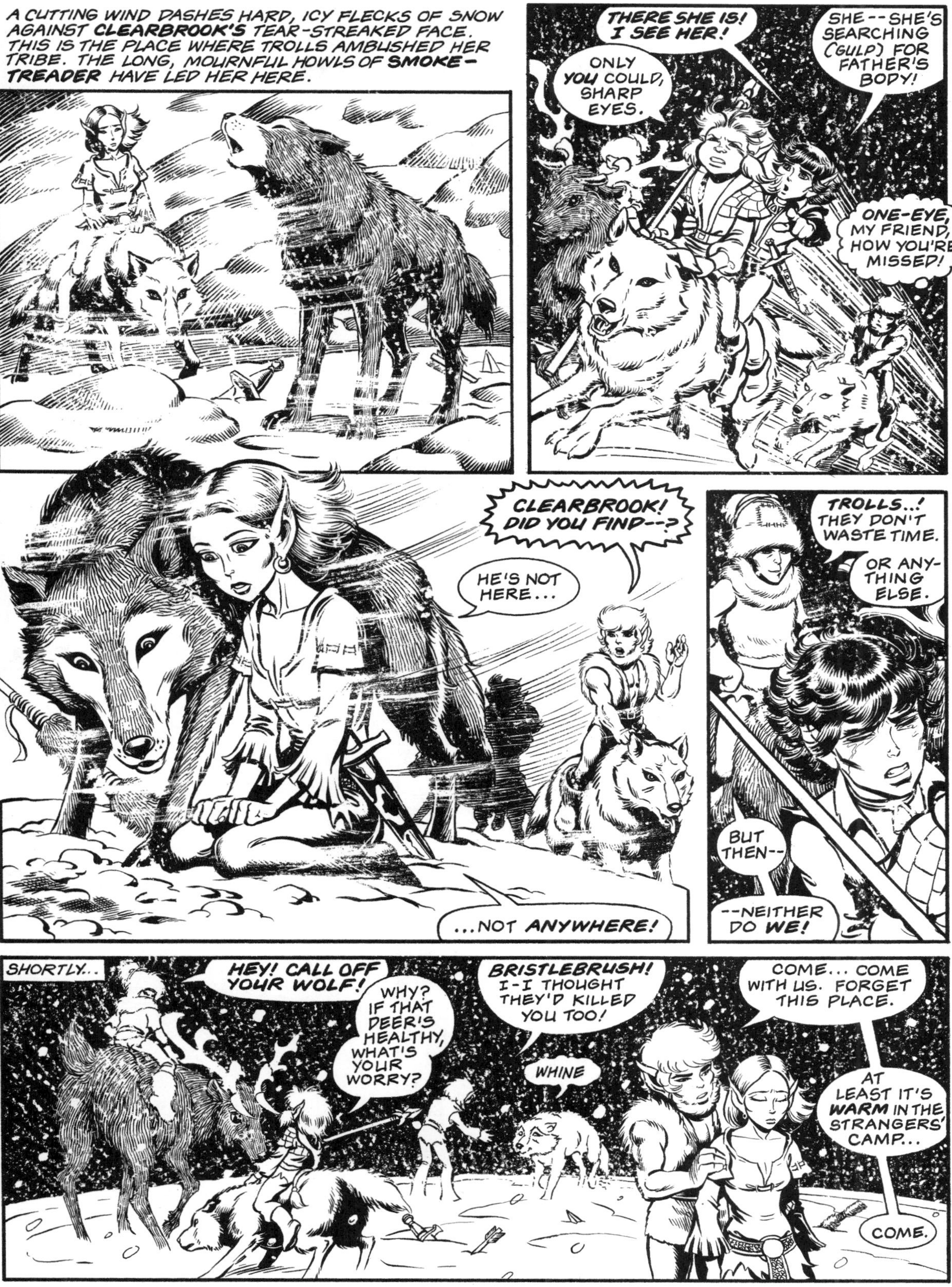

A CUTTING WIND DASHES HARD, ICY FLECKS OF SNOW AGAINST CLEARBROOK'S TEAR-STREAKED FACE. THIS IS THE PLACE WHERE TROLLS AMBUSHED HER TRIBE. THE LONG, MOURNFUL HOWLS OF SMOKE-TREADER HAVE LED HER HERE.
THERE SHE IS! I SEE HER!
ONLY YOU COULD, SHARP EYES.
SHE -- SHE'S SEARCHING (GULP) FOR FATHER'S BODY!
ONE-EYE, MY FRIEND, HOW YOU'RE MISSED!
CLEARBROOK! DID YOU FIND--?
HE'S NOT HERE...
...NOT ANYWHERE!
TROLLS..! THEY DON'T WASTE TIME.
OR ANYTHING ELSE.
BUT THEN--
--NEITHER DO WE!
SHORTLY...
HEY! CALL OFF YOUR WOLF!
WHY? IF THAT DEER'S HEALTHY, WHAT'S YOUR WORRY?
BRISTLEBRUSH! I-I THOUGHT THEY'D KILLED YOU TOO!
WHINE
COME... COME WITH US. FORGET THIS PLACE.
AT LEAST IT'S WARM IN THE STRANGERS' CAMP...
COME.

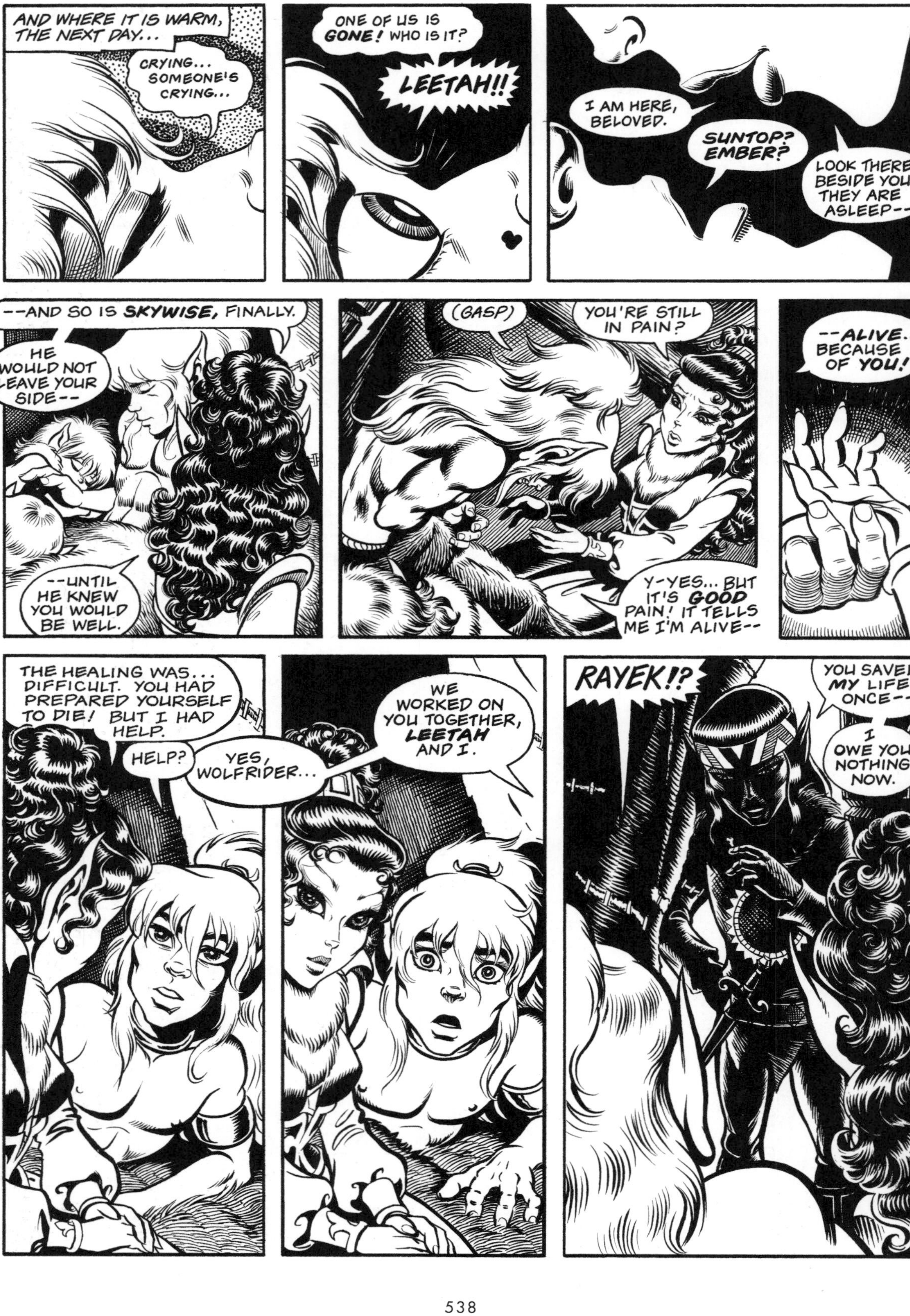

AND WHERE IT IS WARM, THE NEXT DAY...
CRYING... SOMEONE'S CRYING...
ONE OF US IS **GONE!** WHO IS IT?
LEETAH!!
I AM HERE, BELOVED.
SUNTOP? EMBER?
LOOK THERE, BESIDE YOU. THEY ARE ASLEEP--
--AND SO IS **SKYWISE,** FINALLY.
HE WOULD NOT LEAVE YOUR SIDE--
--UNTIL HE KNEW YOU WOULD BE WELL.
(GASP)
YOU'RE STILL IN PAIN?
Y-YES... BUT IT'S **GOOD** PAIN! IT TELLS ME I'M ALIVE--
--**ALIVE...** BECAUSE OF **YOU!**
THE HEALING WAS... DIFFICULT. YOU HAD PREPARED YOURSELF TO DIE! BUT I HAD HELP.
HELP?
YES, WOLFRIDER...
WE WORKED ON YOU TOGETHER, **LEETAH** AND I.
RAYEK!?
YOU SAVED **MY** LIFE ONCE--
I OWE YOU NOTHING NOW.

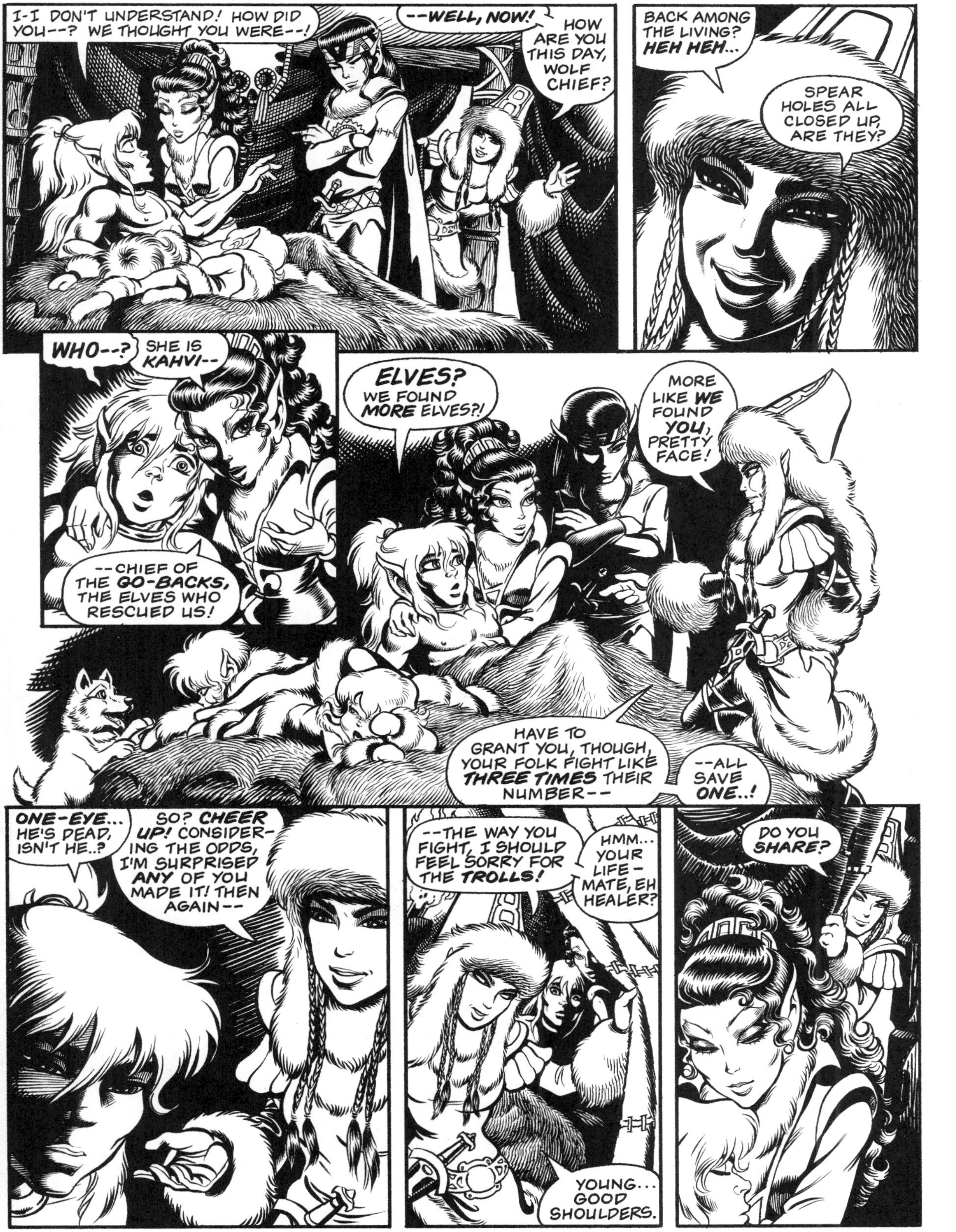

I-I DON'T UNDERSTAND! HOW DID YOU--? WE THOUGHT YOU WERE--!
--WELL, NOW!
HOW ARE YOU THIS DAY, WOLF CHIEF?
BACK AMONG THE LIVING? HEH HEH...
SPEAR HOLES ALL CLOSED UP, ARE THEY?
WHO--?
SHE IS KAHVI--
--CHIEF OF THE GO-BACKS, THE ELVES WHO RESCUED US!
ELVES? WE FOUND MORE ELVES?!
MORE LIKE WE FOUND YOU, PRETTY FACE!
HAVE TO GRANT YOU, THOUGH, YOUR FOLK FIGHT LIKE THREE TIMES THEIR NUMBER--
--ALL SAVE ONE..!
ONE-EYE... HE'S DEAD, ISN'T HE..?
SO? CHEER UP! CONSIDER-ING THE ODDS, I'M SURPRISED ANY OF YOU MADE IT! THEN AGAIN--
--THE WAY YOU FIGHT, I SHOULD FEEL SORRY FOR THE TROLLS!
HMM... YOUR LIFE-MATE, EH HEALER?
YOUNG... GOOD SHOULDERS.
DO YOU SHARE?

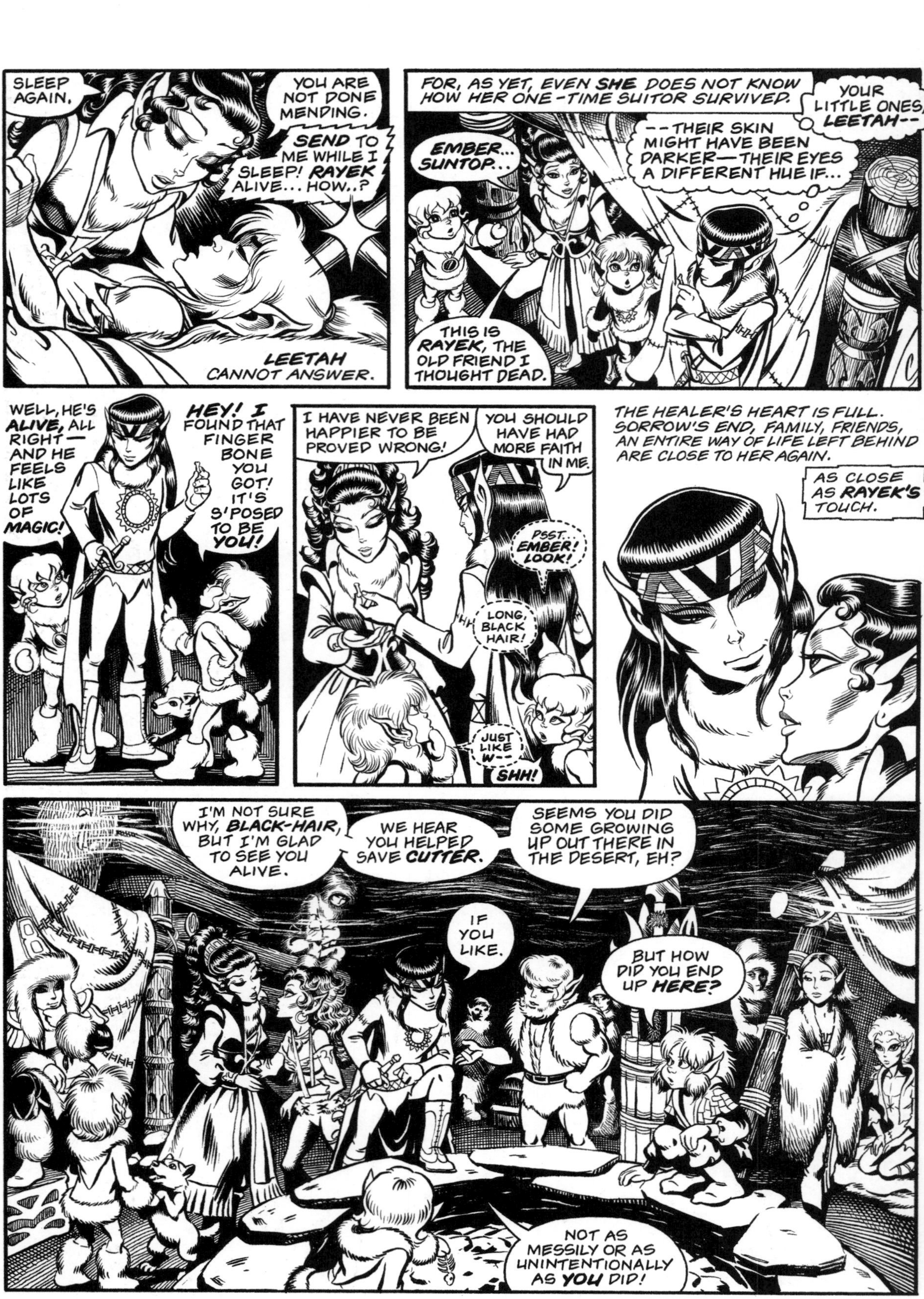
SLEEP AGAIN.
YOU ARE NOT DONE MENDING.
SEND TO ME WHILE I SLEEP! RAYEK ALIVE... HOW..?
LEETAH CANNOT ANSWER.
FOR, AS YET, EVEN SHE DOES NOT KNOW HOW HER ONE-TIME SUITOR SURVIVED.
YOUR LITTLE ONES, LEETAH--
--THEIR SKIN MIGHT HAVE BEEN DARKER—THEIR EYES A DIFFERENT HUE IF...
EMBER... SUNTOP...
THIS IS RAYEK, THE OLD FRIEND I THOUGHT DEAD.
WELL, HE'S ALIVE, ALL RIGHT— AND HE FEELS LIKE LOTS OF MAGIC!
HEY! I FOUND THAT FINGER BONE YOU GOT! IT'S S'POSED TO BE YOU!
I HAVE NEVER BEEN HAPPIER TO BE PROVED WRONG!
YOU SHOULD HAVE HAD MORE FAITH IN ME.
PSST... EMBER! LOOK!
LONG, BLACK HAIR!
JUST LIKE W--
SHH!
THE HEALER'S HEART IS FULL. SORROW'S END, FAMILY, FRIENDS, AN ENTIRE WAY OF LIFE LEFT BEHIND ARE CLOSE TO HER AGAIN.
AS CLOSE AS RAYEK'S TOUCH.
I'M NOT SURE WHY, BLACK-HAIR, BUT I'M GLAD TO SEE YOU ALIVE.
WE HEAR YOU HELPED SAVE CUTTER.
IF YOU LIKE.
SEEMS YOU DID SOME GROWING UP OUT THERE IN THE DESERT, EH?
BUT HOW DID YOU END UP HERE?
NOT AS MESSILY OR AS UNINTENTIONALLY AS YOU DID!

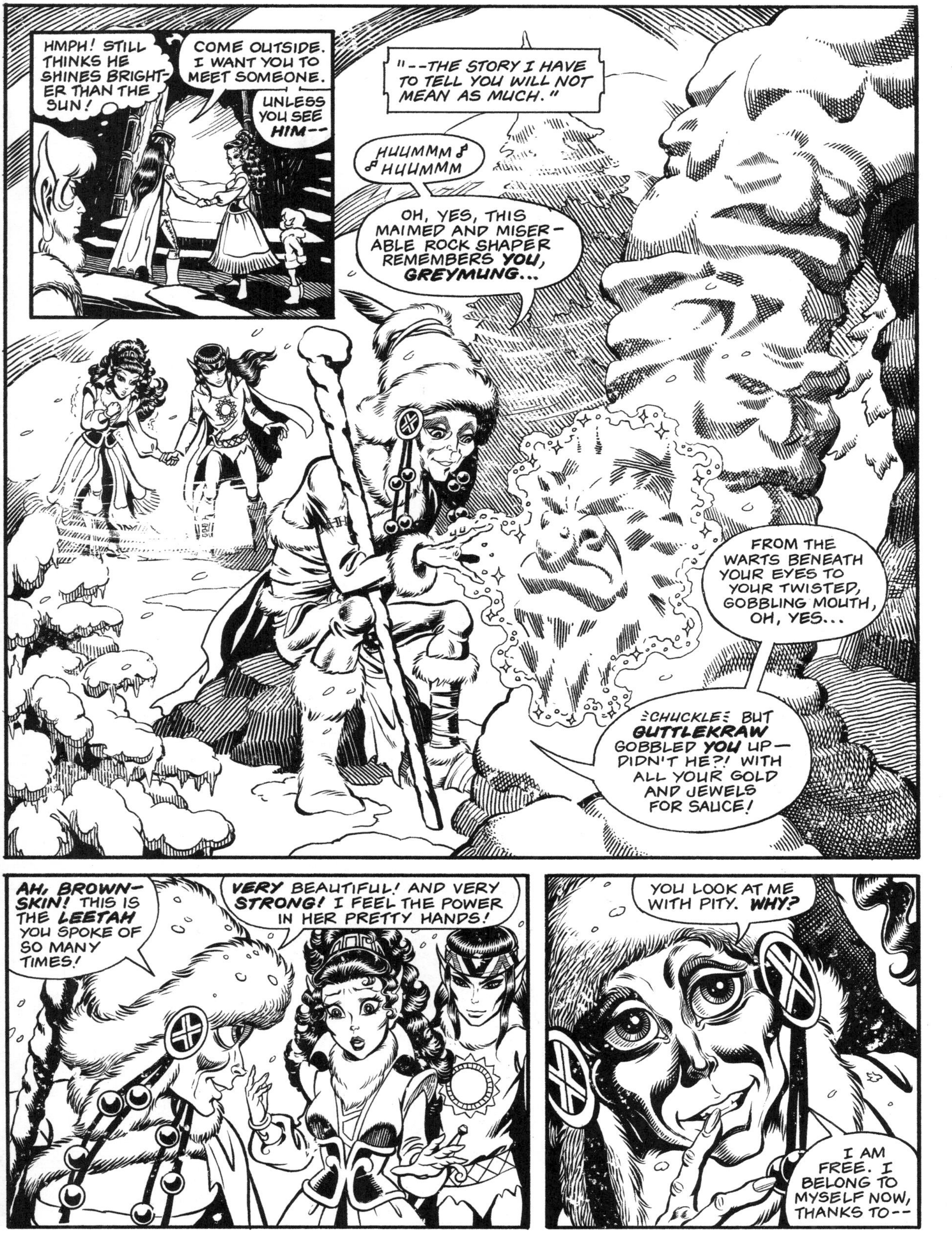
HMPH! STILL THINKS HE SHINES BRIGHTER THAN THE SUN!
COME OUTSIDE. I WANT YOU TO MEET SOMEONE.
UNLESS YOU SEE HIM--
"--THE STORY I HAVE TO TELL YOU WILL NOT MEAN AS MUCH."
HUUMMM HUUMMM
OH, YES, THIS MAIMED AND MISERABLE ROCK SHAPER REMEMBERS YOU, GREYMUNG...
FROM THE WARTS BENEATH YOUR EYES TO YOUR TWISTED, GOBBLING MOUTH, OH, YES...
CHUCKLE BUT GUTTLEKRAW GOBBLED YOU UP-- DIDN'T HE?! WITH ALL YOUR GOLD AND JEWELS FOR SAUCE!
AH, BROWNSKIN! THIS IS THE LEETAH YOU SPOKE OF SO MANY TIMES!
VERY BEAUTIFUL! AND VERY STRONG! I FEEL THE POWER IN HER PRETTY HANDS!
YOU LOOK AT ME WITH PITY. WHY?
I AM FREE. I BELONG TO MYSELF NOW, THANKS TO--

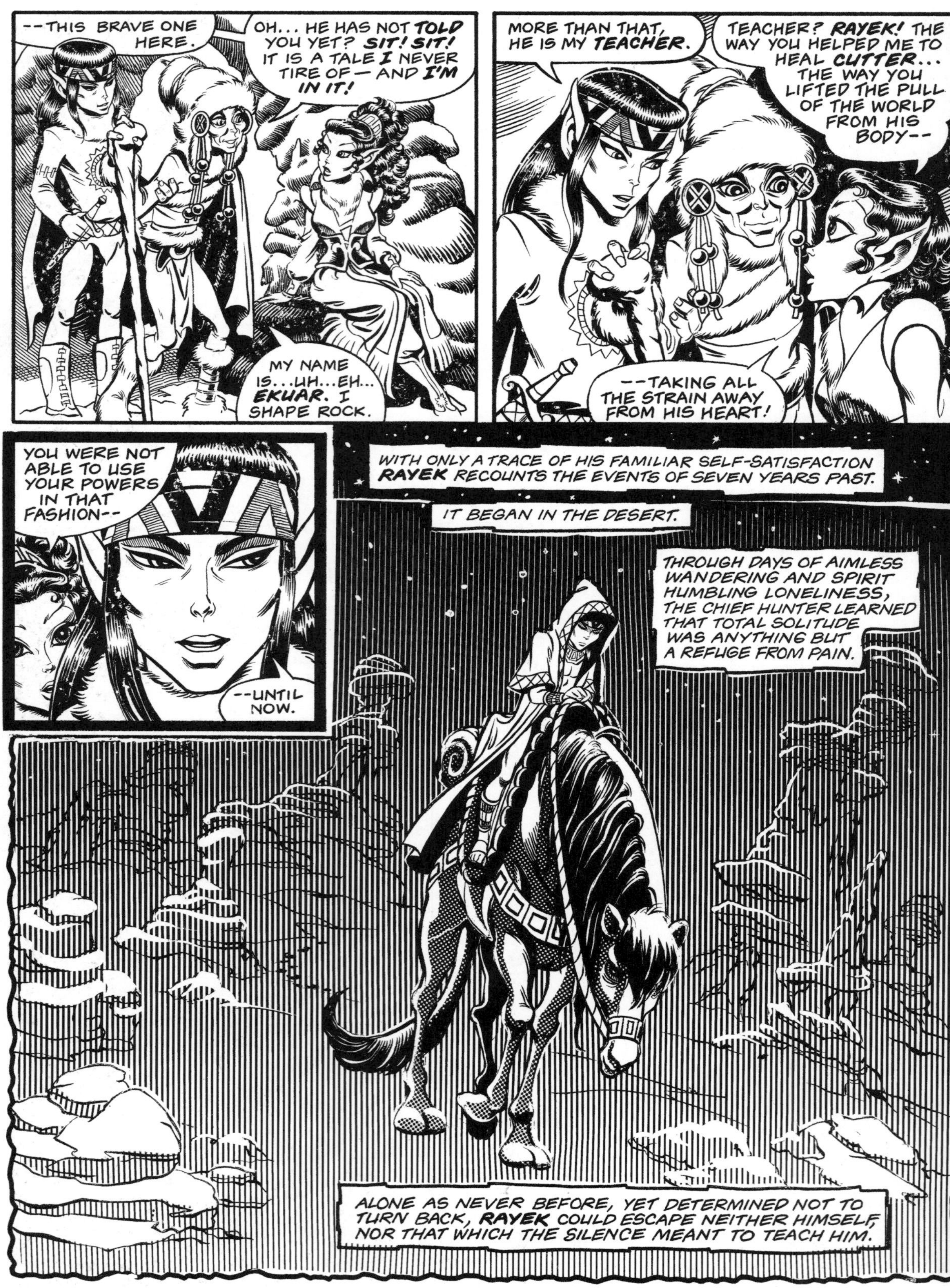

--THIS BRAVE ONE HERE.
OH... HE HAS NOT TOLD YOU YET? SIT! SIT! IT IS A TALE I NEVER TIRE OF — AND I'M IN IT!
MY NAME IS...UH...EH... EKUAR. I SHAPE ROCK.
MORE THAN THAT, HE IS MY TEACHER.
TEACHER? RAYEK! THE WAY YOU HELPED ME TO HEAL CUTTER... THE WAY YOU LIFTED THE PULL OF THE WORLD FROM HIS BODY--
--TAKING ALL THE STRAIN AWAY FROM HIS HEART!
YOU WERE NOT ABLE TO USE YOUR POWERS IN THAT FASHION--
--UNTIL NOW.
WITH ONLY A TRACE OF HIS FAMILIAR SELF-SATISFACTION RAYEK RECOUNTS THE EVENTS OF SEVEN YEARS PAST.
IT BEGAN IN THE DESERT.
THROUGH DAYS OF AIMLESS WANDERING AND SPIRIT HUMBLING LONELINESS, THE CHIEF HUNTER LEARNED THAT TOTAL SOLITUDE WAS ANYTHING BUT A REFUGE FROM PAIN.
ALONE AS NEVER BEFORE, YET DETERMINED NOT TO TURN BACK, RAYEK COULD ESCAPE NEITHER HIMSELF, NOR THAT WHICH THE SILENCE MEANT TO TEACH HIM.

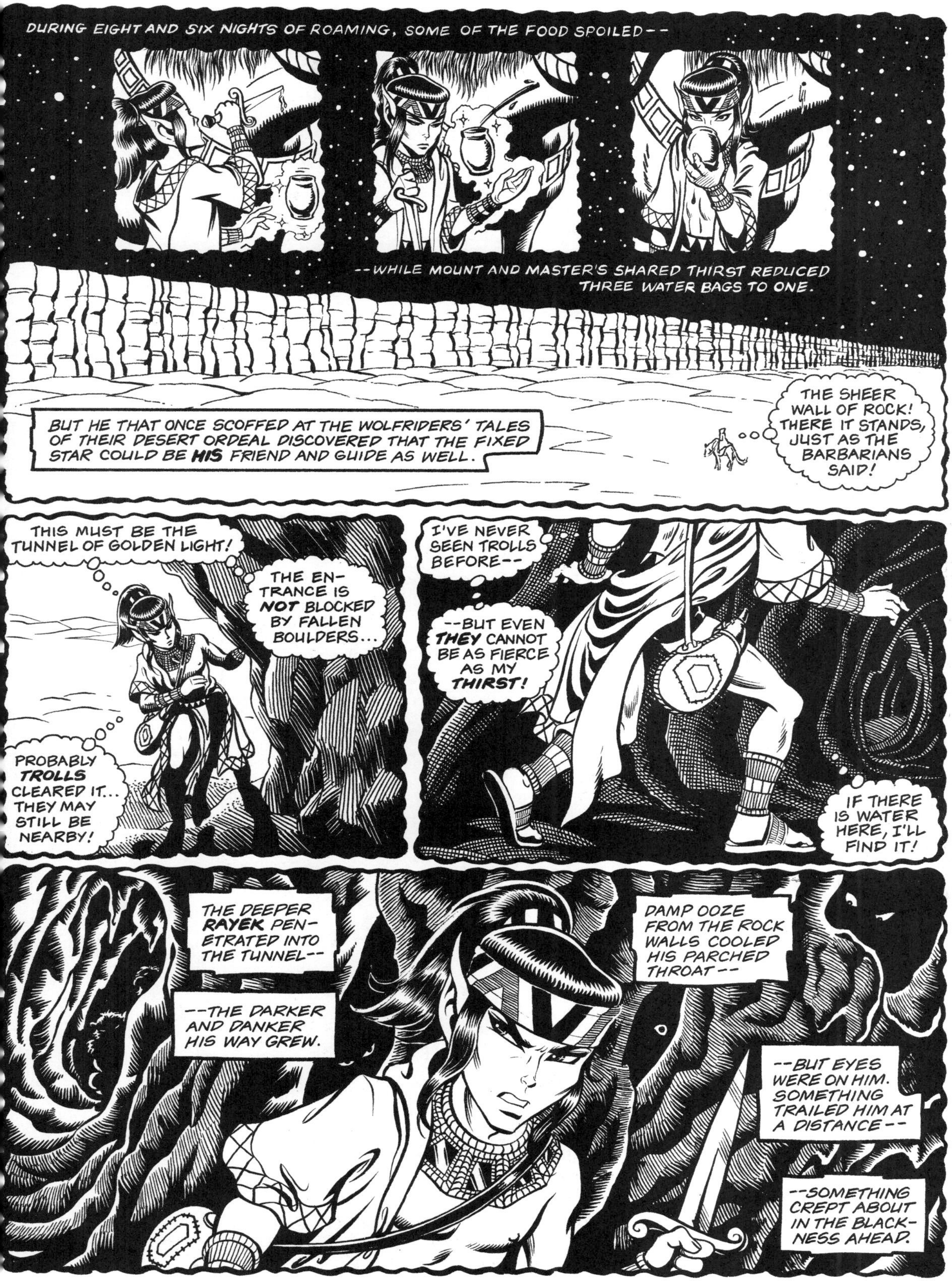
DURING EIGHT AND SIX NIGHTS OF ROAMING, SOME OF THE FOOD SPOILED--
--WHILE MOUNT AND MASTER'S SHARED THIRST REDUCED THREE WATER BAGS TO ONE.
BUT HE THAT ONCE SCOFFED AT THE WOLFRIDERS' TALES OF THEIR DESERT ORDEAL DISCOVERED THAT THE FIXED STAR COULD BE HIS FRIEND AND GUIDE AS WELL.
THE SHEER WALL OF ROCK! THERE IT STANDS, JUST AS THE BARBARIANS SAID!
THIS MUST BE THE TUNNEL OF GOLDEN LIGHT!
THE EN-TRANCE IS NOT BLOCKED BY FALLEN BOULDERS...
PROBABLY TROLLS CLEARED IT... THEY MAY STILL BE NEARBY!
I'VE NEVER SEEN TROLLS BEFORE--
--BUT EVEN THEY CANNOT BE AS FIERCE AS MY THIRST!
IF THERE IS WATER HERE, I'LL FIND IT!
THE DEEPER RAYEK PEN-ETRATED INTO THE TUNNEL--
--THE DARKER AND DANKER HIS WAY GREW.
DAMP OOZE FROM THE ROCK WALLS COOLED HIS PARCHED THROAT--
--BUT EYES WERE ON HIM. SOMETHING TRAILED HIM AT A DISTANCE--
--SOMETHING CREPT ABOUT IN THE BLACK-NESS AHEAD.

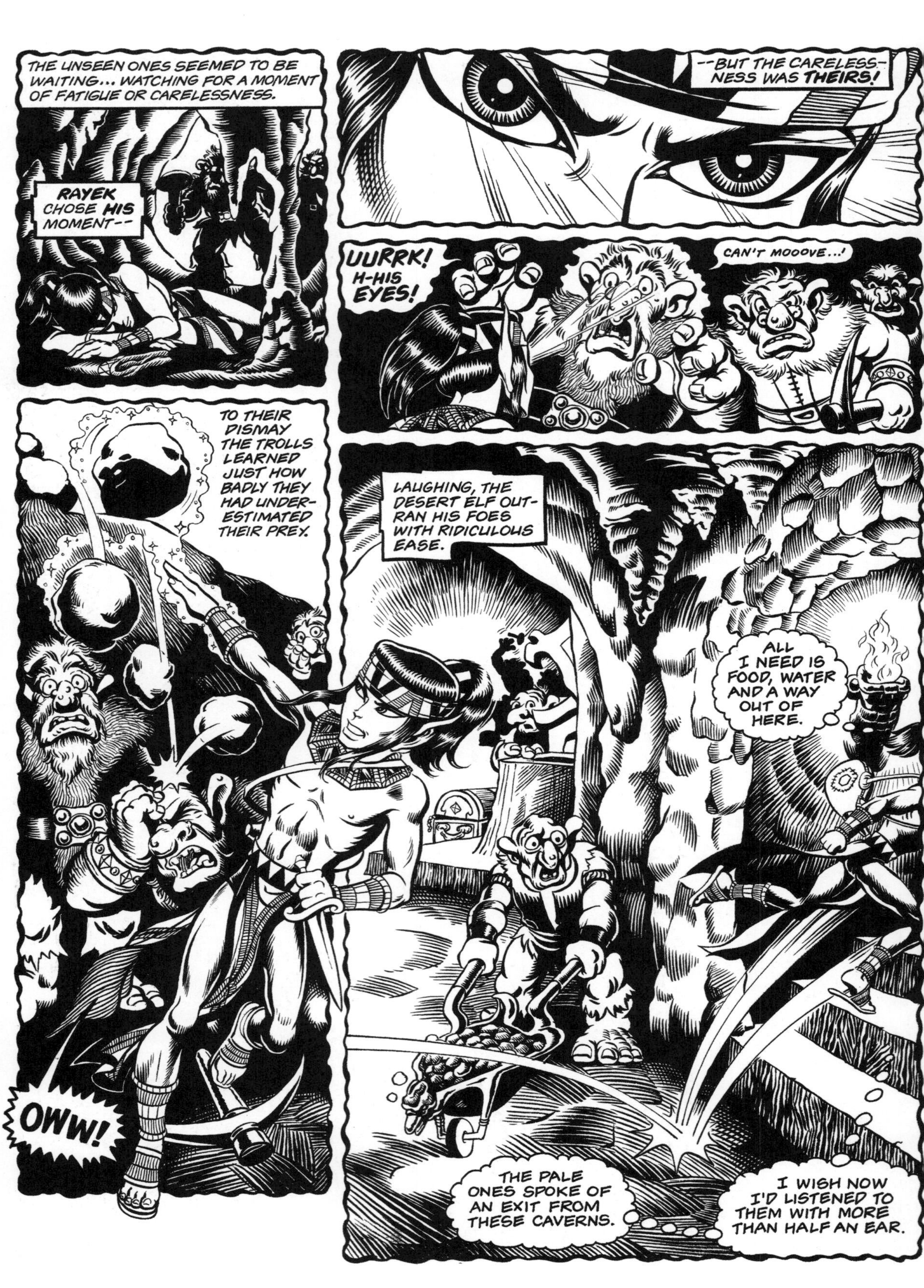
THE UNSEEN ONES SEEMED TO BE WAITING... WATCHING FOR A MOMENT OF FATIGUE OR CARELESSNESS.
RAYEK CHOSE HIS MOMENT--
--BUT THE CARELESSNESS WAS THEIRS!
UURRK! H-HIS EYES!
CAN'T MOOOVE...!
TO THEIR DISMAY THE TROLLS LEARNED JUST HOW BADLY THEY HAD UNDERESTIMATED THEIR PREY.
OWW!
LAUGHING, THE DESERT ELF OUTRAN HIS FOES WITH RIDICULOUS EASE.
ALL I NEED IS FOOD, WATER AND A WAY OUT OF HERE.
THE PALE ONES SPOKE OF AN EXIT FROM THESE CAVERNS.
I WISH NOW I'D LISTENED TO THEM WITH MORE THAN HALF AN EAR.

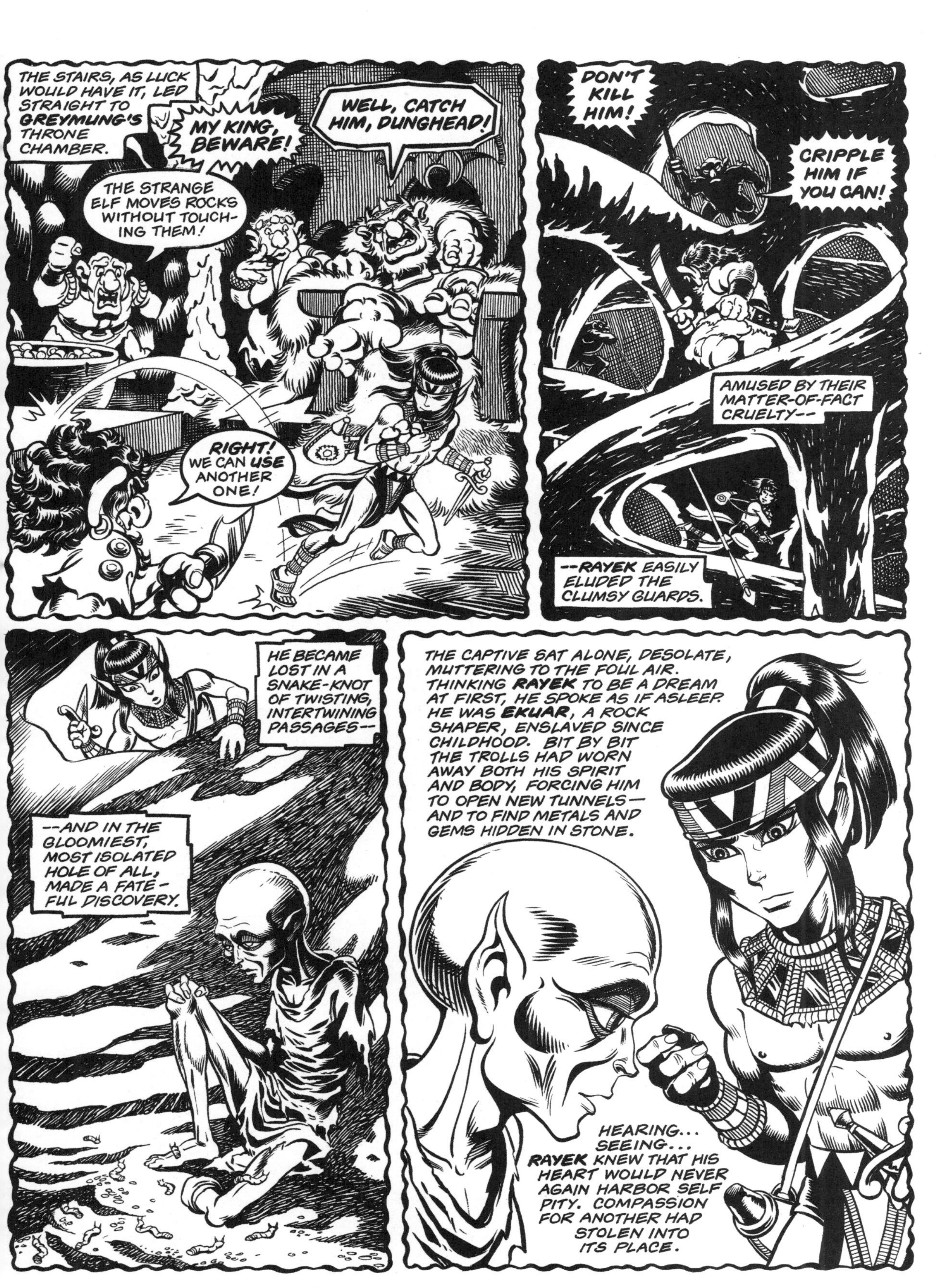
THE STAIRS, AS LUCK WOULD HAVE IT, LED STRAIGHT TO GREYMUNG'S THRONE CHAMBER.
MY KING, BEWARE!
WELL, CATCH HIM, DUNGHEAD!
THE STRANGE ELF MOVES ROCKS WITHOUT TOUCHING THEM!
RIGHT! WE CAN USE ANOTHER ONE!
DON'T KILL HIM!
CRIPPLE HIM IF YOU CAN!
AMUSED BY THEIR MATTER-OF-FACT CRUELTY--
--RAYEK EASILY ELUDED THE CLUMSY GUARDS.
HE BECAME LOST IN A SNAKE-KNOT OF TWISTING, INTERTWINING PASSAGES--
--AND IN THE GLOOMIEST, MOST ISOLATED HOLE OF ALL, MADE A FATE-FUL DISCOVERY.
THE CAPTIVE SAT ALONE, DESOLATE, MUTTERING TO THE FOUL AIR. THINKING RAYEK TO BE A DREAM AT FIRST, HE SPOKE AS IF ASLEEP. HE WAS EKUAR, A ROCK SHAPER, ENSLAVED SINCE CHILDHOOD. BIT BY BIT THE TROLLS HAD WORN AWAY BOTH HIS SPIRIT AND BODY, FORCING HIM TO OPEN NEW TUNNELS— AND TO FIND METALS AND GEMS HIDDEN IN STONE.
HEARING... SEEING... RAYEK KNEW THAT HIS HEART WOULD NEVER AGAIN HARBOR SELF PITY. COMPASSION FOR ANOTHER HAD STOLEN INTO ITS PLACE.

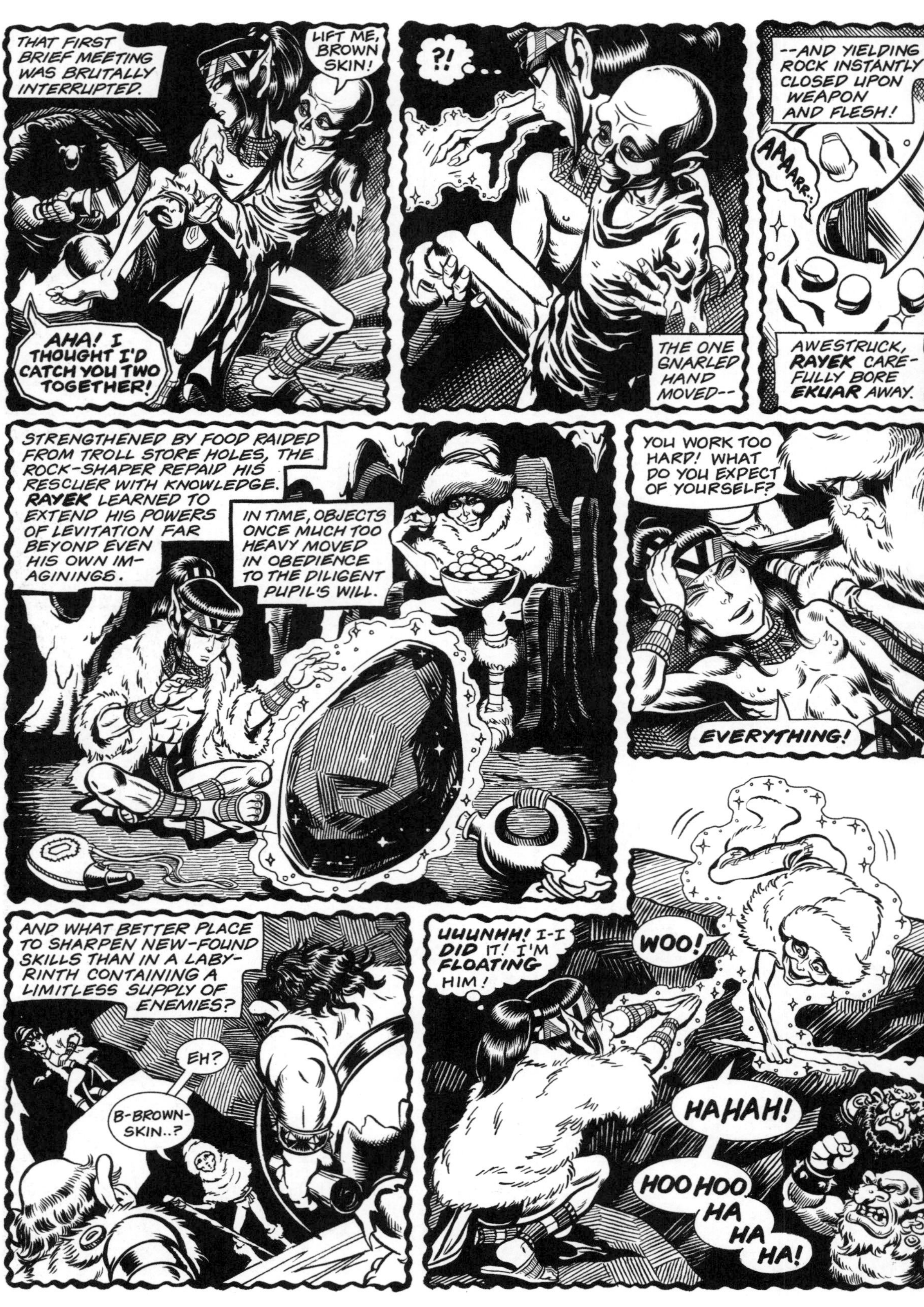
THAT FIRST BRIEF MEETING WAS BRUTALLY INTERRUPTED.
LIFT ME, BROWN SKIN!
AHA! I THOUGHT I'D CATCH YOU TWO TOGETHER!
?! ...
THE ONE GNARLED HAND MOVED--
--AND YIELDING ROCK INSTANTLY CLOSED UPON WEAPON AND FLESH!
AAAAARR..!
AWESTRUCK, RAYEK CAREFULLY BORE EKUAR AWAY.
STRENGTHENED BY FOOD RAIDED FROM TROLL STORE HOLES, THE ROCK-SHAPER REPAID HIS RESCUER WITH KNOWLEDGE. RAYEK LEARNED TO EXTEND HIS POWERS OF LEVITATION FAR BEYOND EVEN HIS OWN IMAGININGS.
IN TIME, OBJECTS ONCE MUCH TOO HEAVY MOVED IN OBEDIENCE TO THE DILIGENT PUPIL'S WILL.
YOU WORK TOO HARD! WHAT DO YOU EXPECT OF YOURSELF?
EVERYTHING!
AND WHAT BETTER PLACE TO SHARPEN NEW-FOUND SKILLS THAN IN A LABYRINTH CONTAINING A LIMITLESS SUPPLY OF ENEMIES?
EH?
B-BROWN-SKIN..?
UUUNHH! I-I DID IT! I'M FLOATING HIM!
WOO!
HAHAH!
HOO HOO HA HA HA!

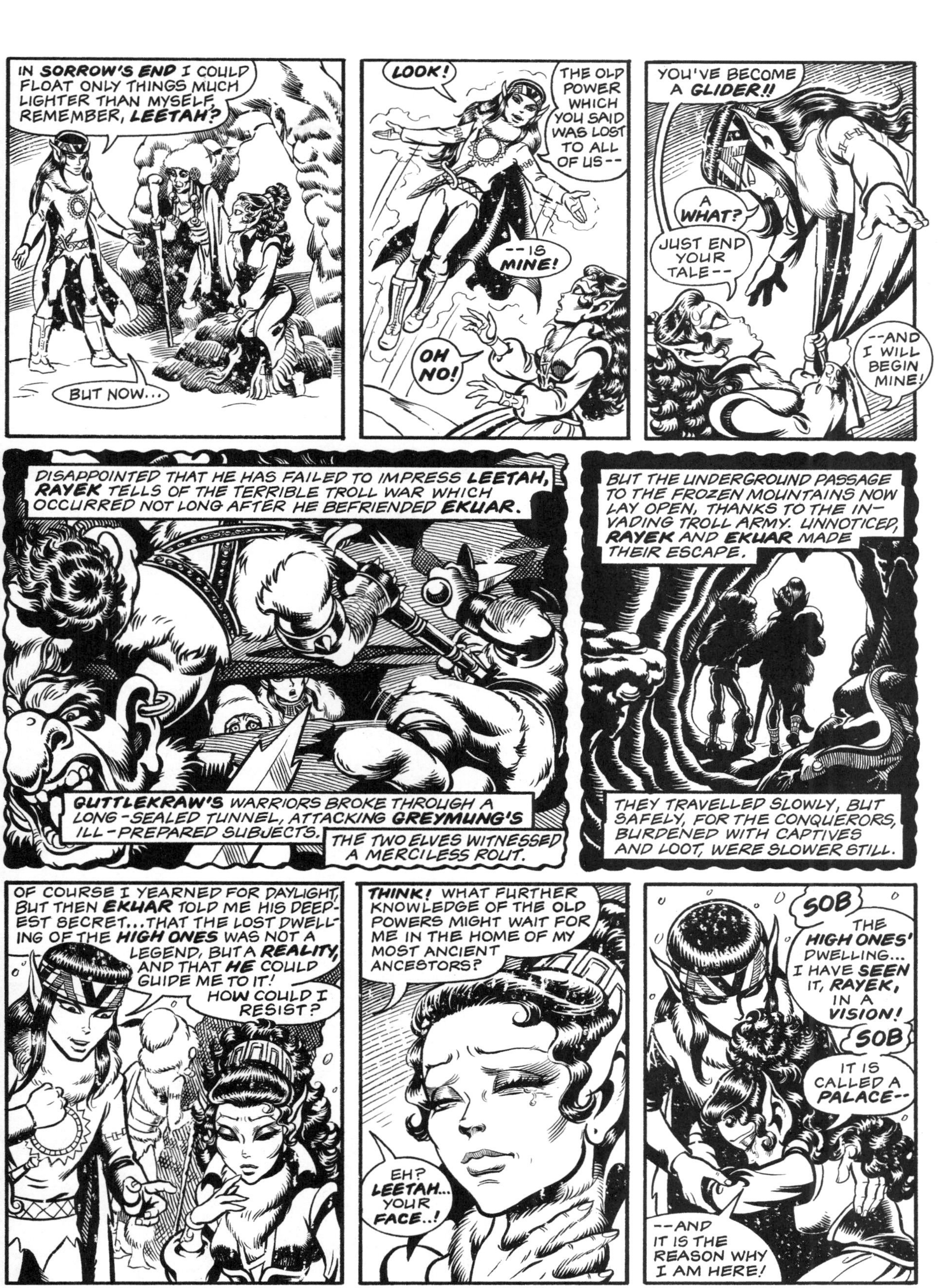

IN SORROW'S END I COULD FLOAT ONLY THINGS MUCH LIGHTER THAN MYSELF, REMEMBER, LEETAH?
BUT NOW...
LOOK!
THE OLD POWER WHICH YOU SAID WAS LOST TO ALL OF US--
--IS MINE!
OH NO!
YOU'VE BECOME A GLIDER!!
A WHAT?
JUST END YOUR TALE--
--AND I WILL BEGIN MINE!
DISAPPOINTED THAT HE HAS FAILED TO IMPRESS LEETAH, RAYEK TELLS OF THE TERRIBLE TROLL WAR WHICH OCCURRED NOT LONG AFTER HE BEFRIENDED EKUAR.
GUTTLEKRAW'S WARRIORS BROKE THROUGH A LONG-SEALED TUNNEL, ATTACKING GREYMUNG'S ILL-PREPARED SUBJECTS.
THE TWO ELVES WITNESSED A MERCILESS ROUT.
BUT THE UNDERGROUND PASSAGE TO THE FROZEN MOUNTAINS NOW LAY OPEN, THANKS TO THE INVADING TROLL ARMY. UNNOTICED, RAYEK AND EKUAR MADE THEIR ESCAPE.
THEY TRAVELLED SLOWLY, BUT SAFELY, FOR THE CONQUERORS, BURDENED WITH CAPTIVES AND LOOT, WERE SLOWER STILL.
OF COURSE I YEARNED FOR DAYLIGHT, BUT THEN EKUAR TOLD ME HIS DEEPEST SECRET...THAT THE LOST DWELLING OF THE HIGH ONES WAS NOT A LEGEND, BUT A REALITY, AND THAT HE COULD GUIDE ME TO IT!
HOW COULD I RESIST?
THINK! WHAT FURTHER KNOWLEDGE OF THE OLD POWERS MIGHT WAIT FOR ME IN THE HOME OF MY MOST ANCIENT ANCESTORS?
EH? LEETAH... YOUR FACE..!
SOB
THE HIGH ONES' DWELLING... I HAVE SEEN IT, RAYEK, IN A VISION!
SOB
IT IS CALLED A PALACE--
--AND IT IS THE REASON WHY I AM HERE!

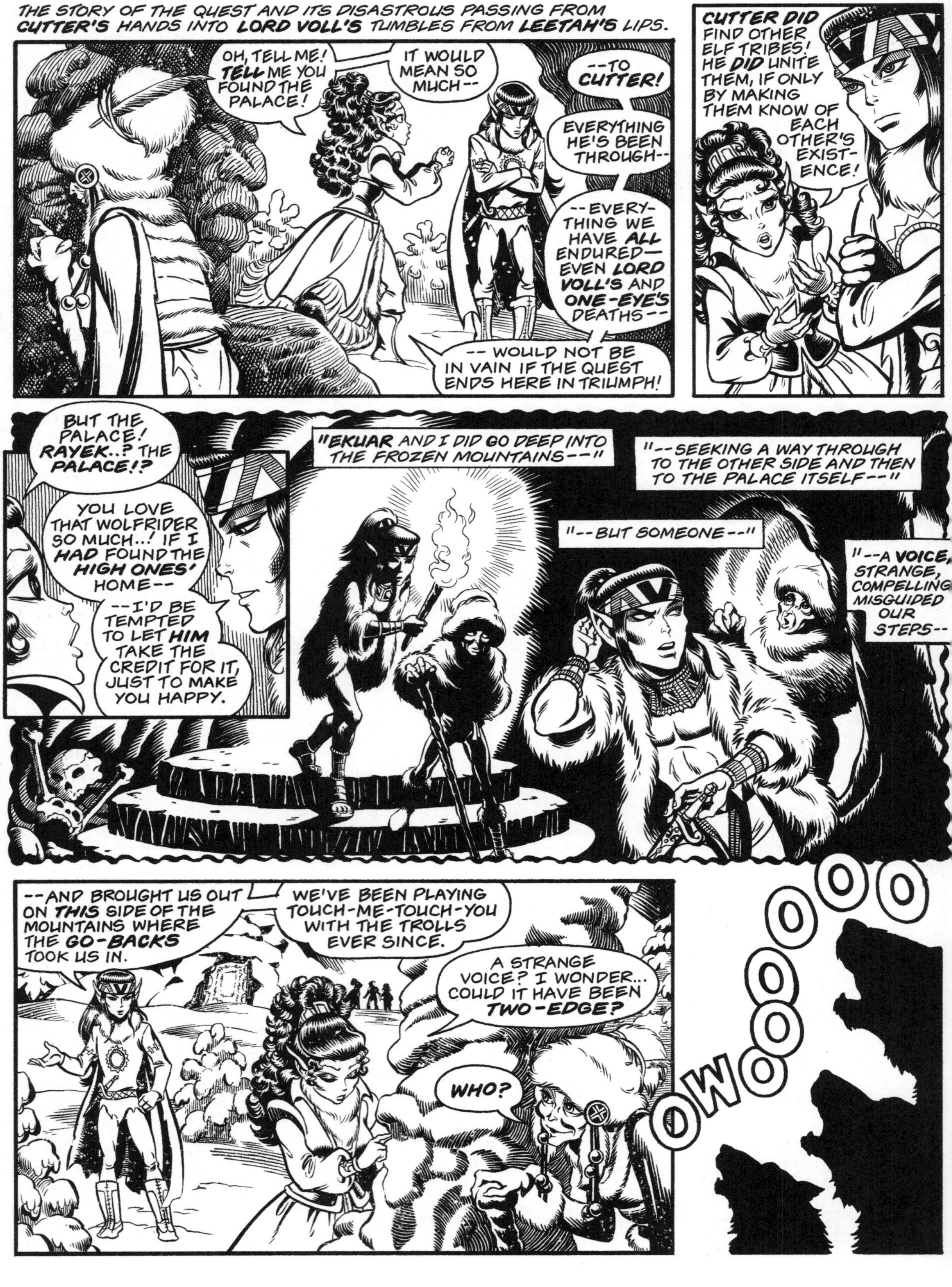
THE STORY OF THE QUEST AND ITS DISASTROUS PASSING FROM CUTTER'S HANDS INTO LORD VOLL'S TUMBLES FROM LEETAH'S LIPS.
OH, TELL ME! TELL ME YOU FOUND THE PALACE!
IT WOULD MEAN SO MUCH--
--TO CUTTER!
EVERYTHING HE'S BEEN THROUGH--
--EVERYTHING WE HAVE ALL ENDURED—EVEN LORD VOLL'S AND ONE-EYE'S DEATHS--
--WOULD NOT BE IN VAIN IF THE QUEST ENDS HERE IN TRIUMPH!
CUTTER DID FIND OTHER ELF TRIBES! HE DID UNITE THEM, IF ONLY BY MAKING THEM KNOW OF EACH OTHER'S EXISTENCE!
BUT THE PALACE! RAYEK..? THE PALACE!?
YOU LOVE THAT WOLFRIDER SO MUCH..! IF I HAD FOUND THE HIGH ONES' HOME--
--I'D BE TEMPTED TO LET HIM TAKE THE CREDIT FOR IT, JUST TO MAKE YOU HAPPY.
"EKUAR AND I DID GO DEEP INTO THE FROZEN MOUNTAINS--"
"--SEEKING A WAY THROUGH TO THE OTHER SIDE AND THEN TO THE PALACE ITSELF--"
"--BUT SOMEONE--"
"--A VOICE, STRANGE, COMPELLING MISGUIDED OUR STEPS--
--AND BROUGHT US OUT ON THIS SIDE OF THE MOUNTAINS WHERE THE GO-BACKS TOOK US IN.
WE'VE BEEN PLAYING TOUCH-ME-TOUCH-YOU WITH THE TROLLS EVER SINCE.
A STRANGE VOICE? I WONDER... COULD IT HAVE BEEN TWO-EDGE?
WHO?
OWOOOOOOO

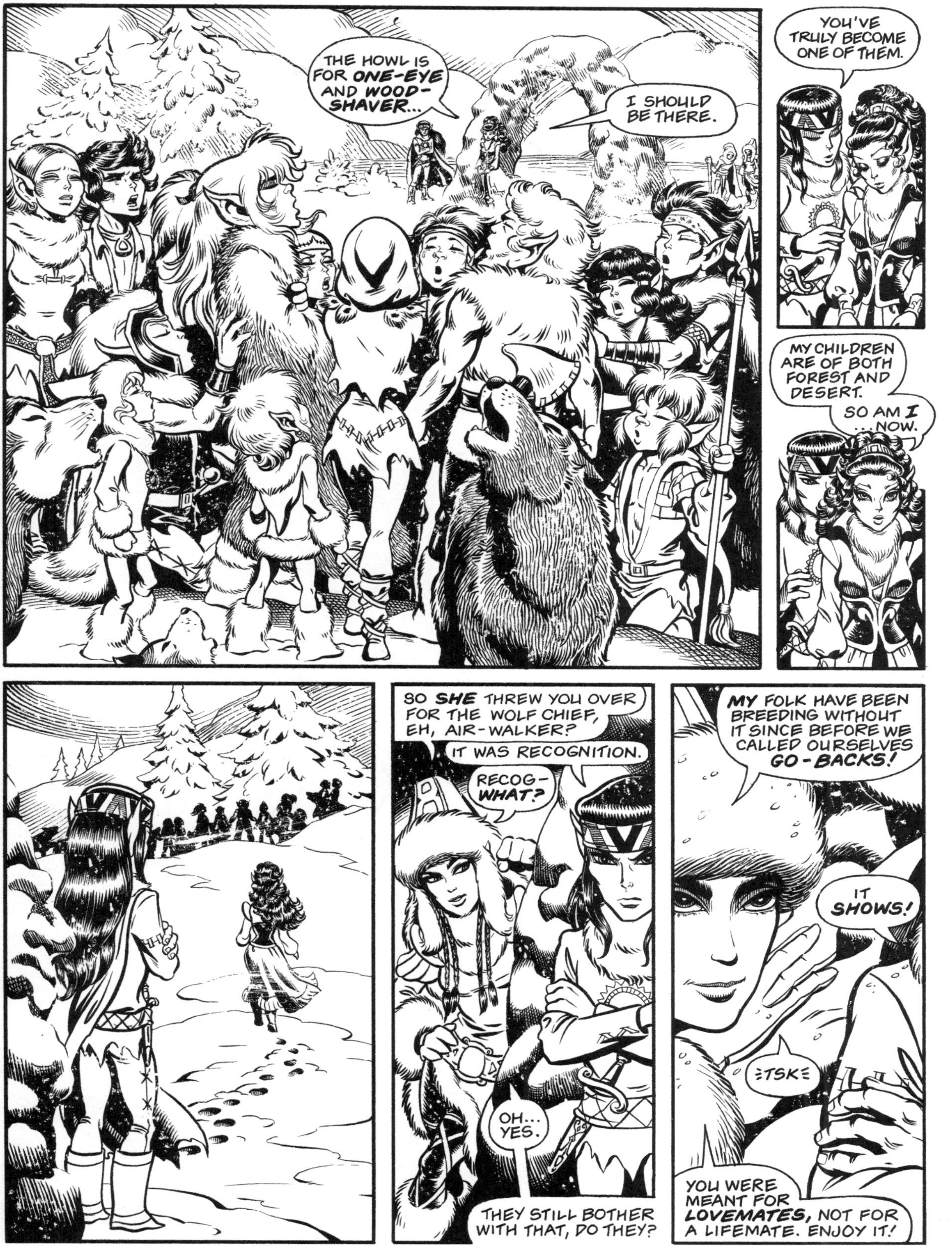
THE HOWL IS FOR ONE-EYE AND WOOD-SHAVER...
I SHOULD BE THERE.
YOU'VE TRULY BECOME ONE OF THEM.
MY CHILDREN ARE OF BOTH FOREST AND DESERT.
SO AM I ...NOW.
SO SHE THREW YOU OVER FOR THE WOLF CHIEF, EH, AIR-WALKER?
IT WAS RECOGNITION.
RECOG-WHAT?
OH... YES.
THEY STILL BOTHER WITH THAT, DO THEY?
MY FOLK HAVE BEEN BREEDING WITHOUT IT SINCE BEFORE WE CALLED OURSELVES GO-BACKS!
IT SHOWS!
TSK
YOU WERE MEANT FOR LOVEMATES, NOT FOR A LIFEMATE. ENJOY IT!

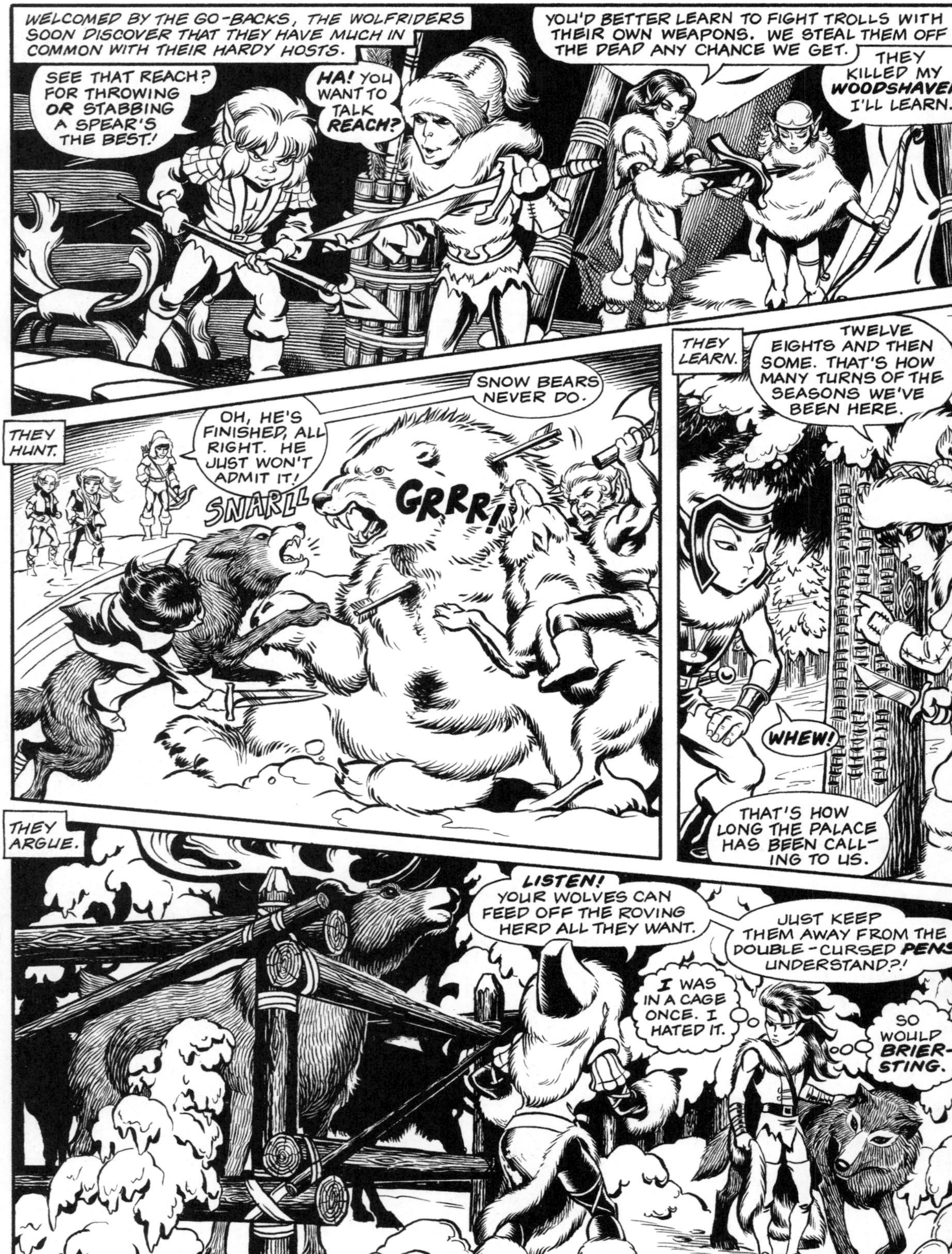
WELCOMED BY THE GO-BACKS, THE WOLFRIDERS SOON DISCOVER THAT THEY HAVE MUCH IN COMMON WITH THEIR HARDY HOSTS.
SEE THAT REACH? FOR THROWING OR STABBING A SPEAR'S THE BEST!
HA! YOU WANT TO TALK REACH?
YOU'D BETTER LEARN TO FIGHT TROLLS WITH THEIR OWN WEAPONS. WE STEAL THEM OFF THE DEAD ANY CHANCE WE GET.
THEY KILLED MY WOODSHAVER. I'LL LEARN.
THEY HUNT.
OH, HE'S FINISHED, ALL RIGHT. HE JUST WON'T ADMIT IT!
SNOW BEARS NEVER DO.
SNARLLL
GRRR!
THEY LEARN.
TWELVE EIGHTS AND THEN SOME. THAT'S HOW MANY TURNS OF THE SEASONS WE'VE BEEN HERE.
WHEW!
THAT'S HOW LONG THE PALACE HAS BEEN CALLING TO US.
THEY ARGUE.
LISTEN! YOUR WOLVES CAN FEED OFF THE ROVING HERD ALL THEY WANT.
JUST KEEP THEM AWAY FROM THE DOUBLE-CURSED PENS, UNDERSTAND?!
I WAS IN A CAGE ONCE. I HATED IT.
SO WOULD BRIER-STING.

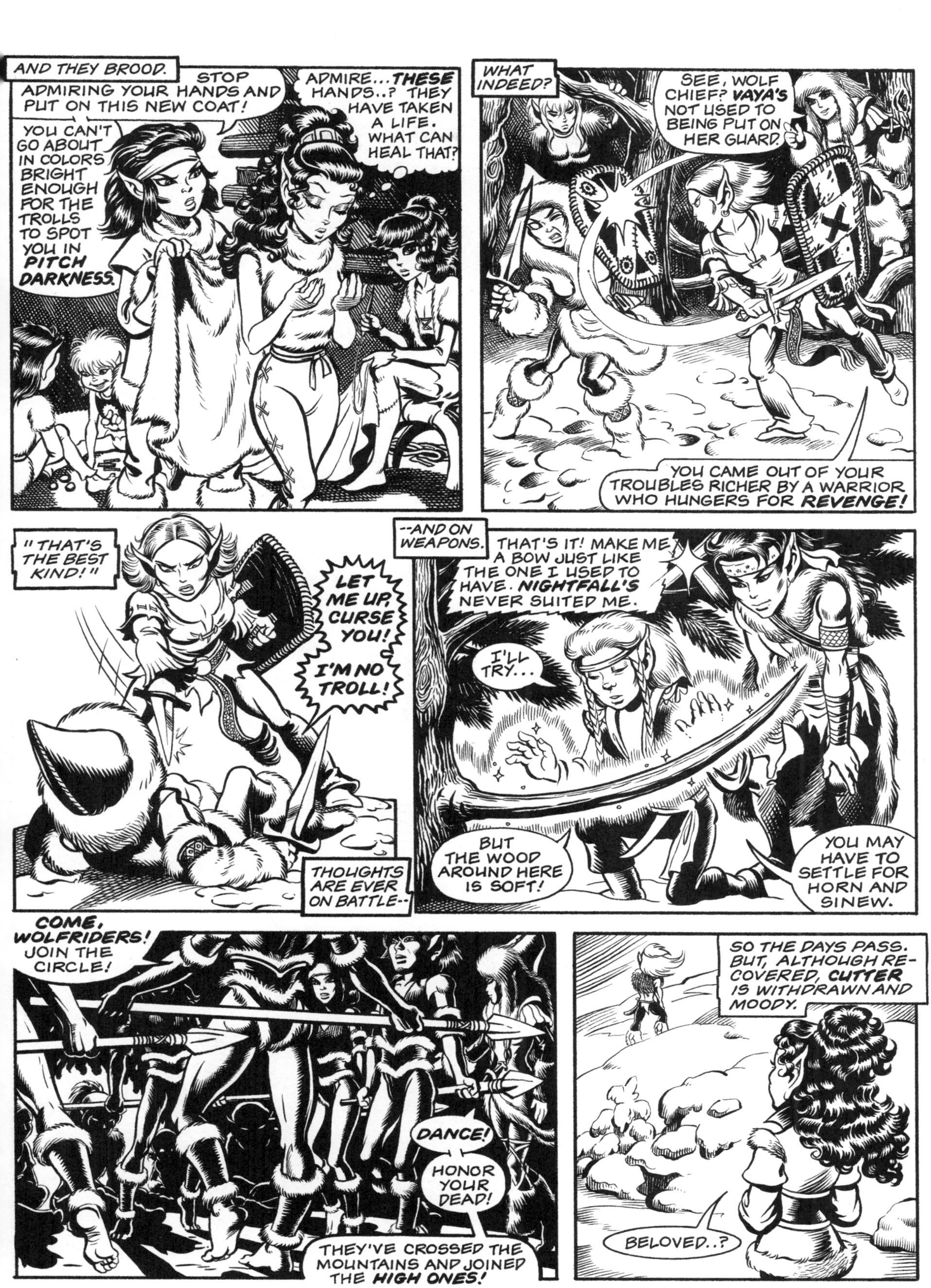

AND THEY BROOD.
STOP ADMIRING YOUR HANDS AND PUT ON THIS NEW COAT!
YOU CAN'T GO ABOUT IN COLORS BRIGHT ENOUGH FOR THE TROLLS TO SPOT YOU IN PITCH DARKNESS.
ADMIRE... THESE HANDS..? THEY HAVE TAKEN A LIFE. WHAT CAN HEAL THAT?
WHAT INDEED?
SEE, WOLF CHIEF? VAYA'S NOT USED TO BEING PUT ON HER GUARD.
YOU CAME OUT OF YOUR TROUBLES RICHER BY A WARRIOR WHO HUNGERS FOR REVENGE!
"THAT'S THE BEST KIND!"
LET ME UP, CURSE YOU!
I'M NO TROLL!
THOUGHTS ARE EVER ON BATTLE--
--AND ON WEAPONS.
THAT'S IT! MAKE ME A BOW JUST LIKE THE ONE I USED TO HAVE. NIGHTFALL'S NEVER SUITED ME.
I'LL TRY...
BUT THE WOOD AROUND HERE IS SOFT!
YOU MAY HAVE TO SETTLE FOR HORN AND SINEW.
COME, WOLFRIDERS! JOIN THE CIRCLE!
DANCE!
HONOR YOUR DEAD!
THEY'VE CROSSED THE MOUNTAINS AND JOINED THE HIGH ONES!
SO THE DAYS PASS. BUT, ALTHOUGH RE-COVERED, CUTTER IS WITHDRAWN AND MOODY.
BELOVED..?

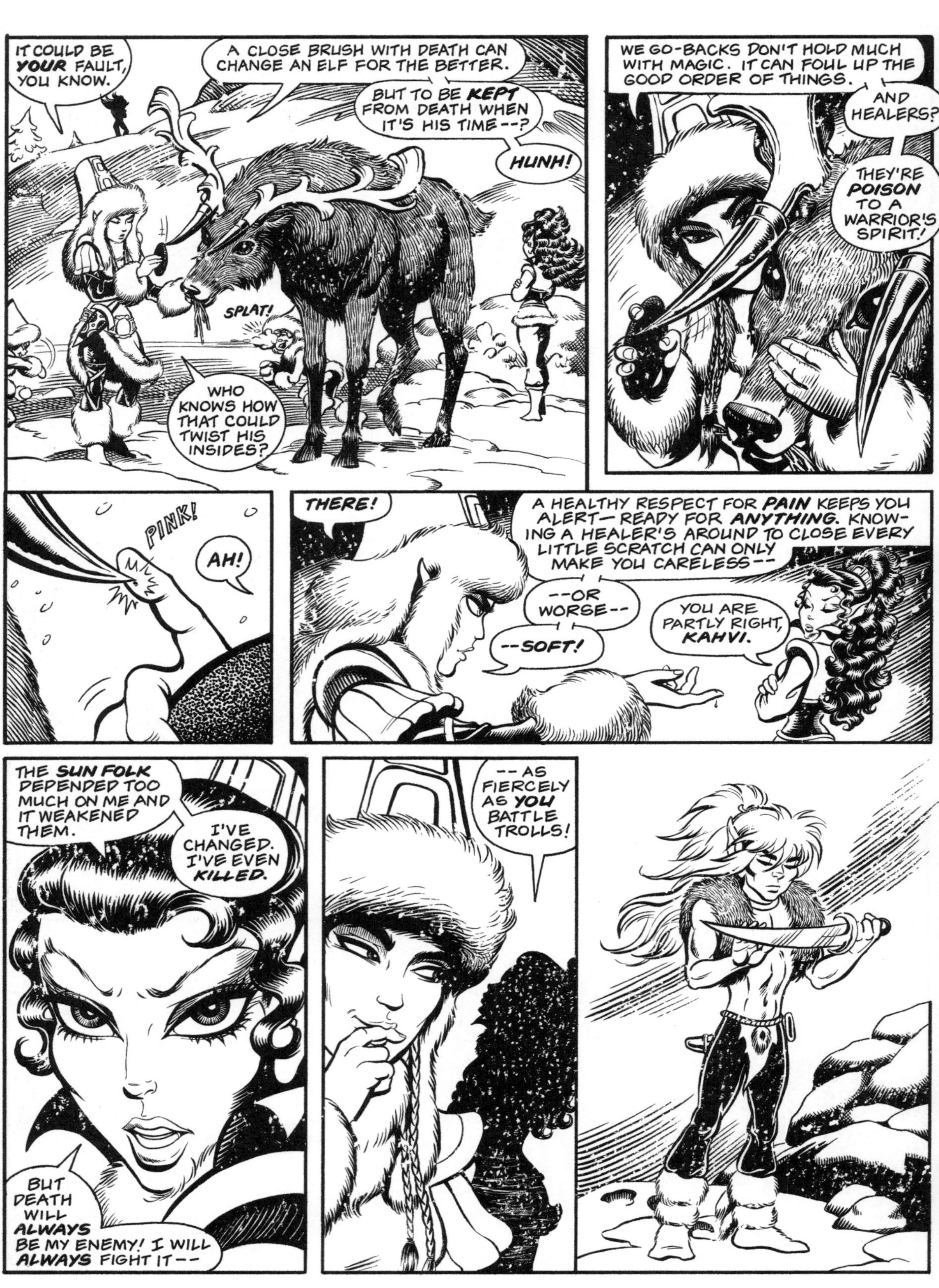
IT COULD BE YOUR FAULT, YOU KNOW.
A CLOSE BRUSH WITH DEATH CAN CHANGE AN ELF FOR THE BETTER.
BUT TO BE KEPT FROM DEATH WHEN IT'S HIS TIME--?
HUNH!
SPLAT!
WHO KNOWS HOW THAT COULD TWIST HIS INSIDES?
WE GO-BACKS DON'T HOLD MUCH WITH MAGIC. IT CAN FOUL UP THE GOOD ORDER OF THINGS.
AND HEALERS?
THEY'RE POISON TO A WARRIOR'S SPIRIT!
PINK!
AH!
THERE!
A HEALTHY RESPECT FOR PAIN KEEPS YOU ALERT— READY FOR ANYTHING. KNOWING A HEALER'S AROUND TO CLOSE EVERY LITTLE SCRATCH CAN ONLY MAKE YOU CARELESS--
--OR WORSE--
--SOFT!
YOU ARE PARTLY RIGHT, KAHVI.
THE SUN FOLK DEPENDED TOO MUCH ON ME AND IT WEAKENED THEM.
I'VE CHANGED. I'VE EVEN KILLED.
BUT DEATH WILL ALWAYS BE MY ENEMY! I WILL ALWAYS FIGHT IT--
--AS FIERCELY AS YOU BATTLE TROLLS!

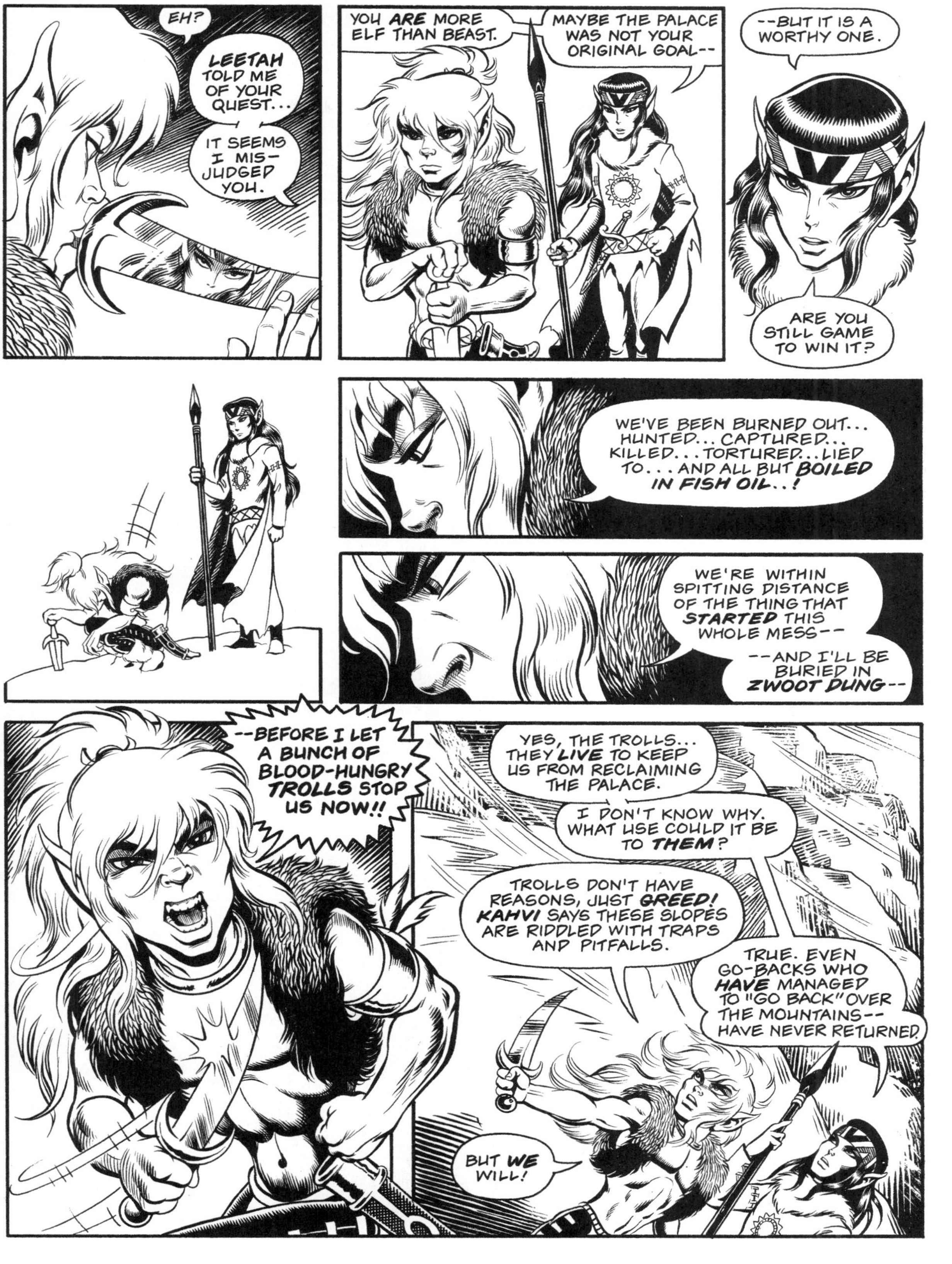

EH?
LEETAH TOLD ME OF YOUR QUEST...
IT SEEMS I MIS-JUDGED YOU.
YOU ARE MORE ELF THAN BEAST.
MAYBE THE PALACE WAS NOT YOUR ORIGINAL GOAL--
--BUT IT IS A WORTHY ONE.
ARE YOU STILL GAME TO WIN IT?
WE'VE BEEN BURNED OUT... HUNTED... CAPTURED... KILLED... TORTURED... LIED TO... AND ALL BUT BOILED IN FISH OIL..!
WE'RE WITHIN SPITTING DISTANCE OF THE THING THAT STARTED THIS WHOLE MESS--
--AND I'LL BE BURIED IN ZWOOT DUNG--
--BEFORE I LET A BUNCH OF BLOOD-HUNGRY TROLLS STOP US NOW!!
YES, THE TROLLS... THEY LIVE TO KEEP US FROM RECLAIMING THE PALACE.
I DON'T KNOW WHY. WHAT USE COULD IT BE TO THEM?
TROLLS DON'T HAVE REASONS, JUST GREED! KAHVI SAYS THESE SLOPES ARE RIDDLED WITH TRAPS AND PITFALLS.
TRUE. EVEN GO-BACKS WHO HAVE MANAGED TO "GO BACK" OVER THE MOUNTAINS-- HAVE NEVER RETURNED.
BUT WE WILL!

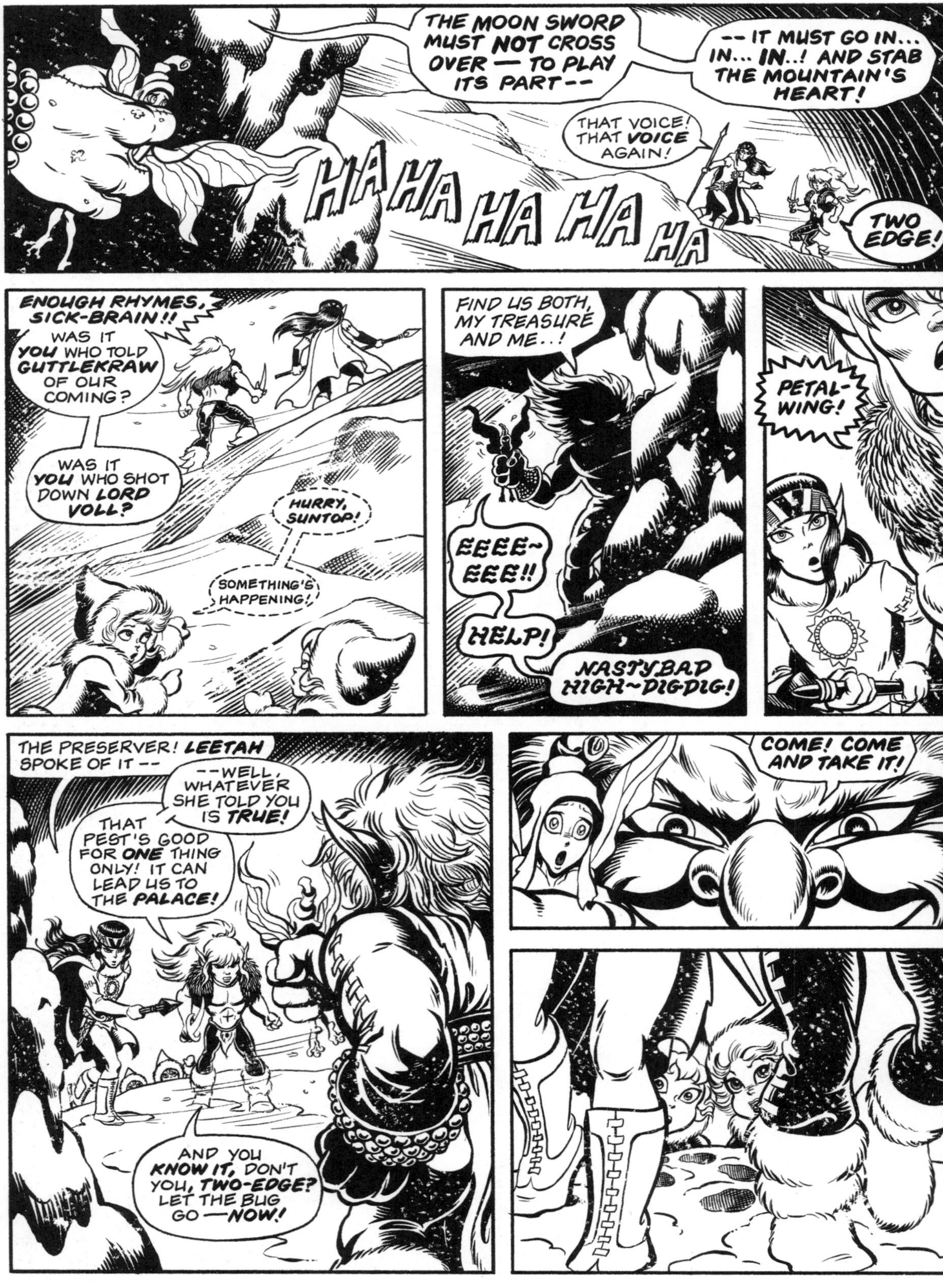
THE MOON SWORD MUST NOT CROSS OVER — TO PLAY ITS PART --
-- IT MUST GO IN... IN... IN..! AND STAB THE MOUNTAIN'S HEART!
THAT VOICE! THAT VOICE AGAIN!
HA HA HA HA HA HA HA
TWO EDGE!
ENOUGH RHYMES, SICK-BRAIN!!
WAS IT YOU WHO TOLD GUTTLEKRAW OF OUR COMING?
WAS IT YOU WHO SHOT DOWN LORD VOLL?
HURRY, SUNTOP!
SOMETHING'S HAPPENING!
FIND US BOTH, MY TREASURE AND ME..!
EEEE-EEE!!
HELP!
NASTYBAD HIGH-DIGDIG!
PETAL-WING!
THE PRESERVER! LEETAH SPOKE OF IT --
--WELL, WHATEVER SHE TOLD YOU IS TRUE!
THAT PEST'S GOOD FOR ONE THING ONLY! IT CAN LEAD US TO THE PALACE!
AND YOU KNOW IT, DON'T YOU, TWO-EDGE? LET THE BUG GO —NOW!
COME! COME AND TAKE IT!

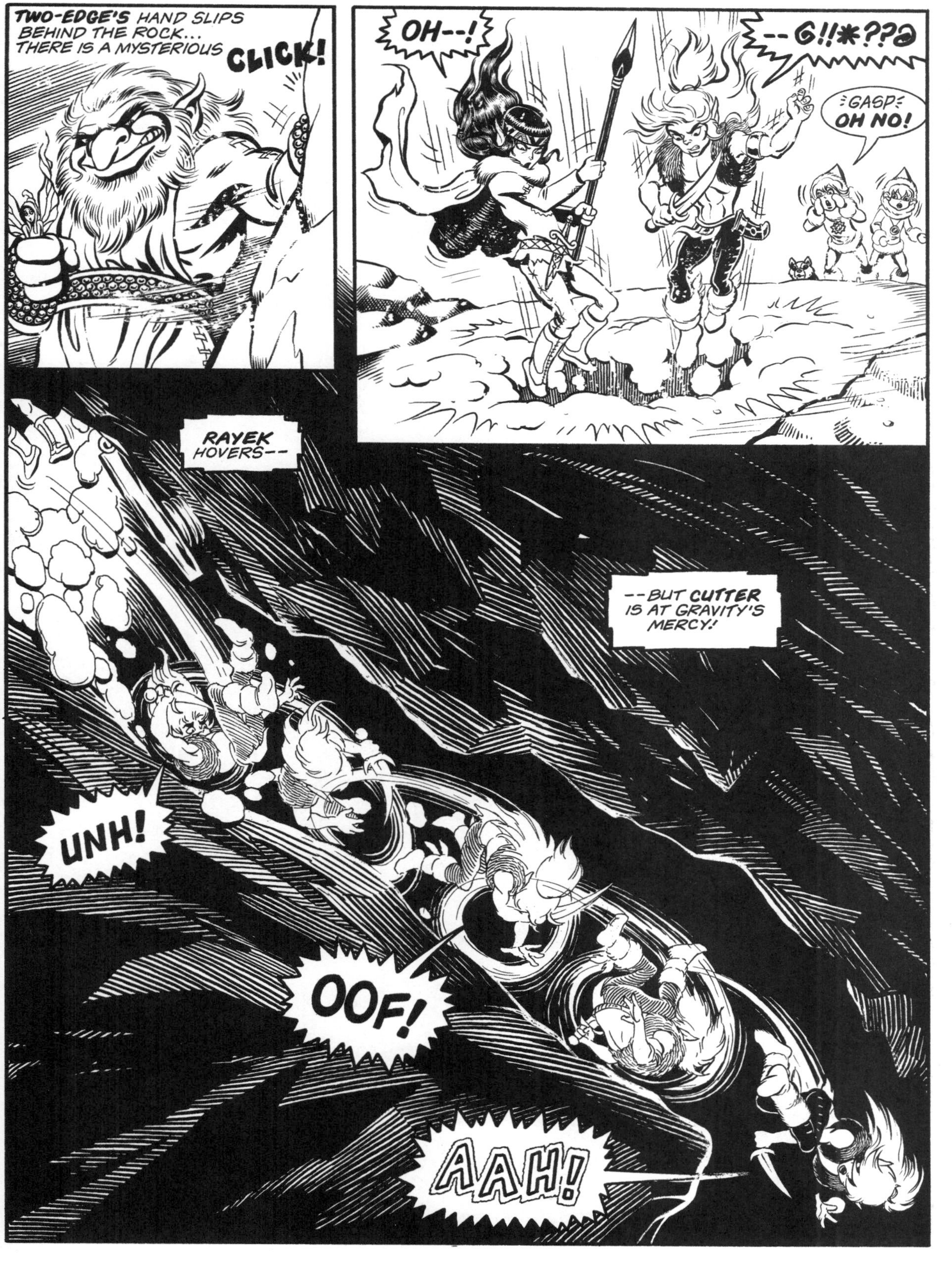

TWO-EDGE'S HAND SLIPS BEHIND THE ROCK... THERE IS A MYSTERIOUS CLICK!
OH--!
--G!!*??@
GASP OH NO!
RAYEK HOVERS--
--BUT CUTTER IS AT GRAVITY'S MERCY!
UNH!
OOF!
AAH!

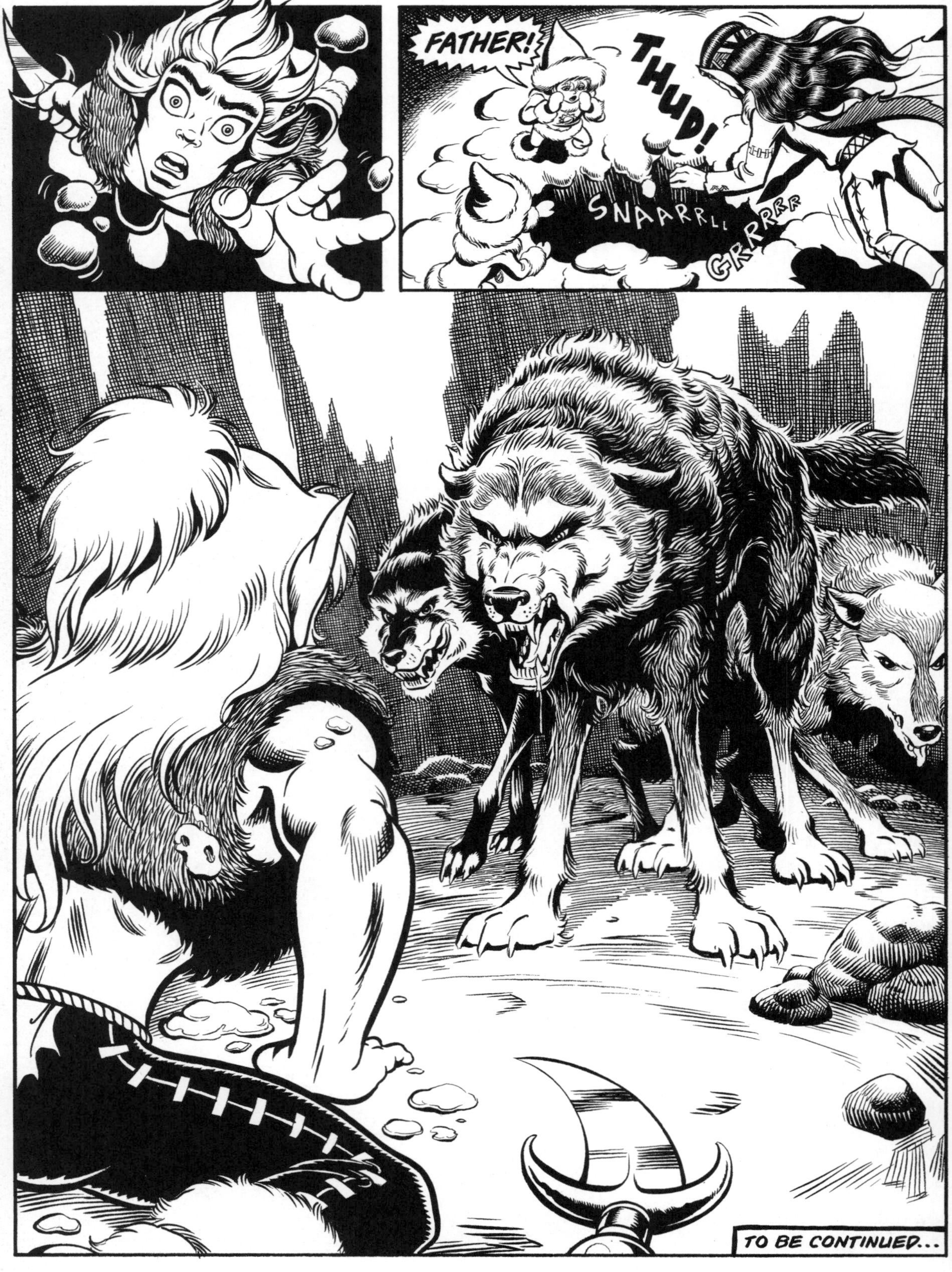
FATHER!
THUD!
SNAARRLL
GRRRRR
TO BE CONTINUED...

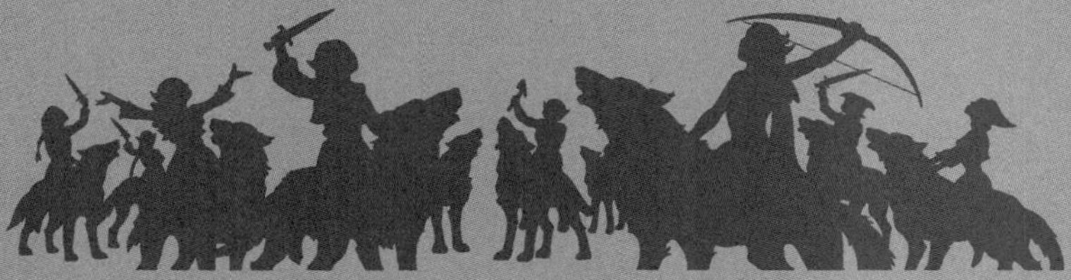

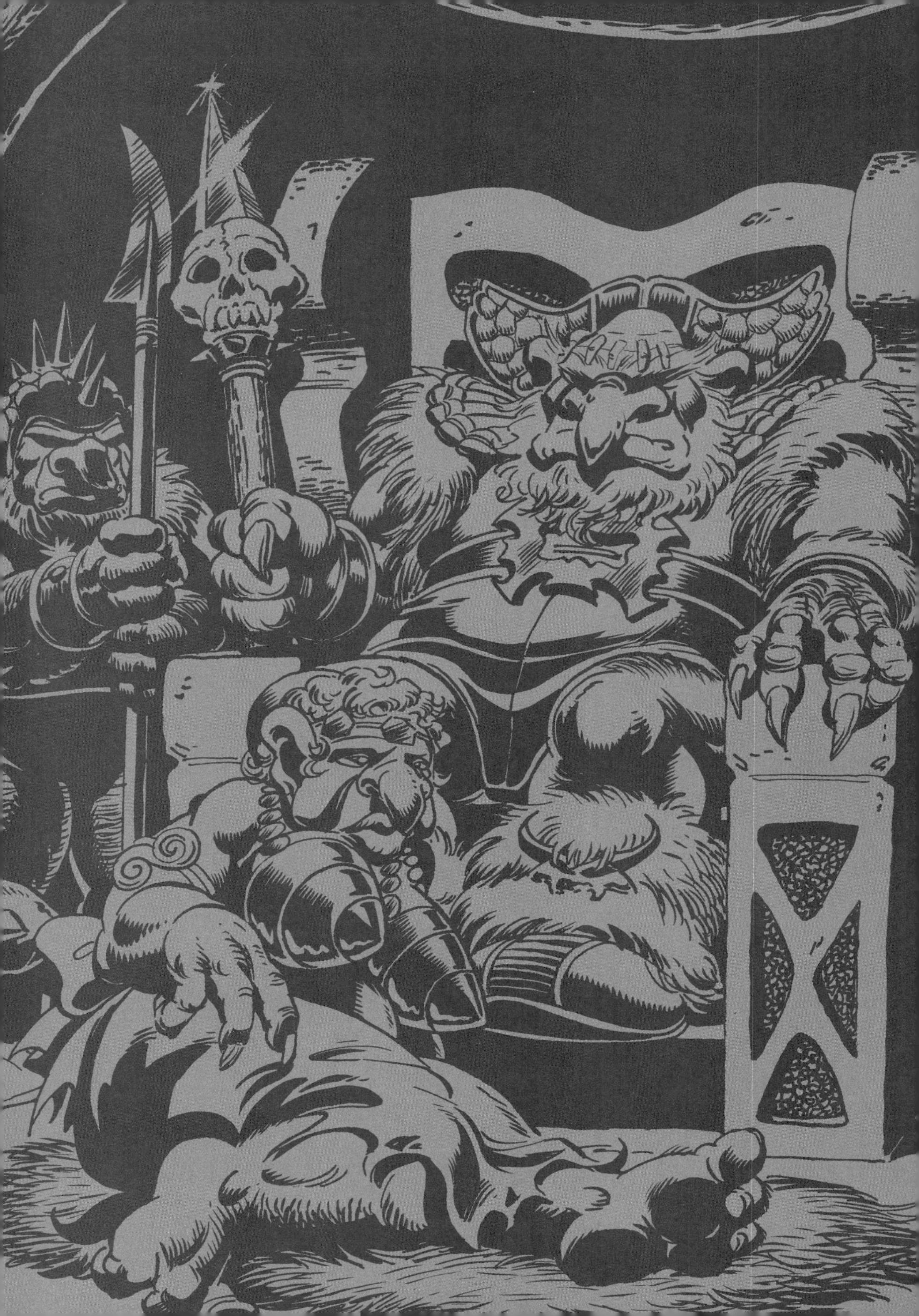

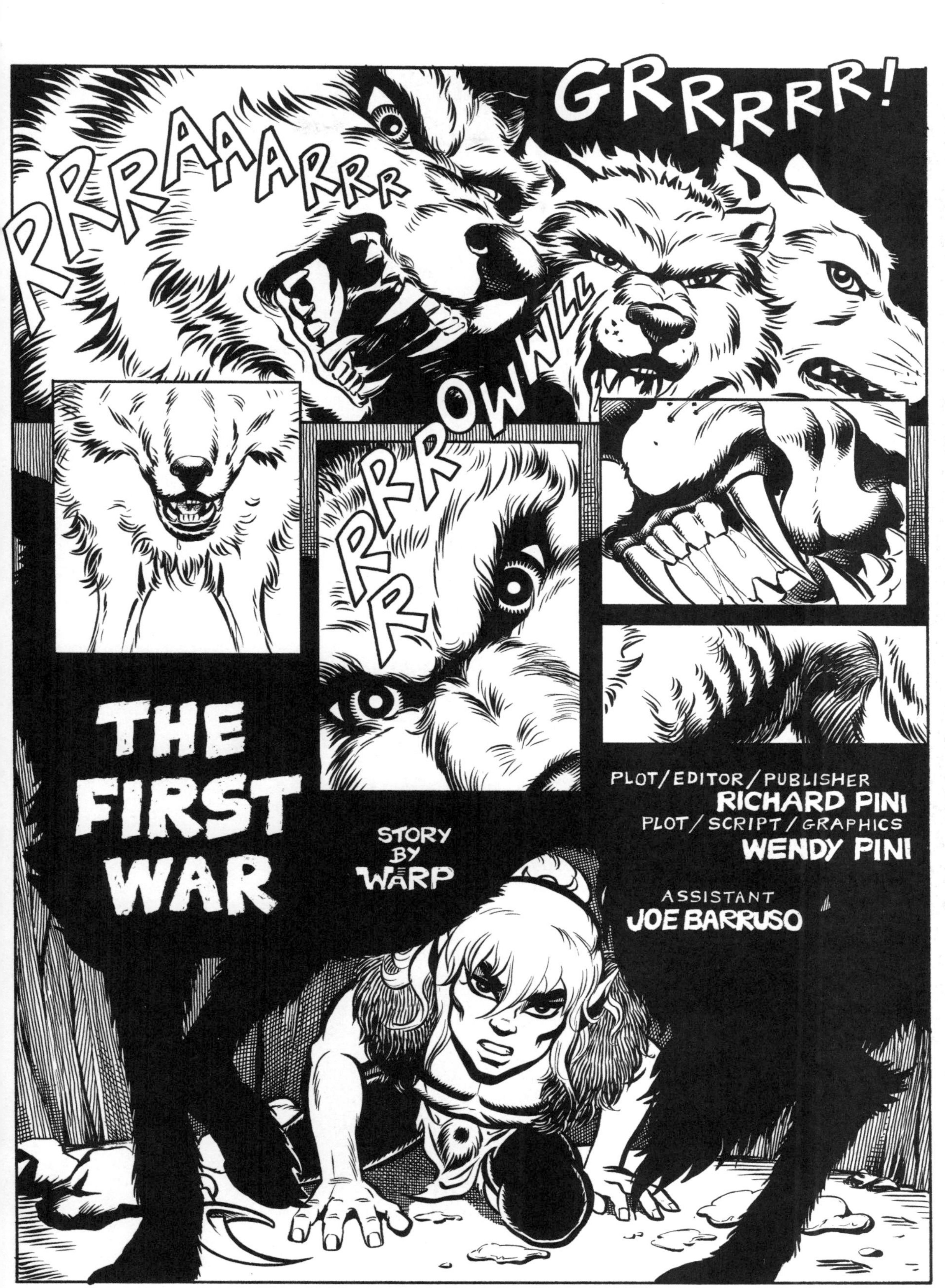
RRRAAAARRR
GRRRRRR!
RRROWWLL
RRRRR
THE FIRST WAR
STORY BY WARP
PLOT/EDITOR/PUBLISHER
RICHARD PINI
PLOT/SCRIPT/GRAPHICS
WENDY PINI
ASSISTANT
JOE BARRUSO

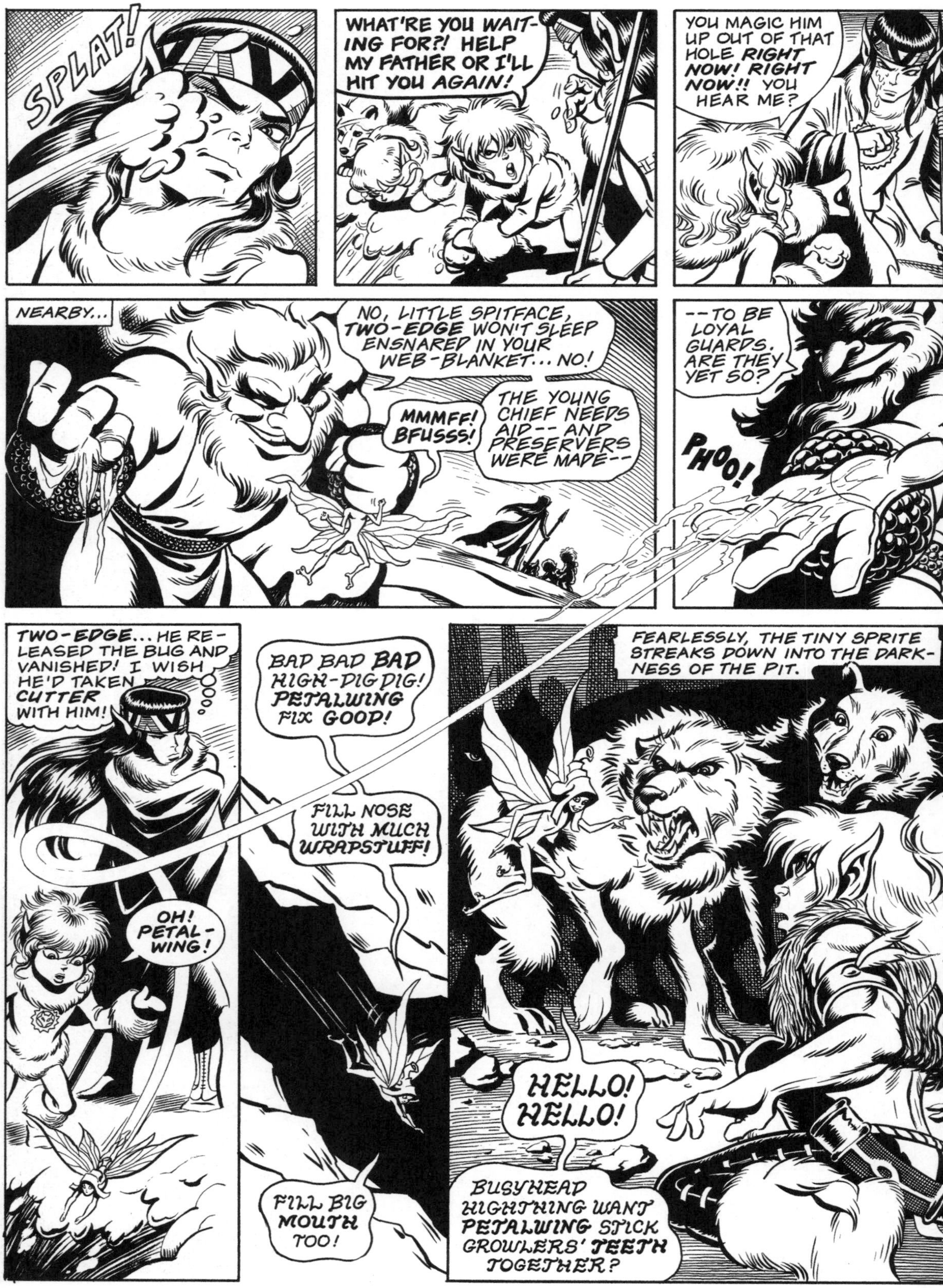
SPLAT!
WHAT'RE YOU WAITING FOR?! HELP MY FATHER OR I'LL HIT YOU AGAIN!
YOU MAGIC HIM UP OUT OF THAT HOLE RIGHT NOW! RIGHT NOW!! YOU HEAR ME?
NEARBY...
NO, LITTLE SPITFACE, TWO-EDGE WON'T SLEEP ENSNARED IN YOUR WEB-BLANKET... NO!
MMMFF! BFUSSS!
THE YOUNG CHIEF NEEDS AID-- AND PRESERVERS WERE MADE--
--TO BE LOYAL GUARDS. ARE THEY YET SO?
PHOO!
TWO-EDGE... HE RELEASED THE BUG AND VANISHED! I WISH HE'D TAKEN CUTTER WITH HIM!
BAD BAD BAD HIGH-DIG DIG! PETALWING FIX GOOD!
FILL NOSE WITH MUCH WRAPSTUFF!
OH! PETALWING!
FILL BIG MOUTH TOO!
FEARLESSLY, THE TINY SPRITE STREAKS DOWN INTO THE DARKNESS OF THE PIT.
HELLO! HELLO!
BUSYHEAD HIGHTHING WANT PETALWING STICK GROWLERS' TEETH TOGETHER?

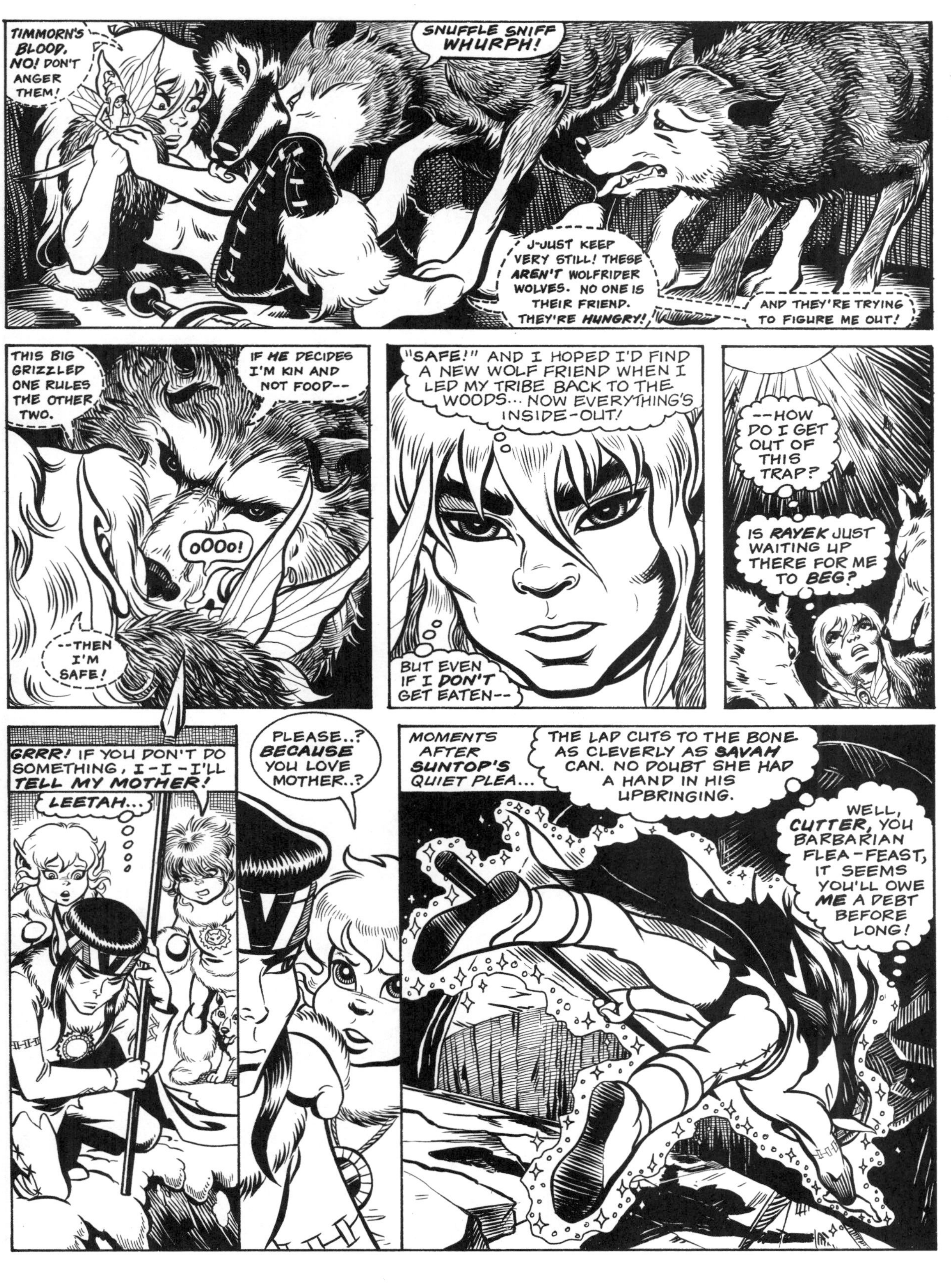
TIMMORN'S BLOOD, NO! DON'T ANGER THEM!
SNUFFLE SNIFF WHURPH!
J-JUST KEEP VERY STILL! THESE AREN'T WOLFRIDER WOLVES. NO ONE IS THEIR FRIEND. THEY'RE HUNGRY!
AND THEY'RE TRYING TO FIGURE ME OUT!
THIS BIG GRIZZLED ONE RULES THE OTHER TWO.
IF HE DECIDES I'M KIN AND NOT FOOD--
OOOO!
--THEN I'M SAFE!
"SAFE!" AND I HOPED I'D FIND A NEW WOLF FRIEND WHEN I LED MY TRIBE BACK TO THE WOODS... NOW EVERYTHING'S INSIDE-OUT!
BUT EVEN IF I DON'T GET EATEN--
--HOW DO I GET OUT OF THIS TRAP?
IS RAYEK JUST WAITING UP THERE FOR ME TO BEG?
GRRR! IF YOU DON'T DO SOMETHING, I-I-I'LL TELL MY MOTHER!
LEETAH...
PLEASE..? BECAUSE YOU LOVE MOTHER..?
MOMENTS AFTER SUNTOP'S QUIET PLEA...
THE LAD CUTS TO THE BONE AS CLEVERLY AS SAVAH CAN. NO DOUBT SHE HAD A HAND IN HIS UPBRINGING.
WELL, CUTTER, YOU BARBARIAN FLEA-FEAST, IT SEEMS YOU'LL OWE ME A DEBT BEFORE LONG!

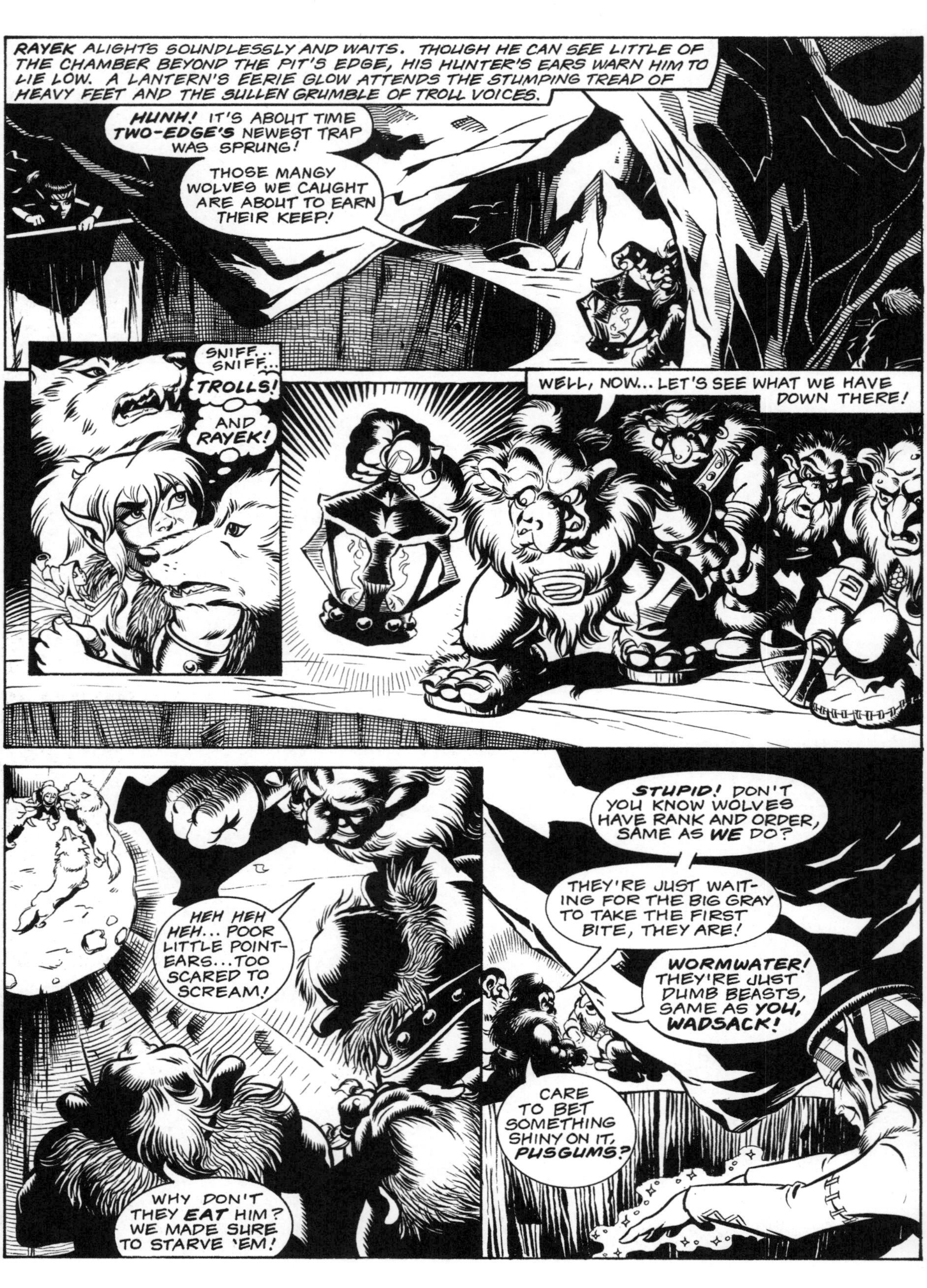
RAYEK ALIGHTS SOUNDLESSLY AND WAITS. THOUGH HE CAN SEE LITTLE OF THE CHAMBER BEYOND THE PIT'S EDGE, HIS HUNTER'S EARS WARN HIM TO LIE LOW. A LANTERN'S EERIE GLOW ATTENDS THE STUMPING TREAD OF HEAVY FEET AND THE SULLEN GRUMBLE OF TROLL VOICES.
HUNH! IT'S ABOUT TIME TWO-EDGE'S NEWEST TRAP WAS SPRUNG!
THOSE MANGY WOLVES WE CAUGHT ARE ABOUT TO EARN THEIR KEEP!
SNIFF... SNIFF... TROLLS!
AND RAYEK!
WELL, NOW... LET'S SEE WHAT WE HAVE DOWN THERE!
HEH HEH HEH... POOR LITTLE POINT-EARS... TOO SCARED TO SCREAM!
WHY DON'T THEY EAT HIM? WE MADE SURE TO STARVE 'EM!
STUPID! DON'T YOU KNOW WOLVES HAVE RANK AND ORDER, SAME AS WE DO?
THEY'RE JUST WAITING FOR THE BIG GRAY TO TAKE THE FIRST BITE, THEY ARE!
WORMWATER! THEY'RE JUST DUMB BEASTS, SAME AS YOU, WADSACK!
CARE TO BET SOMETHING SHINY ON IT, PUSGUMS?

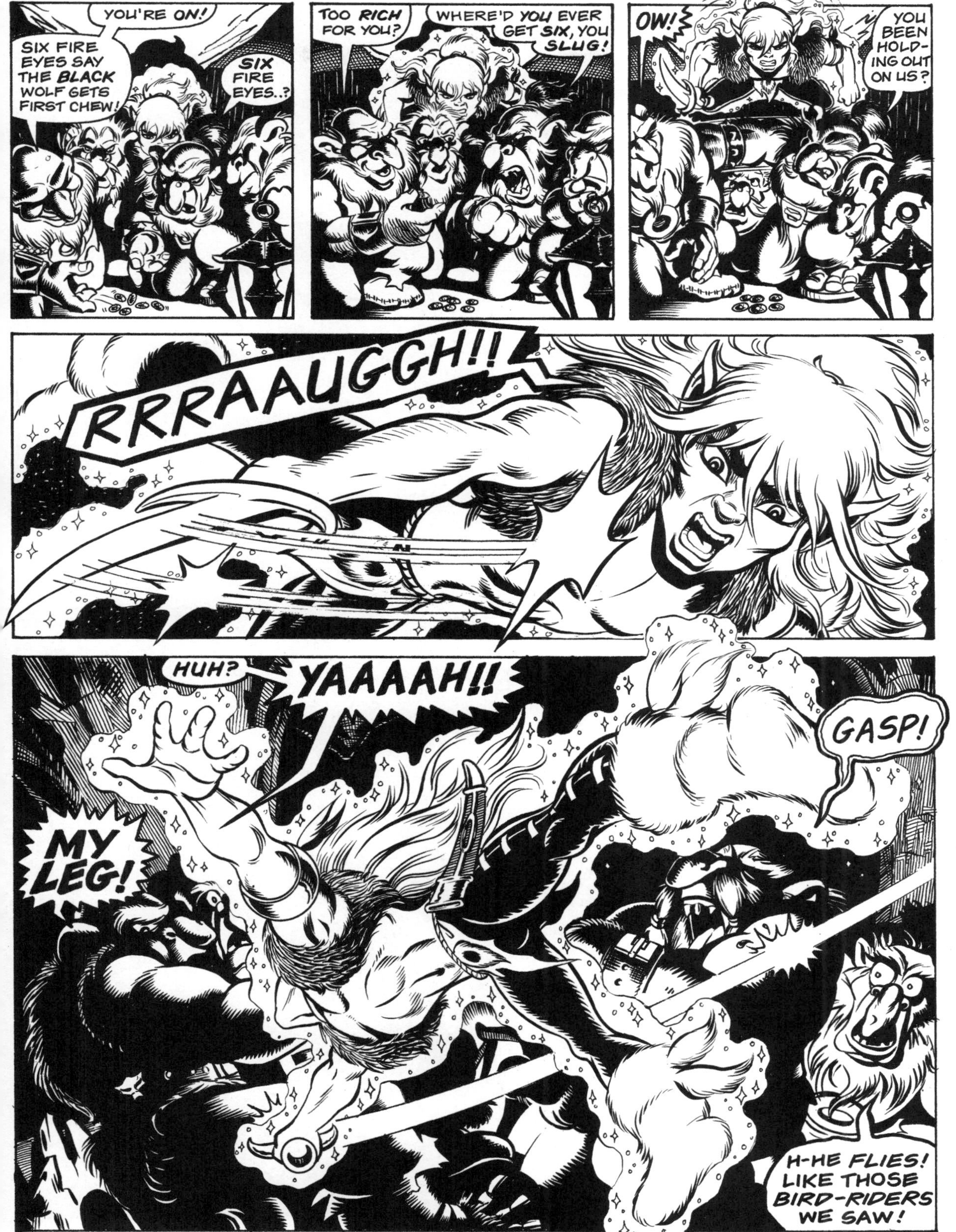

SIX FIRE EYES SAY THE BLACK WOLF GETS FIRST CHEW!
YOU'RE ON!
SIX FIRE EYES..?
TOO RICH FOR YOU?
WHERE'D YOU EVER GET SIX, YOU SLUG!
OW!
YOU BEEN HOLD-ING OUT ON US?
RRRAAUGGH!!
HUH?
YAAAAH!!
GASP!
MY LEG!
H-HE FLIES! LIKE THOSE BIRD-RIDERS WE SAW!

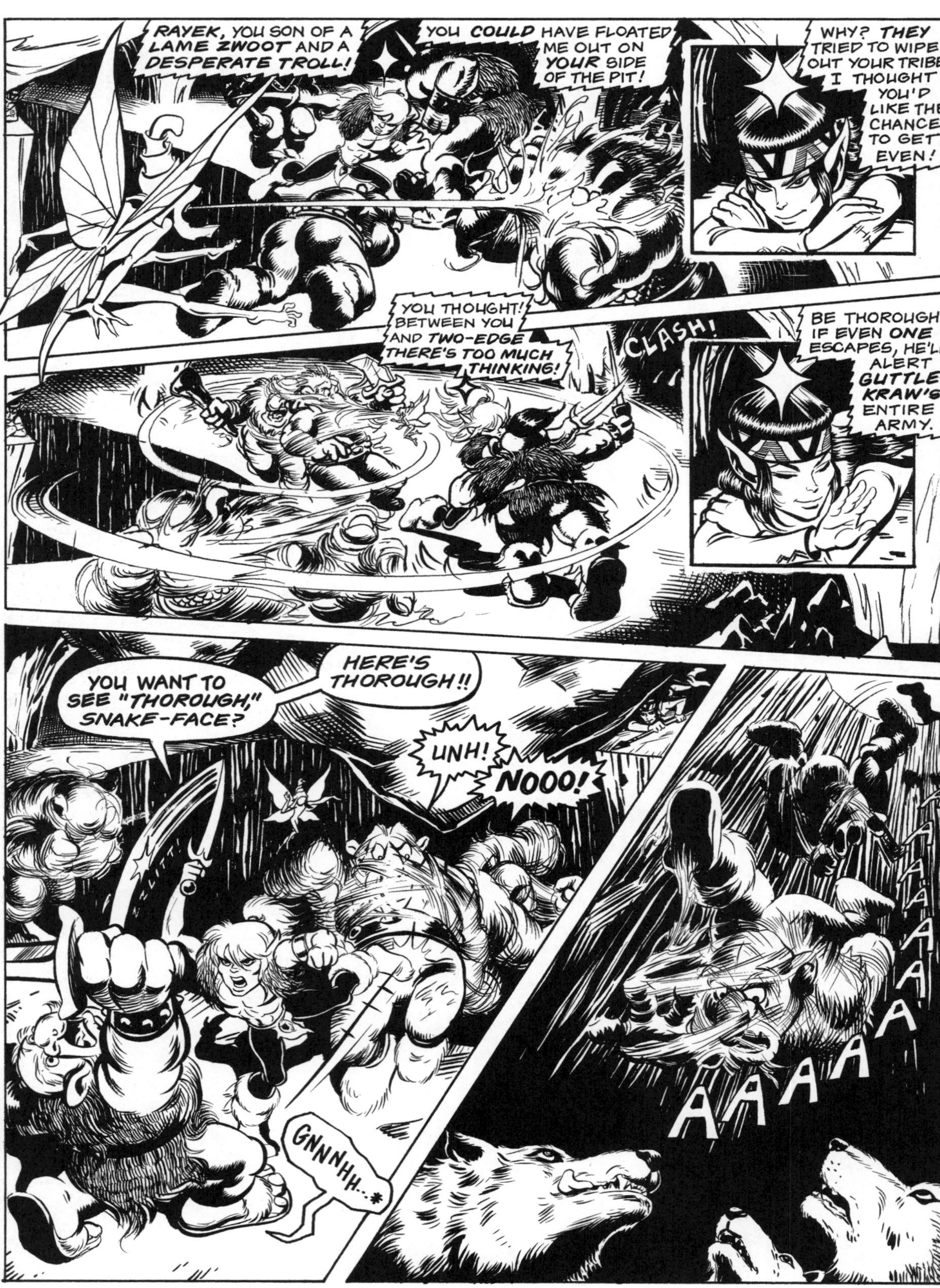

RAYEK, YOU SON OF A LAME ZWOOT AND A DESPERATE TROLL!
YOU COULD HAVE FLOATED ME OUT ON YOUR SIDE OF THE PIT!
WHY? THEY TRIED TO WIPE OUT YOUR TRIBE. I THOUGHT YOU'D LIKE THE CHANCE TO GET EVEN!
YOU THOUGHT! BETWEEN YOU AND TWO-EDGE THERE'S TOO MUCH THINKING!
CLASH!
BE THOROUGH. IF EVEN ONE ESCAPES, HE'LL ALERT GUTTLEKRAW'S ENTIRE ARMY.
YOU WANT TO SEE "THOROUGH," SNAKE-FACE?
HERE'S THOROUGH!!
UNH!
NOOO!
GNNNHH...*
AAAAAAAAAAAAAAAAA

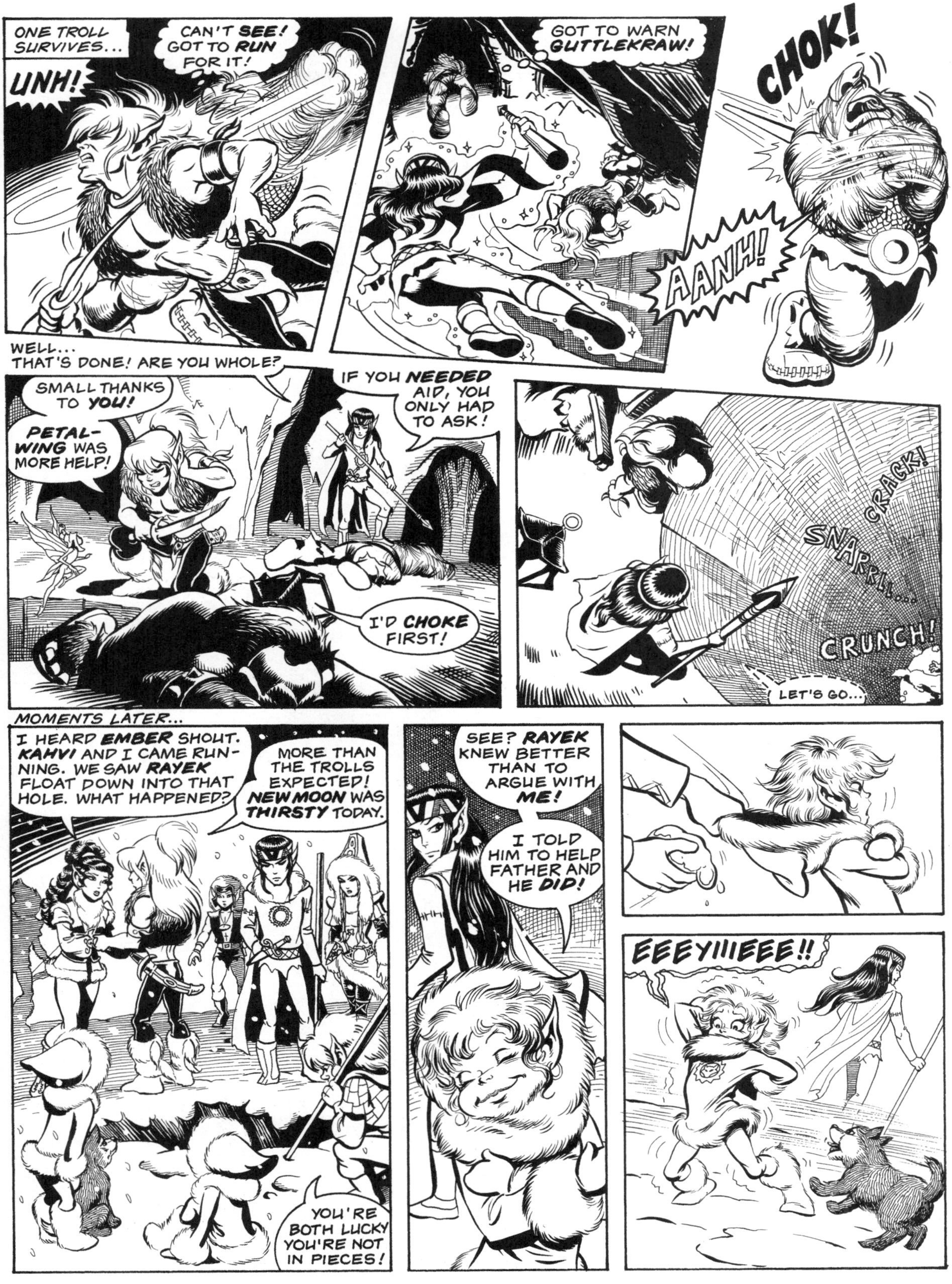
ONE TROLL SURVIVES...
CAN'T SEE! GOT TO RUN FOR IT!
UNH!
GOT TO WARN GUTTLEKRAW!
CHOK!
AANH!
WELL... THAT'S DONE! ARE YOU WHOLE?
SMALL THANKS TO YOU!
PETAL-WING WAS MORE HELP!
IF YOU NEEDED AID, YOU ONLY HAD TO ASK!
I'D CHOKE FIRST!
CRACK!
SNARRLL...
CRUNCH!
LET'S GO...
MOMENTS LATER...
I HEARD EMBER SHOUT. KAHVI AND I CAME RUN-NING. WE SAW RAYEK FLOAT DOWN INTO THAT HOLE. WHAT HAPPENED?
MORE THAN THE TROLLS EXPECTED! NEW MOON WAS THIRSTY TODAY.
YOU'RE BOTH LUCKY YOU'RE NOT IN PIECES!
SEE? RAYEK KNEW BETTER THAN TO ARGUE WITH ME!
I TOLD HIM TO HELP FATHER AND HE DID!
EEEYIIIIEEE!!

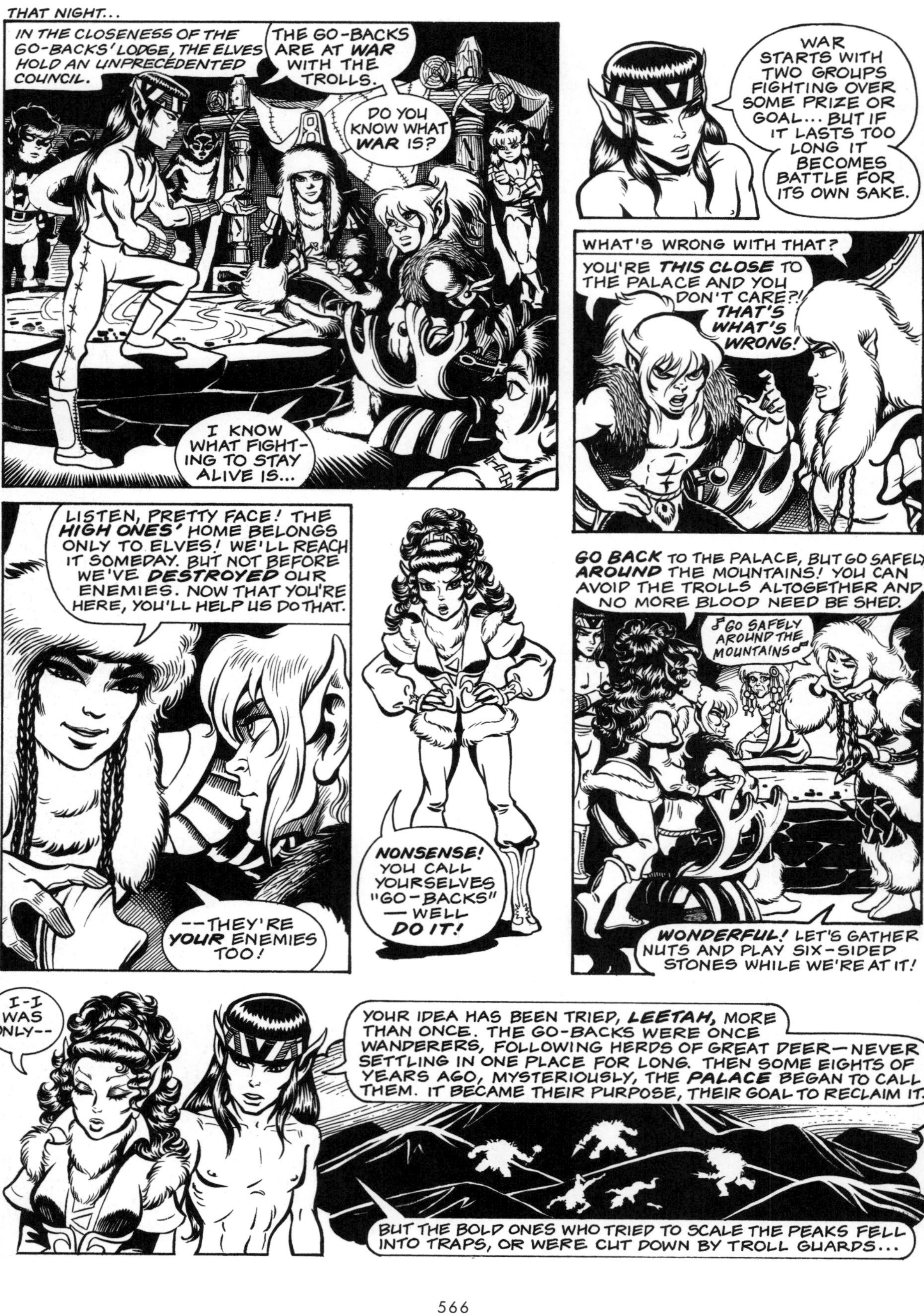
THAT NIGHT...
IN THE CLOSENESS OF THE GO-BACKS' LODGE, THE ELVES HOLD AN UNPRECEDENTED COUNCIL.
THE GO-BACKS ARE AT WAR WITH THE TROLLS.
DO YOU KNOW WHAT WAR IS?
I KNOW WHAT FIGHTING TO STAY ALIVE IS...
WAR STARTS WITH TWO GROUPS FIGHTING OVER SOME PRIZE OR GOAL... BUT IF IT LASTS TOO LONG IT BECOMES BATTLE FOR ITS OWN SAKE.
WHAT'S WRONG WITH THAT?
YOU'RE THIS CLOSE TO THE PALACE AND YOU DON'T CARE?! THAT'S WHAT'S WRONG!
LISTEN, PRETTY FACE! THE HIGH ONES' HOME BELONGS ONLY TO ELVES! WE'LL REACH IT SOMEDAY. BUT NOT BEFORE WE'VE DESTROYED OUR ENEMIES. NOW THAT YOU'RE HERE, YOU'LL HELP US DO THAT.
--THEY'RE YOUR ENEMIES TOO!
NONSENSE! YOU CALL YOURSELVES "GO-BACKS" — WELL DO IT!
GO BACK TO THE PALACE, BUT GO SAFELY, AROUND THE MOUNTAINS! YOU CAN AVOID THE TROLLS ALTOGETHER AND NO MORE BLOOD NEED BE SHED.
♪GO SAFELY AROUND THE MOUNTAINS♪
WONDERFUL! LET'S GATHER NUTS AND PLAY SIX-SIDED STONES WHILE WE'RE AT IT!
I-I WAS ONLY--
YOUR IDEA HAS BEEN TRIED, LEETAH, MORE THAN ONCE. THE GO-BACKS WERE ONCE WANDERERS, FOLLOWING HERDS OF GREAT DEER—NEVER SETTLING IN ONE PLACE FOR LONG. THEN SOME EIGHTS OF YEARS AGO, MYSTERIOUSLY, THE PALACE BEGAN TO CALL THEM. IT BECAME THEIR PURPOSE, THEIR GOAL TO RECLAIM IT.
BUT THE BOLD ONES WHO TRIED TO SCALE THE PEAKS FELL INTO TRAPS, OR WERE CUT DOWN BY TROLL GUARDS...

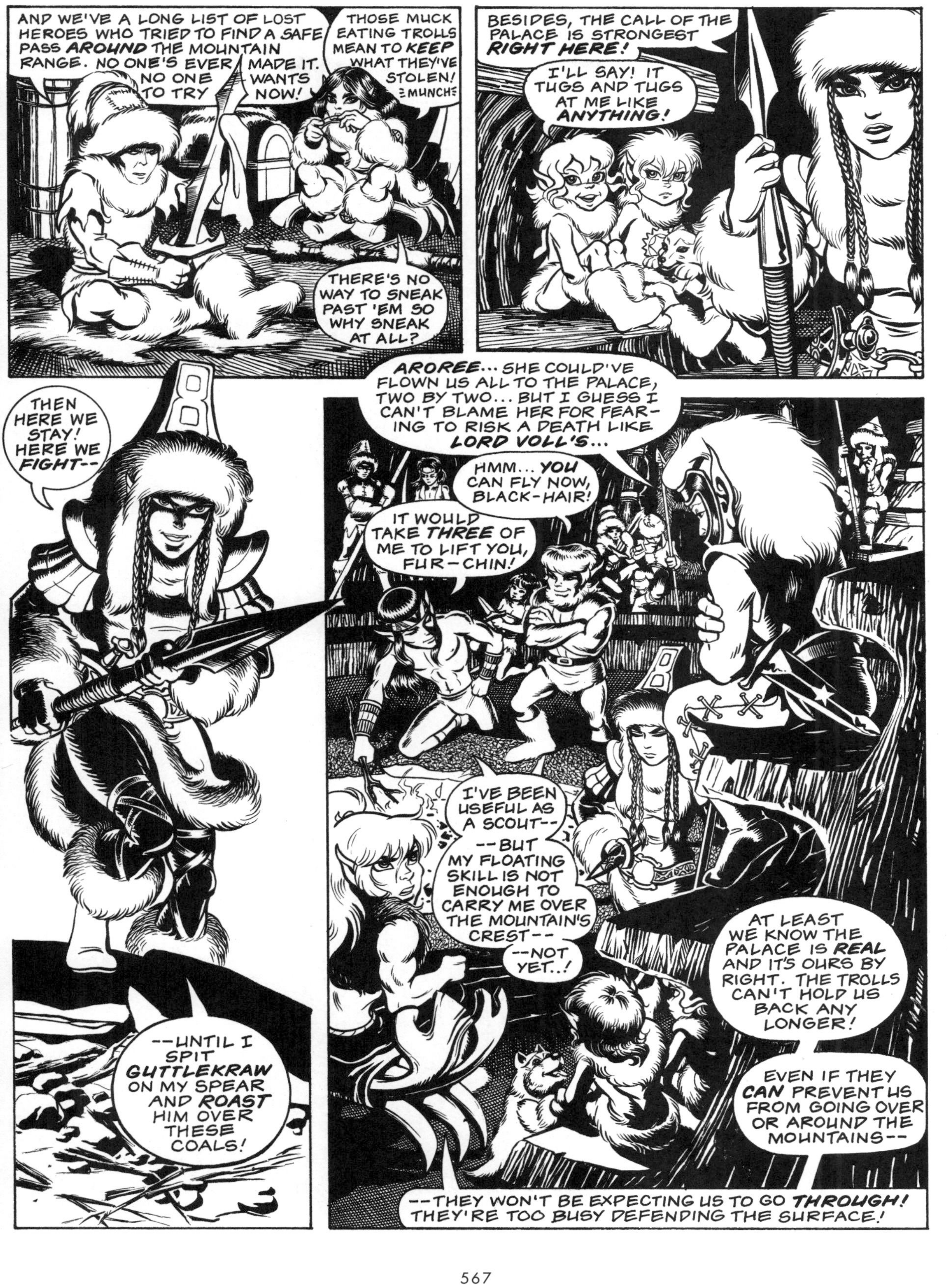
AND WE'VE A LONG LIST OF LOST HEROES WHO TRIED TO FIND A SAFE PASS AROUND THE MOUNTAIN RANGE. NO ONE'S EVER MADE IT.
NO ONE WANTS TO TRY NOW!
THOSE MUCK EATING TROLLS MEAN TO KEEP WHAT THEY'VE STOLEN!
MUNCH
THERE'S NO WAY TO SNEAK PAST 'EM SO WHY SNEAK AT ALL?
BESIDES, THE CALL OF THE PALACE IS STRONGEST RIGHT HERE!
I'LL SAY! IT TUGS AND TUGS AT ME LIKE ANYTHING!
THEN HERE WE STAY! HERE WE FIGHT--
--UNTIL I SPIT GUTTLEKRAW ON MY SPEAR AND ROAST HIM OVER THESE COALS!
AROREE... SHE COULD'VE FLOWN US ALL TO THE PALACE, TWO BY TWO... BUT I GUESS I CAN'T BLAME HER FOR FEARING TO RISK A DEATH LIKE LORD VOLL'S...
HMM... YOU CAN FLY NOW, BLACK-HAIR!
IT WOULD TAKE THREE OF ME TO LIFT YOU, FUR-CHIN!
I'VE BEEN USEFUL AS A SCOUT--
--BUT MY FLOATING SKILL IS NOT ENOUGH TO CARRY ME OVER THE MOUNTAIN'S CREST--
--NOT YET..!
AT LEAST WE KNOW THE PALACE IS REAL AND IT'S OURS BY RIGHT. THE TROLLS CAN'T HOLD US BACK ANY LONGER!
EVEN IF THEY CAN PREVENT US FROM GOING OVER OR AROUND THE MOUNTAINS--
--THEY WON'T BE EXPECTING US TO GO THROUGH! THEY'RE TOO BUSY DEFENDING THE SURFACE!

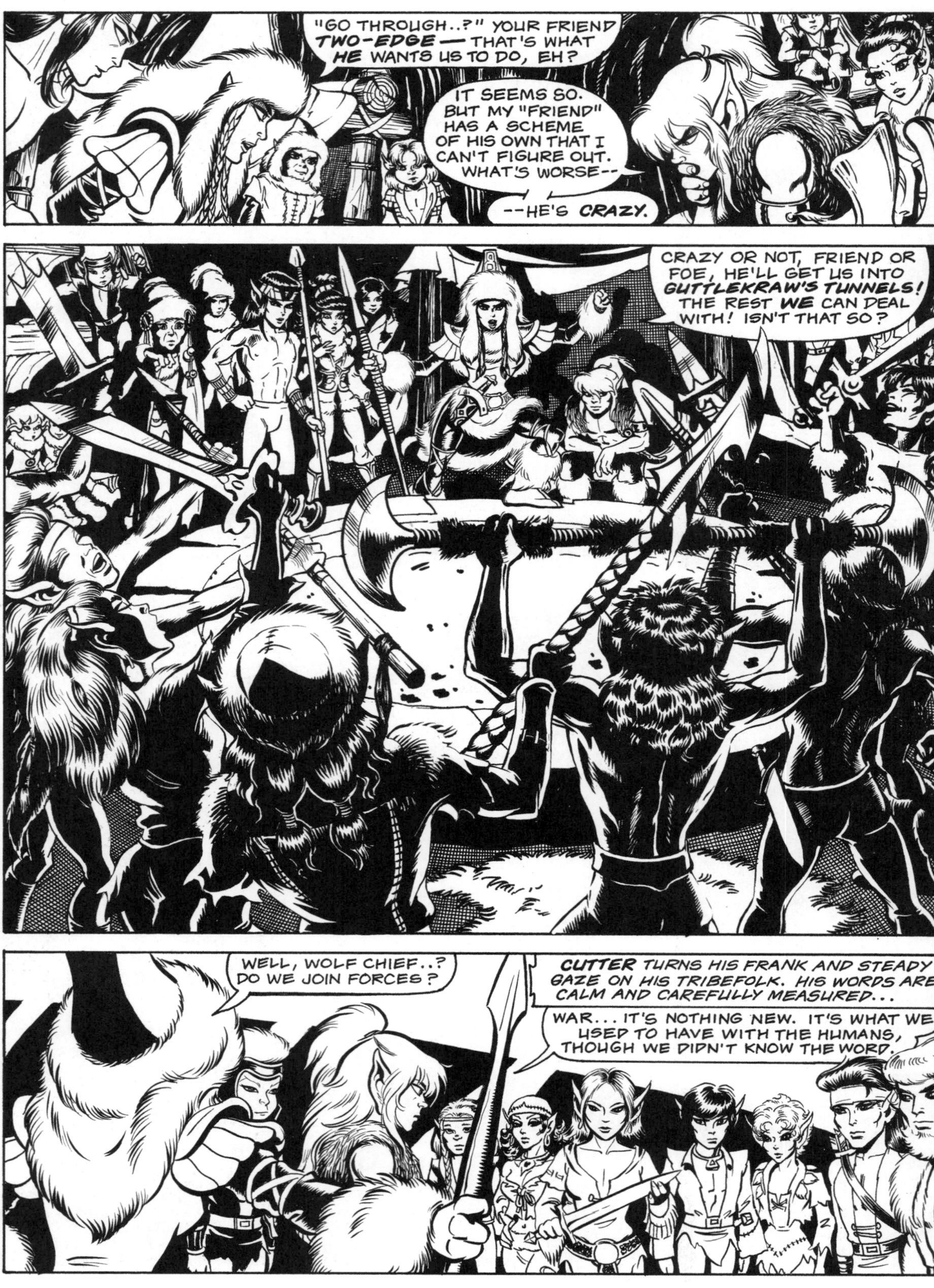
"GO THROUGH..?" YOUR FRIEND TWO-EDGE — THAT'S WHAT HE WANTS US TO DO, EH?
IT SEEMS SO. BUT MY "FRIEND" HAS A SCHEME OF HIS OWN THAT I CAN'T FIGURE OUT. WHAT'S WORSE--
--HE'S CRAZY.
CRAZY OR NOT, FRIEND OR FOE, HE'LL GET US INTO GUTTLEKRAW'S TUNNELS! THE REST WE CAN DEAL WITH! ISN'T THAT SO?
WELL, WOLF CHIEF..? DO WE JOIN FORCES?
CUTTER TURNS HIS FRANK AND STEADY GAZE ON HIS TRIBEFOLK. HIS WORDS ARE CALM AND CAREFULLY MEASURED...
WAR... IT'S NOTHING NEW. IT'S WHAT WE USED TO HAVE WITH THE HUMANS, THOUGH WE DIDN'T KNOW THE WORD.

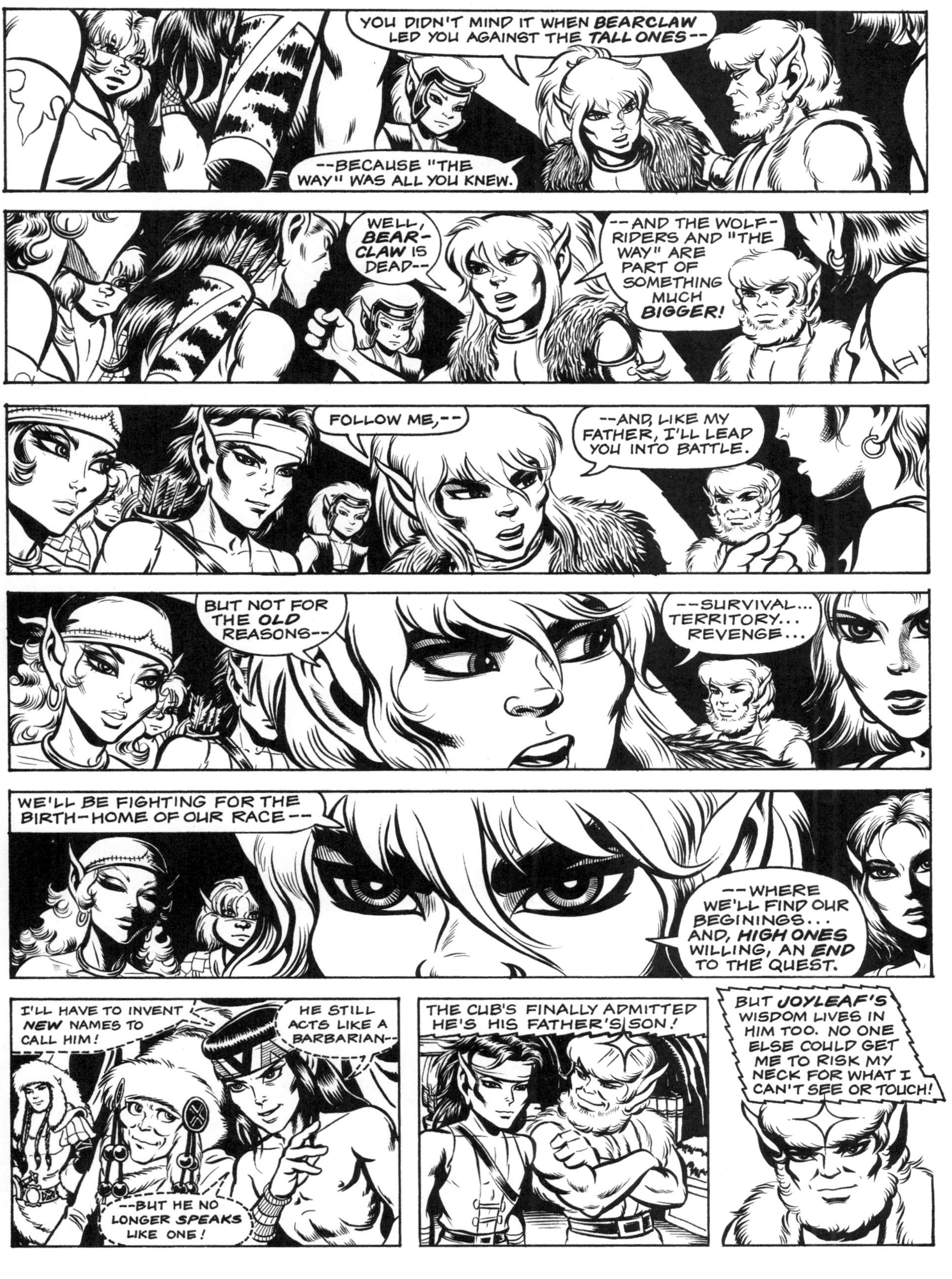
YOU DIDN'T MIND IT WHEN BEARCLAW LED YOU AGAINST THE TALL ONES--
--BECAUSE "THE WAY" WAS ALL YOU KNEW.
WELL, BEARCLAW IS DEAD--
--AND THE WOLF-RIDERS AND "THE WAY" ARE PART OF SOMETHING MUCH BIGGER!
FOLLOW ME,--
--AND, LIKE MY FATHER, I'LL LEAD YOU INTO BATTLE.
BUT NOT FOR THE OLD REASONS--
--SURVIVAL... TERRITORY... REVENGE...
WE'LL BE FIGHTING FOR THE BIRTH-HOME OF OUR RACE--
--WHERE WE'LL FIND OUR BEGININGS... AND, HIGH ONES WILLING, AN END TO THE QUEST.
I'LL HAVE TO INVENT NEW NAMES TO CALL HIM!
HE STILL ACTS LIKE A BARBARIAN--
--BUT HE NO LONGER SPEAKS LIKE ONE!
THE CUB'S FINALLY ADMITTED HE'S HIS FATHER'S SON!
BUT JOYLEAF'S WISDOM LIVES IN HIM TOO. NO ONE ELSE COULD GET ME TO RISK MY NECK FOR WHAT I CAN'T SEE OR TOUCH!

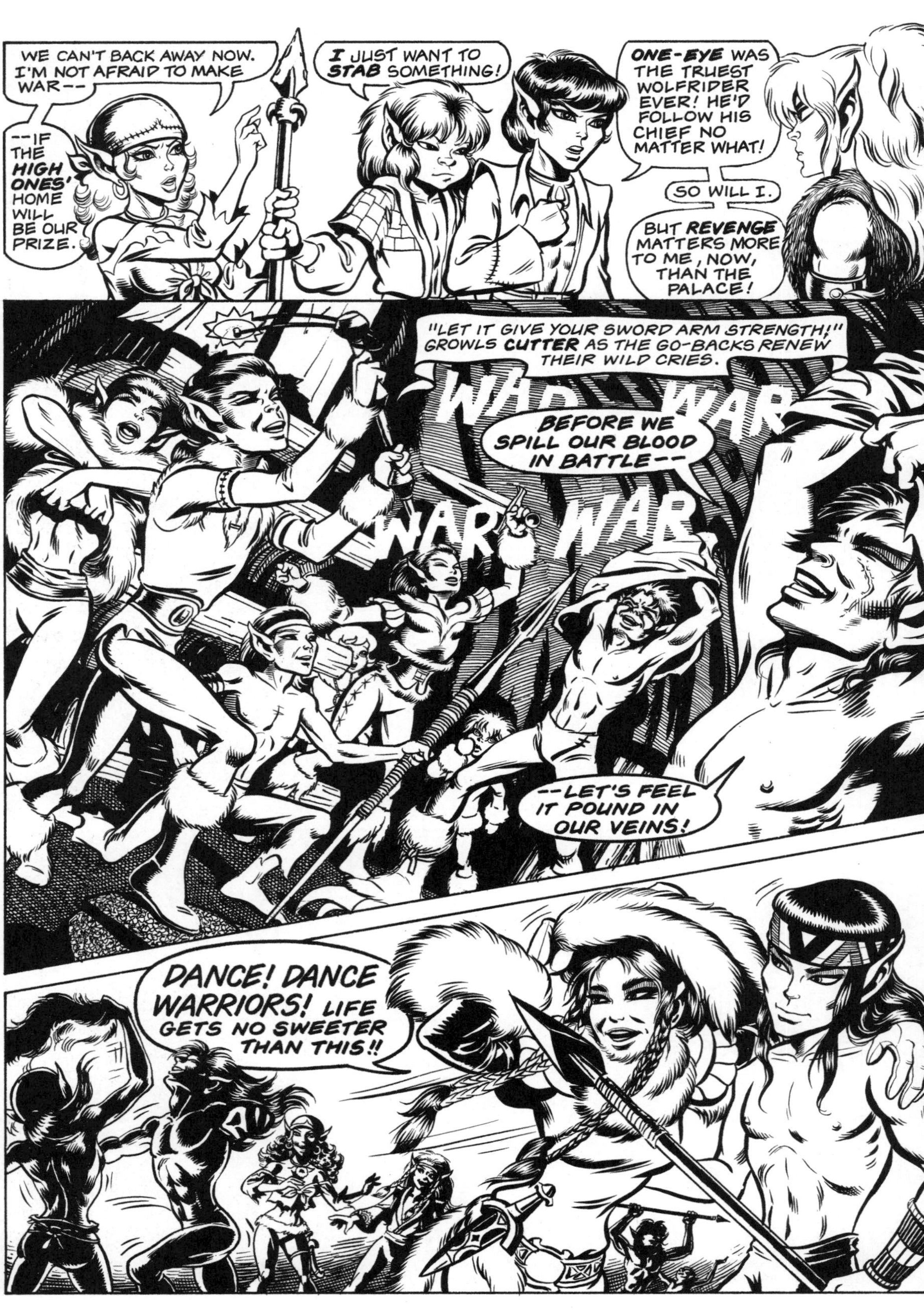
WE CAN'T BACK AWAY NOW. I'M NOT AFRAID TO MAKE WAR--
--IF THE HIGH ONES' HOME WILL BE OUR PRIZE.
I JUST WANT TO STAB SOMETHING!
ONE-EYE WAS THE TRUEST WOLFRIDER EVER! HE'D FOLLOW HIS CHIEF NO MATTER WHAT!
SO WILL I.
BUT REVENGE MATTERS MORE TO ME, NOW, THAN THE PALACE!
"LET IT GIVE YOUR SWORD ARM STRENGTH!" GROWLS CUTTER AS THE GO-BACKS RENEW THEIR WILD CRIES.
WAR WAR
BEFORE WE SPILL OUR BLOOD IN BATTLE--
WAR WAR
--LET'S FEEL IT POUND IN OUR VEINS!
DANCE! DANCE WARRIORS! LIFE GETS NO SWEETER THAN THIS!!

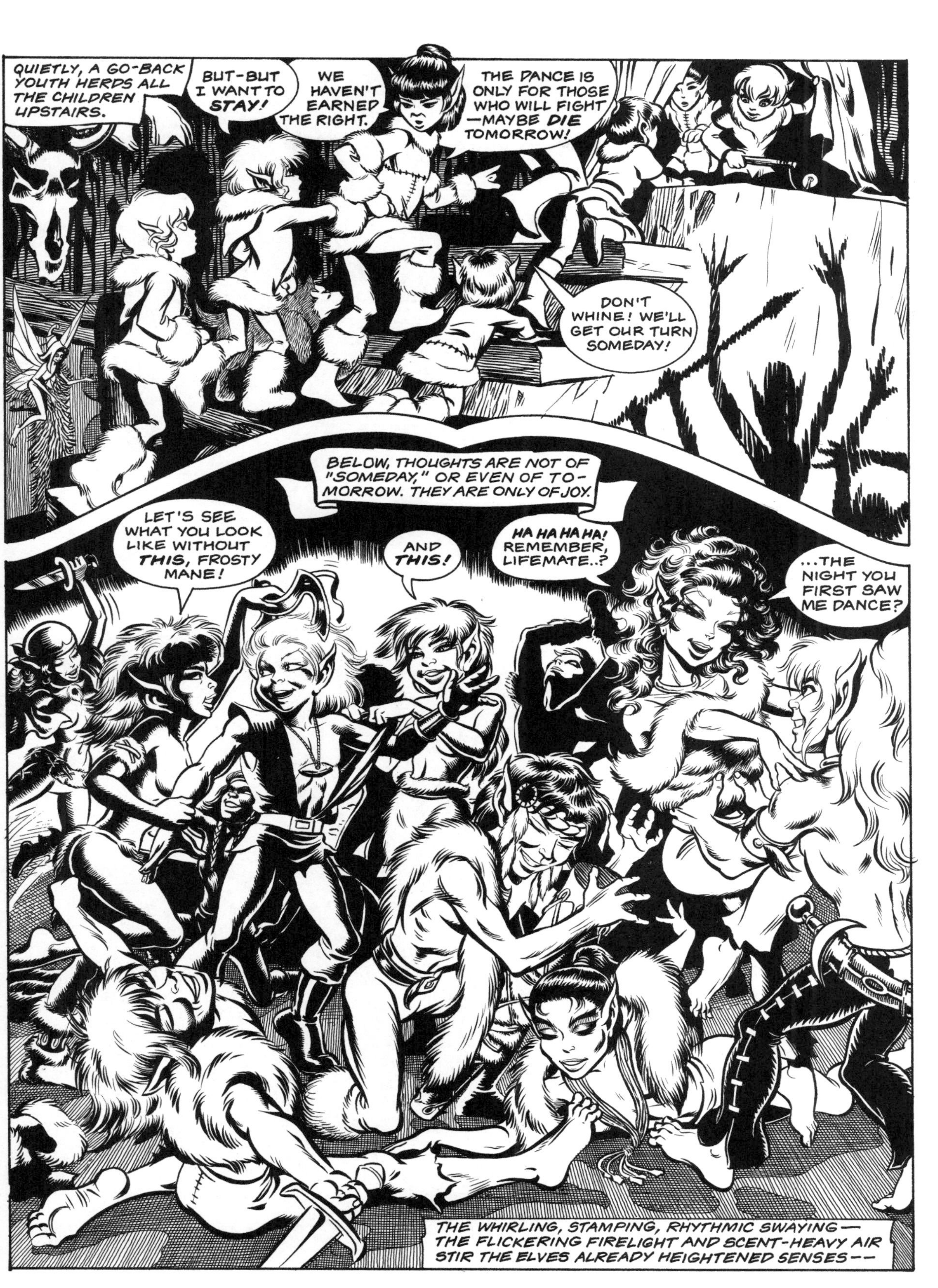
QUIETLY, A GO-BACK YOUTH HERDS ALL THE CHILDREN UPSTAIRS.
BUT-BUT I WANT TO STAY!
WE HAVEN'T EARNED THE RIGHT.
THE DANCE IS ONLY FOR THOSE WHO WILL FIGHT —MAYBE DIE TOMORROW!
DON'T WHINE! WE'LL GET OUR TURN SOMEDAY!
BELOW, THOUGHTS ARE NOT OF "SOMEDAY," OR EVEN OF TO-MORROW. THEY ARE ONLY OF JOY.
LET'S SEE WHAT YOU LOOK LIKE WITHOUT THIS, FROSTY MANE!
AND THIS!
HA HA HA HA! REMEMBER, LIFEMATE..?
...THE NIGHT YOU FIRST SAW ME DANCE?
THE WHIRLING, STAMPING, RHYTHMIC SWAYING— THE FLICKERING FIRELIGHT AND SCENT-HEAVY AIR STIR THE ELVES ALREADY HEIGHTENED SENSES--

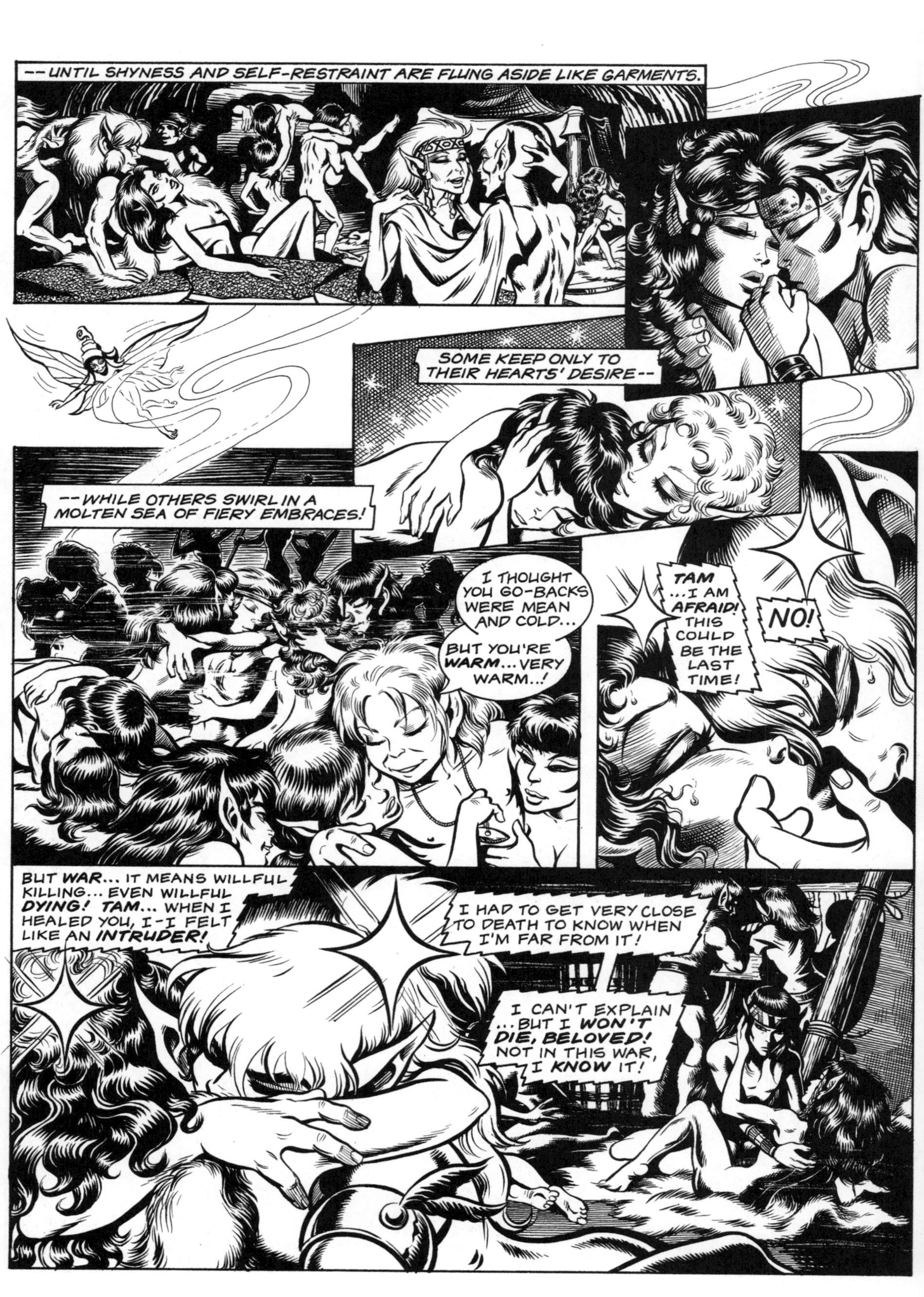

--UNTIL SHYNESS AND SELF-RESTRAINT ARE FLUNG ASIDE LIKE GARMENTS.
SOME KEEP ONLY TO THEIR HEARTS' DESIRE--
--WHILE OTHERS SWIRL IN A MOLTEN SEA OF FIERY EMBRACES!
I THOUGHT YOU GO-BACKS WERE MEAN AND COLD...
BUT YOU'RE WARM... VERY WARM...!
TAM ...I AM AFRAID! THIS COULD BE THE LAST TIME!
NO!
BUT WAR... IT MEANS WILLFUL KILLING... EVEN WILLFUL DYING! TAM... WHEN I HEALED YOU, I-I FELT LIKE AN INTRUDER!
I HAD TO GET VERY CLOSE TO DEATH TO KNOW WHEN I'M FAR FROM IT!
I CAN'T EXPLAIN ...BUT I WON'T DIE, BELOVED! NOT IN THIS WAR, I KNOW IT!

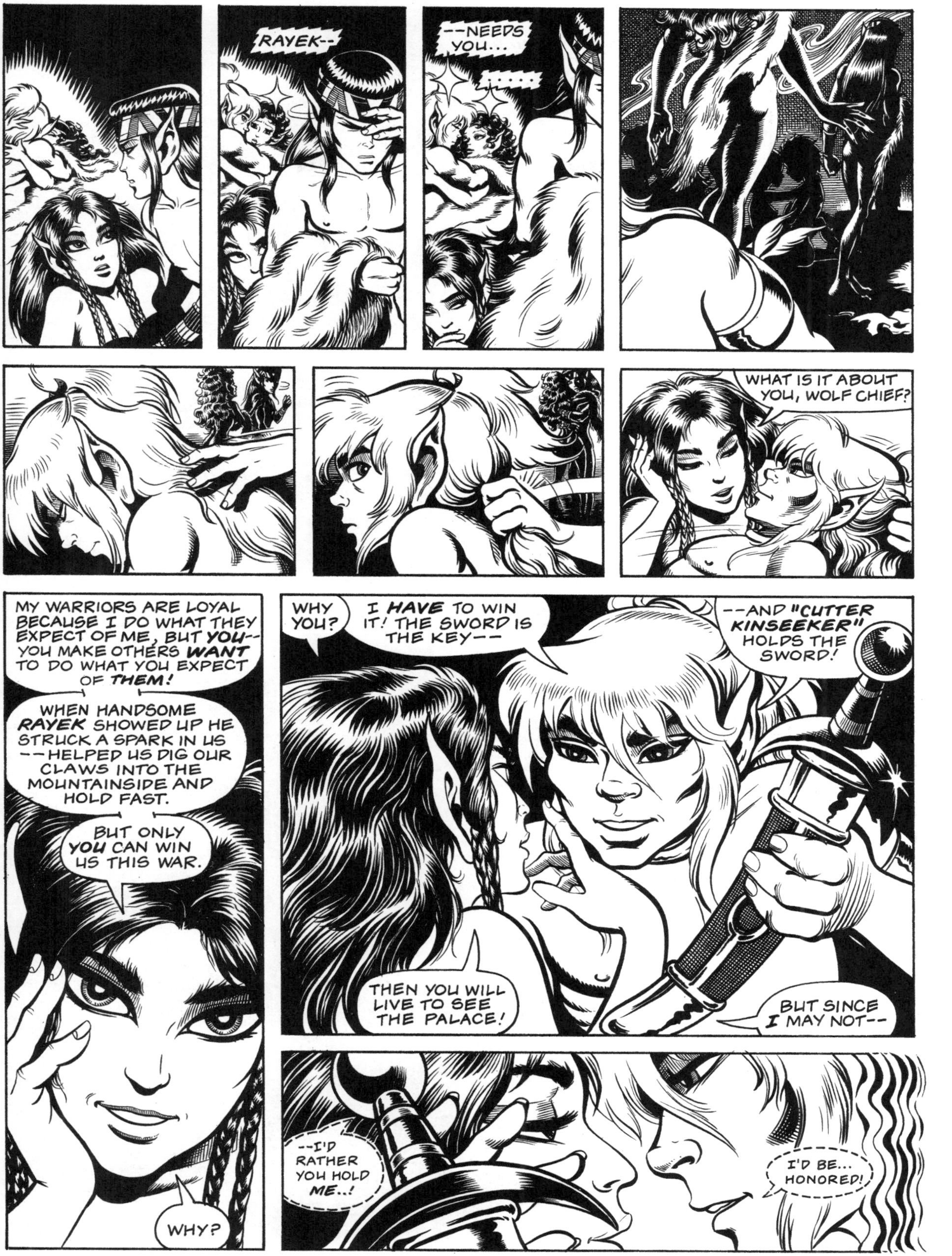

RAYEK--
--NEEDS YOU...
......
WHAT IS IT ABOUT YOU, WOLF CHIEF?
MY WARRIORS ARE LOYAL BECAUSE I DO WHAT THEY EXPECT OF ME, BUT YOU-- YOU MAKE OTHERS WANT TO DO WHAT YOU EXPECT OF THEM!
WHEN HANDSOME RAYEK SHOWED UP HE STRUCK A SPARK IN US --HELPED US DIG OUR CLAWS INTO THE MOUNTAINSIDE AND HOLD FAST.
BUT ONLY YOU CAN WIN US THIS WAR.
WHY?
WHY YOU?
I HAVE TO WIN IT! THE SWORD IS THE KEY--
--AND "CUTTER KINSEEKER" HOLDS THE SWORD!
THEN YOU WILL LIVE TO SEE THE PALACE!
BUT SINCE I MAY NOT--
--I'D RATHER YOU HOLD ME..!
I'D BE... HONORED!

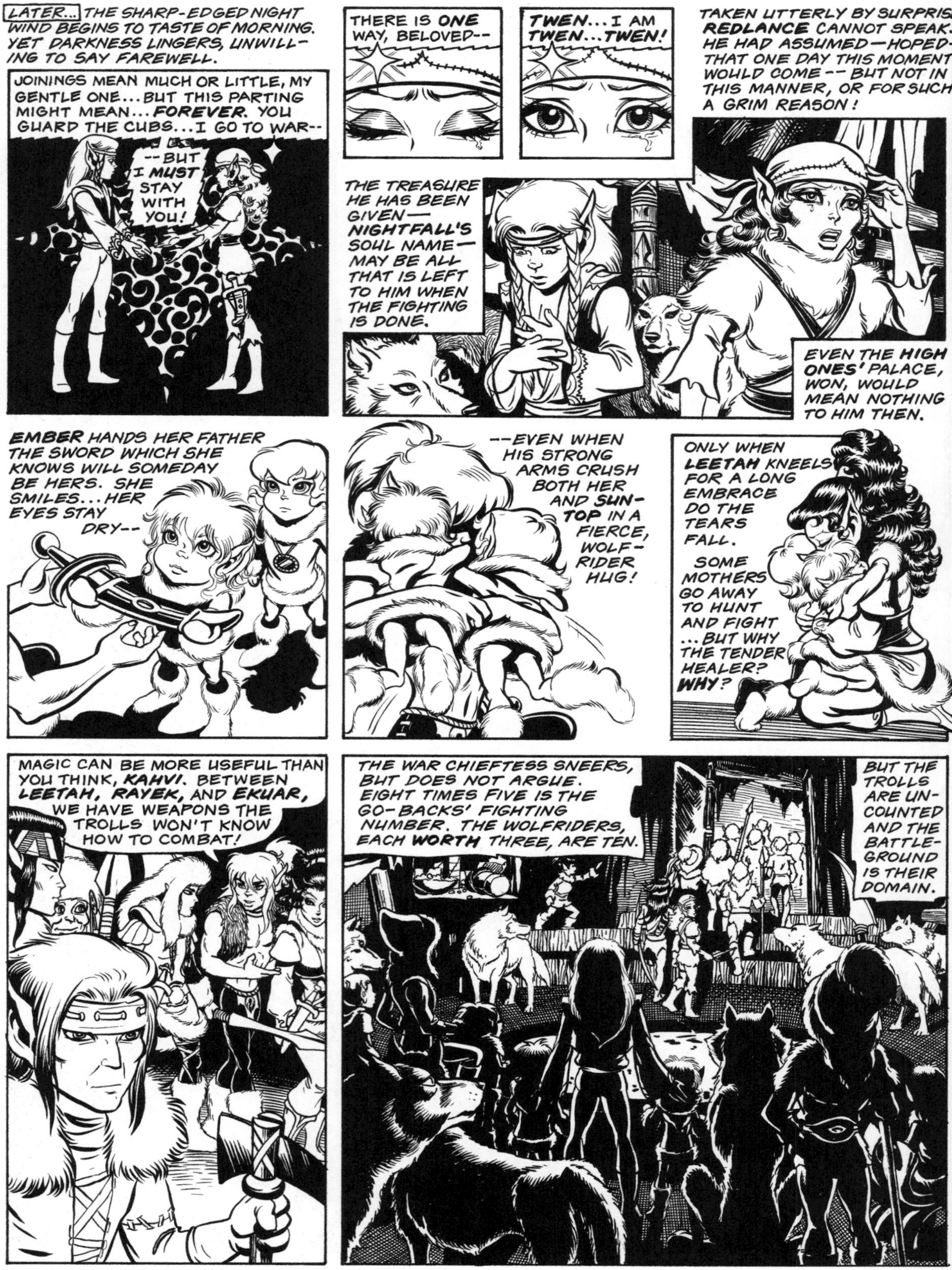
LATER... THE SHARP-EDGED NIGHT WIND BEGINS TO TASTE OF MORNING. YET DARKNESS LINGERS, UNWILLING TO SAY FAREWELL.
JOININGS MEAN MUCH OR LITTLE, MY GENTLE ONE... BUT THIS PARTING MIGHT MEAN... FOREVER. YOU GUARD THE CUBS... I GO TO WAR--
--BUT I MUST STAY WITH YOU!
THERE IS ONE WAY, BELOVED--
TWEN... I AM TWEN... TWEN!
TAKEN UTTERLY BY SURPRIS
REDLANCE CANNOT SPEAK. HE HAD ASSUMED—HOPED—THAT ONE DAY THIS MOMENT WOULD COME -- BUT NOT IN THIS MANNER, OR FOR SUCH A GRIM REASON!
THE TREASURE HE HAS BEEN GIVEN—NIGHTFALL'S SOUL NAME—MAY BE ALL THAT IS LEFT TO HIM WHEN THE FIGHTING IS DONE.
EVEN THE HIGH ONES' PALACE, WON, WOULD MEAN NOTHING TO HIM THEN.
EMBER HANDS HER FATHER THE SWORD WHICH SHE KNOWS WILL SOMEDAY BE HERS. SHE SMILES... HER EYES STAY DRY--
--EVEN WHEN HIS STRONG ARMS CRUSH BOTH HER AND SUN-TOP IN A FIERCE, WOLF-RIDER HUG!
ONLY WHEN LEETAH KNEELS FOR A LONG EMBRACE DO THE TEARS FALL.
SOME MOTHERS GO AWAY TO HUNT AND FIGHT ... BUT WHY THE TENDER HEALER? WHY?
MAGIC CAN BE MORE USEFUL THAN YOU THINK, KAHVI. BETWEEN LEETAH, RAYEK, AND EKUAR, WE HAVE WEAPONS THE TROLLS WON'T KNOW HOW TO COMBAT!
THE WAR CHIEFTESS SNEERS, BUT DOES NOT ARGUE. EIGHT TIMES FIVE IS THE GO-BACKS' FIGHTING NUMBER. THE WOLFRIDERS, EACH WORTH THREE, ARE TEN.
BUT THE TROLLS ARE UNCOUNTED AND THE BATTLEGROUND IS THEIR DOMAIN.

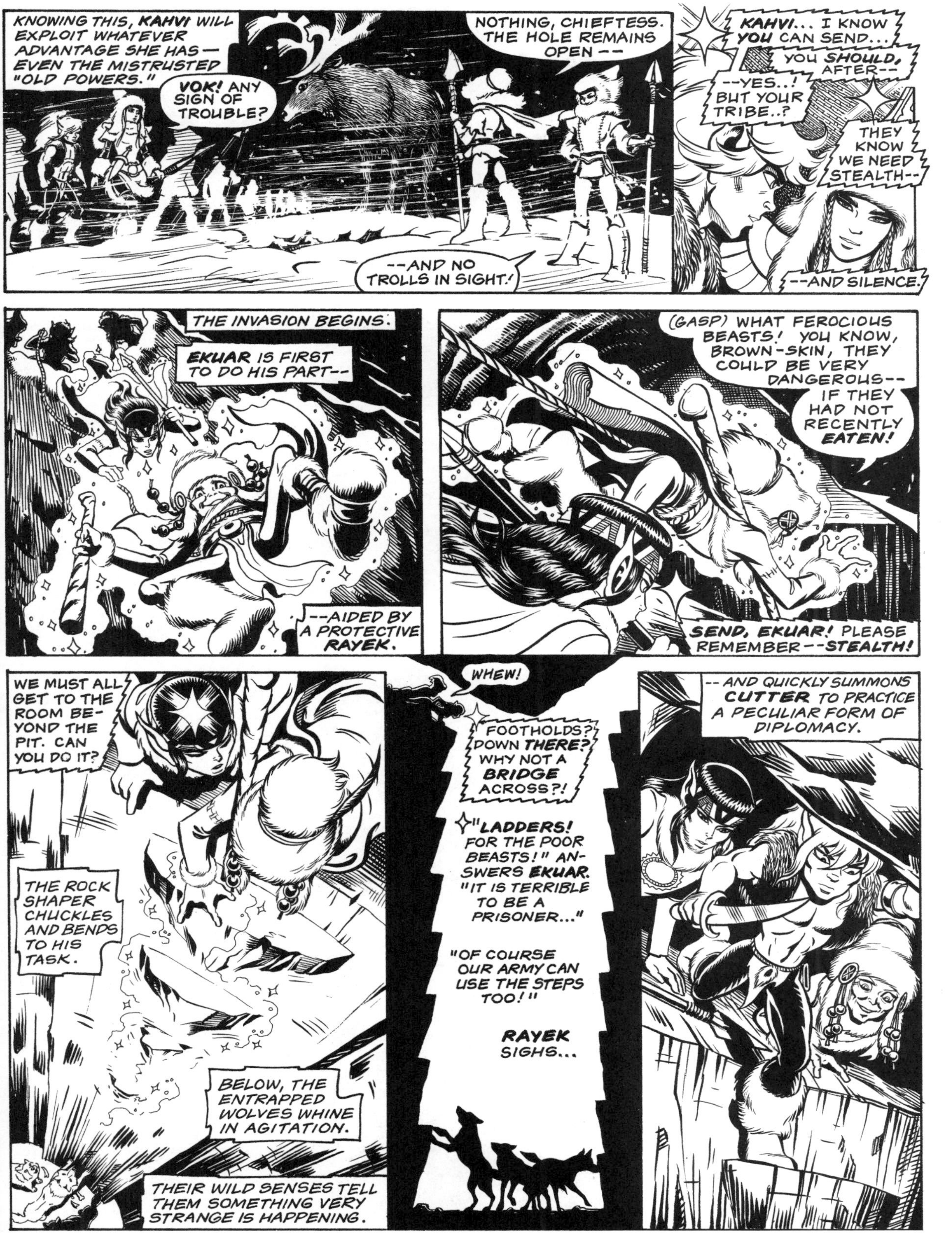

KNOWING THIS, KAHVI WILL EXPLOIT WHATEVER ADVANTAGE SHE HAS— EVEN THE MISTRUSTED "OLD POWERS."
VOK! ANY SIGN OF TROUBLE?
NOTHING, CHIEFTESS. THE HOLE REMAINS OPEN --
--AND NO TROLLS IN SIGHT!
KAHVI... I KNOW YOU CAN SEND...
YOU SHOULD, AFTER--
--YES..! BUT YOUR TRIBE..?
THEY KNOW WE NEED STEALTH--
--AND SILENCE.
THE INVASION BEGINS.
EKUAR IS FIRST TO DO HIS PART--
--AIDED BY A PROTECTIVE RAYEK.
(GASP) WHAT FEROCIOUS BEASTS! YOU KNOW, BROWN-SKIN, THEY COULD BE VERY DANGEROUS-- IF THEY HAD NOT RECENTLY EATEN!
SEND, EKUAR! PLEASE REMEMBER--STEALTH!
WE MUST ALL GET TO THE ROOM BEYOND THE PIT. CAN YOU DO IT?
THE ROCK SHAPER CHUCKLES AND BENDS TO HIS TASK.
BELOW, THE ENTRAPPED WOLVES WHINE IN AGITATION.
THEIR WILD SENSES TELL THEM SOMETHING VERY STRANGE IS HAPPENING.
WHEW!
FOOTHOLDS? DOWN THERE? WHY NOT A BRIDGE ACROSS?!
"LADDERS! FOR THE POOR BEASTS!" ANSWERS EKUAR. "IT IS TERRIBLE TO BE A PRISONER..."
"OF COURSE OUR ARMY CAN USE THE STEPS TOO!"
RAYEK SIGHS...
-- AND QUICKLY SUMMONS CUTTER TO PRACTICE A PECULIAR FORM OF DIPLOMACY.

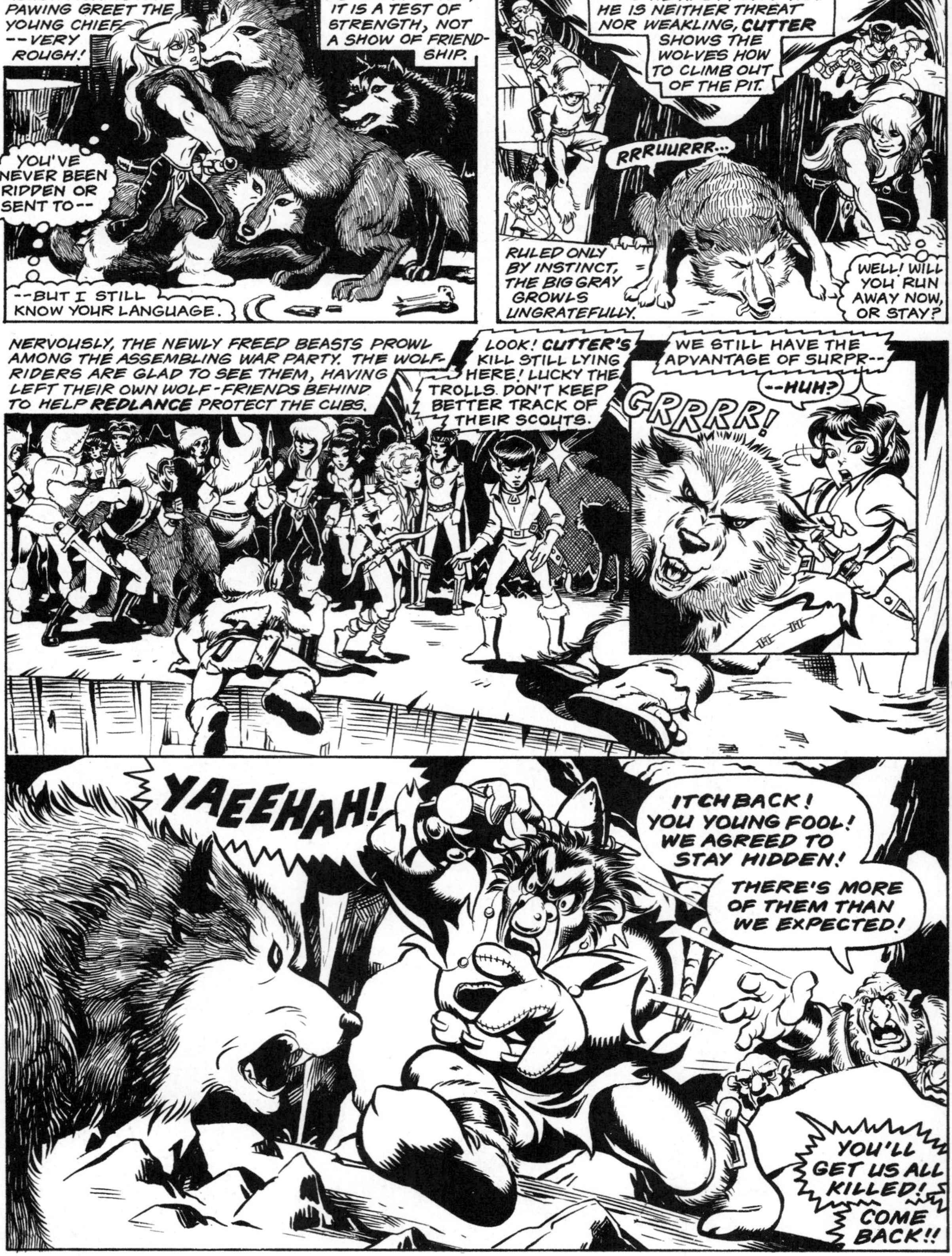
ROUGH LICKING AND PAWING GREET THE YOUNG CHIEF --VERY ROUGH!
AS HE EXPECTED, IT IS A TEST OF STRENGTH, NOT A SHOW OF FRIENDSHIP.
YOU'VE NEVER BEEN RIDDEN OR SENT TO--
--BUT I STILL KNOW YOUR LANGUAGE.
ONCE HE HAS PROVED THAT HE IS NEITHER THREAT NOR WEAKLING, CUTTER SHOWS THE WOLVES HOW TO CLIMB OUT OF THE PIT.
RRRUURRR...
RULED ONLY BY INSTINCT, THE BIG GRAY GROWLS UNGRATEFULLY.
WELL! WILL YOU RUN AWAY NOW, OR STAY?
NERVOUSLY, THE NEWLY FREED BEASTS PROWL AMONG THE ASSEMBLING WAR PARTY. THE WOLF-RIDERS ARE GLAD TO SEE THEM, HAVING LEFT THEIR OWN WOLF-FRIENDS BEHIND TO HELP REDLANCE PROTECT THE CUBS.
LOOK! CUTTER'S KILL STILL LYING HERE! LUCKY THE TROLLS DON'T KEEP BETTER TRACK OF THEIR SCOUTS.
WE STILL HAVE THE ADVANTAGE OF SURPR--
GRRRR!
--HUH?
YAEEHAH!
ITCHBACK! YOU YOUNG FOOL! WE AGREED TO STAY HIDDEN!
THERE'S MORE OF THEM THAN WE EXPECTED!
YOU'LL GET US ALL KILLED!
COME BACK!!

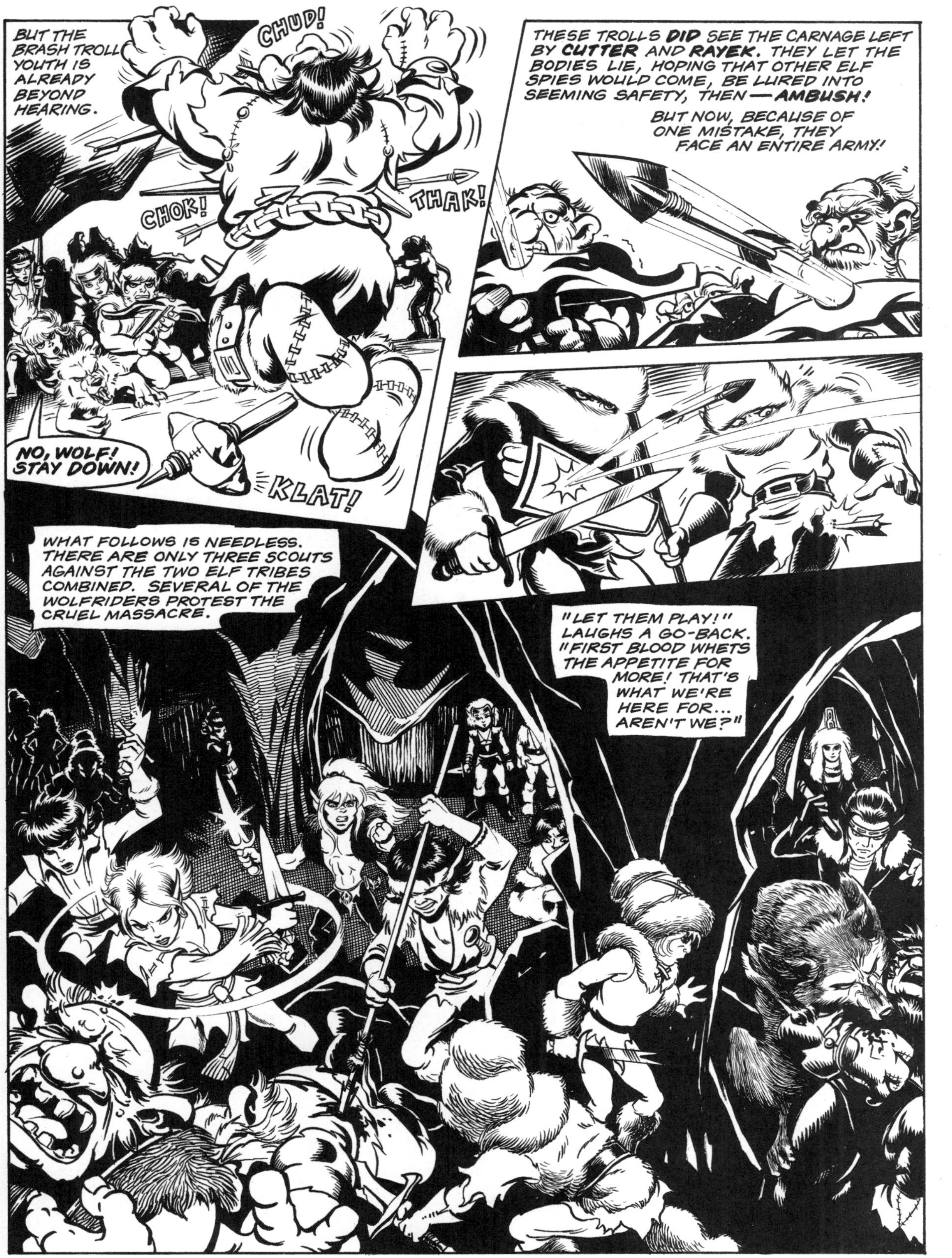
BUT THE BRASH TROLL YOUTH IS ALREADY BEYOND HEARING.
CHUD!
CHOK!
THAK!
NO, WOLF! STAY DOWN!
KLAT!
THESE TROLLS DID SEE THE CARNAGE LEFT BY CUTTER AND RAYEK. THEY LET THE BODIES LIE, HOPING THAT OTHER ELF SPIES WOULD COME, BE LURED INTO SEEMING SAFETY, THEN — AMBUSH!
BUT NOW, BECAUSE OF ONE MISTAKE, THEY FACE AN ENTIRE ARMY!
WHAT FOLLOWS IS NEEDLESS. THERE ARE ONLY THREE SCOUTS AGAINST THE TWO ELF TRIBES COMBINED. SEVERAL OF THE WOLFRIDERS PROTEST THE CRUEL MASSACRE.
"LET THEM PLAY!" LAUGHS A GO-BACK. "FIRST BLOOD WHETS THE APPETITE FOR MORE! THAT'S WHAT WE'RE HERE FOR... AREN'T WE?"

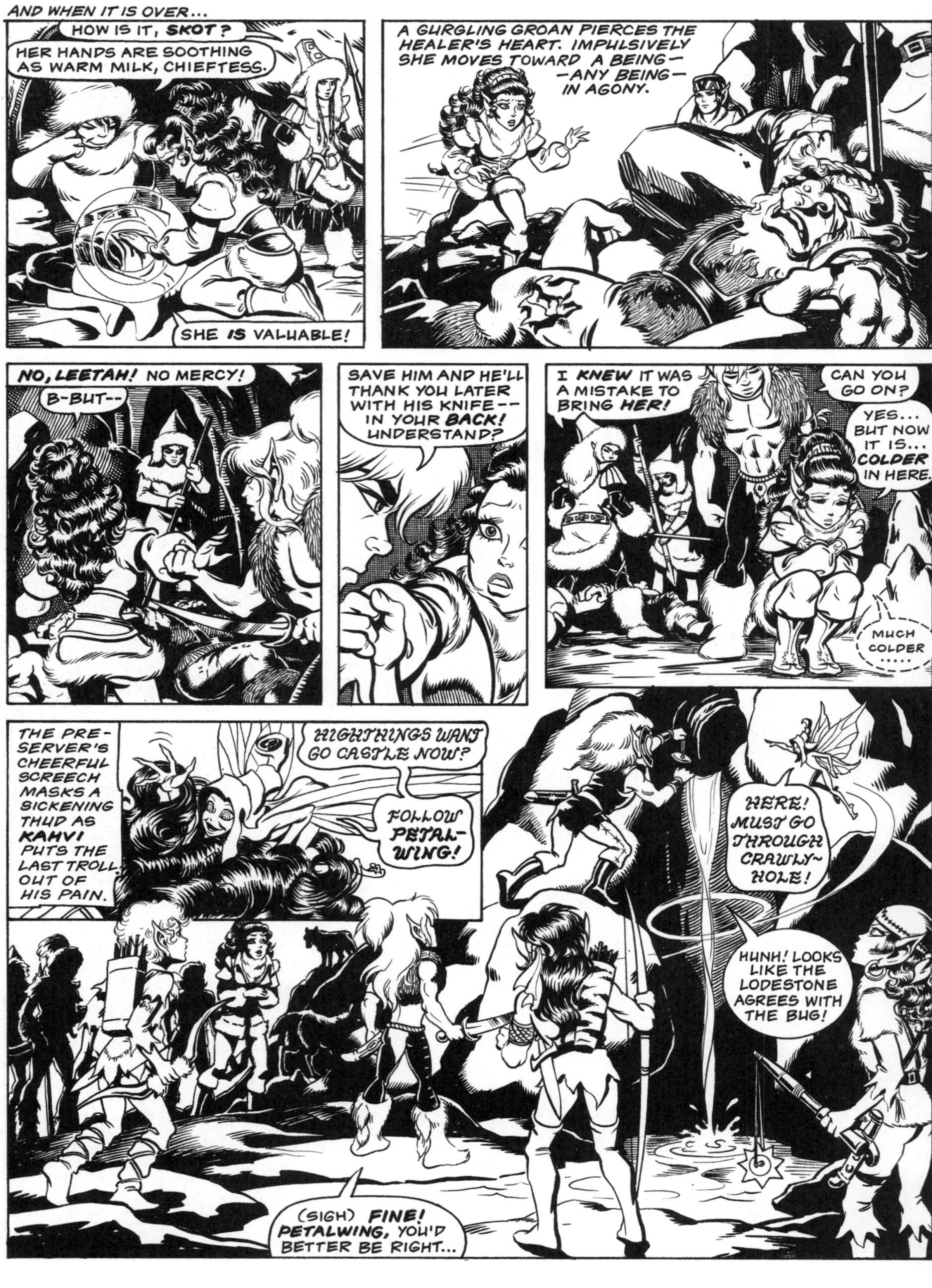
AND WHEN IT IS OVER...
HOW IS IT, SKOT?
HER HANDS ARE SOOTHING AS WARM MILK, CHIEFTESS.
SHE IS VALUABLE!
A GURGLING GROAN PIERCES THE HEALER'S HEART. IMPULSIVELY SHE MOVES TOWARD A BEING— —ANY BEING— IN AGONY.
NO, LEETAH! NO MERCY!
B-BUT--
SAVE HIM AND HE'LL THANK YOU LATER WITH HIS KNIFE-- IN YOUR BACK! UNDERSTAND?
I KNEW IT WAS A MISTAKE TO BRING HER!
CAN YOU GO ON?
YES... BUT NOW IT IS... COLDER IN HERE.
MUCH COLDER .....
THE PRESERVER'S CHEERFUL SCREECH MASKS A SICKENING THUD AS KAHVI PUTS THE LAST TROLL OUT OF HIS PAIN.
HIGHTHINGS WANT GO CASTLE NOW?
FOLLOW PETALWING!
HERE! MUST GO THROUGH CRAWLY-HOLE!
HUNH! LOOKS LIKE THE LODESTONE AGREES WITH THE BUG!
(SIGH) FINE! PETALWING, YOU'D BETTER BE RIGHT...

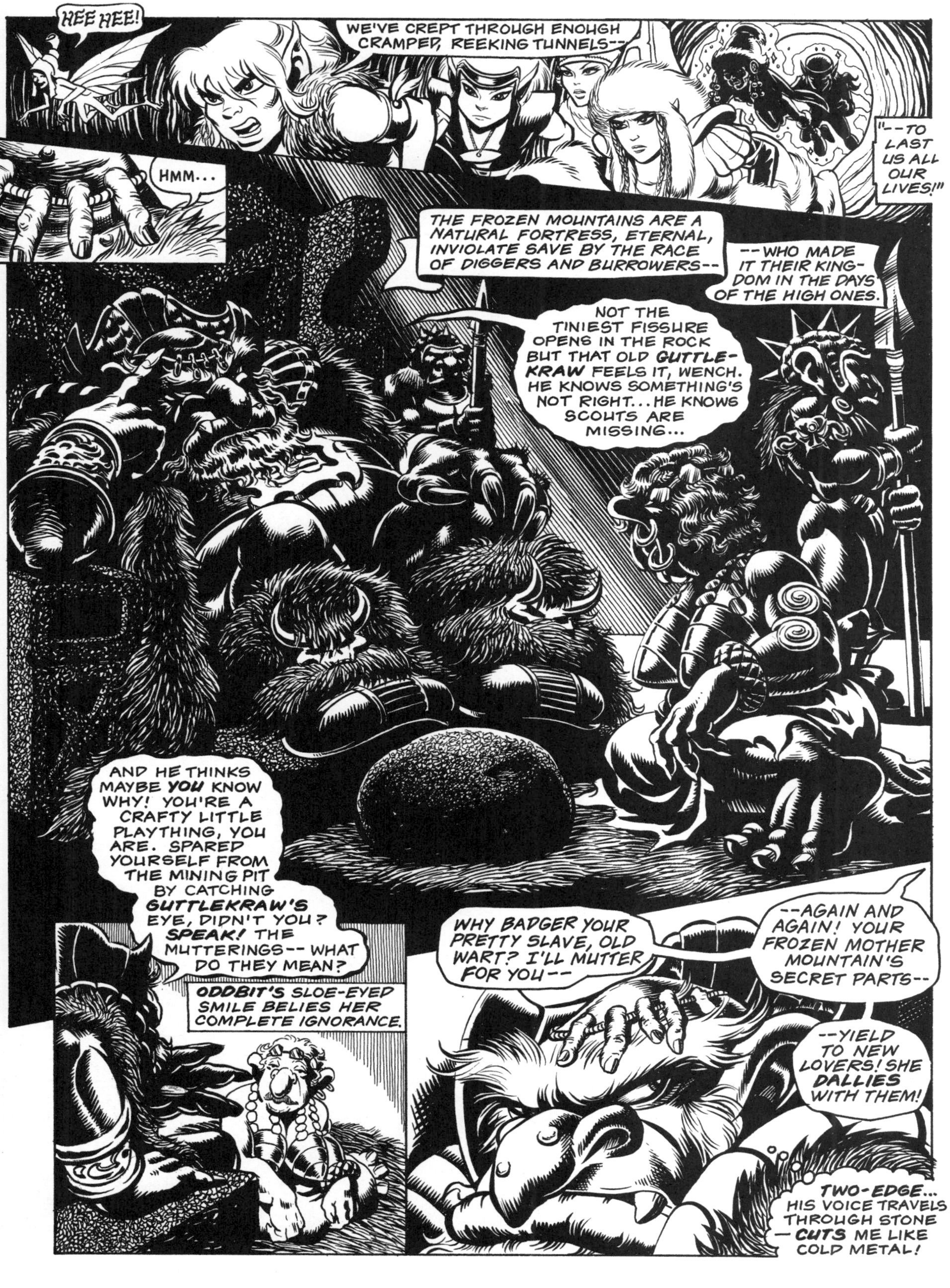
HEE HEE!
WE'VE CREPT THROUGH ENOUGH CRAMPED, REEKING TUNNELS--
"--TO LAST US ALL OUR LIVES!"
HMM...
THE FROZEN MOUNTAINS ARE A NATURAL FORTRESS, ETERNAL, INVIOLATE SAVE BY THE RACE OF DIGGERS AND BURROWERS--
--WHO MADE IT THEIR KINGDOM IN THE DAYS OF THE HIGH ONES.
NOT THE TINIEST FISSURE OPENS IN THE ROCK BUT THAT OLD GUTTLEKRAW FEELS IT, WENCH. HE KNOWS SOMETHING'S NOT RIGHT... HE KNOWS SCOUTS ARE MISSING...
AND HE THINKS MAYBE YOU KNOW WHY! YOU'RE A CRAFTY LITTLE PLAYTHING, YOU ARE. SPARED YOURSELF FROM THE MINING PIT BY CATCHING GUTTLEKRAW'S EYE, DIDN'T YOU? SPEAK! THE MUTTERINGS-- WHAT DO THEY MEAN?
ODDBIT'S SLOE-EYED SMILE BELIES HER COMPLETE IGNORANCE.
WHY BADGER YOUR PRETTY SLAVE, OLD WART? I'LL MUTTER FOR YOU--
--AGAIN AND AGAIN! YOUR FROZEN MOTHER MOUNTAIN'S SECRET PARTS--
--YIELD TO NEW LOVERS! SHE DALLIES WITH THEM!
TWO-EDGE... HIS VOICE TRAVELS THROUGH STONE —CUTS ME LIKE COLD METAL!

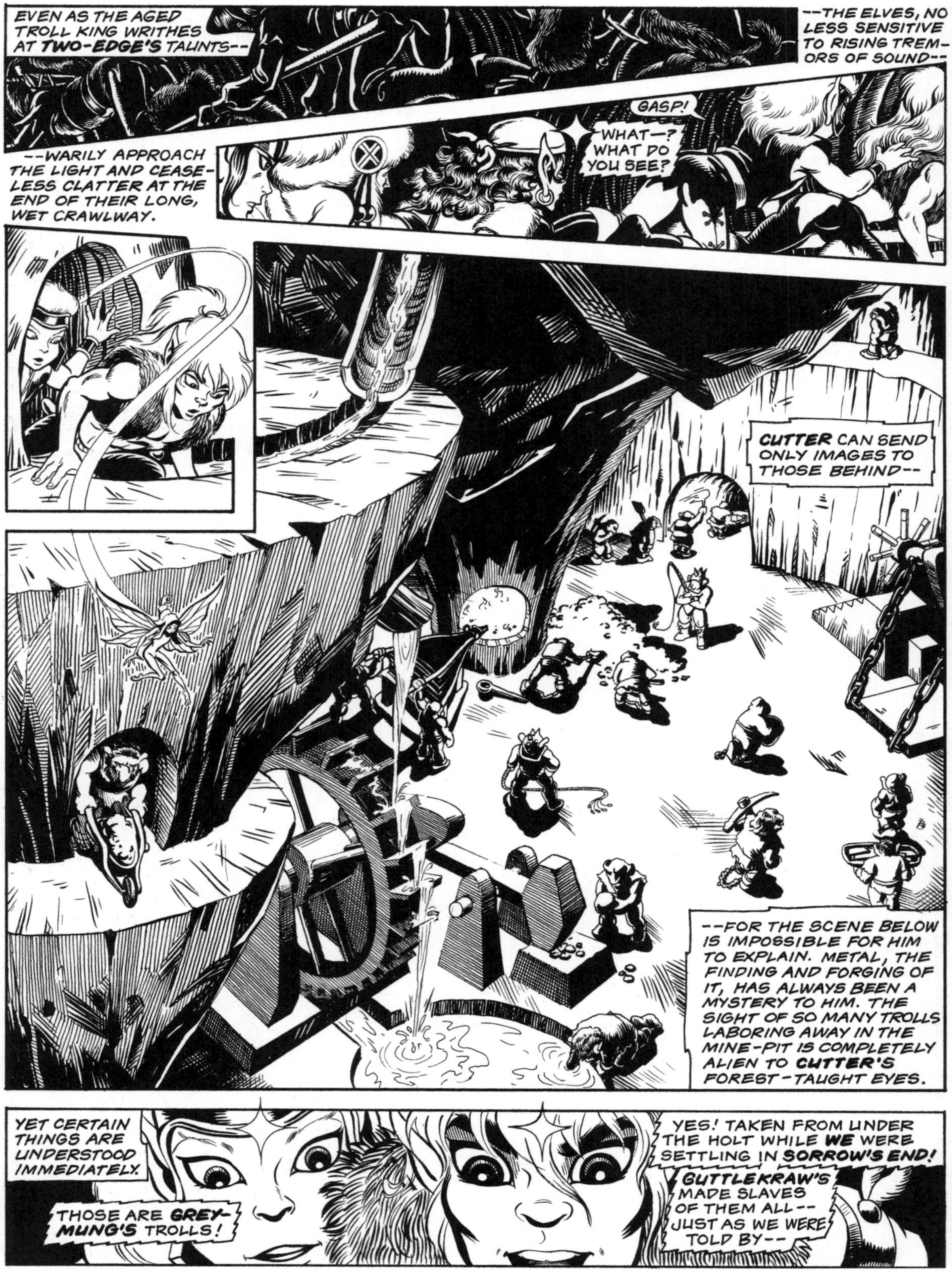
EVEN AS THE AGED TROLL KING WRITHES AT TWO-EDGE'S TAUNTS--
--THE ELVES, NO LESS SENSITIVE TO RISING TREMORS OF SOUND--
GASP!
WHAT--? WHAT DO YOU SEE?
--WARILY APPROACH THE LIGHT AND CEASELESS CLATTER AT THE END OF THEIR LONG, WET CRAWLWAY.
CUTTER CAN SEND ONLY IMAGES TO THOSE BEHIND--
--FOR THE SCENE BELOW IS IMPOSSIBLE FOR HIM TO EXPLAIN. METAL, THE FINDING AND FORGING OF IT, HAS ALWAYS BEEN A MYSTERY TO HIM. THE SIGHT OF SO MANY TROLLS LABORING AWAY IN THE MINE-PIT IS COMPLETELY ALIEN TO CUTTER'S FOREST-TAUGHT EYES.
YET CERTAIN THINGS ARE UNDERSTOOD IMMEDIATELY.
THOSE ARE GREYMUNG'S TROLLS!
YES! TAKEN FROM UNDER THE HOLT WHILE WE WERE SETTLING IN SORROW'S END!
GUTTLEKRAW'S MADE SLAVES OF THEM ALL-- JUST AS WE WERE TOLD BY--

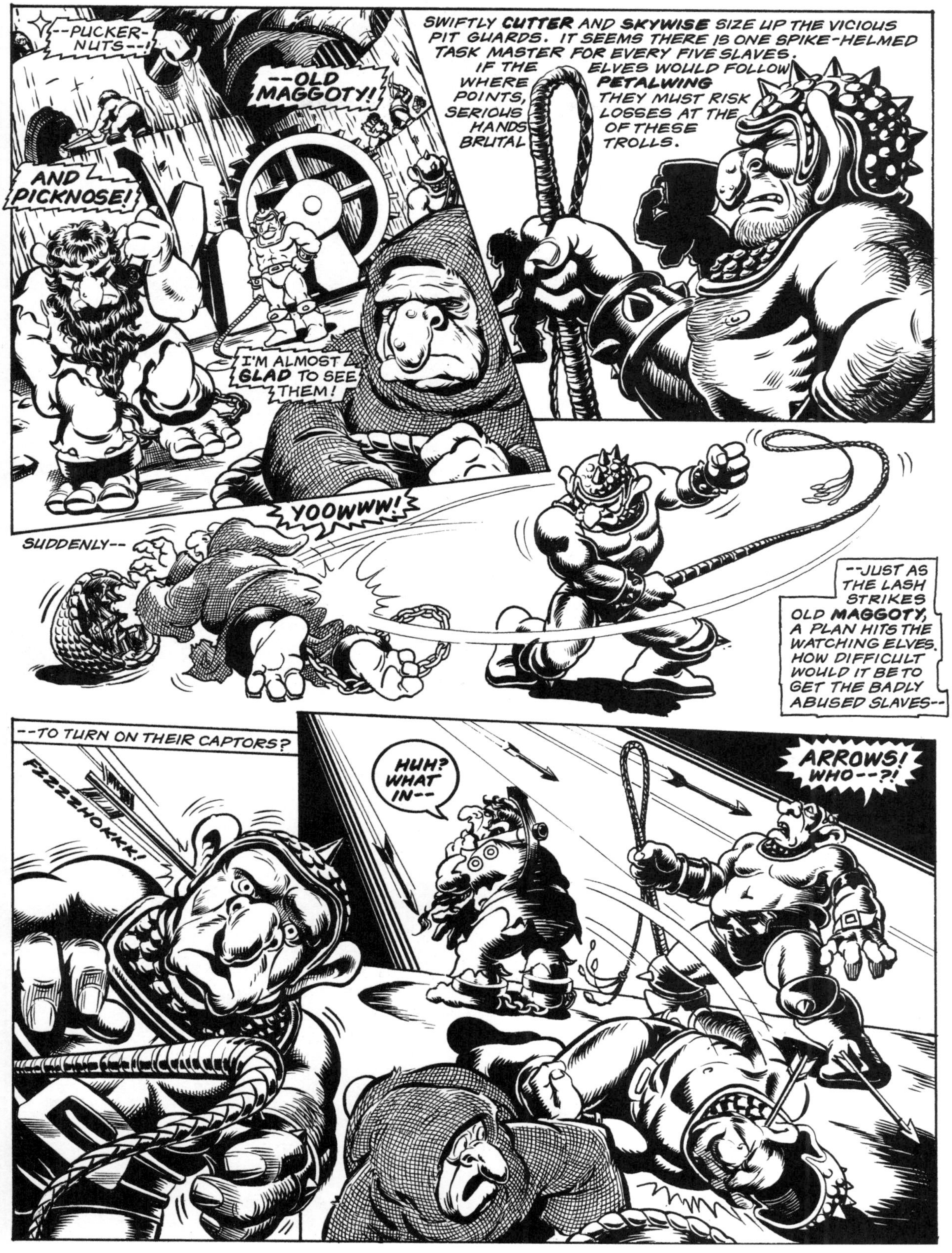
--PUCKER-NUTS--!
--OLD MAGGOTY!
AND PICKNOSE!
I'M ALMOST GLAD TO SEE THEM!
SWIFTLY CUTTER AND SKYWISE SIZE UP THE VICIOUS PIT GUARDS. IT SEEMS THERE IS ONE SPIKE-HELMED TASK MASTER FOR EVERY FIVE SLAVES.
IF THE ELVES WOULD FOLLOW WHERE PETALWING POINTS, THEY MUST RISK SERIOUS LOSSES AT THE HANDS OF THESE BRUTAL TROLLS.
SUDDENLY--
YOOWWW!
--JUST AS THE LASH STRIKES OLD MAGGOTY, A PLAN HITS THE WATCHING ELVES. HOW DIFFICULT WOULD IT BE TO GET THE BADLY ABUSED SLAVES--
--TO TURN ON THEIR CAPTORS?
FZZZHOKKK!
HUH? WHAT IN--
ARROWS! WHO--?!

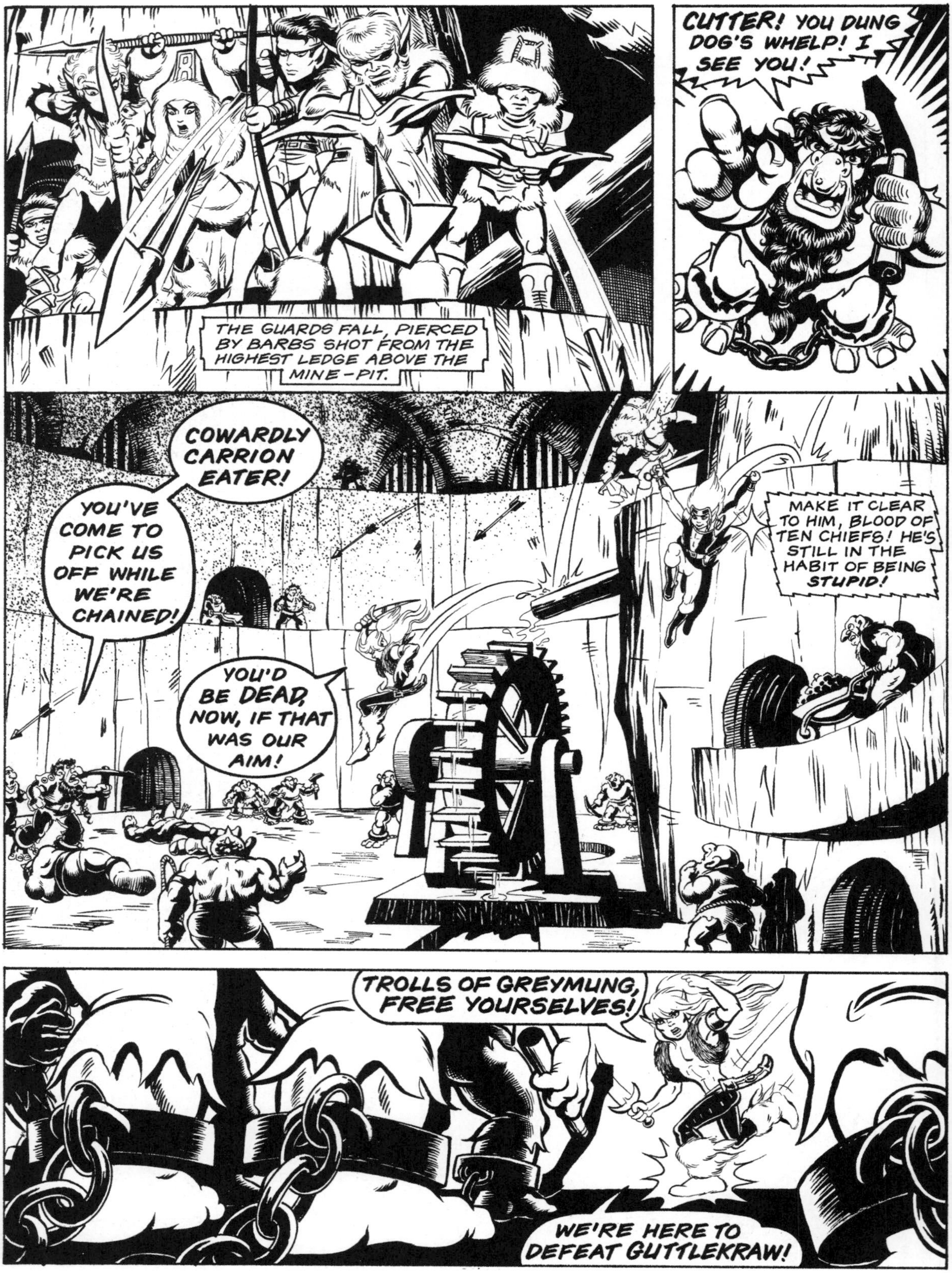
THE GUARDS FALL, PIERCED BY BARBS SHOT FROM THE HIGHEST LEDGE ABOVE THE MINE-PIT.
CUTTER! YOU DUNG DOG'S WHELP! I SEE YOU!
COWARDLY CARRION EATER!
YOU'VE COME TO PICK US OFF WHILE WE'RE CHAINED!
YOU'D BE DEAD, NOW, IF THAT WAS OUR AIM!
MAKE IT CLEAR TO HIM, BLOOD OF TEN CHIEFS! HE'S STILL IN THE HABIT OF BEING STUPID!
TROLLS OF GREYMUNG, FREE YOURSELVES!
WE'RE HERE TO DEFEAT GUTTLEKRAW!

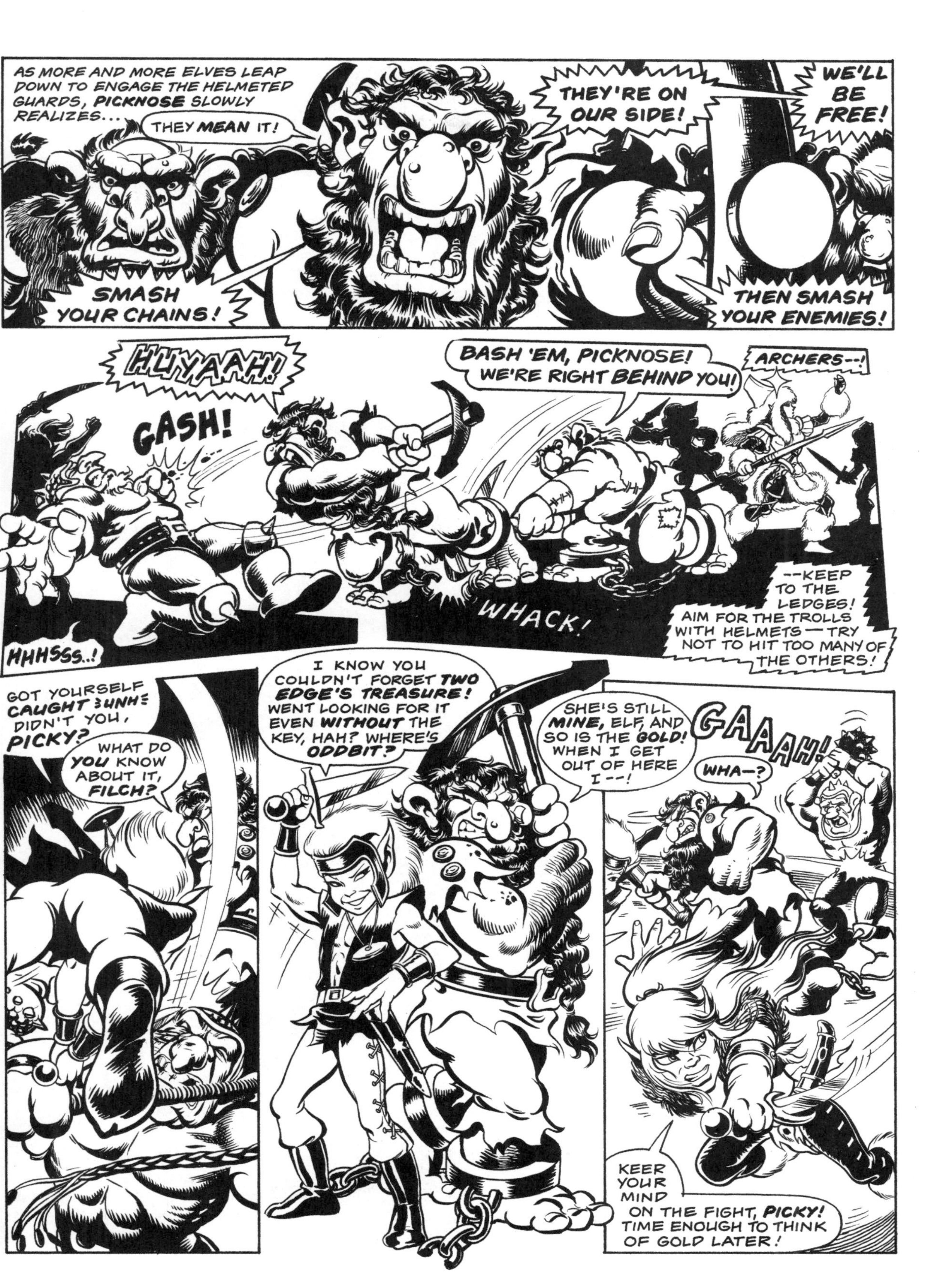
AS MORE AND MORE ELVES LEAP DOWN TO ENGAGE THE HELMETED GUARDS, PICKNOSE SLOWLY REALIZES...
THEY MEAN IT!
THEY'RE ON OUR SIDE!
WE'LL BE FREE!
SMASH YOUR CHAINS!
THEN SMASH YOUR ENEMIES!
HUYAAAH!
GASH!
BASH 'EM, PICKNOSE! WE'RE RIGHT BEHIND YOU!
ARCHERS--!
--KEEP TO THE LEDGES! AIM FOR THE TROLLS WITH HELMETS — TRY NOT TO HIT TOO MANY OF THE OTHERS!
WHACK!
HHHSSS..!
GOT YOURSELF CAUGHT UNH DIDN'T YOU, PICKY?
WHAT DO YOU KNOW ABOUT IT, FILCH?
I KNOW YOU COULDN'T FORGET TWO EDGE'S TREASURE! WENT LOOKING FOR IT EVEN WITHOUT THE KEY, HAH? WHERE'S ODDBIT?
SHE'S STILL MINE, ELF, AND SO IS THE GOLD! WHEN I GET OUT OF HERE I --!
GAAAAH!
WHA--?
KEEP YOUR MIND ON THE FIGHT, PICKY! TIME ENOUGH TO THINK OF GOLD LATER!

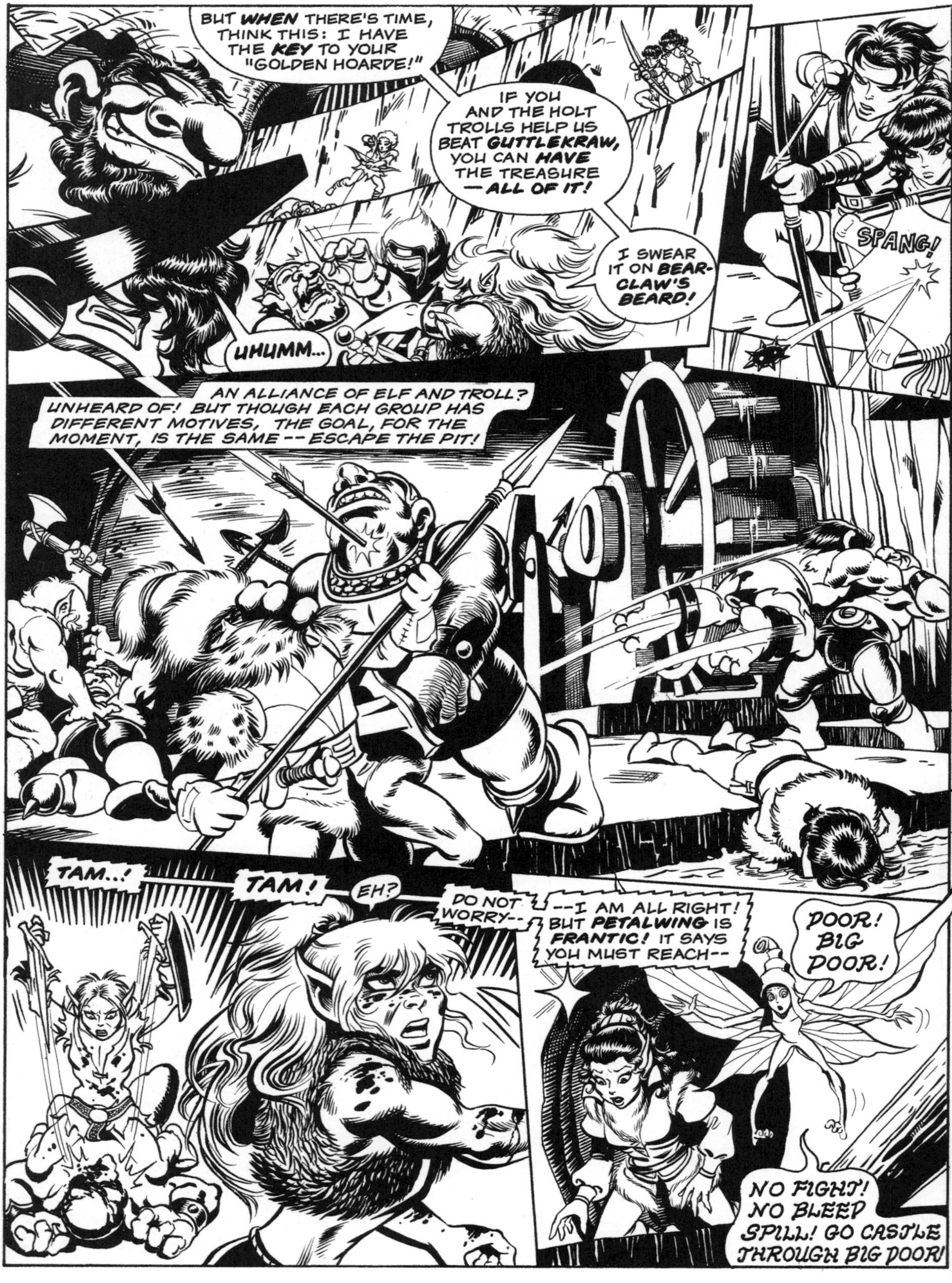

BUT WHEN THERE'S TIME, THINK THIS: I HAVE THE KEY TO YOUR "GOLDEN HOARDE!"
IF YOU AND THE HOLT TROLLS HELP US BEAT GUTTLEKRAW, YOU CAN HAVE THE TREASURE —ALL OF IT!
I SWEAR IT ON BEARCLAW'S BEARD!
UHUMM...
SPANG!
AN ALLIANCE OF ELF AND TROLL? UNHEARD OF! BUT THOUGH EACH GROUP HAS DIFFERENT MOTIVES, THE GOAL, FOR THE MOMENT, IS THE SAME -- ESCAPE THE PIT!
TAM...!
TAM!
EH?
DO NOT WORRY--
--I AM ALL RIGHT! BUT PETALWING IS FRANTIC! IT SAYS YOU MUST REACH--
DOOR! BIG DOOR!
NO FIGHT! NO BLEED SPILL! GO CASTLE THROUGH BIG DOOR!

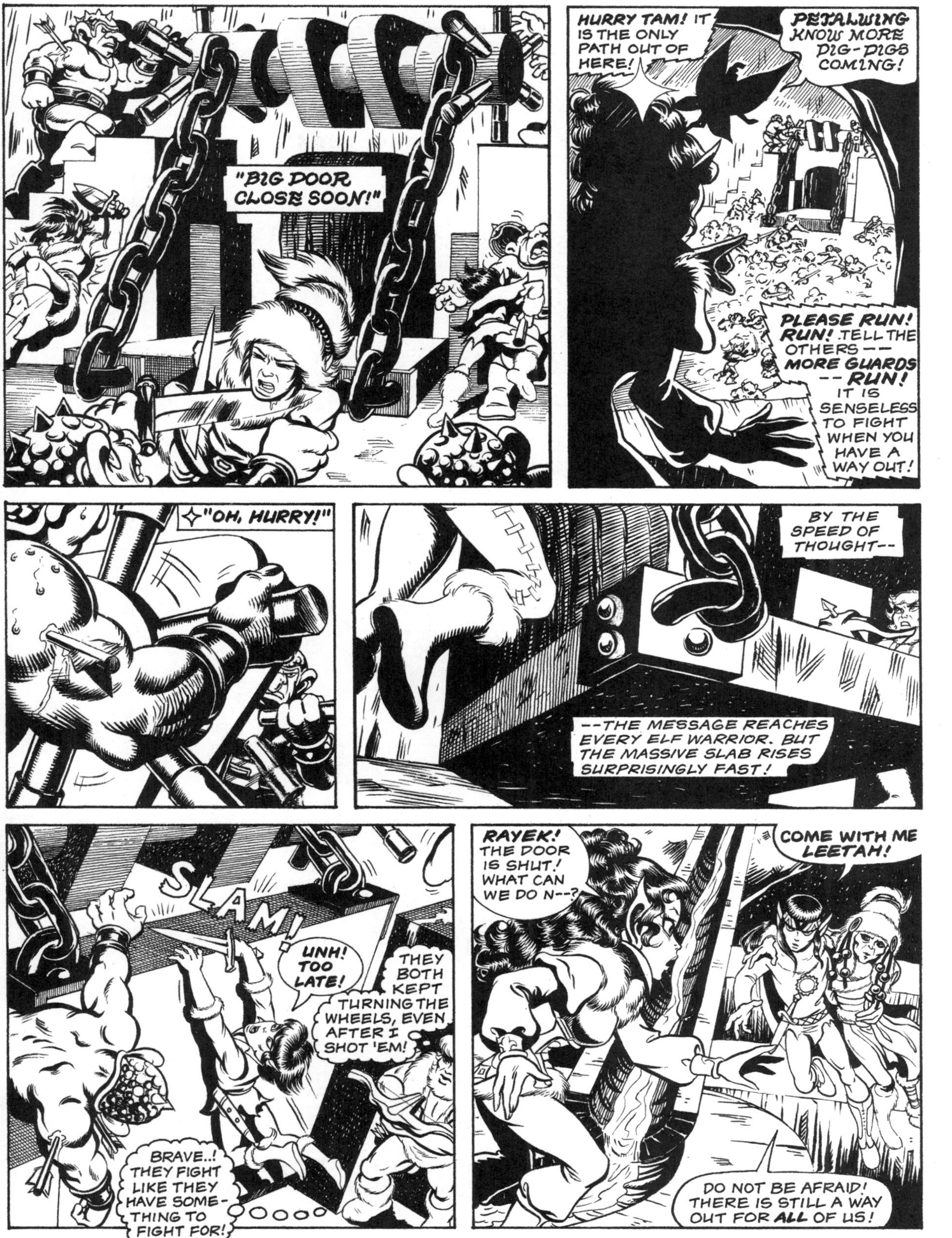
"BIG DOOR CLOSE SOON!"
HURRY TAM! IT IS THE ONLY PATH OUT OF HERE!
PETALWING KNOW MORE DIG-DIGS COMING!
PLEASE RUN! RUN! TELL THE OTHERS -- MORE GUARDS -- RUN! IT IS SENSELESS TO FIGHT WHEN YOU HAVE A WAY OUT!
"OH, HURRY!"
BY THE SPEED OF THOUGHT--
--THE MESSAGE REACHES EVERY ELF WARRIOR. BUT THE MASSIVE SLAB RISES SURPRISINGLY FAST!
SLAM!
UNH! TOO LATE!
THEY BOTH KEPT TURNING THE WHEELS, EVEN AFTER I SHOT 'EM!
BRAVE..! THEY FIGHT LIKE THEY HAVE SOME-THING TO FIGHT FOR!
RAYEK! THE DOOR IS SHUT! WHAT CAN WE DO N--?
COME WITH ME LEETAH!
DO NOT BE AFRAID! THERE IS STILL A WAY OUT FOR ALL OF US!

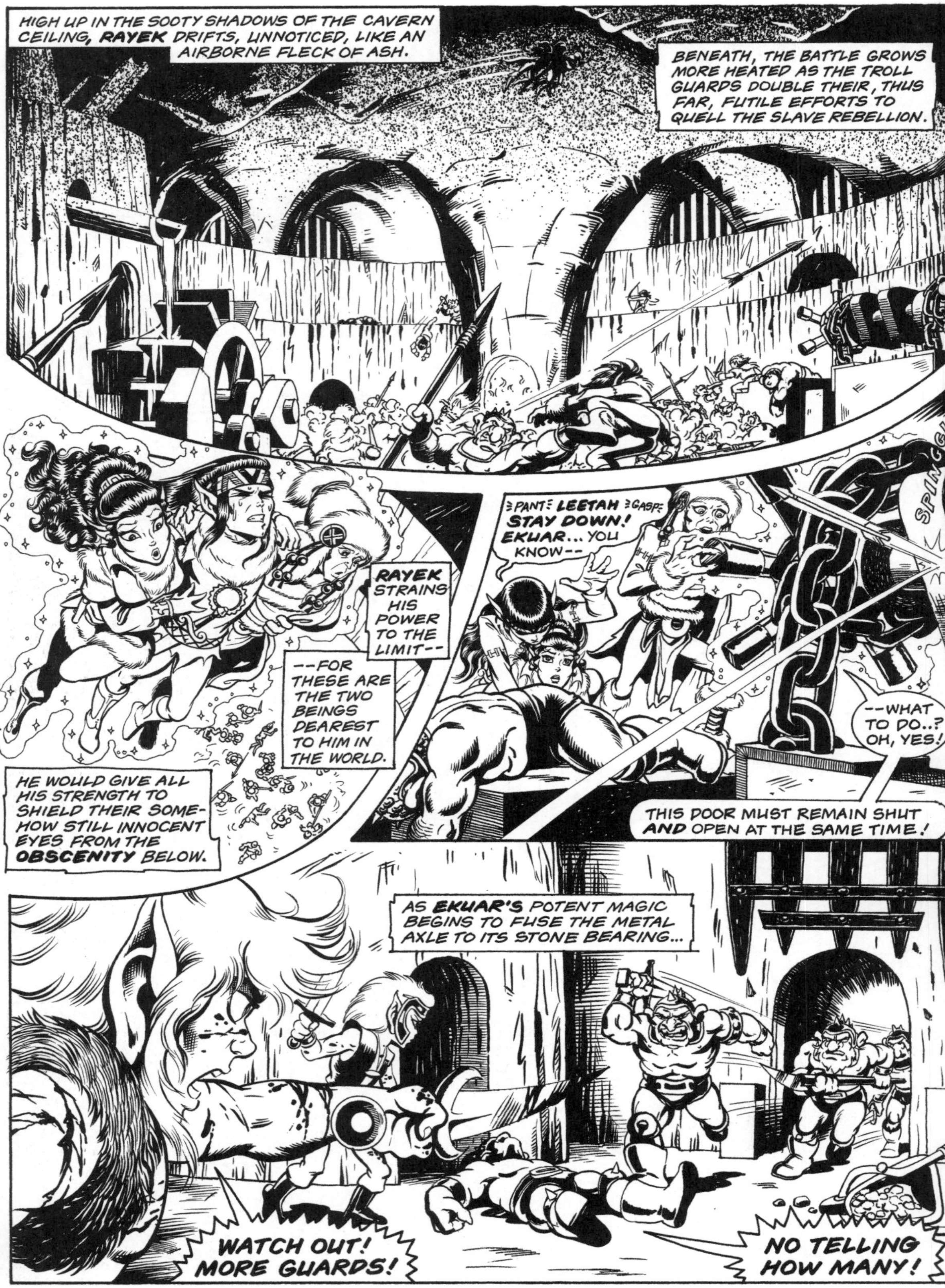
HIGH UP IN THE SOOTY SHADOWS OF THE CAVERN CEILING, RAYEK DRIFTS, UNNOTICED, LIKE AN AIRBORNE FLECK OF ASH.
BENEATH, THE BATTLE GROWS MORE HEATED AS THE TROLL GUARDS DOUBLE THEIR, THUS FAR, FUTILE EFFORTS TO QUELL THE SLAVE REBELLION.
RAYEK STRAINS HIS POWER TO THE LIMIT--
--FOR THESE ARE THE TWO BEINGS DEAREST TO HIM IN THE WORLD.
HE WOULD GIVE ALL HIS STRENGTH TO SHIELD THEIR SOMEHOW STILL INNOCENT EYES FROM THE OBSCENITY BELOW.
PANT LEETAH GASP STAY DOWN! EKUAR... YOU KNOW--
SPINGG!
--WHAT TO DO..? OH, YES!
THIS DOOR MUST REMAIN SHUT AND OPEN AT THE SAME TIME!
AS EKUAR'S POTENT MAGIC BEGINS TO FUSE THE METAL AXLE TO ITS STONE BEARING...
WATCH OUT! MORE GUARDS!
NO TELLING HOW MANY!

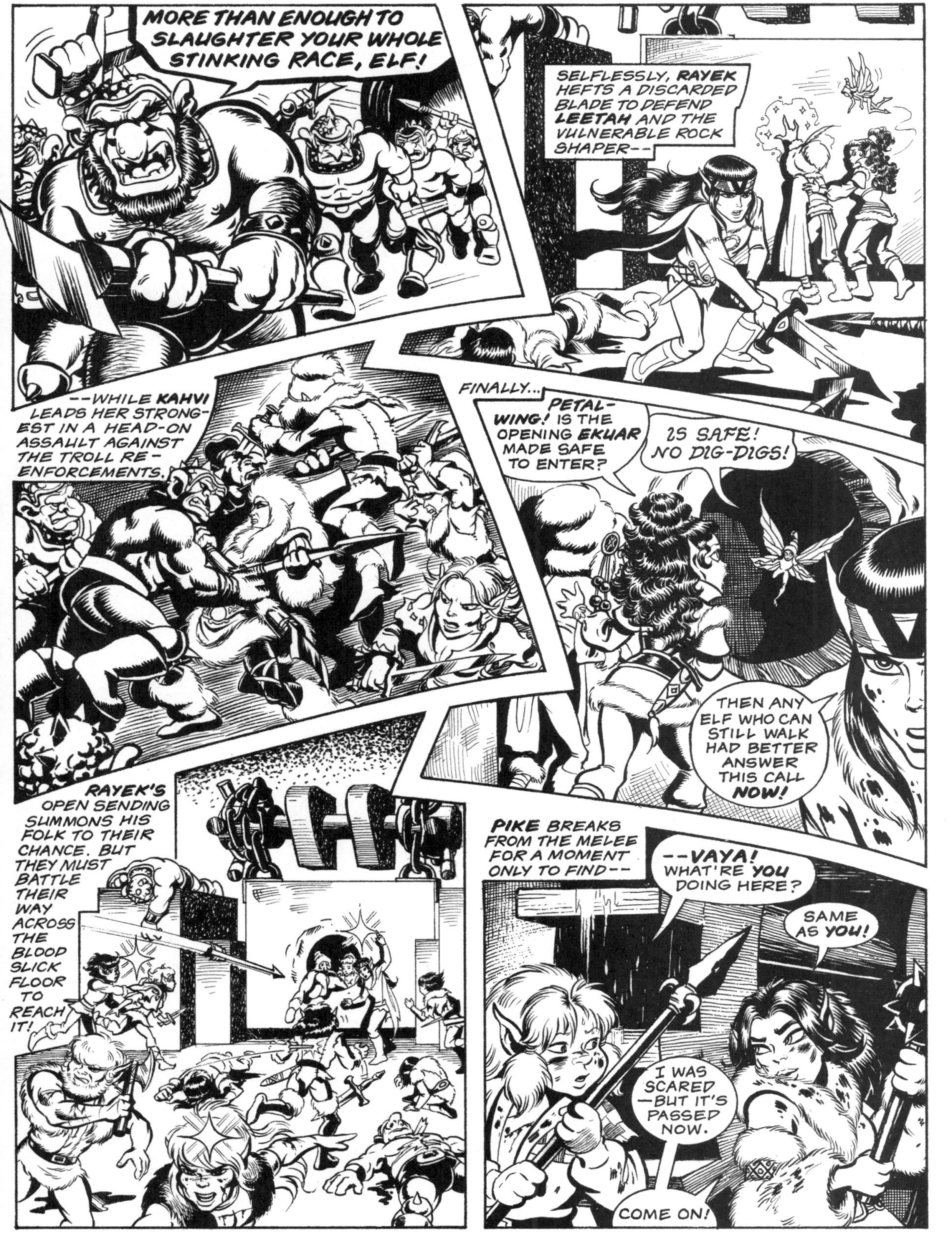
MORE THAN ENOUGH TO SLAUGHTER YOUR WHOLE STINKING RACE, ELF!
SELFLESSLY, RAYEK HEFTS A DISCARDED BLADE TO DEFEND LEETAH AND THE VULNERABLE ROCK SHAPER--
--WHILE KAHVI LEADS HER STRONGEST IN A HEAD-ON ASSAULT AGAINST THE TROLL RE-ENFORCEMENTS.
FINALLY...
PETALWING! IS THE OPENING EKUAR MADE SAFE TO ENTER?
IS SAFE! NO DIG-DIGS!
THEN ANY ELF WHO CAN STILL WALK HAD BETTER ANSWER THIS CALL NOW!
RAYEK'S OPEN SENDING SUMMONS HIS FOLK TO THEIR CHANCE. BUT THEY MUST BATTLE THEIR WAY ACROSS THE BLOOD SLICK FLOOR TO REACH IT!
PIKE BREAKS FROM THE MELEE FOR A MOMENT ONLY TO FIND--
--VAYA! WHAT'RE YOU DOING HERE?
SAME AS YOU!
I WAS SCARED —BUT IT'S PASSED NOW.
COME ON!

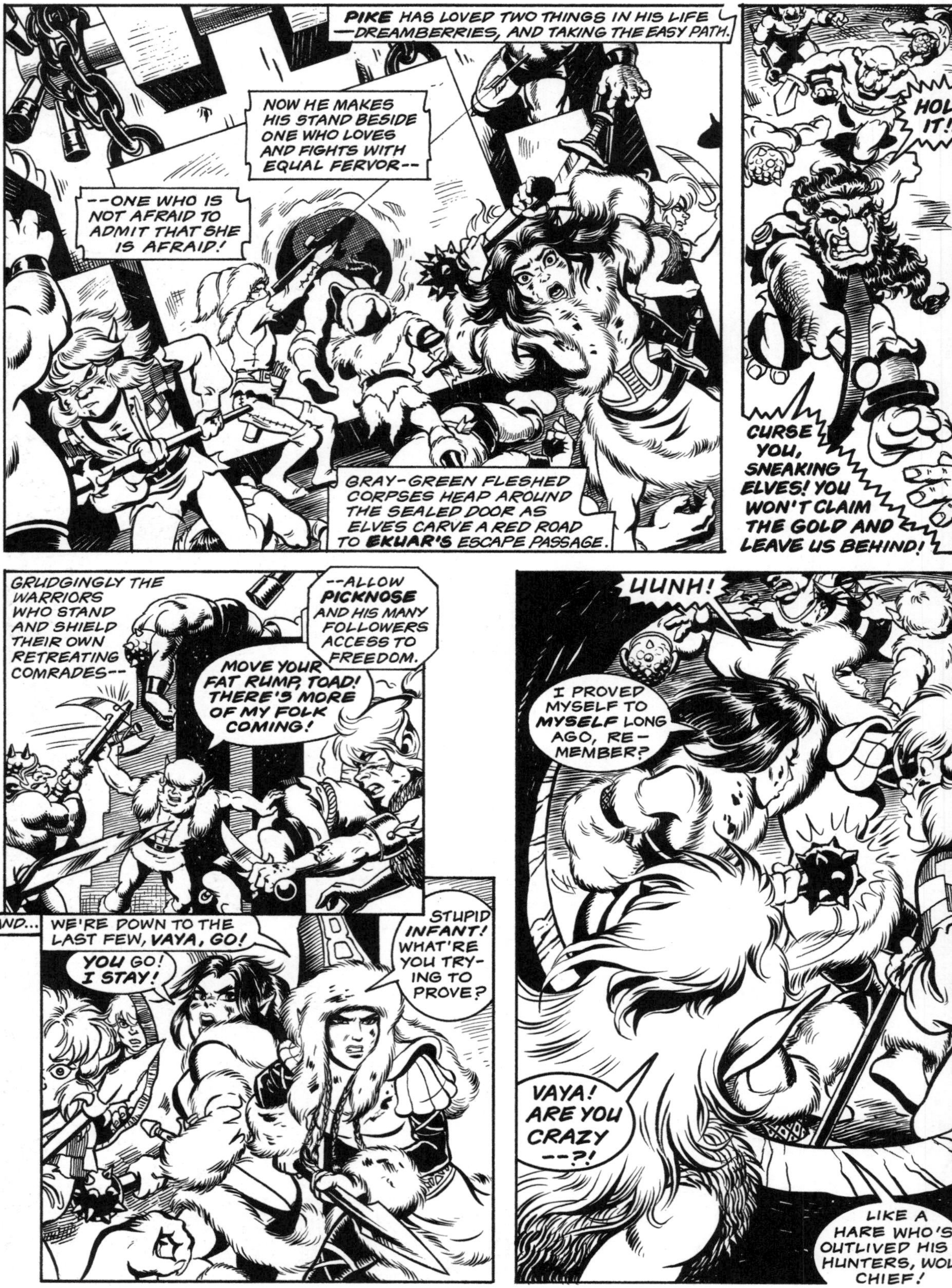
PIKE HAS LOVED TWO THINGS IN HIS LIFE —DREAMBERRIES, AND TAKING THE EASY PATH.
NOW HE MAKES HIS STAND BESIDE ONE WHO LOVES AND FIGHTS WITH EQUAL FERVOR--
--ONE WHO IS NOT AFRAID TO ADMIT THAT SHE IS AFRAID!
GRAY-GREEN FLESHED CORPSES HEAP AROUND THE SEALED DOOR AS ELVES CARVE A RED ROAD TO EKUAR'S ESCAPE PASSAGE.
HOLD IT!!
CURSE YOU, SNEAKING ELVES! YOU WON'T CLAIM THE GOLD AND LEAVE US BEHIND!
GRUDGINGLY THE WARRIORS WHO STAND AND SHIELD THEIR OWN RETREATING COMRADES--
--ALLOW PICKNOSE AND HIS MANY FOLLOWERS ACCESS TO FREEDOM.
MOVE YOUR FAT RUMP, TOAD! THERE'S MORE OF MY FOLK COMING!
AND...
WE'RE DOWN TO THE LAST FEW, VAYA, GO!
YOU GO! I STAY!
STUPID INFANT! WHAT'RE YOU TRY-ING TO PROVE?
UUNH!
I PROVED MYSELF TO MYSELF LONG AGO, RE-MEMBER?
VAYA! ARE YOU CRAZY --?!
LIKE A HARE WHO'S OUTLIVED HIS HUNTERS, WOLF CHIEF!

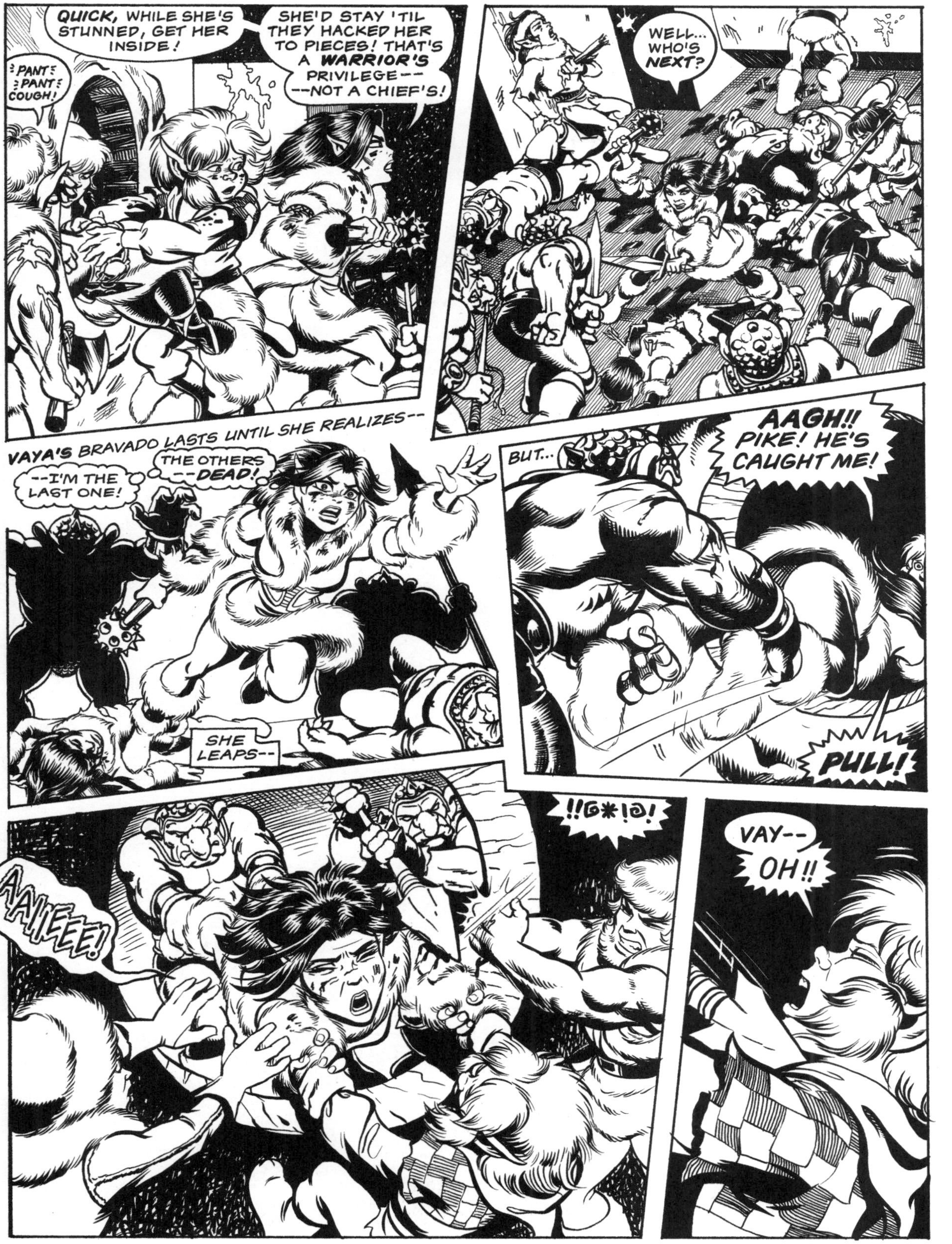
QUICK, WHILE SHE'S STUNNED, GET HER INSIDE!
PANT PANT COUGH!
SHE'D STAY 'TIL THEY HACKED HER TO PIECES! THAT'S A WARRIOR'S PRIVILEGE-- --NOT A CHIEF'S!
WELL... WHO'S NEXT?
VAYA'S BRAVADO LASTS UNTIL SHE REALIZES--
THE OTHERS --DEAD!
--I'M THE LAST ONE!
SHE LEAPS--
BUT...
AAGH!! PIKE! HE'S CAUGHT ME!
PULL!
AAIIEEE!
!!@*!@!
VAY-- OH!!

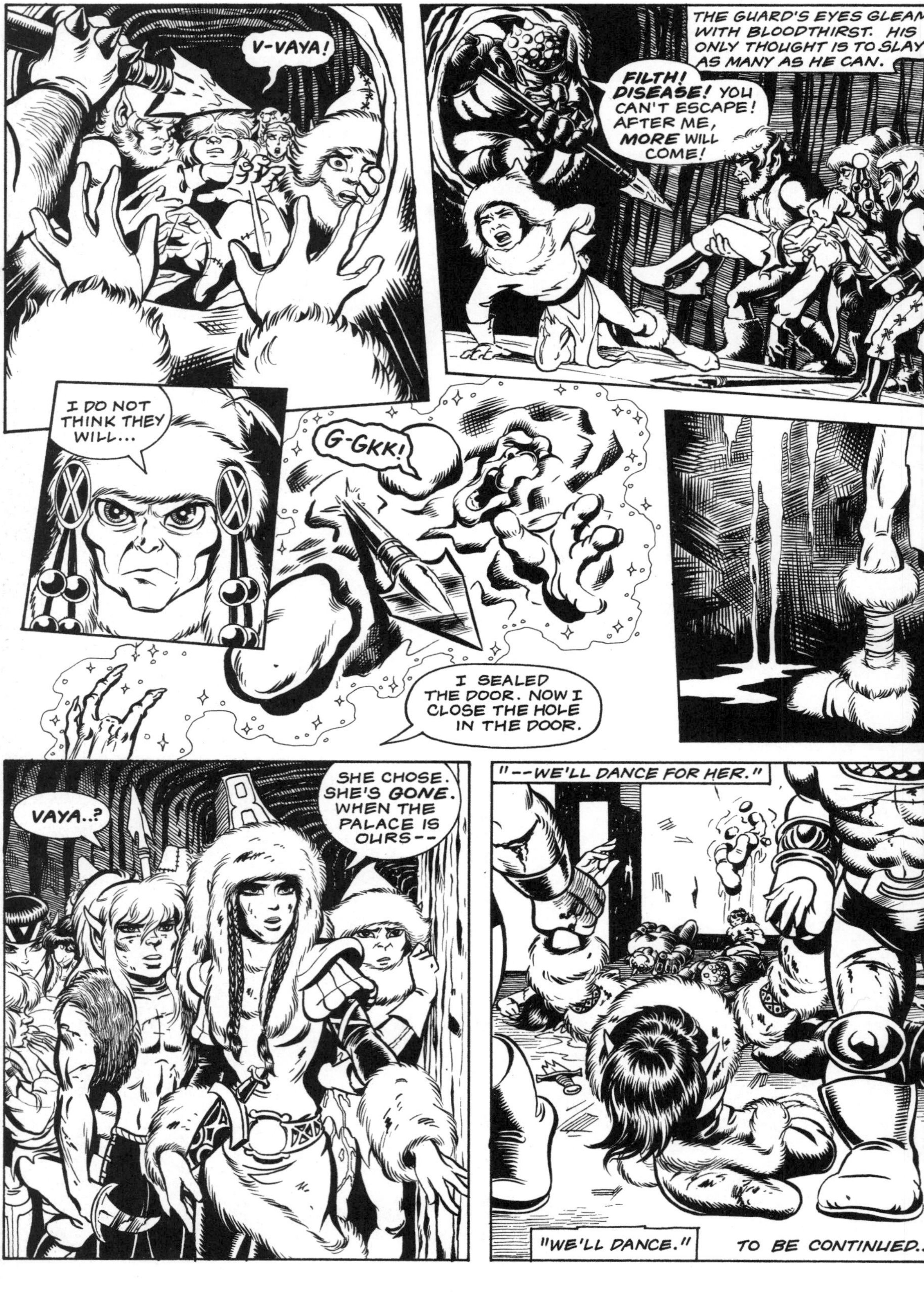
V-VAYA!
THE GUARD'S EYES GLEAM WITH BLOODTHIRST. HIS ONLY THOUGHT IS TO SLAY AS MANY AS HE CAN.
FILTH! DISEASE! YOU CAN'T ESCAPE! AFTER ME, MORE WILL COME!
I DO NOT THINK THEY WILL...
G-GKK!
I SEALED THE DOOR. NOW I CLOSE THE HOLE IN THE DOOR.
VAYA..?
SHE CHOSE. SHE'S GONE. WHEN THE PALACE IS OURS--
"--WE'LL DANCE FOR HER."
"WE'LL DANCE."
TO BE CONTINUED...

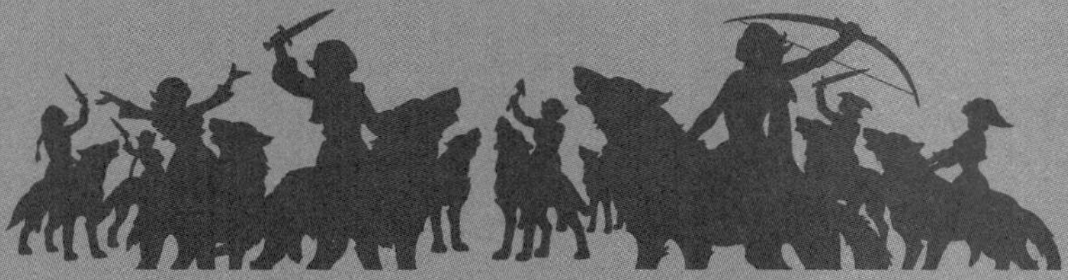

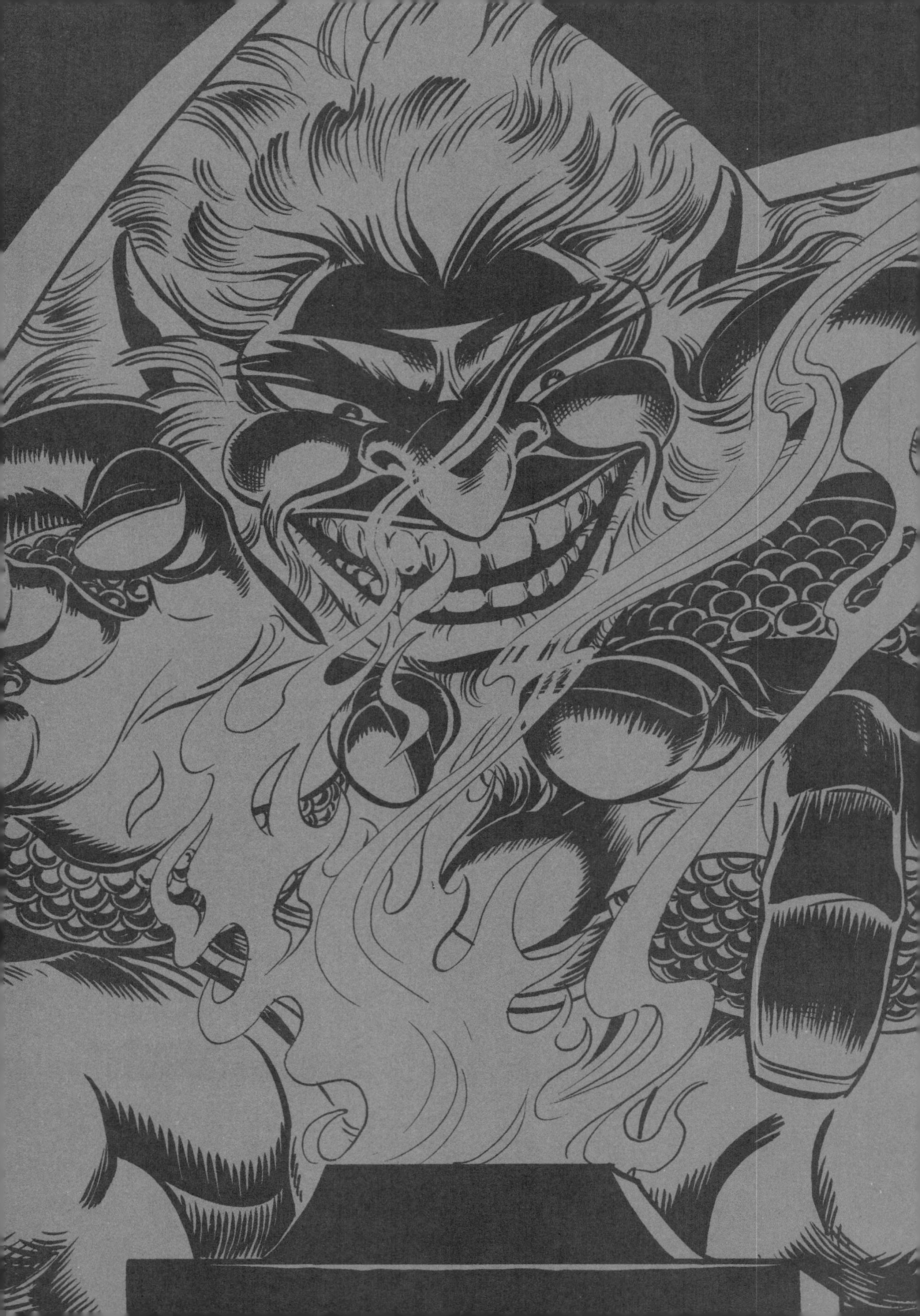

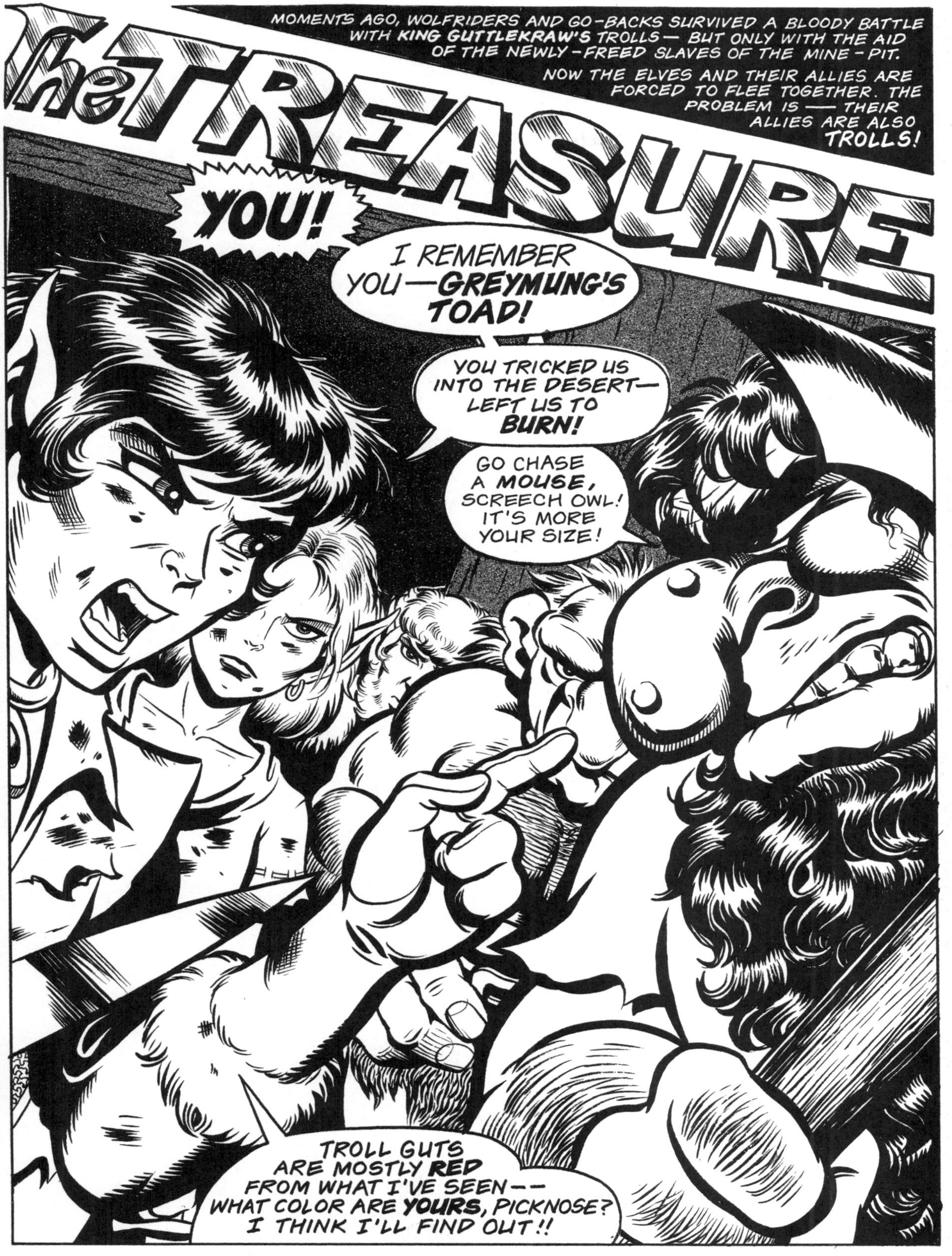
The TREASURE
MOMENTS AGO, WOLFRIDERS AND GO-BACKS SURVIVED A BLOODY BATTLE WITH KING GUTTLEKRAW'S TROLLS— BUT ONLY WITH THE AID OF THE NEWLY-FREED SLAVES OF THE MINE-PIT.
NOW THE ELVES AND THEIR ALLIES ARE FORCED TO FLEE TOGETHER. THE PROBLEM IS —— THEIR ALLIES ARE ALSO TROLLS!
YOU!
I REMEMBER YOU—GREYMUNG'S TOAD!
YOU TRICKED US INTO THE DESERT— LEFT US TO BURN!
GO CHASE A MOUSE, SCREECH OWL! IT'S MORE YOUR SIZE!
TROLL GUTS ARE MOSTLY RED FROM WHAT I'VE SEEN-- WHAT COLOR ARE YOURS, PICKNOSE? I THINK I'LL FIND OUT!!

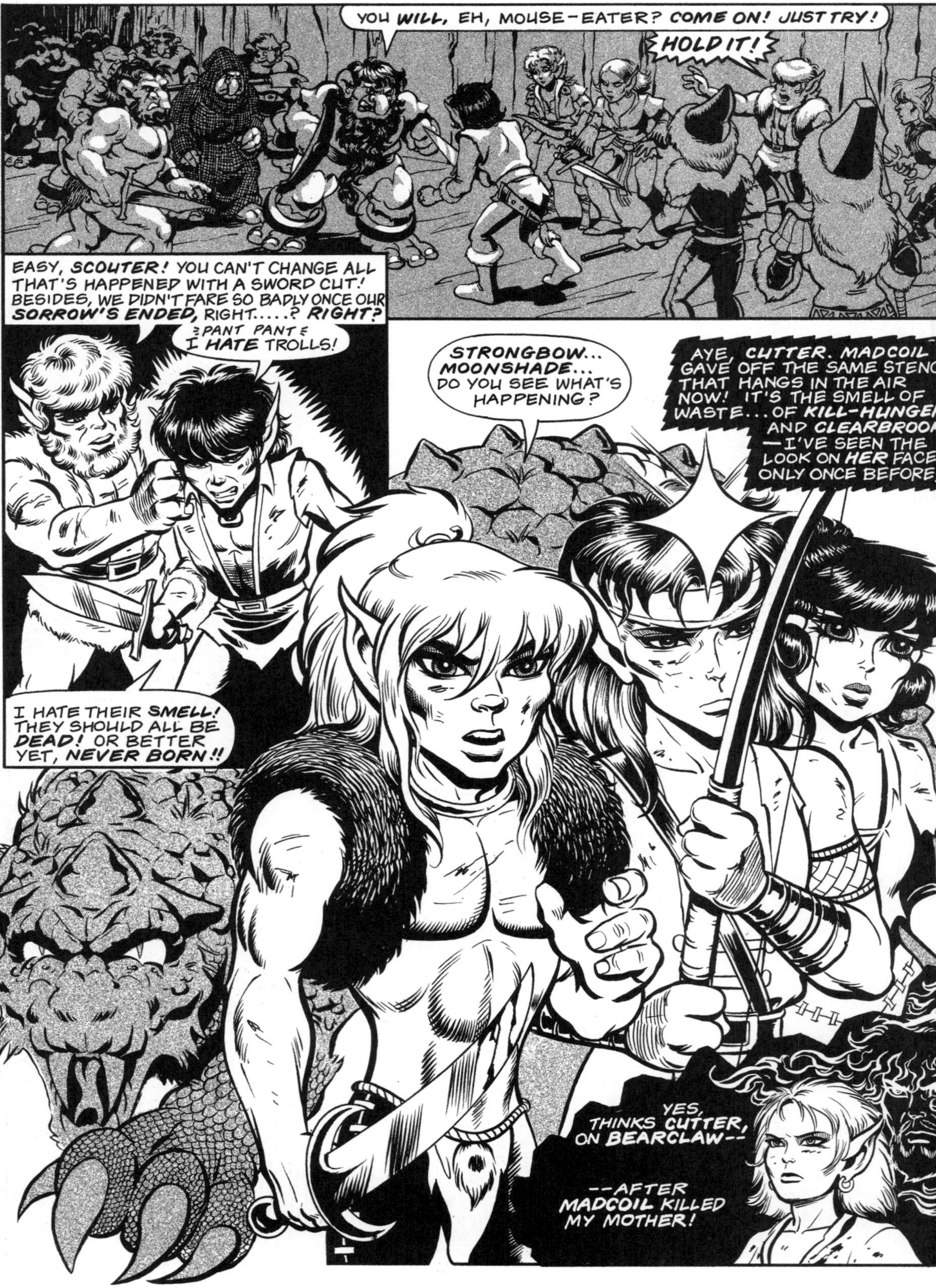

YOU WILL, EH, MOUSE-EATER? COME ON! JUST TRY!
HOLD IT!
EASY, SCOUTER! YOU CAN'T CHANGE ALL THAT'S HAPPENED WITH A SWORD CUT! BESIDES, WE DIDN'T FARE SO BADLY ONCE OUR SORROW'S ENDED, RIGHT.....? RIGHT?
PANT PANT I HATE TROLLS!
I HATE THEIR SMELL! THEY SHOULD ALL BE DEAD! OR BETTER YET, NEVER BORN!!
STRONGBOW... MOONSHADE... DO YOU SEE WHAT'S HAPPENING?
AYE, CUTTER. MADCOIL GAVE OFF THE SAME STENCH THAT HANGS IN THE AIR NOW! IT'S THE SMELL OF WASTE... OF KILL-HUNGER! AND CLEARBROOK —I'VE SEEN THE LOOK ON HER FACE ONLY ONCE BEFORE!
YES, THINKS CUTTER, ON BEARCLAW--
--AFTER MADCOIL KILLED MY MOTHER!

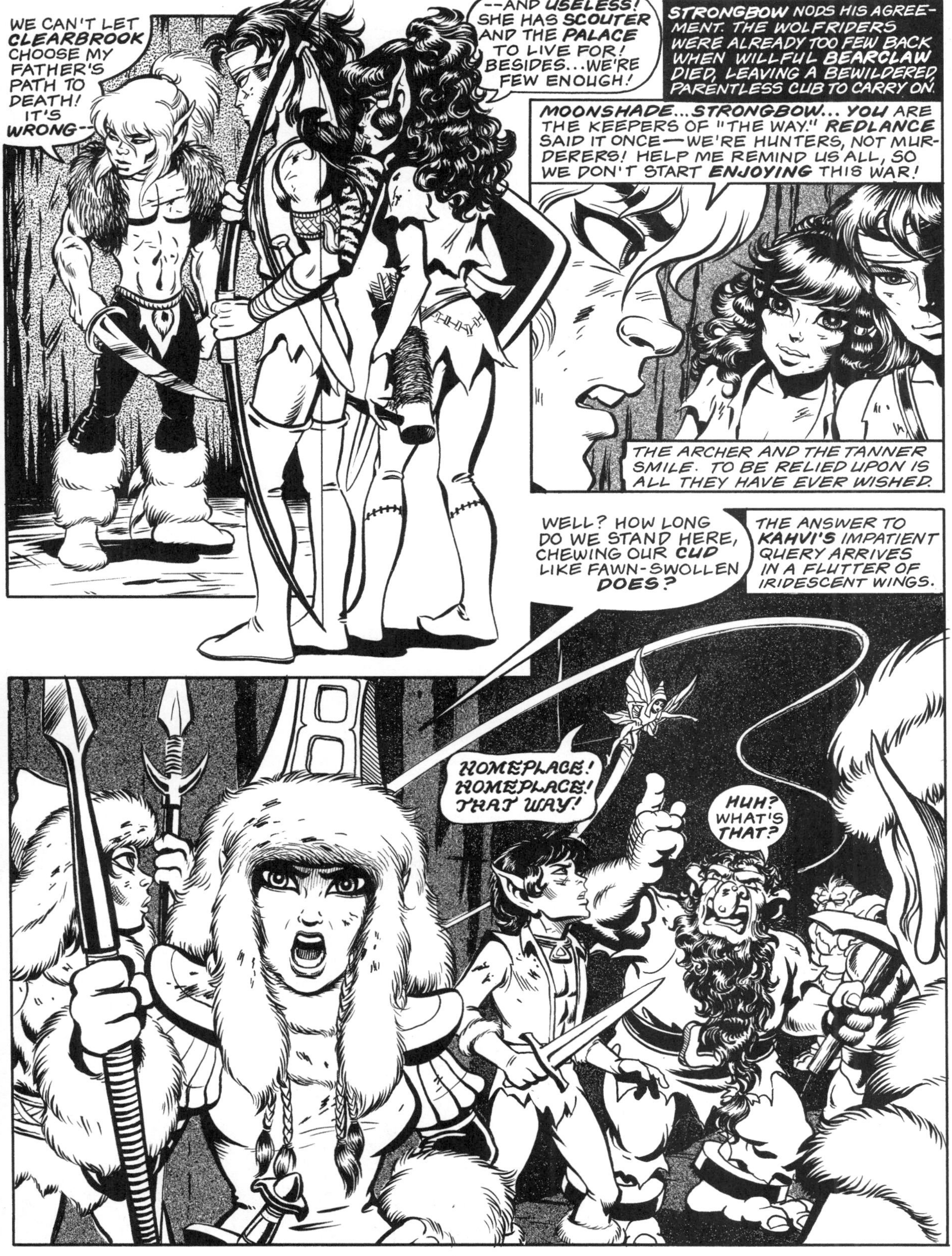
WE CAN'T LET CLEARBROOK CHOOSE MY FATHER'S PATH TO DEATH! IT'S WRONG--
--AND USELESS! SHE HAS SCOUTER AND THE PALACE TO LIVE FOR! BESIDES...WE'RE FEW ENOUGH!
STRONGBOW NODS HIS AGREEMENT. THE WOLFRIDERS WERE ALREADY TOO FEW BACK WHEN WILLFUL BEARCLAW DIED, LEAVING A BEWILDERED, PARENTLESS CUB TO CARRY ON.
MOONSHADE...STRONGBOW...YOU ARE THE KEEPERS OF "THE WAY." REDLANCE SAID IT ONCE—WE'RE HUNTERS, NOT MURDERERS! HELP ME REMIND US ALL, SO WE DON'T START ENJOYING THIS WAR!
THE ARCHER AND THE TANNER SMILE. TO BE RELIED UPON IS ALL THEY HAVE EVER WISHED.
WELL? HOW LONG DO WE STAND HERE, CHEWING OUR CUD LIKE FAWN-SWOLLEN DOES?
THE ANSWER TO KAHVI'S IMPATIENT QUERY ARRIVES IN A FLUTTER OF IRIDESCENT WINGS.
HOMEPLACE! HOMEPLACE! THAT WAY!
HUH? WHAT'S THAT?

GO WAY! NO LIKE NASTYBAD PIG DIGS!

TAKE ONLY SOFT-PRETTY *HIGHTHINGS* TO CASTLE!

PICKNOSE'S EYES GLEAM LIKE CHIPS OF FLINT. HE TWIRLS HIS PICKAXE, WHOSE CURVED BUSINESS END BOTH HIS NOSE AND HIS NAME REFLECT.

SoooOooo... GUTTLEKRAW WAS *RIGHT!*

THE POINT-EARS *ARE* OUT TO CLAIM THAT ROTTING RELIC OF THEIR FANCY ANCESTORS!

HA HA HHAHA! I HAVE TO HAND IT TO YOU ELVES FOR GETTING *THIS* FAR! TOO BAD *GUTTLEKRAW'S* READY FOR YOU! BEATS ME HOW THE OLD STINKWIND KNEW YOU WERE COMING--

--BUT HE'S HAD SLAVES WORKING TO SHIELD THE CASTLE EVER SINCE HE TOPPLED *GREYMUNG!*

LAUGH, MUCK-MOUTH!

BUT IF YOUR HEART'S WITH *GUTTLEKRAW* IN SPITE OF ALL HE'S DONE TO YOU, YOU CAN SAY *FARE WELL* TO *TWO-EDGE'S* HIDDEN TREASURE!

=SPUTTER= YOU SWORE AN *OATH*--

--IN GOOD FAITH! STICK TO *YOUR* PART OF THE BARGAIN — BE OUR ALLIES— AND I'LL STICK TO *MINE!* 'TIL THEN, *I'LL* KEEP THE KEY!

DON'T *DROOL*, DEARIE, JUST BIDE YOUR TIME! *BEARCLAW'S* BRAT WILL END UP *SLICED* THROUGH HIS SKINNY MIDDLE, AND THE KEY WILL FALL FROM HIS DEAD FINGERS INTO YOUR WAITING HANDS!

LET THE LITTLE WOLF MONGRELS TRY FOR THE CASTLE. WITH *OUR* AID, THEY MIGHT VERY WELL *WIN*. BUT EVEN *THAT* WILL POSE NO THREAT TO US.

AFTER ALL...THEY'RE NOT *REAL* ELVES... ARE THEY.

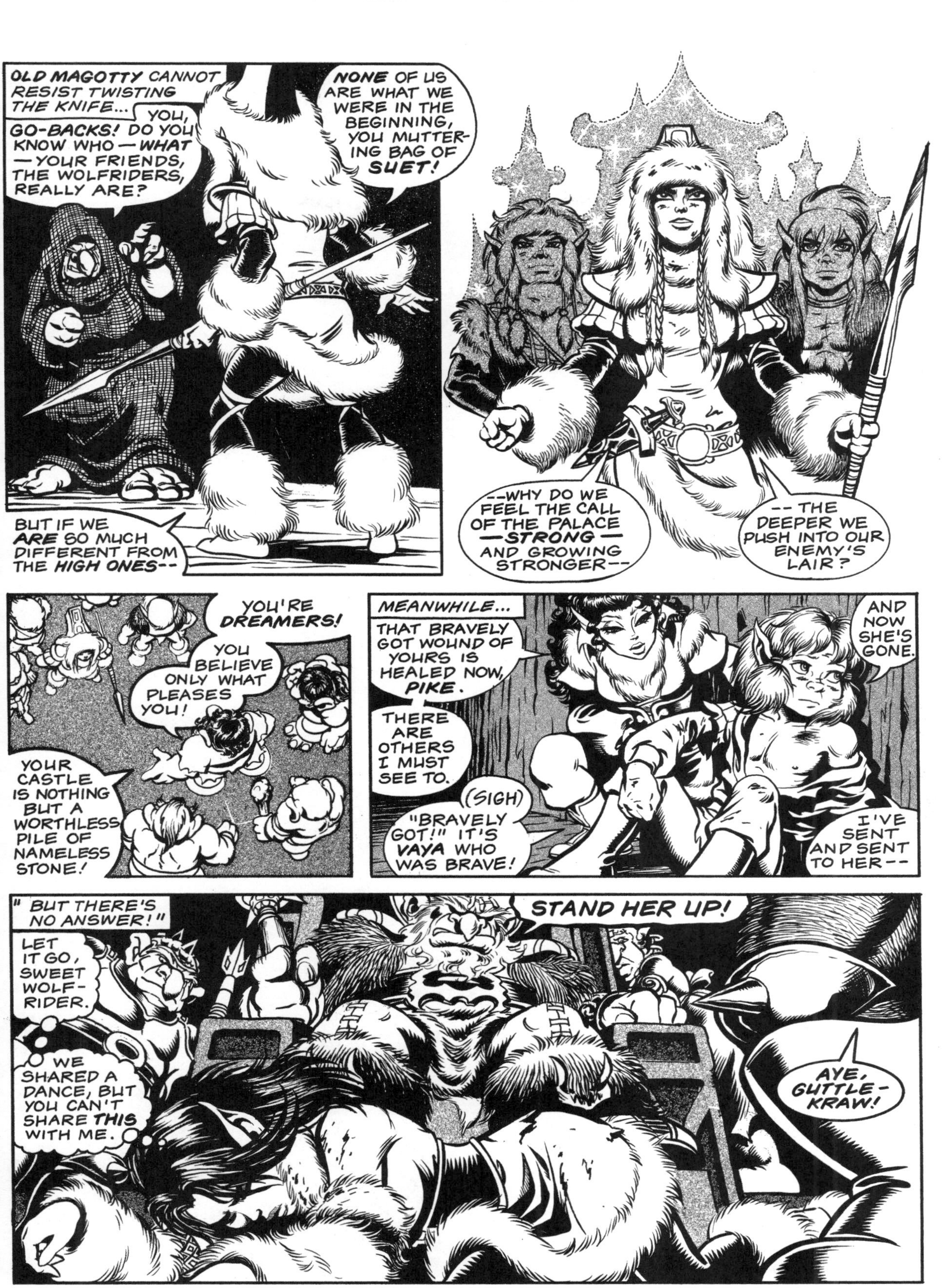
OLD MAGOTTY CANNOT RESIST TWISTING THE KNIFE...
YOU, GO-BACKS! DO YOU KNOW WHO—WHAT—YOUR FRIENDS, THE WOLFRIDERS, REALLY ARE?
NONE OF US ARE WHAT WE WERE IN THE BEGINNING, YOU MUTTERING BAG OF SUET!
BUT IF WE ARE SO MUCH DIFFERENT FROM THE HIGH ONES--
--WHY DO WE FEEL THE CALL OF THE PALACE—STRONG—AND GROWING STRONGER--
-- THE DEEPER WE PUSH INTO OUR ENEMY'S LAIR?
YOU'RE DREAMERS!
YOU BELIEVE ONLY WHAT PLEASES YOU!
YOUR CASTLE IS NOTHING BUT A WORTHLESS PILE OF NAMELESS STONE!
MEANWHILE...
THAT BRAVELY GOT WOUND OF YOURS IS HEALED NOW, PIKE.
THERE ARE OTHERS I MUST SEE TO.
(SIGH)
"BRAVELY GOT!" IT'S VAYA WHO WAS BRAVE!
AND NOW SHE'S GONE.
I'VE SENT AND SENT TO HER--
" BUT THERE'S NO ANSWER!"
LET IT GO, SWEET WOLF-RIDER.
WE SHARED A DANCE, BUT YOU CAN'T SHARE THIS WITH ME.
STAND HER UP!
AYE, GUTTLE-KRAW!

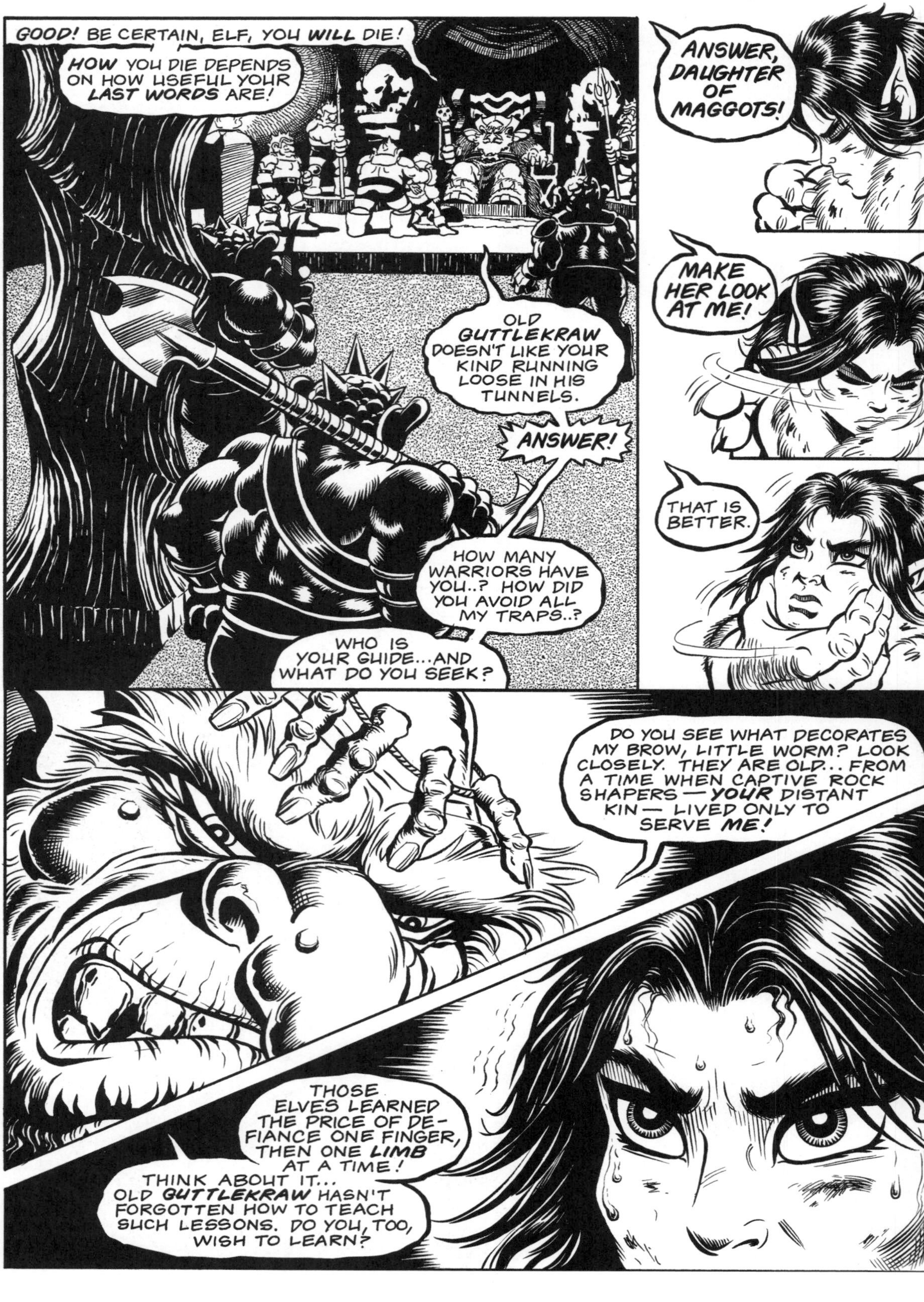

GOOD! BE CERTAIN, ELF, YOU WILL DIE!
HOW YOU DIE DEPENDS ON HOW USEFUL YOUR LAST WORDS ARE!
OLD GUTTLEKRAW DOESN'T LIKE YOUR KIND RUNNING LOOSE IN HIS TUNNELS.
ANSWER!
HOW MANY WARRIORS HAVE YOU..? HOW DID YOU AVOID ALL MY TRAPS..?
WHO IS YOUR GUIDE...AND WHAT DO YOU SEEK?
ANSWER, DAUGHTER OF MAGGOTS!
MAKE HER LOOK AT ME!
THAT IS BETTER.
DO YOU SEE WHAT DECORATES MY BROW, LITTLE WORM? LOOK CLOSELY. THEY ARE OLD... FROM A TIME WHEN CAPTIVE ROCK SHAPERS — YOUR DISTANT KIN — LIVED ONLY TO SERVE ME!
THOSE ELVES LEARNED THE PRICE OF DEFIANCE ONE FINGER, THEN ONE LIMB AT A TIME!
THINK ABOUT IT... OLD GUTTLEKRAW HASN'T FORGOTTEN HOW TO TEACH SUCH LESSONS. DO YOU, TOO, WISH TO LEARN?

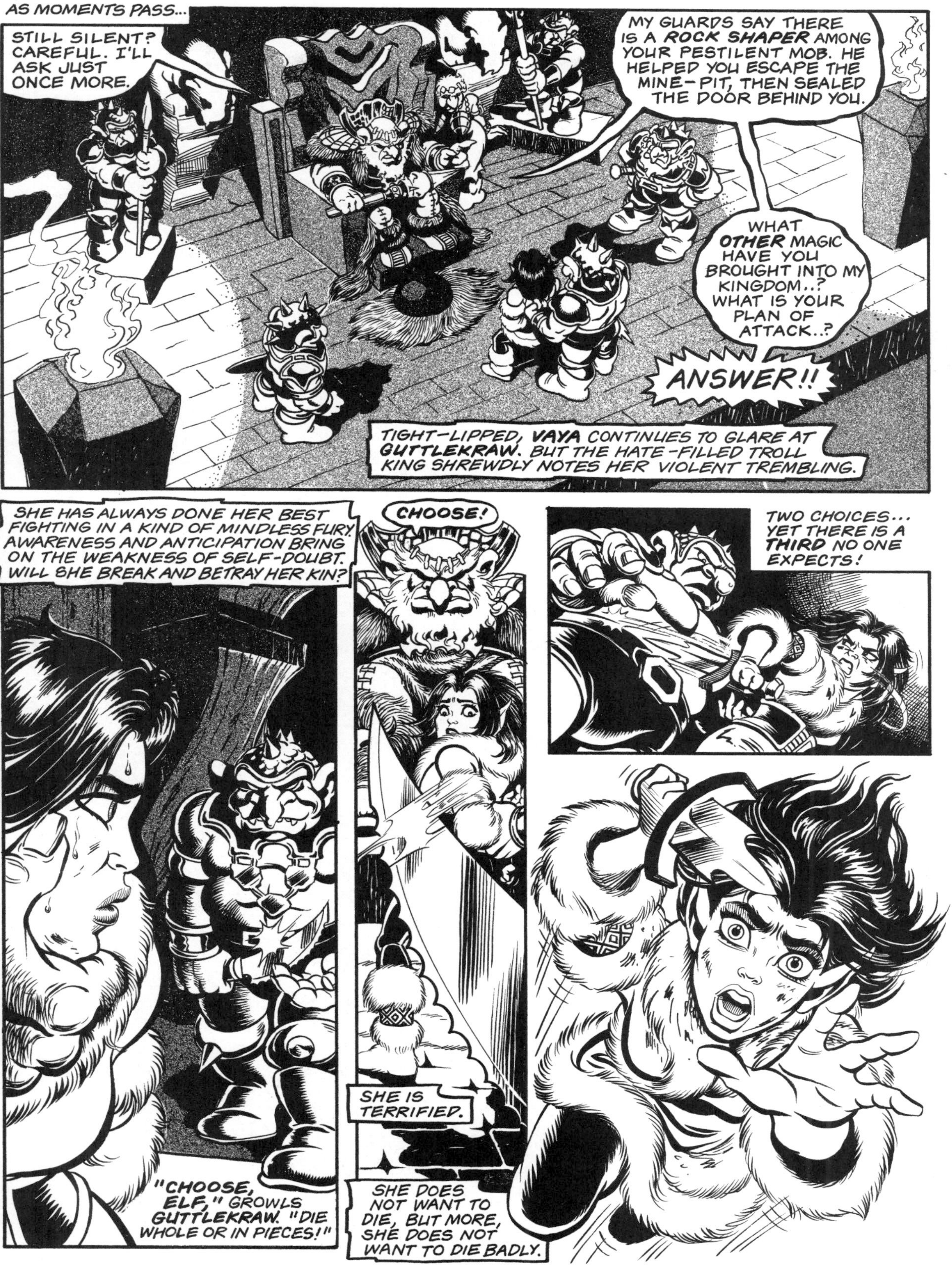
AS MOMENTS PASS...
STILL SILENT? CAREFUL. I'LL ASK JUST ONCE MORE.
MY GUARDS SAY THERE IS A ROCK SHAPER AMONG YOUR PESTILENT MOB. HE HELPED YOU ESCAPE THE MINE-PIT, THEN SEALED THE DOOR BEHIND YOU.
WHAT OTHER MAGIC HAVE YOU BROUGHT INTO MY KINGDOM..? WHAT IS YOUR PLAN OF ATTACK..?
ANSWER!!
TIGHT-LIPPED, VAYA CONTINUES TO GLARE AT GUTTLEKRAW. BUT THE HATE-FILLED TROLL KING SHREWDLY NOTES HER VIOLENT TREMBLING.
SHE HAS ALWAYS DONE HER BEST FIGHTING IN A KIND OF MINDLESS FURY. AWARENESS AND ANTICIPATION BRING ON THE WEAKNESS OF SELF-DOUBT. WILL SHE BREAK AND BETRAY HER KIN?
"CHOOSE, ELF," GROWLS GUTTLEKRAW. "DIE WHOLE OR IN PIECES!"
CHOOSE!
SHE IS TERRIFIED.
SHE DOES NOT WANT TO DIE, BUT MORE, SHE DOES NOT WANT TO DIE BADLY.
TWO CHOICES... YET THERE IS A THIRD NO ONE EXPECTS!

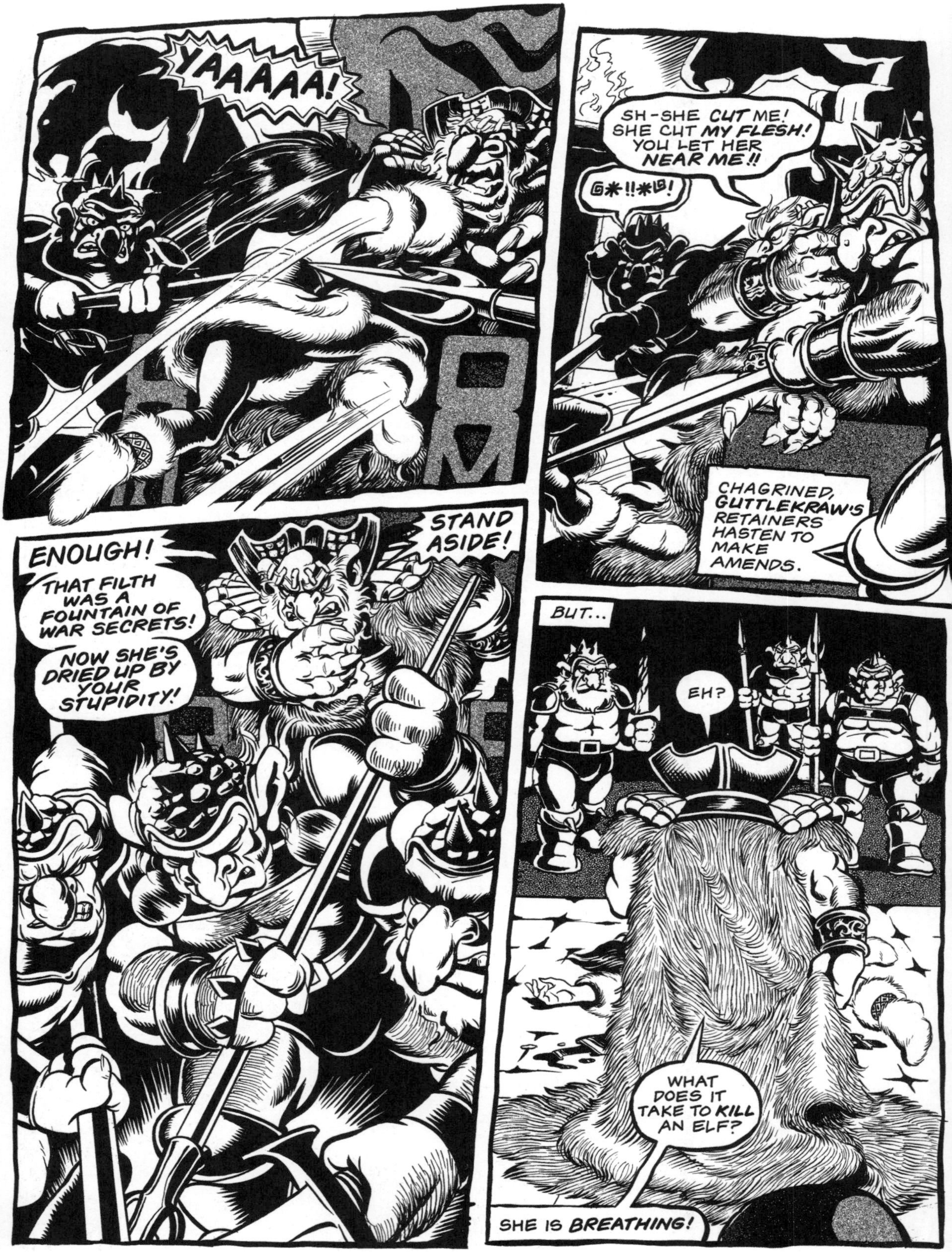

YAAAAA!
SH-SHE CUT ME! SHE CUT MY FLESH! YOU LET HER NEAR ME!!
@✱!!✱@!
CHAGRINED, GUTTLEKRAW'S RETAINERS HASTEN TO MAKE AMENDS.
ENOUGH!
THAT FILTH WAS A FOUNTAIN OF WAR SECRETS!
NOW SHE'S DRIED UP BY YOUR STUPIDITY!
STAND ASIDE!
BUT...
EH?
WHAT DOES IT TAKE TO KILL AN ELF?
SHE IS BREATHING!

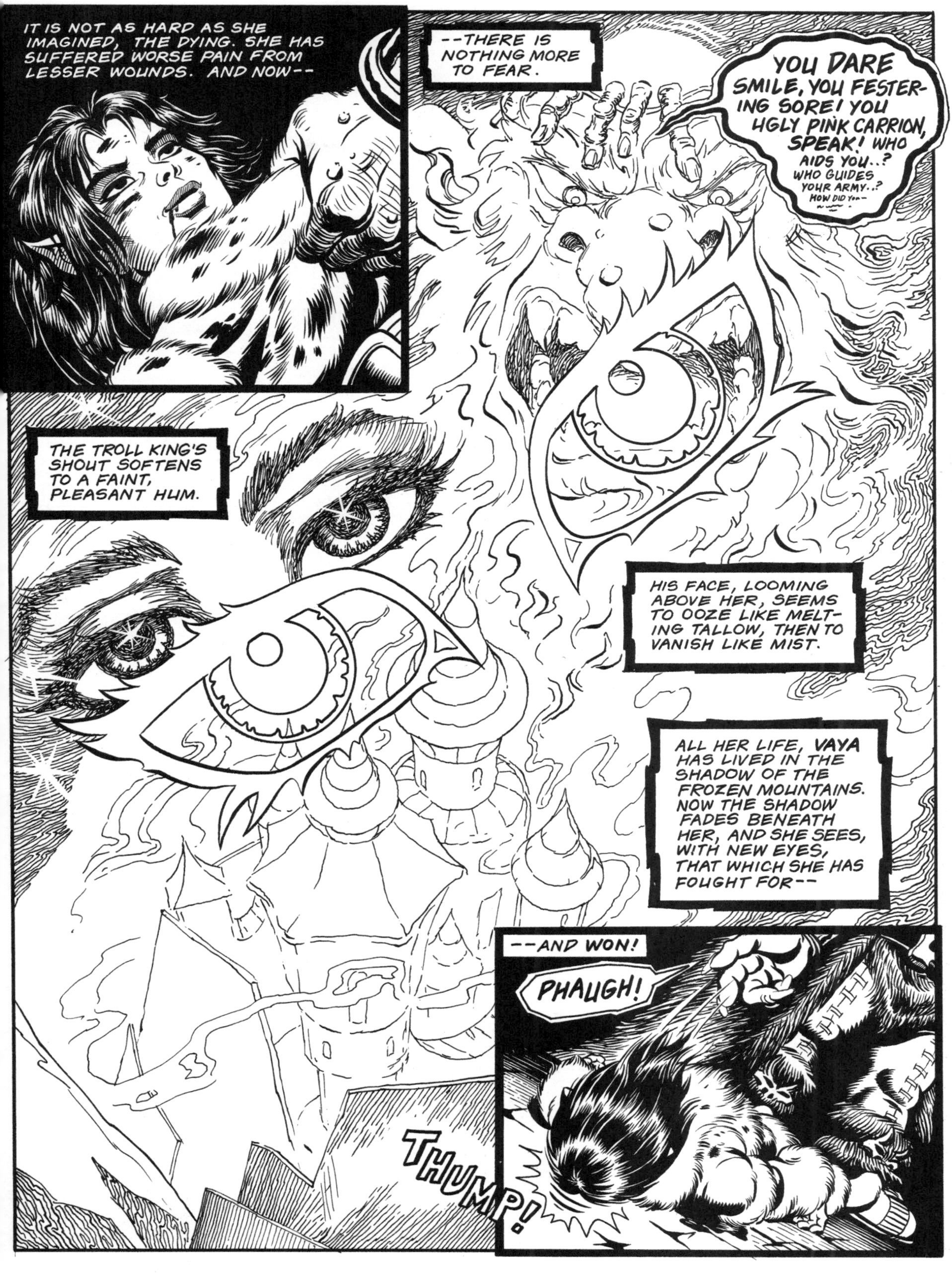
IT IS NOT AS HARD AS SHE IMAGINED, THE DYING. SHE HAS SUFFERED WORSE PAIN FROM LESSER WOUNDS. AND NOW--
--THERE IS NOTHING MORE TO FEAR.
YOU DARE SMILE, YOU FESTERING SORE! YOU UGLY PINK CARRION, SPEAK! WHO AIDS YOU..? WHO GUIDES YOUR ARMY..? HOW DID YOU--
THE TROLL KING'S SHOUT SOFTENS TO A FAINT, PLEASANT HUM.
HIS FACE, LOOMING ABOVE HER, SEEMS TO OOZE LIKE MELTING TALLOW, THEN TO VANISH LIKE MIST.
ALL HER LIFE, VAYA HAS LIVED IN THE SHADOW OF THE FROZEN MOUNTAINS. NOW THE SHADOW FADES BENEATH HER, AND SHE SEES, WITH NEW EYES, THAT WHICH SHE HAS FOUGHT FOR--
--AND WON!
PHAUGH!
THUMP!

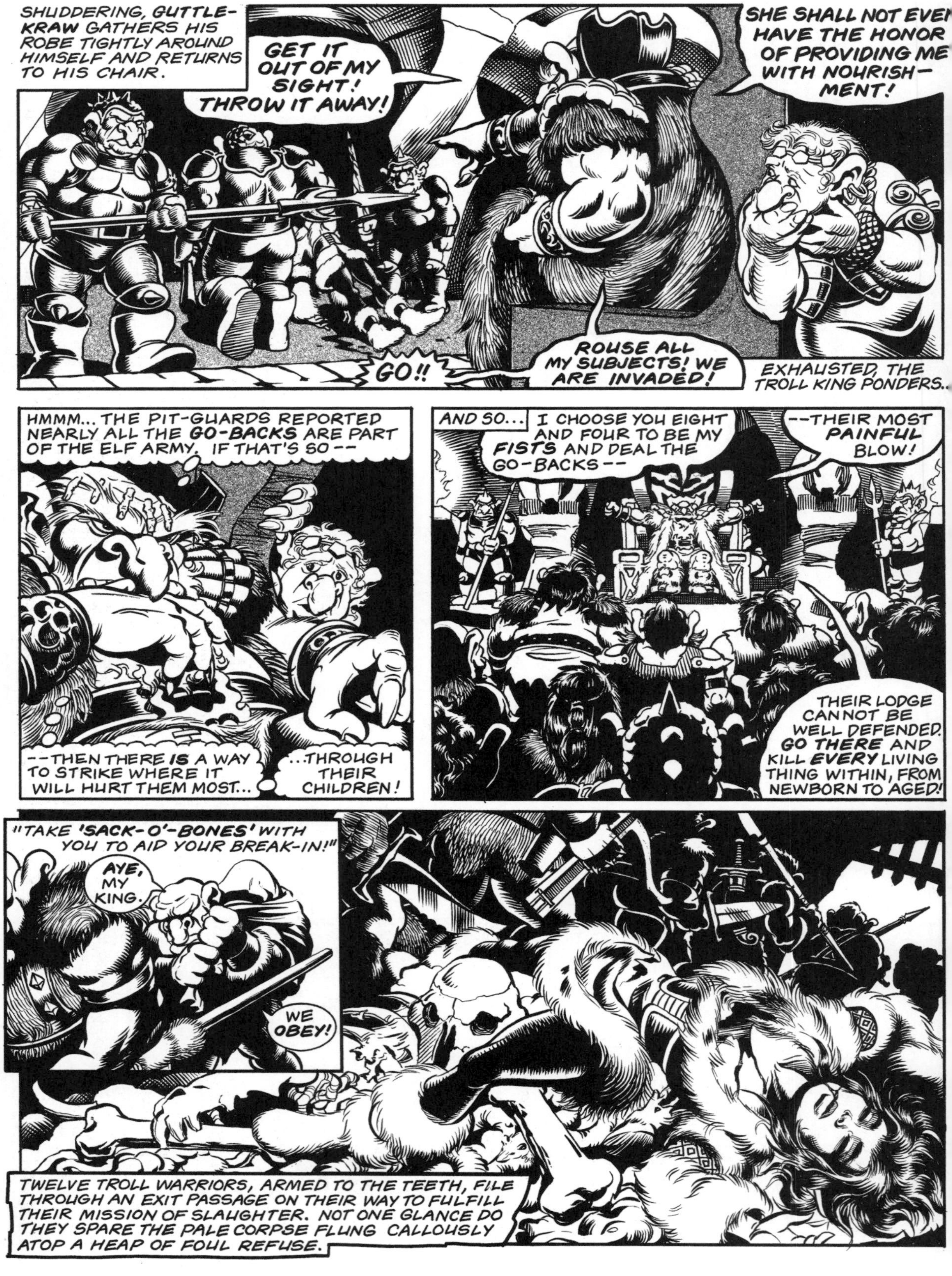

SHUDDERING, GUTTLEKRAW GATHERS HIS ROBE TIGHTLY AROUND HIMSELF AND RETURNS TO HIS CHAIR.
GET IT OUT OF MY SIGHT! THROW IT AWAY!
SHE SHALL NOT EVEN HAVE THE HONOR OF PROVIDING ME WITH NOURISHMENT!
GO!!
ROUSE ALL MY SUBJECTS! WE ARE INVADED!
EXHAUSTED, THE TROLL KING PONDERS..
HMMM... THE PIT-GUARDS REPORTED NEARLY ALL THE GO-BACKS ARE PART OF THE ELF ARMY. IF THAT'S SO --
--THEN THERE IS A WAY TO STRIKE WHERE IT WILL HURT THEM MOST...
...THROUGH THEIR CHILDREN!
AND SO...
I CHOOSE YOU EIGHT AND FOUR TO BE MY FISTS AND DEAL THE GO-BACKS --
--THEIR MOST PAINFUL BLOW!
THEIR LODGE CANNOT BE WELL DEFENDED. GO THERE AND KILL EVERY LIVING THING WITHIN, FROM NEWBORN TO AGED!
"TAKE 'SACK-O'-BONES' WITH YOU TO AID YOUR BREAK-IN!"
AYE, MY KING.
WE OBEY!
TWELVE TROLL WARRIORS, ARMED TO THE TEETH, FILE THROUGH AN EXIT PASSAGE ON THEIR WAY TO FULFILL THEIR MISSION OF SLAUGHTER. NOT ONE GLANCE DO THEY SPARE THE PALE CORPSE FLUNG CALLOUSLY ATOP A HEAP OF FOUL REFUSE.

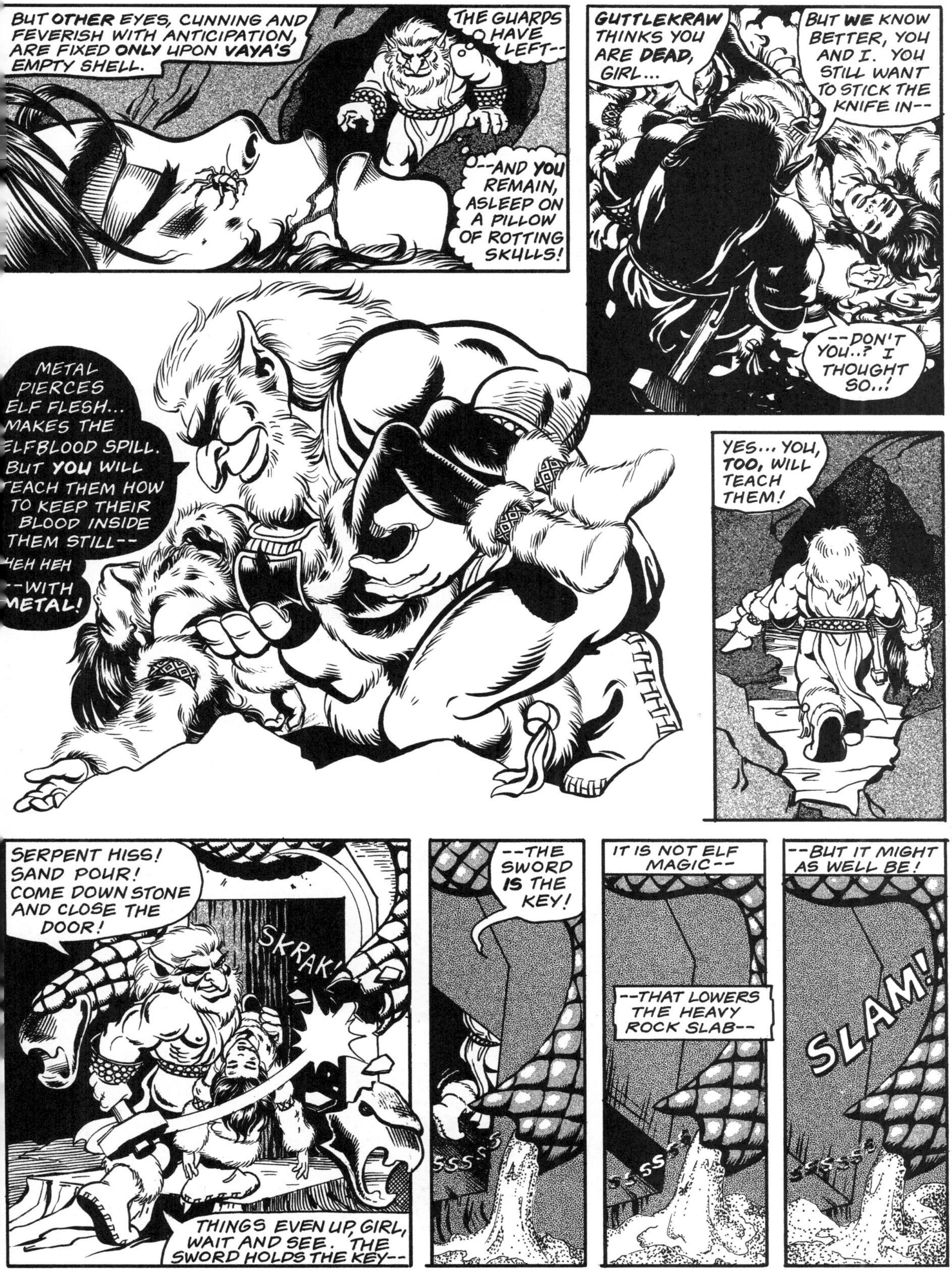
BUT OTHER EYES, CUNNING AND FEVERISH WITH ANTICIPATION, ARE FIXED ONLY UPON VAYA'S EMPTY SHELL.
THE GUARDS HAVE LEFT--
--AND YOU REMAIN, ASLEEP ON A PILLOW OF ROTTING SKULLS!
GUTTLEKRAW THINKS YOU ARE DEAD, GIRL...
BUT WE KNOW BETTER, YOU AND I. YOU STILL WANT TO STICK THE KNIFE IN--
--DON'T YOU..? I THOUGHT SO..!
METAL PIERCES ELF FLESH... MAKES THE ELF BLOOD SPILL. BUT YOU WILL TEACH THEM HOW TO KEEP THEIR BLOOD INSIDE THEM STILL-- HEH HEH --WITH METAL!
YES... YOU, TOO, WILL TEACH THEM!
SERPENT HISS! SAND POUR! COME DOWN STONE AND CLOSE THE DOOR!
SKRAK!
THINGS EVEN UP, GIRL, WAIT AND SEE. THE SWORD HOLDS THE KEY--
--THE SWORD IS THE KEY!
IT IS NOT ELF MAGIC--
--THAT LOWERS THE HEAVY ROCK SLAB--
--BUT IT MIGHT AS WELL BE!
SLAM!

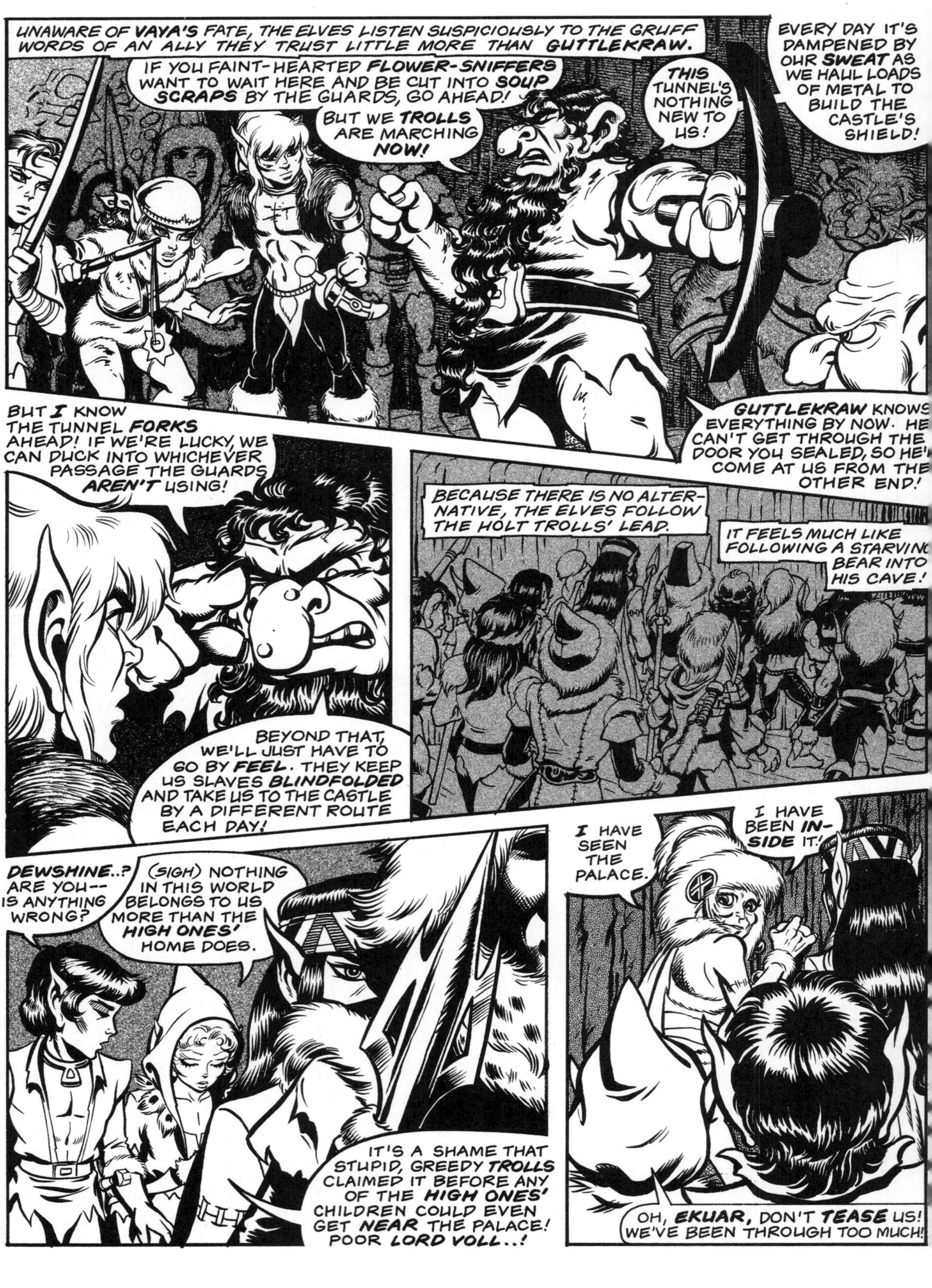

UNAWARE OF VAYA'S FATE, THE ELVES LISTEN SUSPICIOUSLY TO THE GRUFF WORDS OF AN ALLY THEY TRUST LITTLE MORE THAN GUTTLEKRAW.
IF YOU FAINT-HEARTED FLOWER-SNIFFERS WANT TO WAIT HERE AND BE CUT INTO SOUP SCRAPS BY THE GUARDS, GO AHEAD!
BUT WE TROLLS ARE MARCHING NOW!
THIS TUNNEL'S NOTHING NEW TO US!
EVERY DAY IT'S DAMPENED BY OUR SWEAT AS WE HAUL LOADS OF METAL TO BUILD THE CASTLE'S SHIELD!
BUT I KNOW THE TUNNEL FORKS AHEAD! IF WE'RE LUCKY, WE CAN DUCK INTO WHICHEVER PASSAGE THE GUARDS AREN'T USING!
BEYOND THAT, WE'LL JUST HAVE TO GO BY FEEL. THEY KEEP US SLAVES BLINDFOLDED AND TAKE US TO THE CASTLE BY A DIFFERENT ROUTE EACH DAY!
GUTTLEKRAW KNOWS EVERYTHING BY NOW. HE CAN'T GET THROUGH THE DOOR YOU SEALED, SO HE' COME AT US FROM THE OTHER END!
BECAUSE THERE IS NO ALTERNATIVE, THE ELVES FOLLOW THE HOLT TROLLS' LEAD.
IT FEELS MUCH LIKE FOLLOWING A STARVING BEAR INTO HIS CAVE!
DEWSHINE..? ARE YOU-- IS ANYTHING WRONG?
(SIGH) NOTHING IN THIS WORLD BELONGS TO US MORE THAN THE HIGH ONES' HOME DOES.
IT'S A SHAME THAT STUPID, GREEDY TROLLS CLAIMED IT BEFORE ANY OF THE HIGH ONES' CHILDREN COULD EVEN GET NEAR THE PALACE! POOR LORD VOLL..!
I HAVE SEEN THE PALACE.
I HAVE BEEN INSIDE IT!
OH, EKUAR, DON'T TEASE US! WE'VE BEEN THROUGH TOO MUCH!

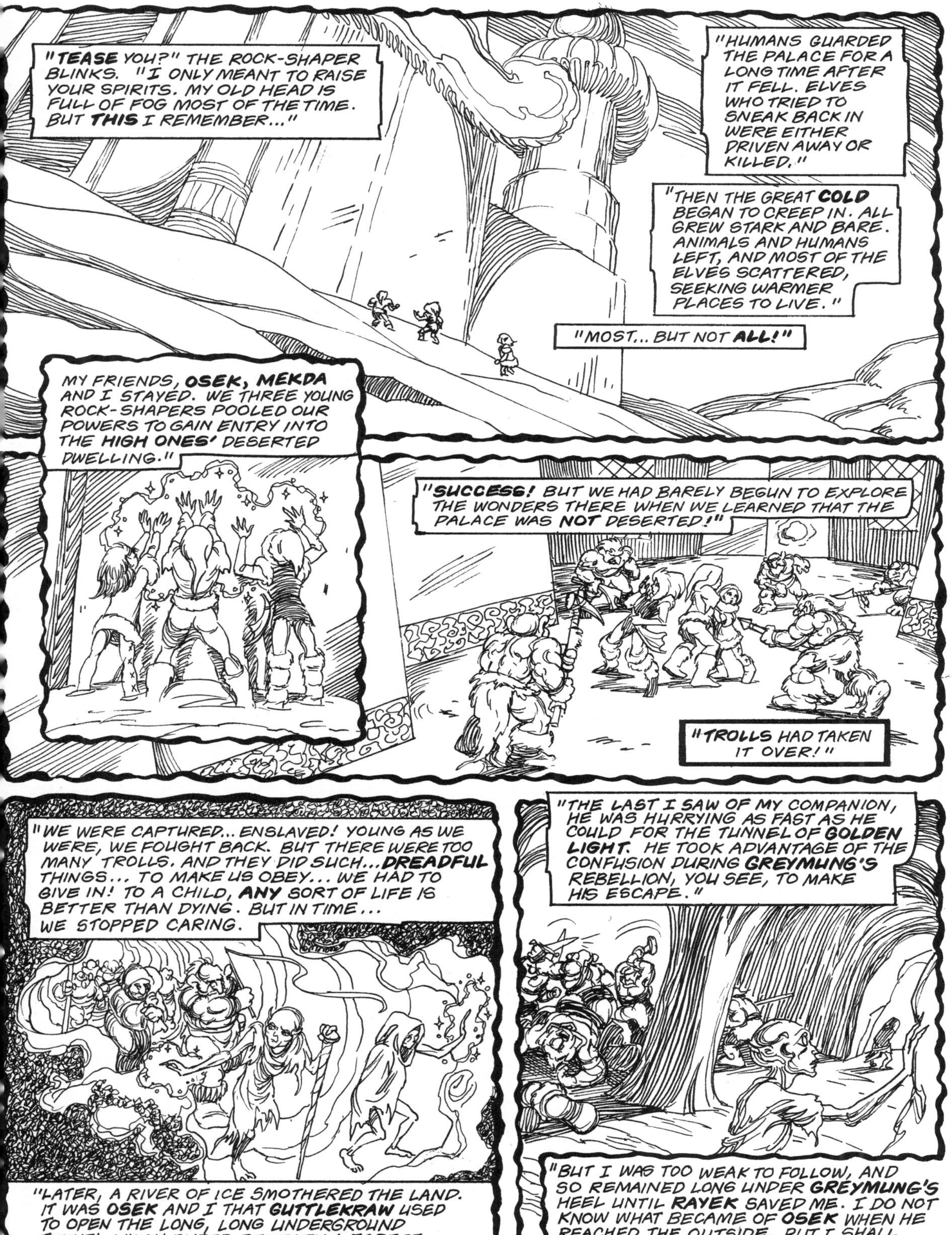
"TEASE YOU?" THE ROCK-SHAPER BLINKS. "I ONLY MEANT TO RAISE YOUR SPIRITS. MY OLD HEAD IS FULL OF FOG MOST OF THE TIME. BUT THIS I REMEMBER..."
"HUMANS GUARDED THE PALACE FOR A LONG TIME AFTER IT FELL. ELVES WHO TRIED TO SNEAK BACK IN WERE EITHER DRIVEN AWAY OR KILLED."
"THEN THE GREAT COLD BEGAN TO CREEP IN. ALL GREW STARK AND BARE. ANIMALS AND HUMANS LEFT, AND MOST OF THE ELVES SCATTERED, SEEKING WARMER PLACES TO LIVE."
"MOST... BUT NOT ALL!"
MY FRIENDS, OSEK, MEKDA AND I STAYED. WE THREE YOUNG ROCK-SHAPERS POOLED OUR POWERS TO GAIN ENTRY INTO THE HIGH ONES' DESERTED DWELLING."
"SUCCESS! BUT WE HAD BARELY BEGUN TO EXPLORE THE WONDERS THERE WHEN WE LEARNED THAT THE PALACE WAS NOT DESERTED!"
"TROLLS HAD TAKEN IT OVER!"
"WE WERE CAPTURED... ENSLAVED! YOUNG AS WE WERE, WE FOUGHT BACK. BUT THERE WERE TOO MANY TROLLS. AND THEY DID SUCH... DREADFUL THINGS... TO MAKE US OBEY... WE HAD TO GIVE IN! TO A CHILD, ANY SORT OF LIFE IS BETTER THAN DYING. BUT IN TIME... WE STOPPED CARING.
"LATER, A RIVER OF ICE SMOTHERED THE LAND. IT WAS OSEK AND I THAT GUTTLEKRAW USED TO OPEN THE LONG, LONG UNDERGROUND TUNNEL WHICH ENDED BENEATH A FOREST -- YOUR HOLT, AS I HAVE LEARNED."
"THE LAST I SAW OF MY COMPANION, HE WAS HURRYING AS FAST AS HE COULD FOR THE TUNNEL OF GOLDEN LIGHT. HE TOOK ADVANTAGE OF THE CONFUSION DURING GREYMUNG'S REBELLION, YOU SEE, TO MAKE HIS ESCAPE."
"BUT I WAS TOO WEAK TO FOLLOW, AND SO REMAINED LONG UNDER GREYMUNG'S HEEL UNTIL RAYEK SAVED ME. I DO NOT KNOW WHAT BECAME OF OSEK WHEN HE REACHED THE OUTSIDE. BUT I SHALL NEVER FORGET THAT WE ONCE STOOD TOGETHER IN THE HALLS OF THE HIGH ONES."

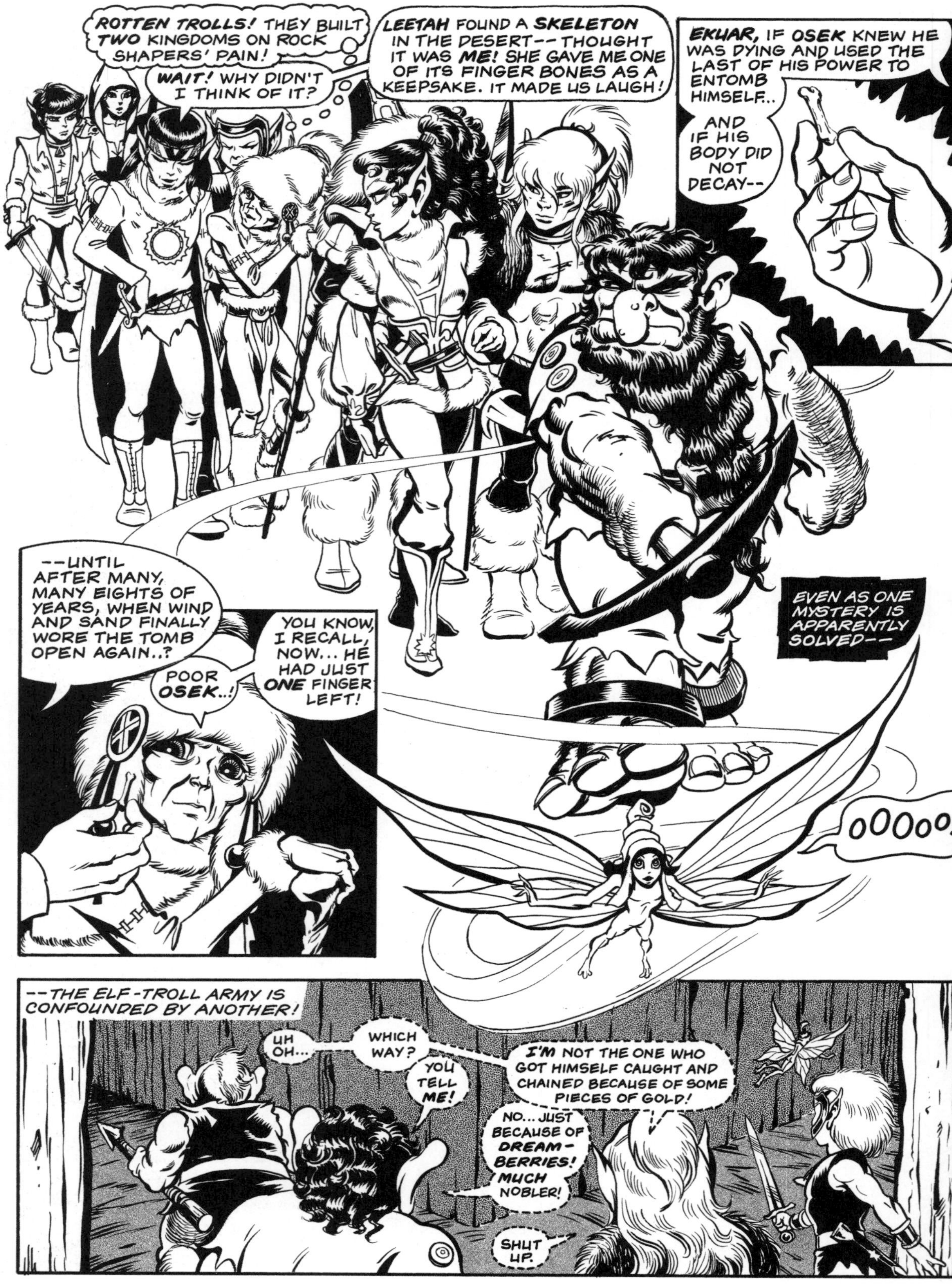
ROTTEN TROLLS! THEY BUILT TWO KINGDOMS ON ROCK SHAPERS' PAIN!
WAIT! WHY DIDN'T I THINK OF IT?
LEETAH FOUND A SKELETON IN THE DESERT--THOUGHT IT WAS ME! SHE GAVE ME ONE OF ITS FINGER BONES AS A KEEPSAKE. IT MADE US LAUGH!
EKUAR, IF OSEK KNEW HE WAS DYING AND USED THE LAST OF HIS POWER TO ENTOMB HIMSELF..
AND IF HIS BODY DID NOT DECAY--
--UNTIL AFTER MANY, MANY EIGHTS OF YEARS, WHEN WIND AND SAND FINALLY WORE THE TOMB OPEN AGAIN..?
POOR OSEK..!
YOU KNOW, I RECALL, NOW... HE HAD JUST ONE FINGER LEFT!
EVEN AS ONE MYSTERY IS APPARENTLY SOLVED--
OOOOO!
--THE ELF-TROLL ARMY IS CONFOUNDED BY ANOTHER!
UH OH...
WHICH WAY?
YOU TELL ME!
I'M NOT THE ONE WHO GOT HIMSELF CAUGHT AND CHAINED BECAUSE OF SOME PIECES OF GOLD!
NO... JUST BECAUSE OF DREAM-BERRIES! MUCH NOBLER!
SHUT UP.

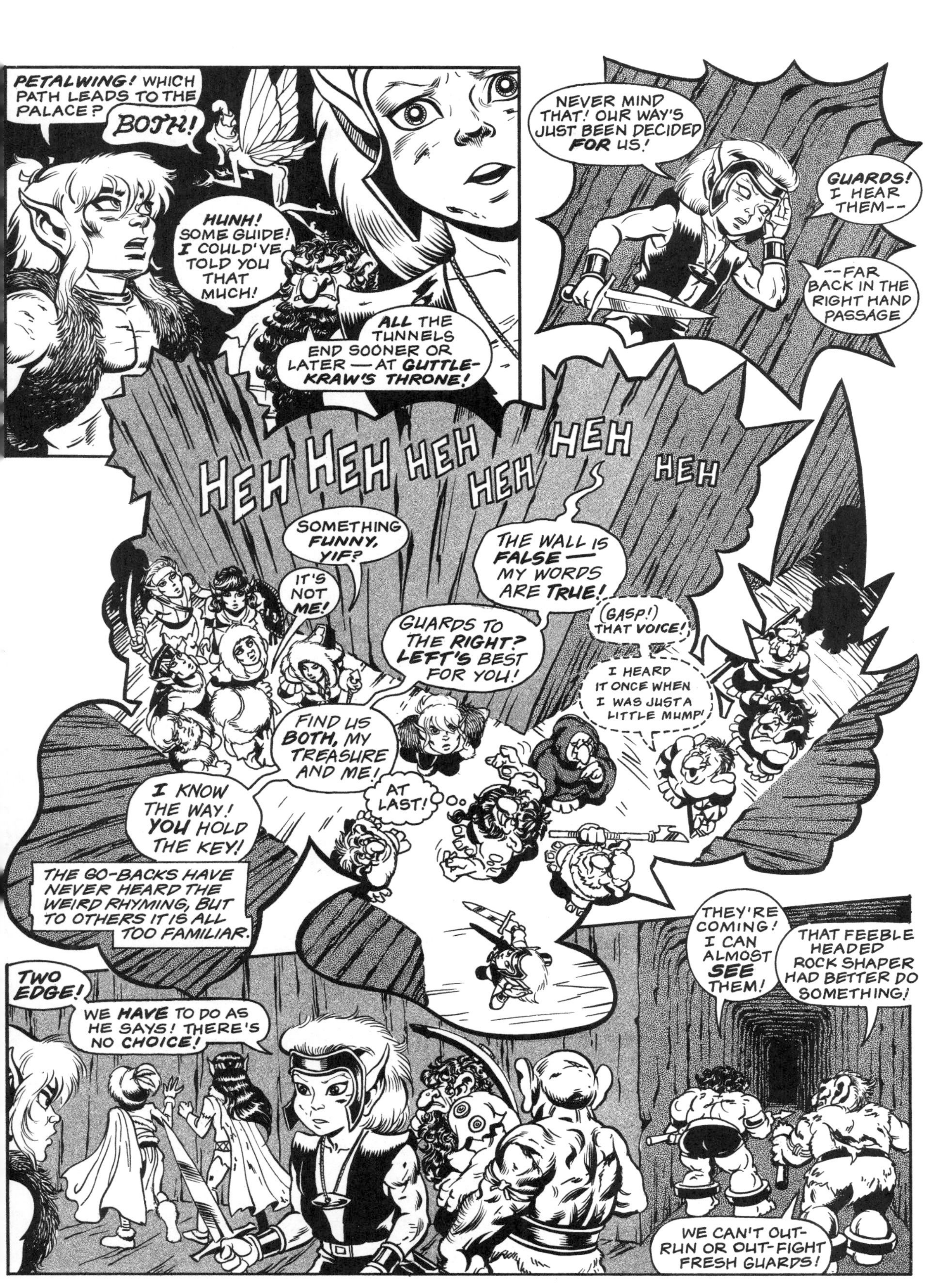
PETALWING! WHICH PATH LEADS TO THE PALACE?
BOTH!
HUNH! SOME GUIDE! I COULD'VE TOLD YOU THAT MUCH!
ALL THE TUNNELS END SOONER OR LATER — AT GUTTLE-KRAW'S THRONE!
NEVER MIND THAT! OUR WAY'S JUST BEEN DECIDED FOR US!
GUARDS! I HEAR THEM--
--FAR BACK IN THE RIGHT HAND PASSAGE
HEH HEH HEH HEH HEH HEH
SOMETHING FUNNY, YIF?
IT'S NOT ME!
THE WALL IS FALSE— MY WORDS ARE TRUE!
GUARDS TO THE RIGHT? LEFT'S BEST FOR YOU!
(GASP!) THAT VOICE!
I HEARD IT ONCE WHEN I WAS JUST A LITTLE MUMP!
FIND US BOTH, MY TREASURE AND ME!
I KNOW THE WAY! YOU HOLD THE KEY!
AT LAST!
THE GO-BACKS HAVE NEVER HEARD THE WEIRD RHYMING, BUT TO OTHERS IT IS ALL TOO FAMILIAR.
TWO EDGE!
WE HAVE TO DO AS HE SAYS! THERE'S NO CHOICE!
THEY'RE COMING! I CAN ALMOST SEE THEM!
THAT FEEBLE HEADED ROCK SHAPER HAD BETTER DO SOMETHING!
WE CAN'T OUT-RUN OR OUT-FIGHT FRESH GUARDS!

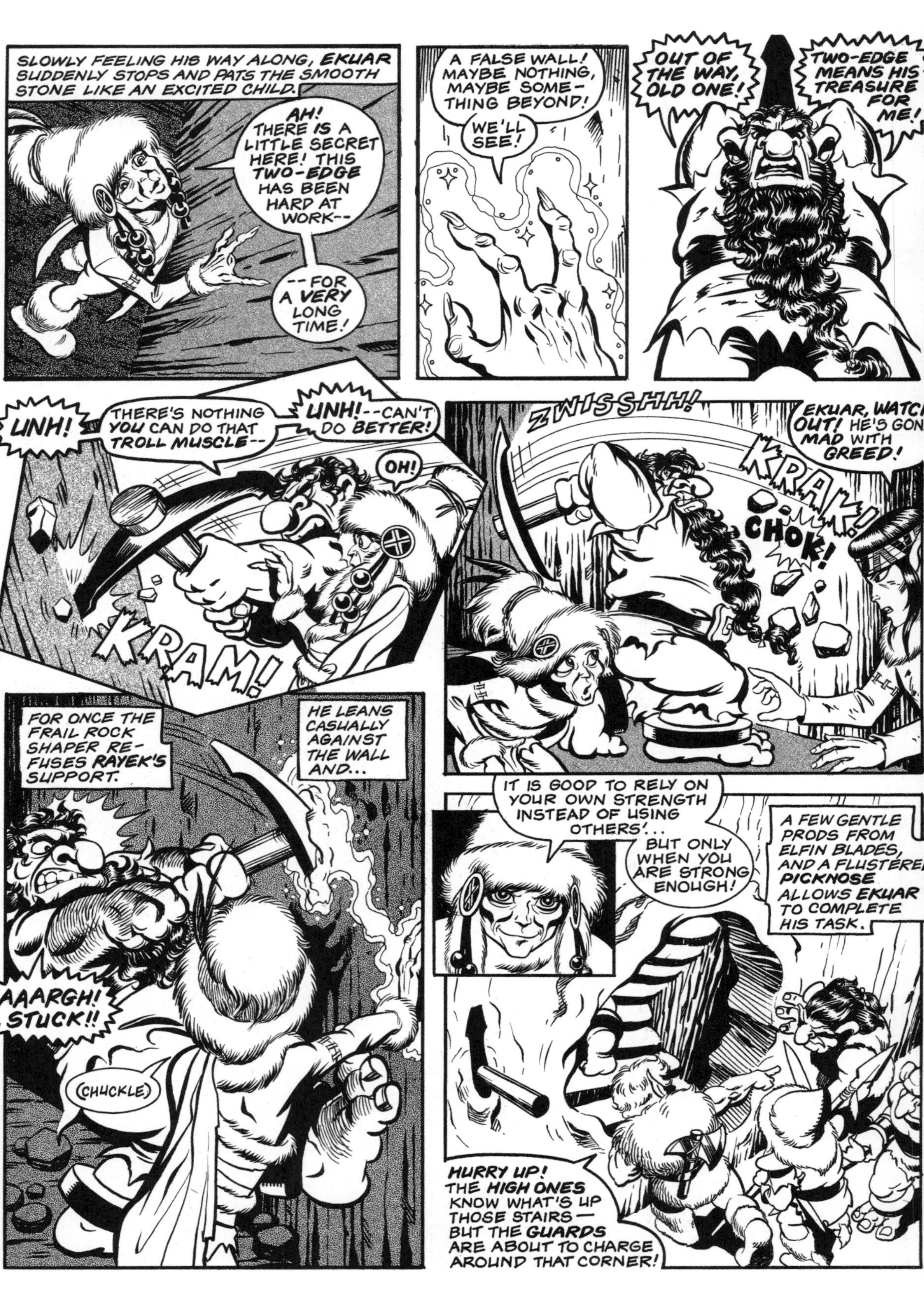

SLOWLY FEELING HIS WAY ALONG, EKUAR SUDDENLY STOPS AND PATS THE SMOOTH STONE LIKE AN EXCITED CHILD.
AH! THERE IS A LITTLE SECRET HERE! THIS TWO-EDGE HAS BEEN HARD AT WORK--
--FOR A VERY LONG TIME!
A FALSE WALL! MAYBE NOTHING, MAYBE SOME-THING BEYOND!
WE'LL SEE!
OUT OF THE WAY, OLD ONE!
TWO-EDGE MEANS HIS TREASURE FOR ME!
UNH!
THERE'S NOTHING YOU CAN DO THAT TROLL MUSCLE--
UNH!--CAN'T DO BETTER!
OH!
KRAM!
ZWISSHH!
EKUAR, WATCH OUT! HE'S GON MAD WITH GREED!
KRAK!
CHOK!
FOR ONCE THE FRAIL ROCK SHAPER RE-FUSES RAYEK'S SUPPORT.
HE LEANS CASUALLY AGAINST THE WALL AND...
AAARGH! STUCK!!
(CHUCKLE)
IT IS GOOD TO RELY ON YOUR OWN STRENGTH INSTEAD OF USING OTHERS'...
BUT ONLY WHEN YOU ARE STRONG ENOUGH!
A FEW GENTLE PRODS FROM ELFIN BLADES, AND A FLUSTERED PICKNOSE ALLOWS EKUAR TO COMPLETE HIS TASK.
HURRY UP! THE HIGH ONES KNOW WHAT'S UP THOSE STAIRS— BUT THE GUARDS ARE ABOUT TO CHARGE AROUND THAT CORNER!

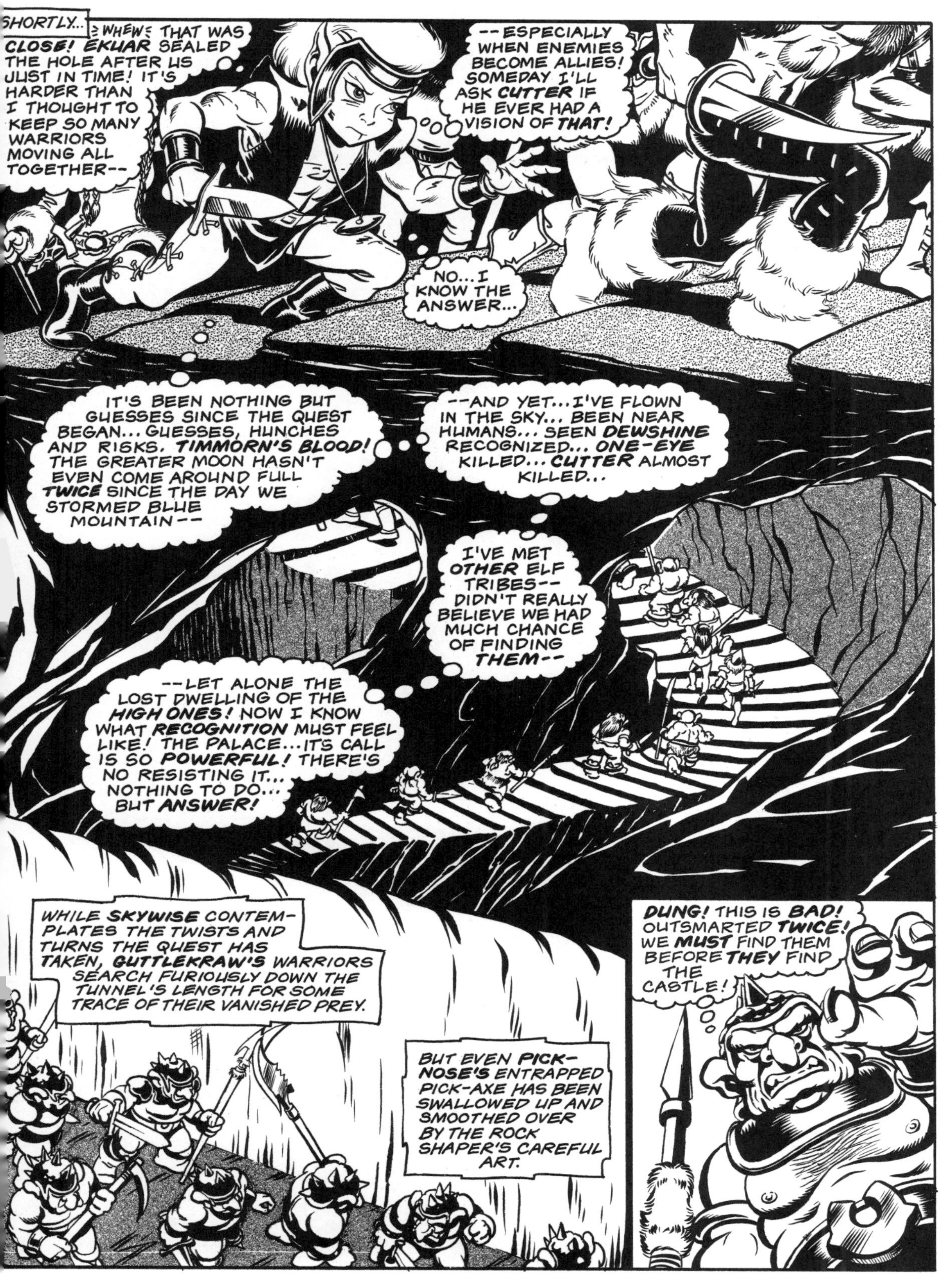
SHORTLY...
WHEW! THAT WAS CLOSE! EKUAR SEALED THE HOLE AFTER US JUST IN TIME! IT'S HARDER THAN I THOUGHT TO KEEP SO MANY WARRIORS MOVING ALL TOGETHER--
--ESPECIALLY WHEN ENEMIES BECOME ALLIES! SOMEDAY I'LL ASK CUTTER IF HE EVER HAD A VISION OF THAT!
NO... I KNOW THE ANSWER...
IT'S BEEN NOTHING BUT GUESSES SINCE THE QUEST BEGAN... GUESSES, HUNCHES AND RISKS. TIMMORN'S BLOOD! THE GREATER MOON HASN'T EVEN COME AROUND FULL TWICE SINCE THE DAY WE STORMED BLUE MOUNTAIN--
--AND YET... I'VE FLOWN IN THE SKY... BEEN NEAR HUMANS... SEEN DEWSHINE RECOGNIZED... ONE-EYE KILLED... CUTTER ALMOST KILLED...
I'VE MET OTHER ELF TRIBES--DIDN'T REALLY BELIEVE WE HAD MUCH CHANCE OF FINDING THEM--
--LET ALONE THE LOST DWELLING OF THE HIGH ONES! NOW I KNOW WHAT RECOGNITION MUST FEEL LIKE! THE PALACE... ITS CALL IS SO POWERFUL! THERE'S NO RESISTING IT... NOTHING TO DO... BUT ANSWER!
WHILE SKYWISE CONTEMPLATES THE TWISTS AND TURNS THE QUEST HAS TAKEN, GUTTLEKRAW'S WARRIORS SEARCH FURIOUSLY DOWN THE TUNNEL'S LENGTH FOR SOME TRACE OF THEIR VANISHED PREY.
BUT EVEN PICK-NOSE'S ENTRAPPED PICK-AXE HAS BEEN SWALLOWED UP AND SMOOTHED OVER BY THE ROCK SHAPER'S CAREFUL ART.
DUNG! THIS IS BAD! OUTSMARTED TWICE! WE MUST FIND THEM BEFORE THEY FIND THE CASTLE!

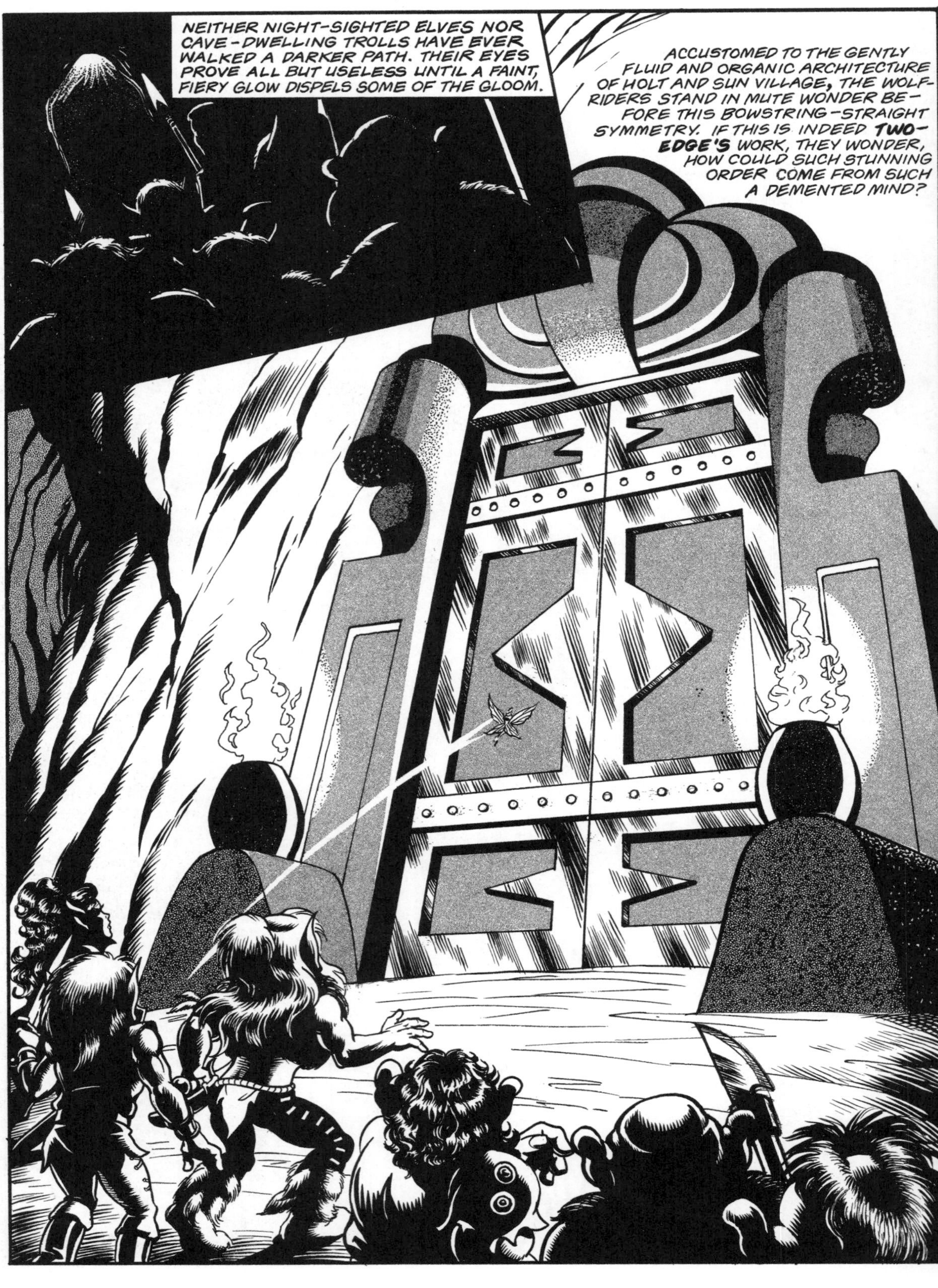
NEITHER NIGHT-SIGHTED ELVES NOR CAVE-DWELLING TROLLS HAVE EVER WALKED A DARKER PATH. THEIR EYES PROVE ALL BUT USELESS UNTIL A FAINT, FIERY GLOW DISPELS SOME OF THE GLOOM.
ACCUSTOMED TO THE GENTLY FLUID AND ORGANIC ARCHITECTURE OF HOLT AND SUN VILLAGE, THE WOLF-RIDERS STAND IN MUTE WONDER BEFORE THIS BOWSTRING-STRAIGHT SYMMETRY. IF THIS IS INDEED TWO-EDGE'S WORK, THEY WONDER, HOW COULD SUCH STUNNING ORDER COME FROM SUCH A DEMENTED MIND?

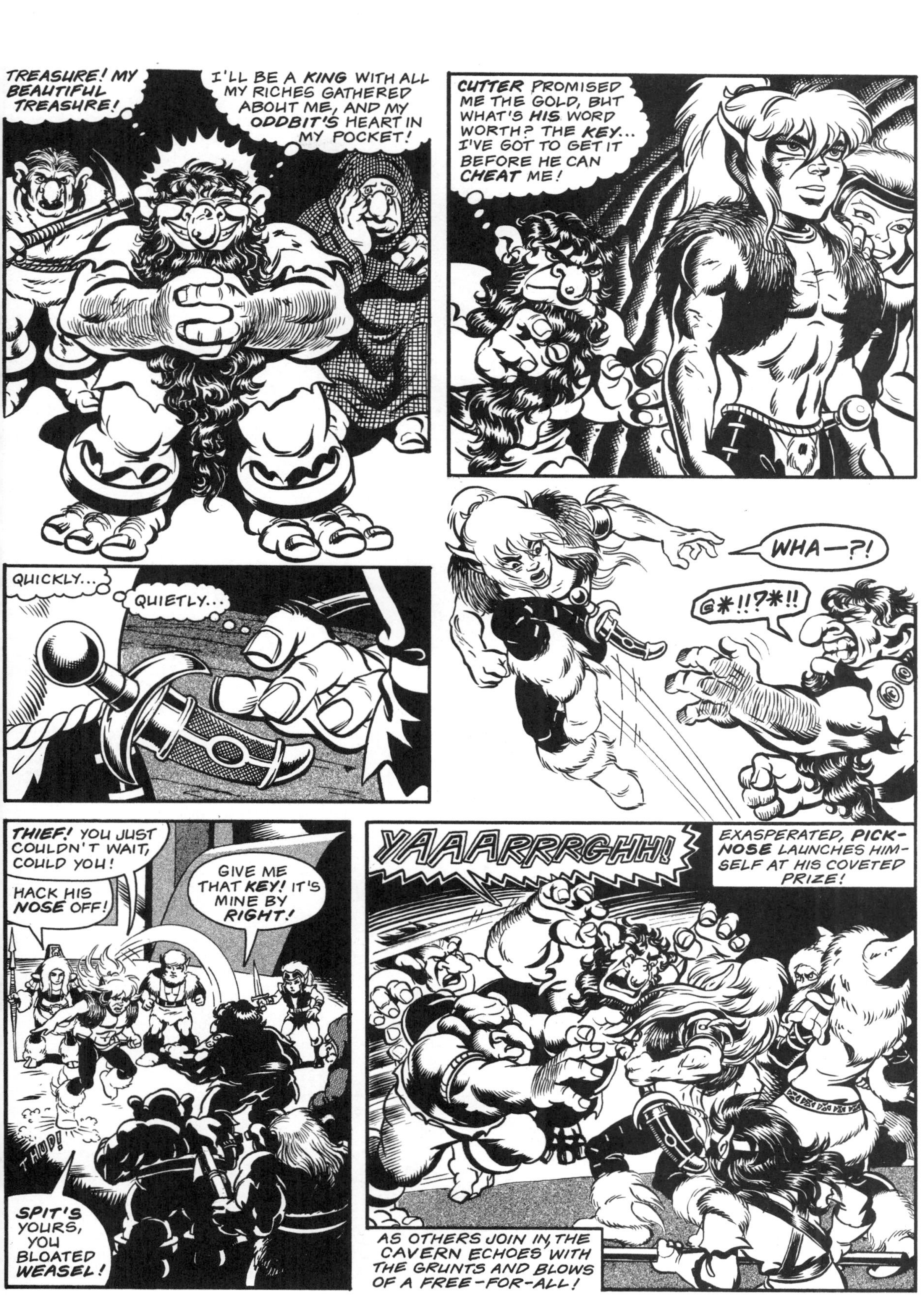
TREASURE! MY BEAUTIFUL TREASURE!
I'LL BE A KING WITH ALL MY RICHES GATHERED ABOUT ME, AND MY ODDBIT'S HEART IN MY POCKET!
CUTTER PROMISED ME THE GOLD, BUT WHAT'S HIS WORD WORTH? THE KEY... I'VE GOT TO GET IT BEFORE HE CAN CHEAT ME!
QUICKLY...
QUIETLY...
WHA--?!
G*!!?*!!
THIEF! YOU JUST COULDN'T WAIT, COULD YOU!
HACK HIS NOSE OFF!
GIVE ME THAT KEY! IT'S MINE BY RIGHT!
THUD!
SPIT'S YOURS, YOU BLOATED WEASEL!
YAAARRRGHH!
EXASPERATED, PICK-NOSE LAUNCHES HIMSELF AT HIS COVETED PRIZE!
AS OTHERS JOIN IN, THE CAVERN ECHOES WITH THE GRUNTS AND BLOWS OF A FREE-FOR-ALL!

CUTTER! THROW *NEW MOON* TO ME!

WHIT WHIT WHIT

HA HAH!

GOT IT!!

THE TUSSLE GOES ON AS SKYWISE BOUNDS FOR THE TOWERING VAULT DOOR. ALL HE KNOWS IS THAT KEYS--

"--OPEN THINGS..." BUT *HOW?*

HOW CAN SOMETHING SO SMALL MAKE SUCH A HUGE DOOR OPEN?

CURIOUS, HE NOTICES MANY SYMBOLS CARVED INTO THE STONE PORTAL. HOPING TO FIND A CLUE, HE STUDIES THEM CLOSELY--

--AND TO HIS *DELIGHT,* HE RECOGNIZES A FAMILIAR DESIGN.

UH HUMM!

BUT MERELY PRESSING THE KEY TO THE RECESSED CARVING BRINGS NO RESULT.

IT'S GOT THE RIGHT *SHAPE*... HOW DOES IT *WORK?*

UH OH! HERE COMES GOOD OLD *PICKY!* GOT TO FIGURE THIS OUT *FAST!*

HALF BY REASON, HALF BY GUESS *SKYWISE* JAMS THE KEY INTO A TINY, RECTANGULAR HOLE.

COME ON! COME ON!

CLICK!

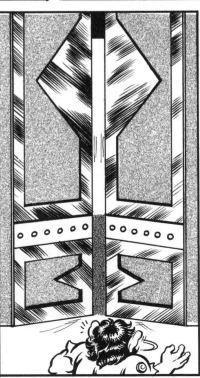

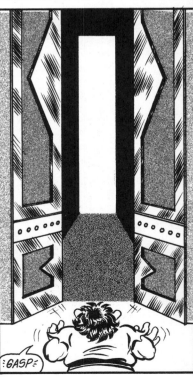

:GASP:

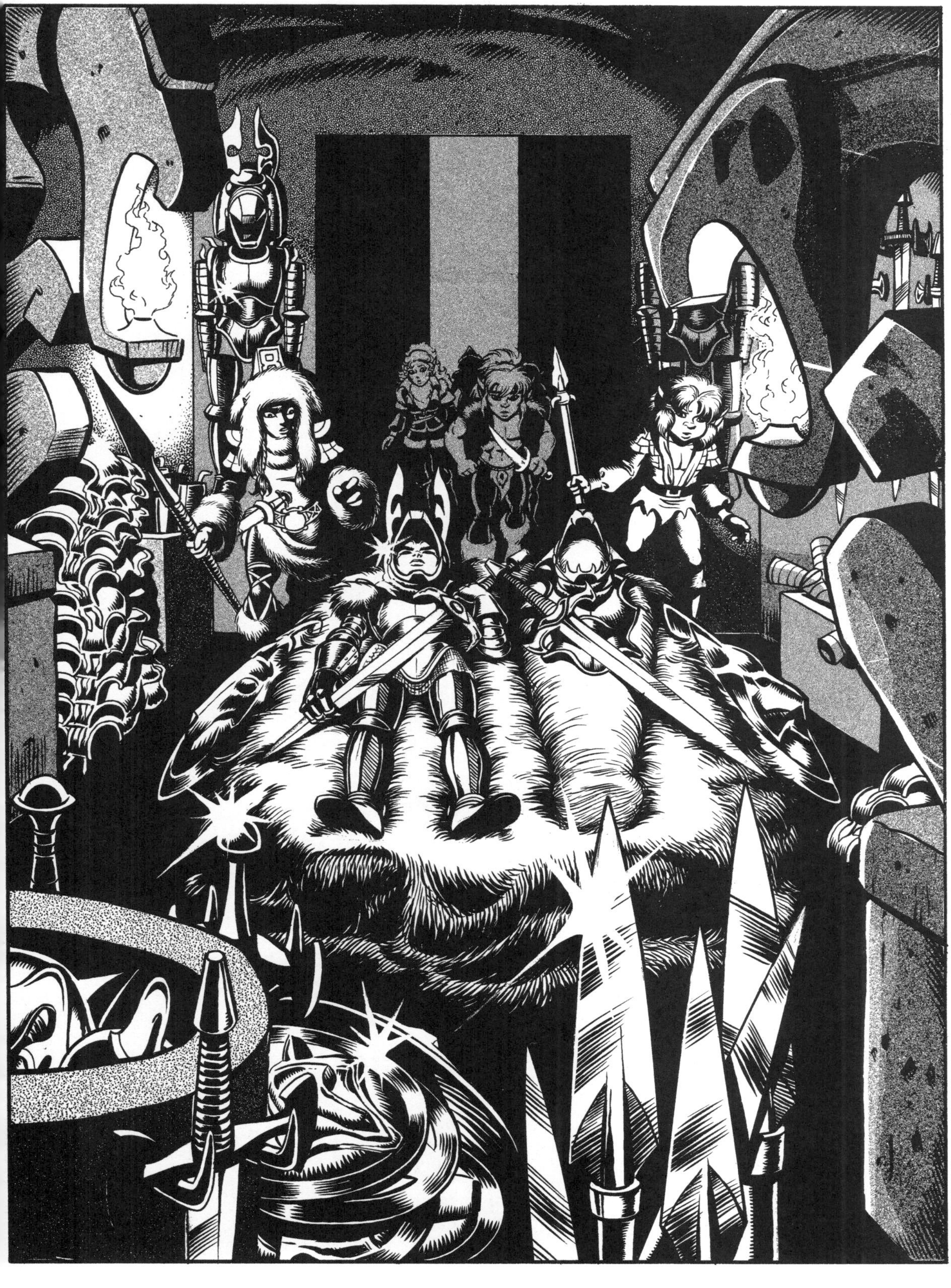

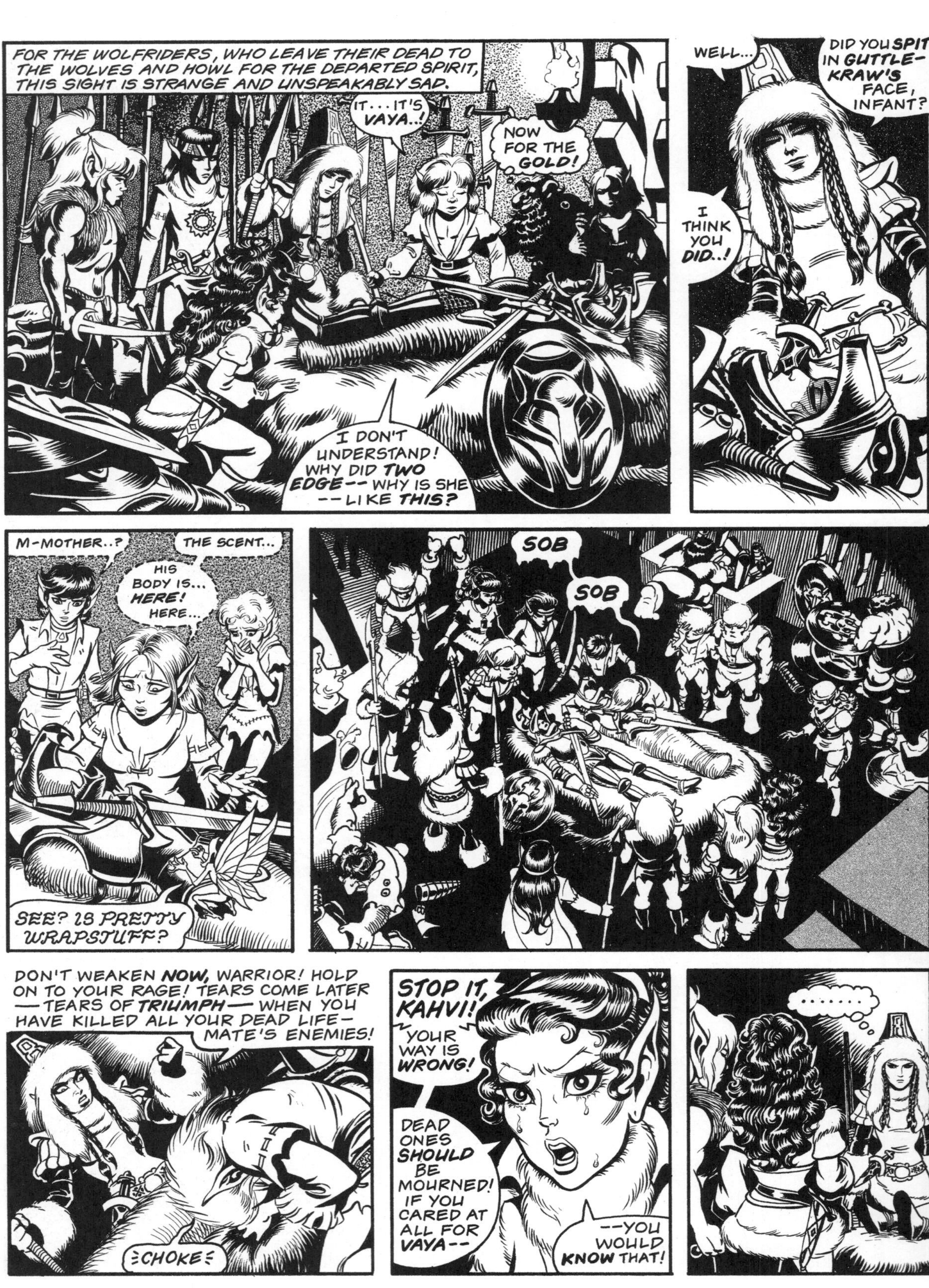
FOR THE WOLFRIDERS, WHO LEAVE THEIR DEAD TO THE WOLVES AND HOWL FOR THE DEPARTED SPIRIT, THIS SIGHT IS STRANGE AND UNSPEAKABLY SAD.
IT... IT'S VAYA..!
NOW FOR THE GOLD!
I DON'T UNDERSTAND! WHY DID TWO EDGE-- WHY IS SHE --LIKE THIS?
WELL...
DID YOU SPIT IN GUTTLE-KRAW'S FACE, INFANT?
I THINK YOU DID..!
M-MOTHER..?
THE SCENT...
HIS BODY IS... HERE! HERE...
SEE? IS PRETTY WRAPSTUFF?
SOB
SOB
DON'T WEAKEN NOW, WARRIOR! HOLD ON TO YOUR RAGE! TEARS COME LATER — TEARS OF TRIUMPH— WHEN YOU HAVE KILLED ALL YOUR DEAD LIFE-MATE'S ENEMIES!
CHOKE
STOP IT, KAHVI!
YOUR WAY IS WRONG!
DEAD ONES SHOULD BE MOURNED! IF YOU CARED AT ALL FOR VAYA--
--YOU WOULD KNOW THAT!
....

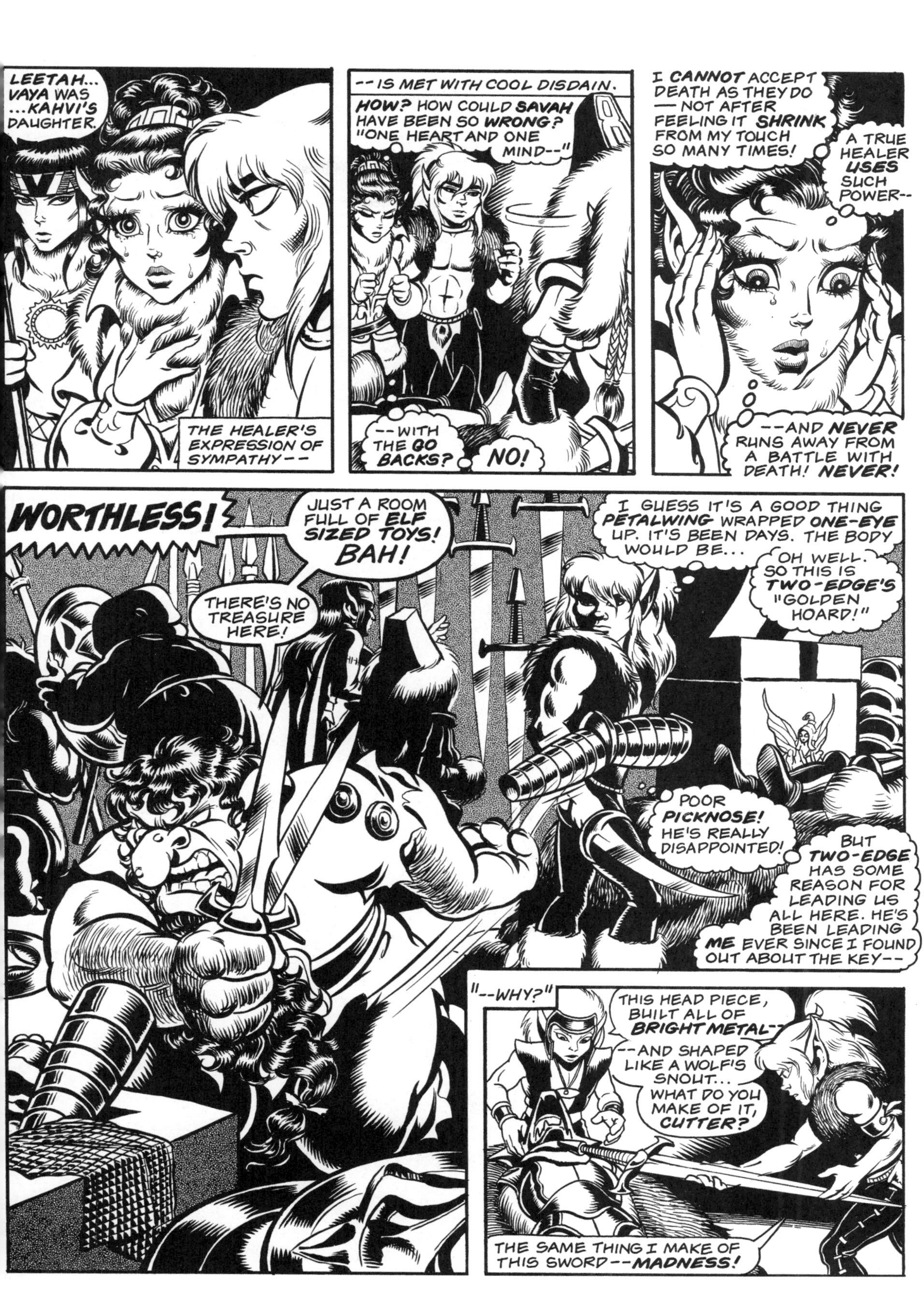

LEETAH... VAYA WAS ...KAHVI'S DAUGHTER.
THE HEALER'S EXPRESSION OF SYMPATHY--
--IS MET WITH COOL DISDAIN.
HOW? HOW COULD SAVAH HAVE BEEN SO WRONG? "ONE HEART AND ONE MIND--"
--WITH THE GO BACKS?
NO!
I CANNOT ACCEPT DEATH AS THEY DO — NOT AFTER FEELING IT SHRINK FROM MY TOUCH SO MANY TIMES!
A TRUE HEALER USES SUCH POWER--
--AND NEVER RUNS AWAY FROM A BATTLE WITH DEATH! NEVER!
WORTHLESS!
JUST A ROOM FULL OF ELF SIZED TOYS! BAH!
THERE'S NO TREASURE HERE!
I GUESS IT'S A GOOD THING PETALWING WRAPPED ONE-EYE UP. IT'S BEEN DAYS. THE BODY WOULD BE...
OH WELL. SO THIS IS TWO-EDGE'S "GOLDEN HOARD!"
POOR PICKNOSE! HE'S REALLY DISAPPOINTED!
BUT TWO-EDGE HAS SOME REASON FOR LEADING US ALL HERE. HE'S BEEN LEADING ME EVER SINCE I FOUND OUT ABOUT THE KEY--
"--WHY?"
THIS HEAD PIECE, BUILT ALL OF BRIGHT METAL--
--AND SHAPED LIKE A WOLF'S SNOUT... WHAT DO YOU MAKE OF IT, CUTTER?
THE SAME THING I MAKE OF THIS SWORD--MADNESS!

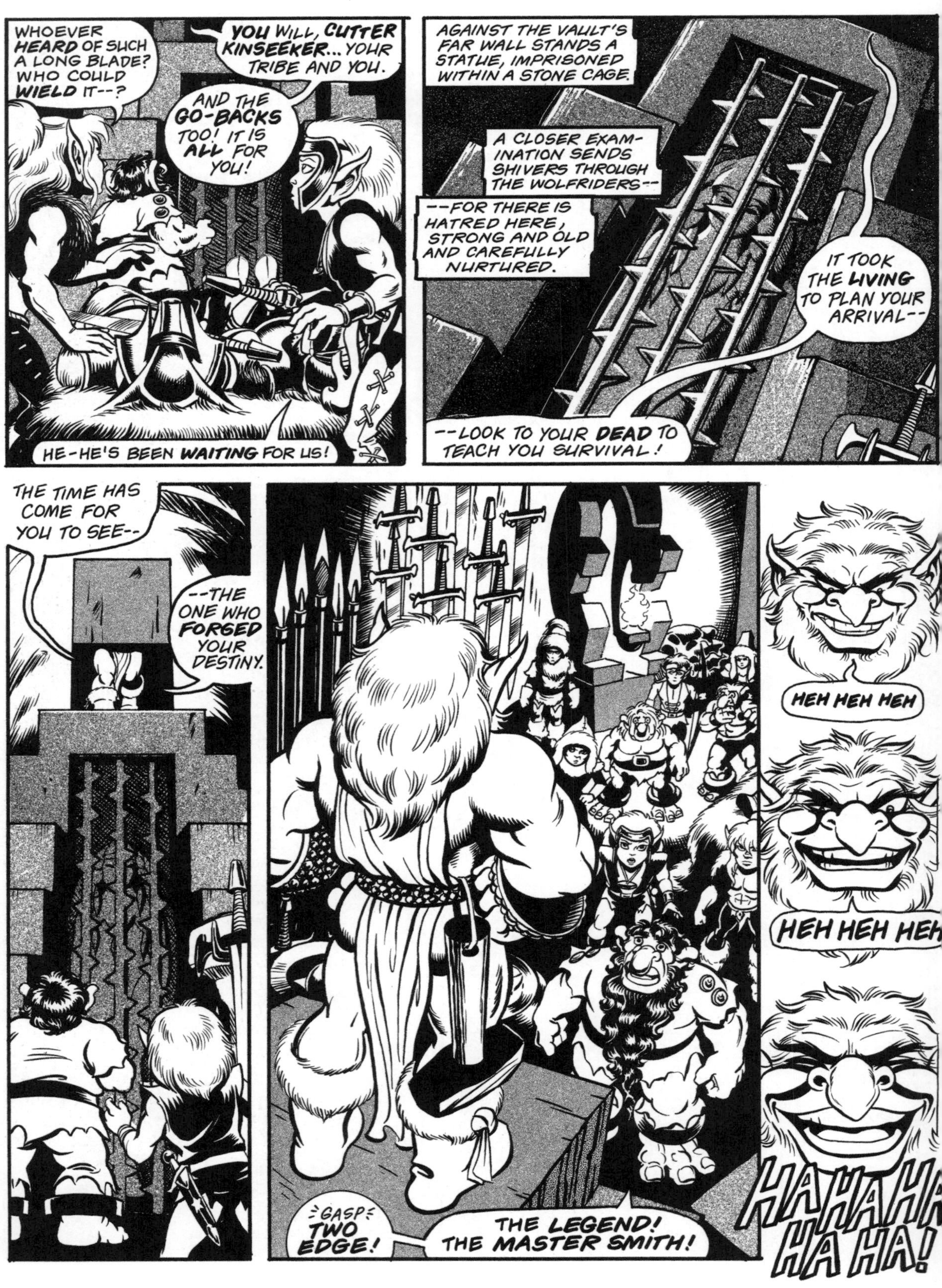
WHOEVER HEARD OF SUCH A LONG BLADE? WHO COULD WIELD IT--?
YOU WILL, CUTTER KINSEEKER... YOUR TRIBE AND YOU.
AND THE GO-BACKS TOO! IT IS ALL FOR YOU!
HE-HE'S BEEN WAITING FOR US!
AGAINST THE VAULT'S FAR WALL STANDS A STATUE, IMPRISONED WITHIN A STONE CAGE.
A CLOSER EXAMINATION SENDS SHIVERS THROUGH THE WOLFRIDERS--
--FOR THERE IS HATRED HERE, STRONG AND OLD AND CAREFULLY NURTURED.
IT TOOK THE LIVING TO PLAN YOUR ARRIVAL--
--LOOK TO YOUR DEAD TO TEACH YOU SURVIVAL!
THE TIME HAS COME FOR YOU TO SEE--
--THE ONE WHO FORGED YOUR DESTINY.
GASP TWO EDGE!
THE LEGEND! THE MASTER SMITH!
HEH HEH HEH
HEH HEH HEH
HAHAHA HA HA!

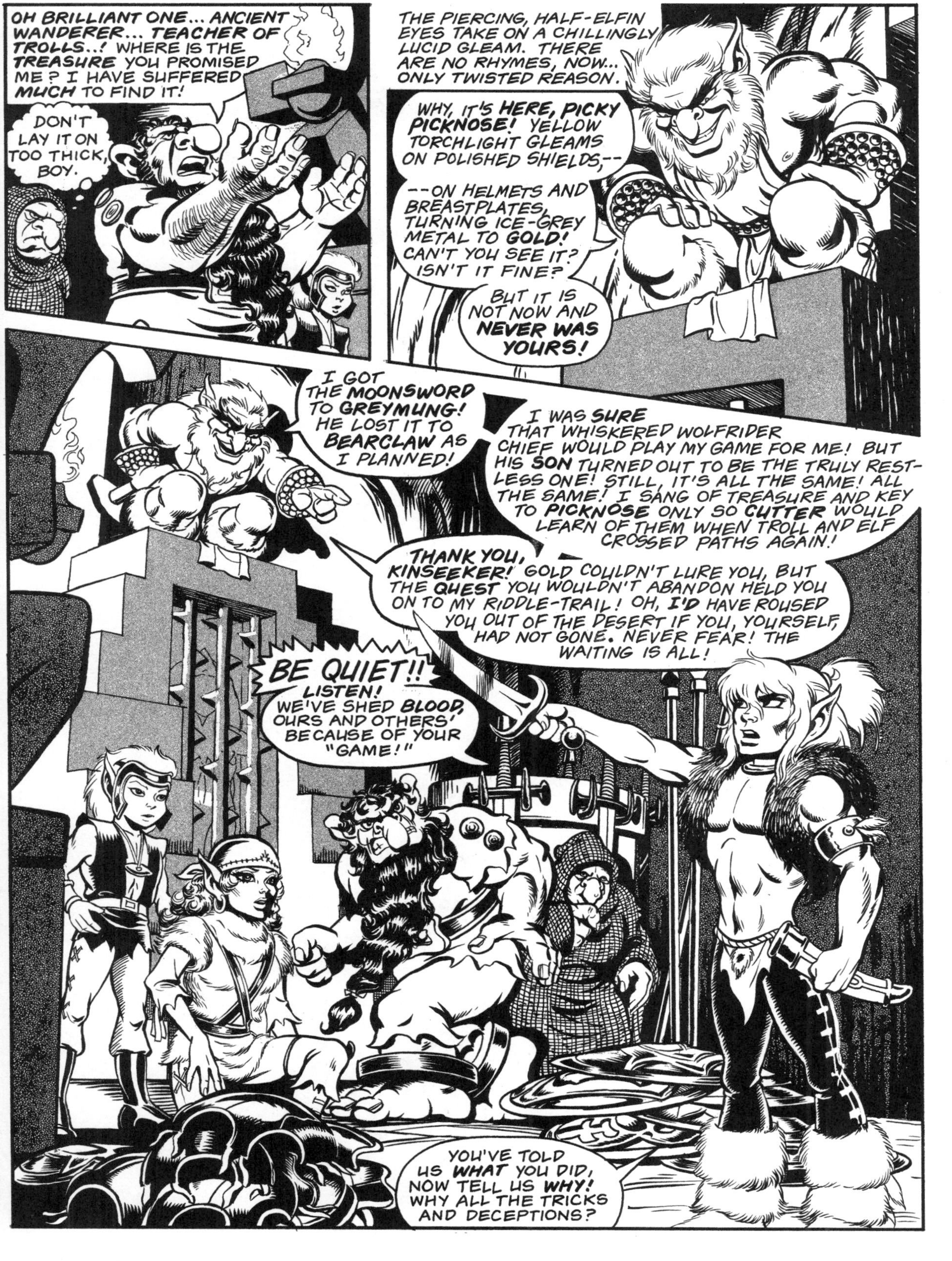

OH BRILLIANT ONE... ANCIENT WANDERER... TEACHER OF TROLLS..! WHERE IS THE TREASURE YOU PROMISED ME? I HAVE SUFFERED MUCH TO FIND IT!
DON'T LAY IT ON TOO THICK, BOY.
THE PIERCING, HALF-ELFIN EYES TAKE ON A CHILLINGLY LUCID GLEAM. THERE ARE NO RHYMES, NOW... ONLY TWISTED REASON.
WHY, IT'S HERE, PICKY PICKNOSE! YELLOW TORCHLIGHT GLEAMS ON POLISHED SHIELDS,--
--ON HELMETS AND BREASTPLATES, TURNING ICE-GREY METAL TO GOLD! CAN'T YOU SEE IT? ISN'T IT FINE?
BUT IT IS NOT NOW AND NEVER WAS YOURS!
I GOT THE MOONSWORD TO GREYMUNG! HE LOST IT TO BEARCLAW AS I PLANNED!
I WAS SURE THAT WHISKERED WOLFRIDER CHIEF WOULD PLAY MY GAME FOR ME! BUT HIS SON TURNED OUT TO BE THE TRULY RESTLESS ONE! STILL, IT'S ALL THE SAME! ALL THE SAME! I SANG OF TREASURE AND KEY TO PICKNOSE ONLY SO CUTTER WOULD LEARN OF THEM WHEN TROLL AND ELF CROSSED PATHS AGAIN!
THANK YOU, KINSEEKER! GOLD COULDN'T LURE YOU, BUT THE QUEST YOU WOULDN'T ABANDON HELD YOU ON TO MY RIDDLE-TRAIL! OH, I'D HAVE ROUSED YOU OUT OF THE DESERT IF YOU, YOURSELF, HAD NOT GONE. NEVER FEAR! THE WAITING IS ALL!
BE QUIET!! LISTEN! WE'VE SHED BLOOD, OURS AND OTHERS' BECAUSE OF YOUR "GAME!"
YOU'VE TOLD US WHAT YOU DID, NOW TELL US WHY! WHY ALL THE TRICKS AND DECEPTIONS?

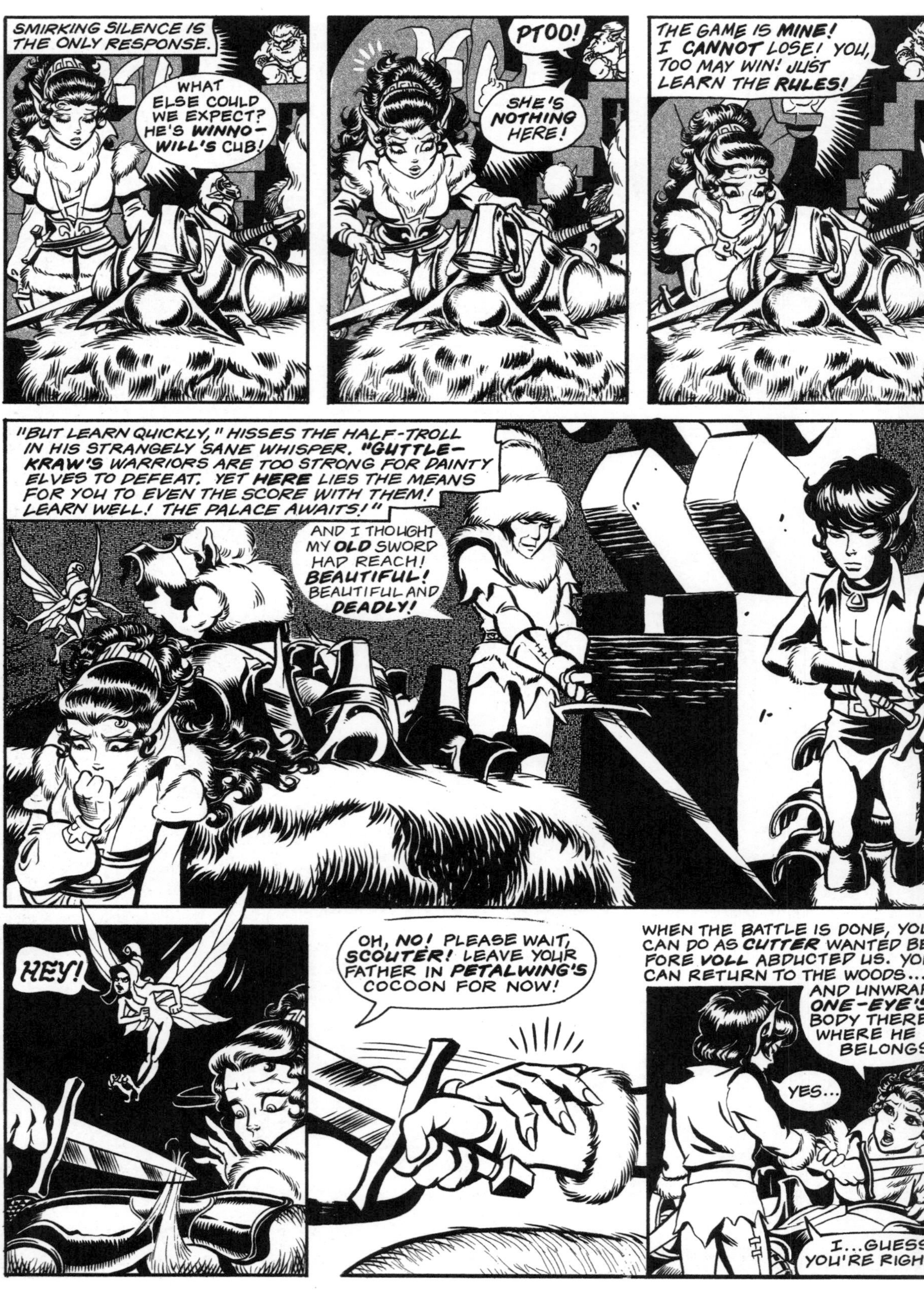
SMIRKING SILENCE IS THE ONLY RESPONSE.
WHAT ELSE COULD WE EXPECT? HE'S WINNOWILL'S CUB!
PTOO!
SHE'S NOTHING HERE!
THE GAME IS MINE! I CANNOT LOSE! YOU, TOO MAY WIN! JUST LEARN THE RULES!
"BUT LEARN QUICKLY," HISSES THE HALF-TROLL IN HIS STRANGELY SANE WHISPER. "GUTTLEKRAW'S WARRIORS ARE TOO STRONG FOR DAINTY ELVES TO DEFEAT. YET HERE LIES THE MEANS FOR YOU TO EVEN THE SCORE WITH THEM! LEARN WELL! THE PALACE AWAITS!"
AND I THOUGHT MY OLD SWORD HAD REACH! BEAUTIFUL! BEAUTIFUL AND DEADLY!
HEY!
OH, NO! PLEASE WAIT, SCOUTER! LEAVE YOUR FATHER IN PETALWING'S COCOON FOR NOW!
WHEN THE BATTLE IS DONE, YOU CAN DO AS CUTTER WANTED BEFORE VOLL ABDUCTED US. YOU CAN RETURN TO THE WOODS...
AND UNWRAP ONE-EYE'S BODY THERE, WHERE HE BELONGS!
YES...
I...GUESS YOU'RE RIGHT.

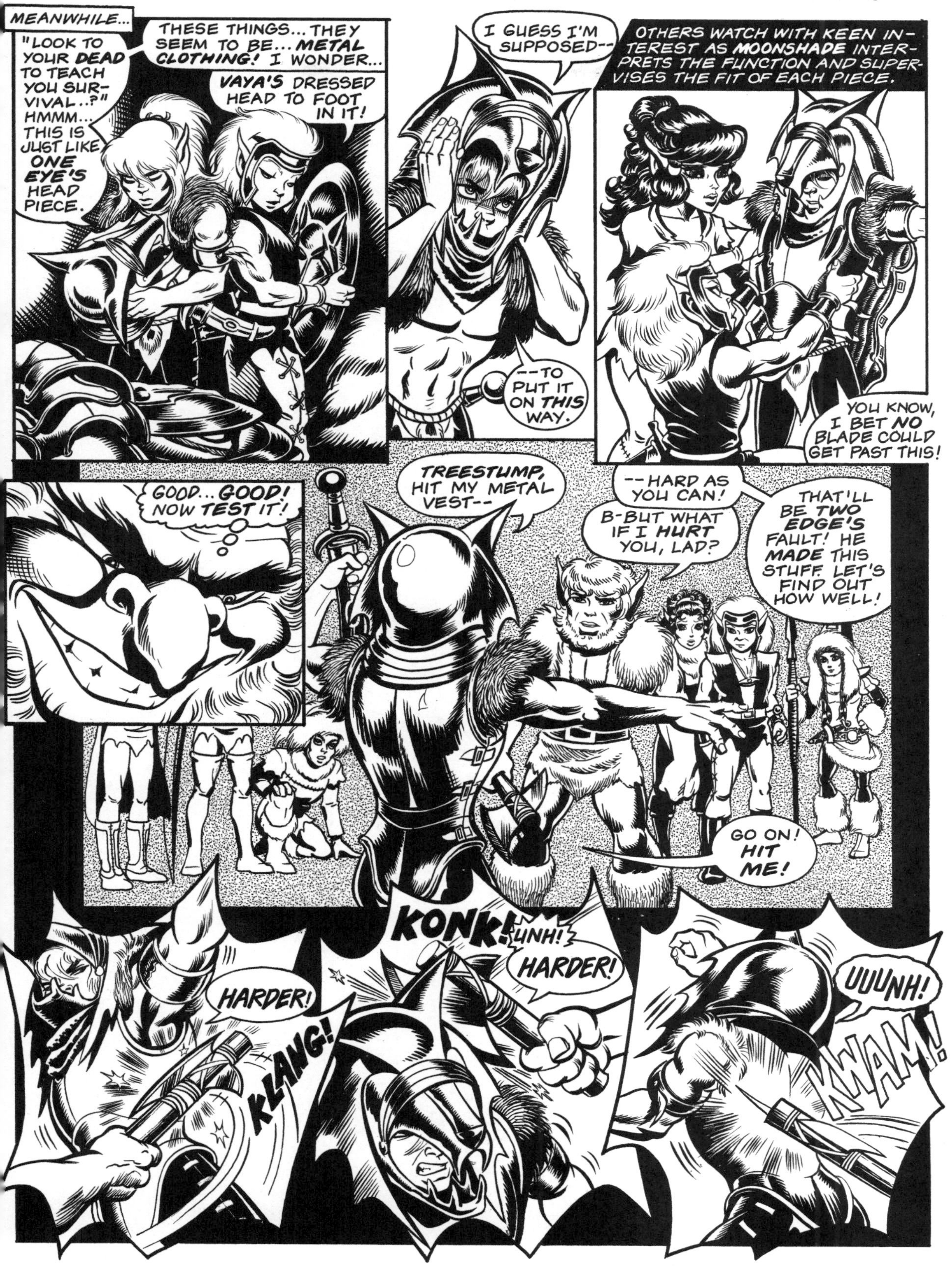
MEANWHILE...
"LOOK TO YOUR DEAD TO TEACH YOU SURVIVAL..?" HMMM... THIS IS JUST LIKE ONE EYE'S HEAD PIECE.
THESE THINGS... THEY SEEM TO BE... METAL CLOTHING! I WONDER...
VAYA'S DRESSED HEAD TO FOOT IN IT!
I GUESS I'M SUPPOSED--
--TO PUT IT ON THIS WAY.
OTHERS WATCH WITH KEEN INTEREST AS MOONSHADE INTERPRETS THE FUNCTION AND SUPERVISES THE FIT OF EACH PIECE.
YOU KNOW, I BET NO BLADE COULD GET PAST THIS!
GOOD... GOOD! NOW TEST IT!
TREESTUMP, HIT MY METAL VEST--
--HARD AS YOU CAN!
B-BUT WHAT IF I HURT YOU, LAD?
THAT'LL BE TWO EDGE'S FAULT! HE MADE THIS STUFF. LET'S FIND OUT HOW WELL!
GO ON! HIT ME!
HARDER!
KLANG!
KONK!
UNH!
HARDER!
UUUNH!
KWAM!

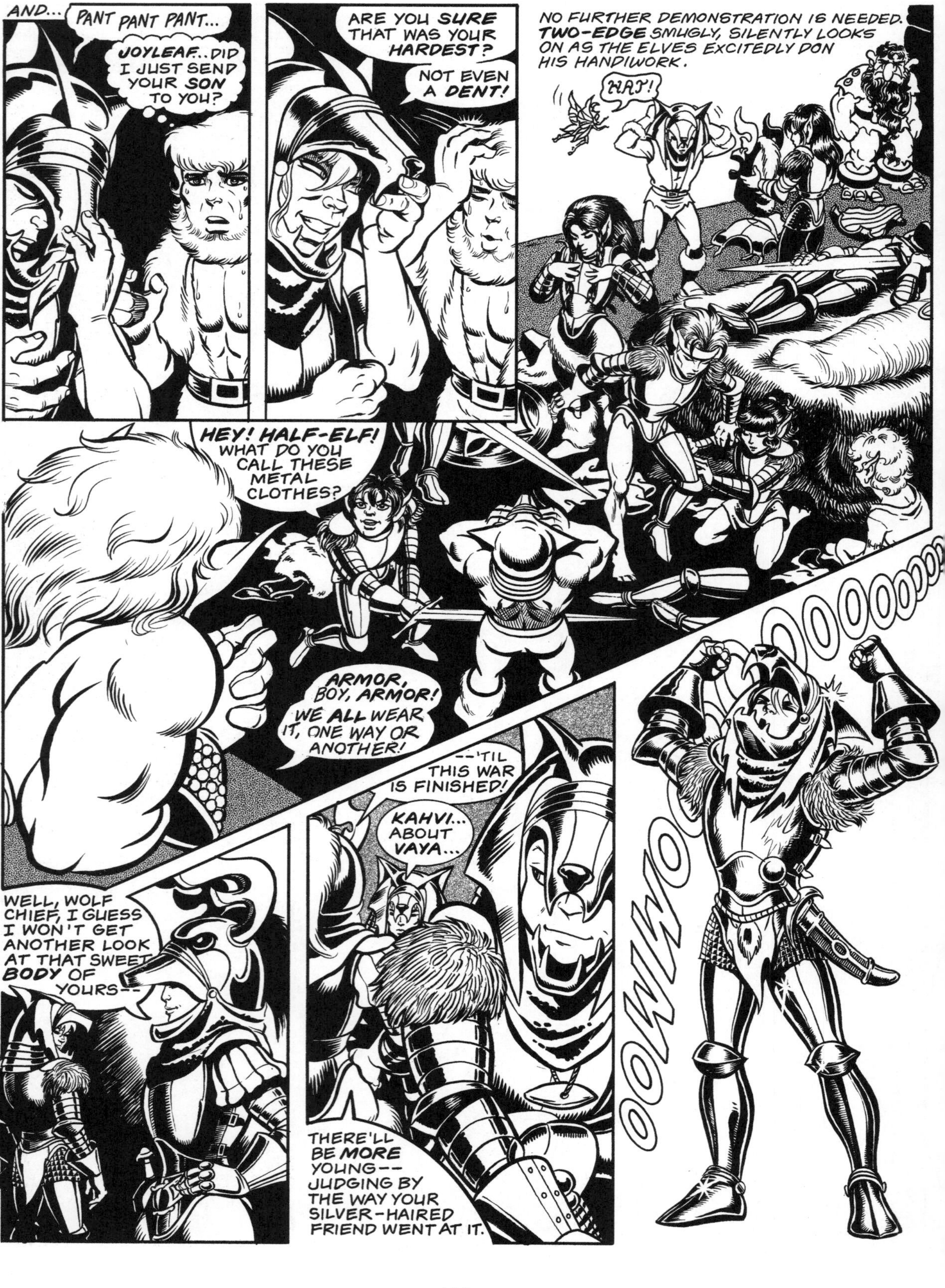

AND...
PANT PANT PANT...
JOYLEAF...DID I JUST SEND YOUR SON TO YOU?
ARE YOU SURE THAT WAS YOUR HARDEST?
NOT EVEN A DENT!
NO FURTHER DEMONSTRATION IS NEEDED. TWO-EDGE SMUGLY, SILENTLY LOOKS ON AS THE ELVES EXCITEDLY DON HIS HANDIWORK.
HAI!
HEY! HALF-ELF! WHAT DO YOU CALL THESE METAL CLOTHES?
ARMOR, BOY, ARMOR! WE ALL WEAR IT, ONE WAY OR ANOTHER!
--'TIL THIS WAR IS FINISHED!
KAHVI... ABOUT VAYA...
WELL, WOLF CHIEF, I GUESS I WON'T GET ANOTHER LOOK AT THAT SWEET BODY OF YOURS--
THERE'LL BE MORE YOUNG-- JUDGING BY THE WAY YOUR SILVER-HAIRED FRIEND WENT AT IT.
OOWWOOOOOOOOOOOOO

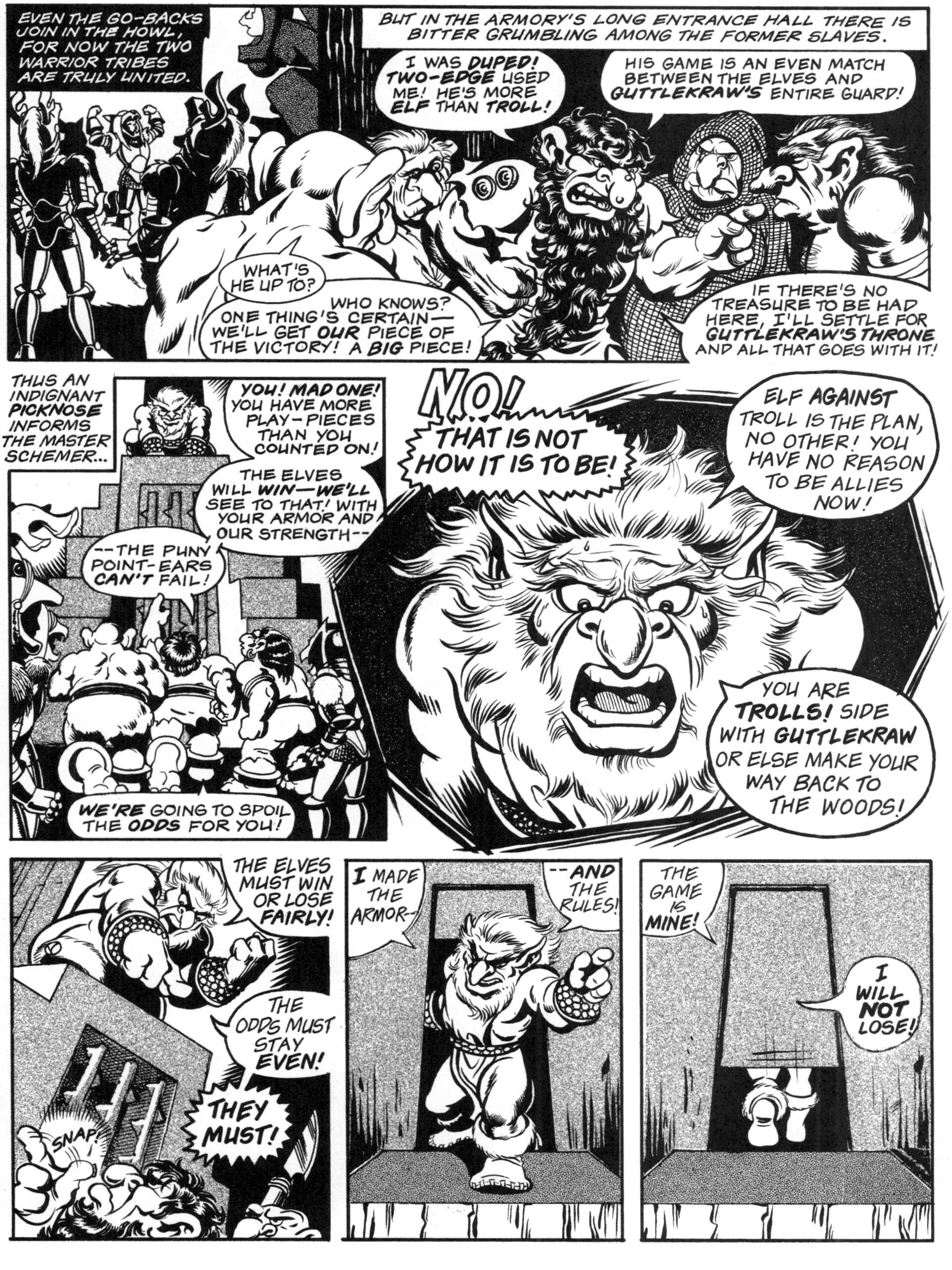
EVEN THE GO-BACKS JOIN IN THE HOWL, FOR NOW THE TWO WARRIOR TRIBES ARE TRULY UNITED.
BUT IN THE ARMORY'S LONG ENTRANCE HALL THERE IS BITTER GRUMBLING AMONG THE FORMER SLAVES.
I WAS DUPED! TWO-EDGE USED ME! HE'S MORE ELF THAN TROLL!
HIS GAME IS AN EVEN MATCH BETWEEN THE ELVES AND GUTTLEKRAW'S ENTIRE GUARD!
WHAT'S HE UP TO?
WHO KNOWS? ONE THING'S CERTAIN— WE'LL GET OUR PIECE OF THE VICTORY! A BIG PIECE!
IF THERE'S NO TREASURE TO BE HAD HERE, I'LL SETTLE FOR GUTTLEKRAW'S THRONE AND ALL THAT GOES WITH IT!
THUS AN INDIGNANT PICKNOSE INFORMS THE MASTER SCHEMER...
YOU! MAD ONE! YOU HAVE MORE PLAY-PIECES THAN YOU COUNTED ON!
THE ELVES WILL WIN—WE'LL SEE TO THAT! WITH YOUR ARMOR AND OUR STRENGTH--
--THE PUNY POINT-EARS CAN'T FAIL!
WE'RE GOING TO SPOIL THE ODDS FOR YOU!
NO! THAT IS NOT HOW IT IS TO BE!
ELF AGAINST TROLL IS THE PLAN, NO OTHER! YOU HAVE NO REASON TO BE ALLIES NOW!
YOU ARE TROLLS! SIDE WITH GUTTLEKRAW OR ELSE MAKE YOUR WAY BACK TO THE WOODS!
THE ELVES MUST WIN OR LOSE FAIRLY!
THE ODDS MUST STAY EVEN!
THEY MUST!
SNAP!
I MADE THE ARMOR--
--AND THE RULES!
THE GAME IS MINE!
I WILL NOT LOSE!

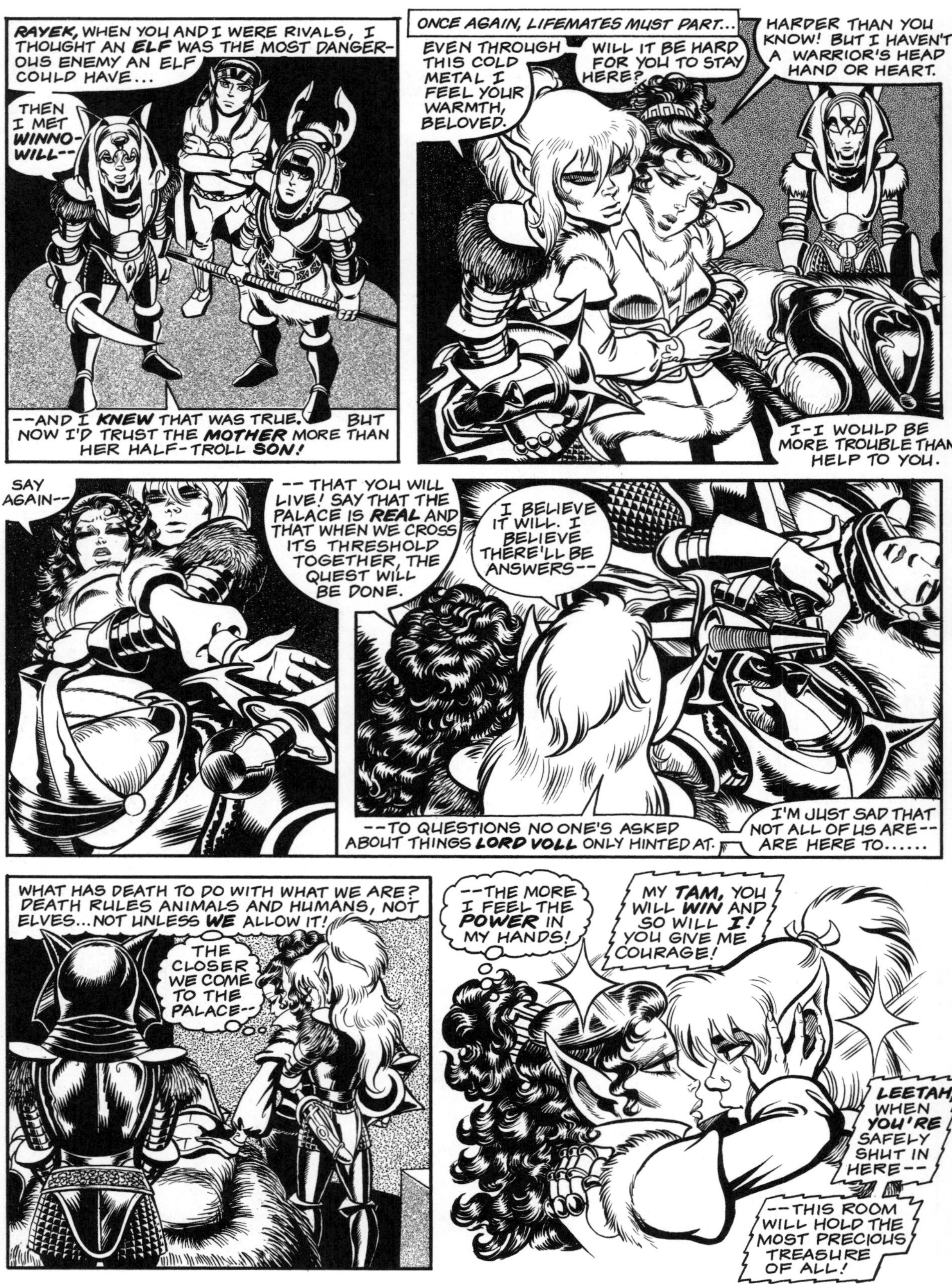
RAYEK, WHEN YOU AND I WERE RIVALS, I THOUGHT AN ELF WAS THE MOST DANGEROUS ENEMY AN ELF COULD HAVE...
THEN I MET WINNOWILL--
--AND I KNEW THAT WAS TRUE. BUT NOW I'D TRUST THE MOTHER MORE THAN HER HALF-TROLL SON!
ONCE AGAIN, LIFEMATES MUST PART...
EVEN THROUGH THIS COLD METAL I FEEL YOUR WARMTH, BELOVED.
WILL IT BE HARD FOR YOU TO STAY HERE?
HARDER THAN YOU KNOW! BUT I HAVEN'T A WARRIOR'S HEAD HAND OR HEART.
I-I WOULD BE MORE TROUBLE THAN HELP TO YOU.
SAY AGAIN--
--THAT YOU WILL LIVE! SAY THAT THE PALACE IS REAL AND THAT WHEN WE CROSS ITS THRESHOLD TOGETHER, THE QUEST WILL BE DONE.
I BELIEVE IT WILL. I BELIEVE THERE'LL BE ANSWERS--
--TO QUESTIONS NO ONE'S ASKED ABOUT THINGS LORD VOLL ONLY HINTED AT.
I'M JUST SAD THAT NOT ALL OF US ARE--ARE HERE TO......
WHAT HAS DEATH TO DO WITH WHAT WE ARE? DEATH RULES ANIMALS AND HUMANS, NOT ELVES...NOT UNLESS WE ALLOW IT!
THE CLOSER WE COME TO THE PALACE--
--THE MORE I FEEL THE POWER IN MY HANDS!
MY TAM, YOU WILL WIN AND SO WILL I! YOU GIVE ME COURAGE!
LEETAH, WHEN YOU'RE SAFELY SHUT IN HERE--
--THIS ROOM WILL HOLD THE MOST PRECIOUS TREASURE OF ALL!

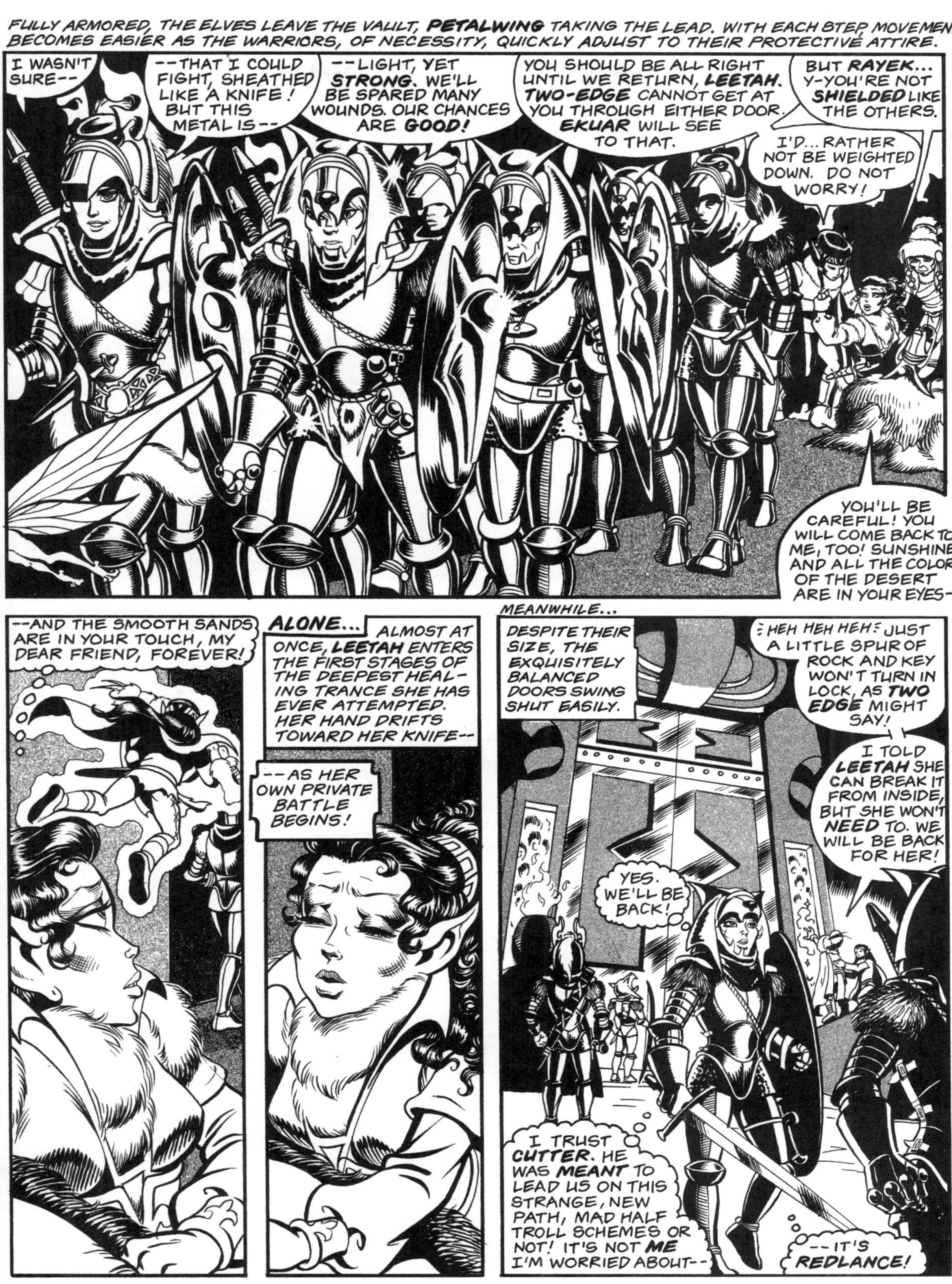

FULLY ARMORED, THE ELVES LEAVE THE VAULT, PETALWING TAKING THE LEAD. WITH EACH STEP MOVEMENT BECOMES EASIER AS THE WARRIORS, OF NECESSITY, QUICKLY ADJUST TO THEIR PROTECTIVE ATTIRE.
I WASN'T SURE--
--THAT I COULD FIGHT, SHEATHED LIKE A KNIFE! BUT THIS METAL IS--
--LIGHT, YET STRONG. WE'LL BE SPARED MANY WOUNDS. OUR CHANCES ARE GOOD!
YOU SHOULD BE ALL RIGHT UNTIL WE RETURN, LEETAH. TWO-EDGE CANNOT GET AT YOU THROUGH EITHER DOOR. EKUAR WILL SEE TO THAT.
BUT RAYEK... Y-YOU'RE NOT SHIELDED LIKE THE OTHERS.
I'D... RATHER NOT BE WEIGHTED DOWN. DO NOT WORRY!
YOU'LL BE CAREFUL! YOU WILL COME BACK TO ME, TOO! SUNSHINE AND ALL THE COLORS OF THE DESERT ARE IN YOUR EYES--
--AND THE SMOOTH SANDS ARE IN YOUR TOUCH, MY DEAR FRIEND, FOREVER!
ALONE... ALMOST AT ONCE, LEETAH ENTERS THE FIRST STAGES OF THE DEEPEST HEALING TRANCE SHE HAS EVER ATTEMPTED. HER HAND DRIFTS TOWARD HER KNIFE--
--AS HER OWN PRIVATE BATTLE BEGINS!
MEANWHILE...
DESPITE THEIR SIZE, THE EXQUISITELY BALANCED DOORS SWING SHUT EASILY.
HEH HEH HEH! JUST A LITTLE SPUR OF ROCK AND KEY WON'T TURN IN LOCK, AS TWO EDGE MIGHT SAY!
I TOLD LEETAH SHE CAN BREAK IT FROM INSIDE, BUT SHE WON'T NEED TO. WE WILL BE BACK FOR HER!
YES. WE'LL BE BACK!
I TRUST CUTTER. HE WAS MEANT TO LEAD US ON THIS STRANGE, NEW PATH, MAD HALF TROLL SCHEMES OR NOT! IT'S NOT ME I'M WORRIED ABOUT--
--IT'S REDLANCE!

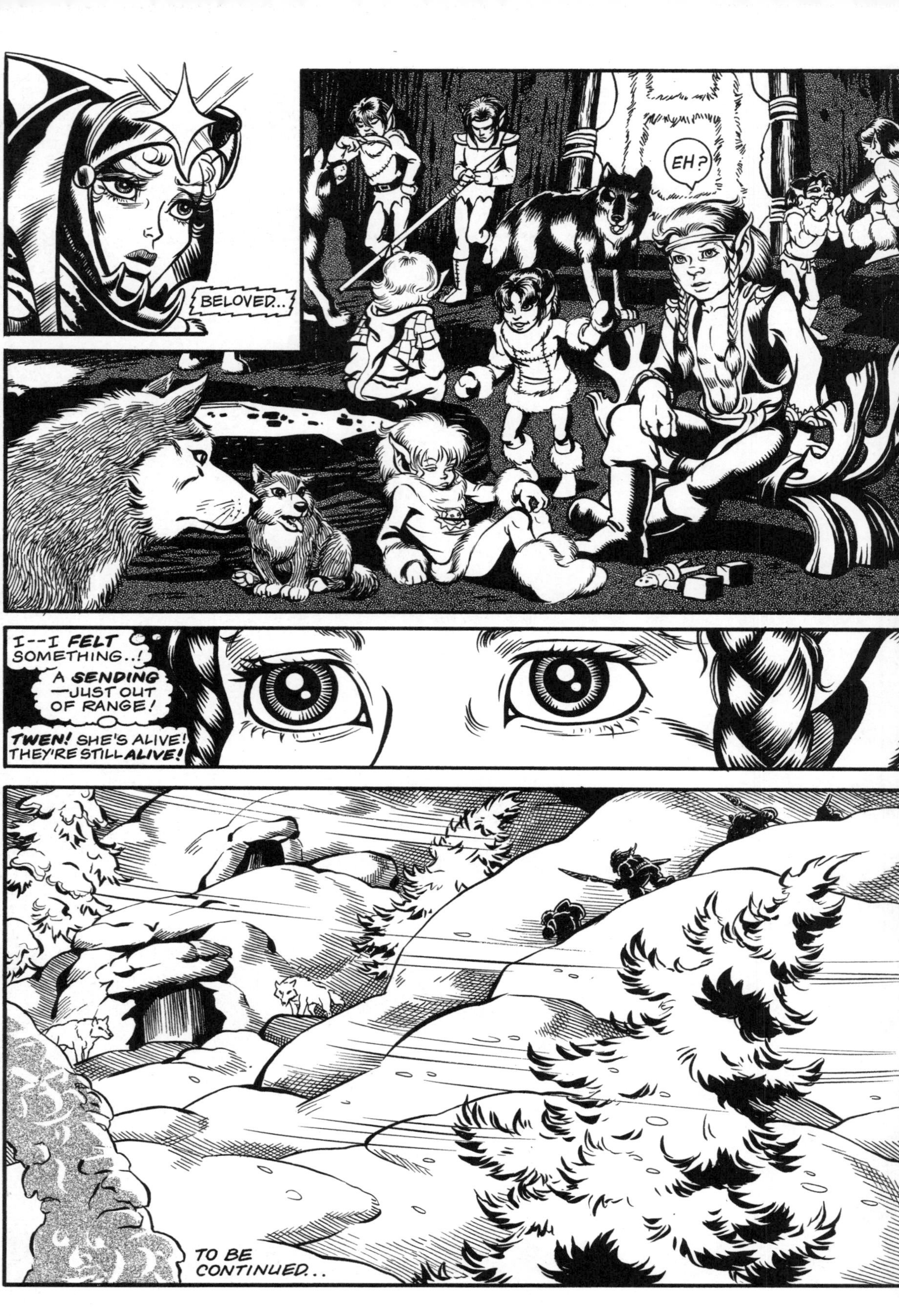
BELOVED...
EH?
I--I FELT SOMETHING..!
A SENDING—JUST OUT OF RANGE!
TWEN! SHE'S ALIVE! THEY'RE STILL ALIVE!
TO BE CONTINUED...

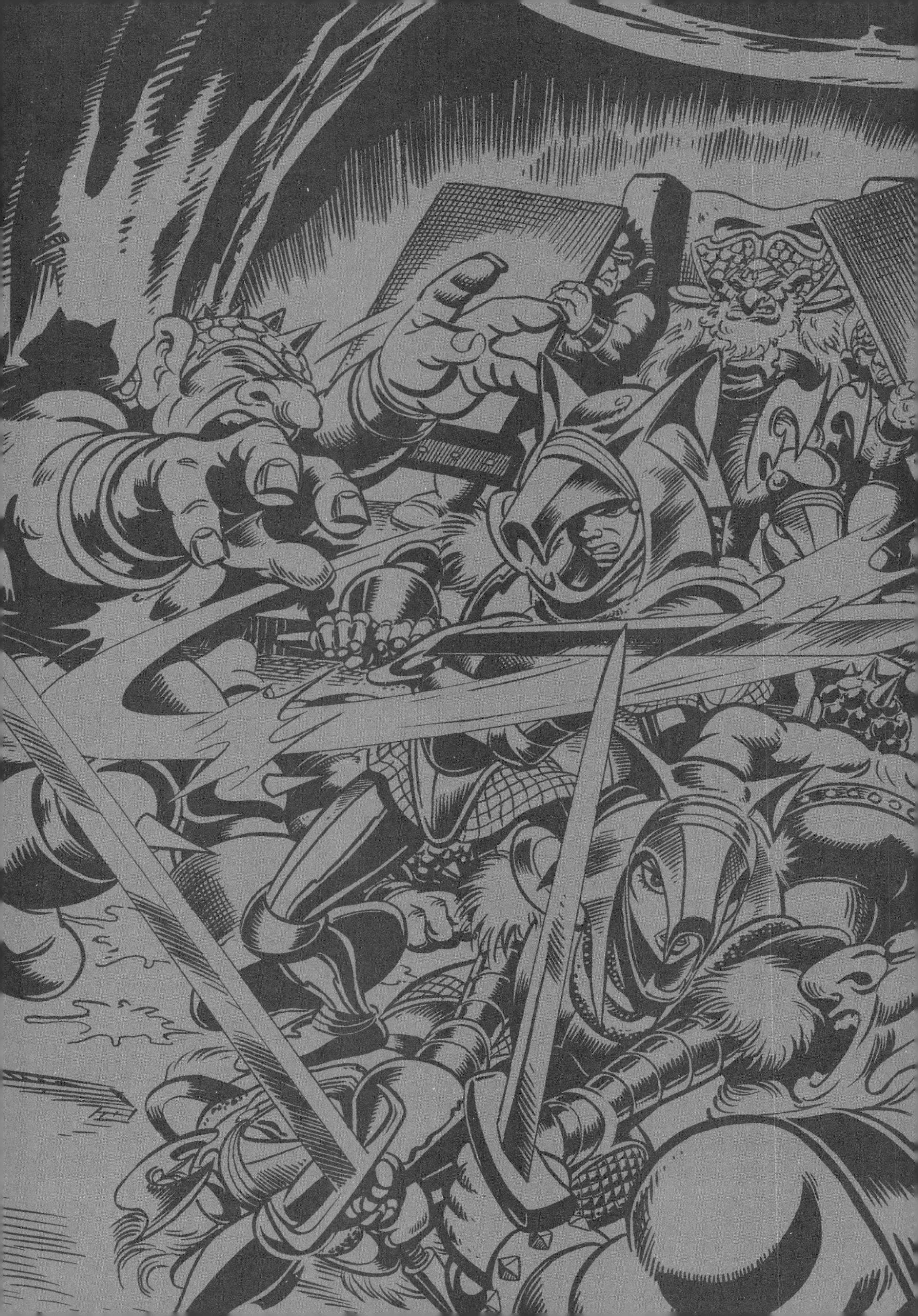

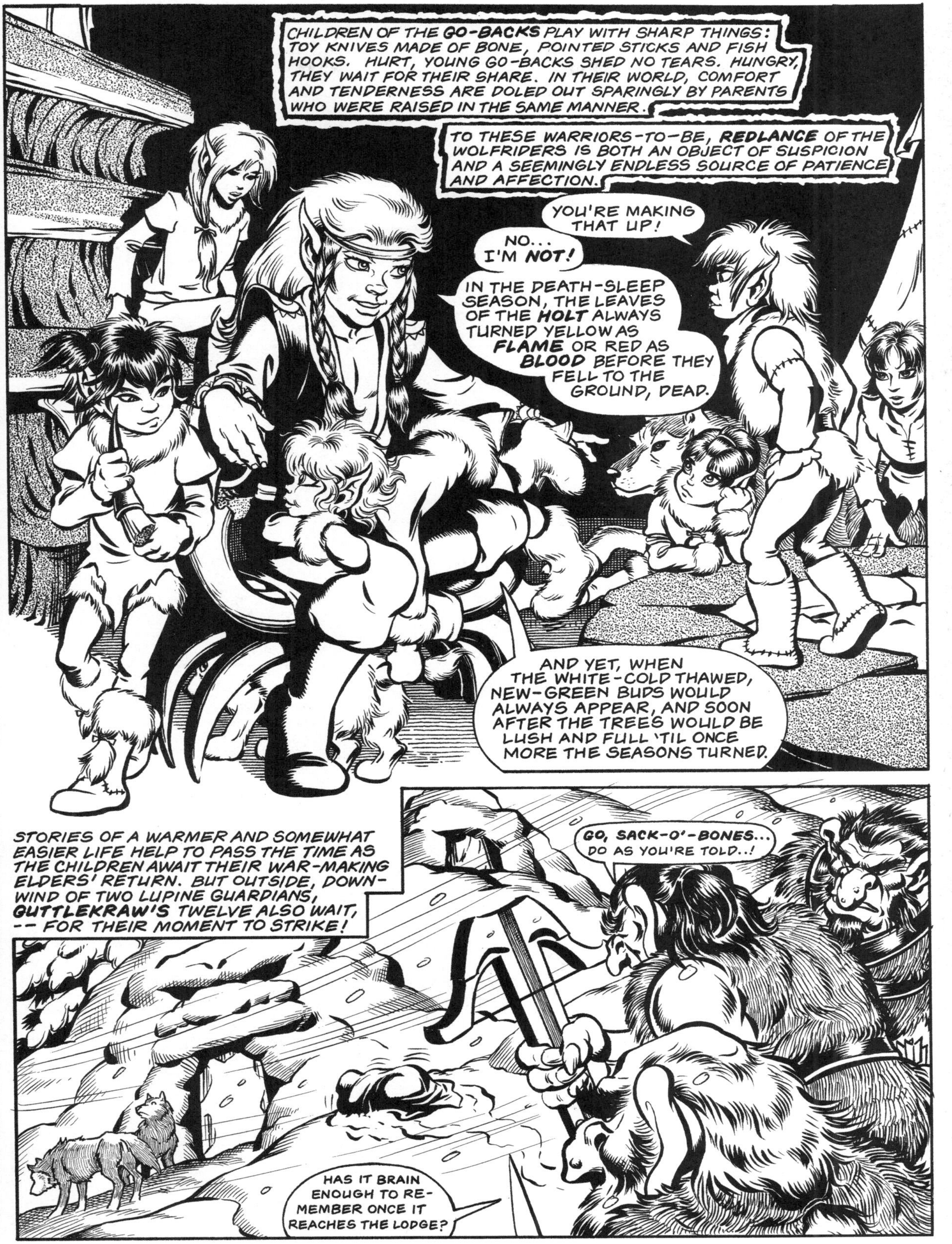
CHILDREN OF THE GO-BACKS PLAY WITH SHARP THINGS: TOY KNIVES MADE OF BONE, POINTED STICKS AND FISH HOOKS. HURT, YOUNG GO-BACKS SHED NO TEARS. HUNGRY, THEY WAIT FOR THEIR SHARE. IN THEIR WORLD, COMFORT AND TENDERNESS ARE DOLED OUT SPARINGLY BY PARENTS WHO WERE RAISED IN THE SAME MANNER.
TO THESE WARRIORS-TO-BE, REDLANCE OF THE WOLFRIDERS IS BOTH AN OBJECT OF SUSPICION AND A SEEMINGLY ENDLESS SOURCE OF PATIENCE AND AFFECTION.
YOU'RE MAKING THAT UP!
NO... I'M NOT!
IN THE DEATH-SLEEP SEASON, THE LEAVES OF THE HOLT ALWAYS TURNED YELLOW AS FLAME OR RED AS BLOOD BEFORE THEY FELL TO THE GROUND, DEAD.
AND YET, WHEN THE WHITE-COLD THAWED, NEW-GREEN BUDS WOULD ALWAYS APPEAR, AND SOON AFTER THE TREES WOULD BE LUSH AND FULL 'TIL ONCE MORE THE SEASONS TURNED.
STORIES OF A WARMER AND SOMEWHAT EASIER LIFE HELP TO PASS THE TIME AS THE CHILDREN AWAIT THEIR WAR-MAKING ELDERS' RETURN. BUT OUTSIDE, DOWN-WIND OF TWO LUPINE GUARDIANS, GUTTLEKRAW'S TWELVE ALSO WAIT, -- FOR THEIR MOMENT TO STRIKE!
GO, SACK-O'-BONES... DO AS YOU'RE TOLD..!
HAS IT BRAIN ENOUGH TO RE-MEMBER ONCE IT REACHES THE LODGE?

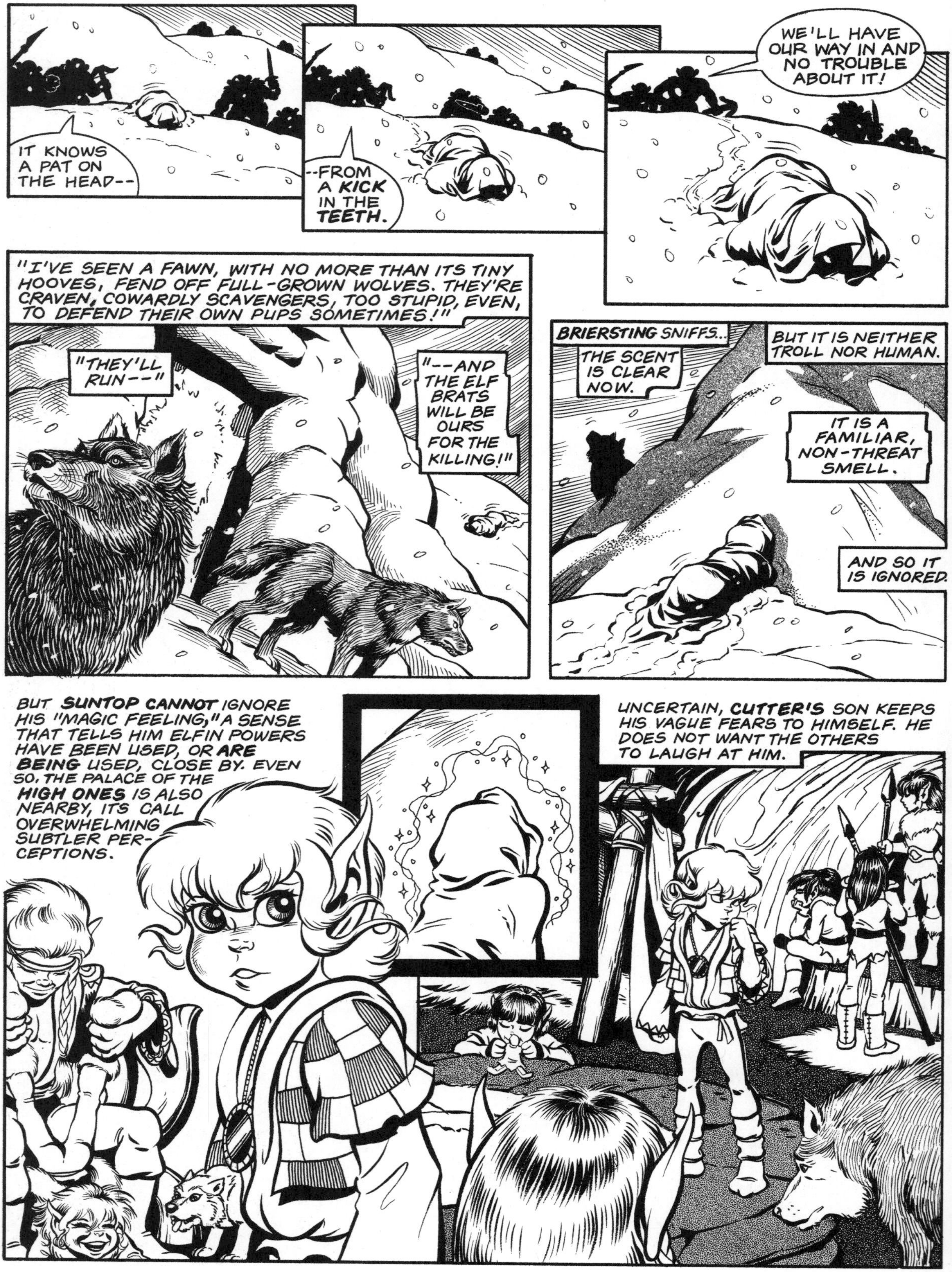
IT KNOWS A PAT ON THE HEAD--
--FROM A **KICK** IN THE **TEETH**.
WE'LL HAVE OUR WAY IN AND NO TROUBLE ABOUT IT!
"I'VE SEEN A FAWN, WITH NO MORE THAN ITS TINY HOOVES, FEND OFF FULL-GROWN WOLVES. THEY'RE CRAVEN, COWARDLY SCAVENGERS, TOO STUPID, EVEN, TO DEFEND THEIR OWN PUPS SOMETIMES!"
"THEY'LL RUN--"
"--AND THE ELF BRATS WILL BE OURS FOR THE KILLING!"
BRIERSTING SNIFFS...
THE SCENT IS CLEAR NOW.
BUT IT IS NEITHER TROLL NOR HUMAN.
IT IS A FAMILIAR, NON-THREAT SMELL.
AND SO IT IS IGNORED.
BUT **SUNTOP CANNOT** IGNORE HIS "MAGIC FEELING," A SENSE THAT TELLS HIM ELFIN POWERS HAVE BEEN USED, OR **ARE BEING** USED, CLOSE BY. EVEN SO, THE PALACE OF THE **HIGH ONES** IS ALSO NEARBY, ITS CALL OVERWHELMING SUBTLER PERCEPTIONS.
UNCERTAIN, **CUTTER'S** SON KEEPS HIS VAGUE FEARS TO HIMSELF. HE DOES NOT WANT THE OTHERS TO LAUGH AT HIM.

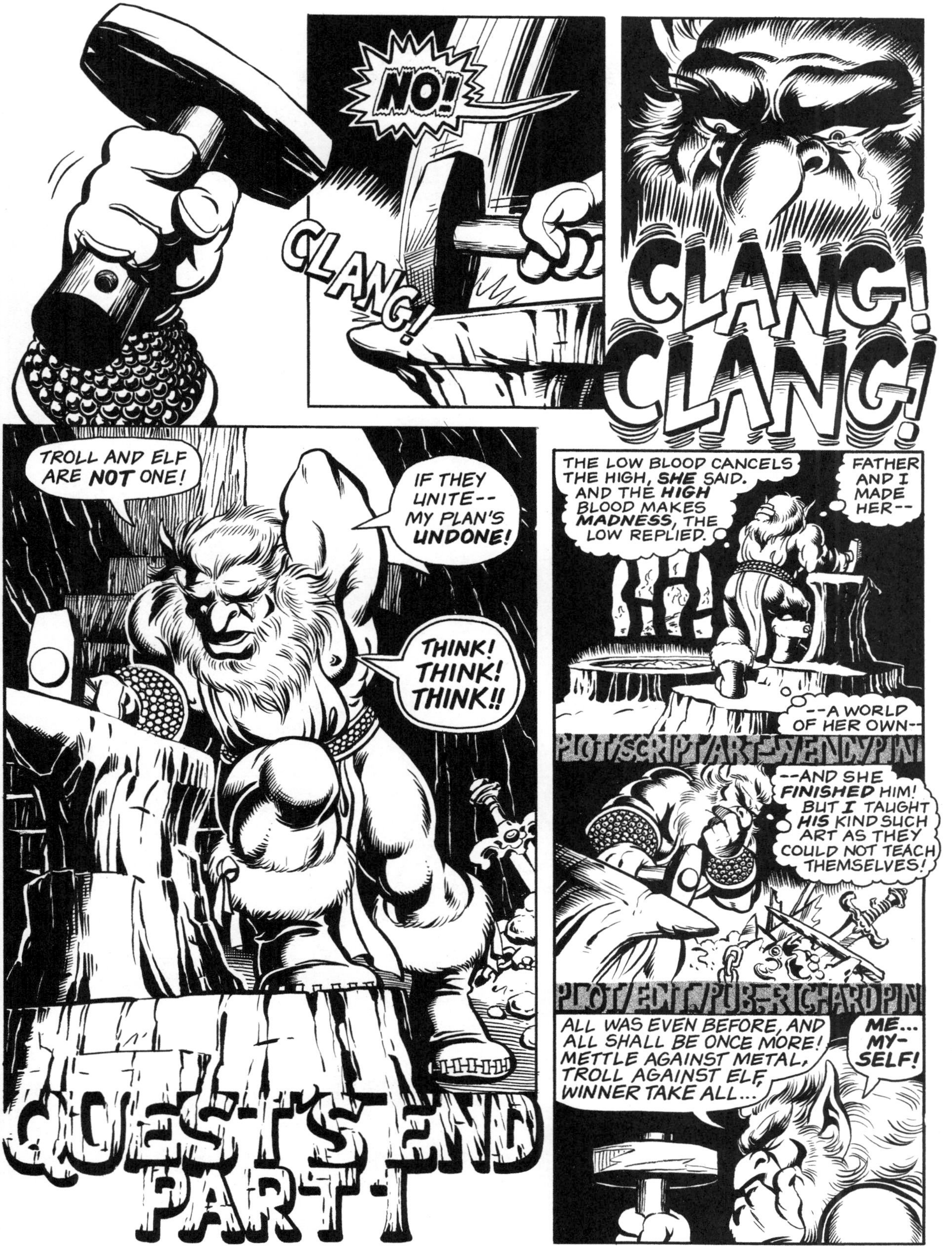
NO!
CLANG!
CLANG! CLANG!
TROLL AND ELF ARE NOT ONE!
IF THEY UNITE-- MY PLAN'S UNDONE!
THINK! THINK! THINK!!
QUEST'S END PART I
THE LOW BLOOD CANCELS THE HIGH, SHE SAID. AND THE HIGH BLOOD MAKES MADNESS, THE LOW REPLIED.
FATHER AND I MADE HER--
--A WORLD OF HER OWN--
PLOT/SCRIPT/ART-WENDY PINI
--AND SHE FINISHED HIM! BUT I TAUGHT HIS KIND SUCH ART AS THEY COULD NOT TEACH THEMSELVES!
PLOT/EDIT./PUB.-RICHARD PINI
ALL WAS EVEN BEFORE, AND ALL SHALL BE ONCE MORE! METTLE AGAINST METAL, TROLL AGAINST ELF, WINNER TAKE ALL...
ME... MY-SELF!

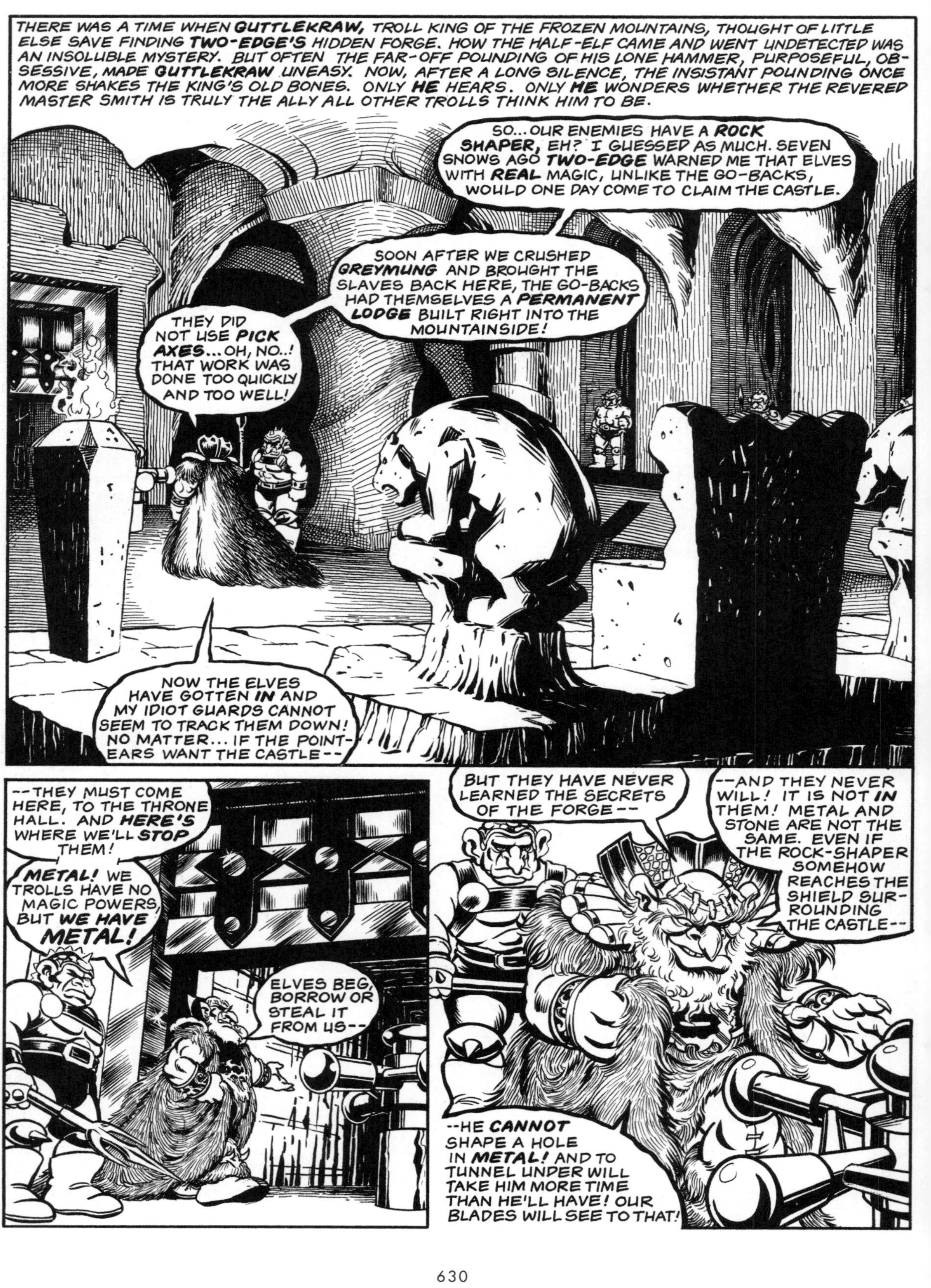
THERE WAS A TIME WHEN GUTTLEKRAW, TROLL KING OF THE FROZEN MOUNTAINS, THOUGHT OF LITTLE ELSE SAVE FINDING TWO-EDGE'S HIDDEN FORGE. HOW THE HALF-ELF CAME AND WENT UNDETECTED WAS AN INSOLUBLE MYSTERY. BUT OFTEN THE FAR-OFF POUNDING OF HIS LONE HAMMER, PURPOSEFUL, OBSESSIVE, MADE GUTTLEKRAW UNEASY. NOW, AFTER A LONG SILENCE, THE INSISTANT POUNDING ONCE MORE SHAKES THE KING'S OLD BONES. ONLY HE HEARS. ONLY HE WONDERS WHETHER THE REVERED MASTER SMITH IS TRULY THE ALLY ALL OTHER TROLLS THINK HIM TO BE.
SO... OUR ENEMIES HAVE A ROCK SHAPER, EH? I GUESSED AS MUCH. SEVEN SNOWS AGO TWO-EDGE WARNED ME THAT ELVES WITH REAL MAGIC, UNLIKE THE GO-BACKS, WOULD ONE DAY COME TO CLAIM THE CASTLE.
SOON AFTER WE CRUSHED GREYMUNG AND BROUGHT THE SLAVES BACK HERE, THE GO-BACKS HAD THEMSELVES A PERMANENT LODGE BUILT RIGHT INTO THE MOUNTAINSIDE!
THEY DID NOT USE PICK AXES... OH, NO..! THAT WORK WAS DONE TOO QUICKLY AND TOO WELL!
NOW THE ELVES HAVE GOTTEN IN AND MY IDIOT GUARDS CANNOT SEEM TO TRACK THEM DOWN! NO MATTER... IF THE POINT-EARS WANT THE CASTLE--
--THEY MUST COME HERE, TO THE THRONE HALL. AND HERE'S WHERE WE'LL STOP THEM!
METAL! WE TROLLS HAVE NO MAGIC POWERS, BUT WE HAVE METAL!
ELVES BEG, BORROW OR STEAL IT FROM US--
BUT THEY HAVE NEVER LEARNED THE SECRETS OF THE FORGE--
--AND THEY NEVER WILL! IT IS NOT IN THEM! METAL AND STONE ARE NOT THE SAME. EVEN IF THE ROCK-SHAPER SOMEHOW REACHES THE SHIELD SURROUNDING THE CASTLE--
--HE CANNOT SHAPE A HOLE IN METAL! AND TO TUNNEL UNDER WILL TAKE HIM MORE TIME THAN HE'LL HAVE! OUR BLADES WILL SEE TO THAT!

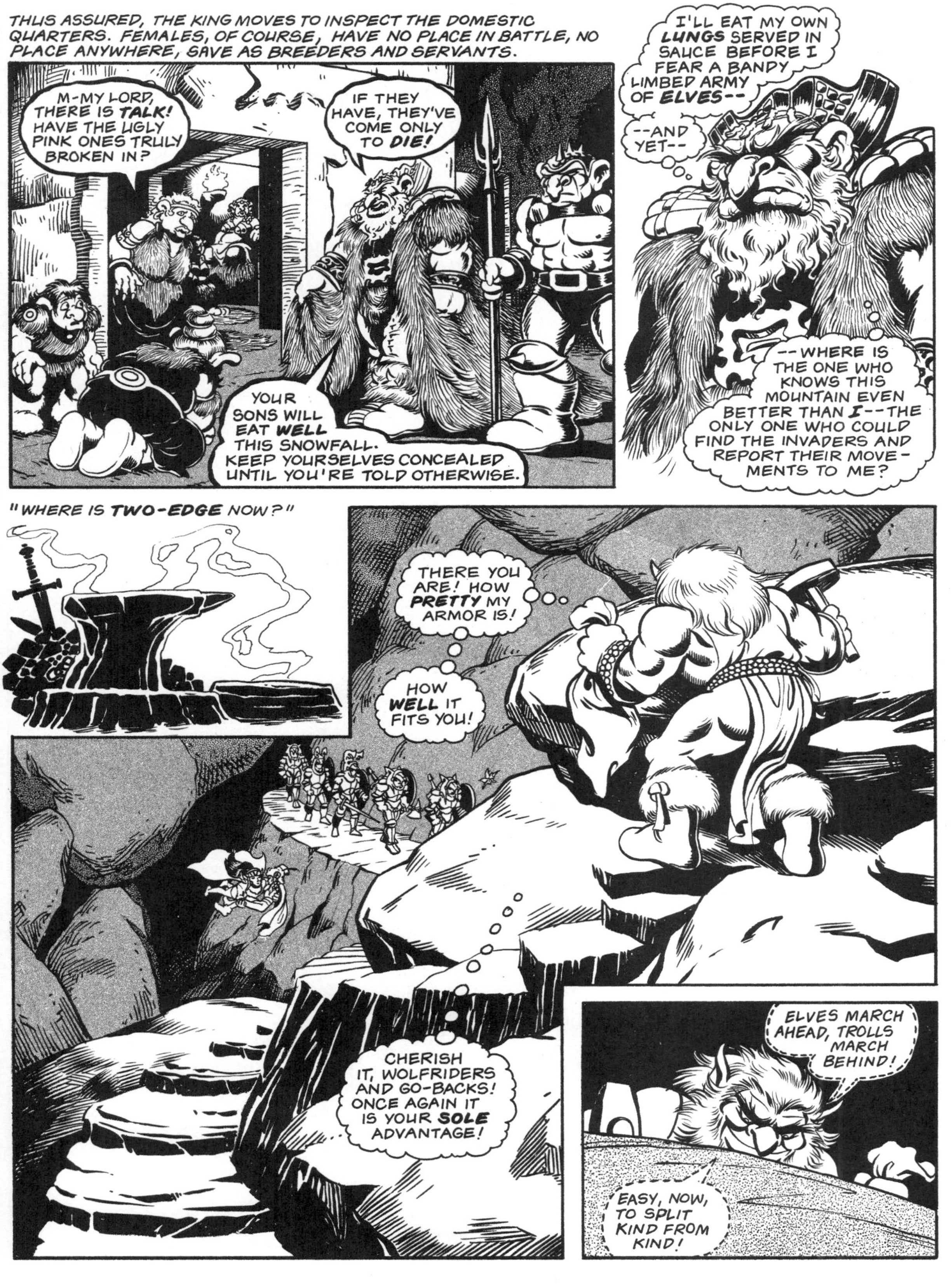
THUS ASSURED, THE KING MOVES TO INSPECT THE DOMESTIC QUARTERS. FEMALES, OF COURSE, HAVE NO PLACE IN BATTLE, NO PLACE ANYWHERE, SAVE AS BREEDERS AND SERVANTS.
M-MY LORD, THERE IS TALK! HAVE THE UGLY PINK ONES TRULY BROKEN IN?
IF THEY HAVE, THEY'VE COME ONLY TO DIE!
YOUR SONS WILL EAT WELL THIS SNOWFALL. KEEP YOURSELVES CONCEALED UNTIL YOU'RE TOLD OTHERWISE.
I'LL EAT MY OWN LUNGS SERVED IN SAUCE BEFORE I FEAR A BANDY LIMBED ARMY OF ELVES--
--AND YET--
--WHERE IS THE ONE WHO KNOWS THIS MOUNTAIN EVEN BETTER THAN I--THE ONLY ONE WHO COULD FIND THE INVADERS AND REPORT THEIR MOVE-MENTS TO ME?
"WHERE IS TWO-EDGE NOW?"
THERE YOU ARE! HOW PRETTY MY ARMOR IS!
HOW WELL IT FITS YOU!
CHERISH IT, WOLFRIDERS AND GO-BACKS! ONCE AGAIN IT IS YOUR SOLE ADVANTAGE!
ELVES MARCH AHEAD, TROLLS MARCH BEHIND!
EASY, NOW, TO SPLIT KIND FROM KIND!

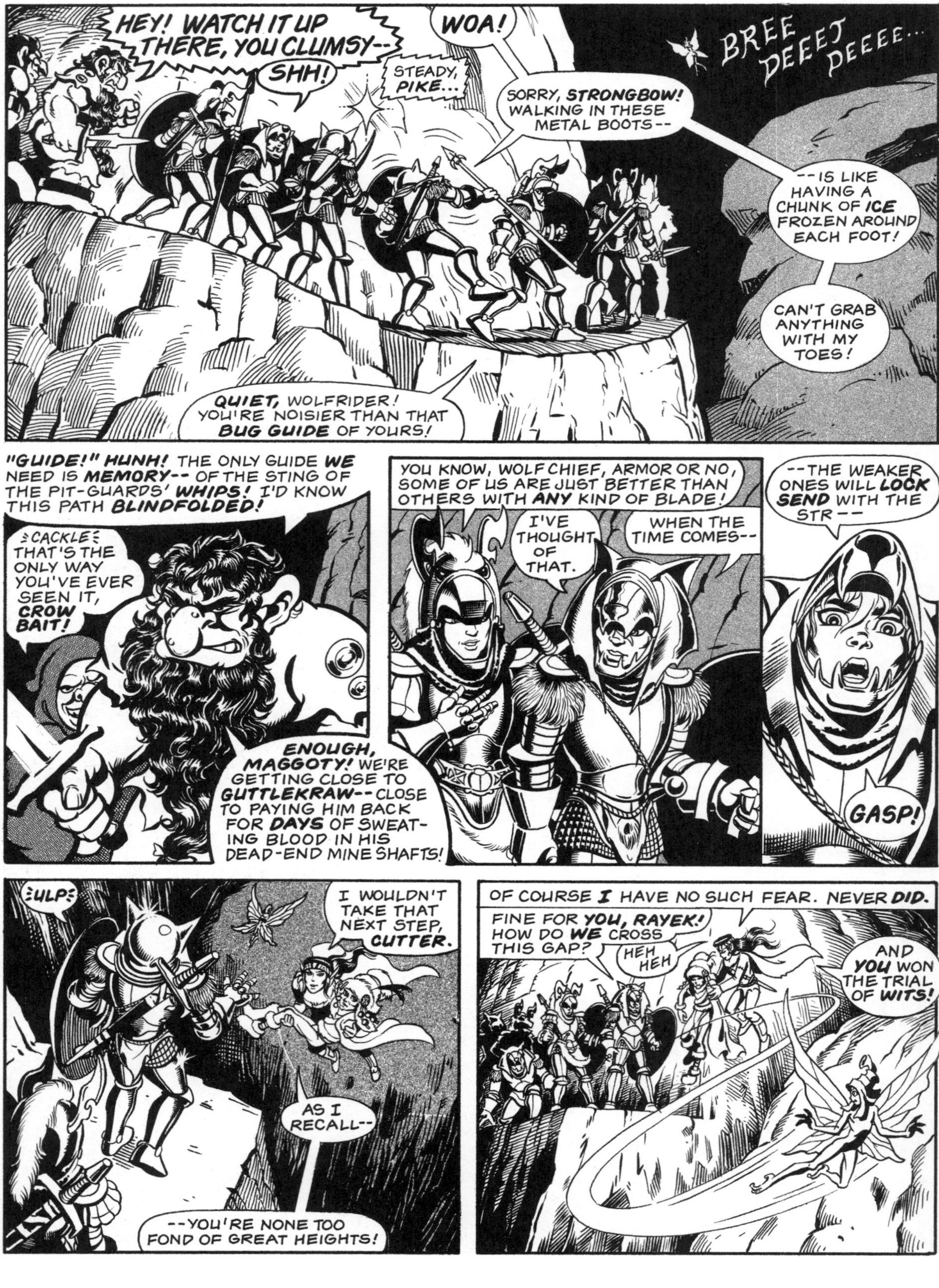
HEY! WATCH IT UP THERE, YOU CLUMSY--
SHH!
WOA!
STEADY, PIKE...
SORRY, STRONGBOW! WALKING IN THESE METAL BOOTS--
BREE DEEET DEEEE...
--IS LIKE HAVING A CHUNK OF ICE FROZEN AROUND EACH FOOT!
CAN'T GRAB ANYTHING WITH MY TOES!
QUIET, WOLFRIDER! YOU'RE NOISIER THAN THAT BUG GUIDE OF YOURS!
"GUIDE!" HUNH! THE ONLY GUIDE WE NEED IS MEMORY-- OF THE STING OF THE PIT-GUARDS' WHIPS! I'D KNOW THIS PATH BLINDFOLDED!
CACKLE THAT'S THE ONLY WAY YOU'VE EVER SEEN IT, CROW BAIT!
ENOUGH, MAGGOTY! WE'RE GETTING CLOSE TO GUTTLEKRAW-- CLOSE TO PAYING HIM BACK FOR DAYS OF SWEATING BLOOD IN HIS DEAD-END MINE SHAFTS!
YOU KNOW, WOLF CHIEF, ARMOR OR NO, SOME OF US ARE JUST BETTER THAN OTHERS WITH ANY KIND OF BLADE!
I'VE THOUGHT OF THAT.
WHEN THE TIME COMES--
--THE WEAKER ONES WILL LOCK SEND WITH THE STR--
GASP!
ULP
I WOULDN'T TAKE THAT NEXT STEP, CUTTER.
AS I RECALL--
--YOU'RE NONE TOO FOND OF GREAT HEIGHTS!
OF COURSE I HAVE NO SUCH FEAR. NEVER DID.
FINE FOR YOU, RAYEK! HOW DO WE CROSS THIS GAP?
HEH HEH
AND YOU WON THE TRIAL OF WITS!

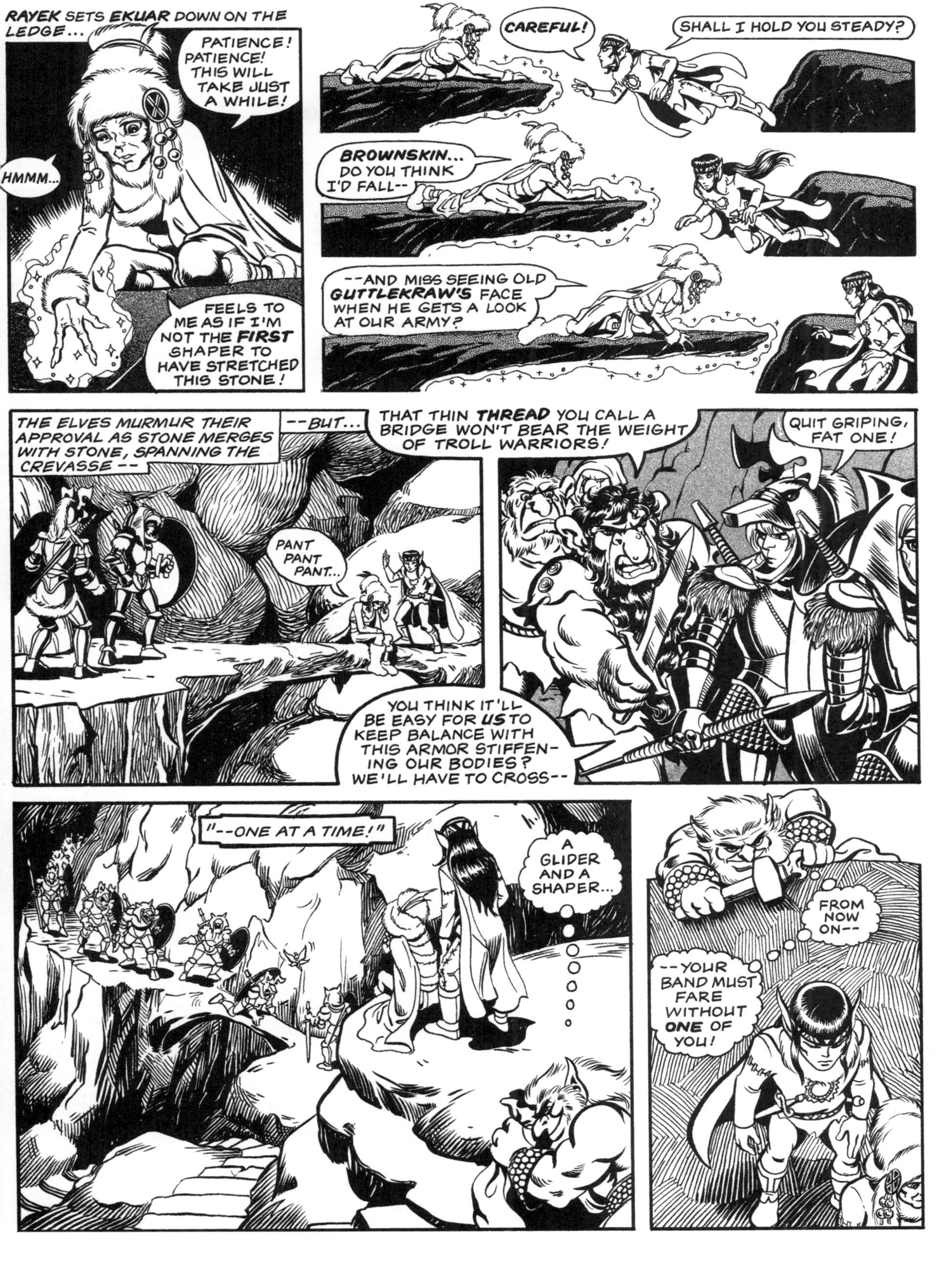
RAYEK SETS EKUAR DOWN ON THE LEDGE...
PATIENCE! PATIENCE! THIS WILL TAKE JUST A WHILE!
HMMM...
FEELS TO ME AS IF I'M NOT THE FIRST SHAPER TO HAVE STRETCHED THIS STONE!
CAREFUL!
SHALL I HOLD YOU STEADY?
BROWNSKIN... DO YOU THINK I'D FALL--
--AND MISS SEEING OLD GUTTLEKRAW'S FACE WHEN HE GETS A LOOK AT OUR ARMY?
THE ELVES MURMUR THEIR APPROVAL AS STONE MERGES WITH STONE, SPANNING THE CREVASSE--
PANT PANT PANT...
--BUT...
THAT THIN THREAD YOU CALL A BRIDGE WON'T BEAR THE WEIGHT OF TROLL WARRIORS!
QUIT GRIPING, FAT ONE!
YOU THINK IT'LL BE EASY FOR US TO KEEP BALANCE WITH THIS ARMOR STIFFENING OUR BODIES? WE'LL HAVE TO CROSS--
"--ONE AT A TIME!"
A GLIDER AND A SHAPER...
FROM NOW ON--
--YOUR BAND MUST FARE WITHOUT ONE OF YOU!

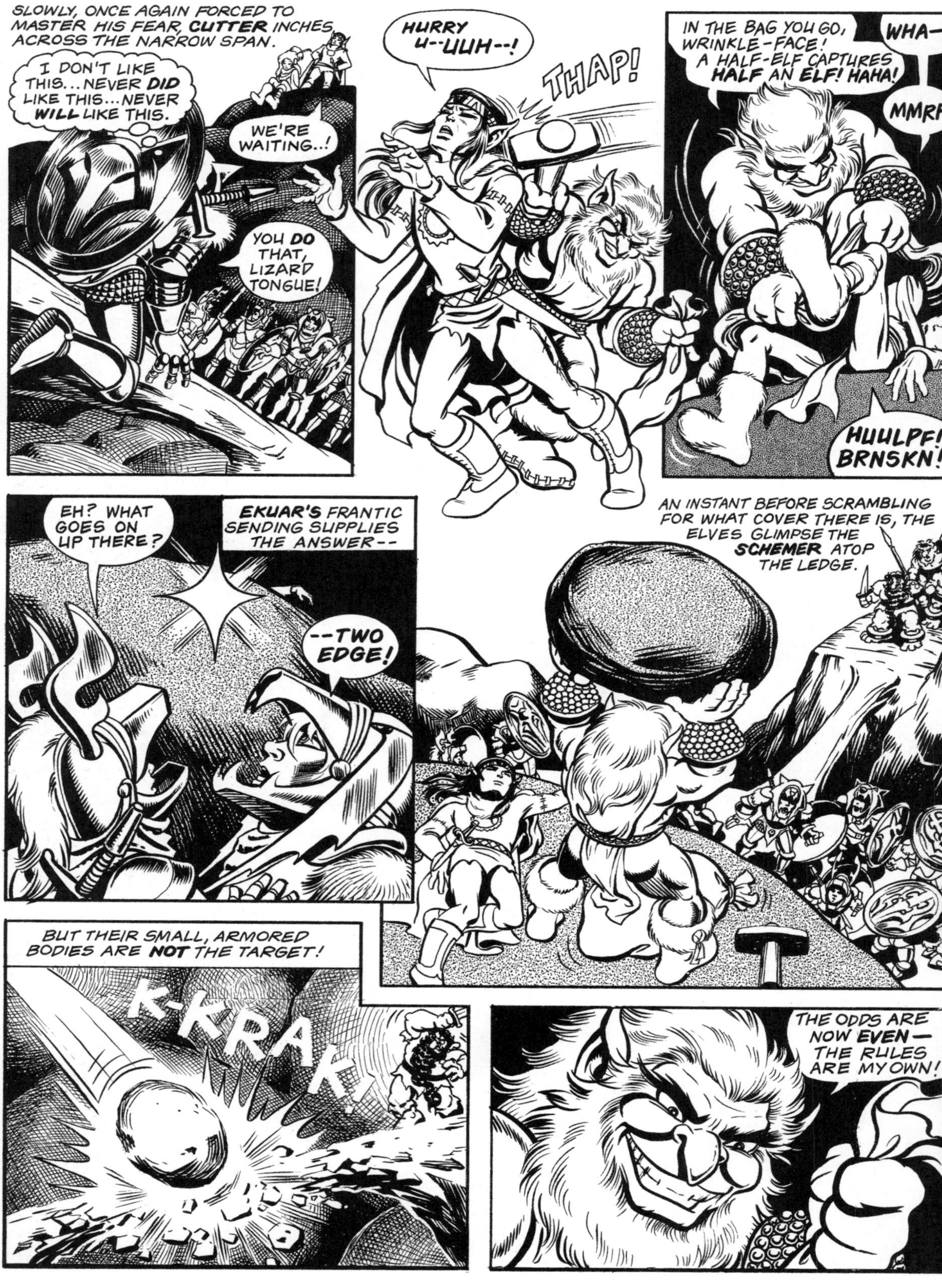
SLOWLY, ONCE AGAIN FORCED TO MASTER HIS FEAR, CUTTER INCHES ACROSS THE NARROW SPAN.
I DON'T LIKE THIS... NEVER DID LIKE THIS... NEVER WILL LIKE THIS.
WE'RE WAITING..!
YOU DO THAT, LIZARD TONGUE!
HURRY U--UUH--!
THAP!
IN THE BAG YOU GO, WRINKLE-FACE! A HALF-ELF CAPTURES HALF AN ELF! HAHA!
WHA--?
MMRF
HUULPF! BRNSKN!
EH? WHAT GOES ON UP THERE?
EKUAR'S FRANTIC SENDING SUPPLIES THE ANSWER--
--TWO EDGE!
AN INSTANT BEFORE SCRAMBLING FOR WHAT COVER THERE IS, THE ELVES GLIMPSE THE SCHEMER ATOP THE LEDGE.
BUT THEIR SMALL, ARMORED BODIES ARE NOT THE TARGET!
K-KRAK!
THE ODDS ARE NOW EVEN— THE RULES ARE MY OWN!

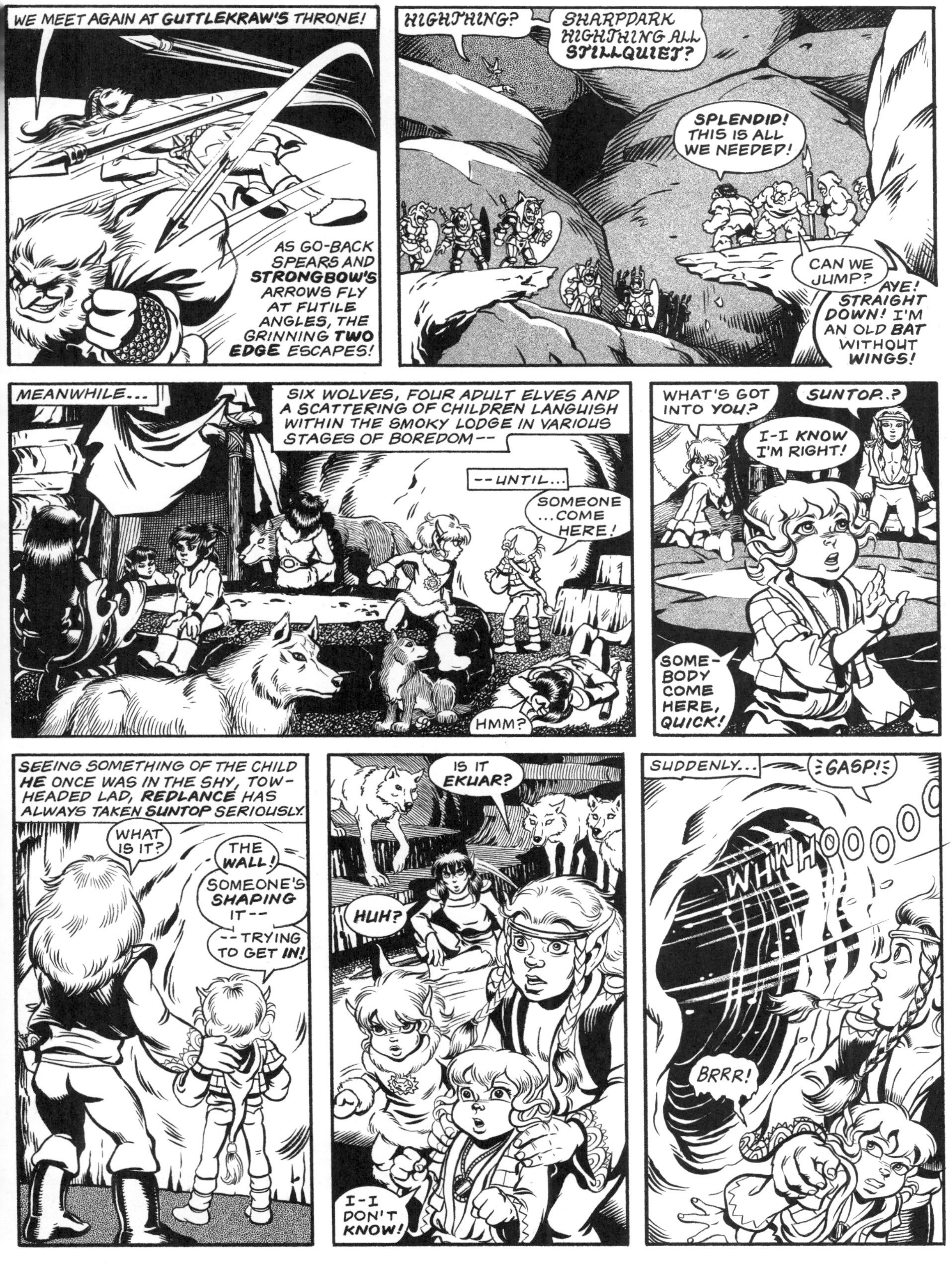

WE MEET AGAIN AT GUTTLEKRAW'S THRONE!
AS GO-BACK SPEARS AND STRONGBOW'S ARROWS FLY AT FUTILE ANGLES, THE GRINNING TWO EDGE ESCAPES!
HIGHTHING?
SHARPDARK HIGHTHING ALL STILLQUIET?
SPLENDID! THIS IS ALL WE NEEDED!
CAN WE JUMP?
AYE! STRAIGHT DOWN! I'M AN OLD BAT WITHOUT WINGS!
MEANWHILE...
SIX WOLVES, FOUR ADULT ELVES AND A SCATTERING OF CHILDREN LANGUISH WITHIN THE SMOKY LODGE IN VARIOUS STAGES OF BOREDOM--
--UNTIL...
SOMEONE ...COME HERE!
HMM?
WHAT'S GOT INTO YOU?
SUNTOP..?
I-I KNOW I'M RIGHT!
SOME-BODY COME HERE, QUICK!
SEEING SOMETHING OF THE CHILD HE ONCE WAS IN THE SHY, TOW-HEADED LAD, REDLANCE HAS ALWAYS TAKEN SUNTOP SERIOUSLY.
WHAT IS IT?
THE WALL!
SOMEONE'S SHAPING IT--
--TRYING TO GET IN!
IS IT EKUAR?
HUH?
I-I DON'T KNOW!
SUDDENLY...
GASP!
WHWHOOOOOO
BRRR!

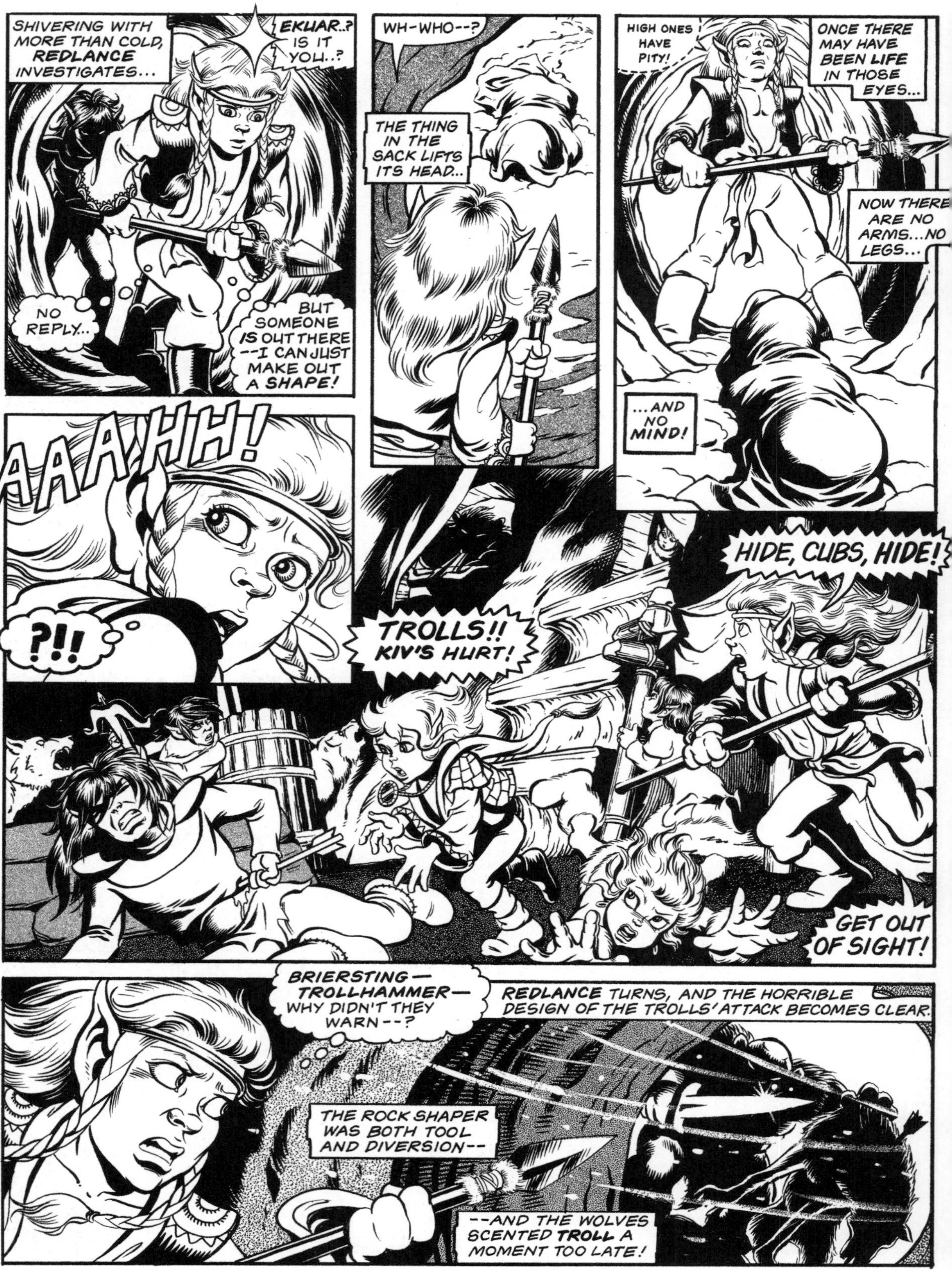

SHIVERING WITH MORE THAN COLD, REDLANCE INVESTIGATES...
EKUAR..? IS IT YOU..?
NO REPLY...
BUT SOMEONE IS OUT THERE --I CAN JUST MAKE OUT A SHAPE!
WH-WHO--?
THE THING IN THE SACK LIFTS ITS HEAD...
HIGH ONES HAVE PITY!
ONCE THERE MAY HAVE BEEN LIFE IN THOSE EYES...
NOW THERE ARE NO ARMS...NO LEGS...
...AND NO MIND!
AAAHH!
?!!
TROLLS!! KIV'S HURT!
HIDE, CUBS, HIDE!
GET OUT OF SIGHT!
BRIERSTING— TROLLHAMMER— WHY DIDN'T THEY WARN--?
REDLANCE TURNS, AND THE HORRIBLE DESIGN OF THE TROLLS' ATTACK BECOMES CLEAR.
THE ROCK SHAPER WAS BOTH TOOL AND DIVERSION--
--AND THE WOLVES SCENTED TROLL A MOMENT TOO LATE!

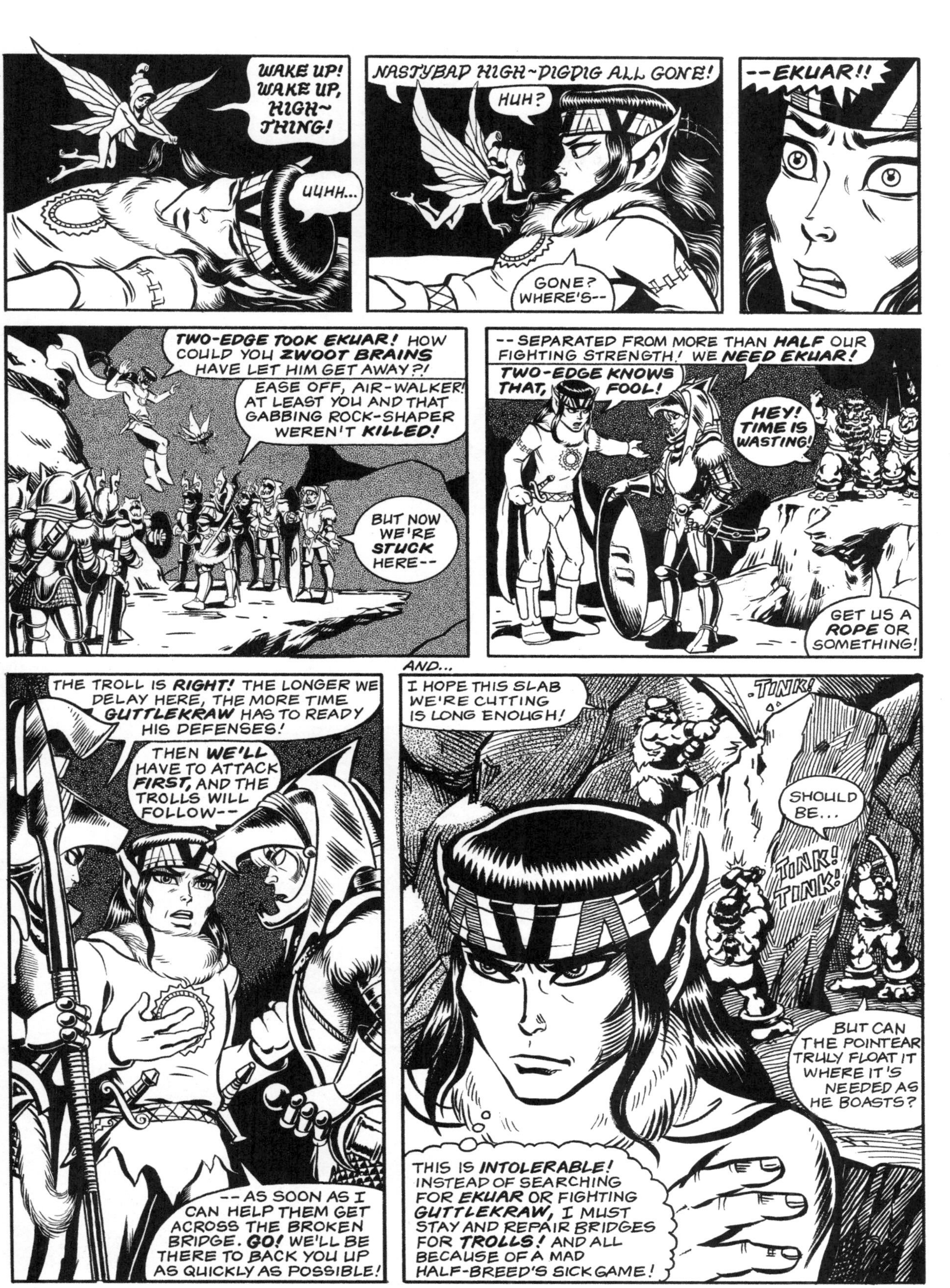
WAKE UP! WAKE UP, HIGH~THING!
UUHH...
NASTYBAD HIGH~DIGDIG ALL GONE!
HUH?
GONE? WHERE'S--
--EKUAR!!
TWO-EDGE TOOK EKUAR! HOW COULD YOU ZWOOT BRAINS HAVE LET HIM GET AWAY?!
EASE OFF, AIR-WALKER! AT LEAST YOU AND THAT GABBING ROCK-SHAPER WEREN'T KILLED!
BUT NOW WE'RE STUCK HERE--
--SEPARATED FROM MORE THAN HALF OUR FIGHTING STRENGTH! WE NEED EKUAR!
TWO-EDGE KNOWS THAT, FOOL!
HEY! TIME IS WASTING!
GET US A ROPE OR SOMETHING!
AND...
THE TROLL IS RIGHT! THE LONGER WE DELAY HERE, THE MORE TIME GUTTLEKRAW HAS TO READY HIS DEFENSES!
THEN WE'LL HAVE TO ATTACK FIRST, AND THE TROLLS WILL FOLLOW--
--AS SOON AS I CAN HELP THEM GET ACROSS THE BROKEN BRIDGE. GO! WE'LL BE THERE TO BACK YOU UP AS QUICKLY AS POSSIBLE!
I HOPE THIS SLAB WE'RE CUTTING IS LONG ENOUGH!
TINK!
SHOULD BE...
TINK! TINK!
BUT CAN THE POINTEAR TRULY FLOAT IT WHERE IT'S NEEDED AS HE BOASTS?
THIS IS INTOLERABLE! INSTEAD OF SEARCHING FOR EKUAR OR FIGHTING GUTTLEKRAW, I MUST STAY AND REPAIR BRIDGES FOR TROLLS! AND ALL BECAUSE OF A MAD HALF-BREED'S SICK GAME!

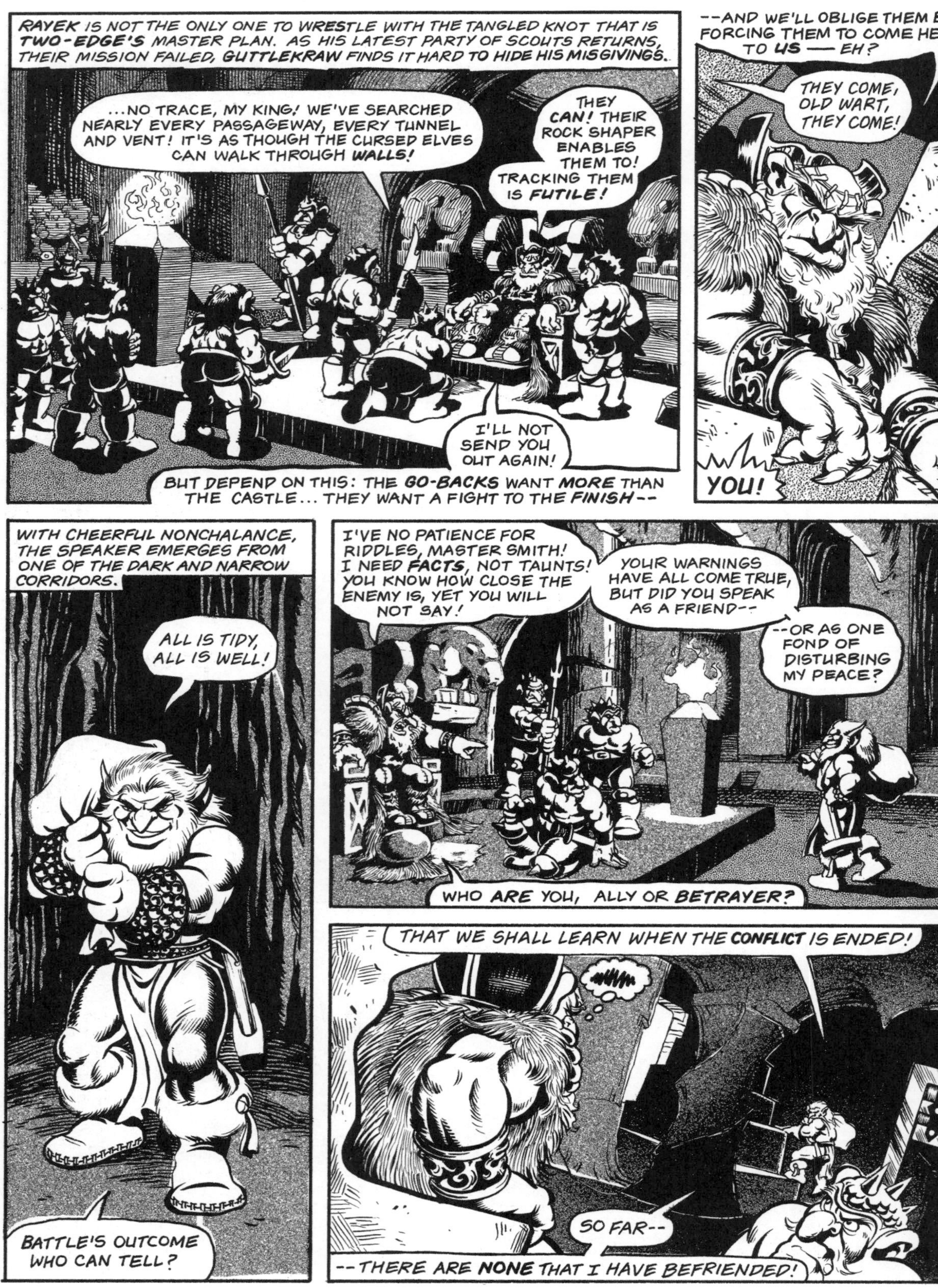
RAYEK IS NOT THE ONLY ONE TO WRESTLE WITH THE TANGLED KNOT THAT IS TWO-EDGE'S MASTER PLAN. AS HIS LATEST PARTY OF SCOUTS RETURNS, THEIR MISSION FAILED, GUTTLEKRAW FINDS IT HARD TO HIDE HIS MISGIVINGS.
...NO TRACE, MY KING! WE'VE SEARCHED NEARLY EVERY PASSAGEWAY, EVERY TUNNEL AND VENT! IT'S AS THOUGH THE CURSED ELVES CAN WALK THROUGH WALLS!
THEY CAN! THEIR ROCK SHAPER ENABLES THEM TO! TRACKING THEM IS FUTILE!
I'LL NOT SEND YOU OUT AGAIN!
BUT DEPEND ON THIS: THE GO-BACKS WANT MORE THAN THE CASTLE... THEY WANT A FIGHT TO THE FINISH--
--AND WE'LL OBLIGE THEM BY FORCING THEM TO COME HERE TO US — EH?
THEY COME, OLD WART, THEY COME!
YOU!
WITH CHEERFUL NONCHALANCE, THE SPEAKER EMERGES FROM ONE OF THE DARK AND NARROW CORRIDORS.
ALL IS TIDY, ALL IS WELL!
BATTLE'S OUTCOME WHO CAN TELL?
I'VE NO PATIENCE FOR RIDDLES, MASTER SMITH! I NEED FACTS, NOT TAUNTS! YOU KNOW HOW CLOSE THE ENEMY IS, YET YOU WILL NOT SAY!
YOUR WARNINGS HAVE ALL COME TRUE, BUT DID YOU SPEAK AS A FRIEND--
--OR AS ONE FOND OF DISTURBING MY PEACE?
WHO ARE YOU, ALLY OR BETRAYER?
THAT WE SHALL LEARN WHEN THE CONFLICT IS ENDED!
SO FAR--
--THERE ARE NONE THAT I HAVE BEFRIENDED!

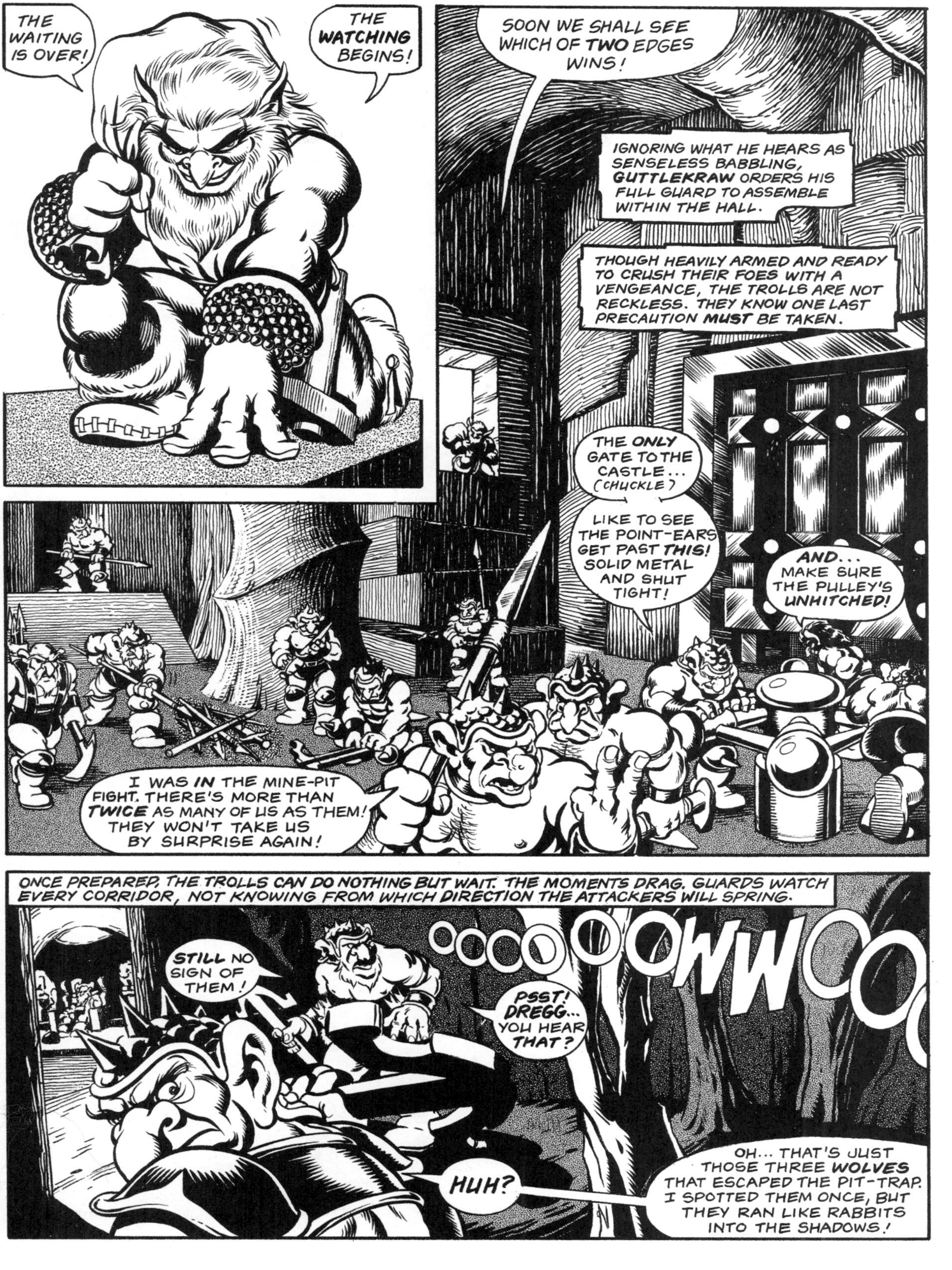
THE WAITING IS OVER!
THE WATCHING BEGINS!
SOON WE SHALL SEE WHICH OF TWO EDGES WINS!
IGNORING WHAT HE HEARS AS SENSELESS BABBLING, GUTTLEKRAW ORDERS HIS FULL GUARD TO ASSEMBLE WITHIN THE HALL.
THOUGH HEAVILY ARMED AND READY TO CRUSH THEIR FOES WITH A VENGEANCE, THE TROLLS ARE NOT RECKLESS. THEY KNOW ONE LAST PRECAUTION MUST BE TAKEN.
THE ONLY GATE TO THE CASTLE... (CHUCKLE)
LIKE TO SEE THE POINT-EARS GET PAST THIS! SOLID METAL AND SHUT TIGHT!
AND... MAKE SURE THE PULLEY'S UNHITCHED!
I WAS IN THE MINE-PIT FIGHT. THERE'S MORE THAN TWICE AS MANY OF US AS THEM! THEY WON'T TAKE US BY SURPRISE AGAIN!
ONCE PREPARED, THE TROLLS CAN DO NOTHING BUT WAIT. THE MOMENTS DRAG. GUARDS WATCH EVERY CORRIDOR, NOT KNOWING FROM WHICH DIRECTION THE ATTACKERS WILL SPRING.
OOOOOOWWOO
STILL NO SIGN OF THEM!
PSST! DREGG... YOU HEAR THAT?
HUH?
OH... THAT'S JUST THOSE THREE WOLVES THAT ESCAPED THE PIT-TRAP. I SPOTTED THEM ONCE, BUT THEY RAN LIKE RABBITS INTO THE SHADOWS!

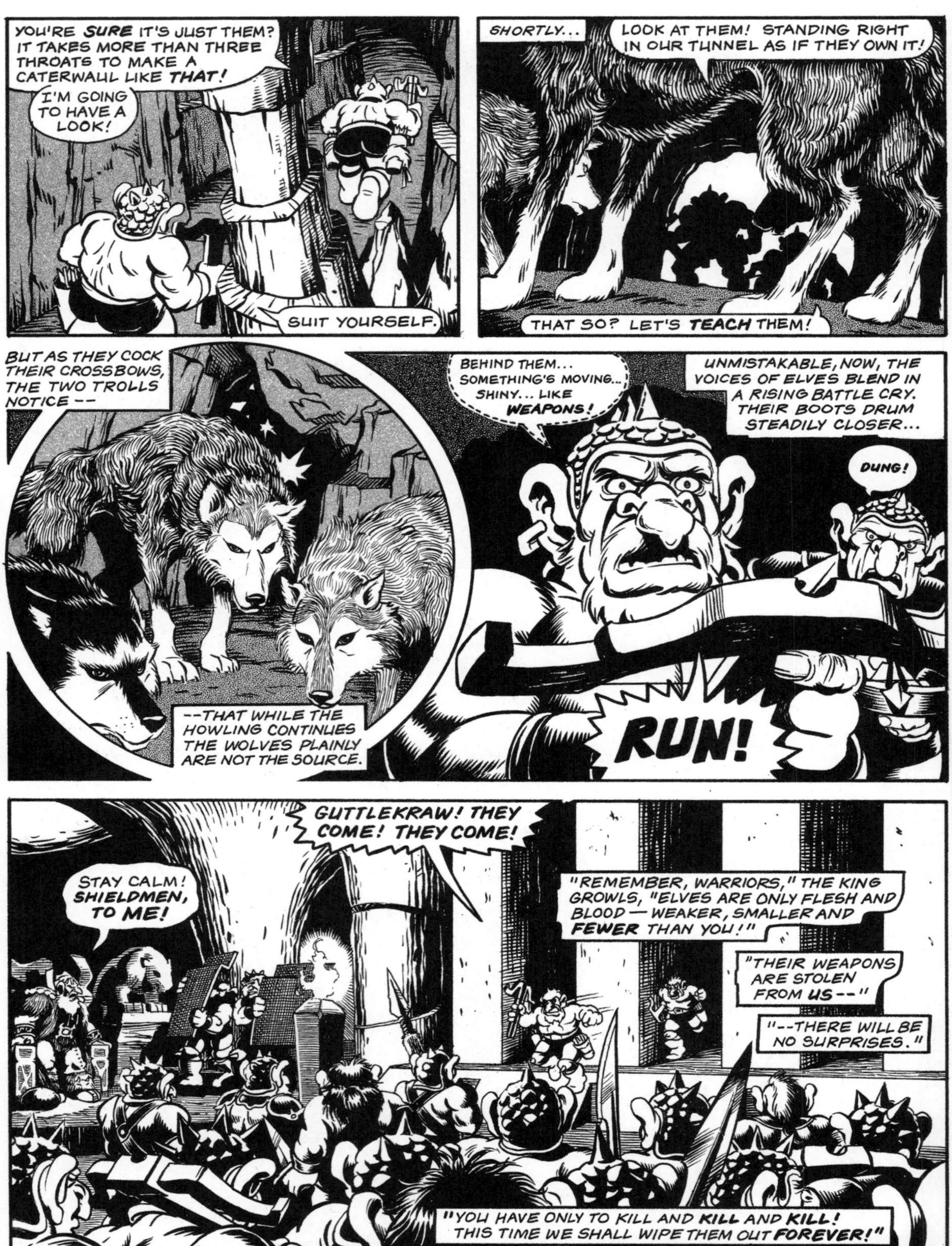

YOU'RE SURE IT'S JUST THEM? IT TAKES MORE THAN THREE THROATS TO MAKE A CATERWAUL LIKE THAT!
I'M GOING TO HAVE A LOOK!
SUIT YOURSELF.
SHORTLY...
LOOK AT THEM! STANDING RIGHT IN OUR TUNNEL AS IF THEY OWN IT!
THAT SO? LET'S TEACH THEM!
BUT AS THEY COCK THEIR CROSSBOWS, THE TWO TROLLS NOTICE --
--THAT WHILE THE HOWLING CONTINUES THE WOLVES PLAINLY ARE NOT THE SOURCE.
BEHIND THEM... SOMETHING'S MOVING... SHINY... LIKE WEAPONS!
UNMISTAKABLE, NOW, THE VOICES OF ELVES BLEND IN A RISING BATTLE CRY. THEIR BOOTS DRUM STEADILY CLOSER...
DUNG!
RUN!
GUTTLEKRAW! THEY COME! THEY COME!
STAY CALM! SHIELDMEN, TO ME!
"REMEMBER, WARRIORS," THE KING GROWLS, "ELVES ARE ONLY FLESH AND BLOOD — WEAKER, SMALLER AND FEWER THAN YOU!"
"THEIR WEAPONS ARE STOLEN FROM US --"
"--THERE WILL BE NO SURPRISES."
"YOU HAVE ONLY TO KILL AND KILL AND KILL! THIS TIME WE SHALL WIPE THEM OUT FOREVER!"
ACROSS THE ROOM, TWO-EDGE SIGHS WITH DEEP SATISFACTION.

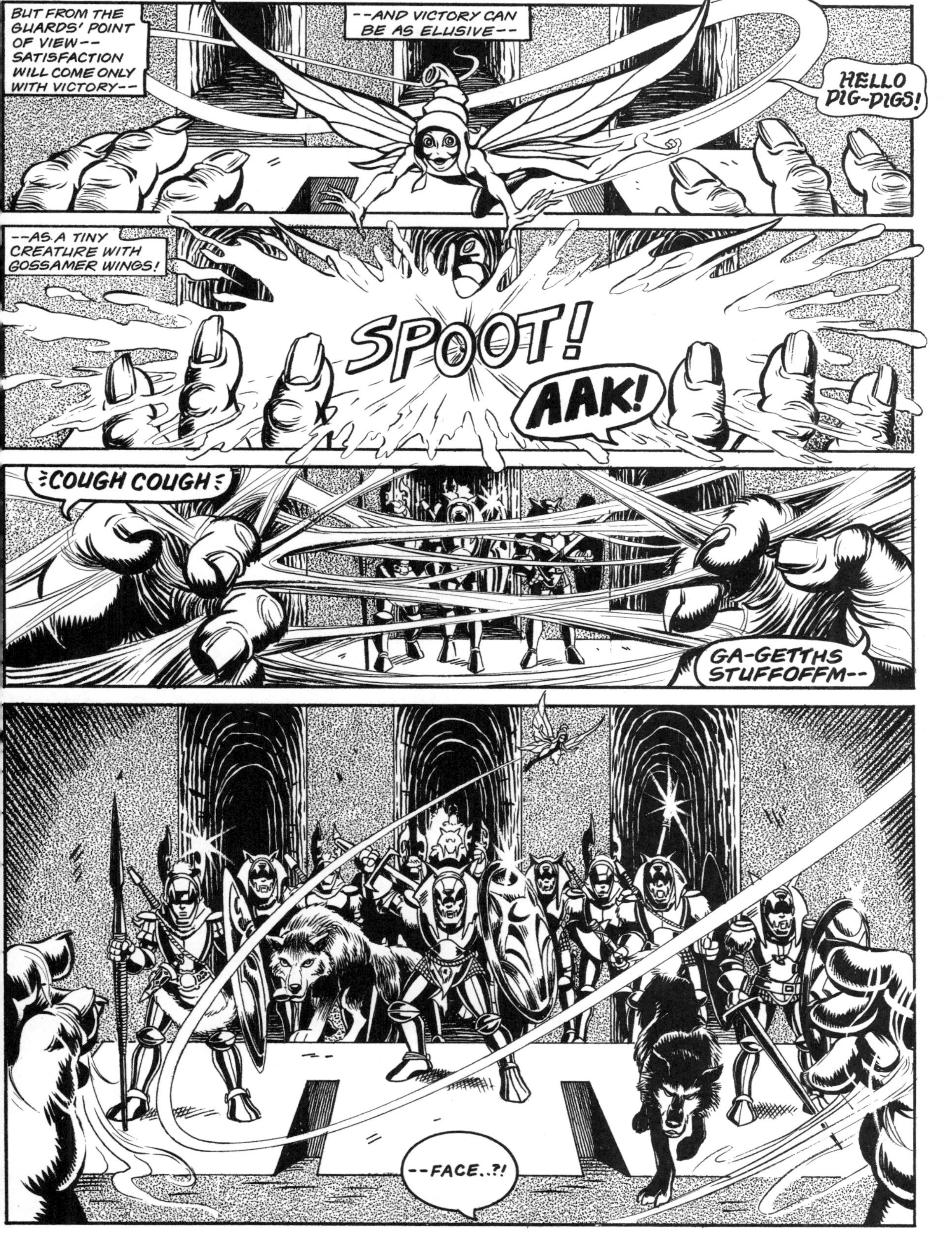
BUT FROM THE GUARDS' POINT OF VIEW-- SATISFACTION WILL COME ONLY WITH VICTORY--
--AND VICTORY CAN BE AS ELUSIVE--
HELLO PIG-PIGS!
--AS A TINY CREATURE WITH GOSSAMER WINGS!
SPOOT!
AAK!
COUGH COUGH
GA-GETTHS STUFFOFFM--
--FACE..?!

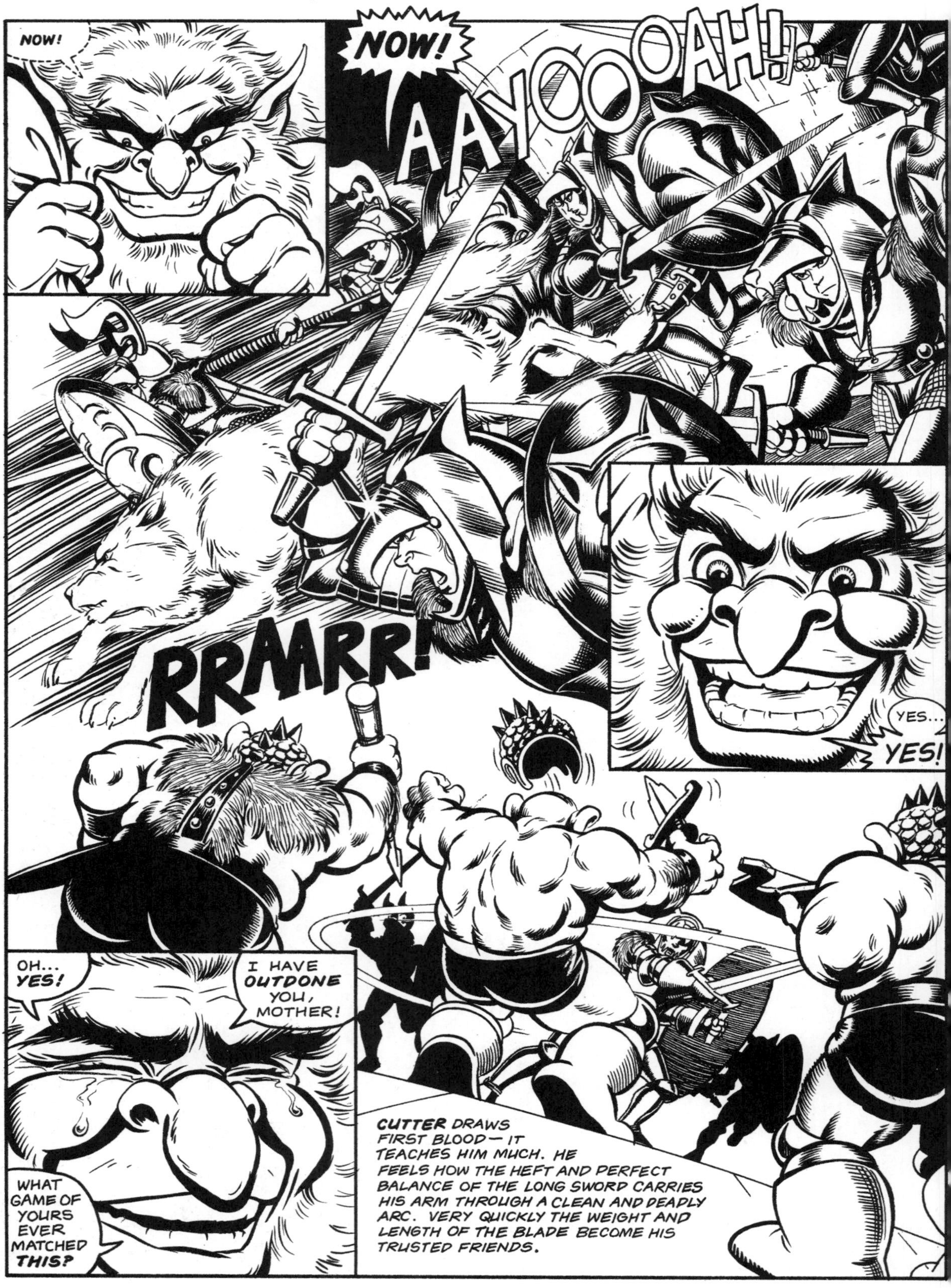
NOW!
NOW!
AAYOOOAH!!
RRAARR!
YES... YES!
OH... YES!
I HAVE OUTDONE YOU, MOTHER!
WHAT GAME OF YOURS EVER MATCHED THIS?
CUTTER DRAWS FIRST BLOOD—IT TEACHES HIM MUCH. HE FEELS HOW THE HEFT AND PERFECT BALANCE OF THE LONG SWORD CARRIES HIS ARM THROUGH A CLEAN AND DEADLY ARC. VERY QUICKLY THE WEIGHT AND LENGTH OF THE BLADE BECOME HIS TRUSTED FRIENDS.

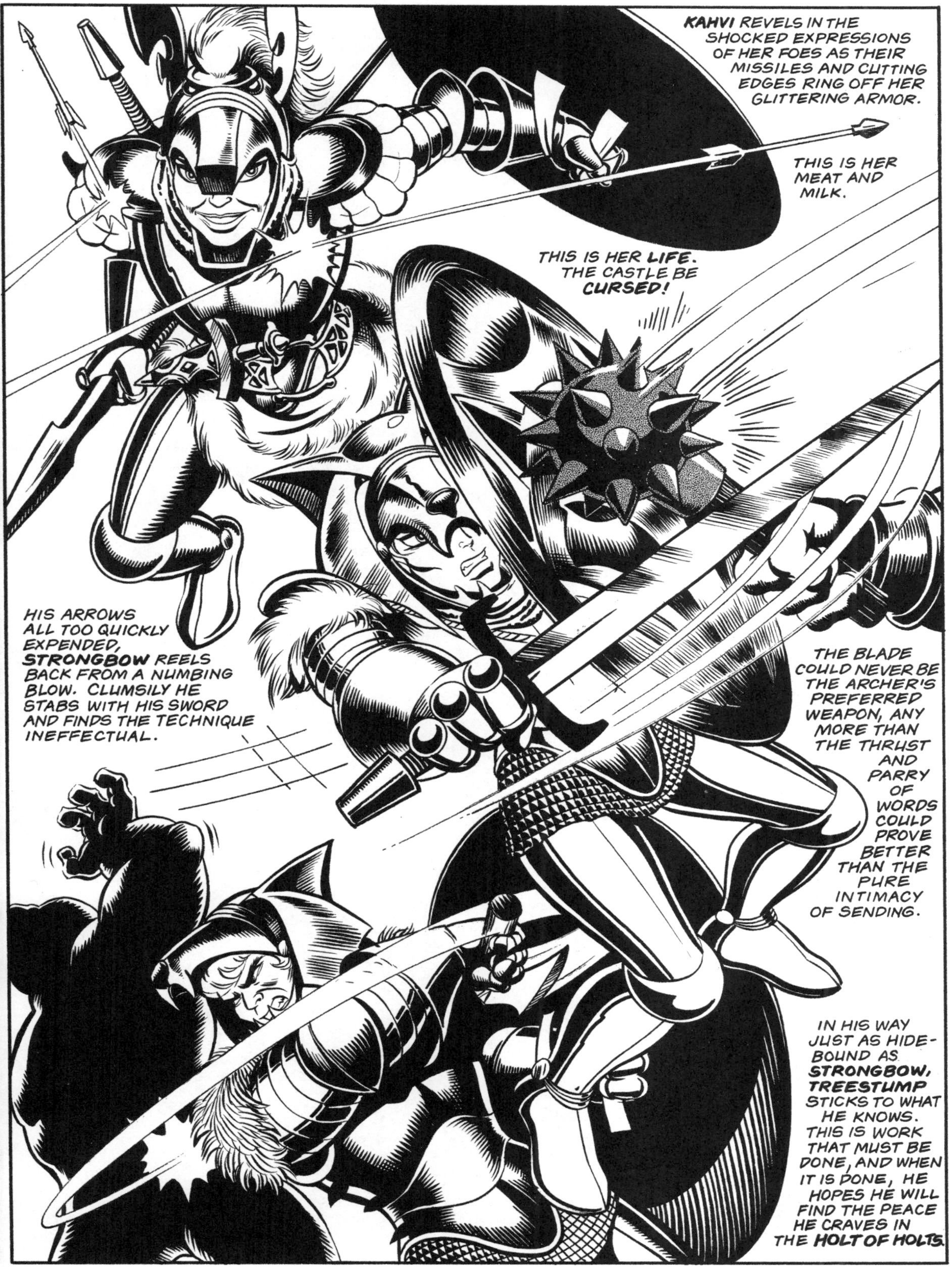
KAHVI REVELS IN THE SHOCKED EXPRESSIONS OF HER FOES AS THEIR MISSILES AND CUTTING EDGES RING OFF HER GLITTERING ARMOR.
THIS IS HER MEAT AND MILK.
THIS IS HER LIFE. THE CASTLE BE CURSED!
HIS ARROWS ALL TOO QUICKLY EXPENDED, STRONGBOW REELS BACK FROM A NUMBING BLOW. CLUMSILY HE STABS WITH HIS SWORD AND FINDS THE TECHNIQUE INEFFECTUAL.
THE BLADE COULD NEVER BE THE ARCHER'S PREFERRED WEAPON, ANY MORE THAN THE THRUST AND PARRY OF WORDS COULD PROVE BETTER THAN THE PURE INTIMACY OF SENDING.
IN HIS WAY JUST AS HIDE-BOUND AS STRONGBOW, TREESTUMP STICKS TO WHAT HE KNOWS. THIS IS WORK THAT MUST BE DONE, AND WHEN IT IS DONE, HE HOPES HE WILL FIND THE PEACE HE CRAVES IN THE HOLT OF HOLTS.

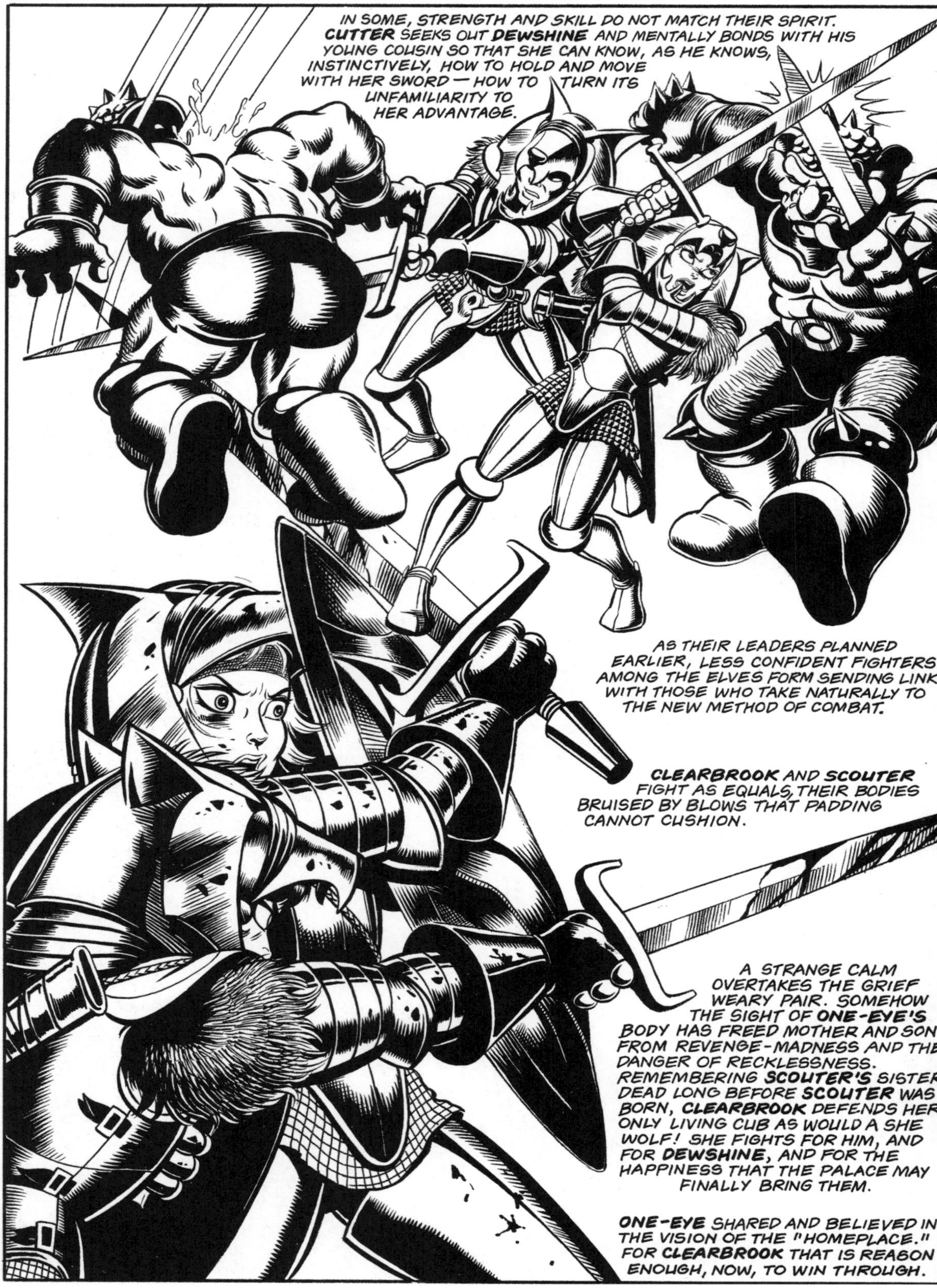
IN SOME, STRENGTH AND SKILL DO NOT MATCH THEIR SPIRIT. CUTTER SEEKS OUT DEWSHINE AND MENTALLY BONDS WITH HIS YOUNG COUSIN SO THAT SHE CAN KNOW, AS HE KNOWS, INSTINCTIVELY, HOW TO HOLD AND MOVE WITH HER SWORD — HOW TO TURN ITS UNFAMILIARITY TO HER ADVANTAGE.
AS THEIR LEADERS PLANNED EARLIER, LESS CONFIDENT FIGHTERS AMONG THE ELVES FORM SENDING LINKS WITH THOSE WHO TAKE NATURALLY TO THE NEW METHOD OF COMBAT.
CLEARBROOK AND SCOUTER FIGHT AS EQUALS, THEIR BODIES BRUISED BY BLOWS THAT PADDING CANNOT CUSHION.
A STRANGE CALM OVERTAKES THE GRIEF WEARY PAIR. SOMEHOW THE SIGHT OF ONE-EYE'S BODY HAS FREED MOTHER AND SON FROM REVENGE-MADNESS AND THE DANGER OF RECKLESSNESS. REMEMBERING SCOUTER'S SISTER, DEAD LONG BEFORE SCOUTER WAS BORN, CLEARBROOK DEFENDS HER ONLY LIVING CUB AS WOULD A SHE WOLF! SHE FIGHTS FOR HIM, AND FOR DEWSHINE, AND FOR THE HAPPINESS THAT THE PALACE MAY FINALLY BRING THEM.
ONE-EYE SHARED AND BELIEVED IN THE VISION OF THE "HOMEPLACE." FOR CLEARBROOK THAT IS REASON ENOUGH, NOW, TO WIN THROUGH.

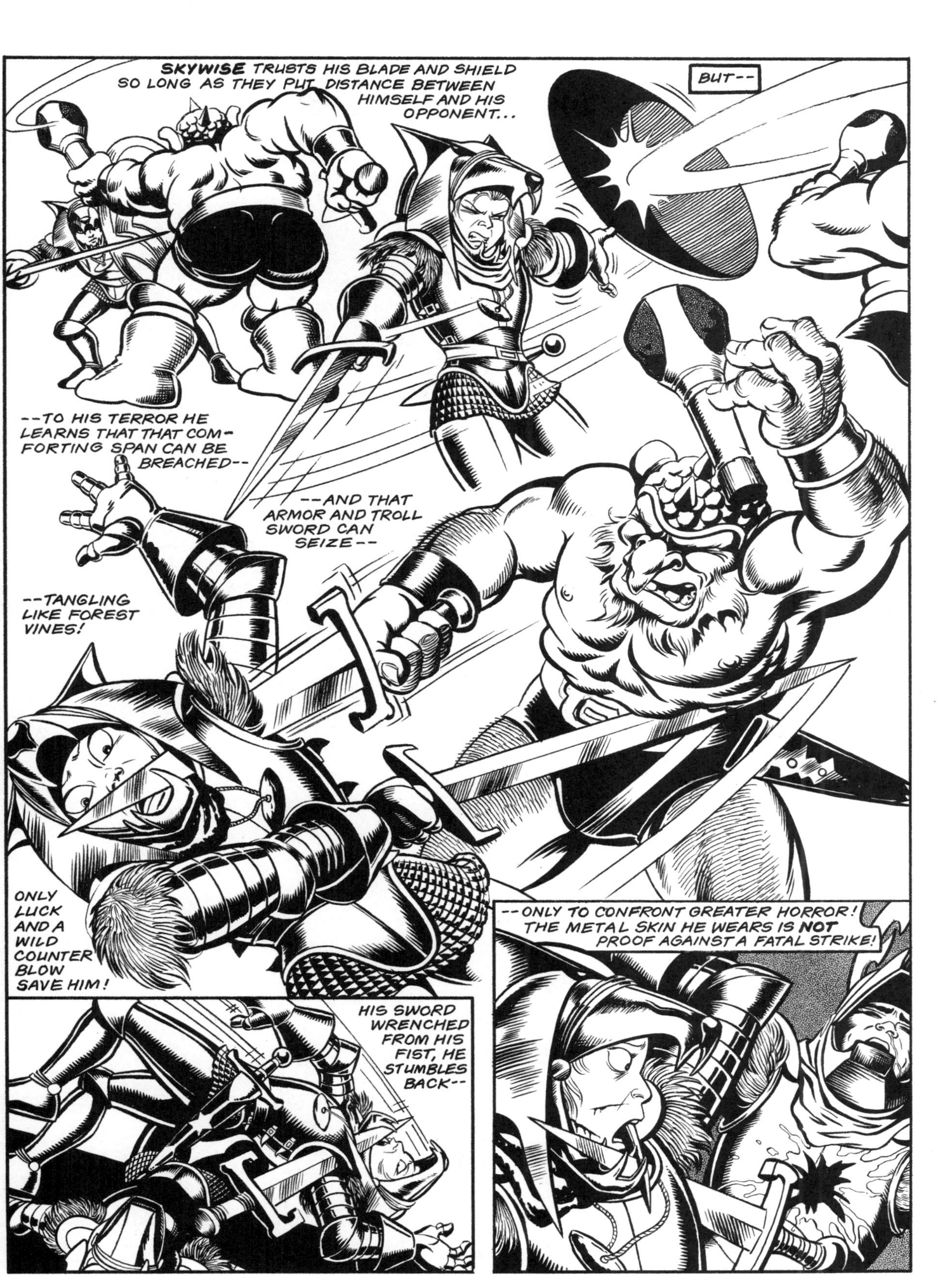
SKYWISE TRUSTS HIS BLADE AND SHIELD SO LONG AS THEY PUT DISTANCE BETWEEN HIMSELF AND HIS OPPONENT...
BUT--
--TO HIS TERROR HE LEARNS THAT THAT COM-FORTING SPAN CAN BE BREACHED--
--AND THAT ARMOR AND TROLL SWORD CAN SEIZE--
--TANGLING LIKE FOREST VINES!
ONLY LUCK AND A WILD COUNTER BLOW SAVE HIM!
HIS SWORD WRENCHED FROM HIS FIST, HE STUMBLES BACK--
--ONLY TO CONFRONT GREATER HORROR! THE METAL SKIN HE WEARS IS NOT PROOF AGAINST A FATAL STRIKE!

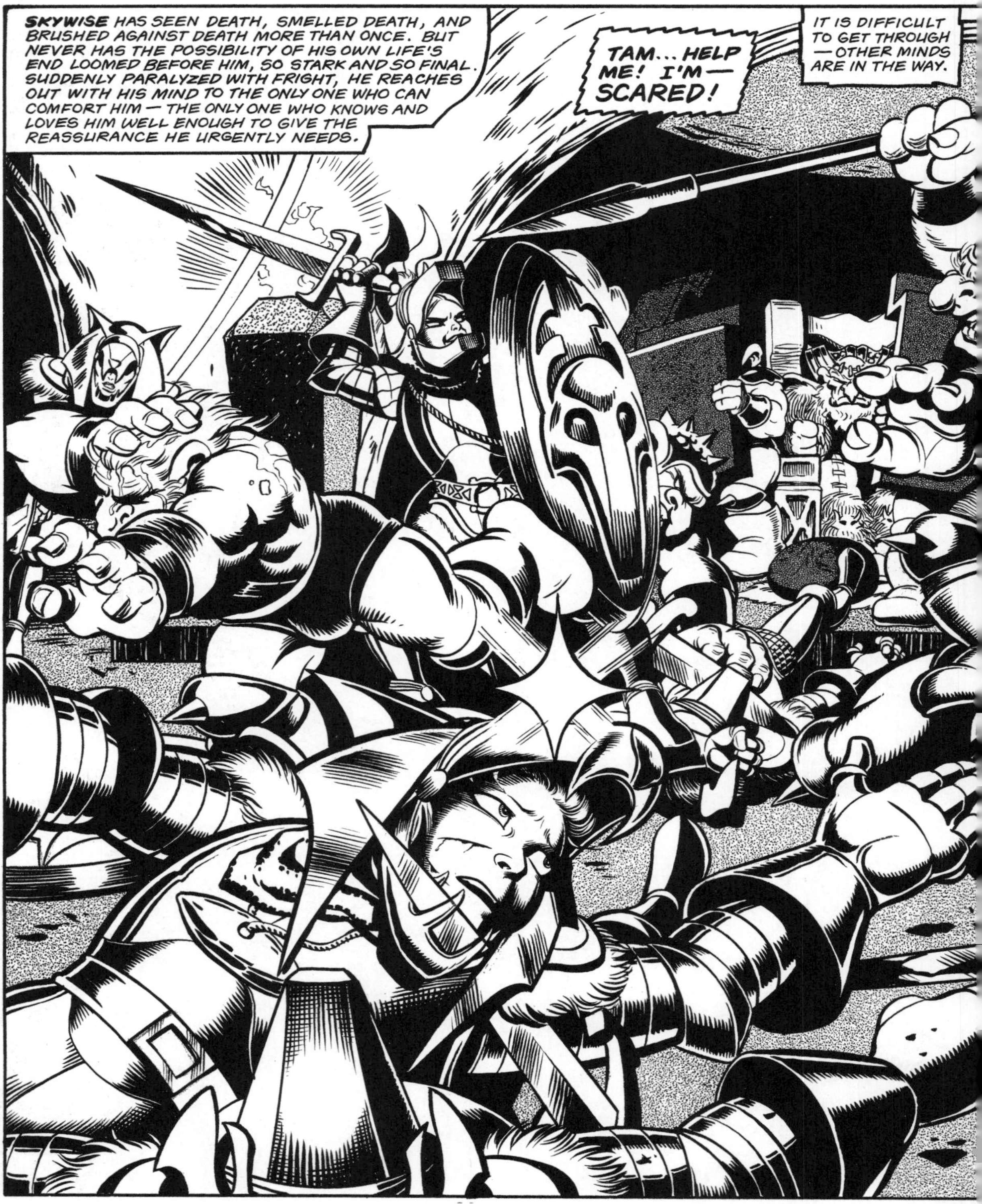

SKYWISE HAS SEEN DEATH, SMELLED DEATH, AND BRUSHED AGAINST DEATH MORE THAN ONCE. BUT NEVER HAS THE POSSIBILITY OF HIS OWN LIFE'S END LOOMED BEFORE HIM, SO STARK AND SO FINAL. SUDDENLY PARALYZED WITH FRIGHT, HE REACHES OUT WITH HIS MIND TO THE ONLY ONE WHO CAN COMFORT HIM — THE ONLY ONE WHO KNOWS AND LOVES HIM WELL ENOUGH TO GIVE THE REASSURANCE HE URGENTLY NEEDS.
TAM... HELP ME! I'M— SCARED!
IT IS DIFFICULT TO GET THROUGH —OTHER MINDS ARE IN THE WAY.

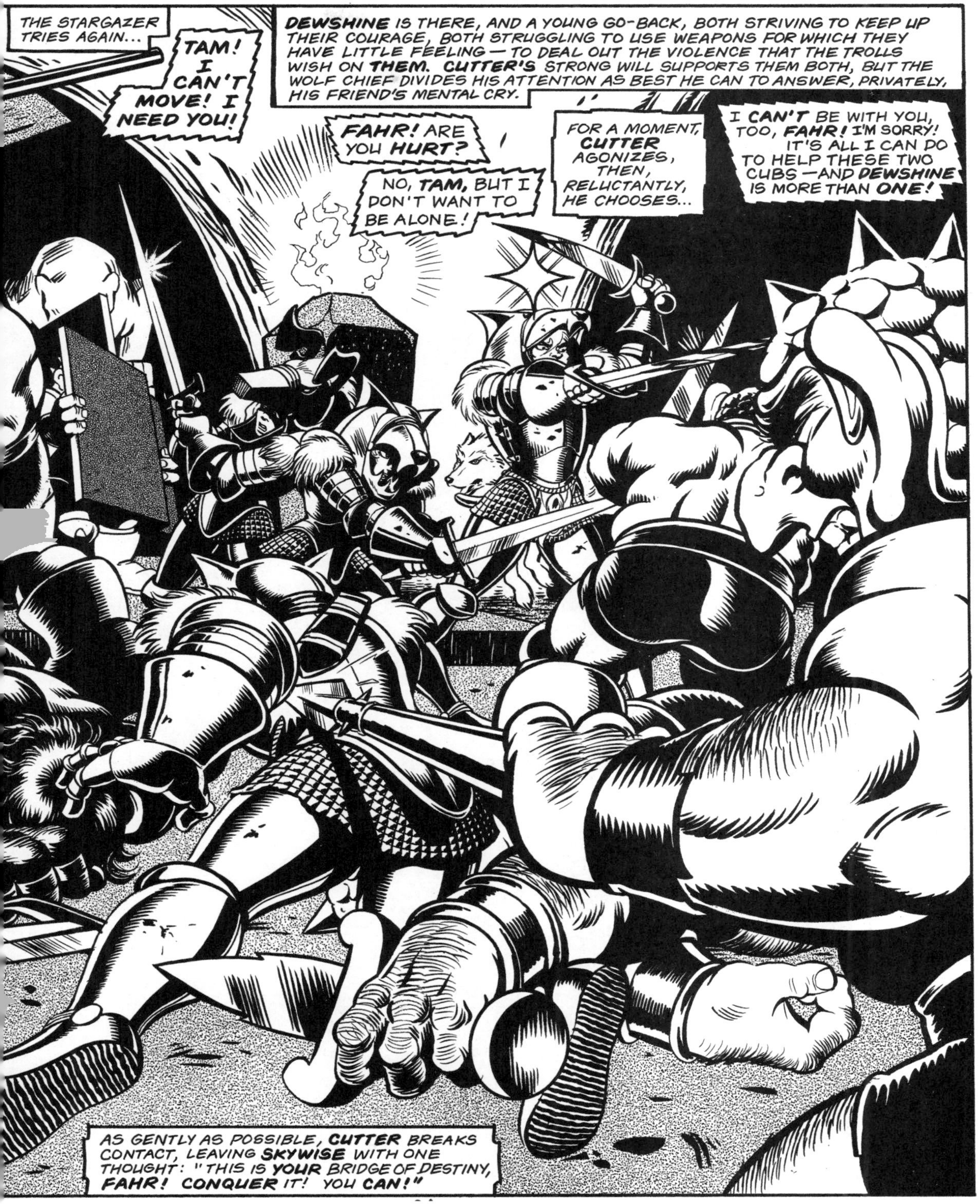

THE STARGAZER TRIES AGAIN...
TAM! I CAN'T MOVE! I NEED YOU!
DEWSHINE IS THERE, AND A YOUNG GO-BACK, BOTH STRIVING TO KEEP UP THEIR COURAGE, BOTH STRUGGLING TO USE WEAPONS FOR WHICH THEY HAVE LITTLE FEELING — TO DEAL OUT THE VIOLENCE THAT THE TROLLS WISH ON THEM. CUTTER'S STRONG WILL SUPPORTS THEM BOTH, BUT THE WOLF CHIEF DIVIDES HIS ATTENTION AS BEST HE CAN TO ANSWER, PRIVATELY, HIS FRIEND'S MENTAL CRY.
FAHR! ARE YOU HURT?
NO, TAM, BUT I DON'T WANT TO BE ALONE!
FOR A MOMENT, CUTTER AGONIZES, THEN, RELUCTANTLY, HE CHOOSES...
I CAN'T BE WITH YOU, TOO, FAHR! I'M SORRY! IT'S ALL I CAN DO TO HELP THESE TWO CUBS — AND DEWSHINE IS MORE THAN ONE!
AS GENTLY AS POSSIBLE, CUTTER BREAKS CONTACT, LEAVING SKYWISE WITH ONE THOUGHT: "THIS IS YOUR BRIDGE OF DESTINY, FAHR! CONQUER IT! YOU CAN!"

THAT'S IT, SOUL BROTHER?

"I'M SORRY?"

THAT'S ALL YOU HAVE FOR ME?

THOUGH HIS HEAD UNDERSTANDS *CUTTER'S* REFUSAL -- *SKYWISE'S* HEART BEGINS TO HARDEN WITH THE FIRST STIRRINGS OF RESENTMENT.

UP STARGAZER! THE TROLLS ARE ON OUR BACKS HARDER THAN EVER!

NIGHTFALL... THANKS!

I... CAN FIGHT ALONE!

ELSEWHERE *REDLANCE,* TOO, LEARNS THAT NO MATTER HOW MANY FRIENDS ONE FIGHTS BESIDE, MOMENTS OF TRUTH ARE ALWAYS FACED ALONE.

THE CUBS WILL NOT STAY HIDDEN --

--THEY WANT TO HELP! AND LIKE THE CHIEF'S DAUGHTER SHE IS, *EMBER* SUCCEEDS!

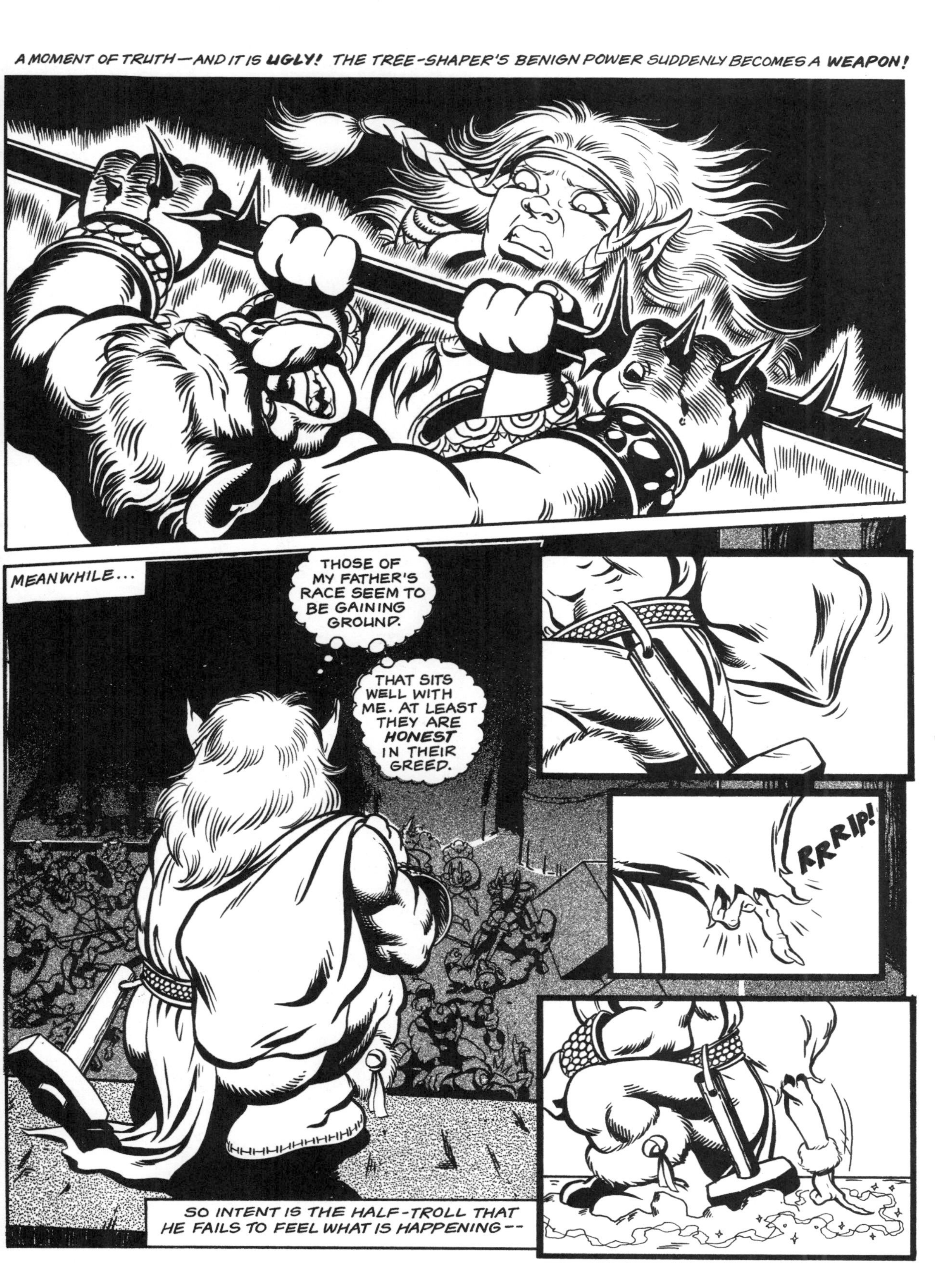
A MOMENT OF TRUTH—AND IT IS UGLY! THE TREE-SHAPER'S BENIGN POWER SUDDENLY BECOMES A WEAPON!
MEANWHILE...
THOSE OF MY FATHER'S RACE SEEM TO BE GAINING GROUND.
THAT SITS WELL WITH ME. AT LEAST THEY ARE HONEST IN THEIR GREED.
RRRIP!
SO INTENT IS THE HALF-TROLL THAT HE FAILS TO FEEL WHAT IS HAPPENING--

--UNTIL...

GAAAH! MY FEET!

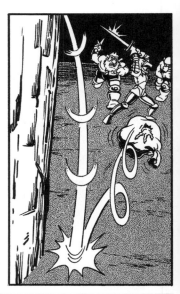

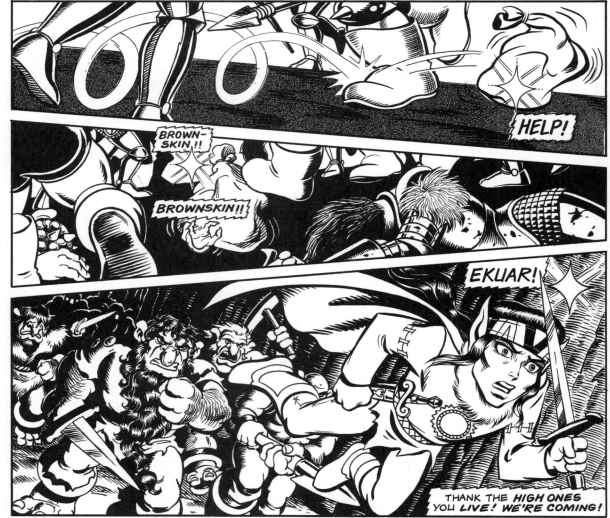

HELP!

BROWN-SKIN!!

BROWNSKIN!!

EKUAR!

THANK THE *HIGH ONES* YOU *LIVE!* WE'RE *COMING!*

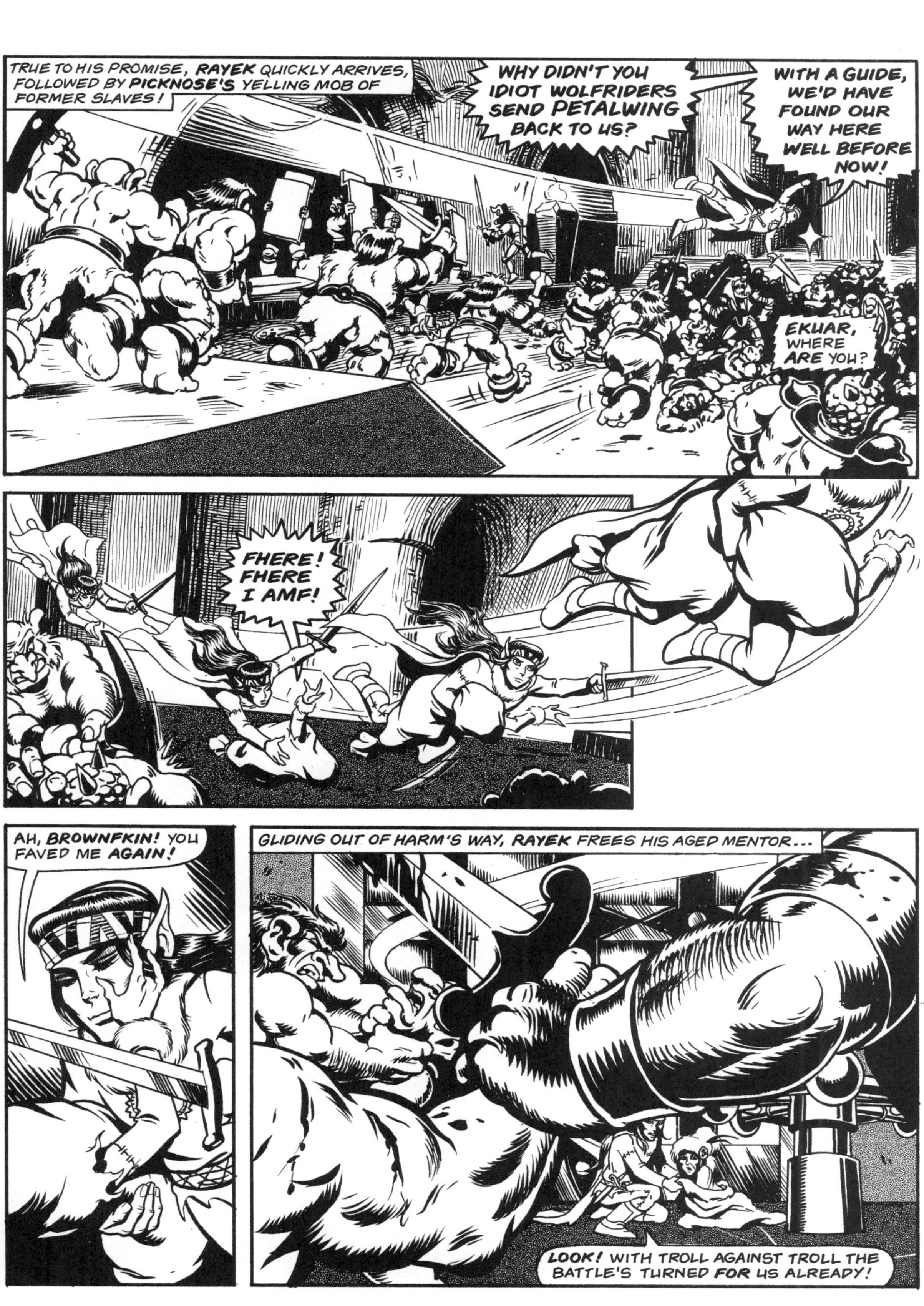

TRUE TO HIS PROMISE, RAYEK QUICKLY ARRIVES, FOLLOWED BY PICKNOSE'S YELLING MOB OF FORMER SLAVES!
WHY DIDN'T YOU IDIOT WOLFRIDERS SEND PETALWING BACK TO US?
WITH A GUIDE, WE'D HAVE FOUND OUR WAY HERE WELL BEFORE NOW!
EKUAR, WHERE ARE YOU?
FHERE! FHERE I AMF!
AH, BROWNFKIN! YOU FAVED ME AGAIN!
GLIDING OUT OF HARM'S WAY, RAYEK FREES HIS AGED MENTOR...
LOOK! WITH TROLL AGAINST TROLL THE BATTLE'S TURNED FOR US ALREADY!

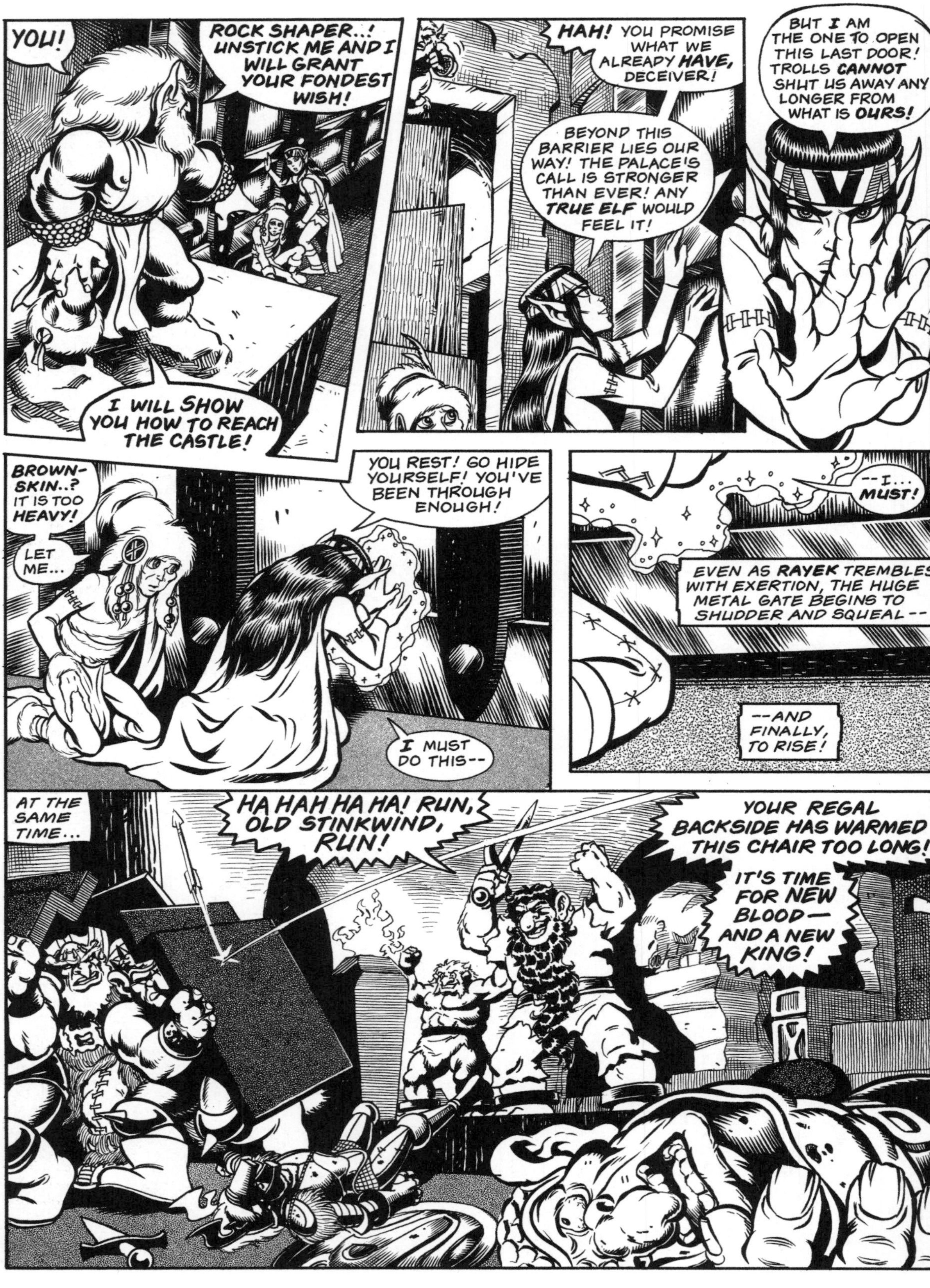
YOU!
ROCK SHAPER...! UNSTICK ME AND I WILL GRANT YOUR FONDEST WISH!
I WILL SHOW YOU HOW TO REACH THE CASTLE!
HAH! YOU PROMISE WHAT WE ALREADY HAVE, DECEIVER!
BEYOND THIS BARRIER LIES OUR WAY! THE PALACE'S CALL IS STRONGER THAN EVER! ANY TRUE ELF WOULD FEEL IT!
BUT I AM THE ONE TO OPEN THIS LAST DOOR! TROLLS CANNOT SHUT US AWAY ANY LONGER FROM WHAT IS OURS!
BROWN-SKIN..? IT IS TOO HEAVY!
LET ME...
YOU REST! GO HIDE YOURSELF! YOU'VE BEEN THROUGH ENOUGH!
I MUST DO THIS--
--I... MUST!
EVEN AS RAYEK TREMBLES WITH EXERTION, THE HUGE METAL GATE BEGINS TO SHUDDER AND SQUEAL--
--AND FINALLY, TO RISE!
AT THE SAME TIME...
HA HAH HA HA! RUN, OLD STINKWIND, RUN!
YOUR REGAL BACKSIDE HAS WARMED THIS CHAIR TOO LONG!
IT'S TIME FOR NEW BLOOD— AND A NEW KING!

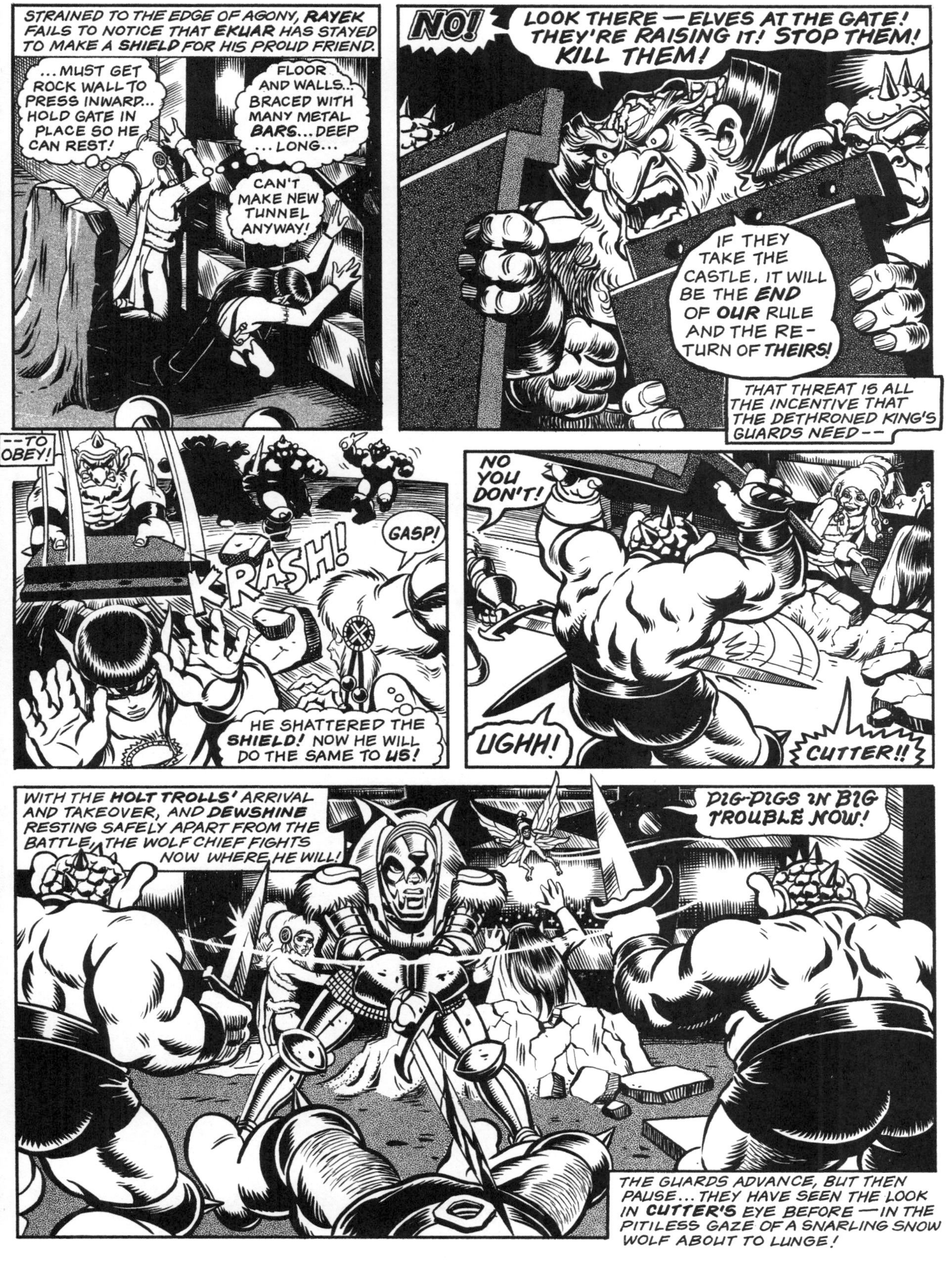

STRAINED TO THE EDGE OF AGONY, RAYEK FAILS TO NOTICE THAT EKUAR HAS STAYED TO MAKE A SHIELD FOR HIS PROUD FRIEND.
...MUST GET ROCK WALL TO PRESS INWARD... HOLD GATE IN PLACE SO HE CAN REST!
FLOOR AND WALLS... BRACED WITH MANY METAL BARS... DEEP ...LONG...
CAN'T MAKE NEW TUNNEL ANYWAY!
NO!
LOOK THERE — ELVES AT THE GATE! THEY'RE RAISING IT! STOP THEM! KILL THEM!
IF THEY TAKE THE CASTLE, IT WILL BE THE END OF OUR RULE AND THE RE-TURN OF THEIRS!
THAT THREAT IS ALL THE INCENTIVE THAT THE DETHRONED KING'S GUARDS NEED --
--TO OBEY!
KRASH!
GASP!
HE SHATTERED THE SHIELD! NOW HE WILL DO THE SAME TO US!
NO YOU DON'T!
UGHH!
CUTTER!!
WITH THE HOLT TROLLS' ARRIVAL AND TAKEOVER, AND DEWSHINE RESTING SAFELY APART FROM THE BATTLE, THE WOLF CHIEF FIGHTS NOW WHERE HE WILL!
DIG-DIGS IN BIG TROUBLE NOW!
THE GUARDS ADVANCE, BUT THEN PAUSE... THEY HAVE SEEN THE LOOK IN CUTTER'S EYE BEFORE — IN THE PITILESS GAZE OF A SNARLING SNOW WOLF ABOUT TO LUNGE!

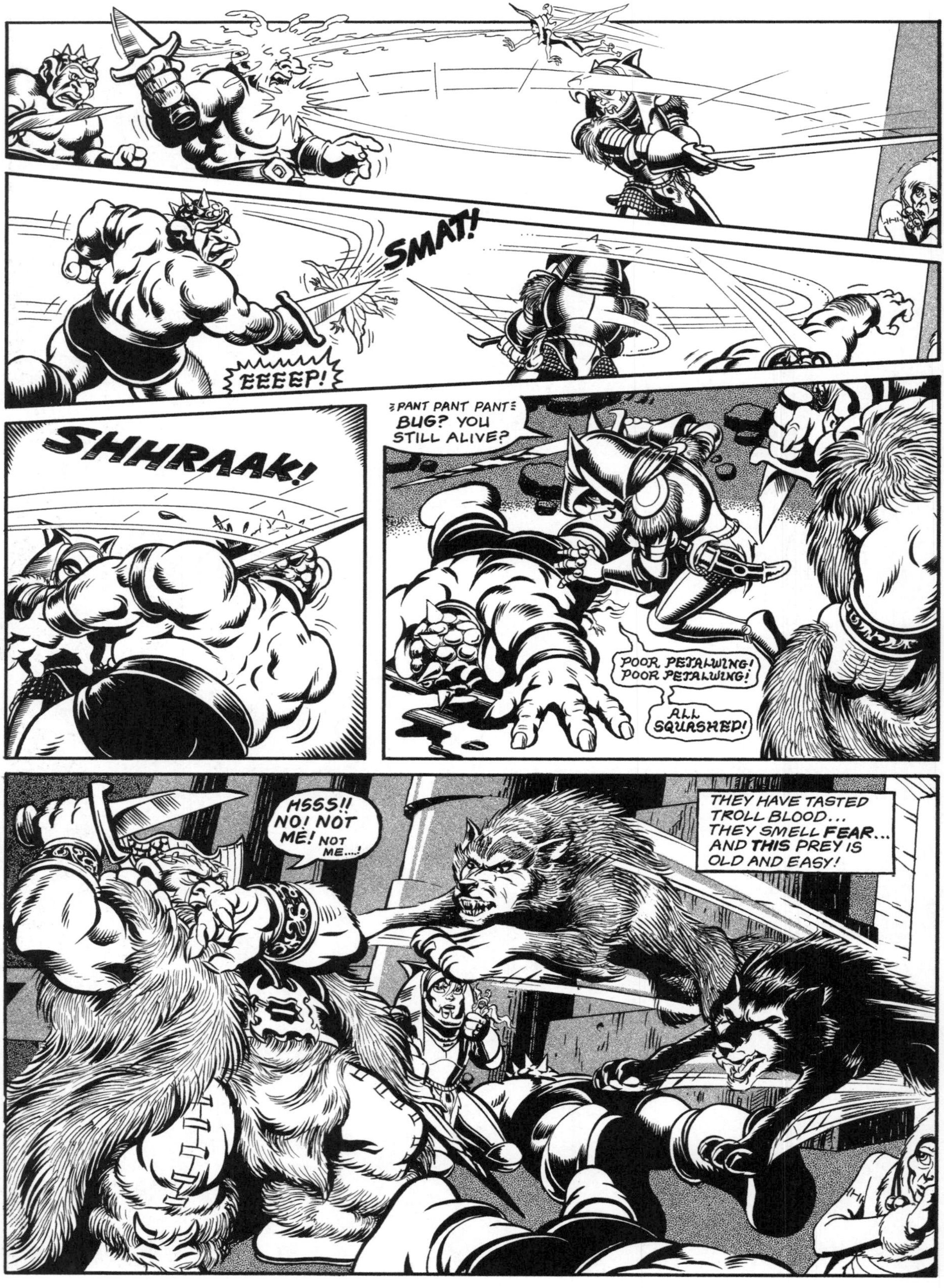
SMAT!
EEEEP!
SHHRAAK!
PANT PANT PANT
BUG? YOU STILL ALIVE?
POOR PETALWING! POOR PETALWING!
ALL SQUASHED!
HSSS!! NO! NOT ME! NOT ME...!
THEY HAVE TASTED TROLL BLOOD... THEY SMELL FEAR... AND THIS PREY IS OLD AND EASY!

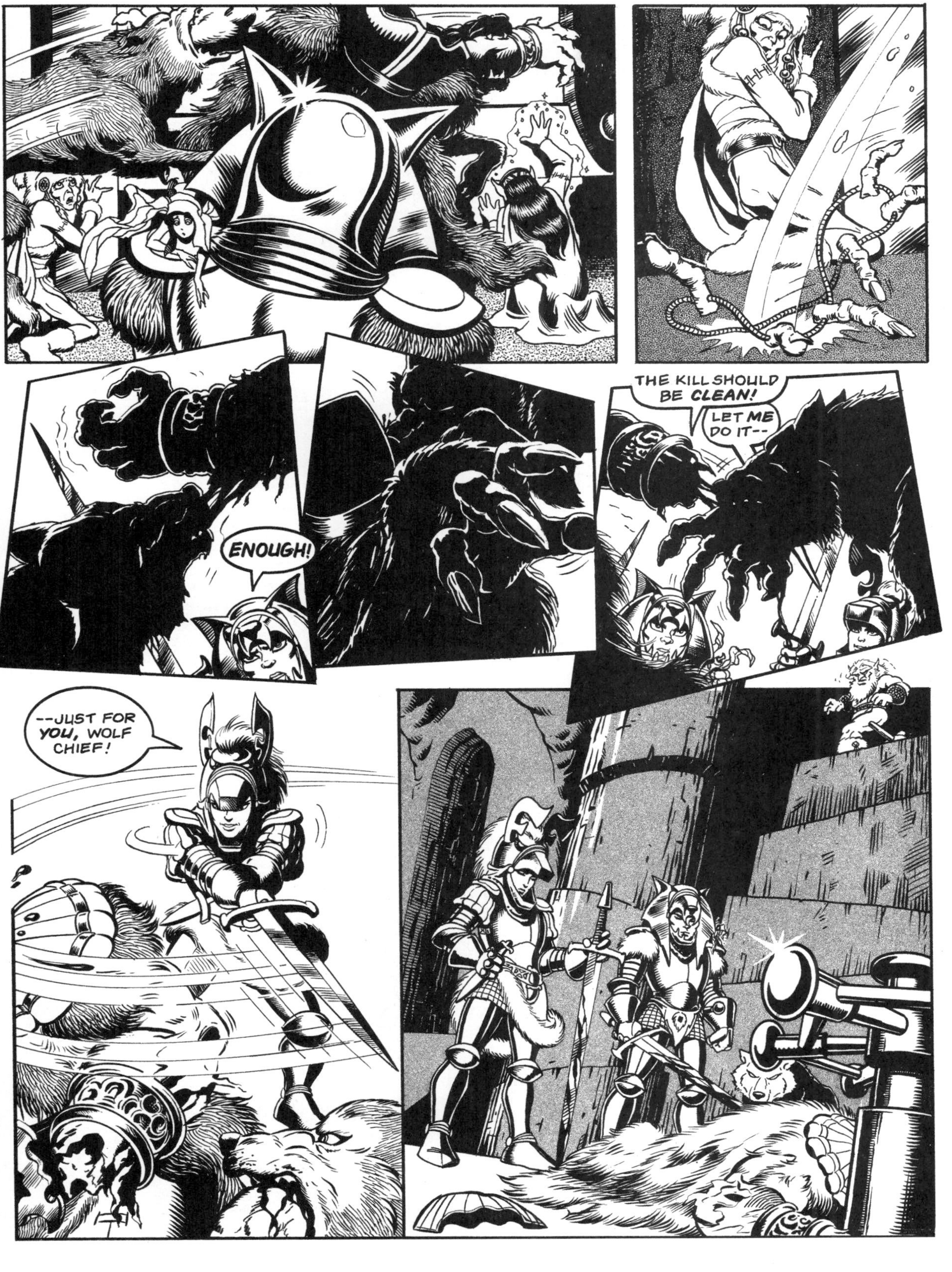

ENOUGH!
THE KILL SHOULD BE CLEAN!
LET ME DO IT--
--JUST FOR YOU, WOLF CHIEF!

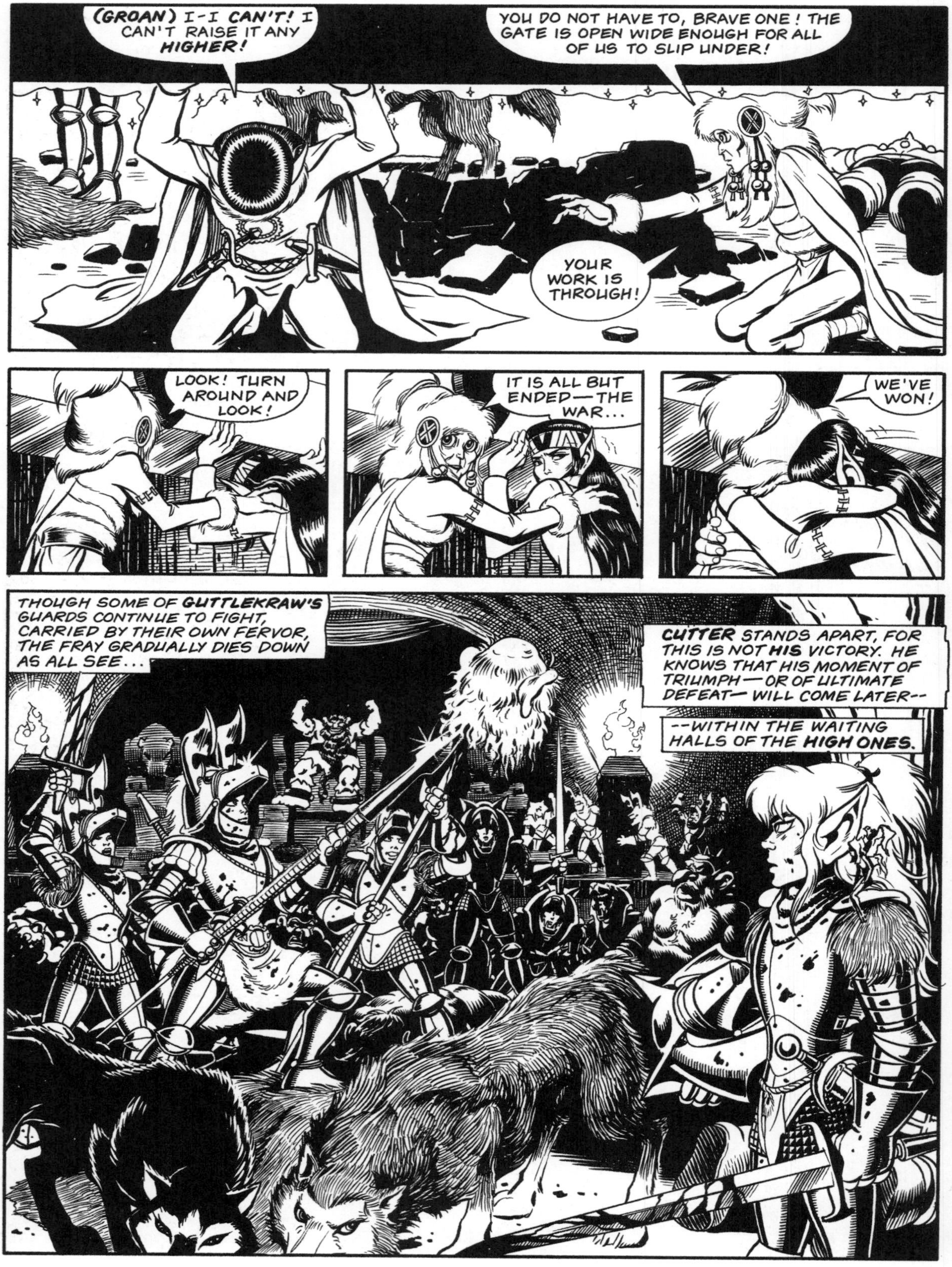
(GROAN) I-I CAN'T! I CAN'T RAISE IT ANY HIGHER!
YOU DO NOT HAVE TO, BRAVE ONE! THE GATE IS OPEN WIDE ENOUGH FOR ALL OF US TO SLIP UNDER!
YOUR WORK IS THROUGH!
LOOK! TURN AROUND AND LOOK!
IT IS ALL BUT ENDED—THE WAR...
WE'VE WON!
THOUGH SOME OF GUTTLEKRAW'S GUARDS CONTINUE TO FIGHT, CARRIED BY THEIR OWN FERVOR, THE FRAY GRADUALLY DIES DOWN AS ALL SEE...
CUTTER STANDS APART, FOR THIS IS NOT HIS VICTORY. HE KNOWS THAT HIS MOMENT OF TRIUMPH—OR OF ULTIMATE DEFEAT—WILL COME LATER--
--WITHIN THE WAITING HALLS OF THE HIGH ONES.

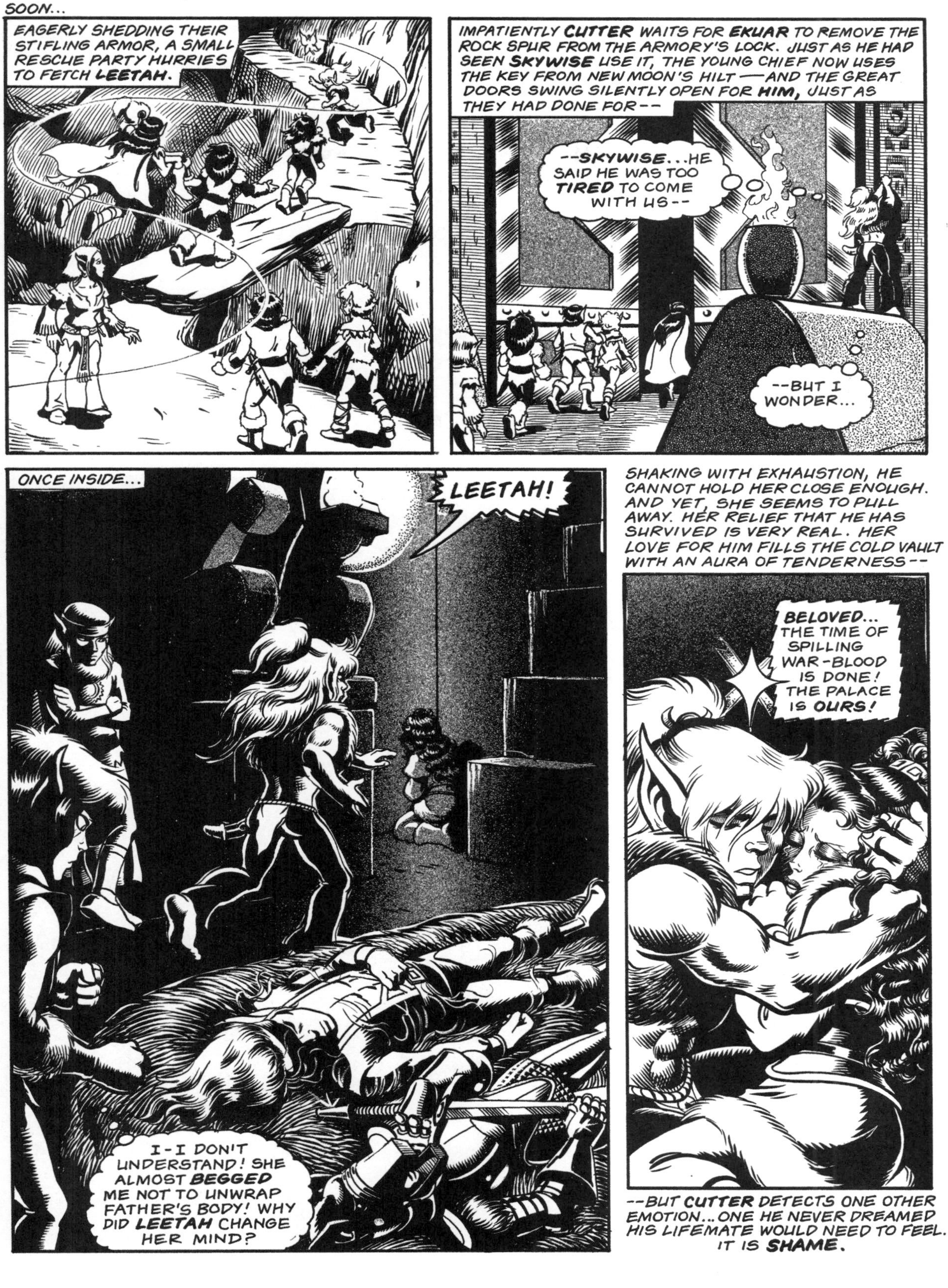
SOON...
EAGERLY SHEDDING THEIR STIFLING ARMOR, A SMALL RESCUE PARTY HURRIES TO FETCH LEETAH.
IMPATIENTLY CUTTER WAITS FOR EKUAR TO REMOVE THE ROCK SPUR FROM THE ARMORY'S LOCK. JUST AS HE HAD SEEN SKYWISE USE IT, THE YOUNG CHIEF NOW USES THE KEY FROM NEW MOON'S HILT — AND THE GREAT DOORS SWING SILENTLY OPEN FOR HIM, JUST AS THEY HAD DONE FOR--
--SKYWISE...HE SAID HE WAS TOO TIRED TO COME WITH US--
--BUT I WONDER...
ONCE INSIDE...
LEETAH!
I-I DON'T UNDERSTAND! SHE ALMOST BEGGED ME NOT TO UNWRAP FATHER'S BODY! WHY DID LEETAH CHANGE HER MIND?
SHAKING WITH EXHAUSTION, HE CANNOT HOLD HER CLOSE ENOUGH. AND YET, SHE SEEMS TO PULL AWAY. HER RELIEF THAT HE HAS SURVIVED IS VERY REAL. HER LOVE FOR HIM FILLS THE COLD VAULT WITH AN AURA OF TENDERNESS--
BELOVED... THE TIME OF SPILLING WAR-BLOOD IS DONE! THE PALACE IS OURS!
--BUT CUTTER DETECTS ONE OTHER EMOTION...ONE HE NEVER DREAMED HIS LIFEMATE WOULD NEED TO FEEL. IT IS SHAME.

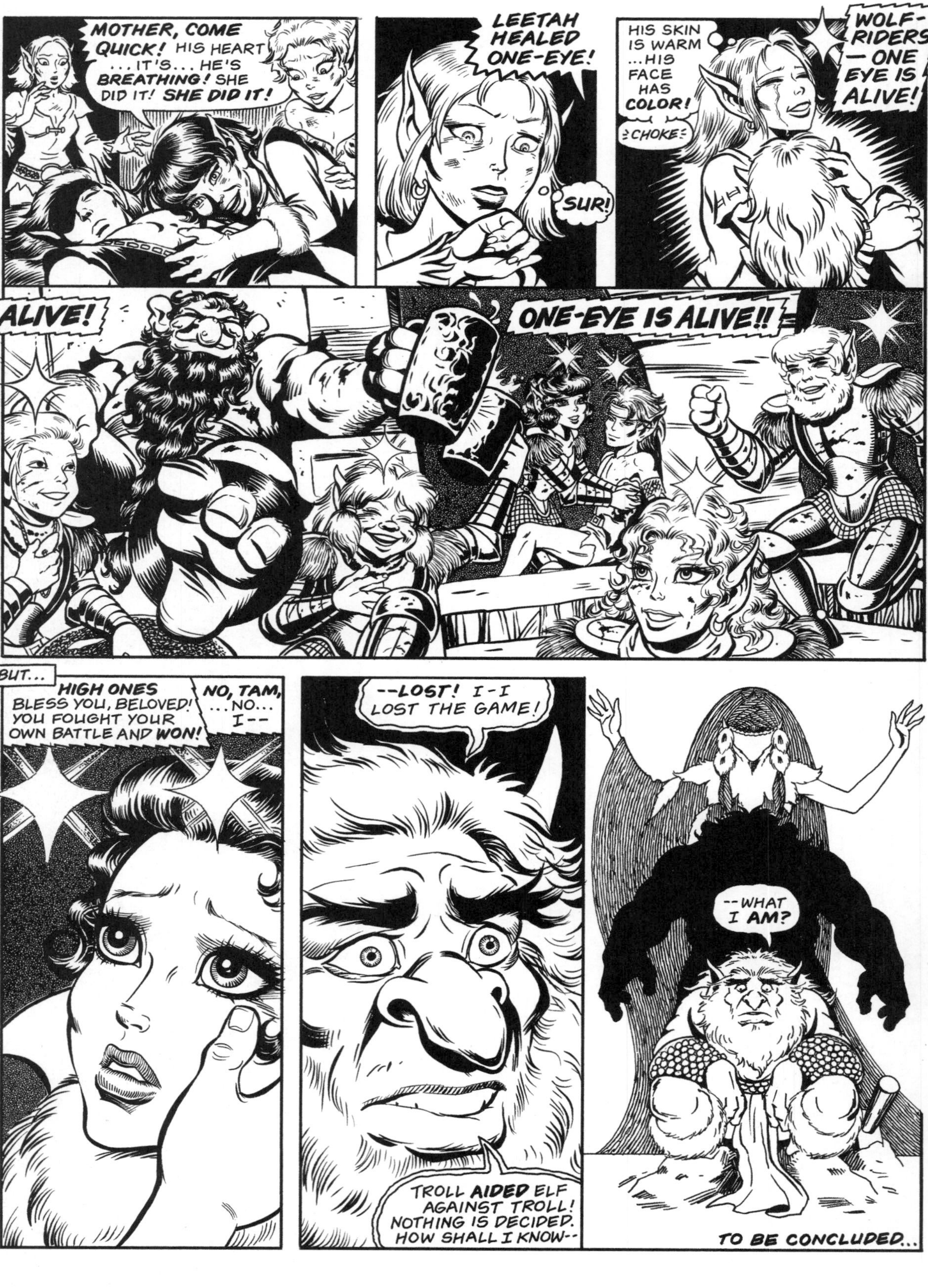

MOTHER, COME QUICK! HIS HEART . . . IT'S . . . HE'S BREATHING! SHE DID IT! SHE DID IT!
LEETAH HEALED ONE-EYE!
SUR!
HIS SKIN IS WARM ...HIS FACE HAS COLOR!
CHOKE
WOLF-RIDERS — ONE EYE IS ALIVE!
ALIVE!
ONE-EYE IS ALIVE!!
BUT...
HIGH ONES BLESS YOU, BELOVED! YOU FOUGHT YOUR OWN BATTLE AND WON!
NO, TAM, . . . NO . . . I--
--LOST! I-I LOST THE GAME!
TROLL AIDED ELF AGAINST TROLL! NOTHING IS DECIDED. HOW SHALL I KNOW--
--WHAT I AM?
TO BE CONCLUDED...

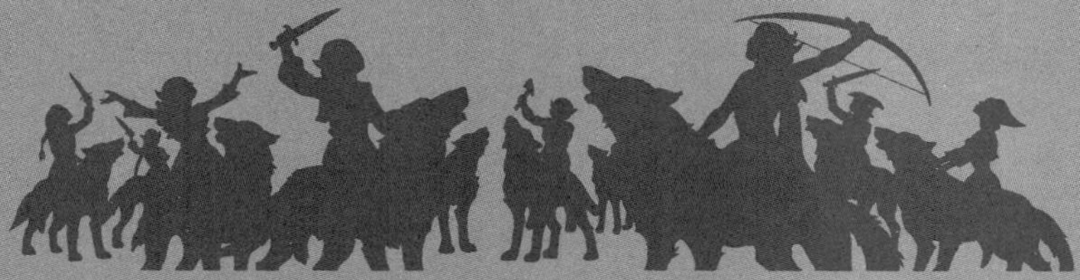

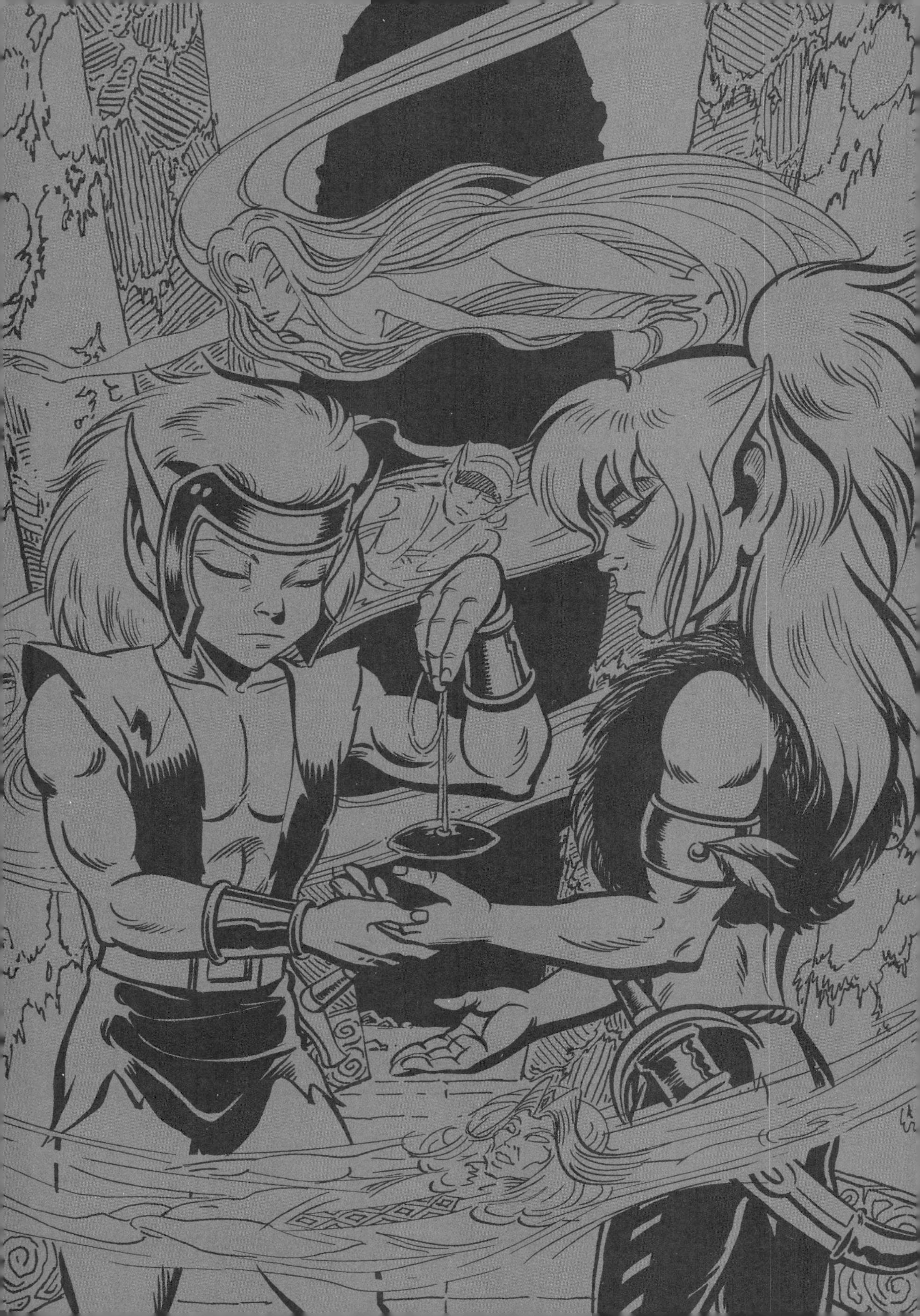

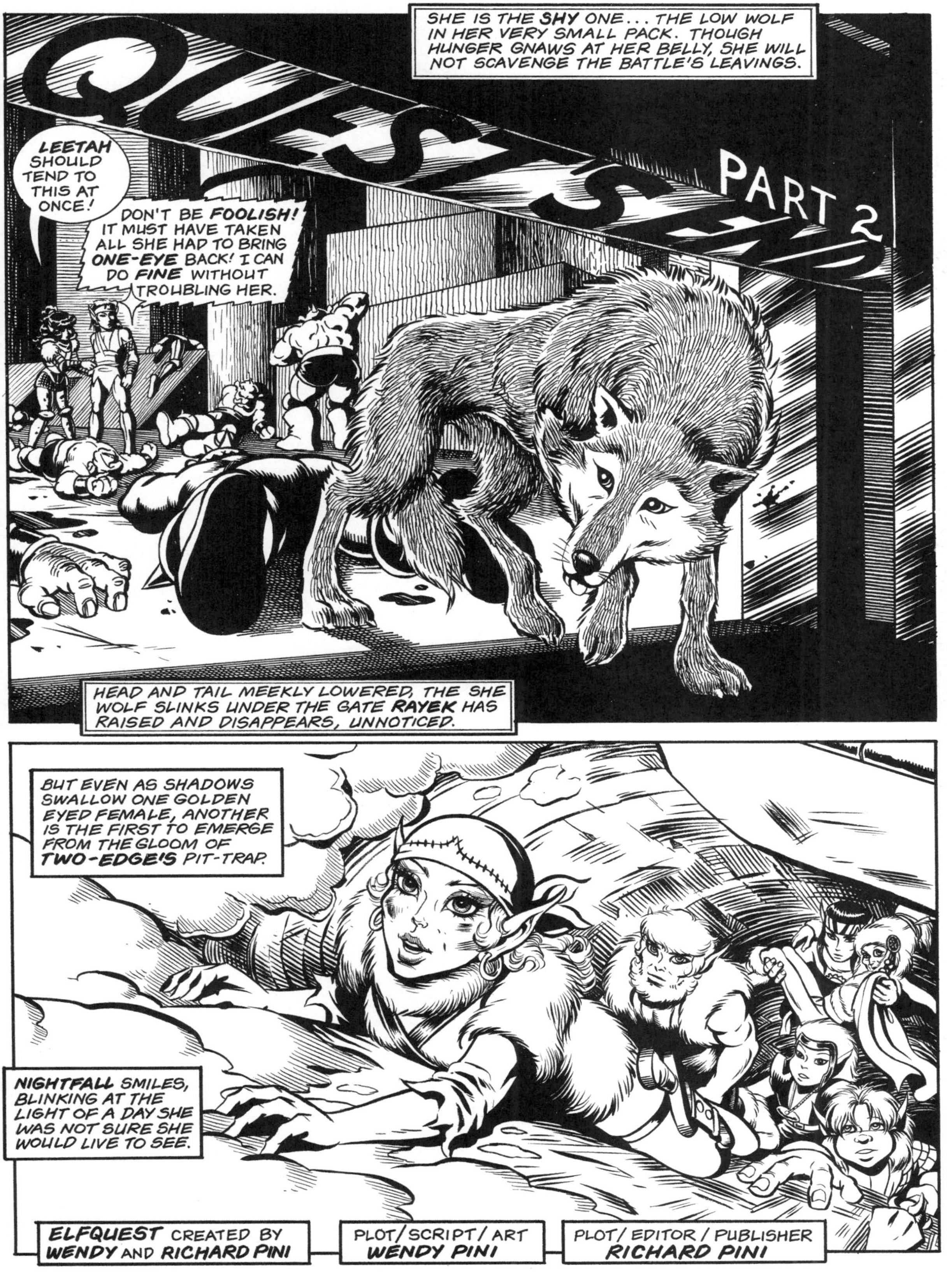
QUEST'S END PART 2
SHE IS THE SHY ONE... THE LOW WOLF IN HER VERY SMALL PACK. THOUGH HUNGER GNAWS AT HER BELLY, SHE WILL NOT SCAVENGE THE BATTLE'S LEAVINGS.
LEETAH SHOULD TEND TO THIS AT ONCE!
DON'T BE FOOLISH! IT MUST HAVE TAKEN ALL SHE HAD TO BRING ONE-EYE BACK! I CAN DO FINE WITHOUT TROUBLING HER.
HEAD AND TAIL MEEKLY LOWERED, THE SHE WOLF SLINKS UNDER THE GATE RAYEK HAS RAISED AND DISAPPEARS, UNNOTICED.
BUT EVEN AS SHADOWS SWALLOW ONE GOLDEN EYED FEMALE, ANOTHER IS THE FIRST TO EMERGE FROM THE GLOOM OF TWO-EDGE'S PIT-TRAP.
NIGHTFALL SMILES, BLINKING AT THE LIGHT OF A DAY SHE WAS NOT SURE SHE WOULD LIVE TO SEE.
ELFQUEST CREATED BY WENDY AND RICHARD PINI
PLOT/SCRIPT/ART WENDY PINI
PLOT/EDITOR/PUBLISHER RICHARD PINI

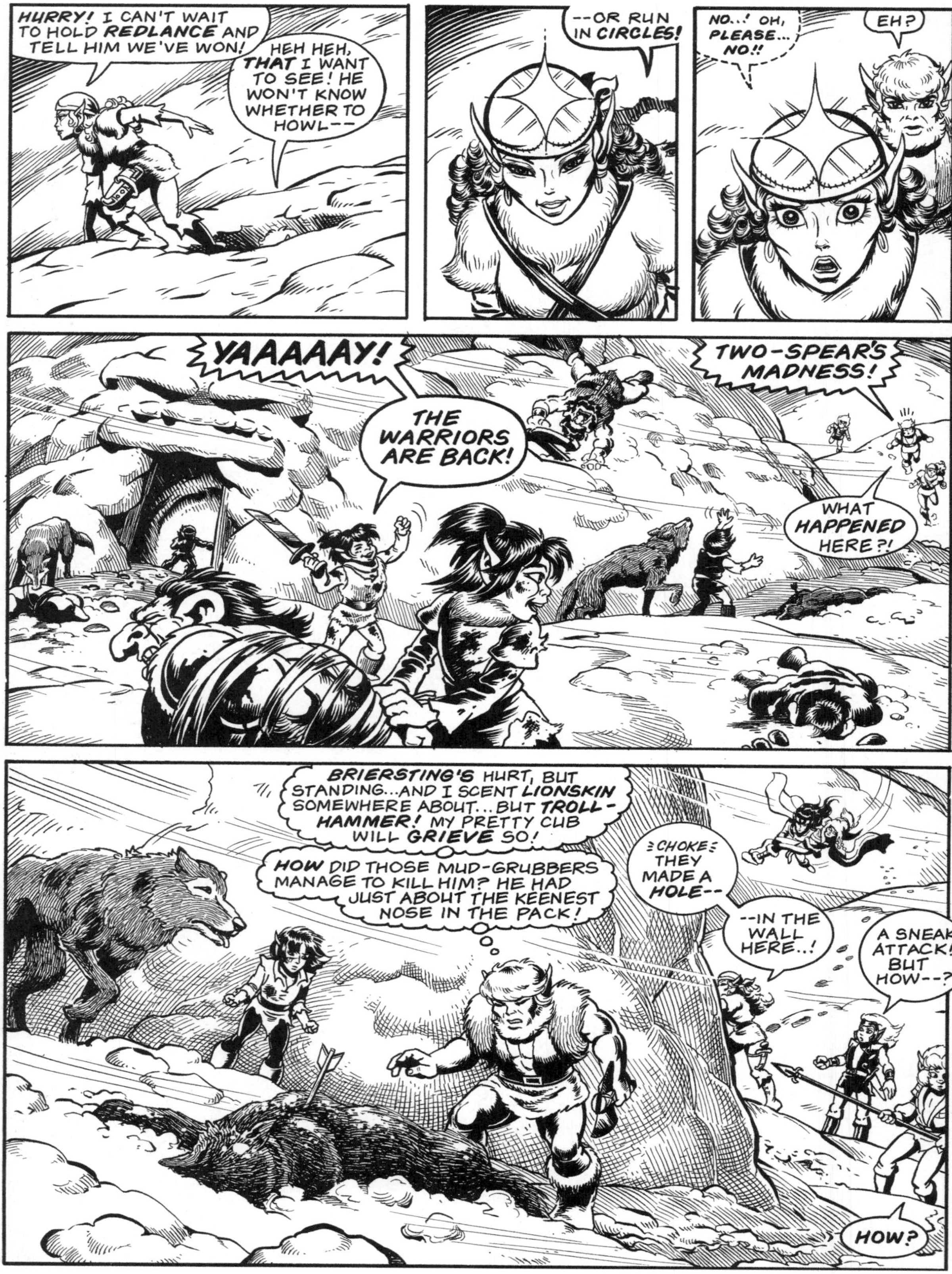
HURRY! I CAN'T WAIT TO HOLD REDLANCE AND TELL HIM WE'VE WON!
HEH HEH, THAT I WANT TO SEE! HE WON'T KNOW WHETHER TO HOWL--
--OR RUN IN CIRCLES!
NO...! OH, PLEASE... NO!!
EH?
YAAAAAY!
THE WARRIORS ARE BACK!
TWO-SPEAR'S MADNESS!
WHAT HAPPENED HERE?!
BRIERSTING'S HURT, BUT STANDING...AND I SCENT LIONSKIN SOMEWHERE ABOUT... BUT TROLL-HAMMER! MY PRETTY CUB WILL GRIEVE SO!
HOW DID THOSE MUD-GRUBBERS MANAGE TO KILL HIM? HE HAD JUST ABOUT THE KEENEST NOSE IN THE PACK!
CHOKE THEY MADE A HOLE--
--IN THE WALL HERE...!
A SNEAK ATTACK! BUT HOW--?
HOW?

ROCK SHAPER'S WORK! OH, *BROWNSKIN!* GUTTLEKRAW'S POWER HOLDS BEYOND DEATH!

HE STILL HAS ONE OF US!

HAD ONE OF US...I THINK...

THEY'RE *CARELESS* WITH THEIR TOOLS, THESE TROLLS!

SHUDDERING, *EKUAR* KNEELS BESIDE THE FROZEN LUMP WRAPPED IN BRITTLE DOESKIN. THE HOOD CRACKLES AS HE RAISES IT TO GAZE INTO SIGHTLESS, STARING EYES.

MEKDA!

AND INSIDE THE LODGE... REDLANCE!?

NIGHT-FALL..? UM...

OH, HIGH ONES! ƎUNHƎ MOVE AWAY, CUBS!

STARJUMPER! YOU *MADE* IT!

OH, HIGH ONES! ƎUNHƎ MOVE AWAY, CUBS!

TH-THE TROLL... UM... SEE HE...HE SCREAMED AND ...FELL OVER...

UM... HE'S TOO BIG...C-CAN YOU..?

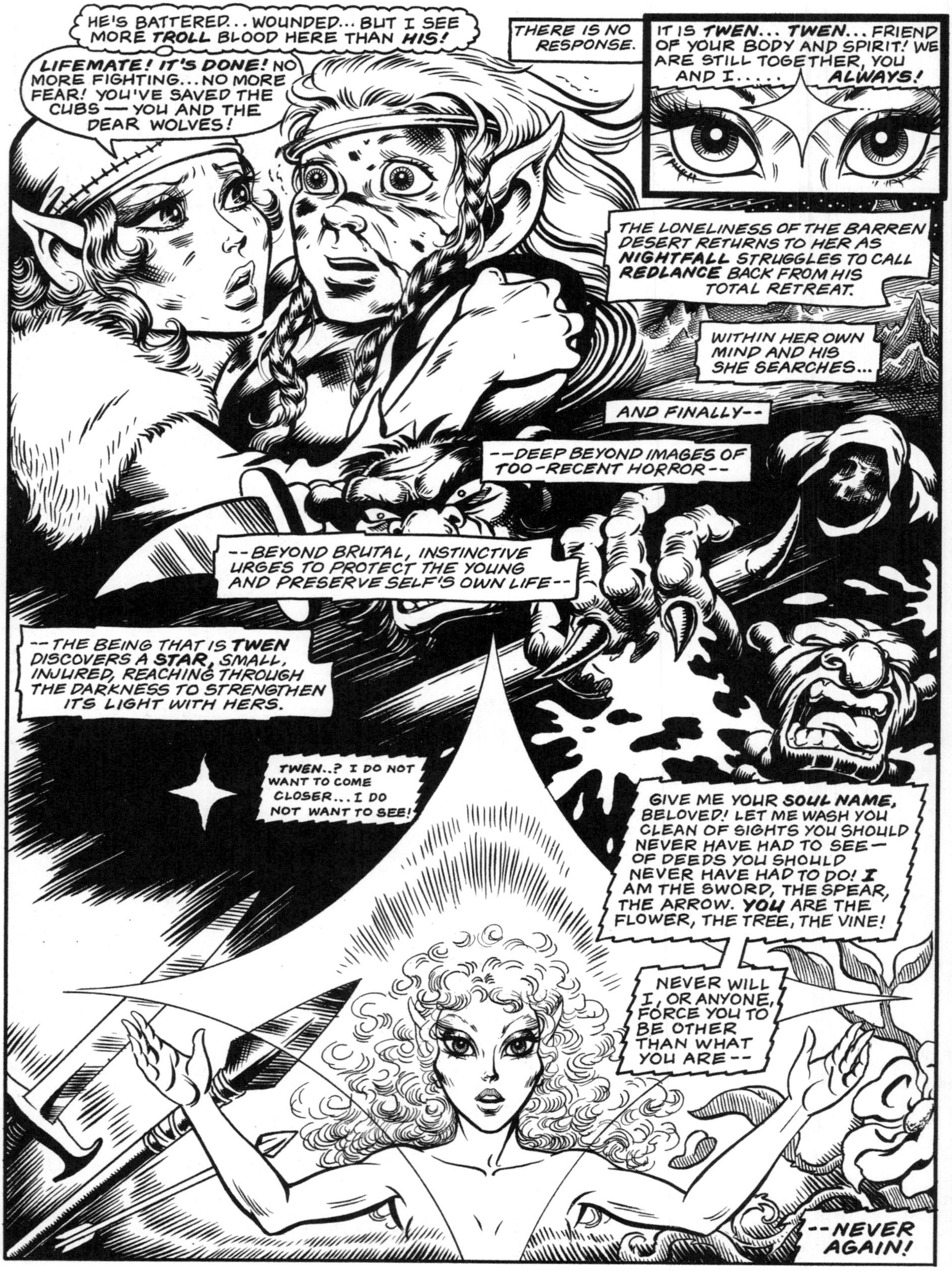
HE'S BATTERED... WOUNDED... BUT I SEE MORE TROLL BLOOD HERE THAN HIS!
LIFEMATE! IT'S DONE! NO MORE FIGHTING... NO MORE FEAR! YOU'VE SAVED THE CUBS — YOU AND THE DEAR WOLVES!
THERE IS NO RESPONSE.
IT IS TWEN... TWEN... FRIEND OF YOUR BODY AND SPIRIT! WE ARE STILL TOGETHER, YOU AND I..... ALWAYS!
THE LONELINESS OF THE BARREN DESERT RETURNS TO HER AS NIGHTFALL STRUGGLES TO CALL REDLANCE BACK FROM HIS TOTAL RETREAT.
WITHIN HER OWN MIND AND HIS SHE SEARCHES...
AND FINALLY--
--DEEP BEYOND IMAGES OF TOO-RECENT HORROR--
--BEYOND BRUTAL, INSTINCTIVE URGES TO PROTECT THE YOUNG AND PRESERVE SELF'S OWN LIFE--
--THE BEING THAT IS TWEN DISCOVERS A STAR, SMALL, INJURED, REACHING THROUGH THE DARKNESS TO STRENGTHEN ITS LIGHT WITH HERS.
TWEN..? I DO NOT WANT TO COME CLOSER... I DO NOT WANT TO SEE!
GIVE ME YOUR SOUL NAME, BELOVED! LET ME WASH YOU CLEAN OF SIGHTS YOU SHOULD NEVER HAVE HAD TO SEE— OF DEEDS YOU SHOULD NEVER HAVE HAD TO DO! I AM THE SWORD, THE SPEAR, THE ARROW. YOU ARE THE FLOWER, THE TREE, THE VINE!
NEVER WILL I, OR ANYONE, FORCE YOU TO BE OTHER THAN WHAT YOU ARE--
--NEVER AGAIN!

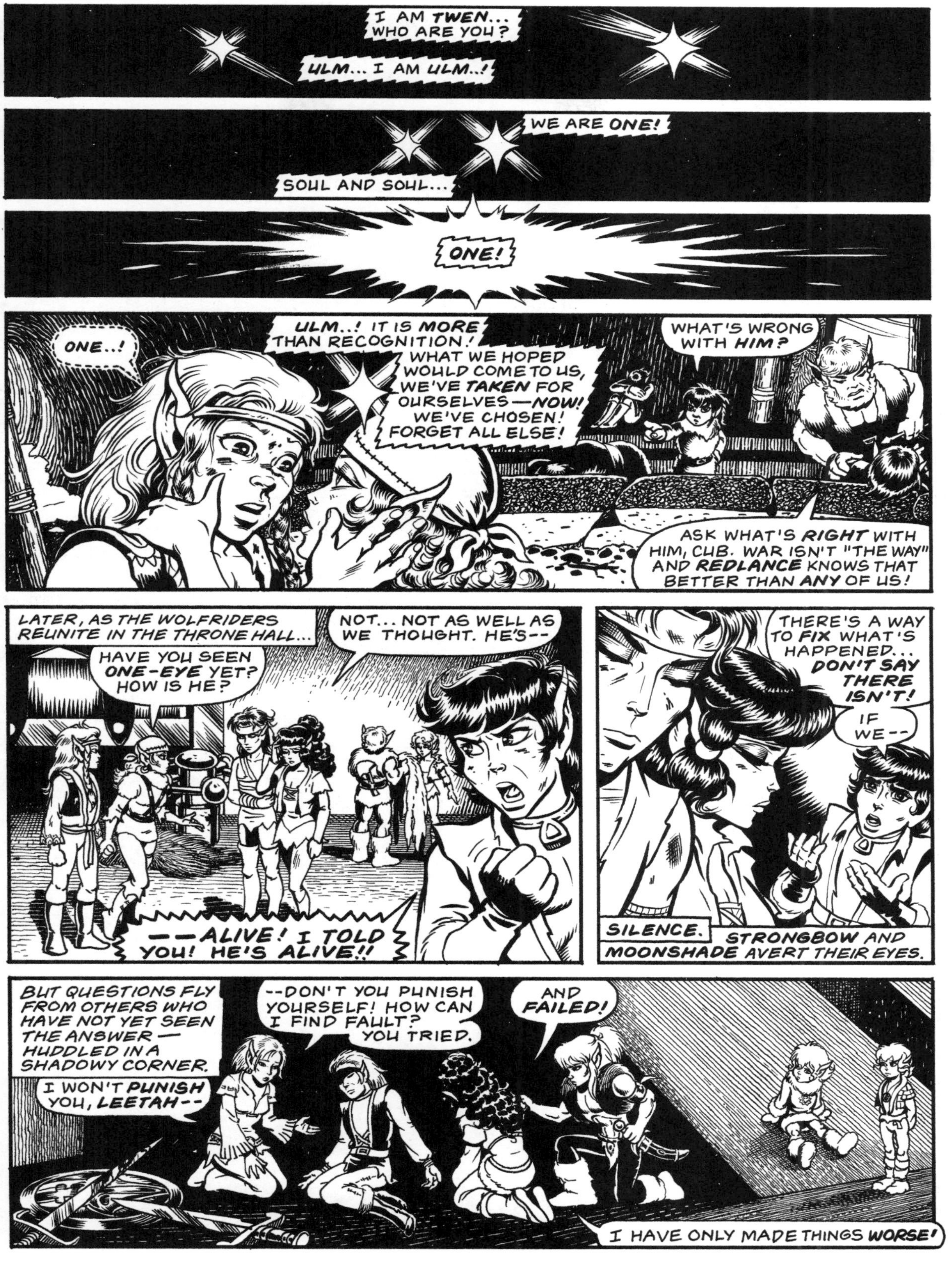

I AM TWEN... WHO ARE YOU?
ULM... I AM ULM..!
WE ARE ONE!
SOUL AND SOUL...
ONE!
ONE..!
ULM..! IT IS MORE THAN RECOGNITION!
WHAT WE HOPED WOULD COME TO US, WE'VE TAKEN FOR OURSELVES—NOW! WE'VE CHOSEN! FORGET ALL ELSE!
WHAT'S WRONG WITH HIM?
ASK WHAT'S RIGHT WITH HIM, CUB. WAR ISN'T "THE WAY" AND REDLANCE KNOWS THAT BETTER THAN ANY OF US!
LATER, AS THE WOLFRIDERS REUNITE IN THE THRONE HALL...
HAVE YOU SEEN ONE-EYE YET? HOW IS HE?
NOT... NOT AS WELL AS WE THOUGHT. HE'S--
--ALIVE! I TOLD YOU! HE'S ALIVE!!
THERE'S A WAY TO FIX WHAT'S HAPPENED... DON'T SAY THERE ISN'T!
IF WE--
SILENCE.
STRONGBOW AND MOONSHADE AVERT THEIR EYES.
BUT QUESTIONS FLY FROM OTHERS WHO HAVE NOT YET SEEN THE ANSWER—HUDDLED IN A SHADOWY CORNER.
I WON'T PUNISH YOU, LEETAH--
--DON'T YOU PUNISH YOURSELF! HOW CAN I FIND FAULT? YOU TRIED.
AND FAILED!
I HAVE ONLY MADE THINGS WORSE!

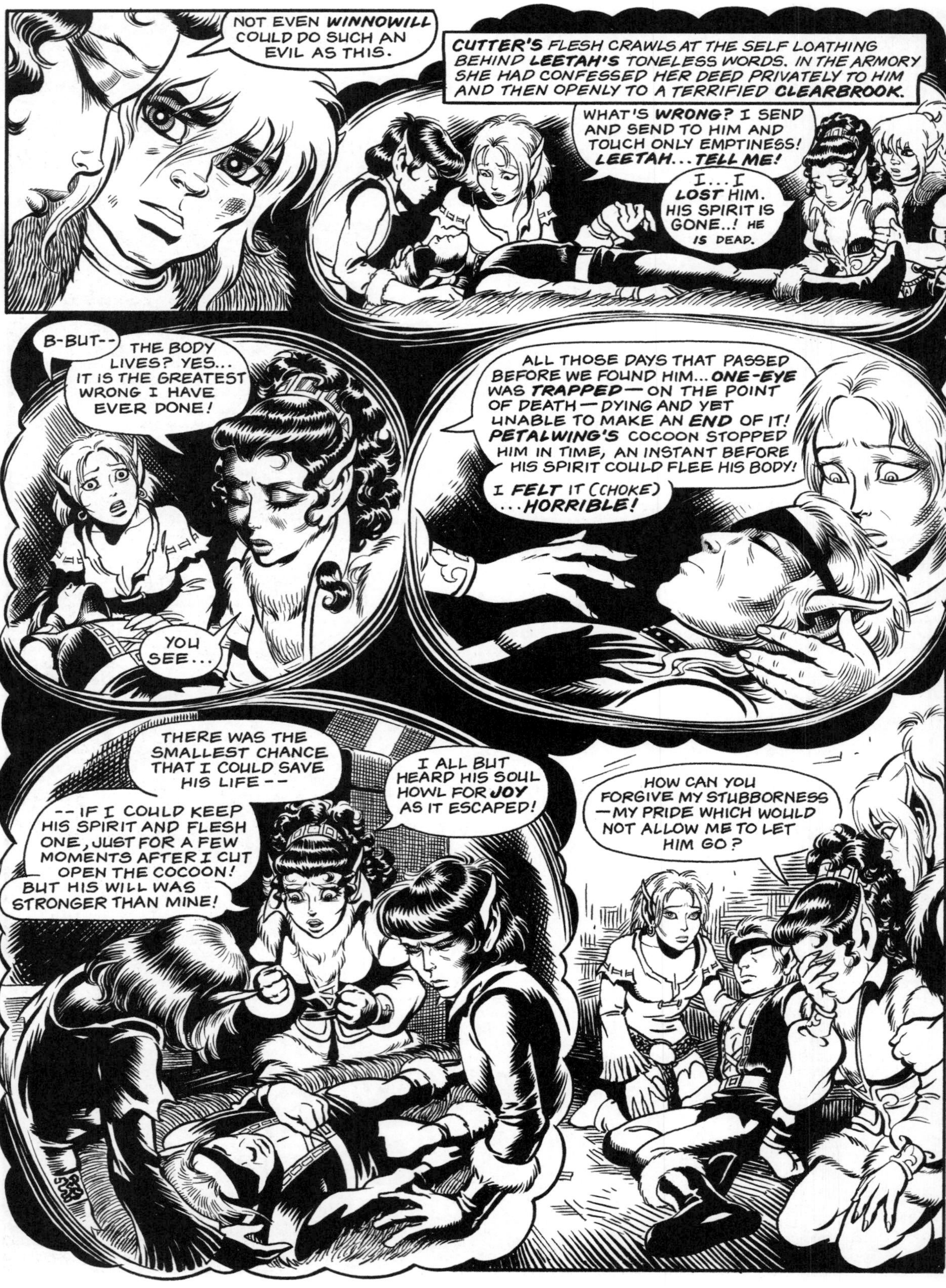
NOT EVEN WINNOWILL COULD DO SUCH AN EVIL AS THIS.
CUTTER'S FLESH CRAWLS AT THE SELF LOATHING BEHIND LEETAH'S TONELESS WORDS. IN THE ARMORY SHE HAD CONFESSED HER DEED PRIVATELY TO HIM AND THEN OPENLY TO A TERRIFIED CLEARBROOK.
WHAT'S WRONG? I SEND AND SEND TO HIM AND TOUCH ONLY EMPTINESS! LEETAH... TELL ME!
I... I LOST HIM. HIS SPIRIT IS GONE..! HE IS DEAD.
B-BUT--
THE BODY LIVES? YES... IT IS THE GREATEST WRONG I HAVE EVER DONE!
YOU SEE...
ALL THOSE DAYS THAT PASSED BEFORE WE FOUND HIM... ONE-EYE WAS TRAPPED — ON THE POINT OF DEATH — DYING AND YET UNABLE TO MAKE AN END OF IT! PETALWING'S COCOON STOPPED HIM IN TIME, AN INSTANT BEFORE HIS SPIRIT COULD FLEE HIS BODY!
I FELT IT (CHOKE) ...HORRIBLE!
THERE WAS THE SMALLEST CHANCE THAT I COULD SAVE HIS LIFE --
-- IF I COULD KEEP HIS SPIRIT AND FLESH ONE, JUST FOR A FEW MOMENTS AFTER I CUT OPEN THE COCOON!
BUT HIS WILL WAS STRONGER THAN MINE!
I ALL BUT HEARD HIS SOUL HOWL FOR JOY AS IT ESCAPED!
HOW CAN YOU FORGIVE MY STUBBORNESS — MY PRIDE WHICH WOULD NOT ALLOW ME TO LET HIM GO?

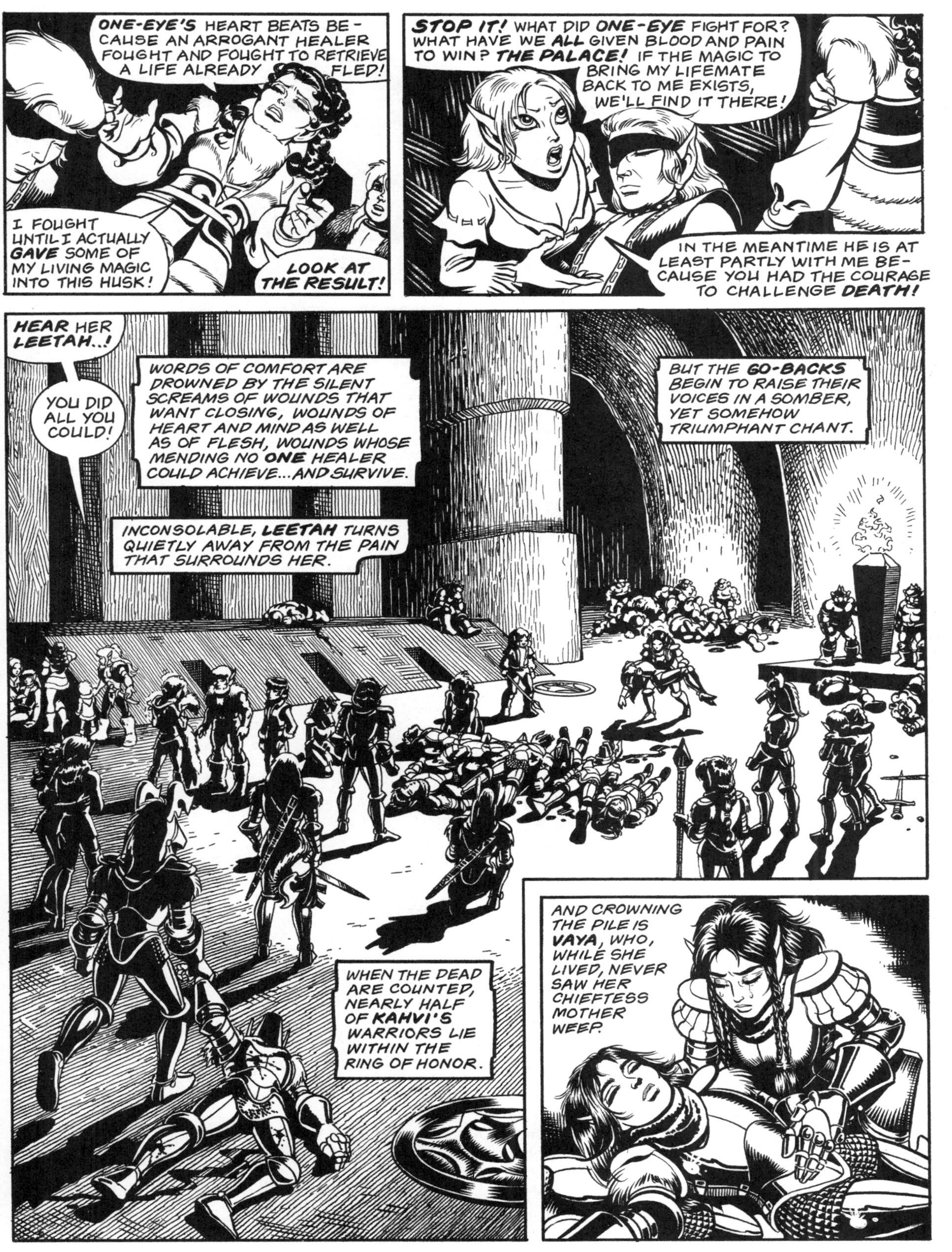
ONE-EYE'S HEART BEATS BECAUSE AN ARROGANT HEALER FOUGHT AND FOUGHT TO RETRIEVE A LIFE ALREADY FLED!
I FOUGHT UNTIL I ACTUALLY GAVE SOME OF MY LIVING MAGIC INTO THIS HUSK!
LOOK AT THE RESULT!
STOP IT! WHAT DID ONE-EYE FIGHT FOR? WHAT HAVE WE ALL GIVEN BLOOD AND PAIN TO WIN? THE PALACE! IF THE MAGIC TO BRING MY LIFEMATE BACK TO ME EXISTS, WE'LL FIND IT THERE!
IN THE MEANTIME HE IS AT LEAST PARTLY WITH ME BECAUSE YOU HAD THE COURAGE TO CHALLENGE DEATH!
HEAR HER LEETAH..!
YOU DID ALL YOU COULD!
WORDS OF COMFORT ARE DROWNED BY THE SILENT SCREAMS OF WOUNDS THAT WANT CLOSING, WOUNDS OF HEART AND MIND AS WELL AS OF FLESH, WOUNDS WHOSE MENDING NO ONE HEALER COULD ACHIEVE...AND SURVIVE.
INCONSOLABLE, LEETAH TURNS QUIETLY AWAY FROM THE PAIN THAT SURROUNDS HER.
BUT THE GO-BACKS BEGIN TO RAISE THEIR VOICES IN A SOMBER, YET SOMEHOW TRIUMPHANT CHANT.
WHEN THE DEAD ARE COUNTED, NEARLY HALF OF KAHVI'S WARRIORS LIE WITHIN THE RING OF HONOR.
AND CROWNING THE PILE IS VAYA, WHO, WHILE SHE LIVED, NEVER SAW HER CHIEFTESS MOTHER WEEP.

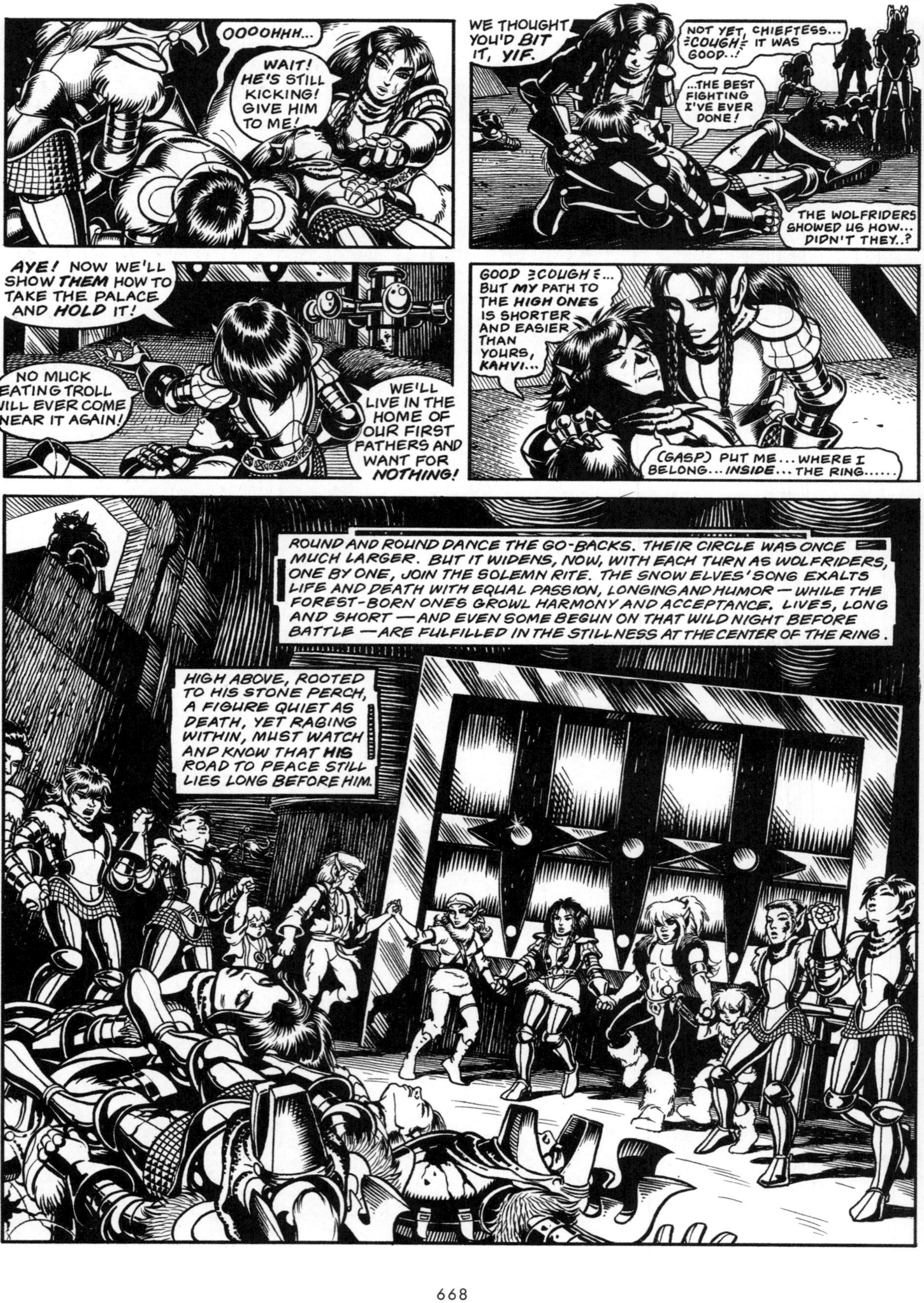
OOOOHHH...
WAIT! HE'S STILL KICKING! GIVE HIM TO ME!
WE THOUGHT YOU'D BIT IT, YIF.
NOT YET, CHIEFTESS... COUGH IT WAS GOOD..!
...THE BEST FIGHTING I'VE EVER DONE!
THE WOLFRIDERS SHOWED US HOW... DIDN'T THEY..?
AYE! NOW WE'LL SHOW THEM HOW TO TAKE THE PALACE AND HOLD IT!
NO MUCK EATING TROLL WILL EVER COME NEAR IT AGAIN!
WE'LL LIVE IN THE HOME OF OUR FIRST FATHERS AND WANT FOR NOTHING!
GOOD COUGH... BUT MY PATH TO THE HIGH ONES IS SHORTER AND EASIER THAN YOURS, KAHVI...
(GASP) PUT ME... WHERE I BELONG... INSIDE... THE RING......
ROUND AND ROUND DANCE THE GO-BACKS. THEIR CIRCLE WAS ONCE MUCH LARGER. BUT IT WIDENS, NOW, WITH EACH TURN AS WOLFRIDERS, ONE BY ONE, JOIN THE SOLEMN RITE. THE SNOW ELVES' SONG EXALTS LIFE AND DEATH WITH EQUAL PASSION, LONGING AND HUMOR — WHILE THE FOREST-BORN ONES GROWL HARMONY AND ACCEPTANCE. LIVES, LONG AND SHORT — AND EVEN SOME BEGUN ON THAT WILD NIGHT BEFORE BATTLE — ARE FULFILLED IN THE STILLNESS AT THE CENTER OF THE RING.
HIGH ABOVE, ROOTED TO HIS STONE PERCH, A FIGURE QUIET AS DEATH, YET RAGING WITHIN, MUST WATCH AND KNOW THAT HIS ROAD TO PEACE STILL LIES LONG BEFORE HIM.

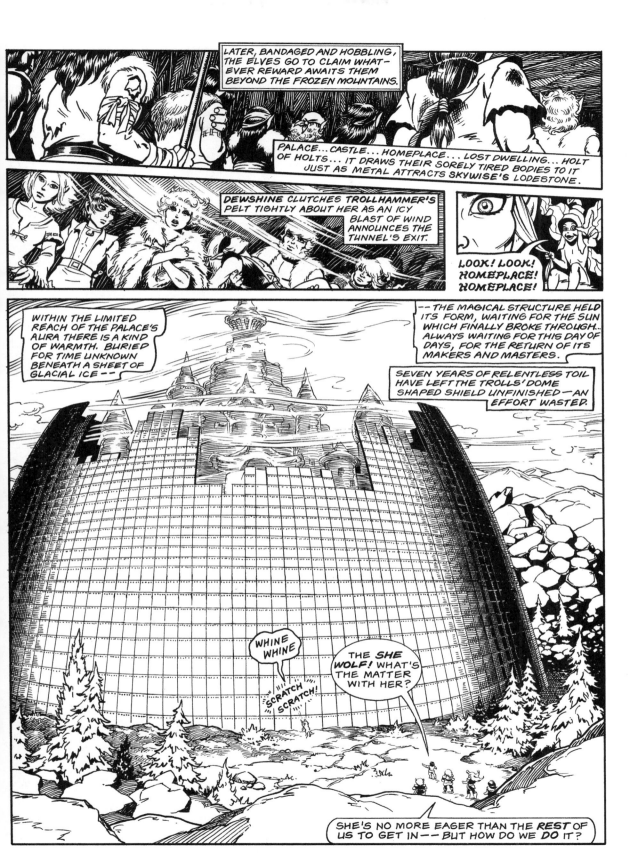

LATER, BANDAGED AND HOBBLING, THE ELVES GO TO CLAIM WHAT-EVER REWARD AWAITS THEM BEYOND THE FROZEN MOUNTAINS.

PALACE... CASTLE... HOMEPLACE... LOST DWELLING... HOLT OF HOLTS... IT DRAWS THEIR SORELY TIRED BODIES TO IT JUST AS METAL ATTRACTS SKYWISE'S LODESTONE.

DEWSHINE CLUTCHES TROLLHAMMER'S PELT TIGHTLY ABOUT HER AS AN ICY BLAST OF WIND ANNOUNCES THE TUNNEL'S EXIT.

LOOK! LOOK! HOMEPLACE! HOMEPLACE!

WITHIN THE LIMITED REACH OF THE PALACE'S AURA THERE IS A KIND OF WARMTH. BURIED FOR TIME UNKNOWN BENEATH A SHEET OF GLACIAL ICE --

-- THE MAGICAL STRUCTURE HELD ITS FORM, WAITING FOR THE SUN WHICH FINALLY BROKE THROUGH... ALWAYS WAITING FOR THIS DAY OF DAYS, FOR THE RETURN OF ITS MAKERS AND MASTERS.

SEVEN YEARS OF RELENTLESS TOIL HAVE LEFT THE TROLLS' DOME SHAPED SHIELD UNFINISHED — AN EFFORT WASTED.

WHINE WHINE

SCRATCH SCRATCH!

THE SHE WOLF! WHAT'S THE MATTER WITH HER?

SHE'S NO MORE EAGER THAN THE REST OF US TO GET IN -- BUT HOW DO WE DO IT?

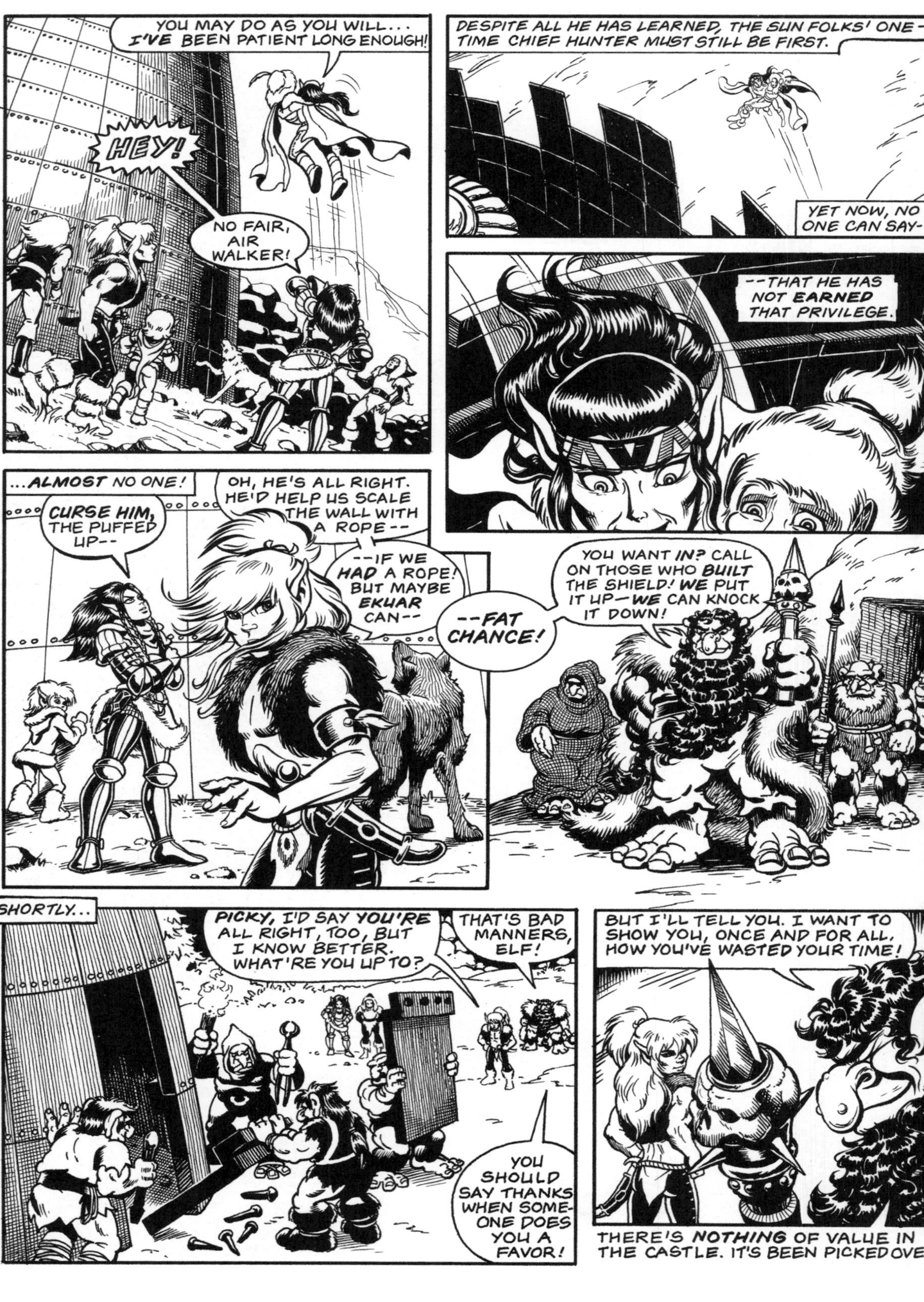
YOU MAY DO AS YOU WILL... I'VE BEEN PATIENT LONG ENOUGH!
HEY!
NO FAIR, AIR WALKER!
DESPITE ALL HE HAS LEARNED, THE SUN FOLKS' ONE-TIME CHIEF HUNTER MUST STILL BE FIRST.
YET NOW, NO ONE CAN SAY--
--THAT HE HAS NOT EARNED THAT PRIVILEGE.
...ALMOST NO ONE!
CURSE HIM, THE PUFFED UP--
OH, HE'S ALL RIGHT. HE'D HELP US SCALE THE WALL WITH A ROPE--
--IF WE HAD A ROPE! BUT MAYBE EKUAR CAN--
--FAT CHANCE!
YOU WANT IN? CALL ON THOSE WHO BUILT THE SHIELD! WE PUT IT UP—WE CAN KNOCK IT DOWN!
SHORTLY...
PICKY, I'D SAY YOU'RE ALL RIGHT, TOO, BUT I KNOW BETTER. WHAT'RE YOU UP TO?
THAT'S BAD MANNERS, ELF!
YOU SHOULD SAY THANKS WHEN SOME-ONE DOES YOU A FAVOR!
BUT I'LL TELL YOU. I WANT TO SHOW YOU, ONCE AND FOR ALL, HOW YOU'VE WASTED YOUR TIME!
THERE'S NOTHING OF VALUE IN THE CASTLE. IT'S BEEN PICKED OVER!

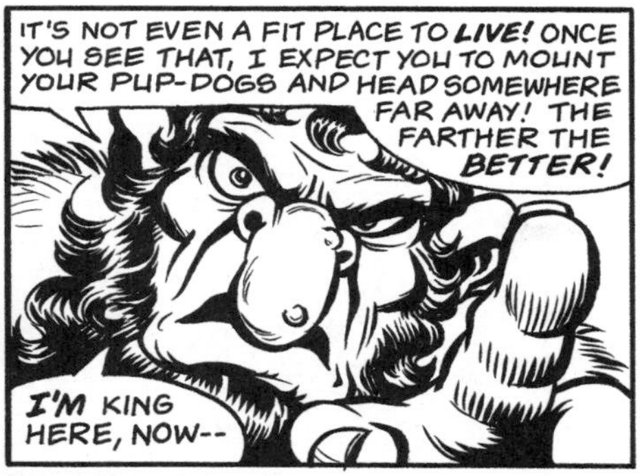
IT'S NOT EVEN A FIT PLACE TO LIVE! ONCE YOU SEE THAT, I EXPECT YOU TO MOUNT YOUR PUP-DOGS AND HEAD SOMEWHERE FAR AWAY! THE FARTHER THE BETTER!
I'M KING HERE, NOW--

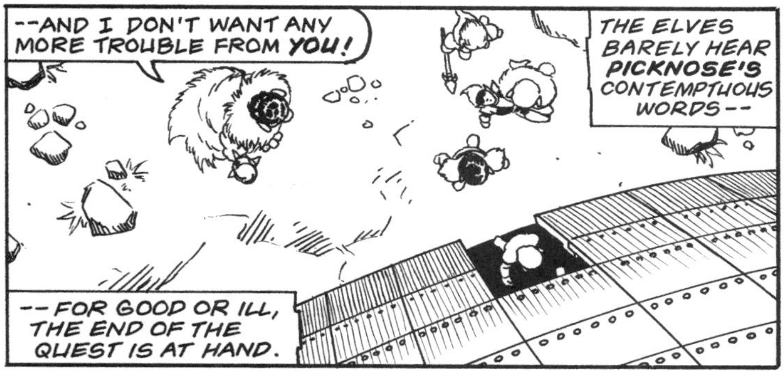
--AND I DON'T WANT ANY MORE TROUBLE FROM YOU!
THE ELVES BARELY HEAR PICKNOSE'S CONTEMPTUOUS WORDS--
--FOR GOOD OR ILL, THE END OF THE QUEST IS AT HAND.

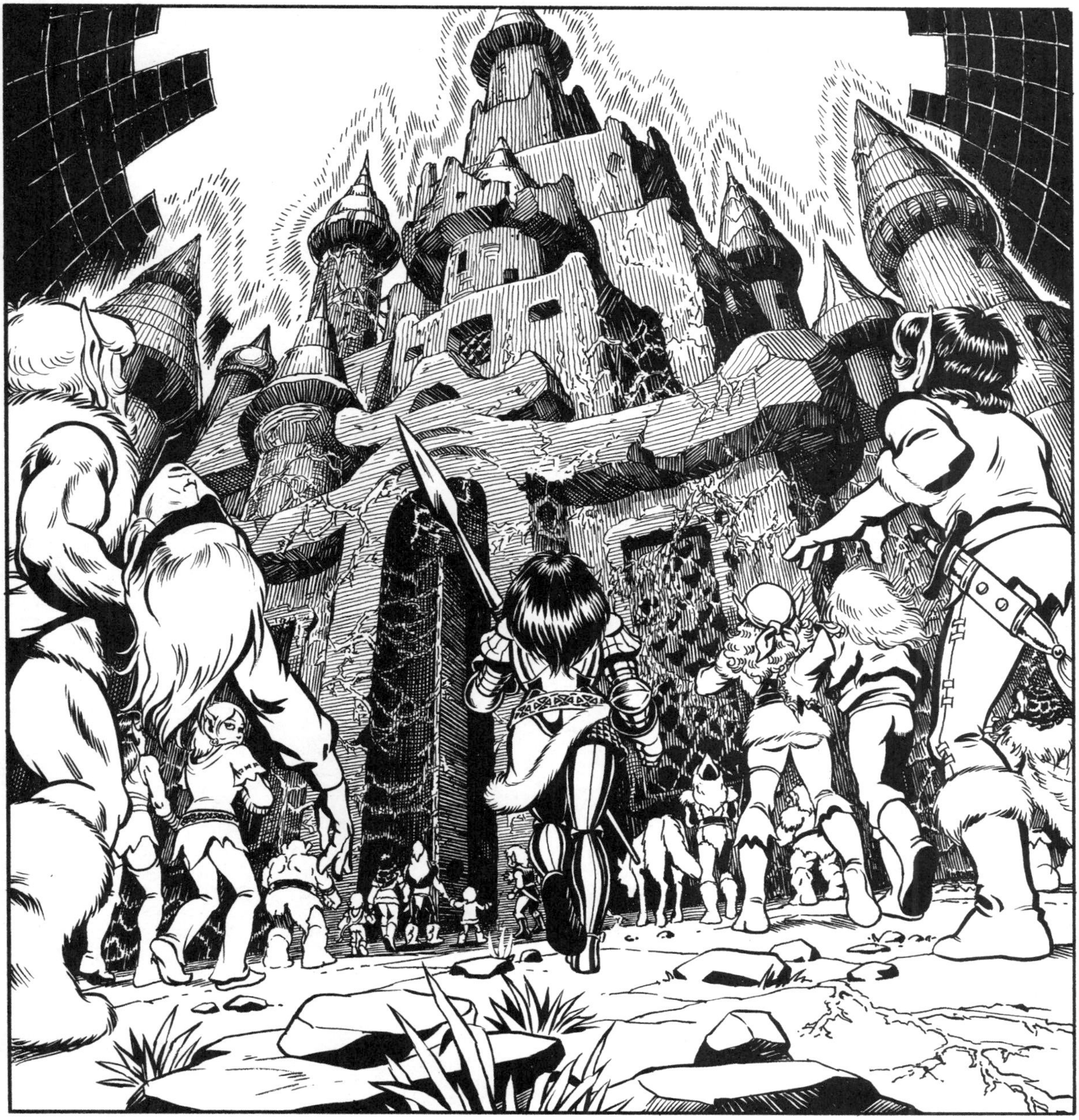

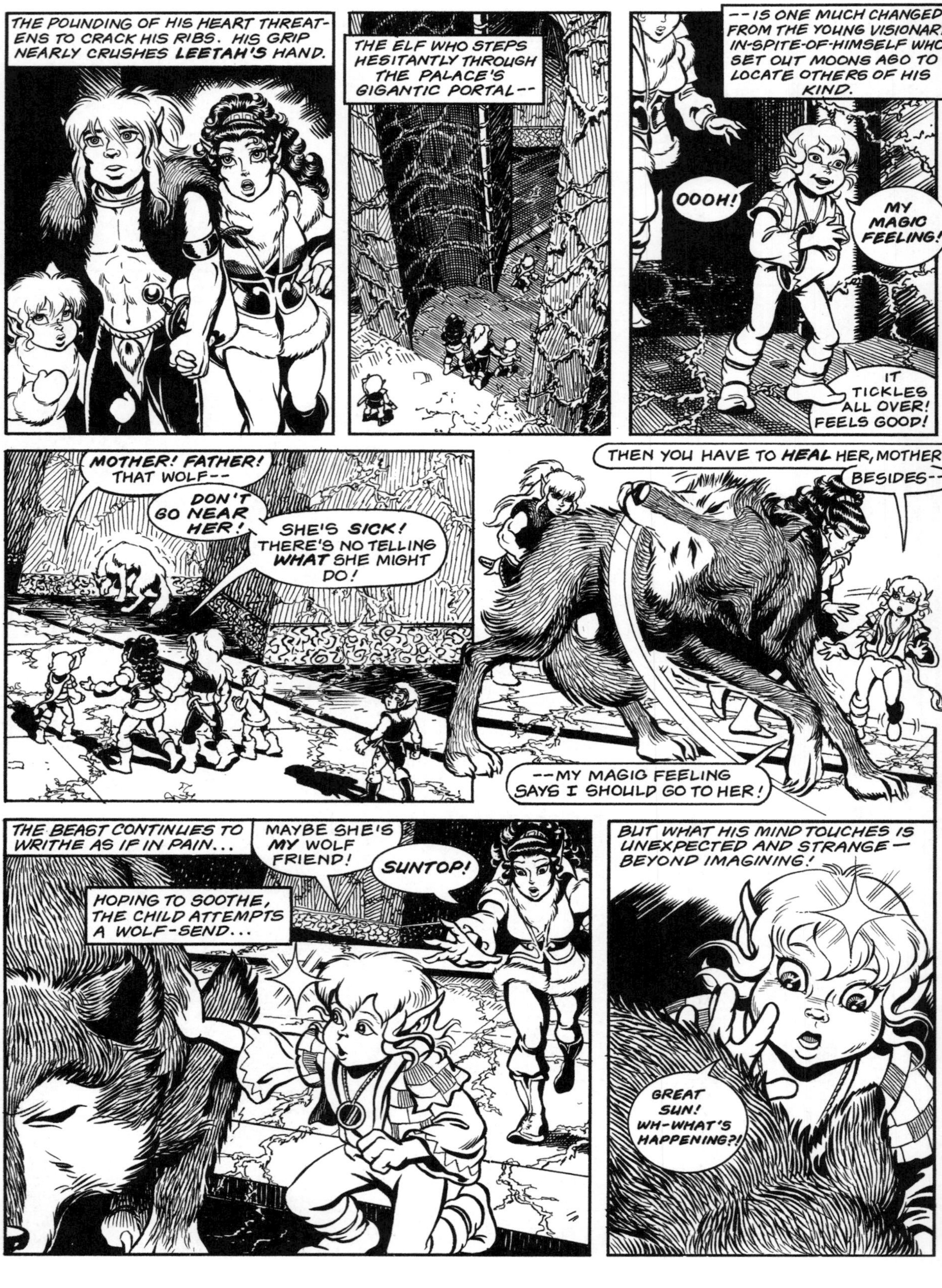
THE POUNDING OF HIS HEART THREATENS TO CRACK HIS RIBS. HIS GRIP NEARLY CRUSHES LEETAH'S HAND.
THE ELF WHO STEPS HESITANTLY THROUGH THE PALACE'S GIGANTIC PORTAL--
--IS ONE MUCH CHANGED FROM THE YOUNG VISIONARY IN-SPITE-OF-HIMSELF WHO SET OUT MOONS AGO TO LOCATE OTHERS OF HIS KIND.
OOOH!
MY MAGIC FEELING!
IT TICKLES ALL OVER! FEELS GOOD!
MOTHER! FATHER! THAT WOLF--
DON'T GO NEAR HER!
SHE'S SICK! THERE'S NO TELLING WHAT SHE MIGHT DO!
THEN YOU HAVE TO HEAL HER, MOTHER!
BESIDES--
--MY MAGIC FEELING SAYS I SHOULD GO TO HER!
THE BEAST CONTINUES TO WRITHE AS IF IN PAIN...
MAYBE SHE'S MY WOLF FRIEND!
SUNTOP!
HOPING TO SOOTHE, THE CHILD ATTEMPTS A WOLF-SEND...
BUT WHAT HIS MIND TOUCHES IS UNEXPECTED AND STRANGE— BEYOND IMAGINING!
GREAT SUN! WH-WHAT'S HAPPENING?!

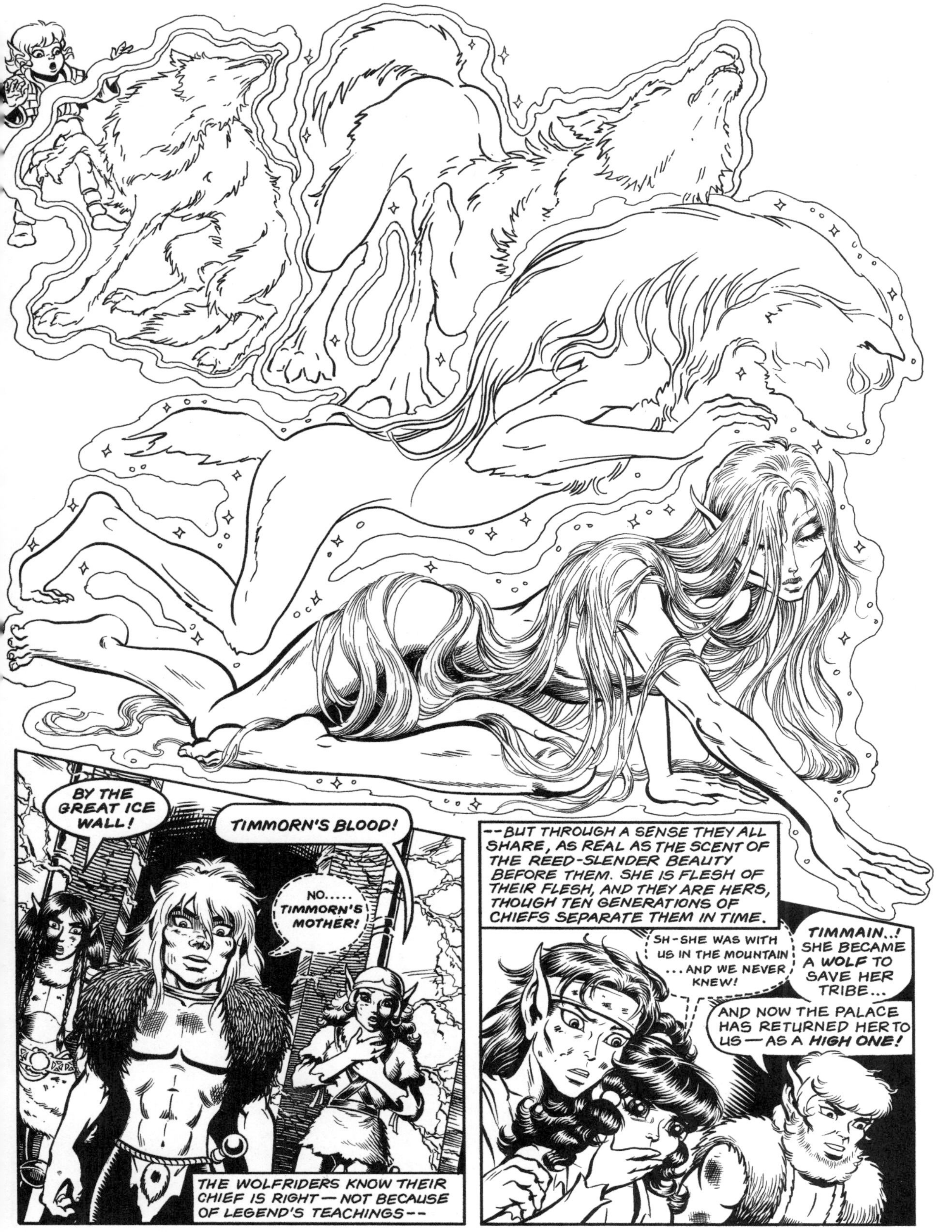
BY THE GREAT ICE WALL!
TIMMORN'S BLOOD!
NO..... TIMMORN'S MOTHER!
THE WOLFRIDERS KNOW THEIR CHIEF IS RIGHT — NOT BECAUSE OF LEGEND'S TEACHINGS--
--BUT THROUGH A SENSE THEY ALL SHARE, AS REAL AS THE SCENT OF THE REED-SLENDER BEAUTY BEFORE THEM. SHE IS FLESH OF THEIR FLESH, AND THEY ARE HERS, THOUGH TEN GENERATIONS OF CHIEFS SEPARATE THEM IN TIME.
SH-SHE WAS WITH US IN THE MOUNTAIN ...AND WE NEVER KNEW!
TIMMAIN..! SHE BECAME A WOLF TO SAVE HER TRIBE...
AND NOW THE PALACE HAS RETURNED HER TO US — AS A HIGH ONE!

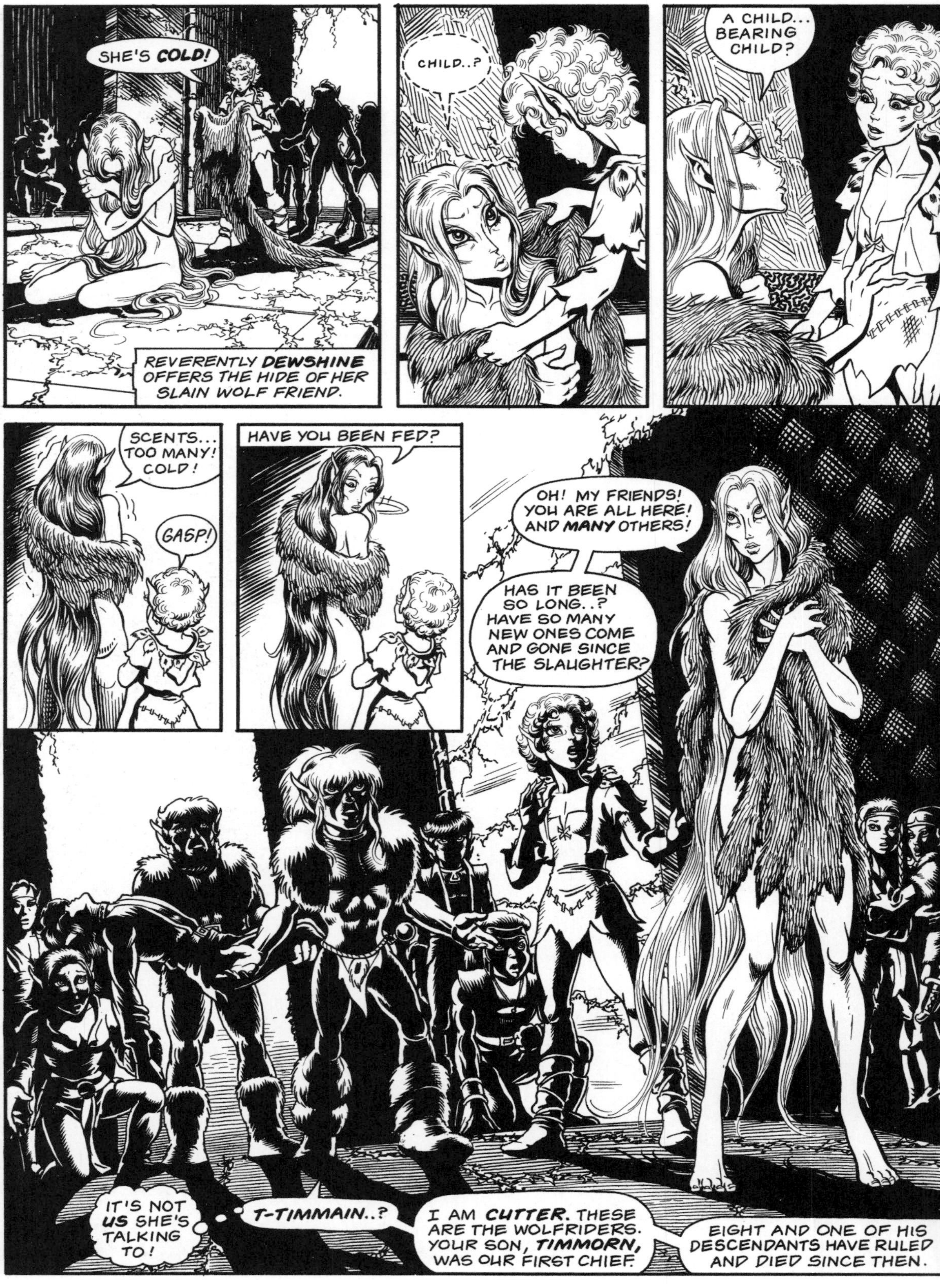
SHE'S COLD!
REVERENTLY DEWSHINE OFFERS THE HIDE OF HER SLAIN WOLF FRIEND.
CHILD..?
A CHILD... BEARING CHILD?
SCENTS... TOO MANY! COLD!
GASP!
HAVE YOU BEEN FED?
OH! MY FRIENDS! YOU ARE ALL HERE! AND MANY OTHERS!
HAS IT BEEN SO LONG..? HAVE SO MANY NEW ONES COME AND GONE SINCE THE SLAUGHTER?
IT'S NOT US SHE'S TALKING TO!
T-TIMMAIN..?
I AM CUTTER. THESE ARE THE WOLFRIDERS. YOUR SON, TIMMORN, WAS OUR FIRST CHIEF.
EIGHT AND ONE OF HIS DESCENDANTS HAVE RULED AND DIED SINCE THEN.

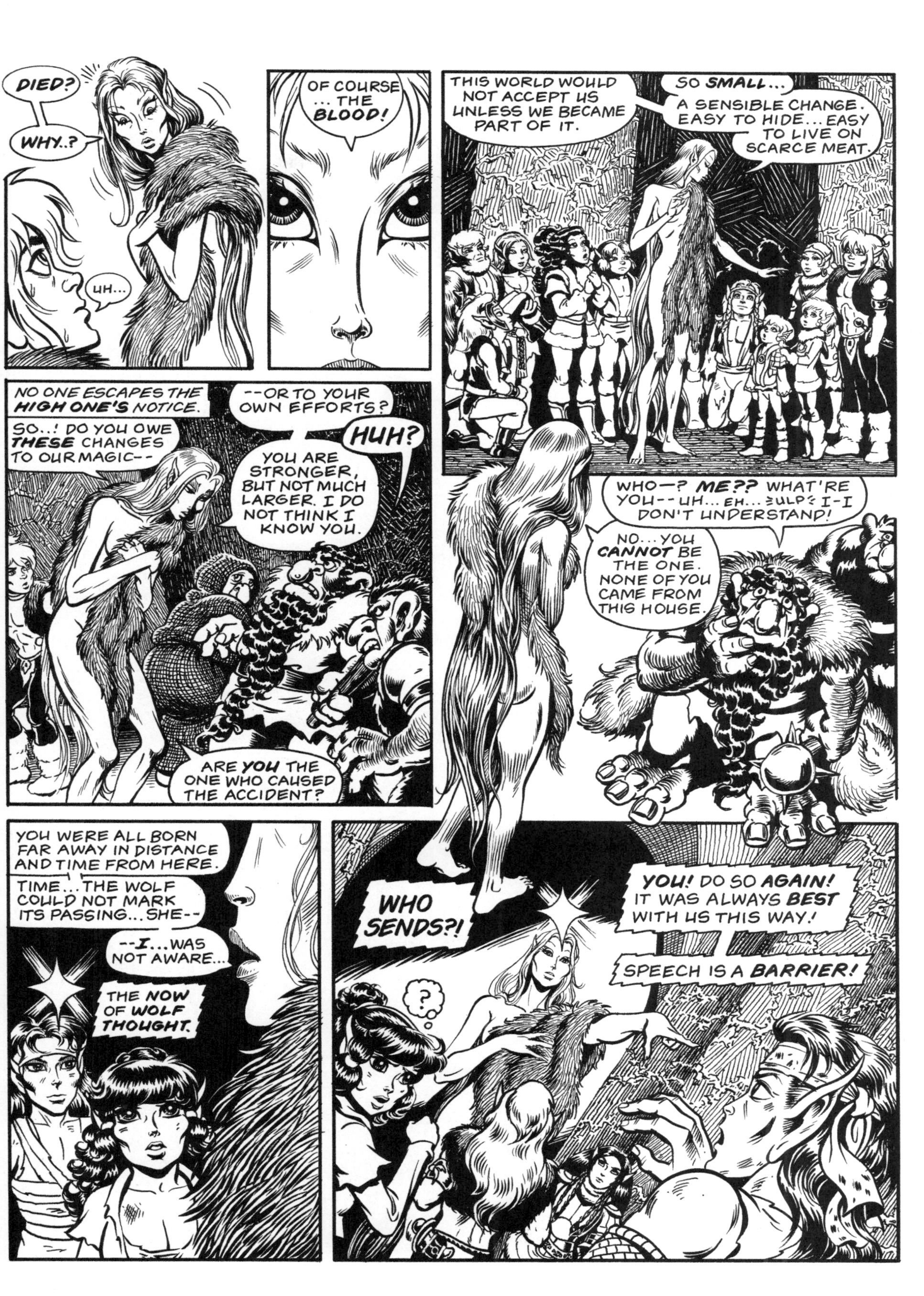
DIED?
WHY..?
UH...
OF COURSE ... THE BLOOD!
THIS WORLD WOULD NOT ACCEPT US UNLESS WE BECAME PART OF IT.
SO SMALL...
A SENSIBLE CHANGE. EASY TO HIDE... EASY TO LIVE ON SCARCE MEAT.
NO ONE ESCAPES THE HIGH ONE'S NOTICE.
SO..! DO YOU OWE THESE CHANGES TO OUR MAGIC--
--OR TO YOUR OWN EFFORTS?
HUH?
YOU ARE STRONGER, BUT NOT MUCH LARGER. I DO NOT THINK I KNOW YOU.
ARE YOU THE ONE WHO CAUSED THE ACCIDENT?
WHO--? ME?? WHAT'RE YOU--UH... EH... GULP? I-I DON'T UNDERSTAND!
NO... YOU CANNOT BE THE ONE. NONE OF YOU CAME FROM THIS HOUSE.
YOU WERE ALL BORN FAR AWAY IN DISTANCE AND TIME FROM HERE.
TIME... THE WOLF COULD NOT MARK ITS PASSING... SHE--
--I...WAS NOT AWARE...
THE NOW OF WOLF THOUGHT.
WHO SENDS?!
YOU! DO SO AGAIN! IT WAS ALWAYS BEST WITH US THIS WAY!
SPEECH IS A BARRIER!
?

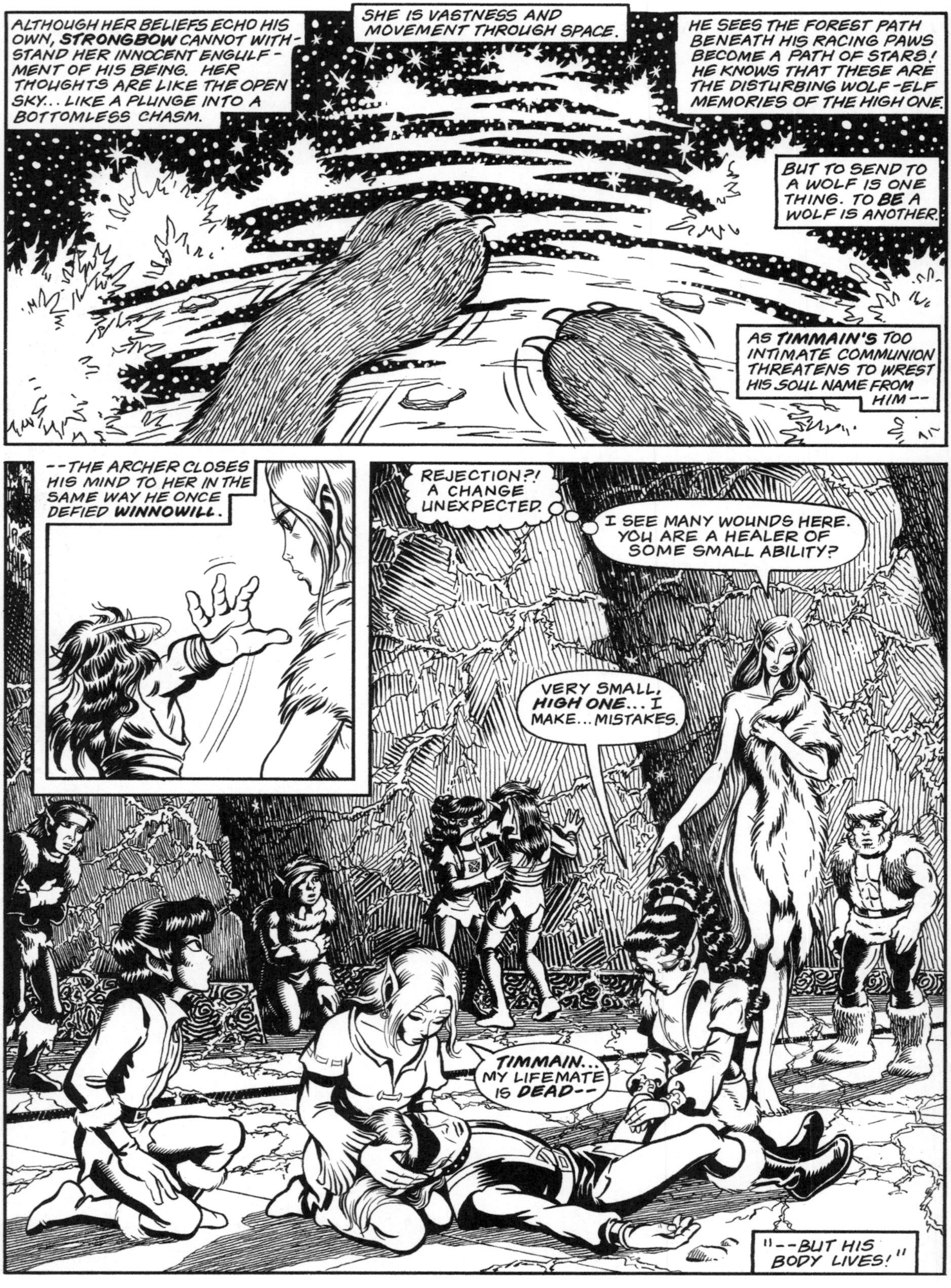
ALTHOUGH HER BELIEFS ECHO HIS OWN, STRONGBOW CANNOT WITH-STAND HER INNOCENT ENGULF-MENT OF HIS BEING. HER THOUGHTS ARE LIKE THE OPEN SKY... LIKE A PLUNGE INTO A BOTTOMLESS CHASM.
SHE IS VASTNESS AND MOVEMENT THROUGH SPACE.
HE SEES THE FOREST PATH BENEATH HIS RACING PAWS BECOME A PATH OF STARS! HE KNOWS THAT THESE ARE THE DISTURBING WOLF-ELF MEMORIES OF THE HIGH ONE.
BUT TO SEND TO A WOLF IS ONE THING. TO BE A WOLF IS ANOTHER.
AS TIMMAIN'S TOO INTIMATE COMMUNION THREATENS TO WREST HIS SOUL NAME FROM HIM--
--THE ARCHER CLOSES HIS MIND TO HER IN THE SAME WAY HE ONCE DEFIED WINNOWILL.
REJECTION?! A CHANGE UNEXPECTED.
I SEE MANY WOUNDS HERE. YOU ARE A HEALER OF SOME SMALL ABILITY?
VERY SMALL, HIGH ONE... I MAKE... MISTAKES.
TIMMAIN... MY LIFEMATE IS DEAD--
"--BUT HIS BODY LIVES!"

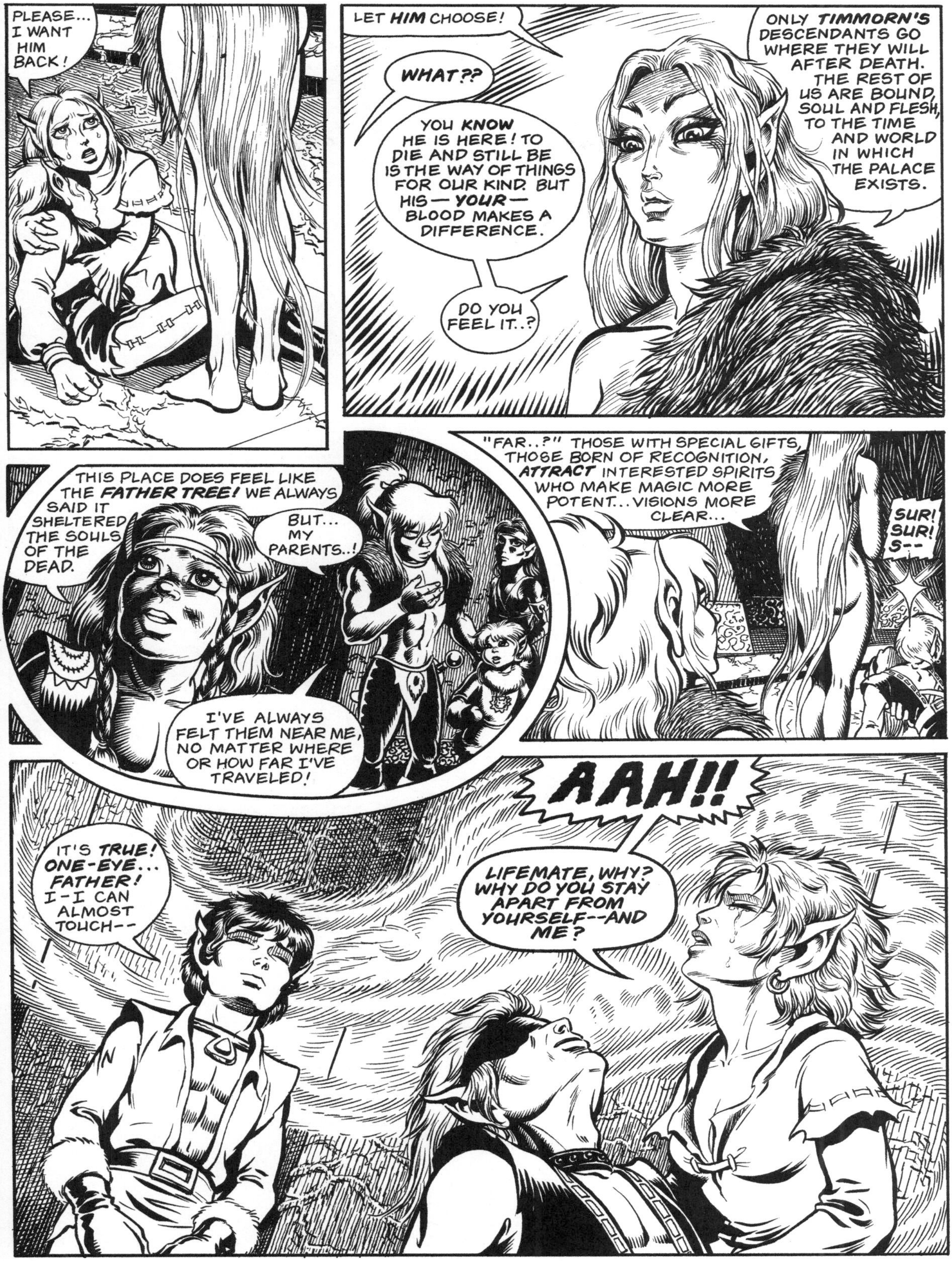

PLEASE... I WANT HIM BACK!
LET HIM CHOOSE!
WHAT??
YOU KNOW HE IS HERE! TO DIE AND STILL BE IS THE WAY OF THINGS FOR OUR KIND. BUT HIS — YOUR — BLOOD MAKES A DIFFERENCE.
DO YOU FEEL IT..?
ONLY TIMMORN'S DESCENDANTS GO WHERE THEY WILL AFTER DEATH. THE REST OF US ARE BOUND, SOUL AND FLESH, TO THE TIME AND WORLD IN WHICH THE PALACE EXISTS.
THIS PLACE DOES FEEL LIKE THE FATHER TREE! WE ALWAYS SAID IT SHELTERED THE SOULS OF THE DEAD.
BUT... MY PARENTS..!
I'VE ALWAYS FELT THEM NEAR ME, NO MATTER WHERE OR HOW FAR I'VE TRAVELED!
"FAR..?" THOSE WITH SPECIAL GIFTS, THOSE BORN OF RECOGNITION, ATTRACT INTERESTED SPIRITS WHO MAKE MAGIC MORE POTENT... VISIONS MORE CLEAR...
SURI! SURI! S--
AAH!!
IT'S TRUE! ONE-EYE... FATHER! I--I CAN ALMOST TOUCH--
LIFEMATE, WHY? WHY DO YOU STAY APART FROM YOURSELF--AND ME?

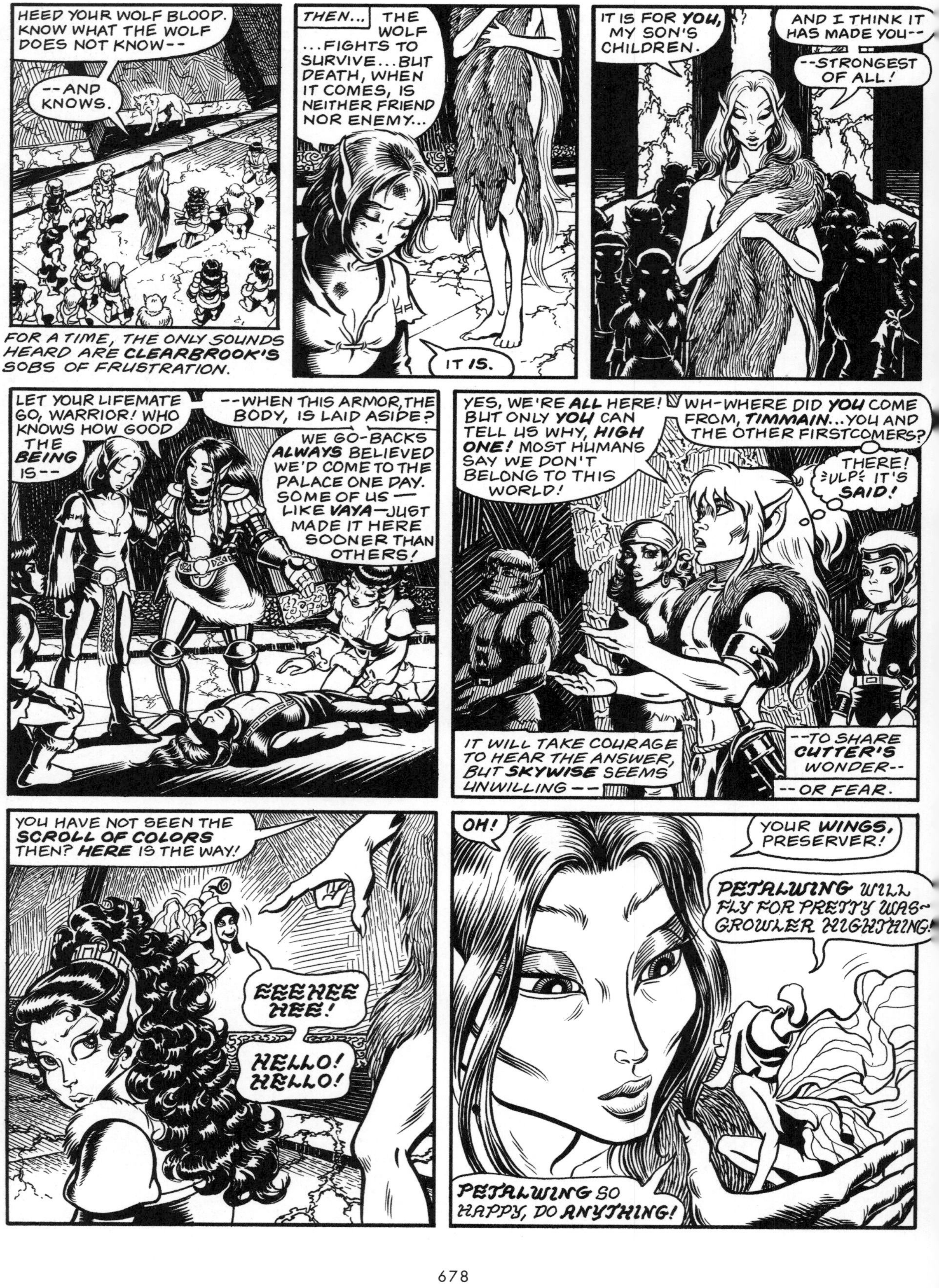
HEED YOUR WOLF BLOOD. KNOW WHAT THE WOLF DOES NOT KNOW--
--AND KNOWS.
FOR A TIME, THE ONLY SOUNDS HEARD ARE **CLEARBROOK'S** SOBS OF FRUSTRATION.
THEN...
THE WOLF ...FIGHTS TO SURVIVE... BUT DEATH, WHEN IT COMES, IS NEITHER FRIEND NOR ENEMY...
IT **IS.**
IT IS FOR **YOU,** MY SON'S CHILDREN.
AND I THINK IT HAS MADE YOU--
--STRONGEST OF ALL!
LET YOUR LIFEMATE GO, WARRIOR! WHO KNOWS HOW GOOD THE **BEING** IS--
--WHEN THIS ARMOR, THE BODY, IS LAID ASIDE?
WE GO-BACKS **ALWAYS** BELIEVED WE'D COME TO THE PALACE ONE DAY. SOME OF US— LIKE **VAYA**—JUST MADE IT HERE SOONER THAN OTHERS!
YES, WE'RE **ALL** HERE! BUT ONLY **YOU** CAN TELL US WHY, **HIGH ONE!** MOST HUMANS SAY WE DON'T BELONG TO THIS WORLD!
WH-WHERE DID **YOU** COME FROM, **TIMMAIN**... YOU AND THE OTHER FIRSTCOMERS?
THERE! *ULP* IT'S **SAID!**
IT WILL TAKE COURAGE TO HEAR THE ANSWER, BUT **SKYWISE** SEEMS UNWILLING--
--TO SHARE **CUTTER'S** WONDER--
--OR FEAR.
YOU HAVE NOT SEEN THE **SCROLL OF COLORS** THEN? **HERE** IS THE WAY!
EEEHEE HEE!
HELLO! HELLO!
OH!
YOUR **WINGS,** PRESERVER!
PETALWING WILL FLY FOR PRETTY WAG-GROWLER HIGHTHING!
PETALWING SO HAPPY, DO **ANYTHING!**

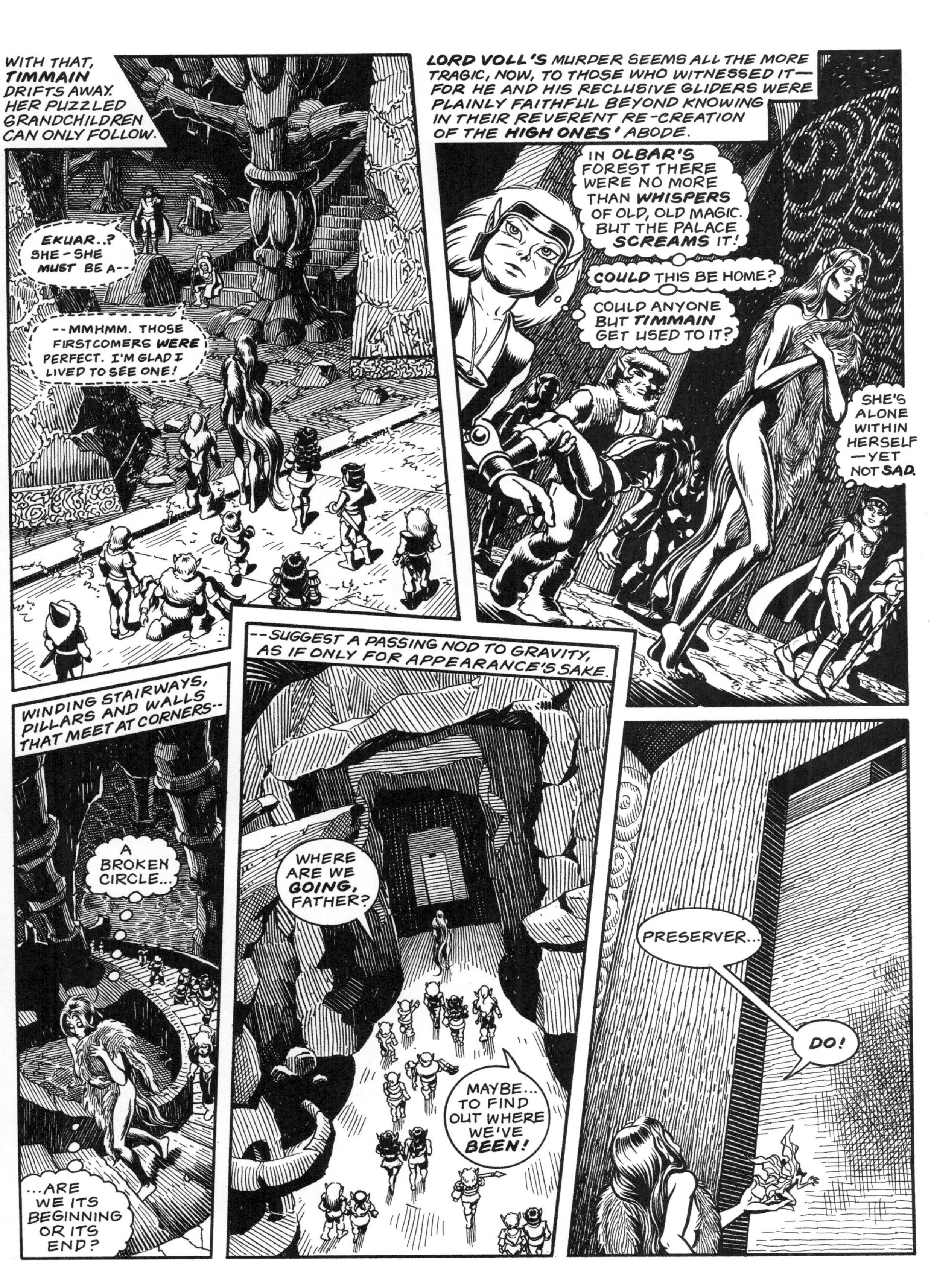
WITH THAT, TIMMAIN DRIFTS AWAY. HER PUZZLED GRANDCHILDREN CAN ONLY FOLLOW.
EKUAR..? SHE-SHE MUST BE A--
--MMHMM. THOSE FIRSTCOMERS WERE PERFECT. I'M GLAD I LIVED TO SEE ONE!
LORD VOLL'S MURDER SEEMS ALL THE MORE TRAGIC, NOW, TO THOSE WHO WITNESSED IT-- FOR HE AND HIS RECLUSIVE GLIDERS WERE PLAINLY FAITHFUL BEYOND KNOWING IN THEIR REVERENT RE-CREATION OF THE HIGH ONES' ABODE.
IN OLBAR'S FOREST THERE WERE NO MORE THAN WHISPERS OF OLD, OLD MAGIC. BUT THE PALACE SCREAMS IT!
COULD THIS BE HOME?
COULD ANYONE BUT TIMMAIN GET USED TO IT?
SHE'S ALONE WITHIN HERSELF --YET NOT SAD.
WINDING STAIRWAYS, PILLARS AND WALLS THAT MEET AT CORNERS--
A BROKEN CIRCLE...
...ARE WE ITS BEGINNING OR ITS END?
--SUGGEST A PASSING NOD TO GRAVITY, AS IF ONLY FOR APPEARANCE'S SAKE.
WHERE ARE WE GOING, FATHER?
MAYBE... TO FIND OUT WHERE WE'VE BEEN!
PRESERVER...
DO!

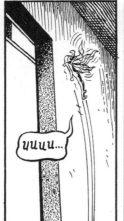
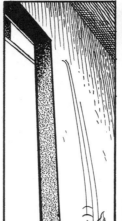YUUU...
YUUUH...
AWW!

WINGS STILL ALL SCRUNCHED! CAN'T FLY GOOP!

SORRY... SORRY...

UNDERSTANDING, **TIMMAIN** ATTEMPTS THE SAME FEAT--

--BUT SHE, TOO, IS CRIPPLED-- HER WOLF FORM HAS BEEN TOO LONG A SLAVE TO THE DOWNWARD PULL OF THE WORLD.

HIGH ONE, ALLOW ME!

AAH..!

WHAT MUST I DO?

THE PRESERVER ...PLACE IT IN THE OPENING ABOVE THE RIM!

LITTLE DOOR FOR ME BIG DOOR FOR YOU!

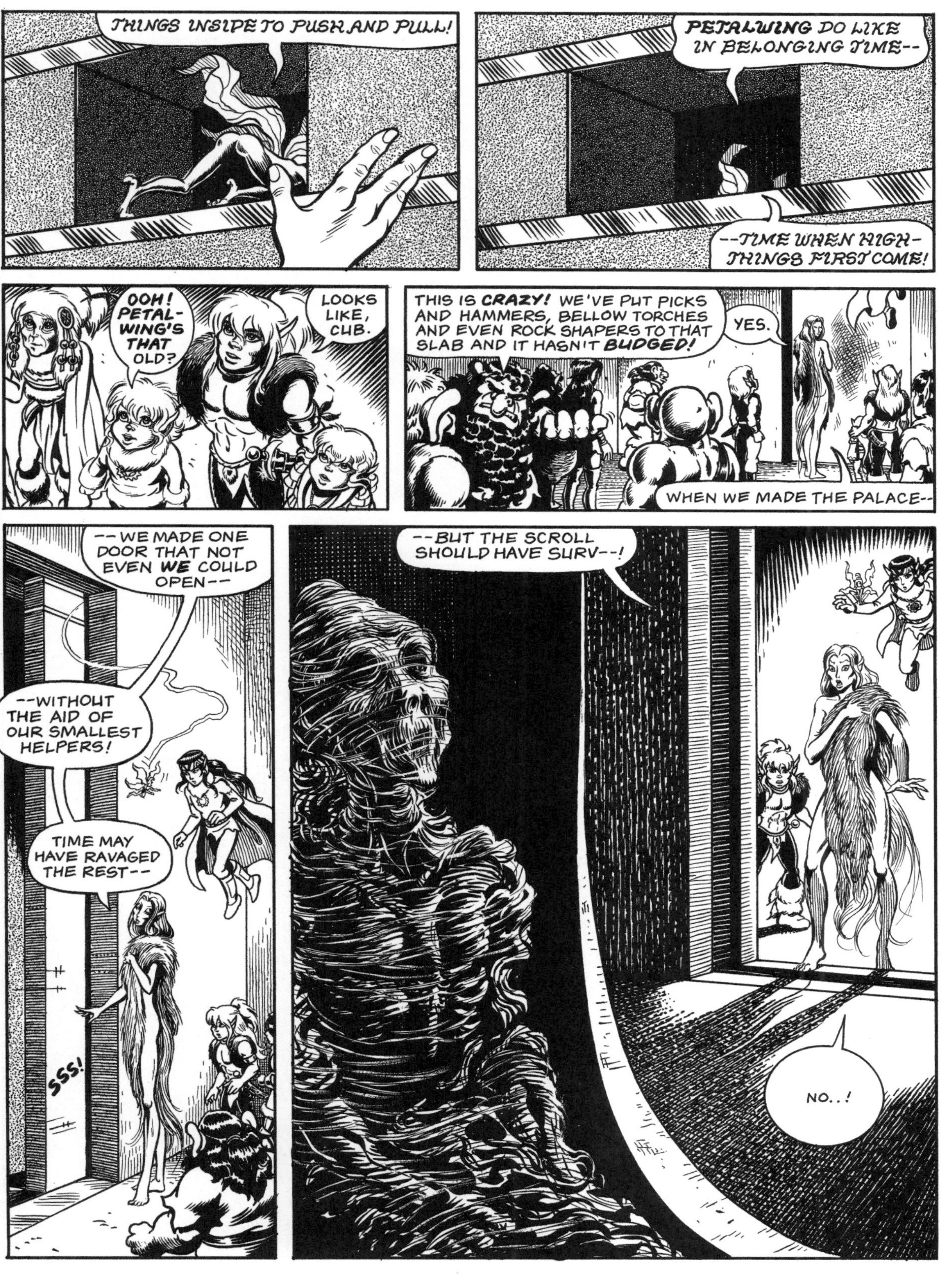
THINGS INSIDE TO PUSH AND PULL!
PETALWING DO LIKE IN BELONGING TIME--
--TIME WHEN HIGH-THINGS FIRST COME!
OOH! PETALWING'S THAT OLD?
LOOKS LIKE, CUB.
THIS IS CRAZY! WE'VE PUT PICKS AND HAMMERS, BELLOW TORCHES AND EVEN ROCK SHAPERS TO THAT SLAB AND IT HASN'T BUDGED!
YES.
WHEN WE MADE THE PALACE--
--WE MADE ONE DOOR THAT NOT EVEN WE COULD OPEN--
--WITHOUT THE AID OF OUR SMALLEST HELPERS!
TIME MAY HAVE RAVAGED THE REST--
SSS!
--BUT THE SCROLL SHOULD HAVE SURV--!
NO..!

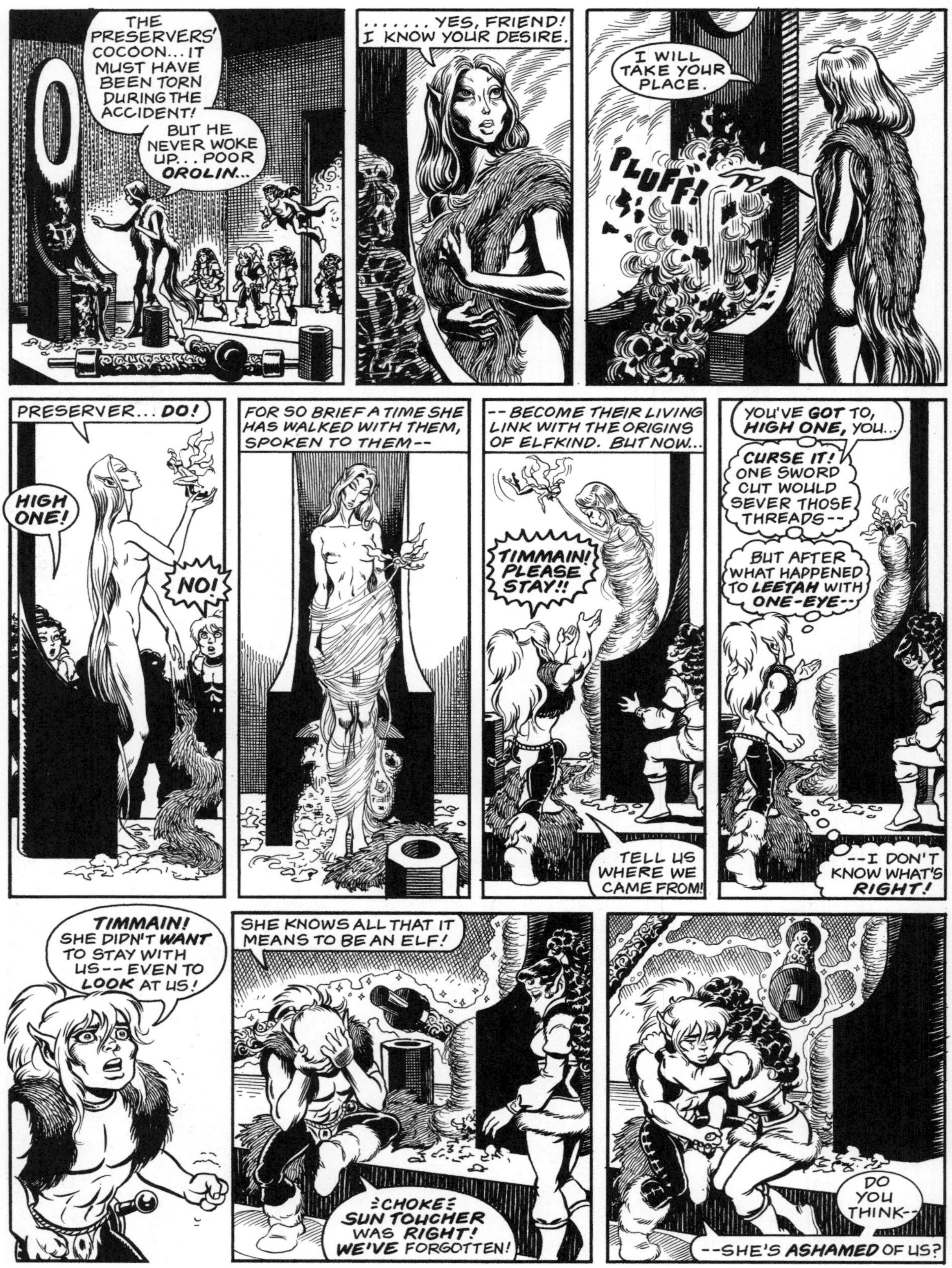

THE PRESERVERS' COCOON... IT MUST HAVE BEEN TORN DURING THE ACCIDENT!
BUT HE NEVER WOKE UP... POOR OROLIN...
.... YES, FRIEND! I KNOW YOUR DESIRE.
I WILL TAKE YOUR PLACE.
PLUFF!
PRESERVER... DO!
HIGH ONE!
NO!
FOR SO BRIEF A TIME SHE HAS WALKED WITH THEM, SPOKEN TO THEM--
--BECOME THEIR LIVING LINK WITH THE ORIGINS OF ELFKIND. BUT NOW...
TIMMAIN! PLEASE STAY!!
TELL US WHERE WE CAME FROM!
YOU'VE GOT TO, HIGH ONE, YOU...
CURSE IT! ONE SWORD CUT WOULD SEVER THOSE THREADS--
BUT AFTER WHAT HAPPENED TO LEETAH WITH ONE-EYE--
--I DON'T KNOW WHAT'S RIGHT!
TIMMAIN! SHE DIDN'T WANT TO STAY WITH US-- EVEN TO LOOK AT US!
SHE KNOWS ALL THAT IT MEANS TO BE AN ELF!
CHOKE SUN TOUCHER WAS RIGHT! WE'VE FORGOTTEN!
DO YOU THINK--
--SHE'S ASHAMED OF US?

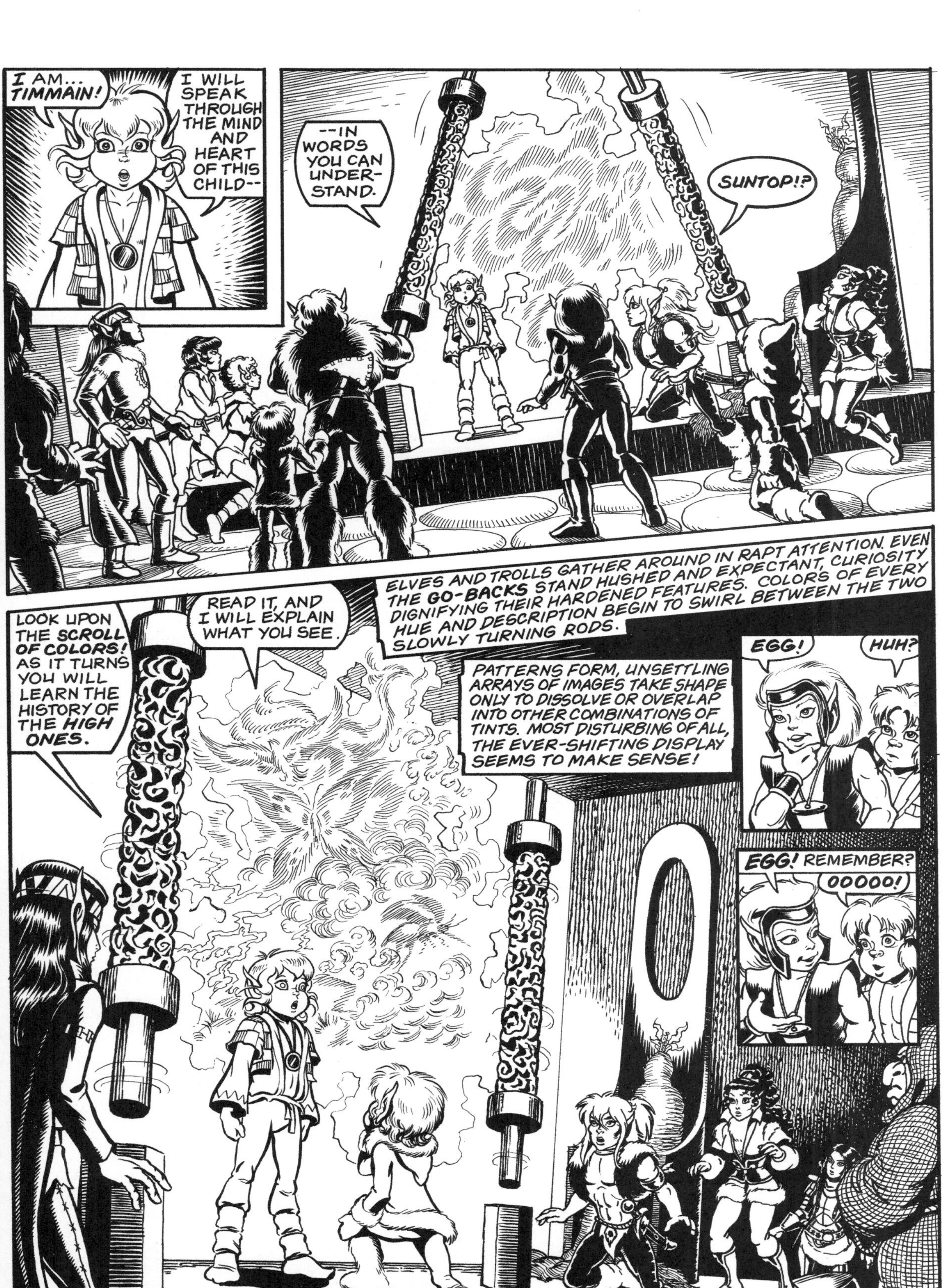
I AM... TIMMAIN!
I WILL SPEAK THROUGH THE MIND AND HEART OF THIS CHILD--
--IN WORDS YOU CAN UNDER-STAND.
SUNTOP!?
ELVES AND TROLLS GATHER AROUND IN RAPT ATTENTION. EVEN THE GO-BACKS STAND HUSHED AND EXPECTANT, CURIOSITY DIGNIFYING THEIR HARDENED FEATURES. COLORS OF EVERY HUE AND DESCRIPTION BEGIN TO SWIRL BETWEEN THE TWO SLOWLY TURNING RODS.
LOOK UPON THE SCROLL OF COLORS! AS IT TURNS YOU WILL LEARN THE HISTORY OF THE HIGH ONES.
READ IT, AND I WILL EXPLAIN WHAT YOU SEE.
PATTERNS FORM, UNSETTLING ARRAYS OF IMAGES TAKE SHAPE ONLY TO DISSOLVE OR OVERLAP INTO OTHER COMBINATIONS OF TINTS. MOST DISTURBING OF ALL, THE EVER-SHIFTING DISPLAY SEEMS TO MAKE SENSE!
EGG!
HUH?
EGG! REMEMBER?
OOOOO!

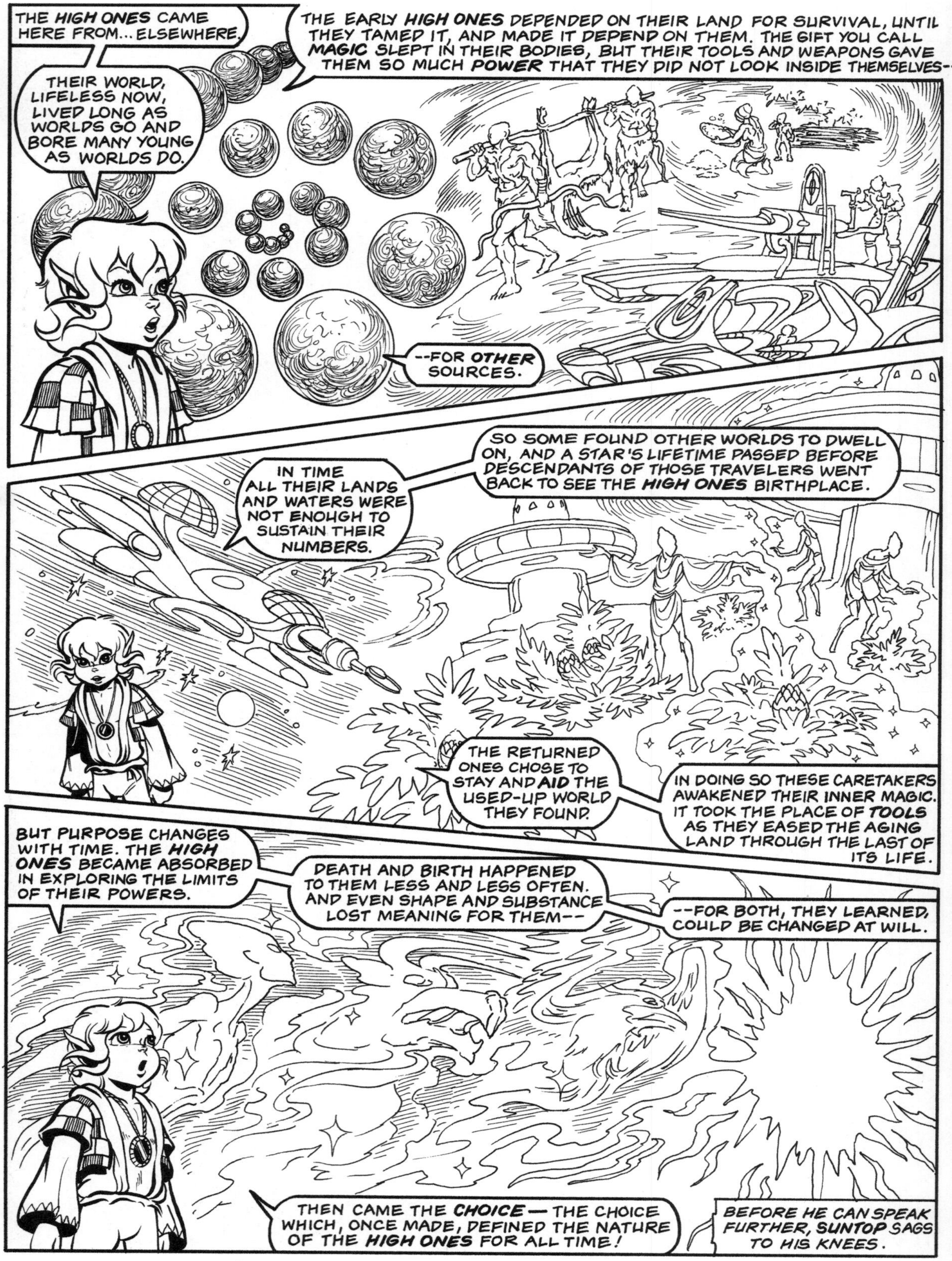

THE HIGH ONES CAME HERE FROM... ELSEWHERE.
THEIR WORLD, LIFELESS NOW, LIVED LONG AS WORLDS GO AND BORE MANY YOUNG AS WORLDS DO.
THE EARLY HIGH ONES DEPENDED ON THEIR LAND FOR SURVIVAL, UNTIL THEY TAMED IT, AND MADE IT DEPEND ON THEM. THE GIFT YOU CALL MAGIC SLEPT IN THEIR BODIES, BUT THEIR TOOLS AND WEAPONS GAVE THEM SO MUCH POWER THAT THEY DID NOT LOOK INSIDE THEMSELVES--
--FOR OTHER SOURCES.
IN TIME ALL THEIR LANDS AND WATERS WERE NOT ENOUGH TO SUSTAIN THEIR NUMBERS.
SO SOME FOUND OTHER WORLDS TO DWELL ON, AND A STAR'S LIFETIME PASSED BEFORE DESCENDANTS OF THOSE TRAVELERS WENT BACK TO SEE THE HIGH ONES BIRTHPLACE.
THE RETURNED ONES CHOSE TO STAY AND AID THE USED-UP WORLD THEY FOUND.
IN DOING SO THESE CARETAKERS AWAKENED THEIR INNER MAGIC. IT TOOK THE PLACE OF TOOLS AS THEY EASED THE AGING LAND THROUGH THE LAST OF ITS LIFE.
BUT PURPOSE CHANGES WITH TIME. THE HIGH ONES BECAME ABSORBED IN EXPLORING THE LIMITS OF THEIR POWERS.
DEATH AND BIRTH HAPPENED TO THEM LESS AND LESS OFTEN. AND EVEN SHAPE AND SUBSTANCE LOST MEANING FOR THEM--
--FOR BOTH, THEY LEARNED, COULD BE CHANGED AT WILL.
THEN CAME THE CHOICE— THE CHOICE WHICH, ONCE MADE, DEFINED THE NATURE OF THE HIGH ONES FOR ALL TIME!
BEFORE HE CAN SPEAK FURTHER, SUNTOP SAGS TO HIS KNEES.

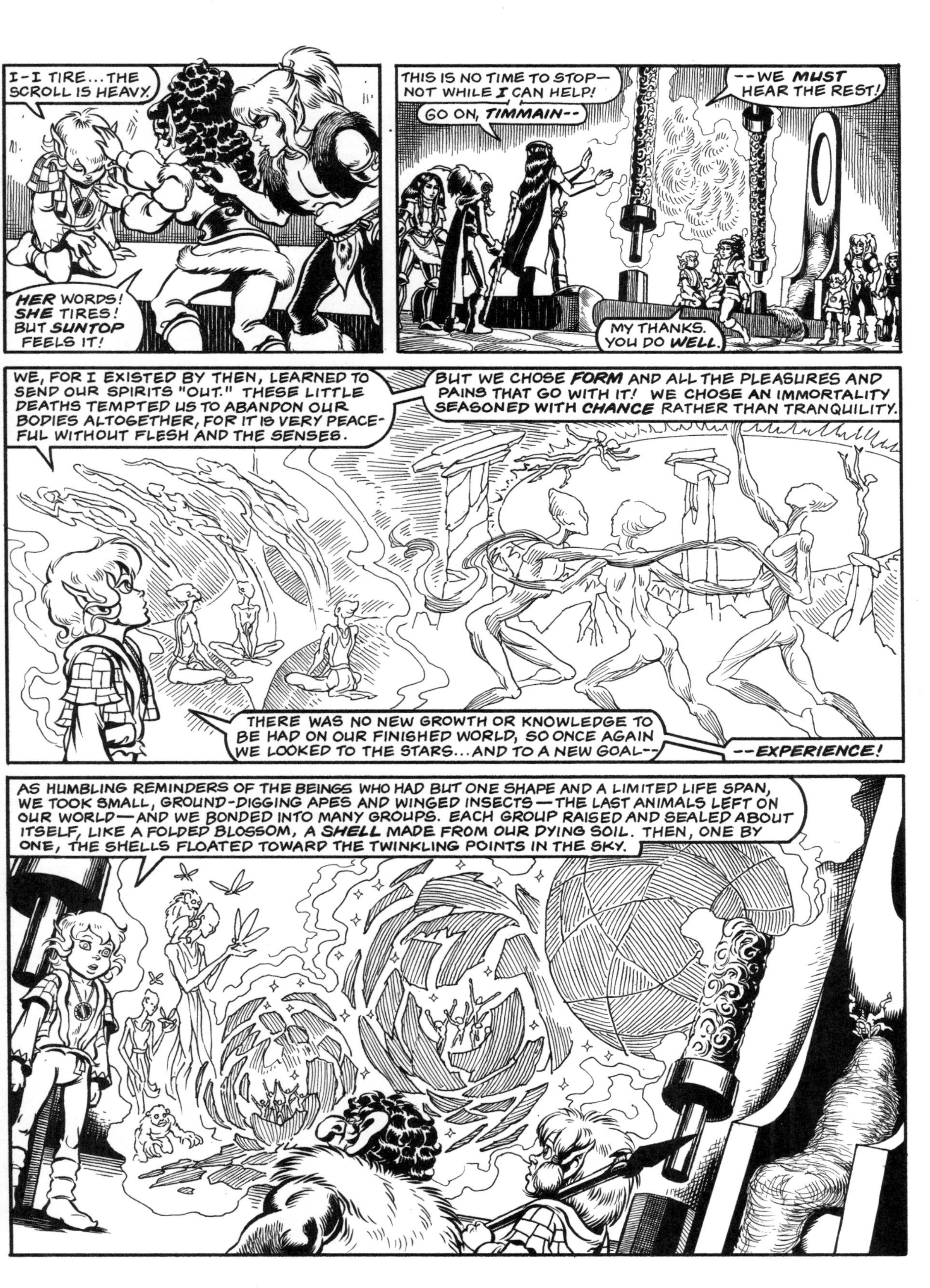
I-I TIRE... THE SCROLL IS HEAVY.
HER WORDS! SHE TIRES! BUT SUNTOP FEELS IT!
THIS IS NO TIME TO STOP— NOT WHILE I CAN HELP!
GO ON, TIMMAIN--
--WE MUST HEAR THE REST!
MY THANKS. YOU DO WELL.
WE, FOR I EXISTED BY THEN, LEARNED TO SEND OUR SPIRITS "OUT." THESE LITTLE DEATHS TEMPTED US TO ABANDON OUR BODIES ALTOGETHER, FOR IT IS VERY PEACEFUL WITHOUT FLESH AND THE SENSES.
BUT WE CHOSE FORM AND ALL THE PLEASURES AND PAINS THAT GO WITH IT! WE CHOSE AN IMMORTALITY SEASONED WITH CHANCE RATHER THAN TRANQUILITY.
THERE WAS NO NEW GROWTH OR KNOWLEDGE TO BE HAD ON OUR FINISHED WORLD, SO ONCE AGAIN WE LOOKED TO THE STARS... AND TO A NEW GOAL--
--EXPERIENCE!
AS HUMBLING REMINDERS OF THE BEINGS WHO HAD BUT ONE SHAPE AND A LIMITED LIFE SPAN, WE TOOK SMALL, GROUND-DIGGING APES AND WINGED INSECTS—THE LAST ANIMALS LEFT ON OUR WORLD—AND WE BONDED INTO MANY GROUPS. EACH GROUP RAISED AND SEALED ABOUT ITSELF, LIKE A FOLDED BLOSSOM, A SHELL MADE FROM OUR DYING SOIL. THEN, ONE BY ONE, THE SHELLS FLOATED TOWARD THE TWINKLING POINTS IN THE SKY.

"IT IS FAR FROM DEAD, THE VAST SEA WHERE ALL STARS SWIM. ANYTHING WE NEEDED, FROM AIR TO BREATHE TO FOOD TO EAT, WE MADE FROM THE MATTER WE COLLECTED FROM THE BLACKNESS BETWEEN SUNS. AND THOSE SUNS GAVE WARMTH TO DIFFERENT WORLDS—SOME TEEMING WITH LIFE. WE VISITED MANY, ALWAYS IN SECRET, SHAPING OURSELVES TO LOOK LIKE AND MINGLE WITH THE CREATURES WE MET. THE SCROLL OF COLORS WILL TELL YOU OF ALL THESE ADVENTURES SOMEDAY, BUT NOW YOU MUST LEARN WHY MY BOND GROUP CAME TO THIS WORLD OF TWO MOONS AND HOW WE BECAME EXILES IN THE WRONG PLACE--"

"--AND TIME!"

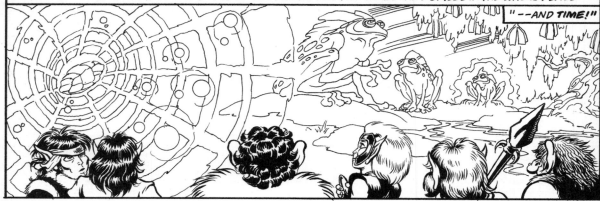

RAYEK FEELS HIS CONTROL OVER THE SPINNING SCROLL MOMENTARILY OVERTAKEN BY TIMMAIN. THE RODS WHIRL RAPIDLY, THEN SLOW TO THEIR ORIGINAL PACE.

I DON'T UNDERSTAND!

HOW CAN SHE CONTINUE TO USE HER POWERS--

--WHILE WRAPPED IN A COCOON THAT STOPS TIME?

HEE HEE! THINK~DO MAGIC NEVER STOP, WRAPSTUFF OR NO! PRESERVERS TAKE GOOD CARE OF STILLQUIET GUIDERS—ONES WHO MAKE CASTLE FLY!

NO NEED FOOD~ NO NEED MOVE--

--JUST THINK~ DO!

LIKE DOOR AND BRACE, ONLY WORSE! IS THAT IT, PETALWING?

IF THAT'S WHAT YOU'RE FOR--

AAWWW... IS GOOD, WRAPSTUFF! PRETTY WAS~GROWLER HIGH THING SAY SO!

GOOD?! A LIVING DEATH IS MONSTROUS! IT'S--

HUSH! SUNTOP'S TALKING AGAIN! WATCH THE SCROLL!

OUR TRAVELS CARRIED US SO FAR AND SO LONG THAT WE SAW MANY GENERATIONS OF OUR LITTLE PETS COME AND GO. OUR SHELL, SUFFUSED WITH SHAPE CHANGING MAGIC, COULD NOT HELP BUT AFFECT THEM. EVENTUALLY THEY BECAME AS LONG-LIVED AS WE!

THE BURROWERS AND WINGED ONES EVOLVED, GAINED THOUGHT AND SPEECH. BUT WHILE THE PRE-SERVERS WERE WILLING HELPERS, THOSE YOU CALL TROLLS WERE WILLFUL AND INDEPENDENT.

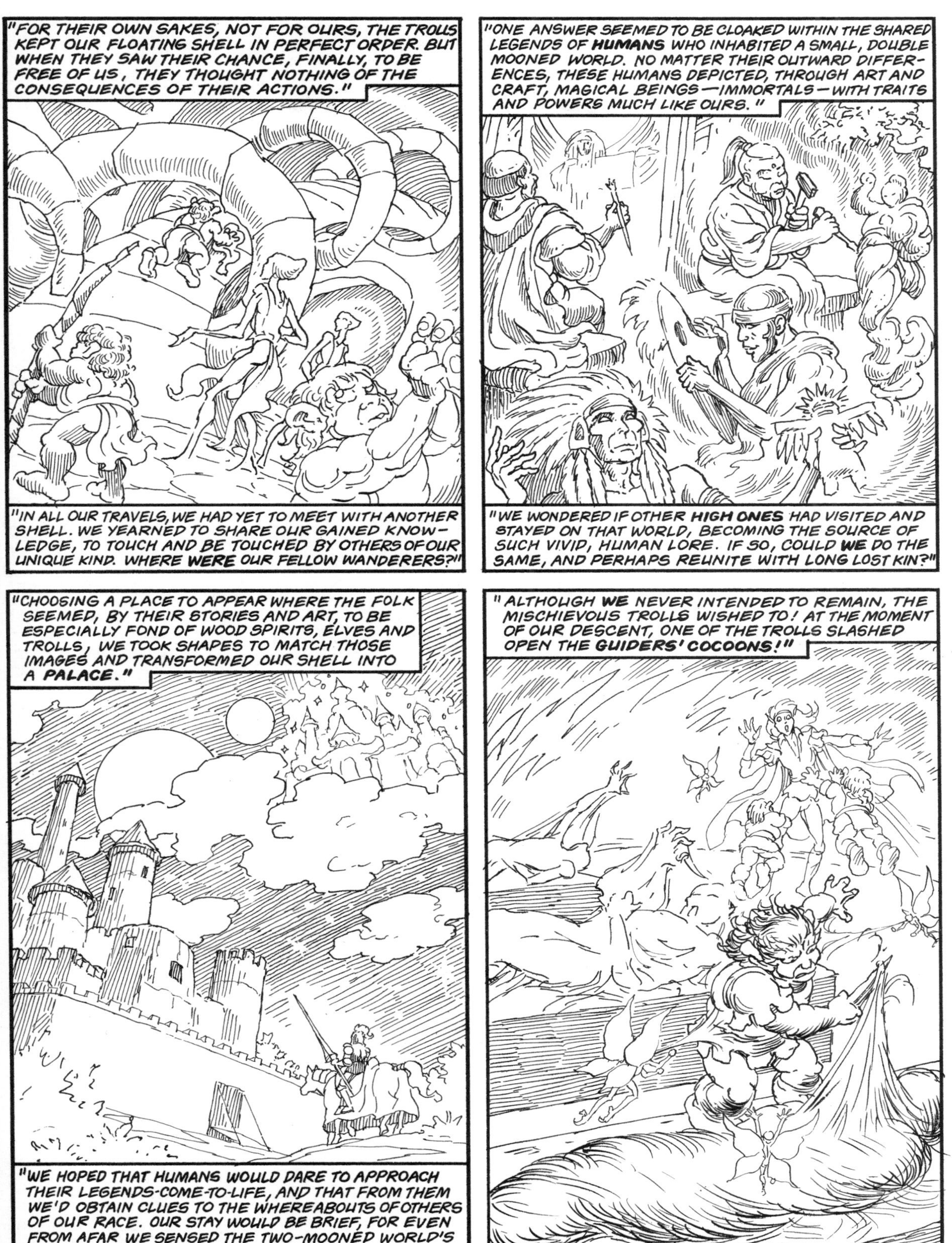

"FOR THEIR OWN SAKES, NOT FOR OURS, THE TROLLS KEPT OUR FLOATING SHELL IN PERFECT ORDER. BUT WHEN THEY SAW THEIR CHANCE, FINALLY, TO BE FREE OF US, THEY THOUGHT NOTHING OF THE CONSEQUENCES OF THEIR ACTIONS."
"IN ALL OUR TRAVELS, WE HAD YET TO MEET WITH ANOTHER SHELL. WE YEARNED TO SHARE OUR GAINED KNOW-LEDGE, TO TOUCH AND BE TOUCHED BY OTHERS OF OUR UNIQUE KIND. WHERE **WERE** OUR FELLOW WANDERERS?"
"ONE ANSWER SEEMED TO BE CLOAKED WITHIN THE SHARED LEGENDS OF **HUMANS** WHO INHABITED A SMALL, DOUBLE MOONED WORLD. NO MATTER THEIR OUTWARD DIFFER-ENCES, THESE HUMANS DEPICTED, THROUGH ART AND CRAFT, MAGICAL BEINGS—IMMORTALS—WITH TRAITS AND POWERS MUCH LIKE OURS."
"WE WONDERED IF OTHER **HIGH ONES** HAD VISITED AND STAYED ON THAT WORLD, BECOMING THE SOURCE OF SUCH VIVID, HUMAN LORE. IF SO, COULD **WE** DO THE SAME, AND PERHAPS REUNITE WITH LONG LOST KIN?"
"CHOOSING A PLACE TO APPEAR WHERE THE FOLK SEEMED, BY THEIR STORIES AND ART, TO BE ESPECIALLY FOND OF WOOD SPIRITS, ELVES AND TROLLS, WE TOOK SHAPES TO MATCH THOSE IMAGES AND TRANSFORMED OUR SHELL INTO A **PALACE**."
"WE HOPED THAT HUMANS WOULD DARE TO APPROACH THEIR LEGENDS-COME-TO-LIFE, AND THAT FROM THEM WE'D OBTAIN CLUES TO THE WHEREABOUTS OF OTHERS OF OUR RACE. OUR STAY WOULD BE BRIEF, FOR EVEN FROM AFAR WE SENSED THE TWO-MOONED WORLD'S DRAINING EFFECT ON OUR POWERS."
"ALTHOUGH **WE** NEVER INTENDED TO REMAIN, THE MISCHIEVOUS TROLLS WISHED TO! AT THE MOMENT OF OUR DESCENT, ONE OF THE TROLLS SLASHED OPEN THE **GUIDERS' COCOONS**!"

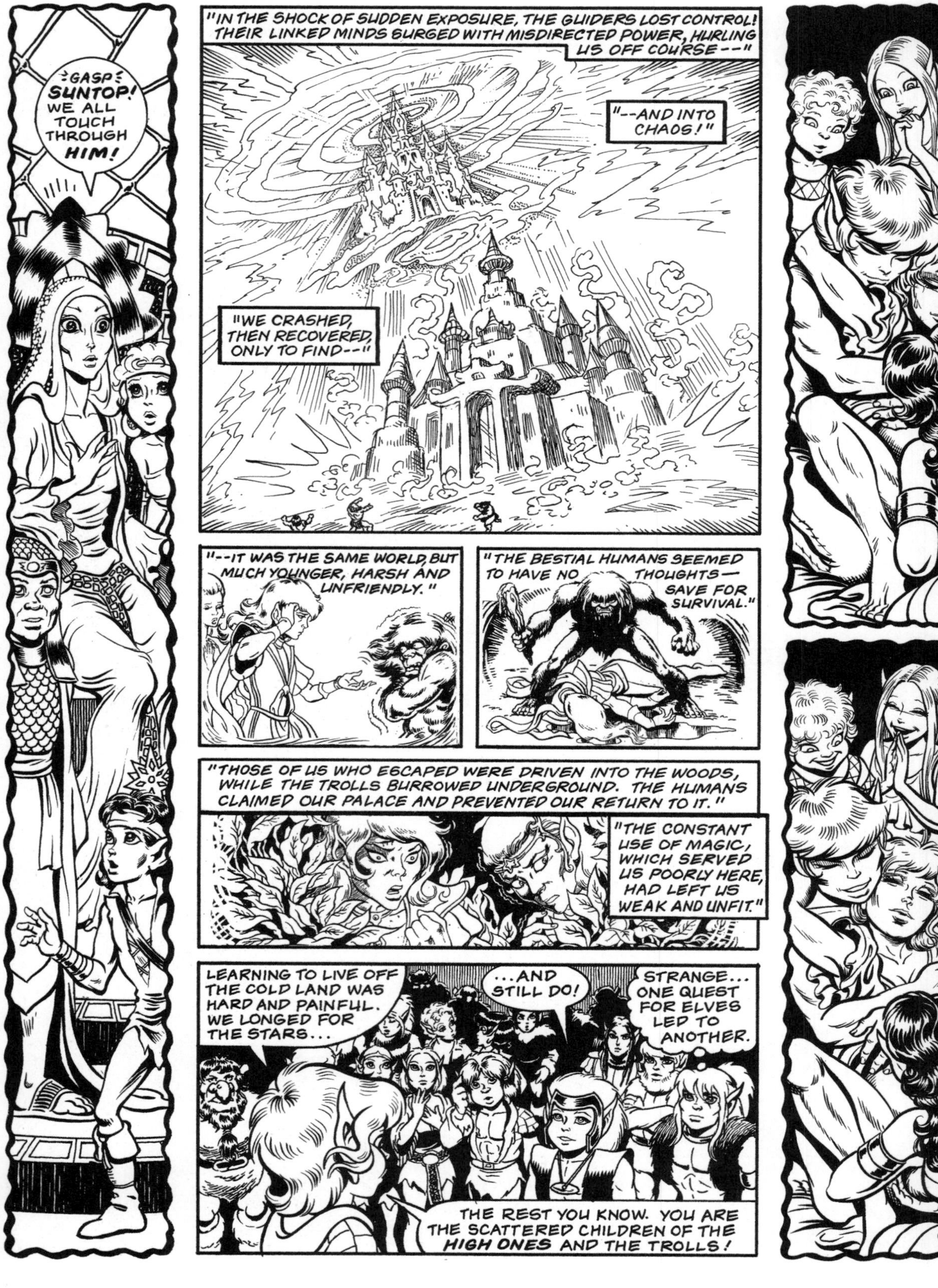

≷GASP≶ SUNTOP! WE ALL TOUCH THROUGH HIM!
"IN THE SHOCK OF SUDDEN EXPOSURE, THE GLIDERS LOST CONTROL! THEIR LINKED MINDS SURGED WITH MISDIRECTED POWER, HURLING US OFF COURSE--"
"--AND INTO CHAOS!"
"WE CRASHED, THEN RECOVERED, ONLY TO FIND--"
"--IT WAS THE SAME WORLD, BUT MUCH YOUNGER, HARSH AND UNFRIENDLY."
"THE BESTIAL HUMANS SEEMED TO HAVE NO THOUGHTS— SAVE FOR SURVIVAL."
"THOSE OF US WHO ESCAPED WERE DRIVEN INTO THE WOODS, WHILE THE TROLLS BURROWED UNDERGROUND. THE HUMANS CLAIMED OUR PALACE AND PREVENTED OUR RETURN TO IT."
"THE CONSTANT USE OF MAGIC, WHICH SERVED US POORLY HERE, HAD LEFT US WEAK AND UNFIT."
LEARNING TO LIVE OFF THE COLD LAND WAS HARD AND PAINFUL. WE LONGED FOR THE STARS...
...AND STILL DO!
STRANGE... ONE QUEST FOR ELVES LED TO ANOTHER.
THE REST YOU KNOW. YOU ARE THE SCATTERED CHILDREN OF THE HIGH ONES AND THE TROLLS!

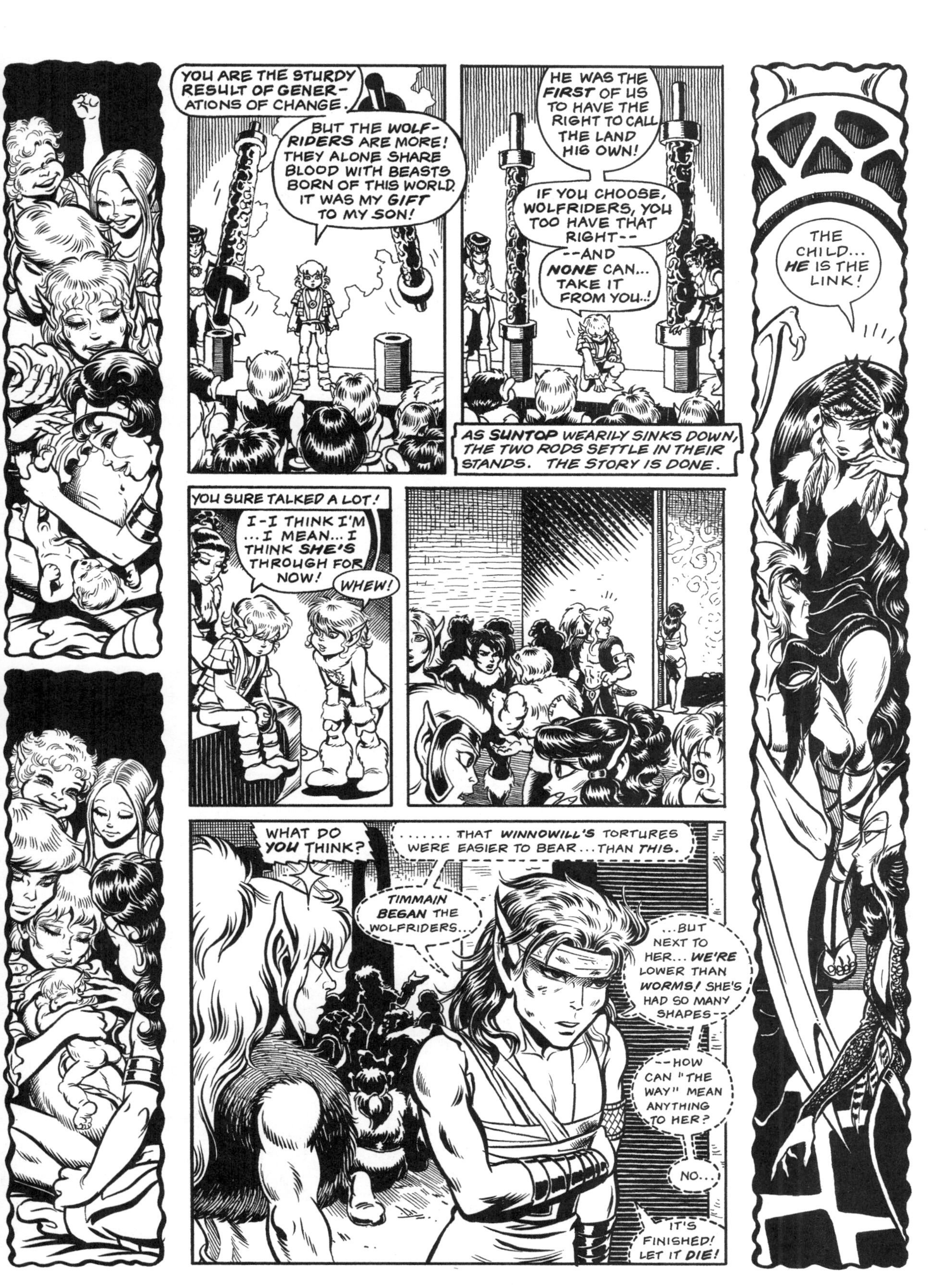

YOU ARE THE STURDY RESULT OF GENER-ATIONS OF CHANGE.
BUT THE WOLF-RIDERS ARE MORE! THEY ALONE SHARE BLOOD WITH BEASTS BORN OF THIS WORLD. IT WAS MY GIFT TO MY SON!
HE WAS THE FIRST OF US TO HAVE THE RIGHT TO CALL THE LAND HIS OWN!
IF YOU CHOOSE, WOLFRIDERS, YOU TOO HAVE THAT RIGHT--
--AND NONE CAN... TAKE IT FROM YOU..!
AS SUNTOP WEARILY SINKS DOWN, THE TWO RODS SETTLE IN THEIR STANDS. THE STORY IS DONE.
THE CHILD... HE IS THE LINK!
YOU SURE TALKED A LOT!
I-I THINK I'M ...I MEAN... I THINK SHE'S THROUGH FOR NOW!
WHEW!
WHAT DO YOU THINK?
......THAT WINNOWILL'S TORTURES WERE EASIER TO BEAR...THAN THIS.
TIMMAIN BEGAN THE WOLFRIDERS...
...BUT NEXT TO HER... WE'RE LOWER THAN WORMS! SHE'S HAD SO MANY SHAPES--
--HOW CAN "THE WAY" MEAN ANYTHING TO HER?
NO...
IT'S FINISHED! LET IT DIE!

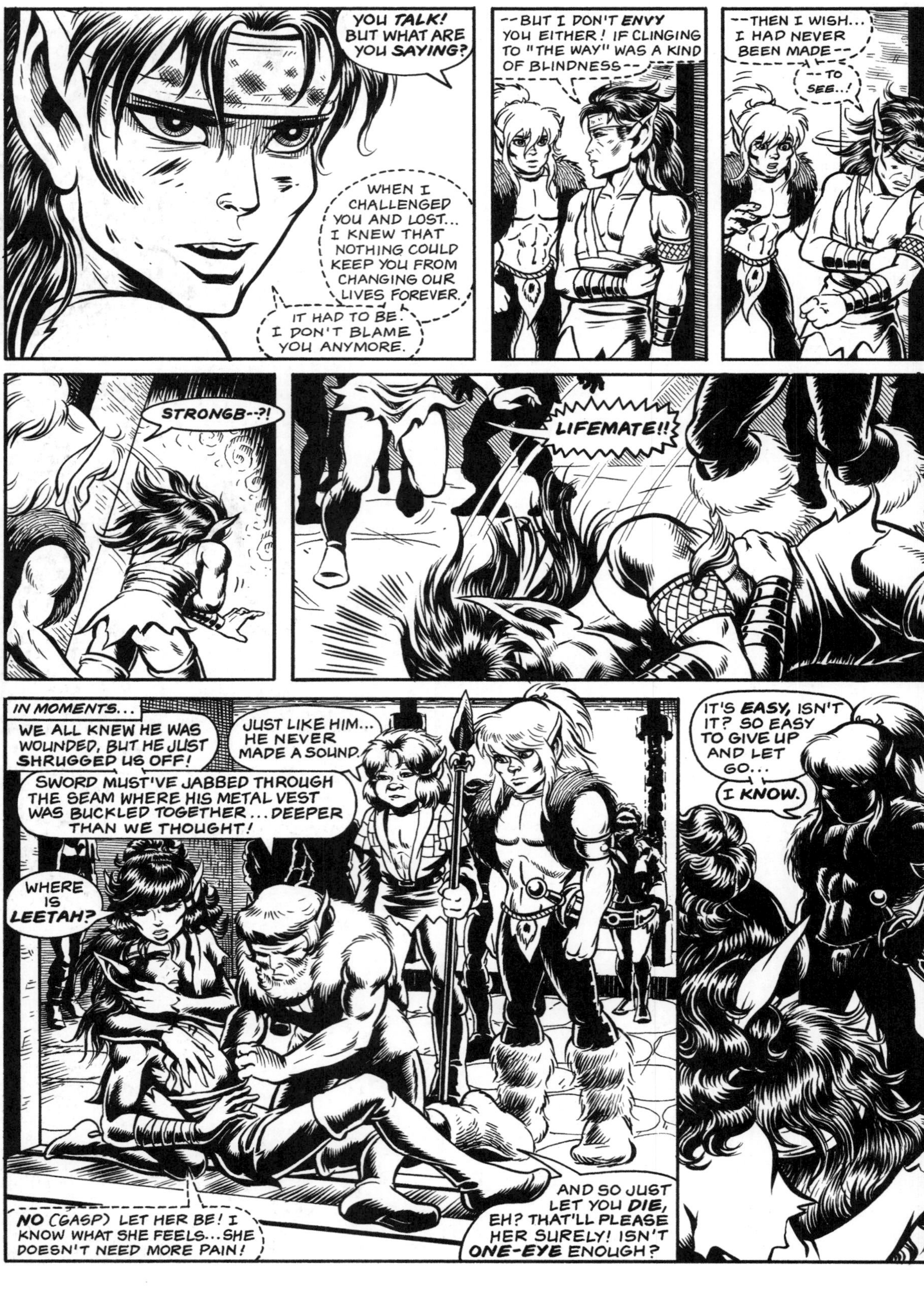

YOU **TALK!** BUT WHAT ARE YOU **SAYING?**
WHEN I CHALLENGED YOU AND LOST... I KNEW THAT NOTHING COULD KEEP YOU FROM CHANGING OUR LIVES FOREVER.
IT HAD TO BE. I DON'T BLAME YOU ANYMORE.
--BUT I DON'T **ENVY** YOU EITHER! IF CLINGING TO "THE WAY" WAS A KIND OF BLINDNESS--
--THEN I WISH... I HAD NEVER BEEN MADE--
--TO SEE...!
STRONGB--?!
LIFEMATE!!
IN MOMENTS...
WE ALL KNEW HE WAS WOUNDED, BUT HE JUST **SHRUGGED** US OFF!
JUST LIKE HIM... HE NEVER MADE A SOUND.
SWORD MUST'VE JABBED THROUGH THE SEAM WHERE HIS METAL VEST WAS BUCKLED TOGETHER ... DEEPER THAN WE THOUGHT!
WHERE IS **LEETAH?**
NO (GASP) LET HER BE! I KNOW WHAT SHE FEELS... SHE DOESN'T NEED MORE PAIN!
AND SO JUST LET YOU **DIE,** EH? THAT'LL PLEASE HER SURELY! ISN'T **ONE-EYE** ENOUGH?
IT'S **EASY,** ISN'T IT? SO EASY TO GIVE UP AND LET GO...
I KNOW.

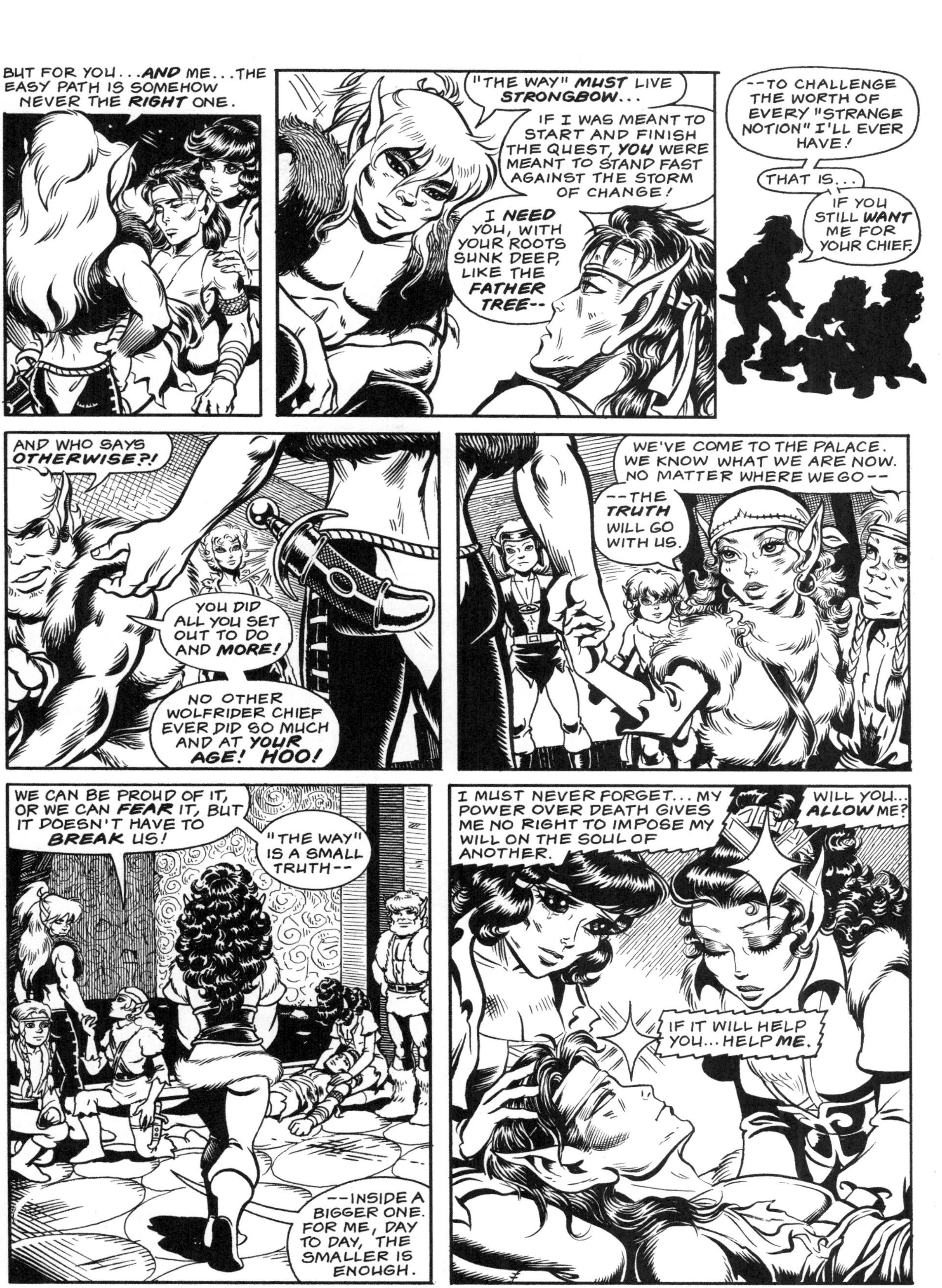

BUT FOR YOU . . . AND ME . . . THE EASY PATH IS SOMEHOW NEVER THE RIGHT ONE.
"THE WAY" MUST LIVE STRONGBOW . . .
IF I WAS MEANT TO START AND FINISH THE QUEST, YOU WERE MEANT TO STAND FAST AGAINST THE STORM OF CHANGE!
I NEED YOU, WITH YOUR ROOTS SUNK DEEP, LIKE THE FATHER TREE--
--TO CHALLENGE THE WORTH OF EVERY "STRANGE NOTION" I'LL EVER HAVE!
THAT IS . . .
IF YOU STILL WANT ME FOR YOUR CHIEF.
AND WHO SAYS OTHERWISE?!
YOU DID ALL YOU SET OUT TO DO AND MORE!
NO OTHER WOLFRIDER CHIEF EVER DID SO MUCH AND AT YOUR AGE! HOO!
WE'VE COME TO THE PALACE. WE KNOW WHAT WE ARE NOW. NO MATTER WHERE WE GO--
--THE TRUTH WILL GO WITH US.
WE CAN BE PROUD OF IT, OR WE CAN FEAR IT, BUT IT DOESN'T HAVE TO BREAK US!
"THE WAY" IS A SMALL TRUTH--
--INSIDE A BIGGER ONE. FOR ME, DAY TO DAY, THE SMALLER IS ENOUGH.
I MUST NEVER FORGET . . . MY POWER OVER DEATH GIVES ME NO RIGHT TO IMPOSE MY WILL ON THE SOUL OF ANOTHER.
WILL YOU . . . ALLOW ME?
IF IT WILL HELP YOU . . . HELP ME.

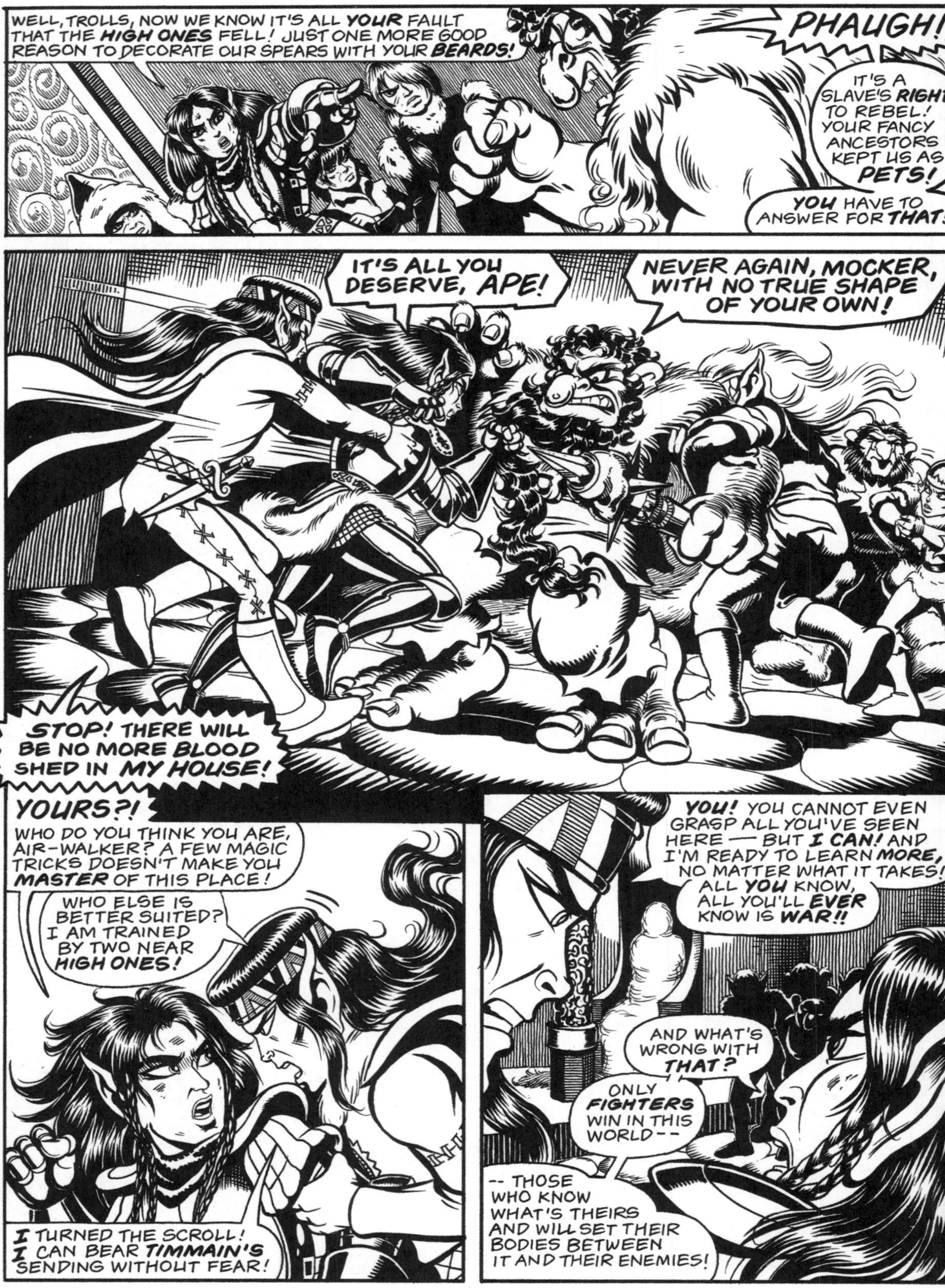
WELL, TROLLS, NOW WE KNOW IT'S ALL YOUR FAULT THAT THE HIGH ONES FELL! JUST ONE MORE GOOD REASON TO DECORATE OUR SPEARS WITH YOUR BEARDS!
PHAUGH!
IT'S A SLAVE'S RIGHT TO REBEL! YOUR FANCY ANCESTORS KEPT US AS PETS!
YOU HAVE TO ANSWER FOR THAT!
IT'S ALL YOU DESERVE, APE!
NEVER AGAIN, MOCKER, WITH NO TRUE SHAPE OF YOUR OWN!
STOP! THERE WILL BE NO MORE BLOOD SHED IN MY HOUSE!
YOURS?!
WHO DO YOU THINK YOU ARE, AIR-WALKER? A FEW MAGIC TRICKS DOESN'T MAKE YOU MASTER OF THIS PLACE!
WHO ELSE IS BETTER SUITED? I AM TRAINED BY TWO NEAR HIGH ONES!
I TURNED THE SCROLL! I CAN BEAR TIMMAIN'S SENDING WITHOUT FEAR!
YOU! YOU CANNOT EVEN GRASP ALL YOU'VE SEEN HERE — BUT I CAN! AND I'M READY TO LEARN MORE, NO MATTER WHAT IT TAKES! ALL YOU KNOW, ALL YOU'LL EVER KNOW IS WAR!!
AND WHAT'S WRONG WITH THAT?
ONLY FIGHTERS WIN IN THIS WORLD--
-- THOSE WHO KNOW WHAT'S THEIRS AND WILL SET THEIR BODIES BETWEEN IT AND THEIR ENEMIES!

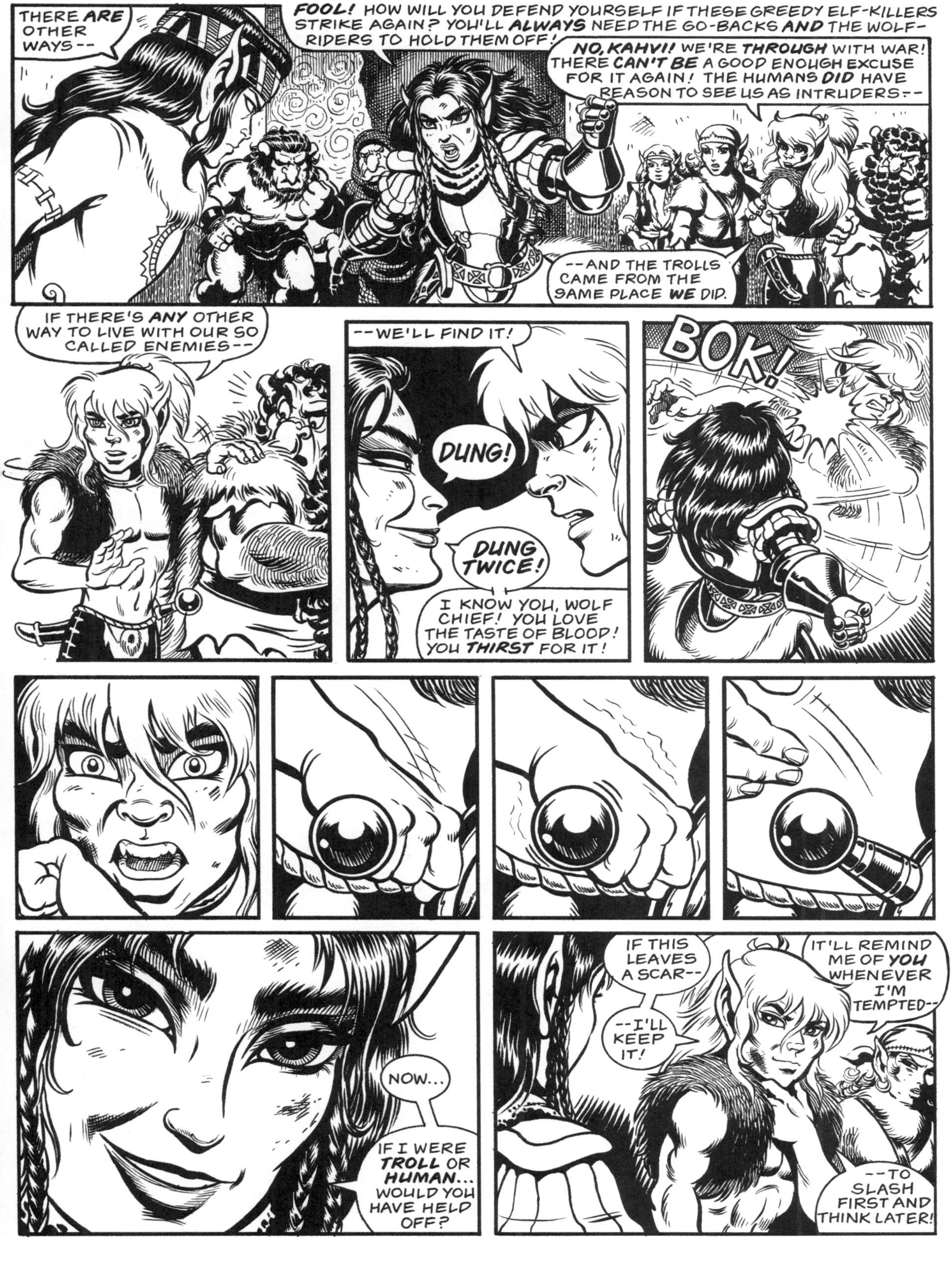

THERE **ARE** OTHER WAYS--
FOOL! HOW WILL YOU DEFEND YOURSELF IF THESE GREEDY ELF-KILLERS STRIKE AGAIN? YOU'LL **ALWAYS** NEED THE GO-BACKS **AND** THE WOLF-RIDERS TO HOLD THEM OFF!
NO, KAHVI! WE'RE **THROUGH** WITH WAR! THERE **CAN'T BE** A GOOD ENOUGH EXCUSE FOR IT AGAIN! THE HUMANS **DID** HAVE REASON TO SEE US AS INTRUDERS--
--AND THE TROLLS CAME FROM THE SAME PLACE **WE** DID.
IF THERE'S **ANY** OTHER WAY TO LIVE WITH OUR SO CALLED ENEMIES--
--WE'LL FIND IT!
DUNG!
DUNG TWICE!
I KNOW YOU, WOLF CHIEF! YOU LOVE THE TASTE OF BLOOD! YOU **THIRST** FOR IT!
BOK!
NOW...
IF I WERE **TROLL** OR **HUMAN**... WOULD YOU HAVE HELD OFF?
IF THIS LEAVES A SCAR--
--I'LL KEEP IT!
IT'LL REMIND ME OF **YOU** WHENEVER I'M TEMPTED--
--TO SLASH FIRST AND THINK LATER!

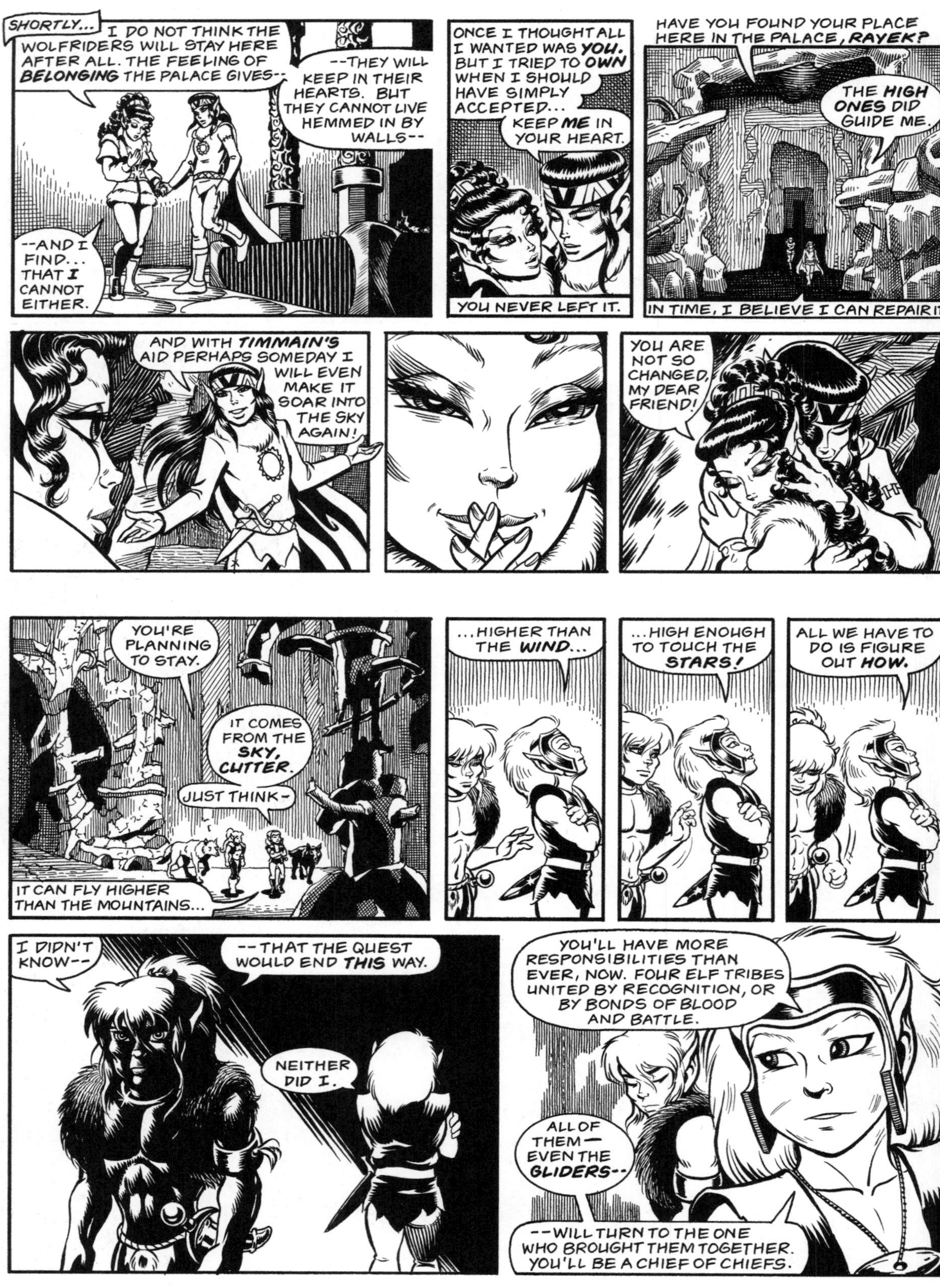

SHORTLY...
I DO NOT THINK THE WOLFRIDERS WILL STAY HERE AFTER ALL. THE FEELING OF BELONGING THE PALACE GIVES--
--THEY WILL KEEP IN THEIR HEARTS. BUT THEY CANNOT LIVE HEMMED IN BY WALLS--
--AND I FIND... THAT I CANNOT EITHER.
ONCE I THOUGHT ALL I WANTED WAS YOU. BUT I TRIED TO OWN WHEN I SHOULD HAVE SIMPLY ACCEPTED...
KEEP ME IN YOUR HEART.
YOU NEVER LEFT IT.
HAVE YOU FOUND YOUR PLACE HERE IN THE PALACE, RAYEK?
THE HIGH ONES DID GUIDE ME.
IN TIME, I BELIEVE I CAN REPAIR IT.
AND WITH TIMMAIN'S AID PERHAPS SOMEDAY I WILL EVEN MAKE IT SOAR INTO THE SKY AGAIN!
YOU ARE NOT SO CHANGED, MY DEAR FRIEND!
YOU'RE PLANNING TO STAY.
IT COMES FROM THE SKY, CUTTER.
JUST THINK-
IT CAN FLY HIGHER THAN THE MOUNTAINS...
...HIGHER THAN THE WIND...
...HIGH ENOUGH TO TOUCH THE STARS!
ALL WE HAVE TO DO IS FIGURE OUT HOW.
I DIDN'T KNOW--
--THAT THE QUEST WOULD END THIS WAY.
NEITHER DID I.
YOU'LL HAVE MORE RESPONSIBILITIES THAN EVER, NOW. FOUR ELF TRIBES UNITED BY RECOGNITION, OR BY BONDS OF BLOOD AND BATTLE.
ALL OF THEM— EVEN THE GLIDERS--
--WILL TURN TO THE ONE WHO BROUGHT THEM TOGETHER. YOU'LL BE A CHIEF OF CHIEFS.

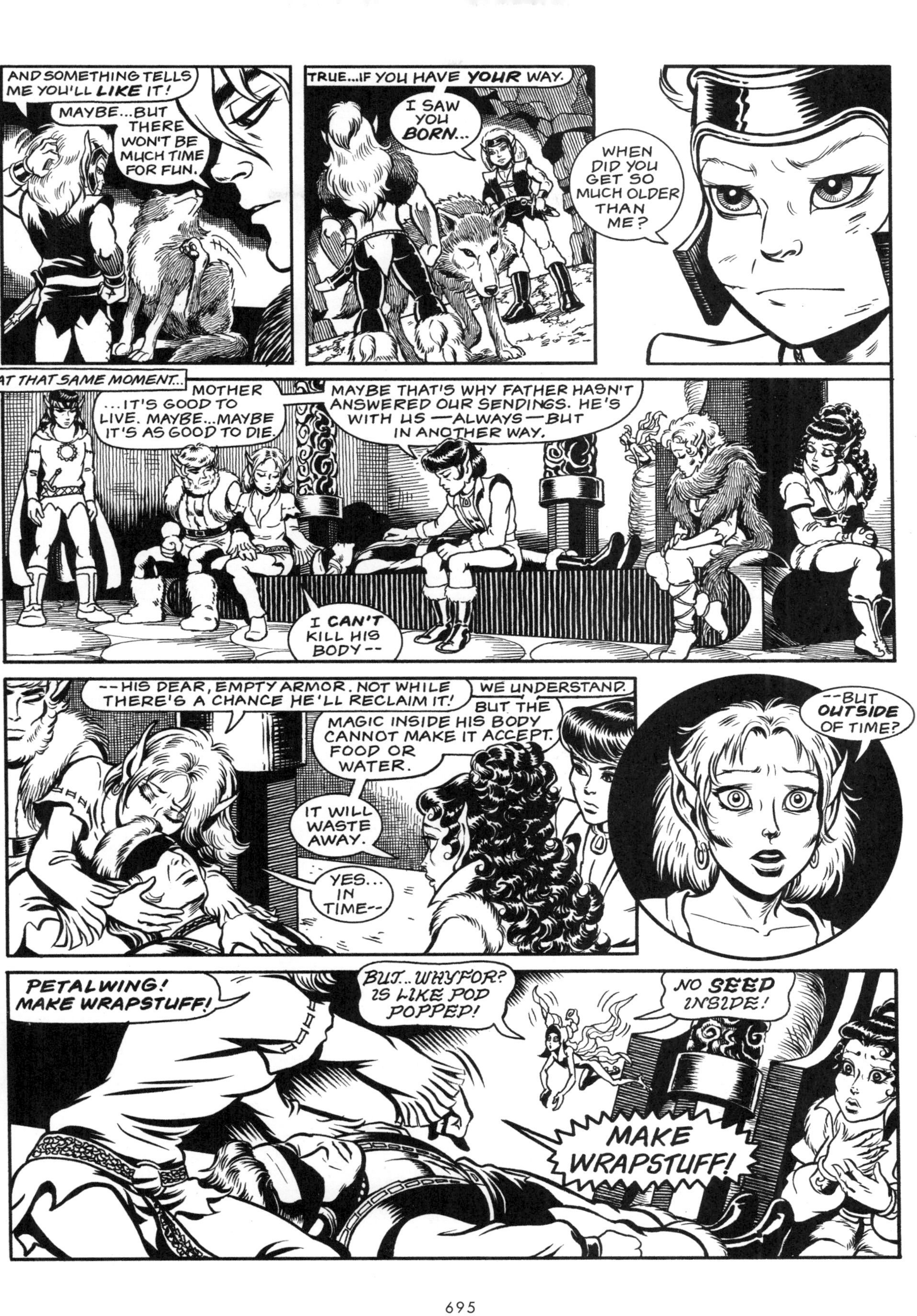

AND SOMETHING TELLS ME YOU'LL LIKE IT!
MAYBE...BUT THERE WON'T BE MUCH TIME FOR FUN.
TRUE...IF YOU HAVE YOUR WAY.
I SAW YOU BORN...
WHEN DID YOU GET SO MUCH OLDER THAN ME?
AT THAT SAME MOMENT...
MOTHER ...IT'S GOOD TO LIVE. MAYBE...MAYBE IT'S AS GOOD TO DIE.
MAYBE THAT'S WHY FATHER HASN'T ANSWERED OUR SENDINGS. HE'S WITH US —ALWAYS— BUT IN ANOTHER WAY.
I CAN'T KILL HIS BODY--
--HIS DEAR, EMPTY ARMOR. NOT WHILE THERE'S A CHANCE HE'LL RECLAIM IT!
WE UNDERSTAND.
BUT THE MAGIC INSIDE HIS BODY CANNOT MAKE IT ACCEPT FOOD OR WATER.
IT WILL WASTE AWAY.
YES... IN TIME--
--BUT OUTSIDE OF TIME?
PETALWING! MAKE WRAPSTUFF!
BUT...WHYFOR? IS LIKE POD POPPED!
NO SEED INSIDE!
MAKE WRAPSTUFF!

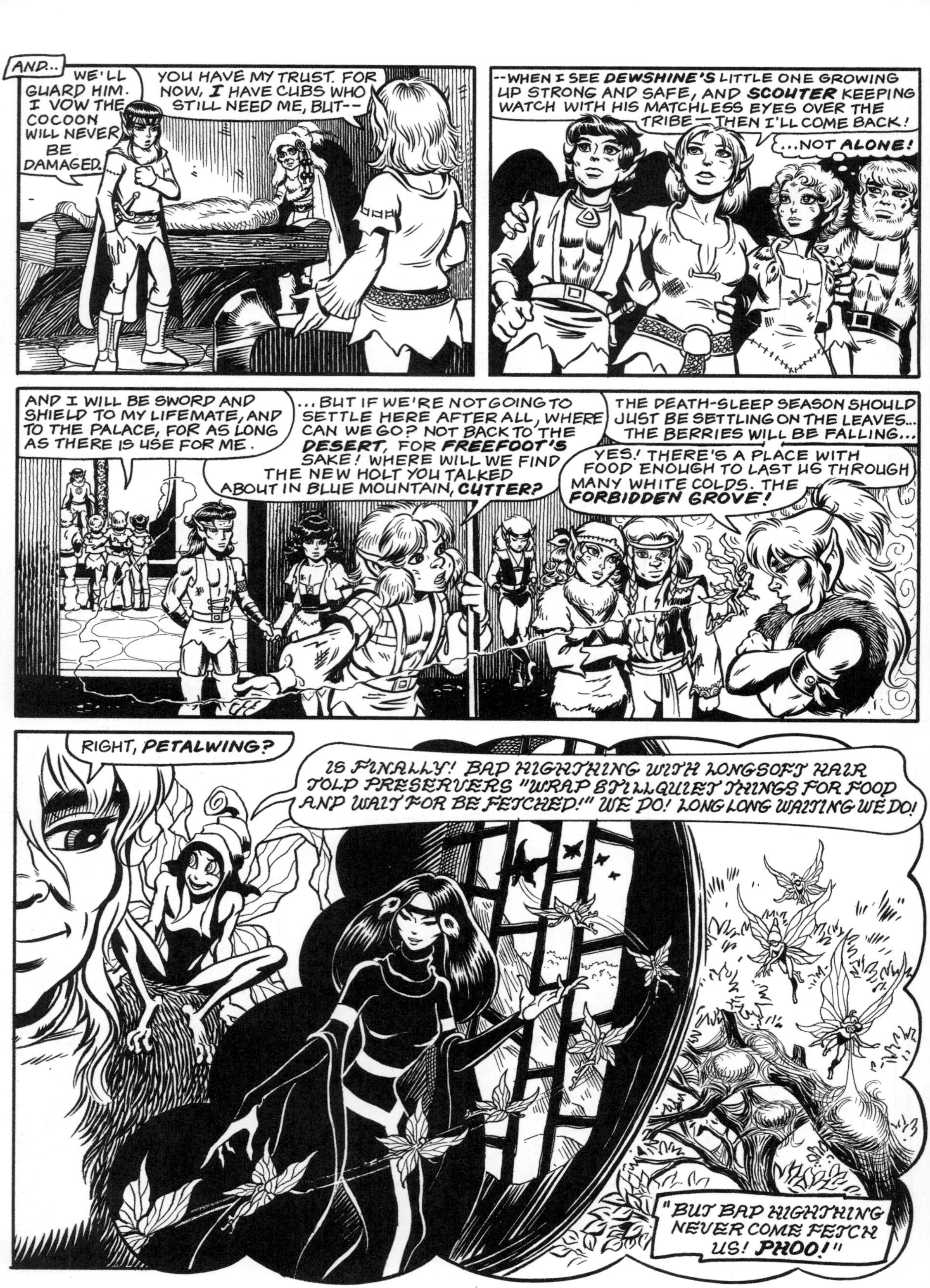
AND...
WE'LL GUARD HIM. I VOW THE COCOON WILL NEVER BE DAMAGED.
YOU HAVE MY TRUST. FOR NOW, I HAVE CUBS WHO STILL NEED ME, BUT--
--WHEN I SEE DEWSHINE'S LITTLE ONE GROWING UP STRONG AND SAFE, AND SCOUTER KEEPING WATCH WITH HIS MATCHLESS EYES OVER THE TRIBE — THEN I'LL COME BACK!
...NOT ALONE!
AND I WILL BE SWORD AND SHIELD TO MY LIFEMATE, AND TO THE PALACE, FOR AS LONG AS THERE IS USE FOR ME.
...BUT IF WE'RE NOT GOING TO SETTLE HERE AFTER ALL, WHERE CAN WE GO? NOT BACK TO THE DESERT, FOR FREEFOOT'S SAKE! WHERE WILL WE FIND THE NEW HOLT YOU TALKED ABOUT IN BLUE MOUNTAIN, CUTTER?
THE DEATH-SLEEP SEASON SHOULD JUST BE SETTLING ON THE LEAVES... THE BERRIES WILL BE FALLING...
YES! THERE'S A PLACE WITH FOOD ENOUGH TO LAST US THROUGH MANY WHITE COLDS. THE FORBIDDEN GROVE!
RIGHT, PETALWING?
IS FINALLY! BAD HIGHTHING WITH LONGSOFT HAIR TOLD PRESERVERS "WRAP STILLQUIET THINGS FOR FOOD AND WAIT FOR BE FETCHED!" WE DO! LONG LONG WAITING WE DO!
"BUT BAD HIGHTHING NEVER COME FETCH US! PHOO!"

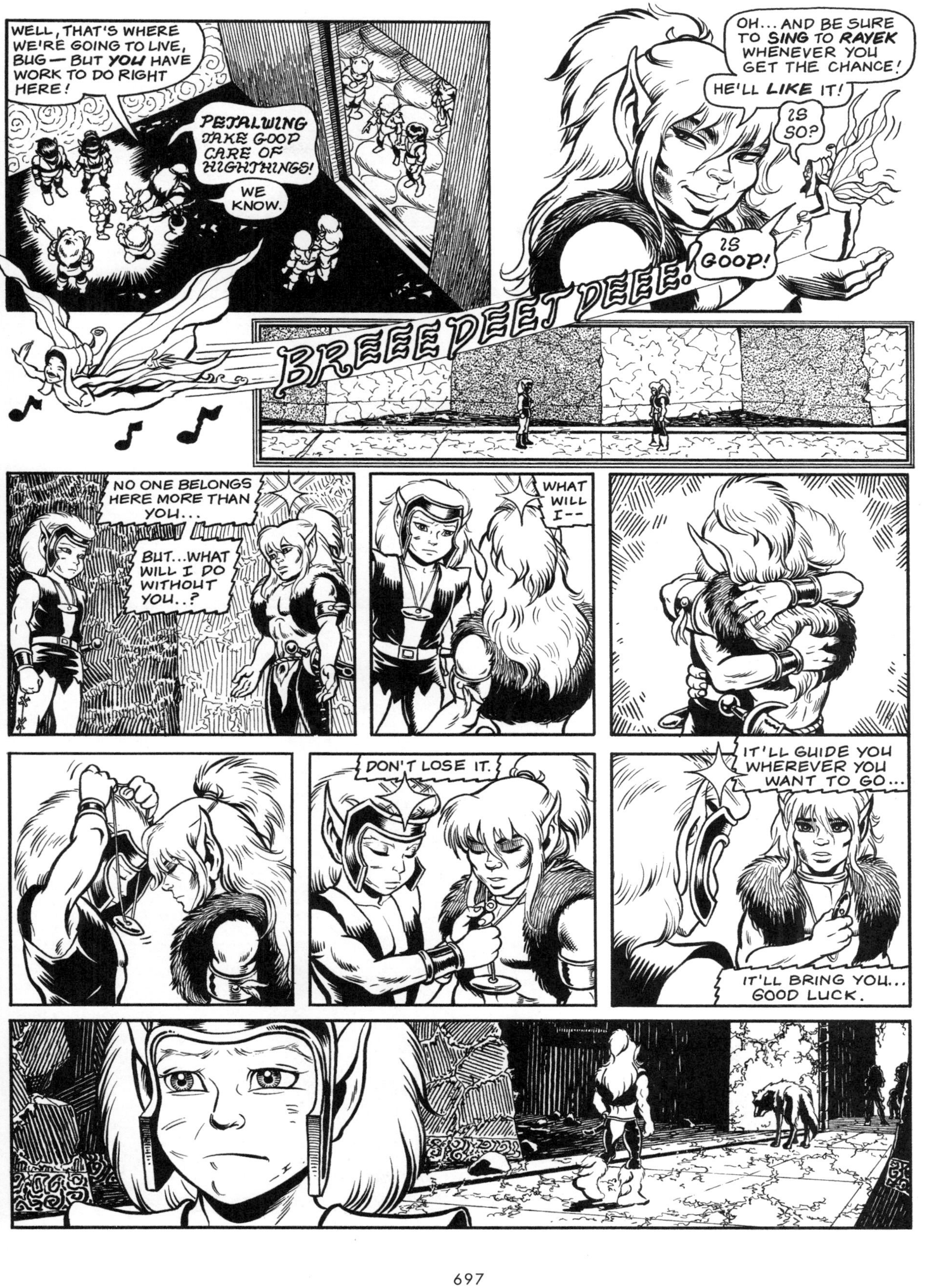
WELL, THAT'S WHERE WE'RE GOING TO LIVE, BUG — BUT YOU HAVE WORK TO DO RIGHT HERE!
PETALWING TAKE GOOD CARE OF HIGHTHINGS!
WE KNOW.
OH... AND BE SURE TO SING TO RAYEK WHENEVER YOU GET THE CHANCE!
HE'LL LIKE IT!
IS SO?
IS GOOD!
BREEEDEET DEEE!
NO ONE BELONGS HERE MORE THAN YOU...
BUT...WHAT WILL I DO WITHOUT YOU..?
WHAT WILL I--
DON'T LOSE IT.
IT'LL GUIDE YOU WHEREVER YOU WANT TO GO...
IT'LL BRING YOU... GOOD LUCK.

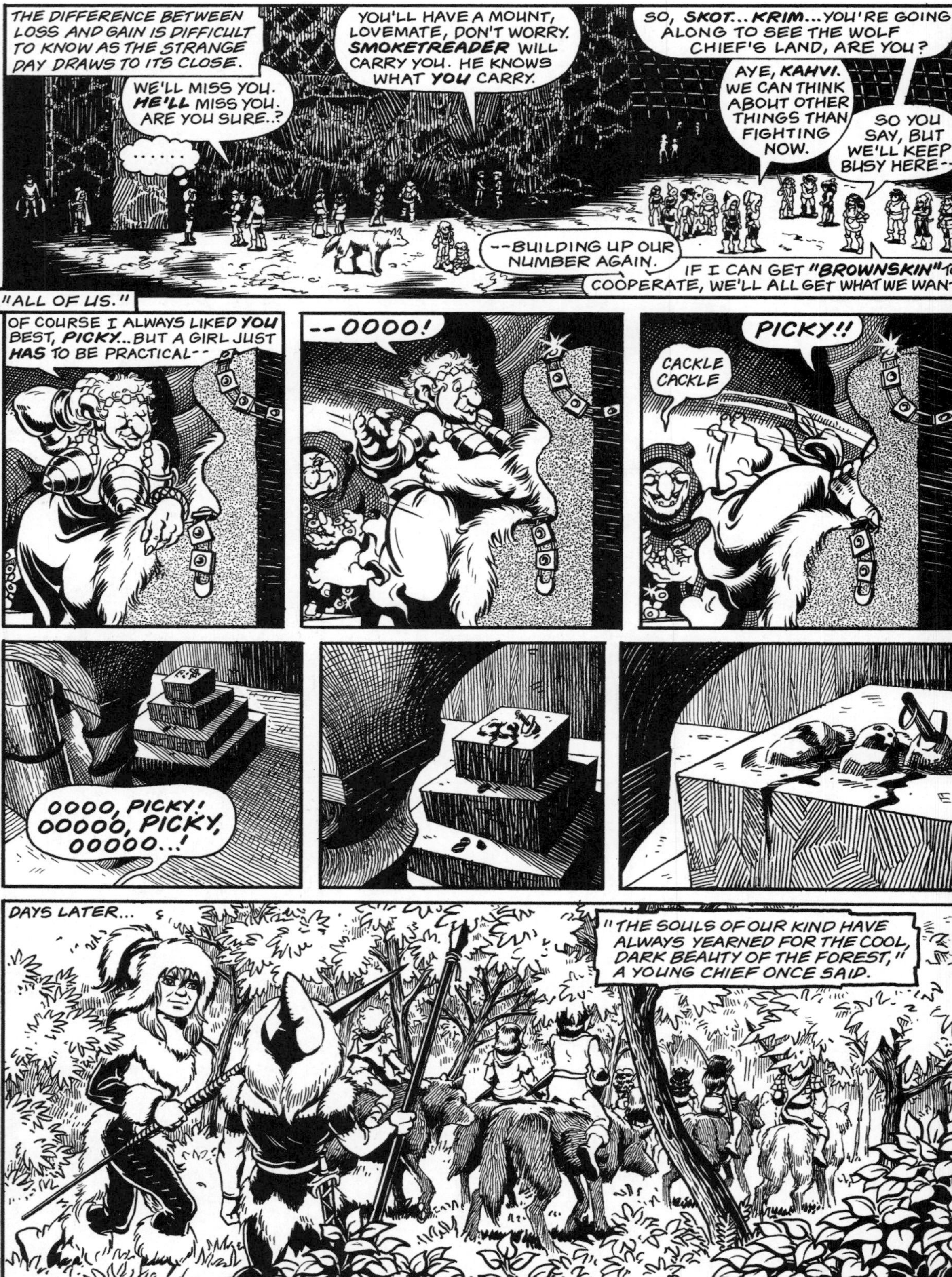
THE DIFFERENCE BETWEEN LOSS AND GAIN IS DIFFICULT TO KNOW AS THE STRANGE DAY DRAWS TO ITS CLOSE.
WE'LL MISS YOU. HE'LL MISS YOU. ARE YOU SURE..?
....
YOU'LL HAVE A MOUNT, LOVEMATE, DON'T WORRY. SMOKETREADER WILL CARRY YOU. HE KNOWS WHAT YOU CARRY.
SO, SKOT... KRIM... YOU'RE GOING ALONG TO SEE THE WOLF CHIEF'S LAND, ARE YOU?
AYE, KAHVI. WE CAN THINK ABOUT OTHER THINGS THAN FIGHTING NOW.
SO YOU SAY, BUT WE'LL KEEP BUSY HERE--
--BUILDING UP OUR NUMBER AGAIN.
IF I CAN GET "BROWNSKIN" TO COOPERATE, WE'LL ALL GET WHAT WE WANT.
"ALL OF US."
OF COURSE I ALWAYS LIKED YOU BEST, PICKY... BUT A GIRL JUST HAS TO BE PRACTICAL--
--OOOO!
PICKY!!
CACKLE CACKLE
OOOO, PICKY! OOOOO, PICKY, OOOOO...!
DAYS LATER...
"THE SOULS OF OUR KIND HAVE ALWAYS YEARNED FOR THE COOL, DARK BEAUTY OF THE FOREST," A YOUNG CHIEF ONCE SAID.

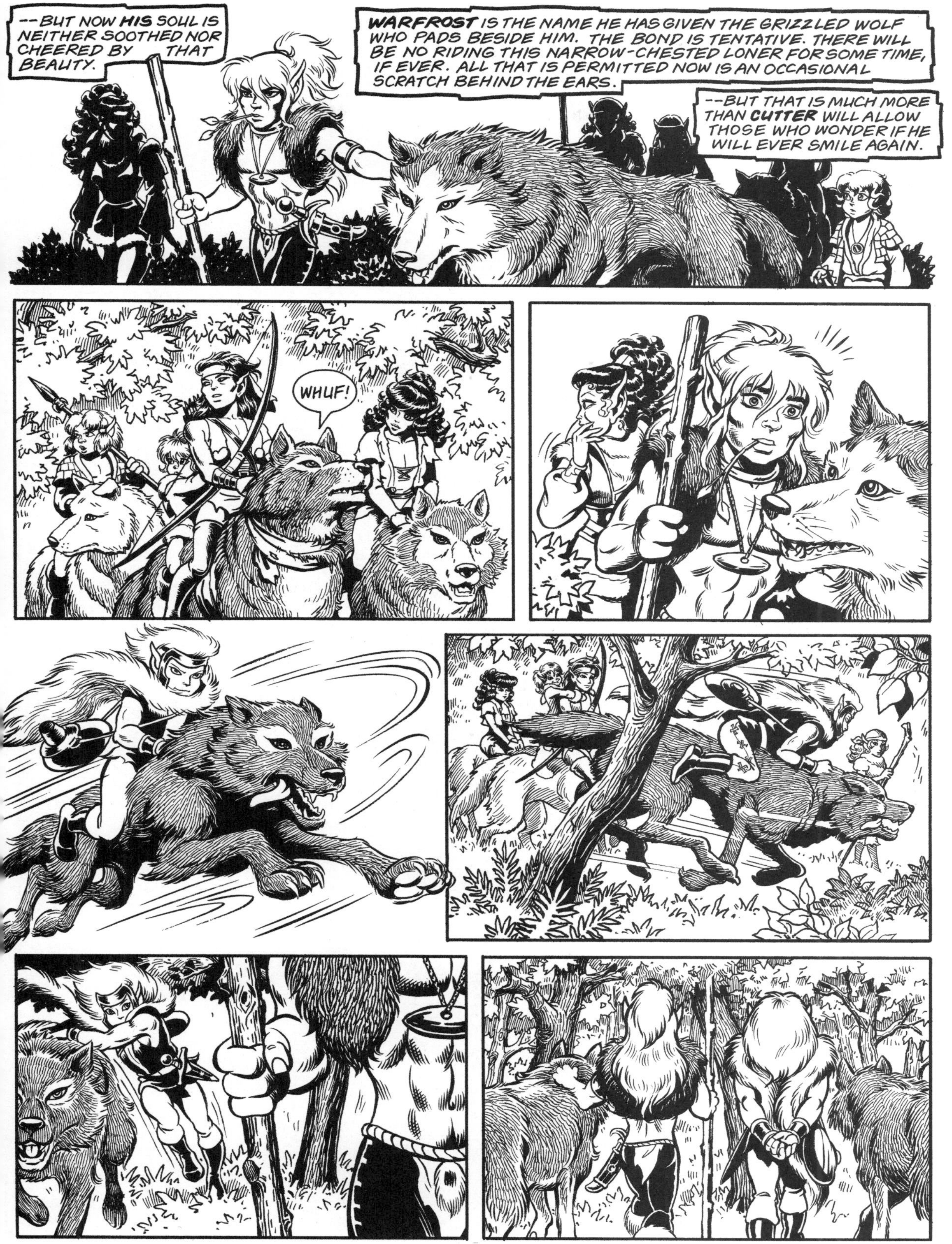

--BUT NOW **HIS** SOUL IS NEITHER SOOTHED NOR CHEERED BY THAT BEAUTY.
WARFROST IS THE NAME HE HAS GIVEN THE GRIZZLED WOLF WHO PADS BESIDE HIM. THE BOND IS TENTATIVE. THERE WILL BE NO RIDING THIS NARROW-CHESTED LONER FOR SOME TIME, IF EVER. ALL THAT IS PERMITTED NOW IS AN OCCASIONAL SCRATCH BEHIND THE EARS.
--BUT THAT IS MUCH MORE THAN **CUTTER** WILL ALLOW THOSE WHO WONDER IF HE WILL EVER SMILE AGAIN.
WHUF!

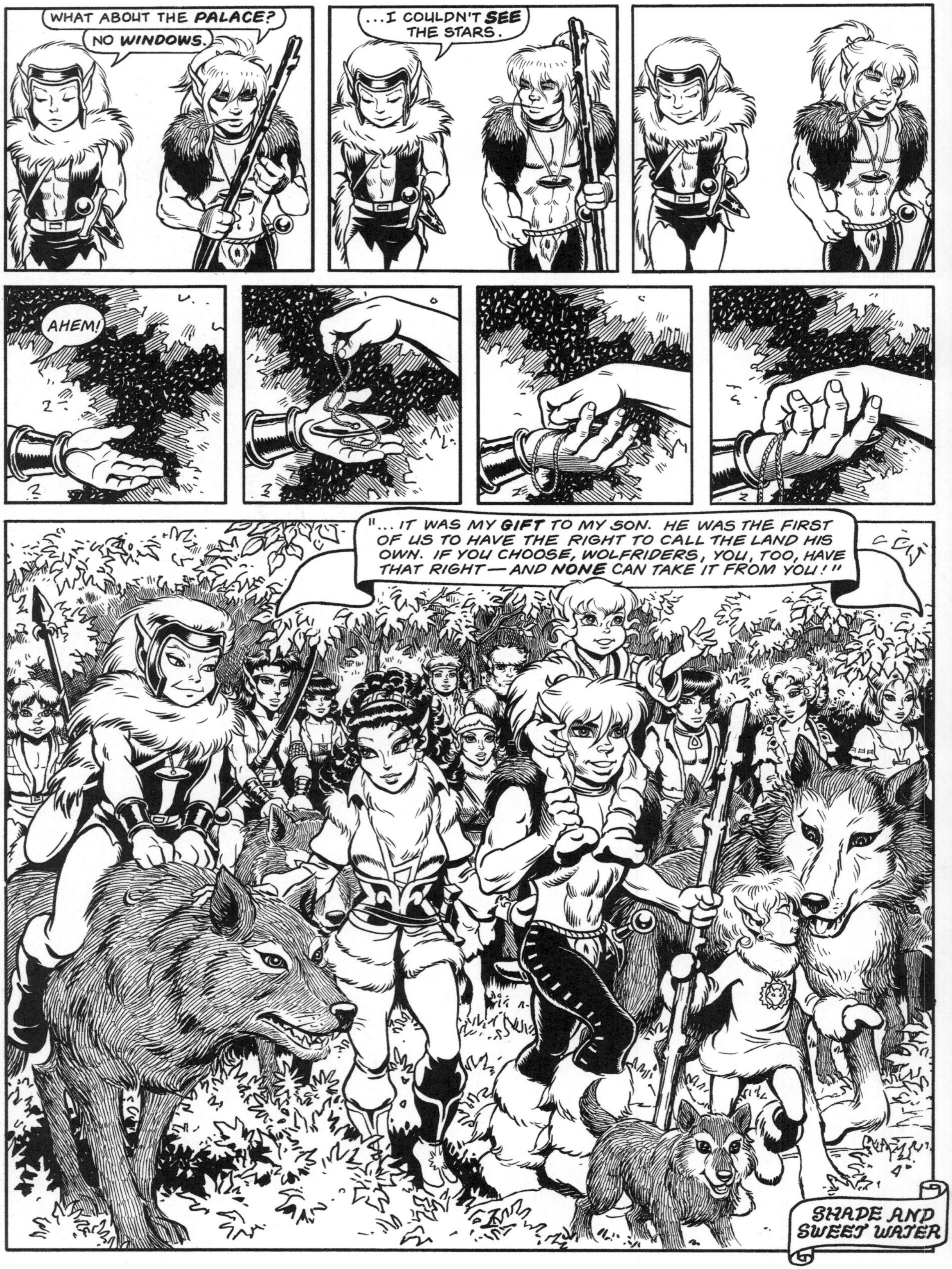
WHAT ABOUT THE PALACE?
NO WINDOWS.
...I COULDN'T SEE THE STARS.
AHEM!
"...IT WAS MY GIFT TO MY SON. HE WAS THE FIRST OF US TO HAVE THE RIGHT TO CALL THE LAND HIS OWN. IF YOU CHOOSE, WOLFRIDERS, YOU, TOO, HAVE THAT RIGHT— AND NONE CAN TAKE IT FROM YOU!"
SHADE AND SWEET WATER

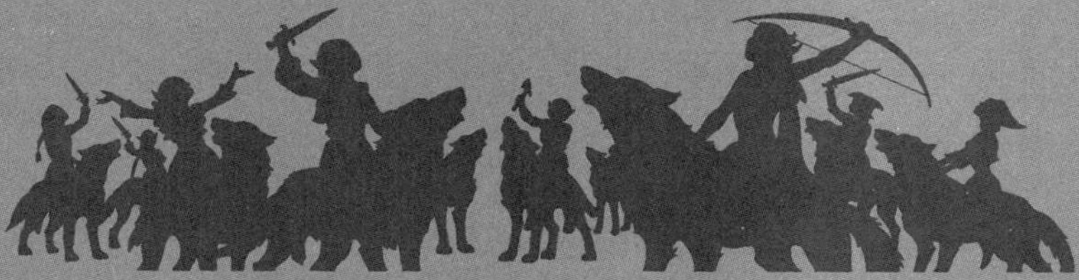

MAKING OF ELFQUEST

COMMENTARY BY WENDY AND RICHARD PINI

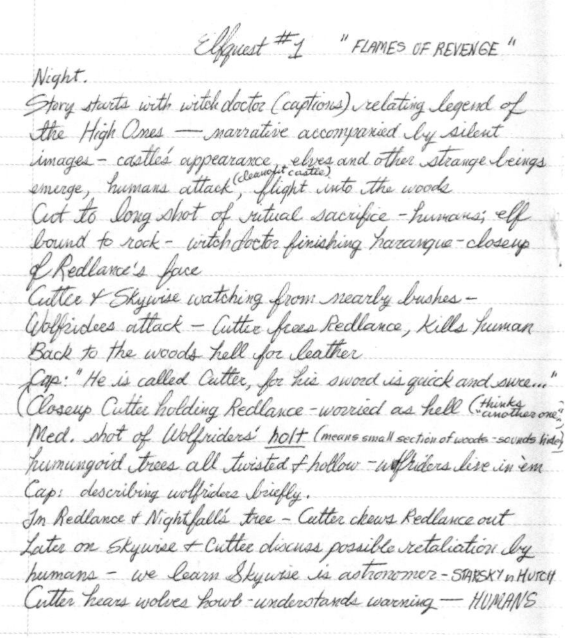

Elfquest #1 "FLAMES OF REVENGE"

Night.

Story starts with witch doctor (captions) relating legend of the High Ones — narrative accompanied by silent images - castle's appearance, elves and other strange beings emerge, humans attack (cleanoft castle), flight into the woods

Cut to long shot of ritual sacrifice - humans; elf bound to rock - witch doctor finishing harangue - closeup of Redlance's face

Cutter & Skywise watching from nearby bushes -

Wolfriders attack - Cutter frees Redlance, kills human

Back to the woods hell for leather

Cap: "He is called Cutter, for his sword is quick and sure..."

(Closeup Cutter holding Redlance - worried as hell (thinks another one)

Med. shot of Wolfriders' holt (means small section of woods - sounds like)

humungoid trees all twisted & hollow - wolfriders live in 'em

Cap: describing wolfriders briefly.

In Redlance & Nightfall's tree - Cutter chews Redlance out

Later on Skywise & Cutter discuss possible retaliation by humans - we learn Skywise is astronomer - STARSKY n HUTCH

Cutter hears wolves howl - understands warning — HUMANS

Even after more than thirty-five years, many readers still don't realize the creative process behind ElfQuest. First, we carefully develop and coplot the story, then Wendy writes the scripts. In 1977, everything, beginning with the story outline, was handwritten on lined binder paper—ultimate low tech! Note that in this first draft, the title of issue #1 was "Flames of Revenge" instead of "Fire and Flight."

The technology has changed, but we still do it the same way in 2014. First, we talk out the plot points for a given issue. Wendy writes a rough script and Richard, as editor, goes over it. Wendy does the pencil (or digital) layouts, the inking, and often the coloring. Together, we fine tune the dialogue and captions once more, and Richard formats and transmits final art and text files to the publisher.

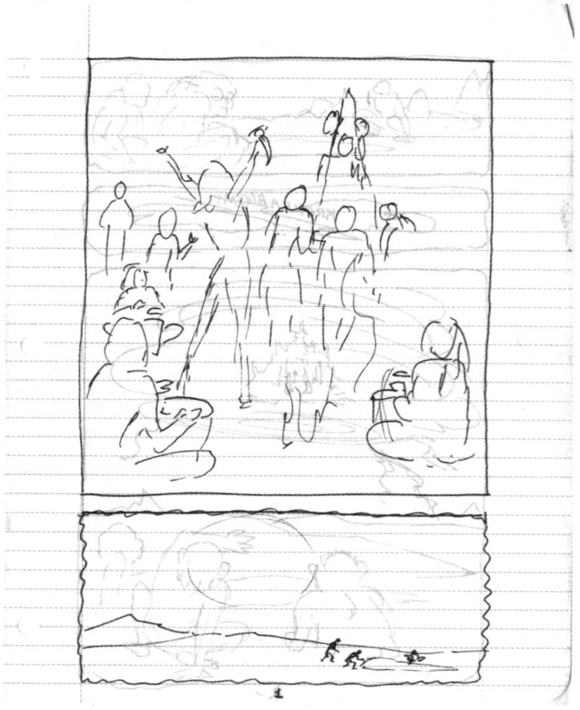

To help Richard visualize what Wendy had in her head and what the script didn't convey, she started doing layouts on that same @#$%^& lined paper. It was time consuming, but necessary to our teamwork. Richard often wears an art director hat too, making useful suggestions about layouts or expressions that Wendy might not have considered.*

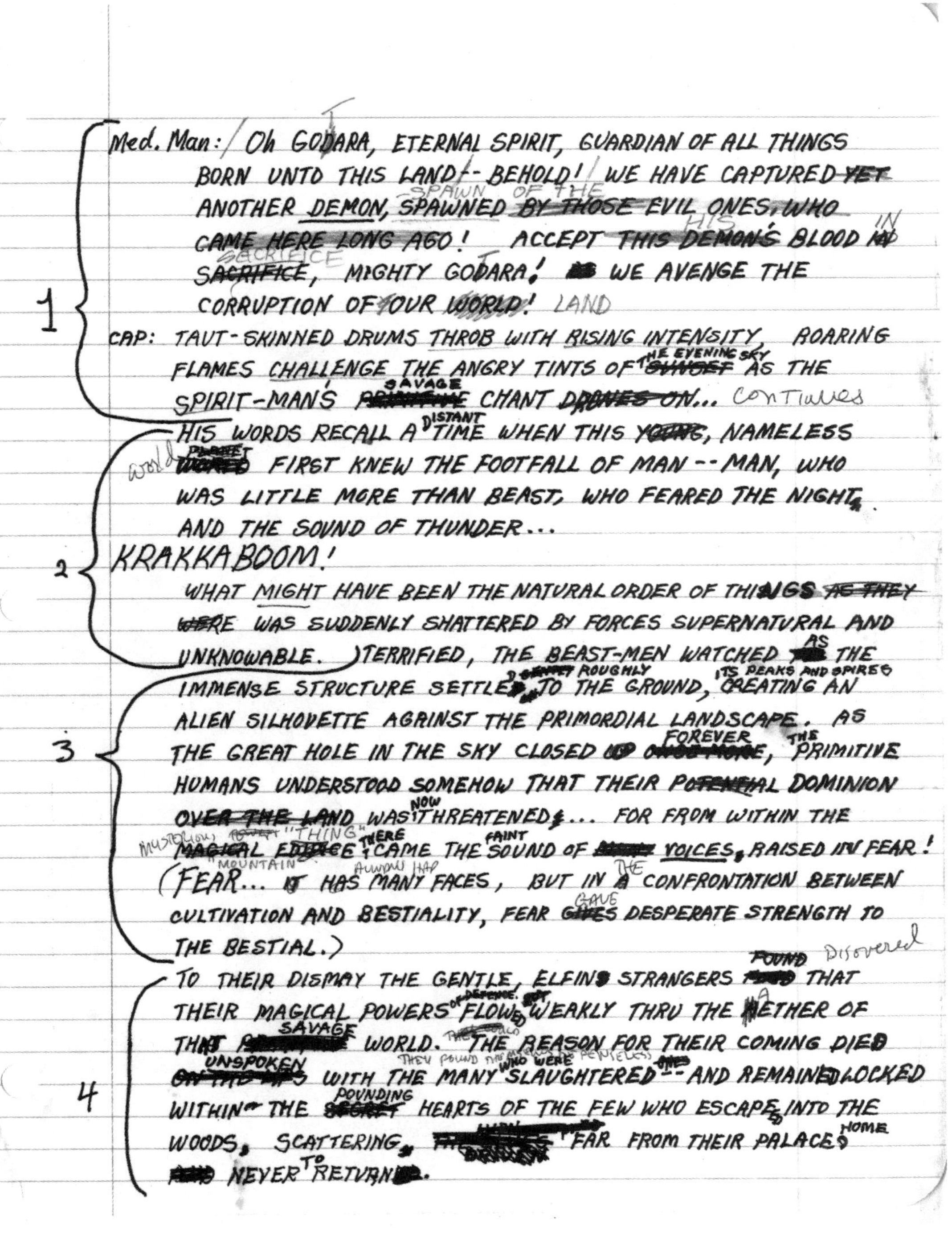

Med. Man: Oh GODARA, ETERNAL SPIRIT, GUARDIAN OF ALL THINGS
BORN UNTO THIS LAND! — BEHOLD! WE HAVE CAPTURED ~~YET~~
ANOTHER DEMON, ~~SPAWNED BY THOSE EVIL ONES, WHO~~ (SPAWN OF THE)
~~CAME HERE LONG AGO!~~ ACCEPT THIS DEMON'S BLOOD ~~IN~~ (IN) (HIS)
~~SACRIFICE~~, MIGHTY GODARA! ~~AS~~ WE AVENGE THE
CORRUPTION OF ~~OUR WORLD!~~ (LAND)

CAP: TAUT-SKINNED DRUMS THROB WITH RISING INTENSITY, ROARING
FLAMES CHALLENGE THE ANGRY TINTS OF ~~SUNSET~~ (THE EVENING SKY) AS THE
SPIRIT-MAN'S ~~PRIMITIVE~~ (SAVAGE) CHANT ~~DRONES ON~~... (CONTINUES)

1

2

HIS WORDS RECALL A ~~DISTANT~~ TIME WHEN THIS ~~YOUNG~~, NAMELESS (WORLD)
~~WORLD~~ (PLANET) FIRST KNEW THE FOOTFALL OF MAN -- MAN, WHO
WAS LITTLE MORE THAN BEAST, WHO FEARED THE NIGHT,
AND THE SOUND OF THUNDER...

KRAKKABOOM!
WHAT MIGHT HAVE BEEN THE NATURAL ORDER OF THINGS ~~AS THEY~~
~~WERE~~ WAS SUDDENLY SHATTERED BY FORCES SUPERNATURAL AND
UNKNOWABLE.) TERRIFIED, THE BEAST-MEN WATCHED ~~AS~~ THE (AS)
IMMENSE STRUCTURE SETTLED ~~GENTLY~~ (ROUGHLY) TO THE GROUND, CREATING AN (ITS PEAKS AND SPIRES)
ALIEN SILHOUETTE AGAINST THE PRIMORDIAL LANDSCAPE. AS

3

THE GREAT HOLE IN THE SKY CLOSED ~~UP ONCE MORE~~, (FOREVER) ~~PRIMITIVE~~ (THE)
HUMANS UNDERSTOOD SOMEHOW THAT THEIR ~~POTENTIAL~~ DOMINION
~~OVER THE LAND~~ WAS ~~NOW~~ THREATENED... FOR FROM WITHIN THE
~~MAGICAL EDIFICE~~ CAME THE ~~FAINT~~ SOUND OF ~~SMALL~~ VOICES, RAISED IN FEAR! (MYSTERIOUS) (NEVER) ("THING") (WERE)
(FEAR... ~~IT~~ HAS MANY FACES, BUT IN ~~A~~ CONFRONTATION BETWEEN (MOUNTAIN) (ALWAYS HAD) (THE)
CULTIVATION AND BESTIALITY, FEAR ~~GIVES~~ DESPERATE STRENGTH TO (GAVE)
THE BESTIAL.)

4

TO THEIR DISMAY THE GENTLE, ELFIN STRANGERS ~~FOUND~~ THAT (FOUND) (DISCOVERED)
THEIR MAGICAL POWERS ~~OF DEFENSE~~ FLOW WEAKLY THRU THE ~~ETHER~~ OF (A)
THAT ~~PRIMITIVE~~ (SAVAGE) WORLD. THE REASON FOR THEIR COMING DIED
~~ON THE LIPS~~ (UNSPOKEN) ~~THEY FOUND THE~~ (AND WERE) (RESTLESS) WITH THE MANY SLAUGHTERED -- AND REMAINED ~~LOCKED~~ (ONES)
WITHIN THE ~~SECRET~~ (POUNDING) HEARTS OF THE FEW WHO ESCAPE INTO THE
WOODS, SCATTERING, ~~FAR~~ FAR FROM THEIR PALACE, (HOME)
~~AND~~ (TO) NEVER RETURN.

Here, on a yellowed piece of binder paper, the myth of the Coming of the High Ones was for the first time essentially set down. We had no idea what these few simple words, hand printed in cheap felt-tip pen, would lead to. (Frankly, Wendy thinks she was just practicing her lettering technique.)

CAP CONT: ~~(IT BEGAN ... WHEN ... ONCE ...)~~ CAME MYSTERIOUSLY ~~TO~~
~~A ... YOUNG ... ON THEIR OWN ... AND ... WERE A~~
~~BUT ... OBLITERATED ... THE HUMANS DROVE THEM~~ DOWN THE GENERATIONS
~~TONS~~, MAN AGAINST SURVIVING ELVES -- ON AND ON, AN UNDYING
FROM THAT FIRST FATEFUL DAY UNTIL -- ENMITY,

SO IT BEGAN. AND SO THE HUNT WENT ON, THRU

CAP: -- NOW.

VOICE OFF: KILL THE DEMON! KILL THE DEMON!

SPIRIT-MAN: COUNTLESS MOONS AGO THE EVIL ONES INVADED OUR LAND,
TWISTING THE SHAPE OF THINGS WITH THEIR FOUL MAGIC!
HEAR, GODARA, THE CRIES OF THIS CHILD OF DEMONS! LET HIS
DEATH-AGONY APPEASE YOUR ~~RIGHTEOUS~~ WRATH!

REDLANCE: YOU'VE HAD YOUR FUN, OLD MAN... GET IT OVER WITH....

~~SKYWISE~~: CUTTER? THOSE SKULLS...

TAM: DON'T WORRY, SKYWISE. ~~ANY~~ REDLANCE'S ~~SKULL~~ WON'T ~~HANG~~ ~~BONES~~
~~ROCK LIKE THE OTHERS~~ HANG AMONG THEM, I SWEAR IT! WOLFRIDERS
READY... ATTACK!!

SPIRIT-MAN: COWARDS! STOP THEM! FIGHT!! GODARA WILLS IT--UNH!!

CUTTER: ~~TO THE HOLT, WOLFRIDERS~~! ENOUGH BLOOD FOR NOW!
I HAVE REDLANCE! ~~MY WARRIORS~~
REMEMBER THIS, HUMAN... NEXT TIME I'LL SKIN ~~CUT~~ YOU LIKE A STAG AND LET ~~FEED~~
THE
~~LET~~ WOLVES PICK YOUR BONES!

CAP: HIS SOUL-NAME IS TAM. THE BLOOD OF TEN CHIEFS PLOWS ~~RUNS~~ IN HIS VEINS. HE IS THE
~~FIERCE~~, YOUNG LEADER OF AN ELFIN TRIBE KNOWN AS THE WOLFRIDERS.
THOUGH HIS FOLK CALL HIM "CUTTER" FOR HIS SKILL WITH A SWORD,
HE IS NO COLD AND MERCILESS DEATH-DEALER ~~OR EVEN~~ CUTTER SMALL
~~HE IS MORE THAN MERE HUNTER~~, MORE IS HE. TAM LOVES HIS ~~MEN~~ TRIBE
SO MUCH, IN FACT, THAT
WITH A STRENGTH BEYOND HIS YEARS;~~ AND~~ THE BITTER BLOOD SHED THIS DAY
MAY AS WELL HAVE BEEN HIS OWN.

SKYWISE: HOW BAD IS HE, ~~CUTTER~~?

CUTTER: I DON'T KNOW. RIDE ON AHEAD, SKYWISE, AND TELL NIGHTFALL:
WE BRING HER LIFE-MATE BACK... SOMEWHAT LESS THAN WHOLE.

CAP: FIREFLIES TWINKLE IN THE PURPLE DUSK, GENTLY ILLUMINATING THE
HOLT OF THE WOLFRIDERS. TREE DWELLERS ~~THEY ARE~~ THESE ELVES ARE, QUIET AND
SECRETIVE, CUTTER'S TRIBE SHUNNING THE DAYLIGHT, RANGING FAR AT NIGHT TO
S

The elves are actually aliens from another star but to the primitive, frightened humans of the World of Two Moons, they are invaders who must be wiped out. We wanted to show that the humans had a side, too—no clichéd good guys vs. bad guys scenario. Cutter's soul name, revealed right away, comes from the legendary Scottish ballad "Tam Lin."

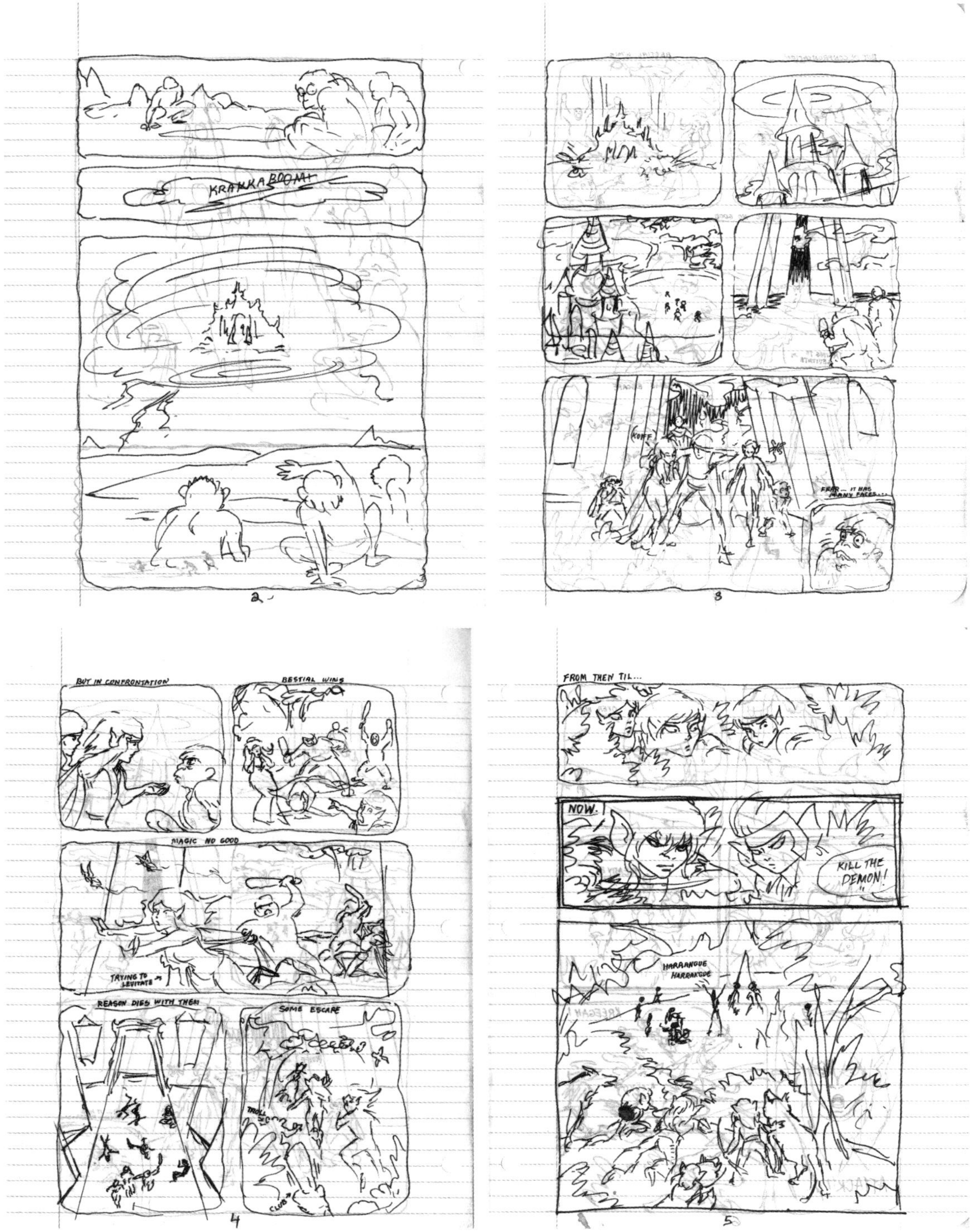
KRAKKABOOM!
KOFF
BUT IN CONFRONTATION
BESTIAL WINS
MAGIC NO GOOD
TRYING TO LEVITATE
REASON DIES WITH THEM
SOME ESCAPE
TROLL
CLUB
FROM THEN TIL...
NOW.
KILL THE DEMON!
HARRANGUE
HARRANGUE

It was important to emphasize, through art design, the extreme differences in body type between the elves and the primitive humans. For Wendy, designing the willowy, lithe elves came easy. But for the bulky, muscle-bound humans she resorted to influences from her first comic book mentor, the incomparable Jack Kirby.

                    AND SING
HUNT WITH THE WOLFPACK. GAME IS PLENTIFUL IN THIS PART OF THE

WOODS, BUT THERE ~~ARE MANY~~ DANGERS ~~AROUND HERE~~. ^AND^ THIS IS NOT THE

FIRST TIME CUTTER HAS BORNE AN INJURED FRIEND HOME.

NIGHTFALL: ~~OH~~, REDLANCE...! OH, NO!

CAP: AT THE SAME TIME....

WOMAN: AIEEE (SOB, SOB) TABAK! ^TABAK!^ MY MAN IS DEAD !! PUNISHMENT!

~~MAN: NO ~~ ~~ONE OF US COULD~~

SPIRIT MAN: THIS IS A SIGN FROM THE SPIRIT~~GODS~~. WE WERE WEAK.

      THE WOLF DEMONS ^ONE OF^ RESCUED THEIR OWN FROM OUR RITUAL. ~~BECAUSE~~

              ~~TABAK LIES DEAD !~~ ~~WE ARE AFRAID!~~ AND

~~WE WERE AFRAID~~ ~~WE RAN FROM THE SACRIFICE~~ ALL

BECAUSE WE WERE AFRAID. ^TO FIGHT^ THE SPIRITS ~~ARE AROUND THE MOUNTAIN, LOOK~~

~~GO TOO~~ ^THEY^ DESPISE~~S~~ OUR COWARDICE AND TURN~~S~~ ^AWAY^ FROM OUR PRAYERS.

WE HAVE ^DELAYED^ ~~WAITED~~ TOO LONG ^IN CARRYING OUT GODARA'S WILL^ ~~TO DO~~ ~~THE DARKLY BIDDING~~. ~~AND THIS~~

~~IS NOW~~ ^NOW^ WE WILL DO WHAT MUST BE DONE, SO THAT TABAK'S ~~SOUL~~ ^SPIRIT^ MAY REST!

REDLANCE: YOU SHOULD HAVE SEEN HIM, CUTTER... THE FINEST, FATTEST BUCK IN ALL

          THE WOODS ! I ALMOST HAD HIM...

TAM: I DON'T CARE HOW SWEET THE GAME ~~WAS~~ ^IS^ NEAR THE HUMANS' CAMP!

     YOU KNOW THAT HUNTING ALONE IS FORBIDDEN! WHY DID YOU

     DISOBEY ME?!

REDLANCE: FORGIVE ME, MY CHIEF... IN THE HEAT OF THE CHASE... I-I FORGOT --

TAM: ^WELL,^ DON'T FORGET AGAIN! YOUR CARELESSNESS ALMOST COST ME MY

     BEST TRACKER! YOU, REDLANCE! ~~DON'T WORRY, NIGHTFALL.~~

     ~~HE'LL MEND IN TIME.~~

NIGHTFALL: CUTTER, WHY MUST THE HUMANS ~~SEEK EVER TO KILL US?~~ ^HATE US SO?^ WE OFFER

           THEM NO HARM.

TAM: HUMANS HAVE ALWAYS HATED OUR KIND, ~~FROM THE FIRST MOMENT~~ ^EVER SINCE^ OUR

      ANCIENT FATHERS, THE HIGH ONES, SET FOOT ON THIS LAND. THERE'S

      ~~IS~~ NO RHYME OR REASON TO IT. THAT'S JUST THE WAY IT IS.

NIGHTFALL: ~~SOMETIMES~~ I WISH WE COULD FIND A PLACE TO LIVE WHERE

           THERE ARE NO HUMANS. ~~BEYOND THE WOODS~~

TAM: ~~DON'T BE~~ I KNOW. BUT ^THIS IS HOME.^ WHAT ELSE IS THERE?

~~SKYWISE~~: SEE, CUTTER? THE GREAT WOLF CHASES THE HUMAN HUNTER ACROSS

        THE SKY. HE'S CLUMSY, THAT HUMAN. ONE DAY HE'LL TRIP AND

        FALL, AND THE WOLF WILL HAVE HIM.

One of our strongest female characters, Nightfall, gets a gentle, thoughtful introduction on this page. Over time she matured into a "knight," Cutter's shield mate in battle and friend to the end. Her mate Redlance remained mild and nurturing, but came into his own powers as a magical tree shaper. Revisions and corrections are in great evidence—no Undo command here!

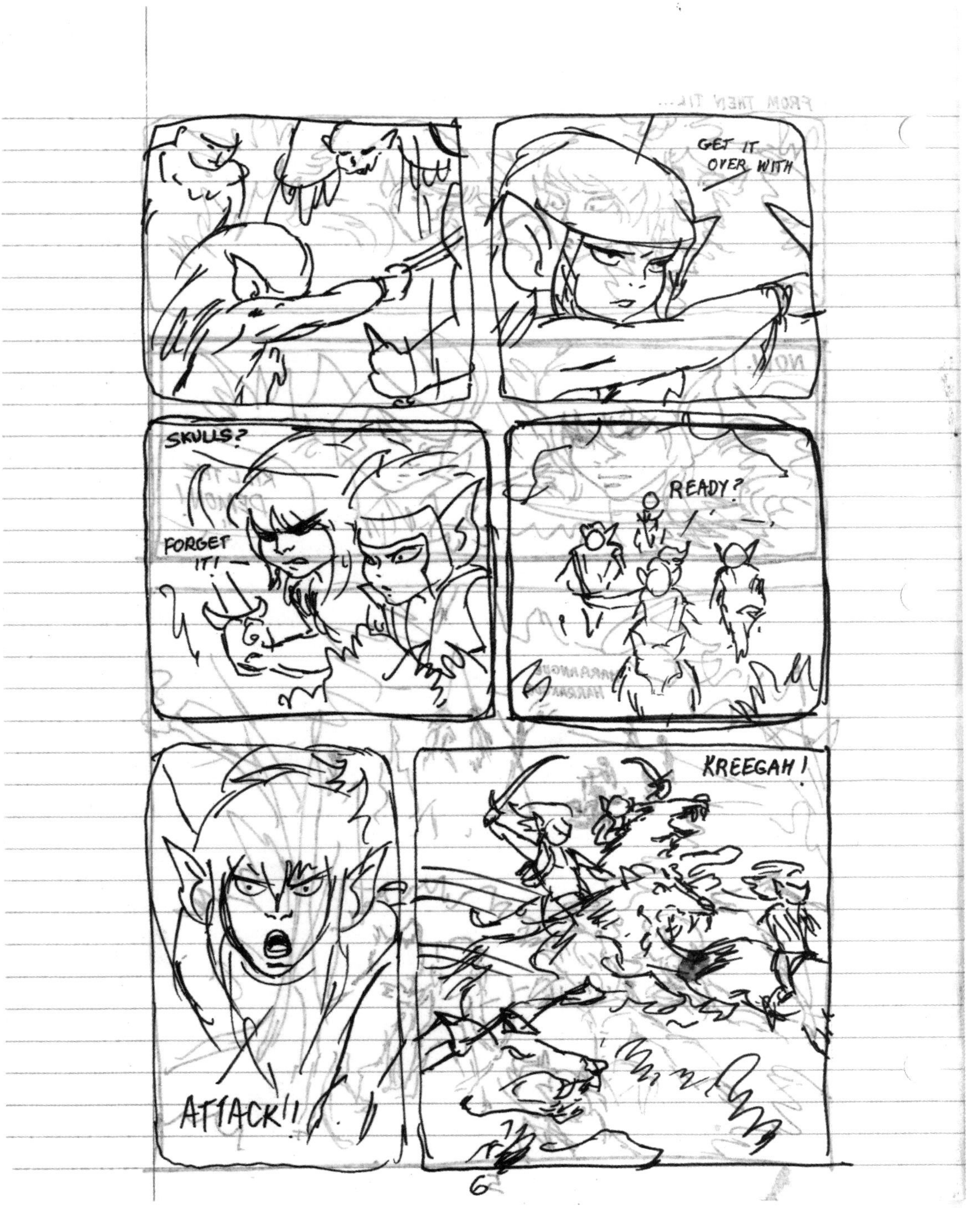
GET IT OVER WITH
SKULLS?
FORGET IT!
READY?
ATTACK!!
KREEGAH!
6

Redlance was the perfect elf to establish sympathy for the Wolfriders as a persecuted, misunderstood race. Yet we also see they are truly one with—and just as scary as— their snarling, lupine mounts. Such contrast creates interest; you never quite know what the elves will do next. We also have fun at the layout stage not taking things too seriously.

D

TAM: YOU SEE ALL THAT UP THERE, SKYWISE? STRANGE... I JUST SEE STARS.

SKYWISE: WHAT'S THE MATTER?

TAM: I... NEVER KILLED A HUMAN BEFORE. DIDN'T THINK IT COULD BE DONE. THEY'LL WANT REVENGE. SOMETHING BAD WILL HAPPEN SOON. I FEEL IT!

SKYWISE: YOU'RE FULL OF DREAMBERRIES! WHAT CAN THE HUMANS DO TO US? THEY'RE AFRAID TO COME NEAR OUR HOLT. REDLANCE WAS CAPTURED ONLY BECAUSE HE STRAYED TOO FAR FROM HOME.

TAM: SHHH! LISTEN! SOME-THING'S WRONG!

~~CAP: SKYWISE LISTENS, HIS KEEN SENSES PROBING FOR A HINT OF DANGER— AND IT IS THERE IN THE WIND, IN THE TREMBLING FOLIAGE...~~

NIGHTRUNNER HOWLS

SKYWISE: THE WOLVES! IT'S ~~IS~~ THEIR WARNING CRY!

TAM: ✧SPEAK, NIGHTRUNNER, MY FRIEND— WHAT HAVE YOU SEEN?

NIGHTRUNNER: ✧ HUMANS. THEY COME. WITH FIRE.

TAM: AH!

CAP: QUICKLY THE UNSPOKEN MESSAGE IS PASSED AMONG THE TRIBE. CUTTER SUMMONS HIS HUNTERS TO DEFEND THE HOLT.

TAM: ✧ ONE-EYE ✧SCOUTER ✧ STRONGBOW ✧ TREESTUMP (SO IT'S FINALLY COME TO THIS, EH?)

NIGHTFALL: LIE STILL, BELOVED, CUTTER DID NOT SUMMON YOU WITH THE OTHERS!

REDLANCE: BUT-BUT THE HUMANS..! THEY MEAN TO DESTROY US ALL!

CUTTER: QUICKLY! ~~DRAW YOUR~~ WEAPONS OUT! NIGHTRUNNER WILL SHOW THE WAY!

CAP: THE WOLFPACK HOWLS AT THE HEELS OF ITS POWERFUL LEADER AS THEY PLUNGE THRU THE MURKWOODS. EACH ELFIN HUNTER IS ONE WITH HIS SHAGGY MOUNT, RIDING HARD TOWARD AN UNCERTAIN FATE!

SKYWISE: LOOK! TORCHES!

CAP: BETRAYED BY THEIR INSTINCTUAL FEAR OF FIRE, THE WOLVES STOP SHORT OF THE CLEARING, BUT CUTTER URGES SNARLING NIGHTRUNNER FORWARD.

TAM: I WARNED YOU OLD MAN... GO AWAY OR WE MUST KILL YOU!

SPIRIT MAN: NO, DEMON! WE SHALL LIVE, BUT YOU AND YOUR KIND WILL BE ASHES BEFORE SUNRISE!

The central relationship of the story—the loving bond of brotherhood between Cutter and Skywise—is set out in a way that also points out their differences. Skywise, the stargazer, dreams of worlds beyond worlds while Cutter, the Wolfriders' barbaric young chieftain, is firmly rooted in the gritty reality of day-to-day survival.

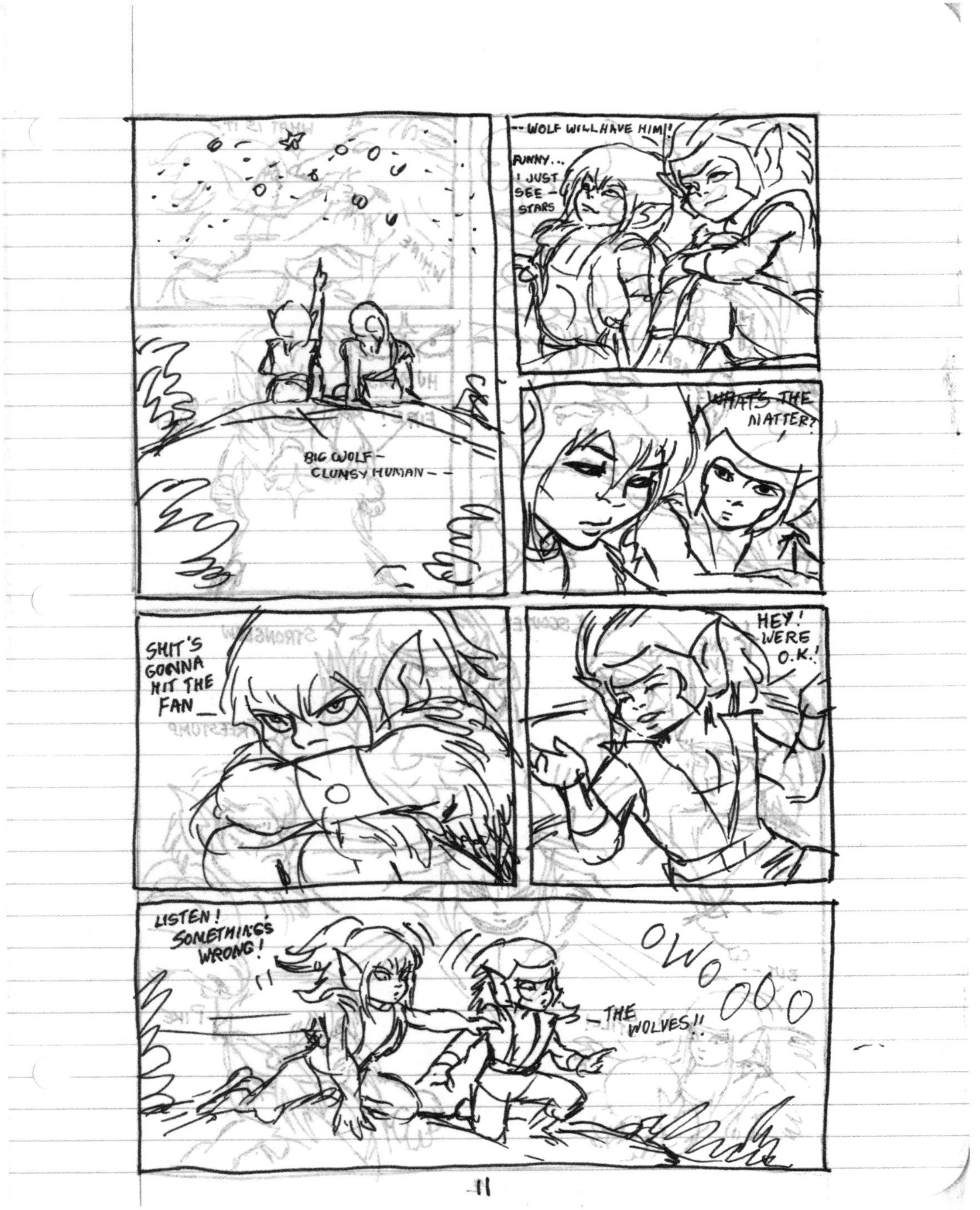
BIG WOLF—
CLUMSY HUMAN— —
— WOLF WILL HAVE HIM!
FUNNY... I JUST SEE— STARS
WHAT'S THE MATTER?
SHIT'S GONNA HIT THE FAN__
HEY! WERE O.K.!
LISTEN! SOMETHING'S WRONG!
—THE WOLVES!!
OWOOOOO
11

Some male readers, experiencing ElfQuest for the first time in the mid-1970s, felt uncomfortable with Cutter and Skywise's intimacy—a new kind of male bonding for the macho, superhero-heavy American comics industry. But Wendy was bitten by the Japanese manga/anime bug decades before it became a craze in the mid-1990s. Strong manga influences informed both her art and storytelling, taking them in a more sensual, feminine direction.

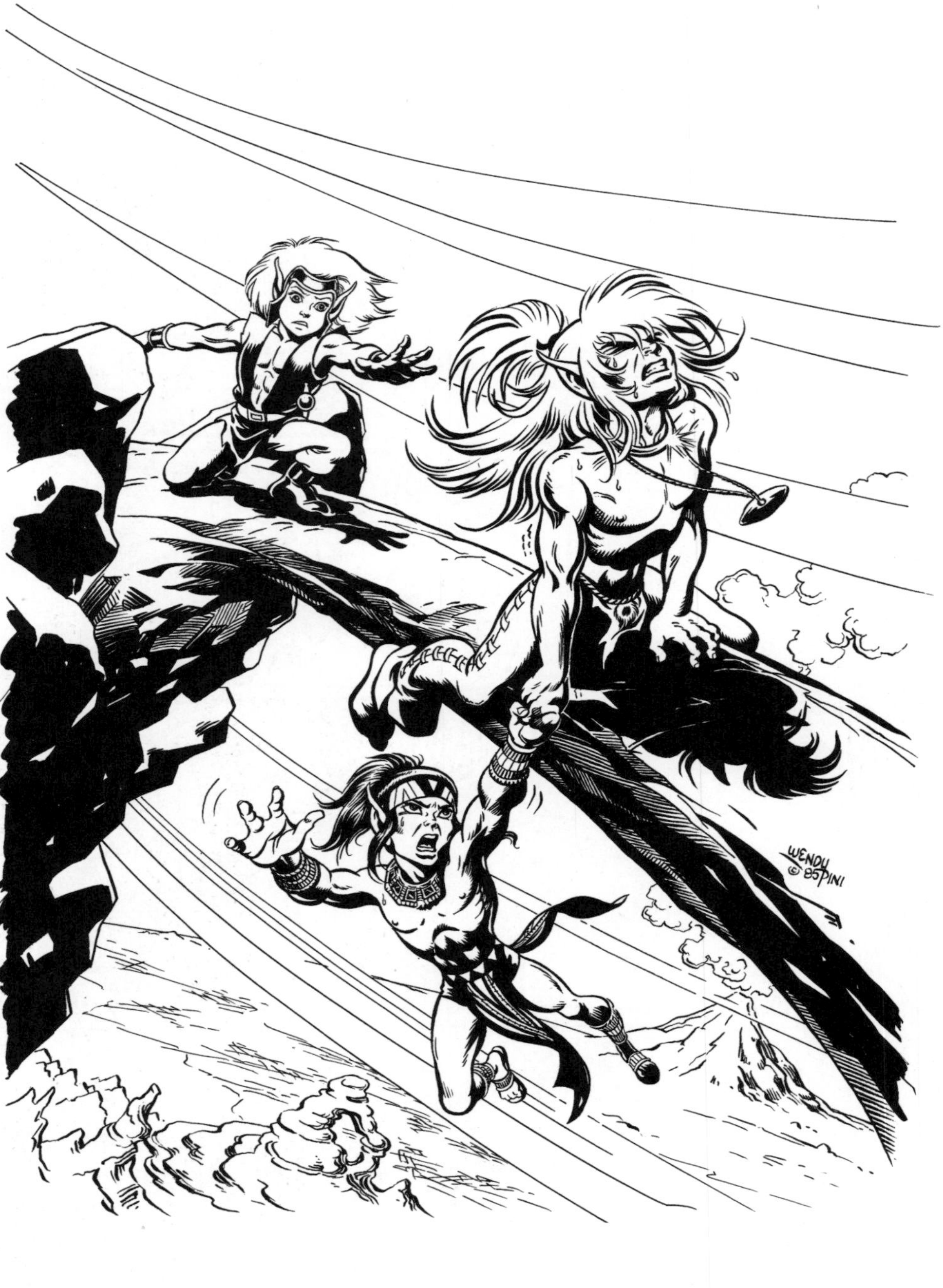
WENDY
© 85 PINI

When Marvel Comics' Epic line reprinted the classic quest for newsstand distribution beginning in 1985, a whole new journey began and we knew we would reach a whole new audience. What follows are a series of Epic covers that were also used as chapter breaks in this collection.

The hero reaching out a hand to rescue his rival or foe has become a much overused trope in comics and especially movies. But back in the 1980s, not so much. Fans really love the love/hate (mostly hate) relationship between Cutter and Rayek to this day. Technical note: Because Warp's comics contained thirty-two pages of story, compared to Marvel's twenty-two, the story often broke in odd places. Wendy then needed to provide cover art referring to different dramatic moments for the new comics.

Our first all-humor story, "The Dreamberry Tales," shocked some readers by deviating so far from the serious mood of past issues. But now it's an all-time favorite. Most everyone can relate to Cutter and Skywise's epic hangover. And the elves' short sojourn with the larcenous trolls, slapstick as it was, also set the stage for momentous events to occur in the story years later.

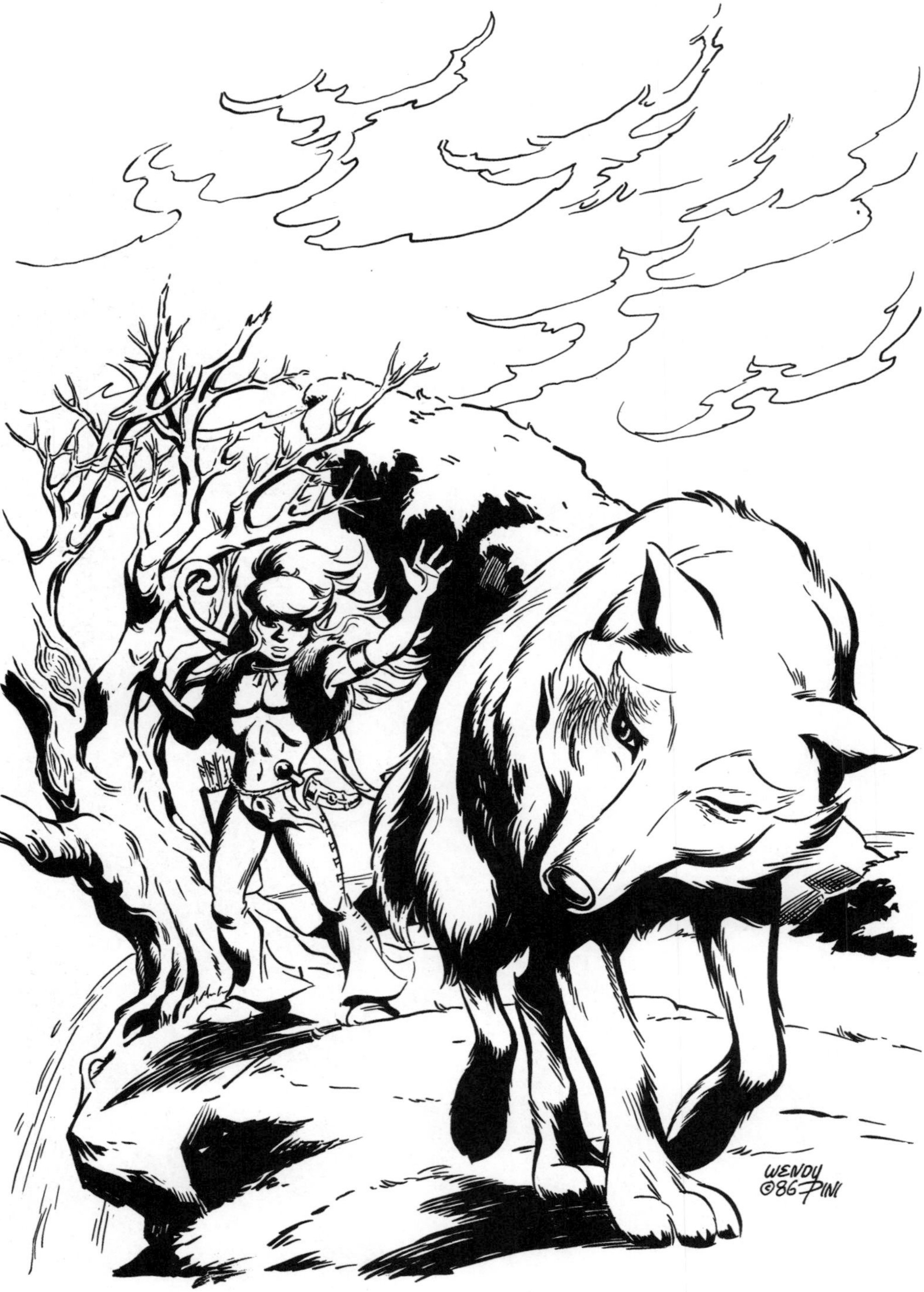
WENDY
©86 PINI

We've been told over the years that the way we handled the death of Cutter's beloved old wolf, Nightrunner, helped many a fan cope with the loss of a pet. There is no higher compliment than to know that a story you've created has gone beyond mere entertainment to touch lives and even transform them.

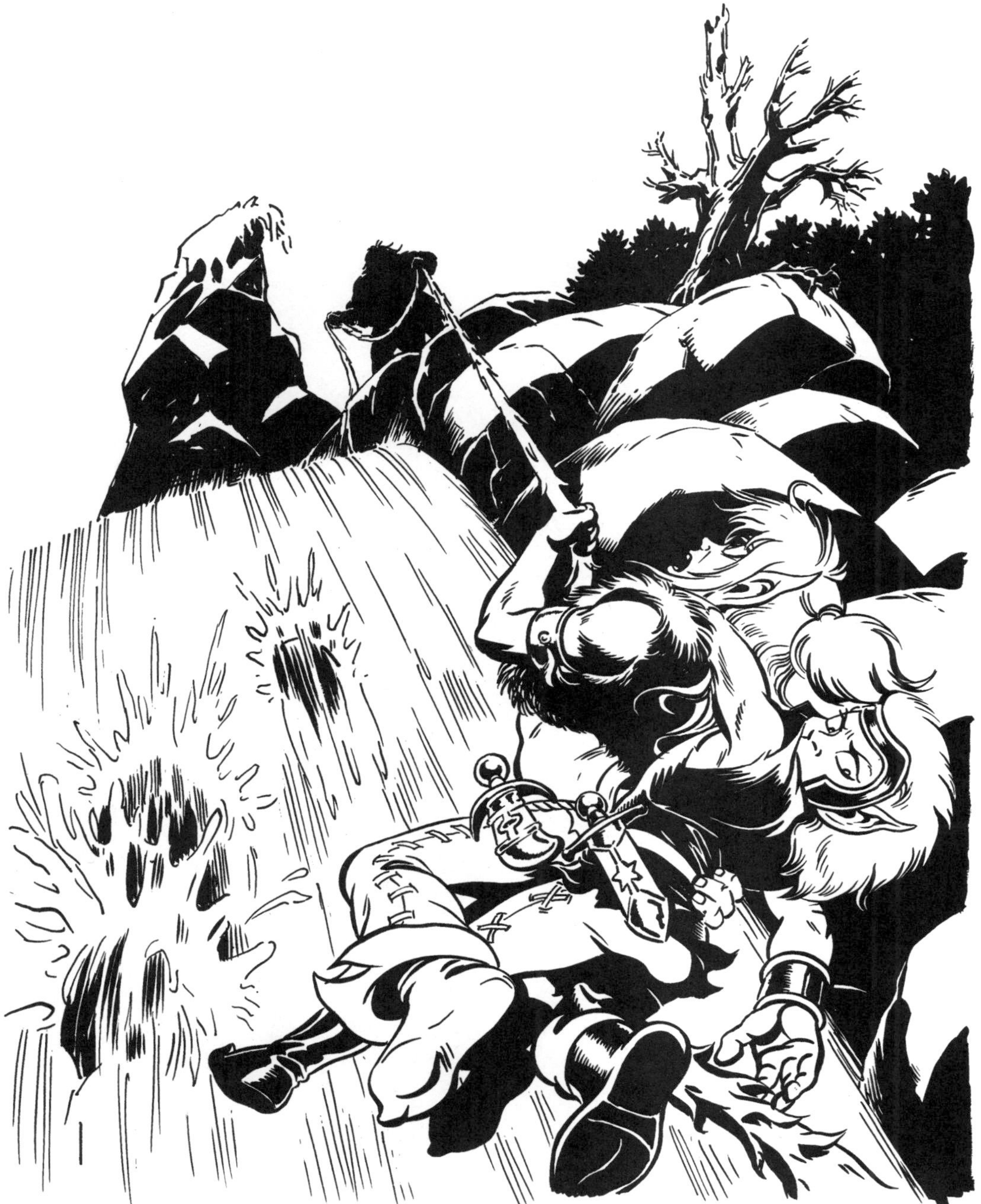

We're going to let you in on a not-so-well-kept secret. Originally, Skywise was slated to die heroically and tragically in Cutter's arms at this point in the story. But Richard would have none of it. "That elf's an astronomer! He's mine! Hands off!" Good thing there was no arguing. Skywise is easily the most popular character in ElfQuest*. This Marvel cover also captures a moment when the elves' perception of humans changes dramatically.*

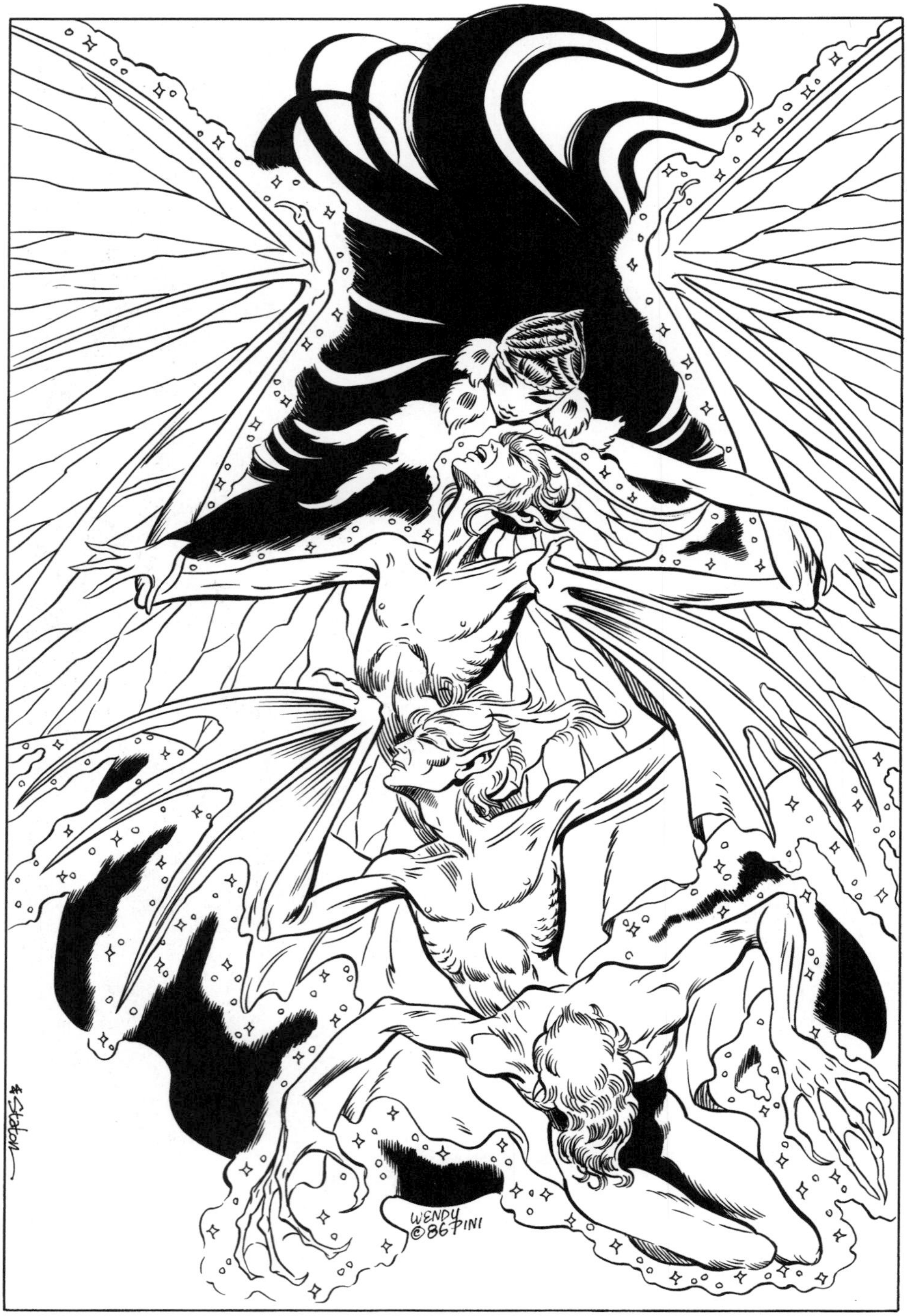

WENDY ©86 PINI

Artistically speaking, the creation of the winged Glider Tyldak is Wendy's favorite of all the new covers she did for Marvel/Epic. It makes strong use of the S curve--the classic "line of beauty." Yet it's a pretty creepy image with disturbing sadistic overtones. Sharp-eyed readers also noticed a slight difference in the look of this cover. Wendy asked veteran artist Joe Staton to do the inks, lending an eerie overtone to the whole.

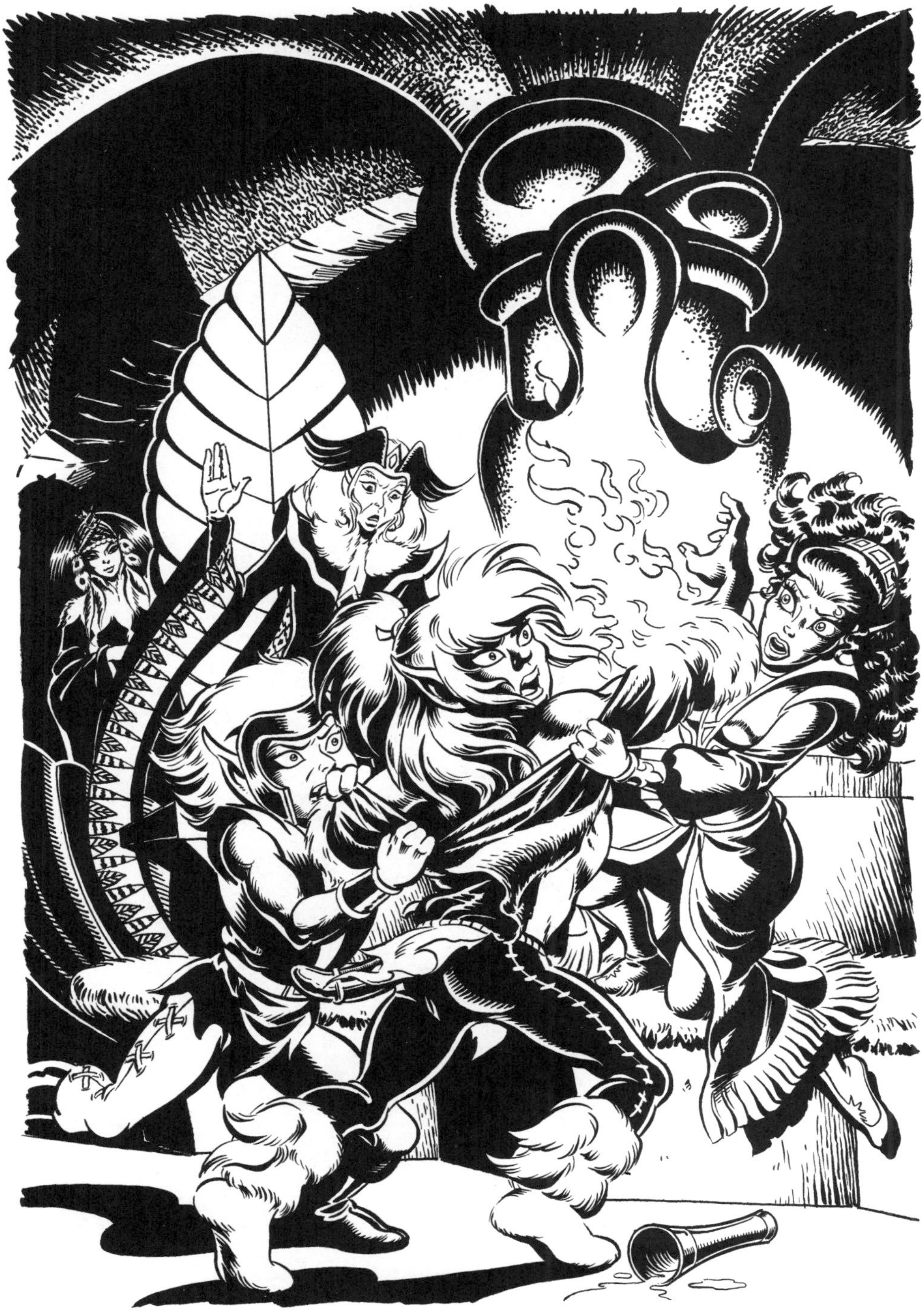

Sometimes you can take a minor story incident, as in this case, and make it look like quite a major disaster. The process is called "desperation to meet the deadline." Again, because of the difference between the Warp and the Epic issue breaks, this event came into more focus than it otherwise might have.

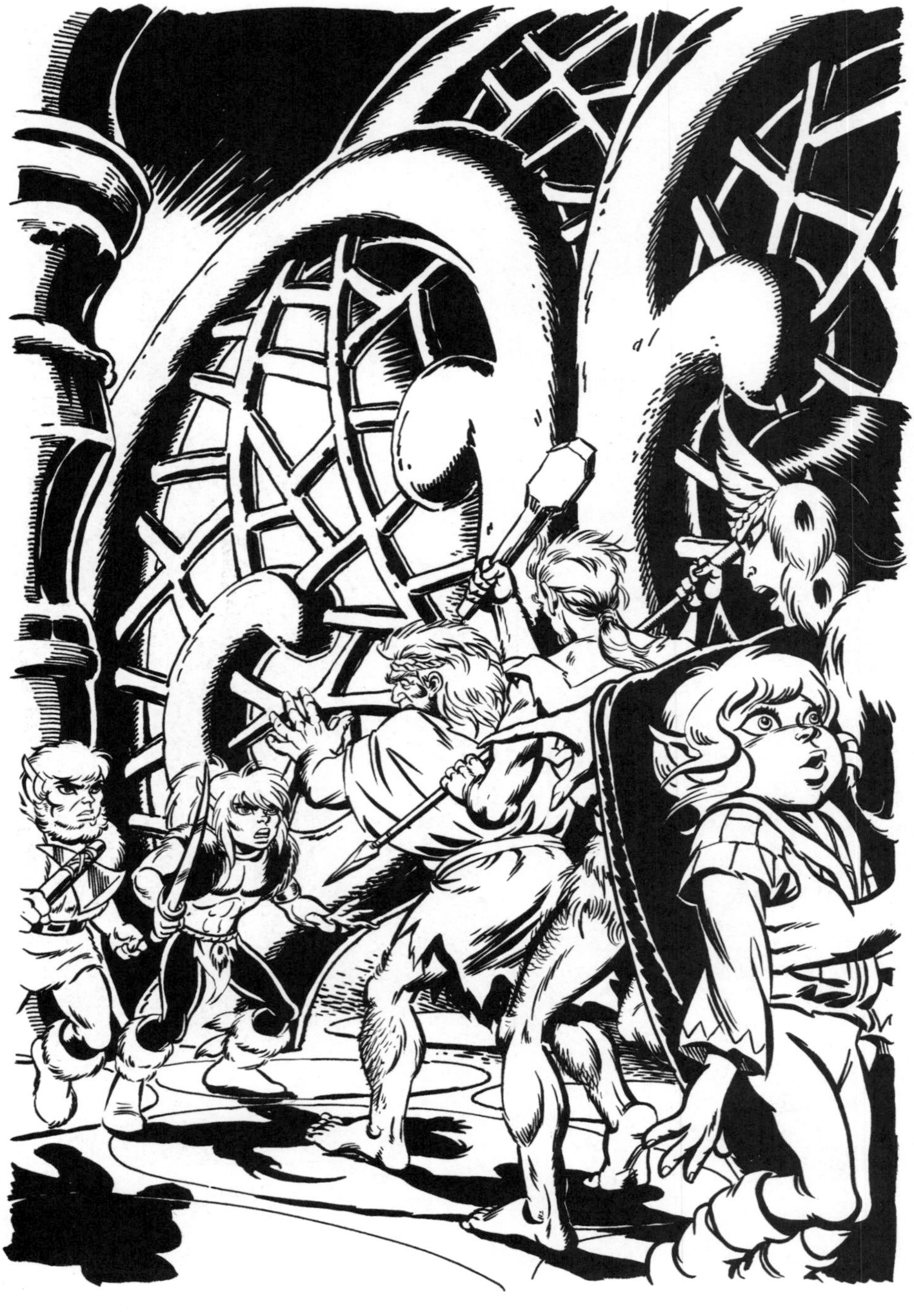

This is one of Wendy's least favorite of the Epic covers. The composition has absolutely no focal point, and you can't really tell what's happening. While there is a lot of tension in this part of the story, it's mostly psychological. There's nothing much physically or visually exciting going on. Oh, well. You can't win 'em all.

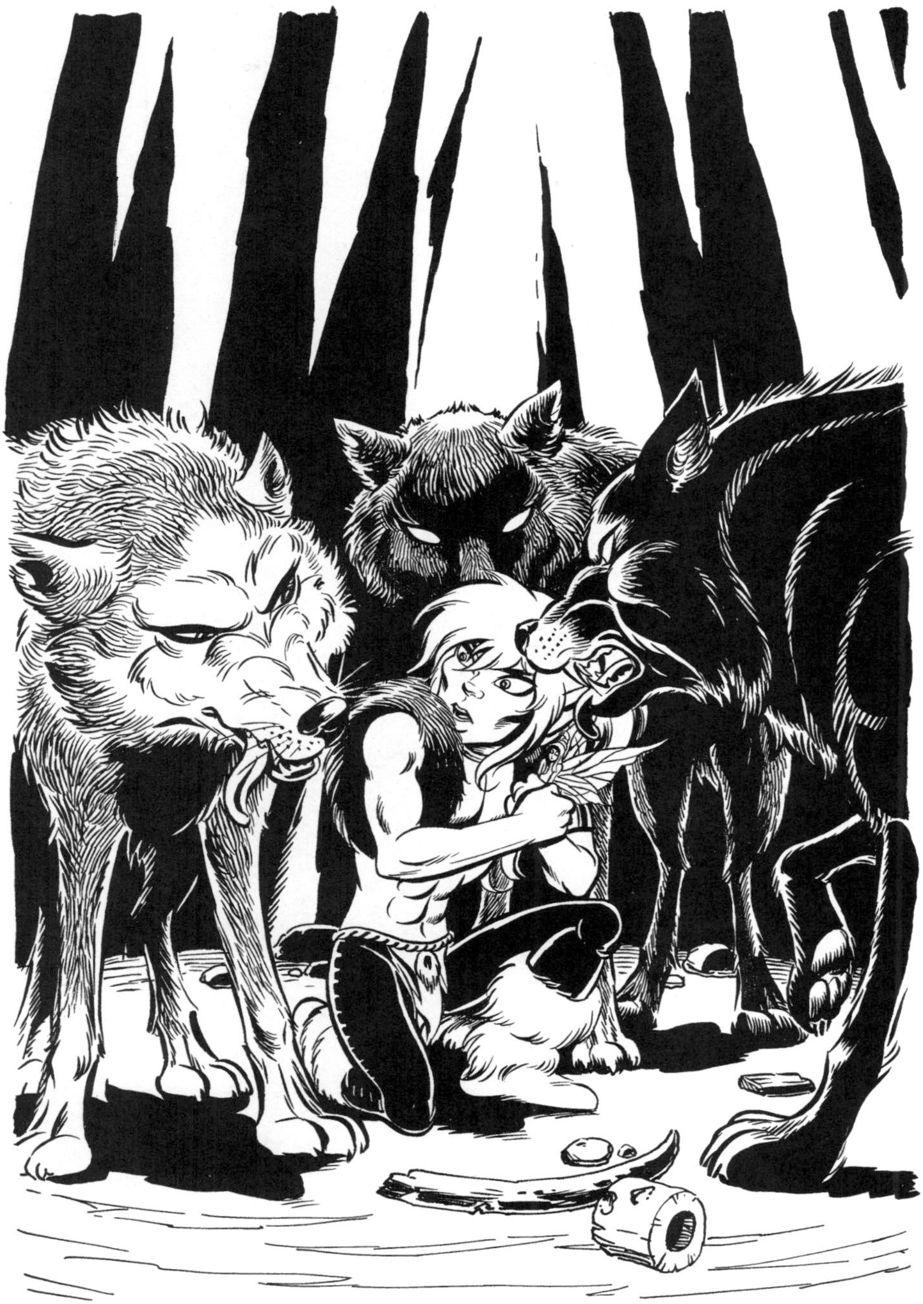

Here, the cliffhanger peril that ended a Warp issue has become the cover for an Epic issue. Not only does Cutter meet his next wolf, Warfrost, after he tumbles into this trollish pit trap, but someone else is there, in the shadows, someone in disguise whom he can't recognize. That mysterious presence will lead him, by quest's end, to knowledge of the very origins of his race . . . and more.

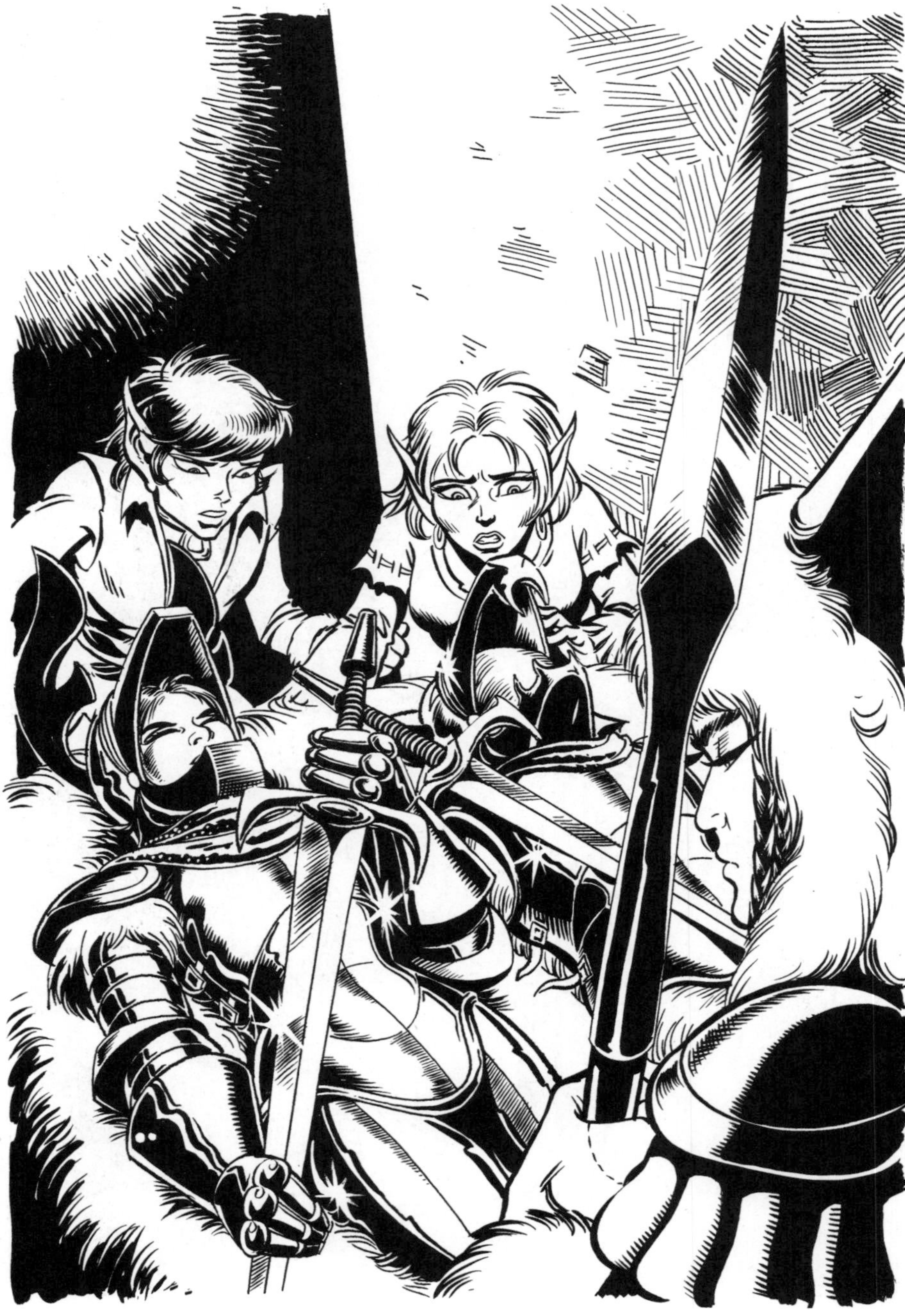

Unlike some other comic book series—and many of today's blockbuster movies—death is final in ElfQuest. *Final, and always meaningful. Nobody resurrects to say, "Fooled ya!" Violence has far-reaching consequences, and major loss is always a real possibility. Death matters as much as life. It's an honor to take a character through the full cycle of his or her journey, however brief or lengthy. We take that responsibility very seriously.*

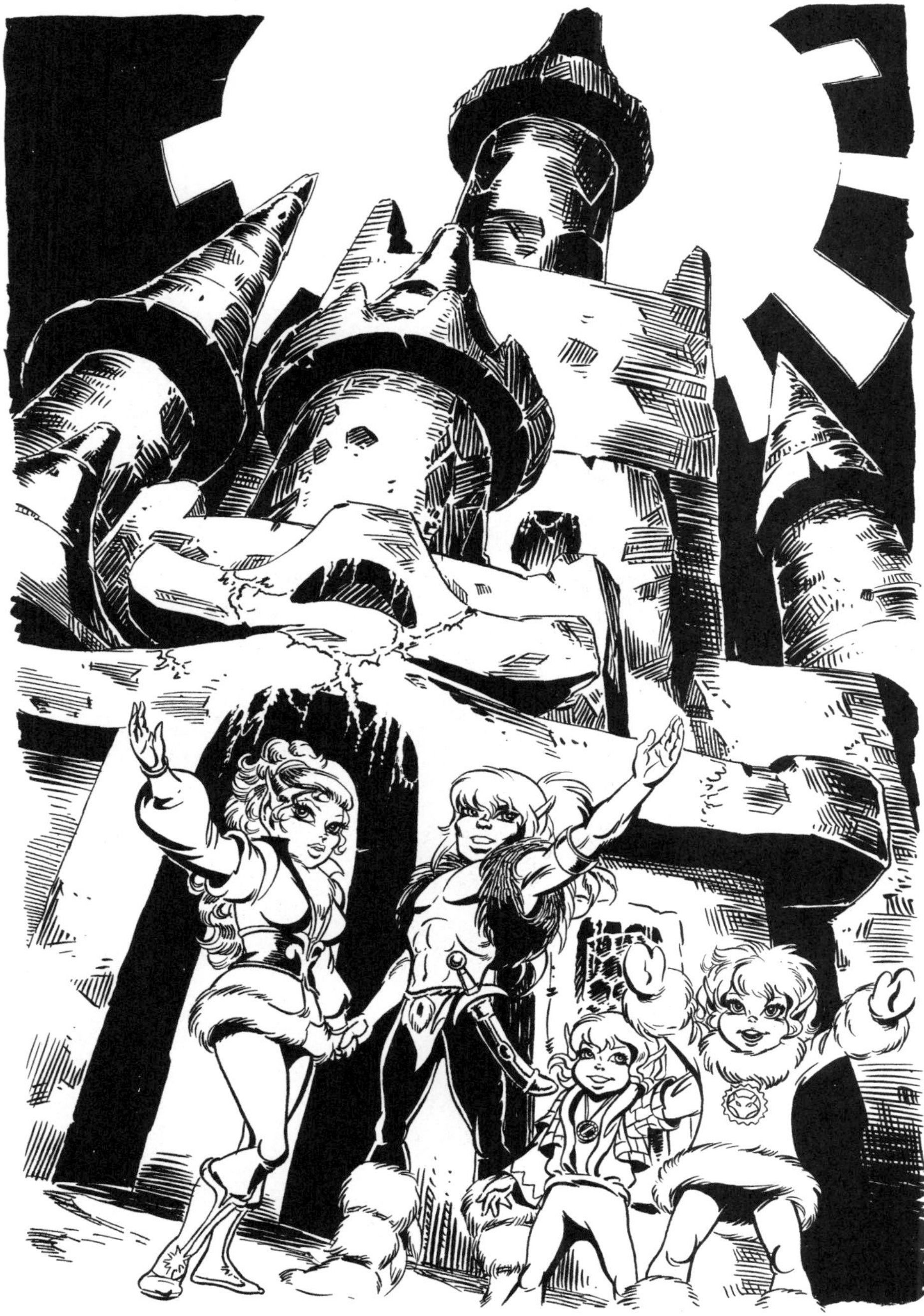

The Palace of the High Ones, long dormant, long hidden. In this, the next-to-last Epic cover, Wendy wanted to welcome the reader to what appeared to be the triumphant victory of the elves. Ah, but the secrets it holds are still being uncovered--especially by Cutter Kinseeker--thirty-six (or ten thousand) years later. What have the elves learned so far? "Be careful what you wish for."

ELFQUEST®

DISCOVER THE LEGEND OF *ELFQUEST*! ALLIANCES ARE FORGED, ENEMIES DISCOVERED, AND SAVAGE BATTLES FOUGHT IN THIS EPIC FANTASY ADVENTURE, HANDSOMELY PRESENTED BY DARK HORSE BOOKS!

THE COMPLETE ELFQUEST
Volume 1: The Original Quest
978-1-61655-407-1 | $24.99

Volume 2
978-1-61655-408-8 | $24.99

Volume 3
978-1-50670-080-9 | $24.99

Volume 4
978-1-50670-158-5 | $24.99

Volume 5
978-1-50670-606-1 | $24.99

ELFQUEST: THE ORIGINAL QUEST GALLERY EDITION
978-1-61655-411-8 | $125.00

ELFQUEST: THE FINAL QUEST
Volume 1
978-1-61655-409-5 | $17.99

Volume 2
978-1-61655-410-1 | $17.99

Volume 3
978-1-50670-138-7 | $17.99

Volume 4
978-1-50670-492-0 | $17.99